Sports activities for men

Sports activities for men

DONALD R. CASADY
PROFESSOR OF PHYSICAL EDUCATION AND CHAIRMAN OF PHYSICAL EDUCATION SKILLS PROGRAM,
DEPARTMENT OF PHYSICAL EDUCATION FOR MEN, THE UNIVERSITY OF IOWA, IOWA CITY

Macmillan Publishing Co., Inc.
New York
Collier Macmillan Publishers
London

GV
341
.C342
1974

Copyright © 1974, Donald R. Casady
Printed in the United States of America

All rights reserved. No part of this book may be reproduced or transmitted in any form or by any means, electronic or mechanical, including photocopying, recording, or any information storage and retrieval system, without permission in writing from the Publisher.

Macmillan Publishing Co., Inc.
866 Third Avenue, New York, New York 10022

Collier-Macmillan Canada, Ltd.

Library of Congress Cataloging in Publication Data

Casady, Donald Rex, (date)
   Sports activities for men.

   1. Physical education and training.   2. Sports.
I. Title.
GV341.C342   613.7'07   73-8581
ISBN 0-02-319920-2

Printing: 1 2 3 4 5 6 7 8   Year: 4 5 6 7 8 9 0

foreword

The first book designed specifically as a textbook for use in required and elective courses in physical education for all college students was published about 1950. For the most part, the book presented the history, rules, fundamental skills, and strategies associated with the activities commonly presented in college programs of physical education for all students.

During the twenty-odd years that have followed, a number of such books have appeared on the scene, attesting to the need for this type of teaching aid in physical education. In each succeeding publication, an attempt has been made to reflect the ever-widening scope of physical education, both in terms of the increased number of activities included in basic programs of physical education and in the social, psychological, and physiological significance of participation in such activities.

This volume, *Sports Activities for Men*, ranks among the most comprehensive textbooks for students in physical education produced to date. It provides detailed information about a widely diversified list of activities. The author of each chapter dealing with an activity is truly an expert in that activity. In addition, the book provides information concerning the significance and meaning of participation in physical activities of a recreational nature.

The book should provide a functional teaching and learning aid for those interested in activities that are basic to a comprehensive physical education program.

Louis E. Alley, Head
Physical Education for Men
The University of Iowa
Iowa City, Iowa

preface

Sports permeate practically all aspects of our lives in some manner. Much of our leisure is spent either engaging in or viewing sports of various kinds or in discussing sports and sporting events. This often intense interest is shared by persons in all segments of society—in America and in other nations. People interested in sports range from the beginner who is just learning how to play tennis or golf, for example, to parents who have a child playing little league baseball, to the President of the United States.

The ways in which our lives are influenced by sports have only recently received serious study. What other kinds of events can attract fifty thousand or more people to often travel long distances to a football stadium in which they are forced to sit in a confined space on uncomfortable seats, and sometimes in unpleasant weather, for three or four hours? What attraction and hold do these sports have on us, causing extremely busy men, including heads of state, high government officials, business executives, and others from all walks of life and of all ages, to deliberately take time each day or several times a week to engage in sports?

Questions of this nature are in the domain of investigators working in the area of the sociology of sport—in fact, an international organization of such investigators was formed a few years ago. This field is still in its infancy; undoubtedly, the findings of authorities will be of significant interest to all sports enthusiasts. For the present time it is perhaps sufficient to emphasize that students at all levels are constantly exposed to a large variety of sports in many situations. Because many physical education programs are largely made up of sports activities, most students are presented with opportunities to learn sports new to them and to improve their previously learned sport skills.

In Part I of this book, an attempt is made to explain the following topics: (1) The meaning of sports, physical education, and education. (2) Why physical education is offered as a part of the school curriculum at almost all levels. (3) The kinds of physical education programs in existence today and how they have evolved to their present form and structure. (4) A selected historical background of physical education in the schools, including the controversial historical concept of physical education as an essential part of education. (5) The increasingly critical need for man to engage regularly in physical activity in view of his strong inclination to lead a sedentary life in our technological space age in which labor-saving devices abound.

In order to support man's need for vigorous physical exercise, examples of various kinds of evidence, mostly positive, are cited. These include man's evolutionary and environmental background and the beneficial effects of exercise that may accrue to his health, both physiologically and psychologically.

Also examined in this part of the book are the reasons why sports are included in physical education programs and why sports have such a high level of universal popularity. Some of the roles that sports play in our modern-day society are also discussed, as are the reasons why people engage in sports and physical activities.

The next section deals with the means by which skill in sports may be efficiently acquired. The effective paths to such acquisition include practicing sound health habits, having a command of fundamental movement skills, utilizing effective training methods, incorporating correct biomechanical principles in performing sports, and utilizing some of the useful principles and theories produced in the field of motor learning.

In the last section of this part of the book some of the considerations that should be weighed in selecting sports in which to participate now and in the near and long-range future are discussed.

Familiarity with the information contained in these sections should permit the reader to understand the role of sports and physical education not only in his school life but literally for his entire lifetime. The reader must, of course, make the final judgment concerning whether or not he wishes to make regular physical activity part of his life style—something that he does or does not want to live without. He must judge the worth of habitual sports participation and, regardless of what others believe, he must evaluate its importance to him and its drawbacks. (It requires some time from each day and some bother in finding available facilities, the opportunity for competition, and teammates.) If the reader decides to increase his skill and knowledge in sports, some information is provided by means of which he can do these effectively. Additional information in choosing sports for further pursuit is provided to those readers who wish to expand their horizon of sports participation.

The author makes no claim that the material presented in the first part is complete; instead, representative information is presented, which is intended to be relatively free of bias. Even this last goal may not be possible because of the author's opinions, experiences, and personal beliefs. At any rate, selected references have been included in appropriate places in order that the reader may gather other ideas and base his judgments on information gleaned from a variety of sources.

D. R. C.

contents

Chapter		Page
	PART I	
	Introduction	
1	Sports, Physical Education, and Education	3
2	Beneficial Effects of Sports Participation	12
3	The Attraction of Sport: Why Man Engages in Sport	25
4	The Efficient Acquisition of Skill in Sports	30
5	Selecting Sports for Participation	44
	PART II	
	Individual and Team Sports	
6	Archery	53
7	Badminton	62
8	Basketball	80
9	Bowling	97
10	Casting and Angling	116
11	Dancing: Social and Square	135
12	Diving: Springboard	151
13	Diving: Skin and Scuba	171

Chapter		Page
14	Fencing	192
15	Football: Flag and Touch	201
16	Golf	217
17	Gymnastics: Apparatus	233
18	Handball	270
19	Racquetball and Paddleball	288
20	Riflery	305
21	Rugby	312
22	Soccer	330
23	Softball	347
24	Speedball	364
25	Swimming	370
26	Table Tennis	383
27	Tennis	399
28	Track and Field	421
29	Trampolining	437
30	Tumbling and Balancing	452
31	Volleyball	471
32	Weight Training and Weight Lifting	489
33	Wrestling	510

part 1

introduction

CHAPTER 1

Sports, physical education, and education

INTRODUCTION

What is the role of general physical education in the curricula of the schools and colleges of the United States? In almost all the states, physical education is required by law in all public secondary schools. Why? Almost all colleges and universities in the United States offer physical education courses on an elective basis, with credit earned in such courses counting toward the bachelor's degree. A recent survey indicated that approximately 85 per cent of the colleges and universities in the United States require their students, before being graduated, to successfully complete specified courses or to demonstrate by examination acceptable levels of proficiency in physical education. Why?

The answer to these questions can be found in the purposes for which our educational systems exist. These purposes are embedded in the philosophy that guides our educational practices in the colleges and universities. Their primary functions are to provide a liberal education and to encourage the student in the fullest possible development of his capacities as a person and as a member of society. The well-rounded development of the individual—intellectually, *physically*, emotionally, and aesthetically—is a fundamental goal of such institutions.

Physical education is included in the basic curricula of our educational institutions because it makes very essential contributions toward the well-rounded development of the individual. Some of these contributions are made in no other area of the curriculum. Physical education and its several facets—school physical recreation activities, club sports, intramural sports, and intercollegiate sports—offer opportunities for developing and maintaining a reasonable degree of physical fitness under proper supervision and guidance. They offer opportunities for developing a wide variety of neuromuscular skills such as correctly timing and stroking a ball, running, and others of use in games and sports. The mastery of a variety of neuromuscular skills enables the body to be handled easily, gracefully, and efficiently. No other area in the formal curriculum provides these opportunities.

The contributions made by physical education toward the well-rounded development of the individual are not limited to those that are purely physical in nature. In physical education opportunities also are provided for practicing and learning a variety of recreational games, sports, and other athletic activities that are of immediate value and that also can be enjoyed throughout life. Physical education offers many opportunities to practice social skills, the mastery of which are requisite to social ease and efficiency in our society. Examples of social skills are cooperation, leadership, and fair play. In addition, knowledge is acquired concerning the rules and strategies of sports, how movement is integrated into purposeful patterns, and how to appreciate expert sports performances. Other contributions include an increased understanding of how the body functions and how one behaves under a variety of situations, thus leading to increased understanding of one's own behavior and living patterns.

Physical education is an integral part of the total educational experience because it makes extremely important contributions toward the accomplishment of the fundamental goal of education: namely, the well-rounded development of the individual. The development of the individual could scarcely be called well-rounded without the contributions made by physical education.

CURRENT STATUS OF GENERAL PHYSICAL EDUCATION

Not many years ago the vast majority of colleges and universities required one or two years—and sometimes even four years—of physical education courses in order to satisfy the requirements for graduation. Recently, however, in some schools and colleges there has been a movement toward either reducing the amount of physical education needed to graduate or else eliminating it as a graduation requirement altogether.

Do these actions indicate a lessening need for college physical education in the modern-day space age? Most authorities agree that the answer to this question is *definitely not*. Man's body and systems, which over untold generations in the past became accustomed to vigorous physical activity on a daily basis, still depend heavily on regular physical activity to remain in optimum regulation during a lifetime. In our present age of labor-saving devices, much of man's work, and his avocational pursuits as well, does not afford him many opportunities for strenuous exercise or vigorous physical activity on a regular basis. The one avenue that is increasingly becoming available to all segments of American society is sports and similar types of physical recreational activity. However, in order for one to engage in these, and especially to enjoy them, it appears necessary that one be taught these kinds of activities and that one practice them (and be coached or tutored in them). Because most adults are somewhat hesitant to engage in a new activity as a beginner—because opportunities for participation and instruction are often limited for unskilled adults, and because many adults, during most of their working life, are quite busy and often believe that they cannot spare time to learn new recreational pursuits—the optimum time to learn physical recreational activities is while one is in school.

Why, then, despite these sobering facts, have some colleges and universities reduced their physical education requirements? Several complex reasons are involved. Many large colleges and universities have had the physical education requirement reduced, or even eliminated, by the personnel within the physical education department. They took this step because they did not have sufficient facilities to handle the thousands of freshmen students who would have been enrolled in required physical education classes. These steps were taken usually quite reluctantly, but physical education personnel believed that they had to be able to give a quality experience to these students or none at all. Probably the outstanding reason for this trend has been the fact that in many colleges and universities in the United States, students and faculty have questioned whether any requirement of a general nature should be applied to all students. Hence, requirements in foreign languages, in writing and speaking, and in core courses in general studies areas have been questioned and many times eliminated. Where the philosophy that no general collegewide requirement should exist, the physical education requirement was often abolished along with others.

An additional reason for reducing or abolishing the physical education requirement that many physical educators as well as faculty members in other disciplines have cited, has been that if students are exposed to good physical education programs in grade schools and in high schools, by the time they reach college status, they should be fairly well physically educated and should have acquired positive attitudes toward physical education and, hence, will regularly engage in physical activity. Therefore, no requirement should be needed by students with such a background. The strongest argument against this position is that those students who probably most need physical activity and have a poor physical education background are the ones who are most apt to avoid physical education if it is offered only on an elective basis. Countering this argument is the possibility that students may not benefit greatly from being required to engage in physical education if they do not wish to do so.

All these observations mirror a growing awareness on the part of the American public in recognizing that college students play an adult role in the functions of society and, hence, should assume the privileges and responsibilities of adults. In such a role, they should have the opportunity to make their own decisions concerning whether or not they wish to take physical education or any other particular subject in college.

Despite this situation, it should be emphasized that most faculty members and college administrators believe that physical education is a highly worthwhile subject; it is supported in almost all colleges and universities, at least on an elective basis, and is a requirement in a significant majority of the colleges and universities in the United States. Accompanying this recognition has been the fact that more and more student services are being offered to college students. Intramural sports have shown a tremendous rise in popularity and participation. Club sports, almost unknown a decade ago, are exceedingly popular in most colleges and universities. All these indicate that college officials recognize that athletics, sports, and physical recreational activity are wholesome and worthwhile for all college students, not just for the elite 5 per cent or so who are sufficiently skilled and talented to make the varsity athletic teams. This recognition, coupled with the fact that intercollegiate athletics are facing severe financial problems—problems which are so serious that it is almost impossible to expand the scope of such programs—either in the number of students participating or in the number of sports included—has lead school and college officials to be aware of the great need for introducing and encouraging a large variety of sports for a diverse group of students who have many different individual needs, interests, and abilities.

One of the problems that sometimes bewilders the college student and the general public is the distinction between physical education and intercollegiate athletics. Some believe that physical education and athletics are the same. Although the two have a very close relationship, this is not at all true. Most believe that the instructional program prepares the student to go at least past the beginner stage and engage in a sport with some skill, to have sufficient knowledge to improve his skill with practice, and to be able to participate enjoyably in the sport. From this broad base, in which a 100 per cent participation by all college students is often cited as the goal, the next step upward is intramural sports and club sports, for which a higher degree of skill is often called, but in which anyone who is really interested can generally find opportunities to participate on a regular basis. The highest level of participation is intercollegiate athletics in which the athletes are highly skilled—they often train twelve months of the year for their particular sport—and they are intensely interested in winning. One philosopher has differentiated sports and athletics in the following way: Sports are played between friends; one wants to give the opponent the same opportunity and chance for winning that one would like the opponent to give him. Sports are mainly played for the fun of playing, and although winning may be important it is not all-important. On the other hand, the foremost goal in athletics is winning. The athletics competitor may not feel at all friendly toward his opponent and usually believes that he is entitled to do anything that the rules allow in order to win. One example of this is that in a friendly sporting match, such as a game of tennis, one does not see a participating player faking an injury in order to gain additional time out between plays, such as may be done in college or professional football.

COMPOSITION OF PRESENT-DAY PHYSICAL EDUCATION PROGRAMS

Today, in America, most general physical education programs at the college (and high school) level are similar in appearance and composition. The main differences that do occur are often the result of differing philosophies concerning what purposes or objectives should be achieved through these programs. When separate programs are operated for men only and for women only, other differences can be found; however, there appears to be a strong trend toward having coeducational programs and classes. In many instances activities and offerings that comprise a physical education program are considered to be tools (means to an end) that can be employed to accomplish other goals: improved social skills and behavioral patterns, an optimum level of physical fitness, how to move one's body gracefully, and so on. Many students in such programs, however, contend that learning and participation in sports and activities bring considerable enjoyment and satisfaction; any other values derived are definitely secondary.

Beginning about five decades ago, physical education programs began to become sports-centered with sports (and games) being the primary vehicle utilized to accomplish various goals and objectives. At the college level, sports are now the heart of most programs of physical education. For several years team sports—in part because they required fewer facilities and accommodated large numbers—constituted a large part of the college program. During the last few years, however, individual and dual sports (the lifetime sports) have predominated many college programs because these are suitable for participation during the remainder of the students' lives.

Programs of physical education for men have often contained special physical fitness or conditioning classes in which the goal has been to attain and maintain a reasonable level of physical fitness. This has often been combined with informative material and lectures designed to give reasons why one should be physically fit and regularly engage in strenuous physical activity. Sometimes this information is included in *foundation courses*, which are designed to acquaint the student with some important physiological and anatomical information about the workings of his body, ways of evaluating its present status, and inculcating sound health practices. Jogging may be one of the outgrowths of this phase.

Although physical education programs for women have been similar in content, markedly more emphasis has been placed on dance, especially modern dance, as a means of expressing one's self and enabling the dancer to interpret and create. In the past, women's programs tended not to emphasize physical fitness; recently, increasing attention has been devoted to form and figure control. In addition, significantly more attention has been given recently to coeducational sports and club and intercollegiate sports competition rather than intramural sports.

For both men and women, more and more programs are focusing on the exotic sports that are usually not offered below the college level. Some of these sports include camping and outdoor living, Hatha Yoga, horseback riding, judo, karate, mountaineering, orienteering, rock climbing, sailing, skating, snow skiing, sport parachuting, water skiing, and even flight training. These kinds of activities often make heavy use of community areas and resources, which are what will be available to the student after leaving college, and traditional scheduling times have often been ignored with increasing use made of evening and night classes, weekends, or week-long periods. In addition, there appears to be a definite trend toward partially or completely exempting college students from any requirement in general physical education if they are able to pass proficiency examinations. A second trend is that of permitting students to elect activities of their choice when they select their physical education classes.

In most college programs of physical education, attempts are usually made to service those students who are temporarily or permanently unable to engage safely in most activities. Special, adaptive, or remedial classes are often formed in order to help such students improve their condition—if this is possible and medically approved—or else engage in activity that is not deleterious to them. Students with certain kinds of heart conditions and asthma, or who are postoperative, or who have unstable knee joints, and the like, are often assigned to classes where they can get individual attention and an individualized program.

In the past, programs of physical education were often composed mainly of calisthenics and gymnastics, which were designed to "improve the student's health and to teach discipline." Student enjoyment of the activities was given little consideration. Much of this program content can be directly traced to its foreign counterpart, from which it was taken. Physical education did not get started in American colleges until after the Civil War ended (about the time intercollegiate athletics began) and then it spread slowly at first. For many years the physical education instructors were MD's who were strongly health oriented. Because America had no native system of physical education, foreign systems of physical education were adopted.

The two chief systems of gymnastics (the modern term would be physical education) at this time were the German system and the Swedish system. German gymnastics involved the use of heavy gymnastic apparatus (such as rings, horizontal bar, and parallel bars) and stunts to sustain interest and present a challenge; games were included, and music could be used. The Swedish system was a set of calisthenic exercises with held positions that were done in unison to voice command in which light apparatus or no apparatus was employed. It was considered quite formal with no individuality permitted, but it was claimed that it corrected posture defects and was medically beneficial.

Immigrants from both of these countries had settled in various parts of the United States. They brought with them and retained their system of "gymnastics." These were gradually adopted by the public schools and especially by the colleges. After 1900, however, these systems were gradually modified and Americanized and slowly evolved into our modern system of physical education, which included games and sports as well as calisthenics.

SPORTS, PHYSICAL EDUCATION, AND EDUCATION

The average person appears to make little distinction between sports, athletics, and physical education. Although it is true that considerable overlap occurs among them, physical educators and other authorities usually consider each of these as serving different and distinct purposes, even though the same kinds of activities may be employed to achieve these separate goals.

Sports and some forms of athletics are often utilized in physical education programs to accomplish implicit or explicit objectives, many of which are often student selected. Physical education activities are considered to be suitable for all to participate in—they are not restricted to the highly skilled athlete who may have received intensive training and coaching for a period of several months or even several years. Numerous opportunities are available in all three of the preceding categories of recreational physical activities for the participant to learn or acquire many worthwhile skills. Such benefits are more often purposefully stressed and consciously sought after in physical education than in sports or athletics, however.

Some of the benefits that may be accrued from the preceding triad include (1) an increased knowledge of the body and how it operates, (2) an enhancing of aesthetic appreciation, (3) learning how to perform effectively the motor skills used in daily living, (4) learning how to cooperate (or compete) in attempting to win or to attain common goals with teammates, (5) acquiring an appreciation for skilled, graceful human movement in everyday life and in art and sports, whether within the individual or in others, and (6) developing sound physiological functioning and organic health through regular vigorous physical activity.

The term *sports* is sometimes restricted to athletic activities in which amateurs (which has the old-time meaning of gentlemen) engage and in which they observe the golden rule, taking no unfair advantage of the opponent, as is usually true when friends compete in a sport (as is epitomized in tennis and volleyball play). This would include calling a rules infraction on oneself. In *athletics*, on the other hand, it is considered acceptable to take the fullest advantage of whatever the rules will allow, with winning being the primary consideration and other aspects being secondary. Although exceptions to this certainly exist, such as in professional golf, this winning at all costs is best epitomized in professional team sports such as football, basketball, and hockey.

Because lifelong participation is the goal that hopefully will result from engaging in physical education, the attitudes and behavior patterns exhibited in sports, rather than in athletics, are the ones that are to be pursued. Such experiences can be truly educational and enriching. This concept will be expanded and further discussed in Chapters 2 and 3.

THE HISTORY OF PHYSICAL EDUCATION AND SPORTS

The concept that the function of education is to promote the well-rounded development of the individual, and that physical education plays an indispensable role in promoting such development, is not, by any means, new. Although the meaning and the function of physical education have varied in past periods of history, man has always engaged in spontaneous and planned physical activities of many types. Such movements as running, throwing, jumping, climbing, striking, and dodging in which most people engage are regarded as fundamental movements and are spoken of by some as basic human activities.

In discussing physical education and its historical background, the reader should keep in mind that the term *physical education* has several meanings and it has been known by several different names in the past. During some periods of history much of education was actually what we now call physical education. Gymnastics, physical training, physical culture, and movement education are some of the labels assigned to physical education; they include intramural sports and interscholastic sports in their broadest definitions.

In prehistoric times physical education was, without doubt, the chief means and kind of education. At that time education was aimed at the cultivation of such specific skills and activities as hunting, warfare, and other pursuits of importance in the life of uncivilized and semi-civilized man.

Man of Western civilization has evolved slowly to his present attitude toward physical education and sports and their role, if any, in formal education and the school curriculum. In the so-called Golden Age of Ancient Greece, physical activities and sports of sundry types were held in high esteem and were considered to be on an equal plane with the other phases of the total education of man. Gymnastics (which today we would call physical education), music, oratory, and academic subjects were all considered necessary in the complete education of the well-rounded citizen. Greek drama contained a significant element of dance. Hence, physical activities and sports were held in high esteem by the citizenry of ancient Greece and were indeed used to worship their gods. The Panhellenic Games, in general, and the Ancient Olympic Games, in particular, were held in honor of various gods. Hence, for more than a thousand years the ancient Greeks considered sports, physical education, and exercise to be of vital importance in the daily life of man. Women and slaves, however, were largely ignored in these considerations.

The Romans, in general, tended to be extremely practical in their views of the purpose of education and the role of physical education within education. If something did not have immediate, practical value, they tended to believe it was of limited worth at best. However, for many years they accorded physical education a high but limited place in education—a common saying in those days was to describe a person who was completely ignorant as being someone who could neither read nor swim.

The citizens of ancient Rome gradually changed in their attitudes and beliefs concerning the importance of sports, physical education, and military training in the everyday life of man and as a part of the school curriculum. In the early days of the Roman Empire, most male citizens believed that it was necessary to have physical education, mainly in the form of military training and exercise, as part of their everyday life. This attitude was partially based on the belief that the citizen should be fit and prepared to be an effective soldier for the Empire. However, the Romans tended to overemphasize military training (and neglect a well-rounded intellectual development) and were not greatly concerned with other aspects of physical education. Even though this belief prevailed for many years, some time after the Roman Empire had expanded over most of the civilized world, a tendency developed for the male citizenry to avoid services with the armed forces, and to depend on other nationals to fulfill this obligation for them. Gradually, many of the citizens of Rome lessened or quit their participation in physical activity and military training and instead preferred to be entertained by large spectacles at the circus and amphitheater, including gladiator fights, men fighting wild animals, and similar forms of brutal entertainment.

During the Dark, or Middle, Ages formal education was withheld from the majority of the people. Those who received a formal education were mainly those who went into the clergy. Because asceticism arose soon after

Sports, Physical Education, and Education 7

Christianity began flourishing in Rome, the Church generally advocated a neglect of the physical self, including nonparticipation in sports and the omitting of unnecessary physical activity. In general, the ascetics believed that in order to glorify the spirit and to worship God to the fullest, the body should be neglected, because it was the seat of worldly desires and a tool of the devil. Consequently, it was common for ascetics to fast several days in a row and in other ways to neglect their bodies. During this time physical education of a sort flourished because of the system of knighthood in which severe physical training of a military nature was imposed on the pages, squires, and others who desired to become knights. For these people all types of combat training and physical activity were part of the regular daily routine.

During this period of time, physical education and sports in the colleges and universities had no formal recognition whatsoever. However, the college students of this era tended to be boisterous, and in addition, often pitted themselves against the townmen. They often engaged in mass football-like games where as many as several hundred players might comprise each side. In addition, they played other games and even rioted, but these were frowned upon by university officials and were in no way considered to be part of the curriculum of a college or university.

During all this time, and until well into the nineteenth century, girls and women were given little consideration and were not generally thought to be worthy of an education. Beginning in the sixteenth and seventeenth centuries, Humanism began to play a role in the thinking of the prominent philosophers, educators, and some of the leaders in the European nations. The Humanists believed that education should prepare one for life in general and not just for a vocation. Some of the leading Humanists began to advocate that while in school children should have physical activity and should engage in some type of physical education in order to be well rounded and to offset the tensions arising from engaging in their studies. These beliefs arose in part because of the writings of the ancient Greek (and Roman) writers and philosophers who often advocated such educational practices. During this period the school existed mainly for the children of the middle class and nobility.

The practice of actually including physical education and sports in the school did not arrive until the beginning of the nineteenth century when a few schools started what we would call a physical education program and sometimes an intramural sports program as part of their school curriculum. Such programs were probably most widespread in what is present-day Germany, Sweden, and Denmark.

The British, who were relatively well insulated on their island and protected by a strong navy, were less compelled than their European neighbors to force their male citizens to engage in and practice military training during much of their adult lives. This fact, coupled with a favorable climate and an early entry into the Industrial Age with some leisure time resulting, enabled the British to develop sports and sports competition, particularly in the private schools and colleges. Thus, interscholastic and intercollegiate competition got an early start in such sports as soccer, track and field, rowing, cricket, and rugby. The players of these school sports and out-of-school sports such as golf and tennis were mainly from the middle and upper classes. In fact considerable effort was made to keep working people (manual laborers and artisans) ineligible to compete in sports and athletics because the muscular strength derived from their work was thought to give them an unfair advantage and because sports were only for "gentlemen." As the working class gained increased leisure time they more and more participated in sports, but their progress was slow. By 1900, they had made marked progress in attaining eligibility and today little distinction is made in most sports concerning class eligibility. However, both in America and Great Britain, some remnants of the past are still thought to remain in the definition of an amateur and in the eligibility rules for competition in the modern Olympic Games.

In the United States, participation in sports and eligibility for such participation has followed a path closely parallel to the one trod in Great Britain. In part because some of the people and schools in the United States adopted gymnastics programs from other European nations, physical education in the schools of America became fairly well established by 1900. This was partly related to the widespread adoption of free public education, including the senior high schools. The colleges and universities tended to be the leaders in this. As related earlier in this chapter, the programs of physical education gradually evolved from the European system of calisthenics to our modern system with its large sports content.

HISTORICAL CONCEPTS: PHYSICAL EDUCATION IS ESSENTIAL

Throughout the history of physical education in all its manifold forms, one fact is of paramount importance: The rulers and leaders of all nations that were endangered by other nations or who planned conquests of other nations desired most ardently to have physically fit male citizens who were able to be strong, well-trained soldiers with excellent combat skills. Because, until recent times, combat consisted of physical encounter, and because during much of man's history only small states, kingdoms, cities, and feudal estates were in existence, a constant need for physically strong soldiers existed. Hence, as a part of military training, physical education, although often not present in the schools or in formal education, was strongly encouraged and often demanded by the rulers and military leaders. Even today, when armies are completely mechanized and the combatants are often remote from one another, physically fit, strong soldiers are still the desired goal. In fact, during periods of wartime, the nations' leaders place great stress on all citizens being physically fit, and the place of physical education in the school curriculum is heavily emphasized.

The growth of nationalism and its emphasis usually gives rise to a nation having a strong physical education and sports program for its citizens. The Russians, for example, have successfully utilized sports competition and the modern Olympic Games to demonstrate the superiority of their athletes and way of life. Hitler also made heavy use of physical education and sports in attempting to forge an all-conquering Third Reich and a superior race.

In ancient times, the Greeks realized and wrote of the need for physical education for their male citizens. The ideas of the Athenians concerning the role of physical education in education were quite similar to the ideas of modern educators. Plato wrote, "The results of a good physical education are not limited to the body alone, but may extend even to the soul itself." Aristotle, a pupil of Plato, theorized that the highest aim of education was to fit people for the right enjoyment of leisure. Aristotle divided the school curriculum into four areas, one of which was gymnastics. Gymnastics included the entire range of physical education activities employed in the training of the Athenian boy. The Greeks believed that engaging in gymnastics was a means of attaining beauty, symmetry of body, grace, and the complete development and harmony of body and soul.

The Humanists arose during the Renaissance; in discussing and studying Greek and Roman civilizations they were impressed with the place of physical man in those societies as compared to his place (or lack of place) in their era. They believed and advocated that the mind and body need recreation and that long hours of study should be interspersed with exercise and play.

The Realist Humanists (sixteenth and seventeenth centuries) believed that instead of Greek and Latin works, the real things of life should be studied; thus paving the way for later scientific study and investigation. They thought that a person should be trained to meet the conditions of society. John Milton, the English poet, proposed that the day of a student should be divided into three parts: studies, exercises, and diet. The Sense Realists advocated education for all—rich and poor and both sexes—and that the purpose of education, which should be through experience not reading, was to develop the faculties of both the mind and the body.

The eighteenth century marked the emergence of educational philosophies that again emphasized the vital role of physical education as an essential phase of the total education of the individual. Jean Jacques Rousseau, the French philosopher who instigated educational reforms in Europe, formulated educational programs that were concerned with the physical as well as the mental aspects of living. He believed it impossible to divide educational activities according to their physical and intellectual values—the two were inseparable to him. John Locke, an English contemporary of Rousseau, made famous the expression, "a sound mind in a sound body," thus giving further emphasis to the need for physical education. The work of these and other educators initiated public acceptance of the idea of the integrated person and the importance of the development of all aspects of the individual.

Johann Heinrich Pestolozzi (1746-1827), the Swiss educator who laid the groundwork for modern pedagogy, believed that mental faculties were sharpened by physical exercises and thus had a positive effect on learning.

Johann Basedom, one of the first physical education teachers in Europe, believed that nature demanded that the child be given time for play and bodily exercise that normal physical growth is more important in early years than mental training—and that there are intellectual and moral values to be derived from the playing of games. He scheduled gymnastics daily at the Philanthropium school, which opened in 1774.

HISTORICAL CONCEPTS: PHYSICAL EDUCATION IS NON-ESSENTIAL

It should be pointed out that physical education has not always been regarded as an essential part of the total education of the individual. In ancient China with the advent of religions such as Confucianism and Buddhism, intellectualism was stressed while physical education and individual development were de-emphasized for all but children and warriors. The only exceptions were dancing in which older students and adults engaged, and Cong Fu medical exercises, which were supposed to keep the organs in good shape, promote long life, and help assure immortality of the soul.

During the centuries of the so-called Dark Ages, physical activities of a recreational type, many games, and most types of physical education as it presently exists were actively discouraged in most European nations, especially in the schools and universities. Educational systems of that time chiefly emphasized the acquisition of knowledge; the Greek and Roman writers were studied mainly for their style, not their content.

Religious teachings also discouraged participation in physical education activities within the school and the Church. Dualism, a concept in which the mind and body are considered to be completely separate and independent of each other, was one of the prevalent beliefs that further encouraged this narrow point of view. Dualism rejected the idea that the physical aspect of the individual should be developed, because this aspect was thought to be unrelated to the individual's mental or spiritual functioning. These beliefs continued to be held until long after the Renaissance. In addition, ascetism has for centuries adversely affected the views of many concerning sport and play. The Church instilled the belief that one should live the "good" life while on Earth, denying oneself all pleasures, in order to reap forever the rewards of Heaven after death. Thus, the physical aspect of life tended to be neglected in favor of the spiritual aspect.

Here in America, the Puritans impeded for quite some time the acceptance of the need for physical activities of a recreational nature. The Puritans believed that play and the recreational use of leisure time were sinful and, hence, avoided such pursuits. Hard work and a faultless spiritual life were their goals. Their influence gradually diminished, until about one century ago educators began to include physical education as a part of the curriculum while recognizing the value of play periods during the school day. Only until recently, however, has the influence of the Puritans been completely dispelled; now it is common practice to schedule sports contests on Sunday (Sabbath Day) and to permit dancing in the schools.

During the Great Depression of the 1930s and during the current era of problems in obtaining adequate school funds, suggestions and outcries were and are being made to reduce or eliminate altogether physical education and sports programs in the schools. Because some people are not convinced of the educational values and the worthiness of these programs they frequently suggest eliminating them to reduce educational expenditures.

Since the turn of the century, scientific advances in such fields as physiology, medicine, psychology, mental health, and sociology have repeatedly emphasized the need and importance of frequent physical activity and of the social experience obtained from participation in sports and physical education. This need has been especially dramatized by the findings of a multitude of studies conducted within the past two decades.

THE NEED FOR PHYSICAL EDUCATION IN THE SPACE AGE

An examination of the evolutionary background of man and the conditions under which he now lives provides evidence that it is more important than ever before that physical education activities be included as a part of the educational experience. The fact that physical activity is a constant need has been engendered by countless generations of our forebears who by necessity had daily to participate in multitudinous physical tasks.

Man's evolution has caused him to adjust to an environment composed of fresh air, sunshine, and much physical activity daily. His evolution better fits him to thrive in an environment of constant physical activity than in one that demands constant mental activity with no relief of stress or tension through the medium of play, exercise, and physical activity.

Recreation, especially physical recreation, seems to be a necessity to wash away, if only briefly, the cares and worries of life. In order to achieve mental relaxation and an accompanying freedom from worry and stress, the best route appears to be physical relaxation or a complete change of pace physically. This can usually be effectively accomplished through play and physical exercise.

Findings in the field of psychosomatic medicine give strong indications that our mind and body are inseparable and that each needs the other. Numerous medical cases have been studied that indicate that a person can be seriously ill even when no organic causes can be found; instead, the illness is unconsciously caused by the person's mind.

Karl Menninger, the renowned psychiatrist, has stated his conviction that the person who cannot play is potentially dangerous to society. Learning how to play often seems to be something that must be achieved before full adulthood is attained.

Like all animals, man has many muscles and they were designed for muscular activity. Thanks to his highly developed nervous system and his amazing control of his movements, particularly trained movements, he is capable of an infinite variety of movements. Man's biological heritage implies a deep need for physical activity and exercise. If he ignores this and fails to exercise, far-reaching implications of changed and reduced physiological functions occur.

The ease and comfort possible in our modern society can cause the physically lazy victim to experience *decreases* in the efficiency (and size) of his muscular system, and in his organic vitality—his heart rate and breathing rate increase and he pays an increased price for the same amount of work or exercise.

In the next chapter appears a discussion of the beneficial long-term effects that result from engaging in vigorous physical activity on a regular basis. These benefits clearly establish the need by man for physical activity in the Space Age.

An article written by Dr. Robert N. Irving, which appeared in the *American College of Sports Medicine Newsletter*, entitled, "Leisure—The Deadly Status"[1] summarizes quite well the dilemma facing the modern American. Dr. Irving writes,

> It has always been a symbol of one's status to avoid physical labor—by hiring others to do it, or, as is the case now, to use machinery. It is commonplace to ride the lawnmower and escalator, or hail the taxi and city bus, to use the family car in place of the four-block walk. This ability to pay for the machinery or to hire others to perform the work of human muscles has reached the proportions of a deadly threat.
>
> The human being has evolved through 250,000,000 years, but he is still a creature possessed of about 40 per cent muscle. He has lungs with which to supply himself with oxygen and a blood supply with which to transport the oxygen. Keeping this apparatus functioning is a biological necessity but most "status-seekers" avoid it and end up in a casket way ahead of their time for their folly.

It seems also very odd that we have more time for leisure now than at any other time in our history but at the same time seem to take less of this available time for our use in self-preservation.

Selected References

The Ancient World: To 300 A.D. Ed. by Paul J. Alexander. New York: Macmillan, Inc., 1968.

Aspects of Contemporary Sport Sociology. Ed. by Gerald S. Kenyon. Chicago: The Athletic Institute, 1969.

Barck, Oscar Theodore, Jr., and Hugh Talmage Lefler. *Colonial America.* New York: Macmillan, Inc., 1968.

Dulles, Foster Rhea. *A History of Recreation: America Learns to Play.* New York: Meredith, 1965.

Five Great Dialogues—Plato. Trans. by B. Jowett and ed. by Louise R. Loomis. New York: Walter J. Block, 1942.

Glader, Eugene A. "A Study of Amateurism in Sports." Unpublished Ph.D. dissertation, University of Iowa, Iowa City, 1970.

Hackensmith, C. W. *History of Physical Education.* New York: Harper, 1966.

Loy, John W., Jr. and Gerald S. Kenyon. *Sport, Culture, and Society: A Reader on the Sociology of Sport.* New York: Macmillan, Inc., 1971.

The Medieval World: 300–1300. 2nd ed. Ed. by Norman F. Cantor. New York: Macmillan, Inc., 1968.

Paterson, Ann, and Edmond C. Hallberg. *Background Readings for Physical Education.* New York: Holt, 1965.

Renaissance and Reformation: 1300–1648. Ed. by G. R. Elton. New York: Macmillan, Inc., 1968.

Rice, Emmett A., John L. Hutchinson, and Mabel Lee. *A Brief History of Physical Education.* 4th ed. New York: Ronald, 1958.

Sage, George H. *Sports and American Society: Selected Readings.* Reading, Mass.: Addison-Wesley, 1970.

Siedentop, Daryl. *Physical Education: Introductory Analysis.* Dubuque, Iowa: Brown, 1972.

Singer, Robert N., David R. Lamb, John W. Loy, Jr., Robert M. Malina, and Seymour Kleinman. *Physical Education: An Interdisciplinary Approach.* New York: Macmillan, Inc., 1972.

Slusher, Howard S. *Man, Sport, and Existence: A Critical Analysis.* Philadelphia: Lea, 1967.

Slusher, Howard S., and Aileene S. Lockhart. *Anthology of Contemporary Readings: An Introduction to Physical Education.* Dubuque, Iowa: Brown, 1970.

Sport in the Socio-Cultural Process. Ed. by M. Marie Hart. Dubuque, Iowa: Brown, 1972.

Van Dalen, Deobold B., and Bruce L. Bennett. *A World History of Physical Education* (second edition). Englewood Cliffs, N.J.: Prentice-Hall, 1971.

---

[1] (Nov. 1967) Vol. 2, No. 4, reprinted with permission from the *Physical Fitness Newsletter*, Series XIII, No. 8.

CHAPTER 2

Beneficial effects of sports participation

In the past few years a multitude of scientific evidence and findings, derived from a variety of sources, has been produced that attest to the values forthcoming from regularly participating in vigorous physical activity. Although this evidence is incomplete, there is considerable support for the viewpoint that meaningful physiological and psychological effects can be derived from regular sports participation.

One assumption is made in presenting this information: that is, that sports participation will be regular and of sufficient duration and/or severity to elicit sweating, even in a cool environment (65°F.), and a heart rate of at least 135 beats per minute. One's heart rate is readily determined by palpating either the radial arterial pulse at the wrist or the carotid arterial pulse at the side of the neck. Using the maximal amount of oxygen that the tissues of the body can consume as an index of physiological stress, the activity must result in a response that is at least 50 per cent of this value. The reader should realize that participation in a wide variety of athletic or physical endeavors can cause most of the benefits discussed in this chapter to accrue to the participant. Because this book is about sports participation and because for most people engaging in sports is a very enjoyable type of physical activity, the reader may safely assume that these benefits will occur because of regular sports participation.

The chapter ends by stating some beneficial effects assumed or claimed to accrue from participation in sports or physical activity but for which little or no scientific documentation has been produced. The reader is invited to draw his own conclusions concerning the worth of these claims.

Of the various studies reviewed, only a brief summary (or overview) and the main findings, not the details, are presented. By no means is an exhaustive review made of all the studies available in these areas; instead, only selected representative investigations have been cited.

The question of how much evidence or proof is needed before a verdict can be fairly reached is an intriguing one, and one for which no general concensus can be attained. As is often true in jury trials, absolute proof is rarely forthcoming; alternative explanations can usually be found. This question particularly applies to research involving people, who are highly complex, individualistic, and have variable backgrounds. The question of the effects of exercise on the human body is complicated because a variety of factors interact simultaneously in determining the body's state of being. Unlike research in some areas, the effect of only one variable, such as exercise, is almost impossible to isolate in order to study it independently of all other variables. Instead, usually several variables—having different possible effects and each perhaps affecting different people in different ways—must be investigated strenuously. Thus, in a study on the effects of strenuous sports participation in reducing excessive amounts of cholesterol in the blood, other factors that may have an effect would include body weight or degree of obesity, daily stress, age, and number of cigarettes smoked each day. Despite these difficulties a significant amount of evidence has been accumulated about this chapter topic.

A further note should be injected for the reader's contemplation. Practically all research deals with small samples which are obtained from large populations. How representative sample findings are of the parent population is always unknown to some degree. Complicating this issue is the fact that medical studies are often conducted on animal subjects, making it particularly difficult to extrapolate the findings and apply them to Homo sapiens.

The final complication worthy of mention is the fact that sample research is based on the findings that apply to the sample group as a whole. Quite often one or more individuals within the group have findings that are contrary to what is true of the group considered as a whole. This means that many of the findings produced in studies of man have individual exceptions—in drug studies these, in some cases, are termed *side effects*. It is almost impossible to predict who will fall into the main group and who may be an exception to the rule. This stumbling block is perhaps truer of psychological research than physiological or medical research and may in part be a reflection of the inability of the investigator to control all the important variables that can have an effect on the outcomes of his study.

A consideration that particularly applies to psychological, social-psychological, and sociological research findings is the fact that some effects (beneficial or otherwise) are practically impossible to measure on an objective scale that is either qualitative or quantitative. The problem is similar to the ones encountered in describing the color red to a person who has been blind all his life, or having a group decide which of two kinds of food tastes best, or in determining whether it is most enjoyable to watch baseball, basketball, or football contests. How can one scientifically measure and evaluate if strenuous sports participation makes one feel better, makes life more worthwhile, or enriches one's life?

NATURE OF SPORTS PARTICIPATION EFFECTS

It should be pointed out that many of the effects of strenuous physical exertion that occur in sports or other physical activities produce transitory effects that may not be long-lasting in nature. This is particularly true of most of the biological effects that result from vigorous exercise. However, the immediate effects of exercise, such as an accelerated heart beat, an increased rate and depth of breathing, and the like, will not be discussed. These immediate exercise responses, which occur almost as soon as strenuous physical activity begins, occur in both the trained and the untrained person, varying mainly in the quality and depth of response. These kinds of responses are akin to eating or sleeping—regardless of how much one eats or sleeps during a given day, one still has hunger and a need for sleep the following day. Instead, the intermediate-range effects and especially the long-term effects of exercise will be presented. Again, however, the persistance of many of these effects has not been repeatedly measured within the same groups of subjects in order to obtain a record of their permanence. The method that has generally been employed is to obtain measurements shortly after long-term sports participation begins, or, especially in psychological and sociological studies, soon after it has ceased.

IMMEDIATE AND DELAYED NEEDS

The long-term benefits that can be derived from regular participation in vigorous sports and exercise are often not of immediate great value to the college-age participant. For this reason he often does not appreciate the protective mechanisms that he may be developing. While in college most students enjoy at least reasonably good physical health, have an abundance of vitality, do not usually have an overweight problem, are reasonably fit and hence unfamiliar with the feeling of being physically unfit, and in general have a zest for life. However, these students are now building the foundations upon which their future well-being will depend in no small measure. Although it is difficult to prepare for a future that is ten, twenty, or more years ahead, this preparation can pay rich dividends. As a bonus, however, as will be shown in this chapter, many immediately useful and enjoyable benefits can be expected to occur; these can be of considerable value to the college student.

PHYSIOLOGICAL HEALTH BENEFITS

In contrast to the sedentary person, the physically active person, including the sports participant, if he regularly obtains a sufficient amount of exercise that requires a strong cardiovascular response (wind or endurance), should, over the long term, benefit in the following ways:

1. An improvement in the feeling of well-being.
2. A reduction in the possibility and in the severity of cardiovascular disorders.
3. A lessened probability of being overweight, obese, or suffering from the diseases associated with being overweight.
4. Increased resistance against stress, fatigue, and neuromuscular tension.
5. Increased muscular strength, flexibility, breathing capacity, and lowered systolic blood pressures and resting heart rates.
6. Less incidence of low back pain.
7. Improved ability to cope with emergencies requiring strength and endurance.
8. An improved physical appearance.

One of the most obvious benefits that can be derived from participating regularly in vigorous sports, exercise, and/or physical activity is in preventing coronary heart disease—and should it occur in lessening its convalescent time or fatality rate. At the present time, it is estimated that 55 to 60 per cent of the people in the United States who die yearly die because of coronary illness. The mechanisms underlying coronary heart disease are many and some are associated in a variety of ways with the sedentary living habits that many adults develop in our technological, labor-saving society, and with the longer life spans experienced by present-day Americans. Such illnesses are often called heart attack, stroke, hypertensive heart disease, congestive heart failure, and similar terms. Coronary heart disease falls under the domain of hypokinetic disease, which seems to be induced by inactivity and results in bodily and emotional ills.

The causes of coronary heart disease apparently develop quite early in life, as evidenced by the results of autopsy studies. For example, autopsies of soldiers (largely in their late teens and twenties) who were killed in combat during the Korean War indicated that most of them showed at least some signs of coronary heart disease. This usually took the form of atherosclerosis, which is a narrowing of the arteries, with an accompanying loss of elasticity of the arterial walls. Similar findings have been found from autopsies performed on Chilian men and women who died in automobile accidents and British pilots who were killed in air crashes.

Dr. Kenneth Cooper, author of *The New Aerobics*, has stated that as many as three-fourths of all people in the United States die of some manifestation of atherosclerosis (hardening of the arteries). This health problem begins to become evident by heart attacks in the thirties age group and it is widespread in the forties and fifties age groups. A much larger incidence of young men are affected than are young women; this difference tends to disappear after women go through their menopause and lose their special hormonal protection.

PHYSIOLOGICAL FACTORS INVOLVED IN HEART DISEASE

The heart, circulatory system, and the blood form the transport system for getting fuel to the body cells. Hemoglobin carries to the tissues of the body the oxygen passed to the blood from the lungs. Oxygen is used by the cells to convert food into chemical energy of a useable form, which energy in turn is utilized when physical work is done. Under normal circumstances, the physical capacity of an individual is limited more by the flow of blood and its distribution to active tissues than by the amount of air inspired by the lungs.

The heart is composed of muscle tissue (myocardium) and it must have a continuous blood supply, which is furnished by the coronary arteries, not from the blood that is pumped through the heart. Deposits of fatty substances along the inside wall of the blood vessels, which are believed to contribute to atherosclerosis, begin to occur early in adult life. These deposits contain cholesterol, which is always present within the blood. The normal amount of cholesterol in the blood stream is between 100 to 250 milligrams per 100 milliliters of blood (mg per cent). Concentrations higher than 250 mg per cent should be a source for concern, because if the coronary arteries become narrower and are eventually plugged by a traveling blood clot (embolism), symptoms associated with a coronary heart attack can result. If the blood supply to a specific area of the myocardium (heart muscle tissue) is reduced, eschemia results, anoxia (lack of oxygen) occurs, and subsequently portions of the cardiac tissue will begin to die (becomes necrotic). A myocardial infarct, or heart attack, then occurs. If an inadequate supply of blood is distributed to the heart, pain often occurs and the individual is unable to continue his present task.

CORONARY HEART DISEASE

A general conclusion resulting from the numerous studies dealing with coronary heart disease—who its most likely candidates are and its causes (especially, the lack of physical activity)—has been incorporated by Drs. Kattus, cardiologist, and Taylor, a long-time investigator in this area, in their Draft Statement for a 1969 White House Conference on coronary heart disease and preventative and rehabilitation measures.

> A considerable body of evidence suggests that exercise lack is a major contributing factor in the pathogenesis of the most widespread degenerative disease entity of our time, namely arteriosclerosis and its most lethal manifestation, ischemic heart disease. Epidomiologic studies suggest that populations that habitually do vigorous exercise have less ischemic heart disease than inactive populations. Thus, there appears to be a primary protective effect of exercise against the development of coronary heart disease. Clinical investigations have demonstrated a favorable effect of judiciously applied exercise in the treatment of coronary occlusive disease, thus indicating a therapeutic role of exercise in the management of heart disease.

REPRESENTATIVE EPIDEMIOLOGICAL STUDIES

Only a selected few epidemiological studies are reported in this chapter. One of the most-cited studies in which an epidemiological (studies of populations) approach was taken is the Morris and Raffle (82) investigation, which was reported in 1954. They compared the total annual incidence of coronary attack between London bus drivers (who sat during their work day) and London bus conductors (who systematically during their work day walked and climbed up and down the steps of the two-story London buses). They continued this study and published additional findings in 1970. When compared to the conductors, the sedentary drivers had a higher incidence of coronary attack (2.7 vs. 1.9 per 1,000), which started at a younger age. Their mortality rate from the coronary heart disease was more severe than in the physically active conductors. One mitigating factor found in the 1970 study was that the drivers were larger than the conductors; consequently, constitutional body types may have influenced the findings. In addition, personality factors that influenced job selection might have played a role in the coronary attacks.

In another study conducted in London (81), autopsy reports for 4,000 noncoronary heart disease deaths indicated that twice as many heart scars (an indication of previous cardiac damage) were found in those males who engaged in light sedentary occupations than those who were involved in strenuous physical labor in their occupations.

Taylor and his co-workers (107), in one of the most carefully controlled studies of this type, studied coronary heart disease in middle-aged men employed in the railroad industry. In this study improved controls were made of men changing occupations and especially changing jobs that differed in the amount of physical labor required. The incidence of deaths as a result of coronary heart disease in section hands, who did hard physical labor, was 2.8 deaths per 1,000; switchmen, 3.9 deaths per 1,000; and clerks, who were quite sedentary, 5.7 deaths per 1,000. One complicating factor was that section hands tended to live in small communities, and were therefore exposed to less stress whereas the others tended to live in larger towns and were probably subjected to increased stress within their community.

Brunner and Manelis (1) conducted several studies in Israel of the relationship between coronary heart disease and physical activity. Here, communal life in the kibbutzim, in which similar environmental conditions and diet prevailed, resulted in samples being taken from the same socioeconomic classes, regardless of occupation. The investigators found that sedentary workers of all age brackets and both sexes had 2.5 to four times as many incidents of heart attacks as did the nonsedentary workers. These findings led to the conclusion that for all kinds of heart disease, physical activity through work tends to prevent ischemic heart in the middle-aged; lack of physical activity tends to enhance the appearance of clinical ischemic heart disease.

In studies conducted in Scotland, Norway, and Austria, the mortality rate from coronary heart disease was about three times higher for sedentary workers than among workers in occupations requiring heavy labor.

Russek and Zohman (98) made a study of coronary patients between the ages of twenty-five to forty years. In comparison to a normal control group, the coronary heart disease patients tended toward (1) having more fat in their diet, (2) obesity, (3) greater incidence of smoking, (4) more occupational stress and strain, and (5) a lesser amount of regular physical activity.

The histories of men in Westchester County, New York, who died suddenly from coronary occlusion were obtained after death by Spain (104). Those subjects who had been in sedentary occupations had a greater death rate from coronary heart disease at a younger age than those who were in physically active occupations. For those subjects under age fifty-five, the following statistics were reported: sedentary occupations, 44 per cent; moderately strenuous occupations, 32 per cent; and physically strenuous occupations, 24 per cent.

In Framingham, Massachusetts, 5,000 adults were observed for more than ten years. Those who were sedentary individuals suffered more heart attacks, and the attacks were more likely to be fatal, than those who were physically active. An additional finding was that a high blood cholesterol content was the best single indication of a coming heart attack.

Approximately 55,000 men were surveyed by the Health Insurance Program of Greater New York. Those whose lives involved more physical activity had a survival rate from heart attacks that was two or three times better than those leading a sedentary life (44).

A corollary finding in support of the studies was reported by Kenneth Cooper (21). He reported that five times more deaths occurred in a group of men whose resting heart rates were 90 and above than in a group whose resting heart rates were between 60 and 70 beats per minute.

In several investigations the incidence of coronary heart disease in athletes has been monitored for several years following the end of athletic competition. The general findings are that participating in vigorous competitive sports does not predispose a person toward coronary heart disease; former athletes who continue to pursue and participate in reasonably strenuous exercise have only a slight risk of heart attack.

On the other hand, a few investigators have reported no significant differences between the incidence of coronary heart disease of sedentary workers and physically active workers. In some instances the differences that were found were not large enough to be statistically significant. Some of these investigators speculated that at least some of the men in sedentary occupations probably engaged in moderately strenuous or vigorous physical activity during their leisure time, thus nullifying the sedentary effects of their job.

The concensus of the findings resulting from epidemological studies are summarized by Kraus and Raab (66) in their book, *Hypokinetic Disease.*

> Heart disease occurs with greater frequency among persons engaged in the physically non-strenuous or completely sedentary occupations such as business managers, professional men, clerks, and so forth, as compared to laborers, farmers, railroad maintenance workers, and the like.

THE RELATIONSHIP BETWEEN PHYSICAL ACTIVITY AND PREVENTION OF CORONARY HEART DISEASE

The actual mechanisms by which exercise of a regular and vigorous type helps to reduce the incidence and severity of coronary heart disease are still under extensive investigation.

Fox and Haskell (39) suggest seven mechanisms that they believe *may* reduce the occurance and/or severity of coronary heart disease when one exercises regularly.

1. Increased coronary vascularization: collateral circulation is increased through exercise at and around the area of coronary restriction.
2. Myocardial function: myocardial efficiency is enhanced.
3. A lowering of serum cholesterol and serum triglyceride levels. (Recent evidence indicates that high levels of triglyceride are associated with coronary disease.)
4. Blood clotting time is favorably affected and fibrinolytic mechanisms are stimulated when physical activity is habitually increased.
5. Systolic blood pressures are reduced through exercise.
6. Physical activity, especially when combined with dieting, is effective in controlling the body weight.
7. Some possibility that mental conflicts be modified or lessened through physical activity.

Improvement in Collateral Circulation

Proper exercise is believed to help develop the coronary blood vessels, and these in turn may provide for a more adequate coronary blood circulation, the phenomena of which is termed *collateral circulation*. Thus, if a heart attack should occur, this would help reduce its severity and would aid in supplying blood to the coronary tissue. The concept is supported by the study of Eckstein (32) (and by other investigators using a variety of animals), who found an improved collateral circulation in exercised dogs in which experimentally induced atherosclerosis was caused by tying off the coronary arteries to induce heart disease.

Reduction of Serum Cholesterol and Serum Triglycerides

In several investigations it was found that (1) loss of body fat through diet and exercise contributes to a lower blood serum cholesterol and triglyceride level, and (2) fat loss through regular exercise appears to be a long-lasting loss. Exercise has been shown to be an important factor in reducing elevated cholesterol levels in other studies. The importance of this is emphasized in the publication *Heart Facts, 1972*, published by the American Heart Association, in which it has been demonstrated that high levels of serum cholesterol are associated with an increased risk of heart disease.

An investigation by Mann (72) revealed that three subjects who doubled their caloric supply did not have any increase in serum lipids as long as the extra caloric intake was controlled by exercise. However, when exercise was restricted, fat deposits occurred and serum cholesterol levels were doubled. Cureton and Phillips (24) showed that serum cholesterol levels were reduced during the first few weeks of physical training. However, during detraining, when no conditioning was done, serum cholesterol levels again rose. In a similar study, Lumsden (70) discovered that a training program, conducted on a treadmill, caused obese individuals to lower significantly their serum cholesterol concentration; however, slim and muscular subjects who performed the same exercises showed no significant change in their serum cholesterol levels. No change in weight or serum cholesterol levels was found in subjects who added 900 calories to their diets with a proportionate rise in fat intake and who walked on a treadmill at 3.5 miles per hour up a 10 per cent incline for two hours daily (an equivalent of 1,280 calories of work).

Golding (46), who has been exercising businessmen for more than a decade, has found that without any change in diet these middle-aged subjects were able to reduce significantly their serum cholesterol levels. This reduction, which was achieved through exercise, was maintained thereafter by continuing to engage in physical activity. In four other studies it was found that exercise undertaken after consuming fat-laden meals can cause a reduction of the lipid levels in the blood. The importance of these findings is emphasized by those of White and Gerdler (114) who found, in Boston, that individuals with heart disease had cholesterol levels of 286 mg/100 ml of blood, whereas those who were considered normal had an average cholesterol level of 224 mg/100 ml of blood.

Russek and Zohman (98) have observed that emotional stress tends to increase lipid levels in the blood. During times of stress, hormones are activated that cause lipids to be released into the circulation. Unless these lipids are used as fuel for working muscle, they can be used to form deposits within blood vessels and ultimately contribute to the development of arteriosclerosis. Russek and Zohman (98) have demonstrated that exercise can aid in minimizing some of the undesirable results of stress and thereby promote improved cardiovascular function.

Cureton (25), in an analysis of the findings of ten studies performed at the University of Illinois, concluded that if exercise were of sufficient length and intensity and involved cardiovascular endurance (running, swimming, cycling, and many competitive sports) a reduction of serum cholesterol resulted. He also concluded that mild forms of exercise were of limited or of no value for this purpose. Bowling, leisurely walking, softball, and similar activities that did not tax the circulation system were assigned to this category.

Reduction of Blood Fibrin

It has also been theorized that atherosclerosis may develop as a result of fibrin (a protein that is the active agent in the coagulation of the blood) being deposited on the inside of the arterial walls. If true, such deposits can cause a diminished blood supply or even block a narrow artery. That exercise does reduce the fibrin levels and thus combat this problem has been demonstrated in two different studies. The end result would be a decrease in the rate of atherosclerotic development. Some studies have shown that chronic exercise may delay the process of clot formation or increase the capacity of the body to lysis (dissolve) clots already formed.

Favorable Control of Body Weight

Exercise and physical activity have been shown in a number of studies to be an effective way of reducing or controlling body weight. If the food intake is held constant, a person who daily does an extra one-half hour of vigorous activity, which he otherwise would not do, could expect to lose twenty to twenty-five pounds of body fat in one year. It appears that engaging in vigorous physical activity does not cause a corresponding increase in appetite. Thus, if at least one hour of daily exercise (this seems to be the minimum required) is performed, caloric intake and caloric expenditure tend to become equalized and a stable body weight will result for most people.

During strenuous exercise stored body fat is used as an energy source and is depleted when the energy requirements exceed the caloric intake of the diet. Conversely, when more energy is consumed than is utilized via activity, the excess is converted into fat and stored in various sites within the body.

Being noticeably overweight is associated with a detrimental body appearance, motor inefficiency, shortened life expectancy, and a predisposition toward functional diseases of the circulatory system. The overweight person tends to have a higher resting heart rate, is inclined to be less active, and has an increased possibility of incurring heart disease than a similar person of normal body weight.

The Metropolitan Life Insurance Company (77) has estimated that 40 to 50 per cent of our citizenry between thirty and sixty years of age have too much fat. Jean Mayer (75), a prominent investigator in nutrition at Harvard University, calls this creeping obesity. According to the Metropolitan Insurance actuary tables, marked obesity results in a 70 per cent higher-than-normal death rate; being moderately overweight, 40 per cent higher.

Reduction of Tension

Many claims have been made that engaging in sports or physical activity will reduce stress or tension. In a study by DeVries (31), in which he employed electromyographic (tracings of microvoltages produced by the muscles) methods, exercise was shown to reduce the level of muscular tension. This in turn is believed to cause an accompanying reduction in mental tension.

Reduction of Low Back Pain

In their book, *Hypokinetic Disease* (disease resulting from physical inactivity) Drs. Kraus and Raab (66) cite the finding that of 5,000 hospital patients checked, almost 80 per cent of those who had low back pains were categorized as having muscular weakness or stiffness. For a period of eight years, 233 cases were followed with the resultant conclusion that their pain symptoms decreased as their muscle strength and flexibility improved. However, regression occurred when therapeutic exercise or physical activity ceased. Therefore it appears that lifelong participation in suitable physical activity gives insurance against low back pain caused by muscular deterioration.

BENEFICIAL PSYCHOLOGICAL AND SOCIOLOGICAL EFFECTS OF SPORTS PARTICIPATION

The psychological and social benefits that may be derived from participating in sports and physical activity have only recently been the focus of serious scientific investigation. Because this area of research is in its infancy, little conclusive evidence has been produced to date. Instead, a patchwork of findings has evolved for which few patterns can be discerned. With this limitation in mind, this writer has chosen to list the possible beneficial effects of sports participation. As is true of education in general, most of these values can be considered opportunities to be grasped. The values that can be obtained from sports participation usually must be consciously striven for; they do not necessarily automatically happen to the participant.

Representative Findings and Claims

Harry Webb (113), a sports sociologist, points out in his paper, "Professionalization of Attitudes Toward Play Among Adolescents," that participation in play and especially sports contributes a major role in shaping the personality of modern urban-industrial man. The socialization processes to which everyone is subjected can be aided through participating in (and watching) sports. Much social interaction occurs in sports:

1. Racial integration.
2. Developing respect for personality differences.
3. Developing both competitive skills and skills of cooperation—these must be kept in balance.
4. Learning acceptable ways to be aggressive but to avoid antisocial behavior.

The learning that can occur in sports can travel along several different paths and requires discrimination of judgment. For example, one can learn to accept authority and yet be independent of authority, and one can learn sportsmanship; however, adults in the business world do not necessarily follow this precept.

Personalities of Athletes

Quite a number of studies have been made of the personality characteristics of athletes and sports participants. The two general conclusions derived from personality studies of successful athletes are that they tend to be stable extroverts (although many exceptions occur), and that athletes in team and individual sports have different personality types. Miraslav Vanek (112), a sports psychologist at the University of Charles, Prague, Czechoslovakia, has published research findings indicating that superior athletes have higher levels of dominance, self-confidence, physiological stability, and anxiety and are more paranoid than the normal population.

Sports and Group Interaction

Sports, games, and play, because they provide opportunities for group interaction, are an important part of, and make important contributions to, culture. Sports can help to promote understanding in an individual of his relationships within a group and to society. As such, they can make an important contribution toward learning social efficiency and in developing secure relationships with others. Sports participation presents opportunities for leadership training and development. In several studies, evidence has been accumulated demonstrating that physical prowess and athletic ability are often important factors in determining a group leader.

The rules governing play of a sport structure it, allowing all to know the terms of play. Learning to observe such rules can develop a restraint on inconsiderate and unfair behavior. This mode of social behavior can be used as a guide in other situations involving interpersonal behavior. It should be understood that participating in sports can be of help in gaining an understanding of the abilities and contributions of others for the group effort.

John Loy (69), a sports sociologist, did a study of outstanding UCLA athletes. He found that athletics appears to foster (and not interfere with) education and that such participation appears helpful in achieving later upward social status. Upward social mobility is one of the most common outcomes claimed as a result of participating in athletics.

Sports and Individual Improvement

Much has been written about the many rewards that may come to the sports enthusiast as a result of his sports participation. A possible explanation is that success in sports may cause one to raise one's level of aspiration; this in turn could lead to setting higher goals in other areas. Complimenting this is the fact that sports encourages self-expression. Sports participation can help foster the healthy development of a comfortable self-concept (how a person regards himself and how he thinks other people feel about him). A person who holds himself in high esteem learns efficiently; he does not distort reality but accepts himself and others as they are. This can be of help in meeting some of the many threats present in life, especially academic life.

Participation in sports can help one become aware of his limitations and capacities. This fact is emphasized by Arthur Jersild, an educational psychologist, who believes that physical education has more potential for self-understanding than any other discipline. Physical education and sports experiences make a person feel better or worse about himself, never neutral. He learns to accept his body or reject it, to be a worthy competitor or a poor one, to identify masculine and feminine roles or reject them, to develop a balance between work and leisure or live under constant stress, to rely on his own resources or be overly dependent. Physical Education has potential for helping to develop creative expression and self-understanding.

Sportsmanship (applying the golden rule)—an understanding of the feelings and rights of others—can be enhanced through sports competition, which also presents opportunities to learn how to win and lose gracefully. In addition, an immediate sense of achievement, satisfaction, and fun can usually be expected.

Some authorities suggest that engaging in sports and similar activities can enhance the cognitive and sensory perceptual functions. Kephart (119) believes that appropriate motor experiences help perceptual organization, which in turn allows the full intellectual potential to be realized. Benoit believes that physical activity is a primary tool in inducing optimum mental development. Some studies have indicated a low, but positive, relationship between physical fitness, or motor proficiency, and general academic achievement.

Gains in (1) knowledge, (2) reasoning ability, (3) ability to make judgments, and (4) development of intellectual powers may be an outcome of sports participation.

Emotional Well-being

The afterglow from mild physical fatigue (as opposed to chronic fatigue that may be a concomitant of boredom and depression) following vigorous physical activity leads to deep relaxation. Sports are a form of diversion in which the participant becomes completely immersed in the activity, thus providing relief to tension and the emotions.

Dr. Barry B. Mongille, a neuropsychiatrist, believes that participating in sports promotes mental health and peace of mind. Sports can offer "freedom from tension, a sense of security and worth, and are very definitely a maturing experience." They can relieve natural hostilities, aggressiveness, competitiveness, and reduce delinquency, crime, and violence.

Kenneth Cooper, M.D. (21), states that engaging in an exercise program results in less depression and hypochondria (imaginary illness) and a better self-image. In psychiatric treatment programs for resident patients, sports participation is one of the commonly used modes of preparing a person to return to normal everyday life. Sports place people together and give them healthy ways in which to interact with and tolerate competition from others.

Dr. Frank D'Elia, a psychiatrist, believes that man has aggressive instincts or impulses and that these have to be expressed. In his opinion the best way to express them is to sublimate them (divert by substituting something else). This can easily and safely be done in competitive sports in which aggressive feelings can be expressed in socially acceptable ways and without appreciable damage. Thus, he believes that brutality and mindlessness, for example, can be sublimated or overcome by sports competition.

Burris Husman, of the University of Maryland, in a paper, "Sport Personality Dynamics," discusses two contradictory theories that have been proposed about aggression. Evidence in different studies and even in the same studies support both the cathartic theory (a lowering of the aggression drive by displacing aggression into socially acceptable channels such as sports participation) and the circular theory (guilt is created by experiencing aggression, which during childhood was punished, causing increased frustration and aggression). Husman speculates that research evidence appears to indicate that during competition a good athlete has his emotions under control—an important trait—because as emotions go up, functioning intelligence goes down.

CONCLUDING STATEMENT

Hans Kraus, M.D. (65), who has long been involved with sports medicine, has written an article in the *New York State Journal of Medicine* entitled, "Preventive Aspects of Physical Fitness." He points out that a lack of physical activity in our overstimulated environment can give rise to such emotional diseases as neurosis, anxiety, depression, compulsion, and maladjustment. He summarizes our need for habitual exercise at all ages as follows.

> Mechanized society deprives man of movement. He cannot react to stimuli but is forced to suppress the defense responses which are elicited by irritations. He lives in chronic imbalance. Underexercise and overstimulation produce stress disease, tension syndrome, overweight, orthopedic disability (painful backs, necks, and so forth), cardiovascular disease, and endocrine and emotional imbalance.

Exercise from cradle to grave, designed to substitute for previously normal everyday activity and serving as a vicarious outlet for tensions, is the simplest preventive measure.

Selected References

(1) Alost, Robert. "A Study of the Effect of Initial Cardiovascular Condition, Type of Training Program, and Frequency of Practice Periods upon Cardiovascular Development of College Males." Unpublished Ed. D. thesis, Louisiana State University, Baton Rouge, 1963.

(2) American Heart Association, "Heart Facts 1972," New York: 1972.

(3) Asmussen, E. "Some Physiological Aspects of Fitness for Sport and Work." *Proceedings of the Royal Society for Medicine,* **62** (1969), 1160.

(4) Beckner, G. L., and T. Winsor. "Cardiovascular Adaptations to Prolonged Physical Effort." *Circulation,* **9** (1954), 835.

(5) Berkson, D., and Associates, "Experience with a Long-Term Supervised Ergometric Exercise Program for Middle-Aged Sedentary American Men." *Circulation,* Supplement 2, **36** (1967), 67.

(6) Biddulph, Lowell G. "Athletic Achievement and the Personal and Social Adjustment of High School Boys." *Research Quarterly,* **25** (March 1954), 1.

(7) Blakeslee, and Stamler. *Your Heart Has Nine Lives.* (summary). Englewood Cliffs, N.J.: Prentice-Hall, 1963.

(8) Breslow, L., and P. Buell. "Mortality from Coronary Heart Disease and Physical Activity of Work in California." *Chronic Disease,* **11** (1960), 421.

(9) Brown, R. G., and Associates. "Coronary Heart Disease: Influences Affecting Its Incidence in Males in the Seventh Decade." *Lancet,* **273** (1957), 1073.

(10) Brumbach, Wayne B. "Changes in the Serum Cholesterol Levels of Male College Students Who Participated in Vigorous Physical Exercise Programs." Unpublished Ph.D. dissertation, University of Oregon, Eugene, 1959.

(11) Brunner, D., and G. Manelis. "Myocardial Infarction Among Members of Communal Settlements in Israel." *Lancet,* (Nov. 12, 1960), 1049.

(12) Brunner, D., and G. Manelis. "Physical Activity at Work and Ischemic Heart Disease." *Coronary Heart Disease and Physical Fitness.* Ed. by O.A. Larsen and R.O. Malmborg. Baltimore: University Park Press, 1971, 244.

(13) Burt, J. J., C. S. Blyth, and H. A. Rierson. "Effects of Exercise on the Coagulation–Fibrinolysis Equalibrium." *Journal of Sports Medicine and Physical Fitness,* **4** (1964), 213.

(14) Calvy, C., and Associates. "Serum Lipids and Enzymes: Their Levels After High Caloric, High Fat Intake and Vigorous Exercise Regimen in Marine Corps Recruit Personnel." *Journal of American Medical Association,* **183** (1963), 1.

(15) Campbell, Donald E. "Effect of Controlled Running on Serum Cholesterol of Young Adult Males of Varying Morphological Constitutions." *Research Quarterly,* **39** (1968), 47.

(16) Campbell, Donald E. "Acute Effects of Physical Activity upon Serum Cholesterol." *Journal of the Association for Physical and Mental Rehabilitation,* **21** (1967), 87.

(17) Cantone, A. "Physical Effort and Its Effect in Reducing Alimentary Hyperlipaemia." *Journal of Sports Medicine and Physical Fitness,* **4** (1964), 32.

(18) Casady, Donald R., Donald F. Mapes, and Louis E. Alley. *Handbook of Physical Fitness Activities.* New York: Macmillan, Inc., 1965.

(19) Chirico, A., and A. Stunkard. "Physical Activity and Human Obesity." *New England Journal of Medicine,* **263** (1960), 935.

(20) *Contemporary Readings in Sport Psychology.* Ed. by William P. Morgan. Springfield, Ill.: Thomas, 1970.

(21) Cooper, Kenneth H. *The New Aerobics.* New York: Bantam, 1970.

(22) *Coronary Heart Disease in Seven countries.* Ed. by Ancel Keys. *Circulation,* Supplement No. 1, **41** (1970).

(23) Creus, J., and E. E. Aldinger. "Effects of Chronic Exercise on Myocardial Function." *American Heart Journal,* **74** (1967), 537.

(24) Cureton, T. K., and E. E. Phillips. "Physical Fitness Changes in Middle-Aged Men Attributable to Equal Eight-Week Periods of Training, Non-Training, and Re-Training." *The Journal of Sports Medicine and Physical Fitness,* **4** (1964).

(25) Cureton, Thomas K. *The Physiological Effects of Exercise Programs on Adults.* Springfield, Ill.: Thomas, 1969, p. 52.

(26) Cureton, Thomas K. "Use of Exercise to Reduce Fat, Cholesterol Triglycerides, and Phospholipids." *Review of Studies to Improve Cardiovascular Fitness.* Urbana: University of Illinois, The Physical Fitness Research Laboratory, 1963.

(27) Daniel, Billy Jo. "The Effects of Walking, Jogging, and Running on the Serum Lipid Concentration of the Adult Caucasian Male." Unpublished Ph.D. dissertation, University of Southern Mississippi, Hattisburg, 1969.

(28) "Dr. Irving's Feature Physical Fitness Articles." *American College of Sports Medicine Newsletter*, 2 (Nov. 1967).
(29) Dawber, T. R., F. R. Moore, and G. V. Mann. "Coronary Heart Disease in the Framingham Study." *American Journal of Public Health*, Supplement No. 47 (1957), 24.
(30) Dawber, T. R., W. B. Kannel, and G. D. Friedman. "Vital Capacity, Physical Activity, and Coronary Heart Disease." Burlington: University of Vermont, *First International Conference on Preventive Cardiology*, 1964.
(31) deVries, H. A. "Immediate and Long-Term Effects of Exercise upon Resting Muscle Action Potential Level: Implications for Relaxation." *Journal of Sports Medicine and Physical Fitness*, 8 (1968), 1.
(32) Eckstein, R. W. "Effect of Exercise and Coronary Artery Narrowing on Coronary Collateral Circulation." *Circulation Research*, 5 (1957), 230.
(33) Enos, W. F., et al. "Coronary Disease Among United States Soldiers Killed in Korea." *Journal of the American Medical Association*, 152 (1962), 1090.
(34) Esko, A., and A. Knottinen. "Effects of Physical Activity on Postprandial Levels of Fats in Serum." *Lancet*, 1 (1962), 1151.
(35) Evans, J. et al. "The Effects of Exercise on the Reduction of Body Weight." *Journal of Physical and Mental Rehabilitation*, 12 (1958), 56.
(36) Falls, Harold B., Earl L. Wallis, and Gene A. Logan. *Foundations of Conditioning*. New York: Academic, 1970.
(37) Flanagan, Lance. "A Study of Some Personality Traits of Different Physical Activity Groups." *The Research Quarterly*, 22 (Oct. 1951), 312.
(38) Fletcher, Gerald F., and John D. Cantwell. *Exercise in the Management of Coronary Heart Disease: A Guide for the Practicing Physician*. Springfield, Ill.: Thomas, 1971.
(39) Fox, Samuel M., and William Haskell. "Physical Activity and the Prevention of Coronary Heart Disease." *Bulletin of the New York Academy of Medicine* (Aug. 1968), 950.
(40) Fox, Samuel M., John P. Naughton, and William L. Haskell. "Physical Activity and the Prevention of Coronary Heart Disease." *Annals of Clinical Research*, 3 (Dece. 1971), 404.
(41) Fox, S. M., J. P. Naughton, and James S. Skinner. "Physical Activity in Prevention of Coronary Heart Disease." *Annals of Clinical Research*, 3 (1971), 404.
(42) Fox, Samuel M., and Paul Oglesby. "Physical Activity and Coronary Heart Disease." *American Journal of Cardiology*, 23 (1969), 298.
(43) Fox, Samuel M., and James S. Skinner. "Physical Activity and Cardiovascular Health." *American Journal of Cardiology*, 14 (1964), 731.
(44) Frank, C. W. "The Course of Coronary Heart Disease: Factors Relating to Prognosis." *Bulletin of New York Academy of Medicine*, 44 (1968), 900.
(45) Friedman, M., and H. Rosenman. "Association of Specific Behavior Patterns with Increase in Blood Cholesterol Blood Clotting Time and Incidence of Clinical Coronary Disease." *Circulation*, 18 (1958), 721.
(46) Golding, Lawrence A. "Cholesterol and Exercise: A Ten-Year Study." *Journal of Physical Education* (March-April 1972), 106.
(47) Golding, Lawrence A. "The Effects of Exercise Training upon Total Serum Cholesterol Levels." *Research Quarterly*, 33 (1961), 499.
(48) Haskell, W. L., and S. M. Fox. "The Possible Place of Stress Testing to Discover and Physical Activity to Prevent Coronary Heart Disease." *Southern Medical Journal*, 59 (1966), 642.
(49) Hellerstein, Herman, et al. "The Influence of Active Conditioning upon Subjects with Coronary Artery Disease." Toronto: *Proceedings of the International Symposium on Physical Activity and Cardiovascular Health*, 1967, p. 758.
(50) Holloszy, J. O. "Biochemical Adaptations in Muscle. Effects of Exercise on Mitochondrial Oxygen Uptake and Respiratory Enzyme Activity in Skeletal Muscle." *Journal of Biological Chemistry*, 342 (1967), 2278.
(51) Hollozy, J. O., and James S. Skinner. "Effects of Six Months of Endurance Exercise on Serum Lipids of Middle Age Men." *American Journal of Cardiology*, 14 (1964), 753.
(52) Hunsicker, Paul. *Physical Fitness. What Research Says to the Teacher*. Washington, D.C.: NEA, 1963.
(53) Iowa State University. "The Role of Exercise and Activity in Weight Control." *Report of the Colloquium on Weight Control*. Ames: Iowa State University Press, 1955.
(54) Johnson, Warren R., Daniel C. Hutton, and Granville B. Johnson, Jr. "Personality Traits of Some Champion Athletes as Measured by Two Projective Tests: Rorschach and H-T-P." *The Research Quarterly*, 25 (Dec. 1954), 484-485.
(55) Kalin, H. "The Relationship of Reported Coronary Heart Disease Mortality to Physical Activity of Work." *American Journal of Public Health*, 53 (1963), 1058.
(56) Kane, J. E. "The Description of Sport Types Using the 16PF." *Research in Physical Education*, London, England, 1 (1967), 1.
(57) Kane, J. E. "Personality and Physical Abilities." Paper presented at the 2nd International Congress of Sport Psychology, Washington, D.C. (Nov. 1, 1968).

(58) Kannel, William B. "The Framingham Heart Study." Public Health Service Publication No. 1515.
(59) Keough, Jack. "Relationship of Motor Ability and Athletic Participation in Certain Standardized Personality Measures." *The Research Quarterly,* 30 (Dec. 1959), 438.
(60) Keys, Ancel, and Associates. "Physical Activity and the Diet in Populations Differing in Serum Cholesterol." *Journal of Clinical Investigation,* 35 (1956), 1173.
(61) Keys, Ancel. "Diet and the Epidemiology of Heart Disease." *Journal of the American Medical Association,* 164 (1957), 1912.
(62) ———. "Physical Activity and the Epidemiology of Coronary Heart Disease." *Medicine and Sport,* Vol. 2, *Physical Activity and Aging,* p. 264. Ed. by D. B. Bruner and E. Jokl. Baltimore, Md.: University Park Press, 1970.
(63) Klouda, M. A., and W. C. Randall. "Subendocardial Hemorrhages during Stimulation of the Sympathetic Cardiac Nerves." *First International Conference on Preventive Cardiology.* Burlington: University of Vermont, 1964.
(64) *Knowledge and Understanding in Physical Education.* Washington, D.C.: American Association for Health, Physical Education, and Recreation, 1969.
(65) Kraus, Hans. "Preventive Aspects of Physical Fitness." *New York Journal of Medicine,* 64 (May 1964), 1182.
(66) Kraus, H., and W. Raab. *Hypokinetic Disease.* Springfield, Ill.: Thomas, 1961.
(67) Lakie, William L. "Personality Characteristics of Certain Groups of Intercollegiate Athletes." *The Research Quarterly,* 33 (Dec. 1962), 566.
(68) Lew, E. A. "Some Implications of Mortality Statistics Relating to Coronary Artery Disease." *Journal of Chronic Disabilities,* 6 (1957), 192.
(69) Loy, John W. "The Study of Sport and Social Mobility: Problems, Patterns, and Prospects." Paper presented at the Symposium on the Sociology of Sport. Madison: University of Wisconsin (Nov. 1968).
(70) Lumsden, T. "Serum Cholesterol Concentrations During Physical Training and During Subsequent Detraining." *The American Journal of the Medical Sciences,* 253 (Feb. 1967), 55.
(71) Mann, G. V., and Associates. "Exercise and Coronary Risk Factors." *Circulation,* Supplement No. 2, 36 (1967), 181.
(72) Mann, G. V., et al. "Exercise in the Disposition of Dietary Calories: Regulation of Serum Lipoprotein and Cholesterol in Human Subjects." *New England Journal of Medicine,* 253 (1955), 349.
(73) Mallerowicz, H. "The Effects of Training on O_2 Consumption of the Heart and Its Importance for Prevention of Coronary Insufficiency." *Health and Fitness in the Modern World.* Chicago: The Athletic Institute, 1961, p. 90.
(74) Mayer, Jean, et al. "Exercise Food Intake and Body Weight in Normal Rats and Genetically Obese Adult Mice." *American Journal of Physiology,* 177 (1954), 544.
(75) Mayer, Jean. "Exercise and Weight Control." *Science and Medicine of Exercise and Sports.* New York: Harper, 1960, p. 301.
(76) McDonald, G. A., and H. W. Fullerton. "Effects of Physical Activity on Increased Coagulability of Blood After Ingestion of High Fat Meal." *Lancet,* 275 (1958), 600.
(77) Metropolitan Life Insurance Company. "Overweight Shortens Life." *Statistical Bulletin,* 32 (1951), 1.
(78) Montoye, Henry J., et al. "The Effects of Exercise on Blood Cholesterol in Middle-Aged Men." *American Journal of Clinical Nutrition,* 7 (1959), 139.
(79) Montoye, Henry J. "Sports and Length of Life." *Science and Medicine of Exercise and Sports.* Ed. by W. R. Johnson. New York: Harper, 1960.
(80) ———. "Summary of Research on the Relationship of Exercise to Heart Disease." *Journal of Sports Medicine and Physical Fitness,* 2 (1962), 35.
(81) Morris, J. N., and M. D. Crawford. "Coronary Heart Disease and Physical Activity of Work." *British Medical Journal,* 2 (1958), 1485.
(82) Morris, J. N., and P. A. B. Raffle. "Coronary Heart Disease in Transport Workers." *British Journal of Industrial Medicine,* 1 (1954), 260.
(83) Naughton, J., and F. McCoy. "Observations on the Relationship of Physical Activity to the Serum Cholesterol Concentration of Healthy Men and Cardiac Patients." *Journal of Clinical Diseases,* 3 (1966), 727.
(84) Nikkila, E. A., and A. Konttinen. "Effect of Physical Activity on Postprandial Levels of Fats in Serum." *Lancet,* 1 (1962), 1151.
(85) Ogilvie, Bruce C. "Personality of the Male Athlete." Academy Papers, No. 1, The American Academy of Physical Education, 1968, p. 45.
(86) Ogilvie, Bruce, and Thomas Tutko. "The Psychological Profile of Champions." *Proceedings of the First International Congress of Sports Psychology.* Ed. by Ferruccio Antonelli. Rome: 1965, 201-203.
(87) Osness, Wayne H. "A Study of Certain Aspects of Lipid Metabolism During Exercise." Unpublished Ph.D. dissertation, Madison: University of Wisconsin, 1966.

(88) Paffenbarger, Ralph S., and Associates. "Work Activity of Longshoremen As Related to Death from Coronary Heart Disease and Stroke." *New England Journal of Medicine,* **20** (1970), 1109.

(89) Phillips, L. "Physical Fitness Changes in Adults Attributable to Equal Periods of Training, Non-Training, and Re-Training." Unpublished Ph.D. dissertation, University of Illinois, Urbana, 1960.

(90) *Physiological Aspects of Sports and Physical Fitness.* Chicago: The Athletic Institute, 1968.

(91) Pollock, Michael L., and Associates. "Effects of Frequency of Training on Serum Lipids, Cardiovascular Function, and Body Composition." *Exercise and Fitness.* Ed. by B. Don Franks. Chicago: The Athletic Institute, 1969, p. 161.

(92) Raab, W. "Training, Physical Inactivity, and the Cardiac Dynamic Cycle." *The Journal of Sports Medicine and Physical Fitness,* **6** (March 1966), 38.

(93) Raab, W. "Degenerative Heart Disease from Lack of Exercise." *Exercise and Fitness.* A collection of papers published by The Athletic Institute, 1960, pp. 10–19.

(94) Robernick, G. N., and Associates. "Effects of Physical Activity on Cholesterol Atherosclerosis." *Proceedings of the Society for Experimental Biology and Medicine,* **96** (1957), 623.

(95) Rook, A. "An Investigation into the Longevity of Cambridge Sportsmen." *British Medical Journal,* **LI** (1954), 773.

(96) Rochelle, R. H. "Blood Plasma Cholesterol Changes During a Physical Training Program." *Research Quarterly,* **32** (1962), 538.

(97) Rushall, Brent S. "An Evaluation of the Relationship Between Personality and Physical Performance Categories." Paper presented at the 2nd International Congress of Sport Psychology, Washington, D.C. (Nov. 1, 1968).

(98) Russek, H. I., and B. L. Zohman. "Relative Significance of Heredity, Diet, and Occupational Stress in Coronary Heart Disease in Young Adults." *Journal of the American Medical Association,* **235** (1958), 266.

(99) Ryan, E. Dean. "Effects of Motor Performance and Learning." *The Research Quarterly,* **33** (March, 1962), 111.

(100) Skinner, James S. "Effect of an Endurance Exercise Program on the Serum Lipids of Middle-Aged Men." Unpublished Ph.D. dissertation, University of Illinois, Urbana, 1963.

(101) Slusher, Howard S., and Aileene S. Lockhart. *Anthology of Contemporary Readings—An Introduction to Physical Education.* Dubuque, Iowa: Brown, 1970.

(102) Slusher, Howard S. *Man, Sport, and Existence: A Critical Analysis.* Philadelphia: Lea, 1967.

(103) ———. "Personality and Intelligence Characteristics of Selected High School Athletes and Non-Athletes." *The Research Quarterly,* **35** (Dec. 1964), 539.

(104) Spain, David M. "Occupational Physical Exertion and Coronary Atherosclerotic Heart Disease." *Journal of Occupational Medicine* (Feb. 1961), 54.

(105) *Sport, Culture, and Society.* Ed. by John W. Loy, Jr. and Gerald S. Kenyon. New York: Macmillan, Inc., 1969.

(106) "Sports Competition Healthy, Psychiatrist Says." *Medicine in Sport Newsletter,* **8** (Sept. 1968).

(107) Taylor, Henry L. "Coronary Heart Disease in Physically Active and Sedentary Populations." *Journal of Sports Medicine and Physical Fitness* (1962), 73.

(108) Taylor, H. L., J. T. Anderson, and A. Keys. "Physical Activity, Serum Cholesterol and Other Lipids in Man." *Proceedings of the Society for Experimental Biology and Medicine,* **95** (1957), 383.

(109) Taylor, Henry J. "Diet, Physical Activity and Serum Cholesterol Concentration." *Minnesota Medicine* (1958), 145.

(110) Tooshi, Ali. "Effect of Three Different Durations of Endurance Training on Serum Cholesterol, Body Composition, and Other Fitness Measures." Unpublished Ph.D. dissertation, University of Illinois, Urbana, 1970.

(111) Ulrich, Celeste. *The Social Matrix of Physical Education.* Englewood Cliffs, N.J.: Prentice-Hall, 1968.

(112) Vanek, Miroslav, and Bryon J. Cratty. *The Psychology of the Superior Athlete.* New York: Macmillan, Inc., 1970.

(113) Webb, Harry. "Professionalization of Attitudes Toward Play Among Adolescents." Paper presented at the CIC Symposium on Sociology of Sport, at Madison, Wisconsin (Nov. 1968).

(114) White, P. E., and M. M. Gertler. *Coronary Heart Disease in Young Adults: A Multi-Disciplinary Study.* Cambridge, Mass.: Harvard University Press, Commonwealth Fund, 1954.

(115) Williams, Harriet G. "Claims for Physical Exercise and Formal Physical Education: Fact and Fancy Concerning Psychological and Sociological Benefits: Learning." Paper presented to the Scientific Foundations Section, American Association for Health Physical Education and Recreation National Convention (March 1968).

(116) Wong, H. Y. C., et al. "Hydrocholesterolizing Effect of Exercise on Cholesterol-Fed Cockerels." *Proceedings of the Federation of American Societies for Experimental Biology,* **17** (1957), 38.

(117) Yater, W. M., and Associates. "Coronary Heart Disease in Men 18-39 Years of Age." *American Heart Journal,* **36** (1948), 334.
(118) Zukel, W. J., et al. "A Short-Term Community Study of the Epidemiology of Coronary Heart Disease." *Journal of Public Health,* **49** (1959), 1630.
(119) Godfrey, Barbara B., and Newell C. Kephart. *Movement Patterns and Motor Education.* New York: Appleton, 1969.

CHAPTER 3

The attraction of sport: why man engages in sport

INTRODUCTION

Information concerning the role of sports and physical education in education, past beliefs concerning the importance of physical education and sports, and the predomination of sports in programs of physical education was presented in the first chapter. Some of the important benefits, such as added insurance against coronary heart disease, other degenerative diseases, and hypokinetic disease, that can be expected as a result of participating regularly in vigorous sports activities are summarized in the second chapter.

Although the first two chapters contain information about the importance of and benefits to be derived from sports participation, they do not answer the question of why man engages in sports. An examination of the theories that have been formulated in answer to this question and of some of the answers given by different individuals should be of interest. The reader will undoubtedly find several that at least partially explain his reasons for participating in sports.

Sports seem to be increasingly occupying a portion of almost everyone's life. The work week, which by 1980 is estimated to average thirty-six hours in length, the increase in three-day weekends for adults, and the advent of long vacation periods and sabbaticals have all combined to give modern man, who probably faces more stress and tension than ever before, the greatest amount of leisure time that has ever been possible.

With this increased leisure time has come the development of many new sports (sky diving, for example) and particularly the common availability of most sports to the majority of youth and adults. This has been augmented by large increases in sports facilities and by the ease of inexpensive transportation to such areas. In addition, the continuing growth of the urban and suburban modes of living, with their accompanying loss of space, has increased man's desire for sports.

Man's preoccupation with and desire for sports may easily be seen by the amount of newspaper coverage given to sports, estimated to be from 8 to 14 per cent of the total amount, 3 per cent of the books published deal with sports, and from the number of television programs devoted to sports, especially on weekends. Close to 100 million people in the United States are estimated to have viewed some of the sports telecasts shown on TV; several hundred million people are believed to have watched sports events such as the modern Olympic Games that have been internationally televised. The fascination with sports of the American public is evident when one realizes that they spend more than 20 billion dollars annually on sports.

WHAT IS SPORT?

Before examining the theories that have been proposed to explain the reasons why man engages in sports, it seems desirable to define sports (commonly referred to by sport sociologists as *sport*, in the singular) and other terms that are similar and that are sometimes used interchangeably. Play, games, and physical education share many common elements with sport; in fact, some authorities do not make large distinctions in the purposes served by the three.

Staley, a physical educator from the University of Illinois, proposed in the 1930s that physical education be called sports education. This was in recognition of the large sport content of physical education programs.

Gunter Erbach (11:23) states that,

> sport is the dominating form of expression of physical culture (planned physical education, sport, physical exercises, and all forms of active leisure pursuits) and signifies the striving to succeed in physical efficiency, on the basis of the norms and rules in contests of all types.

Lüschen, a sports sociologist, states that "sport is a rational, playful activity in interaction, which is extrinsically rewarded." (12:35).

Miller and Russell (4:6) write, "sport is a miniature of real life"; it "intensifies the dynamic process of life itself." They and many others believe that play is a valuable ingredient in sport.

René Maken (10:386) considers sport (and physical training) to be human disciplines with a social function and a contribution to complete personality development.

John Loy (11:56), a sports sociologist, suggests that sport has different meanings for different people. In attempting to clarify the nature of sport he discusses sport as (1) a game occurrence, (2) an institutionalized game, (3) a social institution, and (4) a social situation or social system. Some sport sociologists believe that competitive sports are different from games of chance, dramatic play (mimicry), and activities producing sensations of falling or centrifugal force, which cause vertigo (dizziness).

Functions and Characteristics of Sport

Lüschen (12:31) believes that the usual functions of sport are cultural pattern maintenance and integration into contemporary society. For example, the exposure of children to competitive sports will cause them to become achievement motivated. He raises the question of whether sport participation might, however, work against social control.

Miller and Russell (4) in discussing sport assign four functions or purposes to it: (1) personal, (2) social, (3) cultural, and (4) educational.

Loy (11:56) believes that sports and games have the following common characteristics: they are (1) playful (one or more elements of play are present; they involve voluntary activity and limits of time and space; the outcome cannot be determined ahead of the contest; they are unproductive or nonutilitarian; and they are governed by rules and stand outside of real life), (2) competitive, (3) demand physical prowess, and (4) involve physical skill.

Slusher (9:44) believes that sport in general has the following characteristics: (1) contention of interest (involves a contest or competition), (2) consistency of role (involves choice of performance), (3) utilization-actualization (usually a maximum individual effort is made to improve, and performers have a knowledge of how to perform), and (4) variable unpredictability (the variables that govern the contest and its outcome are not all known).

Sports involvement on a behavior level is spoken of by Kenyon (11) as being of two types: *primary*, which involves actual participation by players and contestants; and *secondary*, which involves the consumption (spectators and TV viewers) and the production (coaches, referees, and promoters) of sports. Even though being a sports fan, being a sport spectator, and in general being a sedentary addict to this form of mass entertainment can be enjoyable and even obsessive, few of the benefits discussed in this book are believed to come to the "person on the sidelines." Instead, the interest is in the sports participant. This viewpoint, which emphasizes the need to engage in sport rather than to view it, is especially well expressed by the well-known newspaper columnist, Sydney Harris.

Participants, Not Spectators*
Sydney Harris

Knowing my strong feelings about the insane emphasis on sports in American society, a friend expressed surprise at seeing me at a school basketball game with three of my children. I dare say he would have been even more surprised to know that I urged one of my sons to try to make his school tennis team.

The mistake most of us make lies in assuming that because someone is against overemphasis, he is against emphasis. Precisely because I am not a lockerroom type, I think it important that my children be exposed to athletics and understand its beneficial value; I would be doing them a grave disservice otherwise.

What is desperately needed is a sense of appreciation of other modes of life, and of the excellence that goes into every phase of doing and becoming. Without this sense, we become rigid, narrow, dull, and intolerant of other modes.

My antagonism to professional sports comes from a feeling that they pre-empt values and interests that should be devoted to a wider development of the whole human personality. But if I scorned and sneered at sports to my children, I would be doing them as much of an injustice as the sports-minded father who ignores or rejects the worlds of creativity, imagination, scholarship, and thought. I would be an intellectual barbarian, just as he is a physical barbarian.

Now, as never before, we need to aim at the whole man—and whole woman, too, of course. But the average sports fan in our society not only snubs knowledge, he also betrays his own body by sitting

---

*The Des Moines Register, Saturday, March 21, 1970. Reprinted by permission of Sydney J. Harris and Publishers-Hall Syndicate.

hunched up in front of a TV set all weekend, watching professionals do his exercise for him. He betrays his children by making interschool team play so important that intramural sports are slighted, and only a handful of pupils get the benefit of competitive athletics, when all should have it.

The sports nut doesn't even truly respect and understand the virtue of his own interest. If he did, he would dismantle those enormous stadiums for 22 players to compete in, and replace them with fields for thousands to play in, where children might develop into sturdy participants rather than turning into shriveled spectators.

WHY PEOPLE ENGAGE IN SPORTS

Many people state that they enjoy working out and that they feel much better after they engage in vigorous physical activity. Several theories have been propounded to explain these feelings and why man engages in physical activity and sport—what values he derives from such participation. Some of these theories overlap one another and, in fact, may be similar except for name. Psychiatrists, sociologists, psychologists, educators, medical doctors, physical educators, and other experts have advanced a number of theories that explain why such participation is a source of enjoyment and produces a sense of contentment. The human organism is highly complex: no single explanation will apply to different people or even the same person. Undoubtedly, many of the reasons listed in these theories are all working together, often on a subconscious level, to motivate and induce sport participation.

Ascetic Theory. Engaging in sports by those who wish high levels of achievement induces them to delay gratification and be able to endure long, strenuous training periods, causing them to punish (temporarily) their bodies.

Aesthetic Theory. By playing and engaging in sports, man's creative imagination is satisfied; he creates beauty through movement and play. Sport itself can possess beauty and artistic qualities.

Catharsis Theory. By yelling, kicking, pushing, and similar actions, man loosens his animal instincts and reduces his animal nature. Through vicarious means he releases tension brought on by various frustrations.

Domination Theory. Sports participation allows one, within certain rules and boundaries, to exercise his desire to dominate, thus fulfilling a basic human desire.

Energy Theory. Man has a surplus of energy that he does not expend in work and that he needs to discharge in a wholesome way—play and sports afford one acceptable way.

Imitation Theory. Play (and sport) is a mimicry, usually in miniature, of actual life experiences and patterns.

Personal Values Theory. Sports add depth and breadth to existence; feelings of personal value and worth are enhanced—all of which enriches one's life.

Preparation for Life Theory. Play (and sports) prepares the young for real-life situations. Personality traits developed or reinforced during play are of value in other phases of life.

Pursuit of Excellence Theory. Engaging in sport is one means by which excellence or outstanding accomplishment can be sought and even attained.

Recapitulation Theory. In sports participation, man recapitulates his cultural history—the dangers and victories of his ancestors—and captures anew old combats and battles.

Recreation Theory. During work man "uses himself up"; play restores him and supplies newly created incentive and energy.

Restraint Theory. Sports permit man, who is thought to be an aggressive organism, a safety valve whereby dangerous types of aggression are funneled and behavior restraints are reinforced.

Stress-seeking Theory (6). Man actively seeks stress-producing situations on his own initiation. Examples are the sports of long-distance running and swimming, mountain climbing, and sports parachuting, and the occupation of professional soldier, as well as certain others. Some of the possible reasons people seek stress are that it (1) promotes ego growth through conquering fear, (2) stimulates a feeling of freedom that cannot be accomplished through pleasure activities, (3) enhances nobility through the will to conquer, (4) is an expression of a usually dominant genetic factor, and (5) recaptures the struggle of life itself.

Sublimination Theory. Sport and play allow man to rid himself of frustrations and disappointments in natural forms of behavior. This permits him to avoid unacceptable behavior forms such as lashing out in anger or sobbing in sorrow.

Vertigo Theory. Vertigo, or giddiness—actually risk—is pursued (but not normally caught) in riskful physical experiences that provide for thrill through acceleration, speed, and sudden changes of direction, or else the participant is exposed to dangerous situations of which he is normally in control.

Will to Power Theory. This theory proposes that man is aggressive in order to win. From infancy on, he demonstrates his superiority and mastery of the environment in an attempt to gain adult strength.

Wish-fulfillment Theory. Play and sports provide a secret way by which people can have their wishes come true.

REASONS FOR ENGAGING IN SPORTS

When an examination is made of the reasons given by various people for engaging in sport and other vigorous physical activity, it is apparent that the preceding theories will fit. Although people almost always will give explanations as to why they play or participate in sports, some question that any legitimate reason (or reasons) need to exist. It has often been observed that children, aboriginal tribesmen, and animals play without having any notion of why they play. The viewpoint that sports and play need fill no end is argued by Johan Huizinga (2), who writes that play ought to be considered for its own sake—it is an end in itself rather than the means to some other end. But most people have logical explanations of why they play; generally, these include health, fun, and social contact. Sports, especially, can give rise to exciting encounters that are enjoyed.

What College Students and Adults Say

The reasons for participating in sports of all kinds, and in other physical activities as well, are quite similar for male college students and male adults. Some typical responses, which have been gathered from a variety of sources, are presented here.

Such participation is done, as would be expected, for many reasons—the sport participant frequently gives several reasons when asked why he participates in sports.

1. To maintain good health and keep physically fit.
2. To produce a better feeling for having exercised.
3. To have fun and enjoyment.
4. To produce a feeling of physical well-being.
5. To keep mentally alert.
6. To relieve tension and stress.
7. To relax the mind from the day's vocation.
8. To sleep better at night.
9. To increase interest in life.
10. To benefit by being out-of-doors.
11. To compete against others.
12. To allow the mind to function with increased clarity.
13. To enjoy the friendship of the other participants.
14. To gain the satisfaction that accompanies effort and achievement.
15. To feel better.
16. For the tonic effect of feeling better physically and mentally.
17. For the fellowship.
18. To meet new people and get acquainted with them.
19. To keep muscles in good tone.
20. To maintain an attractive, wholesome appearance.
21. To develop a good physique.
22. To keep the body weight in proper adjustment.
23. To maintain business and professional contacts in a social atmosphere.
24. To develop a good posture.
25. For the fellowship and association with others.
26. As a diversion from the daily routine.
27. To aid in maintaining an even temperament.
28. As a relief from boredom.
29. To learn to know oneself better.
30. To get some exercise that would not otherwise be obtained.
31. To improve the disposition and feel better.
32. To be able to study better and get more out of it.
33. To increase the life span.
34. To develop resistance to disease.
35. To improve coordination.
36. To improve the ability to work.
37. To aid in keeping the system regulated.
38. To increase emotional stability.
39. To provide a better appetite.

Selected References

(1) *Contemporary Readings in Sport Psychology.* Ed. by William P. Morgan. Springfield, Ill.: Thomas, 1970.
(2) Huizinga, Johan. *Homo Ludens: A Study of the Play Element in Culture.* Boston: Beacon, 1955.
(3) Kretchmar, R. Scott, and William A. Harper. "Why Does Man Play?" *Journal of Health, Physical Education, and Recreation,* (March 1967).
(4) Miller, Donna Mae, and Kathryn R. E. Russell. *Sport: A Contemporary View.* Philadelphia: Lea, 1971.
(5) Parker, Franklin. "Sport, Play, and Physical Education in Cultural Perspective." *Journal of Health, Physical Education, and Recreation,* (April 1965), 29.
(6) Reich, Kenneth E. "Stress-seeking: The Unknown Factor of Human Personality," *Sport Psychology Bulletin* (North American Society for the Psychology of Sport and Physical Activity), **4** (Aug. 1971), 6.
(7) Singer, Robert N., et al. *Physical Education—An Interdisciplinary Approach.* New York: Macmillan, Inc., 1972.
(8) Slusher, Howard S., and Aileene S. Lockhart. *Anthology of Contemporary Readings—An Introduction to Physical Education.* Dubuque, Iowa: Brown, 1970.

(9) Slusher, Howard S. *Man, Sport, and Existence—A Critical Analysis.* Philadelphia: Lea, 1967.

(10) *Sport and American Society.* Ed. by George H. Sage. Reading, Mass.: Addison-Wesley, 1970.

(11) *Sport, Culture, and Society.* Ed. by John W. Loy, Jr. and Gerald S. Kenyon. New York: Macmillan, Inc., 1969.

(12) *Sport in the Socio-Cultural Process.* Ed. by M. Marie Hart. Dubuque, Iowa: Brown, 1972.

(13) Ulrich, Celeste. *The Social Matrix of Physical Education.* Englewood Cliffs, N.J.: Prentice-Hall, 1968.

(14) Van Der Zwaag, Harold J. *Toward A Philosophy of Sport.* Reading, Mass.: Addison-Wesley, 1972.

CHAPTER 4

The efficient acquisition of skill in sports

In one respect our national sports teams in the Olympic Games and in other international sports competitions tend to lag behind those of some European nations: As a rule, the European teams have at least some of the following specialists attached to them on a regular basis who advise the coaches and consult with the athletes in the experts' areas of specialization:

1. A medical doctor in sports medicine.
2. An exercise physiologist.
3. A sports psychologist.
4. A person knowledgeable in biomechanics (principles of mechanics applied to human performance).

These specialists are able to offer help in special areas where many coaches and physical education instructors have little expertise. In the United States this deficiency has been recognized only recently. The primary purpose of this chapter is to provide specific information in the areas of biomechanics applied to sports and the psychology of motor learning, both of which have practical implications for learning sports skills.

In order for the reader to gain an understanding of some of the basic information that has been derived from these areas, and how to apply this information to his own sports performance, this chapter is mainly devoted to an exposition of biomechanics and motor learning.

Some of the important findings and information from the areas of sports medicine, exercise physiology, and sport psychology have already been presented in the first three chapters. An attempt has been and will be made to limit this information and explanations to what will be of *practical value* to the sports learner. Much of the considerable information that has been accumulated in these areas is both interesting and valuable; however, it does not enable the sports performer to improve his skill or overall play—this type of information is not included in these introductory chapters.

Most people would agree that if they are going to invest time and effort in learning the fundamentals of a sport or in improving their level of skill in a sport then his time should be used as wisely and as efficiently as possible. Otherwise, it is time and effort that is lost forever. The material in this chapter has been written with this purpose in mind. Consequently, by following the advice and observing the information and principles presented in the succeeding pages, the reader should progress at the maximum rate possible for his circumstances.

Sound Health Practices

One very important underlying aspect of becoming skilled in a sport is to *not* be distracted or retarded by subnormal physical (or mental) health. If one's health is less than optimal, this can and probably will have a deleterious effect in all endeavors. The possession of sound health is especially important in improving one's sports performance, which usually demands intense concentration and physical effort. To what degree the sound health practices listed below subsequently should be pursued is naturally a decision that must be made by the reader. To whatever extent they are violated will determine the price paid—how much one's future performance and improvement are impaired.

**Duke University
Department of Health and Physical Education
Prescription for your Future***

Introduction—Your health is one of your most valuable possessions. As you look toward the future, keep in mind the fact that the relatively small amount of time it takes to develop and maintain health is the most rewarding time you can spend.

1. Exercise regularly and properly (30 minutes a day at least three times a week of sustained large muscle activity like swimming, jogging, etc.). Include activities which provide for optimum endurance, strength, range of motion, and development of energy reserve.
2. Take time regularly for recreation (something you enjoy doing). Learn skills which are enjoyable and satisfying to you.
3. Adapt your activity and eating patterns to your body type. Select activity in which you can be most successful.
4. Learn to relax (practice relaxation regularly). Gain regular emotional stress release through sports, hobbies, etc.
5. Get enough rest (the average adult needs 6-8 hours daily).
6. Maintain abdominal muscles to prevent lower back pain. (Do exercises for this at least two times weekly.)
7. Don't smoke.
8. Avoid excessive use of narcotics, stimulants, and alcohol.
9. Don't worry—enjoy life. Develop a workable philosophy of life and a realistic self-image. Be concerned for and involved with others. Have creative outlets.
10. Don't overeat. If possible eat five small meals daily rather than three large meals. If you're overweight, reduce—keep your weight at the level it was while you were in college (assuming it was desirable then).
11. Don't eat too much animal (saturated) fat, sugar, or salt. Try to keep diet fats to no more than 20 per cent of total caloric intake.
12. Eat a balanced diet (adequate vitamins, minerals, and proteins).
13. Obtain adequate dental and medical care.

"Add Years to Your Life and Life to Your Years"

*Reproduced by permission of John Friedrich, Department of Physical Education, Duke University, Durham, North Carolina.

INTRODUCTION TO SECTION I

In section I here, "Mechanics of Sports Activities," the principles discussed apply to everyone; however, individual differences are evident in how different athletes and performers apply these principles in specific movements and situations. Evidence accumulated from some research studies indicates that although an actual knowledge of "mechanics" is not vital for an outstanding or a championship performance, beginning sports performers who were taught the correct applications of mechanics improved more rapidly than a similar group who were not given this information. There is the possibility, however, that if too much attention is focused on the correct mechanics of a sport, *initial* skill learning may be retarded for a short time.

For most sports performers the implication of such findings is that they should be taught or coached by someone who is cognizant of these mechanical principles and who will insist that they *not* be violated. The student who can recognize and apply these principles to his own performance is of course able to acquire the skills of a sport correctly and thus does not need to unlearn incorrect skills and then relearn the correct ones—generally a long, tedious process. Lawther (3) lists three ways in which a knowledge of mechanical principles may aid the performer, they: "may add to motivation, may help in the transfer of the learning to similar situations, may help in new learning for individuals with wide background in skills."

Section I: Mechanics of Sports Activities
*James G. Hay**

The University of Iowa

INTRODUCTION

The human body, like all other bodies, either animate or inanimate, functions in strict accordance with certain laws and fundamental concepts of mechanics—that branch of science dealing with the motion of bodies. For this reason a knowledge of these laws and concepts can be helpful in understanding activities involving motion of the human body and this, of course, includes all those sports activities with which this book is concerned.

Specifically, a knowledge of mechanics can be helpful in evaluating the particular problems an activity presents. For example, a student who is having difficulty in executing a forward one-and-one-half somersault dive might consider the mechanical factors relating to initiating rotations, and those relating to the speed (and thus the control) of such rotations in order to overcome his difficulty.

A knowledge of mechanics can be helpful too in evaluating the various alternative methods of performing a particular activity. For some activities there are a large number of styles or techniques that one might use. In high jumping, for instance, there are no less than five named styles—scissors, back layout, eastern cutoff, western roll and straddle—together with particular variations of each, such as the straight western roll and the V- (or dive) western roll, which one might employ.

Too often the decision as to which high-jumping style to use, which grip to use in golf, which type of forward pass or place-kicking technique to use in football, which style to employ when shooting free throws and so on, is based on grounds that are at best questionable. Many look to the established star performer as a model and unquestioningly copy his methods, ignoring two highly relevant points.

First, the style the star performer uses may demand certain physical prerequisites. Some of the shots used by a Wilt Chamberlain or a Lew Alcindor, for example, are in good part related to their unique physical characteristics. Those without similar physical gifts could expect little success using the same methods. Less extreme perhaps but just as valid are those instances where a particular style can be used by a champion because of his high degree of strength, agility, or flexibility. A novice attempting to employ the same methods will inevitably obtain poor results if he does not have the same highly-developed characteristics.

Secondly, to copy blindly the methods of a champion or star performer is to imply either that he has attained perfection in his technique—which is not as likely as might be expected—or that his faults as well as his good points are to be copied. It is very often not realized that most, if not all, champions are champions in spite of certain flaws in their techniques and that they might be able to obtain even higher levels of performance if they could eliminate these flaws. A somewhat extreme illustration of this point might be given by considering the case of Emil Zatopek, the famous Czech distance runner of the late 1940s and early 1950s. Zatopek ran practically every one of his major races looking as if he were undergoing the most inhuman physical torment—his face was distorted in apparent agony, his head and shoulders rolled in a grotesque manner, his eyes looked as if they were ready to fall out at any moment—yet his powerful legs never faltered as he virtually annihilated the world's best runners

---

*Dip., Phys. Ed., University of Otago, New Zealand; M.A., Ph.D., University of Iowa, Iowa City. Dr. Hay, in pursuing the Ph.D. degree, specialized in the study of biomechanics. He has since applied this knowledge to track and field (in which he has excelled for several years) and to other sports. In addition to presenting lectures on the mechanics of sports activities, Dr. Hay has conducted and published several research studies in this area, and has written a textbook on the subject, *The Biomechanics of Sports Techniques,* Prentice-Hall, Inc., 1973.

at distances from three miles to the marathon. This was a case of an athlete succeeding despite very obvious flaws in his technique. Had he chosen to work on eliminating these flaws it can reasonably be expected that he would have performed even greater feats. To have even considered copying Zatopek's technique to the extent of trying to employ the same grotesque gyrations of head and upper body would obviously have been absurd. It is less obvious perhaps, but no less absurd, to copy the champion in any sports activity without first ascertaining whether or not what is being copied is a desirable feature of his technique.

Another danger for the novice, attempting to reach a decision concerning which technique to learn or which particular variation of a technique is best, lies in interpreting what star performers recommend. In some instances (unfortunately far too few!) the star performer is a very astute observer of his activity, has amassed considerable experience in the activity, and has studied the scientific aspects of it. If one were in a position to know just which of the champions fell into this category one might be tempted to put considerable weight on their opinions. However, most often this is not known to the novice and most often, too, star performers have misconceptions as to what they do in performing their activity, and even more misconceptions as to why they do it. In general, they have a very clear conception of how their strokes, pitches, and stunts feel, but this feeling is very often rather inaccurate in terms of what actually happens. For example, a baseball pitcher throwing a curve ball may feel that he is releasing the ball at nearly arm's length in front of his body, and may assume such a pose if asked to describe how he does it. However, a basic knowledge of mechanics is all that is needed to demonstrate that this is just not the case and, in fact, is well-nigh physically impossible.

Very clearly, there are many pitfalls in acquiring a sound technique in any sports activity, one of the first of which is involved in the choice of which technique one should attempt to master. Fortunately mechanics provides us with an excellent means—in fact the final means—for making a decision. Mechanics is the science underlying all considerations concerning techniques in sports just as surely as physiology is the science underlying the training and conditioning of the body for participation in sport. It is to mechanics, therefore, that we must turn to find solutions to all our questions concerning techniques in sports.

An exhaustive discussion of the application of mechanics in the area of sports activities is well beyond the scope of this short chapter. The remainder of this part of the chapter will, therefore, be devoted to a presentation of just some of the basic mechanical laws and concepts that have wide or particularly significant application in the area of sports activities.

SCALARS AND VECTORS

The various physical characteristics of a body (e.g. its mass, weight, density, and specific gravity) and of its motion (e.g. displacement, velocity, and acceleration) and the forces that bring about its motion are classified in mechanics into two distinct categories: scalars and vectors. Scalar quantities have magnitude but no direction (mass, density, and specific gravity). Vector quantities, on the other hand, have both magnitude and direction (displacement, velocity, acceleration, weight, and force).

Vectors can be represented graphically by drawing a straight line to a scale such that the length of the line represents the magnitude of the vectors. The direction in which the line is drawn indicates the direction in which the vector is acting. Two or more such graphically-represented vectors can be summed in order to find their net effect or resultant. Consider, for example, the overhead view of an arrow on its way to the target. See Figure 4-1(a). As the arrow leaves the bow it is moving at a velocity represented by the length of the line OA and in the direction of the bull's eye on the target. On a still day it will not deviate laterally from this course. However, if there is a cross wind blowing, the arrow will be given an additional velocity in the direction of that wind—represented in magnitude and in direction by the line OB in Figure 4-1(b). If the parallelogram of which OA and OB are adjacent sides is now constructed, the diagonal through O represents in magnitude and direction the resultant velocity of the arrow. See Figure 4-1(c). Because this is no longer in the direction of the bull's eye it should be evident that some adjustment needs to be made in the point of aim (that is, the direction in which the arrow is initially fired) in order to obtain the best results. See Figure 4-1(d).

If one considers the effect of changing the length of the line OA (that is, increasing or decreasing the initial velocity of the arrow) on the direction of the resultant, it can be seen that the greater the velocity of the arrow the less it will be diverted from its initial course by a wind of a given velocity. It is this factor that governs the differences in the extent of the adjustments necessary for differing situations. A kicker attempting a field goal in football may have to aim several feet to one side of his target in order to compensate for a strong cross wind, whereas an archer may have to aim only a few inches, and a rifleman perhaps only a fraction of an inch to one side, when shooting from the same distance under identical conditions.

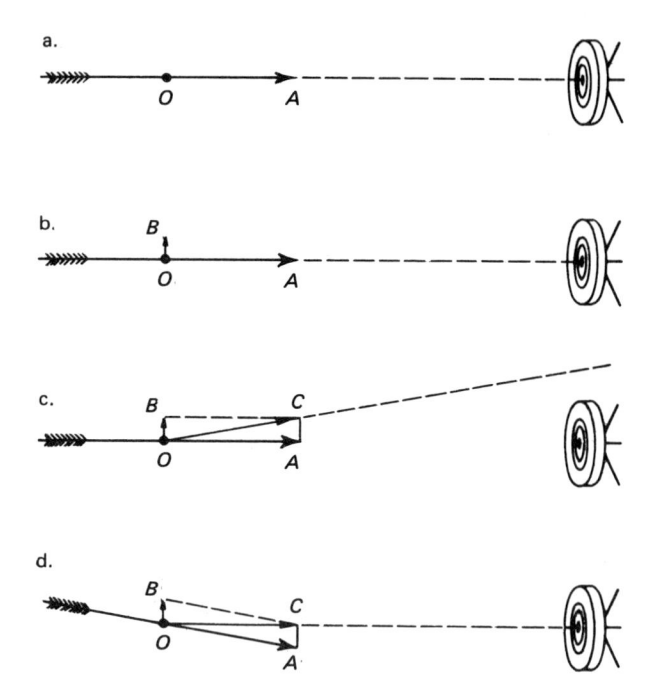

Figure 4-1. Effect of a cross-wind on the point of aim in archery. (*OA* represents the initial velocity of the arrow; *OB* represents the velocity subsequently imparted to the arrow by the cross-wind; and *OC* represents the resultant of these two vector quantities. Note that because both velocities *OA* and *OB* vary with time, actual conditions are simplified.)

PROJECTILES

Success in many sports activities depends largely on the ability of the performer to project a body into the air so that it will land at a desired point. Skill in horseshoe pitching, for example, depends to a large extent on the ability of the pitcher to judge his throw so that the shoe will land right by the stake. A player taking a penalty kick in soccer tries to kick the ball so that it will "land" at some predetermined point. In this case the point at which it is aimed to land the ball will be some point within and in the plane of the goal mouth. Perhaps in the top right-hand corner or maybe knee-high just inside the upright to the goalkeeper's left. In this case the element of time also becomes a factor of considerable importance. Although a hard-driven shot to either of the positions mentioned might reasonably be expected to result in a goal, a high floating lob shot to the same positions would probably be much less successful because the goalkeeper would have more time to cover the shot.

Most sports activities in which the flight of a projectile is important are of this second type, in which both time and position are critical factors. In some cases one or another of these two factors is replaced by another critical factor, the trajectory. In executing a lob in tennis, for example, it is important that the ball be hit so that it will land near the base line in the opponent's court. It is not really too important how long it takes to get there, but it is most important that it not be intercepted early in its flight—as, for example, by a player standing near the net. In this case, then, the two critical factors are those of position and trajectory.

In still more complex cases all three factors—time, position, and trajectory—become of critical importance. For example, the quarterback dropping back to pass has three things to consider in the execution of the pass. He has first to get the ball to a certain position. Secondly, he must not only get the ball to that position but he must get it there at the same time that his receiver's hands get there. Finally, he must release the ball in such a manner that its trajectory will be high enough for it to clear the outstretched hands of the onrushing defensive players. Thus it can be seen that, for the quarterback, time, position, and trajectory must all be considered.

Factors Governing Projectile Motion

The equations that show the basic relationships governing the flights of projectiles shed considerable light on the problems faced by the horseshoe pitcher, soccer and tennis players, and the quarterback. They show quite clearly that, in the absence of wind or air resistance (or in cases where these are negligible), the trajectory, the duration of the flight, and the position of the projectile at any given instant are completely determined by three factors relating to the way in which the projectile is released: (1) the magnitude of the velocity at which the object is released, (2) the angle to the horizontal at which it is released, and (3) the height from which it is released.

To obtain improved performance in activities involving the flight of a projectile depends logically, therefore, on the adjustment of one or more of these three factors. As far as the flight characteristics of the projectile are concerned, all other adjustments, such as alteration of the throwing or striking stance, grip on the object, and so forth, are only of importance insofar as they effect one or more of these three basic factors.

MOMENTUM

Momentum has been defined as the "quantity of motion that a body possesses" and, in the case where the body is moving in a straight line, is equal to the product of the mass of the body and its velocity. Thus, a big man traveling at the same velocity as a smaller man will have greater momentum by virtue of his greater mass.

Similarly, for two men of the same mass (or weight: weight = mass × constant), the one who is moving with the greater velocity will have the greater momentum. This is one of the reasons why speed (that is, the magnitude of the velocity) is of such great importance in activities such as wrestling, blocking in football, shoulder charging in soccer, and tackling in football and rugby.

When the body being considered is moving in a straight line, the momentum it possesses is termed *linear momentum*. On the other hand, if the body is undergoing motion that is rotary in nature (that is, the body is rotating about some axis), its momentum is termed *angular momentum*. In this latter case the magnitude of the body's momentum is equal to the product of its angular velocity (the number of degrees of rotation it undergoes in a given time) and a quantity termed its *moment of inertia*. A body's moment of inertia is a measure not only of the mass of the body but also of the distribution of this mass relative to the axis about which the body is rotating. Consider, for example, the three gymnasts in Figure 4-2. Each of these men is performing a backward somersault. The first is using a tightly tucked position in midflight and because the mass of his body is close to the axis about which his body is rotating, he has a relatively small moment of inertia. The second gymnast is performing his somersault in a piked position in which the mass of his legs and arms is somewhat farther away from the axis of rotation than was the case with the first man. He, thus, has a greater moment of inertia than the man in the tightly tucked position. The third gymnast has, of course, the largest moment of inertia of the three, because he has his limbs almost as far from the axis of rotation as it is possible to get them.

Law of Conservation of Momentum

Under certain conditions in which the effect of external forces can be considered negligible—and this can be said to apply in many situations in sports activities—the momentum that a body or aggregation of bodies possesses is said to be conserved (that is, it cannot be altered). As an illustration of this concept, consider a ball rolling down a bowling alley toward the pins. The ball, by virtue of its mass and its motion, has a certain amount of momentum. The pins, on the other hand, have zero velocity and, hence, zero momentum. When the ball strikes the pins it is slowed down a little (it loses some of its momentum). The pins, however, fly off in all directions, having between them gained the momentum lost by the ball. (Note that because the mass of the pins is considerably less than that of the ball, their increase in velocity is much greater than the velocity lost by the ball.) The total momentum of the system, however, is the same after impact as it was before. That is to say, the momentum of the ball plus the momentum of the pins after impact is equal to the momentum of the ball plus the momentum of the pins before impact.

This law, known in mechanics as the Law of Conservation of Momentum, is of particular significance in sports activities in which the human body is projected into the air. When in the air, the human body behaves in just precisely the same manner as does any other projectile: its trajectory, time of flight, and distance of flight (range) are completely determined by the three factors of speed, height, and angle of take-off (or release) mentioned earlier. However, although the trajectory of a person's body, or more specifically of his center of gravity, is completely determined at take-off, and nothing he does in the air can alter this, he can adjust the position of his body relative to his center of gravity in order to obtain certain desirable results. For example, the long jumper who uses the hitch-kick or running-in-the-air style does so, not to propel himself forward—a physical impossibility—but to position his body so that he can obtain the optimum forward reach of his heels as he lands.

Gymnasts, divers, and—to a lesser extent—track men (especially jumpers) use the principles involved in the Law of Conservation of Momentum frequently. For example, a gymnast executing a tucked forward somersault leaves the ground with a certain amount of angular momentum. By tucking in midflight, he decreases his moment of inertia and, because there can be no change in his angular momentum—it must be conserved in accord with the Law of Conservation of Momentum—this is accompanied by a

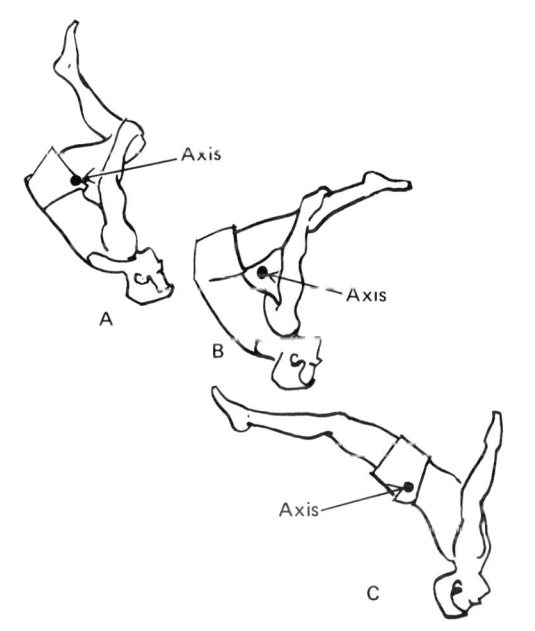

Figure 4-2. Backward somersault positions in order of increasing magnitude of the moment of inertia: (*a*) Tuck, (*b*) Pike, (*c*) Straight.

corresponding increase in his angular velocity. Then, after his body has rotated a certain amount, he increases his moment of inertia by straightening his body and extending his legs. This, in turn, slows his rotation (angular velocity) and puts him in position to make a controlled landing.

The trampolinist attempting the stunt known as a full turntable does essentially the same thing. After landing in a prone (or front drop) position on the bed, he thrusts off vigorously to one side, thereby imparting angular momentum to his body. Then, in order to get the maximum possible rotation from this angular momentum, he tucks up tightly, thus decreasing his moment of inertia and increasing his angular velocity. Just before he has completed 360° of rotation, he extends his body, slows his rotation, and prepares to land once again in a front drop position.

It should by now be apparent that two of the principal factors governing the amount of rotation obtained in any gymnastic or similar activity are the angular momentum with which the body leaves the ground and the adjustments subsequently made in the moment of inertia of the body. If a gymnast needs more rotation for a given stunt (and is already obtaining the optimum height for the stunt in question), he must increase his angular momentum at take-off and/or decrease his moment of inertia during part of the flight.

Transfer of Momentum

Another situation in which the Law of Conservation of Momentum applies is that where the momentum of one part of the body is transferred to the whole body. The racing start in swimming is an illustration of this. At the crack of the pistol the swimmer flings his arms forward and upward. As they approach the anatomical limit of their movement, their velocity is reduced to that of the body. This necessarily means that their momentum is reduced. Because the over-all momentum of the system is unaltered (again assuming that the external forces are negligible), the momentum of the rest of the body is, therefore, increased. Similar use of the arms or legs to transfer momentum from a part of the body to the body as a whole is evident in many activities, including most jumping events, certain gymnastic stunts, such as the kip or upstart, and such specialized movements as the rugby dive pass.

NEWTON'S LAWS

Three other laws of mechanics that can play a very large role in the understanding of human movements are those formulated by Sir Isaac Newton and first published in 1687. Of these three laws only one, Newton's third law, the Law of Reaction, will be considered here. This law states that for every action there is always an equal and opposite reaction; or, the mutual actions of any two bodies are always equal and oppositely directed.

Because every action is accompanied by an equal and opposite reaction, and because there are innumerable actions one might consider, there are, similarly, an endless number of possible examples of this law. To consider just a very few, one might turn first to the movements of walking and running. To propel the body forward in walking or running the driving foot is thrust downward and backward against the ground. This action of the foot against the ground is accompanied by an equal and opposite reaction of the ground against the foot. It is this reaction of the ground against the foot, and not the action of the foot against the ground, that brings about the forward movement. It should be obvious that this is so if one tries to conceive of how a force directed backward could *of itself* result in forward motion. The concept implied here, of motion necessarily being in the direction of the force that produces the motion, is actually embodied in the second of Newton's three laws, his Law of Acceleration.

The mass of the interacting bodies involved greatly influences the effects obtained. For example, one might consider the case of a person walking as a series of actions in which he pushes the ground back and the ground pushes forward. However, because the masses of the two bodies involved (the person and the earth) are so vastly different, the visible effects are also very different. The same force that propels the person forward has an imperceptible effect on the earth.

The influence of the mass of the interacting bodies is perhaps most readily apparent in rifle shooting. When a rifle is fired, the bullet leaves the muzzle at high velocity and the rifle moves in the opposite direction, but at a much lower velocity, because of its considerably greater mass. If the rifle is held loosely against the shoulder, the recoil or reaction will result in the butt of the rifle striking the shoulder a sharp, painful blow. However, if the rifle is held firmly against the shoulder, the effective mass of the reacting body will be that of the rifle plus the man and the reaction, although still the same in magnitude, will be considerably less violent. If the man is firmly braced against the ground—for example, as in shooting from a prone position (Figure 4-3)—the effective mass is further increased.

The Law of Reaction applied to movements executed while the body is in the air deserves special mention. To understand what happens in this situation one must first consider the normal relationship between bones and

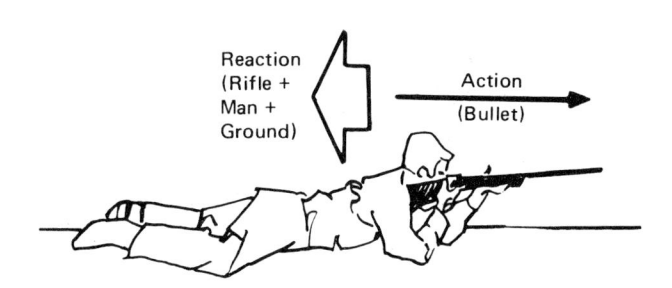

Figure 4-3. Increasing the effective mass of a rifle decreases the velocity of recoil.

muscles. When muscles contract they exert equal and opposite forces on the bones to which they are attached. Consider, for example, the weight lifter curling the dumbbell in Figure 4-4. His biceps muscle, which does a considerable amount of the work involved in this exercise, has two attachments to his scapula (shoulder blade) and one just below the elbow to his radius (one of the two bones of the forearm). As the muscle contracts, the force exerted on his radius is equal in magnitude and opposite in direction to the vector sum (or resultant) of the forces exerted on his scapula. If at this time both of these bones were free to move (that is, if his scapula was not firmly "fixed" by the action of other muscles), they would tend to move toward each other when the muscle contracted. This is essentially what happens when the body is in the air—contraction of a muscle or group of muscles causes the parts of the body to which they are attached to move toward each other.

Figure 4-4. Equal and opposite forces exerted by the biceps muscle.

Figure 4-5. Action and reaction in a leaping overhead smash in tennis.

The long jumper preparing to land is an excellent example of this. Just prior to landing, he contracts his abdominal and hip flexor muscles and swings his legs forward and slightly upward. As he does so, his upper body, acted on by the same muscles, is pulled forward and downward. Generally, the movement of the legs, which, of course, is the jumper's prime concern, is termed the *action* and the resulting movement of his upper body the *reaction*.

Sometimes the muscular analysis becomes quite complex as more and more muscles are involved in producing and controlling a particular movement. The over-all outcome however is essentially the same—the desired action of one part of the body is accompanied by an opposing reaction of some other part. The tennis player making a leaping overhead smash is an example of this. (Figure 4-5) As his racket has been swung downward and forward his legs have come upward and forward in reaction.

CONCLUSION

Possession of a basic knowledge of mechanics and of the application of mechanics to the teaching of sports activities is widely regarded as being an essential tool for physical education instructors.

Students who possess some knowledge of basic mechanical concepts and principles (perhaps as a result of course

The Efficient Acquisition of Skill in Sports

work in mechanics or the related sciences) can also gain considerable insight into the factors governing success in the performance of a sports activity by bringing their knowledge of mechanics to bear on the basic skills involved.

As a starting point, it is suggested that such students attempt to apply the mechanical concepts and principles discussed here, to the particular sports activity or activities with which they are concerned.

Later, as greater insight into the mechanical factors governing success in a sports activity become apparent, other means of applying a knowledge of mechanics to the solution of problems in sports activities should suggest themselves.

For all who participate in sports, and particularly for those who have some background in the science of mechanics, the application of this science to the analysis of sports activities affords excellent opportunities to obtain improved performances through an increased understanding of the nature of the skills involved.

INTRODUCTION TO SECTION II

Only in recent years has adequate attention been devoted to the theories and principles of motor learning in teaching motor skills or in acquiring skills in sports. At the present time, considerable attention and study are being devoted to the conditions under which the efficient practice of sports skills can best be arranged. The knowledge and research findings that are applied to the psychology of teaching and the psychology of coaching can facilitate the rapid, efficient learning of sports and their component skills. Limited research has been completed in motor learning and sports psychology, and as yet considerable gaps still exist in the knowledge available in these areas. Fortunately, however, much of the research completed in these areas has been performed with the use of college students as subjects. Thus, at least the commonly encountered problem of having to attempt to interpolate findings for a population differing in age, background, experiences, intelligence level, and so forth does not exist to the degree that is often encountered in many other areas of research.

One note of warning is in order: The majority of subjects in a sample may change significantly in a certain direction when systematically exposed to a specific learning situation. This still does not necessarily indicate that any given individual who undergoes a similar experience in the future when practicing a sport will necessarily change in that same direction. Although the odds underlying such findings favor this as the best approach to take, it must be remembered that considerable individual differences often prevail between various learners and performers of sports. Therefore, unless he initially has evidence to the contrary, the odds favor the person who follows the path that seems best for the majority.

The amount of evidence that has been accumulated to support various principles contained in this chapter differs. Sufficient evidence has been gathered to date, however, to seriously consider the principles of motor learning and adheres to them when learning a new sport or when attempting to improve one's level of skill in a sport. By recognizing, understanding, and conscientiously applying these principles whenever possible in practicing a sport, the learner should enhance the possibility of improving his skill at an optimum rate.

Section II: Principles of Motor Learning
Dr. Leon Smith*

Upper Montclair State College, New Jersey

SPECIFICITY VERSUS GENERALITY OF SPORTS SKILLS

Physical skills and learning of physical skills, like intelligence, are believed to be quite specific, and not a single general trait. Although "physically gifted" and the "super all-around athlete" are often-heard terms, as are "mentally gifted" or "genius," each person has many, many facets involved with either his physical or his mental abilities. Having an outstanding knowledge of mathematics or an aptitude for learning in this area gives almost no indication of one's knowledge of foreign languages or one's aptitude for learning them. Similarly, one's ability in swimming, for example, is of little value in predicting one's degree of skill or success in learning bowling or tennis. Thus, until a sport is attempted and practiced for some time, most persons will have little indication of how rapidly (or slowly) they will acquire proficiency in that particular sport. As beginners they are unaware of the ultimate level of achievement they may attain relative to themselves or to others. How many potential world champions have never achieved their innate ability because of a lack of training and practice?

Learning, performance, and the retention (remembering) of what has been previously learned are all different aspects of the broad problem facing the person who desires to utilize motor research principles in order to acquire skill in sports or improve skill. *Learning* can be considered to be the relatively permanent changes that take place in behavior (performance) in response to practice. *Motor learning,* which is the broad area in which sport skill acquisition resides, is the relatively stable changes in motor performance or skill that result from practice and largely involve patterned muscular contractions and bodily movements.

Much of the information gained in an attempt to understand motor learning has involved laboratory investigations in which the subjects performed such novel motor tasks as pursuit motor tracking, star drawing while viewing a mirror, and balancing on a stabilometer. Thus, the results of many of these studies have to be interpolated to the practical learning and developing of skills in sports.

LEARNING THEORIES

General psychologists, educational psychologists, and sport psychologists have, in recent years, advanced a number of theories, based on observed facts, principles, and laws of learning, in attempts to explain what learning is and especially how it takes place. As new facts and principles emerge, the theories have been amended, new ones added, and some old ones have lost support. Recently, the field of motor learning has been in considerable flux, causing many of the previously accepted theories and principles to be questioned and reevaluated.

Information processing and cybernetics, which include the study of the feedback loop—a process by which knowledge of results is, for example, obtained and one determines the effectiveness of practice—give rise to practical implications for teaching, coaching, and learning sports skills.

---

*B.Ed., Western Australia University, M.Ed., British Columbia University, Canada; E.D.D., University of California, Berkeley. Dr. Smith, formerly at the University of Iowa, is a well-known authority in the area of motor learning and sport psychology, having published more than forty articles in a variety of research journals in these areas. He has attended, and presented papers in, several national and international symposiums on sport psychology. He has been and is active in many sports; among his achievements are record performances in skin diving in Australia.

The Efficient Acquisition of Skill in Sports

Learning (Performance) Curves

Although the patterns may be similar, different individuals learn the same task at different rates (individual differences) and the same individual shows marked variation in the learning patterns (intraindividual differences) he exhibits for different tasks. Learning is inferred from plotting a performance curve for lengths of times varying from a few seconds to several or more years. These learning (performance) curves display many shapes and, for individuals, are generally irregular in shape. If average scores are used, or if smoothed curves are plotted, or if the performance of a large number of performers is plotted, the following types of curves are often the typical result:

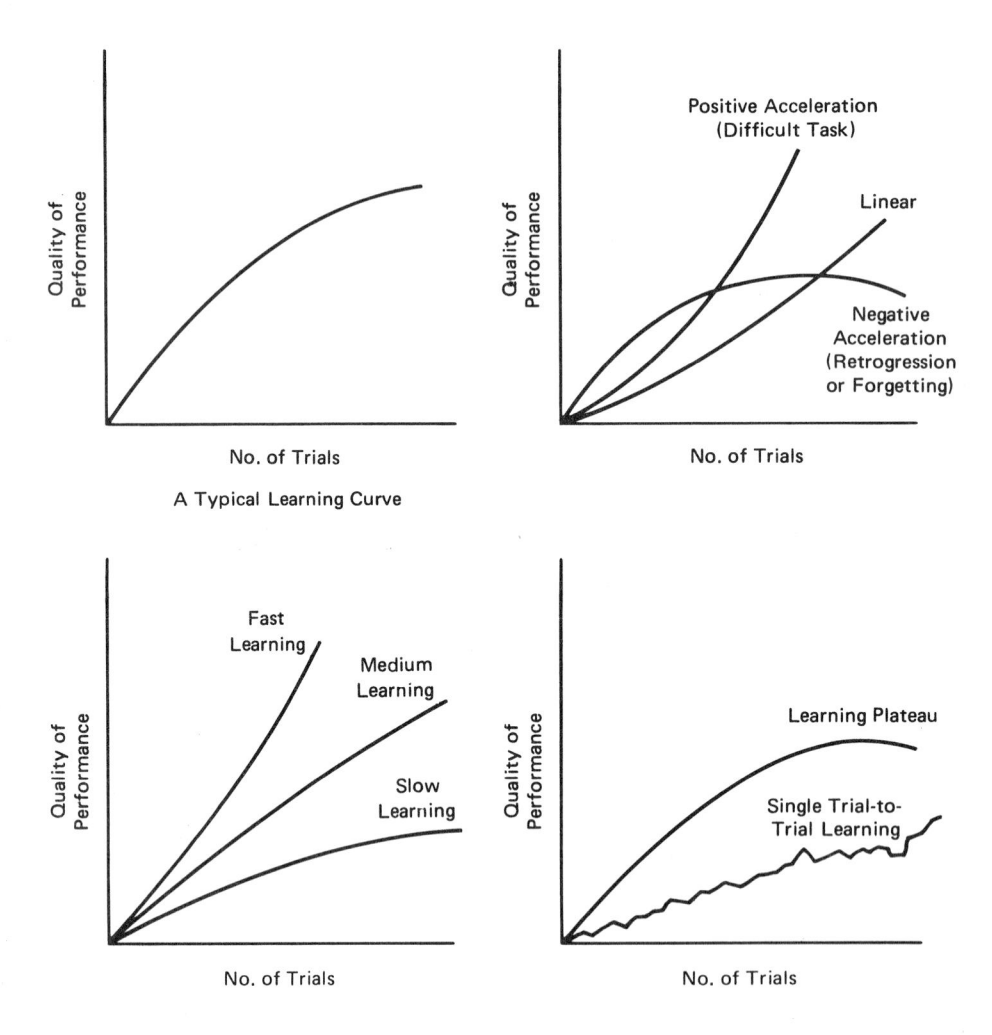

Careful evaluations of learning curves indicate that

1. Early success or failure in skill acquisition provides little indication in predicting later or final achievement.
2. The rate of learning a skill cannot necessarily be predicted from the current level of performance.
3. If conditions of learning are ideal, improvement in learning apparently continues indefinitely; man rarely achieves his ultimate learning potential. In studying the performance displayed during a twenty-year period of doing the same manual task in a factory, an investigator demonstrated that improvement in performance (learning) was still discernible.

At one time, a learning plateau was believed to exist (a period of time when no learning appears to take place despite continued practice during the learning process). Investigators have recently shown, however, that plateaus are not an integral component of learning curves. If the rate of learning temporarily slows or terminates, the soundest advice is that the teacher or coach should suggest new techniques and methods of practice to his students, or else the learner himself should adopt a new approach to his practice.

The *reminiscence phenomenon* (an improvement in performance after a long rest period or layoff without any practice) is often noticed by many sportsmen such as tennis players, bowlers, and golfers. Following a layoff, they often play an excellent first game, after not having played or practiced throughout the winter months, for example. Learning can also occur when the learner is fatigued; thus, while the performance curve temporarily lags during a fatiguing practice period, it may improve in a manner similar to reminiscence during the next session.

Learning Considerations

Singer (8) has pointed out that many variables influence one's rate and amount of learning. Individual variables, such as age, previous experience, and capacity for learning are not amenable to change—the learner must accept them as they are. However, *task variables* (length, difficulty, and the meaningfulness of the material to be learned), which can be controlled, and *method-of-learning variables* (such as the type of practice and how the material is presented to the learner) are both amenable to some manipulation and control by the learner, teacher, or coach. These types of learning variables are the ones discussed in this part of the chapter.

Knowledge of Results

In order for the most effective learning to occur, the learner needs to have an accurate knowledge of his performance. This is often regarded as the most critical factor associated with learning. Two of the most important aspects of knowledge of results are the quality and the rapidity of the feedback following motor performance. In order to obtain a high quality of feedback, especially during early learning, the learner or performer needs a competent observer to observe his performance, to constructively criticize it, and to advise him as to how to correct his mistakes and improve his performance. Thus, competent coaching or teaching is an essential element in learning to improve one's performance. Combined with this requirement is the need or requirement for having an appropriate model whose performance can be emulated. The learner can thus attempt to imitate this model and compare his performance to a concrete standard. Hence, the use of demonstrations, motion picture films, video tapes, and other visual methods are often most helpful for facilitating the rate of learning. For the beginner, especially, slow-motion films and television tapes can be extremely instructive in permitting the learner to see quite clearly each individual facet (or phase) of a skill that he is learning. Obviously, having a knowledge of the correct performance (model) does not necessarily mean that the learner will achieve this ideal goal. Also, there are often wide variations between how a learner actually performs and what he *thinks* he is performing. This fact emphasizes once again the critical need for an observant teacher or coach who is conversant with correct form and can report to the learner the discrepancy (error) between his performance and the learning goal.

In general, the more rapid, specific, and quantitative the feedback, the more meaningful it is to the learner and the greater its possibility of facilitating learning. Therefore, as little time as possible should elapse between each performance and the evaluation of that performance. In most instances, feedback of some kind should occur after each trial, especially in the initial learning stages. As the learner improves (1) his skills, (2) his awareness of the correct model, and (3) his ability to analyze his performance correctly, the need for external constructive criticism is essential. Even the world's best professional golfers frequently have a golf pro watch and analyze their golf strokes. They are particularly apt to seek outside help anytime their game deteriorates or they lose their normal grooved swing. Because these players, who have perhaps been playing golf for twenty or thirty years, still feel the need for someone to evaluate them in their area of expertise, it seems obvious that all learners will continue to need constructive feedback from a competent coach.

Reinforcement of Learning

The reinforcement of learning is based on information that the performer can utilize in checking or confirming his performance. Information feedback, or knowledge of results, is the most wisely used form of reinforcement. Little or no learning takes place unless there is meaningful feedback. Feedback is a mechanism that allows the performer to confirm, correct, or moderate his response to a given task; thus, in essence, he is able to reinforce himself based on his progress. A number of theories have been advanced to explain how and why appropriate feedback enhances the learning process.

Sensory feedback can be intrinsic or internal—it occurs when the person perceives the performance from within; it is a kinesthetic feeling as when a golf swing feels "good" or feels correctly grooved. Sensory feedback also can be extrinsic or external—many types of sports, such as archery and badminton, give immediate external feedback of a visual nature. In order to make the best utilization of the concept of feedback when practicing or playing sports, feedback should (1) be immediate (follow as close to the response or performance as possible); and (2) be as quantitative as possible. Generally, visual feedback (seeing) seems more effective than auditory or verbal instructions (which works well for higher-level motor skills), which in turn seems more effective than manual guidance.

All types of feedback, however, should be utilized whenever they are appropriate in order to acquire skill in a sport at an optimum rate.

Ideal Learning Conditions

The learner often cannot control all the variables in his learning environment that affect how effectively he acquires skill in sports. However, those factors that can be manipulated or controlled by the sports performer can be a valuable asset in assisting the learning task. One individual variable about which a person can take remedial steps is either to have or to develop a command of the fundamental movements (running, throwing, catching, pivoting, and so on) that are normally learned early in life. Skills appear to evolve and to develop in hierarchies, and the higher complex patterns of movement are more difficult to develop if the component parts (simple skills comprising them) have not been previously acquired.

Whole versus Part Learning

In whole learning the entire skill is studied at one time, whereas in part learning specific phases of an activity are practiced before other phases are introduced or the activity is practiced in its totality. Thus, in learning to play tennis, the beginner may learn separately the serve toss, the weight shifting of the body, and the serving swing before practicing the complete act of serving.

In general, no single definitive answer exists concerning the most efficient manner of practicing and learning a sport. For a given person, skill, sport, or situation, one method of practice may be best; the opposite may hold true for a different person, skill, sport, or situation. The best procedure perhaps is to practice the largest whole part of the skill or sport that the learner can grasp and perform. This part should be meaningful to the performer; he should know how it meshes into the over-all skill or sport.

The more skilled the learner, the larger is the whole that can be meaningfully practiced with success. The part method may be better for becoming skilled in or learning a complex skill such as team sports (basketball, football, or volleyball). The whole method of learning may tend to be more efficient for learning sequential material or the difficult skills of individual sports (such as serving the tennis ball) as it is with later practice periods of the same skill or sport (or when the practice periods are distributed over a block of time).

In all skills the learner should begin practice with as large a whole or subwhole as can be perceived within the gross framework of the total activity or sport. Therefore, in learning a new sport the whole, if it is not too difficult, should first be attempted; next, individual parts, which should be large enough and sufficiently difficult to be challenging, should be practiced, provided the learner realizes the role these parts play in the over-all sport. It is vital that the relationship of any part to the whole be clearly understood if practice of that part is to be meaningful and productive. This concept gives rise to what is called a hierarchy of sports skills; that is, at the base are those simple skills on which the more advanced skills are developed. This means that the learner must learn the basic skills of a sport in the proper hierarchical order, proceeding from the simple to complex skills.

Transfer of Learning

The transfer of learning (training) is the process wherein practicing or performing one skill (or sport) influences the learning of a second skill (or sport). It appears to influence all learning. The presence of transfer is obvious, for example, when an experienced musician learns to play a new instrument or a skilled tennis player learns to play badminton. Thus, training acquired in one sport can often be applied to learning other sports.

Transfer seems to be most beneficial when (1) the training conditions underlying two skills are highly similar, (2) the general principles appropriate to the two skills are well understood, (3) motivated and sustained effort is extended during the learning of a series of related skills, and (4) a hierarchy (ordered from easy to difficult) of closely related skills is learned in order. The previously described conditions involve a *positive* transfer of learning in which the near-identical elements of a learned skill have a high probability of being transferred to the new skill being learned. In order for optimum positive transfer to occur, the performer should be motivated to transfer, and he must be taught how to transfer as, for example, how the smash in badminton (new skill) is quite similar in action to the overarm throw in baseball (previously learned skill).

Unfortunately, in certain situations a *negative transfer* of learning can occur, which results in a hinderance to or an inhibition of learning. Examples of this would be the tennis player who attempts to use broad, sweeping, straight-arm strokes when playing racquetball, or the baseball player (an experienced batter who uses a leg hitch when swinging the bat) who attempts to learn the correct golf swing in which a completely different leg and hip action is used.

The term *interference* (negative transfer) is used to describe any inhibition that retards the transfer process. Up to a certain point, highly similar or markedly different skills cause the least amount of negative transfer, whereas moderately similar skills can result in a large amount of interference. Two types of inhibition can occur. *Proactive inhibition* results when a previously learned skill interferes with the learning of a new skill, especially if it is complex. *Retroactive inhibition* results when the learning of a new skill interferes with the retention of a previously learned skill. The impact of the interpolation of intervening activity on retention depends mainly on the similarity or dissimilarity of the two skills and follows the pattern already cited for interference. The implication derived from conditions that favor negative transfer is that in learning or practicing sports, in general, highly similar or quite different skills and sports should be practiced in any given unit of time; a longer time span should separate the practice of moderately similar skills or sports.

Overlearning (Retention or Remembering)

Many periods of appropriate repetitive practices lead to the overlearning of skills, which generally results in effective, long-term retention, particularly if satisfying experiences have been associated with the prolonged practice. For example, once one overlearns how to ride a bicycle or to swim, the skill is rarely forgotten. Interference or negative transfer, of course, plays a role in retention or relearning, which in part depends on the similarity and intensity of the interpolated activity, the length of the layoff period, and the skill level prior to the layoff period. Usually, if initial learning was effective, relearning requires less time and practice than did the original learning.

LEARNING AND COACHING CONSIDERATIONS

1. The learner should have explicit, clear models or standards to imitate (a skilled performer, books, pictures, films, and television are very helpful for this purpose). He also must practice in order to acquire a skill. Playing against a better player or team whenever possible gives the learner an opportunity to learn the techniques, skills, and strategies of the more skilled performers. (A learner should be encouraged to develop his own individual style of performance.)
2. The performer should plan his strategy ahead of time, such as the receiver planning where the serve will be returned in badminton, handball, racquetball, or tennis. Such preplanning allows the receiver the opportunity to respond automatically and correctly.
3. Form the habit of analyzing each play or play series as soon as it is completed; try to determine how a performance or strategy could have been improved.
4. Carefully study the opponent or opposing team and locate weaknesses to exploit and strengths to avoid or counter.
5. Work toward eliminating or protecting weaknesses: for example, if the backhand is weak, take a court position somewhat on the backhand side, thus forcing the opponent to hit a majority of shots to the forehand.
6. The use of appropriate equipment of good quality can often be helpful in improving skill in a sport.
7. The conditions under which learning or practice takes place should simulate real playing conditions as closely as possible. A basketball offensive play should be practiced at regular or full speed—a walkthrough would be valuable only during initial learning.
8. Try to remember the "feel" of doing whatever is being learned.
9. Set high but realistic goals.

Selected References

(1) *Contemporary Readings in Sport Psychology.* Ed. by William P. Morgan. Springfield, Ill.: Thomas, 1970.
(2) Cratty, Bryant J. *Movement Behavior and Motor Learning.* Philadelphia: Lea, 1967.
(3) Lawther, John D. *The Learning of Physical Skills.* Englewood Cliffs, N.J.: Prentice-Hall, 1968.
(4) Oxendine, Joseph B. *Psychology of Motor Learning.* New York: Appleton, 1968.
(5) *Quest.* "Psychology of Sport." Ed. by Margaret A. Mordy. Published by NAPECW and NCPEAM. Monograph XIII, Winter Issue (Jan. 1970).
(6) *Quest.* "A Symposium on Motor Learning." Ed. by Pearl Berlin. Published by NAPECW and NCPEAM. Monograph VI, Spring Issue (May 1966).
(7) *Readings in Motor Learning.* Ed. by Robert N. Singer. Philadelphia: Lea, 1972.
(8) Singer, Robert N. *Motor Learning and Human Performance—An Application to Physical Education Skills.* New York: Macmillan, Inc., 1968.
(9) Singer, Robert N., et al. *Physical Education—An Interdisciplinary Approach.* New York: Macmillan, Inc., 1972.

CHAPTER 5

Selecting sports for participation

The problem of selecting sports in which to participate is generally not a serious problem for the college student or adult. Such factors as degree of interest; amount of skill and past practice; knowledge of, and familiarity with, several sports; the probable enjoyment that will be forthcoming; what facilities and equipment are available; the season of the year; what sports are close friends interested in playing; the availability of an opponent or of teammates and opposing teams; and the amount of leisure time available are all obvious considerations when deciding what sport or sports one wishes to engage in today, next week, next year, or even in a decade.

The contents of this chapter are devoted to a cursory examination of some of the variables one may want to consider in selecting sports to play and especially in selecting previously untried sports in which to receive instruction and coaching in order to play these sports with skill and interest in the future. Most people appear to derive increased satisfaction in playing sports in which they have at least some skill. The beginning golfer may enjoy playing a round of golf, but usually he soon becomes aware of many errors in his performance; as he continues to practice and to play, the sport of golf often increases in enjoyment and fascination for him. Even though mistakes are apt to occur, the beginning skier or scuba diver may find his or her initial efforts to be exhilarating and full of inducement to continue them. In large part, the enjoyment of a sport appears to bear little relationship to one's skill, providing the competition is fairly close or that pleasant companionship or camaraderie are present.

At one time, recreators, based on the findings of a widely publicized survey of recreational pursuits, believed that most enjoyable recreational activities were learned by the age of 12. For sports, at least, this no longer appears to hold true. Most individuals are not exposed to a wide variety of different sports until a later age. Examples of such sports are archery, badminton, sailing, racquetball, and weight lifting. In addition, new sports and sport facilities have only recently become available to the average person; many of these have not yet been introduced into the physical education curriculum. Examples of these sports are judo, rock climbing, scuba diving, snow skiing, and sports parachuting.

Vocational Field and Sports Selection

If one has some idea of his future vocational or professional field, the sports in which he learns and participates can be selected with a view toward being a complete change of pace from the daily routine. Large numbers of doctors and dentists participate in golf and tennis: sports that get them out-of-doors, involve moderately strenuous activity, demand considerable bodily movement, and require distant instead of close-up vision. Those who will encounter more-than-ordinary stress or tension in their occupations would be wise to select tension-reducing sports that permit aggressions to be relieved in acceptable ways. Racquetball and handball are examples of popular activities that can be utilized for this purpose.

The tendency toward a sedentary life that is imposed on students needs to be balanced by sports requiring significant amounts of physical activity. This may help explain the popularity of basketball among college students. Jogging and swimming would also supply this need but, because of the lack of competition and teammates, they may not be as appealing, even though they provide a quick, effective workout.

Actually, so far as this writer knows, there have been few studies made in which sports preferences and vocational fields have been compared. If very large numbers of participants in any sport are examined, many occupational fields will normally be represented. The studies done to date tend to focus on the relationship between socioeconomic class and kind of sports participation, or else on the kinds of occupations that college athletes later go into.

In general such studies indicate that in some sports, such as wrestling and tackle football, the athletes are drawn from lower socioeconomic classes. Their fathers are in less prestigious occupations, whereas the fathers of golf and tennis athletes fall into the upper half of these categories. Observations of sports participation by socioeconomic classes leads to some obvious findings. Yachting, by its expensive nature, is largely confined to the upper class. The immense popularity of basketball in the ghettos has often been discussed.

Body Type and Sports Participation

Some studies have been conducted concerning what types of body build seem to be most effective in various sports. These studies have usually involved college athletes or champion athletes, not the average sports participant. Their purpose was generally to permit coaches to assign effectively playing positions or events to the athlete whose body type seemed best suited for success in that event or position. In many sports, swimming as one example, it was found that there were usually no single types of body builds that were most successful; instead, many factors, several of which were psychological, were involved. This fact is evident when one views the wide variation in body type evident in professional golfers. One tends to associate the tall, slender (ectomorphic) type of build as being the most suitable for basketball playing success. Even here, where this applies better than for most sports, numerous exceptions are apparent at the guard position. For success in most sports, a minimum amount of muscularity (a mesomorphic type of build) and restrictions on the amount of body fat (endomorphy) are usually requisite components.

Some authorities in this area claim that one's basic body type, which is almost always made up of varying amounts of all three types of body structure, never changes throughout life. This means that a person has to live with whatever body build he inherits from his ancestors. This claim that the basic body build never changes is disputed by others, however. In addition, the usual goal is not to be a champion athlete but rather to develop skills and interests in sports that can be enjoyed for many years. Thus, one's body build appears to be a secondary consideration at best in selecting sports for participation. Indeed, the opposite argument might be made: that is, one should select certain sports with the idea of modifying the body build. Distance running or jogging, for example, is an excellent activity, if participation is regular, for getting rid of excess body weight.

PRESENT NEEDS, INTERESTS, AND ENVIRONMENTS

While attending college the students usually have a wide variety of sports from which to choose. Hence, those sports in which one has the greatest interest will probably be uppermost in any selection. However, because college students often have a limited sports background and because they are normally exposed to so many sports in which they can receive instruction and training, the college years appear to be the ideal time to explore and diversify one's sports interests. The average college student has a young, resilient body that is able to endure considerable stress and hard physical work; it responds quickly to training and skill and these can be acquired at an efficient pace.

As is true for junior and senior high school students, team sports possess considerable appeal. These are generally available in the instructional program and are almost always available in club sports and intramural sports programs. Mitigating against choosing team sports is the fact that in most physical education and sports programs previous to college, team sports are heavily emphasized and most students have a larger exposure to them than to nonteam sports. Among the arguments supporting the involvement in team sports is the fact that facilities, teammates, and opponents are easily available; they are scheduled at the most convenient times for a busy college student; and good fellowship and the social benefits derived from being a team member are readily forthcoming.

The British have a system of athletics that Americans could well emulate. A college will have not one soccer team, but rather A, B, C, D, and E, or even more, soccer teams, according to the number and abilities of the students. Each of these teams plays the equivalent-level team from another college whenever a sports contest is held. This pattern is also often followed with community sports teams. Thus, at most levels, many of the sports enthusiasts are actively playing rather than sitting and watching.

Now, while one is enrolled in sports classes in which instruction and coaching are readily available, is an excellent time to learn how to play new sports. Most adults, if they are beginners, do not like to be singled out because of ineptitude. This often happens if special sports instruction or tutoring is sought after leaving college when one may be the only beginner in a group. Many sports classes in the college setting are offered especially for beginners; in this situation the neophyte is just one of many in the class.

FUTURE SPORTS NEEDS AND INTERESTS

It is difficult to predict with much accuracy what one's future environment will be and what facilities will be available for sports participation. For this reason, despite the fact that sports facilities of many types are experiencing a rapid growth in America and other parts of the world, any preparation that is made for future sports participation must be of a general nature. With more and more communities adding or expanding municipal recreation programs, with artificial inland water areas being constantly added, and with the present huge interest in sports, it would appear that the prospects of being able to engage regularly in a wide variety of sports are indeed bright, especially in view of the increasing availability of inexpensive transportation. However, as is true of present sports needs, if one is to enjoy sports on a daily basis, sports facilities must be near by and easily accessible.

Five, ten, twenty, or even forty years after one's college days will produce changes, most of them irreversible, in one's body. Invariably, some fitness and perhaps skill will be lost. The needs and interests of a wife and children will have to be considered as well. One's sports interest may change, although in one study it was found that the recreational habits of young men did not differ greatly in kind from those of older men. These are the kinds of factors for which one should make future plans.

For example, team sports are so constituted that no one player can control the level or intensity of play as can be done with individual and dual sports. This, in turn, can cause them to be somewhat dangerous for the older person, especially if he is out of training, to play. This may be one of the important reasons why, in comparing the sports interests of three thousand men ranging in age from 20 to 59 years, a definite decline with age was found for team sports. The greatest decline in participation and interest in recreational activities (and sports) was in those requiring (1) quick reaction time, (2) physical stamina and endurance, and in those (3) satisfying the romantic and erotic impulses. Those that increased in popularity with increasing age were those that were of a sedentary nature and that were enjoyed when alone or with only a few people.

The physical recreational habits of a group of young adults, who five to ten years ago graduated from a large Midwestern university, were revealed in the results of a survey conducted recently. In the following table the percentages and frequencies of their current participation in sports activities are listed.

Activity	Total Participation (of 226)	Per cent Participating Yearly	Monthly	Weekly
Swimming	154	24	50	26
Golf	132	27	33	39
Dancing, social	97	51	40	7
Conditioning activities (including jogging)	86	7	36	57
Tennis	81	56	32	12
Bowling	76	49	26	25
Basketball	73	45	27	27
Badminton	69	64	32	4
Softball	69	46	30	23
Table tennis	58	59	33	9
Boating	57	44	32	25
Volleyball	57	68	14	18
Hunting	55	27	22	51
Fishing	53	32	43	25
Skiing, water	50	52	34	14

Activity	Total Participation (of 226)	Per cent Participating Yearly	Per cent Participating Monthly	Per cent Participating Weekly
Football, touch	44	43	36	18
Handball	44	41	27	32
Home recreational games	41	17	54	29
Skating, ice	36	42	47	11
Canoeing	35	74	17	9
Riflery	30	47	37	17
Skiing, snow	27	33	33	33
Weight training	27	59	22	19
Diving	25	20	44	36
Horseshoes	21	81	14	5
Archery	17	65	24	12
Dancing, square	17	59	18	24
Track and field	9	56	33	11
Fencing	7	100	0	0
Gym work	7	14	43	43
Wrestling	7	71	14	14
Shuffleboard	6	50	50	0
Squash racquets	6	33	17	50
Trampolining	4	50	50	0
Hiking	3	0	100	0
Judo	3	67	33	0
Paddleball	3	67	33	0
Skating, roller	3	67	33	0
Horseback riding	2	50	50	0

However, another group of adults was questioned concerning the reasons for their unsatisfactory participation in sports, the main reasons given were (1) lack of time, (2) poor health, (3) lack of finances, and (4) lack of facilities.

SPECIAL CONSIDERATIONS FOR THE AVERAGE SPORTS PARTICIPANT

Team sports seem to have special values and they command a high degree of interest up through the college years. Skill in lifetime (lifelong) sports, mainly nonteam sports, in which one can engage for most of one's life should be acquired before leaving college. The popularity of water sports in many forms continues to increase; one should become proficient in swimming before completing college in order to enjoy safely such water sports as sailing, scuba diving, and water polo. Many of the so-called exotic sports, which were not offered in college physical education programs a generation ago, continue to attract large numbers of enthusiasts. College physical education classes now offer opportunities to learn skills in skiing, Hatha yoga, rock climbing, and horseback riding.

Many sports are seasonal in nature. If one is to maintain regular vigorous physical activity via the sports route, careful consideration must be given to this problem. Although most indoor sports (basketball, handball, badminton) can be played the year round, many outdoor sports are of limited duration each year because of climatic conditions (snow skiing, softball, tennis). Other sports, such as swimming and weight training, can be engaged in in either environment. The best solution might be to engage in several sports each year, each in its own season. This scheme, because it would involve not playing a particular sport during its off season (not playing golf during the winter) would tend to preserve a zest for each sport.

Plans should be made to participate in a variety of sports in order that all the important aspects of physical fitness can be developed or maintained (cardio-respiratory endurance, flexibility, agility, strength, and power). Such participation should also assure continued body symmetry and muscle proportionality.

Paul Hunsicker, in his booklet on physical fitness research findings that is published by the AAHPER, list sports that are high in contributing to physical fitness. These include badminton, basketball, handball, swimming, distance running (jogging), and tennis. He also lists the following sports as being less useful in their contribution to physical fitness.

Moderate Contribution
   Baseball
   Softball
   Track sprints
   Volleyball

Fair Contribution
   Archery
   Golf
   Hiking

Poor Contribution
   Bowling
   Croquet
   Dancing (social)
   Horshoes
   Shuffleboard

By no means should the sports in the last three categories be avoided; however, one should be aware that they do not contribute highly to physical fitness or the maintenance of cardiovascular health and that such sports participation thus needs to be regularly supplemented with play in strenuous sports.

One of the problems faced by Americans who wish to participate regularly in a variety of sports is the lack of sufficient near-by facilities for the large numbers of would-be sports participants. Admittedly, there has been a recent wave of construction of indoor and outdoor tennis courts, golf courses, handball and racquetball courts, bike paths, hiking trails, and so on. However, many more sports facilities need to be constructed in the near future. This is something that all citizens can urge and support for their schools, and especially for their communities.

part 2

Individual and team sports

INTRODUCTION TO PART II

The material in this part of the book constitutes the major portion of the over-all contents, and it contains information about the most-often taught sports in college physical education programs. The selection of these sports was based on a survey of physical education programs throughout the United States. Therefore, such specific geographical areas as, for example, the far-northern states, in which winter sports such as snow skiing and ice hockey are popular, or areas near large bodies of water or the ocean, in which water skiing, sailing, or canoeing may be offered, are not included. Instead, those sports activities that are most often taught in general physical education programs in colleges and universities—whether such programs consist of required or elective physical education, or both—have been selected for presentation. Because college physical education curricula are in the process of change, and because more and more classes are being offered on a coed basis and as electives, the student may find that he is enrolled in a sports class not covered in this book. This writer is well aware that many varied and exotic sports are gradually being added to physical education programs. If the continued popularity of such sports is demonstrated, they will be included in future editions of this book.

One of the foremost goals of the student (and of physical education teachers as well) is to become well educated physically. A physically educated person is one who, among other things, possesses a knowledge and understanding about a variety of sports and who has developed some degree of skill in playing these sports. This book will hopefully serve as one means of furthering one's education of the "physical." Because backgrounds, experience, needs, interests, and aptitudes are highly individualistic in nature, the student should preferably have a free and wide range of choice in selecting those sports and activities in which he wishes to develop further skill, knowledge, and interest. It is especially recommended that the reader carefully consider developing some expertise in sports that will be attractive in the postcollege phase of life.

In selecting sports in which to develop skills, interests, and appreciations, the student is most apt to be guided by a consideration of which sports and activities have the most appeal to him in terms of the actual or expected enjoyment derived from playing the sport. If the student is inexperienced in some sports, he may wish to see others participate in these or talk to some who have played the sport in order to decide whether it will prove to be fun, challenging, or otherwise worth the investment of the time demanded to learn the sport.

General guidelines in selecting sports and activities, which should be given consideration in choosing future participation patterns, should undoubtedly include the following category of sports activities.

Lifelong or lifetime sports. Lifelong or lifetime sports should constitute at least one half of one's repertoire in sports. These are usually individual and dual types of sports, although other categories may also qualify. Those sports that a person can play literally for the remainder of his life have many advantages.

Lifelong sports generally do *not* require a high degree of physical fitness for safe participation. Also, the equipment used in playing the sport is usually inexpensive and easily available. Facilities for playing most of these sports are generally located in large numbers in all areas of the United States and elsewhere. Finding a partner or opponent(s) on a temporary or permanent basis can be easily arranged, as can a daily, tri- or biweekly schedule of play. Most lifelong sports can be played with enjoyment with other family members as well as friends—differences in age or size are generally not a serious problem. Such sports as tennis, golf, racketball, bowling, archery, swimming, and even volleyball are examples of sports with lifelong potentiality.

Team sports. Team sports possess characteristics that make them extremely suitable for college-age participants. Teammates and opponents are easily found, playing schedules can be arranged with a minimum of effort, and facilities and playing areas often exist in large numbers in the college and university setting. College-age students normally are sufficiently fit that strenuous team play imposes no serious health hazards. In addition, participation in team sports affords opportunities for developing or enhancing such favorable traits as leadership and followership—the ability to cooperate well with other team members in a united effort, subjugating individual effort for the good of the team, and so forth. Any sport in which there are three or more members on one team is said to be a team sport. Dual sports in one sense could also be considered team sports. Some team sports such as volleyball and softball, especially slow-pitch, have excellent potential as lifelong sports.

Aquatic sports. Aquatic sports are sports performed in or on water. Many water sports such as canoeing, sailing, scuba diving, and springboard diving have excellent recreational value and many aquatic sports are well adapted for a lifetime of enjoyment. Because of safety aspects when engaging in aquatic sports, many physical educators believe that everyone should attain at least an elementary level of swimming skill. Each year the number of water sports enthusiasts grows. It now appears that most adults will spend some of their recreational time in or near the water. Consequently, the student is well advised to master at least one aquatic sport.

Combative sports. The popularity of combative sports, such as self-defense, judo, karate, fencing, and wrestling, seems to increase each year. If combative types of sport have an appeal, increasing opportunities are available for learning them. Aside from some possible personal safety aspects, the decision concerning whether or not to engage in combative sports is very much an individual one.

The sports listed in the second part of this book are in alphabetical order for convenience in locating readily information about them. This appears to this writer to be a better scheme than categorizing the sports as lifetime, team, combative, and so on. Such categories tend to be artificial in nature, because many sports can logically be assigned to two or more such categories.

In general, each sport chapter is composed of the following segments: brief history, description of activity; unique values to be derived; selection of equipment and its care; techniques of participation (fundamental skills and techniques, strategy, safety; basic rules, including courtesies or etiquette; specific training methods; glossary of terms; self-evaluation) and selected references (books and periodicals).

Most of the chapters are written for a range from the beginner who has never before attempted the sport to the person who may have attained an intermediate level of skill. In some of the chapters, portions of the material will be of value to the person who possesses an advanced level of skill. The student should keep in mind the fact that the effectiveness of the strategy that he employs and the type of play that will tend to work best will vary according to the skill level and experiences of the performer (and his partner or teammates) as well as to the degree that the opponent possesses these qualities. What may be excellent strategy for a beginner to employ, for example, might be quite poor strategy for a highly skilled player. Championship tennis players often aim to hit the side line marker whereas, because of lack of accuracy, this is apt to result in a loss of points if attempted by a tennis player of average-or-less tennis skill.

Now, while one is enrolled in college, is an excellent time to learn new sport skills and to improve skills in previously learned sports. This is true for several reasons. Usually, excellent instruction and coaching are readily available, as are the necessary equipment and facilities. The learner is ordinarily young, physically active, and is accustomed to operating effectively in a learning situation. Because the other students in the class generally possess about the same amount of skill (or lack of it) and background in the sport, the learner is not placed in an embarrassing situation because of being a novice.

Perhaps the attitude and philosophy that should guide the sports participant is one that emphasizes the enjoyment to be gained from playing in sports. Often, the more highly skilled the performer, the more he enjoys participation. Little formal evidence exists to support the thesis that an improvement in skill produces an equal increase in the fun of playing the sport. However, when one observes the amount of time and effort that both children and adults are willing to practice in order to improve, this thesis certainly appears to be at least tenable. Rising above this consideration should be the ideal that sports are very much like the games that children play and therefore should be fun and should not be taken with too much seriousness. They should be enjoyed at the time they are played but should not be brooded over for any length of time. One's playing of sports should produce a memory of happy times, the warmth of shared experiences in which the unimportant was important for a short time. This attitude is epitomized by the oft-quoted saying, "It is not that you won or lost, but how you played the game."

When practicing or playing a sport, the student may wish to be guided by the behavior recommended by Pope Pius XII, who had a strong interest in sports.

> Loyalty that excludes taking refuge in subterfuges, docility and obedience to the director charged with training of the team, the spirit of self-renunciation when one has to fade into the background to further the interests of the team, fidelity to obligations undertaken, modesty in victory, serenity in adverse fortune, patience toward spectators who are not always moderate ... and in general that chastity and temperance recommended by the ancients themselves.[1]

Even though this advice was not written with the casual athlete in mind, heeding it may well increase the enjoyment of sports for the college student who views them as a hobby or as only one among many of the facets of his life.

---

[1] "Requiem for a Friend," *Sports Illustrated* (Oct. 20, 1958), p. 27.

CHAPTER 6

Archery

*Tom Stoll**
St. Stephen's School

HISTORY

Archery has played an important role in the prehistory, history, and legend of man. Archeologists have estimated that archery originated from 50,000 to 100,000 years ago. Historical records indicate that in about 5,000 B.C. the Egyptians discovered that for use in warfare the arrow could effectively outrange the slingshot and the spear. The application of this knowledge made it possible for the Egyptians to free themselves from Persian domination. From that time until about A.D. 1600, when it was supplanted by the firearm, the bow was the weapon of first importance in warfare. From the thirteenth to the sixteenth century the practice of archery was compulsory in England. The resulting skill of the English bowman had a definite effect on the history of Western civilization.

In England, archery was first advanced as a sport in 1790 by the Royal Toxophilite Society. The first archery championship was organized in 1844 by the Grand National, which is one of the most important archery groups in the British Isles.

In the United States, the first archery tournament was held in 1879, in Chicago, under the auspices of the National Archery Association of the United States. Annual championship tournaments have been held since that time with the exception of the years during World War II.

---

*B.S., Wisconsin State University—LaCrosse; M.A., University of Iowa, Iowa City. Mr. Stoll, a former archery instructor at the University of Iowa and St. Marks, Dallas, Texas, is archery instructor and athletic director of St. Stephen's School, Bradenton, Florida. Stoll has hunted big game throughout the United States and Canada.

VALUES DERIVED FROM ARCHERY

Archery has something to offer to everyone—the young, the old, the physically handicapped, and the physically gifted. The person who has scored his first gold has just entered an exciting world that may lead to the sport of archery competition or to the bow hunting of deer or other big-game animals. Each year the number of archers of both sexes grows considerably.

The cost of participating in archery is relatively small and the equipment, once purchased, is long lasting. Suitable equipment can be found to fit anyone's budget. Many archers enjoy making their own equipment, which markedly reduces their expenses.

For many people, the mere fact that they are actively participating in an out-of-doors sport such as archery is beneficial. Although the exercise involved cannot be classified as strenuous, the all-around exercise incurred, especially if it is outdoors, is quite stimulating. A novice will soon readily notice the effect of an hour of shooting on his upper-body musculature. Archery is a sport that is readily adaptable to many limitations and thus is widely utilized in special programs of physical education for students who cannot safely engage in strenuous body movements because of medical restrictions.

Archery is definitely a lifelong activity. When a person reaches an age at which he can no longer participate in more strenuous activities, he can continue to use his bow for recreation, in tournaments, or for hunting and fishing. Entire families can participate together in any of these activities. Archery can be an individual sport or a group activity. Many tales are told and stories written about exciting hunting trips, the hunters armed with only bows and arrows, that will never be forgotten by their participants.

Archery 53

DESCRIPTION OF ARCHERY EQUIPMENT AND ITS CARE

The equipment used in archery is generally referred to as tackle. The basic tackle includes a bow, bowstring, and arrows. For increased accuracy and protection, a finger tab or shooting glove should be used. Quivers, bow sights, and range finders are additional items of tackle.

Bows

Wood, fiberglass, steel, and aluminum are the materials most commonly used in constructing the modern bow. (See Figure 6-1.) Steel bows are no longer as popular as they were a few years ago; the fiberglass bow, known for its durability, is becoming increasingly popular. A type of cedar known as yew is the preferred wood in the making of bows. However, osage, orange, lemonwood, and hickory are also widely used.

The laminated recurve bow is becoming the first choice of experienced archers. The fiberglass on the back and belly of the bow adds to its appearance and durability, while the recurve projects the arrow 20 per cent faster than a long bow of comparable weight.

The weight of the bow, which is usually printed on the belly on the upper limb of the bow, is the number of pounds of force required to pull the bow the length of the arrow. In target archery, a bow weight of between eighteen to thirty pounds is recommended for women and a bow weight of twenty-five to thirty-five pounds is recommended for men.

The length of the bow selected depends on the length of the arrows—shorter arrows require a shorter bow and longer arrows a longer bow. The average length of a bow for men is five and one-half feet.

Arrows

The arrow is the most important item of the archer's tackle. (See Figure 6-2.) Without good arrows, consistent results cannot be expected. Arrows are commonly made from wood, fiberglass, or aluminum. Wooden arrows are generally made of Port Oxford cedar, Norway pine, or birch. Birch is the least desirable because it warps very readily. Aluminum arrows are frequently selected by experienced archers because they are light and can be perfectly matched.

A commonly used method for determining the correct length of the arrow is to place the nock of the arrow against the upper end of the sternum (upper center of the chest) and extend both arms forward, parallel to the floor. The point, or pile, of the arrow should barely reach the fingertips. Women commonly use arrows twenty-six inches in length and men, arrows twenty-eight inches in length.

Shooting Gloves and Finger Tabs

Shooting gloves and finger tabs are used for two main reasons. The first is for the protection of the fingers, because the friction created by the bowstring as it is released will quickly irritate unprotected fingers. In addition, their use helps to insure a smoother release. The tab, which generally costs less than the glove, is used by many target archers, whereas the glove appears to be the first choice of the bow hunter and some target archers.

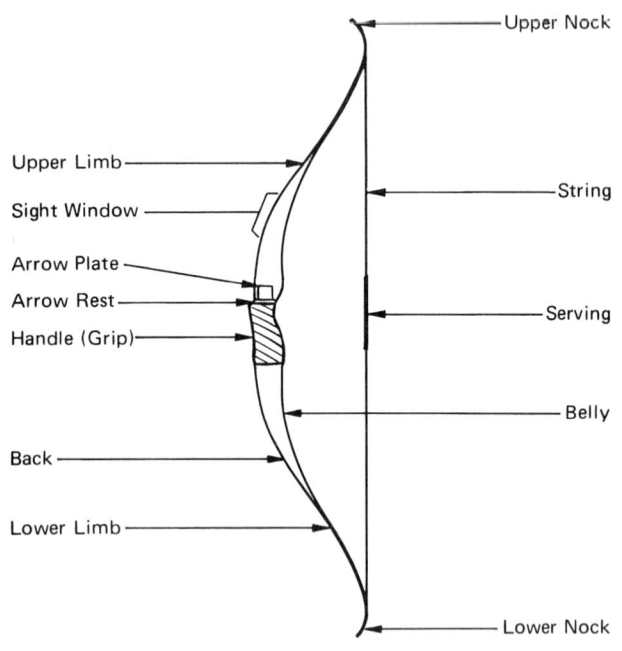

Figure 6-1. Recurve bow.

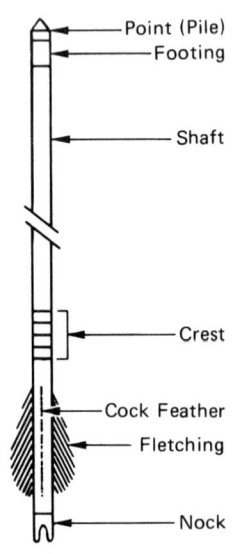

Figure 6-2. Target arrow.

54 *Individual and Team Sports*

Arm Guards

The arm guard has two main functions: to protect the arm from being slapped by the bowstring after it has been released and to hold any clothing out of the path of the passing bowstring.

Quivers

The quiver, of which many different types exist, is used to hold the archer's arrows. The most common include the bow quiver, arm quiver, back quiver, hip quiver, pocket quiver, and the ground quiver.

Targets

Regulation archery targets are forty-eight inches in diameter and four to five inches in thickness. (See Figure 6-3.) The center of the target should be located forty-eight inches above ground level. Targets are usually hung on a tripod stand or on portable carriers. Oilcloth is the preferred material for the target face. There are five concentric circles on the target face. From the center outward the colors are gold, red, blue, black, and white; the respective point values of which are 9, 7, 5, 3, and 1. Indoor archery targets should be located immediately in front of backdrops made of canvas, rugs, or special nylon netting in order that any stray arrows are stopped without damage.

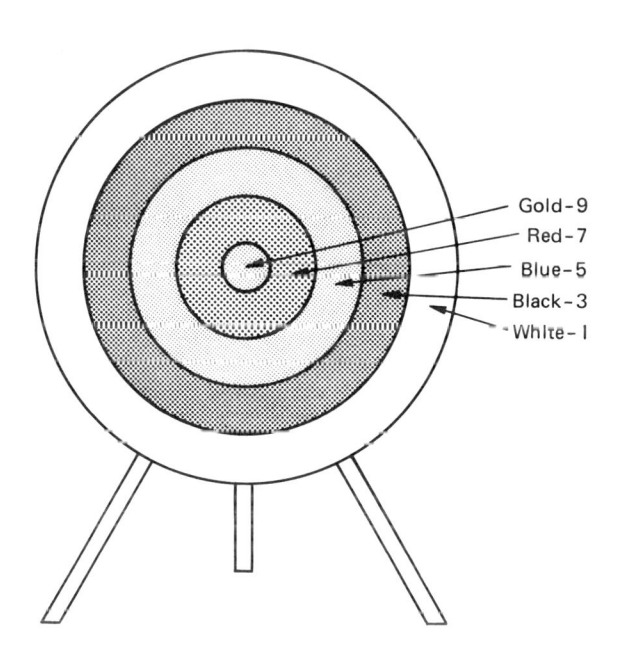

Figure 6-3. The target.

Care of Equipment

Bows

1. Bows should be hung or placed horizontally on a rack.
2. Storage areas should be cool and well ventilated.
3. Bows should be unstrung when not in use.
4. Bows should be cleaned with a good quality of wax.

Bowstrings

1. All bowstrings should be waxed. Beeswax is the kind most frequently used.
2. Bowstrings should be twisted rather than knotted when a shorter string is needed.
3. Frayed bowstrings should be discarded.

Arrows

1. Arrows should be stored in a vertical position.
2. Cracked arrows should be discarded.
3. Nocks, feathers, and points can and should be replaced when damaged.
4. When the feathers have penetrated the target, pull the arrow from behind the target until it passes completely through.

Targets

1. The targets should be stored face down.
2. The targets should be dampened in extremely dry weather.
3. To protect the facing while removing an arrow, the back of one hand should be placed next to the arrow and against the target face while the arrow is pulled out in the direction of its entry by the other hand.

BASIC RULES FOR ARCHERY COMPETITION

1. All archers must straddle the shooting line.
2. A whistle is used to start the shooting.
3. When not shooting, the archers must stand behind the shooting line.
4. Any object used for the point of aim shall not stand over 6 inches above the ground.
5. Six arrows constitute an end. A round is made up of a selected number of ends.
6. If more than six arrows are shot in one end, only the lowest six are scored.
7. The shooting begins at the longest distance and ends at the shortest distance.
8. If an arrow is dropped, it can be shot if it can be reached with the bow.
9. If an arrow in the target touches two colors, the higher value color shall count.

Archery 55

10. An arrow that has so passed through the scoring face that it is not visible from the front shall count 7 at sixty yards or less and 5 for ranges beyond sixty yards. An arrow passing completely through the target, if witnessed, is scored in the same manner.
11. An arrow that rebounds from the scoring face, if witnessed, shall score the same as a pass-through.
12. Arrows having the highest value should be withdrawn first.
13. The arrows must remain untouched until withdrawn by the target captain.
14. Tie scores shall be resolved in favor of the archer who scored the highest score at the longest distance.
15. The scoring shall be witnessed by all archers shooting on the target.
16. If a target falls over during an end, the end is shot over.
17. Any hits on a target not assigned to the archer shooting that target shall not be counted.

SHOOTING FUNDAMENTALS

Bracing

Bracing is the process of stringing the bow in preparation for shooting. (See Figure 6-4.) The two acceptable methods of stringing the bow are the push-pull method and the step-through method. In the push-pull method, the bow is held with the back facing the archer, and the string is placed on the lower nock, which is placed on the instep of the right foot. The upper loop of the bowstring should be on the upper limb of the bow. The right hand should grasp the bow handle and the left hand should be placed on the upper limb. The right hand then pulls while the left hand pushes on the upper limb and slides the loop onto the upper nock. Before drawing the bow, it should be checked to see that the bowstring loops are securely placed on the nocks.

When using the step-through method, the curve of the lower limb of the bow is laid over the left ankle, while the string is held tightly by the left hand. The handle of the bow is placed on the rear of the right thigh, keeping the right knee slightly bent. The right hand, palm open, is placed near the top of the upper limb. The left leg is kept straight. The left heel is then raised off the ground and the right hand pushes forward at the same time the right knee is so locked that the bow bends naturally. The top of the string is slipped in place on the upper nock and the legs are then slowly relaxed. The bowstring loop should be checked to insure that they are securely placed on the nocks before drawing the bow.

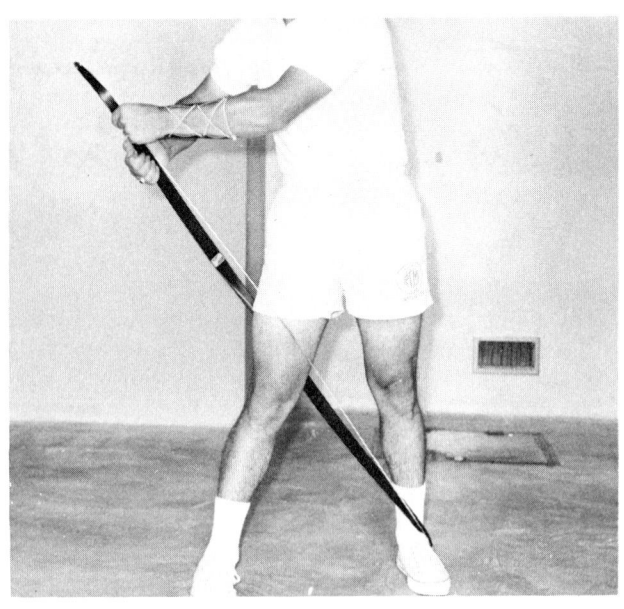

Figure 6-4. Bracing the bow.

To unstring the bow either of the preceding processes should be reversed.

Stance

The archer should, at a right angle to the target, straddle the shooting line. His feet should be about shoulder width apart and his body weight should be evenly distributed on them. His body should exhibit a proper posture, be comfortable, and be relaxed. It is important that the archer return to the same spot to shoot his remaining ends; this procedure eliminates many of the sighting and aiming problems experienced by the beginner.

Grasping the Bow

The archer does not grip or wrap his fingers around the handle of the bow, instead he "shakes hands" with the bow, using his left hand if right handed. The bow should be placed in the V formed by the thumb and fingers while the hand is held in the hand-shaking position. The index finger is then wrapped around the bow handle; the thumb, encircling the bow from the other side, rests on the index finger. The grasp of only the thumb and index finger is needed in order to prevent the bow from falling after the string is released. The other three fingers should be completely relaxed. (See Figure 6-5.)

Nocking the Arrow

When nocking an arrow, the bow is held parallel to the floor with the back of the bow hand facing up. The

56 *Individual and Team Sports*

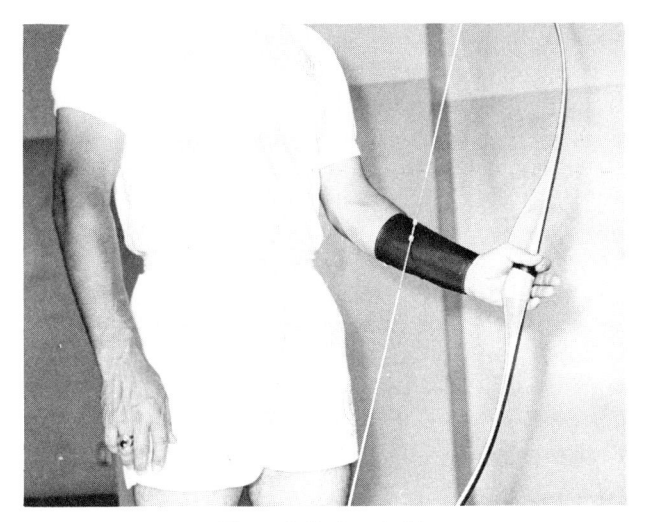

Figure 6-5. Bow hold.

arrow, grasped by the nock with the thumb and index finger (of the right hand if right handed), is placed on the arrow rest with the cock feather facing away from the bow. When properly placed on the string, the arrow forms two right angles with the string. It is important to nock all the arrows at this same spot. The difference of a fraction of an inch in the nocking point will be greatly magnified in the error on the target. Therefore, it is a wise procedure to mark the exact nocking point on the string. Rubber buttons, tape, or ink on the serving help to locate the nocking point readily. (See Figure 6-6.)

Drawing the Bow

After the arrow has been nocked and the bow is still in the horizontal position, the drawing hand (the right hand for right-handed archers) is positioned on the bowstring.

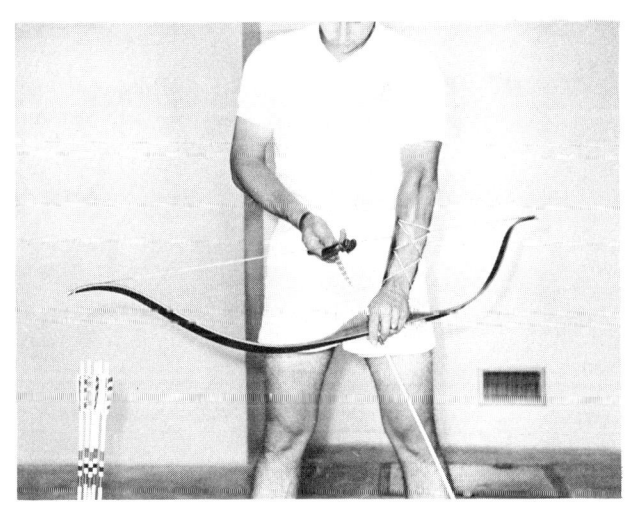

Figure 6-6. Nocking.

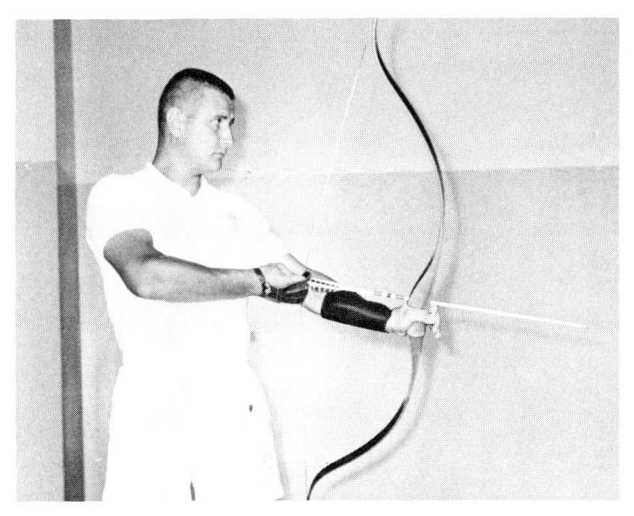

Figure 6-7. Drawing the bow.

The first three fingers, which are used to draw the string back to the anchor point, are placed on the string anywhere up to, but not beyond, the joint formed by the distal and middle phalanges—the first or far joints. If the string is placed inside the first joints, it is difficult to obtain a smooth release and inaccuracy will result. When drawing the string, the middle and far joints of the fingers should be flexed.

The draw involves a simultaneous extension of both arms; hence, as the bow arm moves toward the target, the string arm moves back toward the anchor point. Beginning archers have a tendency to squeeze the arrow nock with the fingers of the drawing hand. This practice should be avoided because it often results in the arrow slipping off the arrow rest, thus destroying an opportunity for an accurate shot. (See Figure 6-7.)

Anchor Point

The anchor point is the point on the archer's face or jaw where he should stop at full draw each time that the bow is drawn. Some archers choose to have the string bisect the chin and nose with the first finger located directly under the chin. Another commonly used anchor point is one in which the first finger touches the corner of the mouth with the thumb resting under the jawbone. Bow hunters commonly use a higher point, such as drawing to a spot just below the prominence of the cheek bone.

The anchor point will vary from individual to individual. The important thing is that the anchor point be the same every time an arrow is shot, regardless of the distance. (See Figure 6-8.)

Archery 57

Figure 6-8. Anchor point.

Aiming

The three methods of aiming most commonly employed in archery are the point of aim, sight shooting, and instinctive methods.

In the point-of-aim method, the archer looks over the point of the arrow when at full draw. At short distances, the point or pile is aimed at a point lower than the actual target. At point-blank distance, the pile will be aimed at the spot where the arrow should land. At longer distances, the point of aim is above the target. (See Figure 6-9.)

In the sight method, a sight—which can be anything from a pin taped to the bow to an expensive bow sight—is attached to the bow. This method is the most accurate to date and is replacing the point-of-aim method.

The sight is placed on the left side of the bow and is aligned with the center of the target. When a shooter groups his arrows outside the center of the target, he adjusts his sight by moving it in the direction of the error. For example, if the grouping is at five o'clock in the white, the pin is moved down and to the right.

In the instinctive method, which is considered the natural method of shooting the bow, no sights are attached to the bow. Instead, the instinctive shooter looks at the target, raises the bow to the position that he feels is the correct one for hitting the target, and then shoots. Because instinctive shooting is designed to hit the target with the first arrow, bow hunters and field archers frequently use this method. The instinctive shooting method obviously requires considerable practice on the archer's part.

Release

Once the archer has reached his anchor point at full draw, has aimed at the target, and becomes relaxed, he is ready to release the bowstring. To obtain a smooth release, the archer simply relaxes his fingers, and let the bowstring slide off their ends. Any movement in excess of this simple action will result in an improper release and probably in an inaccurate arrow.

Follow-through

The follow-through in archery can be likened to the follow-through in riflery. The archer merely holds his position for an instant after the release in order to insure that the bow is not moved until the arrow has left the bow. This might best be described as patience. (See Figure 6-10.)

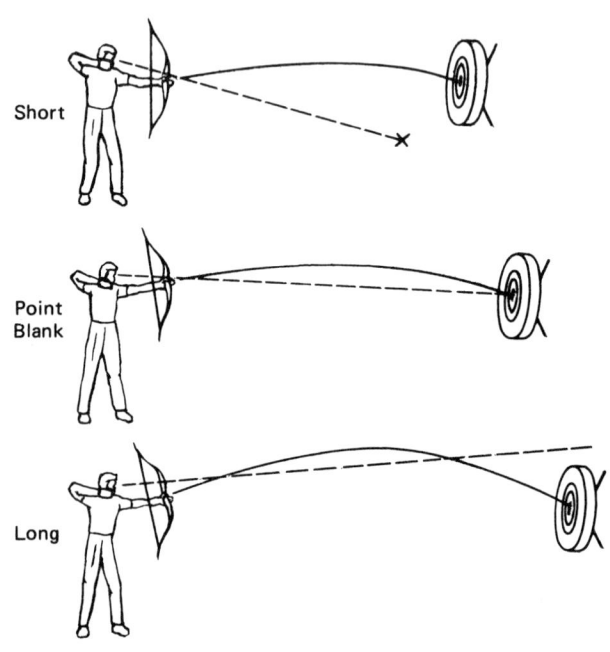

Figure 6-9. Point of aim.

Figure 6-10. Release and follow-through.

Individual and Team Sports

SAFETY

Archery accidents do not just happen—they are caused by ignorance or disregard of safe procedure. The archer should strictly adhere to the following safety rules at all times.

1. Before shooting check the bow for cracks.
2. Make sure the string is not frayed.
3. Check that arrows are not damaged.
4. Never draw a bow without an arrow in it.
5. Make sure that the fistmele is about six inches wide.
6. Arm guards and finger tabs or gloves should be worn when shooting.
7. Loose clothing, watches, bracelets, and pins should not be worn when shooting.
8. All shooters should straddle the shooting line.
9. Be sure no one is in front of the shooting line when the signal to begin is given.
10. Once shooting has started, no one should step completely across the shooting line.
11. No one should stand directly in front of a target while the arrows are being withdrawn.
12. Never shoot an arrow straight up into the air.
13. Never point a loaded bow at anything you do not intend to shoot.
14. Common sense should prevail at all times.

COMMON ARCHERY ERRORS AND THEIR CAUSES

Error: Shooting to the Left

Possible Causes
1. Aiming too far to the left.
2. Hunching the left shoulder.
3. Sighting with the left eye while shooting right-handed.
4. Shifting the weight to the right foot.
5. Sight set too far to the right.
6. Anchor point too far to the right.
7. Moving the bow arm to the left during release.
8. Pulling the bowstring to the right on release.
9. Locked or tensed bow arm.
10. Wind blowing from right to left.

Error: Shooting to the Right

Possible Causes
1. Aiming too far to the right.
2. Elbow of the string hand too high.
3. Sight set too far to the left.
4. Bending the bow arm during release.
5. Anchor point too far to the left.
6. Tilting the upper bow limb to the right.
7. Wind blowing from left to right.

Error: Shooting Too High

Possible Causes
1. Aiming too high.
2. Arrow nocked too low.
3. Body leaning backward.
4. Overdrawing.
5. Jerking the string hand back during the release.
6. Sight set too low.
7. Opening the mouth before release.
8. Lifting the bow arm during release.
9. Bow may be overstrung.
10. Wind blowing toward target.

Error: Shooting Too Low

Possible Causes
1. Aiming too low.
2. Dropping the bow arm.
3. Anchor point too high.
4. Sight set too high.
5. Not using full draw.
6. Creeping during the release.
7. Body leaning forward.
8. String hitting the bow arm.
9. Arrow nocked too high.
10. Bow may be understrung.
11. Wind blowing toward archer.

VARIATIONS OF ARCHERY

Clout Shooting

In clout shooting, the archer shoots at a circular target, which is marked on the ground with white lines. The proportions of a standard target are reproduced by a ratio of one foot to the inch, making the clout target forty-eight feet in diameter. The center of the target is usually indicated by a triangular or rectangular flag, which is mounted on a stake and is three to five feet above the ground.

The rules and scoring of target archery are applicable to clout shooting, with the exception that rebounds are scored from the place at which the point of the arrow comes to final rest. Thirty-six arrows are shot from a single distance, which for men is 180 yards; for women, 120 or 140 yards; for students, from 80 to 100 yards.

Wand Shooting

Wand shooting involves shooting at a vertical soft-wood slat, two inches wide, six feet in height, that is securely inserted into the ground. A strip of tape or paper can be placed on a regulation target in order to achieve the same effect. Thirty-six arrows are shot in competition in which the rules of conduct applying to target shooting are applicable. Only those arrows that are actually embedded in the wand, or are witnessed rebounds, are counted as hits. The wand-shooting distance for men is 100 yards; for women, 60 yards; and, for students, a modified distance is generally used.

Archery Golf

Archery golf is usually played on a regular golf course. Any large area can, however, be utilized, providing that adequate safety procedures are observed. In place of the "hole" used in regular golf, a round target is used in archery golf, which is about twelve inches in diameter and is divided into three rings. Surrounding this target is a marked distance of ten yards from which the archers do their "putting."

In scoring archery golf the total score for each hole is the number of shots taken to get into the ten-yard circle plus the putting score. When each of the archers has shot his arrow within the ten-yard circle, each one then shoots one arrow (putt) at the twelve-inch target. A hit in the center ring adds one point to the score for the hole; a hit in the next ring, two points; and a hit beyond that adds three points. The object of archery golf is to "go around" the course (nine or eighteen holes) in as few shots or points as possible.

Field Archery

A standard field course consists of fourteen target faces of varying sizes. Shooting in groups of three to five, each archer shoots four arrows at each of the fourteen target layouts. At ten of the layouts the archer shoots four arrows each time from a single post, and at the remaining four layouts he shoots each of the four arrows from different posts—or else he shoots at different target faces from the same post.

The target face consists of two concentric rings. The outside ring is black and the bull is white with a black spot in its center. Five points are scored for a bull and three for a hit in the outer black ring.

The *Handbook of Field Archery,* published by the National Field Archery Association, provides a fruitful source of information about field archery.

Glossary of Terms

Address: To prepare to shoot.
Anchor point: A certain spot on the archer's face to which the stringhand comes on the draw.
Archery golf: An adaptation of golf to the sport of archery.
Arm guard: A device, worn on the forearm, used to protect the arm from the bowstring.
Arrow plate: A piece of material attached to the upper portion of the bow's limb, which is located immediately above the handle.
Arrow rest: The portion of the bow's upper handle that contains a shelf or rest for the arrow to pass over.
Arrow rack: A device for storing arrows.
Back: The side of the bow facing away from the archer.
Backed bow: A bow that is reinforced on its back with a strengthening substance.
Belly: The side of the bow facing the archer.
Blunts: Blunt-tipped arrows—often used on small game.
Bow arm: The arm that holds the bow.
Bow rack: A device used to hold and store bows.
Bow sight: A device on the bow used for sighting.
Bowman: Another term for an archer.
Bowyer: A person who makes bows.
Braced bow: A bow that is strung and ready for shooting.
Broadhead: A tip used on hunting arrows.
Butt: A backstop for halting arrows shot at a target.
Cant: To hold the bow tilted while shooting.
Cast: The distance that a bow can shoot an arrow.
Clout: A target on the ground that is used in clout shooting.
Clout shooting: Long-distance shooting at a circular target laid out on the ground.
Cock feather: The feather at right angles to the nock.
Creeping: Allowing the shooting hand to edge forward before the release.
Crest: Colored marks placed on the arrow for identification.
Draw: To pull the bowstring back into the anchor position.
Drawing arm: The arm that draws the bowstring back.
Drift: The natural deflection of an arrow due to outside factors such as the wind.
End: Six arrows shot in succession.
Eye: The loop at the end of a bowstring.
Field archery: A competitive round shot at various distances on a course laid out like a golf course.
Field arrow: A heavy arrow that is primarily used in field archery.
Finger tab: A small tab, usually leather, worn on the shooting hand for protection and for a smoother release.
Fistmele: An approximate measuring unit consisting of a clenched fist with the thumb raised. This indicates the approximate correct distance between the bow and the bowstring at the handle.
Fletcher: A person who makes arrows.

Fletching: The feathers on an arrow.
Flight: The path of the arrow.
Flight shooting: Shooting an arrow for maximum distance.
Grip: The handle of the bow.
Group: Arrows placed in the target in close proximity.
Hand: Shooting four arrows in field archery.
Head: The tip, point, or pile of an arrow.
Hen feathers: The two feathers on an arrow that are not at right angles to the nock.
Hold: To hesitate at full draw.
Home: An arrow that is at full draw.
Instinctive shooting: Aiming and shooting arrows instinctively.
Jerking: Letting the shooting hand jerk backward as the string is released.
Kick: The recoil of the bowstring and bow after the arrow is shot.
Laminated bow: A composite bow, usually of wood and fiberglass.
Limbs: The two ends of a bow, from the handle out.
Longbow: A bow with no recurve.
Loose: To shoot an arrow.
Nock: The groove in the end of an arrow in which the bowstring fits. Also, the grooves at both ends of the bow that hold the bowstring.
Nocking point: The place on the bowstring where the arrow is placed before drawing and shooting.
Overbowed: Using a bow that is too strong for the individual.
Overdraw: Drawing the arrow so far back that the point passes the belly of the bow.
Overstrung: A bow that has too short a bowstring.
Petticoat: Any part of the target outside the white ring.
Pile: The tip of an arrow.
Point: The tip of an arrow.
Point-blank range: The only distance from the target at which the point of aim is directly at the target.
Point of aim: A method of aiming.
Quiver: A device for holding arrows that can be worn or attached to the archer.
Range: The distance to be shot.
Range finder: A device to aid in locating the correct aiming point.
Recurve: A bow curved on the ends.
Reflexed bow: A bow where the limb ends curve toward the back rather than the belly of the bow.
Release: To let the bowstring slip off the string fingers.
Scatter: To hit the target in different places rather than in the same general area.
Self-arrow: An arrow made entirely of one piece of wood.
Self-bow: A bow made entirely of one piece of wood.

Serving: The reinforcement on the string where the arrow is nocked.
Shaft: The middle section of an arrow.
Shelf: The place on the bow where the arrow rests.
Shooting line: The line that the target archer straddles while shooting at targets.
Sinking: The gradual loss of a bow's power.
Stagger: The erratic flight of an arrow.
String fingers: The three fingers used to draw back the bowstring.
Strung bow: A bow that is ready to shoot.
Tackle: The equipment used in archery.
Target arrow: A lightweight arrow with a target point.
Throwing: Moving the bow hand to the left while shooting.
Timber: A warning, in field archery, to let others know that an arrow is being shot.
Understrung: A bow that has too long a bowstring.
Vane: A feather on an arrow.
Weight: The amount of pull (in pounds) required to draw the bow to full draw.
Windage: The amount of drift in the flight of an arrow caused by wind.
Wobble: The erratic motion of an arrow in flight.

Selected References

BOOKS

Burke, Edward. *Archery Handbook.* New York: Arco, 1954.

DGWS. *Archery Rules.* Washington, D.C.: AAHPER. Current.

Hougham, P. C. *The Encyclopedia of Archery.* New York: A. S. Barnes, 1958.

McKinney, W. C. *Archery.* Dubuque, Iowa: Brown, 1966.

NAA. *Archery Rules—Target.* Santa Ana, Calif.: The National Archery Association. Current.

NFAA. *Archery Rules—Field.* Redlands, Calif.: The National Field Archery Association, 1953.

Niemeyer, Roy D. *Beginning Archery.* Belmont, Calif.: Wadsworth, 1969.

PERIODICALS

Archery. Official Publication of the National Field Archery Association, Box H, Palm Springs, California 92262.

The Archer's Magazine. 1200 Walnut Street, Philadelphia, Pennsylvania 19107.

Bow and Arrow. 550-A South Citrus Avenue, Covina, California 91722.

Bow Hunting. Eastern Bowhunter, Inc., Riderwood, Maryland 21139.

CHAPTER 7

Badminton
Donald R. Casady*
The University of Iowa

HISTORY

The origin of badminton is obscure. Some evidence indicates that a badmintonlike game was played in England as early as the twelfth century. Early versions of badminton were later played in China and Poland. Some authorities credit present-day badminton as originating in India, where it was called Poona. English army officers learned the game while stationed there and introduced it into England in around 1870. The sport attracted little interest until the Duke of Beaufort launched it at his home, "Badminton," in Gloucestershire.

The original Indian rules governed the game until 1887, when the Bath Badminton Club formulated its basic regulations. These were revised in 1890 and supplemented and completed by the Badminton Association of England, which was established in 1895. The current rules are derived from these.

The early courts were sometimes shaped like an hourglass, and their dimensions varied widely. Some courts were as large as present-day volleyball courts and four players constituted a team.

Badminton was brought to Canada in the 1890s and to the United States shortly thereafter. Although it spread widely at first, its popularity in the United States waned, and the game had few followers until a second wave of popularity, starting in 1929, carried it to its present status. It is now popular throughout the United States and has an especially strong following in California.

As a result of its present popularity, the American Badminton Association (ABA), which now controls the sport and sanctions all badminton tournaments in the United States, was formed in 1936. It is affiliated with the International Badminton Association (IBA), which was founded in 1934 and has its headquarters in England. The Thomas Cup is awarded to the male international championship team and is usually won by a Far Eastern nation—badminton is the national game in such countries as India, Indonesia, and Malaysia.

VALUES OF THE GAME

Badminton is a recent addition to the family of sports played widely in America. Despite the late date of its recognition as a valuable leisure-time activity, its popularity has recently grown by leaps and bounds as a result of its adaptability. It is one game that can be played fast or slow, hard or easy, in or out-of-doors; by men, women, and children; young or old, fat or thin.

The game of badminton affords healthy exercise and enjoyment and an opportunity for the participants to lose themselves in excitement, physical exuberance, fun, and companionship. It is an easy game to play and the beginner can have an enjoyable time while learning the game. Because of the speed with which the shuttlecock passes back and forth across the net, and because of the quick changes of direction that a player must make, badminton is an excellent conditioner for other sports. For these reasons many athletes play badminton during the off-season of their sport in order to stay in condition.

---

*Dr. Casady, who received his B.S., M.A., and Ph.D. from The University of Iowa, was introduced to the game of badminton while attending college. The author later won the all-university badminton championship. While athletic director at the Atlanta Athletic Club, he was exposed to the finer points of the game by the badminton pro, R. S. Jackson, a former national badminton champion in England. Casady, a member of the ABA, has taught many classes in badminton to college students and has had the pleasure of playing the game with players from several countries, including England, Norway, India, Indonesia, and Malaysia.

When properly played, badminton requires considerable speed, endurance, and power. The team play of partners in doubles demands the utmost in cooperation, concentration, and initiative in the use of strokes.

The game has two disadvantages: when played out-of-doors, badminton requires that there be little or no wind (because of the light weight of the shuttlecock)—a condition often not existing—and the difference in the score does not necessarily reflect the difference in playing ability between the players. A slight superiority in playing ability can result in a one-sided game.

DESCRIPTION OF THE GAME

The game of badminton is played either by two players (one on each side), called singles, or four players (two on each side), called doubles. The object of the game is to hit the shuttlecock back and forth across and above the net without permitting it to land on the floor in bounds. The side failing to return the shuttlecock legally across the net commits a fault, resulting in the loss of a point or service. A point can only be scored by the serving side. If the receiving side wins a rally, the serve passes either to them or, in the case of doubles, to the server's partner if he has a service turn coming. The shuttlecock can be hit only once in attempting to return or serve it.

EQUIPMENT AND ITS CARE

The game equipment needed for badminton ordinarily includes only three items: the net and its supports, the rackets, and the shuttlecock (commonly called a shuttle).

Net

The net is usually made of fine tanned cord of one-quarter-inch mesh and supported on the upper side by a light rope or small steel cable. It should be firmly stretched from post to post and should be two feet, six inches in depth. The top of the net should be five feet in height from the floor at the center, and five feet, one inch at the supports. The net is vulnerable to damage as a result of improper care and rough usage. One common improper use of the net is its serving as the object of a player venting his ire by hitting it with his racket after making a poor play or missing a shot. The net should serve only one purpose: to stop shuttles that are not played sufficiently high to pass over it.

Racket

The size and weight of a badminton racket are not officially specified. In selecting a racket the main considerations are to get one that is light and strong and flexible in the shaft. Most rackets weigh approximately five ounces when strung. Special lightweight rackets, which are preferred by champion players but which are not so durable, that weigh less than four ounces when strung, are available. Many rackets are constructed with steel shafts and some with metal heads. Nylon strings of various grades are most commonly used, but top competitors usually prefer a good grade of gut string. Because the badminton racket is lightly constructed, and therefore easily damaged, it should receive the best of care. When not in use, wooden rackets should be kept in a press to prevent the racket head from warping. The racket should not be hit against the leg or other objects, nor should it ever be thrown.

Shuttlecock

The specifications for the indoor shuttlecock are that it should weigh between seventy-three and eighty-five grains (the exact weight depends primarily on the temperature and altitude of the playing site) and be constructed of a leather-covered cork base in which fourteen to sixteen feathers, two and one-half to two and three-quarter inches long, are inserted at regularly spaced intervals. Some of the new varieties of plastic shuttles have proven quite satisfactory and are recommended for class and casual play. An outdoor shuttle has a heavier base (it weighs approximately eighty-five grains) than the one used indoors. The shuttlecock is deemed to be of the correct pace if a player of average strength, hitting from above a back boundary line with a full underhand stroke, drives it upward and parallel to a sideline to not less than one foot or more than two and one-half feet short of the other back boundary line. To get the most service from any type of shuttle, the following rules concerning its care should be practiced: (1) remove it from the container base first and replace it in the same manner, (2) put the shuttle in play with an underhand stroke—otherwise the racket may hit the feathers and damage them, (3) straighten the feathers after each rally, and (4) do not kick or knock the shuttle along the floor or ground; instead, pick it up and throw or bat it to the desired location.

Facilities

Badminton can be played on any flat, level surface—a feature that makes it highly suitable for outdoor play. (See Figure 7-1.) The size of the playing area need not be

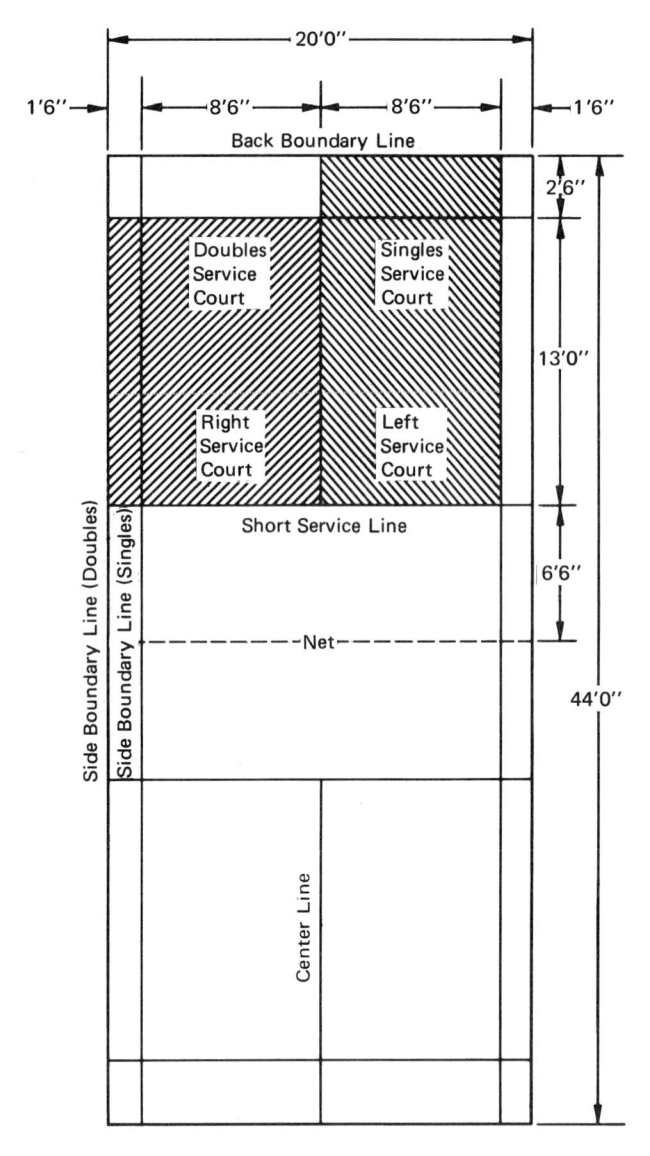

Figure 7-1. Badminton court diagram.

The ceiling should be at least twenty-five feet high. The lines should be heavily painted (white, black, or any other easily distinguishable color) on the floor, one and one-half inches wide. Pressure-sensitive tape can be used to form the lines.

BASIC RULES AND ETIQUETTE

The game is started by the side winning the toss. For this purpose a coin can be tossed or a racket can be spun. The opponent calls heads or tails, rough or smooth, or trademark up or down. The winner of the toss can choose one of the following options: (1) to serve first, (2) to receive, or (3) to select the side of the court on which he wants to play.

The server must stand within the boundaries of his service court while in the act of serving, and the receiver must stand within his service court while the serve is being made. A serve is considered delivered as soon as the shuttle is struck by the server's racket. The server should not serve until the receiver is ready—attempting to return the service is a declaration of being ready. Both players must keep both feet on the ground and may not in any way feint or intentionally balk their opponents either before or during the serve. The partners of the server and of the receiver can take any position they choose, provided that they do not interfere with the view of the server or receiver or otherwise obstruct an opponent. After the serve is delivered, both the server and the receiver can occupy any position that they wish on their side of the net.

If the shuttle touches and passes over the net during a service or rally, the shuttle remains in play. If the shuttle hits the floor, or becomes suspended in the net, or does not pass over it, the shuttle is out of play.

Doubles Play

If the serving side ("in" side) wins the point after legally serving, the server then serves from his left service court to the left service court of his receiver ("out" side). The receiver is now the partner of the opponent served to previously. Thus, the serve is alternated back and forth to the opponents by the original server until he loses his serving turn. The players on the side just losing the serve (now the "out" side) remain in the court positions they held at the beginning of the last rally.

When a doubles team loses the serve, it goes to the opponent located in the right service court who in turn serves to the man in the diagonally opposite right service court; this server continues to serve alternately to each service court and each opponent until he loses the

much larger than a regulation court. However, an additional few feet around the perimeter of the court are needed in order to provide sufficient room to swing the racket safely.

The court can be made of almost any material. A macadam driveway is a good place to play because the court markings can be drawn quickly. The lawn has proven to be a popular place for playing badminton, where a light line of lime or a small rope serves well for marking the court.

Indoor courts are by far the most popular for badminton play. When possible, they should be located in rooms with indirect lighting in order to eliminate any possible glare, which might create a blind spot thus causing the player to lose sight of the shuttle while it is in flight.

64   *Individual and Team Sports*

service. The side beginning the game has only one serving turn (or hand) at the start of the game, but thereon both partners on each side serve before the service passes to their opponents. Once the receiver has returned the service before the shuttle strikes the floor, either player on either team can return the shuttle from any position on their court. In doubles the first serve by either side is always made from the right service court regardless of the score. For either side, if their score is an even number (for example, 2 or 8), the players are located in the half court from which they started the game; if their score is an odd number, they are located in the opposite half court.

Serving out of turn or from the wrong service court is called a let if the serving side wins the rally, provided it is allowed before the next service is delivered. This rule also holds true for a player standing in the wrong service court and receiving the service, provided his side wins the rally. If the side at fault loses the rally, the mistake stands and the players' positions are not corrected.

Singles Play

The rules for singles are the same as for doubles with these exceptions: (1) the serve is from the right service court whenever the server's score is an even number, and the serve is from the left service court whenever the server's score is an odd number; (2) both players change service courts after a point is scored; and (3) the alleys in the doubles court are out-of-bounds in the singles game, and the right and left service courts extend to the back boundary line. This makes the singles service court longer and narrower than the doubles service court.

Faults in Badminton Play

It is a fault and the offender (1) loses a point when his side is receiving or (2) loses the service when his side is serving, if:

1. The service is overhand—the shuttle is hit at any point higher than the server's waist, or any part of the head of the racket is higher than any part of the server's hand at the instant the service is made.
2. The shuttle falls into the wrong service court.
3. The server does not stand in the correct service court at the time of service, or stands on the lines of the correct service court.
4. The receiver does not stand in the proper service court at the time of receiving the service.
5. During the service, the server or his partner makes a preliminary feint or otherwise balks the opponent.
6. The shuttle, while in play, is struck before it crosses the net and goes into the striker's side of the net.
7. The shuttle is caught or slung instead of being hit with the racket head.
8. The shuttle lands outside the court boundaries or passes through or under the net, or is otherwise not returned over the net and into the correct court area; or touches the roof, side walls, or dress of the player.
9. The net or supports are touched with a racket or by a player or his dress when the shuttle is in play.
10. The shuttle is hit twice on one side before being returned.

Scoring

Men's doubles and singles games can consist of either 15 or 21 points, as preferred. In a game of 15, if the score becomes 13-all, the side that first reaches that score has the option of setting the game at 5 or leaving game at 15 points. The same is true if the game reaches 14-all, except that the option is setting the game at 3 points. In either instance, after the game is set the score is called love-all and the side wins that first scores 3 or 5 points, depending on the point at which the game was set. In a game of 21 points, setting to either 5 or 3 is done when the score is 19 or 20, instead of 13 or 14. A side can reject setting at 13 or 19 and then elect to set at 14 or 20 if it is so desired.

A match consists of two out of three games, unless otherwise specified. The players change courts at the end of the first game and the second game. If a third game is required to settle the match, the players must change sides when the leading score is one point more than half the total required to win the game.

Figure 7-2. Legal serve.

The official rules of badminton are governed by the ABA. Official information can be obtained by writing to the American Badminton Association, 333 Saratoga Road, Buffalo, New York 14226.

Badminton Etiquette

The badminton player should be a gentleman when playing—this means that he must be considerate of his opponent (and doubles partner). On a close shot, the call of whether or not a shot landed in bounds should be made by the player in that court. The courteous call is to give the benefit of the doubt to the opponent. If an extremely close one cannot be called, the point can be replayed, but this should be necessary only rarely. The player committing a fault (such as a sling or carry) or a let (such as interference by a player from another court) should call it immediately. If the server calls the score each time before serving, no confusion should arise concerning the correct score. The server should avoid rushing the service before the receiver is ready. If any doubt exists, the server should say "Service" or ask "Ready?" before serving. In tournament play, white comfortable clothing is the usual attire.

FUNDAMENTAL SKILLS OF BADMINTON

The directions for performing the skills comprising badminton play are given for right-handed players. Left-handed players must, when necessary, reverse these directions.

The Grips

Forehand Grip (Figure 7-3). To acquire the proper grip for a *forehand stroke*, hold the badminton racket by the shaft in the left hand, with the face of the racket perpendicular to the floor, and shake hands with the handle with the right hand. After the racket is positioned in this manner, an alternate method is to place the right palm on the strings and slide the hand down to where the handle can be gripped. Grasp the handle lightly in the palm and fingers with the little finger just above the leather base and with the forefinger (as if pulling a trigger) slightly separated from the others. Be careful to grasp the handle near the end, or else the proper wrist and forearm action during the stroke will be hindered. The thumb should be on the left side of the handle, with the V formed by the thumb and forefinger being on top of the handle and slightly to the rear. Basically, this grip (sometimes called a pistol grip) should permit the palm of the hand to be parallel to the face of the racket.

Backhand Grip (Figure 7-4). For the *backhand stroke*, most players use a grip similar to the forehand grip, except that the thumb is placed up on the upper left corner. To take this grip, extend the racket in front of the body, turn the top edge of the racket frame over slightly to the right, and place the thumb along and parallel to the wide side of the handle. Many badminton players, however, do not rotate the racket for a backhand stroke; instead they hold the racket with a forehand grip for all shots, rotating the forearm when necessary. As with the forehand stroke, the V formed by the thumb and forefinger is slightly behind the top of the racket. The power of the thumb is thus added to that of the body, arm, and wrist on the snap during the forward swing of the racket. This grip allows a long reach, increased power, and, in strokes where the shuttle must fly long distances, increased accuracy.

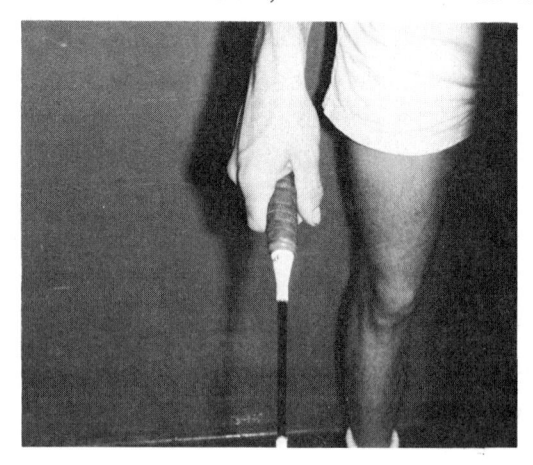

Figure 7-3. Forehand grip. (Photograph by courtesy of the American Badminton Association, R. Stanton Hales, photographer.)

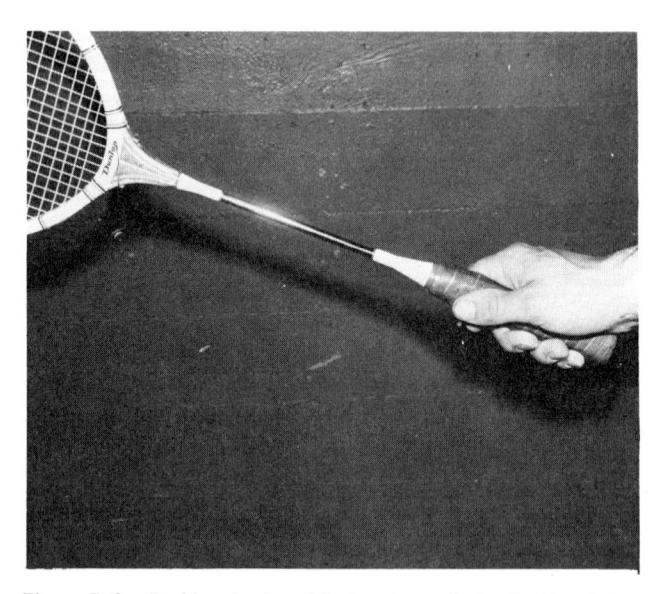

Figure 7-4. Backhand grip with thumb up the back side of the handle. (Photograph by courtesy of the American Badminton Association, R. Stanton Hales, photographer.)

Many beginners tend to grip the racket too tightly. Actually, the palm of the hand does *not* grip the racket; the fingers grip and have control over it. Therefore, the fingers should be spread slightly and not be bunched together. The arm should *not* be stiff during the backhand stroke, and the wrist should be flexible and cocked.

Frying Pan or Hammer Grip. Some players, when playing close to the net, use a grip in which the racket face is parallel to the net. This grip is attained by placing the racket on the floor directly in front (pointing forward), bending over, and picking it up.

Wrist Action

The correct action of the wrist when coupled with forearm rotation permits a powerful shot and allows proper direction and deception. At the beginning of any stroke, forehand or backhand, the wrist is hyperextended (flexed backward) by pointing the racket head away from the point of probable contact between the bird (shuttle) and the racket. Just before the bird is hit, the racket head is whipped through, and, at the time of contact between the bird and the racket, there should usually be a straight line formed by the shoulder through the elbow and wrist to the end of the racket. At the same time the forearm is rotated in the direction of the stroke in order to compliment the stroking action.

Footwork

Almost all shots in badminton should be made with the body at right angles to the net. On the forehand shot, the left foot should be nearer the net than the right foot; on backhand shots, this foot position is reversed. In executing shots, the weight of the body should be transferred from the rear foot to the forward foot if the player has sufficient time. This transfer of weight toward the net adds power and control to the stroke. However, on many shots, particularly when they are made close to the net in a fast game, the player merely goes to the bird and strokes it without moving his feet during the stroking action. When moving about the floor, it is best to start with short steps and end with long steps. This allows a quick start and moves the player into position to execute his shot. In moving to the rear of the court, the player should pivot and shuffle sideward. If the player has inadequate time to pivot and shuffle, he "back pedals" in a style similar to that of a drop-back quarterback passer. Either method permits the player to watch the shuttle constantly.

Body Control and Position

Coupled closely with the proper footwork is the ability to have the body under control and in the proper position on the court, if skillful badminton play is to develop at a rapid pace. One of the most common errors made by beginners in badminton is that of moving too close to the shuttle before making a shot. This results in a faulty bent-arm swing and a poor return. Moving toward the bird and playing it as soon as it crosses the net is preferable to waiting for the shuttle to come directly to the player. One should move rapidly into stroking position and into the proper position on the court in order to make as accurate a controlled return as possible. Normally, the player should hit the shuttle as soon as possible (while it is high) in order to make an attacking shot before the opponent is set. After every shot, the player should return to approximately the center of the court (in singles this is about midway between the net and back line) and assume a position of readiness while awaiting the return. When awaiting a return or a serve, the player should be in a ready position, or on-guard position, which means that the racket is held diagonally across the upper part of the body and is grasped with a forehand grip. The racket head or shaft may rest lightly on the palm of the left hand, if desired. The legs at the knee joint should be slightly bent, the left foot may be slightly in front of the right foot, and the weight of the body is on the balls of the feet. The elbows should be held a comfortable distance from the body, and the body should be crouched slightly.

Service

The serve is an underhand stroke, which is often made on the forehand side of the body. Because the serve is primarily a defensive-type shot that is hit to a waiting opponent, it is essential for the server to use as much deception as possible in order to outwit his opponent. Thus, all types of serves should be made with identical action, if possible.

Figure 7-5. Ready to serve. (Photograph by courtesy of the American Badminton Association, R. Stanton Hales, photographer.)

Description. The shuttle is held with the thumb and fingers of the left hand encircling the feathers, or with the thumb and forefinger gripping the feathers on one side. The server stands with his left foot in front of the right, his body facing the net, and the left shoulder pointing in the direction in which the bird is to travel. With the shuttle held at an arms-length distance the racket is swung back in an arc, the wrist is cocked, and the body weight is shifted to the rear foot. The shuttle can be held between waist and shoulder height and dropped several inches before impact, or it can be held at knee level or slightly above and "hit" out of the holding hand. As the racket swings forward, the shuttle is dropped on it, and the weight can be shifted to the forward foot. Just before the moment of impact between the shuttle and racket, the wrist can be snapped and the forearm rotated, thus uncocking the wrist and sending the shuttle away sharply. If a short serve is desired, little or no wrist action is used. The wrist action, or lack of wrist action, is the factor that permits a deceptive serve, as all other motions of the serve are retained in both the long and short service.

There are three common service flights (Figure 7-6): (1) a low, short serve in which the shuttle should just clear the net and fall a few inches inside the short service line of the opponent's court (the most common serve in doubles play); (2) a deep (long), high serve in which the shuttle must be so placed that it travels above the receiver's reach and falls within six inches of the rear boundary line (the most common serve in singles play); and (3) a drive serve, generally made by a quick flick of the wrist and arm, which is just above net height and travels almost parallel to the floor. This last serve is especially effective when made from the right-hand service court to the receiver's left-hand deep corner.

Backhand Serve (Figure 7-7). A short, low serve made with a backhand stroke in which the shuttle is held below the waist has several advantages and can be a confusing serve for the opponents to return. The wrist-flicking action used in this serve can occasionally be increased to drive the serve overhead and to the rear of the court.

Figure 7-7. Backhand serving position.

Serving Drills. The player should practice each of the preceding serves many times. Each type should first be practiced separately. Concentrate on placing the shuttle in either corner and closely adjust the flight path in order that it just clear the net for the short and drive serves. Finally, the various serves should be mixed, attempting to mask the type of serve until after the shuttle has been stroked.

Receiving the Serve (Figure 7-8). The badminton student will probably need to mix practicing the various strokes and shots described in the next section with practicing serving and receiving (returning) the serve.

The receiver should assume a stance and court position that will enable him to best return any type of serve. He

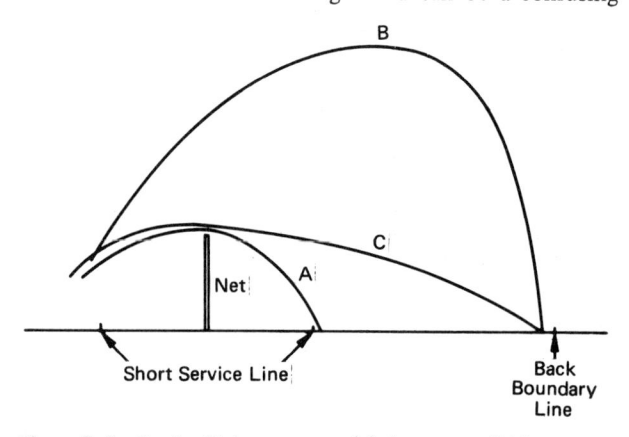

Figure 7-6. Service flight patterns: (a) short serve, (b) long serve, (c) drive or flick serve.

Figure 7-8. Ready position for receiving the serve.

68   *Individual and Team Sports*

should carefully watch the server in order to determine and anticipate as early as possible the type of serve being made. In addition, he should cultivate the habit of planning ahead where the serve should be returned and the type of shot to be utilized. In time this can become automatic, requiring little conscious thought.

The ready, or on-guard, position of the receiver when awaiting the serve is quite similar to that position during a rally. Increased emphasis is placed on moving up and back; therefore, one foot is farther in front of the other than for the rally-ready position. In addition, the racket is usually held upward near the body and in a forehand position, with the racket head about head level. The basic court position is one in which the receiver is best prepared to cover all areas of the service court. (See Figure 7-9.) Because the doubles service court is thirty inches shorter, but eighteen inches wider, than the singles service court, the doubles receiver stands slightly forward of the singles position. The receiver should be especially prepared to move toward the net on a low serve in order to attempt to play the shuttle before it drops below the level of the net. The type of stroke best suited to returning the serve is determined by the type of serve, the player's strengths and weaknesses, and the court position and weaknesses of the opponent(s). A short service barely clearing the net and dropping just inside the receiving court can be returned either by an easy cross-court drop shot just clearing the net, by a straight-ahead drive shot, by a high, clear deep lob to the back court, or by a semi-smash shot executed by the receiver rushing the net and smashing the shuttle before it falls below the net level. If the shuttle is below net level, then a straight-ahead net shot is best, in which the racket head is angled upward and the bird is cut. A long serve can be returned either by a high clear, a drive, a smash, a half-smash, or a drop shot. The high clear is usually the best one in this situation because it moves the opponent away from the net. However, the returns should be varied in order to deceive the opponent and prevent him from accurately anticipating the type and location of the return shot. Whenever the opponent serves the shuttle head high or higher and no farther back than the middle of the receiving court, the smash, if accurately executed, will often end the rally.

Drills. The beginning player should repeatedly practice returning the same type of serves, systematically alternating the type of return shot used and the placement of the shuttle. When some ability in receiving the various serves has been gained, the beginner should drill by returning a mixture of serves, attempting to anticipate the kind of serve being made.

Forehand Strokes

The forehand strokes are very similar to the movements used in throwing a ball. overhead smash equals overhead pitch; forehand drive equals sidearm pitch; and underhand shots equal underhand pitch. (See Figure 7-10). In these strokes, however, the backswing is less pronounced, and the wrist action and forearm rotation become more

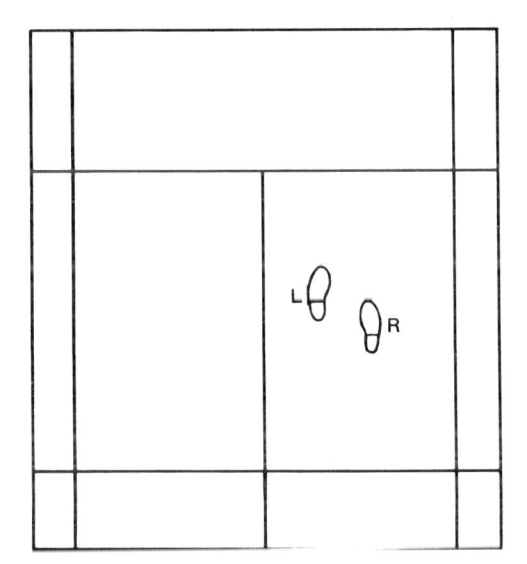

Figure 7-9. Court position for receiving the singles serve.

Figure 7-10. Forehand stroke. (Photograph by courtesy of the American Badminton Association, R. Stanton Hales, photographer.)

important than when throwing a ball. The left foot usually points in the direction that the shuttle is hit, and the body weight is ordinarily shifted to the rear foot during the preparatory backswing. As the forehand stroke is initiated, the weight shifts to the forward foot and the arm comes forward with the wrist hyperextended. The racket head should follow behind the armswing. Just before the racket head contacts the bird, the racket head is whipped forward and the wrist is flexed sharply as the forearm is rotated naturally. The swing should be adjusted according to the position, relative to the player, of the shuttle coming toward him.

Backhand Strokes

Basically, backhand strokes are the reverse of the forehand strokes. (See Figure 7-11.) With the backhand grip on the racket, the right foot is placed in the direction of the net. As the racket is cocked to the rear, the weight is transferred to the forward foot. Again, the racket head trails the movement of the arm until just before the racket contacts the bird, when the wrist is forcefully extended and the forearm is rotated, as in the forehand stroke.

Figure 7-11. Backhand stroke. Body *fully* turned so back is to net; arm extended, racket up and high. (Photograph by courtesy of the American Badminton Association, R. Stanton Hales, photographer.)

Figure 7-12. Overhead stroke. (Photograph by courtesy of the American Badminton Association, R. Stanton Hales, photographer.)

Overhead Stroke

The overhead stroke is basically the same as the forehand stroke, except that the racket is first swung back and down behind the shoulder. (See Figure 7-12.) As the arm swings forward, the racket describes an arc over the head, and the shuttle is stroked with considerable wrist and forearm action. Overhead shots can also be executed with a backhand stroke.

Drill. As for serving and receiving, the player should regularly drill in stroking the shuttle several times with one type of stroking action before proceeding to another type and finally proceed to mix them.

Shots Common to Badminton Play
(See Figure 7-13.)

Clear. The clear shot is a defensive one, ordinarily used when a player is in difficulty—such as when he is off-balance or out of position—or when it is desirable to move the opponent away from the net. The clear shot can be made with either a backhand or forehand stroke, from any part of the court, and with the shuttle at any height that is within reach—although it is preferable to play the shuttle while it is still high above the court. It is important that the shuttle be hit forcefully upward in order that it travel high and deep into the opponent's court, landing

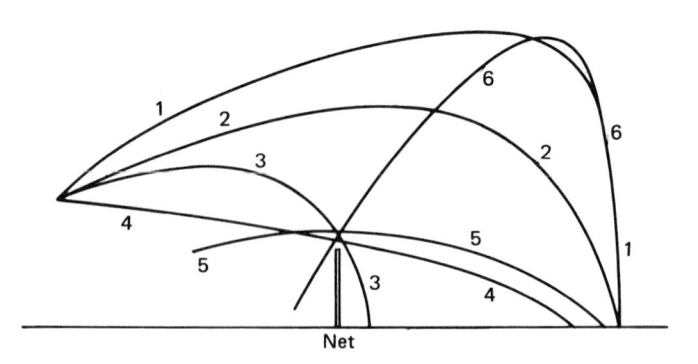

Figure 7-13(a). Various badminton shots: (1) defensive clear, (2) attacking clear, (3) overhead drop shot, (4) smash, (5) drive, (6) underhand clear.

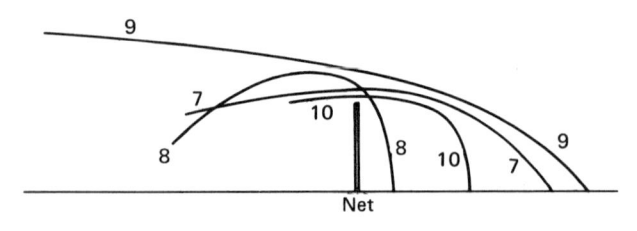

Figure 7-13(b). Various badminton shots: (7) midcourt drive, (8) underhand drop shot, (9) half smash, (10) push shot.

70 *Individual and Team Sports*

just inside the back boundary line, and descend in nearly a vertical direction. The racket face should be facing squarely toward the target area when the shuttle is contacted, and the shuttle should travel above the opponent's reach. The backhand clear shot may require considerable practice before it can be hit to the opposite back-boundary line. The player may need to turn his back somewhat to the shuttle on the backswing and use considerable wrist action and forearm rotation when hitting as he steps toward the net.

Smash. The smash is primarily an attaching or offensive shot, but it can be turned against a player standing in the back court by immediately returning the shuttle with a short net shot. The smash is forcefully made with a complete arm action in which the shuttle is stroked at a height that can be reached comfortably and sufficiently in front of the player so that his arm and racket shaft almost form a straight line. Maximum wrist action and forearm rotation should be employed. Because of the power required, the feet should be placed slightly farther apart, and the body may be twisted slightly more away from the net than for other types of shots. The shuttle should be stroked when at the extreme limit of one's upward reach and when slightly in front of the right shoulder, in order to hit the bird downward as well as forward. When the overhand stroke is executed, the right foot should step forward during the follow-through in order to maintain correct body balance. The bird should clear the net by no more than 1 foot. The smash is usually aimed toward mid-court, along one of the side lines, or directly toward an opponent—usually toward his playing arm side between waist and shoulder height. A smash should not be attempted while moving backward, as the stroke may not have adequate power, and the recovery to play the return shot will be delayed. Only the strong, skilled player should regularly attempt a smash from the back court and expect to win the rally. Because the shuttle slows down rapidly, hitting the shuttle at a downward angle is more important than hitting it extremely fast. The smash is not ordinarily executed with a backhand stroke by the average player because it is difficult to hit the shuttle with sufficient speed for it to be effective.

Drop Shot. A drop shot is any shot that drops immediately after crossing the net and in which the shuttle does not travel more than a few feet beyond the net. The drop shot can be a defensive or an offensive shot; it is generally used to change the pace of the game and to upset the opponent's timing. The overhand drop shot should be made to resemble a smash or clear until the shuttle is struck, and the underhand drop shot should resemble the underhand clear shot. It is difficult to so execute a drop shot that it simulates a drive, or to hit it at the same angle as a drive made from the back court. The overhand drop is the easiest to stroke and can be quite deceptive. Beginners, however, may have increased success with the underhand drop shot. Even though struck very lightly and gently, the drop shot requires some wrist and forearm action if accuracy is to be obtained. A follow-through should be made in order to add to the deception and accuracy of the drop shot. This is an excellent shot to use when the opponent is deep in his back court.

Net Shot (Figure 7-14.) If a drop shot is played from a position close to the net, the shot is referred to as a net shot. It requires little power and is controlled almost exclusively by wrist and forearm action, or by cutting the shuttle with the racket face. Footwork and body position are not as important, because less power is needed and the player often has little time to position himself; hence, the right foot is often forward during the stroke, permitting an increased reach. It can be played while facing the net, and should be played from above or as near the level of the top of the net as possible. However, if the bird drops some distance below the net before being stroked, the net shot, especially if it just clears the top of the net, is normally the most deceptive and most difficult shot for the opponent to return effectively. The angled, cross-court shot (hook or hairpin shot) is the easiest and safest to use if the bird is hit when it is well below the top of the net. When hitting net drop shots, the shuttle is stroked lightly with a guided lifting motion in which a looping shuttle flight results. This shot, when coupled with a clear shot and a low straight-ahead net shot, which can be cut or

Figure 7-14. Net shot. Perfect form to hit drop shot at net. body fully extended, racket *high* near net level. (Photograph by courtesy of the American Badminton Association, R. Stanton Hales, photographer.)

the racket head angled, permits a net game in which the opponent must move quickly for some distance and make accurate returns.

Drive. The drive is a fast, low, flat shot that is second only to the smash as an attacking shot. The drive must be hit forcefully, either with a forehand or a backhand stroke, with the shuttle just passing over the net. This shot is used to pass or to run the opponent to one side. It should be used with caution when the opponent has a good chance of intercepting it near the net, because such a quick return is difficult to retrieve and the rally may well be lost.

Drills. Each of the basic shots of badminton should be singly practiced with backhand and forehand strokes before combining more than one type of shot in a drill. Accuracy and good form should be the primary emphasis. Rallies in which only one type of shot is used can be played. During a drill, full concentration can be given to perfecting a shot without any outside distractions—a condition that is never present during game play.

CORRECTIONS OF COMMON ERRORS

The beginning student, especially, is often apt to make many errors while learning and mastering the fundamental skills of badminton and integrating them into a complete game. One of the greatest values in having an instructor is in his pointing out the mistakes being made and explaining the corrections. The student often has difficulty in recognizing many of the mistakes that he makes and often must examine the symptoms of the errors (such as repeatedly hitting the shuttle into the net during a smash, or consistently being caught out of position) in order to deduct the cause of the symptoms—the errors themselves. Some of the more common errors made by beginning badminton players and a few checks for determining the cause of these errors follow.

Grip

Choking the Racket. Be sure that the little finger is at the very end of the racket.

Locking the Wrist. Check to see that the entire arm is not locked or held rigidly during the stroke; instead, wrist action and forearm rotation should be an integral part of the stroking action. This can be accomplished by cocking the wrist before stroking toward the net. Attempting to hit the shuttle hard often cures this mistake.

Serving

Having the Serve Killed. Check the height at which the shuttle is held and the height at which it is struck. Check the distance of the shuttle from the server when it is struck as well as the angle at which the racket contacts the shuttle. Too much or too little wrist action can be a source of difficulty and should be checked. All the above can result in a short serve that is too high.

Holding the Shuttle Incorrectly. Observe that the shuttle should be held with the thumb and fingers around the feathers for a drop serve and with the tips of the thumb and forefinger for a held serve. Also observe the distance that the shuttle is held away from the body.

Serving Out-of-bounds. Check to see that the server's body, particularly his left shoulder and left foot, is pointed in the proper direction.

Hitting into the Net. Check to see that the shuttle is not too close to the body, that the body is not bent too much, and that the shuttle is not held or struck at too low a height.

Returning the Serve

Hitting to the Opponent. Determine whether or not the body is in the proper position when the shuttle is contacted. The player should practice deliberately aiming for a different part of the opponent's court on each return, and he should try to anticipate where the serve will be made and reason ahead of time what is the best return for that serve.

Repetitious Stroking Action. Although the same pattern should be followed for a stroke, the amount of wrist and forearm action should be varied in order to deceive the opponent's anticipation concerning the direction of the shot, and particularly the distance that the shuttle will travel. Repeatedly using the same shot permits the opponent to anticipate successfully how to return it and where.

Being Out of Position

Not Maintaining the Ready Position. Check to see that a crouch position, with the weight forward on the balls of the feet, is the basic stance.

Standing Still After Stroking. After each shot the player immediately returns to or toward a position near the middle of the court.

Backing Up. When moving backward, the player must quickly pivot and quickly shuffle or *back pedal* to where the shuttle will be played while watching the shuttle all the time.

Not Anticipating the Opponent's Return. The student should plan every shot in advance and anticipate the opponent's possible and probable return of his shots.

General Play of Shots

Pushing a Shot. The badminton player while still a novice should not be overcautious or try too hard to do the right thing when stroking the shuttle. Instead, he should try to relax and employ a full backswing and wrist action on most shots.

Too Close to the Shuttle. When playing the shuttle the player should get his body sufficiently away from the bird in order that his arm can be fully extended, or nearly so, when the racket makes contact with the shuttle.

Indecisiveness in Stroking. Once a shot has been initiated, it should be finished; changing the shot at the last second will cause difficulty for the beginner, although the highly skilled player may be successful with this tactic. Thinking ahead and anticipating the opponent's return should result in few indecisions when playing.

Poor Wrist Action. Check the grip to see if free wrist action and forearm rotation are permitted. Deliberately limit the arm movement and practice stroking in which mainly wrist action is used.

Poor Backhand. Check to see that the thumb is behind the racket on all backhand shots. The student should stand with his feet and body at right angles to the net in order that a full preliminary backswing can be taken that will allow full body and wrist action on the backhand stroke. Do not face the net for a backhand stroke.

Clear Shot Resulting in a Setup. The player should attempt to get full power into his clear shot by snapping the wrist, rotating the forearm, and aiming for the back boundary line. A full preliminary backswing is a necessity.

Hitting Wood Shots. The shuttle should be watched until it is contacted with the racket; the player should actually see the contact. Particularly during the learning stages, he should not watch the opponent or the place he wishes to hit the bird. With experience these can be seen with peripheral vision.

Hitting a Smash into the Net. The player should not be too far behind the shuttle; he should make contact at the proper time; he should hit the shuttle with his arm fully extended, or almost so.

BADMINTON STRATEGY

The strategy in badminton is to place the shuttle in the opponent's court where he cannot reach it or where he will have difficulty making an adequate return and hence may be forced to make a defensive stroke. Although there is no set sequence of shots that can be relied on to win a rally, some situations highly favor a specific shot or a placement to a particular area of the court; other situations negate the use of certain shots and placements.

There are also certain principles concerning the use of the body that make for a more effective game and permit some shots and placements to be employed with maximum effectiveness. Because individuals vary in ability and playing skill, the effectiveness of certain shots often depends heavily on the skill and ability of the player—what works well for one player may not work nearly as well for another.

Basic to good badminton play is the ability to serve well, which is usually dependent on practice, instruction, and perhaps coaching. Points can only be scored when serving. Both low-short and deep-high serves should be mastered; in executing these, the same basic motion should be employed. The server should use both types of serves in order to keep the opponent from anticipating the type of serve he will receive, and, hence, occupying the most advantageous court position before the serve is made.

General Strategy

What is sometimes good strategy to use by or against a novice player may be poor strategy for use by or against a skilled player. The strengths and weaknesses of the opponent, as well as those of the player, should be tested and learned early in order to utilize the most appropriate strategy. When anticipating or guessing the opponent's return (or serve), always remember to recover to a basic body and court position after each stroke, instead of holding the last position while watching the opponent (being a spectator). This is a must if playing skill and strategy are to improve rapidly.

Because hitting the shuttle upward is usually a defensive shot, the player should try to get in such a position that he can hit down on the shuttle. If the shuttle has to be hit upward, it should generally be hit high and deep or low and soft, just passing over the net. An occasional semidrive shot down a side line can also be effective if the opponent is positioned to one side of the court.

The player should be ready for a return at all times. He should attempt to assume the position of readiness and the proper floor position on the court as soon as possible after stroking the shuttle. He should as a rule return the shuttle as quickly as possible in order to give his opponent the minimum time in which to get set.

The shuttle should usually be placed where the opponent cannot hit it cleanly and hence will be forced to make a weak return. The weakest stroke for many players and for most beginners is the backhand stroke; consequently, returns should be aimed there often. Because many players overplay the court position or otherwise cover up their weak backhand, a shot first to their forehand side may force them out of a strong backhand court position.

The beginner must learn early to avoid the natural tendency to hit the shuttle always at the opponent (a ready-made target) rather than to vacant spots on the opponent's court.

The player should learn to change the pace of the game by mixing his shots. In addition, it is important to avoid having a set pattern of shot placements such as up, back, up, back; right side, left side, right side, left side; or constantly to the rear backhand corner. Instead, the shuttle should be hit to one spot two to four times (setting up an apparent pattern) and then placed to another spot once or twice, then perhaps back to the original spot. These practices tend to keep the opponent off-balance, make him move, and upset his timing.

Smashing indiscriminately from the base line is not a good idea. This is tiring and it makes the shuttle fairly easy to return because by the time it crosses the net it is moving relatively slowly. It is also often difficult to recover in time to play a return drop or net shot, particularly if it is well placed.

Shots attempted while moving are apt to be poorly executed and poorly aimed shots. A basic principle to follow is, if possible, to get set first and then hit.

Singles Strategy

Serve long most of the time unless the opponent is playing back, in which situation serve short and also make an occasional drive serve. A long serve puts the server and the receiver on equal terms because it is difficult to drop shot accurately from the back court, and it requires considerable power and accuracy to smash from there. The clear shot also requires power. Therefore, to some extent, the more long shots a receiver has to make, the more tired and less efficient he will become.

Return a high, deep serve with a drop or clear shot. A smash should not be used unless the serve is not too deep or the opponent has a weak smash defense. Because half smashes, which are hit downward with less speed than a regular smash and often involve slicing the shuttle, require less time in which to recover, they are often used more frequently than regular smashes. Drop shots to the opponent's forehand or backhand and clears to his backhand are probably the most difficult for him to handle. The returns should, however, be varied.

The safest return of a short serve is usually the clear because it forces the opponent deep and his return may set up a rally-ending shot. If the opponent moves backward after executing his short service, countering with an underhand drop shot will probably catch him off-balance. The player must always be alert and have a ready racket and body position in order to rush a short serve, driving it down one side line or toward the opponent, if the shuttle can be played above net level. If the shuttle is below net level, a net shot to either side (made by tilting the racket head back with the handle under the head or by angling the racket face to one side) or a clear shot to a rear corner should be the usual return.

Attempt to put the shuttle in the spot the opponent has just vacated as often as possible. Recovering to this vacated position requires extraordinary speed and agility. By "holding" the shot, that is, appearing to hit or starting to hit the shuttle while it is high, but instead waiting and stroking when the shuttle is lower, will often cause the opponent to commit himself. The shuttle should then be placed away from the direction in which he is moving. Its occasional use tends to force the opponent to hold his court position a maximum length of time. If one is moving on the court at the time the opponent plays a shot, he will probably place the shuttle in the vacated position. Therefore, be alert to this possibility and be ready to reverse directions.

Other than shots played directly at the opponent (most of which are aimed at his playing shoulder or below it), the bird should usually be aimed to within one foot of the boundary lines.

A player's game should be built on the basis of drop and clear and net shot, with the half smash, smash, and drive used whenever the openings occur. Make the opponent run back and forth and from side to side.

A cross-court shot (drive) is dangerous unless the shot is a probable winner. The safest drives are those passing the opponent on the side lines. However, cross-court drives should occasionally be used in order to avoid having the opponent guess where a drive shot will be placed. This also applies somewhat to smashes, in that a cross-court smash travels a long distance, slows down markedly, and usually requires the opponent to move a decreased distance to reach it. Again, the cross-court smash should be used sufficiently to disrupt the opponent's anticipation and smash placement.

In singles play the player's basic court position is modified according to the opponent's court position. If the opponent is playing the shuttle from one side of the court, the player should move over one to three feet toward that side since a shot down that side line arrives much sooner than a cross-court shot that can often be cut off at the middle of the court. Because a short shot, particularly a net shot, is in the air only a brief time, if the opponent is playing up toward the net, the player must in turn move his ready court position forward toward the net.

Doubles Strategy

Basic to doubles strategy is a knowledge of court position. In doubles the server should stand close to the inside front corner of the serving court with his partner straddling the line several feet in back of him. (See Figure 7-15.) If he serves short he should go to the net to cover the return. (This system is used by many teams and is basic to the up-and-back system and, on occasion, to the rotation system, both of which are described subsequently.) There are several systems of playing doubles: the side-by-side, the up-and-back, and the rotation system are frequently used. Any system of doubles play generally requires much practice if the partners are to coordinate their efforts well and develop a common understanding of how they will play the system.

Side-by-side System. The side-by-side system is often best for beginners because each player is responsible for his half of the court and there is little chance of becoming confused as to the responsibility for returning a shot—this is determined by the line running down the middle of the court. Frequently, however, both players are caught in the back court or close to the net, leaving a large unguarded area. In addition, the team is vulnerable to shots directed to their backhand side (the left side if both are right handed). Confusion also results when the shuttle is hit to an area midway between the two players: there may be indecision as to which player should take the shot (usually the player with the forehand shot takes it). Under this system, the receiver (or server) plays whatever half court in which he begins play; his partner automatically covers the other half court.

Figure 7-15. Doubles formation. Far side on offense: smasher back, partner up front; near side on defense: side-by-side. (Photograph by courtesy of the American Badminton Association, R. Stanton Hales, photographer.)

Up-and-back System. This system is the one normally used when playing mixed doubles or sometimes when two partners are of unequal ability. The woman (if the weaker player) is primarily responsible for covering the front area (short service line forward) whenever possible, while the partner covers the rest of the court. When the partners are equal in playing ability, the server often takes the forecourt and never goes back. When receiving, the receiver plays to whichever area the serve is made and his partner automatically covers the other. It is important that the front player not back up to take an overhead shot that the back player can move forward to take.

Rotation System. Various rotation systems that combine some of the features of the other two systems have been devised. They are not recommended for beginners because they are complicated and require considerable practice to perfect. Under one type of rotation system the partners should remember and stress (1) holding the court position or else moving only counterclockwise to take a shot, and (2) that whenever one partner moves, the other partner must move an equal distance, always in a counterclockwise direction, allowing the next shot by the opponents to determine whether court positions are to be shifted. The players rotate in a counterclockwise direction whenever either one is forced out of position by a placement. So, instead of returning to the original position, the players continue in the direction taken in playing the shot.

The objectives of rotation systems are to (1) place the partners where they can best cover all areas of the court, especially the net areas, (2) permit a maximum of forehand and a minimum of backhand strokes, (3) require a minimum of movements for taking each shot, (4) use a strategy that causes a minimum of confusion as to which partner takes what shot, and (5) use a system that can be learned without too much difficulty.

Regardless of the system of doubles play used, certain basic elements constitute good strategy, particularly for inexperienced players:

1. Do not change systems in the middle of a winning game; confusion will generally result.
2. Make most serves short and low, preferably to the corners. Use a drive or high, deep service (just over his reach) only when the opponent usually rushes the serve or stands near the front service line. Low, long serves, particularly to the receiver's backhand area, are often effective.
3. Rush short serves by standing close to the service line with the left foot forward. As soon as the bird is served, step or shuffle forward. Turn the racket face parallel with the net, and push the right arm forward, hitting or pushing the bird

while it is still above the level of the net. Hit it down. If, in this situation, the served bird falls below the net level before it can be stroked, the bird should be hit with an overhand stroke (as in a smash), but no wrist action is used. Thus, the hand is ahead of the racket head and the bird is lobbed over the net in a short net shot. Because the receiver rushes the net for this shot, the opponent has a tendency to step back, making this a particularly effective return. Otherwise, a cross-court net shot can be hit.

4. Usually smash a long serve (because the partner is up to handle block shots and net shots), but occasionally play a drop or clear shot for variation.
5. Always make an attacking shot unless any other shot would leave you, your partner, or both out of position for the return. All shots should be hit down whenever possible.
6. Call to say who should take a shot, whether or not it will go out of bounds, and so on.
7. Play for the partner. Hopefully the return shot will then leave an opening for the partner to play his best shot and possibly finish the rally.
8. Make placements to the least obvious spots.
9. Once at the net, stay there until the bird is cleared by either side, then return to position.
10. If the serving team is playing a front and back formation, the best return of a low service is a half-court shot down the side boundary line. A series of net shots is often effective against a team using the side-by-side system. A drive clear to the backhand corner is probably the best return against the side-by-side system.
11. If the opponents are playing side-by-side, draw one player to the net and then play to his backhand on the next shot.
12. Shots near the center line should be taken by the player who can play it on his forehand. The left-court player in the side-by-side system should return these shots.
13. If trouble develops in stroking the bird, concentrate on hitting only the cork or base.
14. A winning strategy is often to play safe shots and allow the opponents to make the errors.
15. When playing skillful opponents, no move should usually be made until they stroke the shuttle; otherwise, they will fake their shots and often hit away from the direction of travel.
16. When playing opponents who hit angle shots with great skill, a down-the-middle game will decrease the angle at which they can hit their shots.

ADVANCED BADMINTON SKILLS

No clear-cut distinction exists between elementary and advanced badminton skills. In fact, what may be an elementary skill for some players may be an advanced skill for others and vice versa. Some of the skills presented in the "Fundamental Skills" section might properly be considered advanced skills. These include the low, fast drive (or flick) serve, the half smash, and holding the shuttle (appearing to start to stroke it but then waiting a short time). Even though a sound game of badminton could be played in which only fundamental skills and shots were utilized, the strategic use of an advanced skill or shot may result in a definite advantage.

Half Smash

The half smash will usually accomplish as much for the player as the full smash, and it has the extra advantages of being directed downward at a steep angle and requiring less effort or time to recover to a ready position. The half smash usually involves a cutting or slicing action on the shuttle, which means that the racket face is angled to the path of the racket head and involves considerable forearm rotation or wrist action, either clockwise or counterclockwise, immediately before the shuttle is struck. This causes the shuttle to be cut or sliced to a different part of the front court than the spot to where it is apparently aimed. The cutting or slicing action used in the half smash can also be employed when striking drop shots and clear shots.

Backhand Smash

The backhand smash is executed as a forehand smash except from the backhand side. It is important that the player quickly get into position, that his playing shoulder face the net (many players have their backs initially facing the net), and that he use a full straight or almost straight-arm action with a significant degree of forearm rotation and wrist action. Because the player has many opportunities to utilize this shot it should be practiced often.

Round-the-head Smash

(See Figure 7-16.) This stroke is like the overhead stroke, except that the arm is bent at the elbow and the body must be inclined to the left in order that the shuttle be struck when above the left shoulder. Players having a weak backhand smash may find this one an ample substitute. Most of the force of a drive or a smash can be obtained from this position. This shot is used primarily

Figure 7-16. Round-the-head smash. (photograph by courtesy of the American Badminton Association, R. Stanton Hales, photographer.)

for returning shots that are at least head high on the backhand side and when there is not sufficient time to move far enough to the left to make a regular forehand smash or drive, or else the player would get too far out of position. The player may also hit clear and drop shots with the round-the-head stroke. He should avoid overusing it because he can lose court position.

Cut Serve

The low serve can be cut by slicing across the shuttle from right to left or vice versa, while stroking forward. This causes the shuttle to make a looping flight, which is disconcerting to the inexperienced receiver. With practice the cut serve can be accurately placed. The same type of cutting action can be employed when hitting net shots, especially when the bird is close to the net and below the top of it.

Backhand Drop

A drop shot hit from the backhand side is frequently unexpected and, therefore, is often effective in deceiving the opponent. Although such a shot must be practiced a great deal, some players develop unusual skill with it. The backhand underhand drop shot to the opposite front corner is an especially effective shot if the opponent believes a clear shot is being made.

SPECIFIC TRAINING METHODS

Drill

As is true of any sport, considerable practice and drill in the fundamental skills of badminton, interspersed with playing the complete game, are necessary for the over-all most efficient improvement of the skill. A single facet of a skill (such as a backhand drop shot) should be practiced to the point of overlearning, thus requiring no conscious thought processes to execute it (except for making corrections). These should be gradually mixed and combined when practicing or training until each skill in the entire repertoire can be done whenever the proper occasion arises during a game.

Game Play

The aspiring player usually improves his game most effectively when he plays against a better player or team. This forces him to evaluate his skills and strategy critically and improve them. The skilled player can increase the degree of competition by playing against a doubles team, by restricting his game to certain shots (such as playing only net and drop shots), or by not using shots such as smashes.

Supplementary Training Methods

Badminton, when well played by skilled players, can be exhausting. Therefore, engaging in activities designed to enhance those basic qualities that underlie rapid movement, stopping and starting, and quick changes in directions should improve one's over-all playing ability. Increasing the degree of flexibility, agility, cardiorespiratory endurance, strength, speed of movement, and reaction time should be done concurrently with regular badminton play. Specific training methods (such as circuit training, running activities, and weight training) are described and their uses are discussed in the companion publication by Macmillan, Inc., *Handbook of Physical Fitness Activities*, by D. Casady, D. Mapes, and L. Alley.

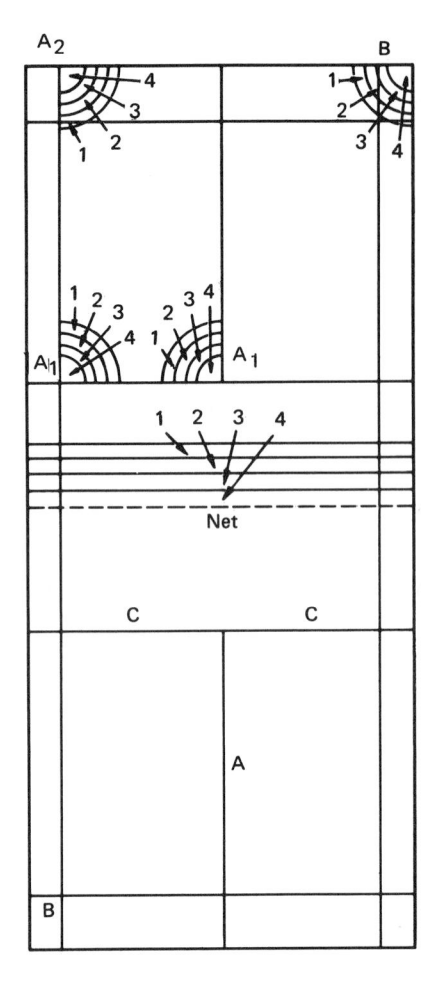

Figure 7-17. Sample badminton evaluation tests. A_1: Short-serve test. A_2: Long-serve test (a rope 10 feet high can be suspended above the receiver's position; the shuttle must pass over it). B: Backhand clear test. C: Net-shot test (often the shuttle must pass below a rope suspended 1 foot above the top of the net.)

SELF-EVALUATION

Tournaments

Tournaments—such as ladder or pyramid, random, double elimination, round robin, and consolation—are frequently used in classes and between classes to evaluate and obtain a ranking of over-all badminton playing ability.

Tests

Different drills or tests, which can be diagnostic as well as evaluative, can be utilized to assess both current skill and areas in need of improvement. Several tests and scoring systems have been devised for these purposes. An example of these appears in Figure 7-17, in which for each type of shot or serve, ten to twenty repeated attempts are made and the total score is recorded.

Written tests can be useful to evaluate knowledge of rules, performance of various skills, strategy, and the like.

Glossary of Terms

The following terms are commonly used in the game of badminton.

ABA: American Badminton Association.
Ace: A serve executed so well that it cannot be returned.
Alley: Eighteen-inch extension on either side of the singles court, used for doubles play only.
Balk: A feint by the server or receiver; it is illegal.
Base: A spot near the center of the court or slightly forward of it to which the player goes after a shot.
Bird: The shuttlecock or shuttle.
Block: Positioning the racket in front of the shuttle from which it rebounds over the net.
Carry (sling or throw): Momentarily catching the shuttle on the racket while stroking; it is illegal.
Cross-court shot: A shot in which the shuttle crosses the net at a sharp angle to it.
Deception: Skillfully outwitting the opponent by deceptively changing the speed and/or direction of the shuttle at the last instant.
Double hit: Hitting the shuttle twice during a stroke; it is illegal.
Drive: A hard-hit shuttle that travels net high and parallel to the floor to near the base line.
Driven serve: A serve similar in flight pattern to that of a drive shot.
Drop: A shot executed like a smash or clear but which is hit softly at the last instant in order that it just clears the net and drops quickly.
Fault: Any error or violation contrary to the rules that results in the loss of a point or the serve.
Flick: A quick snap of the wrist (wrist flexion) that speeds up the badminton shot.
Forecourt: The area between the net and short service line.
Game point: A point that, if made, will win the game.
Hairpin net shot: A shot in which the shuttle is hit from below and close to the net, just clears it, and then drops downward at a sharp angle.
Hand down: The loss of the serve.
High clear: A high, deep shot that forces the receiver to play the shuttle near the back line.
IBF: International Badminton Federation.

Inning: The period during which a player or team has the service.

Long: A serve or shot that goes beyond the back boundary line.

Kill shot: A smash hit so hard and so well placed that it is usually not returned, thus it kills, or ends, a rally.

Match point: The last point of a game, which will determine the victor of a best two-out-of-three games match.

No shot: Call made by a player who carries the shuttle.

Out-of-hand serve: A serve in which the bird, instead of being dropped on the racket, is hit out of the hand.

On-guard stance: The position of readiness while waiting for a serve or a return; ready position.

Push shot: A shot executed by pushing the shuttle easily across the net.

Rally: Hitting the bird back and forth either in a game or during a warm-up before a game.

Set-up: A poor serve or a return that is a perfect candidate for a smash or kill shot.

Setting: The term applied when determining for how many points to play when the game becomes tied.

Smash: An overhead shot returned fast, hard, and at a sharp, downward angle.

Toss serve: A serve in which the bird is tossed or dropped and then hit.

Wood shot: A shot in which the shuttle is struck with the racket frame; it is legal.

Selected References

Badminton, U.S.A. 333 Saratoga Road, Buffalo, New York 14226.

This is the official periodical of the ABA and contains tournament news and instructional articles and comments about the sports.

Friedrich, John, and Abbie Rutledge. *Beginning Badminton.* Belmont, Calif.: Wadsworth, 1962.

Written by two long-time badminton players and instructors, this booklet is especially written for the student who is learning the game.

Poole, James. *Badminton.* Pacific Palisades, Calif.: Goodyear, 1969.

James Poole, a men's singles national championship holder, describes and instructs the various phases of badminton through an advanced skill level.

Rogers, Wynn. *Advanced Badminton.* Dubuque, Iowa: Brown, 1970.

This booklet is designed to be of value specifically to the advanced badminton player and is a companion to the booklet listed below. It is written by a former Thomas Cup player and coach.

Varner, Margaret. *Badminton.* Dubuque, Iowa: Brown, 1966.

The author, a former national and international champion, has written a well-illustrated book of considerable value to the badminton player who wants to improve his game.

CHAPTER 8

Basketball

*Gary Hansen**
The University of Iowa

HISTORY

The game of basketball is the only major sport that has its origin and development in the United States. Basketball was devised in 1891 at the international Young Men's Christian Association (YMCA) Training School in Springfield, Massachusetts, by Dr. James A. Naismith, who was a student-instructor at the time. He developed the game as the result of an assignment given by a senior instructor to develop a recreative-type game for indoor play during the winter months. Dr. Naismith first attempted to modify the existing games of lacrosse and football to an indoor situation. He soon abandoned this idea and proceeded under the assumption that the game should involve the skill of passing rather than carrying the ball. He also incorporated the idea that the goal should be horizontal rather than vertical to insure an arc in the flight of the ball on the try for a score. This concept was introduced in order to eliminate the congregation of the defense around the goal.

The first goals were peach baskets that were hung at the ends of the gymnasium at a height of ten feet. A soccer ball was utilized as the game ball. Later, the peach basket was replaced by a hoop and net and the soccer ball by the larger official basketball. The game of basketball was an immediate success from the day that the eighteen members of Dr. Gulick's class in Springfield first played the game. It spread rapidly throughout the United States in the public schools, colleges, and YMCA programs. The growth of the game was so rapid that, by 1892, Geneva College, Beaver Falls, Pennsylvania, had already played a scheduled game, as had the University of Iowa, Iowa City, Iowa. Yale University played the first intercollegiate basketball schedule in 1896. The state of Indiana conducted a state high school basketball tournament as early as 1905. The growth of basketball was somewhat retarded in South America and in Europe, as the game was first introduced there as a game for girls.

The first rules of the game have been modified considerably since the original thirteen rules were posted on a bulletin board in Springfield, Massachusetts. These rules called for eight players on a team (three forwards, three guards, and two centers). This was probably because the class in Springfield consisted of eighteen members. The number of players was soon reduced to seven and later to five. The dribble and personal foul rules were two of the earliest modifications to the original list. The major rules changes that have occurred since then, in the evolution of the game, follow:

1. 1923: The player fouled must shoot the free throw.
2. 1930: Ten-second rule in which the ball must be advanced past the mid-court line in the designated length of time.
3. 1936: Three-second rule involving the length of time an offensive player is allowed to stay in the offensive free-throw lane.
4. 1937: Elimination of the center jump after each successful field goal.
5. 1957: Widening of the free-throw lane to twelve feet from the original 6 feet.
6. 1967: Elimination of the dunk shot.

---

*B.A., M.A., and Ph.D., The University of Iowa, Iowa City. Dr. Hansen coached the varsity basketball team at University High School of the University of Iowa for several years and was head basketball coach for two years at Shimer College, Illinois. He competed in basketball at Daina College, Blair, Nebraska, and has played several seasons of basketball on winning teams in the Army and AAU basketball leagues.

Prior to 1915, the YMCA, the Amateur Athletic Union (AAU), and the National Collegiate Athletic Association (NCAA) each had a different set of rules for basketball. In 1915, these organizations formed a joint committee and standardized the rules of basketball. At the present time the rules of the game are determined by the National Basketball Committee of the United States and Canada. This committee is formed by representatives from the NCAA, the National Federation of State High School Athletic Association, the National Junior College Athletic Association, the YMCA, the Canadian Intercollegiate Athletic Union, and the Canadian Amateur Basketball Association.

NATURE OF THE GAME

Basketball is played by two teams of five players each on an area called a court. Each team is composed of two guards, two forwards, and a center. The objective of the game is to score more points than the opposing team by shooting the ball through a hoop at one end of the court while attempting to prevent the other team from shooting the ball through the hoop located at the opposite end. Scoring is accomplished by shooting field goals, which count two points each, and free throws (awarded as a result of fouls or rule infractions) from the free-throw line, which count one point each.

The game is started at the center jump circle with a jump ball between any two players of the teams opposing each other. The ball is tossed in the air between them by an official. The team that gains possession of the ball is called the offensive team, and it attempts to score a field goal by shooting the ball into its own goal. The ball is advanced toward the goal by passing the ball between team members or by dribbling it. Dribbling is the act of slapping or striking the ball with one hand in such a manner that control of the ball is maintained while moving about the court.

The defensive team can gain possession of the ball in a number of ways. The most common are rebounding the ball after a missed shot attempt, intercepting a pass, securing the ball from a jump-ball situation, and when the offensive team commits a violation.

The length of playing time for games varies with the age level or type of competition. The professional teams play four twelve-minute quarters, college teams play two twenty-minute halves, high school teams play four eight-minute quarters, and junior high school teams play four quarters that range from four to six minutes in length. The length of time between the halves of the game ranges from fifteen minutes for the professional and college teams to ten minutes for high school and junior high school teams.

Basketball is acclaimed to be the most popular sport in the world today. It is played in more than sixty countries, and it is estimated that forty million people annually participate in some form of basketball. This popularity is attributable to the following factors: a small amount of equipment is needed, the playing area does not need to be large, the teams can be composed of more or fewer than five players, the rules are easily learned, the game can be played at any tempo desired by the participants, it is a sport that is relatively free from serious injury, and it is a sport that has great spectator appeal because it involves rapid and constant action. The sport of basketball has become a chief source of recreational activities during winter months and is the most successful intramural activity offered in high schools and colleges.

UNIQUE VALUES DERIVED FROM PARTICIPATION IN BASKETBALL

Basketball combines the skills of several other sports; it is an excellent activity for developing fitness, coordination, and teamwork. The game is flexible and can be modified to meet the needs or interests of the persons participating or the area that is available to play the game. Shooting baskets alone or with a partner has a great deal of appeal to both sexes. The game is played and enjoyed by teams composed of more or fewer than the official number. In addition, the skill of the participants need not be highly developed in order for them to enjoy playing the game. Basketball has proved to be an excellent sport for interscholastic, intercollegiate, and professional competition from the standpoint of both the participants and the spectators.

Basketball is a sport that can be played the year around—out-of-doors as well as indoors. Many outdoor tennis courts now have basketball goals placed at their ends and lights installed in order that basketball can be played at night. Basketball also provides highly suitable family recreational activity, as it is easy to install a basketball goal on a garage or house and to use the driveway or patio as the playing court.

Basketball is an activity in which participants of all ages and sizes can play. Because of the large number of skills and the differences in skill required of the different positions, short players as well as tall players can participate with enjoyment. Short players often perfect ball handling and shooting skills to the extent that they can contribute to the team as effectively at the guard position as do the tall and relatively slow players who utilize their height to rebound and score at the center or forward positions. An important element of basketball, regardless of the size or skill of the players, is the demand for teamwork if the team is to be successful. Strategy is another important aspect of the game.

CARE OF FACILITIES AND EQUIPMENT

Court

The playing court for basketball is a rectangular area that is free from obstructions. The regulation width for all courts is fifty feet. The length is eighty-four feet for high schools and ninety-four feet for colleges. The most common surface for basketball courts has been a hardwood flooring. In recent years synthetic materials have gained in popularity because they can be utilized for a large variety of activities and they are easy to maintain.

The playing court is marked with side lines, end lines, a center division line, a center jump circle, and two free-throw lanes—all marking lines are two inches in width. The playing court should be as clean as possible; this is normally done by wiping it with wet towels. Only soft-soled athletic shoes should be worn when playing on a wooden court.

Backboards

The backboards, which are located at the ends of the court, are fan-shaped for high school and rectangular for college. They can be made of a transparent material or of any rigid material, which can then be painted white. The rims must be securely attached to the backboard ten feet from the floor as measured from the top of the rim. Regulation rims have an inside diameter of eighteen inches. Glass backboards can be broken if too much stress is placed on the rim; therefore, players should not hang on the rims or nets. The resultant stress can break the glass backboards or bend the rims.

Ball

The regulation color of the spherical basketball is an approved shade of orange or natural tan. The ball covering is made of leather or, if agreeable to both teams, it can be a composition cover. For college competition the circumference of the ball must be not less than twenty-nine and one-half inches and not greater than thirty inches. For high school competition, the circumference of the ball must be at least twenty-nine inches and not greater than twenty-nine and one-half inches. The balls should be kept at the correct air pressure in order to keep the seams from cracking. They should be cleaned frequently with a ball cleaner in order to remove the dirt that accumulates on them.

Uniforms

Basketball uniforms are made in many styles, colors, and materials. Each jersey is numbered on both the back and front. Each player should wear gym shoes with soles that will provide for good traction. Players should wear at least one and preferably two pairs of white athletic socks of a good quality.

BASIC RULES OF BASKETBALL

Officials

The basketball officials are a referee and an umpire who are assisted by two timers and two scorers. A single scorer and timer can be used if they are acceptable to the referee. Some colleges and universities are experimenting with the use of three court officials in an attempt to have them in better positions to referee the game.

The referee's responsibility is to inspect and approve all equipment and facilities, which include the court, baskets, backboards, and the basketball. He is also responsible for notifying each captain three minutes before each half is to begin. He will not permit a player to wear equipment that, in his judgment, is dangerous to other players. The referee tosses the ball at the center jump circle to start the game. He makes the decision as to whether a goal counts if the officials disagree. He also has the power to forfeit a game when in his opinion conditions warrant a forfeiture. At the end of each half he checks and approves the score. He also makes decisions on issues not specifically covered in the rules.

The scorers record the field goals made, the free throws made and missed, and they keep a running summary of the points scored. They record the personal and technical fouls called on each player and notify the referee when a player is charged with his last personal foul, thus fouling out. They also record the number of time-outs each team has taken and report to the coach and the team whenever that team has taken their last time-out without penalty. The scorebook of the home team is the official book unless the referee rules otherwise.

The timers are responsible for notifying the referee more than three minutes before each half is to start in order to give him the opportunity to notify the teams at the three-minutes time. The timer also keeps the time during the playing of the game by starting and stopping the clock according to the rules of the game and the signals of the referee and umpire.

Players and Substitutes

A team consists of five players, one of whom is designated as the captain. The captain represents his

82 *Individual and Team Sports*

team in any official matter of interpretation. Any player, may, however, address an official to request a time-out for permission to leave the court. A substitute player who desires to enter the game must report to the official scorers by giving his number and the number of the player he will replace. After a substitute reports to the scorer, he must remain outside the boundary of the court until he is beckoned onto the court by a court official. A substitute cannot replace a player who is a free-throw shooter or who is involved in a jump-ball situation (unless he has been severely injured).

Scoring and Timing Regulations

A goal is scored when a live ball enters the basket from above and remains in or passes through the basket. A goal scored from the field counts two points for the team into whose basket the ball enters. A goal made on a free throw is credited to the shooter and counts one point for his team. The try for a free throw by a player must be made within ten seconds after the ball is awarded to the player by a court official. In the case of a technical foul, any player can shoot the free throw, including a substitute entering the game at that time.

Each team is allowed five time-outs for each game, during which time the timers stop the clock. The clock is also stopped when an official signals a foul, a held ball, a rules violation, or an injury; wants to confer with the scorer or timer; there is unusual delay in getting a dead ball alive; or for any emergency. After time has been out, the game clock is started when the official signals. If an official should neglect to signal the clock to start, the timer is authorized to start the clock, unless the official specifically signals that the time-out should be continued. When play is resumed the clock is started when the tossed or thrown-in ball is legally touched by an inbounds player. When a free-throw attempt is not successful and the ball remains alive, the clock is started when the ball is first touched by a player.

Jump Balls

The beginning of the game and all succeeding periods of play are started by a jump ball in the center jump circle. A jump ball is also called when two players from opposite teams have simultaneous possession of the ball; it takes place in the jump circle nearest the spot where the held ball occurred. For any jump ball, each jumper must have one or both feet on or inside of the jumping circle. A jumper cannot leave the jumping circle until the ball has been tapped, nor can he catch the ball before it has touched another player. The eight nonjumpers must not have either foot in or on the restraining circle until the ball has been tapped. Teammates may not occupy adjacent positions around the restraining circle if an opponent indicates a desire to be between them before the official is ready to toss the ball for the jump situation.

Out-of-bounds and Throw-in

A player is out-of-bounds when he touches the floor or any object on or outside a boundary. The ball is considered out-of-bounds when it touches a player who is out of bounds; any other person, floor, or any object on or outside of a boundary; the supports or back of the backboard; the ceiling; or the overhead equipment and basket supports. If a ball is simultaneously touched by two opponents, or if the officials disagree, the ball is put in play at the nearest jump circle as a jump ball between the two players involved.

The ball is awarded out-of-bounds to the other team after a violation, a free throw for a technical foul, a field goal, a successful free throw, or an awarded goal. The throw-in starts when the ball is placed at the disposal of a player entitled to the throw-in. He is allowed five seconds to pass the ball into the court. Until a passed ball has crossed the plane of the boundary on a throw-in: (1) the thrower shall not leave the designated throw-in spot; (2) no player shall have any part of his person over the boundary line; and (3) teammates shall not occupy adjacent positions near the boundary if an opponent desires one of the positions.

Free Throw

When a free throw is awarded, the official takes the ball to the free-throw line of the offended team and, before giving the ball to the shooter, allows the other players a reasonable amount of time to take their positions along the lane. The defensive team occupies the first space on each side of the lane with the teams alternating for the second and third positions. The free-throw attempt must be made by the offending player unless he is injured or disqualified. If this occurs, his substitute will attempt the free throw.

A ball is in play after a missed free-throw attempt unless there is a multiple free throw, a technical foul, or a false double foul. After a technical foul the ball is given to the offended team at mid-court. After a false double foul the ball is put into play by a jump ball at mid-court between any two members of the opposing teams.

Violations and Penalties

A violation occurs if a free thrower steps on or over the line before the ball goes through the basket or hits the rim. It is also a violation if he does not shoot the ball within ten seconds after the referee makes it available to him. The players are not allowed to disconcert the free-throw shooter. The rebounding players on the lane may not cross the lane until the ball strikes the rim or the basket. If the defensive team violates one of the preceding rules, the offensive team is awarded another opportunity to shoot the free throw. If the offensive team violates a rule, the point does not count and the ball is awarded out-of-bounds to the defensive team.

It is a violation of the throw-in to move from the designated throw-in spot, to fail to pass the ball directly into the court, to consume more than five seconds from the time the throw-in starts until it touches or is touched by a player on the court, to carry the ball onto the court, to touch the ball in the court before it has touched another player, or to so throw the ball that it enters a basket before touching anyone. It is a violation to run with the ball, kick it intentionally, strike it with the fist, or cause it to enter and pass through the basket from below. It is also a violation to dribble a second time after the first dribble has ended, unless control has been lost because of a try for a goal or the ball is batted away by an opponent.

It is also a violation (1) for an offensive player to remain in the lane area of the free-throw area for more than three seconds, (2) to maintain continuous control of a ball in the back court for more than ten consecutive seconds, (3) to swing the arms or elbows excessively, even though no contact is made with an opponent, and (4) to touch the ball or the rim when the ball is on or above the cylinder or the ball is on a downward flight after a shot attempt.

Fouls and Penalties

Team technical fouls are called when the game is delayed by preventing the ball from being made alive, allowing the game to be an actionless contest, when an excessive number of time-outs is taken, or when more than five squad members participate simultaneously.

Technical fouls can be called on a player, substitutes, coach, or fans for unsportsmanlike conduct. The most common reason for the technical foul is for disrespectfully addressing an official or making objectionable gestures. Technical fouls can be called on players for participating after having been disqualified, wearing an illegal number, grasping a rim or net, leaving the court for an unauthorized reason, or for failure to report to the scorer.

Personal fouls are charged when a player holds; pushes; charges; or trips, by extending an arm, shoulder, hip, or knee, or by bending the body into other than a normal position. A dribbler commits a foul when he makes contact with an opponent who has established a defensive position in the path of the dribbler. In order to be legal, a screen must be set no closer than a normal step behind the defensive player; if it is set at the side or front of a stationary opponent, contact must not be made.

The complete rules of basketball are available from the official rule books listed at the end of the chapter.

FUNDAMENTAL SKILLS AND TECHNIQUES

Body Balance

Before learning the fundamental offensive and defensive skills and other techniques of basketball, it is necessary to be able to assume and understand the importance of body balance. In order to maintain proper body balance, the legs of the player are shoulder width apart with the weight evenly distributed on the balls of both feet. The knees are relaxed and slightly flexed. The arms are up with the wrists above the waist and the fingers are spread and relaxed. The players bend forward slightly at the waist in order to permit quick movements. When in the defensive position, the player keeps the feet well spread with one foot slightly behind the other. The defensive player must keep his arms and hands out from his body in order to deflect passes, discourage the dribble, and block shot attempts.

Receiving the Pass

For effective catching of the ball, the hands are positioned above the waist with the fingers spread and relaxed. The ball is received with the fingers rather than the palms of the hands. The player reaches for the ball as it approaches and then gives slightly as the ball touches his fingers in order to cushion the shock. When the ball is caught above the waist, the thumbs are pointed toward each other with fingers pointed upward. When the ball is received below the waist, the thumbs are pointed away from each other with the fingers pointed downward. It is essential that the player watch the flight of the ball until it has been caught.

Passing the Ball

Passing the ball effectively is the most important skill to be mastered in the game of basketball if the player is to become an effective team member. Many types of passes need to be learned before one can become a complete basketball player. Each player must learn to make a variety of passes, both in the stationary position and while moving. When passing, attempt to pass the ball at chest height and away from the defensive man.

Individual and Team Sports

The push pass can be made with one or both hands. It is executed with both hands when made from the front of the body and with one hand when made from the side. The pass begins at chest height with the elbows flexed and close to the body. The fingers are spread comfortably on the sides of the ball, with the thumbs directly behind the ball. The ball is released by an extension of the elbows and a quick snap of the wrists, which will cause the player to move slightly forward as the ball is released. Right-handed players should step forward with the right foot while pushing off from the left foot.

The bounce pass is an effective pass to use near the basket to feed a cutting teammate or for getting the ball to the postman. This pass can be thrown with one or both hands. The ball should strike the floor approximately two thirds of the distance to the receiver and reach him at a height slightly above his knees. It is important that the ball be sharply bounced on the floor to initiate a quick pass and to insure that the ball will bounce to the proper receiving height. The execution of the two-handed bounce pass is the same as for the push pass, except that the ball is bounced on the floor. To execute the one-handed bounce pass the player steps forward and sideward and then passes the ball under the arms and hands of the defensive player.

The baseball pass (Figure 8-1) is effective for a long-distance pass and for getting the ball to an outlet man on the fast break. The pass is made with one hand and resembles the throw made by a baseball player. To execute this pass the ball is held in both hands for control until it is overhead. The throwing hand is directly behind the ball. The fingers of both hands point upward while the thumbs point toward the head. The power for the pass is mainly generated by the cocked wrist and finger snap.

The hook pass is a valuable pass to use when being closely guarded from one side or for getting the ball out quickly to start a fast break. The pass can be made while on the move or from a stationary position. The hook pass is made by jumping, turning in the air, and hooking the ball over the head with the throwing arm extended. The major impetus to the ball is applied by the wrist and finger action. After the pass is completed, the passer should come back to the floor facing the direction in which the ball has been passed; his feet should be spread and his knees bent so that he can move quickly in any direction.

The two-hand overhead pass (Figure 8-2) is the most versatile of all passes used in setting up offensive plays. It is particularly useful for tall players and for quick return passes. When making this pass both hands are positioned slightly behind the ball with the fingers pointed upward and the thumbs pointing toward each other. The ball is carried straight up and over the head. The ball receives its impetus from a strong wrist snap and finger action.

The two-hand underhand or shovel pass is an effective pass with which to feed the ball to a cutting teammate when in close quarters or when closely guarded. The body is in a crouched position with the ball held close to the hips with both hands. The elbows are away from the body with the hands slightly behind the ball and the fingers well spread. The ball is released by taking a step forward and making a full forward swing of the arms. The wrists and fingers provide the final impetus to the ball. When the ball is released the fingers are pointing upward.

Figure 8-1. Baseball pass.

Figure 8-2. Two-hand overhead pass.

Shooting

Shooting the basketball is a skill that requires, at a minimum, a considerable amount of practice and coaching to perfect. The good player must as a rule master a wide variety of shots. Because scoring is the objective of the game, each individual player should spend a great deal of time practicing this skill. Shooting percentages have been improved significantly in recent years because of the development of improved shooting techniques and different types of shots.

The one-hand set shot is usually employed for free-throw shooting and for taking shots from a distance of 15 feet or farther. The body is in a crouched position with the foot on the side of the shooting hand a few inches forward of the other foot. The ball is held near the chest in both hands. The shooting hand is placed directly behind the ball, while the supporting hand is placed on the side and slightly under the ball. The fingers of the shooting hand are spread behind the ball and the elbow is pointed directly at the floor. The ball is shot by a quick extension of the forearm with a strong wrist and finger flexion. The last finger to have contact with the ball is the index finger. The lead foot supplies impetus to the shot along with an extension of the legs, which causes the feet to leave the floor slightly. The feet come back to the floor slightly forward of the take-off position. This shot requires coordination of the legs, arms, wrists, and fingers to produce a smooth shot that is consistently accurate.

The jump shot (Figure 8-3) has marked similarities to the one-handed set shot, but it is more versatile, as it can be shot after a quick stop while being closely guarded. The ball is brought to the shooting position and held in the same manner as for the set shot. The major exceptions between the two shots are that the shooter jumps into the air from both feet prior to the release of the ball, and the ball is raised to an increased height before the shooting motion. The jump should be natural and without too much strain in order to maintain body rhythm and control. The shooter should attempt to jump vertically rather than horizontally, although the body will move slightly forward from the spot of the take-off. The ball should be released just before the player reaches maximum height. The hand, wrist, and finger action are the same as for the set shot.

The lay-up shot is a high-percentage shot that players strive to get as often as possible. It is a close-in shot that should be banked from the backboard whenever possible. The ball is protected by keeping it on the side of the body away from the defensive man. The jumping leg is the leg opposite the shooting arm. The jump is directed vertically rather than horizontally when shooting this shot, as it is taken while on the move. The ball is brought up to shoulder level with both hands. The shooting hand should be directly behind the ball with the fingers well spread and pointed straight upward just before the ball is released. The ball is then shot by a flip of the wrist and fingers. Another acceptable way of shooting the ball is to hold the ball in the palm of the shooting hand with the fingers pointed straight forward; the ball is then released by a flip of the wrist and fingers. The fingers will be pointing upward after the ball is released. In either case the ball should be laid against the backboard as softly as possible. The place where the ball should be placed on the backboard is determined by the angle from which the shooter is approaching the basket. This can only be learned by practicing the shot from many different angles.

The hook shot (Figure 8-4) is used most often by pivot men but can be used by any player who is close to the basket and guarded by a defensive man who is between him and the basket. The shot is most effective when the player fakes in one direction and then moves in the opposite direction and shoots. The players should, with the foot on that side of the body, step in the direction of the shot. He should attempt to step behind and beyond the leg of the defensive player, if possible, in order to move more directly toward the basket. The ball is carried in both hands until it reaches shoulder level. The shooting arm is straight with the ball held as far from the defensive man as possible. The shot is executed by so sweeping the extended arms over the head that the biceps muscle of the upper arm touches the ear. The ball is then released with a flip of the wrist and fingers in which the fingers and hand are directly behind the ball. The ball should be shot or laid on the backboard as softly as possible. The shooter drives from the foot opposite the shooting hand and turns toward the basket as the shot is being made.

Figure 8-3. Jump shot.   Figure 8-4. Hook shot.

Individual and Team Sports

The one-hand free throw (Figure 8-5) is similar to the one-hand set shot in regard to the hand and wrist actions. The major exception is that the feet of the shooter do not as a rule leave the floor after the shot is taken; instead he rises onto his toes in order to obtain the necessary follow-through. The shooter should develop a definite rhythm in order for the shot to become a reflex action. The shot differs from other shots in that it is always taken from the same distance and there is no defensive pressure while the shot is taken. A free-throw shooter should be as relaxed as possible before taking the shot. Most players develop a routine by dribbling the ball a few times in order to relax before attempting the free throw.

Dribbling

The dribble is an effective offensive weapon if used correctly. Its most effective use is to advance the ball down the court, to drive for a lay-up, and as a device to get out of trouble. Many players and teams have abused the dribble by overusing it. The remedy for this is to remember that a pass is quicker than a dribble and is preferred in most cases. The complete basketball player must be able to dribble the ball effectively with either hand, without watching the ball, in order to drive in either direction and to make accurate and properly timed passes to his teammates.

The low dribble (Figure 8-6) is utilized to get out of trouble when a player is in a congested area or to move toward the basket. The body is in a crouched position with the head up. The ball is dribbled with the hand that is away from the defensive man. The ball should not be dribbled higher than knee high, and it should be dribbled slightly ahead of the body. The elbow of the dribbling hand is held close to the body with the forearm parallel to the floor. The fingers are well spread and in a cupped position. The ball is tapped to the floor by the action of the wrist and fingers.

The high dribble is used when a player gets past the defensive man and is driving toward the basket or is advancing the ball when he is not closely guarded. The body is in an upright position with the hand, forearm, and elbow in front of the body. The ball is tapped ahead of the body by the action of the wrist and fingers. The elbow is parallel to the floor with the ball being dribbled at approximately waist height.

Rebounding

Rebounding is an essential fundamental of basketball as more possessions of the ball come from missed shots than from any other means. Generally speaking, the team that controls the rebounding is in control of the game and usually wins it.

Figure 8-5. Free throw.   **Figure 8-6.** Low dribble.

Defensive rebounds are best achieved when the rebounder positions his body between his offensive man and the basket immediately after a shot has been taken. The first move of the defensive rebounder after a shot is taken is to take a step toward the offensive player and pivot in such a manner that he has his back toward the offensive player while watching him. When the offensive player commits himself to a path toward the basket, the defensive rebounder, who is in a crouched position, moves into this path. His feet are well spread with the hands at shoulder level, elbows away from the body, and fingers pointing upward. The defensive rebounder then turns his head, locates the ball, and moves toward it. The jump for the ball is so timed that the ball is contacted with both hands as the elbows are fully extended at the height of the jump. After the player has the ball in both hands, the legs should be spread apart and the ball should be pulled into the chest to protect it from the offensive players. The feet are well spread on the landing for increased balance, and the elbows are extended to help protect the ball.

Offensive rebounds (Figure 8-7) are difficult to obtain because the defensive player is generally between the offensive player and the basket. Therefore, the offensive player must try to outmaneuver the defensive player in order to get the rebounds. If the offensive player cannot outmaneuver the defensive rebounder he must attempt to tip the ball back to himself or must try and tip the ball into the basket. Tipping the ball is best accomplished by one hand as this allows the players to reach higher than if two hands are used. When the offensive rebounder attempts to tip the ball into the basket he should begin

Figure 8-7. Rebound positions.

with his hands at shoulder level with his fingers up and palms facing toward the basket in order to avoid fouling the defensive rebounder. The act of tipping the ball is accomplished by jumping as high as possible and stretching one hand toward the ball. The ball should be tapped by an action of the wrist and fingers rather than by batting at the ball.

FAKING (FEINTING)

Faking, or feinting, is an important aspect of the game for both the offensive and the defensive player. When a player makes a fake it should be followed by a quick move in order to gain an advantage over an opponent. The accomplished player is able to fake when he does not have the ball as well as when he has it.

The head and shoulder fake is accomplished by a movement of the head and shoulders in one direction, which is followed by a quick movement in the opposite direction.

The ball fake is accomplished by moving the ball in one direction and then quickly moving it to another position.

The eye fake is made by the eyes looking or glancing in one direction and then quickly bringing the accompanying faking foot back to the original position and faking in the opposite direction for a shot, pass, or dribble.

Pivoting

The pivot is an offensive fundamental that helps the offensive player to protect the ball from the defensive man as well as to turn and face the basket in order to gain an offensive advantage. The pivot foot can be either foot, but it is usually the foot opposite the dominant hand. The pivot is performed from a low body position with the ball held close to the body in order to protect it from the defensive man. The feet are well spread to maintain balance. The pivot consists of stepping one or more times in any direction with one foot while the other remains in contact with the floor and turns. The pivot can be a partial turn or it can be a complete turn of the body.

Screening

A screen is a legal maneuver by the offensive man that checks the progress of a defensive man who wants to go in a chosen direction. When an efficient screen is set by the offensive man on a teammate's defensive man, the defense is usually forced to switch men. Very often a switch will create an advantage for the offense, as a small man will be forced to guard a tall man who is near the basket.

The outside screen is made by an offensive guard passing the ball to a forward, who is in a forward position, and cutting close to him on the outside in order that the defensive guard cannot follow him. The forward then hands the ball to the guard who attempts to drive toward the basket if the defensive forward does not switch men. After the offensive forward hands the ball to the guard he pivots toward the basket in such a manner that he is always watching his teammate (the guard) with the ball. The offensive forward then breaks for the basket for a possible return pass from the guard if a switch has been created. The defensive guard will usually be behind the offensive forward as he moves to the basket for a possible return pass from his guard teammate.

The inside screen is made by an offensive guard passing the ball to an offensive forward, who is in the forward position. The offensive guard then sets a screen on the defensive man. The screener stops, facing the defensive forward at arms' length distance. The offensive forward then attempts to drive over the screen to the middle of the court for a lay-up or shoots the shot over the screen. To make this screen effective, the offensive forward must pivot and face the basket as soon as he gets the ball in order to be in a position to drive or shoot as the screen is being set.

INDIVIDUAL DEFENSE

A basketball player spends approximately one half of his playing time attempting to prevent the opposition from scoring. Basically, the defensive player attempts to

88 *Individual and Team Sports*

stay between his man and the basket. Therefore, the defensive player must learn a great many different techniques and skills to stop the many patterns and skilled moves that have been developed by the offensive players. The jump shot has made the defensive players' assignment much more difficult, as many players are now capable of jump shooting accurately when twenty feet or more from the basket.

Defensive Mental Requirements

In order to become a skilled defensive player, pride must be developed in a person's defensive ability. He must develop an aggressive attitude and try to dominate the offensive player whenever possible. He must be alert at all times and concentrate on the requirements of his task. Hustle is the key word at all times for the defensive player.

Defensive Physical Requirements

Quickness is the most important physical asset of the defensive player. Quickness is basically an innate quality, but it can be improved with dedication and hard work. Height is another important factor in defensive play, but a lack of height can be overcome to some extent by quickness and the proper mental attitude.

Defensive Body Position

The distance that the offensive player is from the basket and whether or not he has the ball determine the floor position of the defensive player. Any time that the offensive player has the ball within twenty feet of the basket, he must be closely guarded by the defensive player to prevent an unmolested shot attempt. When a defensive player is guarding a man who does not have the ball and who is fifteen or more feet from the basket, he should sag away from his man, toward the basket and slightly toward the ball in order to prevent his opponent from breaking quickly toward the basket. The defensive player must be able to watch both his man and the ball simultaneously. One hand is pointed toward the ball and the other toward the man he is guarding. When the offensive player attempts to cut toward the basket, the defensive man must force him away from it by moving between him and the basket. A player receiving a pass in the offensive zone should always be forced to catch the ball going away from the basket.

When an offensive man (usually the pivot man) is within eight feet of the basket, the defensive player should play in front of him or between him and the ball. This defensive position will discourage other offensive players from passing the ball to him. A player who gets the ball within eight feet of the basket is very difficult to stop from scoring. Therefore, the purpose of the defense is to keep the ball from being passed to anyone near the basket.

TEAM DEFENSE

The essence of a sound team defense is five players who play as a unit. In order to play as a team it is essential that players talk to each other—teammates should be warned of screens and potential screens, or should help a man who has gotten away from another teammate. With many of the full-court pressing defenses presently utilized, efficient teamwork is becoming even more important than it has been in the past.

Man-to-man Defense

Man-to-man defense is the most common type of defense used in basketball. Each defensive player is assigned a specific offensive player to guard. The defensive assignments are usually made by matching up defensive players with offensive players of equal size, quickness, and ability. The best defensive player is usually assigned to the best offensive player if there is not too much discrepancy in size.

In the *tight man-to-man*, each man is assigned a specific man to guard and will switch only when absolutely necessary. The defensive men play on the basis that if a switch occurs, they have made an error. This type of defense requires a considerable amount of body checking and fighting through screens and will usually create a significant amount of fouling.

In the *switching man-to-man* defense, the defensive men switch men by calling out the switch when a screen is made. It allows the defense to have increased rebounding strength and improved position for a patterned fast break. The weakness of this defense is that a mismatch in size will often occur after a switch has been made.

Zone Defenses

The basic theory of the zone defense is to make the defensive player responsible for a man or men in an area, rather than for a specific man who may move to other areas of the court. The purpose of the zone defense is to make the area close to the basket a compact formation of defensive players who prevent the offensive team from passing the ball inside for close shots and to stop players driving to the basket. The zone is essentially designed to force teams to shoot the ball from long range.

The 2:3 zone defense was one of the earliest zone defenses utilized; it presents a very strong defense near the area of the basket. The jump shot has, however, minimized the effectiveness of this defense. Its advantages, in addition to its very strong defense in the area of the basket, are that it provides strong rebounding and it covers the base line well. The weaknesses of this defense are that the foul-line area is not covered adequately, a weakness exists between the two lines of the defense, and the middle defensive man has difficulty rebounding (as he is too near the basket).

The 2:1:2 zone defense is one of the most popular zone defenses today. The advantages of this defense are that it is strong on the foul line, provides a good rebounding position, and compliments a good fast-breaking attack. The weaknesses of this defense are that it is not strong against a good outside shooting team, and it does not stop the base-line shot.

The 1:3:1 zone defense was developed early, but it is still quite popular today. Its advantages are that it is very strong in the middle, and it provides for a good coverage on the outside shot. Its weaknesses are that good rebounding position is not achieved and corner shooting is possible.

The 3:2 zone defense was a popular defense in the early stages of basketball as it stopped the outside shooting. The advantages of this defense are that it is strong against outside shooting and it provides good fast break opportunities. The weaknesses of this defense are that it is weak in the corners, it is weak when the ball penetrates the front line, and it is not a strong rebounding defense.

The 1:2:2 zone defense is very similar to the 3:2 zone defense and has the same strengths and weaknesses.

Pressure Defense

Pressure defense is an attempt by the defense to put constant pressure on each offensive player. The defense attempts to cut off the passing lanes, puts pressure on the ball handler, and does not allow the offensive team to set up offensive patterns. The defense attempts to tie up the ball handler and to force the offensive team into making bad passes and committing violations. The defense should not attempt to steal the ball from the ball handlers, but rather force them into making ball-handling errors.

Zone Press. The full, three-quarter, and one-half court zone presses have become popular in modern basketball. Some forms of zone presses utilize double teaming the ball, whereas others utilize zone principles with man-to-man defense used by the defenders in these zones. The most popular formations for the zone press are the 2-2-1, 1-2-1-1, and the 1-3-1. The objective of the zone press is to force the ball to the side of the court where the ball handler can be two-timed effectively, as he has lost several of his passing lanes. The defensive players keep their hands high over their heads to encourage the offensive man to make a lob or bounce pass that can be intercepted by a teammate. The ball can most effectively be two-timed in a corner of the court or near the mid-court line.

Man-to-man Pressure. The full-court press utilizing full-court man-to-man pressure is a very effective defense, as constant pressure can be applied at all times on each offensive player. This defense causes the offense to make many ball-handling errors as well as forcing the offense out of its offensive pattern. Each defensive man must overplay his offensive man when he does not have the ball in order to make each pass difficult. In this defense if an offensive player should get past his defensive man, the other members of the defensive team must quickly pick up the loose man until the defensive man can recover and again pick up his man.

TEAM OFFENSE

The type of offensive pattern that a team employs is dependent on the players and the coach of the team. The physical attributes and capabilities of the players available are the determining factor in the selection of the offense by the coach. It is generally conceded, however, that it is not what offense is used that is important, but rather how well the offense that is used is executed. No offensive system can be successful without the players being well skilled in the fundamentals of basketball.

For any offensive system to be successful, proper floor balance must be maintained by the players in order to keep the defense spread and to provide rebounding strength. The most important element of team offense is having five players working as a unit. In addition, the players must be in excellent physical condition, as basketball is an extremely strenuous sport.

Fast-break Offense

The fast-break offense has been used by more and more teams in recent years as both the fans and players enjoy a fast-moving game. (See Figure 8-8.) For many teams, 50 per cent of the shot attempts are obtained from the fast break. The fast break is used after a defensive rebound, a missed free throw by the opposition, a stolen ball, a jump ball, and after the opponent scores. Many ways are utilized to set up a fast-break pattern, but all fast-break patterns use the same basic principles. Three players form the first line of attack and fill the fast-break lanes. The lanes are the two sides of the court and the middle of the court. A fourth player acts as a trailer and

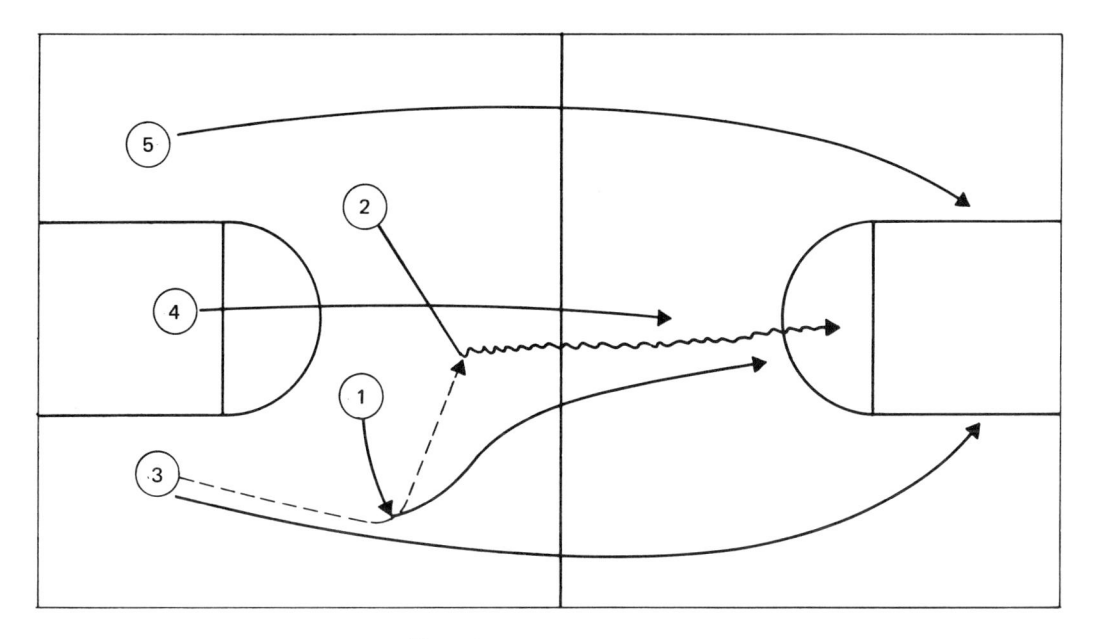

Figure 8-8. Fast-break pattern.

comes down the middle of the court behind the ball for a pass or for rebounding. The fifth player proceeds down the court behind the trailing player and provides the defensive balance in case the ball is lost to the other team.

When fast breaking, the ball should be passed to the middle man as soon as possible, because he can then return the ball to either side or feed the trailer as he breaks by him. The middle man on the fast break should stop at the offensive free-throw line unless he can drive all the way for a lay-up shot.

Man-to-man Offense

It is necessary to develop an effective offensive attack against the man-to-man defense as this is the most common basketball defense. The basic principles involved in the man-to-man offense are the ability of the players to beat other players in one-on-one situations, the ability to use screens, the ability to cut toward the basket, and (most important) the ability to pass the ball accurately.

Single-post Offense

The single-post offense is the most common offense used today. In this offense the guards take positions beyond the top of the circle. The forwards take a position along each side of the court opposite the free-throw line. The center plays in either the high- or low-post position. In the high-post position the center stands in front of the free-throw line; in the low-post position he stands near the basket and just outside of the free-throw lane. This offensive set works well when the team has a tall center, because much of the offensive play is initiated by passing the ball to the center. The center also sets screens for the forwards and guards, both to and away from the ball. Two simple plays utilized in the single-post offense are diagrammed in Figures 8-9 and 8-10.

Double-post Offense

The double-post offense is most commonly used by teams that have two tall men in the starting line-up. The

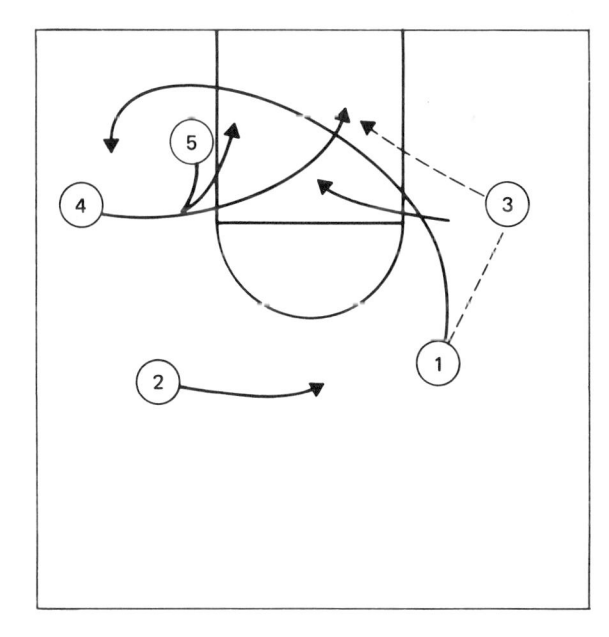

Figure 8-9. Single-post offense.

Basketball 91

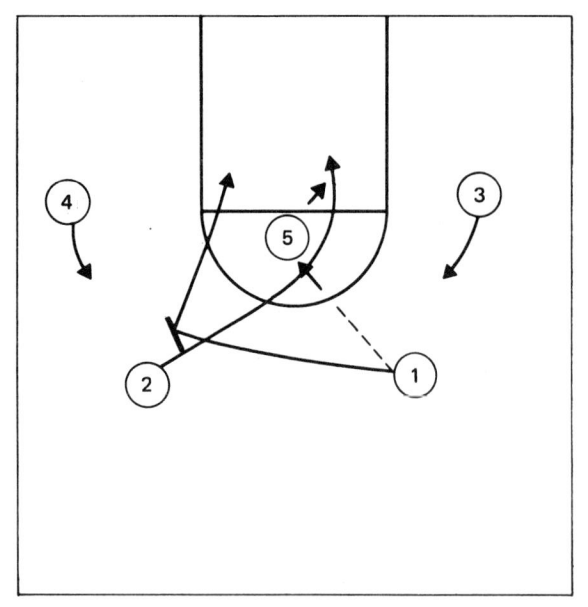

Figure 8-10. Single-post offense.

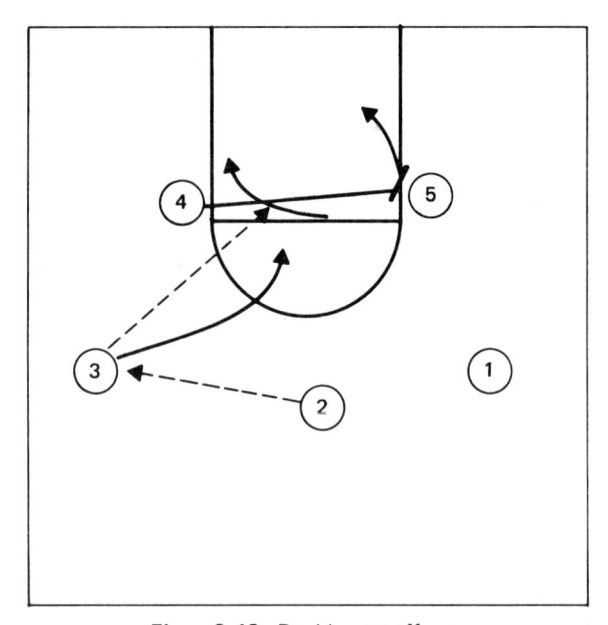

Figure 8-12. Double-post offense.

two tall men, who are called the post men, position themselves on each side of the lane. The position of the post men on the lane varies; both men may play in high post, or one man may play low post and the other high post. The other three players on the team are designated as a point man and two wing men. This offense is established by the point man, who does much of the ball handling, screening, and feeding for the post men. The post men also screen for each other in order to free themselves to get the ball and to set up good shots for themselves. Two simple plays from the double-post offense are diagrammed in Figures 8-11 and 8-12.

Shuffle Offense

In recent years, the shuffle offense has been extremely popular in all sections of the country. This offense is unique in that the players are not designated by positions; instead, the players rotate through all five positions as a part of the offense. This type of offense works very well for a small quick team of nearly equal size, as it provides for considerable movement from all the players. This offense is set up by quickly changing the floor balance of the players from one side of the court to the other. It involves quick cuts, screens, and changes of position by all or several players in each offensive pattern. Two simple plays from the shuffle offense are diagrammed in Figures 8-13 and 8-14.

Zone Offense

A great variety of zone offenses has been used to combat zone defenses. Some coaches prefer to have a separate offensive set to attack each zone defense. Other coaches use a basic offensive set to attack all zones. Still other coaches will modify the team man-to-man offense and use it to attack the zone. Most coaches now prefer to use their own variation. At one time it was believed that the best way to attack the zone was to pass the ball quickly around until an open shot could be taken from the outside. The philosophy of how to attack the zone has changed considerably in recent years. Now, most teams attempt to attack the zone by getting the ball near the basket by cutting and screening.

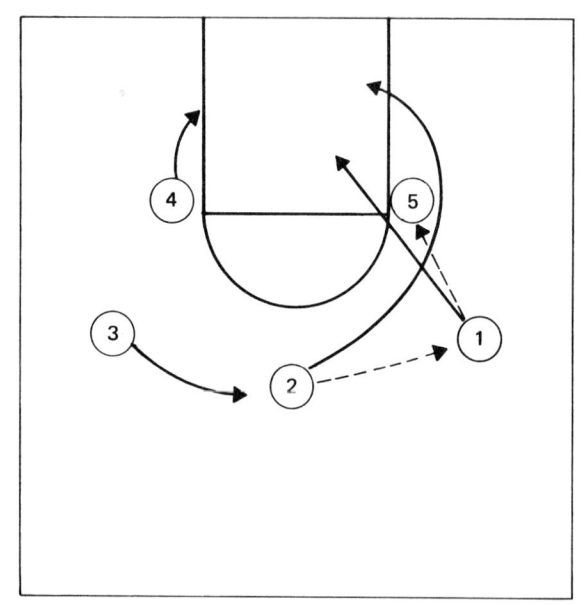

Figure 8-11. Double-post offense.

92 *Individual and Team Sports*

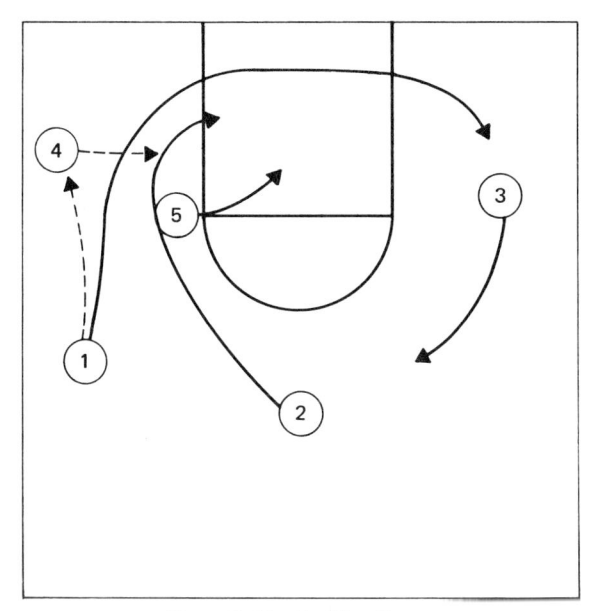

Figure 8-13. Shuffle offense.

1:3:1 Zone Offense. One of the most common zone offenses in use today is the 1:3:1 attack. The positions consist of a point man, two wing men, a high-post man, and a base-line man. The post man is the key man in this offense as he will handle the ball frequently and is expected to score. A simple play from the 1:3:1 zone offense is diagrammed in Figure 8-15.

SAFETY

The game of basketball was originally intended to be a noncontact sport. As a result of rule changes, improved offensive and defensive techniques, and a faster-moving game than a few years ago, considerable contact does occur. Therefore, the number of injuries to participants has increased as the amount of contact and the speed of the game have increased. Most injuries occur from players colliding, scrambling for a loose ball, and as a result of falls. The players should, by a strict observance of the rules, avoid unnecessary roughness when attempting to secure the ball. Deliberate pushing, tripping, or swinging of the elbows should never be done.

The most important items of equipment are the shoes and socks that the player wears. Each player should wear two pairs of socks of good quality to help protect the feet. The socks should be washed each time they are used in order to keep them clean and soft. The shoes should be of a good quality with a cushioned heel, and they should provide support for the arch. The shoes must fit properly, and they should be laced snugly to keep the ankle from becoming twisted and blisters from developing. During the early season special attention must be given to the feet while they are being toughened in order to prevent the occurrence of painful blisters. Poorly fitted shoes and inadequate socks are the most common cause of blisters. Painting benzoin on the feet during early practice sessions is helpful in toughening the skin. If blisters do develop, they should be treated immediately to avoid infections. Skins and scrapes on the body should be protected by bandaging or padding in order to prevent additional injury.

Rings or other items of jewelry should be removed before playing basketball to avoid injury to teammates or opponents. Fingernails must be trimmed relatively short to avoid scratching opponents and to protect the nails

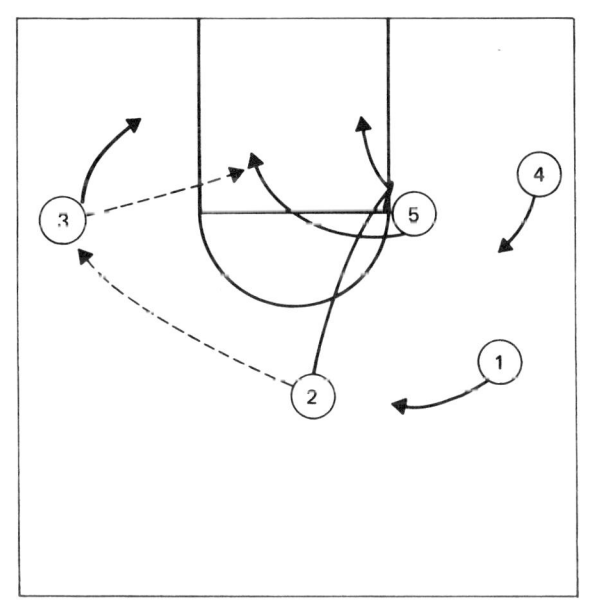

Figure 8-14. Shuffle offense.

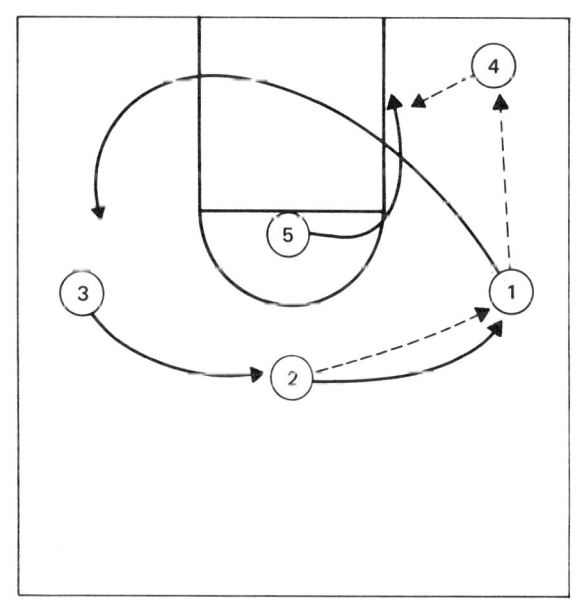

Figure 8-15. 1:3:1 zone offense.

Basketball

from being bent back or broken. Care should be taken to keep the floor free from dust and dirt. Walls and other obstructions near the playing court should be well padded to prevent injury to the players.

DRILLS

Baseball-pass Drill

Two squads of players are lined up on each side of the court at the mid-court line. A_1 passes to B_1 who is cutting toward the basket to receive the ball and shoot the lay-up. A_1 then goes to the end of line B while B_1 retrieves the ball and passes it to A_2 and goes to the end of line A. This drill can be speeded up by using two balls. (See Figure 8-16.)

Hook-pass Drill

A_1 dribbles forward fifteen feet and makes a hook pass to A_2. A_1 returns to the end of the line. (See Figure 8-17.)

On-the-spot Push-pass Drill

A_1 lines up fifteen feet in front of the other players. A_1 and A_2 each have a ball. A_1 passes to A_3 and then receives a pass from A_2. A_1 returns the pass to A_4 and receives a return pass from A_3. (See Figure 8-18.)

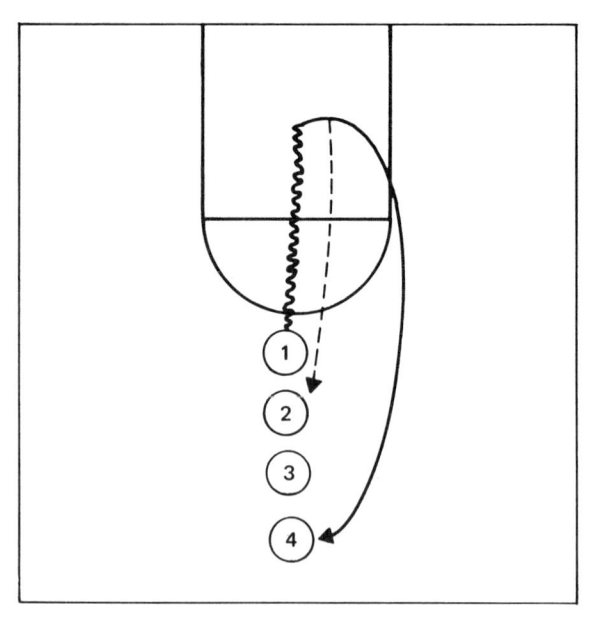

Figure 8-17. Hook-pass drill.

Two-line Multiple-passing Drill

A_1 passes the ball to B_1 and goes to the end of line B. B_1 passes the ball to A_2 and goes to the end of line A. This drill works well for push passes, bounce passes, and shovel passes. (See Figure 8-19.)

Weave Dribble Drill

Player 1 dribbles the ball around player 2 and each of the other players until he reaches the end of the line.

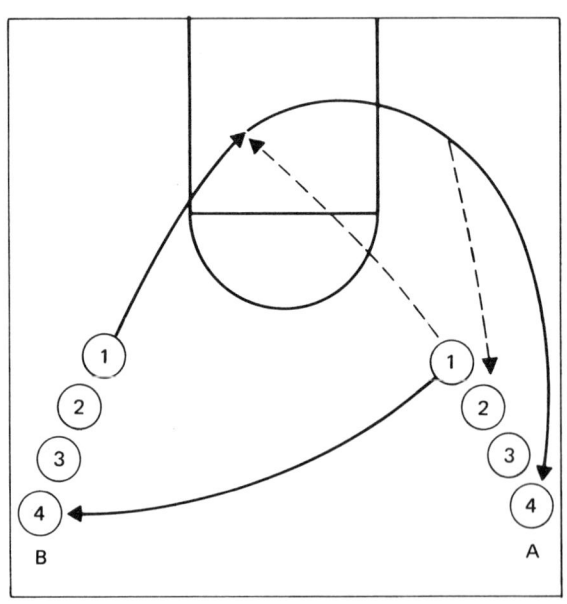

Figure 8-16. Baseball-pass drill.

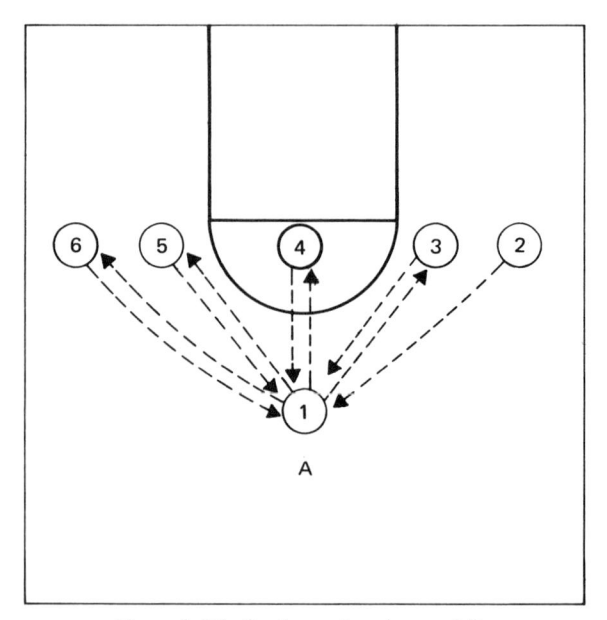

Figure 8-18. On-the-spot push-pass drill.

94 *Individual and Team Sports*

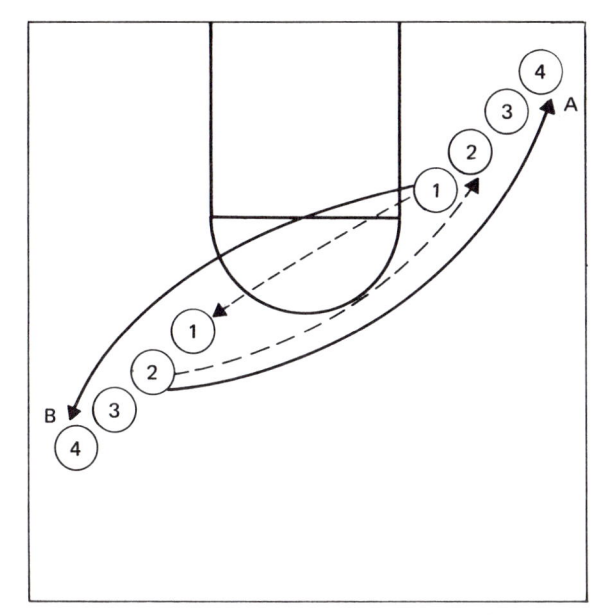

Figure 8-19. Two-line multiple-passing drill.

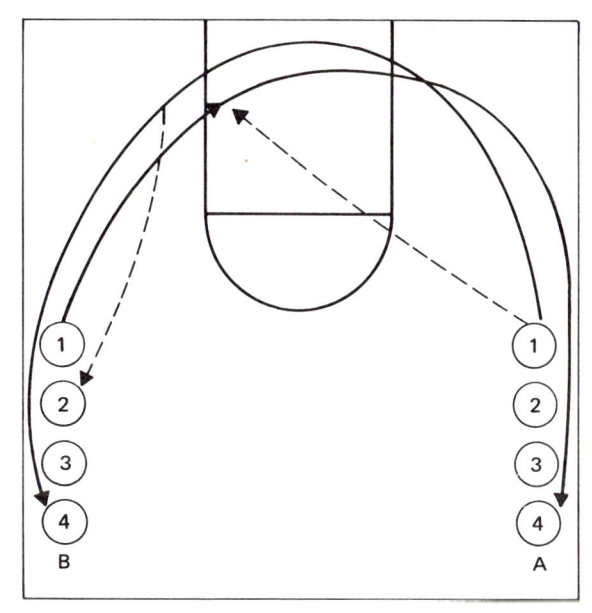

Figure 8-21. Lay-up drill.

Player 1 then passes the ball to player 2 and takes his place at the end of the line. The low dribble, the high dribble, and dribbling with alternate hands can be practiced in this drill. (See Figure 8-20.)

Lay-up Drill

A_1 passes the ball to B_1 who shoots the lay-up. A_1 then rebounds the ball and passes it to B_2 who shoots the lay-up. A_1 goes to the end of line B while B_1 goes to the end of line A. This drill is used from any position on the court. (See Figure 8-21.)

Jump-shot Drill

The number 1 player in each of the five squads begins with a ball approximately twelve feet from the basket. The number 1 player in each of the squads then shoots a jump shot and rebounds the ball. He then passes the ball to the number 2 player of his squad and returns to the end of his squad line. The squads rotate to each of the five positions. (See Figure 8-22.)

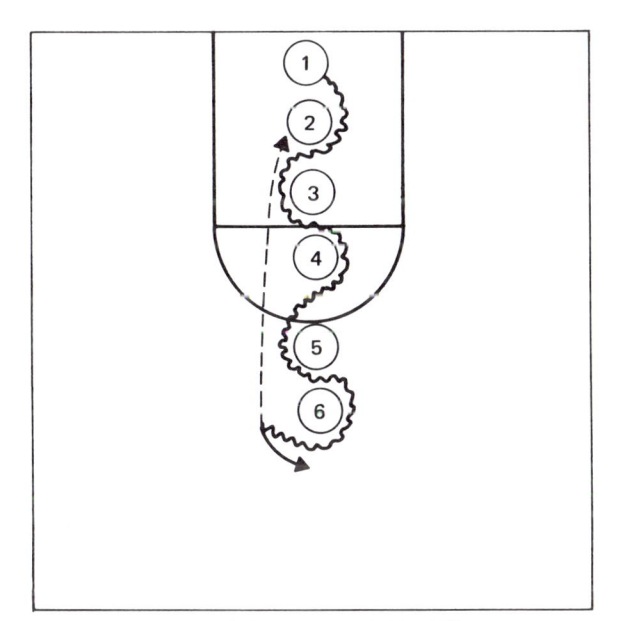

Figure 8-20. Weave dribble drill.

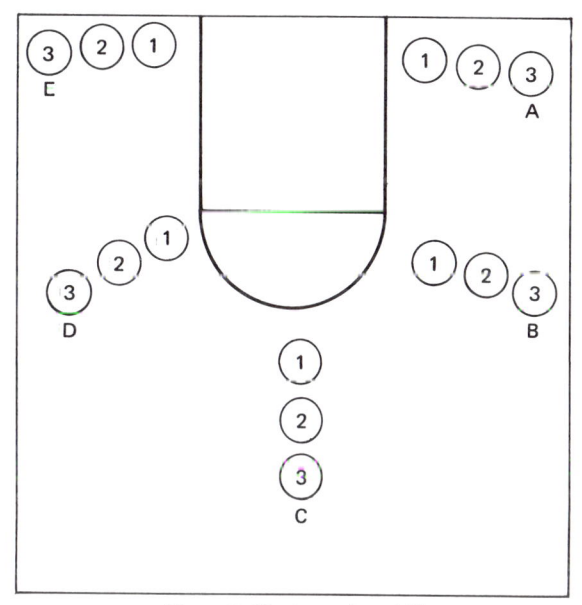

Figure 8-22. Jump-shot drill.

Basketball 95

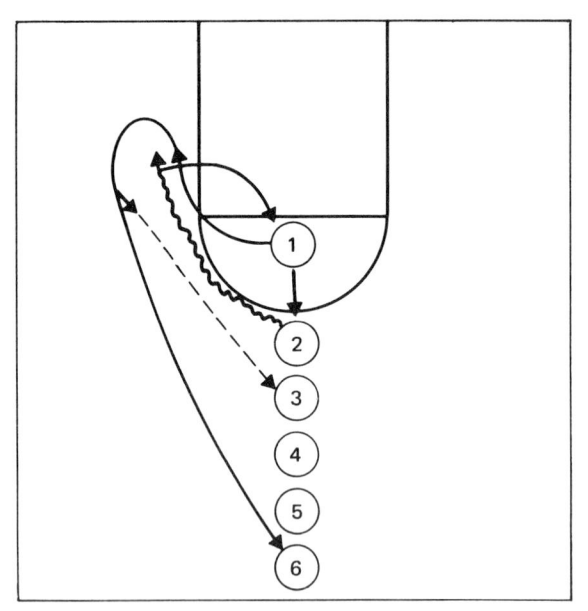

Figure 8-23. Defensive one-on-one drill.

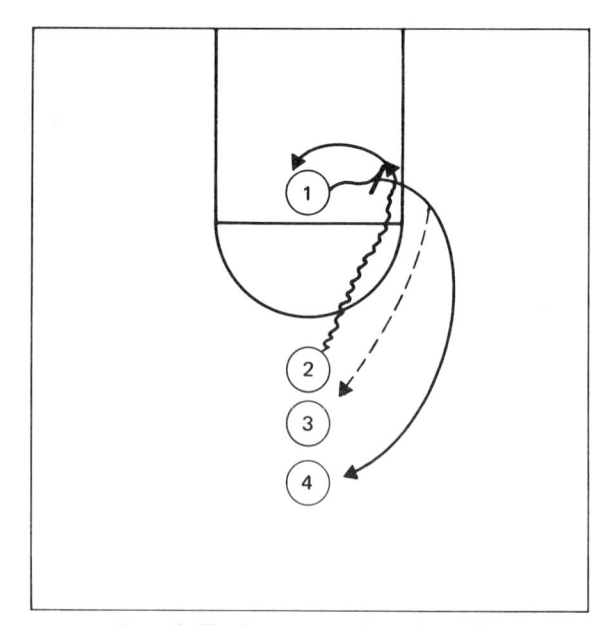

Figure 8-25. One-on-one rebounding drill.

Defensive One-on-one Drill

Player 1 passes the pass to player 2 and then plays defense on him. Player 2 can shoot a shot from the top of the circle or he can drive toward the basket while player 1 attempts to stop him. This one-on-one game between players 1 and 2 continues until player 1 gets the ball or a basket is made by player 2. Player 1 then goes to the end of the line and player 2 passes the ball to the number 3 man and plays defense on him. (See Figure 8-23.)

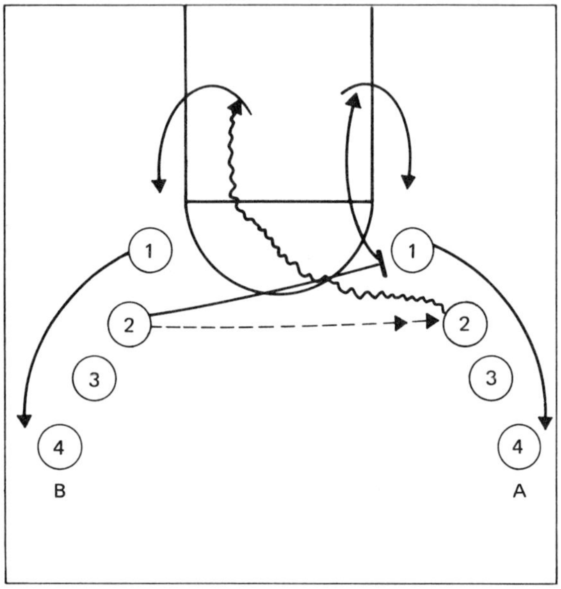

Defensive Two-on-two

The number 2 men in squads *A* and *B* begin with the ball while the number 1 men play defense on the number 2 men. The number 2 men attempt to score by passing, screening, or cutting while the number 1 men attempt to stop them. This drill continues until one of the number 1 men gains possession of the ball or a basket is made. The number 1 men then go to the end of the line and the number 2 men become the defensive men for the number 3 men. (See Figure 8-24.)

One-on-one Rebounding Drill

Player 1 passes the ball to player 2 who takes a dribble and shoots the ball. Player 1 then blocks off the offensive shooter and rebounds the ball. Player 2 attempts to rebound the ball if the shot is not made and will continue to shoot if he regains the offensive rebound. Player 1 then goes to the end of the line and player 2 becomes the defensive rebounder. (See Figure 8-25.)

Selected References

Basketball Rules. AAU of U.S. New York, latest edition.
Basketball Rules Book. Chicago: National Federation of State High School Athletic Association, latest ed.
Junker, Edward. *Cincinnati Power Basketball.* Englewood, N.J.: Prentice-Hall, 1962.
Newell, Pete, and John Bennington. *Basketball Methods.* New York: Ronald, 1962.
Official Basketball Guide. New York: NCAA, latest ed.
Samavas, Robert T. *Blitz Basketball.* West Nyack, N.Y.: Parker, 1966.

Figure 8-24. Defensive two-on-two drill.

Individual and Team Sports

CHAPTER 9

Bowling

*Philip L. Reuschlein**
Michigan State University

Figure 9-1. Modern bowling establishment. (The courtesy of the Brunswick Corporation for permission to reproduce this photograph is gratefully acknowledged.)

HISTORY

Man has engaged in games related to modern-day bowling for longer than he has been recording his history. During this vast period of time, the bowling-type games have been modified gradually until the modern game of tenpin bowling and similar bowling games have evolved.

Stone Age artifacts indicate that prehistoric cave men bowled large pebbles at bones or pointed stones. The ancient Polynesians rolled round stones at flat stone discs. Stone balls that appeared to have been rolled at stone bars or slabs or at pottery were found in the tomb of an Egyptian boy who lived more than seven thousand years ago. Before the time of Christ, the Romans of northern Italy had a bowling game with marked similarities to the present Italian lawn bowling game of *bocce ball*.

---

*B.S., Wisconsin State College, LaCrosse; M.S., Ph.D., University of Wisconsin. Professor Reuschlein has taught bowling and related activities to students at the elementary, secondary, and college levels, including teaching assignments at the Universities of Wisconsin, Iowa, and Western Michigan. A league bowler since 1950, he served as an assistant bowling clinician for the Lifetime Sports Foundation and as cochairman of a committee that wrote the revised edition of *Ideas for Bowling Instruction* for the Lifetime Sports Foundation. He was coeditor of the same manual.

Antecedents of Today's Bowling Games

The modern game of tenpins appears to have originated in monasteries in central Europe in which parishioners engaged in a religious ritual of rolling a large stone or ball at a wooden club, which represented Evil or the Devil. The clerics judged the devoutness of the parishioner by whether he missed the club or hit it. The bowling game called kegel was soon developed from this ritual, and it is considered to be the origin of the game of bowling at a single pin. As time passed additional pins were added and people of nobility and wealth began to engage in the game. These and other bowling games spread throughout Europe and later in England. Originally, outdoor grassy areas were used for bowling, but later clay alleys and finally wooden boards were used for the bowling lanes. As interest in the game of bowling increased, these alleys were covered and later wooden indoor bowling alleys were built. During this entire era no standardized equipment or rules existed, however. Martin Luther is credited with fixing the number of pins at nine and standardizing the rules of ninepins bowling.

Bowling games became popular over much of Europe, with each national area developing its own type of bowling game, such as curling in Scotland and *quilles* in France. The game of ninepins was brought to Manhattan Island by the Dutch in the early seventeenth century. Pin bowling quickly became the most popular game in the Colonies, although lawn bowling attained popularity in certain areas. The German immigrants especially spread the game of ninepins, which reached its top popularity in the 1840s, particularly in New York City. Gamblers gradually began to assume control of bowling in order to win the heavy wagers that were often placed on the game; this resulted in the game of ninepins being outlawed in various Eastern states. Before long, however, the game of tenpins was invented and the law was circumvented. In this game the pins were arranged in their present triangular formation, rather than in the diamond formation previously used in ninepins.

The popularity of tenpins spread rapidly. However, bowling equipment and rules varied from area to area thus creating many problems. In 1875, the National Bowling Congress and, in 1890, the Amateur Athletic Bowling Union were organized for the purposes of standardizing the rules of bowling. Both were short-lived. In 1895, the American Bowling Congress was formed and this organization today promotes bowling, formulates specifications for bowling equipment and lanes, and supervises bowling in the United States.

As the game of bowling evolved, so did bowling establishments and bowling equipment. (See Figure 9-1.) Originally, bowling pins were wooden clubs that were tapered at the top; later, small cones were employed that were soon replaced by small cake-shaped pins that were flat on the bottom and top. The champagne-bottle shape was eventually adopted as the standard shape for bowling pins. From the original small round stones, bowling balls evolved through wooden ones, rubber ones, truly round and smooth-surfaced balls shaped on lathes, and finally the hard rubber composition ball. Recently, plastic bowling balls have become quite popular.

Figure 9-2(a). Placement of pins on pin deck. (The courtesy of the American Machine and Foundry Company for permission to reproduce this photograph is gratefully acknowledged.)

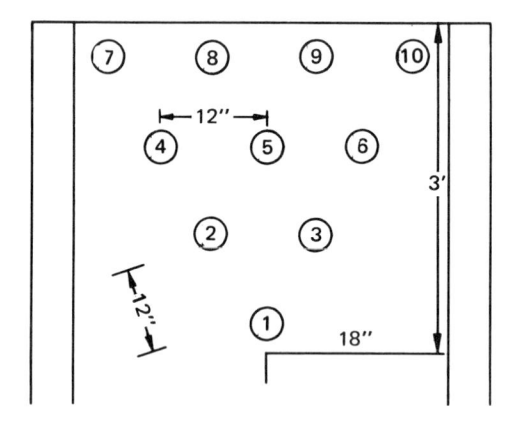

Figure 9-2(b). Placement of pins on pin deck.

DESCRIPTION OF BOWLING

Although a bowling game can utilize candle pins, duck pins, and so on, the most popular by far is tenpin bowling in which a large ball containing three finger holes and weighing between ten and sixteen pounds is employed to bowl at ten pins arranged in the shape of a triangle sixty feet from the foul line. The object in bowling is to knock down as many pins as possible in a game of ten frames. In each frame, a bonus is awarded when all ten pins are knocked down with two balls (a spare). A higher bonus is awarded when all pins are knocked down with the first ball (a strike). (See Figure 9-6.)

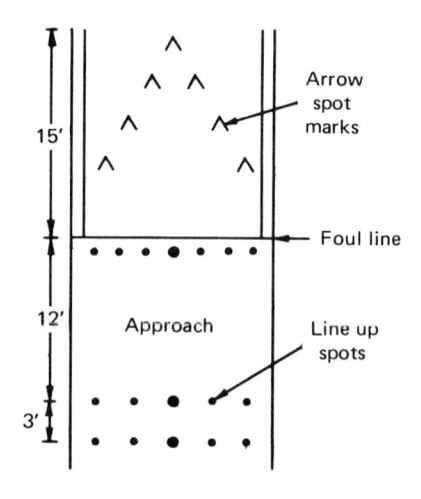

Figure 9-2(c). Layout of the approach area.

98 *Individual and Team Sports*

UNIQUE VALUES OF BOWLING

Bowling lends itself readily to lifelong participation because it is a sport that can be engaged in by people of all ages, by both sexes, and by widely mixed groups. Bowling establishments are located all over the United States; therefore, almost any time that any one wishes to bowl, bowling establishments are readily accessible during the popular times of the day and evening.

Bowling is truly a lifelong sport that can be successfully enjoyed by the preteen child to the older person who has lost some of his physical vigor and attributes. Bowling is a family game that offers enjoyment to the entire family—one of the few sports for which this is true—to students and adults of mixed sex, or to league bowlers who are quite homogeneous in bowling skills and interests. Bowling provides a mild physical workout that is not overly fatiguing and that can be accommodated by most people, including those who suffer from several forms of physical disability.

Bowling is a relatively inexpensive sport, especially when costs are shared by several friends bowling together. No special personal equipment is required of the bowler. The bowler who bowls regularly often saves money by purchasing his own bowling shoes; however, well-fitting shoes can be rented for a nominal fee at any establishment. Until the bowler has developed a fair degree of proficiency, he probably will not want to purchase a bowling ball, whose initial cost is somewhat expensive. However, as with shoes, a bowling ball will last for many years.

Bowling requires a minimum of instruction for successful participation, and even with almost no instruction, the beginning bowler can derive considerable satisfaction and enjoyment from his first attempts at the game. Regardless of the amount of bowling instruction and practice that the bowler has had, a challenge is always before him to improve his game and to perfect his bowling form and skills.

For the person who wants to bowl on a regular schedule, league bowling of various types is readily available and, as a rule, new bowlers are enthusiastically received in most leagues. Bowling affords the participants an opportunity for companionship, pleasant conversations, and a maximum of social interchange with the other members of his bowling team and his opponents under favorable circumstances.

SELECTION OF EQUIPMENT

Fitting the Ball

Several factors need to be considered when selecting a ball, whether it is one furnished by the bowling establishment or it is a personal ball being purchased by the bowler. Most male bowlers in college classes prefer a heavyweight bowling ball, usually a sixteen-pound ball, if they can control it. The heavier ball has greater momentum and is more effective in knocking down pins than a lighter one. However, some male bowlers prefer to bowl with a ball as light as fourteen pounds, and a few may use a ball that weighs twelve pounds or less. In order to have maximum control of the ball during all phases of the bowling approach and delivery, it is essential that the ball properly fit the bowler's hand. The correct diameter of the finger and thumb holes is essential. The finger holes should be of sufficient diameter that the thumb and fingers can slip in and out of the ball easily and without sticking or causing a popping sound. However, these finger holes should be small enough to permit the bowler to easily retain his grip on the ball. Another important consideration is the span between the thumb hole and finger holes. Because most beginning bowlers will use a ball with a regular grip in which the thumb and two middle fingers are utilized, the span should be such that when the ball is gripped, a pencil or little finger can just be inserted between the ball and the palm of the bowling hand. Another method of checking the span is to insert the thumb into the bowling ball the proper distance to see that the middle joint of each of the two fingers extends approximately one-half inch past the inside edge of the finger holes.

Figure 9-3. Fitting the ball. (The courtesy of the Brunswick Corporation for permission to reproduce this photograph is gratefully acknowledged.)

Almost all house balls have the finger holes drilled at a neutral angle (pointing directly to the center of the ball), because this is the kind used by most bowlers. Such neutral finger-hole angles should be present in the ball used by the bowler until he has had a reasonable chance to adjust to such balls. The beginner who wants to bowl seriously and achieve maximum success in the game may eventually want to try a semifinger tip or fingertip ball, after becoming experienced with a regular ball. Similarly, special bowling gloves are available that enable the bowler to place increased spin on the ball and thus increase the hooking action or the consistency of the hook. This type of equipment is for use only by the advanced bowler.

Shoes

Bowling shoes can be rented at any bowling establishment; they should be comfortable, light, and well fitting. If one buys one's own shoes, then the shoe opposite the bowling hand (the left shoe for the right-handed bowler) should have a leather tip on the sole, or an all-leather sole, in order to facilitate the slide on the last step of the delivery (house bowling shoes are made with all-leather soles on both feet). The clothes worn by the bowler should be comfortable and in accord with what is normally worn at the bowling establishment. As a rule, considerable freedom exists in what is worn for casual or class bowling.

Pin and Lane Dimensions

The dimensions of the bowling pin and the bowling lane are depicted in Figure 9-5. The dimensions of the bowling

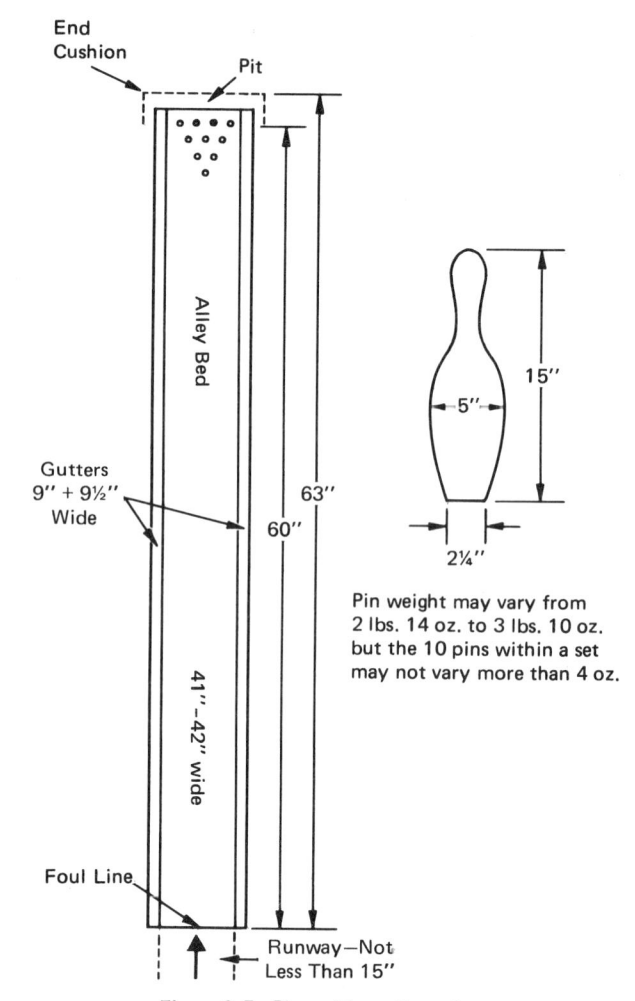

Figure 9-5. Pin and lane dimensions.

lane, except for the length of the approach, are quite exact and permit little variation from lane to lane.

RULES AND COURTESIES OF BOWLING

Rules

The rules of bowling are few and uncomplicated; the average bowling student has little difficulty in learning them. When delivering the bowling ball, a foul is committed when any part of the body passes beyond the foul line during delivery of the ball. Ordinarily, fouls are committed by sliding the front foot past the foul line; however, a bowler who loses his balance or trips during his approach or release and extends a hand past the foul line and onto the bowling alley commits a foul. For a complete set of the rules of bowling, an up-to-date copy can be obtained from the American Bowling Congress in Milwaukee, Wisconsin, or in a more complete book on bowling.

Figure 9-4. Bowling shoes, bags, and balls. (The courtesy of the Brunswick Corporation for permission to reproduce this photograph is gratefully acknowledged.)

Scoring (Figure 9-6). Scoring in bowling is not complicated and is quickly learned by most college students after a short period of practice. The game of bowling consists of ten frames. The pin fall for each frame is usually recorded in the two small squares within the large frame. A cumulative total is kept in the large frame in order that the running score at the completion of each frame is known. In each frame the bowler has a maximum of two balls to deliver, and unless he commits a foul, his score is the number of pins felled with the two balls. The exceptions are that when all ten pins are felled with the first ball (a strike), only one ball is delivered for that frame. When a strike is made, the bowler receives, in addition to 10 for the ten pins knocked down, a bonus of the pin fall for the next two balls rolled. If all the pins are knocked over with two balls in one frame (a spare), the bowler is awarded the pin fall for that frame (10) plus a bonus of the pin fall for the next ball rolled. In the tenth frame the bonus rule still applies. Therefore, if a mark is made (either a strike or a spare), the bowler must roll a total of three balls in the tenth frame.

In the event that the bowler commits a foul, this counts as a ball rolled, but he receives no pin fall for the ball rolled when the foul was committed. Thus, if a foul is committed on the first ball, all the pins are reset and the best he can do is score a spare if all the pins are knocked down with the second ball. If the foul is committed during the second ball of the frame, then only the pin fall for the first ball in that frame is counted. A sample game is scored and explanations given in Figure 9-6. The scoring of the sample game should be carefully studied in order that it is completely understood.

Team and League Bowling. Many bowlers progress to bowling in a team or league situation, which often enhances their enjoyment of the game. When bowling against another team, the actual score may be counted whereby one team must achieve a higher total score than the other team in order to win the game. The usual practice, however, is to award handicaps on the basis of bowling averages previously achieved by the bowlers (and team) in order to somewhat equalize the difference in bowling ability. The usual rule is to find the sum of the averages for each team, subtract the difference, and award to the team with the smaller sum two thirds of the difference. Thus, if the sum of the average scores for one team was 600 and the sum for the other team was 700, the difference is 100; two thirds of this difference is 66 2/3. Because fractions of a pin are not counted, the second team would be awarded a handicap score of 66. At the completion of each game they would receive 66 additional pins to be added to their game score. In team or league bowling competition, generally one point is awarded for

Frame	Pins Down First Ball	Pins Down Second Ball	Bowling Term for Frame	Score for That Frame	Running Score
1	7	2	Error	9	9
2	6	4	Spare	10 + 0	19
3	0	9	1st ball—Gutter Ball	9	28
4	10		Strike	10 + 10 + 8	56
5	10		Strike	10 + 8 + 2	76
6	8	2	Spare	10 + 0	86
7	0	10	1st Ball—Foul 2nd Ball—Spare	10 + 8	104
8	8	2	1st Ball—Split 2nd Ball—Spare	10 + 0	123
9	9	0	Error (see below)	9	132
10	7	3	Spare	10 + 8	150
	8				

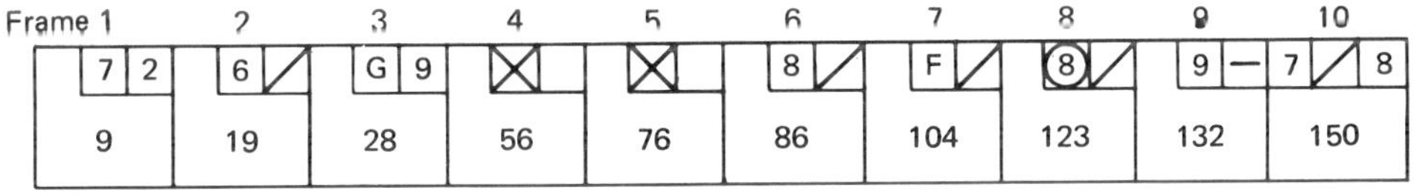

Frame	1	2	3	4	5	6	7	8	9	10
	7 2	6 /	G 9	X	X	8 /	F /	⑧ /	9 —	7 / 8
	9	19	28	56	76	86	104	123	132	150

Figure 9-6. Scoring in bowling.

each of the three games won plus one point for the total score; therefore, a team could win by a score as high as 4-0 (four points won, none lost). If a game or total pin score is tied, usually a half point is awarded to each team.

Courtesies of Bowling

Etiquette in bowling is really just a matter of common sense—treating another bowler as you would like him to treat you when you bowl. The main objective is not to disturb a bowler when he is bowling on your lane or an adjacent one. This includes not talking to the bowler when he is on the approach or when he is delivering the ball. If a bowler on a lane is ready to bowl, a bowler in the adjacent lane should stay off his approach area. When two bowlers are simultaneously getting ready to bowl, the usual rule is that the bowler on the right has precedence. Sometimes this rule is so modified that the person bowling the second ball has precedence over a bowler who has not yet delivered the first ball in a frame. Most bowling establishments permit the bowlers to drink beverages or eat snacks while sitting in the scoring area awaiting their turn to bowl.

BOWLING TECHNIQUES

Warm-up

Most bowlers warm up by rolling a few balls before competing in a game in order to get the feel of the ball. They study the conditions of the alleys in order to determine whether an alley is slick and will cause the ball to hook less than usual or if the alley will cause the ball to hook more than usual. Such a warm-up usually helps the bowler attain the proper frame of mind to review the correct techniques of bowling delivery and release and to concentrate on the points most in need of attention.

FUNDAMENTAL SKILLS OF BOWLING

The techniques and skills that are most commonly advocated by bowling authorities are presented in this chapter. In some cases more than one method or technique is presented when both appear to be acceptable and of nearly equal value. Each bowler must employ those techniques that seem to suit him best, because individual variations and abilities must definitely be taken into account in any sport or physical activity. The discussion of the fundamental skills of bowling is presented for the right-handed bowler. The left-handed bowler should reverse these directions as appropriate.

Stance or Ready Position

In the stance taken by the bowler preparatory to taking his approach and delivering the ball, the bowler can do several things to help insure a consistent approach and delivery and to best prepare himself to deliver an accurately rolled ball. The nonbowling hand is normally positioned under the ball when in the stance in order to help

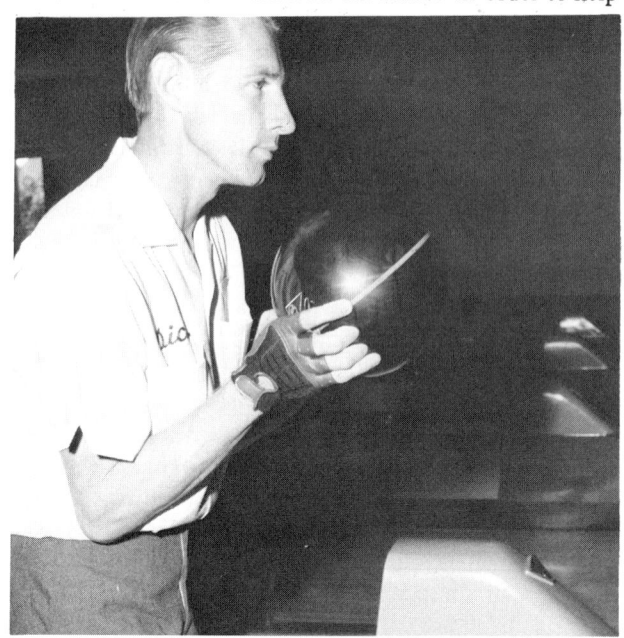

Figure 9-7(a). Stance or ready position. (The courtesy of the American Machine and Foundry Company for permission to reproduce this photograph is gratefully acknowledged.)

Figure 9-7(b). Another stance or ready position. (The courtesy of the Brunswick Corporation for permission to reproduce this photograph is gratefully acknowledged.)

support its weight and thus avoid unduly tiring the bowling arm or hand. The recommended height of the bowling ball when in the starting stance is between waist and chest height. Although a few bowlers start with the ball in a lower or higher position than this, these unorthodox positions often cause problems in properly timing the approach and the swing of the ball as well as introducing problems in releasing the ball down the lane at an optimum speed. While in the stance the ball is kept fairly close to the body and is centered in front of the right shoulder. A common variation is to center the ball in the center of the body. However, this position often introduces an extraneous factor that must be corrected when the ball is pushed away from the body during the approach: the path of the ball is out of the plane of movement formed by the right shoulder and the target. For this reason, and because an extra effort is needed to correct this out-of-plane movement, most beginning bowlers will do best by centering the ball in front of the bowling-arm shoulder during the stance.

While in the stance the body and legs are as relaxed as possible, and the body and legs are slightly bent. Although the position of the feet is an individual matter, most bowlers seem to prefer to have one foot slightly in front of the other. Usually, the forward foot is the one with which the first step is taken, although this depends somewhat on the number of steps taken in the approach and whether the bowler is a beginner who has not yet fixed his stance position. If one foot is in front of the other, the bulk of the body weight normally rests on the rear foot so that the front foot can be easily moved forward when the first step is taken.

When in the stance, the body is so positioned on the alley that it is squarely facing toward the target. In addition, the body is often positioned somewhat on the right side of the approach area. The exact lateral position depends on the type of ball delivery used and other factors. Most right-handed bowlers like to start with their left foot on the dot immediately to the right of the center dot (that is, five boards to the right of the center). Other bowlers may want to start with the left foot two dots to the right of the center dot, thus releasing the ball near the right-hand channel. Whatever body position is chosen, it should be comfortable and one from which the bowler has confidence that he can repeatedly make a consistent ball delivery.

The position of the bowling hand is usually one in which the thumb is located between a nine and twelve o'clock position on the ball. The exact position depends on the type of ball delivery that is utilized.

Because the stance is the first phase in executing a consistent and accurate delivery of the ball, it must be one that the bowler can easily and consistently assume each time before delivering the ball, and one in which all the preceding points are integrated into a smooth and relaxed position.

Approach

The approach consists of the movements made by the bowler as he moves toward the foul line while delivering the ball. A consistent approach that is properly executed can be of immense value in assuring an accurately delivered ball of the proper speed. The main consideration in the approach is that the correct timing of the feet movement and the arm swing of the ball is achieved together with the maintenance of good body balance throughout the approach. The chief objective of the approach is to permit the bowler to smoothly and easily generate sufficient speed while approaching the foul line so that the ball can be delivered without undue effort and with accuracy and consistency.

Even though the length of the approach will vary somewhat according to the type of ball delivery, the bowler's body build, and other factors, most of the fifteen feet available on the approach deck of the bowling lane ordinarily should be used. During the initial learning stages, some bowlers may experiment briefly with a one-step approach while learning the correct timing of the last step, forward arm swing, and release of the ball. Some bowlers may need to then practice a two-step approach, and a few bowlers, because of physical handicaps and/or difficulty in coordinating a complex approach with an increased number of steps, may stay with a one- or two-step approach. There appears to be little reason to encourage the use of a three-step approach except for those bowlers for whom it has been firmly entrenched and who would have marked difficulty in changing to a four- or five-step approach.

Many male bowlers tend to start their approach with too speedy and too long a first step; hurrying this step causes some control of the ball's delivery to be lost. The entire approach must be one that is quite deliberate and one in which the final step or two is no faster than a normal walking pace. For these reasons the four-step approach is the one normally recommended for most beginning bowlers, although many professional bowlers use a five-step approach.

When the bowler has determined how many steps he will use in his approach, he needs to locate the spot on the approach deck (or runway) at which he will regularly assume his stance in order to begin his approach. Two methods are commonly employed for this purpose. One is to start with the back to the pins with the heel of the rear foot approximately six inches "in front of" the foul line. From this position the bowler takes his regular approach away from the pins and marks the spot where his forward foot stops. Another method sometimes used is to start from the foul line and walk normally away from the pins the number of steps that will be used in the approach. From this stopping point a half step more is added. Either method should result in the bowler locating approximately the same position from the foul line from which he should always begin his approach.

The approach, as is true of the complete cycle of the arm swing of the bowling arm when delivering the ball, is an integrated movement that cannot actually be fragmented. For purposes of instruction, however, the timing of the arm swing and the steps in the delivery are sometimes broken up into separate components in order to enhance the student's understanding of what the correct timing should be. Because this is artificial and can result in negative learning, this fragmenting of the arm swing and steps in the approach should only be employed for the minimum time needed to gain an understanding of what is expected to occur during the approach. As soon as this understanding has been achieved, a unified and coordinated approach and arm swing should be practiced.

Again, if a consistent and accurate delivery is to be made, the arm swing needs to be a consistent one that starts the same, has the same range and plane of motion during its execution, and finishes the same each time. The arm swing is not forced but instead, after the initial pushaway of the ball, the weight of the ball furnishes the primary impetus until the ball release takes place. Thus, considerable practice is also needed in order to properly coordinate the timing of the approach.

The recommended arm swing is a "pendulum swing" (a swing in one plane similar to that of the pendulum in a grandfather clock). One way of visualizing this is to think of the ball being suspended by a rope inserted to the shoulder. Consequently, after the ball has been started into motion, the bowling arm plays no part in changing the plane of motion that has been initiated. This concept will enable the bowler to see that the ball should swing about as far to the rear of his shoulder as it was carried forward at the initial pushaway. The weight of the ball causes both gravity and inertia to play an important role throughout the completion of the arm swing.

The first phase of the arm swing is the pushaway (Figure 9-8). This is exactly what its name implies it to be—the pushing forward (and downward) of the ball toward the target, the action of which starts the arm swing. The nonbowling hand assists in this initial pushing movement.

As soon as the ball is pushed as far forward as the completely extended bowling arm permits, the backswing, which begins as a down swing, is started immediately. The backswing should be a natural one; the ball should not be forced downward or backward (or upward at the end of the backswing). A fair range of motion should be

Figure 9-8. Start of the pushaway. (The courtesy of the American Machine and Foundry Company for permission to reproduce this photograph is gratefully acknowledged.)

employed in the backswing in order that the bowling arm is almost parallel to the floor at the time that the backswing is completed. During the backswing (and all phases of the arm swing) the shoulder alignment should remain essentially perpendicular to the lane direction (or parallel to the foul line). As the backswing is completed, and without any forcing movements or muscular effort being exerted, the forward swing is started by the weight of the ball.

In the forward swing no undue force should be used to propel the ball forward, nor should there be any particular hurry to initiate the forward swing of the ball and bowling arm. The pendulum-swing concept should definitely be retained during this phase of the arm swing, and a side-arm action should be avoided. This can be done with relative ease if the bowler does not rush his approach, keeps his shoulders parallel with the foul line, does not try to force the ball forward ahead of its natural movement, or does not apply undue force to the ball.

Timing of Steps and Arm Swing

The timing of the steps with the swing of the bowling arm varies somewhat according to the individual bowler,

Figure 9-9. Timing of last step and forward arm swing. (The courtesy of the American Machine and Foundry Company for permission to reproduce this photograph is gratefully acknowledged.)

Figure 9-10. Releasing the ball. (The courtesy of the American Machine and Foundry Company for permission to reproduce this photograph is gratefully acknowledged.)

his style of bowling, his speed of delivery, and his approach to the foul line. The one unviolable principle is that the last step must be initiated at the same time that the ball is started on the forward swing. (See Figure 9-9.) In addition, with most bowlers the backswing and the next to the last step occur together. Although the arm position at various steps can be broken down step by step, this artificial type of practice has little transfer value to actual bowling. A better procedure is to practice and perfect the timing for a one-step approach. Then, perhaps, if difficulty is encountered, the two-step approach can be practiced and the timing of the arm swing and release can be perfected for it. From this practice the beginning bowler should, while using a four- or five-step approach, attempt to retain the feel and timing previously achieved.

When using the four-step approach it is essential that the bowler initiate the pushaway simultaneously with or slightly before taking his first step. Almost always, when the first step is taken before the ball is pushed away, the bowler either starts his last step while the ball is still in its backswing or else he skips while approaching. Consequently, the approach finishes before the forward arm swing, and the bowler loses most of the momentum and timing that should be achieved during the approach. To compensate, the bowler then uses considerable muscular effort to deliver the ball at the regular speed, the practice of which forces him to side arm the ball—a highly inaccurate style of delivering the ball. Instead, the bowler must fight initiating the pushaway before starting his first step and he must not hurry his approach. Only rarely will the bowler find that his arm-swing timing is ahead of his steps.

Releasing the Ball

As the bowler completes his last step with the foot opposite the bowling hand, the forward arm swing of the ball carries it past the sliding forward foot. At this instant the ball is smoothly released, usually by permitting it to roll onto the lane surface—the ball should not be dropped or thrown. Instead, the bowler should feel the ball being placed on the lane. (See Figure 9-10.)

Finish Position

After releasing the ball, the bowling hand continues its forward and upward motion to about a head-high

Figure 9-11. Finish position. (The courtesy of the American Machine and Foundry Company for permission to reproduce this photograph is gratefully acknowledged.)

Bowling

position. At the completion of the follow-through, the bowling hand should point directly at or above the target. After releasing the ball, the bowler should retain his finish position for a short time in order to check to see that he has completed his delivery (1) in the correct finishing position, (2) at the proper distance from the foul line, and (3) with his body in good balance.

During the approach and finish, the nonbowling arm is positioned directly sideward and is used to maintain balance. At the finish, the body should face directly toward the pins and be in balance without any need to hop or touch either hand to the floor. The rear foot finishes behind the front foot and often somewhat to the side away from the bowling hand. By flexing his hips and knees, but keeping his trunk erect, the bowler can lean forward in a low position for the release and finish. To achieve consistency and minimize the number of variables that must be controlled during the delivery, the delivery must be completed in the same finish position each time.

Because bowling is a relatively simple skill compared with many games, the beginning bowler will need to review this section and work diligently toward achieving a consistent workable stance, approach, arm swing, and finish. If this is achieved, the problem of delivering the ball accurately to the target should not be major because all the preliminary phases will have been stabilized.

TYPES OF BALL DELIVERIES

Two types of ball deliveries are normally utilized by the beginning bowler. Several considerations must be weighed in deciding which is the most appropriate for an individual bowler; even then, as the bowler achieves increased skill and ambition, he may decide to revise his ball delivery.

Choosing a Ball Delivery

A number of bowling instructors advocate that beginning bowlers use a straight-ball delivery in which the ball travels in a straight line from its point of release to its impact on the pins. The straight-ball delivery has a number of advantages and some disadvantages. Because the straight-line direction of travel can be easily envisioned, this delivery is relatively easy to aim. Because the amount of hooking (curving) action that a hook ball will take varies from delivery to delivery, it is often quite difficult to achieve a consistent hook from one lane to another, from different positions starting on the same lane, or from one day to another. Thus, the straight ball is a much simpler ball to bowl with consistency. Because the different locations on the approach from which the second (or spare) ball in a frame is delivered causes the amount of hooking action to differ, the straight ball is easier to aim and control when attempting to pick up spares than is a

Figure 9-12. Paths for the straight, hook, and curve ball. (The courtesy of the Brunswick Corporation for permission to reproduce this photograph is gratefully acknowledged.)

106 *Individual and Team Sports*

hook ball. In addition, the hook-ball bowler must roll his ball with more accuracy than the straight-ball bowler when picking up spares, particularly when rolling for a tenpin spare. The hook-ball bowler must practice regularly if he is to achieve a consistent amount of hook on his ball with each first-ball delivery. The once-a-week or occasional bowler can, therefore, generally have better scores with a straight ball than with a hook ball.

The straight-ball delivery, however, has several disadvantages as compared to the hook ball. An attempted straight-ball delivery may hook slightly or even back up, thus missing the target. After a certain degree of bowling skill has been achieved, a controlled hook ball will result in a larger proportion of strike hits and a smaller proportion of split hits than will a controlled straight ball. As one increases in bowling skill, this factor becomes increasingly important. Even though the hook ball may be a little more complicated to aim, practice can enable the hook ball to be aimed as accurately as the straight ball.

The beginner should never deliberately practice throwing a back-up ball (sometimes called a reverse hook ball), which curves toward the side of the body from which it is delivered. Although some success may be achieved with a back-up ball, it requires lengthy practice and a good, consistent delivery—traits that should assure even more success with a recommended type of ball delivery. A right-handed bowler should deliver a back-up ball from the left side of the approach if the ball is to approach the pins from a favorable angle, but this approach is a difficult one to make. In addition, with a back-up ball more splits and fewer strikes will occur than usual because of the small angle at which the ball goes into the head pin pocket. Sometimes a beginner will inadvertently throw a back-up ball because he rotates his forearm in a clockwise direction during the delivery. This can happen when throwing a straight ball because during the back swing the bowler inadvertently permits his forearm to rotate in a counterclockwise direction; consequently, the forearm uncocks with a clockwise rotation during the forward swing as a correction is made. A back-up ball may occur when the fingers are too far under the ball during the carry, causing the ball to rotate clockwise when the fingers are released. A tight thumb hole, which causes the thumb to come out late, can sometimes be the cause of a back-up ball.

Straight-ball Delivery

When making a straight-ball delivery, the bowler keeps the thumb of his bowling hand at the twelve o'clock position throughout the approach and release. By having the finger positioned directly toward the rear of the ball, no side rotation is imparted to the ball when the thumb or the fingers are withdrawn from the finger holes. Consequently, the ball maintains a straight line throughout its travel to the pins. The straight-ball bowler starts from the right-hand side of the approach and finishes in a straight line toward the target, still on the right side of the alley. The usual starting position is five to ten boards in from the right-hand channel.

Because the straight-ball delivery requires the thumb to remain at approximately the twelve o'clock position at all times during the delivery, some people experience considerable difficulty in consistently rolling a straight ball. If this is true, a hook-ball delivery should be considered. If during the backswing, the thumb position varies because the hand rotates, the attempted straight ball may have a slight hook or back-up. If this curving action is slight and consistent, the bowler may want to retain this delivery. For some bowlers, however, this curving motion may be considerable and variable from ball to ball, thus resulting in an unreliable, inconsistent ball delivery.

Hook-ball Delivery

An advantage of the hook ball is that a more natural type of grip is employed—a so-called suitcase grip—that is easier to assume and requires less effort to maintain than does the straight-ball grip. The usual thumb position for the hook-ball grip is at about ten o'clock. This may vary from nine o'clock to eleven o'clock for a natural hook-ball delivery in which no wrist action or forearm rotation is employed in an effort to induce increased side rotation on the ball during the release. The V formed by the thumb and forefinger should point directly toward the pins throughout the approach and release of the hook ball. With the bowling hand in this position, the thumb comes out of the ball first and the fingers, being located to one side of the center of the ball, impart a sideward spinning action to the ball. As a result, the ball curves away from the side of the body from which the ball was delivered. For a right-handed bowler this curving motion is toward the left. Because the ball is delivered with some speed it slides a distance before it begins rolling (because of its inertia when first set down on the lane), the curling action on the ball is not apparent until the ball is approximately halfway down the lane. When throwing a hook ball the bowler as a rule forcefully lifts his hand while releasing the ball. The more forceful this lifting motion, the more side spin imparted to the ball. The bowler does not need to take any special precautions to remove his thumb from the bowling ball first, because this natural action requires no conscious effort, provided that the ball is properly fitted. Some advanced bowlers attempt to achieve increased hooking action by special means, the techniques of which are discussed later.

The approach position for the hook-ball delivery is usually near the center of the alley, commonly ten to fifteen boards in from the right-hand side of the approach. This distance varies from bowler to bowler; some bowlers prefer to deliver the hook ball from the center of the approach, hoping to avoid a tenpin leave.

A curve-ball delivery, in which the ball begins curving almost as soon as it is released, should be avoided because of the wide sweeping arc and the difficulty in controlling the ball. A hook ball that first slides some distance also avoids the problem of having a ball lose its hooking action before it reaches the pins, thus coming into the pins as if it were a straight ball.

AIMING METHODS

Two methods are commonly employed for aiming the ball at the target. With either aiming method, the target should be the same for the *first* ball in each frame, the so-called strike ball. This same target may sometimes be the point of aim for the second ball—the spare ball. Regardless of the aiming method used, however, for all first balls the bowler has a spot from which he should consistently start his approach, a spot at which he should consistently end his approach, and a target at which he is aiming. The bowler should check after each delivery to see that the line formed by his approach crosses these three spots in a straight line. He should especially note where his front foot finished. In addition, he should occasionally have someone else check to see that his entire approach was straight and not a zigzag (in which he steps to one side on the next-to-last step and toward the other side on the last step).

Pin-aim Method

The simplest aiming method is to aim directly at the target—the pins themselves. For the first ball in any frame—the strike ball—the aim for a right-handed bowler is the center of the 1-3 pocket or slightly in (high) toward the head pin. The bowler should concentrate on focusing his vision at this target during his approach and release.

If the bowler is throwing a hook ball, then he must experiment to see how much his ball is hooking in order to find the target at which to aim the ball. Depending on the amount of hook achieved, the hook-ball bowler, if pin aiming, may need to aim directly at the number 6 pin if the ball is to hook into the 1-3 pocket as desired. With more hook, the 6-10 pocket and, with less hook perhaps, the 3-6 pocket may be the aiming points.

Spot-aim Method

When using the spot-aim method the bowler really has four spots on which he must focus his attention. The fourth spot is normally one a short distance down the lane at which the bowler aims to roll his ball. The spot is usually located on one of the darts on the range finder, which is a series of darts across the alley in an inverted Vee formation several feet in front of the foul line. (See Figure 9-13.) If aiming at a particular dart does not result in the ball going into the 1-3 pocket, the bowler may have to move his aiming spot one or two boards to the left or right of that particular dart. The spot-aiming

Pin-aim Method
with Straight
Ball Delivery

Spot-aim Method
with Hook Ball
Delivery

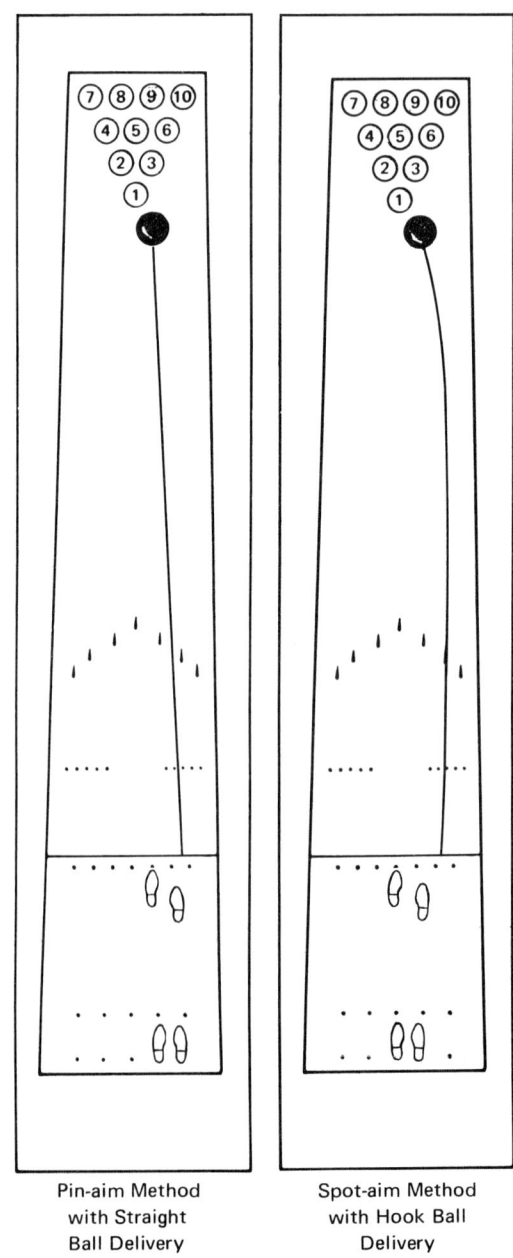

Figure 9-13. Pin-aim and spot-aim methods.

method has the advantage of giving the bowler a fairly close target at which to aim. When hook-ball bowling, this spot may change from lane to lane, depending on the amount of hooking action produced on the ball.

Aiming for Spare Balls

The second ball of a frame may have to be delivered from a different starting and finishing position (thus in a different line) than that used for the strike ball. When spare-ball bowling, the usual principle followed is that of utilizing the maximum alley angle. Thus, for pins in the vicinity of the strike-ball target zone, the same starting and finishing positions are employed as when a first ball is delivered. For right-side pins, the spare bowler bowls from the left side of the approach, and for left-side pins, from the right side of the approach.

When spare bowling, the main target is the pin closest to the bowler (the lowest-numbered pin). When spare bowling, the bowler can pin aim or spot aim—the choice usually coincides with the technique used for strike-ball bowling.

Strike-ball Aiming. When the target pins are the 1, 2, 3, 5, 8, or 9 pins, the bowler will generally bowl a strike ball in which he aims at or near the 1–3 pocket.

Right-side Leaves. When the target pins are the 3, 6, 9, or 10 pins, the bowler usually moves to the left side of the alley and makes his approach directly toward the target pin. The actual aiming point may be into the 3–6 pin pocket, directly at the 6 pin, between the 6–10 pin pocket, or directly at the 10 pin. Some bowlers prefer to modify their regular strike-ball approach only slightly when bowling at right-side spares that do not include the 10 pin. (The approach is started from the right side.) This seems to be a matter of personal preference; the individual bowler should use whatever method works best for him.

Left-side Leaves. The 4, 7, and 8 pins, and sometimes the 2, 5, and 9 pins, are considered to be left-side spare leaves for which the approach is moved to the right of the first ball approach in order to utilize a maximum angle toward the target pin. The target is usually the 1–2 pocket, the 2–4 pocket, or directly at the 4 or 7 pin.

Full-pin Hits. In three spare leave situations the target pin needs to be hit full because a pin is standing directly behind it. Other pins may or may not be standing. The 2–8, the 3–9, and the 1–5 pin leaves require that the ball hit the center of the target pin almost squarely in order to carry the rear pin.

Split Leaves. The nemesis of all bowlers is the split leave—a leave in which one or more pins are missing between two standing pins. Some of these leaves, such as the baby split (the 4–5 pins or the 9–10 pins, for example), are not too difficult to pick up because the ball can carry the pins. Other leaves in which the ball must barely hit the target pin in order to deflect it at almost a right angle are extremely difficult to pick up and take a very exact hit if they are to be converted to a spare. The most difficult splits involve various combinations of the 4, 7, 6, and 10 pins. The odds of making this difficult a split are so stiff that most bowlers believe that they will score higher in the long run by aiming directly at the biggest target, taking the 4 and 7 pins and leaving the 10 pin, for example. Which strategy to follow in this circumstance is in part dependent on how accurate the individual bowler is and what the circumstances are. If in the tenth frame of a league game a mark is needed to win, then it is worth taking a slim chance in an attempt to make the conversion.

The general rule followed in converting splits is that, whenever possible, one should let the ball be deflected by the front pin into the back pin, as with a 3–10 pin leave. If this is not possible, the front pin should be deflected into the other standing pins. The bowler should usually attempt to play the type of shot that gives him the best chance of knocking down the most pins in case he misses the target.

At frequent intervals the bowler, depending on his temperament and related factors, must periodically remind himself not to rush his delivery of the ball. Many bowlers, when in difficulty or when bowling poorly, unconsciously speed up their approach and "muscle" their delivery. This tendency must be consciously resisted.

Using the Straight- or Hook-ball Delivery. The student should decide as soon as possible which type of delivery he will use when bowling. Some authorities used to recommend that all bowlers bowl a straight-bowl delivery for the first year or so of their careers. Then they could decide whether they should go to a hook-ball delivery (if their interest and skills indicated that this might be profitable for them). However, principles of motor learning and general learning indicate that much negative transfer can take place when a person learns one technique and then changes to another, and that considerable interference in learning takes place under these circumstances. Thus, before habits become ingrained, the bowler should decide which type of delivery he will use and then stay with that decision. The main questions to answer in making this decision are (1) will the bowler be bowling regularly (at least three games a week) and (2) does he have sufficient skill, timing, coordination, and ability to throw a hook-ball delivery with adequate control? A "yes" answer to these questions indicates that a hook-ball delivery should be chosen. The bowler who knows that he will bowl irregularly with long intervals in between, or who realizes that he is quite a bit below average in his timing and coordination, will find that the straight-ball delivery may result in his bowling a higher average than the hook-ball delivery.

IMPROVING THE BOWLING GAME

The main strategy in bowling is to knock down as many pins as possible each time the ball is delivered. Although this important concept can never be overlooked, other points of strategy are often involved in the game.

In most situations, especially when in class, the bowler should take the long-range viewpoint and deliver the type of ball that will ultimately result in the best bowling game for him. Thus, the bowler should avoid the mistake of developing an unorthodox approach or delivery in order to make a slightly higher score at the moment, knowing that in the long run this will prevent him from developing his full potential in bowling.

The bowler should never overlook the importance of skillful spare bowling. Without making a mark of any kind, the maximum score that a bowler can make is 90 points. Without striking at all, but converting a spare on every frame, the maximum score the bowler can achieve is 190 points, a score that is well above the average of most league bowlers. The bowler should therefore strongly concentrate on converting each spare leave. The bowler who makes very few strikes can still achieve a respectable score by making most of the spares.

On any spare-ball attempt, the bowler should keep in mind the fact that he has a fairly large target at which to roll the ball, particularly if only a single pin remains standing. The size of target for a single pin involves a five-inch width for the pin, plus the width of the bowling ball on either side of the edge of the pin, approximately eight and one-half inches. Consequently, the target area for the ball is a twenty-two inch zone. For this reason the spare-ball attempt should usually result in a mark being scored, unless a split leave or a large number of pins were left standing.

Some bowlers, when bowling their spare ball, deliberately refrain from lifting their hand vigorously upon releasing the ball, resulting in less hook being placed on the ball. This seems to work well when the lift for both the strike and the spare ball can be differentiated and each accurately controlled. This technique reduces the problem of picking up corner leaves, especially the 10 pin.

SPECIFIC TRAINING METHODS FOR BOWLING

Practice Deliveries Without a Ball

The first step in acquiring skill in bowling for the beginner is to practice his delivery without a bowling ball in order to concentrate on the steps in the approach and to begin to time the arm swing and steps. Beginners need to practice this for only a short time, but it should enable one to focus on starting the delivery with the correct foot, not rushing the straight-line approach, and starting and finishing in the correct spots behind the foul line. The beginner can profitably practice the one-step delivery several times before moving on to the four- or five-step delivery. Only after these phases are completed should a bowling ball be delivered at the completion of the approach.

Practice Delivery Without Pins

When the bowler has achieved the ability to make a smooth, coordinated approach in a straight line he should next practice delivering the bowling ball during his approach, aiming at about the center of the lane—but without any pins on the pin deck. Practicing the delivery without pins helps avoid the temptation to be concerned about knocking down pins; instead, the bowler can concentrate on perfecting his approach, delivery, ball release, and the other basic skills that are fundamental to developing a consistent delivery and bowling skill.

If needed, the bowler can practice delivering the ball with a one-step delivery for several deliveries. When he achieves a feeling of swinging the ball forward as he steps forward, the bowler is ready to move directly to his regular delivery. Should the bowler have difficulty in mastering a four- (or five-) step approach, he may need to practice for a while on an intermediate two-step approach. Once he masters the fundamentals of the approach and ball delivery, he should bowl with pins on the pin deck. If possible, only the 1 and 3 pins should be placed on the pin deck, because this is the target at which the bowler usually bowls. A 1-3 pin setup enables the bowler to integrate a proper approach and delivery with rolling the ball directly at the target area. Hopefully, he will make the adjustments necessary to roll the ball consistently into the 1-3 pocket, before proceeding to bowl with all ten pins set up as in the regular bowling game. For quite some time, however, the bowler should not be concerned with the number of pins knocked down. He should concentrate his efforts on getting a grooved pattern in his approach and ball delivery.

Spare Bowling

One successful method of improving one's bowling average is to spare bowl in those bowling establishments where special pin leaves can be set up. Several balls can be delivered in which only the 10 pin is set up—a common leave that many bowlers have difficulty in converting. Other frequent leaves at which the bowler can practice include the 1-5 pins, the 5 pin, the 5-8 pins, the 5-9 pins, and the 3-10 split.

When practicing or when bowling, the bowler should keep his full attention on his bowling; he should not allow his mind to become occupied with extraneous thoughts. By devoting his complete attention to the various components of bowling, he should improve at an optimum rate, if he practices regularly. Many bowlers and almost all beginning bowlers universally find that they need someone else to watch their approach and ball delivery in order to spot some of the numerous faults that are apt to be committed. Faults, of which the bowler may be completely unaware, may be obvious to an experienced bowler or instructor. In addition, even though the bowler may realize that he is committing one or more faults (such as side arming or being off-balance at the completion of the delivery), he may have no idea of what is causing this. A bowling instructor or an expert bowler can often quickly pinpoint the causes and can offer definite help to the bowler in correcting such faults.

CORRECTING COMMON ERRORS

Rushing the Delivery

Many male bowlers, often without being aware of it, rush their delivery, which can impair their accuracy. Some bowlers habitually do this; others hurry their approach and delivery when their game is going poorly. The correction for this is to slow the approach deliberately, concentrating on making the approach slower than what seems to be normal speed. The purpose of the approach is mainly to help the bowler stay in balance while smoothly accelerating during his arm swing.

Some bowlers, during the entire forward arm swing, exert muscular effort in order to increase the speed with which the ball is delivered. The correction for this is to let gravity pull the ball downward and to let inertia continue its path forward, thus making little conscious muscular effort. Any unusual efforts can interfere with the accuracy of the ball; the hooking action of the hook ball can also be adversely affected by such an effort. Many bowling authorities believe that a ball delivered with too much speed does not allow the pins sufficient time to fall sideward and present a broad face to the other pins. This decreases the possibility of these pins knocking over the standing pins that are not taken out by the ball.

Poor Timing of Approach and Ball Delivery

Several reasons exist as to why the approach is not coordinated correctly with the ball delivery. The usual reasons are that the approach is too fast or else that the pushaway of the ball was started too late. For most bowlers the usual correction for this fault is to start the pushaway before the first step is taken. Some bowlers find that they have to start the pushaway and let the ball actually start dropping downward, with the bowling arm completely extended, before the first step is taken. The recommended correction, however, is to concentrate on taking slow, short steps.

Roundhousing or Sidearming the Ball

When the ball is roundhoused or sidearmed the bowler may have completed his last step and slide while the ball is still in the backswing or is just starting the downswing. Because the bowler's timing and momentum have been lost, he often roundhouses or sidearms the ball in trying to hurry it or to apply extra speed to it. If the ball remains centered on the middle of the body during the pushaway, the plane of movement of the pendulum swing may be to the left or right of the target, causing the bowler to sidearm the ball in an attempt to correct its alignment with the target. One correction is to start the pushaway sooner, the first step later, and to take slower steps. Another correction is to so push the ball forward that it is directly in front of the right shoulder on the pushaway.

Dropping the Bowling Shoulder

Dropping the bowling shoulder during the delivery often occurs because of poor timing or because the pushaway of the ball is not sufficient to cause the bowling arm to be completely extended before the ball is dropped (causing the weight of the ball to be suddenly taken up by the bowling arm). The bowler should take care that he is extending the bowling arm all the way forward during the pushaway.

Stepping or Sliding over the Foul Line

The bowler who fouls probably is not beginning his approach a sufficient distance behind the foul line. Tripping or stumbling can be caused by a dirty approach surface or dirty shoe soles. Both should be checked and wiped clean if needed. In addition, the bowler should take some practice approaches to accustom himself to the approach (and lane) conditions before actually delivering the ball. He should develop the habit of completing his approach a few inches behind the foul line in order to allow for a margin of error during the delivery.

Delivering a Back-up Ball

A straight-ball bowler may inadvertently rotate his forearm during the backswing. The correcting clockwise forearm rotation on the forward swing causes the ball to back up. The bowler should concentrate on keeping his thumb consistently at twelve o'clock and his fingers directly underneath throughout the delivery. If this difficulty persists, an instructor or classmate can stop and hold the ball in position at the end of the backswing in order to check the thumb position. The bowler will need to become sensitive to the feel of where his thumb is positioned throughout the delivery.

Bowler Being Off-balance During the Release

Several different factors can be responsible for the bowler being off-balance when releasing the ball. An off-balance position is indicated if the right-handed bowler has to move his rear leg far to the left (or right) after releasing the ball. Faulty timing in the delivery can be a cause; slowing the approach and speed of delivery is often the remedy. If a crooked approach is made toward the foul line, this can throw the player off balance. One way of correcting this is to focus the vision on the finish spot behind the foul line for the first couple of steps and then shift the vision to the point of aim.

Delivering the Ball to the Right or Left of the Intended Target

During his approach, the right-handed bowler may have traveled to the right or left of the line to the target, or his pendulum swing may have been off the target line. This fault can have many causes. A right-handed bowler using a ball with finger holes that are too loose may drop the ball early on the release because of an insecure grip. If the ball travels to the left of the target, the hook-ball bowler, instead of lifting his hand on the release, may push the ball to the left with his hand and fingers and thus miss the target to the left. Instead, the bowler should concentrate on lifting upward when releasing the ball. If the finger holes are too tight, the bowler may not be able to release his fingers as soon as intended, causing the ball to travel to the left of the intended target. The solution here is to use a ball with finger holes of the proper span and diameter for the bowler's thumb and fingers.

Zigzag Approach

An approach in which the bowler steps to the left and/or right of the line to the target often goes unnoticed; it is frequently caused by a failure to concentrate on making a straight approach. With an observer present, or while watching a crack between the boards on the approach, the bowler should practice his approaches until he is able on any step to detect a deviation to the left or right.

Missing the Point of Aim

Several reasons why the point of aim might be missed, and their corrections, have been cited in the previous sections. The first check point to note is whether the usual starting or finish positions are assumed with each delivery. The idea is to develop and maintain an unchanging approach and delivery. If these positions remain constant, a zigzag approach is sometimes the cause of missing the target area. At times, a lack of intense concentration is the cause.

Obtaining Varied Amounts of Hook on the Ball

At times the hook-ball bowler finds that he obtains varying amounts of hook on the ball when rolling it on the same lane. A common cause for this is sometimes forcefully lifting the bowling hand during the release and failing to lift the hand at other times. This results in different amounts of finger lift being placed to the side of the ball, which determines how much the ball will hook. Another reason for varying amounts of hook may be the ball being carried with different hand positions. The bowler should ensure that the V formed by his hand and forefinger points directly toward the target, and that his thumb remains in the same position (unless a forced hook by means of forearm rotation is utilized) throughout the delivery (usually a nine or ten o'clock position). When releasing the ball, variance in the hooking action will occur if the fingers push to the left rather than remain in place or lift directly upward. It is normal to obtain different degrees of hooks on the same lane when different angles are rolled. A right-handed bowler rolling a ball from left to right will get significantly less hook than when rolling from right to left. As noted previously, the same delivery and hooking action will often produce varying degrees of hooking action on two different lanes.

ADVANCED SKILLS OF BOWLING

Adjusting for Alley Conditions

To be successful, the hook-ball bowler needs to develop the ability to determine rapidly how much the hooking action on the ball is affected by the conditions of the lane. Naturally, he also needs to learn how to adjust for these various lane conditions. The recommended method of making these adjustments is to adjust the point of aim. The start and finish of the approach remain the same, but the target (the alley dots, the range finder, arrows, or the pins) must be shifted slightly until the correct point of aim is found. Instead of changing the point of aim, some bowlers change their starting and finishing position on the approach (roll a different line). One method that is not recommended, but which some bowlers attempt, is to vary the speed of the ball delivery in order to adjust for lane conditions when using the hook ball. This technique is the antithesis of maintaining consistency—the key to good bowling.

Different Kinds of Hook-ball Deliveries

The method previously described for hooking the ball produces a natural hook delivery. Advanced bowlers who bowl frequently employ other methods. The tournament bowlers of today seem to favor a minimal hook rather than try for a maximal hook, which was in vogue at one time. The theory of the minimal hook is that it can be controlled readily, it gives a consistent action from lane to lane, it is reliable for picking up spares, and it does not often leave the 10 pin standing on first-ball hits.

One method of hooking the ball is to rotate the forearm counterclockwise as the ball is being released. This means that the bowler is apt to either hold the ball with the thumb in a twelve to two o'clock position, or else rotate his forearm clockwise on the backswing and counterclockwise on the forward swing.

Another method of placing increased hooking action on the ball is to increase the amount of lift, perhaps combining this with a counterclockwise rotation of the forearm during the last phase of the delivery. Although these hooking methods are successful for the bowler who bowls several lines almost daily, the average bowler is apt to find that they result in too inconsistent a delivery.

Some bowlers wear a special bowling glove in order to increase or better control the amount of hook placed on the ball. Many bowling authorities believe that the average bowler will not be helped by a special glove, a semi- or finger-tip ball, or a ball with a built-in hook. Some bowlers, after passing the novice stage, may want to experiment with such devices, however.

SELF-EVALUATION

The ease with which bowling can be scored, the scores recorded, and averages calculated, makes evaluating one's progress in bowling a fairly simple matter. The bowling averages of various groups of male college bowlers have been reported. Depending on the amount of class instruction and their backgrounds in bowling, beginning bowlers usually have an average score of 100 to 115. Those enrolled in advanced bowling class typically have a minimum score of around 125, whereas the mean average score is apt to be 140 to 145.

First-ball Score

Until one becomes fairly proficient in bowling, an excellent method of evaluating progress and accuracy is to record first-ball scores; that is, the number of pins knocked down by the first ball in each of the ten frames. This indicates how accurately the first ball is being delivered and is much less subject to chance or luck than is a regular bowling score. A first-ball game score of 70 is fair, 80 is good, and 90 is excellent.

Running Averages

When bowling on a team or in a league, running averages are usually kept for all team members. This is the mean score, which is computed by summing the scores achieved for all games bowled to date for the season and dividing this total by the number of games bowled. A comparison of weekly running averages easily enables the bowler to see if his average is going up, remaining constant, or declining. The more games bowled, the less impact any one game score will have on the running average. For this reason a three- or five-game moving average can be kept, which better reflects daily or weekly fluctuations in bowling skill. To compute a three-game moving average, the bowler finds the mean for the first three games bowled and plots it on a chart. When game number 4 is bowled, the score for games 2, 3, and 4 are totaled, divided by 3 and charted for game 3. Thus, with each new game bowled the third-to-the-last game score is dropped and the most recent game score is added to the other two game scores in computing the moving average. Maintaining a plot or graph of a three- or five-game moving average yields an accurate indication of one's bowling progress.

Other devices that can be used for self-evaluation are class tournament results, class comparison with bowling averages, and written-test scores. Written tests are valuable in assessing the student's understanding of what to do when bowling and how to make basic corrections.

Glossary of Terms

ABC: American Bowling Congress, the governing body for most organized bowling in the United States.
Anchor: The player who bowls last on a bowling team.
Approach: The area between the beginning of the lane and the foul line on which the delivery is made, which is sometimes called the runway. The approach also refers to the footwork and style used when delivering the bowling ball.
Baby split: A split in which only the 2 and 7 pins or the 3 and 10 pins remain standing.

Back-up ball: A ball that curves toward the side of the bowler's body from which it was delivered—a back-up ball curves to the right when delivered by a right-handed bowler.

Ball rack: The rack on the side of the lane approach to which the bowling balls are returned from the pit and where bowling balls are stored between turns.

Bed posts: A split in which only the 7 and 10 pins remain standing. This is sometimes called goal posts or 7–10 railroad.

Big four: A split in which the 4, 6, 7, and 10 pins remain standing.

Blow: A failure to knock down the remaining pins with the second ball when there is no split. This is sometimes called an error.

Brooklyn: Hitting the side of the head pin opposite the side of the body from which the ball is delivered. This is often called a crossover.

Cherry: Knocking down the front pin or pins on a spare setup, but leaving the back pin or pins standing. This is sometimes called a chop.

Count: The number of pins knocked down by the first ball delivered after a spare has been made.

Curveball: For a right-handed bowler a ball that travels toward the right edge of the alley and then curves or breaks in toward the center of the alley.

Dead ball: An ineffective ball that does not mix the pins.

Division boards: That area on the alley where the light and dark colored boards intersect, approximately twenty feet in front of the foul line.

Double: Two successive strikes in a game.

Fast lane: A highly polished lane bed that resists the hooking action of the ball. This is sometimes called a slow or holding lane.

Foul: A rule infraction for which the bowler is penalized by the loss of the pins knocked down on that roll.

Frame: A tenth part of the game as indicated by each of the ten large squares on the score sheets.

Full, or square, hit: A ball that strikes a target pin on its center.

Gutter: A hollow trough on either side of the lane bed that catches the ball if it rolls off the side. The modern term is channel.

Head pin: The number 1 pin.

High hit: A strike ball that comes into the pins on the headpin side of the 1–3 pocket.

Inning: Each bowler's turn during the game. Usually called a frame.

King pin: The number 5 pin; sometimes the head pin is referred to as the king pin.

Lane: That portion of the alley between the foul line and the pit. Another name for the alley bed, which is often referred to as the alley.

Leave: The pin or pins that remain standing after the first ball is scored.

Light hit: Hitting the target pin low or thin.

Line: A game of bowling, which consists of ten frames.

Lofting: Releasing the ball above the alley bed; thus, throwing it some distance beyond the foul line during the delivery.

Mark: To make a strike or spare.

Open frame: A frame without a mark after both balls have been delivered.

Pit: The space behind the lane bed into which the pins fall after being struck by the ball.

Pocket: The space between any two pins. The usual pockets referred to are the 1–3 or 1–2 pockets.

Runway: The space between the front of the lane and the foul line, in which the delivery is made. Also called the approach.

Sleeper: A pin directly behind another pin that is not readily seen from the approach.

Slow lane: A lane on which the ball readily hooks (in some locations it has the opposite meaning). A running alley.

Spare: Knocking down all the remaining pins with the second ball of a frame.

Split: This occurs when two or more pins remain standing after the first ball has been delivered; the number 1 pin and at least one pin is down between or ahead of the remaining pins.

Spot: A mark or location on the lane at which the bowler aims during the delivery.

Striking out: Getting three strikes in the last frame.

Turkey: Making three successive strikes during the game.

Working ball: A ball with lots of spin that mixes the pins around when it strikes them, causing a large number of pins to fall.

Selected References

BOOKS

American Bowling Congress Rule Book, latest ed.
   The latest official rules for bowling are contained in this publication.

Bellisimo, Lou. *The Bowler's Manual.* Englewood Cliffs, N.J.: Prentice-Hall, 1965.
   A recognized bowling authority and master bowler presents his views concerning how to improve one's bowling. The discussion of bowling techniques is thorough and interesting.

Casady, Donald R., and Marie Liba. *Beginning Bowling.* (Wadsworth Sports Skills Series). Belmont, Calif.: Wadsworth, 1968.
   This booklet, the first of the series to be written for college students, covers the important concepts of bowling and cites relevant research findings to support various recommended bowling techniques.

Kidwell, Kathro, and Paul Smith, Jr. *Bowling Analyzed.* Dubuque, Iowa: Brown, 1960.
   This excellent book gives especially useful information concerning spot bowling; analysis of errors; hook, curve, and back-up balls; and lead-up games to bowling.

Mackey, Richard T. *Bowling*. Palo Alto, Calif.: National Press Books, 1967.

The book is outstanding for its illustrations and photographs. The section on bowling in competition is excellent.

Schunk, Carol. *Bowling*. (Saunders Physical Activities Series). Philadelphia: Saunders, 1970.

This booklet, which is profusely illustrated, covers all the important phases of bowling. The chapters on scoring and handicaps, bowling organizations, and tournaments and games are quite informative.

PERIODICALS

Bowling (American Bowling Congress). Mount Norris, Ill.: Kable Printing Company.

Issued monthly, this magazine presents the current happenings in bowling in America.

CHAPTER **10**

Casting and angling
E. A. Scholer*
University of New Mexico

HISTORY

The origins of fishing are lost in antiquity; however, it is generally accepted that since earliest times man has fished for food. Early fishermen, in all probability, caught their fish by hand. According to Menke[1] the spearman might well be considered the first true fisherman. The practice of fishing with a hook and line probably originated much later with the ancient Egyptians, for it is known that these people used a crude line of woven animal hair and a sharpened bone for a hook. They also used poles to extend their reach and to provide additional leverage for landing the fish.

Fishing historians accept a funeral epigram of Sappho's (written about 600 B.C.) as the key to early writing on fishing.[2] The best surviving Greek work on fishing is Oppian's *Halleutica* (written in A.D. 169), a hexameter poem in five books. Oppian classified four methods of fishing: hook and line, net, weels, and tridents. He further distinguished between fishing with a rod and fishing with hand lines. The literature of the ancient Greeks contains many additional references to fishing and, in particular, refers to the person fishing as an angler, not as a fisherman. In the Odyssey, Scylla comments, "As when an angler on a jutting rock sits with his tapered rod and casts his bait."[3]

Figure 10-1. A young angler.

During this same period of history, Aellan, an Italian (A.D. 170-230), is credited by Menke[4] with writing for the first time about fly casting; however, Radcliffe, in his book, *Fishing From the Earliest Times*, gives this credit to Martial, a Roman author (A.D. 10-20), who wrote, "who has not seen the scarus rise, decoyed and killed by fraudful flies."[5]

The reel, according to fishing historians, was introduced in the fifteenth century, but there is no agreement as to when or where it was introduced. The earliest English

---

*Dr. Scholer, an avid fishing enthusiast for most of his life, is the coordinator of the recreation program, Department of Health, Physical Education, and Recreation at the University of New Mexico, Albuquerque. He was the chairman of the Recreation Leadership Program at The University of Iowa for nine years. He has worked with tackle manufacturers in promoting casting and angling in schools and colleges, is a field tester for the Shakespeare Tackle Company, and is a member of the Outdoor Writers of America Association and the Outdoor Education and Camping Council.

[1] Frank G. Menke. *The Encyclopedia of Sports* (New York: A. S. Barnes, 1947), p. 17.
[2] John McDonald. *Origins of Angling* (Garden City, N.Y.: Doubleday, 1963), p. 273.
[3] Henry Marion Hall. *Idylls of Fishermen* (New York: Columbia U. P., 1914), p. 5.
[4] Menke, loc. cit.
[5] William Radcliffe, *Fishing From Earliest Times*, 2nd ed., London: J. Murray, p. 45.

116 *Individual and Team Sports*

description of the reel appears in *The Art of Angling*, by T. Barker in 1651. However, Dr. John T. Bonner, Chairman of the Department of Biology at Princeton University, refutes this accepted introduction of the reel with evidence of the use of the reel by the Chinese in the thirteenth century or earlier. Bonner refers to a painting by the celebrated Chinese artist, Ma Yaun, known to have painted in the period of A.D. 1190-1230, which depicts a fisherman using what clearly resembles a reel.[6]

The first writing in English on the subject of fishing was printed in the second book of St. Albans in A.D. 1496. The person purported to be the author of this work, "The Treatise of Fishing with an Angle," was Dame Julianna Berners who, according to legend, was a nun and an avid sportswoman in the fifteenth century. This treatise was a manual containing ideas and deportment as well as of the techniques of fishing. It taught a type of life in fishing in which the concept of chivalry was transformed into a code of good and quiet manners. The treatise mentions other "books of credence," which would suggest earlier writings that are now lost.

"The Treatise of Fishing" has no known antecedents in history and indicates for the first time a distinctive sporting attitude toward fishing. Furthermore, the publication serves as the beginning source of reference for the origin of modern angling.[7] Of particular interest to anglers of today are the regulations quoted in the "Treatise," which are similar to contemporary ones: seek permission, be careful of property, shut gates, don't take more fish than you can use, and, finally, practice conservation.

In the second book on angling, *Arts of Angling*, author unknown, the sport of angling is treated as an art and a science.[8] In 1590, Leonard Mascall wrote *A Book of Fishing with Hooke and Line*, and this publication, even today, is held in high esteem in the field of fish conservation.

The Art of Angling (1651) followed John Denney's *Secrets of Angling* (1613). Izaak Walton, the author of *The Compleat Angler* (1653), is considered to be the father, or patron saint, of anglers. With the publication of his book, angling gained acceptance as a sport. During Walton's lifetime five editions were published, and since that time there have been another forty editions. Walton borrowed freely from *The Art of Angling* but failed to credit the author in any manner. He was the first person to write of a reel and to invent new trout flies to add to the twelve described in "The Treatise."

As a result of the popularity of Walton's book, many angling clubs were formed in England; however, this type of fishing body did not gain popularity in America until 1732, when the Schuykill Fishing Company was founded in Philadelphia.

The Colonist brought the sport of angling to the United States in the eighteenth century, and during the years adapted fishing tackle and skills to the new country. In the late 1700s, settlers in Kentucky developed a new method of fishing for the popular black bass. They cast with a cane pole playing the line out from loops held in the hand. It was from this type of angling that George Snyder saw the need for a simpler device, and in the early nineteenth century he developed the forerunner of the modern casting reel.

Current Status

Today the opportunities for fishing are greater than at any time in the past. With the increase of leisure and the technical skill in the manufacture of fishing tackle, far more people can now enjoy the sport than ever before.

According to the *National Survey of Fishing and Hunting*, as conducted by the Bureau of Sports, Fisheries, and Wildlife, Fish and Wildlife Service, United States Department of the Interior, in 1970, over 29,363,000 fresh water fishermen spent approximately $3,734,178,000 or $127 per person over a period of 592,494,000 man days in pursuit of the wily fish. Their counterpart, the salt water fisherman, of which there were 5,010,000, spent approximately $636,380,000 or $129 per person for a period of 61,032,000 man days.[9]

The Federal government estimates that approximately 20,358,000 fishermen in the United States are licensed while 2,800,000 are not and of the combination of these figures, 5,345,000 are young sportsmen in the age bracket of 9, 10, and 11 years. This composite group of fishermen spent approximately $5,000,000,000 in 1970.[10] The Sport Fishing Institute estimates, however, that there are over 60,000,000 fishermen in the United States and the American Tackle Manufacturers Association claims that fishing is the number one participant sport in the nation today.

Purposes of Casting and Angling

With increased leisure in today's society, the necessity of learning activities of the "carry-over variety" is essential. One of the cardinal principles that has long been accepted

---

[6] "Fishing Reel Depicted in Chinese Art of 13th Century," *The Izaak Walton Outdoor American*, Glenview, Ill.: Izaak Walton League of America (July 1967), p. 6.
[7] McDonald, loc. cit.
[8] Ibid.

[9] *1970 National Survey of Fishing and Hunting*. Washington, D.C. Supt. of Documents, U.S. Printing Office, pp. 9, 10.
[10] Ibid. pp. 26, 32.

by educators is of increased importance today. Casting and angling are ideal carry-over activities that can bring satisfaction to people of all ages and interests. Casting and angling can instill lifelong ideals of sportsmanship and conservation in the participant. Here, too, is an activity in which the mentally or physically handicapped person can participate freely, an activity that will afford him a rewarding and enriching outdoor experience.

The person who regularly participates in angling and casting should (1) have his interests in the out-of-doors stimulated, (2) be encouraged in the wise use of our natural resources through intelligent conservation practices, (3) live a life of increased health because of the acquisition of skills and interests adaptable for continued participation, (4) enhance his mental and physical fitness through participation, and (5) acquire a knowledge of the safe use and maintenance of casting and angling equipment.

BASIC METHODS OF SPORT FISHING

Regardless of innovations and changes through the years, only three basic types of fishing exist.

Still Fishing

The simplest form of fishing, and thus quite often the initial type of fishing experience, is still fishing. The basic equipment required is a rod, a length of line, a float or bobber, a hook, and—depending on the depth of the water—a weight. A natural bait normally is impaled on the hook and lies static beneath the surface of the water until a fish strikes.

Trolling

In trolling, the bait—natural or artificial—is drawn through the water by a slow moving boat. When a fish strikes the bait, the motor is stopped until action ceases. Trolling is practiced in salt water and on lakes or rivers of sufficient depth and width to allow the lure unobstructed passage.

Casting

The art of casting is to employ the action of the rod in such a manner as to "throw" an artificial lure or live bait over the water and then so retrieve it that the lure imitates the action of live and natural bait. The principal casting techniques are bait, spin, and fly casting for all manner of freshwater and salt water fish. Ocean fishing, although it utilizes similar equipment, is termed *surf casting*.

Because of the fun and increased sport when catching a fish by casting, it is by far the most widely employed method of fishing today. The angler is able to place his lure in strategic "hot" spots unavailable when still fishing or trolling and, because of the ability to place the lure, his opportunity to hook a trophy catch is considerably improved.

Because of the importance of casting, the succeeding sections will cover each of the four methods currently in vogue: bait casting, spinning (or push-button casting), and fly casting.

BAIT CASTING

Bait casting is considered by many experts to be the best all-weather method of casting because it is not handicapped by stormy or windy conditions and provides the greatest lure accuracy. The objective is to place the lure where desired without causing a backlash of the line.

Rods

The bait casting rod is five and one-half to six and one-half feet in length. It has considerable power and is still the favorite rod when fishing for large fish. Some bait-casting rods are in two pieces but the majority are in one piece with a detachable handle. The reel, a revolving spool type, is usually seated in an offset reel seat, which allows the caster to use his thumb naturally and without strain when it is necessary to thumb the spool.

Figure 10-2. Bait casting. (Courtesy of Shakespeare Company)

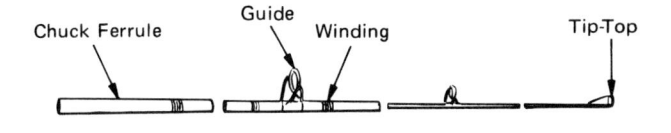

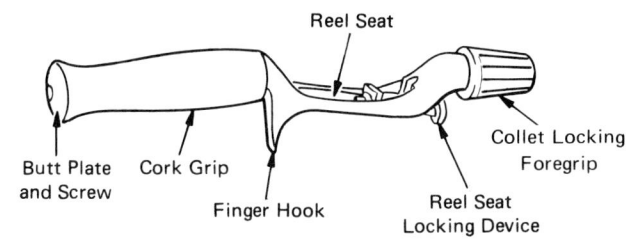

Figure 10-3. Bait-casting rod. (Drawing—Courtesy of Shakespeare Company)

Reels

A standard level-winding bait-casting reel is one of the most commonly used reels currently in use. The bait-casting reel operates with spiral gears, usually on a 4-to-1 ratio (four turns of the spool for each turn of the handle). The reel should include a free spool, a device that disengages the spool to revolve and the level winder to operate without the reel handle or related gears moving. This device also allows for smoother and longer casts and provides the caster with the ability to use a wide range of lures. Many reels include an antibacklash device; however, it is recommended that a beginner learn to cast without such a device in order that he learn to control the revolutions of the spool on a cast and thus prevent the tangle in the line (backlash). Regardless of the antibacklash device, the thumb control (or "educated thumb") is essential in adjusting for the force of the cast and to place the lure on the target. Many reels have a metal, cord, or plastic arbor, which is placed over the spool to permit it to be filled without using excess amounts of line.

Line

The lines for bait casting can either be braided nylon or monofilament; however, the latter should be used only on those reels (monoreels) designed especially for its use. The standard method of classifying line is to refer to the pound test of the line. This refers to the dead weight a line or leader will support without breaking. Pound test should be in relation to the rod action and the weight of the lures used.

Bait-casting Techniques

When practicing casting, tournament or practice plugs—three-eighths to five-eighths of an ounce—should be utilized, as they have no hooks that can cause injury.

The Overhead Cast. The principal cast to master is the overhead cast, which is used more than 90 per cent of the time because it is safer, easier, and more accurate than other types. When preparing to do an overhead cast, stand in a comfortable position, facing the target with the right foot slightly forward. Grasp the rod in a natural manner, reel handles up, palm down, thumb on spool, and elbow close to the body. Allow the lure to dangle about two to six inches below the rod tip. Begin the cast with the rod pointing at the target at approximately the two o'clock position. Quickly bring the rod back, always in vertical plane, with a snappy wrist action until the tip approaches a perpendicular twelve o'clock position. Stop the rod abruptly as it reaches this point so that the weight and momentum of the plug will bow it to the rear and then immediately begin the forward cast. This should be twice as fast as the back cast, and it should be performed in one continuous motion. Keep a light thumb pressure on the spool throughout the cast, but when the cast approaches the ten o'clock position, release the thumb tension. When the plug reaches the target, reapply sufficient thumb pressure to stop the spool completely. This will aid in removing the slack from the line and allow the lure to drop easily.

After casting, cup the reel in the left hand with the thumb on the spooled line. In this manner, the thumb is always ready to aid in "setting the hook" and to control the run of the fish. The thumb thus serves as a brake and can supplement the "brake" or star drag on the reel, which in turn can be set to a lighter pressure.

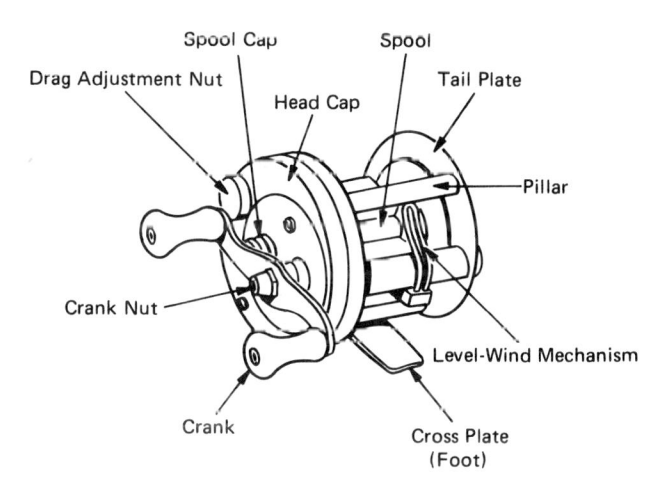

Figure 10-4. Bait-casting reel. (Drawing—Courtesy of Shakespeare Company)

Casting and Angling 119

Figure 10-5. Bait-casting techniques. (Drawing—Courtesy of Shakespeare Company)

SPINNING

Spinning (casting with a stationary spool reel) has been in vogue in Europe for many years, but it did not become popular in the United States until after World War II. Spinning as a fishing technique is believed to have originated in France, but the word itself was coined in the United States when this method of casting was introduced. Since then it has achieved tremendous popularity, as it allows for ease of casting with minimal backlash, even with light artificial lures and live bait—which is a decided advantage for the neophyte caster.

Rod

A spinning rod six to seven feet in length is the most popular length of rod with the spinning fisherman. The rods are primarily made of tubular glass fiber. The line guides on the spinning rod are quite different from those on the bait or fly rod because they are extra large and resemble an elongated cone when one sights through them from the butt of the rod. Two principal types of reel seats are used on the spinning rod. The simplest is nothing more than two sliding metal rings, or winch bands, that are forced over the reel foot, holding the reel in place on the handle. Another type has a fixed reel seat that encompasses a locking system to assure nonmovement of the reel.

Reel

There are two types of reels, the open-face spool and the closed-face spool. With the open-face reel the line is wound back onto the spool by a full bail, a revolving finger, or a manual roller. In contrast, the line pickup on the closed-face reel is accomplished by a pin or lug, which in turn engages the line inside the reel housing. The spool on which the line is coiled has no cover on the

Figure 10-6. Spinning. (Courtesy of U.S. Forest Service)

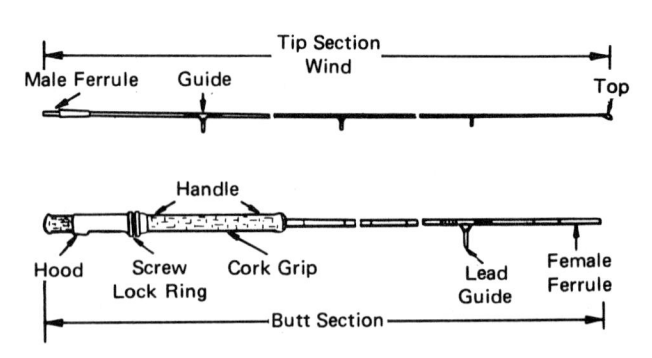

Figure 10-7. Spinning rod. (Drawing—Courtesy of Shakespeare Company)

120　*Individual and Team Sports*

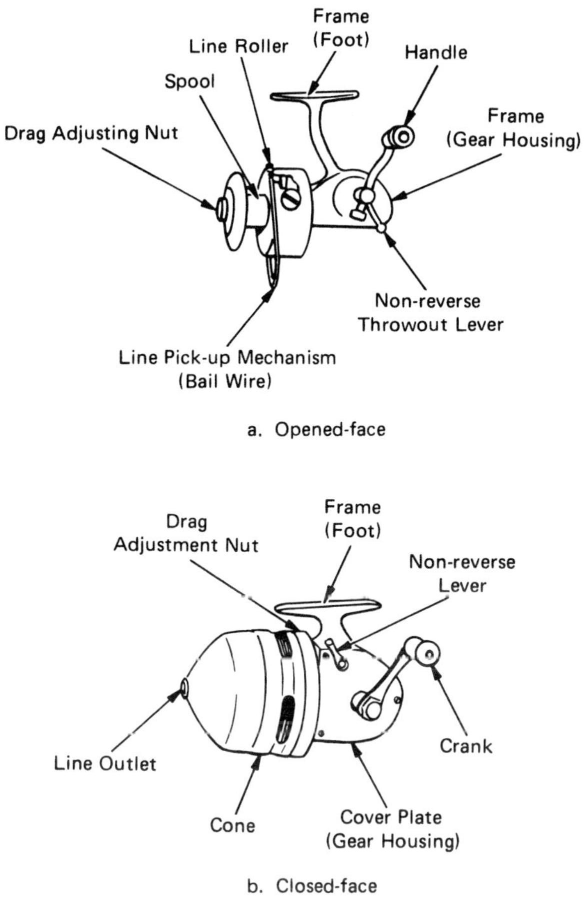

Figure 10-8. Spinning reels. (Drawing—Courtesy of Shakespeare Company)

open-face reel, whereas the closed-face reel has a (housing) cover that protects the spool and line. The closed-face reel has a hole directly in the front of the spool shaft axis; this allows the line to move freely during the cast.

Line

The spinning outfit utilizes monofilament line. The test poundage of the line should be in direct relationship to the weight and stiffness of the rod selected and the type of fishing proposed. A line of from six to ten pound test is considered the most practical for beginning fishermen and use in casting classes.

The Overhead Cast. The overhead cast, which is similar to the overhead bait cast, is by far the most popular and allows for greater accuracy at longer distances then other types. When casting with an open-face spinning outfit, face the target and stand relaxed with the weight on the forward foot. Grasp the rod loosely. Set the antireverse lever in the off position and leave two to six inches of line from rod tip to lure. With the index finger, pick up the line, open the bail, and pinch the line gently against the rod handle. See Figures 10-9 (*a*) and (*b*). Begin the cast with rod sighted in on the target and slightly above it and holding the line relaxed with the index finger. See Figure 10-9 (*c*). Lift the rod in a single easy motion, cocking the wrist back at the same time until the rod reaches the twelve o'clock position. When the rod reaches the vertical position, the momentum of the back cast will force it to bend backward. As the rod reaches its maximum flexion, using the wrist only, drive the rod forward, keeping the elbow close to the side. When the rod reaches the original position on the cast (approximately two o'clock), release the line by simply straightening the index finger. Be certain to follow through by pointing the rod directly toward the target as the line spins out from the reel. The caster can control the line in flight by placing the index finger on the edge of the spool, by trapping the line with the forefinger (Figure 10-9[*d*]), or by turning the reel handle to close the bail for retrieving. If the lure shoots high into the air, the line has been released too soon.

Although the overhead cast is the one most commonly employed, others such as the side or bow and arrow can be practiced by the caster (when learning accuracy is more important than distance). Therefore, it is best to perfect one type of cast and as skill increases the others will develop naturally.

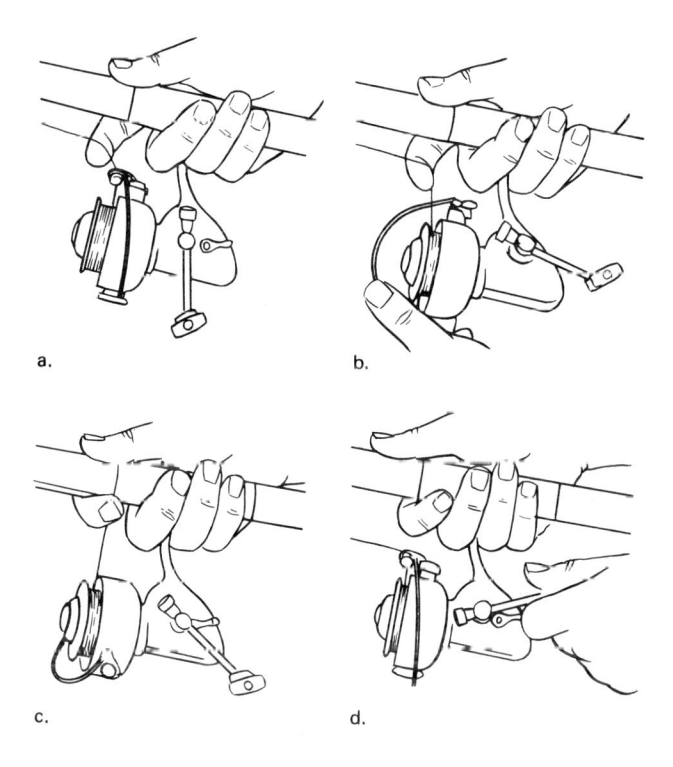

Figure 10-9. Overhead or overhand cast. (Drawing—Courtesy of Shakespeare Company)

Casting and Angling **121**

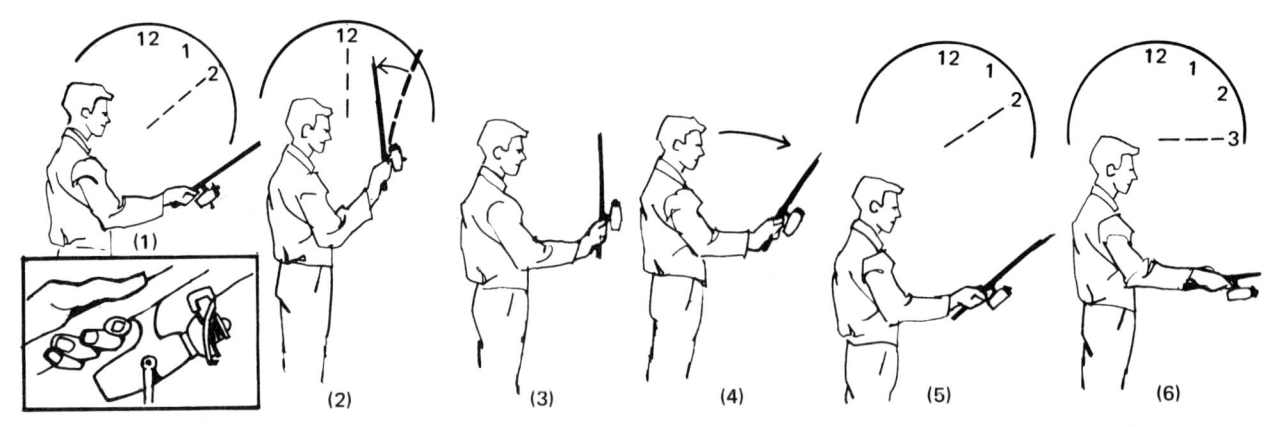

Figure 10-10(a). Overhead cast with open-faced spinning reel. (Drawing—Courtesy of Shakespeare Company)

Figure 10-10(b). Side cast. (Drawing—Courtesy of Shakespeare Company)

Side Cast (Figure 10-10). As for the overhead cast, keep the upper arm close to the body and point the rod toward the target. Using the wrist and forearm, bring the rod sideways and downward. Utilizing the bend in the rod created by this sideward motion, bring the rod forward and slightly upward, releasing the line when the rod reaches a position at approximately a 45° angle over the target. Control the line and retrieve as with the overhead cast. The sideward cast, although not as accurate as the overhead cast, is particularly effective in brush country or on windy days.

Bow-and-arrow Cast (Figure 10-11). The rod produces the force for the bow-and-arrow cast. The length of line from the rod tip to the lure should be long enough for the hand to hold the lure easily. Grasp the lure with the free hand and bend the rod by drawing the lure backward. To keep the line from unwinding, hold the line against the rod with the forefinger. When the rod is aimed at the target, release the lure and line; the straightening of the rod will project the line and lure. This cast is effective when standing in overhanging brush as it allows the caster to make a fairly accurate and long cast when in a cramped area. However, care should be taken in using this cast.

Figure 10-11. Bow-and-arrow cast. (Drawing—Courtesy of Shakespeare Company)

122 *Individual and Team Sports*

Figure 10-12. Spin or push-button casting. (Courtesy of U.S. Forest Service)

SPIN OR PUSH-BUTTON CASTING

Spin casting, or push-button casting as it is also known, is by far the easiest method to learn and master. In essence, it is spinning with a modified rod. One decided advantage of spin casting is that a backlash is virtually impossible. It is also easy to make long casts with little practice.

Rods

Beginning fishermen often use a bait-casting rod with the push-button reel. A push-button rod, one that has been designed exclusively for "balance" with the new reels, is different from the typical bait-casting rod in that it is longer (averaging from six to seven feet, which allows for lighter action and the use of lighter lures or live baits). It is two piece and the guides are usually the large spinning variety.

Reels

The push-button reel combines the best features of both the casting and spinning reel. The caster uses the thumb lever to release the line in order to make the cast. After the cast, the crank is turned to prevent additional line from being released and to begin the retrieve.

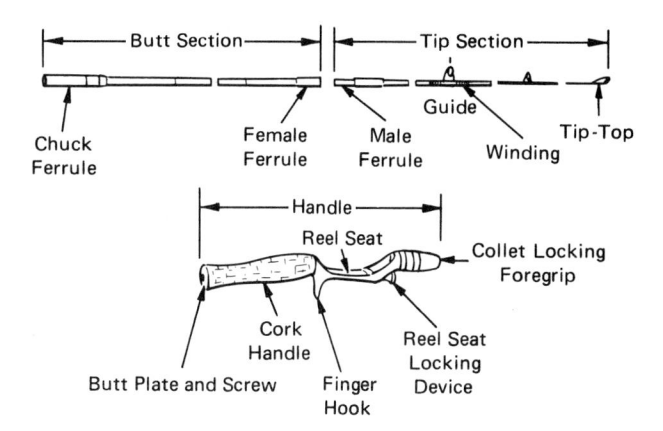

Figure 10-13. Push-button rod. (Drawing—Courtesy of Shakespeare Company)

Lines

As for the spinning outfit, all line should be of monofilament, as it has the advantage of being strong, wear resistant, and rot and mildew proof. The pound test, as with a spinning line, will be in direct relationship to the weight and stiffness of the rod selected, the type of lures used, and the type of fishing proposed.

Push-Button Casting Techniques

Push-button casting procedures are for the most part identical to those used in bait casting. The one principal exception is that the caster does not have to control a revolving spool. As for the overhead bait-casting technique, the lure dangles approximately two inches from the tip of the rod. Hold the rod in a natural position with the thumb on the push button and so rotate the wrist that the

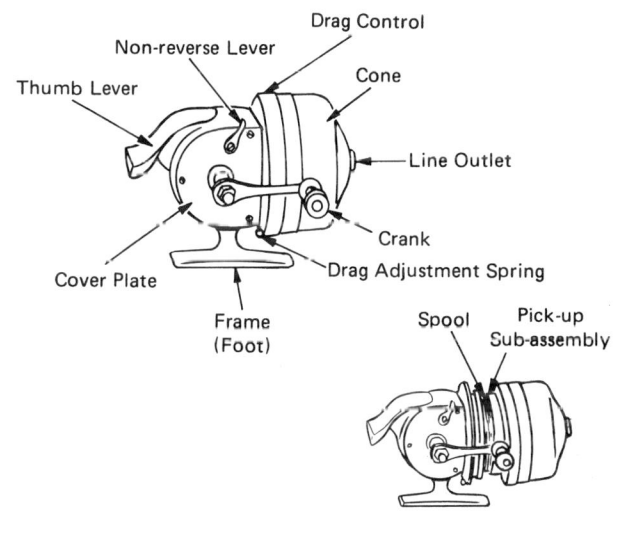

Figure 10-14. Push-button reel. (Drawing—Courtesy of Shakespeare Company)

Casting and Angling 123

crank handles are up. Depress the push button and hold it down firmly while aiming over the rod tip toward the target. Keep the elbow close to the body and bring the rod back to twelve o'clock with a motion of the forearm and wrist. Keep the arm close to the body and begin the forward motion twice as fast as the backward motion, utilizing a snap action. Be certain that the push button is still down. When the rod approaches the two o'clock position, release the thumb pressure on the push button. When the lure strikes the water, transfer the rod to the left hand (if right-handed), grasp the reel handle, and turn the crank to begin the retrieve. Always retrieve the line under tension through fingers.

As for all the previously mentioned casting techniques, it is the spring of the rod and not the movement of the caster's arm that projects the lure toward the target. "Let the rod do the work."

FLY FISHING

Fly fishing has long been considered the aristocrat of fishing techniques. Originally it was used only for taking salmon and trout; however, before long fishermen discovered that it was the most sporting way to take any fish that would strike an artificial lure.

In fly casting, it is important to remember that it is *not* the lure (fly) that is being cast but rather the *line*. The very weight of the line when it is cast behind the caster bends the rod and the power of the rod, as activated by the caster's forearm, thrusts the line forward, and in the process takes the leader and lure with it. The fly used in fly casting can be a lightweight insect or an artificial lure; if the latter, it can be classified as a dry fly, which floats on the surface, or a wet fly, which sinks beneath the surface of the water.

Figure 10-15. Fly fishing. (Courtesy of U.S. Forest Service)

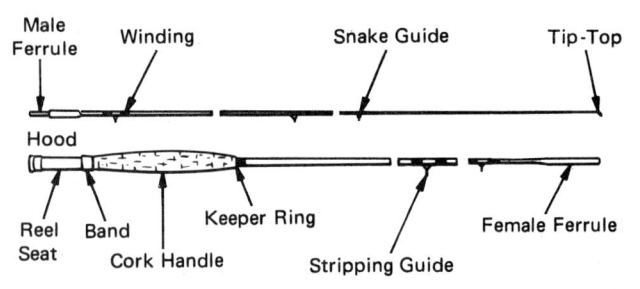

Figure 10-16. Fly rod. (Drawing—Courtesy of Shakespeare Company)

Rods

Because the line is cast rather then the lure, the selection of a rod for fly fishing is of the utmost importance. Modern fly rods are primarily of fiberglass and are light in weight, but the better ones retain the benefits of quality split bamboo rods, which are considered to be ideal by some fishermen.

The rod in fly casting is in essence a lever that is utilized to give momentum to the line. When cast, the weight of the line bends the rod and employs its flexibility. Fly rods are usually seven to nine feet in length and have a reel seat located below the hand grasp in order to enable the caster to strip the line from the reel with his free hand. The rod is usually composed of two sections and has a series of guides commencing with a stripping guide thirteen inches above the hand grasp on the butt section of the rod and ending with a loop guide at the rod tip or tip top. The average weight of a fly rod is from three to six ounces. For the beginning fly caster, a rod weighing four ounces or less is recommended.

Reels

The fly-casting reel is not used for casting; however, it is more than a mere line holder. There are two main types of fly reels: the single-action reel and the automatic reel.

The single-action reel is hand-operated. On most models one turn of the handle rotates the reel spool once. Thus, the single action is not a multiplier reel, as are the bait- and spin-casting reels.

The automatic fly reel is spring-operated. This results in the caster literally winding the spring as he strips the line from the reel. To retrieve the line, the caster merely depresses the brake lever and the spring activates the spool to take up the line.

Lines

Fly-fishing lines are of plastic coating over nylon core. The lines are of three basic types: level, double tapered, and weight forward or forward taper. Each is used for a specific purpose.

124 *Individual and Team Sports*

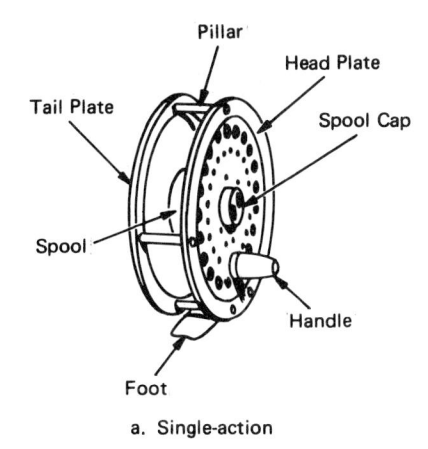

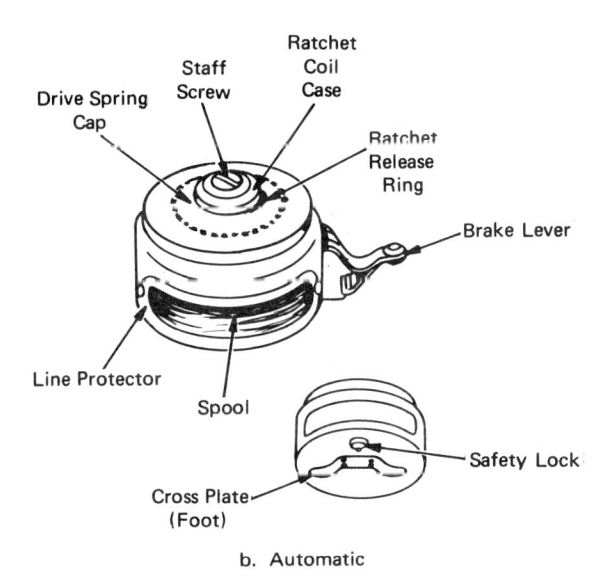

Figure 10-17. Fly reels. (Drawing—Courtesy of Shakespeare Company)

The level line (of the same diameter and weight throughout the line), is ideal for use by beginning fly casters as it is the least expensive, but more difficult to master. Weight forward is easiest to learn and master.

The double tapered line has a heavy, level center section that tapers toward both ends, with the result that the line provides exactly the same action and taper when reversed. The heavier center section provides the necessary weight for casting, whereas the tapered end allows for smaller knots on the end, better fly delivery, and lends itself to more varied casts.

The weight forward, or forward taper, has a short section of small diameter line, which leads quickly to a heavier line to provide the proper casting weight. This heavier dimension line is then reduced to approximately sixty feet of "running," or hand, line. This type of line is perhaps the best distance casting line. After the torpedo section is out of the rod guides it serves to carry the running line out. The weight-forward line has all the advantages of the double taper except that it cannot be reversed.

Balanced tackle is of importance in fly casting. The rod must be matched with a fly line of the proper weight. Because the weight of the fly line with rod action casts the fly, performance is best when the rod and line are balanced. The American line manufacturers and the National Association of Angling and Casting Clubs (now the American Casting Association, ACA) in cooperation with the International Federation of Casters worked two years preparing a set of universal fly-line standards.

These standards are based on the weight of the working part of the fly line (the front section). Exclusive of any tip on a taper, the first thirty feet of line are weighed.

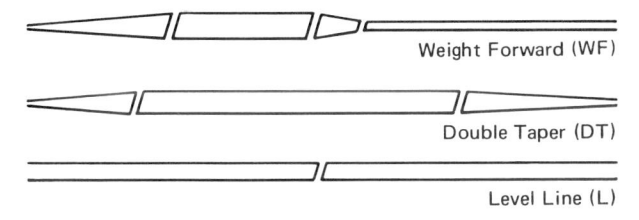

Figure 10-18. Different types of fly lines.

Leaders

In fly fishing the purpose of a leader is to reduce the visible connection between the fly and the line. The leader, being somewhat translucent, absorbs and reflects the color of the background. Standard leaders are of seven and one-half to twelve feet in length. It is important to keep the leader as light as the conditions warrant. The tapered leader is the most suitable for accurate and easy casting.

Fly-Casting Techniques

Fly casting requires more initial skill and concentration than do the other types of casting. However, practice should permit a mastery of these techniques.

Overhead Cast. The timing and rhythm of the fly cast are entirely different from that of spinning or bait casting. First, the fly caster stretches twenty-five to thirty feet of line out on the ground in front of him. He stands in a relaxed manner and faces the target. He firmly holds the rod handle, reel down, with his thumb either on top of the handle or along the side—whichever is most comfortable. For the right-handed caster, the left hand is termed the line hand, as it is used to hold the extra line in readiness for the forward cast or to collect the line for the retrieve. The slack in the line is taken up with the line

Casting and Angling

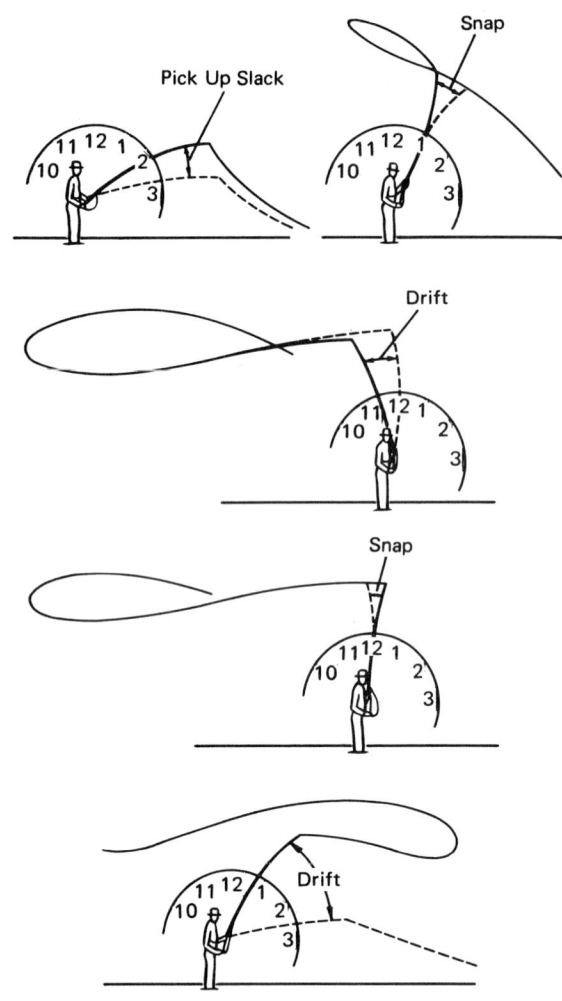

Figure 10-19. Overhead fly casting. (Drawing—Courtesy of Shakespeare Company)

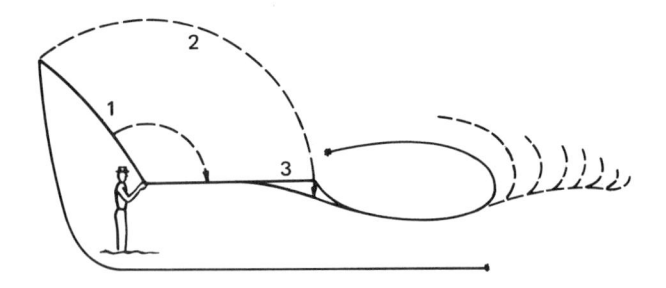

Figure 10-20. Making the roll cast.

hand and the cast is begun with the rod. With a sharp upward stroke with the forearm (wrist stiff), the caster should try to send the line high and behind him. The line should form a loop that quickly straightens out behind the caster. As with all overhead back casts, the rod is stopped at the twelve o'clock position. When the loop straightens out, the rod should drift slightly to the rear. A slight pull will be felt at the tip and on the line held in the left hand. At this time the forward cast should be started, and like the backward cast the loop should be allowed to straighten out in front. The forward motion of the rod should be halted at the two o'clock position. The slack line in the left hand is released and the rod is permitted to drift downward as the line shoots forward. When the lure touches the target, the slack is gathered with the left hand and preparations are made to repeat the cast.

It is most important that all phases of the cast, backward and forward, are so blended together as to constitute a continuous motion. Using a steady one, two, three, four count will aid in the development of the correct timing—one, take up the slack line; two, make the distinct upward and backward cast; three, allow the loop to straighten out behind; and four, begin the forward cast.

While casting on the water, the same procedure is followed, except that the backward and forward casts will be made in the air without allowing the line to touch the water. These are called false casts and are used to measure distance, to dry the fly, or to extend the line and hence give increased distance to the final casts.

The majority of beginning fly casters fail to bring their line and leader to the surface of the water before beginning the back cast. Lifting a sunken line overloads the rod and a clean, high backward cast is virtually impossible.

Roll Cast. The roll cast is an ideal way to pick up the line or to enable the caster to fish out the cast to a boat or bank. To do the roll cast, retrieve the line until the rod is overhead at approximately a one o'clock position, or a 45° degree angle, and the line droops beside the caster. (See Figure 10-20 [1].) Bring the rod over and down sharply, as if hammering a nail (Figure 10-20 [2]); the line should sail upward from behind and forward in a perfect loop. End the cast by lifting the rod tip (Figure 10-20 [3]) in order that the fly hits the water first.

The hand retrieve allows the caster positive control when a fish strikes, or allows for the pick up of the line for a new cast at any time. (See Figure 10-21.)

BALANCED FISHING TACKLE

The term *balanced tackle* indicates that the fishing rod, reel, line, and lure are matched to one another for maximum performance as a complete unit. The literature of the tackle manufacturers generally recommends the reel, test weight of line, and lure weight for the various rod models manufactured by them. The fisherman or sport caster who follows the recommendations of the tackle manufacturer can expect maximum results from his equipment.

Individual and Team Sports

Thumb and first finger grab

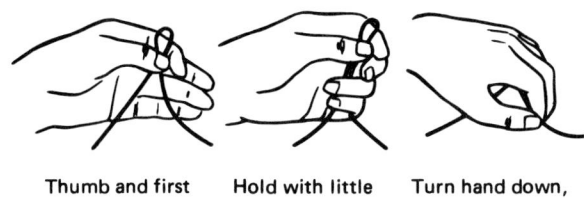

Hold with little finger plus index

Turn hand down, pick up next "bite"

Fold it in with the first loop

Repeat the process, gradually releasing the old loops

Figure 10-21. Easy-to-learn hand retrieve.

Knots

It is important that the caster know certain basic fishing knots. A knowledge of the correct knot to use when tying a fly to a leader, joining the line to a lure or hook, or tying one monofilament line to another can be the difference between a limit in the creel or no fish at all. The basic fishing knots are illustrated in Figure 10-22.

FISHING LAWS

Because the fishing laws, length of season, cost of license, and so on, vary from state to state, the casting and angling student is advised to obtain a current copy of the fishing laws of the state(s) in which he plans to fish.

ACA RULES GOVERNING CASTING EVENTS ACCURACY BAIT AND FLY RULES (ADAPTED FOR SCHOOL USE)[11]

Accuracy Bait

The rod, reel, and line are used unrestrictedly.

Bait. For use with level-wind type reels, either a three-eighths or a five-eighths of an ounce practice plug; for use with spinning rods and reels, a one-quarter ounce practice plug. In competition all casters should use the same type of equipment and the same size plugs.

Targets. There should be five targets scattered at random on the water or lawn, at distances unknown to the caster. The target nearest to the casting box should not be

[11] This material is published through the courtesy of Mr. Paul N. Jones, Executive Secretary of the American Casting Association, P.O. Box 51, Nashville, Tennessee 37202.

nearer than forty feet or farther than forty-five feet. The target farthest from the casting box (which is often the second target) should not be farther than eighty feet or nearer than seventy-five feet. The remaining three targets should be placed at irregular intervals in the intervening space. The targets should not be bunched or placed in line with one another. There can be one station for the five targets, five stations for five pairs of targets, or ten stations for ten targets.

Casting. (Single-handed). Ten casts, two at each target, are to be made in the order directed.

Method of Casting and Scoring. The plug must fall within or on the target, in order to be scored perfect. For each foot or fraction thereof that the plug falls without the target 1 demerit is scored. In case of a broken line, the cast will be scored where the plug falls, except that no cast is scored unless the plug falls in front of the casting box. A penalty of 1 demerit is scored for each false cast in excess of three, and such demerits are designated separately on the caster's score sheet. One hundred, a score of ten perfect casts, less the number of demerits, constitutes the score.

After a caster steps into the box, he is responsible for the result, and takes for his score whatever he makes. No fouls are allowed unless they are caused by outside interference. In no case is a caster given more than 10 demerits on any one cast.

A *false cast* refers to a caster making a cast in the general direction of the target when not casting for score, ostensibly to clear loose line from the reel. When false casting toward a target, the judge should be notified that such is the caster's intention.

The differences between this bait accuracy game and the Skish Bait Accuracy are in the scoring system and the number of casts required to complete the target course. The tackle used and target arrangement are the same in both games.

In the Skish Bait Accuracy, two casts are required to be made at each target, a total of twenty in all. The caster must build his score from zero, by credits of 6 points for each first cast striking in or on the target, and 4 points for each second cast hitting the target. Each cast that misses the target is scored zero. For a novice, a final score of 40 is creditable, 56 is very good, and anything above 66 is excellent.

In the ACA Accuracy Bait, only one cast is made at each target—ten casts complete the course. The caster begins with a theoretical score of 100, or perfect, and is demerited one point for each foot or fraction of a foot each target is missed, and the demerit count is entered on the score card at each target. A perfect cast, one that strikes in or on the target, is scored zero—that is, no demerits. When the caster has completed the ten targets, his demerits are totaled and deducted from 100, the result being

Casting and Angling 127

This knot is used primarily for securing a hook or a leader to a line at a point other than the very end.

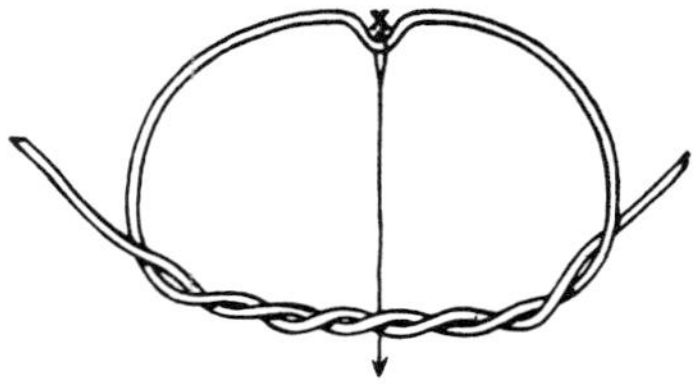

FIG. 1: Make a loop with 5 or 6 turns—at any desired point on your line, as shown.

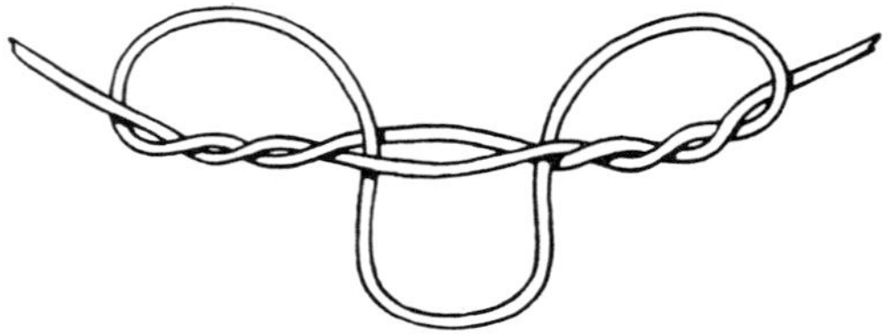

FIG. 2: Thrust center of loop down thru the turns and hold securely.

FIG. 3: Draw knot up while holding loop. Pull tight.

c. Blood Dropper Loop

This knot has proven to be the best for tying one monofilament line to another.

FIG. 1: Overlap the ends of your 2 strands that are to be joined and twist them together about 10 turns.

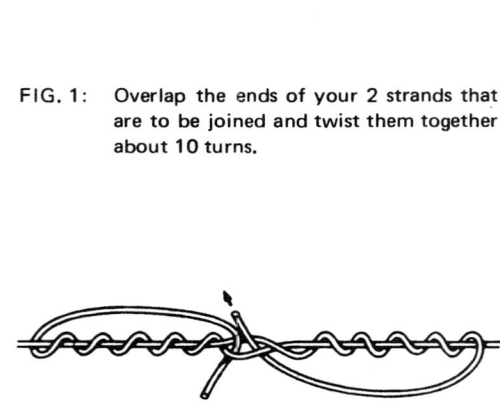

FIG. 2: Separate one of the center twists and thrust the two ends thru the space as illustrated.

FIG. 3: Pull knot together and trim off the short ends.

b. Improved Blood Knot

A very highly recommended knot for monofilament line when joining line to lure, hook or fly.

FIG. 1: Thrust end of line thru eye of hook and double back. Loop around standing part of line 5 or 6 times.

FIG. 2: Thrust end back up between the eye and the coils then back thru the big loop.

FIG. 3: Pull up tight and trim end.

a. Improved Clinch Knot

128 *Individual and Team Sports*

Exceptionally strong loop knot for end of monofilament line.

FIG. 1: Make a "U-Bend" in line about 4" long, as shown.

FIG. 2: Fold the U-bend back and loop it around itself about 5 times.

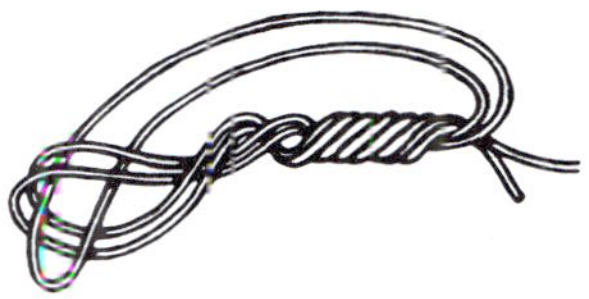

FIG. 3: Insert the end back thru opening made by the backward turn. Pull up tight. Trim short ends.

d. Improved End Loop

This knot is used to tie a leader to a fly line or a monofilament backing to a fly line.

Notice a small piece of monofilament (about 10" long) is used in tying this knot. This piece is needed in addition to your fly line and leader.

This knot is preferred by most fly fishermen because there is no bulky loop in the fly line itself.

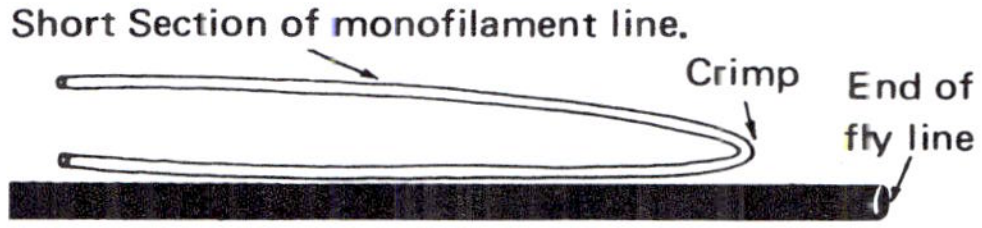

FIG. 1: Crimp the short section of monofilament and hold in place next to fly line, as illustrated.

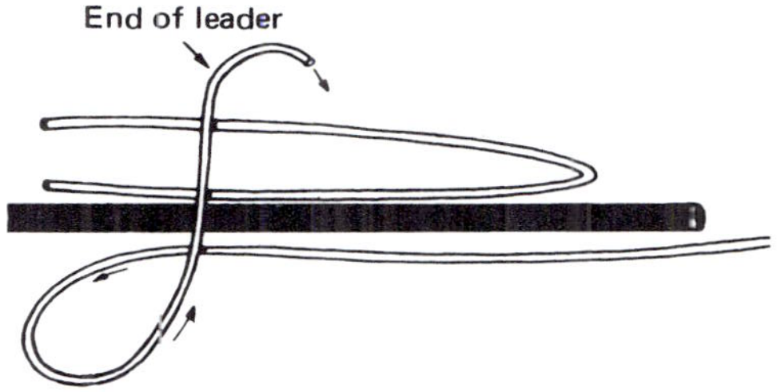

FIG. 2: Bring end of leader up next to fly line and form a loop as shown. Hold in place with thumb and forefinger of left hand.

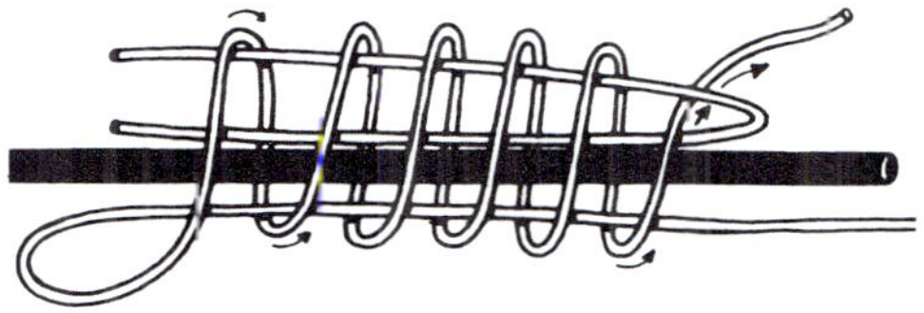

FIG. 3: Make approx. 6 turns with end of leader, as illustrated. Bring end of leader out thru loop in short section of monofilament.

e. Fly Line Knot

FIG. 4: While holding loops together with thumb and forefinger, grasp both ends of short section with other hand and pull entire piece, along with end of leader, back thru your 6 loops as shown. Discard short section of mono.

FIG. 5: Pull leader from both ends to tighten around body of fly line.

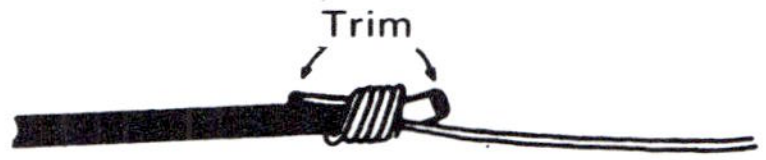

FIG. 6: Trim the ends of fly line and leader at 1/8". Be sure knot is pulled up tight before trimming.

e. (Continued)

Figure 10-22. Basic fishing knots.

Casting and Angling 129

his score. Not more than ten demerits can be charged to any one target, no matter how far it may have been missed. This game usually gives the caster a gratifying score, because it is possible to cast the entire course without hitting a target and still have a score in the mid-80s by coming reasonably close to each one; in the Skish version of this game, under the same circumstances, the score would be a disheartening zero.

The Bait Accuracy games, either ACA or Skish, can be cast using either the five-eighths of an ounce plug and levelwind reel; three-eighths of an ounce plug and either levelwind or enclosed spin-cast type reel; or the one-quarter ounce plug with open face or enclosed spinning reel and rod. The method of casting and scoring is identical with each kind of equipment. For competitive purposes, however, all contestants should use the same size plug.

Accuracy Fly

In accuracy fly, the rod, reel, and line used are unrestricted and the leader must be at least six feet in length.

The fly is a tied approved dry fly style on size 10 hook, with the hook cut off at the beginning of the curve (an ACA official fly is recommended). The fly is not oiled or treated; only one fly can be attached to the leader. A fly can be changed or a lost fly replaced at any time.

Targets. One or more stations of five targets each are scattered at random on the water or land at distances unknown to the caster. If more than one station is used, the targets are arranged to provide similar conditions for all casters. The target nearest the casting box should not be nearer than twenty feet nor farther than twenty-five feet. The target farthest from the casting box should not be farther than fifty feet nor nearer than forty-five feet. The remaining three targets should be placed at irregular intervals in the intervening space. The targets should not be bunched or placed in line with each other.

Casting (Single-handed). Ten casts at targets are to be made in order.

Time. The caster must complete his casts within eight minutes. The time starts when the caster steps onto the casting box; no time out is allowed except in the case of outside interference. A penalty of 5 demerits is scored for each minute or fraction of a minute overtime.

Method of Casting and Scoring. The caster starts with the fly in either hand and with no length of line or leader extending beyond the length of the rod. The line is extended to the respective targets by stripping. In general, stripping is done while the fly is in the air. After starting, the caster is permitted to hold any loose line in either hand. The caster lifts line and leader from the water. No stripping or pulling of line or leader on the water is permitted unless the rod is in motion retrieving a fly. A penalty of 2 demerits shall be scored for each such improper strip or pull. Whenever the fly strikes the water in front of the caster on a forward cast, it is scored a cast. The fly floats and is left floating a few seconds, then the judges call "score;" the line is retrieved (while the judge announces the score to the scorer). A penalty of 2 demerits shall be scored for each time the line is improperly retrieved before the judges call "score."

Should the fly fail to float, or sink and rise to the surface, before judges call "score," it shall be scored a "sunken fly." Penalty of 5 demerits is charged for each "sunken fly."

Should the line, leader, or fly strike the water (or lawn) on a retrieve, it is not scored a cast but a *tick* for a penalty of 5 demerits. The caster should not allow the fly to dangle and be blown over a target before dropping a fly. A penalty of 2 demerits is scored for each such improper cast.

No cast is scored without a fly. The judges notify a caster whenever they notice that the fly is off.

The fly should fall within or on the target to be scored perfect (zero). For each foot or fraction thereof that the fly falls without the target, 1 demerit is scored. One hundred, a score of ten perfect casts, less the number of demerits, constitutes the final score. In no cast can more than ten demerits be scored on any one cast, except that the demerits for penalties are additional.

The object of the game is to simulate average fly-fishing conditions with a dry fly, in which accuracy, delicacy in presentation of the fly, and limited time in which to cast a feeding fish are important factors. Before making the delivery cast at a given target, the caster first makes one or more false casts to that target, in order to measure the distance and direction of the cast. If on a false cast the fly leader or line touches the water, it is scored a tick, it being assumed that under actual fishing conditions this disturbance would have put down a feeding fish. As soon as the caster is satisfied that he has extended the proper amount of line to reach the desired target, and his false casts are consistently over the target, he should deliver the next cast. This is done by executing the backcast prior to delivery in the same manner as the preceding backcasts, but on the forward casts instead of stopping the rod at ten o'clock position, it should follow on through to a horizontal or nine o'clock position, allowing the fly to settle gently on the water's surface. If this is done properly, the fly will float; if delivered too forcefully, or if the leader is too heavy, the fly may sink, with the resulting sunken-fly penalty of five demerits.

Unnecessary false casting is not recommended. Beyond its use in extending or retrieving line, changing direction

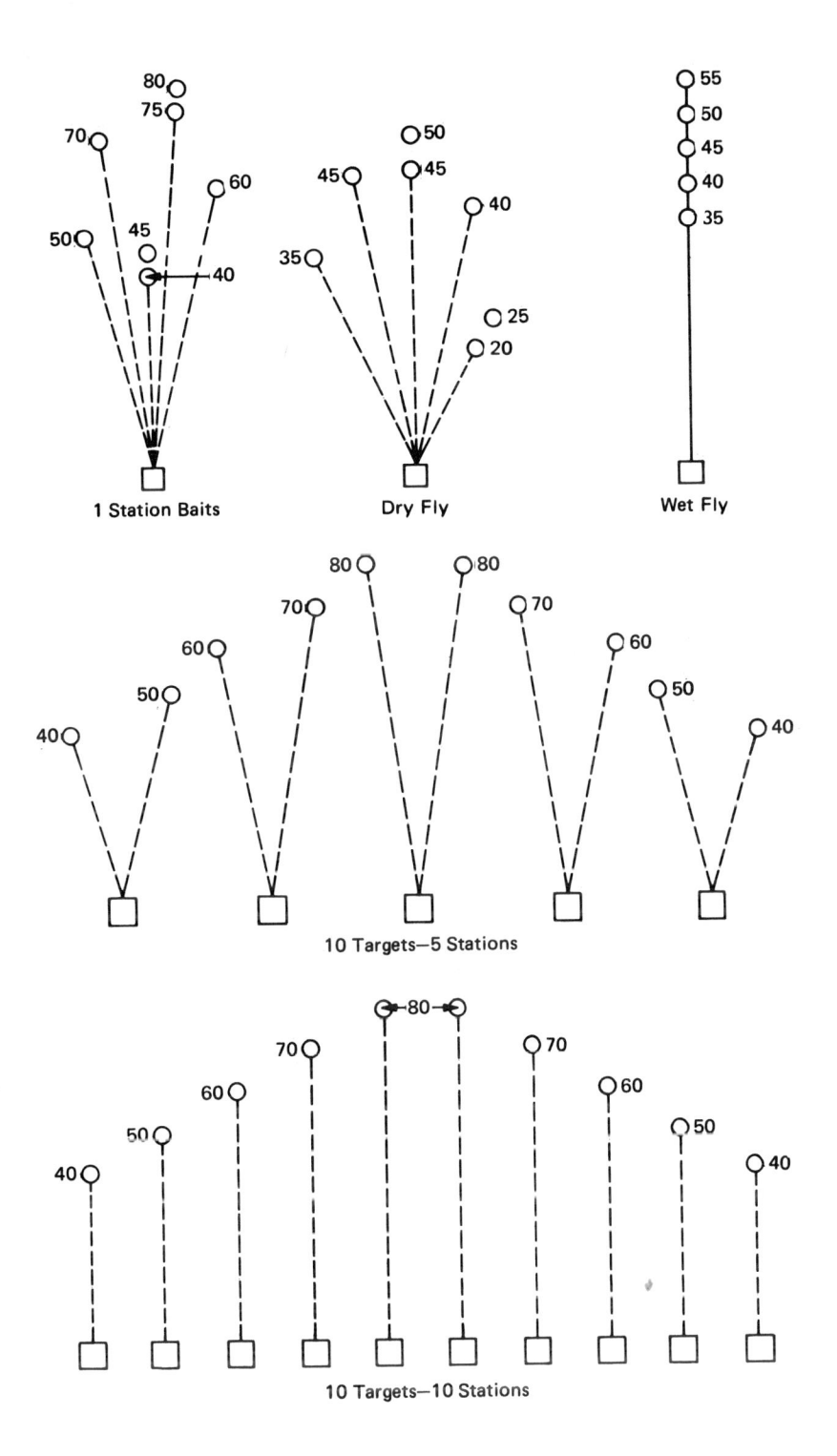

Figure 10-23. Target setups.

Casting and Angling 131

of the cast, and drying the fly from a preceding cast, it serves no purpose whatever except to tire the caster and consume time.

There are practically no restrictions as to tackle used in this game, the following is quite satisfactory:

1. Rod: 8, 8½ feet in length. Avoid selection of a rod with "soft" or "slow" action. Such a rod will not cast a dry fly properly.
2. Line: Level weight-forward line works best with most rods of the recommended length. A tapered line will permit a smoother and better turnover, and a more delicate delivery of the fly.
3. Leader: A tapered leader is most desirable in this type of casting, especially if a tapered line is used. A tapered leader with a heavy butt, tapering down to a 3 or 4 pound test at the tip, works quite well. A leader with a minimum length of 6 feet is required, and one longer than 7½ feet is not recommended.

The accuracy fly event is one of the most fascinating of all casting games to watch and to cast. It is not nearly as difficult as it appears from reading the rules, and these rules are not as complicated as they appear. From a practical standpoint, a beginner who learns to cast this game well will have mastered the essentials for enjoyable fly fishing: balance of tackle and the skill to use it efficiently.

THE AMERICAN CASTING ASSOCIATION (ACA)

The ACA (a member of the ICF, the Amateur Athletic Club Union, and the U.S. Olympic Association) is the only nationally recognized organization concerned primarily with tournament casting and related activities. The composition of the ACA is of individual casting and angling clubs, regional club associations, and individual memberships. First organized in 1906 as the National Association of Scientific Angling Clubs, the name was changed in 1939 to the National Association of Angling and Casting Clubs. In 1961, the present name was adopted.

The principal objectives of the ACA are to serve as the recognized organization in the regulation of organized competitive bait and fly casting and, to publish and disseminate the rules governing the various recognized angling and casting activities. Other activities of the ACA, which, although incidental to the primary functions are of equal importance, are cooperation with the fishing tackle industry in the development of improved tackle, the promotion of angling and casting on the educational level, the youth program, and the development of sportsmanship and conservation by all fisherman.

Casting and angling students should first learn accuracy bait casting as outlined by the ACA. The American Casting Association, P. O. Box 51, Nashville, Tennessee 37202, not only supplies booklets and pamphlets for tournament casting and instruction materials for the formation of casting clubs for all ages, but also has a complete line of supplies other than tackle.

SKISH

Skish, which is similar to the accuracy game already described, and which is popular for tournaments and in college casting and angling classes, is also widely participated in. The ACA rules governing Skish events can also be obtained from the Nashville address.

Introduction

Skish is a game dedicated especially to the improvement of fly, bait, and spin casting among fishermen as a recreational sport between fishing trips that makes for more enjoyable angling on lake or stream. In back of Skish are many volunteer expert casters who are devoting much of their time and effort toward making better casters of fishermen so that they will become better fishermen.

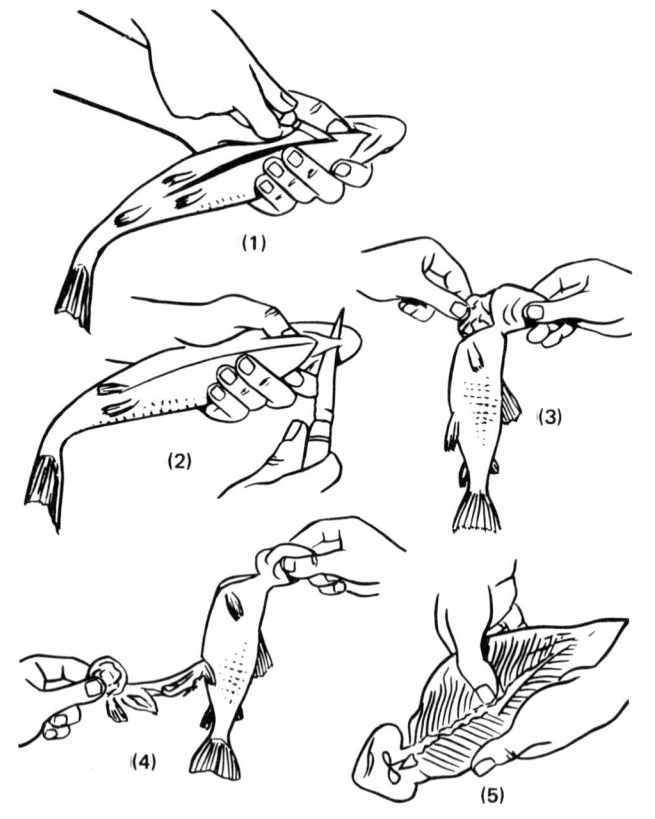

Figure 10-24. Cleaning fish.

132 *Individual and Team Sports*

CLEANING FISH

1. Fish should be cleaned as soon as possible after being caught.
2. Hold the fish in the palm of the hand, stomach up. Place the thumb and forefinger in the gills of the fish to assure a sturdy grip.
3. Insert the knife at the vent and slit the skin to the gills. Make a cut across the head to sever the lower junction of the gills from the skin.
4. Grasp the gills and pull outward and downward removing the gills and intestines. Do not leave any of the gills in the fish as they tend to hasten spoilage.
5. With thumbnail remove all dark material located along the backbone. This too adds to spoilage, so be sure it is all removed.

Glossary of Terms

GENERAL TERMS

Balanced tackle: All units of a fishing outfit—rod, reel, line, and lures—matched to one another for maximum performance as to complete unit.
Bow-and-arrow cast: Used in spinning or fly casting where there is insufficient room for a backcast. The lure is held by the hook in one hand and drawn back to tighten the line and bend the rod tip. When the lure is released, the rod snaps straight and shoots the lure forward.
Casting: The act of sending the line and bait or lure out into the water, whether by use of a fly, spinning, bait casting, or surf rod, or merely the twirl-and-throw method of a hand line.
Dry-fly fishing: Fishing with an artificial fly that floats on the surface of the water.
False cast: Fly cast in which the line and fly are not allowed to drop to the water. Used to dry the line or fly and to work out line in order to lengthen the cast.
Fly casting: A method of casting extremely light lures by means of a long rod and line, the weight of the line providing the momentum to carry the lure out.
Forward cast: Cast made in front of the caster. Actual fishing cast.
Roll cast: A fly cast made by slowly raising the rod tip without picking the line off the water, then snapping the rod down and forward to roll the backcast out. Useful where space does not permit a backcast.
Thumbing: Term applied to the act of controlling a reel spool by thumb pressure, either in casting or playing a fish.
Trolling: Fishing by towing a lure or strip of bait behind a propelled boat, usually at a low speed.
Wet fly fishing: Fly fishing with flies that sink below the water surface.

RODS

Angle offset: A bait-casting rod grip with the handle at an angle to the rod.
Butt: The handle of a salt-water rod; the bottom end of a freshwater rod.
Casting rod: Used for propelling a lure some distance, as opposed to a trolling rod.
Ferrule: The plug and socket used at the joint of a rod; some refer to the socket alone as the ferrule.
Fly rod: A light rod with the reel seat below the handle; the function of the fly rod is to cast a weighted line to which lures can be attached.
Guides: A series of rings through which the line passes as it progresses from the reel to the tip top.
Reel seat: The area of the handle to grip where the reel rests; it is generally provided with a device to hold the reel in place.
Spinning rod: A slender rod of from 6 to 8 or more feet in length with a long cork handle and a series of graduated guides, with a very large one near the handle.

REELS

Antibacklash: A reel with a device to keep the spool from overrunning and tangling line.
Arbor: A cork, wood, or plastic supplementary core placed on a reel spool to occupy space in order that the spool can be filled with a lesser amount of line.
Automatic fly reel: A spring-actuated fly reel that will take up line automatically when a trigger is pressed.
Bail: A hinged loop on the front of a spinning reel that picks up the line for retrieving; used instead of a pickup finger.
Backing: A filler line placed under the fishing line proper to fill out the spool and to provide sufficient line to fight strong running fish.
Backlash: Tangle or snarl caused by the reel spool revolving faster than line passes off it.
Bait-casting reel: A reel revolved by the spool when the line is cast or retrieved; used for casting heavy artificial lures with a short rod.
Drag: A brake on a reel.
Finger: The curved pickup device on some types of spinning reels.
Fly reel: A single-action reel used on a fly rod.
Level wind: A mechanism on bait-casting and some salt-water reels that winds the line evenly over the spool.
Line capacity: The amount of a certain size and kind of line that a reel spool will contain; sometimes used as a designation of the size of a reel.

Selected References

ACA Manual for Tournament Fly and Bait Casting. Nashville, Tenn.: National Association of Casting and Angling Clubs.

Accuracy Bait and Fly Rules: Adapted for Use in Schools. Nashville, Tenn.: ACA National Association of Casting and Angling Clubs.

Bates, Joseph D., Jr. *Elementary Fishing.* New York: Popular Library, 1967.

Garcia Fishing Annual. Teaneck, N.J.: The Garcia Corporation, annually.

How to Catch Fish in Fresh Water. Chicago: Fisherman's Information Bureau.

McNally, Tom. *Fisherman's Bible.* Chicago: Follet, 1970

Shakespeare, Henry. *Secret of Successful Fishing.* New York: Dell.

Shakespeare, Henry. *Fishing Tackle Catalog.* Kalamazoo, Mich.: Shakespeare Company, annually.

Smith, Julian W. *Outdoor Education Project.* Washington, D. C.: American Association for Health, Physical Education and Recreation.

Sport Fishing USA. Washington, D. C.: The United States Department of the Interior, Bureau of Sports, Fisheries and Wildlife, Fish and Wildlife Service, 1972.

Tying Knots with Trilene. Spirit Lake, Iowa: Berkley and Company.

Wolff, Dick. *Fishing Tackle and Techniques.* New York: Dutton, 1961.

CHAPTER 11

Dancing— social and square

*John Kautz**
Davenport Public Schools

Even the turtle has to stick its neck out in order to get someplace!

INTRODUCTION

I didn't think I could "hack" it, but it has been fun.
Quite a workout!
Dancing usually has "bugged" me, but I'm willing to try more.

These are a few off-the-cuff statements made by male high school and college students concerning dance instruction. Such fellows have participated either in evening recreational gatherings or credit-bearing workshops in which forms of social and square dancing have been presented by this writer. Many males seem to harbor a sense of inferiority and lack of confidence in their own ability within the area of dance. Needless to say, this nurtures a reluctance to participate in any form of dance instruction. This reluctance can often be traced to either a meager dance experience or none at all in the elementary and secondary grades. Furthermore, the presentation of dance activities at those levels is entrusted primarily to women instructors, causing an initial appraisal that dance must be strictly for girls. Dance should no more remain in the domain of women than should jumping and skipping rope.

---

*B.S., University of Michigan, Ann Arbor, M.A., Northwestern University, Evanston, Ill. Mr. Kautz, the coordinator of physical education in the Davenport public schools, has spent the past twenty-three years in the field of education, including two years of civilian residence in Germany. He was a staff member of the annual Rhythm Workshop at Golden, Colorado, for five years, serving as director in 1963. Specializing in conducting recreational dance mixers, he has appeared at various college workshops and summer school sessions.

Very few other activities have the potential to unify people as do the various forms of social and square dance. Because man apparently has an inborn desire for expression by means of music, rhythm, and sociability, these activities should certainly be investigated by anyone with an interest in expressing himself or in identifying with others.

HISTORY

No one actually knows when man first danced. People throughout the world and over generations have always engaged in some form of dancing. From the paintings and drawings made by cavemen on the walls of their caves, archeologists believe that these people expressed their hopes and desires, in reference to hunting and war, through figures leaping and springing in dance rituals. Similar activities are portrayed on Egyptian tombs, as well as dances in honor of gods, royal functions, and the highlights in lives of important personages, such as birth, marriage, and death. The writings of the ancient Greeks and Romans reveal the important part that dance activity played in their lives. This importance has been emphasized by the abundant evidence of dancing depicted in sculptured reliefs, frescoes, and vase paintings.

Thousands of years prior to the Christian era, Chinese dancing was a cultivated art. The Cong Fou cult of gymnastic dancers taught health and philosophy through dancing. In the Middle Ages, the Roman Catholic Church played an important part in nurturing dance throughout Europe. During this era the folk dance came into being.

Other forms of dance—ballet, square, ballroom, tap, and modern—were to follow. In this chapter those forms of social and square dancing that have proven their popularity over the years are presented. It is assumed that class instruction and instructor explanation and demonstration are available to the student.

SOCIAL FORMS OF DANCE

Social forms of dance include traditional singing and party games, square and round dances, international folk dances, and contemporary social dance.[1] Practically all social forms of dance can be categorized as folk dances, for they are those that "evolve from the people—those which are danced and enjoyed by the people."[2]

Some of the early motives for dancing (as part of religious ceremonies, and to implore favors from the gods, for example) have not survived. Modern man dances primarily for recreation. Social dancing provides a healthful outlet for leisure-time activity and it considerably broadens one's social experiences. A person who practices and engages in social dancing usually becomes increasingly at ease not only on the dance floor but in other formal and informal social gatherings as well. Exchange students from foreign countries are reported to seek out dance instruction because active dance participation provides them with increased opportunities for meeting people and for getting acquainted than almost any other means.

Fads

Social dance on college campuses today is dominated by fads. To present the footwork used would be a prodigious task! Questioned about the dance steps he used, one college youth replied, "I just listen to a song and picture what steps go with the beat." Recently and currently popular dances, such as the Twist, the Bop, the Monkey, the Watusi, the Frug, the Jerk, the Grinder, and others, truly offer young men and women a most fertile field for creative expression. As Clark states, "The new move in social dance is away from partners and toward individual and/or group dances. The movement base has shifted from foot patterns to body motions, or in other words, from locomotor movement to essentially axial movement."[3]

[1] Elizabeth Halsey and Lorena Porter, *Physical Education for Children* (New York: Holt, Rinehart & Winston, Inc., 1963).
[2] Anne Schley Duggan, Jeanette Schlottmann, and Abbie Rutledge, *The Teaching of Folk Dance* (New York: A. S. Barnes & Co., Inc., 1948).
[3] Sharon L. Clark, "The Changing Scene in Social Dance," *Journal of Health, Physical Education and Recreation* (March 1967), p. 89.

These dancers certainly have challenged the old concept that Occidental dancing is from the waist down and that Oriental dancing is from the waist up.

These fads, or novelty dances, will probably go the way of the Charleston, the Big Apple, and the Jitterbug and not be popular in more than a few years from now. Yet, they should not be ignored, because in addition to the pleasure they bring the dancer, they can create an appreciation for other forms of social dance. In this section, however, traditional rather than contemporary dance steps and patterns will be presented.

Suggestions for the Male Dance Student

1. It is important to be a strong leader.
2. Listen carefully to the music before attempting to learn a specific step.
3. It is probably best to learn a step on an individual basis before practicing with a partner.
4. Get the basic movements well in mind before attempting to get the details perfected.
5. Travel on the dance floor is generally counter-clockwise.
6. As steps are mastered in couple movement, creative expression within the pattern of the dance can be explored.
7. Dancing is a partnership; each partner must know his part.
8. When dancing, the dancer should be relaxed yet be in control.

The Dance Walk

1. Listen carefully to the explanation of the dance walk, and watch the demonstration closely; it resembles the ordinary walking step. Clapping hands to the music is helpful in learning the rhythm of the dance walk.
2. The leg swings directly forward and backward from the *hip*.
3. Keeping with the music, practice walking forward and backward alone. Then practice the dance walk with a partner.
4. Practice turning, using the dance walk.

Closed Position

1. The closed dance position is one in which the partners face each other with their shoulders parallel.
2. The partners look over each other's right shoulders and turn their heads slightly to their left.

Figure 11-1. Closed position.

3. The gentleman places his right arm around his partner with his right hand just below the lady's left shoulder blade. He holds his right elbow away from his body and a little below shoulder level.
4. The lady's left arm rests *lightly* on the gentleman's right arm. Her left arm is placed on his right shoulder, or just below it on his upper arm. She should have a fairly firm grip with her left hand to enable her to sense her partner's lead with increased ease.
5. The lady extends her right arm sideward and just below shoulder level. The palm of the hand should be down and the arm relaxed.
6. The gentleman takes hold of the lady's right hand with his left. The palm of his hand is down with only his thumb touching the underside of the lady's hand.
7. The gentleman steps forward with his *left* foot. The lady steps backward with her *right* foot.
8. The gentleman should practice this dance position by himself, keeping his head up so that he will not look at his feet.
9. Practice the dance walk in couples, progressing counterclockwise around the floor.

The Two-step

Every man should have one dance combination that he has mastered and can dance to both slow and fast music. The two-step is admirably suited for this kind of versatility. One of the two ways in which it is done is to do the combination on the left side and then repeat the same combination on the right side. The other approach is to repeat one pattern on the same side each time, which is the easiest for beginners to learn. Beginner dancers should not practice both steps at first because they are apt to become confused. The men should first receive and practice their instructions while alone. Then each can practice with a woman partner. Practicing turns should follow a similar pattern. A corner is turned by using the same basic step with a quarter turn.

Man	Count	Woman
Step diagonally, forward, L	1	Step diagonally backward R
Close R to L	2	Close L to R
Step diagonally forward L	3 (4)	Step diagonally backward R
Step diagonally forward R	1	Step diagonally backward L
Close L to R	2	Close R to L
Step diagonally forward R	3 (4)	Step diagonally backward L

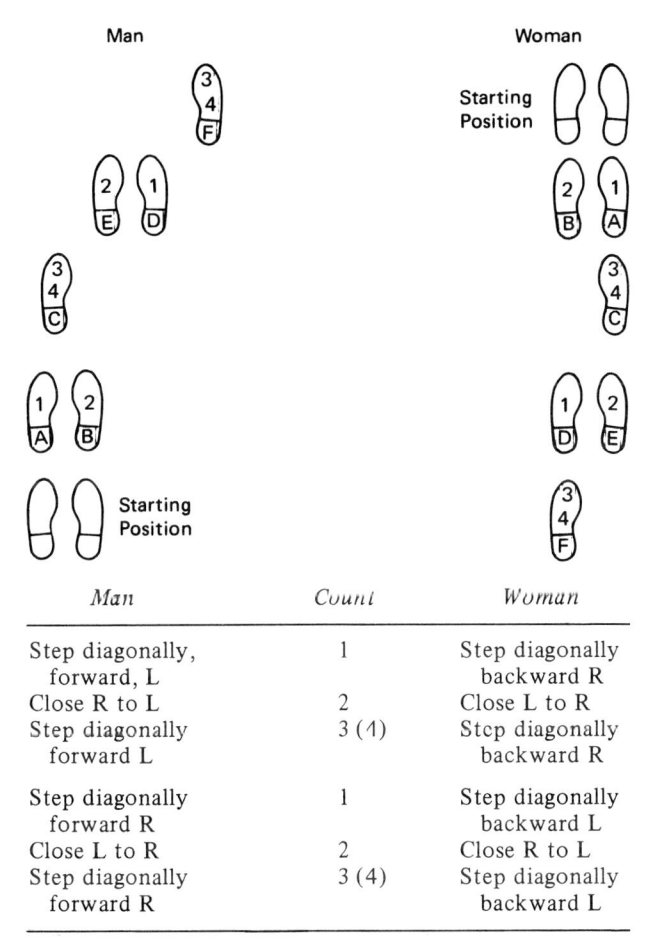

Figure 11-2. Two-step.

Basic Step Pattern

The basic step pattern consists of two slow, large steps and two small steps. Long, long, short, short. (See Figure 11-3.)

Man	Count	Woman
Step forward on L	1	Step backward on R
Step forward on R	2	Step backward on L
Step aside on L quickly	3	Step aside on R quickly
Draw R up to L quickly, weight on R	4	Draw L up to R quickly, weight on L

Dancing: Social and Square

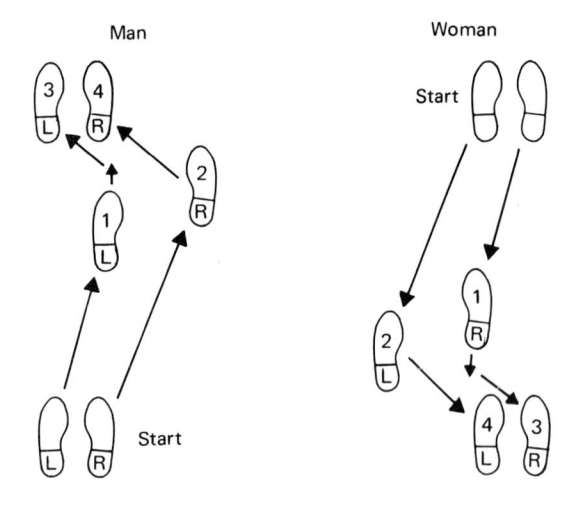

Figure 11-3. Basic step pattern.

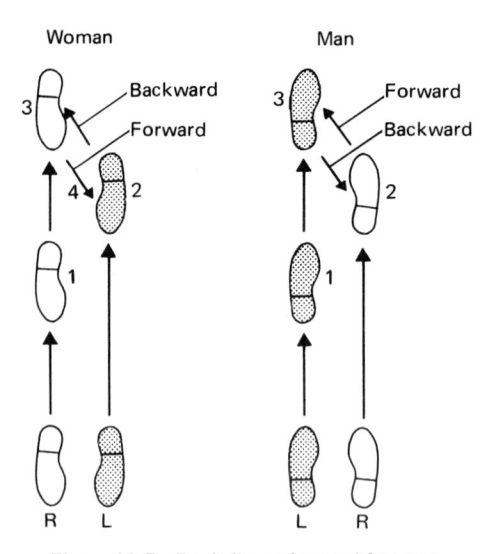

Figure 11-5. Rock-figure-forward fox trot.

Fox Trot—Basic Figure

Timing: Even rhythm 1, 2, 3, 4, or slow, slow, slow, slow. This can be done to various tempos.

Remarks: The dancer should be aware of how he is moving and should take pride in the way that he moves.

Rock-figure-forward Fox Trot

Timing: Each step is given the same amount of time in order that all four steps be even. Steps 3 and 4 are the rock.

Remarks: This figure depends a great deal on the dancer's ability to control his body as it rocks back and forth. Develop balance.

Open-figure Fox Trot

Timing: This is the same as for the basic fox trot.

Remarks: This figure is done to the side from the starting position, but the dancer should turn away from his partner a little toward an open position. When this is done both partners are moving on a diagonal. The dancer should become aware of the change of direction and changes of position. If this figure is to be repeated several times in succession, the partners should not go back to the closed position, but bring their feet together, remaining in the open position.

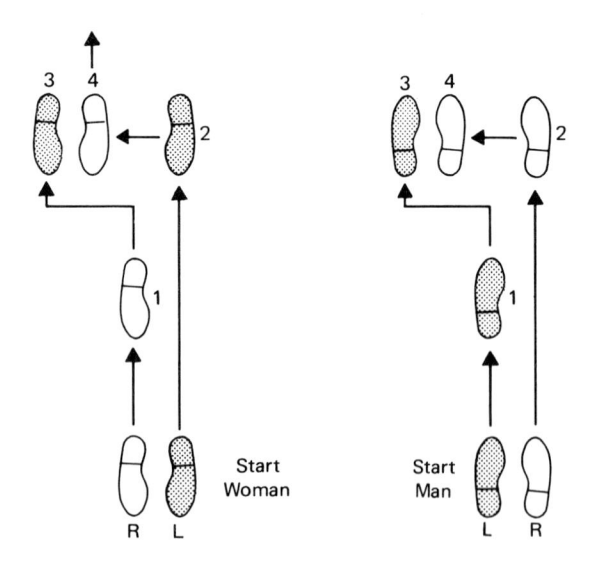

Figure 11-4. Fox trot—basic figure.

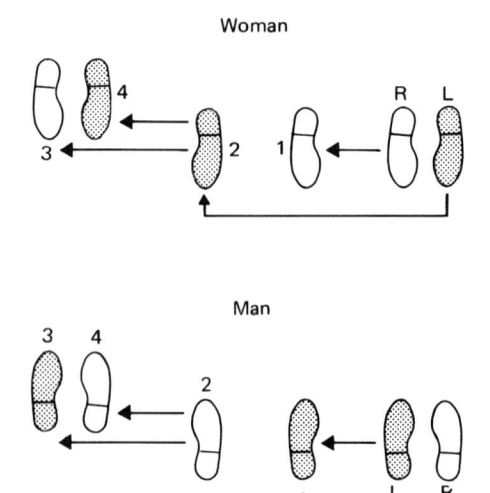

Figure 11-6. Open-figure fox trot.

138 *Individual and Team Sports*

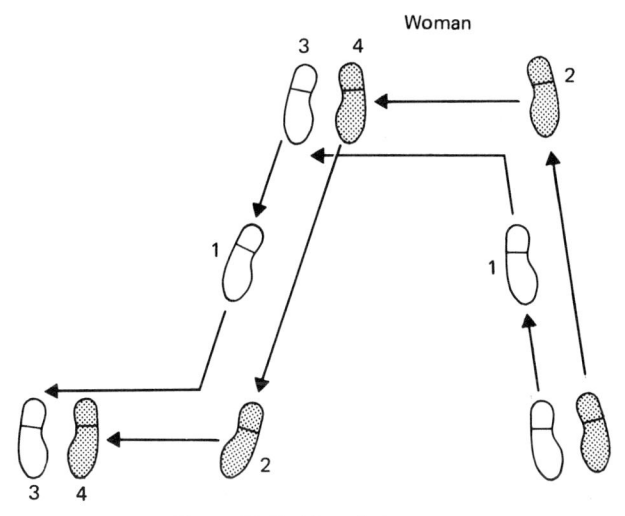

Figure 11-7. Victoria fox trot.

Victoria Fox Trot

Timing: Same as the basic step of the fox trot.

Remarks. The relationship of the partners to each other in this figure and the change of direction make this an interesting dance step if followed distinctly and with confidence. On the first 1 and 2 the couple is in the right reverse position. On 3 and 4 they step in a closed position. The next 1 and 2 is a left reverse and the 3 and 4 is closed.

Rock-pivot-forward

Timing: Same as for the rock-figure-forward.

Remarks for men: This figure is best done with small steps and a slight turning on each pivot. Decide whether to rock a few or many times. Note that the pivot is on the back foot and that the front foot always goes straight ahead. (Just the opposite is true for the woman.)

Tip: Be alert and ready to start with the correct foot.

The Waltz

Incredible as it may seem to the beginner, the waltz step is actually the basis for most of the fox trot combinations. (See Figure 11-9.)

Man	Count	Woman
Step forward L	1	Step backward R
Slide diagonally forward R	2	Slide diagonally backward L
Close L to R	3	Close R to L
Step forward R	1	Step backward L
Slide diagonally forward L	2	Slide diagonally backward R
Close R to L	3	Close L to R

When stepping forward, the *opposite* shoulder is brought slightly *forward*. When stepping *backward* with either foot, the opposite shoulder is similarly brought slightly *backward*.

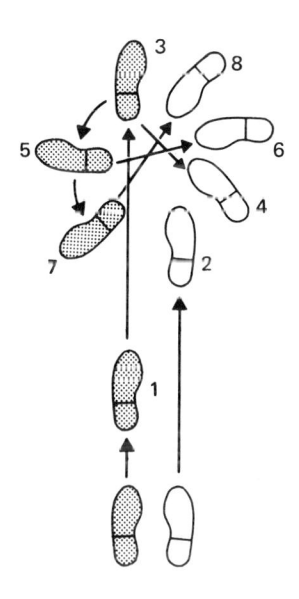

Figure 11-8. Rock-pivot-forward.

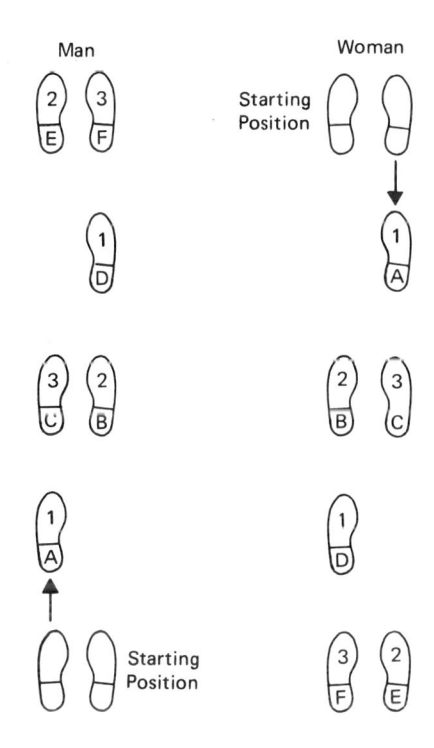

Figure 11-9. Waltz.

Dancing: Social and Square

A large step should be taken on the first count of each measure to give the feeling of an *accent*. The diagonal slide is smaller and is taken almost directly forward. Experienced dancers take two steps directly forward and close on count 3. "Step, slide, close" are appropriate descriptive words to remember.

Left-waltz-turn

When learning the left-waltz-turn, the men should receive their instructions separately from the women. Then the step can be practiced by couples without music, and finally with music.

Men	Women
Turn $\frac{1}{4}$ L and waltz forward L	Turn $\frac{1}{4}$ L and waltz backward R
Turn $\frac{1}{4}$ L and waltz backward R	Turn $\frac{1}{4}$ L and waltz forward L
Turn $\frac{1}{4}$ L and waltz forward L	Turn $\frac{1}{4}$ L and waltz backward R
Turn $\frac{1}{4}$ L and waltz backward R	Turn $\frac{1}{4}$ L and waltz forward L
(one measure for each waltz)	

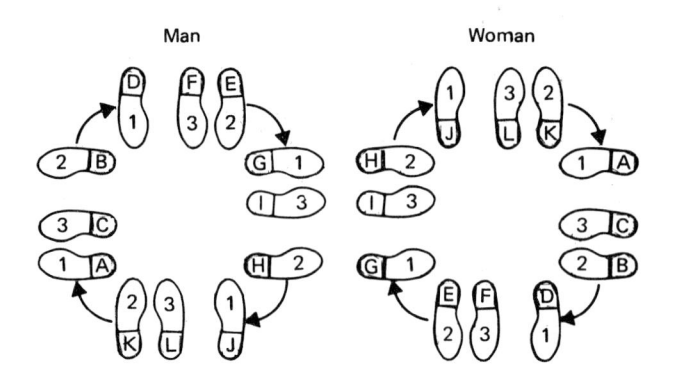

Figure 11-10. Left-waltz-turn.

The waltz turn can be done to the right by reversing the instructions for the left-waltz-turn.

The Hesitation

The hesitation is a pause in which a step is taken on the accented beat of the measure and is then held throughout the measure, while the free leg swings forward or backward. No weight is transferred onto the foot that is pointing. The modern hesitation is not an exaggerated position. There is a feeling of "hold" as the free leg

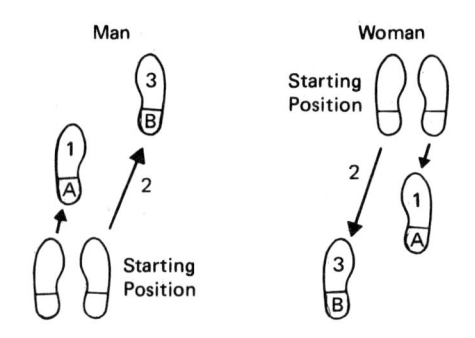

Figure 11-11. Hesitation forward and backward.

swings forward. When transferring his weight on the first count of the measure, the man applies pressure with his right arm and hand, which is accompanied by a slight lift of both arms. This pressure is held throughout the measure and prevents the lady from stepping backward or forward.

Man	Count	Woman
Step forward L Swing R leg directly forward	1 (2)	Step backward R Swing L leg directly backward
Touch R toe to floor slightly in advance of the L foot	3	Touch L toe to floor slightly beyond R foot
The toe is turned outward (no weight)	4	The toe is turned outward (no weight)
(Repeat going backward. Step back R, point L. Do not put weight on L foot.)		(Repeat going forward. Step forward L, point R. Do not put weight on R foot.)

Open Position

The instructions for the open position are as follows:

1. The partners face the same direction.
2. To assume the open position from the closed position, the man turns to his left and the lady to her right. The man's right side and the lady's left side are touching.
3. The relative position of the arm is the same as for the closed position.
4. The angle of the open position may vary from a full open position, in which the partners are facing squarely in the same direction, to a slight deviation from the closed position.

140 *Individual and Team Sports*

Figure 11-12. Open position

5. The man steps forward with his *left* foot while the lady steps forward with her *right* foot. The description of the step pattern for the lady's part is the same as for the man's, except that she starts with her right foot.

Conversation Position

The only difference between the conversation position and the regular open position is that the man's left arm and the lady's right arm are dropped to their sides rather than extended forward.

Position-practice Routine

The student should practice changing from the basic step pattern of long, long, short, short (L,L,S,S)—or the two-step—to the open position and then back to the closed position by observing the following instructions:

1. The basic step pattern (L,L,S,S) is done twice.
2. At the end of the second one (S,S), the man uses pressure with the heel of the right hand, accompanied by a turn of the shoulders to the left and turns the lady to the side. The lady's left side and the man's left side are touching and they are facing in the same direction.
3. While in this open position, two more basic steps (L,L,S,S) are done.
4. At the end of the second basic step (S,S), the man brings the lady back to the closed position by using pressure with his high right hand.
5. Practice two basic steps, open position, two basic steps, closed position, repeatedly, while dancing with a partner.

The Dip

Both the man and woman should be able to dip forward or backward on either foot. The explanation given subsequently pertains to the man dipping backward left and the woman forward right. To avoid interference of the knees in a dip, the man turns his bent knee slightly outward. A dip is often held for the entire measure. When the dip is done to waltz tempo, two counts are used for the dip and one count for the recovery. Practice is necessary to insure smoothness and balance. The use of

Figure 11-13. Conversation position.

Figure 11-14. Dip.

Dancing: Social and Square 141

the descriptive words dip and up will at first aid in establishing the proper rhythm. On the count preceding a backward dip, the man applies pressure and a slight downward movement of his right arm and hand. This gently pulls the woman forward into the dip. The relaxing of the pressure of his arm and the hand will aid in the recovery from the dip.

Movements and Timing of the Dip

Man	Count	Woman
Step backward L, bending the knee. The R leg is extended directly forward, the toe turned outward and just touching the floor.	1	Step forward R, bending the knee. The L leg is extended backward, the toe turned outward and just touching the floor.
The body weight is directly over the L foot. There is a straight line from the head through the hips and the L ankle	2	The body weight is directly over the R foot. There is a straight line from the head through the hips and the R ankle
Step forward onto the R foot (recovery).	3	Step backward onto the L foot (recovery).

In learning the dip, the following practice routine is helpful:

1. Practice the dip without a partner.
2. Practice the dip in couples without music.
3. Without music do two two-steps (or L,L,S,S) and a dip, then two two-steps.
4. Do the preceding combinations to music.

Pivot Turn

The pivot turn is a right- or left-about turn; the pivot turn to the right is used most often by men. It is done by alternately transferring the weight from one foot to the other while turning. The turn can be done in place or while progressing. Any number of steps from two to eight can be taken to complete a pivot turn. The man places the inside of his right foot close to, and parallel with, the inside of his partner's right foot. Then, the right is the pivoting foot, and the partners' feet remain in the same relative position. When done in place, the partners pivot on the spot, each keeping the left foot well in back of the right one. A common fault to be avoided is to swerve the left foot to the side while pivoting on the right. For the progressive pivot turn, a pivot is made on each foot and the steps are of equal length. In this turn only two pivots are taken to complete the turn.

Figure 11-15. Pivot.

To learn to pivot smoothly, beginners should practice stepping forward on the heel of the pivoting foot and then transferring the weight to the toe of that foot.

Practice Routine for the Pivot Turn. (1) Step forward onto the right heel. Transfer the weight to the right toe. Step backward left. This can be done using the descriptive words: *heel, toe, step.* This pattern is done several times forward, then turning slowly to the right. A pivot is made on the right toe just before the weight is transferred to the left foot. The right toe is turned outward, the left toe inward. (2) The partners face each other and hold elbows. The man steps forward right and the lady backward left, with the insides of their feet parallel and close together. They practice in place, transferring the weight from one foot to the other, and then turn slowly to the right. (3) The partners assume the social dance position and first practice in place and then turn slowly to the right. The right feet are kept close together, and the left are extended backward. The knees must remain relaxed (but not bent) throughout the turn, to prevent the appearance of rocking from one foot to the other. The weight of the body should be kept over the pivoting foot. The man tightens his right arm and hand-hold and swings his partner into the pivot.

The Grapevine Step

When dancing the grapevine step the body should turn to accomodate the crossing feet. If the right foot crosses in back of the left, the body turns right; if the right foot crosses in front of the left, the body turns left. The man usually crosses in back first. It is easier for him to lead into the grapevine by so turning the lady that she crosses

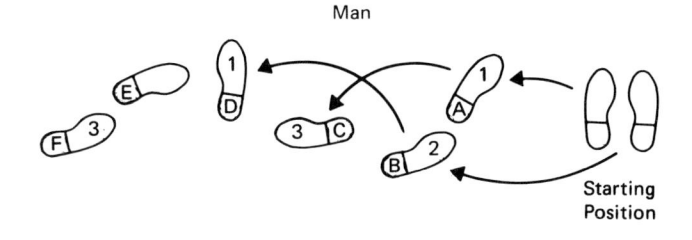

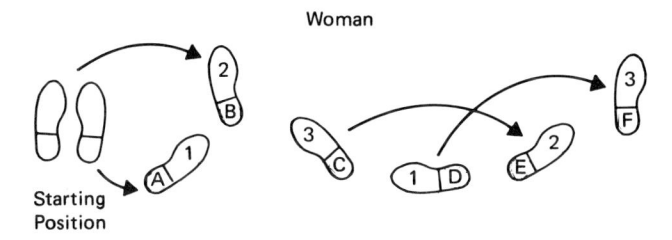

Figure 11-16. Grapevine.

in front. Descriptive words that can be said silently are "sideward, backward, sideward, forward" or "side, back, side, front." For the waltz rhythm, the words are *slow, fast, fast.*

On the first "step sideward left," the man turns his shoulders toward the right and applies pressure with the heel of his right hand. This turns the lady toward her right and indicates that she is to cross in front with her left foot. On the second "step, sideward left," the man turns his shoulders toward the left and applies pressure with the finger tips of his right hand, while he pulls the lady's right arm forward with his left hand. This turns the lady toward her left and indicates that she is to cross in back with her left foot.

Practice Routine for the Grapevine Step. (1) The dancer, by himself, does the grapevine with music. (2) The grapevine is practiced with a partner but without music. (3) Step 2 is repeated with fox trot music. (4) The partners do two two-steps (or L,L,S,S), grapevine, and then two two-steps (or L,L,S,S). (5) The partners next use all the steps combined by two-steps (or L,L,S,S). In between they use the open and closed positions and dip, pivot, and turn. (6) The partners do this same step combined with two waltz steps before and after each step. (7) The partners do a free choice of combinations.

SELF-EVALUATION

Man appears to possess an instinct to express rhythm; through dance he can develop poise, grace, timing, balance, and enhance his personality development. Dance for most people is an integral part of modern life. The male social dancer should keep the following pointers in mind when on the dance floor.

1. Keep your body relaxed enough to feel the rhythm.
2. Move counterclockwise on the dance floor.
3. Keep your head and shoulders up.
4. Keep slightly to your partner's left.
5. Move your legs from the hips and not the knees.
6. Let your feet respond smoothly and easily to music.
7. Keep your feet close together.
8. Refrain from watching your feet.
9. Keep your weight over one foot at a time—never over both feet.
10. Point the way in every step with your big toe leading.
11. Start backward with your left foot.
12. Turn by making the first step shorter.
13. Learn a variety of steps and practice them alone and with a partner.
14. Be natural.
15. Be an enjoyable partner through meticulous personal hygiene habits and appropriate dress.

A dancer should observe the following etiquette:

1. Request a dance politely.
2. Greet the host and express appreciation at the end of the evening.
3. Introduce friends correctly.
4. Cooperate with group activity.
5. Be an interesting conversationalist, avoid argumentative subjects, and be a good listener.
6. Be considerate of your partner and stay with her.
7. Attempt to enjoy dancing.

The tall dancer should

1. Keep his elbows low.
2. Let his knees bend slightly without altering his natural standing position.
3. Prevent himself from leaning forward in order to appear smaller.
4. Take pride in his height by reflecting it in his dance carriage.

The short dancer should

1. Imagine that he is touching the ceiling with his head.
2. Hold his elbows high.
3. Place his hand firmly on his partner's back.

FOLK DANCE

Folk dances are traditional movement patterns related to traditional airs that have been handed down through the years. These dances often tell a story or dramatize some occupation. They reflect many cultural values and touch a number of facets of human experience.

In this section those steps that an adult can expect to find woven into many successful informal dance parties in the guise of mixers are introduced. "These are dance patterns designed to move people to new partners so that socialization can be better assured, for socialization is one purpose of teaching dance." Neuromuscular skills are developed in the basic, or fundamental, steps and dance figures of folk dance. Included are the walk, run, skip, slide, jump, two-step, the waltz in all its variation, and various types of polka, schottische, step-hop, jig, and buzz steps. Because all forms of dance were ultimately derived from folk dance, the neuromuscular skills developed in this particular activity afford a natural carry-over into the skillful performance of other types of dance, including modern, ballroom, and tap. For most people, however, the main attraction of folk dancing lies in its social and recreational values.

Box Waltz

The box waltz is done in 3/4 time, which consists of three steps done in even rhythm. The following actions comprise the basic movements of the box waltz:

Count 1	Step forward on the L foot.
Count 2	Bring the R foot alongside the L foot and then directly out to the side.
Count 3	Close the L foot to the R foot.
Count 1	Step backward on the R foot.
Count 2	Bring the L foot alongside the R and then directly out to the side.
Count 3	Close the R foot to the L foot.

These movements may be practiced alone, with a partner, or in a double-circle formation with the men's back to the center of the circle and with the women holding hands and facing the men. The man begins forward left (and the woman begins backward right). The use of the descriptive words, *step, side–close; step, side–close*, will be beneficial at first.

To add the balance step, clasping the right hand to the partner's right hand, the movements are

Count 1	The man steps on the L foot.
Counts 2 and 3	The man swings the R foot across in front of the L foot. At the same time, the woman steps on the R foot and swings the L foot across and in front of the R foot.

Polka

The polka, which is similar to a two-step with the addition of a hop–hop, step, step (uneven rhythm)–is done in 2/4 time. It can be practiced in a double circle formation with the men's backs to the center of the circle. The partners face each other with the right hand of the man clasping the left hand of his partner. Using the method called sliding into the polka, everyone moves in a counterclockwise direction; the man slides with the left foot and the woman with the right. The trailing foot is drawn up to this leading foot, another sliding step is made, and, then, while still holding hands, the partners turn away from each other (the man to the left; the lady to the right). The hop has automatically taken place and the partners are now in a back-to-back position, ready to start a new sliding step. The man leads with his right foot and the lady leads with her left foot. A series of face-to-face and back-to-back sequences are alternated until the movement becomes natural to the dancers. The dancers can call out the pattern:

A face to face and a back to back.
A face to face and a back to back.

And a polka step and a polka step.
And a polka step and a polka step.

And a hop, step, step and a hop, step, step.
And a hop, step, step and a hop, step, step.

The partners can polka while in a closed dance position, both of them starting with the same foot. The hop is utilized as a means of changing direction.

Schottische

The schottische is performed in a smooth, even rhythm in 4/4 time. It consists of three walking or running steps followed by a hop. An example is step left, step right, step left, and hop on left. The entire pattern or dance usually followed is:

Step	Step	Step	Hop
L	R	L	L
Step	Step	Step	Hop
R	L	R	R
Step-hop	Step-hop	Step-hop	Step-hop
L L	R R	L L	R R

The schottische can be practiced with a turn variation. Standing in a double circle and facing counterclockwise, the men have their partners on their right side. They hold inside hands and both start with the left foot:

1. Schottische forward—run, run, run, hop. Run, run, run, hop.
2. Turn away from each other with a step-hop, step-hop, step-hop, step-hop.
3. Schottische forward—run, run, run, hop. Run, run, run, hop.
4. Dishrag turn—holding the inside hand, turn under each other's arms as a step-hop, step-hop, step-hop, and step-hop are executed.

Varsovienne

The varsovienne is done in 3/4 time. In the varsovienne position both the man and woman execute the same steps.

Part 1: Do a brush step by swinging the left foot (bent at knee) in front of the right leg. Step left, close right to left with the weight on the right foot.
Part 2: Repeat.
Part 3: Brush with the left foot. Step left, right, left, and point right to the right.
Part 4: Same as Part 1, beginning with the brush with the right foot.
Part 5: Repeat Part 4.
Part 6: Brush with the right foot. Step right, left, right, and point the left toe to the left.

Using a crossover, alternate Parts 3 and 4 four times. Beginning with the left foot, with three steps, the man shifts his partner across in front of him to his left side. Then, using the right foot, she is shifted back to his right side.

Figure 11-17. Varsovienne.

Obtaining and Interchanging Partners

The dancer will benefit by leading many partners. He can do his part to increase the success of each practice session by quickly following any instructions concerning a change in partner or routine.

Several methods of obtaining or exchanging partners are commonly employed. To secure a partner:

1. The men form a line on one side of the dance area and the women on the opposite side—both lines facing the same end of the room. As music is played, the leader of each line proceeds around the room until he meets the leader of the other line. They proceed down the center of the hall and each succeeding "matching" couple follows.
2. The men form a circle, facing counterclockwise. The women, facing clockwise, construct a second circle around the men. When the music is played each circle walks in the opposite direction. When the music is stopped, the men and women face one another and take the closest partner. All remaining persons raise their hands and look for an unclaimed partner.
3. With all the dancers forming one large circle in which the men and women are alternated, the instructor calls out, "Take the lady on your left," or "lady on your right," or "second lady on your left."
4. Starting in the same arrangement as for step 3, on command, the men turn right, and the ladies turn left. The right hands are extended and a grand right and left to the music commences. When the music stops, the persons facing each other become partners.

To exchange partners:

1. The couples are asked to promenade around the hall and then down the center in fours. When fours have been formed, the men in each foursome exchange partners.
2. As a dance is in progress, the instructor calls out, "Exchange partners." Those having difficulty raise their hands and seek out a new partner.
3. A counterclockwise double circle of partners is formed with the men on the inside. All promenade forward until the music stops. The instructor calls out, "Men remain where you are, women advance three places."
4. In square dance sets:
   a. The head ladies can change with the side ladies.
   b. The men of one set can exchange partners with the men of another set.
   c. The men can move one position to the left or right.

Dancing: Social and Square

SQUARE DANCE

The origin of square dancing dates back to the earliest days of America. The most popular square dance during Colonial days was the quadrille. This originated from a square formation with four couples standing on the sides of an imaginary square. It is quite likely that the use of this formation gave rise to the name square dance. The round dance, forerunner of our social couple dancing, developed as a result of twosomes breaking away from the regular set and dancing alone.

The beginning dancer who develops sufficient interest in square dancing may eventually want to seek membership in a local square dance club, where he can receive further instruction and practice in this form of dancing.

Basic Movements

A large, single-circle formation in which the men and women are alternated is usually employed when a class or a large group of mixed persons are learning the fundamentals of square dancing. The gentleman's partner will be the lady on his right-hand side. The lady on his left side is his corner lady. The names of the basic movements used in square dancing are listed subsequently, together with a description of the movements.

Honor. The partners face each other. With his feet together, the gent places his right hand over his heart and, with his left hand at his side, he bows slightly to his partner. This is done from the waist. The lady steps back and curtsies. The same movement can be done with the corner lady.

Do-sa-do. (Also referred to as Do-Si-Do, and Dos-A-Dos.) Depending on the call, the partners either face each other or their corners. The dancers advance and pass each other, right shoulder to right shoulder. Each takes one step to the right in back of the other person and, without turning, moves backward into place.

Allemande Left. The gentleman and his designated lady join left hands, walk around each other and back to position. Allemande right is the same movement, except that the right hands are joined.

Grand Right and Left. All couples in the circle face their partners and grasp right hands. As the men walk counterclockwise and the women walk clockwise, the left hand is extended to the next person and then the right hand to the second next person, and so on until the partner is met. Usually a promenade follows but this is up to the caller.

Promenade. This is done by couples in a counterclockwise direction with the gentleman on the inside and the lady on his right. The hands are held in a skater's position, right to right and left to left, with the right hands on top.

Varsovienne Promenade. The man places his right arm around the lady's right shoulder and holds her right hand in his right hand. The left hands are joined in front of the body at approximately waist height.

Balance. The partners face each other. Holding right hands, they perform a step swing (the gentleman steps left and swings his right foot in front of his left leg; the lady does the same).

Swing. The partners face each other and assume a waltz position, placing the outside of the right foot against that of the partner. The partners then lean back and swing clockwise, using the ball of the right foot as a pivot, and pushing as if on a scooter with the left foot. Usually, two complete swings are sufficient. After these two turns, the lady is released out to the right so that both partners are facing the inside of the circle.

Left-hand or Right-hand Swing. Depending on the call, the partners join left or right hands and walk around each other. This can also be done with the corners. More vigor is exerted than in an allemande left or right.

Left-elbow Swing or Right-elbow Swing. Depending on the call, the partners or corners hook left or right elbows and walk around each other.

Forward and Back. Either the men or the ladies will be called to walk forward (four steps) and then retire to place by walking backward the same number of steps.

After the preceding movements have been individually learned, the next task is to follow a sequence developed by a caller. Different combinations of these simple figures can be challenging for the beginner to follow. The square dancers will probably first walk slowly through various figures without music. Two sample practice calls of this nature might be

Honor your partner and your corner too
Swing your lady and promenade the ring
All join hands and go forward next
When you back up just circle left
Now circle to the right and when you're home
Do a right elbow swing and promenade the ring.

Balance your partner and swing your corner
Do-si-do your partner and balance your corner
A left-hand swing with your partner now
A Do-si-do with your partner
Allemande left your corners all
A grand right and left around the hall
As you meet partners promenade
When home again, swing your maid.

As proficiency is developed, simple dances (circle formation) should be attempted as soon as possible. Examples of such dances, with the directions listed for men, are given subsequently:

All join hands and circle the ring
   (join hands and circle left)
Stop where you are, give your partner a swing
   (all swing their partners)
Swing that gal behind you
   (gents swing the lady on the left)
Now swing your own if she's not flown
   (men swing their own partners)
Allemande left your corner pal and do-si-do your own
   (allemande the corner lady and do-si-do the partner)
Now all promenade with that corner maid
   (gents take the corner lady as their new partner)
Singing Oh Johnny, Oh Johnny, Oh!
   (all join in singing this last line before repeating the dance)

Captain Jinks (Mixer)

Docey 'round your partners now, your partners now, your partners now
   (men do-si-do around their partners)
Docey with your corners now, for this is done in the navy
   (men do-si-do with the corners)
Allemande left your corners now, your corners now, your corners now
   (men allemande left with the corner ladies)
Allemande right with your partners now, for this is done in the navy
   (men allemande right with their partners)
Balance with your corners now, your corners now, your corners now
   (corners face and join right hands, both take a small step to the left and swing the right foot in front of the left leg; step to the right and swing left; repeat again)
Swing your corner lady now and promenade the hall.
   (gentleman promenades with his corner who becomes his new partner)

The Actual Square Dance Set

1. Four couples comprise a set. Each couple stands on one of the sides of an imaginary square, facing the couple across from them. The distance across the set is roughly eight to ten feet.
2. The lady is always on the right side of her partner.
3. The couple with their backs to the source of music is designated as couple one. Counting counterclockwise around the set, the others are couple two, three, and four.
4. The couples facing each other are looking at their "opposites."
5. The starting position occupied by a couple is known as their home position. When promenading, all the couples eventually stop at their home positions. In exchanging dances, a gentleman will take his new lady (partner) to *his* home position.

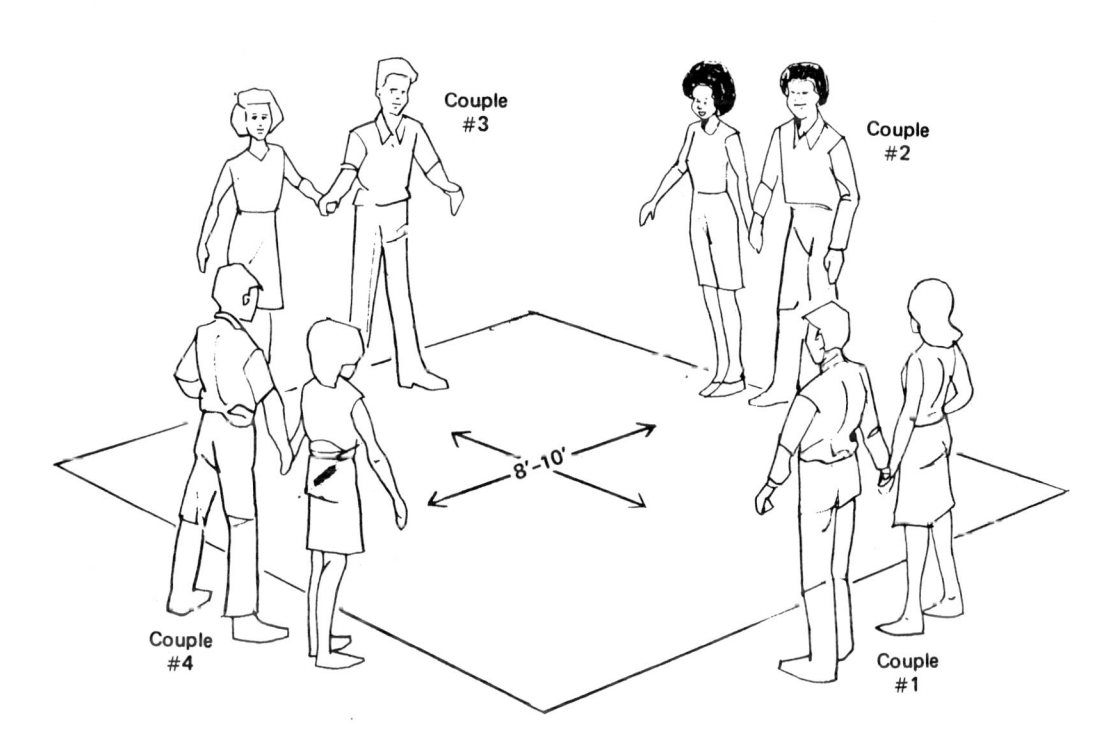

Figure 11-18. Square dance set.

Dancing: Social and Square **147**

6. The basic step used in square dancing is not a skip, but a graceful walk that almost resembles a shuffle.
7. A gentleman's corner is the lady on his left, whereas the lady's corner is the gentleman on her right.

At this stage it would be helpful to learn several additional movements before progressing to some simple square dances.

Right and Left Through. Two couples face each other, extending right hands to their opposites. Both couples walk by (pass through) their opposites, passing right shoulders. Upon passing through, each dancer gives his left hand to his partner and the man places his right hand and arm around his lady's waist. In this position the gentleman continues to turn his lady around counterclockwise until the couples face each other once again. A "right and left back" is now executed so that both couples can return to their initial positions.

Ladies Chain. Opposite ladies grasp right hands in the center of the set and then exchange partners by giving the opposite gent their left hand. The gents receive opposite ladies and repeat the counterclockwise turn (as described in "right and left through") with the right hand around the lady's waist. Each gent finishes by placing his lady on his right side facing her old partner across the set. If the call "chain right back" is given, the action is repeated.

Four-ladies Chain. The four ladies join right hands at shoulder height in the center of the set and commence to walk clockwise until they meet their opposite gents with a left-hand shake. The right-arm-waist turn is once again executed, and if the call "chain them back" is given, the four ladies meet with their right hands again, walk clockwise, and extend the left hand to their initial partner. A final right-arm-waist turn brings all the couples in the set back to their original positions and facings.

Sashay (Chassé). Either the men or the women (sometimes both) move sideward, using sliding steps.

Right-hand Star. The couples involved walk to the center of the set and place their right hands together at shoulder level. They walk clockwise until the next call is given. If the dancers are directed to "left hand back" they simply turn, place their left hands together, and commence walking counterclockwise.

Circle Left or Right. All eight dancers join hands, forming a circle, and walk in the direction called.

Composition of a Square Dance

The *introduction* will probably consist of honoring the partner and/or the corner, all joining hands and circling left and/or right, and possibly swinging the corner and/or the partner. Occasionally, an allemande left followed by a grand right and left will complete the introduction.

The *figure* varies in each dance, and the name of the dance is usually derived from this figure. In most instances couple one is singled out to react to the call, with the other couples following in sequence. Sometimes, the head couples will move simultaneously. Occasionally, the four gentlemen or the four ladies will work as a unit.

The *chorus, or break,* is sometimes referred to as *trimmings* or *fill-ins.* These calls are used after each couple (or all couples) has completed its portion of the figure and has returned to the home position.

Let's Dance

Each person presenting instruction in square dancing will use his own approach. Nothing can be compared to a "live" caller, who can adjust his calling to the ability and response of the group.

Beginning students will appreciate music that is slow to medium in speed, thus permitting them to follow the calls and master the movements with increased ease and decreased frustration. The speed of a record (the number of steps per minute that the dancers are expected to take) should not exceed 128 for beginners. The calls and figures presented on the following pages are arranged in graduated difficulty and include the basic fundamentals of square dancing.

The dancers are advised to walk through the figures slowly without the music until the figures are thoroughly understood.

"Around That Couple and Take a Little Peek"

Introduction. All join hands and circle to the left, break, and promenade back.

Figure.

First Couple lead to the right
Around that couple and take a little peek
Back in the center and swing your sweet
Around that couple and peek once more
Back in the center and round up four
Do-si-do, one more do and on you go.

(The first couple then repeats the figure three more times with the remaining couples. This completes the change or set.)

Chorus Break.

All do-si-do with the corner
And a grand right and left all the way.

Now the second couple lead to the right
Now the third couple lead to the right
Now the fourth couple lead to the right.

148 *Individual and Team Sports*

Explanation. As the first couple leads out to the right they separate and go to either side of couple number two and peek around at each other. They then walk to the center and swing once. They peek once again around couple number two and walk to the center, join hands with couple two, and walk around in a circle. They execute a do-si-do twice and move on to the next couple and repeat the entire figure.

"I'll Swing Your Gal and You Swing Mine"

Introduction.

All join hands and circle left, once around
The other way back single file
Lady in the lead Indian style.

Figure.

Head couple balance and now you swing
Lead right out to the right of the ring
I'll swing your gal and you swing mine
I'll swing my gal half the time
Four hands up and around you go
Now you break with a do-si-do
On to the next and away you go.

(The first couple then repeats the figure two more times with couples three and four.)

Chorus Break

Left hand to your corner and right to your own
Grand right and left and when you meet her promenade home.

Now the second couple balance and now you swing
Now the third couple balance and now you swing
Now the fourth couple balance and now you swing.

Explanation. The first couple bows to each other, then swings. Then they walk over to couple number two and the men change partners and swing once. They change back and swing their partners once. Then the two couples join hands and circle four and break with a regular back-to-back do-si-do. The first couple then moves on to the next couple and repeats the figure.

"Split the Ring and Balance Corners"

Introduction.

Do-si-do your partners all
Do-si-do your corners all
Allemand left, when you come 'round
Now swing your partner 'round and 'round.

Figure.

First couple lead out down the center
The lady goes right, the gent goes left
And balance to your corners all
Balance corners up and down
And swing your partners 'round and 'round
Allemande left with the corner maid
Now take your own and promenade.

(The first couple then repeats the figure two or more times with couples three and four.)

Chorus Break.

Now promenade two by two
Once around and then you're through.

Now the second couple lead out down the center
Now the third couple lead out down the center
Now the fourth couple lead out down the center.

Explanation. The first couple goes across the set and between couple three. They then turn separately around the outside, the lady going right and the man going left; then they go back to their place. Then they balance to the corner lady and swing the partner. Finally, there is an allemande left with the corner and a promenade around the set with the partner.

A follow-up on this basic instruction can be obtained by means of the records listed here, which contain singing calls:

Fun While You Learn—EZ Albums, #LP Sol, 502.
Marching Thru Georgia, *MacGregor*, 004-2A.
Pistol Packin' Mama, *MacGregor*, 004-2B.
Sally Goodin, *Old Timer Record Co.*, 8023.
Nellie Gray, *MacGregor*, Jonesy Album 7.
El Rancho Grande, *Old Timer*, 8020.
       MacGregor, Jonesy Album 7.
Wabash Cannonball, *MacGregor*, Jonesy Album 7.
Texas Star, *Honor Your Partner*, Album 8.
Turkey in the Straw, *MacGregor*, 656-B.
Hurry, Hurry, Hurry, *MacGregor*, 656-A.
If You Knew Susie, *MacGregor*, 682-A.
Too Old to Cut the Mustard, *MacGregor*, 682-B.
Modern Square Dancing, Kimbo Album 4060.

Dancing: Social and Square

Selected References

BOOKS

Duggan, Anne Schley, Jeanette Schlottman, and Abbie Rutledge. *The Teaching of Folk Dance.* New York: A. S. Barnes, 1948.

Durlacher, Ed. *Honor Your Partner.* New York: Berin-Adair, 1949.

Harris, Jane A., Anne Pittman, and Marlys S. Waller. *Dance a While.* Minneapolis, Minn.: Burgess, 1965.

Kirkell, Miriam H., and Irma K. Schaffnit. *Partners All—Places All.* New York: Dutton, 1951.

Waglow, I. F. *Social Dance for Students and Teachers.* Dubuque, Iowa: Brown, 1953.

PERIODICALS

Journal of the American Association of Health, Physical Education and Recreation. 1201 Sixteenth St., N.W. Washington, D. C. 20036.

CHAPTER 12

Diving: springboard

Don Casady*
The University of Iowa

Dale Mood[†]
University of Colorado

HISTORY

Springboard diving, which originated in England, has existed as a competitive sport since shortly after the beginning of the twentieth century. Diving, in which the take-off is from a springboard or a rigid platform, is an outgrowth of aerial acrobatics and tumbling. It has been a national and international event for many years, and was first introduced into the modern Olympic Games in 1904.

The United States has dominated springboard and platform diving in the modern Olympic Games. Until the early 1960s, many of the male Olympic divers had their collegiate diving competition at the Ohio State University under the coaching of Mike Peppe. In general, divers from the "Big Ten" (Western Intercollegiate) Conference have tended to dominate the National Collegiate Athletic Association (NCAA) diving championships.

The equipment for this sport has undergone considerable change in the past few decades. In the early 1930s the springboard consisted of a semirigid wooden plank, which was covered with coca matting and sloped upward at a considerable angle. This type of equipment encouraged the use of *standing* forward dives. Now, springboards are made of fiberglass and wood, stainless steel, or most commonly, aluminum alloys.

---

*B.S., M.A., Ph.D., University of Iowa, Iowa City, Iowa. Don Casady was the varsity diving coach at the University of Iowa for six years. In addition, he has taught numerous classes in diving to college students and others.

[†]Dale Mood, a letter winner in diving at the University of Iowa, was later the varsity diving coach there for five years. In between these two periods he was the diving coach at East High School and the Swim Club of Rockford, both located in Rockford, Illinois. At the University of Colorado, he has taught several diving classes.

UNIQUE VALUES OF DIVING

To become a proficient diver, the aspirant must either possess, or more often, further develop and refine, a wide variety of mental and physical abilities. Among these are the following: (1) to coordinate and synchronize two or more complex movements—especially somersaulting and twisting, (2) to perceive and grasp quickly body position and its relationship to the water, (3) to visualize through mental imagery the complete sequence of movements involved in many dives, (4) to be aware of the position of the body parts by means of visual and kinesthetic perception, (5) to coordinate with precision a variety of body movements and to control such movements with little apparent effort, and (6) to analyze a diving performance and develop an awareness of mistakes made and perhaps why they occurred.

Diving from a springboard can also contribute to the development of strength, power, and flexibility. It can aid in developing poise and self-discipline. Most divers (and former divers) view the challenge of attempting to perfect a dive or a list of dives as a rewarding and pleasurable experience.

DESCRIPTION OF DIVING

The diver attempts to make a relatively high take-off, which is initiated from either a stationary standing position or from a forward walking approach that terminates with the hurdle to the end of the board. The flight of the diver's center of gravity in the air describes a parabola that does not project the diver very far from the end of the board. While in the air the diver may twist, somersault, or bend his body in order to perform graceful but controlled

Diving: Springboard 151

aerial maneuvers, maintaining good body form. While still in the air, the diver fully extends his body and positions it for a head-first or a feet-first entry into the water, attempting to cause a minimum of splashing. An expert diver makes even the difficult dives look easy and effortless—sometimes described as poetry in motion—while exhibiting an awareness of his body position, the board, and the water at all times. Because a wide variety of dives can be performed from four basic types of take-off, and because several of the recognized dives are extremely difficult to control and perform while maintaining proper body form and position, the diver is constantly challenged to master additional dives or to perfect those dives he knows.

DIVING EQUIPMENT

The only necessary equipment the diver must furnish is a pair of diving trunks. These should be made of an elastic type material to facilitate stretching and twisting movements. Some divers prefer high-waisted trunks, believing that they enhance their appearance while diving. Some divers wear ear plugs, and/or nose plugs to avoid possible distress. However, most divers can quickly learn how to tolerate the unpleasant sensations that may be associated with submergence in chlorinated water.

Most diving boards are made of an aluminum alloy and have considerable flexibility, great strength, and long life. Their surface is treated or covered in order to make them less slippery. They often are equipped with a rubber cushion on the diving end for added safety. Diving boards, which are usually sixteen feet long and twenty inches wide, are normally located one meter (three and one-third feet) or three meters (ten feet) above the water surface. Most diving standards have a movable fulcrum that permits the amount and speed of the rebound of the board to be adjusted to the diver's weight and preference. Dives can also be performed from fixed platforms that are five, seven and one-half, or ten meters in height.

SAFETY

As is true of many sports, part of the challenge of diving lies in the fact that it does present a potential danger to the diver. Performing well despite such danger can be a satisfying experience. At no times, however, should the diver take unnecessary chances. He should be cognizant of the possible dangers and how best to avoid them. Observing the following safety rules should insure a maximum of safety:

1. Master the basic skills of a correct approach, hurdle, take-off, and entry before attempting complicated dives.
2. Have a complete mental picture of how a dive is performed and of all the individual movements comprising it before attempting the dive.
3. When first learning a dive, deliberately take it out away from the board a short distance.
4. Once the take-off has started, complete the intended dive—do not attempt to change the dive when in the air.
5. If a diver gets "lost" and has no idea where he is, he should tuck and remain in this position until after he enters the water. (He can also place his hands over his ears to avoid any possible damage to the eardrums.)
6. Above all else, avoid landing on the side of the head because of the danger of injuring the eardrum.
7. After completing a dive, move away from in front of the diving board.
8. Do not begin a dive until the previous diver surfaces and is out of the way.

RULES OF DIVING

Degree of Difficulty

For both the one-meter and the three-meter board, each dive is assigned a degree of difficulty. This number ranges from 1.2 to 3.0 and increases as the difficulty of the dive increases. The degree of difficulty is multiplied by the sum of the judges' awards. The total score for each dive is the product of the degree of difficulty and the sum of the judges' awards. When the total scores for each dive performed are added, the final score is obtained. The diver with the highest final score is the winner.

The degree of difficulty for each dive is reviewed each year by a national committee. The value assigned to each dive can be found in the NCAA *Official Swimming Guide,* which is published yearly and which is the official rule book for college swimming and diving competition.

Dives Performed

In dual meets the diver does one required and five optional dives (one of each class); in championship meets, five required and six optional dives are performed.

The diver positions his body in one or more of the following four positions during a dive: (1) tuck, in which the body is made as compact as possible by tucking it into a ball; (2) pike, in which the body is bent at the hips only; (3) layout, in which the body is maintained straight throughout the dive; and (4) free, which is used only in certain twisting dives in which it is necessary to change from one body position to another during the dive. An example of the free position is the forward 1½ somersault with one twist in which the diver begins in a pike position, changes to a layout position during the twisting movement, and then reverts to the pike position as the twist is completed.

Diving Judges

Three diving judges are commonly employed to judge each dive, and each judge bases his score on the complete dive, not one portion of it. Usually, in championship meets, five qualified judges score each dive. The highest and lowest scores are eliminated, the middle three are added together, and the resulting sum is multiplied by the degree of difficulty.

Awarding of Points

Points for a dive are awarded a value of from 10 to 0 (including half points) according to the opinion of the judges and the following table:

$$\begin{align*}
10 &= \text{perfect} \\
9\text{-}9\tfrac{1}{2} &= \text{very good} \\
7\text{-}8\tfrac{1}{2} &= \text{good} \\
5\text{-}6\tfrac{1}{2} &= \text{satisfactory} \\
3\text{-}4\tfrac{1}{2} &= \text{deficient} \\
\tfrac{1}{2}\text{-}2\tfrac{1}{2} &= \text{unsatisfactory} \\
0 &= \text{completely failed}
\end{align*}$$

When judging a dive, only the approach, hurdle, and dive are considered, without regard to the movements made in getting to the starting position. The points considered are the run, the take-off, the technique and grace of the dive during the passage through the air, and the entry into the water. The forward approach must include at least three steps plus the hurdle. For back take-offs, which are initiated from a standing stationary position, the diver is not permitted to lift his feet (hop) above the board before the take-off.

When doing a dive the diver should be a safe distance from the board. If he touches the board or goes to one side of it, the judges deduct points from their awards. Another cause for deducting points is an entry in which the diver's body is not in a vertical position.

In the event a diver stops during his forward approach, he has committed a balk, which carries the penalty of a loss of one third of the score from each judge. Should a dive position be partially broken or altered, the maximum judge's award is 4½ points; if completely broken or altered, the maximum is 2 points. If the diver performs a dive other than the dive listed for him, or if he does it in a different position than the one listed, he receives zero points.

THE MECHANICS OF DIVING

Mechanical Principles of Rotation

In accordance with Newton's Laws of Motion, a body will remain at rest unless acted on by an external force. In the case of a diver, there are three forces acting on him prior to the instant of take-off from the board:

1. The weight of the body, which can be considered constant and acting through the center of gravity.
2. The force exerted by the recoil of the board on the feet of the diver.
3. The friction between the board and the feet of the diver.

The force causing the diver to be projected from the board is the resultant of the latter two forces plus the momentum generated during the approach, if one is made. If the line of action of the resultant force passes through the diver's center of gravity, a parabolic trajectory [⌒] without a somersault type of rotation occurs. If the line of action of the resultant force does not pass through the center of gravity, the diver will be projected on a parabolic trajectory and will have rotational inertia such that his body rotates in the direction of the lean at the time of the take-off.

Stated in another way, anytime the center of gravity of an object moves to a position outside the object's base of support, a moment of force is created that tends to rotate that object in the direction of the lean. Thus, during take-off, the greater the distance that a diver's center of gravity is away from his feet (base of support), the greater is the force causing him to rotate or somersault while in the air.

The amount of angular inertia that a diver possesses is determined only by the arrangement of forces exerted on the diver at take-off. Once he loses contact with the board, the angular inertia is fixed throughout his trajectory and the path described by his center of gravity cannot be changed.

Amount of Body Lean During Take-off

The body position at the instant of take-off is probably the most crucial instant in the performance of a dive. However, the amount by which the body of the diver leans as it drops to the board and depresses it differs with each dive. In executing forward dives, there must be sufficient lean to permit the center of gravity to pass just

Diving: Springboard 153

beyond the base of support while the feet are on the end of the board. The proper amount of lean should not be confused with the common fault of beginning divers of falling off the board during the take-off. If the diver is falling forward during the take-off, a dramatic reduction in the amount of height and body control (balance) is the usual result. In forward and back dives (actually one-half somersaults) and somersaulting dives, the center of gravity of the diver should be slightly ahead of the base of support at the take-off. No further action on the part of the diver is necessary to achieve the correct line of flight if the amount of lean is correct at the take-off. However, during the descent of the hurdle, most novice divers often introduce more lean than is necessary, and height is lost while distance is gained. As a rule, only through much practice will the diver learn to obtain the correct lean for the type of dive performed. Consequently, as the diver attempts increasingly difficult dives, he must consciously resist the tendency to hurry the hurdle and take-off, which results in an inefficient take-off and a poorly performed dive.

Angular Velocity

The speed with which a diver rotates around his center of gravity is a function of his radius. A diver will rotate (somersault) around the horizontal axis of his center of gravity faster when in a tuck position than when in a layout position. He will rotate (twist) around his vertical axis with increased speed if his arms are brought close to his body.

The path taken by the diver's center of gravity during a dive, which is determined by the body position and lean during the take-off, and the rotation of the diver's body around its center of gravity are the two key principles involved in skillful and consistent diving.

DIVING SKILLS

The Approach

In becoming a successful diver, the approach, hurdle, and take-off are important basic skills underlying a consistent performance. The approach consists of two parts: (1) the starting position and (2) the run. (See Figure 12-1.)

The diver should always start the front approach from the same location on the board. In the starting position the head should be held erect, the chin in, and the chest up. The center of gravity should be located over the balls of the feet, the back should be straight, and the arms should be at the sides with the palms at the sides of the thighs. The eyes should be focused on the end of the diving board (without lowering the head to do so). While in the starting position, the diver should be concentrating on the dive that he is going to perform.

The run must consist of at least three and not more than six steps. The name is a misnomer, because it should resemble a walk rather than a run. The diver should be relaxed during his "run" to the end of the board. The steps should be approximately the same length, or perhaps

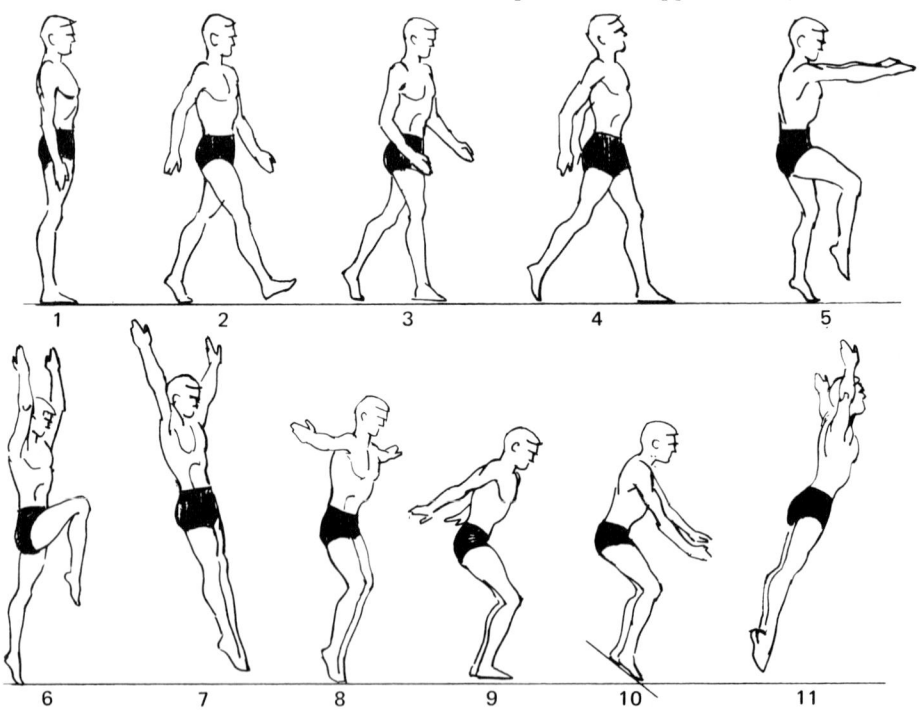

Figure 12-1. Approach, hurdle, and take-off.

should gradually increase in length. The last step of the approach, which sets up the hurdle, should end approximately eighteen to thirty inches (depending on the diver's height and speed of approach) from the end of the diving board. If an uneven number of steps is taken, a right-footed person should initiate the approach with the right leg. The arms swing naturally as in walking, except that at the beginning of the hurdle step both arms should be ready to come forward from behind the hips.

The Hurdle

The purpose of the hurdle is to change the direction of the momentum obtained during the approach from a forward direction to an upward direction. The higher the center of gravity can be raised in the hurdle, the more force will be available with which to depress the diving board, thus resulting in the increased height of the trajectory of the dive. The added potential energy stored in the deflected board then propels the diver upward. With additional height, the diver has increased time in which to perform the dive correctly. The difficult part of the hurdle lies not only in raising the center of gravity as high as possible, but also in maintaining proper balance and body position when returning to the diving board before the take-off. (See Figure 12-1.)

When placing the foot on the board on the last step (assume it to be the right) before the hurdle, the body continues to move forward until the center of gravity is over the ball of the right foot. The right leg is slightly flexed at the knee. A powerful upward swing is made by straightening the right leg and extending the right ankle. At the same time the left leg, which should be bent at the knee to form a 90° angle, is lifted until the thigh is at least parallel to the diving board. As the legs are performing these movements, the arms should move forward and upward from slightly behind the hips. The head should be sufficiently forward so that the eyes can maintain their focus on the end of the board. As the diver continues rising in the hurdle, the left leg should be stretched downward alongside the right leg in somewhat of a stair-climbing action. By the time that the diver reaches the highest point in the hurdle, both the legs and body should be stretched straight and aiming for the end of the diving board.

In the descent from the hurdle, the arms are delayed until just prior to the contact between the diver's toes and the diving board. The arms should then be forcefully driven downward slightly behind the hips, moved forward alongside the hips, and then lifted upward.

The balls of the feet should contact the diving board first. As the feet come in contact with the diving board, the diver should attempt (which will be unsuccessful) to keep his heels off the board. After the ankles flex, the knees and hips should also flex, serving to break the fall and to prepare for the leg extension at the take-off.

The extension of the knees and hips should begin as the diving board approaches the fullest depression caused by the weight of the diver settling on it. The extension should cause the diving board to be even further depressed as the diver attempts to drive the end of the board toward the water.

As the diving board recoils, the knees and hips should be continuing to extend. After the knees and hips have extended and the diving board has recoiled completely, the ankles of the diver extend vigorously as the take-off begins.

The action of the arms during the descent from the hurdle helps in the control of body balance and aids in further depressing the board and in the upward lift. As the body begins to drop to the board, the arms should be outstretched with the hands slightly more than shoulder width apart above the head. The palms should be facing forward and slightly downward. During the descent of the body to the diving board, the arms should remain in this position and start a slow outward motion. As the body nears the board, the motion is converted into a rapid downward swing slightly to the rear of the body. The hands should reach hip level just as the diving board is being depressed.

The arms should continue downward to a position immediately alongside the rear of the hips. They then are drawn forward and upward with the palms of the hands facing the hips. The upward action of the arms causes an equal and opposite downward reaction through the feet onto the board. As the hands are passing the hips, the diver should be extending the legs against the diving board. As the board is being depressed to its fullest extent, the arms should begin lifting upward so that by the time the diving board begins to recoil the arms reach shoulder level. The arms continue upward to the position necessary to guide the dive.

The Take-off

As contact with the diving board is lost, the diver's arms should extend forward and upward at an angle that is dependent on the dive to be performed. The eyes should be focused on the end of the board while the diver is in the hurdle. However, after contact is made with the board, the focus usually shifts to the far wall of the pool as the board is being depressed. During the take-off the focus of the eyes remains briefly on this target.

Drills

Walk through a three-step approach on the pool deck several times, noting the proper mechanics. Walk through

Diving: Springboard

a four-step approach on the pool deck several times. Determine which approach feels most natural. Next, perform the selected approach in the opposite direction on the diving board in order to determine the approximate starting point. Finally, spend some time practicing the approach and hurdle (doing a front jump or front dive into the water).

Common Errors

1. Not concentrating on the correct mechanics.
2. Not starting at the same place each time.
3. Walking too fast in the approach.
4. The last step or steps becoming too long.
5. Steps not the same size.
6. Incorrect arm movement (timing) during the hurdle.
7. Too much forward or backward lean at the take-off.
8. Arms not overhead during the hurdle and take-off.
9. Not extending the body as high as possible in the hurdle.
10. Incorrect head position during the approach, hurdle, or take-off.

Diving Entries into the Water

The point of entry into the water should be slightly forward of the center of gravity of the body, and on a line with the descending flight of the body. The diver's body should ordinarily continue down the line of flight to the bottom of the pool.

In the feet-first entry, the ankles should be extended so that the feet point downward, the body is straight, the arms are along the sides of the body with the palms of the hands on the front of the thighs, and the eyes are focused straight ahead, not downward.

In the head-first entry, the diver should spot the entry point and stretch while his arms and hands attempt to reach through the spot for the bottom of the pool. The hands should be clasped together, one over the other with the thumbs interlocked, and the arms should be held tightly against the head. This position helps streamline the body, reduces the amount of splash, and lessens the impact of the water on the head. The head should be in such a position that the eyes can just see the hands and the head is in line with the body. The back should be as straight as possible when the entry is made.

As a general rule, a diver should enter the water about as far from the board as the height that his center of gravity rises above the board. The diver, on all entries into the water, should stretch his body as much as possible, keeping it straight and not arched.

REQUIRED DIVES

When first beginning to dive, or later, the diver may work only on a one-meter board; he may alternate between a one- and a three-meter board, or, as is usually done, he will learn a dive first on a one-meter board before attempting it from the three-meter height. In making the transition from the one- to the three-meter board, the diver must remember that for the same dive he is in the air an increased length of time when using the three-meter board; hence, he must avoid a tendency to go long on the dive. The following pointers should aid in having the correct amount of rotation when diving from the three-meter board:

1. Little can be done to prevent going long once the diver leaves the board.
2. To avoid going long keep the head up and do not over-lean during the take-off.
3. Do not look for the water (and entry spot) too quickly.
4. To correct for being short the diver needs only to pike his body.

Forward Dive

The forward dive is probably the most commonly performed dive. When done in layout position it is commonly called the swan dive and in the pike position, the jackknife. When performing this dive, in order to avoid too much forward lean during the take-off, the eyes should be focused on the wall at the far end of the pool rather than on the water. Most beginning divers tend to go out too far from the board and enter the water at a flat angle, rather than enter the water vertically at a point approximately four to five feet from the end of the board.

The Forward Dive, Pike (Figure 12-2). The forward dive, when done in a pike position, is usually easy to perform because the amount of pike and length of time the pike is held can be controlled; thus, the amount of somersaulting action can be easily adjusted.

1. On the take-off the arms are moved forward and downward from the overhead position to the feet.
2. The diver should feel the hips lift as the hands go down for the touch.
3. The touch of the feet is made at the peak of the dive and when the legs are perpendicular to the water.
4. As the diver begins to descend, the legs are moved rearward.
5. The eyes spot the entry point and the entire body (including the arms, legs, and feet) is stretched for the entry.

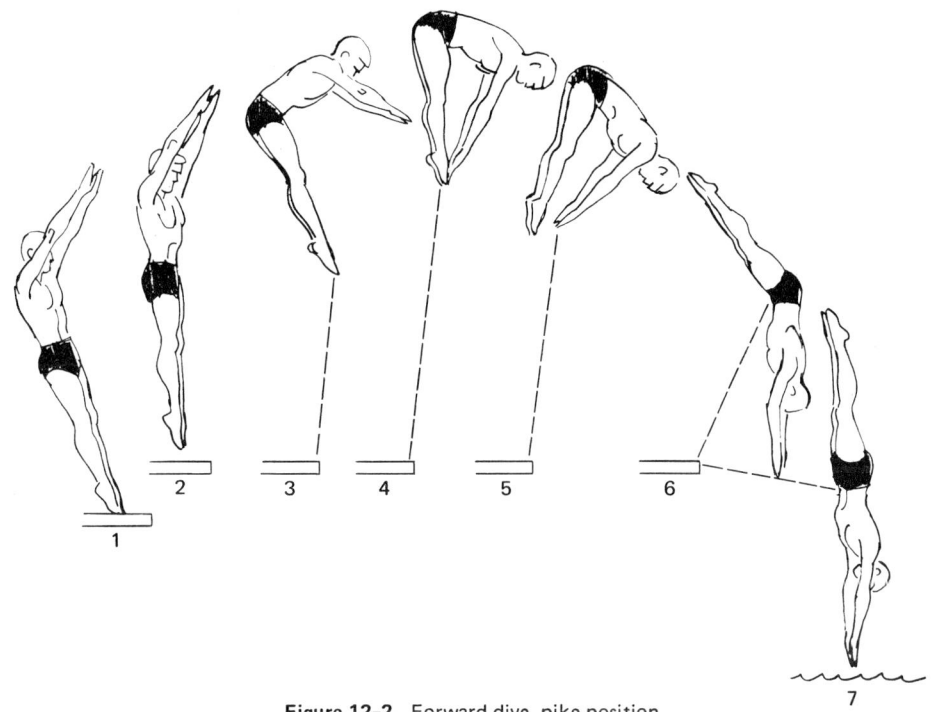

Figure 12-2. Forward dive, pike position.

The Forward Dive, Layout

1. As soon as the take-off begins, the eyes are focused on the front wall.
2. The diver should have the feeling of the feet moving backward as the body ascends.
3. The hands, after reaching up for height, are brought down, keeping the arms extended, until they are in line with the shoulders.
4. The dive rotates around the hips. A common mistake is to rotate the dive around the head, which is usually caused by not focusing the eyes on the front wall. This causes the dive to go long.
5. As the descent begins the diver focuses his eyes on the entry spot, the arms are again brought overhead, and the body is stretched.

The Back Dive

For dives in which a backward take-off is made (back and inward dives), no approach steps are utilized in the take-off.

The Stance. The feet are positioned on the board with only the heels off the end of the board and with the center of body weight over the balls of the feet. The heels are level with the board.

The Back Press. In a simultaneous action, the arms, which remain straight, move laterally up the side of the body and the feet are extended at the ankles. During this movement, the center of gravity remains over the balls of the feet but rises because the body and arms are raised. At the completion of this movement, the diver is in a position analogous to that of the top of the hurdle used with forward approaches, although his feet are still in contact with the board. As the arms begin to descend, the knees flex, and then the ankles flex. In a rounded action near the hips, the downward action of the arms is suddenly changed to an upward action. At the same time the knees and ankles extend as the arms lift upward for the take-off.

Drills. Back jumps, back presses, and take-offs should be regularly practiced, using a feet-first entry and emphasizing obtaining height and proper timing.

The Back Dive, Pike (Figure 12-3).

1. On the take-off the arms are stretched upward and stopped just in back of being vertically extended.
2. The completely extended legs are immediately lifted toward the hands by contracting the abdominal and thigh muscles.
3. The head is prevented from jerking back in an early attempt to see the water by first focusing on the wall behind the board and then watching the touch of the feet to the hands.
4. The touch is made as the diver reaches his peak height.
5. As the descent begins, the legs are held in the vertical position and the head and arms are dropped backward; the entry is then spotted.
6. The body is stretched for the entry.

Diving: Springboard

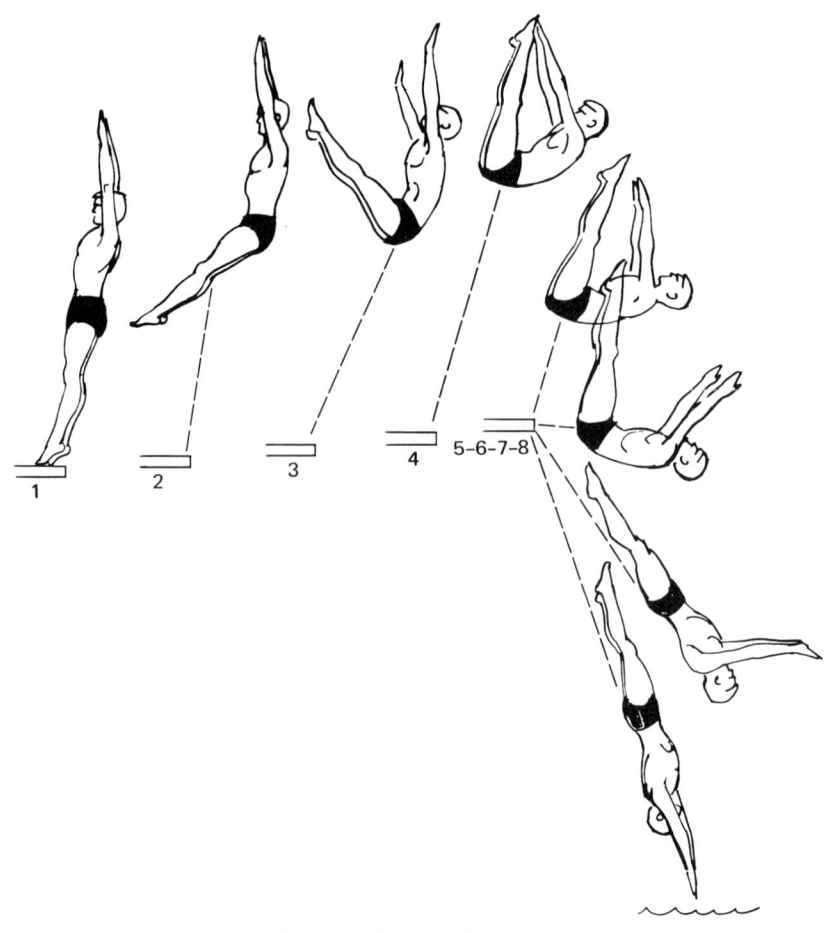

Figure 12-3. Back dive, pike.

The Back Dive, Layout

1. As the body leaves the board, the focus of the eyes shifts from the back wall to the ceiling immediately overhead.
2. The arms, after reaching upward on the take-off, are brought to the same position as in the front dive, layout.
3. As the peak of the dive is approached, the back arches, the arms begin to go overhead together, the eyes then begin to focus on the entry point, and the body stretches.

The usual mistake when first learning this dive is to focus the eyes on the water immediately after the take-off. This error invariably causes a back lean and the dive goes far from the board and is often long.

Forward Dive, One-half Twist, Layout

In order to acquire a feeling for the forward dive (Figure 12-4) with one-half twist (layout position), the diver should first stand on the end of the board with the arms extended laterally. The eyes are focused straight ahead. He falls forward and at the same time brings one arm to the front and the other arm to the rear. When the hand being brought forward is seen, keeping the eyes focused straight ahead, the water should also be seen beyond the hand. The eyes continue to remain focused on the water while the half-twist is completed by continuing the action of the rear hand by bringing it on around to the front.

1. The take-off is the same as for the front dive (layout position), except that the arms immediately perform the same motion as done in the drill described here.
2. The eyes should not see the water until after the peak height of the dive has been attained.
3. At the peak of the dive the diver should have the feeling that he is doing a swan dive on his side.
4. As the diver begins to descend, the arms are brought together, the back should be slightly arched, and the eyes "spot" the entry.

158 *Individual and Team Sports*

5. As the dive goes in with the body stretched, it should feel very much like a back dive.
6. The most common mistakes made in learning this dive are probably looking for the water too soon and not lifting the legs vigorously enough from the board at the take-off.

Inward Dive

Although it is one of the simplest dives to perform, the inward dive requires self-confidence because of an initial fear of hitting the board. Actually, because of the flexibility of the board and a built-in instinct to lean away from it, the chance of hitting the board is minimal. For consistent success, the diver needs to remain closer to the board in performing inward dives than when doing the dives in the other four groups.

Inward Dive, Pike (Figure 12-5). Mechanically, this dive is the same dive as the piked forward dive, except that the inward dive is done from a back take-off.

1. At the take-off the arms are vigorously moved from the overhead position down toward the feet.
2. The legs should be in a vertical position as the hands contact the feet. If the legs are in front of a vertical

Figure 12-4. Forward dive with one-half twist (layout position).

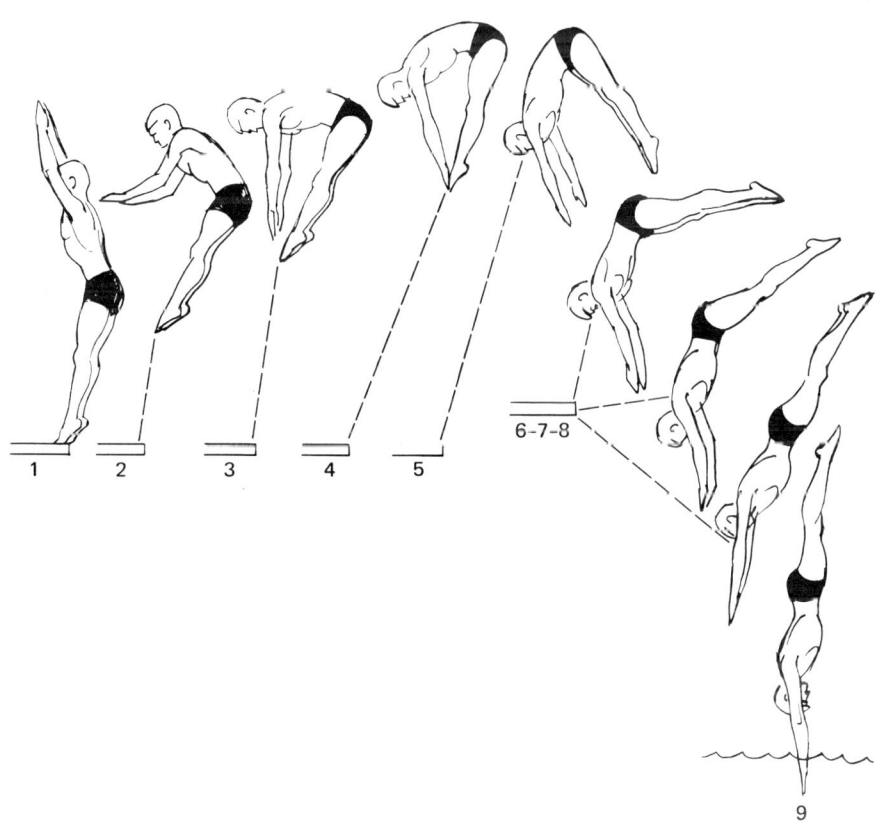

Figure 12-5. Inward dive, pike.

Diving: Springboard 159

position, the dive will probably be short. (The legs actually do move forward slightly in reaction to the arm movement, but because the entire body is rotating slightly it appears that the legs remain vertical.)

3. The eyes should see the touch and then focus on the water as the hands remain in the vertical position and the legs sweep backward and upward.
4. The body stretches for the entry.

The most common error made by novice divers is to lean backward before the take-off, which brings the legs in front of the desired vertical position, thus causing the dive to be short.

Inward Dive, Layout. The inward dive in a layout position is more difficult than a front dive, layout, because less height is obtained from the back press than from the front take-off.

1. The main emphasis during the take-off is the pushing up and backward movements of the legs and hips.
2. The arm movement is identical to that of the front dive, layout.
3. The head and eyes should remain focused forward until the peak of the dive is reached.
4. As in the front dive, layout, the diver rotates about the hips, not the head; however, he should have the feeling of rotating around the shoulders.

5. As the descent starts, the arms are brought together, the eyes are focused on the entry spot, and the body is stretched for the entry.

If the head is lowered too early in the layout inward dive (a common tendency because the diver feels he is going to be short), the legs will finish shorter than if this action had not been done.

Reverse Dive

Although not a difficult dive to do mechanically, the reverse dive is challenging because the diver cannot, during the initial stages, see the water for the entry. An excellent way to "get the feeling" of the dive and to see the importance of getting the legs up is to run off the board, kick an imaginary football (getting both legs as close to vertical as possible), and then drive the head back to look for the water. A towel on the end of a long stick held about ten feet in front of and eight feet above the end of the board gives the diver a target to kick at with both feet. He then extends the head back for the entry.

Reverse Dive, Pike (Figure 12-6).

1. This is actually the same dive as the back dive, pike, except that it is done with a front approach.
2. During the take-off the eyes are focused straight to the front.
3. Upon taking off, the arms are lifted overhead, stopping just slightly behind the vertical position.

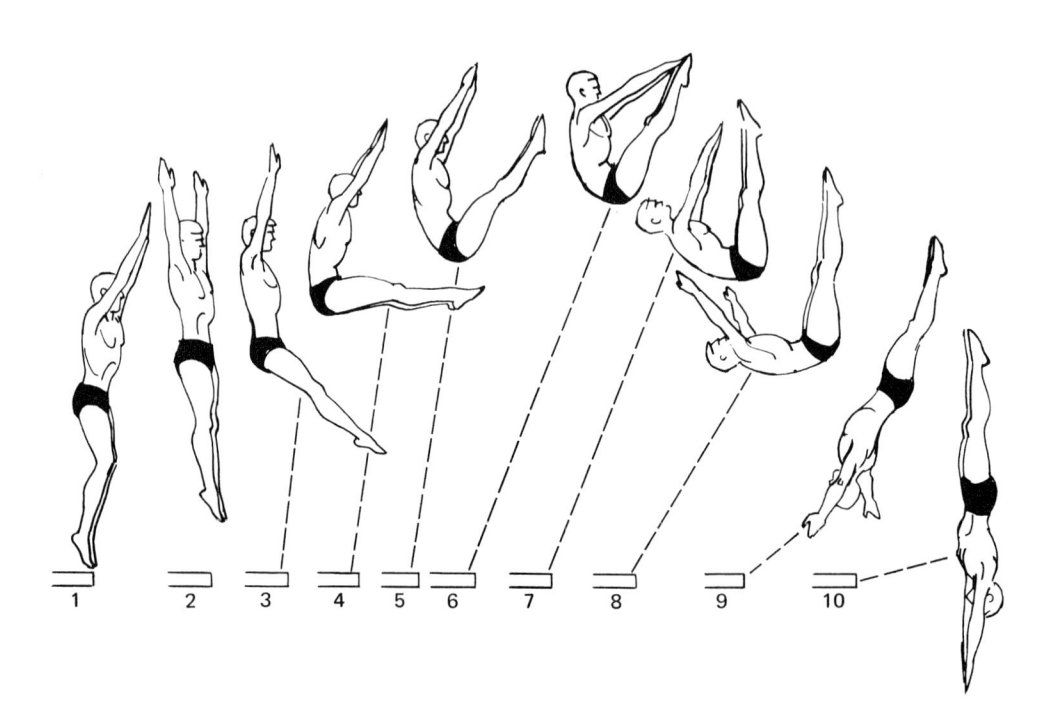

Figure 12-6. Reverse dive, pike.

4. The legs are immediately lifted (knees straight) to the hands by contraction of the abdominal and thigh muscles.
5. The eyes should see the feet touch the hands almost directly overhead.
6. The feet are then held in the vertical position as the head and arms drop back for the entry.
7. The body is stretched for the entry.

A common error made by beginning divers is the failure to raise the legs to the position for the touch. The farther in front of a vertical position the touch is made, the shorter the dive will probably be.

OPTIONAL DIVES

Form in Diving

Beginning with his first diving efforts, the diver should be conscious of his body position and form on each dive. He usually needs the help of an observer to tell him whenever he breaks form, such as allowing his legs to come apart, bending his knees during the entry (a common fault), or losing the point of his feet. In between dives and at other times, the diver should practice pointing his feet to the maximum, squeezing his legs together, and vigorously stretching his body.

Saving Nonvertical Entries

By the time the novice diver has attained sufficient diving proficiency to practice optional dives, he should have acquired some feel of whether his entries are about vertical or whether they are long or short. If a head-first entry is long, the diver may reach farther out from the board than usual with his hands in a save attempt, doing the opposite when he is short on an entry.

Many experienced divers attempt to save head-first dives by moving their legs forward or backward, as appropriate, as soon as their hips go under the water. The amount of saving action that can be done by this method is increased if the diver does a piked somersault immediately under the surface of the water. If long, he unpikes his legs (while they are still above the water) as he somersaults. If he is short, he increases the pike formed by his legs and body. This leg movement in the air is possible because of the resistance the water offers to the portion of the body underneath the surface. Considerable practice is needed to save dives correctly.

Selective Vision While Diving

During the first several attempts of a somersaulting or twisting dive, many beginners either close their eyes during most of the dive or else they see only a blur. Instead, the diver should keep his eyes open and focus his attention on seeing only preselected target areas (including the entry spot) during portions of the dive. For example, on a forward two and one-half somersault dive, the diver should focus on the far wall on the take-off; after completing one and one-half to one and one-quarter somersaults he should focus on the water near his entry point; then after completing two to two and one-half somersaults he should focus on the entry spot. By looking only for specific targets, the diver does not get lost during the dive, and he also has reassurance that the dive is properly timed for a correct entry.

FORWARD OPTIONAL DIVES

Mechanics Involved in Forward Optional Dives

In first attempting dives that require one or more forward somersaults, beginners tend to forget everything they have learned about the approach and hurdle. Some common mistakes include running much too fast in the approach, landing on the end of the board preparatory to take-off with too much lean, failing to get the arms overhead for the take-off, and stomping the board—all of which reduce the height of the take-off and the chances of executing a successful dive.

Forward Somersault, Tuck

1. Before the feet leave the board, the hands must already have been driven up for height; as the diver leaves the board the arms sweep forward and downward in an arc to the shins.
2. As the arms go toward the legs the head is tucked downward. These two motions increase the speed of rotation.
3. While ascending from the board, the diver assumes a tuck position by bringing the chest (and head) downward toward the bending knees. This position is held through the peak of the dive.
4. On the descent, the diver opens his position by extending the legs at the knees but stays flexed at the hips. This gives him a momentary appearance of sitting in mid-air.
5. The legs are then brought in line with the trunk by extending them at the hips, and the body is stretched for the entry. The arms are placed alongside the body before the entry occurs.

Forward Somersault, Pike

1. The arm movement at the take-off is the same as for the forward somersault, tuck.

Diving: Springboard 161

2. As the arms, head, and chest drive downward, the hips are raised.
3. The legs are grasped behind the knees (legs are straight), and the diver pulls the head as close to the knees as possible.
4. Again, on the descent, the "sitting in mid-air" position is attained, except that the legs point more toward the vertical than the horizontal.
5. As the descent continues, the legs are positioned perpendicular to the water, the arms slide up the legs to the thighs, and the body stretches for the entry.

Forward One and One-half Somersault, Tuck

1. This dive (Figure 12-7) is essentially the same as the forward somersault, tuck, except that increased effort is made to lift the hips and to somersault the body.
2. The tucked position is held longer than when doing only a full somersault, permitting an additional one-half somersault to be done.
3. The diver begins to extend from the tuck after about one and one-quarter somersaults have been completed.

In a mistaken effort to obtain increased height, the beginner often stomps the board, which results in the correct timing being missed.

Forward One and One-half Somersault, Pike

1. This dive bears the same relationship to the forward somersault, pike, as the forward one and one-half somersault, tuck, does to the forward full somersault, tuck.

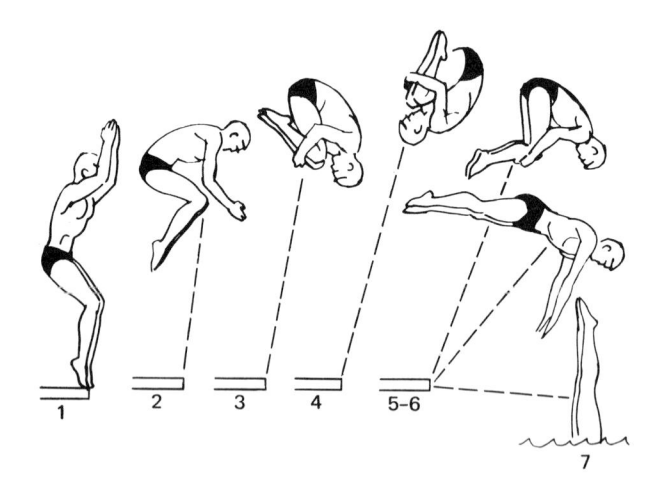

Figure 12-7. Forward one and one-half somersault dive, tuck.

2. On the take-off, the arms and head are driven down toward the knee as the hips lift upward.
3. The legs are grasped as in the forward somersault, pike, and the pike position is pulled as tight as possible.
4. The unpiking action occurs when the head and upper body are in a horizontal position, facing the water after one and one-quarter somersaults.
5. The legs are extended backward to an overhead position in line with the body; the entire body stretches for the entry.

Forward Double Somersault, Tuck

1. The key to doing a tucked, forward double somersault dive is the increased speed of the arm (and upper body) swing from the reach at take-off to the tuck position.
2. The rapid extension of the legs at the take-off is followed by a snap of the hips and feet in the direction of the rotation (mainly upward). At the same time the arms are thrust downward to the shins and the head and chest are pulled downward.
3. During the dive, centrifugal force attempts to loosen the tuck. The diver must keep the tuck as tight as possible.
4. The come-out should occur as the diver feels the body rotate to a sitting-down position, at which point the body is straightened rapidly.
5. If the diver has sufficient height, last-second adjustments can be made on the entry by controlling the speed of the come-out and the spot on the water surface to which the feet are directed.
6. As the legs go toward the water the toes retain their point, the head is lifted erect, and the hands slide from the shins to the front of the thighs.

Forward Two and One-half Somersault, Tuck

1. Without rushing the take-off, the diver vigorously initiates the forward somersaulting action as for the previously described dives.
2. Holding a tight tuck position for somewhat less than two and one-quarter somersaults, the diver then "opens" for the entry.
3. The body snaps open with the arms shooting downward and the legs extending rapidly backward and upward.
4. The diver should stretch hard for the entry, the action of which aids in the rapid extension of the legs and reduces the angular velocity of the diver's body.

OPTIONAL BACK DIVES

For two reasons back somersault dives are potentially dangerous dives for beginners. If the board is not sufficiently depressed, or if the timing is slow and the diver does not jump off the board until after it has recoiled, the board will not push the diver very far away from it. In addition, because the beginning diver does not see the board while somersaulting, because he does not have much height, and because his head comes to an erect position when under the board, he does not have a natural tendency to lean back during the take-off, as happens on the inward dive, for example. These errors can cause the board to come close to the top of the diver's head as it comes up under the board. The solution is to make sure to push the board down hard during the press and then take off as it is recoiling, not afterward.

Back Somersault, Tuck

1. Aside from being initiated from a back press, another important variation of the back somersault from the forward somersault dive is that the legs move toward the chest during the tucking action, whereas in the forward somersault the chest moves down toward the legs.
2. At the take-off the arms are extended overhead.
3. The tuck is quickly assumed immediately after the take-off.
4. The body passes through the peak of the dive while still in a tuck position.
5. The untuck is made by extending the legs as the trunk is horizontal to the water.
6. As the body stretches for the entry, the hands slide up the legs from the shins to the thighs.

Back One and One-half Somersault, Tuck

1. As the diver leaves the board, the body should extend fully and a complete upward reach should be made with the arms. The temptation to tuck too soon, which reduces height, must be avoided.
2. As the take-off is made, the arms swing forward in front of the face and upward to an overhead position.
3. Immediately afterward, and without any pause, the head lifts upward with the eyes focusing on the hands.
4. The knees are then brought upward toward the hands and, as the knees drive to the chest, the hands grasp the bent legs just below the knees and pull them tightly to the chest.
5. The head pulls in to increase the speed of the rotation of the body.
6. The hands release the legs just as the legs pass the horizontal after completing one and one-quarter somersaults. (The diver often spots the end of the board and extends his legs toward it.)
7. As the legs extend, the arms simultaneously extend laterally and then come overhead while the body straightens for the entry.
8. Between the come-out and the entry into the water, the back arches slightly and the head tilts backward. (See Figure 12-8.)

A common error in executing the come-out of this dive is to throw the head, chest, and arms vigorously away from the tucked legs, which causes the legs to be short (opposite and equal reaction). Instead, the legs should rapidly be first extended at the knee and then held in place as the arms, chest, and head reach back for the entry.

REVERSE OPTIONALS

Reverse Somersault, Tuck

A reverse somersault is actually a back somersault executed from a front approach.

1. Immediately after the take-off the legs are brought to the chest; they are contacted with the hands while the body is close to a vertical position.
2. As the knees come up overhead, the head gradually pulls back to look for the water.
3. The diver passes through the peak of the dive while in a tuck position.
4. As the trunk comes to a horizontal position, the legs shoot out to slow the rotation.
5. The hands slide up from the shins to the thighs as the body stretches for the entry point, which can be seen when still upside down.

Reverse One and One-half Somersault, Tuck

1. During the take-off the arms, which are held shoulder-width apart, swing forcefully forward and upward to a vertical overhead position.
2. The eyes follow the hands.
3. The knees are lifted up to the hands for a tight tuck position.
4. When the knees come to the chest, the tuck is tightened by the pull of the hands just below the knees.
5. The head simultaneously extends back and leads the rotation. (Or else it may flex forward in order to tighten the tuck and increase the velocity of the rotation.)

Diving: Springboard 163

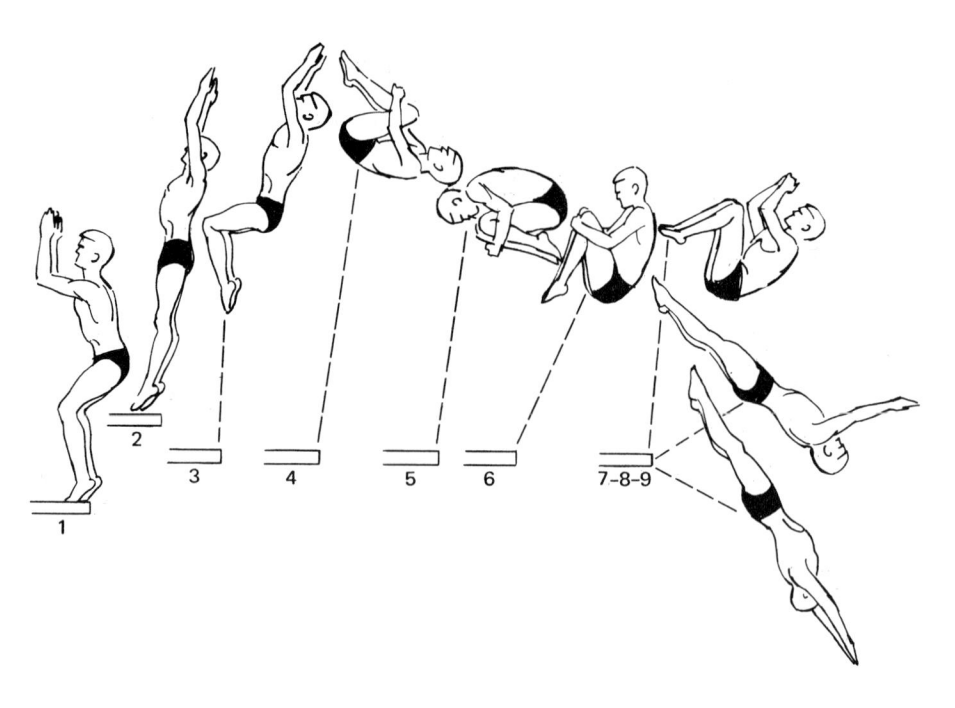

Figure 12-8. Back one and one-half somersault dive, tuck.

6. The opening of the dive comes after one and one-quarter somersaults have been completed.
7. The legs kick out slightly above the horizontal position; the arms reach sideward and then overhead for the entry.
8. The legs should initiate the opening movement by extending and are then held in place while the arms and head reach back for the entry. (See Figure 12-9.)

Beginners commonly make the mistake of keeping the legs tucked while opening the arms and trunk.

INWARD OPTIONAL DIVES

Inward Somersault, Tuck

1. As for the tucked forward somersault, the tucked inward somersault dive is performed by rotating the arms, head, and trunk toward the legs, which are simultaneously bending at the knee for the tuck position.
2. At the take-off the hips are lifted up and slightly back away from the board.
3. The tuck, which should be pulled tight throughout the peak, is released as the sitting-in-mid-air position is reached.
4. As the legs straighten for the entry, the hands slide up to the thighs. (See Figure 12-10.)

Many beginners fail to remain tucked long enough to complete the somersault. Others lean backward too far at take-off.

Inward One and One-half Somersault, Tuck

1. The feeling when performing a one and one-half inward somersault is very similar to that when doing the forward one and one-half somersault.
2. As the hips and legs are lifting from the board, the arms and head are thrust in an arc forward and downward.
3. The tuck must be as compact as possible, because with the maximum height obtained from the back take-off, the speed of rotation must be relatively fast.
4. As the water is spotted, the hands stretch for the water and the legs extend upward.

Errors often made in executing this dive include (1) swinging the arms too vigorously during the take-off, causing a loss of balance and control; and (2) falling or leaning back during the take-off, or pushing the hips away from the board instead of up above the head, both of which reduce the height of the dive.

TWIST OPTION

In twisting dives the twist can occur anytime during the dive, except that the pike must precede the twist for the

164 *Individual and Team Sports*

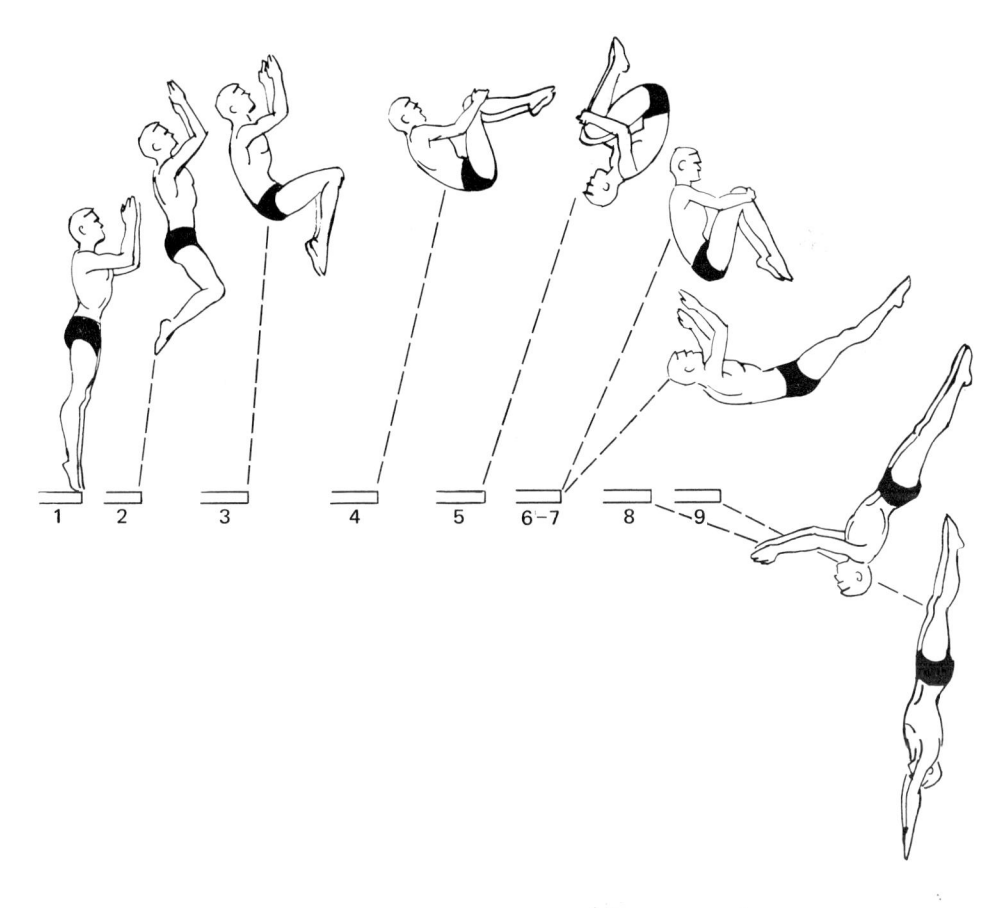

Figure 12-9. Reverse one and one-half somersault, tuck.

Figure 12-10. Inward somersault, tuck.

forward, back, inward, and reverse dives with one-half twist in pike position.

Back Dive, One-half Twist, Layout Position

1. The take-off is the same as for the back dive, layout.
2. As the peak of the dive is approached, with the body in a near-vertical position, the diver rolls over to a face-down position. To roll (twist to the left), the elbow of the left arm is brought behind the back and the right arm is positioned across the chest. At the same time the head is rotated to the left.
3. When the one-half twist is completed, the arms extend outward momentarily.
4. The entry is the same as for the front dive, layout. (See Figure 12-11.)

Reverse Dive, One-half Twist, Layout Position

1. The take-off is identical to that for the reverse dive, layout. The diver should feel he is thrusting his hips toward the ceiling, and he should not look for his point of entry.

Diving: Springboard 165

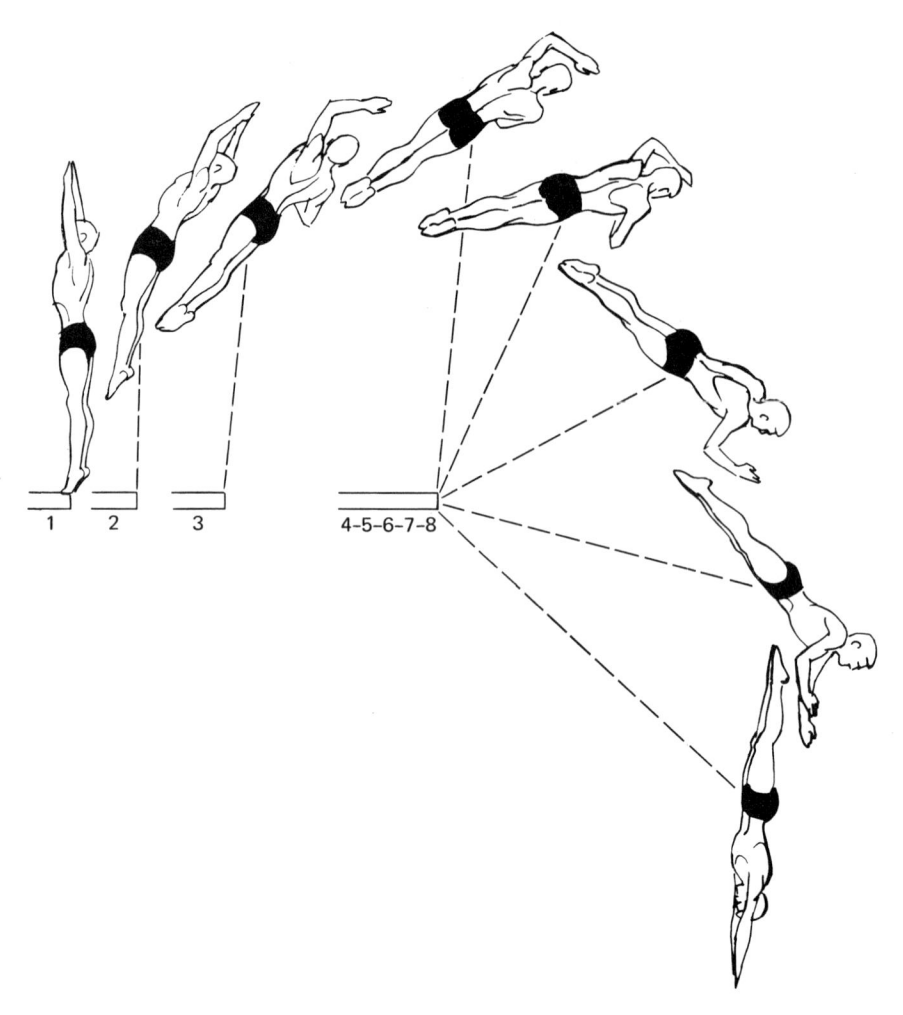

Figure 12-11. Back dive, one-half twist.

2. As the peak of the dive is approached, the diver does a one-half twist to the left in the same manner as for the back dive with one-half twist.
3. The entry is done as for an inward dive, layout, which is similar to that for a forward dive, layout. (See Figure 12-12.)

Forward Dive, Full Twist, Layout Position

1. The take-off is basically the same as for the front dive, layout.
2. The upper body twists slightly before contact with the board is lost.
3. As the dive reaches its peak to twist to the right, the left arm cuts in across the chest and bears downward. The left shoulder is thus lowered.
4. The right arm is immediately raised above the head; it bends at the elbow and the right hand goes behind the head, thus becoming part of the long axis of rotation.
5. The legs must be forced upward during the entire action.
6. During the first one-quarter twist, the eyes focus on the water and remain focused there until the twist is far enough to rotate the head to the side.
7. The initial one-half twist should be completed at the peak of the dive, at which instant the diver should be in a horizontal position. There is no pause in the 360° twisting movement.
8. As the head turns sharply to the right, the right elbow drives backward and the eyes spot the entry point.
9. The left arm extends toward the point of entry and the right arm joins the left arm in stretching for the entry. (See Figure 12-13.)

Forward Somersault with One-half Twist, Free Position

1. As the diver leaves the board, the same mechanics used in the forward somersault, pike are employed.

166 *Individual and Team Sports*

Figure 12-12. Reverse dive, one-half twist.

Figure 12-13. Forward dive, full twist.

Diving: Springboard **167**

2. The hips and feet are snapped toward the ceiling while the legs remain extended.
3. At all times the eyes remain focused on the water—the dive pivots around the head.
4. In order to maintain the focus on the water, the one-half twist must be accomplished while the diver is upside down.
5. The one-half twist is done by swinging one flexed arm in front and the opposite flexed arm in back of the body as the body is proceeding from a pike position at take-off to a layout position at the peak of the dive.
6. As the entry is approached the toes are pointed, the hands are brought to the front of the thighs, and the head is brought to an erect position.

Forward One and One-half Somersault with One-half Twist

1. The take-off and somersaulting portions of the dive are the same as for the forward double somersault.
2. When one and one-quarter somersaults have been completed the opening begins.
3. As the legs straighten, one arm releases from the legs and goes over the head with the same shoulder leading the twist.
4. The other arm extends directly for the water and the eyes focus on the entry spot.
5. The twist is completed as the body goes from a tuck to a layout position.
6. As the diver nears the water the arms are brought together overhead, and the body is stretched for the entry. (See Figure 12-14.)

DIVING TRAINING METHODS

Nondiving Methods of Training

Many divers, during the off-season or early season, supplement their diving skills with a variety of training mediums. Almost daily, they engage in flexibility exercises, doing fifteen to twenty-five repetitions of each exercise and holding each flexed position a few seconds. Forward and backward flexibility at the waist and hips and a high degree of downward flexion of the feet at the ankle joint are especially stressed.

The use of the trampoline is particularly valuable in developing twisting skills from flat front and back drops on the bed (without any somersaulting action), twisting movements combined with front and back somersaults, and front and back somersaults. Safety belts can be used to spot the diver when learning multiple somersaults or twists. When available, the use of a diving board mounted over a sand pit permits the diver to work efficiently on approaches, hurdles, and take-offs.

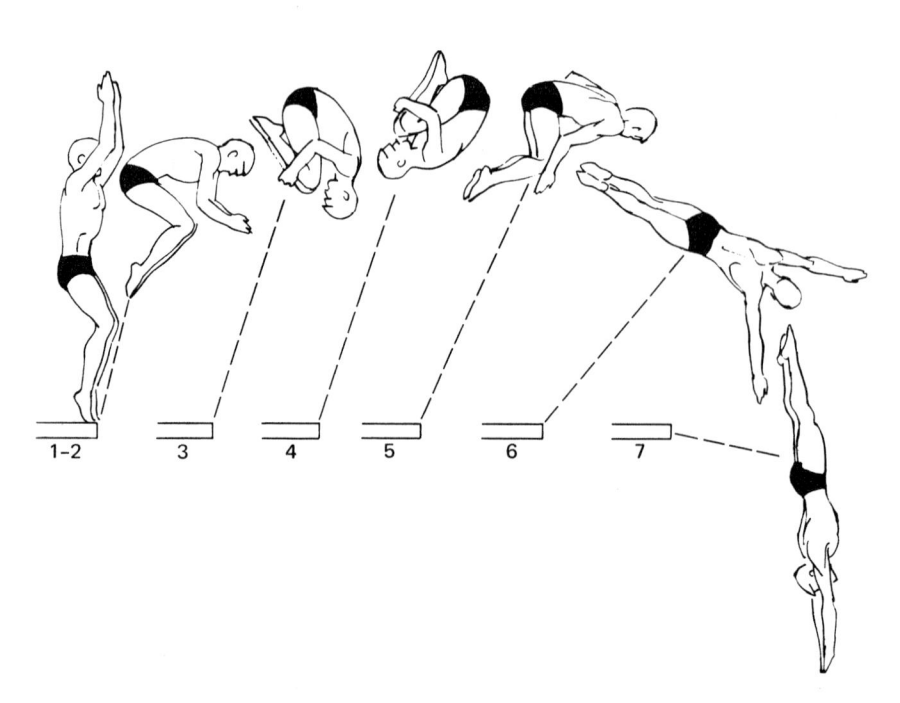

Figure 12-14. Forward one and one-half somersault with one-half twist.

In order to develop over-all strength, or the strength of selected muscle groups, many divers benefit from engaging in weight-training exercises. Strong muscles of the lower back, abdominal area, thighs, and lower leg are especially important for success in diving.

Training for Competitive Diving

Many competitive divers work out twice a day during the season. During the first session they may practice only required dives, and only optional during the second session. Another procedure is to practice one-meter dives at one session and three-meter dives at the other.

When learning or mastering a dive, many divers will practice the same dive several times before proceeding to practice the next one. This permits them to study their diving technique in detail, pinpoint their errors, and attempt to correct them. However, once competition begins, most divers decide on the order in which they will perform their dives and then practice each dive only once or twice before performing the next dive in order. This permits them to simulate closely the conditions that prevail during diving competition.

SELF-EVALUATION

The Diving Skills Score Sheet that appears on the next page is highly useful in evaluating diving skill. Although the diver can periodically score himself on the dives listed, a preferred procedure is to have the dives judged by an experienced diving judge or instructor (or another student). The judging can be done each class period or at a regular interval set aside for that purpose. Whenever he wishes, the diver can repeat the same dive, recording his highest score. If the dives are judged according to the NCAA scoring scale previously listed, a rough evaluation of the total score is as follows:

		Approximate Letter Grade
75 points or higher	=	A
50–74 points	=	B
25–49 points	=	C
10–24 points	=	D
9 or fewer points	=	F

Diving Skills Test Score Sheet

Name _____ Semester _____ Year _____

Dive   *Score*

1. Forward dive .... _____
2. Back press .... _____
3. Back dive .... _____
4. Forward dive, one-half twist .... _____
5. Inward dive .... _____
6. Reverse dive .... _____
7. Forward somersault .... _____
8. Forward one and one-half somersault .... _____
9. Forward double somersault .... _____
10. Forward two and one-half somersault .... _____
11. Back somersault .... _____
12. Back one and one-half somersault .... _____
13. Reverse somersault .... _____
14. Reverse one and one-half somersault .... _____
15. Inward somersault .... _____
16. Inward one and one-half somersault .... _____
17. Back dive, one-half twist .... _____
18. Reverse dive, one-half twist .... _____
19. Forward dive, full twist .... _____
20. Forward somersault, one-half twist .... _____
21. Forward one and one-half somersault with one-half twist .... _____

Total Score _____

Diving Terms

Approach: The three to six steps taken before the hurdle.
Award: The number or score (ranging from zero to 10) awarded by each judge.
Balk: A diver who begins the approach but stops before leaving the board has committed a balk.
Degree of difficulty: A number varying from 1.2 to 3.0, which is assigned to each dive and ranks the dive according to its difficulty.
Final score: The sum of the total scores awarded a diver.
Free position: Any combination of the layout, pike, or tuck positions.
Fulcrum: The bar under the middle of the diving board which, if adjustable, can be used to vary the amount of spring obtained from the board.
Hurdle: The jump following the last step of the approach and preceding the take-off.
Layout position: The body is not bent either at the knees or at the hips, the feet are together, and the toes pointed.
Long: An expression used to denote that a dive entered the water past its intended amount of rotation.
Optional dive: Selected by the diver. (A required dive may not be *repeated* as an optional dive.)

Diving: Springboard

Peak: The point during a dive in which the diver's center of gravity changes from an upward to a downward direction.

Pike position: The body is bent at the hips, but the legs are kept straight at the knees and the toes pointed.

Required dive: Selected from the following list: (1) forward dive, (2) back dive, (3) reverse dive, (4) inward dive, or (5) one-half twist.

Save: A method (tucking or piking while partially underwater) used to make the legs enter the water vertically even though a dive is long or short.

Short: An expression used to denote that a dive entered the water short of its intended amount of rotation.

Take-off: The movements made from the end of the hurdle until the diver loses contact with the board.

Total score: The judges' award multiplied by the degree of difficulty.

Tuck position: The body is as compact as possible with the toes pointed.

Selected References

Armbruster, David A., Robert H. Allen, and Hobert S. Billingsley. *Swimming and Diving.* St. Louis, Mo.: Mosby, 1973.

This classic textbook in the field of swimming contains two chapters (92 pages) on teaching and coaching springboard and tower diving. The author of the chapters, Hobbie Billingsley, has long been recognized as one of the top diving coaches in the world. The illustrations are excellent, as are the advice and information given concerning diving.

Batterman, Charles. *The Techniques of Springboard Diving.* Cambridge, Mass.: MIT Press, 1968.

The author has done an outstanding job of explaining the mechanical principles underlying springboard diving and showing their application to various dives. Excellent explanations and illustrations abound throughout the book, which is all-inclusive in its coverage and, hence, is an extremely valuable reference for the advanced diver.

Billingsley, Hobbie. *Diving Illustrated.* New York: Ronald, 1965.

The author of this well-illustrated book is the diving coach at Indiana University and has produced many national NCAA and AAU diving champions. In the book the methods and techniques utilized in performing all the recognized dives are listed. For each dive, multiple illustrations are keyed to the numbered instructions for performing the dive.

NCAA. *Swimming Guide.* Phoenix, Ariz.: College Athletics Publishing Service, yearly.

This guide, in addition to containing the official NCAA swimming rules and records, also lists the official rules governing NCAA diving competition.

CHAPTER 13

Diving: skin and scuba

*William D. Van Atta**
The University of Wisconsin—La Crosse

Peter R. Francis [†]
Iowa State University

Figure 13-1

INTRODUCTION

The great popularity that skin and scuba diving (self-contained underwater breathing apparatus) has achieved since World War II is the result of the interest focused on it by people seeking adventure. Men, women, and youth with a strong desire for excitement and exploration were quick to take advantage of the opportunity offered by the sport of skin and scuba diving.

---

*B.S., M.A., Ohio State University, Ph.D., University of Iowa. Dr. Van Atta is well qualified to write this chapter on skin and scuba diving. He is undergoing certification to teach scuba diving, and has taught swimming and other aquatic sports classes, including skin and scuba diving, for a number of years. In addition to participating in this sport, Dr. Van Atta has competed several times in long-distance swimming events.

†Certificate of Education, University of Leeds, England; Diploma in Physical Education, Carnegie College, England; B.Sc., University of Durham, England; M.A., University of Iowa. Peter R. Francis is a National Association of Skin Diving Schools Senior Diving Instructor, has a bachelor's degree in Marine Zoology and has had fifteen years of diving experience. During the time that he taught scuba diving at the University of Iowa, Mr. Francis has held advanced scuba certification courses in the Bahamas, Jamaica, and the Cayman Islands. He is continuing these activities at Iowa State University, Ames.

Skin and scuba diving offer the pursuit of a variety of sub-interests. Diving may be pursued by both men and women, and it is also an excellent family activity. Through careful selection of the dive-site, a satisfying experience can be developed for divers ranging from ten to fifty years or more. Spear fishing is probably the most physically demanding of all diving interests, especially if the diver participates as a skin diver in which he must depend on his own breath-holding ability, as opposed to using a self-contained underwater breathing apparatus (SCUBA).

Underwater photography has grown tremendously, originating from an interest on the part of divers to demonstrate to the non-diving world the wonders and beauty of the underwater world. Many non-diving photographers have been attracted to the sport as well.

Scuba diving is utilized in many non-sport pursuits. All branches of the military establishment have highly-skilled diving units that are trained to fulfill a variety of missions ranging from air-sea rescue to reconnaissance infiltration and sabotage. The sciences concerned with underwater explorations and research make extensive use of scuba divers. Several college training programs require scientists in training to acquire diving skills. Oceanography, marine biology, geology, archaeology, and other sciences are broadening their underwater efforts at a great rate. Man will doubtlessly increase the amount of underwater research in the future.

HISTORY

The study of diving from an historical standpoint is an interesting activity in itself. The development of underwater diving can be traced in four major categories: open sea diving, military diving, commercial diving, and sport diving.

Fossil evidence indicates that man made his first move into the underwater world far back in prehistoric times. Piles of oyster and other deep-water shells indicate that thousands of years ago tribes living along sea coasts removed some of their food from the sea by diving. As early as 3,000 B.C. the civilization in Crete was dependent on products of the sea, many of which were undoubtedly gathered by divers. References to oyster and sponge divers are found in Homer's *Iliad* (about 750 B.C.). Open-sea diving has been practiced for thousands of years and is still practiced by native divers in the Pacific and Mediterranean areas.

Military diving has also been practiced for thousands of years. In about 460 B.C., Scyllias, a skillful Greek diver, contributed to the thwarting of a naval assault by the Persians by cutting the cables of several ships during a storm. Historical records since that time are rich with the exploits of military divers. In the first century A.D., Swedish divers contributed to the defeat of the Danish pirate Oddo by cutting holes in the bottoms of Oddo's ships. By the Middle Ages, the use of divers was so common that underwater clashes between divers of warring nations sometimes occurred. During the siege of Malta, about 1565, Turkish and Maltese divers engaged in a bloody battle with hatchets that ended with the retreat of the Turkish divers. Changes in naval warfare brought about by the use of gunpowder resulted in the minimizing of the diver's role in naval operations. However, the Spanish continued to use natural divers for maintenance purposes as late as 1779. With the development of deep sea diving equipment, military divers took on the tasks of ship salvage, harbor clearance, underwater construction, recovery, and research. The development of reliable self-contained underwater breathing apparatus returned divers to combat roles in World War II. Frogmen of many nations were involved in battle activities, including torpedo attacks, mine laying, beach clearance, reconnaissance, and sabotage. The extensive publicity given to the exploits of World War II frogmen had much to do with the rapid rise in popularity of the sport following the war.

Early commercial diving was done by natural divers. Divers were reportedly used to assist with ship salvage before the birth of Christ. Obviously, natural divers were seriously limited in the amount of work that they could accomplish. The development of devices that allowed man to remain underwater for longer-than-normal periods of time can be traced back several hundred years before the time of Christ. Drawings from these early times are sometimes bizarre but are often surprising in the concepts they depict. Early workable diving equipment (Figures 13-2 and 13-3) involved the use of tubes or hoses to the surface. The pressure beyond shallow depths limited man's range with this type of device. In 1680 Giovanni Borelli, an Italian astronomer, made sketches for a recirculating type of apparatus but it was one hundred years before a usable self-contained apparatus was developed.

Diving bells were developed at a somewhat rapid rate. In 1538 man made successful descents in diving bells; an inventor named Becker was able to stay underwater for one hour in 1715. In 1783 wearing leather suits, supplied with air through brass bound leather hoses, divers assisted

Figure 13-2. Early diver using a reed for surface breathing.

Figure 13-3. Early shallow-water breather apparatus.

in the attempted raising of the warship "Royal George." Augustus Seibe made a major contribution to diving in 1819 with the invention of his "open dress" diving suit. Air was pumped from the surface into the diver's helmet and it escaped around the diver's waist. A self-contained diving suit, utilizing a tank of compressed air, was invented by W. H. James in 1825, but because of the lack of high pressure compressors at that time, the development of the suit was not considered important. A closed suit, which first was put into use by Seibe in 1837 became standard dress for about a century.

In 1866, two Frenchmen, Benoust Rouquayral and Captain Denayrouge, designed and built the forerunner of the demand-type regulator used today. H. A. Fleuss developed a self-contained oxygen rebreathing apparatus in 1878 that was further developed and used during World War I as a submarine escape device. The oxygen rebreather incorporated the use of a carbon dioxide absorbant, a steel oxygen flask, and an automatic feed valve. Commander Le Prieur developed, in 1925, a self-contained compressed air device. Divers could now work below the twenty-five to thirty-five foot maximum depth imposed by the oxygen rebreather apparatus. In Le Prieur's device, compressed air was released manually into the face mask from which it escaped into the water (Figure 13-4). The development of the Cousteau-Gagnan Aqua Lung in 1943 proved to be a major break-through in the field of diving. Commercial divers now make extensive use of scuba for much of their work. The light weight, highly reliable, demand-type breathing apparatus available today provides divers with greater flexibility, increased mobility, and requires fewer support personnel and facilities.

Sport diving in the United States underwent an extremely rapid period of growth during the ten to fifteen years immediately following World War II. Returning

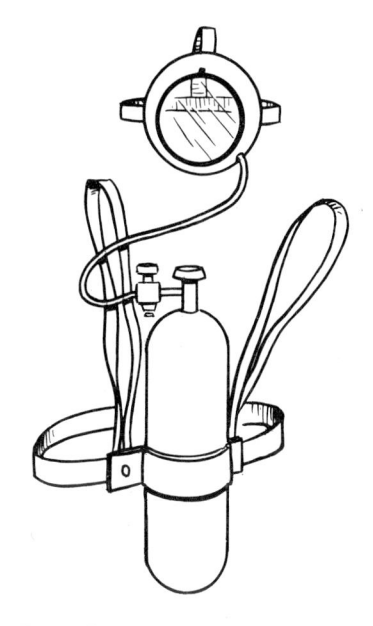

Figure 13-4. Le Prieur diving apparatus.

servicemen from the South Pacific, Mediterranean, and Caribbean areas, where sports diving was popular, introduced sports diving to the warm areas of the country such as the coastal areas of Florida and California. Today sports diving clubs are found across the nation from the lakes and rivers of the northern states to the coastal regions on the East, West, and South.

GETTING STARTED

It should be obvious that to take part in sport diving the individual should be in good physical and mental condition, and he should have acquired certain basic swimming skills. Sport diving includes vigorous activities such as spear fishing and deep diving for extended periods. Further physical and mental demands may be made on the diver during emergency situations. The beginning sport diver should therefore aim to meet the following requirements:

1. Pass a physical examination with special attention given to the condition of the sinuses, ears, heart, and lungs.
2. Swim the front crawl stroke, breast stroke, elementary back stroke, and side stroke in good form.
3. Swim without undue fatigue the front crawl stroke a distance of 440 yards.
4. Float in a relaxed fashion on the front, vertically, or on the back for three minutes.
5. Tread water for three minutes.
6. Demonstrate the ability to "bob" (a drown-proof technique of survival) indefinitely.

Diving: Skin and Scuba

7. Surface dive to a depth of fifteen feet.
8. Swim twenty-five yards underwater without a dive or push-off.

If the swimmer can meet the above requirements the next step is to locate a diving class or private instructor. Skin and scuba classes are regularly offered by YMCA, several universities and colleges, and many skin and scuba diving clubs. In most areas private instruction is available. If interested in private instruction, a competent instructor is a must. Such instructors will have had instructor training and hold NASDS,[1] NAUI,[2] PADI,[3] or YMCA instructor certification.

When a skin and scuba diving class is not available many of the skin diving skills can be practiced while alone. Skills should be thoroughly understood before they are attempted in the water. Having an instruction manual near the pool so that it is readily available for reference when it is needed is helpful. The basic skills listed in the following section are listed in their appropriate order of progression; they may be used for self-instruction.

Before actually starting class work, as much should be read and absorbed about sport diving as possible. The more that the diver knows and understands about the sport, the more enjoyable the sport will be and the more competent the diver will become.

BASIC SKIN AND SCUBA DIVING SKILLS

Sport diving is a relatively safe activity if the sport diver develops a basic pattern of safety. There is no substitute for the basic aquatic skills discussed in the previous section. If one possesses weak aquatic skills, lacks one or two skills or has low endurance, these very important areas should be improved in addition to working on basic skills of skin and scuba diving. Whenever possible, the sport diver should read about the sport, especially in the areas of technology, medical aspects, and safety. A safe attitude based on knowledge, and typified by caution in areas of inexperience will greatly help to ensure the diver's enjoyment of the sport for many years. The remainder of this section includes information about basic skin diving skills, basic scuba diving skills, and selected rescue techniques.

EQUIPMENT

Before discussing the basic skills of sport diving, the basic equipment used should be considered. The minimum equipment for the neophyte sport diver includes a face mask, snorkel, and swim fins.

The Face Mask

The face mask consists of a body, skirt, lens, pressure band, and head strap. The body of the mask should be constructed of medium soft synthetic rubber. A snug fit to the face should be provided by a soft flexible skirt. The lens, which is made of safety glass, should fit into a recess in the interior of the body of the mask and should be held in place by a pressure band. An easily adjustable head strap should be attached to the body of the mask

Figure 13-5. Equipment display—skin- and scuba-diving equipment.

[1] National Association of Skin Diving Schools.
[2] National Association of Underwater Instructors.
[3] Professional Association of Diving Instructors.

174 *Individual and Team Sports*

near the pressure band. Many fine masks at a variety of prices are on the market. Try several different types of masks before purchasing one. Keep in mind that individual facial dimensions will determine the most efficient and comfortable mask. Consider also the relative merits of masks with and without "purge valves."

The Snorkel

The best is the simple "J"-shape snorkel. Avoid mask-snorkel combinations, as experienced divers have found them to be impractical. Also avoid snorkels with valves on the upper end, for the purpose of sealing out water. Flexible snorkels are generally preferred over those made of stiff material. Consider the relative merits of short, wide "barrel" snorkels as compared to the narrow but more easily purged models.

Swim Fins

Fins come in a variety of types and sizes and vary in flexibility. Full-foot fins provide good protection for the diver and are therefore preferred by some skin divers. Scuba divers will find the larger more rigid "Jet" or "Rocket" fins suited to their needs. Flexible fins require less power and are more suitable for smaller, less powerful swimmers. Buoyancy may also be a desirable characteristic of fins. For the diver who occasionally uses a full wet suit, adjustable heel strap fins allow the fins to be used with bare feet, or alternatively, over wet suit booties.

Buoyancy Compensator

As with most other skin diving equipment, there is a wide variety of safety floats or buoyancy compensators available to the sport diver. Included are compact packet floats that snap to the swimmer's suit or an equipment strap; other floats strap around the diver's waist, and still others are of the "Mae West," or vest type. However, buoyancy compensators undoubtedly provide the best protection because they will float an unconscious swimmer face up. In addition, the diver equipped with a buoyancy compensator is able to alter his overall relative density in such a way as to be "neutrally buoyant" at any depth of his choice. This is accomplished by partially inflating or deflating the compensator during diving. The ability of the diver to attain "neutral buoyancy" is undoubtedly one of the most important skills in scuba diving.

Compass

The compass is an essential item of equipment when diving in remote areas, when remaining underwater for extended periods of time, and when diving in open water out of sight of land. The diver's basic compass consists of a neoprene wrist strap, case, liquid fill, and a needle, revolving dial, or directional ball. Appropriate parts of the compass should be coated with luminous paint, and the whole instrument so constructed that it will withstand rigorous usage.

Spears and Spear Guns

Spear hunting with a hand spear is considered more sporting than hunting with a spear gun. Hand spears are of metal or fiber glass construction and are hand or rubber powered. Spear guns provide the underwater hunter with increased power and range. Two basic types of spear guns are (1) elastic powered, and (2) gas powered. There is a great selection of spear guns available on the market. These range from very powerful guns suitable for attacking large, dangerous fish in the open sea to lighter, less powerful, but more easily carried weapons suitable for use with smaller game and in areas where maneuverability is a prime consideration. A variety of spear heads can be used. Single point, pronged, barbed, detachable, and powered heads are all available. The type of hunting to be done and hunter preference determine the type of head to be used.

However, in these days of enlightened consideration of one's environment, fewer and fewer divers engage in activities which damage the beauties of the underwater world and the many creatures which live there. The camera is replacing the spear.

Diver's Knife

The knife consists of handle, blade, and sheath. Sheaths are worn at the waist, on the leg, or on the arm. Heavy duty blades should have both a saw edge and a knife edge. Hence, they may be suitable for scaling fish, digging, cutting heavy rope, and chiseling. "Diving tools" designed more as a lever than a knife are preferred by some experts.

Diving Station

Diving stations serve to carry equipment to the dive site, provide a resting area, and are useful in case of an emergency. The diving float may consist of nothing more than an inner tube rigged with a burlap sack or it may be an elaborately equipped power cruiser. An anchor heavy enough to hold the float on station and an anchor line long enough to reach the bottom are both essential. Seaworthiness and capacity are both of major concern. A diver's flag, consisting of a diagonal white stripe on a red background, should be displayed over the diving station at all times when divers are beneath the surface in the vicinity of the float.

Weight Belt

Weights are necessary for achieving neutral buoyancy when using protective suits. Without a weight belt, divers wearing suits and scuba tend to be buoyed up and indeed may have great difficulty staying at depth. A weight belt consists of a belt of nylon webbing or neoprene, a quick release buckle, and weights. The weights should be removable in order to allow adjustment of the overall weight of the belt. Some belts are fitted with expansion devices that compensate for compression of the diver's wet suit at depth.

Exposure Suits

Exposure suits are necessary when water conditions are such that heat loss to the diver will affect his ability to dive safely. The temperature of the water is not the only important factor to be considered. Exposure time underwater is also a factor. The figures listed in the table below, which have been compiled by the United States Naval Institute, illustrate the effect of temperature and exposure time on the diver.

Water Temperature (Fahrenheit)	Approximate Time to Exhaustion or Unconsciousness (Hours)	Death (Hours)
32	1/4	1/4-1 1/2
50	1/2-1	1-2
60	2-4	6-8
70	3-7	?
80	12	relatively safe

The following time should be used as a guide for the selection of protective clothing.

Water Temperature (Fahrenheit)	Protective Measure
Above 75°	no special suit
65°-75°	sweatshirt
40°-65°	wet or dry suit
below 40°	complete wet or "uni-suit"

Exposure suits may be either full or else "partial" suits. Partial suits, which are of several varieties, are usually of the "wet" type and include vests, short sleeve tunics, and tunic and short combinations. Full suits are either of the "wet" or "dry" type. Wet suits are so called because a layer of water occupies the space between the inside of the suit and the diver's skin. This thin layer of water, which is heated by body heat, acts as an insulating layer. A wet suit is constructed of neoprene ranging in thickness from one-eighth to one-quarter inch. Nylon coverings and linings greatly increase the strength of a suit. Dry suits do not permit the entry of water and depend on a layer of air between the inside of the suit and the diver's skin for insulation; however, they have been largely replaced by the more comfortable wet suit. Brightly-colored suits, yellow or international orange, are useful in dark waters and congested waterways.

Self-Contained Underwater Breathing Apparatus

Two basic types of self-contained underwater breathing apparatus (SCUBA) are presently used. The two types are closed circuit and the open circuit equipment. Closed circuit equipment is considered too dangerous for all but the most highly-trained diver. The latter use pure oxygen as the breathing gas. The closed circuit apparatus consists of an oxygen tank, breathing bag, and carbon dioxide absorbing system. After the oxygen is breathed by the diver it passes through the CO_2 absorbing system into the breathing bag from which it is rebreathed by the diver. Because of the danger of oxygen poisoning at depths beyond twenty-five to thirty-five feet, the use of pure oxygen severely limits the depth to which the diver may descend.

The open circuit diving equipment consists of a tank block and regulator assembly. The tank block includes the tank, tank valve assembly, and the harness, or back pack. The regulator assembly includes an automatic demand regulator, a hose, and a mouth piece. The regulator is the heart of the open circuit diving equipment. It releases air to the diver as he demands it at a pressure equal to the pressure of the water. Modern single-hose regulators have largely replaced the more cumbersome double-hose regulators developed by Cousteau and Gagnan. In addition, the widespread use of submersible pressure gauges attached to single-hose regulators has proved to be an important factor in modern sport diving. The diver is thus provided with visual monitoring of his air supply. All scuba equipment should be rinsed thoroughly in fresh water and stored in a cool dry place following use.

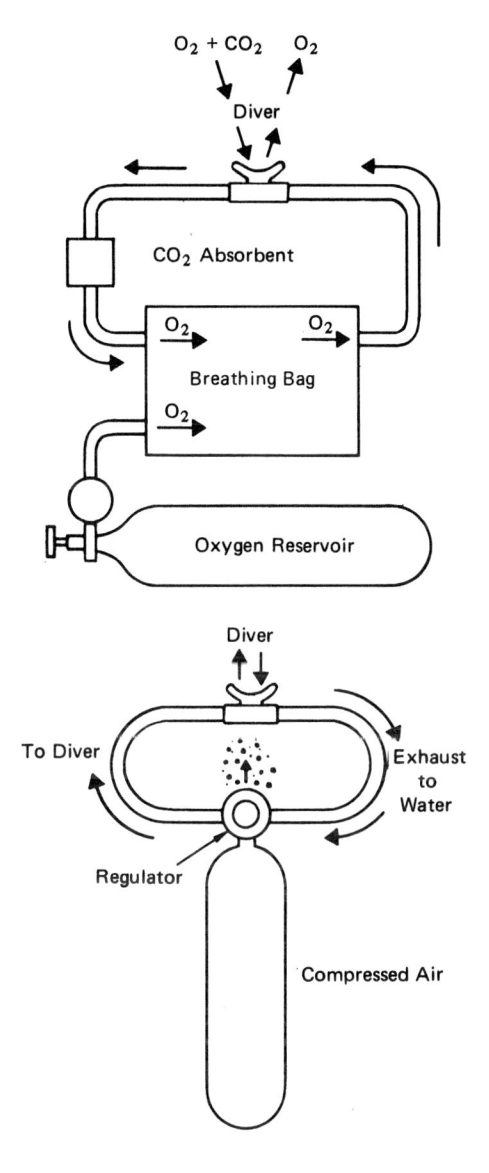

Figure 13-6. Closed- and open-circuit diving apparatus.

A Buddy

The reader may be surprised to find that a list of diving "equipment" includes another diver, or buddy. This is the authors' way of emphasizing that a buddy is an essential, irreplaceable asset to the diver. The individual who dives alone is irresponsible and foolhardy; certain physical situations and equipment malfunctions present little danger to the intelligent, disciplined buddy team, but they may be potentially fatal to an individual who is unaccompanied under the water. It is therefore assumed that all scuba training and diving will be carried out in buddy teams.

SKIN DIVING SKILLS

The skills outlined in this section are considered basic for the skin diver to master. After mastering these skills the use of scuba gear can be undertaken. It is possible to use scuba gear with little training. However, for the development of all-around competence as a sport diver and in order to establish a solid pattern of safety, the mastering of basic skills should precede the use of scuba gear. The most efficient way to attain the required skills is to work with a qualified instructor. It is assumed that the reader will receive initial instruction in a training pool before trying his skills in open water.

Use of the Face Mask

Before putting on the face mask it should be defogged, which prevents the formation of moisture on the inside of the face plate. Defogging can be accomplished by rubbing saliva over the lens and then rinsing the mask lightly. It is also possible to defog by rubbing a potato slice, an apple slice, kelp, cigarette, or a commercial defogging material over the face plate. The diver should then place the mask over eyes and nose and, while holding it in place, inhale. As long as the diver holds the negative pressure inside the mask with the force of inhalation, the mask should remain in place. If the mask does not remain sealed to the face the sport diver should reposition the mask and try again until a position is found that allows the mask to remain sealed against the face. While holding the mask in place

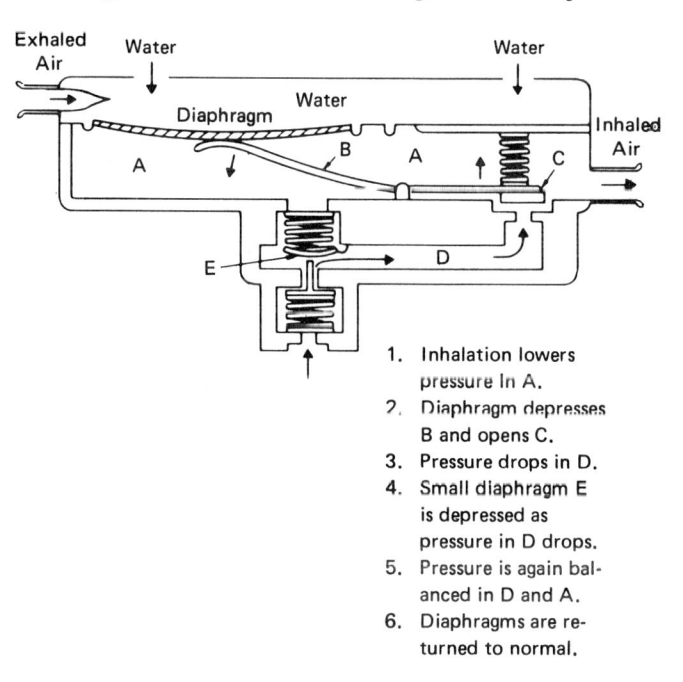

1. Inhalation lowers pressure in A.
2. Diaphragm depresses B and opens C.
3. Pressure drops in D.
4. Small diaphragm E is depressed as pressure in D drops.
5. Pressure is again balanced in D and A.
6. Diaphragms are returned to normal.

Figure 13-7. Two-stage demand regulator (schematic).

Diving: Skin and Scuba

Figure 13-8. Clearing the flooded face mask while in an upright position.

with one hand the diver should place the back of the other hand against the inside of the head band, stretch the head band, slip the head band down over the head, and remove the hand. The diver should check the water tightness of the mask in shallow water.

Clearing the flooded mask is a very important skill. For the skin diver near the surface who experiences face mask flooding, the obvious thing to do is to surface and clear the mask. However, the diver who is in deep water using scuba gear must be able to clear the face mask immediately as a routine matter. To flood the mask, lift one corner of the skirt away from the face. To clear the mask, press the mask against the forehead tightly and exhale vigorously through the nose. (See Figures 13-8 and 13-9.) The clearing process can be accomplished while in an upright position or lying on one's back. Air exhaled from the nose fills the mask and forces water out of it, moving it around the bottom of the skirt. Using a mask with a

Figure 13-9. Clearing the flooded face mask while on the side.

178 *Individual and Team Sports*

"purge valve" facilitates mask clearing. Continuous flooding may be caused by an ill-fitting mask, a loose mask strap, or hair or mustache interfering with sealing.

As the diver descends, discomfort from face squeeze may be experienced. This discomfort can be alleviated easily by exhaling through the nose and into the mask. If not corrected, injury may result to the facial areas enclosed under the mask. Goggles should not be worn for sport diving. It is impossible to equalize pressure inside goggles and thus prevent injury to the eye area from face squeeze.

After use, the mask should be rinsed in clear cold water, dried, and stored in a cool dry place. When the mask will not be used for an extended period of time, it can be dusted with silicone preservative.

Clearing the Ears

When descending beyond normal swimming depths, the diver may experience pain, sometimes severe, in the areas of the ears, forehead, face, and teeth. Pain on descent is the result of pressure differences in the air spaces relative to the pressure of the water. Pressure may be equalized by slowing the rate of descent. If slowing the rate of descent does not alleviate the pain, the diver should "snort" into the mask or press the skirt up against the nose and force air up through the Eustachian tubes into the middle ear. Some masks are fitted with recesses which allow the diver to pinch the nose with thumb and index finger while pressure is gently increased in the Eustachian tubes. Individual divers have often found that a yawning action is sufficient to clear squeeze of the ears. Sinus squeeze usually occurs when the diver has some form of infection. When pain is experienced, the diver should not descend further and in most cases should postpone the dive until the infectious condition disappears. "Tooth squeeze" results from an incomplete dental filling and can be readily cured by a competent dentist. Medical advice should be sought by any diver who suffers from any persistent "squeeze" condition.

Swimming with Fins

After the diver has decided on the type of swim fins best suited to his uses, the correct size should be carefully determined. If the fin is to be worn with a rubber suit the fins should be fitted accordingly. If the fin is fitted to the bare foot it should fit snugly enough to prevent chafing. If the fin is too tight circulation will be impaired, the fin will become uncomfortable, and a cramp may occur in the foot muscles.

Walking in fins is potentially dangerous; therefore, they should be put on as close to the water as possible. If it is necessary to walk on shore, or in shallow water, walk backwards. The fin will slip on easily if dipped into the water prior to putting it on.

When using the fins a relaxed easy flutter kick should be employed. The kick should be from the hip with slight passive knee flexion and extension. The toes should be so pointed that fin blades are aligned with the legs. The diver should experiment to determine which kick will be most efficient for him. All kicking should be done in a relaxed easy fashion. The large surface area of the fins allows good speed through the water even with a slow, steady beat. Too rapid a kick will result in early fatigue of the leg muscles. After use, fins should be rinsed in clear cool water, dried, and stored in a cool dry place. If fins are to be stored for a long period of time, a talcum-type powder or silicone rubber preservative should be applied to them.

Clearing the Snorkel

The shaft of the snorkel should be attached to the left hand side of the head strap, using the small rubber loop that is supplied with all snorkels. (A single hose regulator passes to the right side of the head, and the wise scuba diver keeps his snorkel attached to his mask for immediate usage when he returns to the surface.) The diver should adjust the snorkel so that while swimming face down the snorkel is upright in the water. When cruising along the surface the diver should establish a steady breathing rhythm. While underwater, some water will enter the snorkel. As the diver's head breaks the surface of the water, he should exhale sharply in order to blow water out of the snorkel. The first inhalation should be a cautious one to avoid choking, should any water remain in the tube. Clearing the tube should be repeatedly practiced until it can be accomplished easily. Sucking the tube completely full of water before clearing it provides excellent practice of this important skill.

Entering the Water

There are five basic types of water entry: the wade-in, the feet-first jump, the stride jump, the forward roll, and the backward roll-off (Figure 13-10). All entries should be practiced while wearing a face mask, fins, snorkel, and buoyancy compensator.

The wade-in is the safest method of entry and it should be used whenever possible. The sport diver should remember to either carry his fins or to walk backwards when making a wade-in entry.

When using the front jump the diver holds the mask firmly against his face, jumps clear of the dock or pool edge, and enters the water with both feet together. The front jump allows penetration beneath the surface on the entry.

Figure 13-10. Five methods of entering the water: roll off; forward roll; front jump; stride jump; and climb-in.

In the stride jump entry the diver holds the mask firmly against the face, leans forward with the free arm extended to the side, takes a long stride forward into the water and sweeps the free arm into the water. This entry allows the diver to remain at the surface.

When performing the forward roll entry the diver holds the mask against the face with both hands, tucks the elbows into the chest, dives up and out into a three-quarter forward roll and lands in the water on the shoulders and back.

The backward roll-off is performed from a sitting or squatting position at the edge of the water. The diver holds the mask in place and rolls backward into the water landing on the back. This entry is useful for entering the water from a pitching small craft, especially if scuba gear is worn.

Surface Swimming: Introduction

Equipped with mask, snorkel, buoyancy compensator, and fins, the diver enters the water and cruises along on the surface, using a relaxed steady flutter kick. The diver should practice this stroke until a rhythm can be established that allows sustained swimming for indefinite periods. Surface swimming should also be practiced with the arms extended forward near the surface or with the arms trailing alongside the body. In addition, the diver should practice swimming on the back with the snorkel removed from the mouth.

Diving: Skin and Scuba

Figure 13-11. Head-first surface dive.

Surface Diving: Head First

Surface diving should be practiced while swimming along the surface in the deep area of a pool. The swimmer bends at the waist and directs the head and upper body straight downward. (See Figure 13-11.) As the upper body reaches a 90° bend at the waist, the diver should lift his legs directly over his hips and into alignment with the trunk. The weight of the legs above the surface of the water helps drive the body downward beneath the surface of the water. Breast-stroke type arm pulls and flutter kicking may be used by the diver to continue diving down to the desired depth. (See Figure 13-12.)

Surface Diving: Feet First

The feet-first dive is recommended when visibility is limited and the diver is uncertain about the presence of obstructions in the water. In order to begin the dive, the diver should first lift his body upward, using a downward push of both arms and a scissors kick of the legs. The upward pressure produced by these actions tends to force the diver's upper body out of the water. Then, the weight of the head, chest, and shoulders above the surface forces the diver down beneath the surface of the water. As his downward speed diminishes, the diver should move to a head-downward position; he continues the dive by using a flutter kick. If visibility is limited the arms should be extended forward of the diver in order to protect the face and head.

Swimming Underwater

When swimming underwater a relaxed steady flutter kick should be used with the arms trailing along the sides. If visibility is limited, however, the arms should be extended forward of the body where they can act as "bumpers."

Surfacing

As the diver swims to the surface he should (1) listen carefully, (2) extend a hand above his head, and (3) rotate his entire body continually while looking upwards and around his path of return. A number of accidents have occurred to divers who have collided with boats and other obstacles located at the water surface. Therefore, caution should always be observed when surfacing. (See Figure 13-14.)

Doffing and Donning Equipment

After surface diving and underwater swimming are mastered, the sport diver should practice doffing and donning his equipment while underwater. After surface diving to the bottom the diver should remove the fins and place them neatly on the bottom, remove the mask and snorkel, and place them beside the fins, and then make a safe ascent to the surface. After resting 10 seconds or so the

Figure 13-12. On the way down during head-first surface dive; arm pull completed and flutter kick started.

Figure 13-13. Swimming underwater trailing the arms, utilizing the flutter kick.

180 *Individual and Team Sports*

Figure 13-14. Surfacing.

diver should surface dive to recover his equipment. The mask should be put on and carefully cleared to avoid wasting air. With the mask in place, the diver should place the snorkel mouthpiece in place, make a safe ascent, and then clear the snorkel for surface breathing. After another short rest, a final trip is made to the bottom, the fins recovered, a safe ascent conducted, the snorkel cleared, and surface breathing reestablished. With practice, all equipment can be donned in one breath. The ability to doff and don equipment underwater is important since it helps to develop confidence and self discipline, both of which are necessary ingredients for future success in the fascinating sport of skin and scuba diving.

Towing Another Swimmer

When it becomes necessary to tow another swimmer, first make a quick analysis of the situation. If assistance is within signal range, it should be signaled. If assistance is not available, the victim should be moved ashore or to the diving station, whichever is the most practical under the circumstances. A conscious victim should be approached with great caution. Rescuers should, if possible, avoid direct contact with the victim, especially if he is struggling or is panic-stricken. Towing may be accomplished with an extension device, such as a spear gun or safety float. The rescuer should have the victim inflate his buoyancy compensator and be prepared to inflate his own if necessary.

An unconscious victim should have his buoyancy compensator inflated at once and his mask removed. If the victim is wearing a weight belt, this should be jettisoned immediately. The rescuer should tow the victim, using a cross-chest carry, head carry, or by grasping some item of clothing. The rescuer should keep his own mask and snorkel in place. Keeping the head in the water allows the assisting diver to expend much less energy in towing the victim to safety. Immediately upon reaching the diving station or shore, the rescuer should start the administration of mouth-to-mouth resuscitation.

BASIC SCUBA DIVING SKILLS

Before working with self-contained underwater breathing apparatus the beginning scuba diver should be thoroughly familiar with the functioning of the apparatus. In addition to understanding how it functions, the sport diver should become familiar with how to prepare this equipment for use. The equipment should be checked thoroughly, air pressure in the tank determined, the regulator attached to the tank valve, and both the regulator and the valve "O-ring" should be checked for leaks and proper functioning when the air has been turned on.

Putting on the Scuba Tank in a Training Pool

When it is determined that the apparatus is safe and is functioning properly, the diver should put on his buoyancy compensator, and the diver's buddy should hold the tank up against the diver's back while the harness is secured. The weight belt should next be secured in place. In most cases, only one or two pounds of weight will be required by the diver who is not wearing a suit; hence, in the early stages the weight belt can be disregarded. All belts should be of a quick release type. With the harness secured, the mouthpiece should be positioned for use.

Shallow Water Use

After entering the shallow end of the pool the buddy team should put on their masks, snorkels, and fins and insert the regulator mouthpieces. When the student is confident that the regulator is delivering air sufficiently, he waits until his buddy is also ready and the pair of them sit down on the bottom of the pool. After a brief period on the bottom of the pool the divers may swim around the shallow area of the pool. After the diver can inhale and exhale with no difficulty, removing and replacing the mouthpiece can be practiced. Prior to removing the mouthpiece, the diver should take a deep breath. After replacing the mouthpiece the diver should exhale forcefully and then inhale cautiously. If water remains in the mouthpiece a second forceful exhalation should clear it. Single hose regulators are equipped with a purge button that clears the mouthpiece when it is depressed. A third method of clearing the mouthpiece, called "swishing," entails the movement of air backwards and forwards into the mouthpiece without actually exhaling. All three methods should be practiced.

Diving: Skin and Scuba 181

If a two hose regulator without a nonreturn mouthpiece is used the inhalation hose may become flooded and water may enter the low pressure area behind the diaphragm. Under these circumstances special techniques are required to clear water from the regulator and the inhalation hose. Scuba without nonreturn mouthpieces should be taken out of service until equipped with nonreturn mouthpieces.

Clearing the Mask

The skill of clearing the mask is performed in the same manner as when diving without scuba gear. Roll onto the back, hold the mask tightly against the forehead, and exhale through the nose to force water out of the mask. When using a "purge valve" mask, the face is turned down before exhaling through the nose.

Descending

After developing the ability to clear the mask, clear the mouthpiece and cruise in shallow water with ease, the diver is ready to operate in deeper water. The buddy team should swim into the deep end of the pool from the shallow end. They should then make a gradual descent, equalizing pressure as needed. After swimming around the deep end for a few minutes, the divers should prepare to ascend.

Ascending

The ascent should be accomplished at a rate no faster than one foot per second. Additionally, the diver should exhale during the ascent. Failure to exhale and/or ascend at a slow rate can result in the rupture of air sacs (alveoli) in the lungs. Alveoli rupture, if severe, may be fatal to the diver. Even an ascent, if quite rapid, of only a few feet can cause damage to the delicate tissue of the lungs—if a full breath of air is held in the lungs, causing them to expand beyond their normal limits. This potential hazard will be further discussed in a later section.

Neutral Buoyancy

After developing confidence in deep water the diver should experiment with attaining neutral buoyancy. The total amount of weight on the weight belt should be so adjusted that at the surface the diver floats with the level of the water at about the middle of his mask (in an upright floating position). This is with the tank removed and the buoyancy compensator deflated. After replacing the tank and regulator, and fully inflating the buoyancy compensator, the buddy team enters the water and simultaneously deflate their buoyancy compensators until they begin to descend without swimming. At a predetermined depth each diver removes his mouthpiece, blows some air into his buoyancy compensator and replaces his mouthpiece. Air is then carefully introduced into or vented from the buoyancy compensator until the diver, at mid-inspiration, shows no tendency to either rise or fall in the water.

Entering the Water

Early diving experiences should start with a wade-in entry. After "deep-end" skills are well mastered, other methods of entry should be practiced. The diver should first try stepping in as practiced with the mask and snorkel. When the step-in entry is used, the diver should hold the tank down by grasping the harness behind him. When using a forward-roll entry, the diver should first check that his harness is correctly adjusted; otherwise, the tank may strike the diver on the back of the head. A third method of entry, the roll off, is accomplished by sitting or squatting, back to the pool, at the edge of the pool. The entry is made by rolling backwards into the pool.

Scuba-snorkel Alternate Breathing

The scuba diver should use his snorkel when swimming on the surface. Snorkel surface breathing allows the conservation of compressed air and therefore allows increased diving time. Ascend and exhale into the scuba mouthpiece. As the diver breaks the surface he should drop the scuba mouthpiece, insert the snorkel mouthpiece, clear the snorkel, and start normal breathing by means of the snorkel. To change back to scuba breathing, take a final breath through the snorkel, insert the scuba mouthpiece, clear it, and start normal scuba breathing.

Buddy Breathing

Buddy breathing is a valuable skill that permits two divers to share a single scuba. This skill can be invaluable

Figure 13-15. Buddy breathing.

182 *Individual and Team Sports*

when certain types of emergency conditions prevail. Two divers sit side by side in shallow water. The diver on the left removes his mouthpiece and receives the mouthpiece of the diver on the right. He takes two breaths and returns the mouthpiece so that the diver on the right can then take two breaths. The two divers alternate the use of the regulator and exhale slowly when waiting for the mouthpiece. Continuous exhalation is constantly practiced; thus, in a real emergency, both divers will automatically exhale as they return to the surface. Buddy breathing practiced with divers in changed roles is continued by repeating the process. After buddy breathing has been mastered while sitting on the bottom of the pool, it should be attempted while swimming along the bottom of the pool in the shallow end. Finally the skill should be practiced in deep water, first on the bottom and then during ascent. Each diver confirms that his buddy exhales during that part of the ascent when he is not using the regulator.

Emergency Ascent

To simulate an emergency ascent the diver removes his weight belt, holds it at arm's length before releasing it, removes his mouthpiece, and swims rapidly to the surface while he exhales forcibly. This should be practiced frequently until it can be done correctly without conscious thought.

Doffing and Donning Equipment

Probably the best test of a scuba diver's basic diving ability is that of doffing and donning equipment. The diver enters the water wearing scuba, mask, fins, and weight belt. After entering the water the diver sits on the bottom of the pool, removes his weight belt and drops it across his thighs. With the weight belt in place across the

Figure 13-16. Doffing equipment: swinging the equipment over the head into place.

thighs the diver pulls the quick release buckle on the scuba harness, reaches over the shoulders, grasps the tank, swings it over head and lays it down between his legs. After doffing the scuba tank the diver places the weight belt across the tank to hold it flat on the bottom of the pool. Next, the diver removes his swim fins and slips them under the weight belt. Lastly, the mask is removed and placed beside the regulator. Now the diver moves into a horizontal position facing the regulator. He removes the mouthpiece and swims to the surface while he exhales continuously.

To don his equipment the diver surface dives to a position facing the regulator, places the mouthpiece in his mouth, clears it, and commences normal breathing. With breathing established the diver sits, legs straddling the tank, and moves the weight belt across his thighs. The diver then puts on the mask and clears it, grasps the tank near the valve and swings it up and over his head. With the tank held in place the diver fastens the belt buckle. After putting on his fins and finally the weight belt, the diver stands up. After doffing and donning can be accomplished easily in shallow water, it can be practiced in deep water under the close supervision of an instructor.

SAFETY AND RESCUE SKILLS

Several safety considerations have been mentioned in previous sections of this chapter. Personal safety is the prime requisite for safe diving. The sport diver should have strong basic swimming skills, a high level of endurance, an understanding of his own limits, and a general concern for developing a pattern of safety in his sport diving. Beyond the basic grounding in personal safety, the sport diver should practice sport diving skills until they are second nature, should understand the reasons for safety practices, and should progress through the steps of proficiency with the prime consideration of safe diving. In this section selected safety and rescue skills are presented. The second section, "Diving Technology," also has a direct relationship to safety; hence, it should be carefully studied.

Elementary Forms of Rescue

As with most other persons who spend a great deal of time around the water, the sport diver may find himself confronted with an emergency situation requiring prompt action. Elementary forms of rescue are those rescues that can be made from shore or deck by the rescuer who does not enter deep water but instead reaches or uses some extension device. In making an elementary rescue, the rescuer should analyze the situation quickly, use available means to bring the victim to shore, dock, or boat side and assist the victim out of the water. Caution must be used by the rescuer to prevent being pulled into the water. The American Red Cross textbook, *Life Saving and Water Safety*, is recommended for study.

Special Forms of Rescue

If a victim cannot be reached with an elementary rescue technique another safe rescue method must be attempted at once. Ring buoys should be carried on all diving boats for just such emergencies. Anything that will float and provide support may be thrown or pushed to the victim. If the victim cannot be reached by throwing a floating device to him, the rescuer can swim to the victim with a flotation device, using great care to keep the float between the victim and himself. Once contact is made the victim can be towed to safety using the float as a buffer device. Swimming rescues without a flotation device are very hazardous and should only be undertaken when they are the only means of rescue available.

Small-craft Rescue

If a victim is some distance from shore a boat should be used to effect the rescue. The victim should be approached with caution, so that he is not injured by the rescue craft, from the down wind side. If the rescue craft is small the victim may be guided to the stern of the boat where he can be assisted into the boat.

Towing Another Swimmer with Scuba

If it becomes necessary to tow another diver, he should be approached with great caution. The buoyancy compensator should be inflated, the victim's mask should be removed, and the weight belt dropped. Towing can be accomplished by cupping the victim's chin, or by grasping the hair or some piece of equipment or a strap. A flutter kick or scissors kick and an arm pull with the free arm are utilized for propulsion. The rescuer should utilize his scuba gear or snorkel for breathing during the tow in order to keep low in the water and thus conserve energy.

Artificial Respiration

Sport divers should be proficient at performing artificial respiration both in and out of the water. The most effective means of performing resuscitation is the mouth-to-mouth method. After a drowning victim is removed from the water he should be moved quickly to a back-lying position in which his feet are higher than the head if possible. The mouth should be checked quickly and all visible obstructions such as false teeth, mud, and vomit quickly removed. Tip the head back in order to align the air passage. The operator should now kneel to the right of the victim and pinch the nostrils with the left hand. Now the operator places his mouth over the victim's mouth and blows into it at a rate of from twelve to fourteen times per minute (for the average adult). If it is difficult to blow air in, the victim's mouth and throat should be quickly rechecked for obstruction. As artificial resuscitation gets underway, the victim should be covered in order to retain body heat.

Heart Massage

Extreme caution should be observed if heart massage is attempted. The usual recommendation is that only a person trained in this technique should use it.

Treatment of Shock

In case of a near-drowning or severe injury the victim should be treated for shock. The individual being treated should be placed in a horizontal position with the feet slightly elevated. However, if the victim has a head injury the feet should not be elevated. Cover the victim with blankets, jackets, or whatever is available. Insulation should be placed under as well as over the victim in order to keep him warm. Water can be given to the victim unless he has suffered a penetrating abdominal wound.

Other First Aid Skills

Ideally, sport divers should be skilled in all phases of first aid. A sport diving manual such as *Scuba II* provides information about treating injuries from coral, jelly fish, and other marine hazards that sport divers may encounter. Each sport diver should plan to enroll in and complete a course in first aid at some time early in his career.

DIVING TECHNOLOGY

It is possible to participate safely in sport diving without understanding the various technologies and phenomena related to the sport. However, the sport is much more satisfying and performance is much more effective and efficient when a basic foundation in the technical aspects of the sport is established. Several basic safety considerations have been pointed out in previous sections. The reasons for these and further safety understandings are explained in this section.

Water

Fresh water weighs $62\frac{4}{10}$ pounds per cubic foot; salt water, 64 pounds per cubic foot. As the diver descends the pressure exerted on him is the direct result of the weight of the water "stacked" above him. At sea level the amount of pressure exerted on each square inch of the body by the atmosphere is 14.7 pounds. For each foot of salt water one descends beneath the surface the pressure is increased .445 pound per square inch. The following chart shows the relative increase in pressure as the diver descends to a depth of 132 feet in salt water.

Depth (feet)	Lbs per sq. in.	Atmospheres
Sea level (surface)	14.7	1
33	29.4	2
66	44.1	3
99	58.8	4
132	73.5	5

Air

Air is a mixture of several gases in the following approximate percentages by volume:

Gas	Percentage
Nitrogen	80% (approximate)
Oxygen	20% (approximate)
Carbon dioxide	trace
Inert gases	trace

Air has weight and at sea level it exerts a pressure of 14.7 lbs. per square inch (p.s.i.). The volume of any gas or mixture of gases varies with the pressure extended on it. As stated by Boyle's law, with temperature constant, the volume of a gas varies inversely with the pressure. For example, if the pressure on a volume of gas is doubled the volume is reduced to one half of the original volume. When pressure is decreased, conversely, the volume is increased.

Air is soluble in fluids. Solubility, according to Henry's law, varies with pressure. As pressure is increased greater amounts of gas will be absorbed by the fluid involved. Dalton's law leads to the fact that the gases that make up the air mixture exert pressure independently. The pressures exerted by the components of air are directly proportional to the pressure resulting from increasing depths.

Partial Pressures (pounds per square inch – p.s.i.)

Gas	Sea Level	33 ft.	66 ft.	99 ft.	132 ft.
Nitrogen	11.5 p.s.i.	22.9	34.4	45.9	57.3
Oxygen	3.1 p.s.i.	6.2	9.3	12.3	15.4
Carbon dioxide	.003 p.s.i.	.0069	.0103	.0137	.0171

Air Spaces of the Body and Attached Air Spaces

The air spaces are of major concern in diving. Two types of air spaces are important: internal air spaces and attached air spaces. The internal air spaces that are of concern are the sinuses, the middle ear, the lungs, and the intestines. The attached air spaces are the air spaces contained between equipment and the diver; normally, that which is located in the diving mask. Air spaces create problems for the diver when the air pressure does not equal the pressure of the surrounding water.

Problems of Descent

As the diver descends, air spaces in the body tend to be compressed by the pressure exerted on the body. The air spaces of the skin diver normally achieve a balanced pressure due to the compression of the chest cavity by the pressure of the surrounding water. The increased pressure in the lungs is transmitted to the other air spaces in the body and equalization occurs. As the scuba diver descends, air from the scuba is inhaled at a pressure equal to that of the surrounding water; hence, if the pressure is transmitted to the air spaces, equalization occurs. Several problems may result due to the failure of the diver to equalize pressure as he descends.

Thoracic Squeeze. The skin diver may reach and exceed the depth at which the rib cage reaches its limits of compression. As this occurs the diaphragm is pressed inward and upward, thus balancing the chest cavity pressure until the diaphragm reaches its limits of stretch. If descent is then continued beyond the depth at which lung pressure can be maintained in balance with the pressure of the water, lung damage would result. Blood vessels would rupture and hemorrhage in the lung would occur. However, skin divers are incapable of free-diving to depths at which the effects become significant.

Ear and Sinus Squeeze. When diving, the air spaces in the sinuses and middle ear may not equalize due to swollen mucous membranes, which result in closing off the air passages by which these air spaces are equalized. Relatively low pressure in a sinus cavity or middle ear causes pain in the affected area. If the descent is con-

Diving: Skin and Scuba

tinued, however, the blood vessels will rupture and hemorrhage will occur in the affected area. Divers should be thoroughly familiar with the techniques for equalizing pressure in the sinus and middle ears. One strict rule should always be observed: *divers should not dive with an upper respiratory infection or other conditions that cause inflammation of the mucous membranes in the head region.*

Intestine Squeeze. Air swallowed by the diver and/or gas formed during the dive will usually cause no discomfort during the dive. On ascent, however, expansion of excess gas in the intestine and stomach will cause serious discomfort. Therefore, *carbonated beverages should be avoided just before diving.* Spicy or other gas-producing foods should also be avoided.

Face Squeeze. In order to compensate for the volume change in the mask during descent, the diver must equalize pressure by blowing air through the nose into the mask. If the mask is forced against the face by water pressure, blood vessels in the face and eyes will rupture and hemorrhaging will occur. *Blow air into the mask during descent. Never wear goggles for skin or scuba diving.*

PROBLEMS AT DEPTH

Problems that affect the diver at depth are the indirect results of pressure. Henry's law dictates that greater amounts of a gas are absorbed as pressure is increased. Dalton's law states that the proportion present in the breathing medium will pass into solution. At the surface, there is approximately four times as much nitrogen in the air as there is oxygen. As the diver descends the proportion of gases absorbed by body tissues is maintained; however, due to increased partial pressures the total volume of the gases absorbed within the body is considerably increased.

Nitrogen Narcosis

As the diver descends, the increased pressure of the water causes the amount of nitrogen absorbed into the blood stream to increase as either the depth and/or time increases. Eventually, the increased nitrogen content has narcotic effects upon the diver. With continued descent the narcotic effect of nitrogen increases proportionally. Although there is great individual variation in the susceptability to nitrogen narcosis, the effect produced by nitrogen at a depth of 100 feet has been said to be the same as that produced by the alcohol in two Martinis. The greater the depth, the more pronounced the narcotic effect. For this reason, *sport divers should limit their dives to depths of less than 132 feet.*

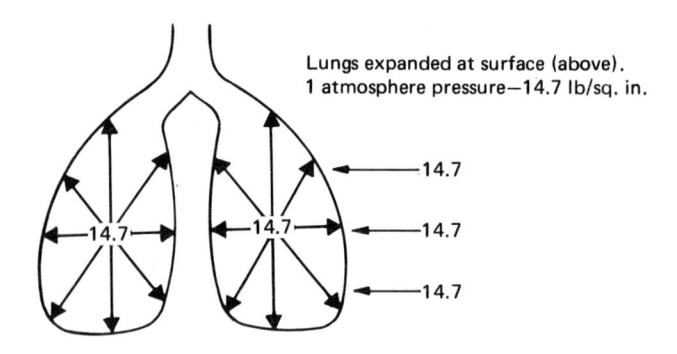

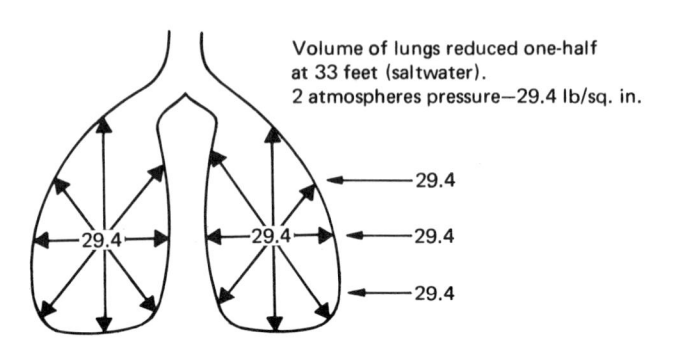

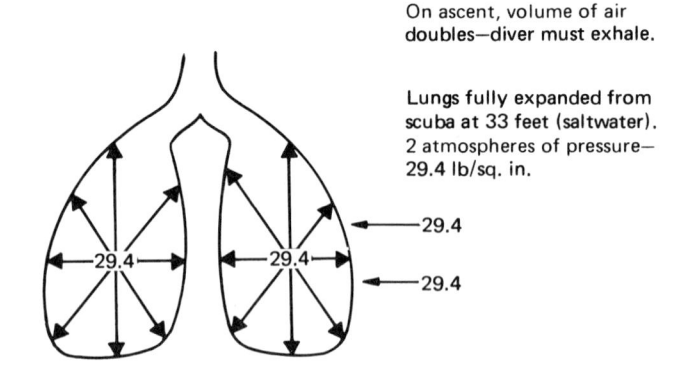

Lungs expanded at surface (above).
1 atmosphere pressure—14.7 lb/sq. in.

Volume of lungs reduced one-half at 33 feet (saltwater).
2 atmospheres pressure—29.4 lb/sq. in.

On ascent, volume of air doubles—diver must exhale.

Lungs fully expanded from scuba at 33 feet (saltwater).
2 atmospheres of pressure—29.4 lb/sq. in.

Figure 13-17. Compression and expansion of air with changes in pressure.

Oxygen Poisoning

The use of closed-circuit scuba is not recommended. Pure oxygen should never be used in open-circuit diving lungs. At depths in excess of twenty-five to thirty-five feet oxygen is toxic and its use may result in unconsciousness and death. *Do not use closed-circuit scuba. Do not use oxygen in open-circuit diving lungs.*

Carbon Dioxide Poisoning

Carbon dioxide poison accidents occur as a result of a malfunction or the failure to use fresh carbon dioxide

(CO_2) absorbant when using closed-circuit scuba. Carbon dioxide poisoning causes dizziness, fatigue, nausea, unconsciousness, cynosis, and even death. *Do not use closed-circuit scuba.*

Carbon Monoxide Poisoning

Carbon monoxide may be present in the diver's air supply because of contamination by fumes from the gasoline-driven compressor or as a result of a breakdown in the lubrication oil of an oil-lubricated compressor. Carbon monoxide is difficult to detect—the first symptom often being the loss of consciousness. Carbon monoxide in the air supply may cause it to "taste bad," but this warning sign cannot be depended upon. If carbon monoxide is suspect the air tank should be "bled" before refilling it. *The diver should refill his tanks only at reputable dive shops. If the diver refills his own tanks, the exhaust fumes should be vented away from the air intake of the compressor.*

Anoxia

Anoxia, a lack of oxygen, is primarily a problem of the skin diver. Skin divers often hyperventilate by breathing deeply several times before a dive. Hyperventilation increases the body's store of oxygen but more importantly it decreases the body's store of carbon dioxide. Breathing, which is normally an automatic mechanism that does not require conscious thought, is initiated by a low partial pressure of oxygen, a high partial pressure of carbon dioxide, or a decreased lung volume. Hyperventilation causes the carbon dioxide to be depleted and oxygen levels to reach dangerously low levels before the urge to breathe occurs. Loss of consciousness under these circumstances can occur with little specific warning. Experimentation with hyperventilation and case studies involving individuals who survived accidents resulting from hyperventilation lead to the conclusion that prolonged or severe hyperventilation is a hazardous practice. *Skin divers should not practice severe or prolonged hyperventilation when diving.*

PROBLEMS ON ASCENT

As the diver ascends, the gas in his lungs expands as the water pressures decrease (Boyle's law). During the ascent the solubility of the nitrogen absorbed by the blood lessens and nitrogen tends to bubble off (Dalton's and Henry's laws). The difficulties that may arise as the diver moves toward the surface are due either to the effects of expanding air within the body or to the effects of decreasing pressure on the gases disolved in the blood and tissue fluids or both effects can simultaneously cause difficulties.

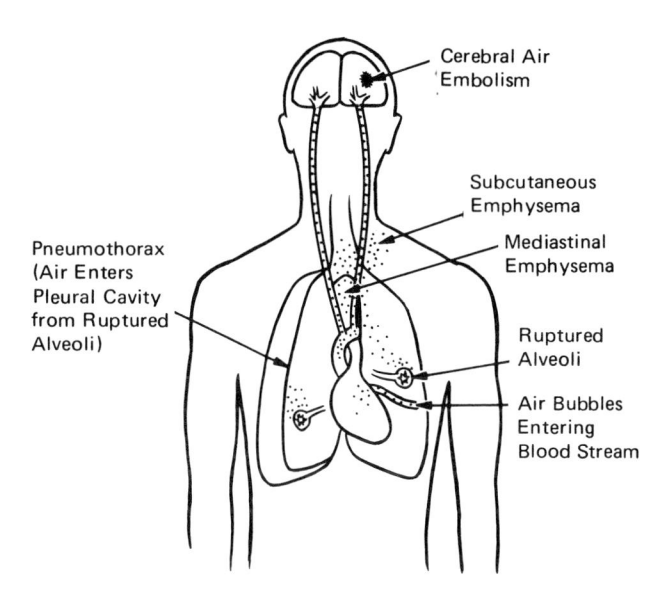

Figure 13-18. Schematic diagram: results of failure to exhale during ascent or ascending too rapidly.

Rapid Ascent

If the diver ascends without exhaling, the expansion of air in the lungs will probably cause the alveoli in the lungs to rupture. If the diver does vent off air, the alveoli may still rupture if the ascent is too rapid to allow venting to keep pace with expansion of the air in the lungs. Air from the alveoli may enter the blood stream, circulate to the head area and produce cerebral air embolism. A diver so afflicted will be quickly rendered unconscious and unless promptly treated, will die. Other results of ruptured alveoli are spontaneous pneumothorax, collapsed lung, and mediastinal emphysema, the collection of air bubbles in the mediastinum tissues and the tissues of the neck. *Always exhale during ascent. Ascend at a rate no faster than one foot per second.*

Expansion of Gas in the Intestine

Gas that is swallowed or that is produced in the intestines may expand and cause serious discomfort during ascent. *Carbonated beverages should be avoided just before diving. Spicy or other gas-producing foods should also be avoided.*

Decompression Sickness (The Bends)

In the discussion of nitrogen narcosis it was pointed out that under the pressure of depth greater quantities of nitrogen are absorbed than are absorbed at surface gas pressure. If enough nitrogen is absorbed into the tissue fluid, it will bubble off into the blood stream as the diver ascends and the pressure decreases. Nitrogen bubbles in the blood may cause pain, obstruction of circulation, dizziness, unconsciousness, and death. The depth of the dive and the duration of the dive are the key factors in the development of decompression sickness. Depths of less than thirty-three feet can be tolerated indefinitely. As the diver descends beyond thirty-three feet, careful checks on time spent at depth must be made. The diver must consult a decompression chart prior to the dive to determine the time that may be spent at the working depth without decompressing. If the working time at the selected depth requires decompression, the diver will be required to stop at certain levels during the ascent in order that the nitrogen in the blood stream can be eliminated through the lungs. Sport divers should avoid situations from which decompression sickness may develop. Avoid long, deep dives requiring decompression stops.

An instrument that automatically computes the level of nitrogen dissolved in the blood is currently available. The "Decompression Meter" is carried by the diver and indicates continuously to the diver how close he is to the need for decompression. When decompression is required the instrument indicates the appropriate depths at which the decompression should be carried out.

Glossary of Terms

Included in this section are those terms, definitions, and formulas that are important to the sport diver. The knowledge represented by an understanding of this information will make the sport increasingly more enjoyable, interesting, and to some degree safer.

Absolute pressure: The total pressure exerted on the diver. The addition of 14.7 p.s.i. to the indicated gauge pressure.

Air: A highly compressable mixture of gases. Approximately 80% nitrogen, 20% oxygen, and trace amounts of carbon dioxide and rare gases.

Air consumption: The volume of air used by a diver. This is usually expressed in cubic feet per minute—C.F.M.—or pounds per square inch per minute when estimated from tank pressure.

Air embolism: A blockage in the circulation of the blood that results from a collection of air bubbles in one of the main blood vessels.

Aqua lung: A brand name that is often used interchangeably with "scuba" and diving lung.

Artificial respiration: Manual or mechanical breathing that is administered to an individual who has stopped breathing. Also called resuscitation.

Atmospheric pressure: The pressure exerted by the pressure of the air. This is usually expressed in pounds per square inch. Sea level pressure is 14.7 p.s.i.

Back pack: A carrying apparatus designed to hold a scuba tank in a stable position on the diver's back.

Bends: The term commonly used for decompression sickness. Decompression sickness results from dissolved nitrogen bubbling off into the blood stream.

Boyle's law: This law states that the volume of a gas, temperature remaining constant, varies inversely with its absolute pressure.

Buddy: Diving partner.

Buddy breathing: A rescue technique in which two divers utilize a single scuba tank and regulator.

Buddy line: A line attaching diving partners.

Buoyancy: The upward force exerted on a floating or immersed body by a fluid.

Buoyancy compensator: An inflatable device that allows the diver to float safely in a face-up position. It also can be used to control buoyancy at any depth.

Carbon monoxide: (CO) a toxic gas that is given off by gasoline engines.

Chokes: A term for one of the symptoms of decompression sickness in which coughing, shortness of breath, and pain on breathing are experienced.

Closed circuit: Diving equipment that is primarily used by commercial and military divers in which pure oxygen, a breathing bag, and a carbon dioxide absorbant are utilized.

Complimental air: The volume of air that can be inhaled after a normal (tidal) inspiration has been taken.

Compressor: A machine, gas or electric driven, that is used to compress gas for use in scuba tanks.

Cylinder: A steel receptacle used to hold the compressed air (gas) employed in sport diving. An air tank.

Dalton's law: Gas in a mixture exerts the same pressure that it would exert if it occupied the same volume alone.

Dead space: The area in the respiratory system wherein the last of the inspired air is contained.

Decompression: The release of nitrogen by body tissues when the surrounding pressure is decreased.

Decompression meter: An instrument which indicates the level of residual nitrogen in the tissues of a diver and which may be used to indicate the stops required for decompression.

Decompression tables: Tables used to determine the number and length of stops, following underwater work.

Doffing equipment: Taking off equipment on the bottom of a body of water. A confidence-building skill.

Donning equipment: Putting on underwater equipment while on the bottom. A confidence-building skill.

Dry suit: An exposure suit made of rubber that covers the body and keeps it completely dry.

Equalizing pressure: The process of balancing pressure in the internal air spaces and attached air space (mask) with the pressure of the water.

Eustachian tube: The tube that connects the middle ear with the nasopharynx.

188 *Individual and Team Sports*

Exhale: To breathe out.
Expiration: Act or process of breathing out.
Face mask: The piece of diving equipment worn over the nose and eyes. It is designed to provide clear vision when underwater.
Fins: The flippers worn on the feet to provide effective propulsion when moving through the water.
Hand signals: Signals with the hand(s) used for underwater communication.
Hemorrhage: Discharge from blood vessels due to injury.
Hyperoxia: Excess of oxygen in the body tissues.
Hyperventilation: Increased rate and/or depth of breathing over and above the needs of the body. This is usually done to delay the urge to breathe when skin diving underwater.
Inhale: To breathe in.
Inspiration: The act of breathing air into the lungs.
Lung diver: A diver who is using a self-contained breathing apparatus.
Mae West: A life jacket used for flotation.
Mediastinal emphysema: A collection of air bubbles in the mediastinum due to ruptured alveoli.
Narcosis: A state of arrested activity, accompanied by dizziness, disorientation, and an inability to think clearly.
Nausea: The feeling of being sick in the stomach.
Nitrogen: The gas composing approximately 80% of the air mixture.
Nitrogen narcosis: Narcosis resulting from the body's absorption of excessive amounts of nitrogen.
Open circuit: A diving apparatus that exhausts exhaled air into the water.
Oxygen: (O_2) a gas composing approximately 20% of the air mixture.
Partial pressure: The pressure exerted by a gas in a mixture of gases, such as the pressure of oxygen in the air.
Perforate: To pierce the surface of.
Physics of diving: The science of matter and motion as related to sport diving.
Physiology of diving: The organic processes and phenomena dealing with life as related to sport diving.
Power head: A spear head containing an explosive charge that detonates after the spear head has penetrated the fish.
Reef: A ridge of sand, rocks, or coral at or near the surface of the water.
Rupture: Breaking or bursting, as can happen to a blood vessel or ear drum.
Safety line: A line attached to the diver and a surface station.
Scuba: Self-contained underwater breathing apparatus. A breathing apparatus free of any attachment to the surface.
Shock: A depressed condition of many of the body functions due to failure of sufficient blood to circulate through the body following serious injury.
Single stage regulator: A regulator in which cylinder pressure is reduced to breathing pressure in one stage.

Sinus: Hollow air-containing spaces in the front part of the bones comprising the skull.
Skin diver: A diver diving without self-contained breathing apparatus.
Spear: A hunting weapon consisting of a head mounted on a long shaft.
Spear gun: Rubber-, spring-, or gas-operated gun used to launch spears.
Spontaneous pneumothorax: A collapsed lung that results when air enters the space between the lung and chest wall after the alveoli rupture.
Sport diver: One who skin or scuba dives for recreational purposes.
Squeeze: Relatively low pressure, in comparison to water pressure, in the internal or attached air space (mask) that results in pain and often hemorrhage.
Staggers: A symptomatic walk that occurs after failing to decompress properly.
Subcutaneous emphysema: A collection of air bubbles under the skin in the neck region, which can result from ruptured alveoli.
Supplemental air: The volume of air that can be exhaled at the completion of a normal (tidal) expiration.
Symptom: A change in the body or body function which indicates disease or injury.
Tidal volume: The volume of air normally inspired and expired.
Toxic: Poisonous.
Two-stage regulator: A regulator in which cylinder pressure is reduced to breathing pressure in two stages.
Vertigo: Dizziness frequently accompanied by nausea.
Vital capacity: The maximum volume of air that can be inhaled following a complete exhalation.
Wet suit: An exposure suit that allows water to form an insulating layer between the suit and the diver's skin.
Weight belt: A belt with adjustable weights utilized for establishing neutral buoyancy in the water.

Useful Formulae

Surface Consumption Rate

$$SCR = \frac{\text{air consumed}}{\text{total pressure} \times \text{time to consume air}}$$

where

air consumed = initial tank pressure − final tank pressure (in p.s.i.)

This information is derived from the diver's submersible pressure gauge.

$$\text{total pressure} = \left[\frac{\text{depth in feet}}{33} + 1 \right] \text{atmospheres}$$

time to consume air = time spent between pressure gauge readings at the chosen depth

For example

A diver used 500 p.s.i. in ten minutes at 33 feet.

$$SCR = \frac{500}{\left[\frac{33}{33} + 1\right] \times 10} = \frac{500}{20} = 25 \text{ p.s.i. per minute}$$

[Note: For any given individual, this would differ under differing work loads.]

Time for Which Available Air Will Last at a Chosen Depth

$$Time = \frac{\text{initial tank pressure}}{\text{total pressure} \times \text{surface consumption rate}}$$

where

initial tank pressure = submersible pressure gauge reading at the outset of the dive in p.s.i.

total pressure = $\left[\frac{\text{depth in feet}}{33} + 1\right]$ atmospheres

surface consumption rate = the value computed from the previous formula (Any serious diver should make occasional checks on his air consumption rate at various work loads.)

For example

The diver making the previous computation wished to know how long his tank of air filled to 2250 p.s.i. would permit him to remain at a depth of 132 feet.

$$Time = \frac{2250}{\left[\frac{132}{33} + 1\right] \times 25} = 18 \text{ minutes}$$

[Note: The diver would of course not plan to dive for the full 18 minutes at 132 feet but would allow a considerable margin of time as a safety factor.] From decompression tables he would be aware that the maximum amount of time he could stay at 132 feet without having to decompress would be *less than 10 minutes*. A list of the maximum times that can be spent at a practical range of depths without having to decompress is a useful guide to the diver. Serious divers will commit the list of no decompression limits to memory. Note that the times listed are "bottom times." Bottom time is defined as the "total time elapsing between the diver leaving the surface at the outset of the dive, until he *begins* his ascent back to the surface."

Maximum Bottom Times Without Decompressing

Depth in Feet	No Decompression Limits (Bottom Time) In Minutes
Less than 35	No limit
35	310
40	200
50	100
60	60
70	50
80	40
90	30
100	25
110	20
120	15
130	10

Selected References

BOOKS AND ARTICLES

American National Red Cross. *Life Saving and Water Safety.* Garden City, N.Y.: Doubleday, 1967.
  Available from American Red Cross chapter offices and book stores. The standard life-saving text for thirty years. Divers should use this text to review their personal safety and basic swimming rescue skills. Coverage is comprehensive and clear. Recommended as a resource for reviewing and studying basic water safety. 248 pp., $.75.

Carrier, Rick, and Barbara Carrier. *Dive: The Complete Book of Skin Diving.* New York: Funk, 1963.
  Thorough, complete coverage of all aspects of sport diving. Well illustrated with more than 200 photographs and line drawings. One of the outstanding features is the suggestions for homemade equipment. A good resource text. 244 pp., $5.95.

Church, Ron. *Beginners Guide to Underwater Photography.* La Jolla, Calif.: Ron Church Productions, 1972.
  An excellent guide for the beginning underwater photographer. Well illustrated with 33 full-color pages and many black and white photographs. Covers all aspects of underwater photography for the beginner. Box 1163, La Jolla. $3.50.

Conference for National Cooperation in Aquatics. *The New Science of Skin Diving and Scuba Diving.* New York: Association Press, 1968.
  Probably the best all-around diving text now available. Excellent for personal reference or as a required text

for a diving course. Authorities on every aspect of sport diving have contributed to the preparation of this excellent work. 208 pp., $2.95.

Craig, Albert B. "Underwater Swimming and Loss of Consciousness." *Journal of the American Medical Association*, Vol. 192, No. 19 (April 19, 1965) 255-58.

A thorough examination of the reasons why swimmers lose consciousness as a result of excessive and/or prolonged hyperventilation. Dr. Craig contends that excessive hyperventilation is hazardous, that unconsciousness can occur without warning, and that hyperventilation should be discouraged.

Cousteau, Jacques Yves. *The Silent World*. New York: Harper, 1953.

A fascinating account of Captain Cousteau's pioneering efforts in the underwater world. A very interesting, exciting, and informative account of undersea diving with self-contained underwater breathing apparatus. 225 pp., $5.79.

Darby, Jim, and George Beardsley. *Scuba Rescue and Recovery*. Hanover Park, Ill.: Illinois Scuba Rescue and Recovery Unit, 1972.

Includes rescue and recovery patterns, underwater signals, ice-diving techniques, and navigation. Well illustrated. The book was written with the cooperation of agencies involved in scuba rescue and is based on many years of practical experience. $2.50.

Duffner, G. J. "Medical Problems Involved in Underwater Compression and Decompression." *Clinical Symposium*, Vol. 10, No. 4 (July-August, 1958), pp. 99-114.

An outstanding article in which Dr. Duffner discusses the causes and treatment of underwater accidents that commonly occur as a result of diving with self-contained underwater breathing apparatus. Highly recommended, especially for instructors.

Hogan, William F. *Safe Scuba*. Minneapolis, Minn.: Printing Inc., 1971.

Hogan, William F., and National Association of Skin Diving Schools. *Safe Scuba*. Long Beach, Calif.: NASDS, 1757 Long Beach Boulevard, 90813.

A profusely illustrated text unique in that it was specifically designed to meet the requirement of a nationally recognized certification course (offered by the National Association of Skin Diving Schools). Recommended for beginners because the emphasis is placed on all aspects of diving safety.

Levitt, Robert O., Richard W. Malpass, Jr., and Joseph G. Strykowski. *SCUBA II*. Bensenville, Ill.: Fairchild Printing Service, 1962.

An excellent manual. The authors are skilled divers and experienced instructors. Information is clearly presented, much of it in outline form. Coverage includes history, underwater physics, medical aspects of diving, marine life, and many other aspects of sport diving. Valuable as a personal reference or as a required text for a skin- and lung-diving course.

Modell, Jerome H. *Drowning and Near Drowning*. Springfield, Ill.: Thomas, 1972.

A book entirely about drowning. Complications, treatment, and physiology are covered. An excellent book for those highly interested in rescue and treatment techniques. $9.50.

Skin and Scuba Diving. Chicago: The Athletic Institute.

Available from book stores and the Athletic Institute Merchandise Mart—Room 805, Chicago, Ill. 60654. An excellent, low-cost manual for sport divers. Six units covering skin and lung diving are included. Each basic fact is illustrated and described in a clear, concise fashion. This serves as the manual for a course designed by The Athletic Institute, but it also serves well for self-teaching and as a general course manual. 81 pp., $.75.

Tillman, Albert A. *Skin and Scuba Diving*. Dubuque, Iowa: Brown, 1966.

This booklet includes information both for the beginner and more skilled diver. Both the "how" and the "why" are covered. Self-evaluation questions afford the reader examples of the understandings and skills he should be acquiring. A booklet that is suitable for use as a course text or for self-instruction and reference. 67 pp., $.95.

U.S. Navy Diving Manual. Washington, D. C.: Superintendent of Documents, Government Printing Office, 1970.

This manual, which is prepared by the United States Navy, is up-to-date, thorough, and technically detailed. It covers the general principles of diving, surface-applied diving, self-contained diving, and diving accessories. An excellent resource for personal or class work. 400 pp., $3.75.

Weeth, John B. "Management of Underwater Accidents." *Journal of The American Medical Association*, Vol. 192, No. 19 (April 19, 1965), 215-19.

An article dealing with five general types of underwater accidents. Accidents resulting from gas and pressure exposure are discussed. Although written primarily for physicians, this is an article of interest to all divers. Informative and described with case study details.

PERIODICALS

Skin Diver Magazine. 8490 Sunset Blvd., Los Angeles, California 90069.

CHAPTER 14

Fencing
*Charles Simonian**
The Ohio State University

HISTORY

From ancient times until the development of firearms, swords were the principal weapons used in battle by soldiers and on the field of honor by gentlemen. Armor was the primary defense against swords and, in order to penetrate armor plate, heavy swords were swung with brute force. As a result, armor kept getting heavier, more cumbersome, and more expensive. Those not rich enough to afford the protection of armor had to develop fencing skills to survive.

In the sixteenth century, while firearms were replacing swords and armor for combat, the Italians were developing the rapier, the sword point was being recognized to be more effective than the cut, and the lunge was coming into use. As armor was discarded, swords no longer had to be heavy, and short court swords were worn both for fashion and as side arms. The use of lighter weapons and the invention of the fencing mask in the eighteenth century further hastened the development of modern fencing.

Fencing today is an international sport and is included in the Olympic Games. In the United States, amateur fencing competition is under the jurisdiction of the Amateur Fencers League of America, which was organized in 1891.

---

*B.S., Fenn College, Cleveland, Ohio, M.A., University of Iowa, Iowa City, Ph.D., The Ohio State University, Columbus, head fencing coach, The Ohio State University, formerly head fencing coach at The University of Iowa. Dr. Simonian has taught fencing at all levels to a large number of classes and individuals. He has been a professional coach of fencing since 1952, and a member, National Fencing Coaches Association of America, since 1954. He is a life member of the Amateur Fencers League of America.

FENCING AND ITS VALUES

The knights of old would be hard put to keep up with the modern fencer because movements now are much faster and blade skills are more highly refined than ever before. The sport of fencing retains all the thrills of dueling without the risks faced in real combat. Two men fencing on the strip are, for all but blood-letting purposes, in combat. Whether it be an informal workout by beginners in a gymnasium or an intensely competitive bout in a major meet, fencing is physically and mentally an exhilerating experience. The mind must be ever alert to plot strategy and to perceive changes in the tactics of the opponent. The body must be conditioned to respond instantly to the attack in order that no scoring opportunity will be lost. Fencing is excellent exercise for anyone, and women are especially attracted to the graceful movements that are an inherent part of the sport.

Some of the advantages of fencing are that it can be practiced in almost any kind of space, outdoor as well as indoor, and it can be practiced well past one's middle age. A full set of fencing equipment is only moderately expensive and it will last many years.

Fencing requires time and practice before any degree of skill can be expected. Competent instruction is usually available in the large cities and in many colleges and universities. For those who have instruction available and the patience to learn, the rewards in fencing are many.

EQUIPMENT

The amount of fencing equipment needed varies with the situation. A competitive fencer is required to wear a complete uniform, which consists of a full jacket, trousers, glove, and mask. The protective needs of a beginner can be met by a mask and half-jacket. Masks are available in small, medium, and large sizes. A properly fitting mask should neither pinch any part of the head nor be so loose that it might fall off while in use. Slight adjustments in the size of the mask can be made by pressing in or pulling out the headspring.

A new foil blade should have a slight downward curve worked into the first quarter of its length. Any other bends or kinks that develop in use must be straightened immediately in order to preserve the life of the blade. If the foil blade is bent too far, it will snap and the broken end will, of course, present a hazard if the blade continues to be used. The replacement of a damaged blade is a simple matter. The pommel is unscrewed at the end of the handle and the handle, thumb pad, and bell are pulled off. The parts are replaced in the same order onto a new blade, and adhesive tape is wrapped around the tip in order to provide a slight cushion. Right-handed foil handles are curved to the right and left-handed handles have their curvature to the left. Therefore, when buying foils it is necessary to specify the type of handle desired.

When purchasing fencing jackets of any type, the buyer should specify whether they are for right- or left-handed fencers and, of course, the sizes desired. Jackets can be laundered without any special care, but the excessive use of bleaches will weaken the material.

GENERAL INFORMATION

Foil

Of the three competitive fencing weapons, the most commonly used is the foil. It is a light, flexible thrusting weapon whose target is the torso, with the arms, legs, and head not considered valid target areas. Being a thrusting weapon, only the point of the foil is used to score touches, and any contacts made with the side of the blade are disregarded. The foil is used by both men and women, whereas the other two weapons are used only by men.

Épée

The épée is also a thrusting weapon and its target area is the entire body. This weapon most closely resembles the old dueling sword, and for this reason it has the fewest rules governing its use. Whichever fencer scores first is awarded the touch, and if two fencers score upon each other simultaneously then each receives a point. This is in marked contrast to the rule of right-of-way that governs the use of the foil and the sabre. This rule will be described later, but briefly it determines which of two fencers established a certain priority of attack and which one was out of the prescribed sequence.

Sabre

The sabre is both a thrusting and a cutting weapon. The target area includes all parts of the body above the hips. Cuts are preferred to thrusts by most sabremen, and this makes for wider actions than when the other two weapons are used, the actions of which are followed with increased ease by uninitiated spectators.

In recent years, in order to reduce human error in judging, electrical scoring devices have been perfected for use with the foil and the épée. Nearly all fencing competitions are now conducted with the use of this equipment.

BASIC FOIL TECHNIQUES

(The instructions are given for right-handed fencers; left-handed fencers must reverse them.)

Grip

The French foil is the type most commonly used by beginning fencers, and this type of handle must be gripped lightly in order that the foil can be manipulated with the fingers. Squeezing the handle will rapidly tire the hand and will not permit fine control of the foil point. The thumb and forefinger should oppose each other on the handle, with the thumb being on the top surface of the handle. The remaining three fingers should rest on the left side of the handle, and the handle should be aligned with the forearm. (See Figure 14-1.)

Attention

Before fencing, the fencer stands at attention and then salutes his opponent. The position of attention is assumed by standing erect and placing the feet at right angles to each other, with the right foot pointed forward and with

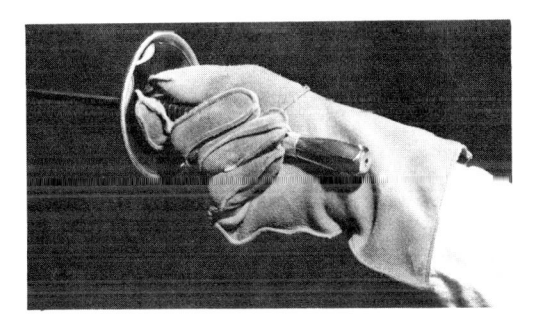

Figure 14-1. Grip.

the right heel in front of and touching the left heel. The mask is held in the left hand and the foil is pointed toward the floor.

Salute

It is traditional to salute one's opponent from a position of attention prior to putting on the mask and beginning to fence. The simple salute is made by bringing the foil bell upward to a position a few inches in front of the face. The palm of the sword hand should be toward the face, and the blade should be held vertically. To complete the salute, the foil is swung smartly back to its original position when at attention. (See Figure 14-2.)

On Guard

The basic stance of "on guard" (Figure 14-3) permits a fencer to make his offensive and defensive movements most effectively. From the position of attention, the sword arm is flexed sufficiently to raise the foil tip to face level while keeping the blade and forearm in alignment. The right thumb should be up and slightly to the right of the vertical. For purposes of balance and proper body position, the left arm should be flexed and lifted until the elbow is at shoulder height. The left forearm should be held vertically, the fingers turned forward, and both shoulders relaxed.

Figure 14-2. Salute: left = 1st position; right = 2nd position.

Figure 14-3. On guard.

With the arms in place, a short step forward is taken with the right foot and the legs are bent at the knees. The weight must be equally distributed onto both feet and the body held in an erect position. The heels should be in line with each other, and the right angle position of the feet must be maintained.

Advance

To move toward an opponent, take a short step forward with the right foot and then take a step of equal length with the left foot. At the completion of the advance, the spacing of the feet should be the same as it was on guard. The length of an advance will vary with the distance that needs to be covered but short, quick advances are preferred to long steps.

Retreat

To back away from an opponent, begin by stepping to the rear with the left foot and then take a backward step of equal length with the right foot. Here, too, it is very important to maintain a consistent spacing of the feet.

Lunge

Because a fencer ordinarily stays well beyond the normal reach of his opponent, the attacker must take an extremely long step forward in order to land a touch. This stretching movement is called a lunge (Figure 14-4) and it is one of the most important single skills to be learned in fencing. The power for the lunge comes from the vigorous extension of the left leg rather than from a forward step with the right foot.

Figure 14-4. Lunge.

The lunge is best learned in three steps. First, the sword arm is extended while the foil tip is directed at the target. In this extension, and throughout the lunge, the sword-hand should be positioned at shoulder height. The second step involves the simultaneous slight lifting of the right foot and the rapid extension of the left leg. The right foot is kept above the floor until the full stretch of the lunge is achieved. Along with the leg action, the left arm should, with the palm up, swing in a rearward and downward arc until it is parallel to the left leg. The rear foot should remain flat on the floor at all times. The third step is the recovery action from the lunge to the on-guard position and it is not an actual part of the lunge itself. To recover, bend at the left knee and push hard with the right foot. The arms are brought to their original on-guard positions.

Engagements

When two fencers have their blades in contact and no particular action is taking place, their blades are said to be engaged. Engagements are identified by number, according to the relative position of the blades to each other. The engagements most commonly used are numbers four and six. A fencer is in the fourth engagement when his opponent's blade is to the left of his own blade and in contact with it. When the opponent's blade is to the right of his own, the engagement number is six. A fourth engagement is sometimes termed an inside engagement, whereas a sixth engagement is also called an outside engagement.

Safety

Although fencing is among the safest of sports, the danger of accidents resulting from horseplay and disregard for some obvious rules of safety always exists. All fencers must wear masks whenever they pair off for practice or bouting. The foil tips should be checked frequently to be certain that the tape has not worn through. A sweatshirt or a similar garment made of soft material is never a safe substitute for a fencing jacket.

ELEMENTARY OFFENSE AND DEFENSE

Direct Lunge

The direct lunge is the simplest of the attacks and it must be thoroughly learned before any advanced actions can be attempted. When first practicing with a partner, the attacker should make a few trial lunges at slow speed in order to measure his distance to the target. The blade should bend in an upward arc when it touches the target. The length of the lunge will vary according to the distance to the opponent but, regardless of the distance, the power should always be supplied by the extension of the left leg.

As a drill, the partners can engage in fourth with one designated as the attacker and the other the defender. The defender gives the signal to lunge by moving his blade to the right, thereby opening his line or target. The attacker then extends his sword arm, lunges, and remains in his lunge while the defender checks his form and suggests needed corrections. As some competence is achieved, the drill can be complicated by having the defender advance or retreat several times before giving the signal to the attacker, who has been following the lead of his partner.

Parry

The defender can avoid being hit by a direct lunge by moving his sword hand and foil horizontally only enough to meet and deflect the attacking blade away from his chest. If the attack is to the inside line, the simple parry will be made by moving the hand to the left and is called a parry four (Figure 14-5). Similarly, an attack to the outside line will be met with a parry six (Figure 14-6), which is made by moving the sword hand to the right to meet the attacking blade. The sword hand should not rotate in parrying, nor should the point or hand rise or fall from its original level in the on-guard position.

Riposte

When an attack is successfully parried, the attacker is momentarily in a poor defensive position and can be easily reached by the counterattack of the defender, which is

Fencing

called a riposte. This return attack is usually accomplished by a simple extension of the sword arm, but if the attacker recovers quickly, the riposte will have to be delivered with a lunge.

Closed-line Engagement

When an engagement is taken in such a way that the defender's target cannot be hit by a direct lunge, his line is said to be closed. The fourth line is closed when a fencer has, in an action resembling a parry four, carried his opponent's blade several inches to the left. A similar movement to the right closes the sixth line.

Disengagement

If a defender has closed his line against direct lunges, the attacker can pass his foil under the defender's blade and lunge into the open line. As the sword arm is being extended, the point should be passed under so quickly that the disengagement is completed by the time the arm is fully extended. The lunge immediately follows the disengagement.

The difficulty of making the disengagement against a simple parry is increased because the disengaging action must be perfectly timed with the parry. To practice disengaging against a simple parry, the fencers should begin in fourth position, but with the blades not engaged. The attacker extends his arm and threatens the open line. As the defender begins to parry in response to this threat, the attacker disengages his blade and lunges into the newly opened line. The disengaging action is best accomplished by moving the point with only the hand and fingers.

As skill is developed, the time between the extension of the sword arm and the beginning of the lunge will become so slight that it will appear to be a simultaneous act. However, the blade should always start its forward travel before the body begins to move.

Compound Parry

Any time that a defender makes a simple parry that fails to contact the opponent's blade, he should reflexively make a second parry in the opposite direction and perhaps step backward. Any combination of two or more parries is termed a compound parry.

One-two

When an attacker determines that his disengagement actions are being repeatedly deflected by the simple parries of the defender, he can add a second disengagement in

Figure 14-5. Parry four.   **Figure 14-6.** Parry six.

the opposite direction of the first and thus deceive the simple parry. The first disengagement thereby becomes a feint intended to draw the parry, and as such it must resemble a real attack. The sword arm remains fully extended following the feint, and the second disengagement, which is accomplished by a lunge, is made in a narrow arc by the use of the fingers.

As skill is developed, the attacker begins his lunge with his feint and does not wait for the defender to make his parry before beginning the second disengagement. Gambling that he has correctly analyzed the defensive pattern, the attacker anticipates that the defender will parry in a predicted manner. It is most important that the attacker not withdraw his arm between the first and second actions. As much as possible, the blade movements should be made with the hand and fingers, because using the entire arm will result in wide and obvious blade movements.

The name of the attack is derived from the number of disengagements involved. If three disengagements had been made, the attack would be called a one-two-three, with the first two being feints to draw compound parries and the third being the scoring attempt.

196 *Individual and Team Sports*

Figure 14-7. Parry seven.

Figure 14-8. Parry eight.

INTERMEDIATE OFFENSE AND DEFENSE

Counterparry Six

In order to add variety to the defense so that the opponent cannot predict the parry to be used, it is necessary to use a counterparry occasionally. The defender should start by closing his sixth line. As the attacker makes a disengagement lunge, the defender circles his blade clockwise and picks up the attacking blade, returning it to the sixth position. The counterparry can also be effectively used against direct lunges. With the partners in the fourth position, but with their blades not engaged, the attacker extends and lunges. The clockwise circling action of the defender will pick up the direct lunge and carry it to the sixth position.

A counterparry four is used less frequently than is the counter six, but it can be practiced by simply reversing the direction of movements used in the counter six. Because a circular parry takes longer to complete than does a simple parry, it may be necessary to take a short step backward to allow more time and room in which to complete the parry. As with all parries, a quick riposte should follow a successful counterparry.

Double

To score a touch against an opponent who uses the counterparry, it is necessary to use a double—a disengagement feint followed by another disengagement that circles around the parry and escapes contact. The starting position from which to practice the double is one with the defender having his sixth line closed. The attacker disengages his blade and threatens the open fourth line. As the defender responds by beginning a counter-six parry, the attacker circles his foil tip around the parry and lunges. The attacking blade must move ahead of the parry and avoid contact—the contact would be construed as a parry. As with the one-two, the blade movements should be narrow, and the elbow must not bend between the first and second actions.

Advance Lunge

Against an opponent who steps back when he is attacked, the offensive fencer must make up the ground by lunging if he hopes to reach the defender. This can be done by combining into one continuous movement an advance and a lunge. Any type of blade action can be used with the advance lunge.

As the advance begins, the sword arm should be extended in order that the lunge can immediately follow. No hesitation should be evident between the advance and the lunge, and the sword arm should remain fully extended throughout the action.

Low-line Parries

When an attack is directed too low to be deflected by the simple high parries four and six, the defender must use one of the low-line parries. The parry seven (Figure 14-7) protects against attacks to the low inside target, whereas the parry eight protects the low outside target. The parries four and seven are both used to cover the inside line, but the point is below the hand level for the parry seven and higher than the hand for the parry four. Similarly, the only real difference between the parries six and eight (Figure 14-8) is that the point is up in the former and down in the latter.

The riposte following a low parry can be to the high or low line of the opponent. An attacker can avoid the low parries by using a modification of the one-two attack; that is, a feint can be made to the low line followed by an attack to the high line.

Beat Attack

If the defender is on guard with his sword arm extended—thus threatening his opponent—the attacker can make a sharp beat on the defender's blade to momentarily deflect

Fencing

it and allow a lunge to be made. The beat should be made by first relaxing the last three fingers of the sword hand and then quickly contracting the fingers in order to cause the blade to forcefully strike the opponent's blade in fourth position. The beat is followed by an extension of the sword arm and a lunge. Because most fencers will reflexively parry a beat, it may be necessary to follow the beat with a disengagement or a one-two. The beat can also be used with a false lunge as a means of getting the opponent to reveal something of his responses.

BOUT STRATEGY

The first attempts at fencing a bout by a beginner will usually be marked by awkwardness, apprehension, and much unnecessary blade movement. Whatever skills and control may have been developed in the lessons to that point are apt to be forgotten in the excitement of combat. For this reason the first few bouts should be quite short.

All too often the beginning fencer will hold his ground and try to parry every attack made against him when, in fact, he would be better off to retreat often. The maintenance of proper distance is one of the most difficult skills or concepts to master, and fencers who are just learning the sport are likely to find themselves either too close together or too far apart much of the time.

To hit and not be hit is one of the oldest principles of fencing, but the accomplishment of this objective requires a considerable degree of skill. For a given attack to score requires that the attacker correctly analyze the defense, choose an attack that will penetrate the defense, pick the right moment to launch the attack, begin from the correct distance, and properly execute the blade action. Along with all these variables, proper consideration must also be given to the unpredictable movements of the defender who, after all, is also trying to hit and not be hit.

As a general rule, the offense should develop from the simple actions to the complex. The attack must be based on the anticipated defensive actions of the opponent. For example, a fencer would be foolish to continue to use a favorite one-two attack when his opponent has been repeatedly using counterparries defensively. Each opponent is different in his tactics, speed, strength, height, and skill; therefore, the fencer must adjust accordingly.

Practice bouts have a different purpose than do competitive bouts; consequently, the fencer must not place winning ahead of learning and improving when he is fencing practice bouts. Because there are no judges in practice fencing, the person who is hit should acknowledge the touch for the benefit of his opponent. The attacker must never call a touch against his opponent. When a phrase (an uninterrupted series of movements of the blades) ends in both fencers being hit, they should pause sufficiently to attempt to decide which one had the right-of-way.

BASIC FOIL RULES

Right-of-way

The rules of right-of-way must be understood by all foil fencers because they define which fencer has priority in any situation. The fencer who attacks first ordinarily has the right-of-way, and the opponent must either defend himself with a parry or retreat. Once having successfully parried, the defender in turn has the right-of-way and is free to riposte. Now the original attacker is obligated to defend himself in some way before resuming the offensive.

For a parry to gain the right-of-way for a defender, it needs only to deflect the attacking blade momentarily. The parry does not have to be held until the threat is completely removed. A riposte must be made immediately if it is to have the right-of-way, and any delay may permit the attacker to resume his attack.

Right-of-way must be decided only when both fencers have landed touches. When only one fencer scores, there is no need to decide on priority. It is possible for both fencers to attack at the same moment, in which case neither would have the right-of-way and no points would be awarded even if one fencer hit off the target and the other hit the valid target.

Fencing Area

The official fencing area is six feet in width and forty-six feet in length; most competitions are held on rubber mats with these approximate dimensions, although the width is sometimes less. A fencer who approaches the end of the mat is warned by the director when his foot reaches the one-meter line. If the fencer then retreats off the end of the mat with both feet, he is penalized one touch, unless in the meantime either fencer scored a point. When a fencer steps off the side of the mat with both feet, the bout is halted and the fencer is replaced on the mat one meter back from the spot where he left the mat.

Scoring

In men's fencing five touches must be made to win the bout, whereas in a women's bout four touches are needed to win. Touches are awarded against the fencer who was hit; hence, the winning fencer is the one with the lowest score.

When time limits are used in fencing competition, a warning is given when only one minute remains in the

198 *Individual and Team Sports*

bout. At the end of the time limit, whichever fencer is leading wins the bout with enough points being added to both scores to bring the losing score up to five. Thus, if the score were 1-3 when time ran out, the final score would be 3-5. If the fencers were tied, the bout score would be raised to 4-4 and the next touch would decide the bout. The time limits vary with the nature of the competition.

Men's intercollegiate fencing meets are decided on the best out of twenty-seven bouts; hence, the team that first wins fourteen bouts wins the meet, although the balance of the bouts are completed. Men's college fencing teams are composed of nine team members (three in each weapon), with each man fencing three bouts. A collegiate women's team has four members and a total of sixteen bouts are fought.

Officiating

A foil jury in nonelectric bouts is made up of four judges and a director, who is in charge of the bout. Two judges flank the fencer to the right of the director and two judges stand on either side of the other fencer. The judges on the right are responsible for seeing touches made on the fencer to the left, and the judges on the left are responsible for seeing touches made on the fencer to the right. The judges should stand a few feet to the side and slightly to the rear of the fencer, and they should move with him in order to maintain this relative position. The director always maintains a central position from which he can observe the fencers and the judges.

The director gives the commands to fence and to halt, looks for touches himself, watches for signals from the judges, and especially observes the blade action so that he is always aware of which fencer had the right-of-way in any given action.

The responsibility of the judge is to raise his hand when he sees a touch land anywhere on the fencer that he is assigned to watch, whether the touch is on or off the target. Upon seeing the judge raise his hand, the director immediately halts the bout.

To aid the judges and contestants, the director verbally reconstructs the action of the phrase in question and indicates which fencer had the right-of-way. He then asks the judges whose fencer had the priority whether a touch landed or not. If that attack failed, the director then asks the opposite pair of judges if any touches landed. The action is thus followed one step at a time until some decision can be reached. Touches that land off the target area invalidate all subsequent touches in that phrase.

Each of the judges has a vote worth one point and the director has a vote worth one and one-half points. The jury members have four types of votes. If the touch hit with the point on valid area, the vote is "yes." If the touch was not on valid area, the vote is "off target." If the attack was parried, missed, or hit flat on the body, the vote is "no." If a judge is not sure of what happened, his vote is "abstain," which has no numerical value in deciding the awarding of the point.

A tie vote, such as might result from an abstention by the director and the disagreeing opinions of the two judges, is termed a *doubtful touch*, and no point is awarded. Whenever one or both judges abstain, the director's vote of one and one-half points can overrule the one judge who may vote.

After the awarding of a point, the fencers return to the center of the mat before resuming fencing. When a bout is halted, but no points are awarded, the fencing resumes at the point at which it stopped.

Glossary of Terms

Beat: A sharp blow to the opponent's blade.
Closed line: An engagement that covers one line against a direct lunge.
Director: The official in charge of the bout and jury.
Disengagement: An attack made by passing the blade under the opponent's foil in order to hit in the opposite line.
Double: An offensive movement used to deceive a counterparry.
Engagement: Any contact of blades not involving action by either fencer.
Feint: Any blade movement that resembles an attack but is not.
Fleche: A running attack sometimes used in place of a lunge.
Infighting: Combat at close quarters. It is permitted so long as the fencers are still able to use their foils and there is no body contact.
Invitation: Any blade action or deliberate exposure of target that is intended to draw an attack.
Line: Target area usually referred to as high or low, inside or outside.
One-two: An attack consisting of two disengagements, the first of which is a feint.
Parry: A deflection of an attacking blade.
Phrase: An uninterrupted series of blade movements by two fencers.
Redoublement: A second blade action in an attack following the failure of the original action.
Remise: An immediate continuation of an attack that has been parried.
Riposte: The return action following a successful parry.

Fencing

Selected References

Castello, Hugo, and James Castello. *Fencing.* New York: Ronald, 1962.

Crosnier, Roger. *Fencing with the Foil.* New York: A. S. Barnes, 1951.

Deladrier, Clovis. *Modern Fencing.* Annapolis, Md.: U.S. Naval Institute, 1948.

Fencing Rules and Manual. New York: Amateur Fencers League of America, latest ed.

Simonian, Charles. *Fencing Fundamentals.* Columbus, Ohio: Merrill, 1968.

CHAPTER 15

Football: flag and touch

*Tom Carlson**
University of Wisconsin-Oshkosh

HISTORY

Football, as it is played in the United States today, had its major origin in similar games played during the times of the ancient Greeks and Romans. The Roman soldiers are believed to have brought the game to Britain where it eventually developed into soccer. Great Britain also gave birth to rugby, a game in which the ball is actually carried as well as kicked. Both of these sports have greatly influenced the development of the modern game of football in America.

The early games of football played in the United States can probably best be described as gang fights over a round ball. The basic rules were gradually formulated, changed, and modified. The first intercollegiate football game in the United States was played between Princeton and Rutgers in 1869. Interest in football spread rapidly, and eventually a majority of the high schools and colleges fielded competitive football teams.

As competition in football increased, a growing number of students not involved in interschool participation began to play the game as a leisure-time activity. Because of a lack of equipment and facilities, the game of touch football was created in which the one- or two-handed touch replaced actual tackling. The blocking rules were also modified by most of the groups who played touch football. This game soon became popular in physical education and intramural sports programs throughout the country. Touch football is played somewhat differently in various locales of the United States because no universal rules have been established and generally accepted. The College Physical Education Association established a set of rules for play; however, these are not followed extensively throughout the country. The size of the areas of play and the numbers of students who desire to participate have also influenced the specific touch football rules a certain locality will adopt.

The idea underlying the game of touch football was to have a game that was similar to regular football but in which play without pads would be relatively safe. This idea often is not achieved—perhaps in part because of little instruction or practice being given to some of the participants and because some participants take their tackle football skills and habits with them to the touch football field.

The exercise, enjoyment, and other values of touch football were recognized by the Armed Forces, who used it during and after World War II as an activity for men in the service.

A recent development in the game of touch football in many areas throughout the country has been the substitution of a flag (which is pulled loose) for a touch. This change in the game has been adopted by the Armed Forces and by several school systems and has resulted in a reduction in accidents and injuries by as much as 80 per cent when compared to that for touch football.[1] Flag

---

*B.A. and M.A., University of Northern Colorado, Greeley; Ph.D., University of Iowa, Iowa City. Dr. Carlson, an associate professor at the University of Wisconsin-Oshkosh, has been active in football for several years. In addition to teaching flag football classes he was a quarterback on the University of Northern Colorado football team for four years, was the freshman football coach at the University of Wisconsin-Oshkosh for one year and is presently the offensive backfield coach at the University of Wisconsin-Oshkosh.

[1] Letter from Charles W. Gasswint, Mason City Tent and Awning Company, Mason City, Iowa, April 14, 1967, manufacturer of Rip Flag flags. D. K. Stanley and I. F. Waglow, *Physical Education Activities Handbook* (Boston: Allyn and Bacon, Inc.) p. 54, (3rd ed.) 1972

football differs from touch football only in that a "tackle" is made by pulling a flag away from the ball carrier instead of making a one- or two-handed touch on him.

The first type of flags were simply handkerchiefs tucked in the belt at the back of each player. The type most commonly used now consists of a belt with two or three colored flags attached to it. (See Figure 15-1.) The flags release from the belt when grasped or jerked by a defensive player.

In addition to the expected decrease in injuries, flag football offers several other advantages over touch football. The task of officiating the game is eased by the use of flags because the decision of whether or not a ball carrier has been legally touched (or tackled) can be made quickly and accurately. Possible disagreement concerning whether or not the touch was made is prevented. Running is a more important part of flag football than it is of touch because a ball carrier can pass closely by a defensive man without being tackled. The passing game is still important in both; therefore, increased scoring generally occurs in flag football. In those schools and organizations in which both the flag and touch football are offered, the flag game is usually the more popular. Both flag and touch football include many of the skills that comprise the primary skills of regular football (passing, receiving, running, carrying the ball, kicking, phases of blocking, and defensive techniques and reactions). Aside from the difference in the way that the ball carrier is tackled, the two games are highly similar in all other aspects.

DESCRIPTION

Flag football is similar to regular tackle football, except that tackling is accomplished by pulling a flag from the belt of the carrier. The ball is dead at the point where the defensive man removed the flag; under some rules the ball is dead at the point where the removed flag is dropped on the ground. The blocking rules of regular football are also modified; the straight-shoulder block from both feet is the only block allowed in flag football. A blocker may not go to his hands or leave his feet during the block, and he is not allowed to use any part of his body except the shoulder throughout the block. These and certain other modifications of the basic tackle-football rules enable the participants of flag football to play safely without padding, while demanding of them most of the skills necessary for playing regular football.

The number of players on a flag football team can vary according to the number of participants available, but in general eight men comprise the official team. The awarding of first downs follows the pattern used in tackle football, but certain modifications are usually specified.

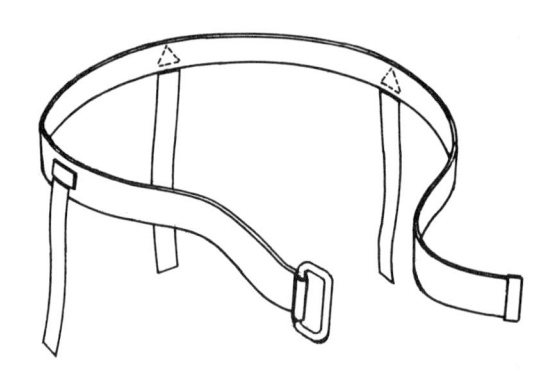

Figure 15-1. Flag belt.

It can be played that when the ball is downed, it is placed on the closest line and then must be advanced ten yards in four or less downs before another first down is awarded. In another version the ball is dead at whatever point possession is gained, and the ball must be moved past the second line (10 + to 19 + yards) before a first down is awarded. At times yard markers are utilized, in which case the ball must be moved ten (or fifteen) yards in four downs.

The game is started with the traditional kickoff. The defense attempts to "tackle" the ball carrier by removing any of his flags (or else touching him). All players, including the center, are eligible to receive passes.

The rules pertaining to punting are also modified. The offensive team must declare its intention to punt, and the defensive team cannot cross the line of scrimmage until the ball has been punted.

The scoring is the same as in tackle football. To prevent a serious injury that could occur because of a lack of protective equipment, a ball that is fumbled is immediately dead and possession goes to the team of the player who last controlled the ball before the fumble occurred.

VALUES

The participant in flag (or touch) football can derive several benefits from the game. Many of the skills of tackle football can be developed through participation in these variant games. The participant has an opportunity to gain an increased understanding of the theory and strategy involved in football. Because of the vigorous activity involved in the game, various facets of physical fitness can be developed. Of primary importance is the value derived from learning to work as a member of a team. For most participants, the sheer enjoyment of playing football is ample reward in itself.

EQUIPMENT

Certain pieces of equipment are necessary to play the game of flag or touch football. The ball used is the regulation football.

The optimal dimensions for the field of play are the same as for regular football—160 by 360 feet. This length includes a 100-yard playing field with 10-yard end zones on both ends. The game can be played on a similar field—sixty yards from goal line to goal line is the minimum length. If down markers are used, the goal lines and boundary lines are the only necessary markings. However, if the usual situation prevails in which no down markers are used and a team has a specified number of plays (downs) in which to advance the ball across a certain line, yard lines (spaced ten yards apart) are also a necessity (see Figure 15-2). If the field goal is to be a part of the game, a goal post must be positioned on the center on each endline. (See Figure 15-2.) In the interest of avoiding a source of possible injuries, the goal posts often are not used. The same reasoning underlies the rule that prohibits the wearing of football cleats.

The only other necessary articles of equipment are whistles for the officials and a stopwatch for timing the various games.

Sets of different colored flags are needed for the participants if flag football is played. Two specially made flags and belts can be obtained for this purpose or a handkerchief (or two) can be tucked in the waistband of a player with a specified length showing.

No special uniforms are required for flag football because the different colored flags distinguish the members of one team from another. If special flags are not available and handkerchiefs or similar pieces of cloth are used, or if touch football is played, the players should wear different colored shirts to distinguish the two teams.

RULES AND REGULATIONS

In general, the National Federation of State High School (NFSHS) Rules (sometimes the Intercollegiate Football Rules) should govern the play in flag football, with the exceptions or modifications noted in this section or those local regulations that may be imposed. Actually several different sets of rules and regulations have been formulated for the play of flag and touch football. The following rules and regulations have been successfully employed in the intramural sports program of a major college.

Eligibility

1. No student who is a member of a Varsity or Freshman athletic squad during the current semester (or quarter) is eligible to play intramural football.
2. No one who lettered in college football is eligible for intramural football (this ineligibility may vary from one year to all years in college, depending on the college or university).

Regulations

1. Eight (8) men constitute a team. A team must have eight eligible men ready to play at game time, but any game can be finished with fewer than eight men on a team.
2. The officials are in complete charge of all contests and have full power to enforce all regulations.
3. The two teams shall each furnish two assistants to the officials; one to keep the scorebook, two to assist with the yardage chains, and one to keep the down box.

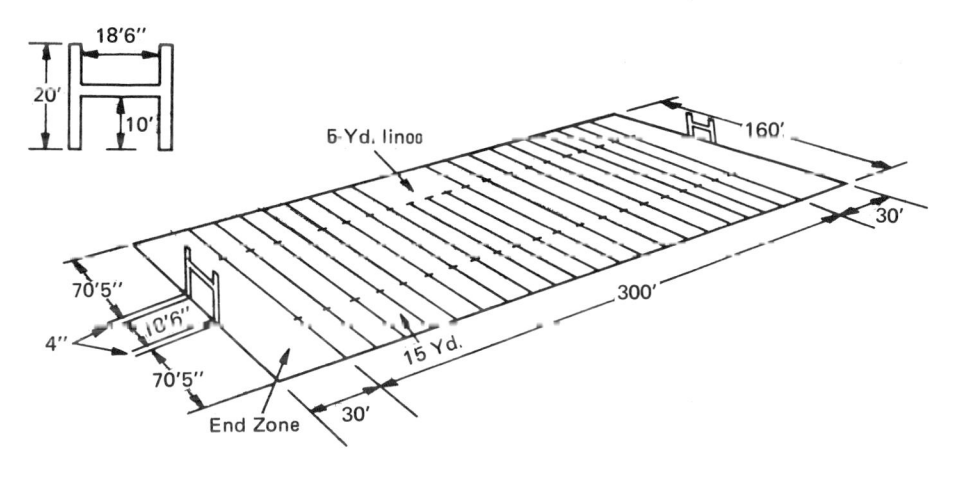

Figure 15-2. Football playing field.

Playing Rules

1. The official Intercollegiate Football Rules shall apply except as hereinafter listed.
2. Teams shall consist of eight players. (Penalty: a team without eight starting players must forfeit.)
3. The offensive team must place five men on the line of scrimmage. (Penalty: loss of five yards.)
4. All players on a team are eligible to receive forward passes.
5. No cleated shoes of any kind can be worn; any basketball or suitable gym shoes are permitted. (Penalty: the offending player is banished from the field and he may not remain in the area.)
6. A team is allowed three downs in which to advance the ball ten yards. (Four downs is the most common rule, however.)
7. Touchdowns shall score 6 points; point-after-touchdown shall score 1 point, and can only be scored by a run or a pass; a safety shall score 2 points; but no provision is made to score field goals.
8. Tackling: a player who has possession of the ball is "tackled" and his forward progress "ceases" when he loses one of his tackle flags, or when any part of his body, except his feet and hands, comes in contact with the ground.
9. Blocking: Only the shoulder block is permitted, and the blocker must have at least one foot on the ground at the moment of contact. Flying, rolling, and cross-body blocks of any kind are prohibited. (Penalty: illegal block, loss of fifteen yards). In blocking, the hands of the blocker must remain in contact with his chest.
10. Defensive players may not use their hands on the opponent's heads. (Penalty: loss of fifteen yards.)
11. A *fumbled ball* that strikes the ground may not be advanced by the players of either team; it belongs to the team that last had possession of it before it struck the ground.
12. *Substitutions* can be made in any numbers and at any time in the game, providing that this does not slow play. A substitute can go onto the field only after the official has secured the ball. (Penalty: if a substitute slows up play, a time-out is charged against his team.)
13. Each game shall consist of two halves, each twenty minutes in duration, with a five-minute intermission between halves. Each team shall be permitted two one-minute time-outs each half. (Note: loss of five yards shall be charged for each excessive time-out, except when an injured player is removed from the playing field.)
14. Games that end in a tie score shall be scored as a one-half game won and a one-half game lost; no tie games shall be replayed or extended to determine a winner.
15. The officials are charged to enforce strictly all playing rules, particularly those concerned with the safety of the players. Penalties of fifteen yards shall be assessed in violations of any of the following: (1) unnecessary roughness in any play and especially in touch- or flag-tackling ball carriers and passers; (2) illegal blocking; (3) kicking, gouging, tripping, piling on, or clipping; (4) illegal use of the hands in blocking or playing a blocker; (5) unsportsmanlike conduct toward either the officials or opponents. (Rough play will not be tolerated.)
16. No protests that are concerned with the rules of play, the interpretations of rules, or the decisions of the game officials will be reviewed. All games are automatically forfeited by a team using an ineligible player.
17. A player shall be suspended for any act of unsportsmanlike conduct, profane language, fighting, harassing officials, or the like.
18. All players must wear gym, basketball, or tennis shoes.

FUNDAMENTAL SKILLS

Stance

Generally one of the marks of an unskilled football player is a poor stance. A good football player, whether playing offense of defense, a lineman or a back, must be able to consistently assume a ready position from which he can quickly move in the desired direction.

Offensive Line Stance (Figures 15-3 and 15-4). An offensive lineman must assume a stance from which he can move forward, laterally, or into a pass-block position at the snap of the ball. He must be able to execute any of these three movements from the same stance in order to avoid tipping the defense to what he will do by the stance he assumes. Most offensive linemen are coached to use a three-point stance, although the four-point stance is sometimes utilized in the offensive line.

Three-point Stance.

1. The feet should be so staggered that the right toe is even with the left instep. This short stagger enables the blocker to step out with equal effectiveness to either the right or the left.
2. With the toes pointed straight ahead, the feet should be spread apart about shoulder width.

Figure 15-3. Three-point offensive lineman stance (Frank Orzel. Wisconsin State University, Oshkosh. All-District Fourteen NAIA Offensive Guard, 1967).

3. The blocker should execute a half squat, bending forward slightly at the waist, rest the left forearm on the left thigh, and let the right arm hang down below the right shoulder.
4. The blocker should rock forward until the weight is on the balls of the feet and the right hand.
5. The back should be parallel to the ground, and the head should be up with the eyes focused straight ahead.
6. If a four-point stance is desired, the blocker should assume a half-squat position and rock forward, placing his weight on both hands. (See Figure 15-4.)

Defensive Line Stance. A defensive lineman may use a three- or a four-point stance. The stance is executed in a manner similar to that for the offensive lineman. Because a defensive lineman generally charges forward initially, he should place increased weight on the hands in his stance.

Offensive Backfield Stance. An offensive back must assume a stance that will enable him to move effectively to the left, right, straight ahead, or up to a pass-block position. These requirements are much the same as for the offensive lineman; therefore, the three-point stance is commonly used by an offensive back. Because the offensive back does not as a rule make contact with an opponent as quickly after the center snap as does the offensive lineman, the offensive back positions more weight on the feet and less weight forward on the hand than does the lineman.

When a single wing or other type of offense is used, in which the center actually snaps the ball to a back behind the line of scrimmage, a two-point stance is generally used by the backfield men who could possibly receive the center hike. In the two-point stance the feet are spread to about shoulder width, the toes point straight ahead, and the weight is uniformly balanced on the balls and heels of the feet. The head is up, the back is straight, and the knees and hips are slightly flexed. The forearms may rest on the thighs (Figure 15-5), or the hands may be placed on the knees with the fingers pointed downward (Figure 15-6).

Regardless of the stance used it is important that the offensive backfield player not indicate in which direction he will go by the stance that he assumes. Before every snap the head should be up and the eyes directed straight downfield.

Defensive Backfield Stance. The linebackers and deep backs on defense should assume a two-point stance in a "ready" position. In order to meet a running play and to cover a pass receiver, these players must be able to move forward, laterally forward, laterally, or backward.

1. The weight should be uniformly distributed on both feet.
2. The feet should be about shoulder width apart, with the toes pointing straight ahead.

Figure 15-4. Four-point offensive lineman stance.

Figure 15-5. Two-point offensive backfield stance—forearms on thighs.

Football: Flag and Touch

Figure 15-6. Two-point offensive backfield stance—hands on knees.

Figure 15-8. Blocking area for shoulder block.

3. The head should be up and back should be straight.
4. The hips and knees should be slightly flexed.
5. The arms and hands should be positioned as shown. (See Figure 15-7.)

Drill for Stances. A stance drill that can be quickly explained and implemented is as follows. The class is divided into several groups, and the groups form lines facing the instructor. The first man in each line is asked to assume a particular stance. Upon command, or a whistle, the men charge forward to a designated distance and then go to the back of their line. All stances and moves are then covered by the entire class. For example, the instructor could say, "Three-point offensive lineman stance, pull right. Ready, Hut!" Different combinations of moves and stances are reviewed.

Figure 15-7. Defensive backfield stance.

Blocking

The two primary objectives of blocking in football are for an offensive blocker to attempt (1) to move a defensive player out of a certain area or (2) to prevent a defensive player from getting into a certain area. If the blockers on an offensive unit fulfill their assignments, the ball carrier should be able to run and advance the football, or the passer should have time to set and throw the football to an eligible receiver. If the blocker fails in his blocking assignment, the play will probably break down. From here evolved the maxim that "good blocking is the key to successful offensive football."

In flag or touch football the only legal block is the shoulder block. The shoulder is generally defined as the surface extending from the side of the blocker's head to the elbow end of the upper arm. (See Figure 15-8.) Only this defined area of either shoulder must make contact if the block in flag or touch football is to be legal. During the block the offensive man must not leave his feet or a penalty is enforced. A blocker may not use his hands in sustaining a block; if such a situation arises, a penalty is assessed against the offensive team. Throughout the block, the hands of the blocker must remain in contact with his chest. Any rolling, flying, cross-body, or crab-type blocks are strictly prohibited. A blocking infraction results in a loss of fifteen yards by penalty.

Straight-shoulder Block (Figure 15-9). The straight-shoulder block is normally used in a running or running-action type of play. The objective in this block is to make contact with the opponent and sustain the block until the defensive man is cleared out of an area or until the ball carrier has advanced downfield beyond the block. Several important points to consider when executing the shoulder block are to

1. Assume a proper stance before the play.

206 *Individual and Team Sports*

Figure 15-9. Shoulder block.

2. Know definitely who to block.
3. Charge on the correct count, stay low, and make contact before the defensive man has gained the advantage of momentum.
4. Use the head as a guide and attempt to make shoulder contact at a point on the opponent that will cause him to be forced out of the play.
5. Keep the feet spread apart about shoulder width throughout the block in order to retain a substantial base and thus preserve the balance.
6. Throughout the block keep the back straight and parallel to the ground and the head up.
7. Use short jab steps to keep the feet moving throughout the block.

Pass Block. The pass block is not used to move a man out of an area but instead to prevent the defensive man from moving into the area around the passer. For this block the following points should be observed:

1. Assume a proper stance.
2. Know who to block.
3. Step in the direction of the defensive man in order to establish initial contact and break his momentum.
4. Keep the feet moving and shoulder width apart in order to maintain balance.
5. Contact the opponent and release; wait for the defensive man to move and then hit him again. Hit and recoil repeatedly until the passer actually passes the ball.

If the purpose of the blocking is to form a "cup" for the passer, the defensive player who is blocked should be forced to the outside or away from the center. He must not be allowed to penetrate.

Drill for Blocking. The class is divided into several groups and each group forms a line. The first man in each line steps forward, and turns and faces the rest of the line—in this position he acts as the defensive man. The second man in line is the blocker, and on the signal he executes the designated block. The drill should at first be of a passive nature and correct form should be emphasized. If a blocking dummy is utilized, the defensive man holds the dummy while the second man blocks.

Tackling (Flagging or Touching)

Tackling in touch football consists of making a two-hand touch (usually above the waist) on the ball carrier or in flag football it consists of pulling off one of the ball carrier's flags. It is a foul to hold the runner while touching him or grabbing the flag; therefore, the skill of making a sure tackle without holding the runner is important to defense and must be learned before success in the game is possible.

1. As the ball carrier approaches the defensive man, he should maintain a solid base with the feet about shoulder-width distance.
2. The feet should be kept in continual motion while taking short, quick steps.
3. The body weight should be kept low to enable a quick change of direction as the runner attempts to evade the tackle.
4. The arms should be in a comfortable, ready position until the reach for the touch or flag is begun.
5. If the ball carrier has two or three flags, the flag nearest the defensive man should be the target.
6. The eyes of the tackler should be focused on the midsection of the ball carrier until the tackle is attempted, then the eyes should shift to the flag or target.
7. If the ball carrier runs straight at the defensive man, the tackler should hold his ground and wait for the runner to commit himself—intentional bulling or running over a defensive man is a foul.
8. The tackler should leave his feet only in a desperation attempt to grab the flag or make the touch. In general, the defensive man should keep his feet and make a second attempt if the runner gets away.

Drill for Flagging (Figure 15-10). The drill is organized in the same manner as for blocking. The first man in line is the defensive man; the second man is the ball carrier. The ball carrier can move only in a restricted lateral area. For example, use the yard lines on the field and allow the ball carrier a width of five or ten yards in which to evade the tackler. Upon the signal, the defensive man attempts to remove a flag from (or touch) the ball carrier.

Football: Flag and Touch

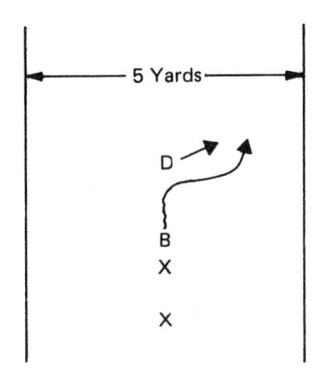

Figure 15-10. Drill for flagging. *B*—ball carrier; *D*—offensive man.

Pass Defense

The importance and heavy use of passing in flag football places an increased premium on the ability to defend against the pass. A good rush on the passer is the best defense; therefore, it is essential for the defensive lineman to pressure the passer into getting rid of the ball quickly.

The defensive back must consider the following several points to cover a receiver properly:

1. A correct stance, as discussed previously, must be assumed before play starts. The defensive back should position himself anywhere from three to seven yards away from the potential receiver he is guarding.
2. The defensive man should maintain a proper base under him; he should keep his weight low in preparation for any necessary quick change of direction that he must make.
3. As the receiver approaches, the defensive man should backpedal quickly enough to maintain approximately a three-yard cushion between himself and the receiver, and with each fake of the receiver he should take another step backward. (See Figure 15-11.)
4. When the receiver makes a definite cut in one direction or another, the defensive man should step with him with the foot nearest the direction of the cut. A crossover step should not be used in moving to the receiver. (See Figure 15-12.)
5. As soon as the ball is passed, the receiver and defender have equal rights to it. Therefore, go to the ball. Keep the eyes on the ball and attempt to either knock it down or intercept it at the highest point possible in order to lessen the chance of the receiver catching it. Remember to go to the ball; however, the rules forbid using the receiver as a stepping stone to the ball. Neither man may interfere with the other in his attempt to catch the ball.
6. As the defender gains experience, he will find that he can use the side line as an aid and play the receiver accordingly. He may also find that a receiver tends to move in one direction better than another, thus easing his task of pass coverage.

Drill for Pass Defense. Form two lines, one line of pass defenders and one of receivers. The players switch from one line to another after defending or receiving. The receiver runs a definite pattern and then watches the moves of the defender who is covering him. At first, form and position should be emphasized with no pass thrown. Later the ball should be thrown, and the defender can attempt to knock down or intercept the pass.

Ball Handling

Because of its shape, a football is more difficult to handle than a round ball. The skill of handling the football properly is essential to sound offensive play.

Receiving a Pass from the Center. Many times in flag football an offensive formation will be used in which the quarterback is set anywhere from three to seven yards

Figure 15-11. Cushion between receiver and defensive back—3 yards.

Figure 15-12. Proper step of defensive back with the receiver after a cut has been made.

208 *Individual and Team Sports*

behind the center. These situations necessitate the receiving of a centered ball in flight. In taking a pass from the center, the offensive back will usually be in a two-point stance. The snap should be aimed somewhere from knee to waist height and will be handled best if the hands are in a fingers-down position. (See Figure 15-13.) The snap should be cushioned by giving with the ball as it contacts the hands. The eyes should be focused on the ball until it is controlled by the hands.

If the play involves running left or right, the offensive back will be in motion before the ball reaches him. He should step with the foot nearest the direction of the play; he still should follow the procedures mentioned here until the ball is under control.

Carrying the Ball. Fumbles are costly, and in a majority of cases they are the result of unnecessary mistakes. The ball should be firmly gripped at all times when running with it. One end of the ball should be forced into the armpit, and the other end should be held and covered by the fingers of the hand. The forearm should be on the outside of the ball to protect it from a defensive man and to help secure it against the body. The ball should be carried in the arm away from the defensive man whenever possible; that is, when running to the right, carry the ball in the right arm and when running left, shift the ball to the left arm. Practice in carrying the ball properly and shifting it quickly from one arm to another is essential.

Drill for Receiving the Center Snap and Carrying the Ball. Two lines are formed: one to center the ball and one to receive the center snap and carry the ball. The instruction "left" or "right" is given, and after a short pause the signal "Hut!" is shouted. The center snaps the ball, the offensive back receives it, puts it in the proper arm, and runs in the specified direction. Practice in changing direction and switching the ball from one arm to another can easily be incorporated into this drill.

Figure 15-13. Position for offensive set back or punter in receiving a pass from center.

Figure 15-14. Execution of handoff.

Handoffs. The handoff (exchanging the ball from one player to another) in a play is an important skill in sound offensive football. In receiving a handoff, it is essential that the arm toward the player from whom the ball is taken be up, and the other arm down, as shown in Figure 15-14. The receiver should, as he contacts the ball, cushion it with his body and secure it with his hands. The quarterback, or whoever executes the exchange, should make sure the ball is placed firmly between the arms of the receiver. He should give the exchange and keep contact with the ball until the receiver has established definite control of it.

T Quarterback Receiving Snap from Center. A correct, fumble-free exchange from the center to the quarterback must be made before any play can function properly. Although many methods of executing the center snap are in existence, the writer believes the following method to be as sound as any.

With the fingers spread and the thumb down, the quarterback should have his left hand under the center's crotch at about a 45° angle. The right hand should be relaxed in order to avoid jamming the fingers. The fingers of the right hand point downward, and the thumb should be next to the thumb of the left hand. The center simply turns the ball a quarter turn to the left as he firmly brings it up to the left hand of the quarterback. As the ball hits the left hand, the quarterback secures it with the fingers of the right hand and begins the play. (See Figure 15-15.) If the quarterback is going to move left or right on the play, he should step out with the foot nearest the direction of the play.

Centering. The center is a vital member of the offensive team because regardless of the formation utilized he starts every play. His execution must be consistent to enable the offense to function effectively.

Football: Flag and Touch 209

Figure 15-15. Center-quarterback exchange.

T-formation Center. For the center to snap the ball effectively to the quarterback, the two players must work closely together. The center should assume a stance much like the four-point stance for an offensive lineman. The only difference is that the hands of the center are closer together and are, of course, on the football. The center should grip the ball in the right hand with the fingers on the portion of the laces toward the front end of the ball. The left hand should be placed on the ball to serve as a guide and to aid the control of the ball. On the proper count, the ball should be turned counterclockwise for a one-quarter turn and lifted firmly into the left hand of the quarterback. The center should strive to lift the ball with the same force each time, and he should be able to complete the turn and the positioning of the ball the same way with each snap. For the proper positioning of the hands for a center snap, see Figure 15-16. The center should keep his head up and concentrate his eyes downfield. He should employ his peripheral vision to spot the man he is to block after making the snap.

Figure 15-16. Positioning of hands for center.

210 *Individual and Team Sports*

Center for Set Backs. In the single wing, shotgun, kicking, or other similar formations, the quarterback does not take the ball directly from the center. Instead, the ball must be centered for a distance of approximately three to fifteen yards. When centering the ball in these circumstances, the center must look backward between his legs to see the man to whom the ball should go. The fact that he cannot immediately see the man he is to block complicates this task, but it is essential that he snap the ball accurately and consistently. The center should grip the ball in the same manner as in a T-formation. The ball should be passed in a spiral, which is created by the action of the right hand. On the snap, the fingers of the right hand should be forced backward and upward in the direction of the intended flight of the ball, imparting a clockwise spin on it. The left hand serves as a guide and control.

The target to which the center snaps the ball depends on the direction of the play. If the play is straight ahead, or if it is a drop-back type play, the centered ball should be aimed directly at the receiving back and at a height slightly above the knees. If the play is to move right or left, the center should lead the receiving back twelve to eighteen inches in the direction of the play. A good center must develop consistency in his performance in numerous ways in order to eliminate fumbles and poor timing at the start of the play. Practice in centering the ball can be incorporated in numerous ways into many different types of basic drills.

Passing

Because of the absence of actual tackling in flag or touch football, running plays in an offensive attack usually do not succeed with any consistency. Because of this the ability to utilize the forward pass successfully is one of the most important skills in flag or touch football. The prospective passer must develop several important understandings and skills if he is to be successful. These include the actual mechanics of throwing the ball, the ability to spot open receivers, and the ability to hit these receivers accurately. The ability to see and then accurately hit a receiver is developed only through consistent practice and repetition after the mechanics of throwing have been mastered.

A basic fundamental that a passer must master is to grip the ball properly and to assume this grip quickly and consistently. In general, the throwing hand should be so placed that it holds as much of the ball as near to its center as the size of the hand allows. The thumb and index finger should be held firmly against the ball until the release is made; the middle finger should normally be placed between the first and second cross laces. The size of the hand naturally determines the actual grip used, but once the correct grip is found, it should be used for every type of pass whether long, short, hard, or soft.

In preparing to pass, the ball should be carried high to allow a high release with the arm up above the head and away from the body. (See Figure 15-17.) This high release decreases the possibility of the pass being blocked by an onrushing defensive lineman. The ball should be gripped by the throwing hand and controlled or guided by the other hand until it starts forward toward the release. A spiral is imparted to the ball by a forward and outward snap of the throwing wrist and fingers. Correct wrist action must be developed to enable a quick snap and to release the ball with optimum force.

To be consistently accurate, a drop-back passer must be set to throw each time that he passes. If right handed, the right foot should be planted and the pass thrown off this foot. A stride in the desired direction of the pass should be taken with the left foot. A proper follow-through with the hips encourages the contribution of a maximum force from the body during the pass. When passing, the passer should concentrate on rotating the wrist of the passing arm and thus cause the ball to be thrown with the front end (or nose) up. This technique makes it easier for the receiver to catch the ball.

A good passer in flag football must have the ability to throw from a run on sprint-out plays to the left or right. Such plays put extreme pressure on the defensive team, because if the defenders pressure the passer, he throws the ball; if they stay with the receivers, the passer runs the ball. Passing should be practiced until the mechanics of setting up, striding, and throwing can be completed in one smooth, quick movement.

Drill for Passing. An initial passing drill includes three lines: one to center, one to pass, and one to receive the ball. The aim of the drill is for the passer to take the snap, to fade back swiftly while carrying the ball high for a quick release, to set up, and to pass to the receiver. Initially, the receiver should be stationary in order that the passer can concentrate on the mechanics of throwing and not be concerned about hitting a moving target. Numerous drills can be created and should be utilized to develop the passing phase of the game.

Receiving

Many important facets of the receiving skill must be developed if receiving is to be on a high level. But it is essential simply to learn to catch the ball every time that it is within reach. Speed is a very valuable asset to a receiver, but lack of speed does not prohibit a player from becoming an effective receiver. Lack of speed may be at least partially offset by extreme concentration on catching the ball, by the ability to run under a condition of controlled relaxation, and by running pass patterns with expertise.

The following general principles are important in receiving or catching the football:

1. The receiver should keep his eyes focused on the ball until he has complete control of it.
2. In general, the ball should be caught with the fingers and not trapped against the body.
3. The hands, arms, and shoulders should be relaxed as much as possible before an attempt is made to catch the ball.
4. When possible, the ball should be caught with both hands.
5. As contact is made with the ball, the receiver should give with it to cushion the catch, and in the same unbroken movement, the ball should be brought against the body and tucked away to prevent an incompletion or a fumble.
6. The position of the ball with respect to the body is a determining factor in how the ball should be caught.

    a. If the ball is about waist height or lower, the catch should be made with the little fingers together and the hands in a palms-up position. (See Figure 15-18.)
    b. If the ball is above the waist and over one shoulder or the other, the catch should be made with the little fingers together and the arms extended beyond the shoulder over which the ball is thrown. (See Figure 15-19.)
    c. If the ball is thrown above the waist and directly at or behind the receiver, the catch should be made with the thumbs together and the fingers up. (See Figure 15-20.)

Figure 15-17. Set position in preparing to pass.

Football: Flag and Touch

Figure 15-18. Position of hands in catching a low pass.

The following important fundamentals should be practiced when running pass patterns.

1. Run under control; a receiver must be able to move according to the way the ball is thrown.
2. If a pass is thrown out in front of the receiver, he should concentrate on running under the ball, using his arms to attain full speed, and not extending them toward the ball until the attempt to catch the ball is made.
3. It is important to use effective fakes in running a pattern in order to keep the defensive back guessing and making his coverage more difficult.
4. With the exception of certain types of pass patterns, a definite cut should be made in the execution of the pattern. This tends to increase the difficulty that the defensive back has in covering the receiver.
5. In some passing plays the receiver simply cannot catch the ball because of the way it is thrown; in these situations he must act as a defensive man and do what he can to prevent an interception.

Figure 15-19. Position for catch over the shoulder.

Figure 15-20. Position for catch of ball passed at or behind a receiver.

The pass patterns depicted in Figure 15-21 are frequently used in football. The patterns that have definite cuts in them (rather than curls or gradual turns) should be learned by emphasizing these cuts as an aid in helping the receiver to break into the open. "Out" or "flag" indicates a pattern toward the side line, and "in" or "post" indicates a pattern toward the center of the field.

Drill for Receiving. In the initial phases the practice of receiving drills should be concentrated on the mechanics of catching the ball while the receiver is in motion. Two lines should be formed: one to pass, and one to receive. The receiver should run a simple pattern and concentrate on the correct arm and hand actions when catching the ball. In the later phases, a center should be used, and on the snap the receiver runs a specific pattern and the passer throws to him. When the mechanics of running patterns catching the ball have been covered, a defensive back could be added to the drill to enable the receiver to practice against an opponent.

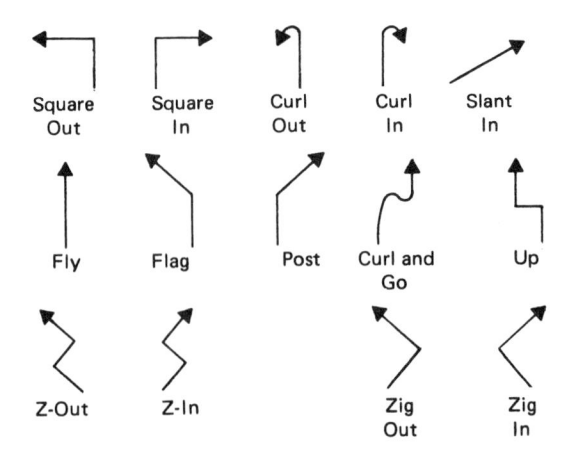

Square Out | Square In | Curl Out | Curl In | Slant In

Fly | Flag | Post | Curl and Go | Up

Z-Out | Z-In | Zig Out | Zig In

Figure 15-21. Pass patterns.

212 *Individual and Team Sports*

Receiving Kicks

In general, the same principles that apply to catching a pass also apply to receiving a kicked ball. The receiver should catch the ball in the hands and then pull it to the body. The eyes should be focused on the ball until it is caught—instead of on the defensive men. The receiver should attempt to keep the ball in flight in front of him in order to ease the task of catching the ball and to increase the possibility of a long kick return. Whenever possible, the receiver should attempt to judge the flight of the ball and catch it on the run while running in the general direction in which he intends to return.

Running with the Ball

The ability to evade would-be tacklers is one of the most important skills for an offensive back in flag or touch football to master. The key to success in carrying the ball is the ability to run under control and to be able to change pace and direction quickly, depending on the positions of the defensive men. A change of direction is achieved by lowering the hips, the action of which lowers the center of gravity and enables sharp turns to be made with increased safety. The outside foot should be firmly planted and used to push off toward the new desired direction. The ability to change direction quickly comes with practice, and ball-carrying drills that demand this execution should be practiced often. The runner must concentrate on changing pace and direction swiftly in order to evade the defensive man in front of him and to prevent a trailing defensive man from catching him.

Another important ability in flag or touch football is that of pivoting or turning after contact has been or is about to be made with a defensive man. This pivot or turn will often cause the opponent to miss the flag or touch and thus permit the ball carrier to continue downfield.

A good ball carrier must also be able to use his blockers effectively. If a teammate blocks an opponent in one direction, the ball carrier should cut or run off the block (in the other direction). A ball carrier can also aid his blocker by helping to set up the defensive man. If the ball carrier fakes in the direction he wants the defensive man to go, he will often cause the opponent to step or lean in that direction and thus aid the blocker in taking the defensive man out of the play.

Kicking

In football, the ability to kick the ball successfully for long yardage is a very important skill in offensive and defensive execution. The team that can kick the ball for distance and for accuracy will have the opportunity to drive the opposing team deep into its own territory and hence make it more difficult for them to generate an effective offense. As the skills are learned, additional players can be used to line up on the line of scrimmage to practice covering the punt after it is kicked.

Punting (Right-footed Kicker). It is important to have at least one member on the flag or touch football team who can consistently kick the ball for long yardage and with accuracy. Punting should be practiced by all team members and the best punter selected for this task. In those situations in which a great deal of yardage must be gained on the last down, or when the team is in poor field position, the kicking phase of the game can play an important role in determining the final score.

The punter normally stands six to twelve yards behind the line of scrimmage to receive the snap from the center. (Because unlimited time in which to kick the ball is the usual rule, this distance is not too important.) The ball should be carefully watched until an easy, relaxed catch (at waist to chest height) is made with both hands. The ball is then generally so rotated that the lace is up and its long axis faces the direction of the kick.

The most popular stepping technique is a short step with the right foot, a full step with the left foot, and then the kick, which is initiated from the hip, with the right foot. The kicking leg swings forward in the direction of the kick with the foot extended (pointed) forward and with a locking or snapping action of the lower leg at the knee as the ball is kicked. A full follow-through should be made.

Before kicking the ball, it is held with the arm extended and with one hand on either side of it—or else with the right hand under and the left hand on top. The hands should guide the ball down to the kicking foot, which contacts the ball at about knee height. The point of the ball is level, or slightly downward, and pointing slightly to the left, the outside part of the instep makes contact with the ball. The kicker should face the direction in which he wants to kick; the ball will generally go in the direction its point is facing. As a general rule, the punter will aim to kick the ball out of bounds as near to the goal line as possible. During and after kicking the ball, both arms should be used to maintain balance.

Place Kicking. A place kick is utilized for three purposes in flag or touch football: (1) for the kickoff at the beginning of each half and after each touchdown or field goal, (2) for the attempted three-point field goal, or (3) for the point-after-touchdown (PAT). In some games, however, purposes (2) and (3) do not apply, because goal posts are not used. For a kickoff, the ball is held upright by a kicking tee, but for field goals and PAT's, the ball must be caught from the center by another member of the offensive team and held upright for the place kicker. A run toward the ball before kicking it gives much of the momentum to the place kick. During a kick-off situation, the kicker can take as long a run as he desires because the amount of time consumed before kicking the ball is relatively unimportant. However, when a field goal or point after touchdown is attempted, the kicker must take only a two- or three-step approach because the ball must be kicked before the rushing opponents have a chance to block it.

A two-step approach is generally used by the right-footed kicker, and the first step is a short one taken with the right foot. The second step is a near-normal step in which the left foot is planted just behind and a few inches to the left side of the ball. The knee of the right leg should be flexed as it starts to kick through to the ball. The ankle should be so locked that the angle between the foot and lower leg is a right angle. When the toes contact the ball, the leg should be fully extended at the knee, and a complete follow-through should be executed in order that, as with the punt, the force of the kicking action of the right leg lifts the entire body off the ground. Throughout the place kick the eyes should be focused on a point slightly below the center of the ball, the point of which is where the toes should contact the ball. The approach should be so executed that the right leg is in a direct line with the desired direction of the kick; the approach should be started immediately after the center snaps the ball. The place kicker should practice his timing with the teammate who is selected to hold the ball, so that the ball is kicked immediately after it is placed down on the ground.

Drill for Place Kicking. The skill of place kicking can be practiced in conjunction with the development of several other skills. Four different lines can be utilized: one to kick, one to hold for the kick, one to center the ball, and one to receive the kick. The drill can be set up to involve both point-after-touchdown and field-goal kicking.

DEFENSE

The ability to prevent the opponent from scoring is an important means to success in flag or touch football. If this objective were always realized, a team could never be beaten; at worst the score would be 0-0. Realistically, this does not happen often, but a team should employ a certain defense with the idea of preventing a score by the opponent. In flag or touch football, it is important to control the run and to prevent the completion of the long pass. If this is accomplished, the opportunities for the opponent to score will be significantly decreased.

The strength of a particular defense depends to a large degree on where the men are placed with respect to the offensive formation. The more defenders that are positioned near the line of scrimmage, the better the chances of controlling the run; the more defenders that are positioned some distance away from the line of scrimmage, the better the chances of controlling the pass. A sensible compromise must generally be reached in order to succeed at team defense.

Personnel

Defensive personnel are commonly classified into three categories. The defensive linemen are lined up on the line of scrimmage in a three- or four-point stance. They have the responsibilities of flagging or touching the ball carrier and rushing the passer. The linebackers, who position themselves just off the line of scrimmage, are responsible for flagging or touching the ball carrier, sometimes rushing the passer, and sometimes covering a potential receiver and preventing a completed forward pass. The third classification includes the deep defensive backs, who line up off the line of scrimmage, and have first the responsibility of defending against the pass and second that of flagging or touching the ball carrier.

The interior defensive linemen have to prevent running plays up the middle, and the exterior linemen must prevent the wide run.

Defensive Formations

Regardless of which type of defense is employed, every receiver must be covered and all running areas must be contained. In Figure 15-22, some other defensive formations that might be utilized in the play of flag or touch football are depicted.

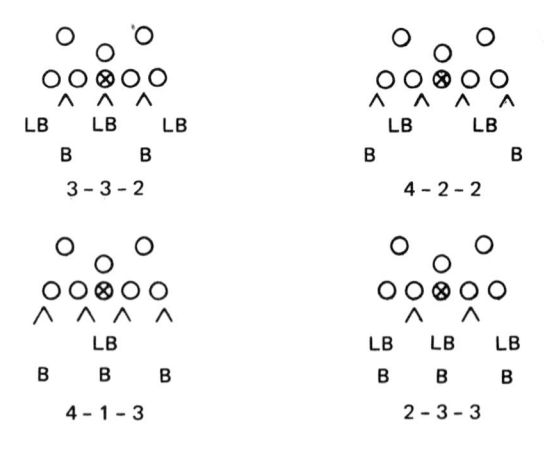

Figure 15-22. Defensive formations.

Numbering Defenses

A specific defense is termed *odd* or *even* depending on the number of defensive linemen. If there are an odd number of defensive linemen, it is an odd defense, and if there are an even number of defensive linemen, it is an even defense. For example, a 3-2-3 defense would indicate three defensive linemen, two linebackers, and three deep backs. Their exact positions depend on the particular offensive formation encountered. (See Figure 15-23.)

Pass Coverage

For pass coverage the linebackers and deep backs can play either man-for-man or zone defense, depending on the offense. It is important that the deep backs cover the faster, more effective receivers and, whenever possible, the linebackers cover the secondary receivers. In a man-for-man coverage, a deep back (or linebacker) is assigned to a specific receiver, whom he covers regardless of where this receiver goes. In a zone-type coverage, each defender is assigned a certain area of the field to cover, and he takes any receiver who comes into his area. If no receiver comes to his zone, he can move to another area and help a teammate.

OFFENSE

A team should have a specific offensive plan that it employs when it gains possession of the ball; this plan or offensive attack should enable the team to move the ball into scoring position, and then to score. Numerous offensive formations can be utilized; normally, a team chooses one or two basic formations, develops specific plays from them, and then puts these plays together into a logical sequence to form their offensive attack. In eight-man flag or touch football, there are five offensive linemen: a center, two tackles, and two ends. These five must be on the line of scrimmage at the start of each offensive play. Three men comprise the backfield, and they must be at least one yard behind the line of scrimmage at the start of each offensive play. (See Figure 15-23.)

Each offensive man must carry out his specific assignment on every play if the play is to have a high chance of being successful. These assignments may involve centering the ball, blocking a defensive man, running with the ball, carrying out a fake, running a pass pattern, passing or catching the ball, or a combination of these. In a well-planned offense these specific assignments are specified for each play. To facilitate the organization and the player's grasp of offensive plays, the running holes and offensive backs are often numbered, as shown in Figure 15-24. Thus, a number such as 26 may be assigned to a play; this indicates that the number 2 back carries the ball through the number 6 hole, and every offensive man has a specific assignment for that play. (See Figure 15-25.)

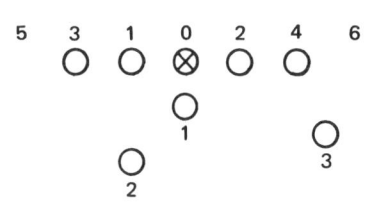

Figure 15-24. Hole and back numbers.

Offensive Formations

The single-wing, double-wing, T, pro, and short-punt formations, which are diagrammed in Figure 15-26, are the ones most commonly used in flag and touch football. Each formation has certain advantages and disadvantages, and the particular formation employed by a team depends primarily on the abilities and weaknesses of the players on that team.

Single Wing. The single-wing formation is a strong formation for running to the wing side. The wing back is in a position to be a strong blocker, which creates this running advantage. The probability of success in running away from the wing is not as great in this formation. It is a strong passing formation because there are two receivers to the wing side who should be able to get out quickly into a pass pattern.

Double Wing. The double-wing formation is a stronger passing formation than the single wing because four prac-

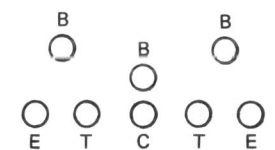

Figure 15-23. Offensive positions: *C*—center, *T*—tackle, *E*—end, *B*—back.

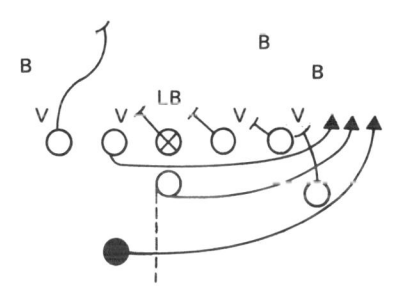

Figure 15-25. Offensive play number 26—number 2 back through 6 hole.

Football: Flag and Touch 215

```
O  O ⊗ O  O
         O
    O O
  Single Wing
```

```
   O O ⊗ O O
 O           O
       O
   Double Wing
   Short Punt
```

```
O  O ⊗ O  O
         O
    O    O
  T-Formation
```

```
O   O ⊗ O O
          O          O
     O
  Pro Formation
```

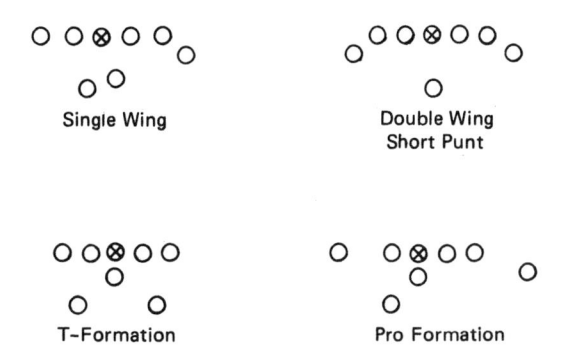

Figure 15-26. Offensive formations.

tical receivers—the two wings and the two ends—are in positions that should enable them to get out and into a pass pattern in a minimum amount of time. This is not a strong running formation because the single set back does not allow for deception in handling the ball and does not enable quick hits to be made at any of the running holes.

T formation. The T-formation allows for running in either direction, allows for deception in ball handling, and enables the team to hit quickly between the tackles. It is not the strongest passing formation because the backs are not in positions from which they can quickly move out on a pass pattern.

Pro. A pro formation is utilized to enable at least three pass receivers to run quickly into a pass pattern. It also enables a quick run to the side of the line near the set or running back, but running wide is difficult because of the way the formation spreads out the defense. Its advantage lies in the fact that it is a strong passing formation and still has a back in an advantageous position for the run.

Regardless of the offensive formation that a team selects, much thought and practice must be employed to devise a numbering system, to define blocking assignments and rules for every man in every play and against every defense, to plan logical plays in a proper sequence, and to master the fundamental skills that are vital to successful performance in flag football.

Selected References

Grombach, John V. *Touch Football.* New York: Ronald, 1958.

Official National College Touch Football Rules. Chicago: The Athletic Institute, latest ed., 805 Merchandise Mart.

Purvis, Chuck. "The Passer." American Football Coaches Association, summer manual, 1962.

Purvis, Chuck. "Training the Passer." *Proceedings of the 43rd Annual Meeting,* American Football Coaches Association. Washington, D. C., 1966.

Shaw, John H. *Selected Team Sports for Men.* Philadelphia: Saunders, 1952.

Stanbury, Dean, and Frank De Santis. *Touch Football.* New York: Sterling, 1961.

CHAPTER 16

Golf

Charles A. Zwiener *
The University of Iowa

HISTORY

Golf, as the game is known today, is one of the world's oldest sports. It is believed to have originated in Scotland during the twelfth century. The first written record of golf dates back to 1457, when the Scottish Parliament of King James II banned golf. Its popularity threatened to interfere with the practice of archery, which was vital for national defense.

Golf was introduced in the United States in about 1887, when the first golf club was established at Foxburg, Pennsylvania. In the United States, the first surge of popularity came in 1913, when a twenty-year-old ex-caddy, Francis Ouimet, won the United States Open Championship. In a play-off at the Country Club of Brookline, Massachusetts, he defeated Harry Vardon and Ted Ray, two of England's finest golfers.

During the Golden Era of sports in the 1920s, the exploits of Robert T. (Bobby) Jones, Jr., did much to popularize golf. He became the only golfer to accomplish the "grand slam" of golf by winning the United States Open and the Amateur and the British Open and Amateur Golf Tournaments all in one year, 1930.

---

*B.A. and M.A., University of Minnesota, Minneapolis. Charles (Chuck) Zwiener has been the varsity golf coach and golf professional at The University of Iowa for fifteen years. His golf classes at the university have always had a heavy enrollment; in addition, he has been unable to accommodate all the people wanting to utilize his services as a golfing pro. Included among his twenty years of teaching golf to groups and individuals are nine years of coaching golf at the high school level. He has been a class A member of the Professional Golfer's Association of America (PGAA) for fourteen years.

VALUES

Golf today has attained tremendous popularity because of its values as a participant sport. The following values ordinarily are derived from the game: (1) Golf has a great carry-over value because it can be played by people of all ages, sizes and physiques. (2) Golf offers numerous opportunities for social and business contacts. (3) It offers mild beneficial exercise coupled with an opportunity to spend time outdoors regularly. (4) It provides an excellent opportunity for clearing the mind of worries and tension and for relaxing while away from the routine of everyday life. (5) To both the duffer and expert, golf offers an equal challenge to improve by competing against oneself and the course. (6) It is a true family game in which men, women, and children can enjoyably play together. (7) After the initial investment, golf is not an expensive game; it can be, and is, played by people from all income brackets.

GOLF EQUIPMENT AND ITS CARE

Two types of clubs are used in golf: woods and irons. As a rule, the woods are distance clubs and the irons are used to approach the green from specific distances less than the maximum range. In a set of golf clubs of good quality the weight, length, shaft flex, and other factors are so coordinated or matched that, with the same uniform swing, the player can obtain a uniform difference in distance between each of the numbered clubs. A brief description of each club, including the length of shaft, loft of club face, and the distance that the ball can be expected

Golf 217

to travel is given subsequently. The distance obtained with each club will vary from golfer to golfer, depending primarily on the power generated in the golfer's swing.

The Woods

No. 1 Wood or Driver: Forty-three inches long, 11° loft, 190 yards and up. Used from the tee for maximum distance and occasionally utilized by the *expert* player for a good lie in the fairway.

No. 2 Wood: Forty-three inches long, 14° loft, 190 yards and up. Used for maximum distance from good lies in the fairway.

No. 3 Wood: Forty-two inches long, 16° loft, 180 yards and up. Used for maximum distance from an average lie in the fairway and on a long approach to the green. A 3 wood is easier to use than a 2 wood.

No. 4 Wood: Forty-one and one-half inches long, 19° loft. Distance: used for maximum distance from tight lies in the fairway and for a long approach to the green.

No. 5 Wood: Forty-one inches long, 24° loft. Distance: used for maximum distance from bad lies in the fairway or rough. It can also be used by the average player instead of the long irons.

Long Irons

No. 1 Iron: Thirty-nine inches long, 18° loft, 180 to 230 yards. A very difficult club to use, but the expert players use it for long approach shots.

No. 2 Iron: Thirty-eight and one-half inches long, 21° loft, 175 to 215 yards. Used for long shots from the fairway and light rough.

No. 3 Iron: Thirty-eight inches long, 24° loft, 165 to 195 yards.

Medium Irons

No. 4 Iron: Thirty-seven and one-half inches long, 27° loft, 150 to 175 yards. Can be used for chip shots from the edge of the green.

No. 5 Iron: Thirty-seven inches long, 31° loft, 135 to 160 yards. Can be used for chip shots from the edge of the green.

No. 6 Iron: Thirty-six and one-half inches long, 35° loft, 120 to 145 yards. Can be used for chip shots from the edge of the green.

Short Irons

No. 7 Iron: Thirty-six and one-quarter inches long, 39° loft, 110 to 135 yards. Also used for pitch and run shots.

No. 8 Iron: Thirty-five and three-quarter inches long, 43° loft, 95 to 120 yards. Also used for pitch-and-run shots.

No. 9 Iron: Thirty-five and one-quarter inches long, 47° loft, 80 to 100 yards. Excellent club for pitch shots and pitch-and-run shots.

Pitching Wedge. Thirty-five and one-quarter inches long, 51° loft, 70 to 90 yards. This pitching wedge is a very versatile club for use around the greens.

Sand Iron. Thirty-five and one-quarter inches long, 55° loft. The sand iron is used from bunkers (sand traps) and can be used for short pitch shots and for short shots from the heavy rough around the greens.

Selection of Equipment

The better quality sets of clubs come in a variety of lengths, weights, shaft flexes, grip styles, grip diameters, lofts, and lies. A person interested in selecting a good set of clubs should consult a qualified professional golfer for advice on which characteristics would be best for his individual needs. A well-matched, proper-fitting set of clubs can considerably increase a person's enjoyment of golf.

A beginning golfer who is not interested in purchasing a complete set of clubs can enjoy the game and markedly improve his golfing skills using only a short, or partial, set, which consists of the 3, 5, 7, and 9 irons, 1 and 3 woods, and a putter. In purchasing any set of golf clubs it is wise to purchase only those clubs made by a reputable manufacturer. They will give longer and better service than the so-called bargain sets.

Care of Equipment

The proper care of golf equipment will do much to increase its life and maintain its value, should the golfer desire to trade them for a newer or better set. The faces of iron clubs should be kept clean and free of dirt. They should be periodically washed with warm water and detergent, using a soft brush—an old toothbrush is excellent for this purpose. The use of steel wool or abrasives, which will destroy the finish and thus allow the faces of the clubs to rust, should be avoided. The woods should be wiped clean with a damp cloth and given a periodical waxing with paste wax.

Leather grips should be cleaned when needed with saddle soap or a special leather conditioner. This keeps them clean and helps retain the tacky feel that prevents the club from slipping in the hands. Rubber grips should periodically be scrubbed with a soft brush in a mild detergent and warm water in order to remove the dirt and grime that accumulates on them.

During the off-season, the clubs should be cleaned thoroughly before being stored in a dry place away from extreme heat. The iron heads can be given a light coat of light oil in order to prevent rusting.

Golf clubs that become broken or in need of minor repairs should be taken to a golf professional for this service. He will either repair them himself, send them to a competent repairman, or return them to the manufacturer for the needed repairs. Many times a club can be repaired and restored to an almost new condition for much less than its replacement.

RULES AND ETIQUETTE

The rules of golf are formulated and published in booklet form by the United States Golf Association (USGA). Rule books are available at most golf courses or can be ordered from the United States Golf Association, 40 East 38th Street, New York, New York 10016. Every golfer should obtain a copy of the current rules and become familiar with them. If the rules are disregarded, the game of golf is not being played. Many of the rules are designed to assist the player; a thorough knowledge of them can be beneficial in many instances.

Golf etiquette should be studied and applied in order that correct conduct on the course becomes a matter of habit. Proper etiquette and conduct on the course are as much a part of the game as the use of clubs and balls.

THE GRIP

The grip taken on the golf club is important because it allows the player to hold the club in the correct position throughout the swing. It is especially important that the club face be square at the instant that it strikes the ball. A proper grip also makes it possible for the golfer to maintain constant pressure on the handle throughout the swing so that the club will be under control at all times. The following instructions for gripping the golf club are for a right-handed golfer.

Left Hand

1. Place the club with the sole on the ground. The fingers of the left hand are extended and joined, and the thumb is so positioned to the hand that a V is formed by the thumb and forefinger.
2. Place the left hand on the club so that the grip runs diagonally across the hand, running from the second joint of the index finger and across the heel of the hand.
3. Close the left hand on the club so that it is held in the hand by the pressure of the fingers.
4. The thumb is about a one-quarter turn to the right of center; the V formed by the thumb and index finger points toward the right shoulder.
5. Only the first three knuckles on the back of the left hand are visible.
6. By means of the fingers, the left hand exerts a counterclockwise pressure on the club handle. An easy way of checking this is to hold the club out in front of the body with the left hand. Grasp the club with the right hand and try to twist it open. If this action is resisted with the left hand, then the proper grip pressure is being exerted by the left fingers.

Right Hand

1. The fingers are extended and joined and the thumb is adjacent to the right hand so that a V is formed by the thumb and forefinger.
2. Position the right hand into a slapping position in which the palm of the hand is square to the leading edge of the club.
3. So position the right hand on the club that the grip on the club handle runs diagonally across from the middle joint of the index finger to the last joint of the little finger.
4. The thumb is turned to the left a quarter turn over the shaft in the opposite direction of the thumb of the left hand. The pad of the right thumb rests on the club.
5. The index finger is extended slightly, farther down the shaft than the thumb. To achieve this position, extend the index finger directly down the shaft, press down with the thumb, and pull the "trigger" with the index finger.
6. The V formed by the right thumb and index finger points toward the right shoulder.
7. The palm of the right hand is in line with the face of the club.

The hands are held snugly together on the club and so positioned that the thumb of the left hand lies in the groove of the palm of the right hand.

Types of Grips

Any one of the three accepted grips can be utilized to grip the golf club. The grip selected depends primarily on the size and strength of the hands.

Overlapping, or Vardon, Grip

1. The little finger of the right hand is taken off the club and hooked into the groove formed by the first and second fingers of the left hand.

Golf 219

2. This is the most popular grip and is suitable for those with normal-sized hands and better-than-average gripping strength.

Interlocking Grip

1. Both the little finger of the right hand and the index finger of the left hand are taken off the club and are interlocked.
2. This grip is recommended for those players with short fingers and small hands.

Full Finger Grip

1. The club is held in all the fingers and no overlapping or interlocking of the fingers is employed.
2. The full finger grip is a valuable grip for beginners and those with small hands and short fingers.

Putting Grip

1. The putting grip differs from the regular golf grip in that the club is held mainly by the fingers, and the thumbs are on top of the shaft. The back of the left hand and the palm of the right hand are lined up with each other and to the face of the putter.
2. Any of the regular grips—overlapping, interlocking, or full finger—can be used.
3. The reverse overlap, in which the index finger of the left hand is overlapped over the fingers of the right hand, is the most popular grip with professional players.
4. The putter is held lightly in the fingers so that a feel of the club head can be maintained throughout the putting stroke. This light finger grip is essential in acquiring a putting touch.

The grip on the club at first will feel strange and unnatural to the beginning golfer, but by regular practice in grasping the club, the grip will become increasingly comfortable. Practice grasping the club as often as possible and check on the components of the proper grip. The grip is one phase of the game of golf that can be self-correcting, because the player can easily see and check his grip before each swing.

THE SHORT GAME

The short game includes all the shots and skills that are utilized in the area around and on the green. A command of these shots is vital to the golfer for the following reasons:

1. A low score demands skill and control in the golf shots played in the area near and on the green.
2. A good short game can make up for errors made between the tee and the green.
3. More than half the shots taken during a round of golf are taken around the green.

PUTTING

Putting is the easiest skill to learn in golf because it involves the least amount of movement and, therefore, fewer possibilities for errors exist. Yet, putting is probably the single most important part of the game. A successful putt can make up for mistakes enroute to the green whereas a poor putt can cancel the finest long shot. An application of the fundamentals of putting and diligent practice will enable almost anyone to become fairly adept at putting.

Objectives in Putting

1. Roll: To roll the ball along the green with overspin so that it will maintain direction and dive into the hole.
2. Direction: To roll the ball in a straight line off the putter head. Every putt should start in a straight line because the putter is swung back and through the ball on a direct line.
3. Distance or speed: To roll the ball up to or slightly past the hole.

These three objectives can be consistently attained by learning and applying the fundamentals of putting. Several factors in putting are individual in nature and vary from golfer to golfer; some factors, however, are fundamental and apply equally to all golfers.

Individual Differences

1. Width of the stance and position of the feet: The most important consideration here is comfort and ease while standing over the ball. The beginning golfer should try to find a stance that feels most comfortable to him.
2. Position of the body: Again, comfort is of primary importance in the body position assumed when putting. As a general rule, a fairly erect position of the trunk is recommended. However, some players putt better from a position in which their trunk has considerable bend.
3. Position of the arms: Most golfers are steadiest if they rest their arms (especially their elbows) against the body when putting. After experimenting, if another arm position feels and works better, it should be adopted.

4. Grip: A comfortable-feeling grip is the most important factor. Any of the accepted golf grips can be used providing that the thumbs are directly on top of the shaft and the putter is held mainly in the fingers. The pressure exerted on the putter shaft should be light in order to insure a sensitive feel throughout the putting stroke. Most skilled golfers use the reverse-overlap grip in which the index finger of the left hand overlaps the fingers of the right hand.

Fundamentals

1. Eye over the ball: When addressing the ball the golfer should position himself so that his eyes are directly over the ball. This position gives him the best perspective of the straight line on which the putt is going to start.
2. Weight on the front foot: During the address, most of the body weight is placed on the inside edge of the front foot. It remains there throughout the entire stroke in order to prevent extraneous body movement and to permit a level stroke. The fundamentals of putting are depicted in Figure 16-1.

Figure 16-1(a). Position at ball when putting—side view.

Figure 16-1(b). Position at ball when putting—front view.

Figure 16-1(c). Completion of backstroke with putter.

The Putting Stroke

A well-executed stroke will have most, if not all, of the following characteristics:

1. The stroke will be fairly short and compact.
2. The stroke will be direct—straight backward and forward through the ball and along the line.
3. The body and head will remain almost motionless during the stroke. This is helped markedly by keeping the weight on the front foot during the stroke.
4. The stroke will be a tapping action similar to that used in tapping a tack with a tack hammer.
5. The hands will lead the putter throughout the forward stroke.
6. There will be little or no wrist action—wrist action leads to indirection and inconsistency in the stroke.

Skills and Techniques

Drills for Learning the Putting Stroke

1. One-hand method:
   a. Weight on the left foot and the eyes over the ball.
   b. Putter gripped with the right hand only.
   c. Swing the putter back and tap the ball on the forward swing, making sure that the fingers of the right hand stay behind the heel of the right hand.
   d. Be sure that the stroke is directly along the line selected.
2. Two-hand method:
   a. Repeat the preceding drill, using both hands.
   b. The right hand is dominant and the left hand is used primarily to steady the putter.
3. Start putting twelve inches from the hole and gradually work away from it in order to learn a feel for distance.

Reading the Green

1. The ball will roll down a slope after it leaves the putter.
2. The ball will be increasingly affected by the slope of the green as it loses speed.
3. The ball will break more on a fast green and less on a slow green; therefore, on a slow green, grip the putter with a firm grip and on a fast green, grip it with a light grip.

Procedure for Long Putts

1. Determine the speed of the green.
2. Determine the slope of the green between the ball and the hole. Pay special attention to the amount or degree of slope in the last few feet of the putt.
3. Pick a line that the ball will probably take to reach the hole.
4. Set the putter down square to this line. Move up to the putter and establish the stance in relation to the putter.
5. Attempt to roll the ball on the line toward the hole, stopping it within a two-foot circle around the hole.

Golf 221

Short Putts

1. Tap the ball with added firmness and try to go past the hole in the event of a miss.
2. On putts of four feet or less, unless the green has a decided slope, play the ball at or inside the hole.

THE CHIP SHOT

The chip shot is used when the ball is just off the green and in a lie where it is not practical to putt the ball, but it is desired to roll the ball up to the hole. For the chip shot, a medium lofted iron (for example, a 6 iron) is used to get the ball up into the air, land it on the green, and let it run to the hole.

Objectives

1. To get the ball up into the air and land it on the green.
2. To roll the ball up to or near the hole so that only a short putt will be required.

Skills and Techniques

1. Using the standard golf grip, grip the club shaft near the lower end of the grip (next to the shaft). Hold the club lightly in the hands and fingers in order to increase the sense of feel during the swing.
2. The stance is open with the feet fairly close together. The weight rests primarily on the front foot.
3. The ball is played two inches inside the front heel.
4. The hands are ahead of the ball with the shaft of the club slanted upward and forward toward the target. The hands should be opposite the inside of the front leg.
5. Square the club face to the line of direction.
6. The club is swung along the line directly back and through the ball. The blade of the club stays square to the line throughout the entire stroke.
7. The club is swung with the hands and arms working as a unit. No wrist action should be employed. Excessive wrist action tends to make the swing erratic and difficult to control.
8. Throughout the stroke the hands lead the club head.
9. The weight remains on the left foot throughout the entire stroke.
10. By keeping the weight on the left foot and the hands ahead of the ball, the ball will be struck a descending blow with the club, allowing the loft of the club to lift the ball into the air.
11. The stroke should be crisp and decisive; it should be kept as short as possible.
12. By developing a solid, direct stroke, the direction of the shot is no longer a problem. Once the mechanics of the stroke are learned, the direction is insured and complete attention can be given to chipping the ball the proper distance.

See Figures 16-2 a, b, c.

Judging Distance

1. Attaining the proper distance is the most important factor on any approach shot. The line or direction of the shot is normally taken care of by the mechanics of the stroking action.
2. Two methods of determining distance—both of which are called spot approaching—can be employed for this purpose.

Figure 16-2(a). Address position for chip shot.

Figure 16-2(b). Chip shot—completion of backstroke.

Figure 16-2(c). Chip shot—impact.

222 *Individual and Team Sports*

a. In the first method, called the single-club method, the same club is always utilized for all chip shots. The number 5 iron is the most popular iron for this purpose. The chip shot is first lined up in much the same manner as for a long putt. Once the line is determined, a spot along the line is selected on which to land the ball and thus have the ball roll from there to a spot near the hole. The ball will normally roll three to four times as far as it flies through the air. The single-club method is illustrated in Figure 16-3.
b. In the second method, called the single-spot method, the same spot, which is usually located two to three feet onto the green, is always used. After the location of the spot is determined, a club is selected that will land the ball on this spot and cause the ball to stop near the hole. The farther the hole is from the edge of the green, the less lofted should be the club that is used. The single-spot method is depicted in Figure 16-4.

Advantages of the Spot Methods

1. Choosing the same approximate spot for all chip shots takes most of the guesswork out of the shot. There is a definite shot planned with which the golfer is experienced.

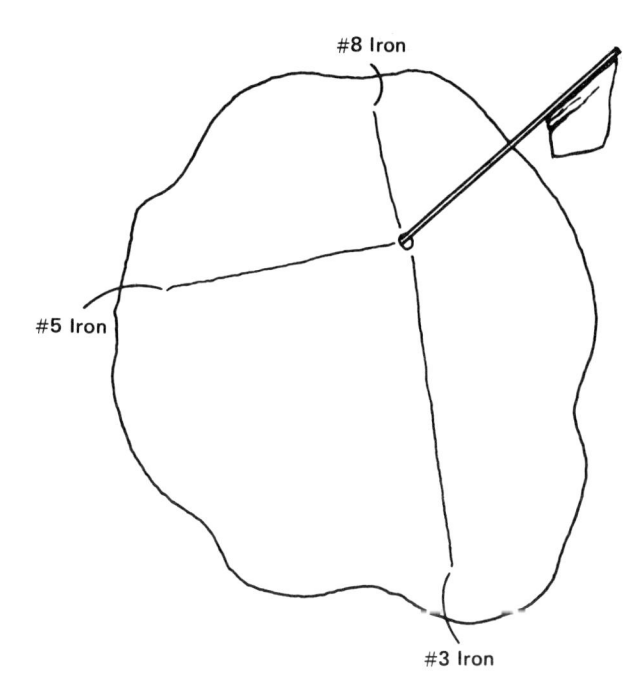

Figure 16-4. Single spot method. The spot aimed at is always two to three feet past the edge of the green. The club selected is the one that will land the ball on this spot and allow it to stop near the hole.

2. Aiming at a spot brings the target closer to the golfer, thus making it easier for him to hit the target.
3. The single-spot method probably works best for the advanced golfer because both the length and force of the stroke for all chip shots can be kept almost constant.
4. The single-club method is recommended for the weekend golfer because its use does not require a full set of clubs and it requires less practice than does the single-spot method.

Practice Methods

1. The mechanics of the stroke for the chip shot should be learned first. Concentrate on the techniques of the shot, and practice one aspect at a time until the complete mechanics of the entire shot are mastered.
2. Once the mechanics are so learned that the correct direction of the shot is automatic, begin to concentrate primarily on the distance that the shot goes. Choose one of the spot methods and practice only that method. To become adept in this method requires time and practice, but it is well worth the effort in improving a person's over-all golf game. After the mechanics of the chip shot are mastered, the pitch shot can be easily learned. The mechanics of the two strokes are quite similar.

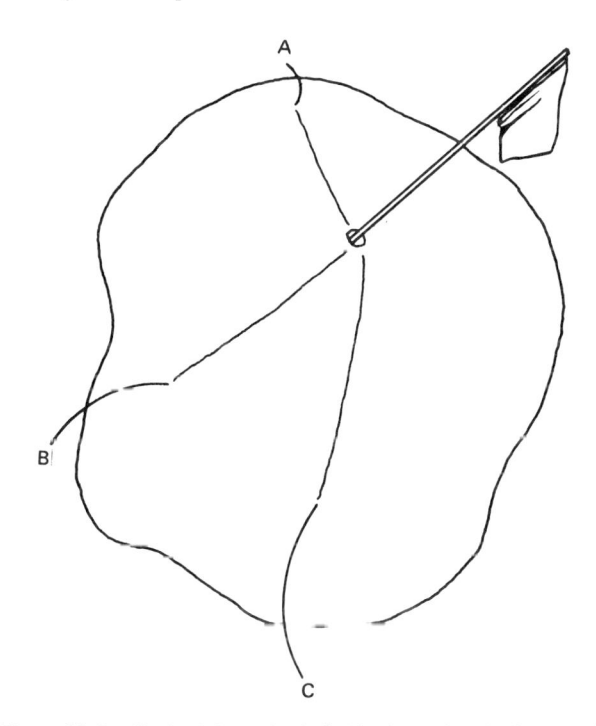

Figure 16-3. Single club method of chipping, using the Number 5 iron. The farther away the ball is from the hole, the further away from the hole is the spot aimed for.

THE PITCH-AND-RUN SHOT

The cardinal rule in approaching is to land the ball on the green whenever possible. If it is not practical to land the ball on the green with the chip shot, or if the ball is in such a position that the chip shot would overshoot the hole or the green, the pitch-and-run shot is used. The pitch-and-run is also used when the ball must be quickly lofted up into the air in order to clear an obstacle such as a bunker or mound.

The pitch-and-run shot is executed with a lofted club such as the number 9 iron or pitching wedge, although it can be played with a less lofted club such as the 7 or 8 iorn. The pitch-and-run shot should be hit with a smooth, rhythmical stroke, as this will reduce the number of misses and yield more uniform results. In hitting this shot a deliberate attempt to put underspin on the ball will cause the stroke to be jerky, which in turn leads to topping or hitting behind the ball. It should be emphasized that this is a pitch-and-run shot. When positioned close to the green, the ball cannot be struck with sufficient force to impart the considerable underspin on it that is required for it to stop quickly after it lands on the green.

Objectives

1. To get the ball up into the air and land it on the green.
2. To roll the ball up to or near the hole, leaving only a short putt.

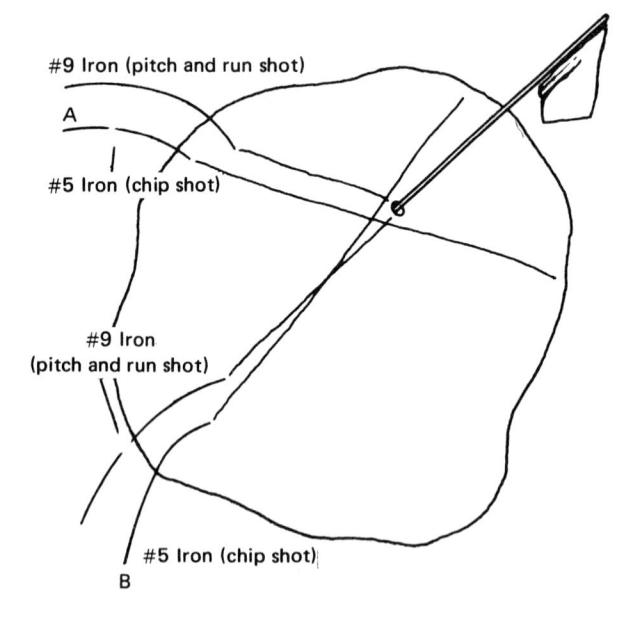

Figure 16-5. Proper use of the pitch-and-run shot. From positions A and B, a chip shot would overrun the hole but a pitch shot would not.

Skills and Techniques

1. The mechanics of the pitch-and-run shot, which are illustrated in Figures 16-6 (*a*) through (*e*), are identical with those of the chip shot, except that the swing is slightly longer because the ball must travel farther in the air than for the chip shot.
2. When playing the pitch-and-run shot the spot method of approaching is utilized. The golfer should attempt to estimate where on the green the ball must land in order to have it stop by the hole after it completes its roll.

Variations in the Pitch-and-run Shot

Depending on the lie, the trajectory and amount of roll placed on the pitch-and-run shot sometimes have to be varied to fit a specific situation.

For a low trajectory shot, which has an increased amount of roll, the ball is played more toward the back foot than normal. The mechanics are the same as for the regular shot, except that a special effort is made to keep the hands well ahead of the club and the club head lower to the ground during the follow-through. A less-lofted club such as the 7 or 8 iron can be used. This type of shot can also be used for shooting into a wind or when there is a strong cross wind. The green should be level with or below the lie of the ball.

A high trajectory shot is used when less roll is desired, when the green is elevated, or when there is an obstacle such as a mound or bunker to be cleared.

1. The ball is played off the front foot.
2. The swing is the same as for the normal shot.

A *low trajectory shot* should be hit when

1. The green is level.
2. The shot is hit into a head wind or a cross wind.
3. There is sufficient room for the ball to run.

A *high trajectory shot* should be hit when

1. The hole is close to the near edge of the green.
2. A mound is in the way.
3. Less run of the ball is desired.

Pitch-shot Practice Methods

1. Learn the mechanics of the shot so thoroughly that the stroke is automatic.
2. Practice pitching to a specific spot on the green.
3. Utilize back-yard practice by shooting to a ground target such as a newspaper, hoop, or an old automobile tire.

Figure 16-6(a). Address position for pitch-and-run shot—side view.

Figure 16-6(b). Address position for pitch-and-run shot—front view.

Figure 16-6(c). Pitch-and-run shot—completion of backstroke.

Figure 16-6(d). Pitch-and-run shot—impact.

Figure 16-6(e). Pitch-and-run shot—completion of follow-through.

4. Practice variations of the pitch shot by setting up a hypothetical playing situation and hitting a shot that fits the situation.

THE SWING

In order to develop an adequate golf swing, the golfer must have an understanding of what the complete swing is like. This understanding requires sufficient knowledge so that a mental picture can be formed of the whole swing and the component actions that make up the whole swing. When the whole-swing picture is understood, the parts or details that combine to make up a sound swing can be integrated into the over-all pattern. Thus, the approach should be to (1) have a good understanding of the swing pattern, and (2) to work the fundamental parts of the swing into the whole pattern, one part at a time.

Over-all Picture of the Swing

A proper golf swing is one that will be the most consistent and will allow the least amount of variation from day to day. It will also serve the so-called weekend golfer because it is simple and will have fewer parts to it that can go wrong. It must incorporate the following factors if it is to be efficient and dependable.

1. The swing is direct and simple. The club is swung in such a manner that all movements are direct and to the point. This is termed the *one-piece swing*.
2. Because the swing is direct it is repetitious. The swing proceeds in a repeating pattern or groove and thus is the same each time.
3. The swing is one in which the movement is fluid and smooth so that the club is accelerated through the ball with a great amount of force and speed. The movement of the swing is smooth and rhythmical, never forced or jerky, thus giving maximum power and distance.
4. The club is swung through the hitting area with the club face squarely facing the ball at contact. This gives the correct direction to the shot and helps to prevent any tendency to hook or slice the ball.

Building the Swing

Once the correct mental picture of the swing has been established, the swing can be developed by integrating the fundamental parts into the whole swing. This is accomplished by working on one part at a time within the swing pattern. An attempt to concentrate simultaneously on more than one part during the swing usually leads to confusion and lack of learning. The swing should be developed slowly and gradually in order that it rapidly becomes automatic and, hence, can be repeated without thinking.

Position at the Ball. Before swinging the club, the golfer must assume a position that makes it possible to swing the club properly. See Figure 16-7 a and b. Because a proper position and posture at the ball make it possible to execute the swing with the least extraneous movement, it will tend to be direct and simple, which is the objective of the swing. A correct position at the ball will also help to insure proper balance and body control throughout the swing. In addition the hands, arms, and club are placed in the proper relationship to the body; consequently, the correct arc and plane of the swing will be established prior to swinging the club. The correct position at the ball can be obtained by following these directions:

1. Stand in a fairly erect position with the feet comfortably spread apart. The left foot points slightly outward and the right foot is square (pointed straight ahead). The ball is slightly inside the left heel.

2. Bend slightly at the hips and place the sole of the club head flat on the ground immediately behind the ball. The left arm is so extended from the shoulder that the arm and shaft of the club form a straight line to the ball.

3. The right arm is bent and so tucked in that the right elbow points to the right hip. The arms are together. In order to assume this position, the right shoulder will be slightly lower than the left. The arms are away from the body, and the only contact with the body is by the upper part of the arms near the armpits. The arms and club form a direct plane that extends through the shoulders.

4. The knees are flexed and the base of the spine is lowered directly downward in order that a feeling of sitting down to the ball is achieved.

5. The weight is placed on the inside of the feet so that a feeling of gripping the ground with the inside of the feet is achieved. The body weight is positioned on the ball of the right foot and slightly toward the heel of the left foot.

6. From the waist upward the upper body is held erect so that the spine is fairly straight. There is a feeling of being up from the waist up, and down from the waist down.

7. The feet, knees, hips, and shoulders are square to the direction in which the aim is being taken.

Arc of the Swing. The club is so swung that the club head describes a wide arc throughout the swing. See Figures 16-8 (a) and 16-8 (b). The radius of the arc is produced through the arms—by the left arm throughout the backswing and downswing through the ball, and by the right arm through the ball contact to the finish. Throughout the backswing the left arm stays straight, but not rigid. It remains straight during the downswing and as the club passes through the ball. After the club passes through the ball, the right arm extends and remains straight until the finish of the swing.

The beginner should practice swinging the club back and through the ball, starting with a short swing and gradually lengthening it into a full arc. He should concentrate on the action of the arms, working for a full extension of the arc made by the club. He should also practice swinging the club with one hand at a time in order to develop the proper feel for the complete swing as well as to develop adequate strength in the arms and hands.

Plane of the Swing. The plane or position of the backswing, which varies according to the body build of the golfer, is determined by the position of the hands, arms, and club when in the address position. A short person will tend to swing in a slightly flat plane that is tilted

Figure 16-7(a). Position at the ball. (Address position for driver.)

Figure 16-7(b). Position at the ball. (Address position with Number 5 iron.)

Figure 16-8(a). Arc of the swing. (Start of backswing—driver.)

Figure 16-8(b). Arc of the swing. (Completion of backswing—driver.)

226 *Individual and Team Sports*

Figure 16-9(a). Plane of downswing when driver is slightly lower and flatter than that of upswing.

Figure 16-9(b). Plane of downswing when driver is slightly lower and flatter than that of upswing.

somewhat toward the horizontal, whereas a tall person will tend to swing in a more upright or vertical plane. The club is swung backward on a plane that extends from the club head through the club shaft, hands, arms and shoulder. The shoulders turn in the same plane as do the hands, arms, and club. The swing back in this plane is quite direct. At the top of the backswing the left arm is fairly straight, and the back of the left hand and the club face are aligned with each other and both are in the plane of the swing. The right arm is bent at the elbow, the right forearm points straight up and down, and the elbow points toward the ground near the right foot.

The plane of the downswing is slightly lower or flatter than that of the upswing. (See Figure 16-9 b.) As the downswing starts, the right elbow returns to the right side and the right arm works inside of and under the left arm. This lowering of the downswing plane allows the club to be swung through the ball and on a direct line toward the target. The club is swung through the ball and to the finish position in which the hands are in a slightly higher position than they were at the top of the backswing. The beginning golfer should practice swinging the club back and through the proper planes. He should occasionally stop at the top of the backswing and check the position of his hands, arms, and club to insure that they are in the proper plane. The player, as he progresses, will develop the feeling that the swing back is a direct, one-piece movement in which a united and simple action occurs.

Axis of the Swing. In order for the swing to function in an effective arc and plane, it must turn or rotate around a center. The center of the swing is the spine, which is referred to as the vertical axis of the swing, and which stays in a vertical position throughout the swing. During the swing this vertical axis should not sway or tip, and both the top and bottom of the spine must remain in position. This holding of a stationary position allows the shoulders and hips to turn on the spine and thus keeps the entire swing centered around the spine. The turning action at the shoulders and hips makes the swing easier to repeat and, because of the correct turning action, the power that is available for the swing is increased.

With the heels of his feet touching and his toes pointing slightly outward, the player should practice swinging the club back and forth. He should gradually spread the feet wider apart until a stance of normal width is attained, but at all times he should be aware of utilizing his spine as the vertical axis of the swing. This is best done by keeping the axis in alignment and in a vertical position and making the arc and planes of the swing turn on this axis. Once the beginning golfer becomes aware of the vertical axis and establishes the feel of a proper turn on it, he will have an excellent start toward building a solid, grooved swing.

Objective of the Swing. One of the attributes of a sound golf swing is to be able to hit the ball with power as well as accuracy. Power is achieved by combining fast club-head speed through the ball with a solid contact of the ball with the club face. The speed of the club head is attained by swinging the club through the ball and to the finish of the swing so that the club head is either accelerating or picking up speed as it passes through the hitting area. The swing through the ball should be crisp and decisive—never hesitant. Thus, the objective of the swing is not just to hit the ball, but to finish the swing completely; that is, to swing through the ball. This can be achieved by thinking in terms of swinging through the ball and upward to the completion of the swing.

Swinging through the ball to a complete finish produces a definite finishing position because of the pull or momentum of the club being swung through the ball and to the finish. (See Figures 16-10(a) through 16-10(e).) In this position the player completes his swinging movement with almost all his weight on his left foot and his body turned toward the target with the belt buckle pointing toward or past the target. The hands and club finish in a high position, and the head comes up and around, facing the target. The right leg so turns that the right knee points to the target and only a minimum of weight is resting on the toe of the right foot. This position is attained primarily only as a result of the swinging action through the ball and to the finish. The player should, in a decisive manner, practice swinging the club through the ball. After each swing he should check to determine that the correct finishing position is achieved. A good golf swing can be heard as well as seen—a definite "swish" of the club head is evident as it accelerates through the ball and continues to the finish position.

Golf

Figure 16-10(a). Swinging through the ball to a complete finish (driver).

Figure 16-10(b). Swinging through the ball to a complete finish (Number 5 iron).

Figure 16-10(c). Swinging through the ball to a complete finish (driver).

Figure 16-10(d). Swinging through the ball to a complete finish (Number 5 iron).

Figure 16-10(e). Swinging through the ball to a complete finish (Number 5 iron).

Head Position. Much has been written and said about the position of the head during the golf swing. The old adages, "Keep your eye on the ball" and "Don't look up, keep your head down," are invariably offered as the magic cure-all for any bad shot. This is mostly poor advice that is glibly offered by the "blind leading the blind." The head position basically should be one of maintaining stability at the top of the vertical axis and not allowing the head to block out or prevent a full swing to the finish. Actually, if the head is kept in a down position too long, it will block the swing to the finish by getting in the way of the right shoulder as it passes under the chin. The head should, however, maintain a fairly steady position throughout the backswing and downswing and until the right shoulder comes in contact with the chin. At this point in the swing-through, the head is allowed to ride up and around with the right shoulder until the head faces the target. This movement is called hitting past the chin. The golfer should practice keeping the head position within the swing, holding the head fairly steady until the right shoulder passes the chin. Although some slight movement of the head will be evident, it will not be noticeable until the head moves up and around to the finish.

Rhythm of the Swing. The correct golf swing, like any movement in sports, must have proper rhythm or cadence. The time required to swing the club back and then through the ball must be the same on each swing if proper rhythm is to be attained. This time length will not be the same for each golfer, however, because of individual differences. Some excellent players have a rather leisurely appearing swing, whereas other equally good players swing the club with increased speed.

If the cadence of the swing is broken down, it should require about the same length of time to swing the club away from the ball and up to the top of the backswing as it does to swing the club from the top of the backswing through the ball and through to the finish. With this knowledge in mind, the cadence or rhythm of the swing can be counted—"one and two" or "back and through." "One" is the swing to the top; "and" is the shifting of gears from the backward to the forward swing; and "two" is the swing from the top to the finish.

The correct rhythm can be developed by counting as the club is swung. With the feet together, practice swinging the club as in the turning drill (which is described in the preceding section, "The Objective of the Swing"). Count the cadence of the swing "one and two, back and through." Start with a short swing and work into a full swing, gradually widening the base by spreading the feet apart. A sense of rhythm will be achieved as the timing becomes integrated with the swing. This drill is also an excellent warm-up and should be done prior to hitting practice balls or playing a round. It will help warm up the muscles and at the same time establish rhythm balance and a proper turn of the body on its vertical axis. The golfer should remember that the rhythm of the swing is an individual matter, but it must be a smooth, fluid move.

Progression of Power. The correct progression of power in the golf swing entails the build-up or stretching of muscle power through the backswing and the violent release of this power through the hitting area and on up to the completion of the swing. An understanding of the sequence of action in both the backswing and swing-through is important in order for the correct mental image of the sequence to be visualized and acted out in the swing.

During the backswing the golfer should attempt to swing the club backward and then upward into the position at the top of the swing so that power is built up through the stretching of the muscles involved in this action. The backswing begins by the hands, arms, and club being swung away from the ball and the shoulders starting to turn on the vertical axis. This is a unified or one-piece movement with the main emphasis on the shoulder turn. At the top of the backswing, the shoulders are so turned in the plane of the swing that the left shoulder is directly under the chin. The muscles are so stretched that they are tense, especially throughout the left side.

The downswing is started by a slight lateral movement in the left hip. The shoulders then start to unwind and are quickly followed by the arms, hands, and club. As the club follows, the hands remain in a fully cocked position. As the swing progresses, the speed of the club head accelerates as it attempts to catch up to the shoulders, arms, and hands. No attempt is made to hit or slap at the ball with the hands or wrists. As the club is swung through the ball it catches up to the hands and arms and without further conscious effort moves through the ball in a violent, forceful manner. As the club is swung to the finish it gradually decelerates to the completion of the swing. (See Figure 16-10a, b, c, d and e.)

The sequence of the swing is practiced by taking the club back and up with the hands, arms, and shoulder turn. On the downswing the hips slide slightly forward and the shoulders, arms, hands, and club follow in that order. This should be practiced with a slow swing at first. The swing is gradually built up into a faster swing, until the proper tempo and rhythm are attained. Concentrate on holding with the hands so that the club is delayed as much as possible. The sequence of action should be worked into the swing pattern until a feeling of power and smoothness is developed.

Position of the Ball and Relationship to Aiming. It is important that the ball be placed in a uniform position in relation to the feet so that the swing is consistent throughout the hitting area. The ideal ball position is one in which the ball is between the left heel and the center line of the body. This ball position forces the golfer to stretch or extend in order to strike the ball. When located in this position, the ball will not be so far forward that it will be difficult to hit. It is of the utmost importance that the ball be properly aimed or aligned with the target. Every shot in golf is hit to a target of some kind; therefore, the accurate aim of a uniformly positioned ball is of prime importance. Positioning the ball and aiming at the target can be done at the same time; they should be performed on every shot so that they become part of the routine prior to swinging the club.

1. In order to position the ball and aim, the golfer should first stand behind the ball so that it is between him and the target. He then establishes the line from the ball to the target—this is the master line or the line of aim.
2. He then moves into a half-open position and squares the club face or leading edge of the club with the master line.
3. With his feet together and the ball in the center of the stance, he next squares himself to the master line and the club. He should check that his feet, knees, hips, and shoulders are along the master line.
4. Lastly, he moves his left foot about two inches toward the target, and he moves his right foot back along the line away from the target until the proper width of stance is achieved. As a rule the stance is wider for the longer-shafted clubs—the woods and long irons—and narrower for the shorter-shafted clubs. The wide stance helps to maintain the proper balance, which can easily be lost because of the long shaft of the wood and the wide arc created by swinging the long club.

Aiming is of the utmost importance because it not only establishes a target, but it helps to force the swing into the proper alignment. Both when practicing and when playing, the golfer should aim on each shot, regardless of its distance. Repeated practice of the aiming routine will cause the proper aim and ball position to become second nature and will hardly require conscious thought.

Unusual Lies

From time to time, and during the course of playing a round of golf, the golfer will be confronted with many lies in which the feet are not on level ground. Because the uneven position of his feet can affect the flight of the ball, the golfer must adjust his feet and the ball position in order to achieve maximum control of the ball.

Uphill Lie. In an uphill lie the ball is on an upslope and the front foot is higher than the back foot. Three adjustments have to be made in order to play the ball with consistent success.

1. The ball is played more toward the front foot because the club reaches the bottom of its arc later in the swing than for a level lie.
2. A less-lofted club is used to negotiate the distance because the uphill lie has the effect of increasing the loft in the club.
3. The ball will have a tendency to hook; therefore, the shot should be aimed to the right of the target.

The Downhill Lie. In a downhill lie the ball is on a downslope and the front foot is lower than the back foot. Thus, the adjustments to be made are the opposite of those for the uphill lie.

1. The ball is played more toward the back foot because the club reaches the bottom of its arc sooner than for a level lie.
2. A more-lofted club is used because the downhill lie has the effect of decreasing the loft in the club—sufficient loft must be used to get the ball into the air, even if distance has to be sacrificed; hence, the low-lofted clubs such as the 3 iron must not be used.
3. The ball will have a tendency to slice; therefore, the shot should be aimed to the left of the target.

Sand Shot

Most courses have sand bunkers located in strategic positions on the fairway, rough, or near the green. When the ball lands on or rolls into a bunker, a special type of shot must usually be employed in order to get the ball out of the bunker and onto the fairway or green. Depending on the location of the bunker in relation to the green, bunker shots fall into different categories and each category must be played in a different manner. In each category, however, the sand bunker is a hazard, and the club cannot touch the ground or sand prior to striking the ball. Nothing can be done to improve the lie of the ball, and the player cannot touch the sand with any part of his body except his feet. After playing the ball out of the sand, the player has a duty to smooth out all footprints and other irregularities he has made in the bunker.

Long Bunker Shots. Long bunker shots are played from bunkers located a considerable distance from the green, such as a fairway bunker. The ball should be sitting up on top of the sand—not buried. To play a long bunker shot the player should

1. Use a club with sufficient loft to get the ball up and out of the bunker. Sacrifice distance, if necessary, but get the ball out.
2. Play the ball a bit more off the front heel than its normal playing position. Wiggle the feet into the sand in order to get a solid, firm footing.
3. Use a shorter backswing than usual. The player should swing through the ball to the finish, picking the ball cleanly off the sand. He should not hit into the sand behind the ball.
4. Aim the ball somewhat to the right because the ball will have a tendency to hook to the left due to the lack of resistance encountered on a clean shot.

Explosion Shot. The explosion stroke is used for short shots when the ball is in a bunker near the green. It is used when the ball is sitting up on—not buried in—the sand. When making an explosion shot the player should

1. Use a sand iron or, if it is not available, the pitching wedge; or a number 9 iron can be used.
2. Play the ball more off the front heel than usual. He should first open the club face by turning the club in his hands. This increases the loft of the club and helps get the ball up into the air.
3. Open his stance by drawing his front foot back and off the line of aim. This stance position compensates for the open club face and permits a normal aim to be taken. The player then digs his feet in the sand in order to obtain a firm footing.
4. Use a short backswing that is fairly upright and direct.
5. Aim at the spot on the sand that is about one inch behind the ball. He swings through the ball and to a complete finish. This aim and swinging action will cause the club head to cut through the sand underneath the ball. The force of the sand exploding against the ball will get the ball up into the air and out of the sand. The player must ensure that he completes the swing to the finish, otherwise the club head will lack sufficient force to cause the ball to come out of the bunker.
6. The club face passes through and under the ball, imparting considerable underspin to it.

Blast Shot. The blast shot is used whenever the ball is buried in the sand or has landed in a depression, thus making it difficult to stroke the ball out of the bunker. The objective of the blast shot is to get the ball out of the bunker and onto the fairway or green. When shooting a blast shot the player should

1. Use a pitching wedge or a number 9 iron. The sand iron should never be used for a blast shot.

2. Close the blade of the club by turning the club in the hands.
3. Play the ball more toward the center of the stance. The feet should be dug in for a firm footing.
4. Use a short backswing and, with considerable force, hit down into the sand, aiming at a spot about an inch behind the ball. Keep the swing going down as long as possible. Because of the resistance of the sand the swing through it will be restricted.
5. The force of the sand against the ball will blast it out of the sand. The ball will have little underspin and it will roll when it hits the green. The blast shot is difficult to control, but the main objective of getting out of the bunker can generally be achieved. If the ball should stop near the hole, this fortunate an out should be considered a bonus.

Other Types of Sand Shots

Other special shots that are sometimes taken from a lie in a sand bunker are described subsequently.

Putting. It is often possible to putt the ball out of a bunker, providing the ball is lying on top of the sand and the bunker is fairly flat and has no lip or sharp edge. To putt the ball from a bunker the ball should be played from a normal putting stance. The ball should be given a sharp tap, hitting it above the center in order to impart top spin to the putt, which will cause the ball to roll up and out of the bunker. This shot involves very little risk and is extremely effective for the average golfer. The percentage in favor of getting on the green is usually quite high.

Chipping or Pitching. Either the chip or the pitch shot can be used when shooting from a bunker, providing the ball is sitting up well on top of the sand. The hands must stay well ahead of the club throughout the stroke and the ball must be contacted first, not the sand. If the sand is contacted before the ball, the chances of even getting out of the bunker are small. As a general rule, pitch and chip shots from a sand bunker are risky. The preferred shot from the bunker is the explosion shot.

THE SPECIAL APPEAL OF GOLF

The same sequence of shots are rarely if ever encountered in two rounds of golf. Undoubtedly, a significant amount of its appeal is that such an endless variety of shots are called for; thus, the golfer is constantly challenged to practice and play a large number of golf shots on successive holes.

Glossary of Terms

Addressing the ball: Positioning the body and club prior to the swing.
Ace: A hole in one.
Approach: A shot played to the green.
Away: The ball farthest from the hole.
Birdie: A score of one below par for a hole.
Bogey: A fixed score that the golfer plays against; this is normally one over par.
Bunker: A hazard filled with sand.
Caddie: A person employed to carry the player's clubs. He can give advice and assistance to the player.
Course: The playing area.
Divot: The turf taken with the club head during a shot. The divot should be replaced and stepped on to press it into the soil.
Dormie: In match play the side or player is as many holes up as there are holes left to play.
Down: The number of holes or strokes that a player is behind.
Driver: The number 1 wood.
Eagle: A score of two under par on a hole.
Face: The area on the club head where the ball is struck.
Fairway: The mowed area between the tee and green. It is usually about thirty-five to forty-five yards wide.
Flag: The flag is attached to the flagstick and is numbered to indicate the number of the hole in which the flagstick rests.
Flagstick: The flagstick is placed in the hole to indicate its location. The flagstick is sometimes erroneously referred to as the pin.
Fore: The warning signal given on a golf course when a player hits a ball toward other players or spectators.
Foursome: A match in which two players play against two other players.
Green: The putting green. The grassy area around the hole that is specially prepared for putting.
Grip: The particular method by which the golf club is held.
Gross score: The actual score shot by a player.
Halved: A tie score for a hole or a match.
Handicap: The strokes subtracted from a player's score in order to equalize the competition.
Hazard: A sand bunker or a water hazard.
Head: That part of the club with which the ball is legally struck.
Heel: The back part of the club head. The part where the neck joins the head.
Honor: The privilege of playing first from the tee.
Hook: For right-handed player, a hook is a shot that curves to the left.
Iron: A golf club with an iron head.
Lie: The position of the ball when it is in play.
Links: A golf course located near the seaside or "links land."
Loft: The angle of the pitch on the club face.

Golf 231

Match play: Hold-by-hole competition between individual players or sides. The winner is determined by the number of holes won and lost.

Par: The score including two putts that expert players would normally be expected to make on a hole.

Rough: The long grass located on each side of the fairway.

Round: The number of holes played. This is usually 18 holes.

Shaft: That part of the club to which the club head is attached.

Slice: For right-handed players a slice is a shot in which the ball curves to the right.

Stance: The position of the feet during the address.

Stroke: Any attempt to hit the ball—whether the ball is struck or not.

Tee: (1) The area on which the teeing ground is located. (2) A tee is the wooden peg used to elevate the ball off the ground.

Teeing ground: The rectangular area that is located between the markers and two club lengths behind them and from which the ball must be played to start play on a hole.

Tee markers: The blocks or spheres that are used to designate the teeing ground.

Toe: The front part of the club head.

Up: The number of holes or strokes by which a player is ahead in a match.

Waggle: The preliminary movements prior to the swing.

Wood: Any club with a head made of wood.

Selected References

BOOKS

Armour, Tommy. *Play Better Golf—The Irons.* New York: The News, 220 East 42nd Street, New York 10017.

Bruce, Ben, and Evelyn Davis. *Beginning Golf.* Belmont, Calif.: Wadsworth, 1968.

Casper, Billy. *Golf Shotmaking.* Garden City, N.Y.: Doubleday, 1966.

Crawford, Peter G. *The Winning Touch in Golf.* New York: Brumhall House, 1961.

The Easy Way to Learn Golf Rules. Chicago: National Golf Foundation, 804 Merchandize Mart.

Golf Digest Magazine. Golfer's Digest: All Annuals. Norwalk, Conn.: Golf Digest, Inc., (The *First Annual* was published in 1966 and one has been published each succeeding year.)

Golf Lessons. Chicago: National Golf Foundation, 1965.

Golf Magazine's Your Long Game. New York: Harper, 1964.

How to Improve Your Golf. Chicago: National Golf Foundation, 804 Merchandize Mart.

Middlecoff, Cary. *Master Guide to Golf.* Englewood Cliffs, N.J.: Prentice-Hall, 1960.

Nance, Virginia L., and E. C. Davis. *Golf.* Dubuque, Iowa: Brown, 1966.

Official Rules of Golf. New York: United States Golf Association, 40 East 38th Street, New York.

Player, Gary. *Gary Player's Golf Secrets.* Englewood Cliffs, N.J.: Prentice-Hall, 1962.

Rosbury, Bob. *The Putter Book.* South Norwalk, Conn.: Golf Digest, 1963.

Snead, Sam. *The Driver Book.* South Norwalk, Conn.: Golf Digest, 1963.

PERIODICALS

Golf. Universal Publishing and Distributing Corporation, 234 East 45th Street, New York, New York 10017 (monthly).

Golf Digest. Golf Digest, Inc., 88 Scribner Avenue, Norwalk, Connecticut 06856 (monthly).

Golf World. Box 2000, Southern Pines, North Carolina 28387 (weekly).

CHAPTER 17

Gymnastics: apparatus[1]

Donald R. Casady*
The University of Iowa

David K. Leslie†
The University of Iowa

HISTORY

The Greeks originated the term *gymnastics,* which means "naked art"—a reference to their practice of performing "gymnastic" activities while unclad. Man has participated in and been entertained by some forms of gymnastics for centuries. However, competition on gymnastics apparatus as we know it today has existed for only somewhat more than a century. Much of its origin is derived from the activities devised by the Germans for their "gymnastics" exercise system. The most famous competition in gymnastics is that provided every four years in the modern Olympic Games, which were revived in Athens, Greece in 1896. At that time gymnastics competition on the side horse, tumbling mat, parallel bars, flying rings, long-horse vault, horizontal bar, and rope climb was held.

Gymnastics competition had a slow beginning in the United States, with the sport being confined mainly to private gymnastics clubs. The high schools and colleges began to participate in this "foreign" sport after the twentieth century arrived, but progress was slow until after World War II ended. In the 1950s and 1960s, gymnastics experienced an especially rapid growth in the United States. Today, high school and collegiate teams, national and international competition, and worldwide coverage of the Olympic Games have exposed this highly entertaining sport to tens of millions. Although the number of gymnastics competitors in the United States is still numbered in the thousands, this sport has attracted millions of participants in Europe, and especially in Russia and Japan. In Russia alone, several million school children and youths annually compete in area and sectional gymnastics competitions, which culminate in the national championships.

INTRODUCTION

The widespread inclusion of gymnastics in programs of physical education and the growth of gymnastics competition in high schools, colleges, private clubs, and at the national level attest to the popularity and the exercise values of this activity as well as to its wide appeal to youths and adults as a competitive event. Its appeal as a spectator sport is demonstrated by the fact that over 100,000 spectators periodically witness huge outdoor gymnastics exhibitions held in Europe. The gymnastics competition for men and women both at the 1968 and the 1972 Olympic Games were purportedly the most popular events televised to a world audience that was estimated to number in the hundreds of millions.

---

[1] The contents of this chapter are, in part, adapted from the books, *Handbook of Physical Fitness Activities,* Chapter 12, "Apparatus and Tumbling Activities," by D. Casady, D. Mapes, and L. Alley, and from the book, *A Guide to Gymnastics,* by F. Musker, D. Casady, and L. Irwin. Permission from Macmillan, Inc., to borrow from these books is gratefully acknowledged.

---

*Donald R. Casady was captain of The University of Iowa gymnastics team. Later, he coached the gymnastics team at Georgia Military Academy for three years and was assistant gymnastics coach at the University of Iowa for one year. He has taught all levels of gymnastics for several years, and is a coauthor of a book on gymnastics for men.

†Dr. David K. Leslie (B.A. and M.A., San Jose State College, San Jose, Calif.; Ph.D., The University of Iowa, Iowa City) taught physical education at Palo Alto High School, California, for eleven years, where he coached gymnastics for seven years. His team had a reputation for having sound fundamentals. He was a gymnastics instructor in the physical education program at The University of Iowa for three years.

THE SPORT OF GYMNASTICS, INCLUDING SELECTED COMPETITIVE RULES

The events comprising gymnastics competition have varied over the years in the United States and in international competition. Currently, at the college level, the usual order of events for dual gymnastics team meets are (1) floor exercise, (2) pommel horse, (3) rings, (4) long-horse vaulting, (5) parallel bars, and (6) horizontal bar. This order may vary in a high school gymnastics meet, which may also include competition on the trampoline but may not include long horse vaulting.

Individual Scores

Four judges normally evaluate each exercise and award scores ranging from 0 to 10, with deductions of whole, half, or 1/10 points for breaks in form or continuity. Of the four scores, the highest and lowest are eliminated and the average of the remaining two is the individual's score for that event.

Evaluation of Exercise

In the evaluation of gymnastics exercise, three factors are taken into consideration:

1. Difficulty   = 3.40 points maximum.
2. Combination = 1.60 points maximum.
3. Execution   = 5.00 points maximum.
                    10.00 points maximum for an exercise.

Difficulty. For the minimum points in all events except long horse, the exercise must be composed of at least eleven parts (six A or main parts, four B parts of medium difficulty, and one C part of superior difficulty). On the long horse, the gymnast must perform either one or two vaults. If he chooses to do the second vault, the first is not scored and the second one must count. A difficult part should never be executed at the expense of correct form or technically correct execution.

Combination. An exercise must be composed of parts and movements typical to the event, and they must be connected with elegance and without extraneous swings.

Execution. Deductions are made for poor position of the feet, legs, body, and so on, and for incorrect technical execution.

Team Scoring

Each team is limited to four (or five) entries per event, three of which must compete in all events. If one or more all-around men fail to compete in any event, they may not be replaced. The best three individual scores for each team in each event are added to determine the event score. The event scores are added to determine the final team score.

In championship meets, the competitors often have to perform a compulsory routine first in each event (everyone does the same prescribed set of parts or exercises). Only those who score highest are permitted to compete in the finals, in which an optional routine of the gymnast's own devising is performed.

UNIQUE VALUES OF GYMNASTICS

It is a common observation that most gymnasts possess remarkably well-developed physiques. Because the gymnastics performer's body serves as the resistance to his movements, he must manipulate a large exercise load each time that he performs a skill; hence, he regularly works against a large overload. Regular participation in gymnastics contributes markedly to the development of a somewhat neglected upper area of the body—especially the musculature of the arms and shoulder girdle. Therefore, a relatively rapid development of muscular strength, flexibility, and other such components of physical fitness can be expected to accrue to the gymnastics performer. Because of the large number and variety of gymnastics stunts and skills, the gymnastics enthusiast is continually challenged to learn new skills and new combinations of exercises; thus, a challenge and a sense of achievement are always present.

Gymnastics possess a strong attraction for many simply because of the fun and challenge that it offers. An example of its universal appeal can be seen in the instinctive drive of small children to tumble, roll, swing, climb, and perform other movements that are duplicated in gymnastics. Because of the many facets of which gymnastics is composed, almost anyone can find one or more events that interest him and in which he has aptitude. If reasonable safety precautions are observed, little danger is involved in practicing most apparatus and tumbling activities. The small risk that is ever present can add significantly to the challenge of practicing and performing gymnastics.

SAFETY IN GYMNASTICS

The performer should first attempt and practice the simple apparatus and tumbling skills and routines before attempting skills and exercises of increased difficulty. Gaining a mastery of lead-up and elementary skills prepares the performer for more difficult skills and exercises that demand increased strength, timing, coordination, and an understanding of their performance. Before performing difficult, hazardous, or strenuous gymnastics skills and routines, the performer should first warm up by performing a few exercises, particularly of the stretching type, and practicing some of the easier gymnastics skills.

Because the performance of certain apparatus activities can be hazardous during the learning state, or when they are performed hurriedly or carelessly, spotters (or assisters) should be ready to assist and safeguard the performer when any hazardous skills or routines are done. The performer should never change his mind in the middle of a stunt, but always follow through as he originally intended. Before performing skills on gymnastics apparatus, the performer should first dust or rub the palms of his hands with carbonate of magnesium chalk to avoid the possibility of his hands becoming moist from sweat, which may cause him to lose his grasp on the apparatus. In addition, carbonate of magnesium chalk provides the correct amount of friction for the grip and thus minimizes the possibility of tearing the skin of the palms when tightly gripping the apparatus. The use of hand straps also helps ensure a safe grip on the apparatus. A fine grade emery cloth should be used periodically to clean the horizontal bar, parallel bars, and rings, as chalk deposits are one of the causes of hand tears. Loose clothing, especially loose-fitting sleeves or pants legs, should not be worn because they may wrap around the apparatus during circling stunts or may get in the way of the hands and fingers and cause an accident. For practically all apparatus work, the thumbs-around-grip should be used: the thumb encircles the apparatus in the opposite direction to the fingers. Some safety rules worth remembering are the following:

1. Always have plenty of mats in place around and under each piece of gymnastics apparatus.
2. Continue to practice the fundamentals and basic elements until these are mastered.
3. Follow a definite progression from the simple to the complex in learning gymnastics skills.
4. Develop confidence in the ability to perform each skill or routine by first having a clear and correct mental picture of what is to be done.
5. Use all available safety devices.
6. Do not continue practicing or working out when very fatigued or ill.
7. Check to be certain that each piece of apparatus and its parts are securely fastened and properly adjusted.
8. Do not engage in horseplay.

Spotting

Spotting is an important consideration. It is concerned with catching, supporting, or adjusting the performer's position to prevent a hard fall or an accident. At least one spotter should stand under the bar or near the apparatus whenever a skill or routine is performed, regardless of the difficulty of the skill being attempted. Spotting serves as a teaching aid and helps speed the learning rate. Spotting can be a learning aid through manual manipulation or the use of a spotting belt in which the student is put or lifted through the proper movements to give him the feel of the skill.

Proper progression in spotting includes the following:

1. Working in the safety belt until the performer has acquired a "muscle feel" for the skill.
2. Assisting by tapping, pushing, lifting, or supporting the performer.
3. Assuming a position of readiness, but giving no support until necessary.
4. Enlisting the confidence of the advanced learner by making him think that he is being assisted but not actually doing so.

All students can learn to spot with practice and coaching from their instructor. Whenever spotting, the following principles should be observed:

1. Protect the performer; he is the primary consideration.
2. Have an active position.
3. Be close to the performer but do not hamper his movements.
4. Two spotters are often needed.
5. Do not allow your attention to be diverted.
6. Do not overspot.
7. Coach the performer.
8. Be ready for instant action and be aware of every movement made by the performer.
9. The spotter should locate himself according to the space required for the execution of a skill or exercise, and at the point where the performer is most likely to lose his grip or have an accident.
10. The falling performer need not be caught; instead, check his fall by protecting his head and shoulders.
11. The spotter should give with the falling performer if he cannot meet him at the top of his fall.

In addition to being spotted, the learner in gymnastics can often avoid accidents or injuries if he knows how to fall properly and how to break his falls should any occur. These skills include learning the proper use of the arms and legs to reduce the momentum of the falling body (doing a reverse push-up, for example); cushioning the fall with other parts of the body; making use of rolling actions; falling forward, if possible, but turning the head and keeping the chin to the side when falling forward; and keeping the fingers pointed forward and the chin on the chest when falling backward.

FORM IN GYMNASTICS

Form (body position) is a basic consideration whenever any gymnastics exercises are performed. From the very beginning the performer should emphasize and attempt to retain as correct a form as possible when learning gymnastics skills and routines. Without form, any apparatus exercise is of limited value at best. Whenever training, the performer should strive for a perfect exercise, which should be presented with elegance, ease, confidence, and in a rhythm and style that are well suited to the aesthetic nature of the exercise. Faults in performance and style are penalized by the deduction of a number of whole or tenths of points.

Good form normally consists of the following:

1. Legs straight and knees together unless the skill or exercise demands otherwise.
2. Toes always pointed.
3. Eyes usually straight ahead and the head in line with the body.
4. Body usually straight when in an extended position, with only a small arch in the back.

PRESENTATION OF APPARATUS ACTIVITIES

Because the scope of gymnastic activity is immense, this chapter has been limited to the five international events that are performed on pieces of gymnastics apparatus. These include the horizontal bar, rings, parallel bars, pommel horse, and long horse. This chapter includes selected apparatus skills that provide a sound foundation for the development of more advanced performance in these events. Some of the gymnastics activities included in this chapter are not ordinarily used in gymnastics competition. However, these activities are of lead-up value and in addition can provide a challenge and enjoyment. The gymnastics activities contained in this chapter are grouped under one of three categories. The reader should understand that these are, in part, categories of convenience to aid him in planning his gymnastics workout; and that although the activity best belongs under the category in which it is placed, some of the skills in any given category could be listed under the other categories as well. These three categories are (1) hanging-type activities, (2) support-type activities, and (3) vaulting activities. To provide a complete workout, skills and routines should be performed from all three categories during each gymnastics workout.

The skills and routines that are listed under each category of each apparatus are placed in their approximate order of difficulty of performance from easiest to hardest according to the amount of timing and coordination required and the complexity of the movements involved.

The directions for performing apparatus skills that can be done in more than one way are given for a right-handed and right-footed performer. However, once a skill is mastered, it often should be learned in the other direction as well. In general, however, the terms *left* and *right* have been used merely to avoid confusion in the explanation of the execution of the various skills. They are not to be interpreted as meaning that the skill is to be performed only in that direction. Because gymnastics terminology has not been standardized in the United States, a gymnastics skill may often be referred to by several terms. As a rule the most common or most descriptive name has been given to each gymnastics skill.

THE PROGRESSIVE APPROACH

The fundamentals in any activity are the essential factors to attaining an advanced level of skill in that activity. One's success in gymnastics lies in large part in the learning of certain movements that are fundamental to a more advanced performance. Safety, also, is largely dependent on thoroughly learning various fundamental skills, especially in gymnastics. The gymnastics performer must be ready to learn—his readiness being dependent on previously learned skills. In learning more complex movements, skills, and routines, the learner must draw on his experience and learning of various elementary skills that are components of the skill being learned. Progression in gymnastics is a process that involves building upon previous experience. Each of the skills included in this manual are either prerequisites to more advanced skills or are in themselves useful elements at later stages of gymnastics. The skills for each apparatus begin with movements of orientation; they terminate with the skills that can be considered the basis of advanced performance. The illustrations depict the performance of each skill at the most critical point(s).

PRESENTATION OF APPARATUS ACTIVITIES AND EXERCISES

For each of the five pieces of apparatus, the skills that are described are separated into categories for convenience in combining them into various routines or exercises. Although one skill must be learned at a time, the student is strongly urged to combine various skills into short routines or exercises as quickly as possible because this is the goal of apparatus work (except for long-horse vaulting). It should also be noted that the same skill often can be performed on two or more kinds of apparatus. For example, a kip can be performed on the horizontal bar, parallel bars, rings, or free-exercise mat. When applicable, the following categories are presented:

1. *Mounting:* A mount is a skill or movement from a position on the floor to a position on the apparatus.
2. *Holding:* A held position on an apparatus is normally one involving balance and it may be preceded by a skill involving a strength move.
3. *Circling or swinging:* Circling or swinging is the concept of the body moving in a 360° circle (or part of a circle) with the apparatus serving as the axis of rotation.
4. *Changing or turning:* This involves changing the grip or a change of direction or movement of the body.
5. *Vaulting:* A vault is a skill or movement that requires the release of both hands in addition to the movement of the body in free flight over the apparatus.
6. *Dismounting:* Dismounting is a skill or movement from a position on the apparatus to a position of attention on the floor.

Gymnastics Routines

A routine or exercise on an apparatus must begin with a mount and end with a dismount. The other categories of skills are employed in between, when composing or performing a gymnastics routine. Naturally, the order of each skill should be so planned that the finishing position of one skill places the performer's body in the correct position to initiate the next skill.

At the end of each apparatus section in this chapter, some sample routines of increasing complexity are presented as examples of routines that might be performed on the apparatus.

HORIZONTAL BAR

The horizontal bar was invented by Friederich Jahn of Germany in 1812. Competition on the horizontal bar was included in the first AAU National Championships, which were held in 1885. A championship routine consists of different kinds of giant swings interspersed with swinging and vaulting movements without holding or stopping. (See Figure 17-1.)

The horizontal bar is often considered to be the most spectacular of all the gymnastic events. The beginner

Figure 17-1. Horizontal bar.

often makes rapid progress and, hence, gains a sense of real achievement. Although strength is an asset in any gymnastic event, the horizontal bar requires less strength than do most of the other events.

A horizontal bar (often called a high bar) is a flexible metal bar, six to eight feet in length and usually one inch in diameter, which is located about eight feet above floor level. Certain horizontal bar skills can be learned and performed with increased safety, ease of spotting, and confidence if first practiced on a horizontal bar about shoulder height. (These are marked with an asterick *).

Three different types of grasps are used when performing on the horizontal bar. The most commonly used grasp is the regular, or overgrip, in which, when the hands are overhead, the palms of the hand face the same direction the performer faces. Unless otherwise specified for a skill, the regular grip is employed. The reverse or undergrip is the opposite of the overgrip. The mixed grasp, one overgrip and one undergrip, is used least of all.

For increased gripping power when performing on the horizontal bar, the thumb is always wrapped around the bar in the direction opposite to that of the fingers. For all circling stunts the performer should maintain a tight grip that permits circling movements on the bar; and in the event that he does not successfully complete a skill, he should flex his body and stay as close to the bar as possible in order to inhibit or stop his swinging motion.

Mounts

Single-knee Upswing.* (Figure 17-2) From a stand under the bar (or from a small swing): (1) jump up, pike, bring knees in front of the bar; (2) hook right knee between hands, keeping the arms straight; (3) swing left leg forward and down; (4) rotate hands forward to a support position; and (5) lift head and shoulders, coming to a sitting position on the bar.

Gymnastics: Apparatus 237

Figure 17-2. Single knee upswing.

Hip Swing Up (Front Hip Pullover).* (Figure 17-3) From a stand under the bar: (1) jump up, flex the arms, extend the head backward, lifting the hips in front of the bar (pike position); (2) continue pulling with the arms while rotating the hands backward and raising the legs; and (3) as the hips move over the bar, lift the head and chest upward and extend the body, coming to a front support position.

Stride Leg Swing-up. (Figure 17-4) From a hang and using a reverse or undergrip: (1) cast by swinging the legs forward and backward, flexing the arms; (2) lift the hips in front of the bar; (3) extend the body upward and forward, extending the arms; (4) at the end of a forward swing bring the right leg between the hands; (5) kick the left leg downward and forward while rotating the hands forward; (6) lift the head and shoulders, keeping the arms straight; and (7) come to a stride position above the bar.

Figure 17-3. Hip swing up (front hip pull over).

Kip. (Figure 17-5) From a hang: (1) cast by flexing at the hips, shooting the legs forward; (2) quickly extend the body and then swing backward; (3) at the end of the forward swing (wait for the "dead point" between the end of the forward swing and the start of the backswing), poke quickly, bringing the toes to the bar; (4) wait in a pike position until the hips pass under the bar; (5) extend the hips upward and forward, tightening the stomach muscles and rotating the hands forward to a support; and (6) lift the head and chest, pushing down on the bar with straight arms.

Common Faults. Common faults are (1) too much swing; (2) extending the hips to the point of straight body position; (3) bending the arms; and (4) bringing the hips to the bar too early.

Figure 17-4. Stride leg swing-up.

238   *Individual and Team Sports*

Figure 17-5. Kip.

Back Uprise. (Figure 17-6) From a hang: (1) cast by swinging the legs forward and backward, flexing the arms; (2) lift hips in front of the bar; (3) extend the body upward and forward, extending the arms; and (4) as the body passes backward under the bar, lift the head and shoulders, keeping the arms straight and pushing down against the bar, coming to a front support position.

Circling and Swinging Skills

Cast. (Figure 17-7) (A cast is used to easily develop a large swinging motion on the horizontal bar.) From a stand three feet behind the bar: (1) jump, grasp the bar, and swing forward; (2) at the end of the backswing, do a pullup while arching the body; (3) immediately flex the hips; (4) pike the legs forward and forcibly extend them upward; and (5) forcefully extend the arms, thus generating a large swing.

*Back Single-knee Circle.** (Figure 17-8) Starting from a stride leg support with the right leg forward: (1) raise the left leg rearward, leaning back (shift the weight rearward) and bending the right leg while stretching the body; (2) as the shoulders pass under the bar, kick the left leg upward and slightly flex the hips and arms; (3) rotate the hands backward to a support position; and (4) extend the hips, lifting the head and chest and extending the arms.

*Front Stride Leg Circle.** (Figure 17-9) From a stride leg support position with the right leg forward and using a reverse or under grip: (1) raise the hips above the bar; (2) fall forward, extending the body; (3) as the shoulders pass beneath the bar, flex the hips slightly; and (4) extend the body, rotating the hands forward to a support position while stretching the right leg forward.

*Back Hip Circle.** (Figure 17-10) From a front support: (1) flex the hips, bending the arms slightly and swinging the legs forward; (2) swing the legs rearward, extending the arms and leaning forward; (3) bring the hips close to the bar and drop backward; (4) as the shoulders pass under the bar, flex the hips slightly, rotating the hands backward to a support; and (5) lift the shoulders and head and extend the hips.

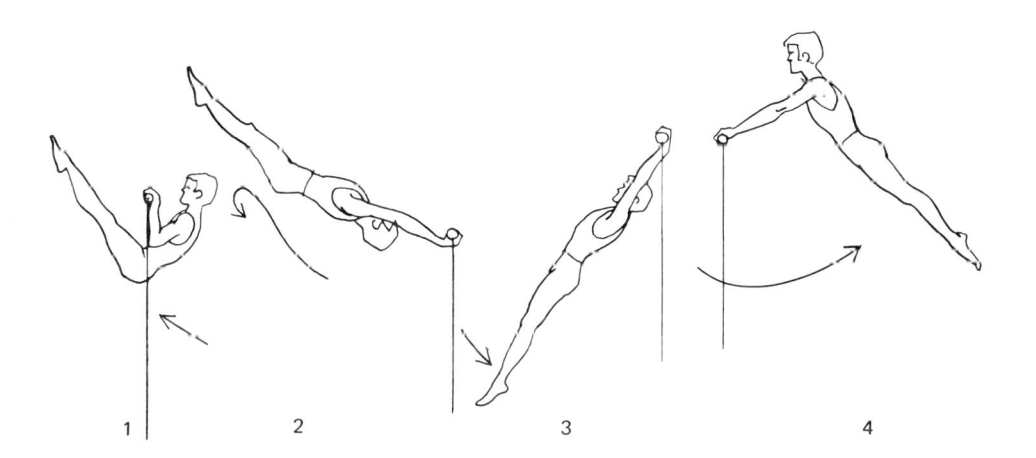

Figure 17-6. Back uprise.

Gymnastics: Apparatus 239

Figure 17-7. Cast.

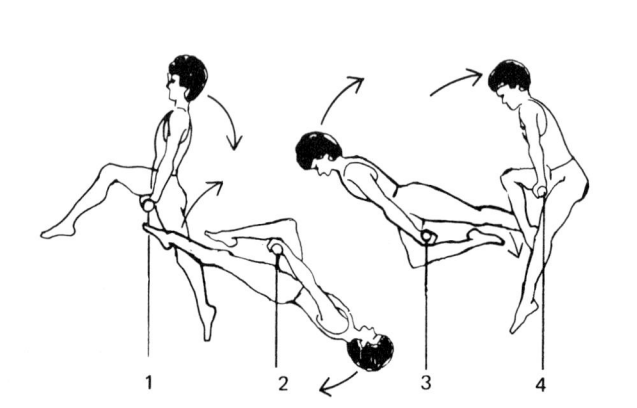

Figure 17-8. Back single-knee circle.

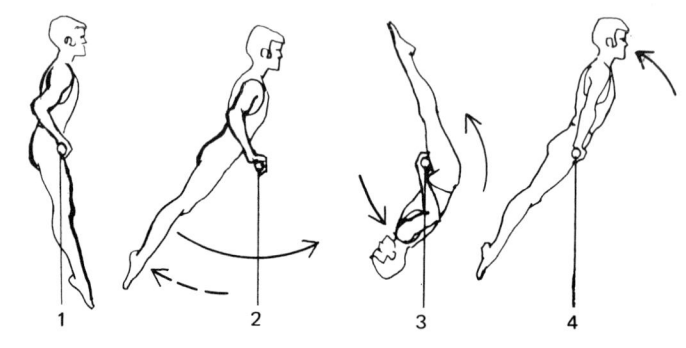

Figure 17-10. Back hip circle.

Common Faults: Common faults are (1) dropping the hips too far below the bar; and (2) not rotating the hands quickly enough.

*Double Knee Circle Forward.** (Figure 17-11) From a sitting position on the bar with a reverse grasp: (1) lift the body and hips as high as possible, pulling the hips back and placing the back of the knees against the bar; (2) drop forward, diving head first; (3) as the upward swing begins, flex the arms and tuck the body; and (4) as the circle is completed, bring the body to an erect position and stop in a sitting position.

Figure 17-9. Front stride leg circle.

Figure 17-11. Double knee circle forward.

240   *Individual and Team Sports*

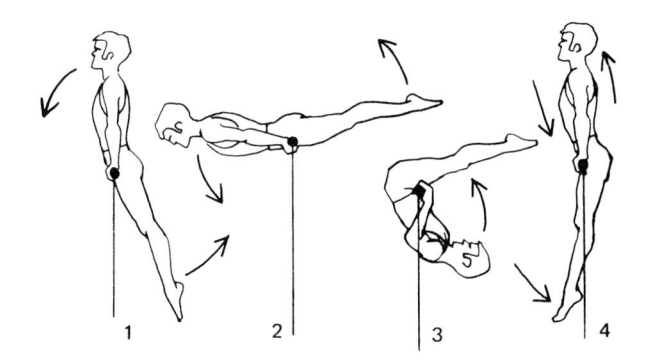

Figure 17-12. Front hip circle.

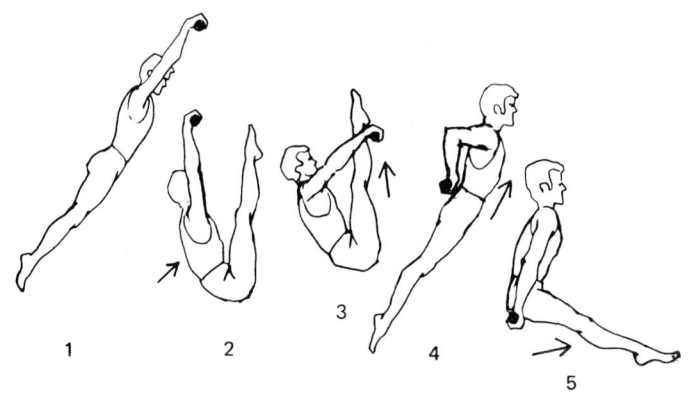

Figure 17-14. Reverse kip.

Front Hip Circle.* (Figure 17-12) From a front support position: (1) lift the hips above the bar, extending the body; (2) fall forward with a straight body and a heads-up position; and (3) as the shoulders drop below the horizontal, pike quickly, rotating the hands forward and leaning over the bar.

Common Faults. Common faults are (1) piking too early; and (2) not rotating hands quickly and simultaneously with the piking action.

Back-seat Circle.* (Figure 17-13) From a rear support: (1) raise the legs to an L position; (2) fall backward (the bar should be midway between the hips and knees); (3) as the shoulders pass under the bar, bring the hips close to the bar; and (4) lift the head and chest, extending the body.

Common Fault. A common fault is dropping the hips too low.

Reverse Kip. (Figure 17-14) Swing forward as for a regular kip: (1) pike the body, raising the extended legs and passing them between the arms and under the bar; (2) with the body piked, the backward swing is started; (3) swing forward and as the hips pass under the bar quickly extend the body over the bar by unpiking at the hips; and (4) flex at the waist and push the hips back and come to a rear-seat position. (If the performer over-shoots past the rear-seat position, he should then do a back-seat circle.)

Back Free Hip Circle.* (Figure 17-15) From a front support position: (1) bend the arms slightly, swinging the legs forward; (2) swing the legs backward while leaning forward and extending the arms; (3) then drop backward, swinging the legs close to the bar; (4) as the shoulders pass under the bar, pike slightly; and (5) lift the hips in front of the bar, rotating the hands backward to a support, and extend the body while lifting the head and shoulders.

Common Faults. Common faults are (1) touching the bar with the hips; (2) extending the body too late; and (3) dropping the hips too low below the bar.

Spotting. The spotter stands slightly in front of the bar and tackles the performer if he reverses his direction because of a lack of circular momentum.

Figure 17-13. Back-seat circle.

Figure 17-15. Back free hip circle.

Gymnastics: Apparatus

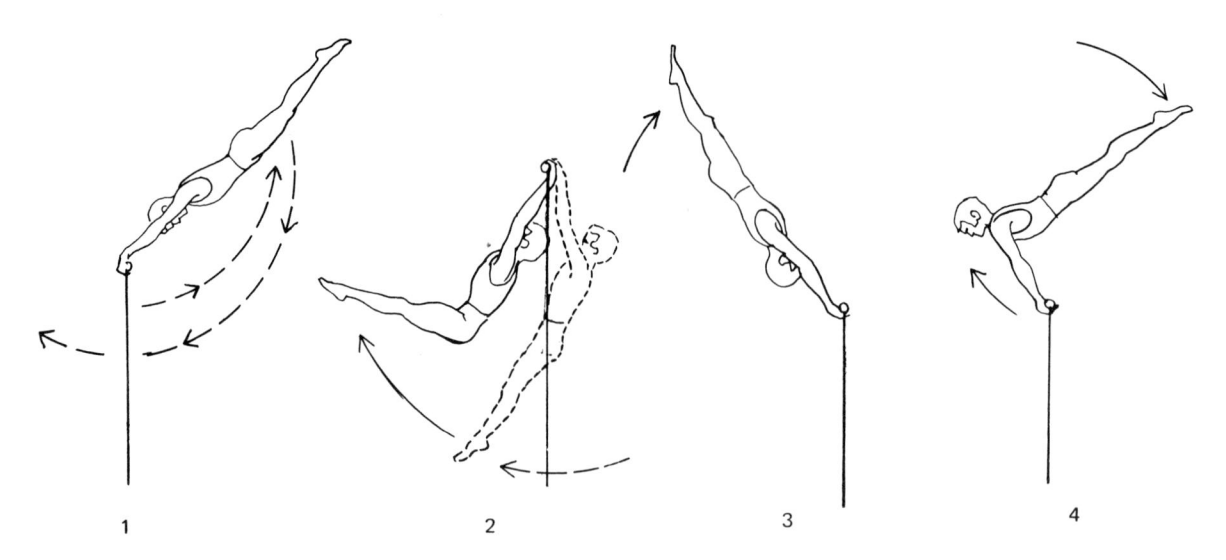

Figure 17-16. Half-back giant (regular grip half-giant swing).

Half-back Giant (Regular Grip Half-Giant Swing). (Figure 17-16) From a front support: (1) take a high cast, going almost to a handstand; (2) swing downward with a straight body, but lead with the chest; (3) as the body begins its upswing, pike slightly; (4) lift or whip the legs and hips upward and forward; and (5) extend the body, rotating the hands backward and lifting the head and shoulders. (Note that the arms should be bent somewhat in passing over the bar.)

Common Errors in Execution. Two common errors in execution are (1) not lifting the hips high enough in front of the bar; and (2) not extending the body.

Spotting. (Same as for the Back Free Hip Circle.)

Three-quarter Front Giant (Reverse Grip Giant Swing). (Figure 17-17) From a support with a reverse or under grip: (1) take a high cast, leaning forward and extending the arms; (2) as the legs near a handstand position, push the shoulders back and overbalance; (3) duck the head between the arms, dropping forward with an extended body; (4) as the body passes under the bar, pike and lift the shoulders, pulling down on the bar; and (5) lean the shoulders forward and come to a front support position.

Spotting. The spotter stands about three feet in back of the bar and to the side of the performer. As the performer's legs pass under the bar, the spotter lifts the thighs of the performer.

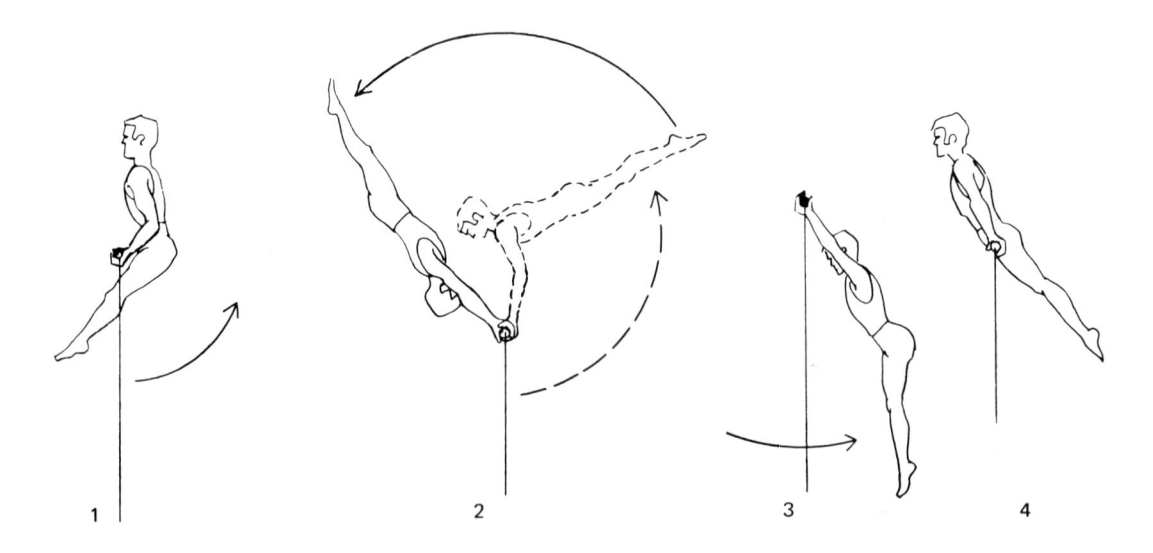

Figure 17-17. Three-quarter front giant (reverse grip giant swing).

242 *Individual and Team Sports*

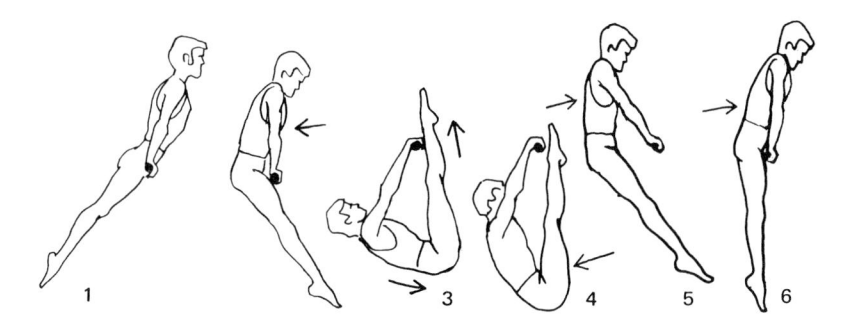

Figure 17-18. Drop kip.

Changing and Turning Skills

*Drop Kip.** (Figure 17-18) From a front-leaning rest position: (1) keeping the arms straight, drop backward, flexing sharply at the hips and raising the insteps to the bar; (2) keeping the legs straight, hold the insteps to the bar until they are directly underneath the bar on the return swing; (3) kip by extending the body rapidly, thrusting the legs forward and downward and pushing down with the hands; and (4) come to a front-leaning rest position on the bar.

Half-twisting Front Swing. (Figure 17-19) Develop a swing: (1) as the body swings under the bar, pike the legs; (2) tightly grasp the bar with the left hand and scissor the right leg over the left leg, twisting the body by means of leg and hip action while pulling with the left hand; (3) release the right-hand grasp and complete the half-twist; (4) regrasp with the right hand and release the left hand grasp; and (5) turn the left hand over and regrasp with it. With practice, several half-twists can be done in succession, twisting on either side of the bar at the end of each front swing.

Figure 17-19. Half-twisting front swing.

One Arm Cut-away. (Figure 17-20) From a hang: (1) execute a small cast; (2) at the end of the front swing lift the hips and pike, bringing the legs between the hands; (3) lift the body upward in back of the bar; (4) at the peak of the upswing, release the left hand and extend the body to the left; and (5) regrasp the bar with the left hand.

Spotting. The spotter stands to the right of the performer and holds the performer's right arm.

Dismounts (Including Vaulting Movements)

(During the learning stages, vaulting dismounts can be initiated from a stand on the floor or from a front leaning rest position on the bar.)

*Single-leg Flank Dismount with One-fourth Turn.** (Figure 17-21) From a stride leg support with the right leg forward and with a mixed grasp (left hand in a regular grip): (1) swing the left leg over the bar, releasing the left hand and leaning to the right; and (2) execute a one-quarter turn to the right and come to a stand.

*Underswing from Stand.** (Long Underswing Dismount) (Figure 17-22) From a stand under the bar. (1) jump, using a one- or two-leg take-off, flex the arms and bring the hips in front of the bar in a piked position; (2) shoot the legs upward and forward; (3) extend the arms and hips; and (4) release the bar and arch, forcing the feet under the body. After some practice the long underswing dismount can be done while swinging.

Spotting. The spotter stands in front of the bar and to one side of the performer. He holds the performer's upper arm and lifts under the small of his back. A towel can be taped to the bar to prevent injury if the head strikes the bar.

Swing with Rear Dismount and One-half Twist. (Short Underswing Dismount with One-half Twist) (Figure 17-23) Do a cast: (1) on the backswing lift the hips to slight pike, push downward and with the arms; (2) release the bar at the peak of the swing when the body is vertical, pushing with one arm and pulling with the other; and (3) drop to a stand, facing away from the bar.

Gymnastics: Apparatus

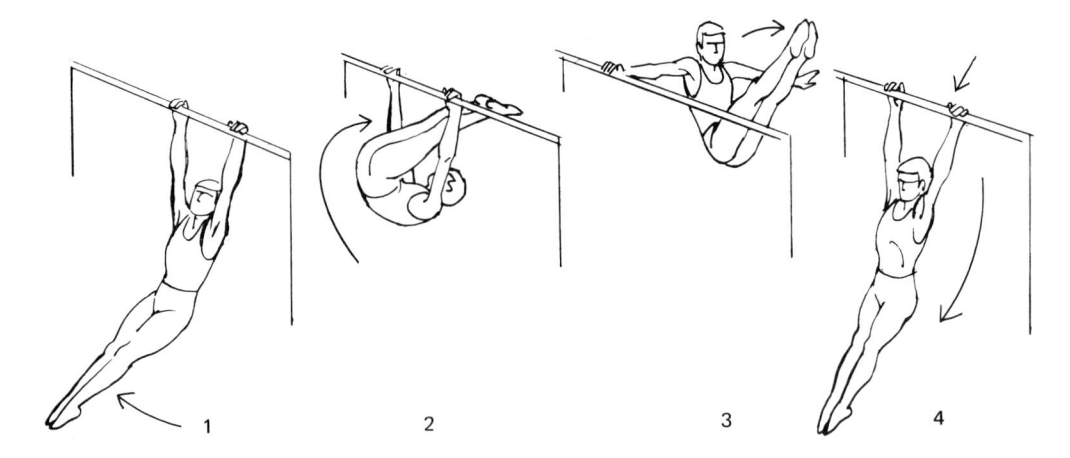

Figure 17-20. One arm cut-away.

Flank Dismount.* (Figure 17-24) From a front support: (1) flex the hips, bending the arms slightly and leaning forward; (2) swing the legs rearward and straighten the arms; (3) lift the hips and legs over the bar and under the left hand, leaning to the right and forward; and (4) release the left hand and drop to a stand with the right side facing the bar.

Heel Circle Forward and Dismount.* From a sitting position on the bar with the legs extended and with a reverse grasp: (1) fully extend the arms and raise the hips, placing the heel tendons against the bar; (2) swing forward and under the bar; and (3) as the body completes its upward swing release the grasp and dismount forward, coming to a stand position in front of the bar.

Spotting. The spotter should carefully spot the arms and shoulders of the performer during his upswing and dismount.

Examples of Horizontal Bar Exercises

1. Cast, two swings, short underswing dismount.
2. Single knee upswing mount, take an undergrip, single knee circle backward, recover leg to front support, drop back to a cast, long underswing dismount.
3. Front pullover, back hip circle, long underswing dismount.
4. Back uprise, back free hip circle, drop kip, cast, undergrip half giant swing, heel circle forward, and dismount.
5. Kip, front hip circle, one-arm cut-away, reverse kip, heel circle forward, and dismount.
6. Single-knee upswing, mount, back-knee circle, front stride leg circle, single-leg flank, dismount with one-fourth turn.

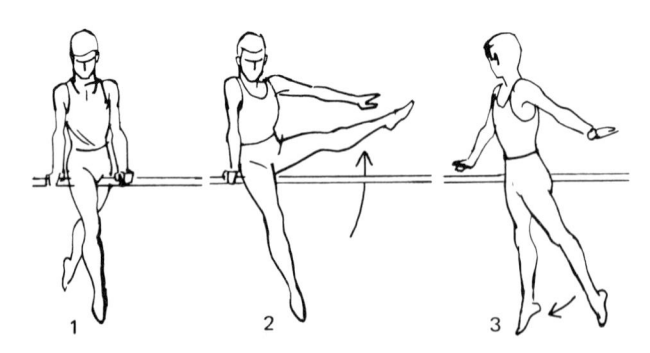

Figure 17-21. Single-leg flank dismount with one-fourth turn.

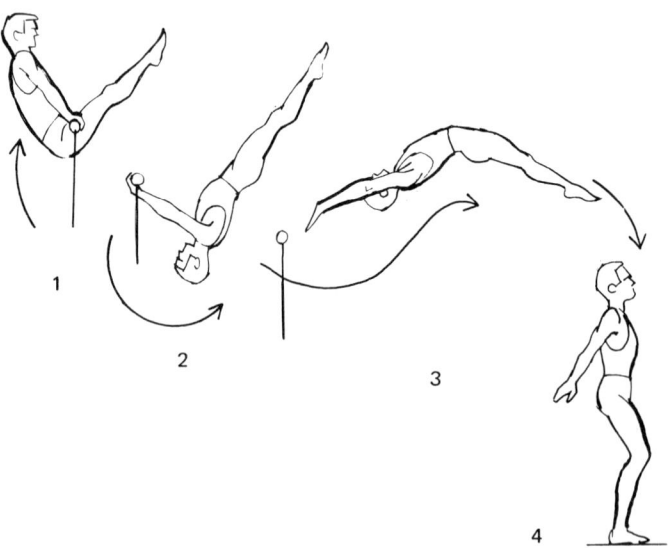

Figure 17-22. Underswing from stand (long underswing dismount).

244   *Individual and Team Sports*

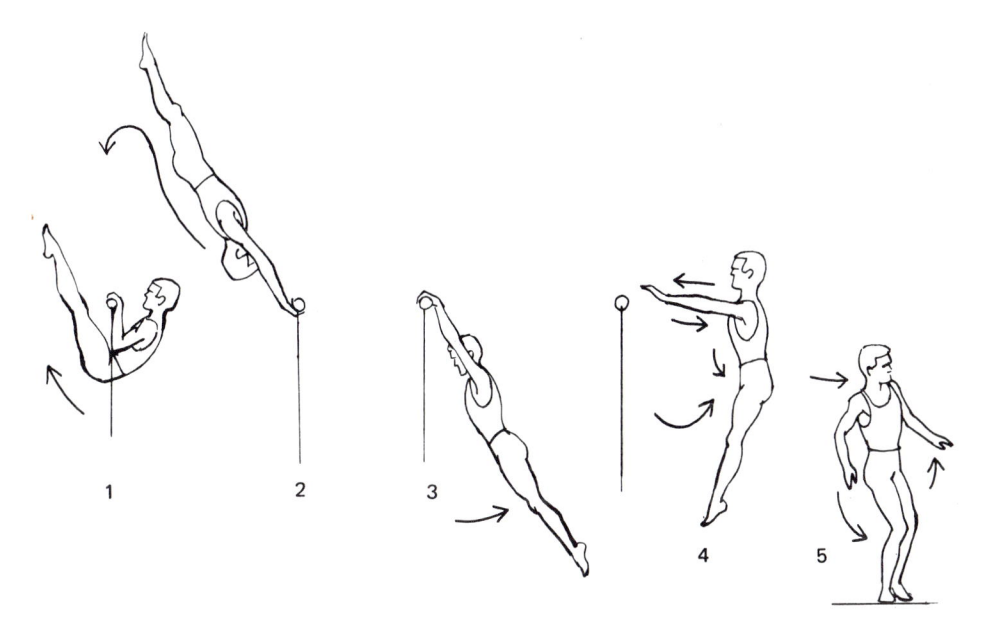

Figure 17-23. Swing with rear dismount and one-half twist (short underswing dismount with one-half twist).

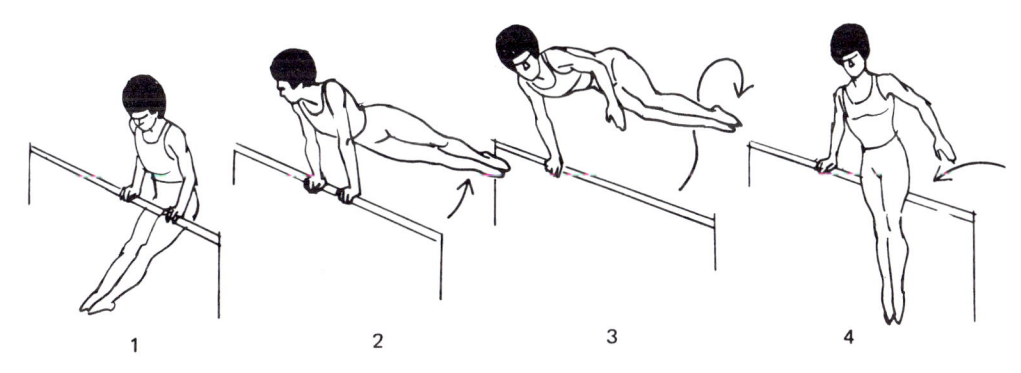

Figure 17-24. Flank dismount.

RINGS

The rings are sometimes referred to as the Roman rings, indicating that they existed in some form in the time of ancient Rome. In 1842, Spies of Germany first described them as they are presently used. *Swinging Ring* competition was first included in the AAU Gymnastics Championships in 1885. The event was changed to the Still Rings in the late 1950s in American collegiate competition. A championship ring routine must contain movements that alternate between swinging, strength, and holding skills. The gymnast must execute two handstands, one with strength, the other with swing, and show one strength part of at least B difficulty. The routine should be performed without the swinging of the rings. (See Figure 17-25.)

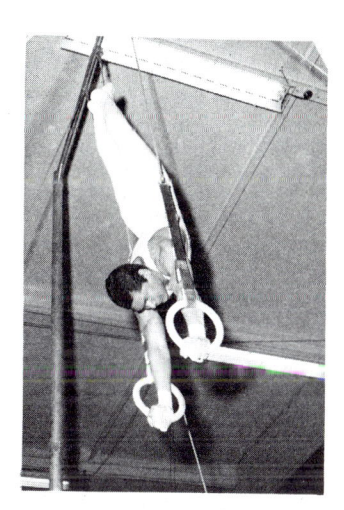

Figure 17-25. Rings.

Gymnastics: Apparatus

Regular Grip   Over Grip or False Grasp

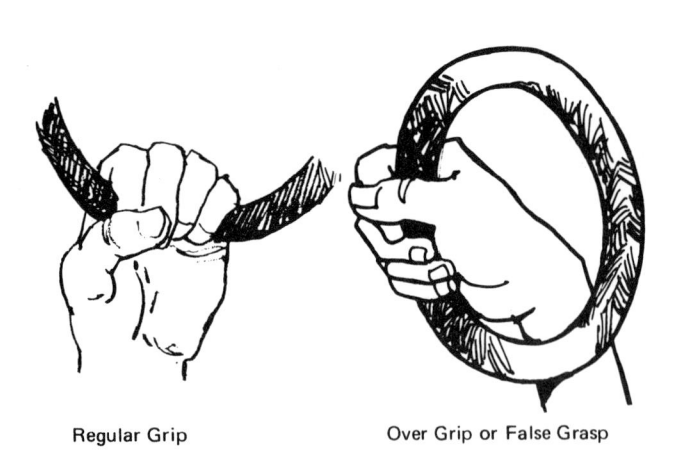

Figure 17-26. Ring grips.

Strength is a most important factor when performing on this apparatus. Regular practice sessions on the rings should help develop this important gymnastic quality. Timing is an important factor in a rings performance. The various skills must be properly timed in order to avoid unnecessary movements of the rings. Still rings exercises require certain positions to be held or swinging-type movements to be made. To insure a safe grip, chalk should be used not only on the palms but also on the palm side of the wrists. Two types of grips are used in performing on the rings. (See Figure 17-26.) The wrist should be placed over the ring in the overgrip or false grasp.

Hanging Positions. (Figure 17-27) In Figure 17-27 various hangs are illustrated from which many skills are initiated on the rings.

Regular or Ordinary Hang   Bent Hip Hang (Basket Hang)   Inverted Hang   Rear Hang or Hang Rearways

Figure 17-27. Hanging positions.

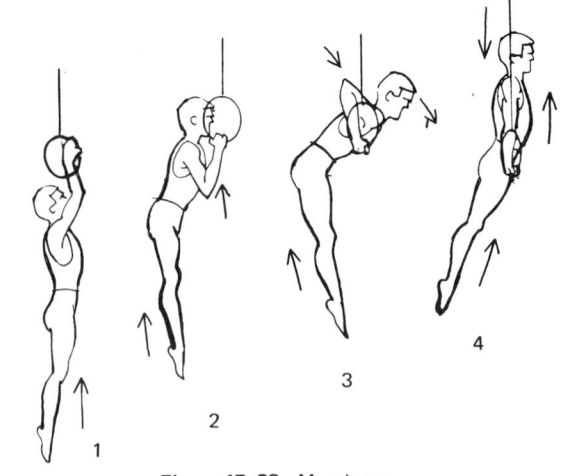

Figure 17-28. Muscle-up.

Mounts

Muscle-up. (Figure 17-28) From a hang with an over-grip: (1) flex the arms until the rings are almost chest level when piking by lifting the hips and leaning forward; (2) quickly turn the elbows outward and backward and turn the hands inward; and (3) without pausing, push to a straight-arm support with the rings behind the buttocks.

Kip. (Figure 17-29) From a bent-hip hang: (1) extend the hips upward and forward, pulling with the arms; (2) push the rings sideward and downward, tightening the stomach muscles; (3) keep the hips even with or above the rings; and (4) lift the head and chest and come to a support position.

Common Faults. Common faults are (1) having the hips too low as the legs kick forward; and (2) kicking too slowly.

Front Uprise. (Figure 17-30) From a hang: (1) on the forward swing pike at the hips as the legs pass under the rings; (2) force the hips forward, flexing the arms and rotating the hands forward; (3) lift the elbows back and keep them close to the body while lifting the chest; and (4) push to a straight-arm support.

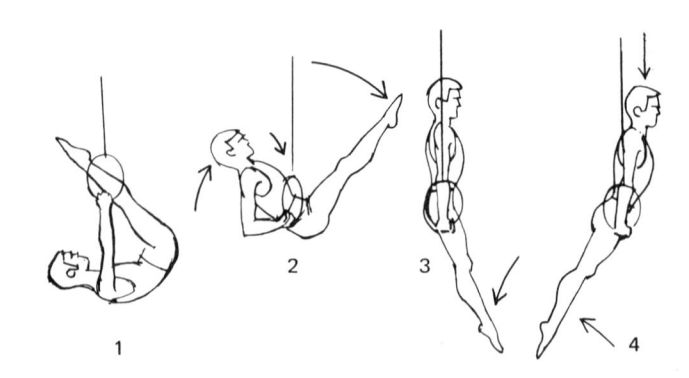

Figure 17-29. Kip.

246 *Individual and Team Sports*

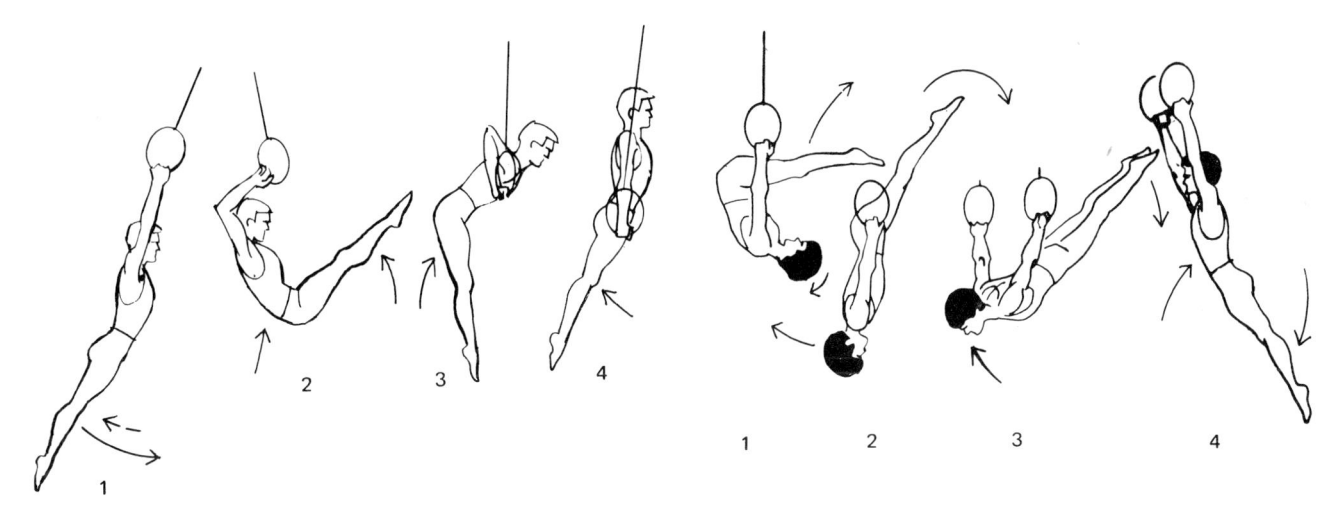

Figure 17-30. Front uprise.

Figure 17-32. Dislocate.

Back Kip (Bird-up). (Figure 17-31) From a hang with an overgrip, or from the forward end of a small swing: (1) raise the legs forward and shoot them upward, flexing the arms; (2) as the hips pass between the straps, lift the head and chest, extending the body and rotating the hands to the sides of the body; and (3) push down on the rings, keeping them close to the hips.

Common Faults. Common faults are (1) failure to raise the hips above the rings; (2) failure to extend the body and push down on the rings simultaneously; and (3) not pulling with the arms throughout the first part of the movement.

Circling or Swinging Skills

Dislocate. (Figure 17-32) From a basket or bent hip hang: (1) quickly extend the body upward and backward (at a 45° angle) and simultaneously push down, forward, and outward on the rings with straight arms, and spread them when shooting the arms sideways, turning the thumbs *backward and out*; and (2) lift the head and chest and swing to a hang.

Common Faults. Some common faults are (1) bending the arms (although this is encouraged in the early learning stages to absorb any shock); (2) extending the body below a 45° angle; and (3) not spreading the hands sufficiently far apart.

Spotting. The spotter lifts the performer's shoulder with one hand while he places the other hand under his thighs to slow the movement.

Inlocate. (Figure 17-33) From a basket: (1) swing forward and downward with a straight body; (2) as the hips pass under the rings, push the rings sideward and pike by lifting the hips; (3) push the rings forward, sideward,

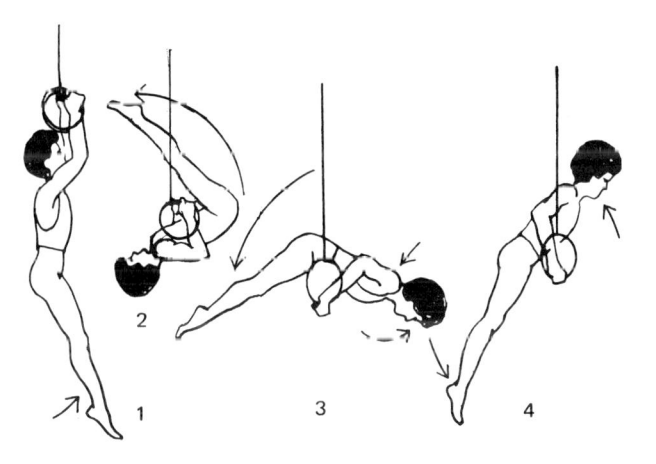

Figure 17-31. Back kip (bird-up).

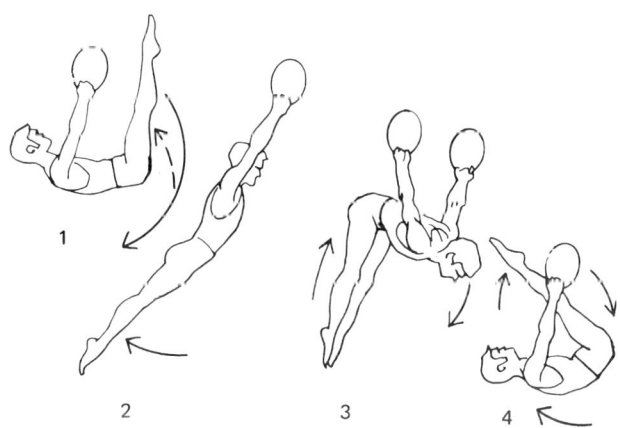

Figure 17-33. Inlocate.

Gymnastics: Apparatus 247

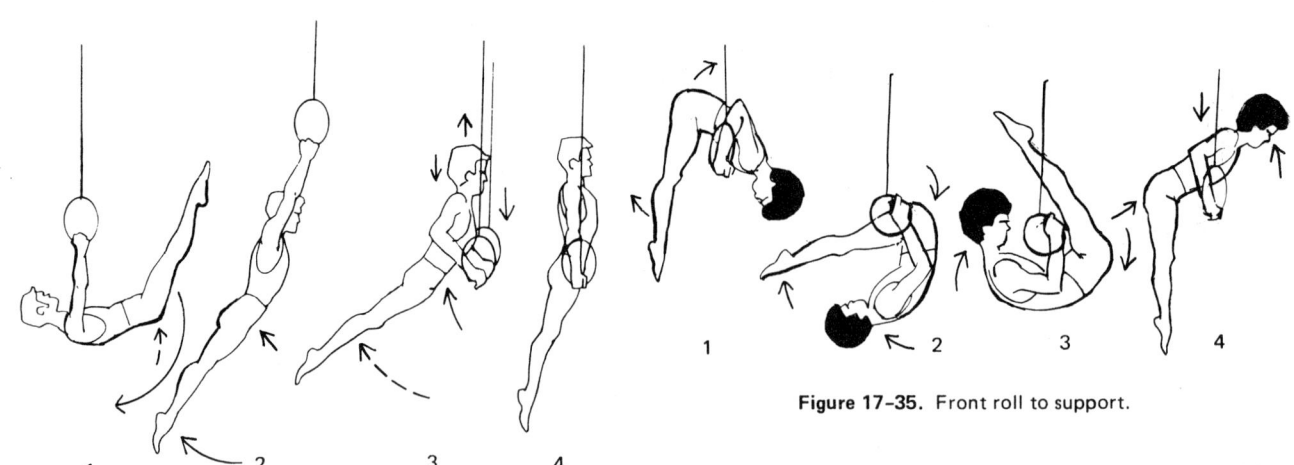

Figure 17-34. Back uprise.

Figure 17-35. Front roll to support.

and backward with the arms straight, and the thumbs turned inward while ducking the head; and (4) maintaining a pike position, return to a basket position.

Spotting. The spotter lifts the performer's shoulders and thighs as the pike is executed.

Back Uprise. (Figure 17-34) From a basket: (1) move to an inverted hang and swing forward and downward while tightly gripping the rings; (2) as the legs pass under the rings, lift the head and chest and thrust the rings sideward; (3) push down vigorously on the rings keeping the body arched; and (4) bring the rings to the side of the body at the top of the rear swing.

Front Roll to Support. (Figure 17-35) From a support: (1) bend the arms and lean forward and pike by lifting the hips; (2) maintain a bent-arm position and overgrip throughout the roll; (3) as the body passes through a basket position, pull the rings to the chest and lean forward, turning the elbows back; and (4) push to a support position.

Forward Cast. (Figure 17-36) From a support: (1) swing the legs forward; (2) then extend the body forward, pushing the rings backward and sideward; and (3) keep arms straight throughout the movement. (During the learning stages, the arms can be bent to cushion any shock.)

Held Positions

L Position. From a support: (1) keeping the legs extended and remaining in a support position, slowly raise the legs forward; and (2) come to a half lever or L position and hold it at least three seconds.

Shoulder Stand. (Figure 17-37) From an L support: (1) slowly bend the arms while leaning forward and lifting the hips; (2) as the hips reach an overhead position, raise the legs to an extended position overhead; (3) keep the elbows close to the body and the shoulders in contact with the rings; and (4) look forward and downward.

Common Faults. Common faults are (1) lifting the legs too early; and (2) not holding the hips in position while in the shoulder stand.

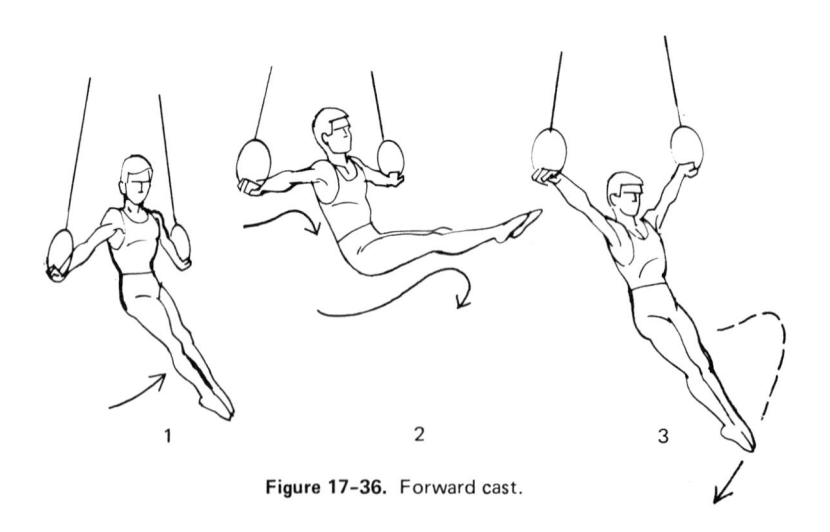

Figure 17-36. Forward cast.

248 *Individual and Team Sports*

Figure 17-37. Shoulder stand.

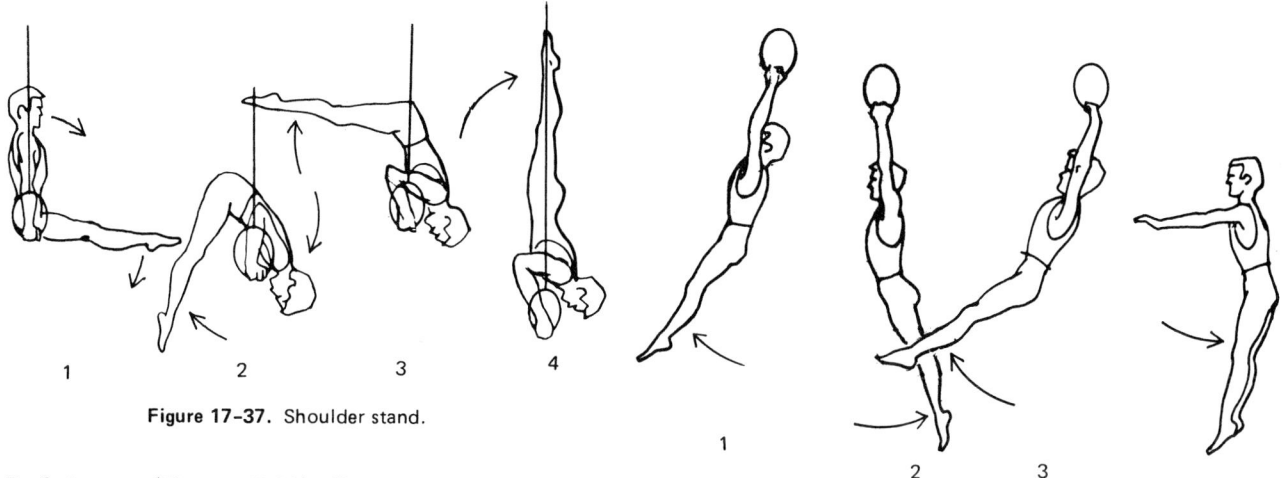

Back Lever. (Figure 17-38) From an inverted hang: (1) slowly lower the extended body rearward; (2) force the arms toward the body, rotating the hands and thumbs inward to the inside; and (3) lock the arms and elbows and hold the body in a horizontal position for at least three seconds.

Dismounts

Swing with Dismount. (Figure 17-39) From a hang: (1) lift the legs forward; (2) stretch the body forward and downward, forcing the rings backward; (3) on the backswing lift the hips and legs, forcing the rings forward; (4) repeat a full swing; and (5) dismount on the backswing by pushing down on the rings and lifting the hips; while keeping the body extended and in a vertical position, release the rings.

Tuck Flyaway (Fold Tumble Rearward). (Figure 17-40) From a hang: (1) swing forward and backward; (2) tuck (or pike) on the next forward swing, pulling with the arms; (3) as the legs pass between the rings release the rings; and (4) lift the head and chest and continue to somersault backward to a stand.

Figure 17-39. Swing with dismount.

Straddle-cut Dismount. (Figure 17-41) From a hang: (1) swing, and on a forward swing, pike; (2) spread the extended legs and lift the hips to a height level with the rings; (3) continue to rotate backward and straddle the legs; (4) just before the crotch contacts the arms, release the rings, lifting the head and chest; and (5) bring the legs together.

Spotting. The spotter holds the performer's upper arm and rotates him if necessary with the free hand.

Forward Double Leg Cut-off. (Figure 17-42) From a basket position: (1) vigorously rock-up onto the arms, (2) just before the legs touch the arms, release the grasp on the rings; (3) chin down and forward; and (4) keep the body tucked after the release until extending the legs directly underneath the hips.

Spotting. The spotter should grasp an upper arm or armpit of the performer and give him whatever assistance is needed.

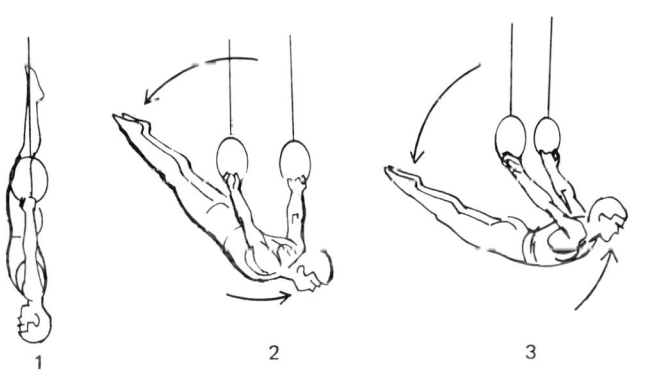

Figure 17-38. Back lever.

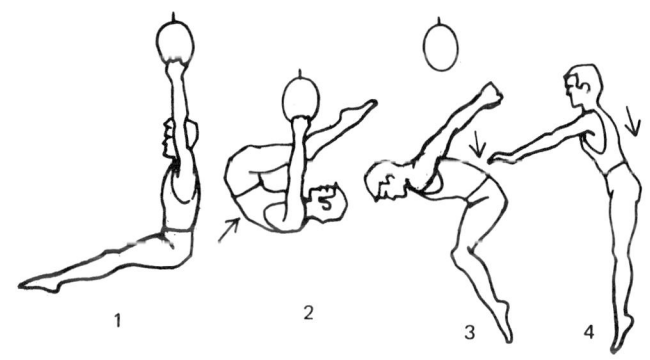

Figure 17-40. Tuck flyaway (fold tumble rearward).

Gymnastics: Apparatus

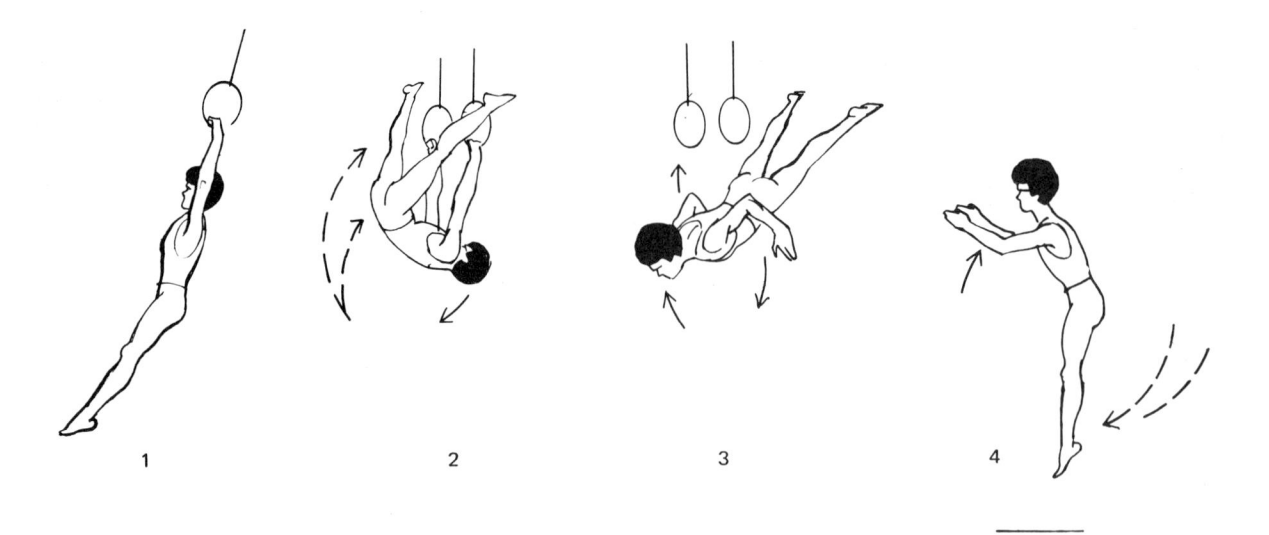

Figure 17-41. Straddle-cut dismount.

Examples of Ring Exercises

1. Inverted hang, back hang, inverted hang, backswing, and dismount.
2. Muscle-up, basket, dislocate, and backswing and dismount.
3. Kip, shoulder stand, basket, dislocate, and tuck flyaway.
4. Front uprise, forward roll to support, L position, forward cast, inlocate, and straddle-cut dismount.
5. Back kip, basket, back lever, basket, forward double leg cut-off.
6. Back kip, L position, shoulder stand, L position, cast, back uprise L position, and straddle-cut dismount.
7. Kip, cast, back uprise, L position, shoulder stand, basket, dislocate, and flyaway.

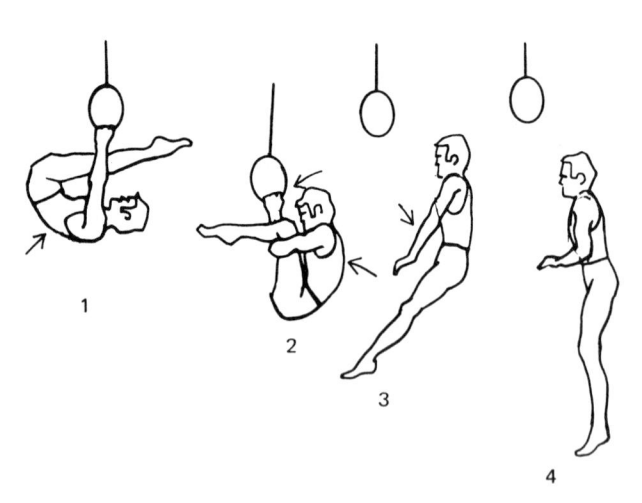

Figure 17-42. Forward double leg cut-off.

PARALLEL BARS

The parallel bars (Figure 17-43) were developed by Friederich Jahn of Germany in 1812. Gymnastics competition on the parallel bars started in the United States in 1885. The parallel bars provide an excellent opportunity for the development of strength and coordination. The muscles of the arms and shoulders in particular can be developed by utilizing this apparatus. Although movements on the parallel bars are mainly of the swinging type, strength and balance movements are also components of a routine. In competitive gymnastics, an exercise or routine on the parallel bars must consist of swinging and flight movements, with not more than three stops (or held positions) and at least one strength part, and one B part either above or below the bars in which the grip of

Figure 17-43. Parallel bars.

250 *Individual and Team Sports*

A
Support Grip

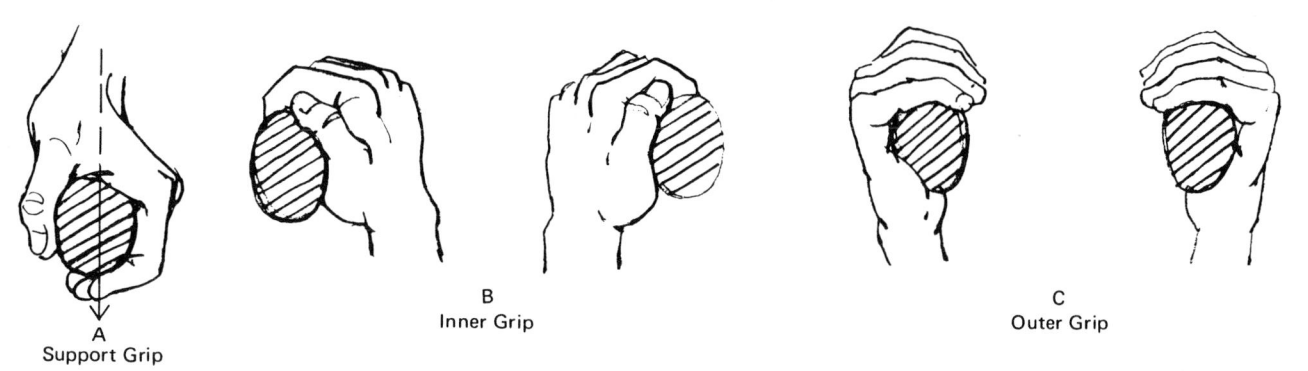

B
Inner Grip

C
Outer Grip

Figure 17-44. Parallel bar grips.

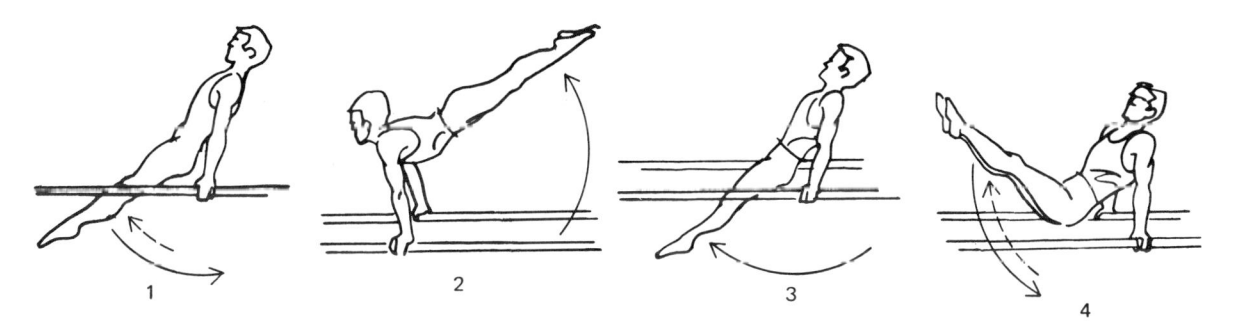

Figure 17-45. Swing.

both hands is released. Most adjustable parallel bars range from approximately 3 to 5½ feet in height and from 10 to 22 inches in width. The width of the parallel bars should be so adjusted that they are shoulder width or slightly wider.

Care should be taken to tighten the adjustments in order to prevent the collapse of the uprights. Gymnastic chalk should be used for all parallel bar skills, and bars should be cleaned periodically with a fine emery cloth.

Low parallel bars (about waist high) should be used to learn skills that do not involve work under the bars or an upper arm support. Such skills are marked with an * (asterisk).

Three grips for parallel bar work are illustrated in Figure 17-44. Note that in support exercises the weight of the body should be in line with the center of each bar.

Basic Fundamentals

Swing. (Figure 17-45) From a support: (1) lift the legs forward, leaning back and keeping the arms straight; (2) swing the legs backward, extending the body and leaning forward; (3) as the hips pass between the hands, pike slightly and lift the legs forward; and (4) extend the body forward and lean back. (With practice the body can be kept straight during all phases of the swing.)

Common Faults. Some common faults are (1) forcing the swing; (2) bending the arms; and (3) sagging at the shoulders.

Mounts

*Front Mount.** (Figure 17-46) From a standing position outside of the middle of the parallel bars and facing

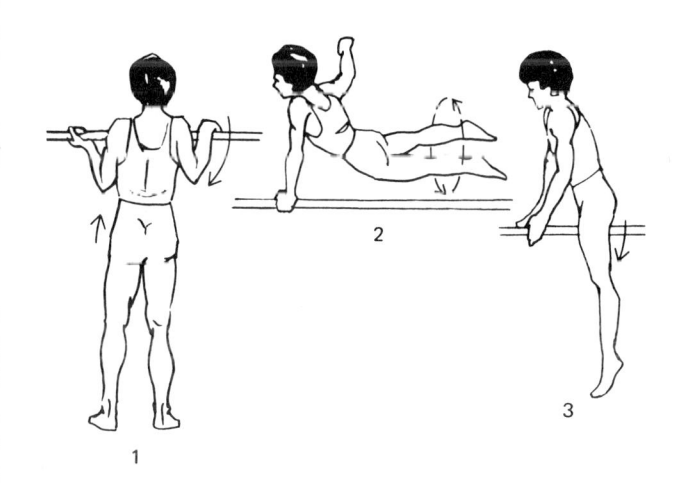

Figure 17-46. Front mount.

Gymnastics: Apparatus 251

Figure 17-47. Underbar kip.

them, using a mixed grasp with the left hand in an undergrip: (1) jump up and lean inward slightly; (2) the left arm is extended to a straight-arm support; (3) swing the extended legs to the right and over the near bar; and (4) grab the far bar with the right hand and come to a support position. (Note that a flank mount and a rear mount are performed in a similar fashion except that either the side or the rear of the body faces the parallel bar when passing over it.)

Underbar Kip. (Figure 17-47) From a stand between bars with straight arms and using an inner grip: (1) jump to a piked position with the hips positioned between the hands; (2) swing forward in a deep pike position; (3) on the backswing extend the hips upward and forward as they pass between the hands, tightening the stomach muscles and pushing down with straight arms; (4) push the hips in front of the hands; and (5) either continue to a straight-arm support or bend the arms and come to an upper-arm support with the elbows out. (In learning this skill a position on the end of the bars facing in is helpful.)

Common Faults. Some common faults are (1) dropping the hips at the beginning; (2) extending the body; (3) bending the arms; and (4) a too-early hip extension.

Underbar Somersault to Upper-arm Support. (Figure 17-48) From a stand between bars with either an inner or an outer grip: (1) jump upward, raising the legs to a pike position; (2) as the hips pass under the hands, raise the head and chest and lift the hips between the hands; (3) vigorously extend the body by lifting the heels upward; (4) as the shoulders rise above the bars release the grip on the bars; and (5) regrasp the bars in an upper-arm support position. (This skill also can be initiated from a support position, dropping backward.)

Common Faults. Some common faults are (1) permitting the hips to rotate behind the hands; (2) not extending the body soon enough; and (3) releasing the bars too early.

Spotting. The spotter stands outside both bars and reaches under them. As the performer begins to extend, the spotter places his hands under the performer's stomach and chest.

Circling, Swinging, or Turning Skills

Single-leg Cut and Catch.* (Figure 17-49) From a support: (1) swing the body backward to a position

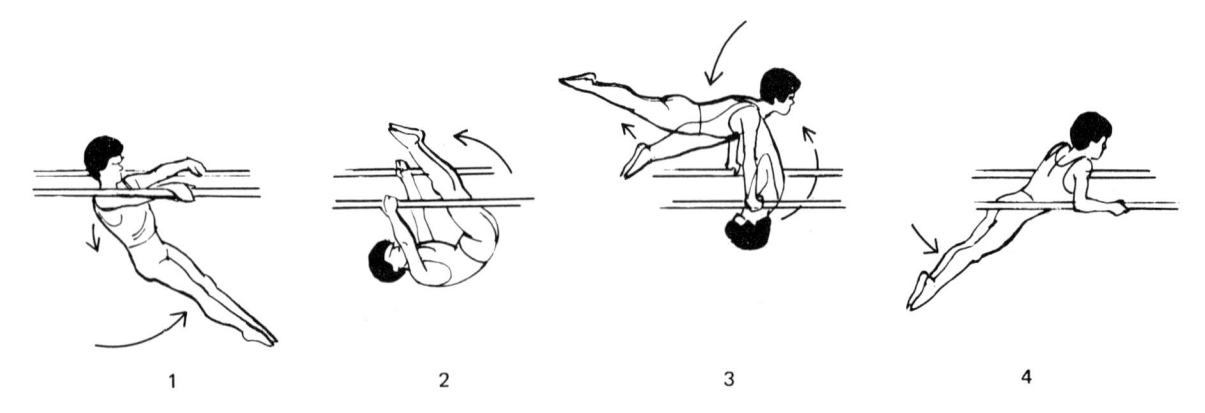

Figure 17-48. Underbar somersault to upper-arm support.

252   *Individual and Team Sports*

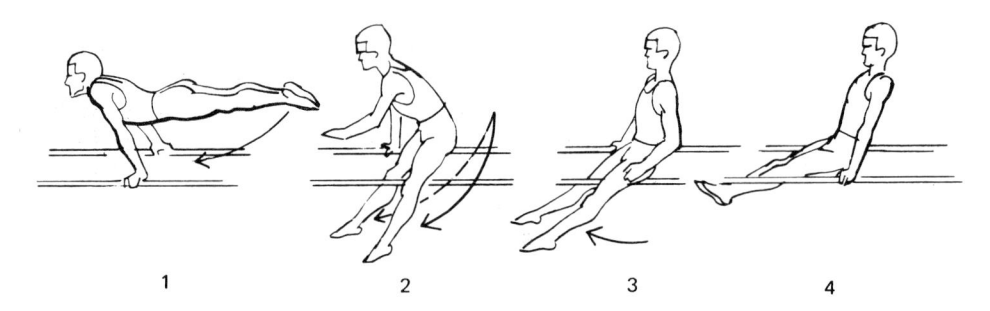

Figure 17-49. Single-leg cut and catch.

slightly higher than the bars; (2) at the end of the backswing, straddle the left leg sideward and forward, flexing the hips and releasing the left hand and leaning on the right hand; (3) swing both legs forward and to the center of the bars, and then quickly regrasp the left bar; and (4) repeat with the right leg.

Common Faults. Common faults are (1) raising the legs too high on the backswing; and (2) swinging the legs forward too slowly.

*Single-leg One-half Turn.** (Figure 17-50) From a swing while in a support position: (1) lean on the left arm on the forward swing, swinging the right leg over the left bar and at the same time releasing the right hand; (2) execute a one-half turn to the left, regrasping with the right hand in rear of the right leg and shifting the weight to the right arm; and (3) transfer the left hand to the opposite bar, swinging the right leg forward to a support position.

*Back Scissors with One-half Turn.** (Figure 17-51) From a swing while in a support position: (1) on the back swing, lean forward and turn to the left by swinging the right leg under the left leg; (2) release the left hand, completing the body turn to the left (facing the opposite direction from that at the start of movement); (3) release the right hand; (4) regrasp the hands behind the legs in a rear straddle support (right hand to left bar and left hand to right bar); and (5) end in a straddle sit position. (With

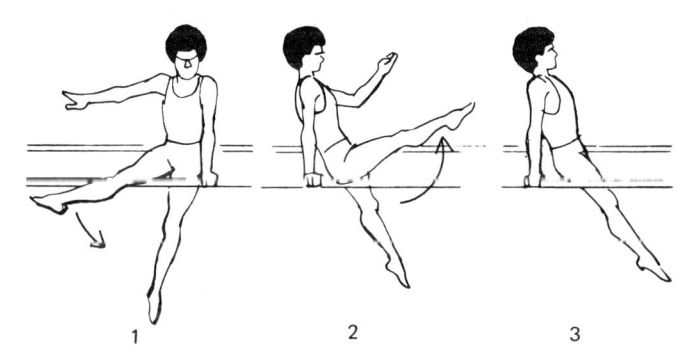

Figure 17-50. Single-leg one-half turn.

practice, the performer can continue his swinging motion, keeping his legs together.)

*Forward Roll from Sit.** (Figure 17-52) From a front straddle support: (1) bend the arms, lean forward, and turn the elbows outward (spreading them as wide as possible) keeping the hands close to the thighs; (2) lift the hips and direct the shoulders down on the bars close to the hands; (3) duck the head, forcing the hips overhead while maintaining pike position throughout and keeping the legs extended and spread as wide apart as possible, then release grasp and then regrasp, having moved the arms in the direction of body rotation, and shift the weight to the arms; (4) release the bars and continue to roll forward; and (5) regrasp the bars and come to a rear straddle support.

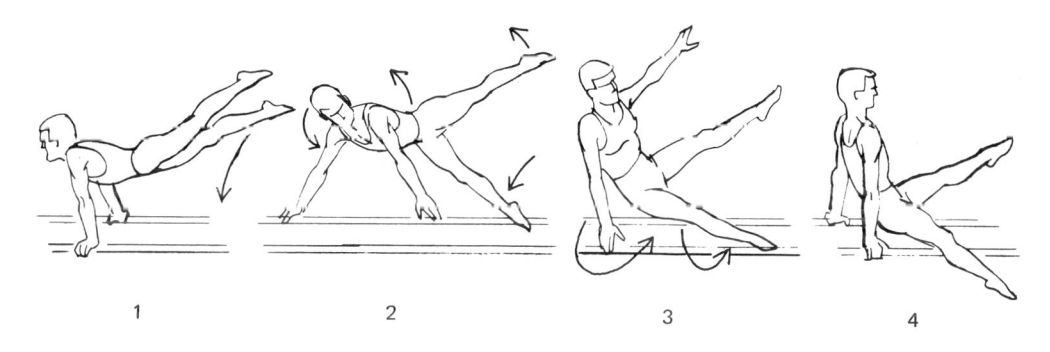

Figure 17-51. Back scissors with one-half turn.

Gymnastics: Apparatus

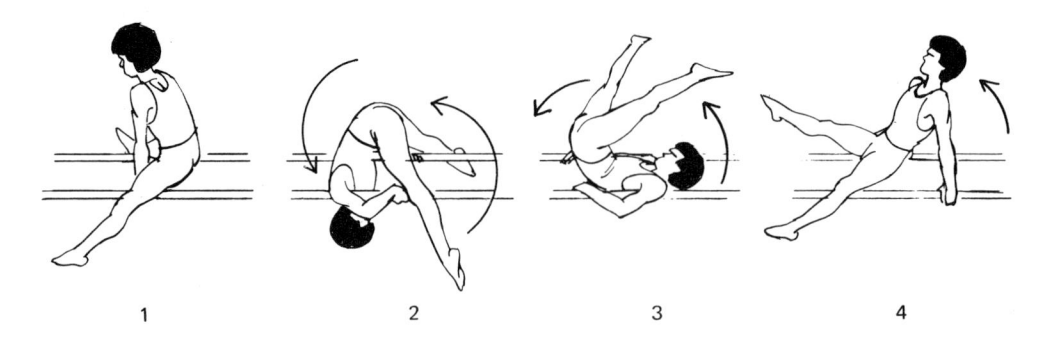

Figure 17-52. Forward roll from sit.

Common Fault. A common fault is extending the body during the forward roll.

Spotting. The spotter reaches under the bars and lifts the performer's shoulders and back during the roll.

*Backward Roll.** (Figure 17-53) From a rear straddle support or an upper-arm hang: (1) pike and lift the hips, falling back and turning the elbows outward; (2) roll backward leading with the legs while lifting the hips overhead (maintain the straddle and pike position); (3) release the bars and regrasp them in front of the legs (allowing gravity to finish the rolling action); and (4) regrasp the bars in rear of the legs.

Spotting. (Same as for the forward roll.)

Upper-arm Kip. (Figure 17-54) From an upper-arm hang position: (1) swing to a pike position with the hips above the bar, keeping the chin on the chest; (2) thrust the legs forward and obliquely upward at a 45° angle; (3) rotate the body around the hips and then extend it coming to a straight-arm support position. (During the learning stages the performer may instead come to a rear straddle seat position.)

Back Uprise. (Figure 17-55) From an upper-arm support: (1) swing forward, lifting the hips above the hands and come to a pike position; (2) swing the legs upward, forward, and downward, extending the body and shifting the shoulders forward close to the hands; (3) as the hips pass under the shoulders, pike slightly; (4) lean forward and shift the weight to the hands, extending the body and pushing down with the hands; (5) extend the arms while lifting the head and chest; and (6) come to a support position.

Front Uprise. (Figure 17-56) From an upper-arm support: (1) on the front swing downward, pike slightly as the hips pass under the shoulders, pulling the shoulders forward to the hands; (2) stretch the legs forward, lifting the hips forward and upward and pike the legs; and (3) at the end of the front swing, push down and back with the hands while lifting the head and chest and extending the body forward and leaning back. The lift of the hips should lift the entire body.

Common Faults. Common faults are (1) allowing the legs to swing too high in front; and (2) dragging the hips on the front swing.

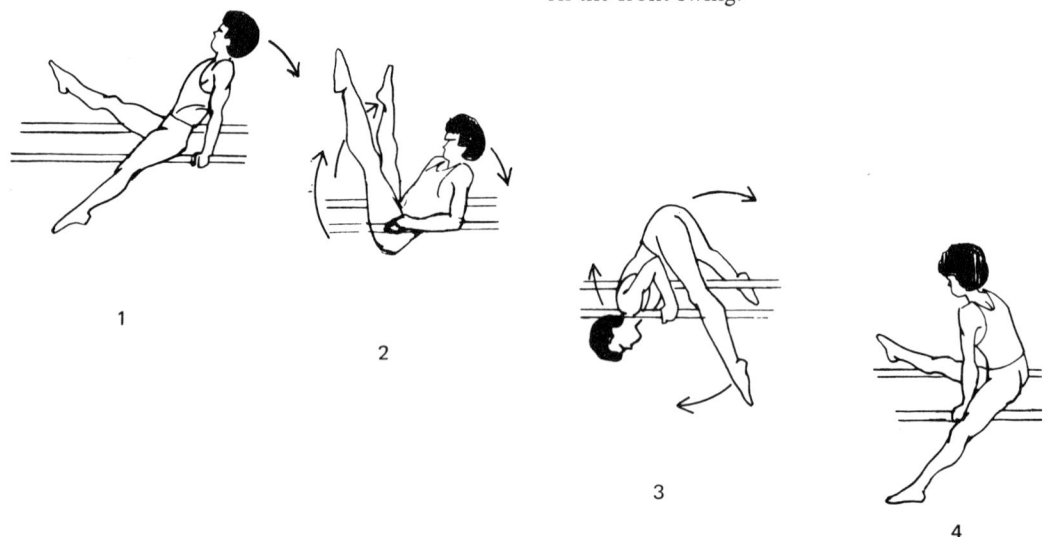

Figure 17-53. Backward roll.

254 *Individual and Team Sports*

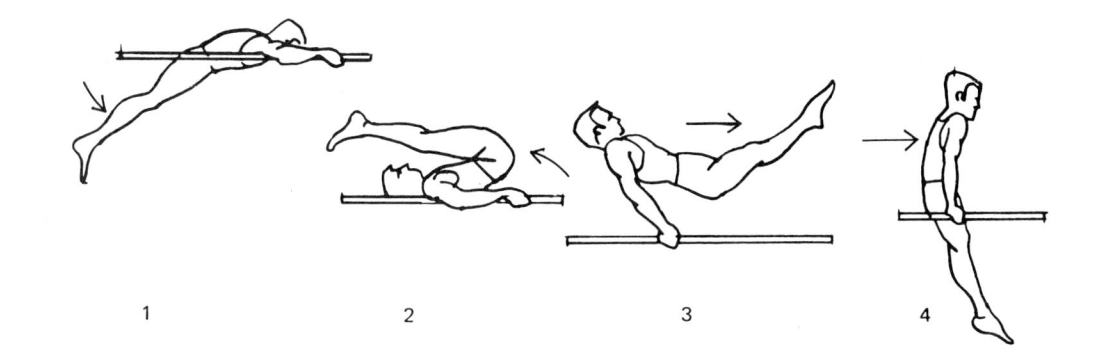

Figure 17-54. Upper-arm kip.

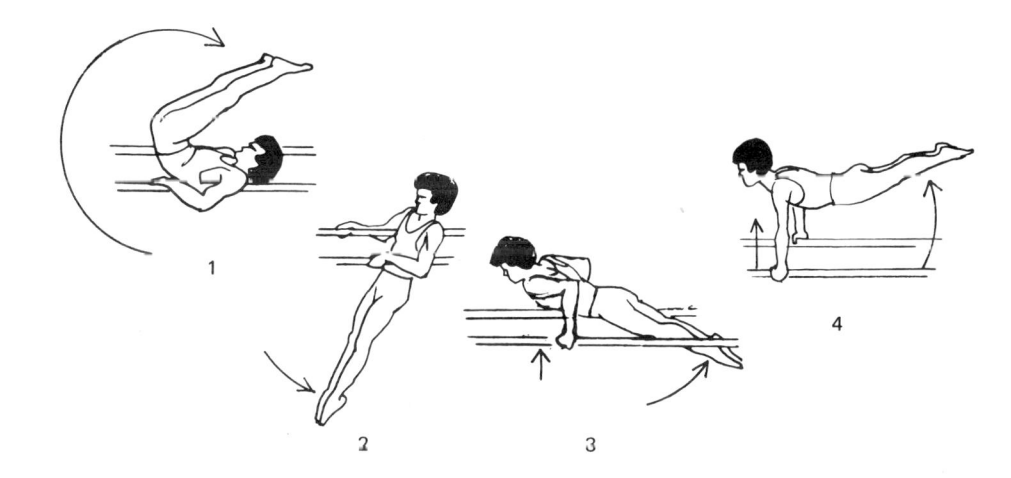

Figure 17-55. Back uprise.

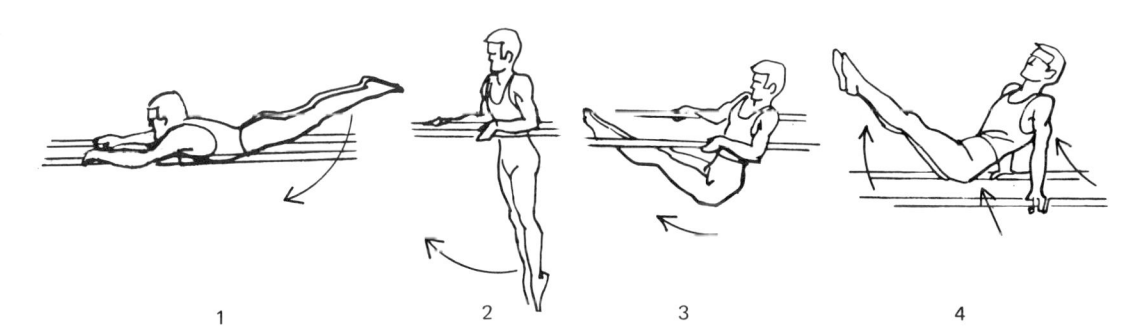

Figure 17-56. Front uprise.

Layout Back Shoulder Roll. (Figure 17-57) From a vigorous swing while in an upper-arm support: (1) pike very slightly on the upswing, pushing down on the bars hard (this skill can be performed with a straight body); (2) as the legs near an overhead position, extend the body, keeping the head back and lifting the chest; (3) release the bars with the hands reaching outward and backward; and (4) on the downswing regrasp the bars.

Spotting. The spotter stands outside the bars and reaches under them and supports the performer's back and shoulders on the upswing.

Undercast (Drop Kip). (Figure 17-58) From a support: (1) at the end of the forward swing fall backward, pushing the hips back and lifting the legs above the bars in a pike position; (2) drop under the bars; (3) as the body swings forward, lift the hips upward above the bars; and (4) as

Gymnastics: *Apparatus* 255

Figure 17-57. Layout back shoulder roll.

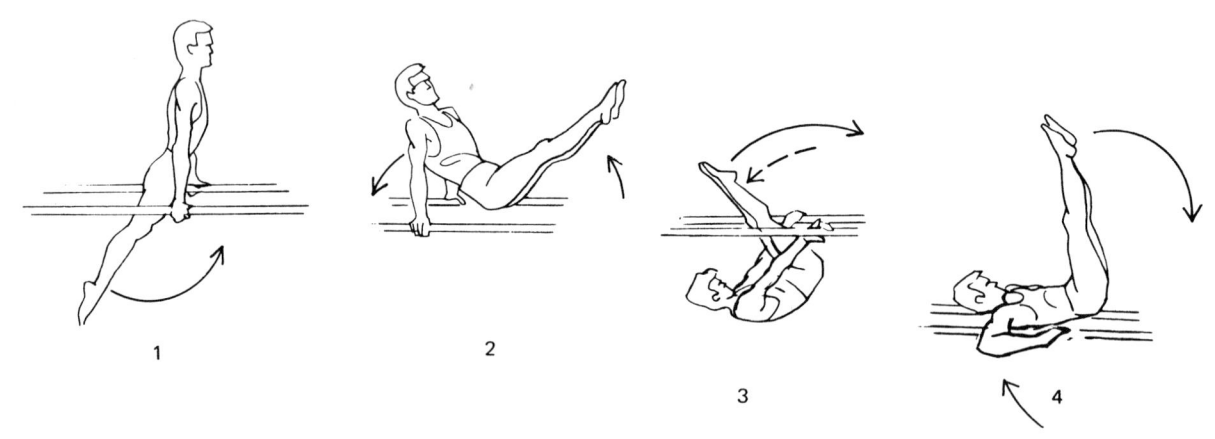

Figure 17-58. Undercast (drop kip).

the shoulders rise above the bars release the grip and regrasp in an upper-arm support with the hips above the hands. (With practice, the performer can come to a support position.)

Spotting. The spotter stands outside bars and reaches under bars. As the performer passes under the bars, the spotter lifts him under his back.

Double Cut and Catch.* (Figure 17-59) The double cut and catch is a straddle vault with a catch, performed from a swing while in a support position. At the end of the backward swing, just as the forward swing begins: (1) push forward and upward with the hands avoiding leaning too far forward; (2) straddle the legs forward, releasing both hands; and (3) as soon as the legs have cleared the bars, regrasp them and swing the legs together and downward with the hands. (This skill can be practiced first by performing a double cut to a rear straddle support position.)

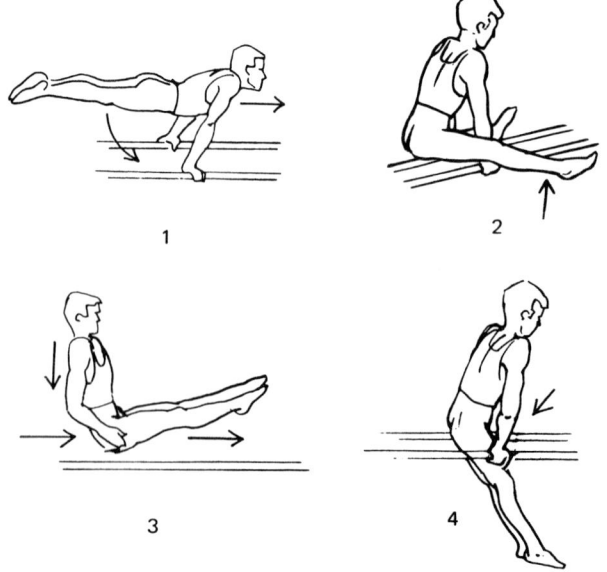

Figure 17-59. Double cut and catch.

256   *Individual and Team Sports*

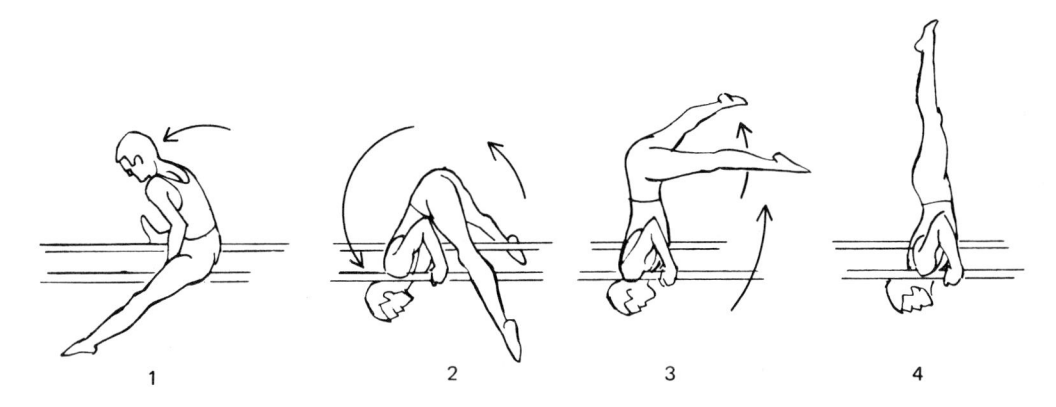

Figure 17-60. Shoulder stand.

Held Positions

Shoulder Stand.* (Figure 17-60) From a front straddle support: (1) bend the arms, turning the elbows outward and lean forward; (2) lift the hips and bring the shoulders down on the bars close to the hands; (3) as the hips reach a position overhead, slowly raise the legs above the hips to an extended body position, keeping the head up by looking directly downward (the weight should be evenly distributed on the hands and shoulders). (Should the performer overbalance and fall forward, he should immediately tuck his body as tightly as possible, extend his arms sideward, and roll forward to an upper-arm hang.)

Half Lever and Pirouette.* From a straight-arm support: (1) assume an L position; (2) shift the weight to the left arm and rotate the legs to the left; (3) grasp the left bar with the right hand while maintaining the L position; (4) release the bar with the left hand and swing the legs back to center of the bars; and (5) grasp the opposite bar with the left hand.

Handstand.* (Figure 17-61) From a support on end of the bars facing out: (1) swing forward and backward several times, rising higher each time, while maintaining a free swing from the shoulders; (2) on the back swing lean forward and pike slightly as the hips pass between the hands; (3) lean forward, extending the body; (4) as the body passes through a three-quarter handstand position, push the shoulders backward; and (5) stretch the body upward in a handstand position. Keep the head up throughout.

Spotting. In case of overbalancing, the performer should execute a one-half turn left or right and pike his legs and come to a stand. The spotter stands to the opposite side of the performer's turn and holds his upper arm.

Dismounts

Front Vault Dismount.* (Figure 17-62) From a swing while in a support: (1) on the backswing lift the body high; (2) push off with the right hand, swinging the legs over the left bar while leaning forward; and (3) as the landing is being made, grasp the left bar with the right hand.

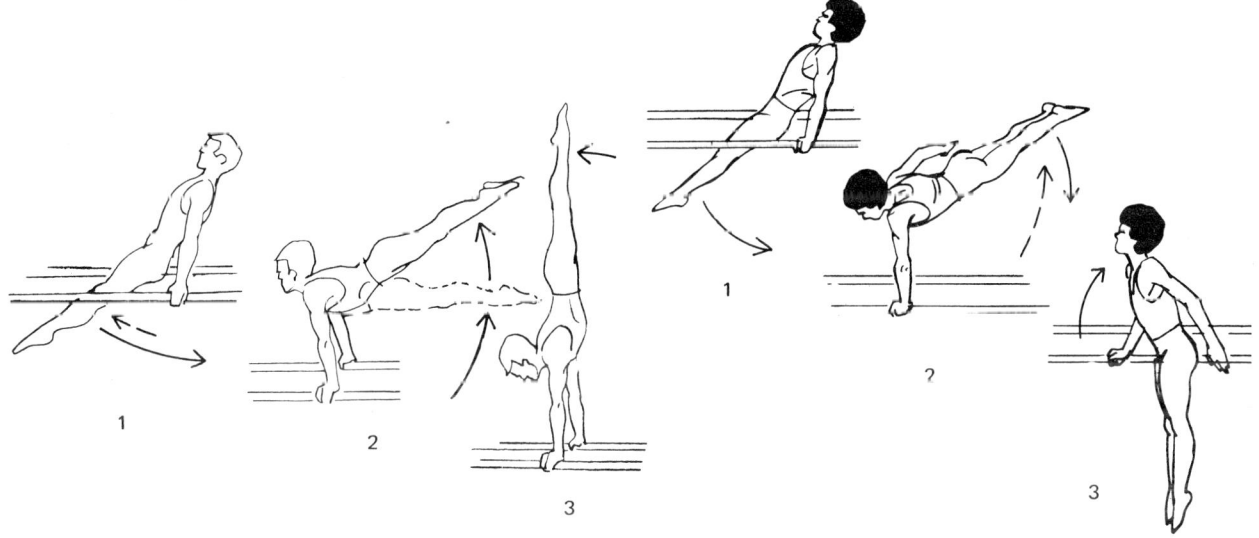

Figure 17-61. Handstand.

Figure 17-62. Front vault dismount.

Gymnastics: Apparatus

Figure 17-63. Rear vault dismount with one-half twist.

Spotting. The spotter stands in front of the performer and grasps him under the arms as he dismounts.

*Triple Rear Dismount.** The fact that the legs cross over the bar three times gives this name to the dismount. From an intermediate swing while in a support: (1) as the body passes the vertical on the backswing, shift the weight to the left leaning on the left arm; (2) raise the hips high, piking while circling the legs counterclockwise over the rear right bar, forward right bar, and then bring the legs under the body in a rear vault as the last movement of the dismount; and (3) as the body passes over the left bar, release the left hand from the bar and regrasp it with the right hand. (The important movement in this skill is to first transfer most of the body weight to the left arm and, as the leg circling movement is started, to move the body to the left and forward.)

*Rear Vault Dismount with One-half Twist.** (Figure 17-63) From a swing while in a support: (1) on the front swing extend the body and lean back; (2) push left with the right hand, swinging the legs over the left bar while extending the body; (3) grasp the left bar with the right hand and immediately turn (roll) the body over toward the right until the chest faces the mat, pushing with the right hand and reaching over the bar with the left hand; and (4) grasp the left bar with the left hand while landing.

*Straddle-cut Dismount (Straddle Vault).** (Figure 17-64) From a swing while in a support position at the end of the bars facing out: (1) on the backswing straddle the legs over the bars, leaning forward hard and keeping the head up; (2) flex the hips and swing the extended straddled legs forward, pushing forward and releasing the bars; and (3) bring the legs together before landing.

Sample Routines on the Parallel Bars

1. Front mount, single-leg cut and catch, front-vault dismount.
2. Flank mount, single-leg one-half turn, rear-vault dismount.
3. Rear mount, back scissors with one-half turn, rear-vault dismount with one-half twist.
4. Underbar kip, upper-arm kip, forward roll, straddle-cut dismount.
5. Underbar kip, front uprise, shoulder stand, backward roll, straddle-cut dismount.
6. Underbar somersault, half lever and pirouette, undercut, triple rear dismount.
7. Underbar somersault, front uprise, handstand, double cut and catch, triple rear dismount.

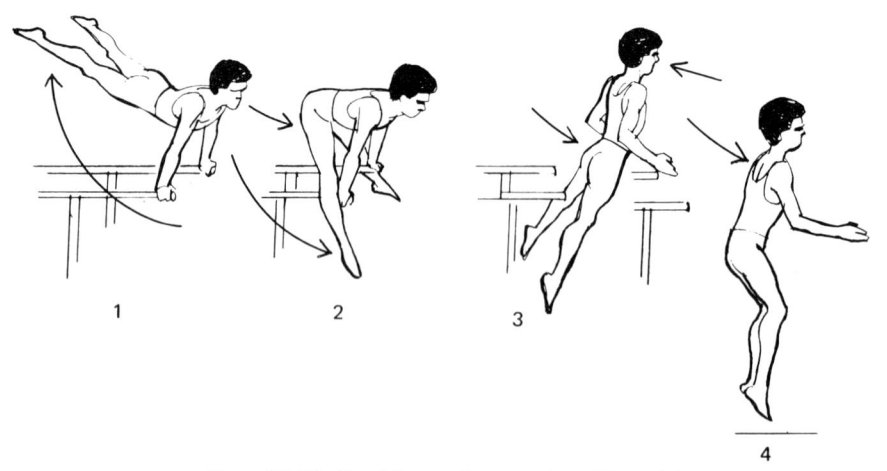

Figure 17-64. Straddle-cut dismount (straddle vault).

258   *Individual and Team Sports*

Figure 17-65. Pommel horse.

POMMEL HORSE

The pommel horse, (Figure 17-65) formerly known as the side horse, was originated as a device to help train knights in armor to mount their horses during the Middle Ages. The first United States competition on the side horse was in 1921. A championship exercise on the pommel horse must be composed of clean swinging movements, without stops, and with double-leg circles predominating. The performer must use all three parts of the horse (both ends and the center), and two scissors must be executed in succession. An entire exercise involves the intricate changing of balance from hand to hand. Major faults include breaks in continuity, touching of the horse with the body, and poorly controlled landings.

The learner's early efforts on the pommel horse may seem ineffectual. However, with patience and many practice sessions the learning curve begins to surge upward. Perhaps the earliest (and most basic) skills are the slowest to be learned, but they are the basis for an advanced performance on this difficult apparatus. Balance is maintained on the horse by shifting the shoulders from side to side and from front to back, as illustrated in Figure 17-66. The arms should be kept straight, while the hands move quickly, regardless of the tempo of the performance. Note that as the legs pass to the left, the right shoulder is well over the right pommel, as depicted in Figure 17-66(*A*).

Figure 17-66(*B*) illustrates the backward lean as the body passes through a rear support, whereas Figure 17-66(*C*) illustrates the forward lean as the body passes through a front support.

For purposes of description, the pommel horse is divided into the three areas shown in Figure 17-67. As the performer faces the horse, the *neck* is to his left and the *croup* is to his right. The area between the pommels is referred to as the *saddle*.

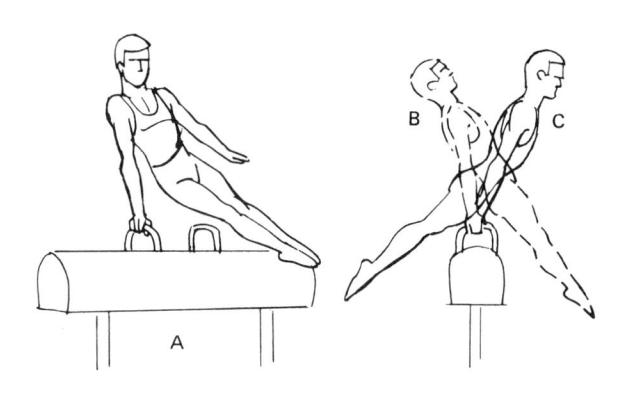

Figure 17-66. Principles of balance.

The pommel horse is generally not considered a hazardous apparatus; however, falls do occur. Therefore, mats should be placed around the apparatus in order that no floor surface is exposed. The body and pommels of the side horse should be free of grease and moisture, and a fine-grade emery cloth should be used on the pommels to rid them of chalk deposits.

Basic Fundamentals
Basic Swing.

From a Rear Support. (1) Shift the body weight from one arm to the other, swinging the legs in opposite directions (the axis of the swing is at the shoulders); (2) release a pommel each time, (3) swing the hips the total distance between the pommels; and (4) maintain balance by keeping the shoulders and head to the rear of the horse. (See Figure 17-66.)

From a Front Support. Execute the preceding procedure with the exception of maintaining balance, which is done by keeping the head and shoulders to the front of the horse.

Mounts
Flank Mount. (Figure 17-68) From a stand facing the horse: (1) jump to a support and then, while leaning to the right release the left hand; (2) swing both legs under the left hand; and (3) regrasp the left pommel and come to a rear-support position with the hips stretched forward.

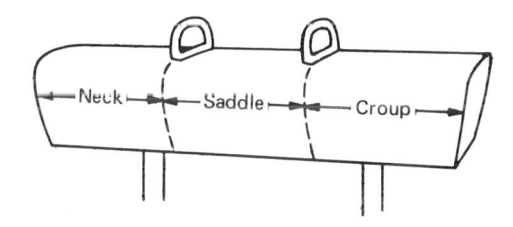

Figure 17-67.

Gymnastics: Apparatus

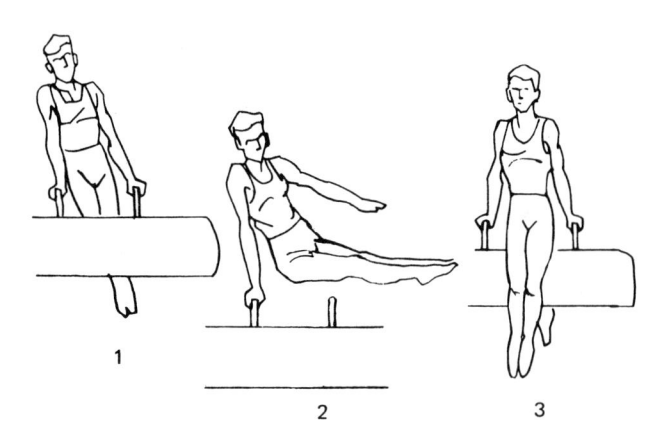

Figure 17-68. Flank mount.

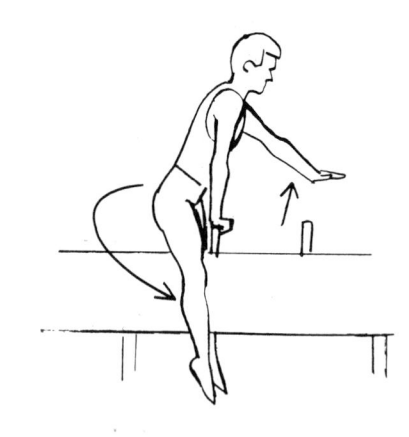

Figure 17-70. Feint balance.

Single-leg Rear Mount. (Figure 17-69) From a stand at the neck with the right hand on the left pommel and the left hand on the neck: (1) jump to a support, swinging both legs under the left hand and leaning back and to the right; (2) raise the legs as the hips pass in front of the right hand, executing a one-half turn to the right; (3) swing the right leg over the far pommel; and (4) grasp the far pommel with the left hand.

Common Faults. Common faults are (1) raising the legs too early; and (2) beginning the one-half turn too early.

Circling, Swinging, or Turning Skills

Feint Balance. (Figure 17-70) From a stand facing the horse, with the hands on the pommels: (1) jump to a support, swinging the right leg over the right pommel; (2) release the left pommel; and (3) come to a balanced position over the right pommel. (The feint-balance position is an excellent one from which to initiate a circling movement.)

Single-leg Flanks (Single-leg Half Circle). (Figure 17-71) From a front support: (1) lean to the left and swing the right leg under the right hand; (2) lean to the right and swing the left leg under the left hand; (3) lean to the left and swing the right leg back under the right hand; and (4) lean to the right and swing the left leg back under the left hand (the movements should be continuous).

Swing with Single-leg Flanks. (Figure 17-72) From a front support: (1) swing the right leg under the right hand; (2) swing the hips to the left, leaning to the right;

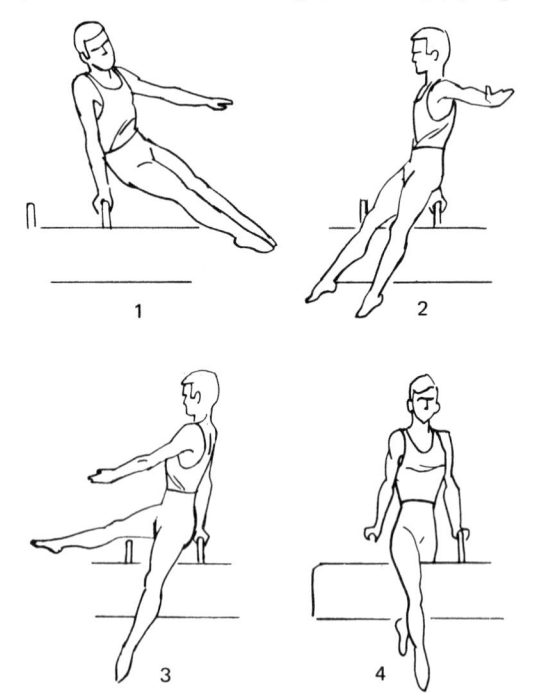

Figure 17-69. Single-leg rear mount.

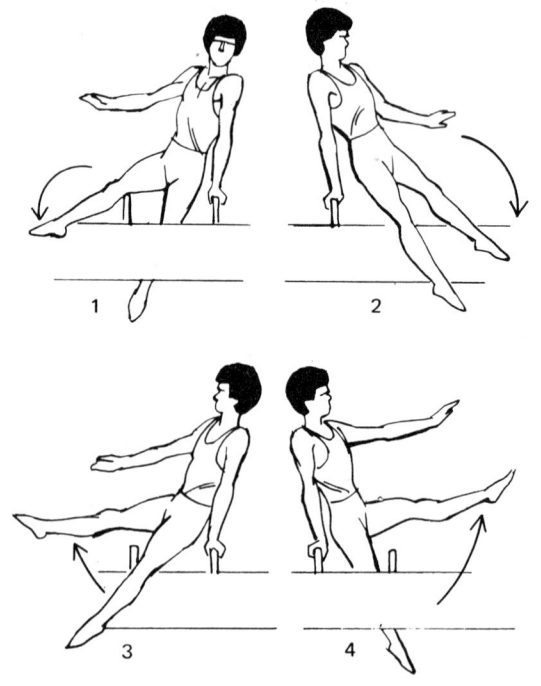

Figure 17-71. Single-leg flanks (single-leg half circle).

260 *Individual and Team Sports*

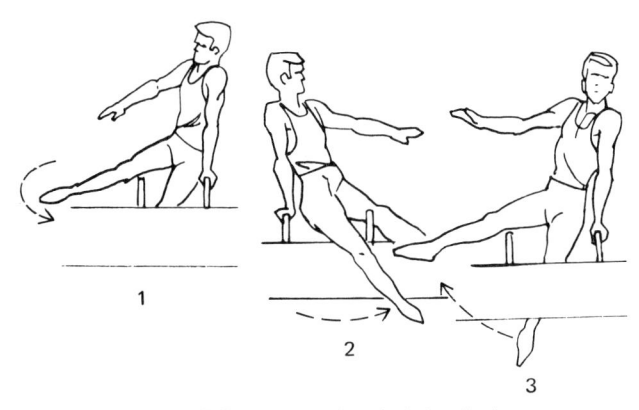

Figure 17-72. Swing with single-leg flanks.

(3) swing the right leg back under the right hand, leaning to the left; and (4) repeat to the opposite side.

Undercuts (Inside Cuts). (Figure 17-73) From a rear support: (1) swing the left leg to the right under the right leg and back under the right hand (pushing the right leg forward); (2) continue circling the left leg under the left hand; (3) end in a rear support; and (4) repeat to the opposite side. The emphasis should be on moving the hips—forward, sideward, and backward.

Single-leg Circle. (Figure 17-74) From a front support: (1) swing the left leg under the left hand, leaning to the right; (2) swing the hips to the right and swing the left leg under the right hand, leaning to the left.

Common Fault. A common fault is twisting the hips to the right as the left leg passes over the right pommel.

Single-leg Travel. (Figure 17-75) From a front support on the croup: (1) swing the right leg under the right hand; (2) swing the left leg to a feint position (needle position) on right pommel; (3) transfer the right hand to the right pommel (in front of the left hand); (4) swing the right leg back; (5) swing the left leg back; and (6) grasp the left pommel with left hand. The movement must be continuous.

Figure 17-74. Single-leg circle.

Double-leg Flank (Double Leg Half-Circle). From a front-support position: (1) repeat the action used to perform the single-leg flanks, except that both legs are kept together and extended; (2) pass them around the horse to a rear support; and (3) reverse the direction of travel of both legs and return to the starting position.

Front Scissors. (Figure 17-76) From a front support: (1) swing the right leg under the right hand; (2) swing the hips to the left; (3) release the left pommel, swinging the left leg forward and the right leg back under the left leg; (4) regrasp the left pommel; and (5) repeat to opposite side.

Common Faults. Common faults are (1) twisting the hips to the left as the legs scissor; and (2) having the hips too low as the legs scissor.

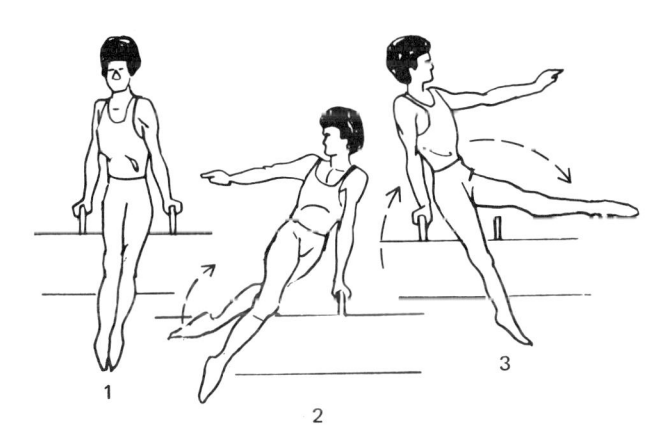

Figure 17-73. Undercuts (inside cuts).

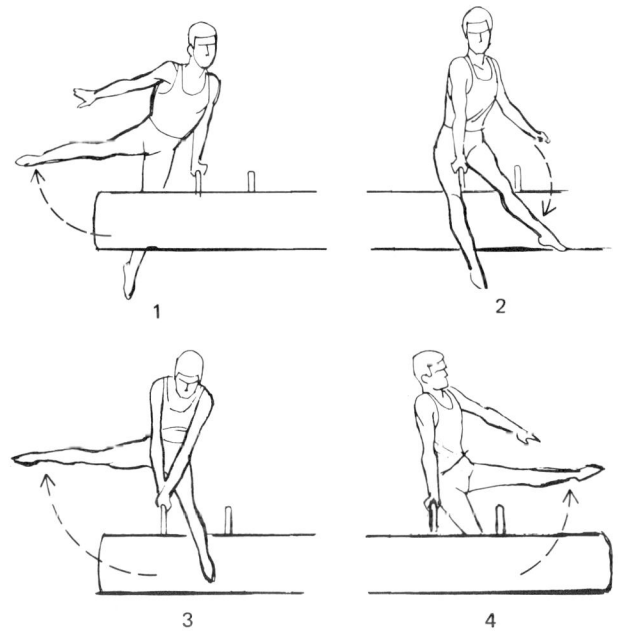

Figure 17-75. Single-leg travel.

Gymnastics: Apparatus **261**

Figure 17-76. Front scissors.

Back Scissor. (Figure 17-77) From a rear support: (1) swing the right leg back under the right hand; (2) swing the hips to the left; (3) leaning to the right, release the left hand and swing the left leg backward and the right leg forward under the left leg; (4) regrasp the left pommel; and (5) repeat to the opposite side.

Low Double-leg Circles. (Figure 17-78) Low double-leg circles are the lead-up skill to free double-leg circles. Advanced horse work is dependent on the latter skill.

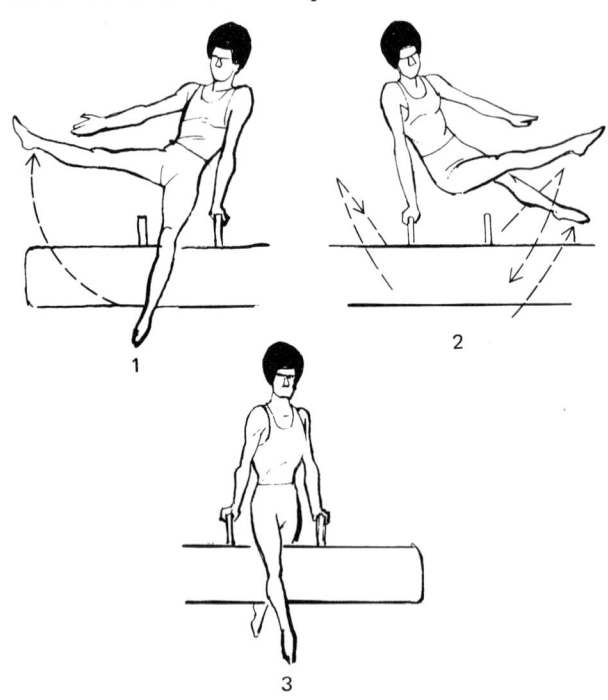

Figure 17-77. Back scissor.

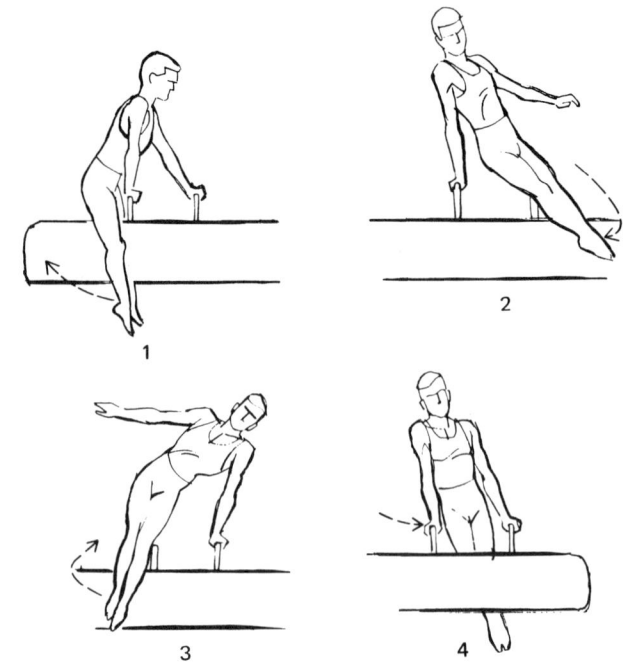

Figure 17-78. Low double-leg circles.

From a feint on the right pommel: (1) swing the right leg back; (2) swing the legs under the left hand, stretching the body to the left and leaning to the right; (3) swing the hips to the right, lifting and twisting them slightly to the left while leaning to the left; (4) swing the legs under the right hand; and (5) repeat movements 1-4.

Common Faults. Common faults are (1) failure to swing the hips wide to the left as the legs pass under the left hand; and (2) permitting the hips to turn to the right.

Double-leg Travel. (Figure 17-79) From a stride leg support with the right leg in front: (1) swing the right leg back under the right hand, leaning to the left; (2) transfer the right hand to the left pommel (in front of the left hand—the head should be above the left pommel); (3) swing the legs left over the neck, leaning to right; and (4) place the left hand on the neck.

Common Faults. Common faults are (1) bending the arms; and (2) not leaning over the horse and over the pommel.

Dismounts

Flank Dismount. From a feint position on right pommel: (1) swing the right leg back; (2) swing both legs to the left under the left hand, leaning to the right; and (3) release the right pommel.

Flank Circle Quarter-turn Dismount. (Figure 17-80) From a front support at the neck with the left hand on the neck and the right hand on the left pommel: (1) feint right and circle the legs under the left hand; (2) release

262 *Individual and Team Sports*

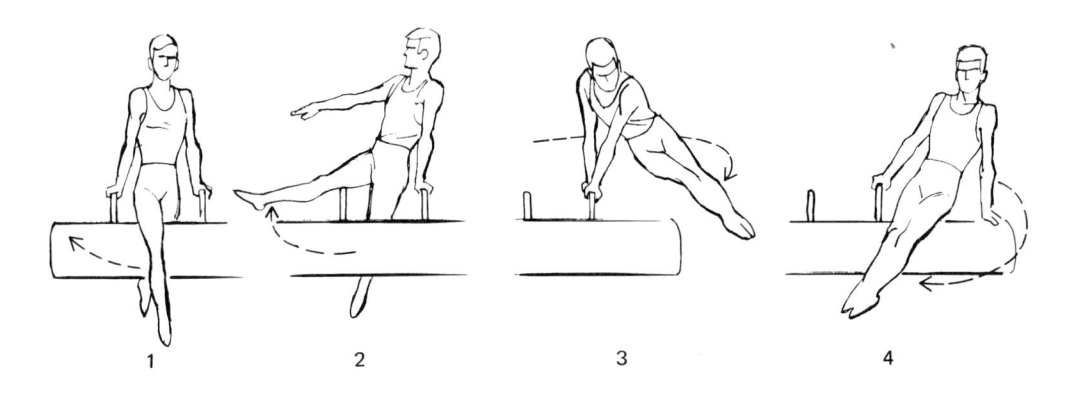

Figure 17-79. Double-leg travel.

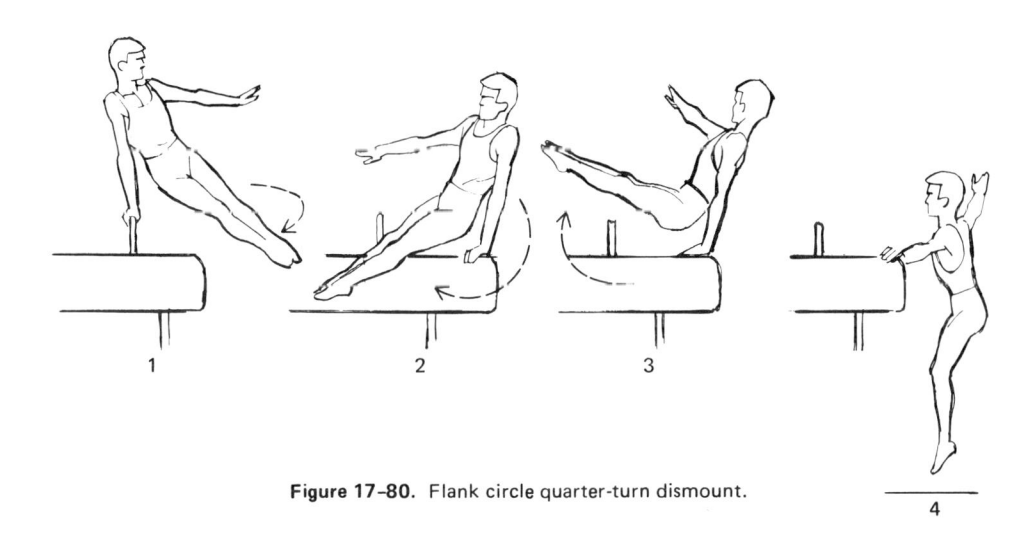

Figure 17-80. Flank circle quarter-turn dismount.

the right hand, shifting the weight to the left arm; and (3) dismount with a one-quarter turn to the right while in a pike position.

Common Faults. Common faults are (1) hips too close to the horse during the circle; and (2) bending the pivot arm.

Double Rear Dismount. (Figure 17-81) From a feint on the right pommel: (1) swing the right leg back; (2) swing both legs under the left hand, leaning back and to the right; (3) raise the legs, executing a one-quarter turn right; (4) as the legs pass over the croup, place the left hand on the croup and release the right hand; and (5) dismount.

Common Faults. Common faults are (1) failure to swing the hips in front of the right pommel when executing the turn; and (2) raising the legs too soon.

Examples of Pommel-horse Exercises

1. Flank mount, double-leg flank, flank dismount.
2. Flank mount, two undercuts, one-half undercut, flank dismount.
3. Feint balance, single-leg flank, double-leg flank, single-leg travel to neck, flank circle quarter-turn dismount.
4. Feint balance, two single-leg circles, single-leg travel to neck, flank circle quarter-turn dismount.

Figure 17-81. Double rear dismount.

Gymnastics: Apparatus **263**

5. Single-leg rear mount, front scissors, double rear dismount.
6. Single-leg rear mount, front scissors, back scissors, feint, double rear dismount.
7. Single-leg rear mount, front scissors to feint, four double-leg circles, double rear dismount.

LONG HORSE (VAULTING)

The first gymnastics competition in the United States in the long-horse event was in 1897. In championship competition the performer is required to execute one vault. If not satisfied with this vault, he can elect a second but different vault, which will be counted, even if inferior to the first. The hand touch on the long horse must occur in specific zones or the performer is penalized. (See Figure 17-82.)

Because the beginner must vault over the length of the long horse, his earliest attempts may prove ineffectual. Therefore, it is necessary first to learn certain lead-up activities that involve the basic principles of vaulting. These are (1) vaulting from a take-off board onto a mat, and (2) vaulting the width of the long horse or the pommel horse (either can be used at first). During the early learning stages, simple vaults can be performed from a stand or a walk. A trampoline or gymnasium springboard are sometimes used to gain additional spring when vaults are practiced.

Vaults on the long horse are performed by "tapping" off the horse with the hands. The long horse is divided into three areas and two penalty zones, as illustrated in Figure 17-83. The croup is the end of the horse nearest the take-off board.

The floor area used for the run should be free of dust or any substance that might be slippery. Rubber-soled gymnastic slippers should be worn during any vaulting activity. Wiping the soles of the slippers on a wet towel will help prevent sliding. A double thickness of mats should be placed well beyond the horse and the area where the performer normally lands. One or two spotters should be positioned on the far side of the horse in order to assist the performer during his flight and landing. The distance of the take-off board from the horse will vary with the vault being performed. However, the board should always be placed so that the performer will not hit the horse on his take-off.

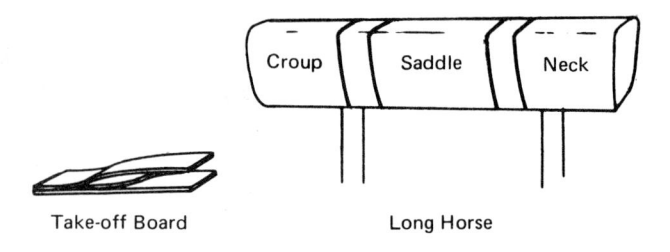

Figure 17-83.

Run and Take-off

A steady stride with increasing velocity should be practiced. The last stride should be about four to six feet in front of the board. The feet must touch down on the board concurrently without contacting it with the heels. As the feet make contact with the board, the knees are slightly flexed and they extend immediately and suddenly. If the last stride of the run is taken far enough in advance of the board, the feet will land on the board slightly ahead of the body, as depicted in Figure 17-84, and the resulting rebound will be such that the body will be carried upward and forward. If the last stride is taken too close to the board, the resulting rebound will carry the performer forward into the horse.

First practice jumping off the board by running a few steps. Then increase the distance of the run, and practice running at a fast pace. Be sure that the last few steps are the fastest of the run. Practice a high jump from the board by reaching for some object held about eight feet high, as shown in Figure 17-85.

Basic Vaults

The basic vaults included in this section are done over the width of the horse. As the performer becomes increasingly proficient, the height of the horse can be increased by stages from about forty-four to fifty-three inches.

When performing the basic vaults a firm and sudden tap-off should be utilized. The head and chest should be lifted, and the body extended prior to the landing.

Figure 17-82. Long horse (vaulting).

Individual and Team Sports

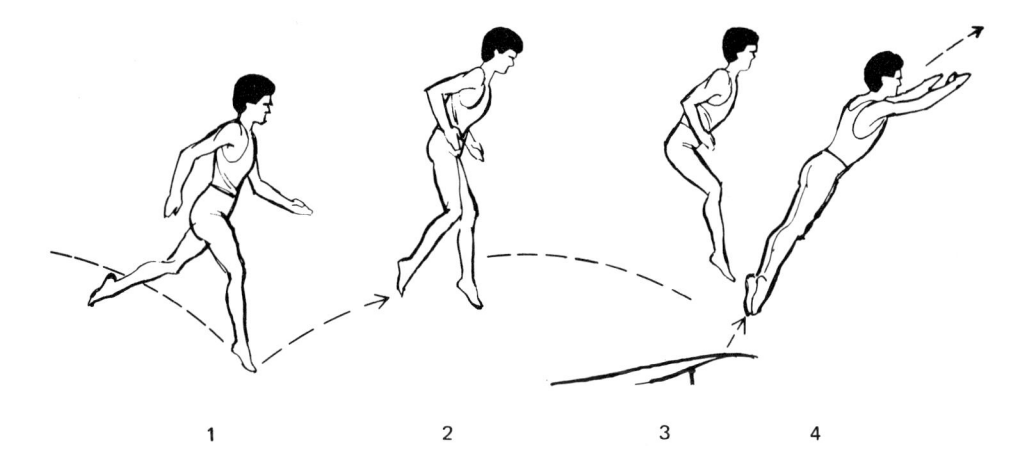

Figure 17-84. The take-off.

Squat Vault On–Leap Off. (Figure 17-86) This vault is performed as depicted in Figure 17-86.

Squat Vault. (Figure 17-87) (1) On the take-off, jump and press upward with the arms; (2) lean forward and tuck the body; (3) press to the rear with the hands; and (4) release the hands after the body passes the apparatus and land on the feet.

Flank Vault. (Figure 17-88) (1) Jump and press upward with the arms; (2) the legs swing left and upward with the weight on the left arm; (3) as the legs swing over the apparatus, release the right arm; (4) as the right arm swings upward and outward, the body assumes an arched position; and (5) flex the hips for the landing.

Figure 17-86. Squat vault on–leap off.

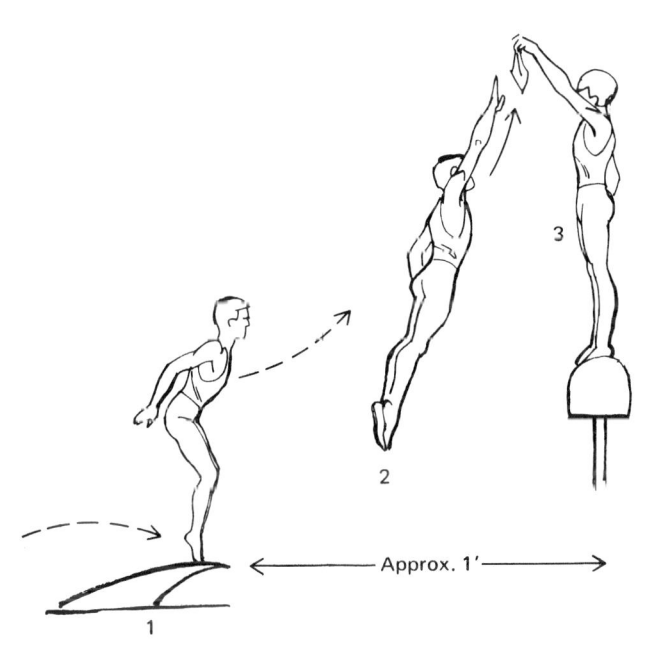

Figure 17-85. Technique for attaining height.

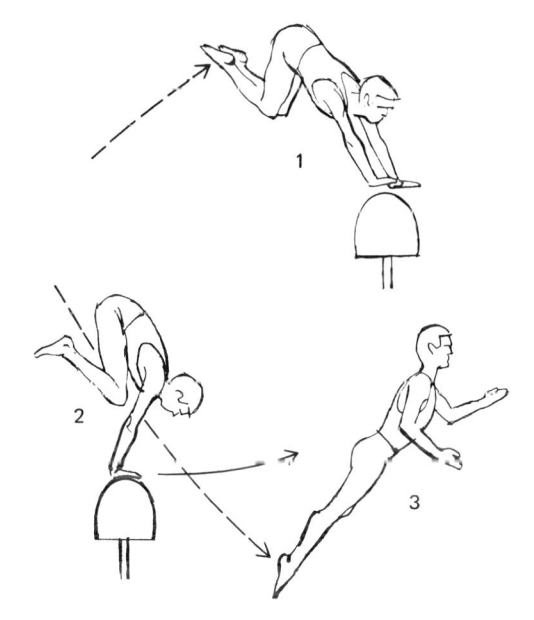

Figure 17-87. Squat vault.

Gymnastics: Apparatus 265

Figure 17-88. Flank vault.

Straddle Vault. (Figure 17-89) The vaulter should first jump to a straddle stand several times. (1) Jump, press down with the arms, pike the hips, and straddle the legs; (2) lean forward and push to the rear with the hands; (3) release both hands as the legs go over the apparatus; and (4) bring the legs together for the landing.

Neck Spring. (Figure 17-90) (1) Jump, press with the arms and pike the hips, keeping the head up; (2) as the hips begin to come overhead, tuck the head under, bend the arms, and place the neck on the horse, supporting the body with the arms; (3) pause in a kip position for an instant; and (4) drop the hips, snap with the arms, and arch to a landing.

Stoop Vault. (Figure 17-91) This is a squat vault except that the legs are straight and together. (1) Jump and execute a high pike; (2) push upward and to the rear with the arms; and (3) extend the body for the landing.

Handspring Vault. (Figure 17-92) (1) During the take-off, keep the head up; (2) attempt to float over the apparatus and come to a handstand position; (3) as the body begins to fall over backward, give a slight push to the rear with the hands and snap the head forward; and (4) maintain an arched position to a landing.

Figure 17-89. Straddle vault.

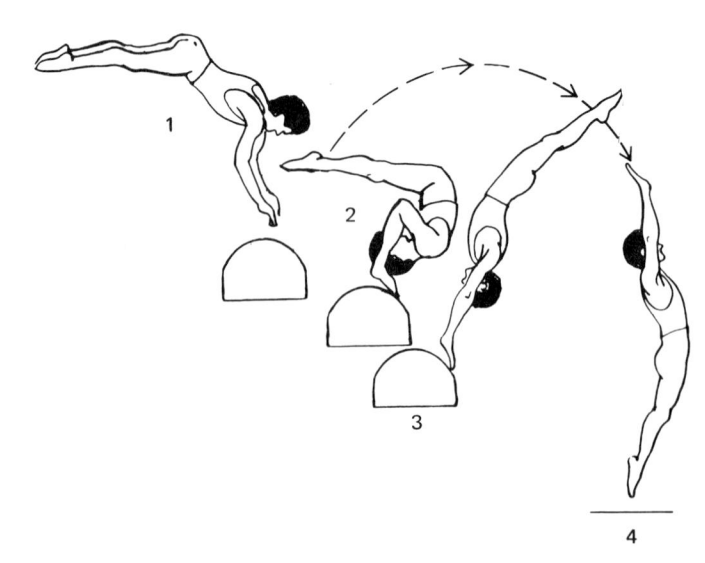

Figure 17-90. Neck spring.

266 *Individual and Team Sports*

Figure 17-91. Stoop vault.

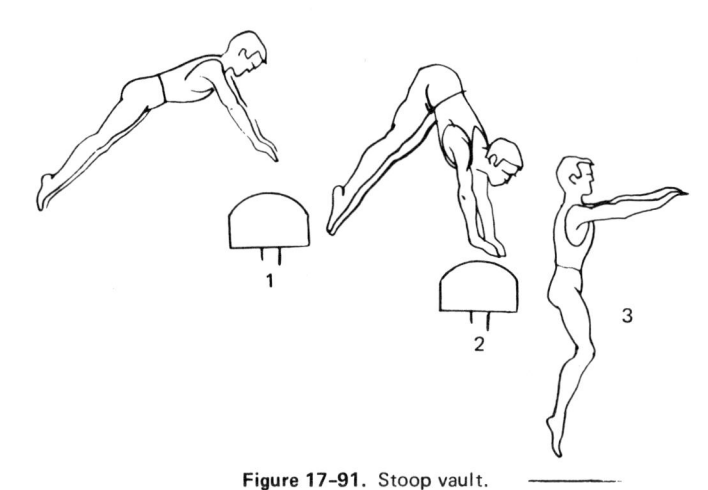

Advanced Vaults

When learning vaults over the length of the horse, its height can be raised by stages from 44 to 53 inches.

Mount to Squat on Neck. (Figure 17-93) (1) From the take-off reach upward and forward toward the neck; (2) lift the hips; (3) bend the legs, ending in a squat support on the neck; and (4) execute a high arched leap dismount.

Squat Vault from Neck. (Figure 17-94) (1) Begin as in the previous vault; (2) tap off with the hands on the neck; and (3) lift the head and chest, extending the body prior to landing.

Straddle Vault from Saddle. (Figure 17-95) (1) From the take-off reach for the saddle, lifting the legs and extending the body; (2) straddle the legs; (3) tap off from the saddle; and (4) lift the head and chest.

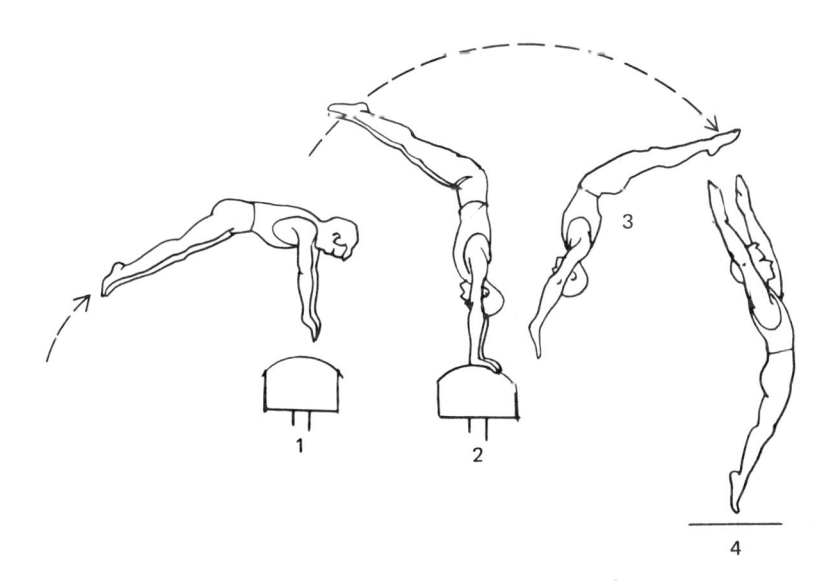

Figure 17-92. Handspring vault.

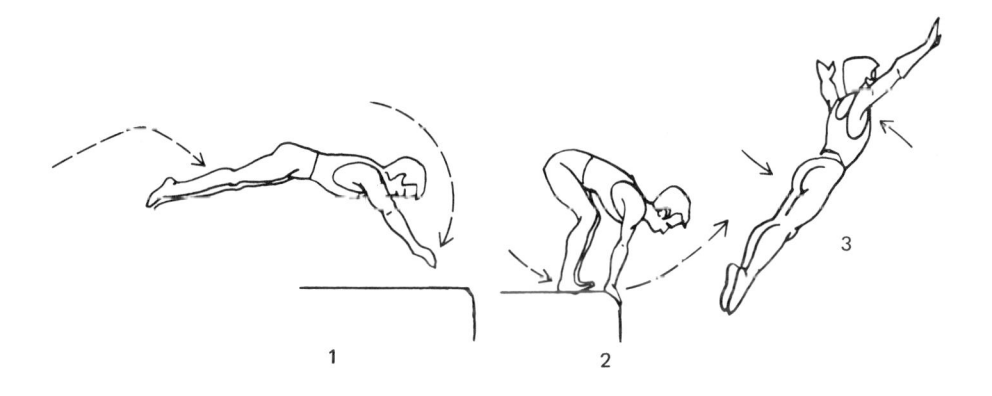

Figure 17-93. Mount to squat on neck.

Gymnastics: Apparatus **267**

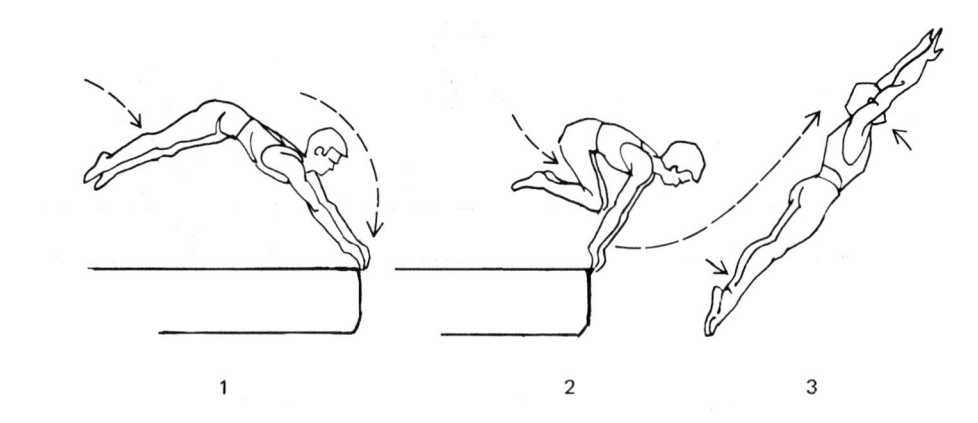

Figure 17-94. Squat vault from neck.

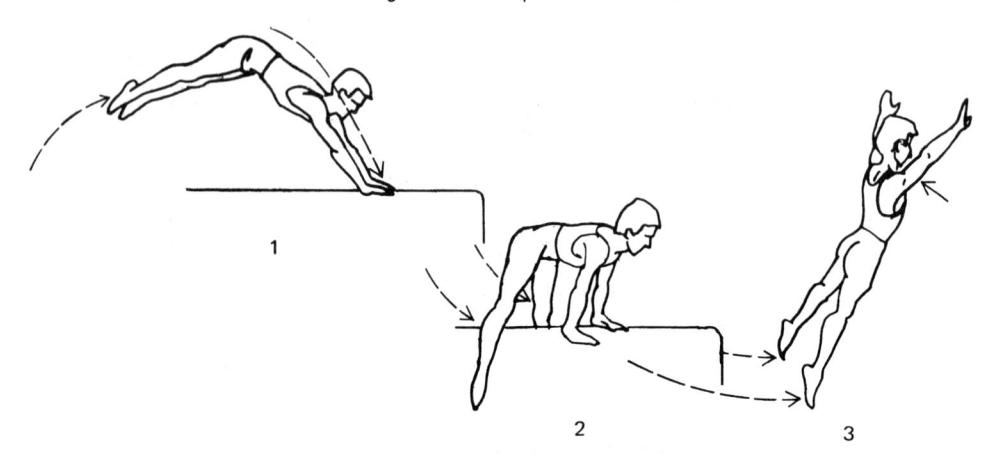

Figure 17-95. Straddle vault from saddle.

Straddle Vault from Neck. (Figure 17-96) This is executed as the previous vault, but the hand contact is on the neck.

Stoop Vault from Saddle with Dismount to Side. (Figure 17-97) (1) From the take-off reach for the saddle, lifting the legs high; (2) pike, flexing the hips upward; and (3) push off to one side of the horse.

Squat Vault from Croup. (Figure 17-98) (1) From the takeoff quickly tap off the croup; (2) lift the hips and tuck the legs; and (3) extend the body prior to landing.

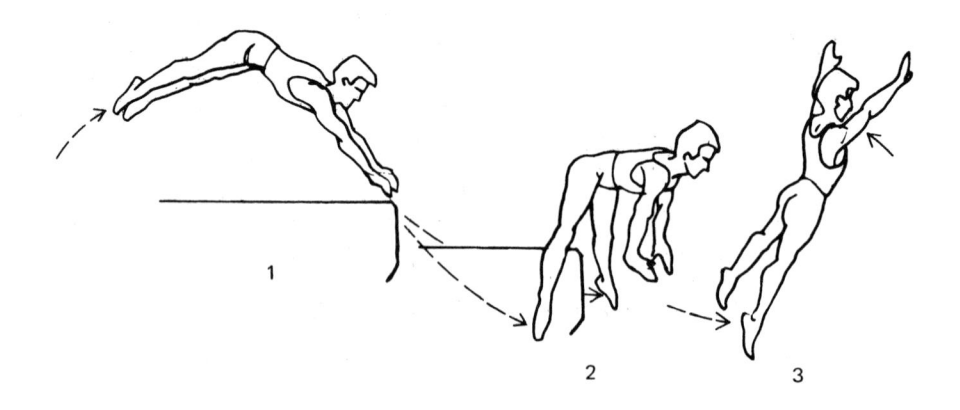

Figure 17-96. Straddle vault from neck.

268 *Individual and Team Sports*

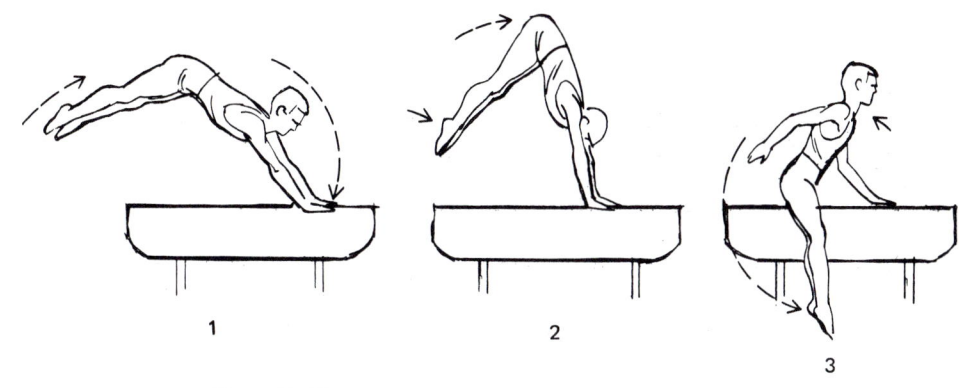

Figure 17-97. Stoop vault from saddle with dismount to side.

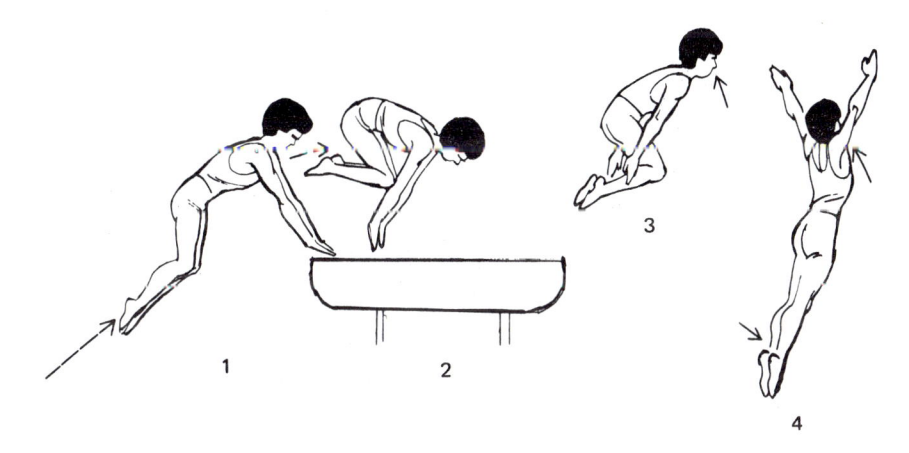

Figure 17-98. Squat vault from croup.

SELF-EVALUATION

The nature of apparatus work is such that the evaluation of the gymnastics performer needs to be made by an instructor or knowledgeable performer. One simple self-evaluation method is to record the number of skills mastered on each piece of apparatus. Another is to self-score (0- to 10-point scale) each apparatus exercise or vault, deducting points for breaks in form and continuity, and keep a running total of the total sum of points achieved on all routines.

Selected References

BOOKS

Baley, James A. *Gymnastics in the Schools.* Boston: Allyn, 1965.

Frey, Harold J., and Charles J. Kenney. *Elementary Gymnastics Apparatus Skills Illustrated.* New York: Ronald, 1964.

Loken, Newton C., and Robert J. Willoughby. *Complete Book of Gymnastics.* Englewood Cliffs, N.J.: Prentice-Hall, 1959.

Musker, Frank F., Donald R. Casady, and Leslie W. Irwin. *A Guide to Gymnastics.* New York: Macmillan, Inc., 1968.

Price, Hartley D., et al. *Gymnastics and Tumbling.* Annapolis, Md.: United States Naval Institute, 1959.

Ryser, Otto E. *A Teacher's Manual for Tumbling and Apparatus Stunts.* Dubuque, Iowa: Brown, 1961.

Taylor, Bruce, Boris Barjin, and Tom Zivic. *Olympic Gymnastics for Men and Women.* Englewood Cliffs, N.J.: Prentice-Hall, 1972.

PERIODICALS

Amateur Athletic Union Official Gymnastics Guide and Handbook. 231 West 58th St., New York, New York 10019.

The Modern Gymnast. P. O. Box 611, Santa Monica, California 90406.

The Official National Collegiate Athletic Association Gymnastics Guide. The National Collegiate Athletic Bureau, New York, New York 10017.

CHAPTER 18

Handball
Donald R. Casady*
The University of Iowa

HISTORY

Games similar to the modern game of handball appear to have been played by man during most of his recorded history. The Egyptians were playing a game in which a ball was batted with the hands at least four thousand years ago. A thousand years later the Greeks played another type of handball game, and later the Romans played a game called Pelota in which a ball was hit against the wall with the bare hands. The forerunner of the modern game of handball is believed to have originated in Ireland nearly one thousand years ago.

Three outstanding early players are commonly listed in the history of modern handball. John Cavanaugh was renowned throughout Great Britain as by far the most superior handball player of the early 1800s. Another Irishman, William Baggs, developed the ability to "hop" and curve the ball, thus enabling him to overcome all opponents in around 1850. Phil Casey, the father of American handball, arrived in Brooklyn in around 1880 and was soon considered the best handball player in the eastern area. He built the first handball courts in the eastern part of the United States and did much to enhance the popularity of the game. Casey won the American Handball Championship in 1888, and soon afterward defeated the Irish handball champion, John Lahr. Casey successfully defended his title on many occasions and retired, in 1900, without ever being defeated. In America, the game of handball deviated from the Irish game in that only the hands (the use of the feet was illegal) could be used to strike the handball.

The beginning of the twentieth century saw the emergence of two types of handball games. The one-wall handball game was particularly popular in New York and along the East Coast, especially at beaches and playgrounds. This game required a minimum of facilities and could be played outside. Because a large, soft handball was used it required no special equipment, not even gloves. The four-wall handball game—the game brought over from Ireland—also continued to develop. Eventually the size of the four-wall handball court was reduced until, shortly after World War II, the present court dimensions of forty feet in length and twenty feet in height and width were established. The first invitational four-wall handball tournament was held in 1915, and the first AAU handball tournament, in which a soft ball was used, was held in 1919.

Another variation of handball, which appeared some time ago, is three-wall handball. In this game modified versions of side walls extend back about one fourth to one half the usual distance, thus enabling a wide variety of shots to be made in which corner kills and side wall-front wall shots are employed.

In 1951, under the auspices and guidance of Robert Kendler, an enthusiastic handball player whose professional business is construction, the United States Handball Association (USHA) was formed as a players' fraternity. This organization has done much to promote and spread the popularity of handball. Handball today is still considered to be primarily an American and Irish game. It is

---

*Dr. Casady first played handball while serving in the Army Air Force during World War II. He has been playing and teaching handball since that time. His accomplishments include singles and doubles all-university handball champion at The University of Iowa, singles champion of the National College Physical Education Association for Men in 1965, singles and doubles champion of the Hawkeye Handball Club in 1969, and doubles champion of the Slick Wall-Sweaty Ball Tournament in 1972. Many of the students previously enrolled in his handball classes are still playing recreational handball and several play tournament handball.

known in some countries as *fives*. In most European nations, the name of *handball* or *team handball* is given to games played on an outdoor field, or indoor court. The games bear some resemblance to soccer, football, basketball, and lacrosse.

Over the years many handball players have achieved considerable fame. During the early 1960s, Jim Jacobs was considered to be the finest all-around four-wall handball player in the United States. Because of a back problem he has, however, during the past few years mainly confined his playing to the doubles game.

Championship handball play is increasingly being presented on television and more and better facilities are being built to accomodate the players and the spectators. Modern exhibition handball courts are now constructed with plate glass walls so that spectators can view the handball players from the sides and the back of the court. Handball appears to be increasing in popularity each year, although the advent of paddleball and racketball has intruded on the use of handball courts for handball play in many areas.

THE GAME OF HANDBALL

Handball can be played either by two players (singles), three players (cut-throat), or four players (doubles). These three types of handball games have many similarities, although each of them has some unique features. To put the ball into play the server, who stands in the service area that is located near the middle of the court, drops the ball to the floor. When it rebounds he hits it against the front wall from which it rebounds and bounces on the floor behind him before striking the back wall. The receiver returns the served ball, making sure that the ball strikes the front wall before it strikes the floor. The opponents in turn alternate returning the ball to the front wall, hitting the ball either on the fly or before it bounces on the floor a second time.

On the serve the ball must clearly strike the front wall before hitting any other surface of the court, all other returns can hit the side walls and ceiling before striking the front wall. The ball must, however, hit the front wall before it hits the floor. In striking the ball, the player can hit it with a clenched fist or with an open hand (usually with the hand in a cup-like position). The only rule here is that the ball must be struck with a portion of the gloved hand and not with the bare skin of the wrist above the handball glove.

During play, the players attempt to make the opponent have as difficult a return shot as possible by using kill shots in which the ball strikes very low on the front wall and has a low bounce before going out of play on the second bounce, or by passing the opponent by hitting the ball along one of the side walls, or by hitting the ball over the opponent's head—the ceiling shot, in which the ball first hits the ceiling and then rebounds to the front wall and then the floor with a resultant high bounce, is often utilized for this purpose. Another widely used shot is to so hit the ball that it rebounds at great speed off the front wall and directly toward the opponent when he is positioned near the front wall.

In singles play the opponents alternate hitting the ball. In cut-throat play, the server opposes the other two players and he must hit the ball every other time. When the server goes out, each player rotates clockwise one position. In doubles play, two players compose a team and either member of the team can hit the ball on that team's turn to strike it.

The game of handball can be played in a four-wall court, which also contains a ceiling. The game is often played out-of-doors on a so-called one-wall court, which consists of a front wall and often small abutments extending a short distance on each side, thus forming extremely modified side walls near the front wall. Three-wall handball is also played in some areas. For the one- and three-wall game, the entire court is often screened in order to avoid chasing far distances after the ball if it is missed by a player.

UNIQUE VALUES OF HANDBALL PLAY

Handball is the favorite game of many amateur and professional athletes, businessmen, and professional men. The one-wall game in which a larger and softer handball is used is also played by some women, although men dominate the game. Handball is a favorite conditioning activity for many men who desire to retain a high level of fitness, because cardio-respiratory endurance, agility, flexibility, speed of movement, and strength are developed and maintained in the game. Many of the American astronauts, for example, play handball with considerable enthusiasm.

Handball is one of the extremely few games that demands extensive use of the nondominant hand and arm. If a ball is traveling quite close to the left-hand wall, the right-handed player must return it with his left hand, because a backhanded right-hand shot is quite difficult to perform. This unique feature of the game of handball is extremely important in developing a bilateral symmetry of the body.

Because the singles, cut-throat, and doubles games are all fun and can be enjoyed by a wide range of players, it is relatively easy to find an opponent or opponents to play handball at about any time of the day (or night). Because many handball courts are indoor, detrimental weather conditions have no adverse effect on the game. Because the speed and intensity of the game can be controlled by the players, the game can be safely played and enjoyed by the unskilled beginner or the player in his sixth or seventh decade of life, who is not able to play a vigorous game. In summary, the game of handball is extremely challenging; the participants rarely seem to tire of playing it.

SELECTION OF EQUIPMENT AND ITS CARE

Because a handball player plays on existing handball courts, there is little need for him to be overly concerned with the court itself, except to know the service-zone area and where the short line and service line are located. The four-wall and one-wall court markings are depicted in Figure 18-1. The two basic pieces of handball equipment

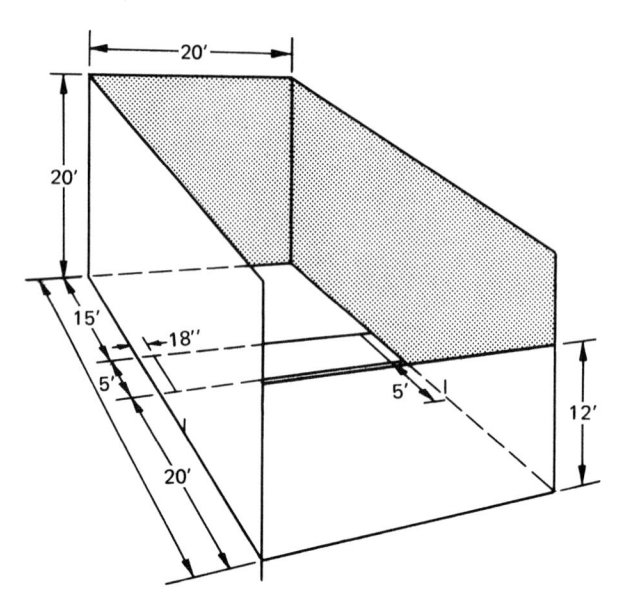

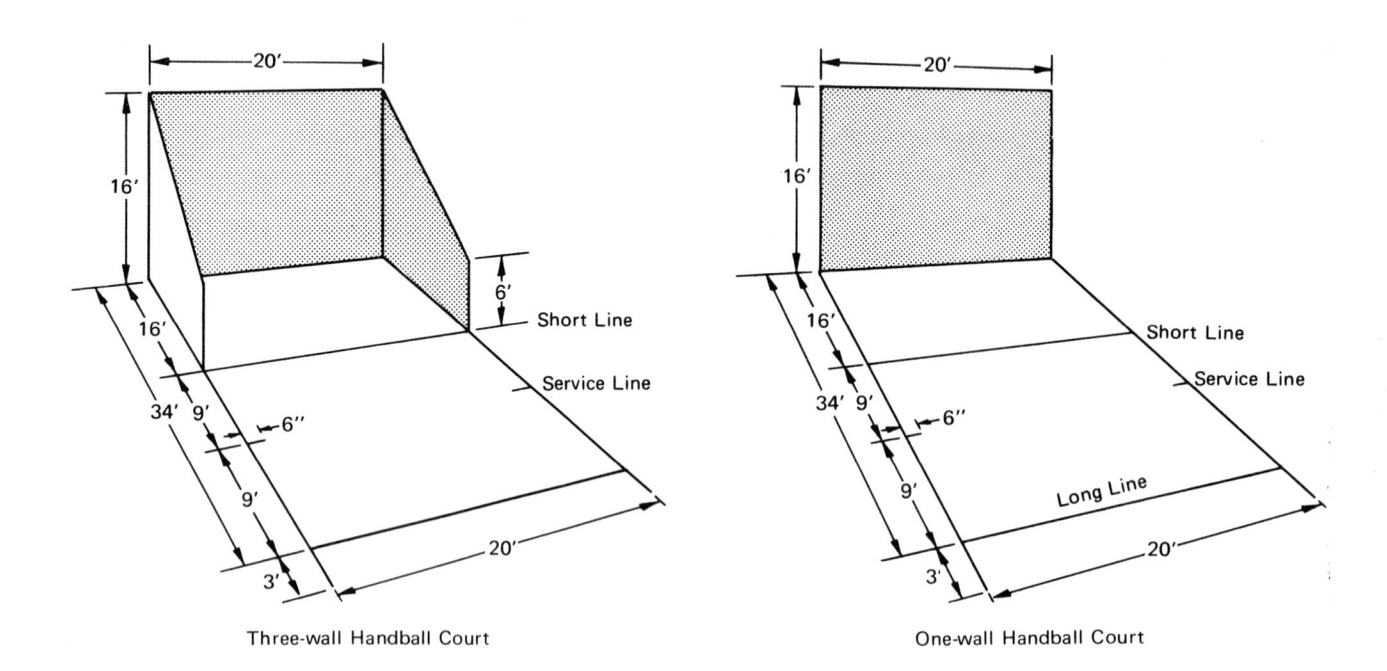

Figure 18-1. Handball court: dimensions and markings.

272 *Individual and Team Sports*

are a pair of handball gloves and the ball. Handball gloves come in a variety of styles but are normally made of leather and may have nylon elastic material on the back of the hand portion; some also have a small nylon webbing inserted around the sides of each finger and thumb. The beginning player often prefers to use a glove that has padding on the palm portion, which helps absorb some of the shock of hitting the ball hard with the palm of the hand. Most advanced players, however, prefer to use unpadded handball gloves. Handball gloves are made with a strap that extends either across the back of the top of the wrist or completely around the wrist in order to hold the glove securely to the hand. The price of handball gloves varies from somewhat less than $3 up to a little over $8. Different kinds of handball gloves are depicted in Figure 18-2.

The handball ($1\frac{7}{8}$ inches in diameter) used in many tournaments today is one made by Spaulding, called the ACE. Seamless also makes a handball of the hard, small variety. A large, soft handball is sometimes used in outdoor play. Another item of equipment that should be considered essential by handball players is the eye guard. Eye guards come in a variety of styles, but all of them serve to protect the eyes from a direct hit by a handball. Eye guards are not only valuable as a safety device—there have been instances of a handball player losing his sight when struck in the eye by a hard-hit handball—they permit the player to watch with safety and for an increased length of time the play of his opponent behind him, thus enabling the player to anticipate with accuracy where his opponent is going to hit his shot.

The usual attire when playing handball normally consists of at least one pair of socks made of a highly absorbent material such as wool (many players prefer to wear two pairs of socks when playing handball); a pair of good quality, low- or high-cut sneakers or gym shoes (special high-cut handball shoes are now marketed); an athletic supporter; and a pair of nonbinding shorts and a T-shirt or knit shirt. Most participants prefer to wear white shorts and a white shirt when playing handball; in tournament competition this is required.

BASIC RULES AND ETIQUETTE

Rules

Several years ago four organizations promoting handball—the AAU of the United States, the YMCAs, the Jewish Community Centers, and the USHA—established a common set of handball rules that were applicable to all organizations. This move did much to simplify and make uniform the rules governing all handball play.

The rules of handball are periodically reviewed and, hence, are subject to change. In order to be certain that up-to-date rules are observed, a copy of the latest rules can be obtained from any of the preceding organizations. The most common rules of handball play include the following.

Serving.

1. The server has two turns in which to make a legal service.
2. A legal service is one in which the served ball first strikes the front wall and rebounds back, striking the floor beyond the short line before hitting the back wall, and which does not hit the ceiling or both side walls before hitting the floor.
3. The server must remain between the short line and the service line while serving the ball. If he starts or steps outside this area during the serve, a foot foul is committed, which results in a serving fault.
4. In doubles play during the serve, the server's partner must remain in the service box located along the side wall. If the server's partner is struck by the served ball while in the box, this is a dead ball and it is served again with no loss of a serving turn. If the server's partner is outside the box and is hit by the struck ball, then this is an out and a loss of a serve is declared.
5. The server may not bounce the ball more than three times before serving it; otherwise, a hand-out occurs.
6. During the first half inning (an inning is a complete turn of service for both sides) only one partner in doubles play is given a serving turn (hand-out). Thereafter, each partner is permitted a turn at serve each time his team has the serve.
7. The receiver may not stand any closer than five feet behind the short line when the ball is served.

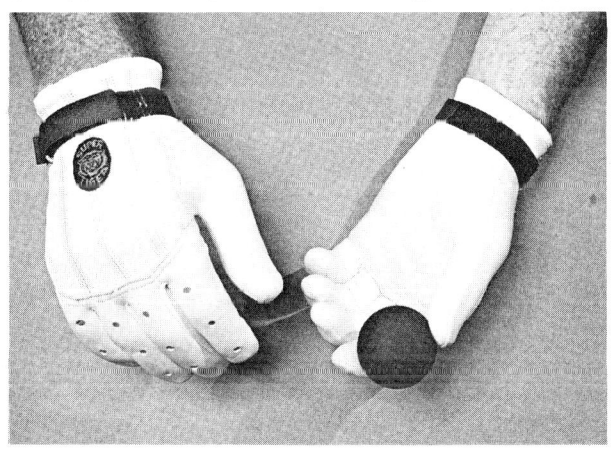

Figure 18-2. Different kinds of handball gloves. (Photographs obtained through the courtesy of the Champion Glove Company, Des Moines, Iowa.)

Ball in Play.

1. The ball is in play so long as it is legally served and is so returned that it strikes the front wall while on the fly. A crotch ball is one that strikes the two surfaces simultaneously from which it often rebounds at an unusual angle. A crotch-ball serve striking the front wall and side wall is no good and results in a loss of serve.
2. The ball can either be hit on the fly, including a served ball, or on its first bounce from the floor. The ball is dead and out of play once it hits the floor a second time.
3. In doubles play the ball can be struck only once by the side returning it. If one partner touches the ball in any fashion (or if the ball touches him), the ball may not be hit by his partner.
4. A ball coming off the front wall that goes into the gallery area at the back top part of the rear court, or strikes the screen covering that area, is a dead ball and is replayed.

Hinders.

1. A hinder occurs whenever the intended player of the ball is unable to go directly to the ball; that is, he must go around an opponent in going to the spot where he intends to hit the ball. A visual hinder occurs when the player's vision of the ball is blocked, at least momentarily, and he is unable to see the ball at some time during his turn to play it. In tournament play a referee will call a hinder whenever a hinder situation arises. In ordinary play the person who is hindered should call the hinder just as soon as it occurs; the play is immediately stopped and the server recovers the ball. A player who suspects that he may have hindered an opponent's path to the ball or his vision of the ball should offer to give the opponent a hinder by asking if he would like one. In cut-throat or doubles play, a player cannot be hindered by his partner. Either partner in doubles play can claim a hinder even though the other partner attempted to or did strike the ball.
2. A hinder occurs when the ball in its path to the front wall strikes an opponent. It is not a hinder, however, if the ball strikes the partner when traveling to the front wall; instead, this is a hand-out or, if the opponents are serving, a point.

Scoring.

1. A game is played to 21 points, and the first player achieving the score of 21 wins the game. There are no deuce games in handball.

2. A point can be scored only by the serving side. If the receiving side wins the play, this results in a hand-out by the player who was serving.
3. A point is scored each time that the serving team wins a play by being the last side to make a legal serve or return of the ball in which no hinder is called.
4. If during the serve the server screens the receiver's view of the ball, a screen or shadow ball is called, a hinder results, and the ball is served again.

Other Rules.

1. It is illegal to hit the ball with both hands. When this occurs the offending player loses the point (or the serve).
2. The ball must be clearly hit with the glove; if the ball strikes any portion of the body other than the gloved hand, a loss of serve (or a loss of point) occurs.

Etiquette

Handball is a game for gentlemen and as such should be played in a gentlemanly fashion. If at any time the question of a possible hinder arises, a player should offer to give his opponent a hinder. In ordinary play, hinders are called less frequently than in tournament play, where whenever a hinder situation arises the referee immediately calls a hinder, regardless of whether or not the player might have actually been able to have gotten to the ball in order to return it. During a friendly game of handball, however, if the player believes he did not have a chance of returning the ball, then he normally does not call a hinder or accept one if it is offered.

Handball is an extremely popular game and often all courts are in use. In these situations if two players are playing singles and other players are waiting to play, an act of courtesy would be to offer to play doubles with them. When handball courts are scheduled on a reservation system, an exception to this practice can be made, but many players make this gesture, knowing that other players have as much love for the game as they do.

The players should determine what local rules prevail when playing in other than their home handball courts. Some local rules, for example, may include replaying the point any time that the ball strikes a bad surface of the court in which there is a crack, or if the door fits loosely, or if a lighting fixture hangs down from the ceiling. On hot, humid days, unventilated or nonair-conditioned courts may develop a film of moisture on the walls. When this condition occurs, the ball often slides rapidly along the wall instead of rebounding out at its usual angle. Before the game begins, the players should determine whether they will continue a ball in play if it slides, or if they will stop and replay all balls that slide. If loose equipment is placed along the back wall or corners, all balls should be replayed that fly or bounce into such equipment.

Different methods are employed for determining who begins the service for the first game. The player who owns the ball that bounces the highest can receive the serve under one method. Another method used is for the players, while standing near the back wall, to throw the ball at the front wall. The one who throws the best kill has his choice of scoring or receiving. Another alternative is to lob the ball for the short line—the player lobbing the closest to it decides whether to serve or receive first. Because points are only scored by the serving side, most players of course prefer the advantage of serving when given the choice. During regular handball play the first turn of service is alternated on each new game. In a friendly game some players prefer to have the loser of the last game start the service for the next game.

A three-game series most commonly is played with the match winner being the winner of at least two of the games. As a rule the ball used in the game is the one with the most bounce. Each player should bring a ball with him and have it available for play.

TECHNIQUES OF PARTICIPATION

Safety

Once a player learns the approximate space encompassed by the handball court and, hence, automatically knows when he is approaching the rear or side walls, and once he learns to avoid his opponents and adjust to his partner's playing position, handball is a relatively safe game. Although the chance of an injury to the eye because of a ball striking it is quite rare, the eye is delicate and extremely vital; therefore, eye guards are essential whenever playing handball.

Whenever the player's path to the ball is blocked by an opponent, the player should immediately call a hinder and avoid physical contact with the opponent, rather than attempt to slide by him and possibly suffer a collision. In competition, especially in tournament play, the handball player may deliberately go to a position on the court where he believes the opponent may return the ball, thus blocking that shot or forcing the opponent to aim toward a different area. In a friendly game of handball, if the opponent is immediately in front of the player, he may call a hinder rather than hit the ball into the opponent when it is obvious that there is little or no chance of missing him.

The little formal research done to date indicates that a warm-up before playing handball is of little or no value in increasing one's accuracy or in avoiding possible injuries (such as pulling a muscle). The available evidence is, however, scanty at best. Consequently, the handball player is urged to spend several minutes in stretching and slowly throwing and easily hitting the ball before proceeding to play all-out handball. Some of the warm-up techniques commonly used are (1) slapping the hands together vigorously several times to increase the blood circulating in them, (2) rotating the arms and swinging them back and forth in order to loosen the shoulder joints, (3) rotating and flexing the trunk forward by doing toe-touches with the legs kept straight, (4) throwing and hitting the ball with either hand while in a variety of court positions, and (5) soaking the hands in hot water for a few minutes before playing.

A sweating player should avoid leaving a film of moisture on the floor, especially if he falls down. If this happens, the floor should be wiped dry before play is continued. Such wet spots can easily cause someone to slip and perhaps take a dangerous fall. If the hands become sore during play or after playing handball (a fairly common experience for beginning players at first), padded gloves should be worn. If needed, a thin sheet of sponge rubber can be inserted between the palm and the glove until the soreness disappears.

FUNDAMENTAL SKILLS AND TECHNIQUES OF HANDBALL PLAY

As with all ball games, it is particularly important that the player always watch the ball closely; if possible, he should watch the ball travel into the hitting hand. As he improves in skill he perhaps tends to not concentrate quite as closely on focusing his vision on the ball, but this basic fundamental should always be closely observed; particularly, any time that a difficult shot has to be made.

Position of Hands

Partly because the hand can be held in more than one position when hitting the ball, most players prefer that their handball gloves fit snugly. The gloves should not be binding nor uncomfortable, but they should also have no slackness in them. The hand position used to hit the ball is normally a semicuplike position in which the fingers are held closely together, the thumb is alongside the index finger, and the hand forms a slight curve. As a player improves in skill and has the increased assurance of not mis-hitting a shot because of his fingers being too relaxed, he tends to hold his hand straight with the fingers almost in a straight line with the palm of the hand.

Handball

Most beginners when playing handball tend to attempt to hit the ball with the palm of their hand, permitting the ball to roll or slide off their fingers. This is probably the safest method of hitting the ball, because a large area of the hand is involved, thus allowing considerable room for error. Advanced players, particularly the champion players, often aim to hit the ball with only their fingers. This allows increased wrist action to be effectively employed.

The fist shot is sometimes used when hitting the ball with the nondominant hand; rarely is a fist shot taken with the dominant hand. With the fist shot the ball is hit with great speed, and accuracy is a secondary consideration. For a fist shot the hand is clenched tightly, a fist is formed, and the ball is hit on the heel of the palm of the hand, just beyond the fingertips of the fist.

Hitting the Ball

The player should, whenever possible, get into a basic hitting position in which he is crouched, his knees are slightly bent, and his body faces a side wall. When hitting the ball the player's weight should be on the balls of his feet and, generally, he should be transferring his weight from his rear foot to his front foot as he strokes the ball. (See Figure 18-3.)

When contacting the ball the ideal position of the ball is ordinarily one that is fairly low, is some distance away from the body (about one half an arm's length should be the goal), and is positioned toward the front of the body. This means that in order to attain an ideal hitting position, the player must move rapidly to get into the proper court location, and he must learn the behavior of the ball when it rebounds off the various surfaces of the court in order to anticipate where he should be positioned. The beginner needs as quickly as possible to establish the habit of recognizing and moving to the court area where he wants to be located when hitting the ball so that he can await its arrival at this site. Before stroking the ball a vigorous backswing should first be taken if time permits. When stroking the ball with the right hand, the player's body should be so positioned that the left shoulder is pointing toward the front wall; if stroking left handed, the right shoulder should ordinarily be pointing toward the front wall. However, on some shots (for example, a low ball coming directly toward the player) the player can directly face the front wall and take an underarm swing similar to a softball pitcher's underarm throw; if the ball is directly overhead the player need not turn to the side quite so much, and he takes a full or three-quarter swing very similar to the overhand throw used in baseball or for a tennis or badminton smash. Whenever possible, the player should take a full swing at the ball and try to contact it when it is even with or somewhat in front of an imaginary line that extends from side wall to side wall and which passes through that part of his body nearest the front wall. If the player is late in getting to the ball, or other circumstances do not permit him to attain the ideal ball-hitting position, he can hit the ball when it is slightly behind and to one side of him. However, success in this shot demands that considerable wrist action be used. In addition, the player is unable to see the front wall with his peripheral vision; thus, he has no target at which to aim.

The beginning handball player should immediately begin cultivating a flexible wrist and use extensive wrist action when hitting the ball. This practice develops the type of hitting most desired when playing handball, and it will enable the player to develop a wide range of possible front-wall hits. As skill develops, the player can make a maximum flexing hand action on some shots and withhold all hand and wrist flexion on other shots, thus confusing the opponent to the last instant concerning to where the ball will be directed.

On those shots for which the player has adequate time to position his body and to watch closely the flight of the ball, he should attempt to place his return shots accurately and should strive for a kill shot or other type of winning shot. If the player has a difficult shot, or is in a poor hitting position, the percentages are against him making a put-away shot; instead, a defensive shot should be made with the objective of not setting up the opponent. In general, the more difficult the shot, the less speed with which the ball should be returned. On extremely difficult shots, such as one that is sliding directly alongside the side wall or is coming off the back wall at a difficult angle, the

Figure 18-3(a). Paul Haber hitting an overhand shot with his off hand. (Photograph obtained through the courtesy of the United States Handball Association.)

Figure 18-3(b). Hitting the ball. (Bob Bourbeau playing Paul Haber.) (Photograph obtained through the courtesy of the United States Handball Association.)

player should do little more than hit the ball with a semi-catching stroke, playing a safe, fairly high shot to the front wall. Although catching or carrying the ball in the hand is illegal, the player should envision almost catching the ball and throwing it rapidly. If this is done with more-than-ordinary speed, then an illegal hit does not result, and the player is able to make a safe play on a difficult return.

The player needs to practice by himself and with others a great deal in order to be able to determine ahead of time about where the ball is going to go and, hence, what court position he should strive to obtain in order to make the best possible return of the ball. The ability to visualize this varies from person to person, but this ability can be mastered if sufficiently practiced.

Very early in his career as a handball player, the student should get into the habit of deciding how he will play the ball and then go ahead and attempt that particular shot, changing his mind only when absolutely necessary. Unless a definite advantage will be gained by waiting to take the shot when it comes off the back wall, or in other similar situations, the player should play the shot as soon as possible in order to allow his opponent less time to get into position for the return.

Whenever attempting to hit the ball low on the front wall, the player should first allow the ball to descend to at least knee-level or below. The importance of this lies in the fact that a ball higher than this must be hit at a considerable downward angle in order for it to hit low on the front wall. However, a ball that is knee level or lower can be aimed approximately parallel with the floor. Thus, if a slight downward error occurs, the ball has less chance of contacting the floor before hitting the front wall than when a downward-angle hit is made. Trying to kill a ball that is waist level or above carries little chance for success for most players. A slight error upward or downward on the ball's path will result in either a hand-out (or point) or the ball coming back "fat," thus permitting the opponent an excellent opportunity for a kill. One of the most deplorable shots in handball is attempting to kill a ball when it is shoulder height or higher, because the overhand stroke must be directed downward similar to the action employed in chopping with an ax. A successful kill from this high position is almost entirely a matter of luck, not skill.

Strokes. The most common stroke in handball is the sidearm stroke, in which the direction of arm and hand travel is approximately parallel to the floor. If the ball is approximately shoulder height or higher when hit, then a three-quarter or full overhead stroke must be employed. If the ball is quite close to the floor, a sidearm stroke can successfully be used if the player crouches his body sufficiently. If he has insufficient time to do this, or if he is

Figure 18-4. Steve August preparing to hit a ceiling shot. (Photograph obtained through the courtesy of the United States Handball Association.)

unable to get as low as he should, then an underhand shot can be utilized in which the ball slides off the palm of the hand and down the fingers. The arm is ordinarily kept in a straight position during the entire underhanded stroking action.

Court Position

Whether playing singles, cut-throat or doubles, the court position assumed by the player during each shot is a highly important facet of successful handball play. For singles play the basic court position is in the center of the court from side to side and slightly toward the front half of the court (usually between the short and the service lines). The faster the player's reactions and speed of movement, and the more accurate his anticipation of where the opponent will place the ball, the closer toward the front wall he can play with success. In doubles play each player plays approximately in the middle of his right or left half of the court and with one slightly ahead of the other.

The exact position in the court that a player should take after hitting the ball is in part dependent on the court position of his opponent when he hits the ball and/or to what area of the court he is going. The lateral position in the court is normally toward the side of the court from which the opponent is hitting the ball. For instance, a shot from the right side of the court can quickly be hit as a drive shot down the right side of the court. If the ball is hit to the left side, it will probably contact the left wall and angle back toward the center of the court. Most players prefer to play slightly in front of their opponent whenever they can. As a result considerable maneuvering takes place during play. The front-court position can often be taken from the opponent by hitting a passing

Figure 18-5(a). Basic court positions.

Figure 18-5(b). Court position for doubles play. (The two players looking back are the opponents.) (Photograph obtained through the courtesy of the United States Handball Association.)

shot or a ceiling shot, forcing him to the back court. Although the front position is ordinarily the desired one, it can be a dangerous position, especially if the opponent is given a set-up that can be killed easily or placed beyond the player's reach.

By raising one arm, turning the head slightly to the side, and watching the opponent out of the corner of the eye until just before he makes his shot, the player should usually anticipate or guess successfully where the opponent is hitting the ball on the front wall and what type of shot he is attempting. However, the player should never turn his body or head to the back wall because this exposes his eyes to the possibility of a direct hit by the opponent's return. Again, the use of eye guards is highly recommended.

Serves

Several different types of serves can be made to start the game. A side-arm, underhand, or even overhand arm action can be employed when serving. The usual goal when serving is to have the served ball rebound quite closely to the side wall while it is in the serving area of the back court. In singles play the server usually serves from

Figure 18-6(a). Bill Yambrick making a basic sidearm serve. (Photograph obtained through the courtesy of the United States Handball Association.)

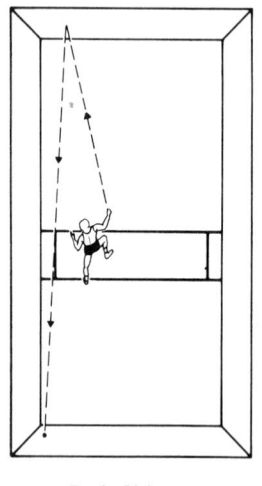

Basic Sidearm Serve Down Left Sidewall

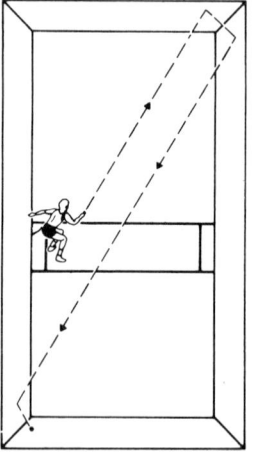

Crisscross Serve

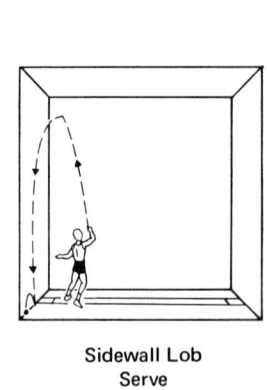

Sidewall Lob Serve

Figure 18-6(b). Various types of serves.

278 *Individual and Team Sports*

near the middle of the court and in doubles play, from either side of the court. Beginning players should strive to develop quickly a low, fast serve in which the ball is so dropped that it rebounds only ten to fifteen inches from the floor and, taking a quick step forward, is hit with a sidearm-underarm action. The ball should strike three to four feet high on the front wall and land on the floor just beyond the short service line. This serve is often directed to the receiver's nondominant hand. Another widely employed serve is the crisscross (zig-zag) serve. While standing near one side wall, the server serves the ball to the opposite front corner, causing the ball to return to his side of the back court. An underhand, sidearm, or overhand stroke can be used; the ball should be aimed about two feet from the corner of the front wall. The lob serve, in which the ball hits high on the front wall and is then lopped barely into the service area, where it dies just short of the back wall, is sometimes used as a change-of-pace serve. When served toward the back corner of the receiver's nondominant hand, it is difficult to make an effective return; often, the return comes directly to the server, who can put it away while the receiver is still in the back court.

Shots

Various shots are utilized in the game of handball; the beginning player should attempt to become as proficient as possible in a variety of them. He will find that some work better than others, but most will require considerable practice before they can be dependently controlled.

Drive Shot. One of the fundamental shots is the drive shot, in which the ball is hit low on the front wall and comes back directly at the opponent or alongside a side wall. The purpose of this shot is either to return the ball before the opponent can get set or else pass him before he can get to the ball. Because the ball moves with great speed, many beginners, especially, have difficulty in successfully returning it.

Ceiling Shot. Another shot that can be used for both defensive and offensive purposes is the ceiling shot. Against advanced players this is mainly a defensive shot, but against players of mediocre skill it often proves to be a winning shot, particularly if it is well placed. An overhand stroke is normally used and the ball is aimed to strike the ceiling three feet or so behind its junction with the front wall. The ball rebounds to the front wall, the floor, and then quickly bounces above the receiver's reach. To successfully play this ball the opponent must either charge forward and hit it as it rebounds upward from the floor, or else he must go back and attempt to hit the ball when it rebounds downward before or after it reaches the back wall. With practice this shot can be so aimed that it falls into the left (or right) rear corner, thus making it an even more difficult shot to return.

Pass Shot. Passing shots can be attempted in which a slide or slight hop (english) is placed on the ball. For a right-handed player a natural sliding shot along the right wall is one which is stroked with a sidearm action by the right hand. The ball is contacted with the palm of the hand and the hand is so pulled toward the body that the ball rolls off the fingers, imparting some spin to the ball and causing it to rebound slightly away from the right side of the right side wall. When this shot is well executed and accurately placed, a ball striking the front wall within four inches of the right side wall will hardly advance toward the side wall during its entire flight toward the back wall, which creates an illusion of the ball sliding alongside the side wall. A left-handed player can

Figure 18-7(a). Jim Jacobs preparing to take a shot off the back wall. (Photograph obtained through the courtesy of the United States Handball Association.)

Figure 18-7(b). Lou Kramberg hitting a kill shot. (Photograph obtained through the courtesy of the United States Handball Association.)

Handball 279

experience considerable success in hitting the same type of shot along the left side wall.

Angle Shot. Whenever the player is in a disadvantageous court position, has a difficult shot, or finds the opponent well positioned for the return, he should so hit the ball at an angle that it rebounds off at least one and preferably two side walls during its backward (or forward) flight. A ball that changes direction once, twice, or even three times while in play is difficult for the opponent to figure out and anticipate the correct court position from which the ball should be returned.

Kill Shot. The shot that all handball players want to master and one that gives the most satisfaction is the kill shot. A kill shot is hit so low on the front wall that it has little or no bounce off the floor after rebounding off the front wall. The perfect kill shot, of course, is a roller, which hits the front wall a fraction of an inch above the floor and rolls back on the floor. Because so many chances for errors exist, handball players usually try to kill the ball two to four inches off the floor; the beginning handball player should probably aim his kills from six to eight inches above floor level.

Corner Kills. Because a ball that changes angles during its flight is difficult to return, the beginner should often attempt to hit kill shots toward either front corner. An inside corner shot is one that first hits the front wall; an outside corner shot is one that first hits the side wall. Both types of corner kill shots can be highly effective and which to use depends in part on the player's court position when hitting and on where the opponent is positioned. A ball that first hits the side wall tends to stay in the front part of the court, whereas a ball that first hits the front wall tends to rebound more toward the back of the court. For a right-handed player, a natural kill shot is to the right outside corner, because the spin imparted by the sidearm stroke causes the ball to ride the side wall with very little drop. For the left-handed player, then, the natural side-corner kill shot is the left side wall.

When attempting kill shots it is extremely important to lower the body into a crouched position, to be in position to hit the ball well ahead of time, and to hit the ball when it is quite low in its flight. When stroking the ball, most players use a sidearm stroke; this writer has found it helpful to hit slightly down on the ball, permitting it to ride upward on the hand, thus imparting a slight cut or chop to the ball. This type of hit permits the player to aim directly at the crack of the floor and front wall; the chopping action on the ball causes it to raise sufficiently to strike the front wall a few inches above the floor. This shot, as is true of most kill shots, works particularly well when made in the front half of the court. When attempting to kill from the back half of the court, the player must either hit the ball with considerable speed or aim high in order to allow for the dropage of the ball during its flight to the front wall.

Another kill shot used successfully by some players is to stand with the body fairly straight and facing directly toward the front wall. As the ball rebounds toward him and is about knee height, the player strokes the ball with a straight-arm, underhand hit, hitting the ball on the palm of the hand and letting it slide downward off the fingers. With this type of stroke the player can with his fingers somewhat guide the ball into a low front-wall hit.

Some players, in trying to kill with the left hand, use a straight-arm, underhand, or combination underhand-sidearm fist-ball hit in which again they try to push the ball into a low position on the front wall, often aiming at one of the front corners.

A kill shot that most advanced players have mastered with their dominant hand (and often with their non-dominant hand as well) is the back-wall kill shot. In this shot the player runs back to within a few feet of the back wall and, facing sideward to the front wall, strikes the ball as it rebounds off. The arm action used is similar to a sidearm throwing action of a combination underhand-sidearm throwing action. Although this shot requires correct court position and excellent timing, the player, especially if he waits until the ball is even with or slightly in front of his body, has peripheral vision of the front wall while watching his hand make contact with the ball. Again, most beginners will probably want to aim for one of the front corners; most right-handed players usually aim this shot at the front right-hand corner. As with any game, however, the placement of the shots should be varied occasionally in order that the opponent cannot always successfully anticipate where the ball will be directed.

Doubles Play

When playing doubles, or cut-throat, it is highly essential that the partners closely coordinate their efforts and court positions. To do this successfully, they normally must play together for some time. When playing doubles the players generally divide the court into two parts in which the left-side player takes approximately three fifths of the court on the left side and the right side player takes about two fifths of the right side of the court. If both players are right handed, as is the usual case, the left-court player will take all shots down the middle. He will be hitting with his dominant right hand, thus negating the need for the right-court player to hit such shots with his left hand.

Some partners divide the court diagonally from the right-hand front corner to the left-hand back corner. Under this scheme the left-side player generally plays about two steps in front of the right-side player, and the left-side player tries to take most returns rebounding in the front court except those that rebound near the right wall. The right-court player, who is playing back somewhat, takes most of the shots off the back wall, although in some doubles teams the left-court player takes those back-wall shots in the left half of the court.

As a rule the better player plays the left side when playing doubles. Whenever there is a question of who should play the ball the partner with the best shot should as quickly as possible yell "Mine," or else "Yours," or "Take it." With practice a player can usually recognize when he should let a shot go in order to permit his partner to take it because he has a better shot. The most difficult decisions usually involve the ball rebounding sharply off the side wall at the instant that the player would have to hit it. If his partner is alert, and if the ball is in the front half of the court and some distance above the floor, the player should depend on his partner to return it.

When playing doubles the usual practice is to direct the ball as much as possible to the weaker player, attempting to force him to make a weak return. This means that the doubles team should work hard to remedy their weak play or else be able to cover it by having the player give up the shot in deference to his stronger partner. However, this introduces the possibility that the strong player on the team will become fatigued, causing the quality of his play to go down. Some doubles teams that are comprised of two players of unequal ability play an up-back formation in which the player with the best shots (or the fastest player) plays in the front court and returns all balls he can reach. The back-court partner returns all balls that get by his front-court partner. This formation is particularly vulnerable to passing shots.

STRATEGY OF HANDBALL PLAY

Patience

As is true of many kinds of ball games, the successful handball player must be patient in his play. If he has poor court position or does not have time to get set for his return shot, he should avoid the temptation of trying to kill the ball or put it away, because if he is somewhat off on his intended shot, he will probably be out of position and, hence, unable to return his opponent's hit. In addition, his problems are compounded by attempting to hit a well-placed shot when in a poor hitting position. Instead, the player should return the ball in such a way (a ceiling shot or a pass shot, for example) that he has time to recover to the basic court position while he avoids setting up his opponent in the front court. Thus, when skilled players play, they often each return the ball several times with the intention of moving the opponent about the court and to avoid giving him a good shot, neither going for a kill shot until both the player and the ball are in excellent court position for a winning shot. This type of game is known as percentage handball.

Placement of Ball

The type of shot to be made and where the ball should be directed are often not clear-cut; the choices will vary depending on the player, the opponent, the strengths and weaknesses of both, and their court positions. The usual strategy employed is to try to direct the ball to the opponent's weakness while avoiding having the opponent do the same. For beginning players, especially, most hits are aimed to the opponent's left hand, if he is right handed. Ceiling shots often force the opponent to move over a considerable part of the court. Ceiling shots and pass shots down the opposite side wall give the opponent little opportunity to take control of the game. Drive shots, hit with considerable speed directly at the opponent when he is in the front court, often force him to make a weak return.

Basic Strategy

The basic strategy employed in either singles or doubles play is to try to pass the opponent(s) if he is up and to kill whenever he is back. The pass shot can be aimed alongside either side wall or be an overhead ceiling shot. Whenever the opponent is in the back court, if the player can get into position, he should go for a kill shot. A corner kill shot works quite well when the opponent is back, but if he is in an in-between position a kill shot down a side wall is often better, because this forces the opponent to go an increased distance to reach the ball. If the opponent is up, the crisscross shot that hits two side walls forces him to run and increases the chances that he will commit an error. If the opponent is standing on one side of the court, then the ball should be hit to the other side (occasionally, however, because the opponent will recover toward the middle of the court, the ball should be hit to the area he is leaving)—the strategy always being to make the opponent run the greatest distance possible. Beginning players often have difficulty in mastering this concept because the natural tendency is to hit to a target—that is, the opponent, instead of hitting where there is no target and forcing the opponent to run and move about. A constant struggle goes on between opponents to get into the best court position and to force the opponent into a poor court position. This strategy can be reinforced by occasionally varying the speed of the return in order to upset the opponent's timing and anticipation.

Effective Serves

When serving it is especially important that the player concentrate fully on serving the ball with maximum effectiveness. The tendency, particularly when tired, to just hit the ball, instead of concentrating on serving in a particular way to a particular spot, should be avoided. Because the server has all the time he desires for getting into the proper body position and to consider fully where he wants to place his serve, he should be more exact with his service than with any other type of shot.

For most players the serve can be a direct source of several points during a game. The main strategy of the serve, however, should be not to score an ace (although this may sometimes occur) but to present the opponent with a difficult shot at which he is apt to make a weak return that the server can put away. In addition, when serving, the server is in the ideal court position, whereas the receiver is forced to hit the ball while in an undesirable court position. This presents the server with a better-than-usual opportunity to place pressure on the receiver and to make a put-away shot of the receiver's return.

Ceiling Shots

The tournament-grade handball players make considerable use of the ceiling shot because it involves little chance for an error, and when hit into a corner it forces the opponent to return the ball when it is quite close to or in contact with a side wall. Although the ceiling shot is primarily a defensive shot, it usually forces the opponent to make a defensive shot in return. Should the opponent make a poor or weak return of the ceiling shot, the player is usually in excellent court position for a kill or pass shot, whereas the opponent is in a disadvantageous court position.

Speed of Return Shot

The champion handball player often hits the ball with considerable speed, thus giving his opponent minimum time in which to get set and make a return shot. Most beginners, until they have had considerable practice, are unable to hit the ball with this much speed. The good handball player, however, frequently hits the ball with different speeds—the change of pace often disconcerts the opponent and upsets his timing. One helpful aspect in hitting the ball fast and in deceptively changing the speed of the hit is to use considerable wrist action. By concentrating on a whiplike wrist action, a player can develop a fast shot that requires little backswing. In addition, this allows the player to inject deception into his shots. If he does wrist through a shot the ball will travel in one direction, whereas with the same arm movement and no wrist action the ball will travel at a different angle, which often fools the opponent.

SPECIFIC TRAINING METHODS

Indirect Training Methods

Observing tournament handball players usually convinces one that the majority are definitely above average in musculature and strength. Therefore, as an indirect method of training, the use of progressive resistance exercises, particularly weight training, can be extremely useful in developing additional strength and musculature, especially in the legs, shoulders, and arms. Another indirect method of training is to develop cardiorespiratory endurance by running. Although running distances, such as running a mile or jogging two miles every day, is quite helpful, training by sprinting fifty to one hundred and fifty yards, walking a short distance, and then repeating the sprint several times simulates quite closely the conditions under which handball games are played, and is most valuable to the player. Games and sports that involve close eye-hand coordination and quick starts and hand and feet movement, such as table tennis, squash racquets, and so on, are also valuable training of an indirect nature. Doing flexibility exercises in order to attain a comfortable low crouch easily is beneficial.

Direct Training Methods

Several direct training methods, which should have maximum transfer of skill value, can be practiced systematically by the handball player who wants to improve his handball-playing ability at a maximum rate. Many players practice the same shot fifty to one hundred times per session and then mass practice another shot. This is particularly helpful at first in mastering ceiling shots, back-wall shots, back-wall kill shots, kill shots from either side wall with either hand, and kill shots with either hand when the ball rebounds off the front wall. Practice of this nature allows the player to concentrate on developing the same actions for each shot, to correct errors noted in previous practice, and to develop a deep feeling of all the movements and facets of each shot. However, it is highly important that the player intersperse this practice with competitive games, because in the game situation he will not often repeat the same shot twice in succession. A good idea is to practice a series of shots of various kinds and then to play a game before engaging in additional practice. During his practice the player can fully concentrate on the correct body position in executing a shot, making sure that he is moving toward the front wall as he executes the shot, and that he takes a full backswing and follow-through. He can also concentrate on attaining complete wrist action, on watching the ball closely until his glove contacts it, and then going to a ready position in the center of the court.

When playing a game the player should intently strive to be aware of his opponent's position at all times, and he should concentrate on developing the ability to sense if the opponent is moving, and if so in what direction, at the time that the player is preparing to make his shot. This ability can be gained with concentrated practice, thus enabling the player to change his shot at the last minute in order to take advantage of his opponent's position. On all kill shots the player should intently practice getting his body in a low crouched position.

Another training method often used as a warm-up is for the player to play himself, trying to keep the ball in the front half of the court or even within ten feet of the front wall. He can play his right hand against his left hand, or just keep the ball in play as long as possible. Some advanced players, in order to sharpen their game and improve their reactions, speed, and endurance, play singles against two players.

ADVANCED TECHNIQUES AND SKILLS OF HANDBALL PLAY

Introduction

Several factors differentiate the champion handball player from the average handball player. Some of these factors are innate and hence are subject to little or no improvement. This includes such items as body size. Most of the champions are in the 5'7" to 6' tall category, although it may be that the quite tall person with above-average body weight is attracted to other sports and hence does not develop his potential for handball play. Although a player may strive to improve his reaction time, speed, and running ability, he is limited by his built-in potential as to how far these traits can be developed. Only a very few people, for example, have the potential ability to develop into a 9.5 or faster 100-yard dash performer. However, most players can—with proper instruction, training, and practice—enhance considerably the various components of their handball play.

Some of the areas in which improvement can be made include (1) developing the ability to hop and slide the ball on the serve and during play; (2) improving running speed, speed of movement, the ability to stop and change direction quickly, and the knack of anticipating an opponent's play and studying his game in detail to detect any weaknesses; (3) developing handball playing strategy until it is second to none; and (4) developing the ability to hustle on every play, together with a strong and accurate off-hand.

Hustling. One difference that often marks the mediocre player from the advanced player is that the latter generally hustles for any possible return that he might be able to get. At times the ball takes a surprising bounce or rides the side wall some distance; the player who has made an all-out effort from the beginning often retrieves what appears to be an impossible-to-get shot. Having the ability to hustle and force the game to the opponent throughout a match places great pressure on the other player and often forces him to play the hustler's type of game. This concept includes a willingness always to assume a correct basic court position immediately after making a shot, trying to take the front-center position away from the opponent at all times, and moving the opponent about the court as much as possible. Along with hustle, patience is sometimes the key in winning a game. Although the player must never overlook an opportunity to go for a winning shot when one is presented, he must on the other hand insure that he and the ball are actually in a position where the probability of making a winning shot is favorable. The temptation to rush or force the shots or attempt to kill a difficult shot when out of position or off-balance should be avoided. Instead, defensive shots that force the opponent out of position should be taken.

Shots with Off-hand. The advanced skills of handball include mastering the common shots with the non-dominant hand. With considerable practice and some instruction, coaching, and self-analysis, the player should eventually be able with his off-hand to kill with at least a modicum of success when in a favorable court position, serve a fairly decent serve, and hit ceiling shots that die in the back corner most of the time. Because the non-dominant hand is usually consistently attacked, the player should strive to become as strong as possible with the shots taken by the nondominant hand, especially the defensive shots. Most champion handball players have practiced so much that it is sometimes difficult to tell which is their dominant hand when watching them play.

When killing the ball with an underhand stroke, especially with the off-hand, the player (as fast as possible) should visualize pushing the ball to the spot on the front wall where he is attempting to direct his kill shot. Some players successfully develop the ability to kill the ball with a straight-arm, underhand, or sidearm fist shot with the nondominant hand. In general the use of the fist shot with the strong hand should be avoided because other types of shots are more accurate.

Hopping the Ball. The ability to cause the ball to hop (angle sharply sideward) after it strikes the floor on a serve (or shot) often disconcerts the receiver, and if an ace does not result, the receiver often makes a weak return that can easily be put away by the server. Different players employ different techniques in attempting to cause the ball to hop. Some work better for some players than for others.

One simple method of hopping the ball is to imagine that it is divided into a right and a left half, each paralleling the right and left half of the court when divided lengthwise. The server drops the ball a short distance, often spinning it slightly backward with thumb and finger motion so that it rebounds off the floor with no spin whatsoever. He then knifes his hand along either the right or left outer side of the ball in order to impart a sideward spin to it. When performing this action with the palm facing toward the body, the server faces somewhat toward the front wall. In cutting the side of the ball facing the server, he stands in a regular side-wall facing position and has the back of his hand facing his body, striking the ball first with the little-finger side of his hand. This method of hopping the ball places minimum hop on it but does have the advantage of causing little or no long-term soreness to the serving arm or shoulder.

The most effective methods of hopping the ball involve a combination forward and sideward direction of the arm swing and a quick wrist snap (forearm rotation) at the time the ball is contacted. The most natural type of hop, which for a right-handed person causes the ball to hop to his left, is one in which the hand travels in toward the body (outside-in) as it travels forward in hitting the ball. The ball is contacted in the palm of the hand near the little-finger side and rotates along the palm of the hand until it contacts the thumb, which is positioned alongside the index finger. The ball rotates off the end of the thumb, thus creating a ball spin that has little apparent effect on the front-wall rebound angle, but that takes a hop as the ball strikes the floor on the first bounce. Most players start this serve with their palm facing slightly down toward the floor and finish with the back of their hand facing the floor. The other type of serving action, which results in less hop, involves a movement in which the hand travels out away from the body while it is moving forward. The palm of the hand faces slightly upward, or at least toward the front wall, and as the ball is struck near the index finger of the palm the hand is rotated down toward the floor and the ball spins off the palm on the little-finger side.

When hitting a maximum-hop ball, the player must employ a maximum of wrist action and arm whip as the hand contacts the ball. The slower the ball is served, the more apparent hop it has, but the more time the receiver has in which to react to the change in the ball path. In making these serves, some players also place some underspin or overspin on the ball, thus causing it to bounce higher or lower than normal.

Slice Serves. Another type of serve, which also involves a whipping action of the arm, is the slice serve, in which most of the english placed on the ball takes effect on the front wall. This type of hit, which is also effective in returning the ball alongside a side wall, involves an outside-in action of the arm and hand as the serve is made, but no wrist rotation need take place. Instead, only a comfortable sidearm stroking action is made, and the ball contacts the palm of the hand and slides sideward off the straight or semiflexed fingers. This action for a right-handed hit causes the ball hit to the right side of the front wall to hop toward the center of the court, thus sliding down the right wall during its flight toward the back wall. If hit to the left side, a right-handed slide shot hops toward the left wall as it rebounds off the front wall. The opposite hopping actions take place when the ball is hit with the left hand.

Fly Kills. A fly kill is a kill shot made while the ball is still rebounding from the front wall and before it has contacted the floor. To fly kill successfully requires quickly getting into position and excellent timing. The fly kill often catches the opponent off-guard and out of position, thus introducing a surprise element that some opponents find disconcerting.

Side-wall Kills. With practice, many handball players become adept at killing the ball from the back court by having it first strike a side wall five to ten feet behind the front wall. In this type of kill the ball strikes the side wall six to twelve inches above the floor, from which it angles to the front wall, contacting it only a few inches above the floor level. For this kill, in which the ball rides up on the side wall, the ball is hit to that side wall to which the hitting arm is nearest (for example, right hand to right side wall). Using a sidearm stroke, the ball should be hit with considerable speed, allowing it to slide off the fingertips. The same hand-same side-wall kill shot works especially well when killing a ball rebounding off the back wall.

In order to take advantage of the unusual angle at which the ball comes off the front wall, some players have perfected a kill shot in which the ball is struck to the side wall opposite the hand hitting the ball. The ball is stroked in the same fashion as for the same hand-same side-wall kill, but the ball must hit very close to the front wall becuase the ball tends to rebound at almost a right angle from the sidewall. For a right-handed shot the ball should hit the left side wall twelve inches or so behind the front wall.

Crotch Balls.
Serves. With practice some players develop a serve in which the ball, after rebounding off the front wall, strikes the side wall and floor simultaneously, which causes it to rebound at an odd, unexpected angle. A crotch-ball serve is sometimes attempted when hopping the ball; using a sidearm or semiunderhand stroke and directing the ball to either side wall.

Kills. A few players develop expertise in making a crotch-ball kill in which the ball simultaneously strikes the side wall and floor. A crotch kill bounces very little, is unanticipated, and is difficult to return. The crotch ball kill normally is aimed at a spot fairly close behind the front wall. This kill shot, which is usually attempted from the front court, can be done with either hand and toward either side wall.

Soft Kill. A winning shot on occasions is the soft kill, in which the ball is semilobbed low to the front wall or corner where it quickly dies. A soft kill shot works especially well if used infrequently when the opponent is in the back court or is moving backward. Very rarely should a soft kill be tried when the opponent is up.

Backward Rebound Shot. A special shot, which is sometimes used when the player can hardly get to the ball and is out of position, is to hit the ball vigorously into the back wall at a slight upward angle. The ball should rebound off the back wall and travel on the fly all the way to the front wall. Care should be taken that the ball is hit with sufficient force and height that the opponent is not presented with a set-up kill-shot opportunity.

Vary Speed of Return. An advanced handball skill is probably a mastery of the ability to vary the speed of the shots. Although outstanding handball players normally hit the ball quite forcefully and vigorously, they still attempt to control the speed of the hit and the distance the ball rebounds. In particular, it is important that the player not hit the ball at the same tempo of speed at all times, thus enabling his opponent to predict successfully how forcefully each shot will be hit and thus anticipate too early where to go to return the shot. Instead, the player should occasionally hit a soft shot and otherwise vary the speed of his returns in order to confuse the opponent as much as possible. This tactic will cause the opponent to not be able to get set too soon for the return shot.

COMMON ERRORS AND THEIR CORRECTIONS

The beginning handball player frequently commits many errors that he must quickly learn to recognize and work conscientiously to overcome if he is to attain success. After each play or rally is concluded, the player should form the habit of reviewing how he played the shots in that particular series and attempt to discover if he committed any errors that could have been avoided.

A common error that even experienced handball players commit, especially if tired, is to fail to return to the base position near the center of the court as soon as possible after making a shot. The unthinking thing after making a shot is to remain standing in that court position and see what happens to the shot just made and to watch the opponent to see what he is doing. Instead, the player must, as soon as he hits a shot, move immediately to the best court position for returning his opponent's probable shot.

Another common error is to hit the ball when it is behind the body. Instead, an extra step should be taken and the ball hit when it is even with, or somewhat in front of, the body. Many players fail to develop the ability to concentrate on making a shot while still recognizing the court positions of their opponents as rapidly as they should. By deliberately concentrating at times on what the opponent is doing, the player can develop the ability to recognize not only where the opponent is but in what direction he is moving just before and while the shot is being made. This ability enables a player to hit behind an opponent who is moving about the court. Often the footsteps of the opponent are sufficiently loud that his court position can be located.

An error frequently encountered is to hit the ball while it is too high, especially when a kill shot is attempted. Instead of hitting a high ball downward, the player should take one or two extra running steps to the rear and make sure that the ball is knee height or below when he contacts it.

Another common error is to attempt to kill the ball when the player cannot get into the correct body or court position and thus has to force a hurried shot. A difficult-to-return kill shot should usually be carefully placed; the player must be in the proper position in order to maximize his chances to do this.

A failure to position the body sideward to the front wall inhibits the full range of the backward and forward arm swing and can result in a poorly directed shot. When shooting with the nondominant hand, the player should especially try to face the side wall before hitting the ball. Except when volleying fast-hit balls in the front part of the court, the player should usually face sideways for most of his strokes.

The beginning handball player needs to focus his attention on keeping his fingers tightly against one another and his thumb alongside his index finger. Otherwise, the ball on some hits is apt to slip between his fingers. Another correction for this is to concentrate on hitting the ball in the palm of the hand until the fingers automatically stay together on all shots.

Some handball players tend to overrely on the fist shot. The main purpose of the fist shot is to hit the ball forcefully, driving it by the opponent before he is set to make a return. Because for most players a fist ball is an inaccurate shot, it should only be used on special occasions.

Handball 285

In doubles play the players must avoid both going for the same ball. The partners must know each other's game to the point where they automatically know who is going to take what ball. In case of any doubt, the partner who wants the ball should quickly call out "Mine," in order to warn his partner away from the ball. However, if a player has a difficult-to-get return, his partner can back him up in case of a miss.

Another common error in doubles play is for the aggressive or strong player on a team to be overly aggressive. This results in this player taking a center court position, thus leaving his partner only one fourth of the court to defend. The overly aggressive player must curb his impulse to take too many shots, and he must trust his partner's ability.

SELF-EVALUATION

The game of handball is one in which a player (or doubles team) can continuously evaluate his play and his progress by comparing his score against the score achieved by others with whom he has played before. However, different players will improve at different rates. The usual method of evaluating progress in handball is to play a given opponent and note whether the match was won or lost and how many points were scored.

Another method of evaluating handball skill and progress is tournament play. The usual types of tournaments involve ladder or pyramid tournaments in which the play is continuous over a period of perhaps several weeks. They are informal in nature. Because of the luck of the draw, single- or double-elimination and consolation tournaments are not as helpful in evaluating one's progress in handball.

The player can attempt several successful shots of the same type and count or record how many of those he succeeds in making within acceptable limits. For example, he might attempt fifteen back-wall kills into the right front corner, or a crisscross serve to the back wall, or a hop serve and note how much the ball hops. Some players evaluate the success of their efforts to develop their nondominant hand by playing a game of dominant hand versus nondominant hand in which they alternate hitting the ball with each hand.

Glossary of Terms

Ace: A serve that is not returned by the receiver.
Avoidable hinder: Avoidable interference to a player who is playing the ball. The penalty for an avoidable hinder is the loss of serve or point.
Back-wall shot: A shot made by hitting the ball after it rebounds off the back wall but before it hits the floor.
Ceiling shot: A shot that hits the ceiling before (or after) it hits the front wall.
Chop: A downward slicing motion on the ball as the hand moves forward.
Crotch ball: A ball that hits the junction of any two surfaces, such as a side wall and the floor, or a side and front wall in a corner.
Dead ball: A ball that goes out of play without penalty.
Defensive shot: A shot made with the purpose of not allowing the opponent to make a put-away or winning shot.
Drive: A forcefully hit low shot that travels quickly into the back court.
Error: The failure to return a playable ball when the possibility exists that it could have been returned.
Fault: An illegally served ball. Two successive faults result in a hand-out.
Fist ball: Hitting the ball on the heel of the hand (or back of the fingers) while the fist is clenched. Occasionally, the ball is hit on the fingers, but this is not recommended.
Fly ball: Hitting the ball while it is still rebounding from the front wall and before it has struck the floor the first time.
Foot fault: Placing or moving the foot or feet outside the service zone while serving the ball. This is against the rules and can result in the loss of the serving turn.
Hand-out: The loss of serve by the server.
Hinder: An accidental interference of the opponent or the flight of the ball during play in which no penalty is invoked.
Hop: A ball that, after it strikes the floor, rebounds more to the right or left than is normally expected.
Kill: A shot hit so low to the front wall that it is unreturnable by the opponent.
Lob: A serve or a shot that is hit high and without much force and that drops at a sharp angle to the floor.
Offensive shot: A shot that either wins the rally or forces the opponent into a poor court position and causes him to make a weak return.
Out: The act of ending the service term of the server. This occurs when the server fails to serve the ball legally or when he fails to return a ball that is legally in play.
Pass shot: A shot that passes the opponent beyond his reach.
Rally: The play that occurs from the time that the ball is served until the ball is not legally returned, thus ending the play.
Service box: An area formed on either side of the service area by a line eighteen inches out from the side wall. The nonserving partner in doubles play must stand in this box while the serve is being made, and his back must be against the wall.
Service line: The line that is five feet in front of the short line.

Service zone: The area of the court that lies between the outside edges of the short line and the service line.

Shadow serve: A serve in which the view of the receiver is momentarily blocked by the server's body or his partner. Shadow (screen) serves are served again without a fault having occurred because they are considered a hinder.

Short serve: An illegal serve that causes a server to lose one serving attempt.

Short line: The line that divides the front and back courts into equal halves.

Side out: Loss of a serving turn by the player or doubles team.

Selected References

BOOKS

Handball Rules. Skokie, Ill.: United States Handball Association.

The latest handball rules can be obtained from the USHA by writing them at 4101 Dempster St., Skokie, Illinois 60076. In addition other information pertaining to handball is included in the booklet.

Phillips, B. E. *Handball: Its Play and Management.* New York: Ronald, 1957.

This was one of the first books to appear that was devoted entirely to the performance of handball skills and techniques and the strategy involved in playing handball. Many of the fundamentals and techniques discussed in this book are still applicable to the game. 120 pp.

Roberson, Richard, and Herbert Olson. *Beginning Handball.* Belmont, Calif.: Wadsworth, 1962.

This booklet might be considered one of the first modern booklets devoted to the play of handball written for college students. The authors are both accomplished handball players and instructors and have much valuable information in their booklet concerning the playing of handball and the application of handball strategy. 62 pp.

Van Goerdt, Carl. *Scientific Handball.* Los Angeles, Calif.: The author, 220 W. 46th Street.

Yessis, Michael. *Handball.* Dubuque, Iowa: Brown, 1966.

This paperback booklet includes an exhaustive treatment of the game and is written by a handball player with a wide knowledge of the game. It is outstanding for its many illustrations and diagrams. 70 pp.

PERIODICALS

Ace Magazine. United States Handball Association, 4101 Dempster St., Skokie, Illinois 60076.

Ace Magazine is devoted to handball and in recent years also to racquetball. Much valuable advice on the play of handball is given in articles written by various handball champions and other recognized authorities of the game. In addition, the results of handball tournaments and local handball news are given. A subscription to *Ace Magazine* is included with membership in the USHA.

CHAPTER 19

Racquetball and paddleball

Donald R. Casady*
The University of Iowa

HISTORY

The games of racquetball and paddleball, while highly similar, are presently played with two sets of equipment and two sets of rules. Paddleball, which is played with a solid paddle, was originated in 1930, at the University of Michigan, by Earl Riskey. Until World War II, the game was chiefly played at that University. Because of the number of servicemen stationed there during World War II and because of the wide appeal of the game, it rapidly spread and is now played at many athletic clubs, YMCAs, colleges, and universities all over the United States. A national paddleball association was formed at the University of Michigan a few years ago. This organization regularly publishes the rules of paddleball.

In recent years a short-handled stringed racket has been adapted for play by many of the YMCAs, colleges, and universities. In 1967, the publishers of *Ace Magazine* ("The Official Voice of Handball") began including articles and other information about paddleball (racquetball) in their publication. Their efforts have resulted in the development of the game of racquetball and the formation of the International Racquetball Association, which has formulated the rules of racquetball. Because both games have traditionally been played in a handball court and because the rules of paddleball and racquetball have been adapted from handball rules, they are highly similar.

Except for the facts that in paddleball a solid paddle (racket) is used and in racquetball a stringed racket is used (both are approximately the same size), and that the official ball for both games differs somewhat, the two games—their skills, techniques, strategies, and rules—are almost identical. Therefore, in this chapter unless a specific difference exists, the term racquetball will be used to designate both games. The game of paddle tennis also makes use of a paddle similar to the ones used in paddleball; however, because paddle tennis is played on a small court with a low net in the middle, it more nearly resembles tennis than it does paddleball or racquetball. Today, racquetball is growing in popularity for many reasons. It appears that in the future racquetball will be quite widespread and its popularity will be limited mainly by a shortage of courts.

THE GAME OF RACQUETBALL

Racquetball, which closely resembles the game of handball, except that paddles or rackets are used to hit the special hollow ball, has a lot of action, and the beginner can play the game with enjoyment during his first session of play. A handball player can, within a few minutes, play a game of racquetball with fair skill and with an understanding of the basic strategy involved.

The ball is put in play by a server who hits it against the front wall. It is returned by the server's opponent, the receiver. The players continue to alternate returning the ball on the fly to the front wall, hitting the ball either on the fly or after the first bounce. Play continues until a

---

*Dr. Casady, a charter member of the International Racquetball Association, has been playing paddleball and racquetball for approximately fifteen years, being introduced to the game by his gymnastics coach, a graduate of the University of Michigan. He is considered by some to be the unofficial University of Iowa singles champion. He has won a number of championships in local tournaments. Dr. Casady has taught the game to many college students. The game of racquetball is introduced to approximately 1,500 college students per year at The University of Iowa.

288 *Individual and Team Sports*

player fails to legally return the ball by making it strike the front wall before it hits the floor. A game normally consists of 21 points. Only the server can score a point by winning the play; if the receiver wins, he wins the serve.

Racquetball can be played by two players (singles), three players (cut-throat), or four players (doubles). In cut-throat the server stands the other two players and when the server loses the play, all players rotate clockwise one position—the left-back-court player then becomes the server. In doubles two players compete against two other players, and the sides alternate hitting the ball, but either player on a side can hit the ball when it is his team's turn. The strokes used in racquetball play resemble those of most racket games, necessitating the use of forearm and backarm strokes as well as underhand and overhead strokes.

UNIQUE VALUES OF RACQUETBALL

Racquetball has many commendable features that highly recommend it to a wide range of potential players. Unlike most games or sports, racquetball can usually be played with enjoyment by beginners on their first attempt. As with other racket games practice adds to the enjoyment (and amount of exercise) that can be derived from playing it. The game can be played by the old or young, by the fit or unfit, by men or women, and at about any pace that the participants desire. The rigorousness of racquetball play and the demands made on the player can be controlled, because the duration of play during a rally is short. This activity is ideally suited for the person who is not physically fit, for the older person, or for mixed play. Yet, racquetball play can be quite intense and very demanding of the most highly skilled and conditioned players. A minimum of equipment is required and courts are usually available in schools, colleges, clubs, YMCAs, and other institutions. A modified game of racquetball can be played on one wall in a gymnasium or other makeshift facilities.

Regardless of the level of ability of the players, racquetball is an enjoyable game that provides a zestful workout but one that is not overly exhausting. Playing the game of racquetball can do much to enhance cardiorespiratory endurance, and it helps in the development of selected motor skills, agility, and—to some extent—flexibility. The player is presented with the opportunity to comprehend situations quickly, select appropriate shots and positions on the court, and apply various kinds of strategy. Doubles play in racquetball helps to develop a high degree of teamwork in which the movements and strategy of the two partners are closely coordinated. Racquetball play helps to develop timing and coordination and the ability to utilize the proper mechanics of movement, especially the placement of the feet in traversing the court.

RACQUETBALL EQUIPMENT

Racquetball, like handball, can be played on one-wall, three-wall, or four-wall handball courts. The dimensions of the one-wall and four-wall court are shown in Figure 19-1. Racquetball can also be played with enjoyment on a squash racquets court in which squash racquets rules are employed, and a shot that hits the metal telltale placed low on the front wall is a fault.

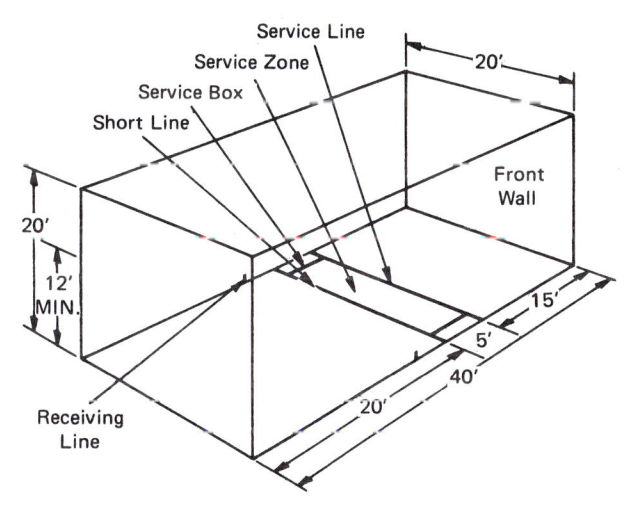

Figure 19-1(a). Standard four-wall court dimensions.

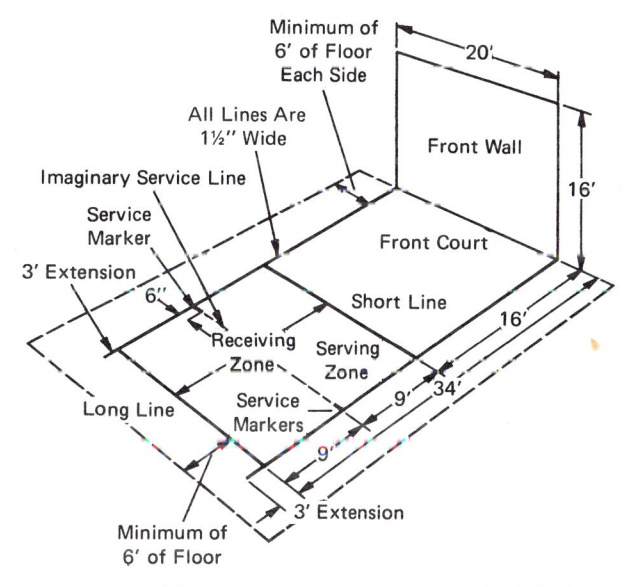

Figure 19-1(b). One-wall court dimensions: 16′ x 20′ x 34′.

Racquetball and Paddleball

The paddle can be a solid one with a wooden or plastic head, which is available in a variety of models. The stringed racket, which somewhat resembles a short-handled tennis racket, is manufactured by several companies. Aluminum rackets are quite popular. In this chapter the term racket will be used to refer to either a paddle or a racket.

Four types of balls are presently used for racquetball play. (1) The official paddleball ball is grayish-purple with a small hole placed in it. (2) A bright blue ball that is somewhat smaller than the official racquetball ball. (3) The pinkish-red ball, which is often called the pinkie, is the ball originally used in paddleball play (it is still used by some players). (4) The official IRA ball is Seamless 558, which is black and bouncy.

The player should wear loose-fitting clothes that permit full movement without binding or restricting him in any way. Shorts and T-shirt are the normal attire, and these are usually white in color. Well-fitting gym shoes should be worn. These can be low cuts or high cuts, depending on the preference of the player. Most players prefer to wear two pairs of socks, because starts and stops and vigorous turns are frequently made in the game of racquetball. The socks should be made of a highly absorbent material such as wool.

A highly recommended item of equipment is the eye guard, which is made of plastic or metal covered with molded rubber. Because the ball can travel with extreme speed, it is well worth the slight discomfort and slight restriction in the range of peripheral vision for the added safety and protection provided by an eye guard.

Players who perspire freely or who play in warm, non-ventilated courts find the use of sweat bands around the wrists and forehead to be worthwhile. Paddleball equipment can be ordered or obtained from most sporting goods stores or from the National Paddleball Organization, Sports Building, Ann Arbor, Michigan 48104. Racquetball equipment is widely sold at sporting goods stores and YMCAs.

BASIC RULES AND ETIQUETTE OF RACQUETBALL

Rules

With few exceptions, the rules of racquetball and handball are identical. One of the exceptions involves having the thong secured around the wrist at all times during racquetball play. The failure to have the thong around the wrist, shifting the grip on the racquetball racket from one hand to the other, or releasing or permitting the racket to slip and fly through the air are all illegal and result in a loss of serve or loss of point. The small restriction on play imposed by wearing the thong is well worth the assurance that no injuries will be caused by the racquet slipping from the player's grasp and hitting another player.

Serving. When serving the server must stand within the service zone during the complete act of serving until the served ball passes the service line. A failure to do so is a foot fault, which is a service violation or illegal serve. Two successive illegal serves result in a serve-out (loss of serve). In doubles play the server's partner must stand in the service box with his back to the side wall. The ball can be served with any kind of serving stroke—underhand, sidearm, or overhead. However, the ball must be dropped to the floor and struck on its first bounce in initiating the serve.

Illegal Serves. A served ball that *on the fly* hits the floor short of or on the short line, hits more than one side wall, or hits the ceiling or back wall is an illegal serve and cannot be played. Two illegal serves of any kind in succession put the server out (hand-out or serve-out).

Serve-out Serves. The following result in a serve-out (loss of serve): (1) the served ball not clearly hitting the front wall first (a crotch serve: for example, the served ball simultaneously hits the side wall and front wall); (2) the ball touching the server's body or clothes during the act of serving; (3) dropping the ball more than once when in the act of serving; and (4) striking at and missing the rebounding ball during the act of serving.

If the server's partner is hit by the served ball when standing outside the box (or outside the side line in one- and three-wall play), a loss of serve results. If hit when standing in the box, a hinder (dead ball) is called, and the ball is served again without the loss of a serving attempt.

Service in Doubles. When starting a game, during the first half of the first inning (an inning consists of one set of service turns by both teams) only one player on a doubles team is permitted a serving turn. Thereafter, both partners on each team are permitted their serving turn in their half of the inning. A serve can be made to any portion of the back court and does not have to be alternated to either side. Serving out of order results in a loss of serving turn, and the same player serving both turns on the doubles team results in a serve-out.

Receiving. The receiver must stay at least five feet behind the service line until the serve is made and he may not invade the service zone in returning the serve. The receiver may, in returning the serve, hit the ball on the fly or on its first bounce off the floor. If the receiver is not ready to receive the serve, he should make no attempt to play it and call out "Not ready." Should the return ball crotch between the front wall and the floor, then it is not legally returned. If the ball appears to roll back when it hits in this area, then it clearly hit the front wall first and is good. If the ball bounces upward after such a hit, it either hit the floor first or the front wall simultaneously. Because it did not clearly hit the front wall first the return is *not* good. On each return during play the ball can be hit only once by a player or a doubles team. However, if a player swings at the ball and misses it, he or his partner can again legally attempt to return the ball. A failure to return the service legally counts as a point for the server.

Play of Ball. If the ball is legally served, the play that follows is termed a volley. During the volley a violation of any of the following rules will result in a serve-out (if the violation is made by the server or his partner) or a point (if the violation is made by the receiver or his partner): (1) the struck ball goes out of the court; (2) both doubles partners simultaneously strike the ball; (3) the ball is struck more than once during a return; (4) hitting the ball with any part of the body, including the hand (only the racket can be used); (5) hitting the ball when the racket is not being held or the safety thong is not around the wrist; (6) deliberately failing to move sufficiently to allow the opponent a fair shot at the ball; or (7) deliberately pushing or blocking the opponent.

Unintentional Hinders. The player is entitled to a clear and unobstructed view of the ball, a clear and unobstructed opportunity to go in a straight line to get into position to play the ball, and a clear or unobstructed opportunity to freely swing his racket in stroking the ball. If for any reason any of these occur, the player is hindered and the point is replayed. Any unnecessary crowding of or interference with the opponent is a hinder. During the service the receiver is entitled to a clear view of the served ball and if his view is obstructed by the server or his partner, the receiver can call a hinder; this situation is called a shadow ball. An unintentional hinder occurs when a returned ball strikes an opponent on the fly on its path to the front wall. If a ball passes between the wall and the server's partner, who is standing in the server's box, a hinder is called, as it usually is anytime a ball passes between the legs of a player (straddle ball). A player, however, cannot hinder his partner. Local playing rules may include unintentional hinder rules concerning dead areas of the court, such as light obstructions, doors that do not fit smoothly on the back wall surface, and so on. The ball (and the racket) must be dry during play. Any time that a ball breaks during play, the point is replayed because a hinder has occurred.

Intentional Hinders. A player who intentionally interferes with an opponent, or in any way deliberately prevents him from having a fair opportunity to hit the ball, has committed an intentional hinder, which results in a point or serve-out—depending on who served the ball. As soon as a player strikes the ball he must immediately give his opponent a fair opportunity to see the ball, get into position to hit it, and to take an unobstructed swing at it.

Scoring. Points are scored by the serving team only, and then only when they win the rally after their serve or else serve an ace. If the receiving team wins the rally, the server loses his service turn (a serve-out in singles play). The game is won by the player first scoring 21 points. A match is ordinarily two out of three games. The serve is determined by a toss of a coin (or by volleying the ball from the back wall, aiming for the best kill, or the lob closest to the short line); the winner chooses whether to serve or receive.

The resumé of the commonly encountered rules of paddleball presented in this section is fairly complete. However, the rules of racquetball are subject to change at any time. Therefore, the latest rules of the National Paddleball Association or the International Racquetball Association should be consulted for the most current rules of the game.

Etiquette

As in most games the golden rule also applies to racquetball. Treat your opponent as you would like him to treat you. In a tournament match a referee is often present to call hinders, faults, and rule violations. However, when friendly competitors play, the contestants themselves must call rule infractions, usually on themselves. The gentlemanly procedure when calling a close decision is to give the benefit of the doubt to the opponent. Often, however, the customary thing to do is to replay a point if a question or disagreement exists as to whether the shot was good, the play was legal, or a rule was violated.

Because racquetball play, particularly in doubles, involves much close contact, the sensible thing is to be extremely generous in granting hinders to the opponent or in requesting them. Almost all players would prefer that a hinder be called rather than attempt a shot and take the risk of hitting an opponent. If the competition is not too intense, it is sometimes customary to ask for a hinder when the opponent is standing directly in front of the player rather than hit him with the ball. In tournament competition, however, some players deliberately play some distance forward of the opponent when he is hitting the ball in order to be in position to block certain shots or else force a different shot direction to be taken. The intensity of the competition and the closeness with which hinders will be called should be discussed before competition begins in a match.

Local rules may involve such items as replaying the point when a ball strikes a wet wall surface and causes the ball to slide, or it strikes a dead or protruding surface on the court, such as light fixtures or cracks.

Safety

As for any sport involving vigorous physical activity, the racquetball player will play with increased comfort and safety if he first warms up. Such informal warm-up methods as performing calisthenics, stretching, and other flexibility exercises can be done to aid the player to achieve a full range of movements. The formal warm-up, which the player begins at a moderate pace, consists of replicating the same types of movements as are employed in regular play. Emphasis is given to stroking the ball, in which, for example, short volleys in the front court, serves, kills, and back-wall shots can each be practiced several times. During the combination warm-up and practice, the player should concentrate on correctly positioning his body before taking each shot.

Other safety aspects of racquetball include (1) purposefully restricting large, sweeping backswings and follow-throughs of strokes to avoid the danger of hitting another player with the racket, (2) being liberal in asking for and calling hinders, (3) avoiding the tendency to crowd the opponent when he is stroking the ball, (4) wearing eye guards, (5) wearing a safety thong around the wrist during all play, and (6) the two partners closely coordinating their shots and efforts when playing doubles. During practice and play the safety thong should be checked frequently to insure that it is securely fastened to the wrist.

If the court is warm and humid, causing much perspiration, it is essential to wipe the floor surface. A person could slip and fall when rapidly stopping, starting, or turning. Whenever the palm or the racket handle becomes moist, the player should carefully dry them before continuing play. The wearing of a sweatband around the wrist can help to prevent this condition.

FUNDAMENTAL SKILLS AND TECHNIQUES OF RACQUETBALL

Although the player can enjoy limited success in utilizing the carry-over skills acquired in playing handball or other racket games such as tennis, squash racquets, or badminton, his success and progress should be enhanced if he studiously practices the fundamental skills that comprise the game of racquetball. The directions for performing these skills are presented for right-handed players; hence, the directions must be reversed for left-handed players.

Grip on Racket

The western grip is most commonly employed for grasping the racket. This grip is used by most players in playing forehand strokes and when serving the ball. This is the familiar shake-hands grip in which the racket head is perpendicular to the floor while the handle is grasped as if shaking hands with it. In this position the thumb is wrapped around the handle and the index finger is often slightly advanced to a triggerlike position. To play the backhand stroke, if sufficient time is available, the racket is rotated counterclockwise toward the thumb a quarter turn. This rotation of the racket places its face perpendicular to the floor and parallel with the front wall when the hand and arm are in their natural position. In playing quick volley shots, particularly when close to the front wall, the player may not have time to shift the racket from the forehand to the backhand position. Instead, he rotates his forearm a quarter turn counterclockwise in order to position the racket at the proper angle.

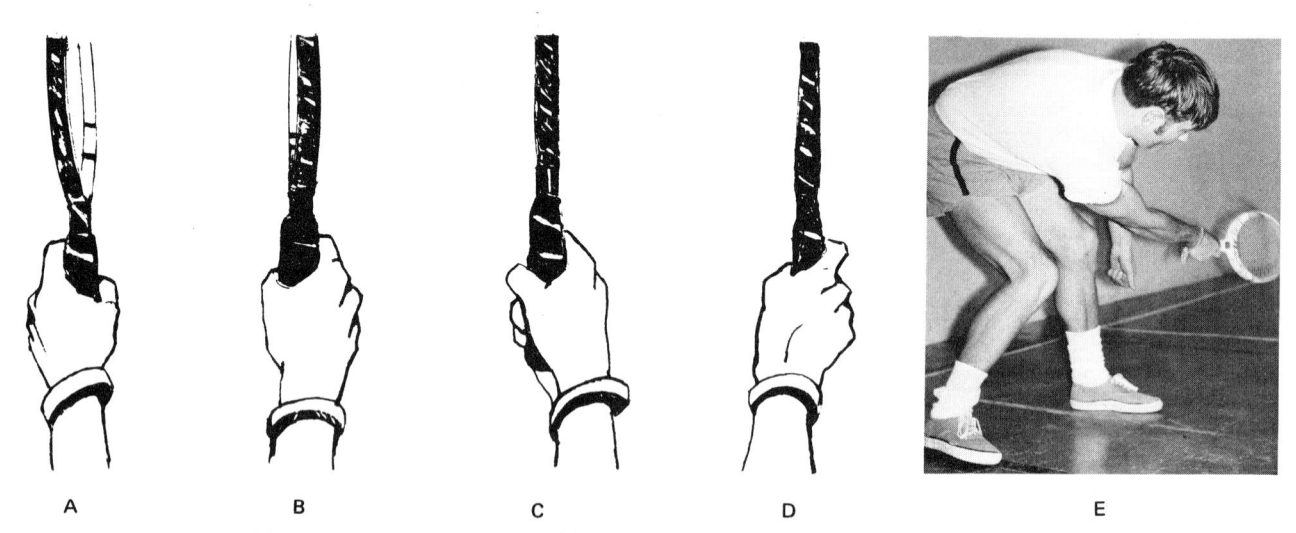

Figure 19-2. (a) Lefthanded continental grip. (b) Righthanded continental grip. (If the continental grip is used, the racket handle need not be rotated for either a backhand or a forehand stroke.) (c) Righthanded forehand grip. (d) Righthanded backhand grip. (e) Western grip (shake hands grip). (This grip permits the player to hit the ball with either a forehand or a backhand stroke by rotating only the wrist or forearm.)

Figure 19-3. Forehand stroke. (Photograph taken just after the ball was stroked.)

Forehand Stroke

The forehand stroke (used to hit a ball that is on the same side of the body as the arm and hand holding the paddle) is quite similar to the stroke used in tennis, except that the backswing is shortened (or sometimes almost eliminated) and the follow-through is usually considerably shortened. The modified backswing distance is necessary for most strokes in racquetball because of the speed with which the ball may be returned to the hitter and to lessen the danger of hitting an opponent with the racket. After hitting the ball the player must immediately come to a ready position facing the front court, ready to stroke his next shot. If little time is available to stroke the ball, it is mainly returned by wrist action. In playing the forehand shot the player normally pivots on his right (or rear) foot and steps toward the front wall with his left (or forward) foot. When executing the forehand stroke, as the ball approaches, the player begins the backswing with the racket, slightly loops it, and then swings it forward. His racket should contact the ball when it is even with or (preferably) slightly in front of his body. The ball can be hit when it is shoulder height or lower, but it is best if the ball is at waist height or lower. Depending on the height of the ball, the body is usually lowered somewhat by crouching the hips and bending the knees.

Backhand Stroke

When executing the backhand stroke the racket is first rotated a quarter of a turn counterclockwise, utilizing the nongripping hand on the throat of the racket to quickly turn it. The nonplaying hand also helps pull the racket back while the player steps back with his left (rear) foot and then during the stroke steps toward the front wall with his right (front) foot. As the ball approaches, the racket is pulled back and then swung forward, contacting the ball when it is even with, or slightly in front of, the body. If little time is available, the backswing and foreswing are considerably shortened and wrist action may be the main source for propelling the ball to the front wall. When time permits, many players will sometimes run an extra distance and then move to a poor court position in order to return the ball with a forehand stroke, which they believe to be much stronger than their backhand stroke. This practice is acceptable if not overdone, but the backhand stroke may always remain weak because of lack of practice.

Overhead Stroke

Either a backhand or a forehand stroke can be used to hit the ball when it is above the head of the player. For most overhead strokes the action resembles the full or three-quarters overhead throw, and the instructions for performing the forehand stroke apply. Quite often, however, instead of hitting an overhead shot, it is more feasible to wait for the ball to rebound off the back wall or to run back a few steps and hit the ball when it is lower—waist level or (preferably) at about knee level.

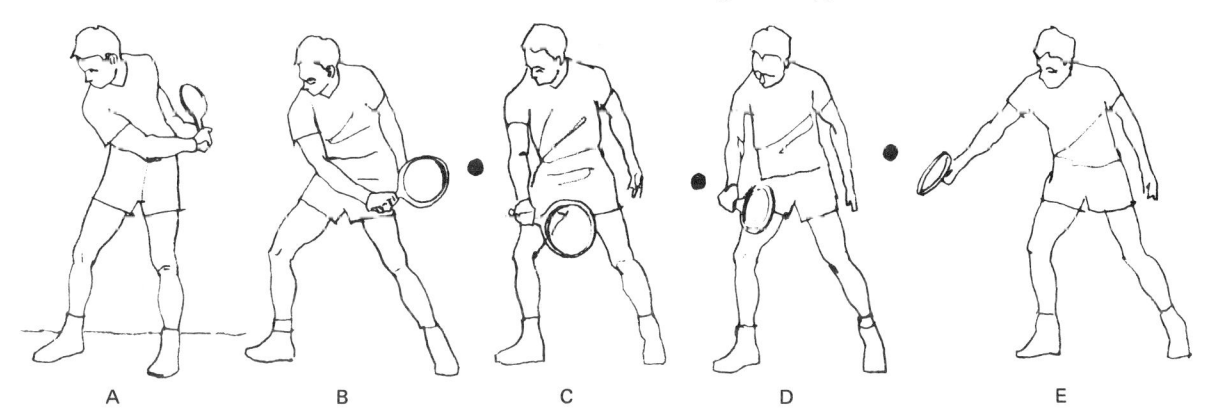

A   B   C   D   E

Figure 19-4. Backhand stroke sequence. (If little time is available in which to stroke the ball, increased wrist action and a decreased arm swing must be employed.)

Racquetball and Paddleball

Underhand Stroke

Many players, while awaiting the ball, stand directly facing the front wall and with their racket held directly under their hitting hand, which is immediately in front of their body. This racket and body position enable them to move quickly to either a backhand or forehand position. When standing in front court, if the ball is low and fast, it often must be hit with an underhand stroke, which somewhat resembles a snappy underarm throw used by a basketball shortstop for a quick throw. In this stroke the racket head is carried through fairly close to the lower legs. Considerable wrist action and little follow-through are usual for this stroke. If the underhand stroke is taken on the backhand side, a pushing type action is often employed.

Serving

The main purpose of the serve is to put the ball into play and hopefully to move the receiver to a disadvantageous court position. Although it is sometimes possible to make an ace serve that eludes the receiver, the server should take advantage of his favorable court position and concentrate on exploiting it and the unfavorable court position of the receiver.

Drive Serve. The drive serve—a low, fast-moving serve that just crosses the short line and usually takes a second bounce before hitting the back wall—is much used in racquetball. This serve is usually directed to the opponent's backhand, and the receiver must often hurriedly return it before being able to get into a good position for stroking the ball. The drive serve is normally hit with a sidearm or underarm type of forehand stroke in which the player strives to accurately place the ball, often on the left side wall. Some players may cut the ball by stroking from the outside in toward their body or from behind their body forward and away from their body in order to put some spin on the ball and cause it to hop or slide slightly.

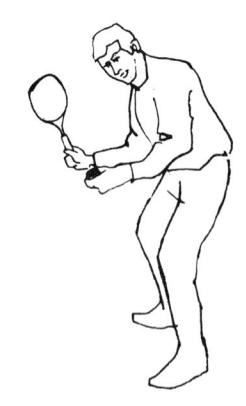

Figure 19-5. Preparing to serve.

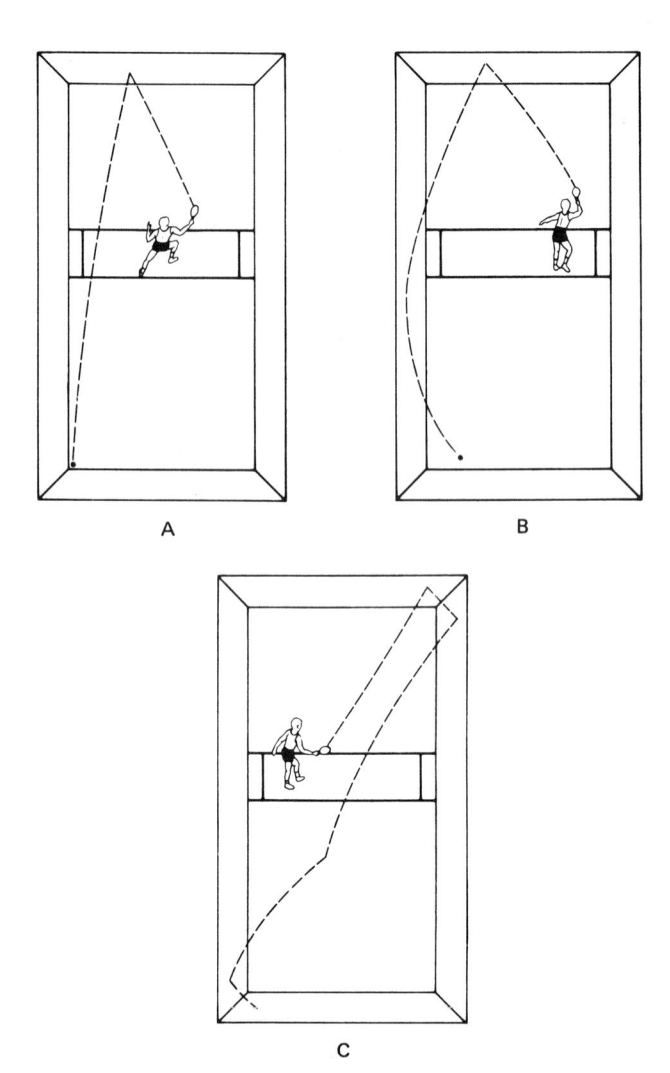

Figure 19-6. (a) Drive serve. (b) Lob serve. (c) Crisscross serve.

Lob Serve. Another frequently used serve is the lob serve, which hits high on the front wall, rebounds back just under the ceiling, and is generally aimed to land on the floor a few feet short of the back wall—where it takes a high bounce and dies just before or after it reaches the back wall. This serve can be hit with an underhand, sidearm, or overhead stroke and is generally aimed along one of the side walls. It has the advantage of holding the receiver in the back court, usually in a corner. In addition to being in an unfavorable area of the court, the receiver is often unable to do much with his return, giving an advantage to the server, who is in a favorable court position.

Crisscross Serve. (Z serve) The crisscross serve, when well placed, usually forces the receiver to return the served ball shortly after it rebounds at a sharp angle from his near side wall, thus giving the receiver little time to play his shot. Standing near one side wall (usually the left), the receiver hits the ball diagonally to the opposite front corner, from which it immediately rebounds to the side wall and angles back to the same side of the court from which it was served. The ball, after hitting the floor, may rebound off the side wall at an unexpected angle and sometimes dies very close to the back wall.

Paddleball Shots

The three factors discussed subsequently are fundamental to the successful and skillful development of the ability to expertly execute paddleball shots.

Always Watch the Ball. A basic axiom of any game in which a moving ball is involved is to always watch the ball when it is in play. This is particularly true in racquetball, especially for the beginning or unskilled player. On every stroke the player should attempt to watch the ball so closely that he sees his racket contact it. This, coupled with attempting to hit all shots when the ball is even with or (preferably) slightly in front of his body, enables the player to glimpse the front wall with his peripheral vision and thus enhance his chances of hitting the shot accurately to the spot where he wants to direct it. An additional advantage of hitting the ball when it is forward of the player is that the opponent's position on the court often can be noted and the ball aimed away from that location. Even for highly skilled paddleball players, the rule should be that, the more difficult the shot, the more closely the ball is watched throughout the entire stroke and play of the ball.

Anticipation

One of the outstanding characteristics of the champion racquetball player is his ability to usually guess correctly where and how his opponent will return the ball. Hence, by anticipating correctly, the champion gets an early start and is not caught out of position. The beginner should at once begin attempting to anticipate his opponent's return shot and begin moving to that position before or as the opponent strokes the ball. With experience most racquetball players can often guess where the return will be hit. This is facilitated by watching the opponent until just before he strokes the ball.

Awareness of Opponent's Court Position

After the player gains some knowledge of the behavior of the ball and how it rebounds off the various surfaces of the court and has learned to hit the various racquetball strokes with some skill, he should consciously strive to develop an awareness of the court position of his opponent(s). Peripheral vision and the sense of hearing can

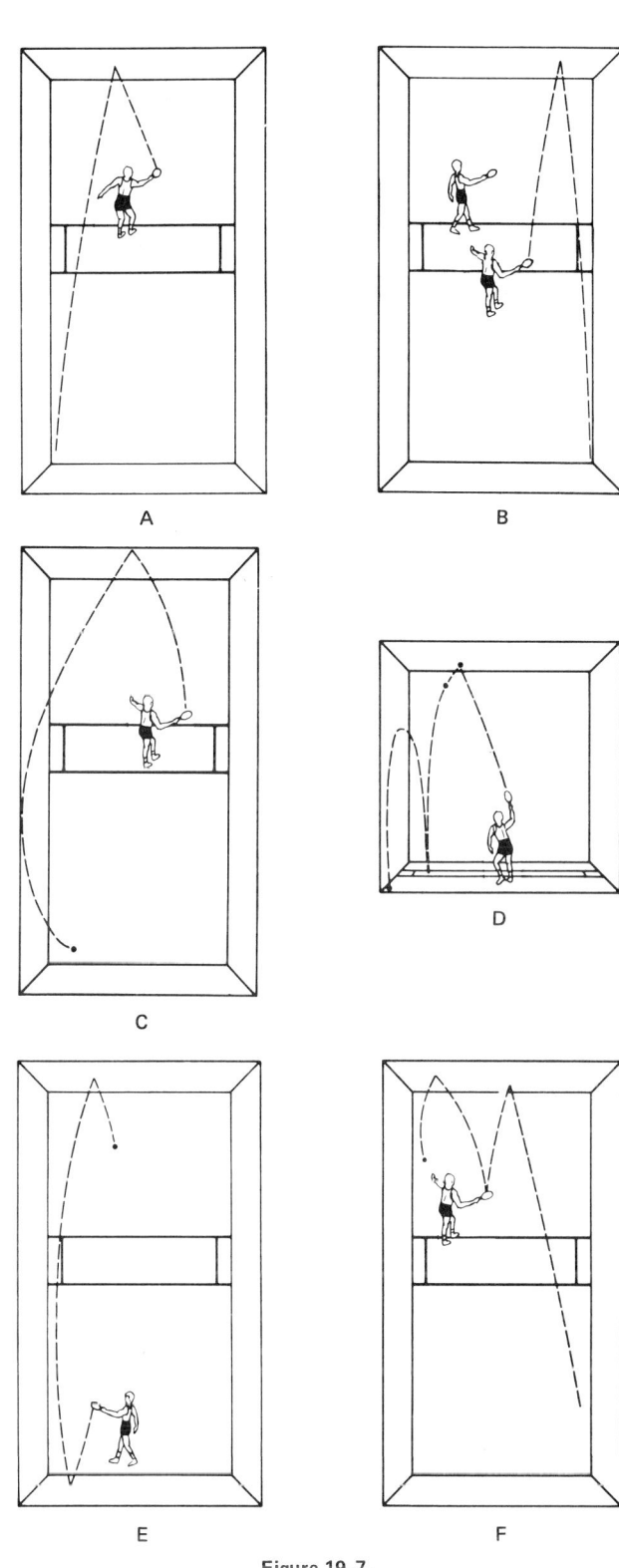

Figure 19-7.
(a) Drive shot.
(b) Pass shot.
(c) Lob shot.
(d) Ceiling shot.
(e) Backwall return shot.
(f) Block shot.

Racquetball and Paddleball

both help locate the opponent as he runs, shuffles, turns, or stops in various positions. With practice the player should gain some expertise in taking advantage of a moving opponent by hitting to the spot just vacated and otherwise catching him unaware by taking advantage of his movements. The player should in general avoid the temptation to aim the shot directly to the opponent—hitting at a target—instead of hitting away from the opponent, where no target exists.

Drive Shot. The drive shot, whether used to pass the opponent or to drive the ball directly at him when he is near the front wall, can be an effective shot in paddleball play. The drive ball can rebound with considerable speed directly at the opponent, catching him unprepared and unable to position his racket for a return, thus forcing him to make a weak return. If the hard-hit drive shot is not aimed to rebound toward an opponent in the front court, the ball is so directed that it slides along a side wall at the instant that it passes the opponent.

Pass Shot. Whenever possible the pass shot is so directed that it passes along the side wall farthest from the opponent or else is directed to his backhand side wall. The ball should not be hit so high or hard that it rebounds off the back wall, giving the opponent additional time and enabling him to move less distance to play the ball.

Lob or Ceiling Shot. A special type of pass shot is the lob shot. It passes over the opponent's head and out of reach if he is positioned in the front court. The ceiling shot is a special type of lob shot in which the hard-hit ball, while traveling to the front wall, hits the ceiling a few feet behind it. The ball comes down at a sharp angle and takes a high bounce to the back court, often bouncing at an unexpected angle. All lob shots, including the ceiling shot, are basically defensive shots that are designed to move the opponent into the back court while giving the player sufficient time to recover to a favorable court position. With many opponents the ceiling pass shot or the lob shot will not be a direct cause of a winning play, but by forcing the opponent out of position, he may make a weak return and set up the player for a winning shot. The lob shot, which is stroked sidearm or overhead with a soft hit, should pass quite close to the ceiling. The lob or ceiling shot is often used when a player is out of position and needs time in which to gain a favorable court position.

Back-wall Return Shots. Quite often, the ball will rebound from the front wall with sufficient speed and height so that it travels to the back wall. With practice, if the player quickly moves to the proper court position his best return is to stroke the ball after it bounces off the back wall and is moving toward the front wall. The player should directly face a side wall (for a forehand stroke his left shoulder faces the front wall) and stroke the ball when it is even with his body and is about two feet out toward the side wall. When first practicing the back-wall return shot, the player should stroke the ball softly, almost catching and carrying it with the racket. As skill develops, the back-wall return shot can be hit when the ball is head height to just above floor level—either a forehand or backhand stroke can be used. The most important factor in hitting this shot with control is that the ball is contacted when it is even with or in front of the body—if possible it should not be hit when it is between the body and the back wall.

In some situations the player will find that he does not have time to run to the back portion of the court and get into the normal position for returning a shot rebounding off the back wall. In these situations the player can attempt a shot in which he hits the ball forcefully toward the back wall, causing it to rebound off the back wall and travel on the fly to the front wall. To accomplish this shot the player should hit the ball with sufficient height and force for it to hit rather high on the front wall and rebound back some distance. This desperation shot will rarely be a winning shot, but it may be a point-saving shot that enables the player to continue the ball in play. The back-wall rebound shot is the only practical one when the player must run fast toward the back wall and cannot stop or shift his body position.

Block Shot. When the player is in the front court and the ball is coming rapidly toward him, he may have time only to place his racket in front of the ball, thus blocking it and allowing it to rebound back to the front wall. Because there is insufficient time to swing the paddle, the ball is returned with little speed. A fast reaction (and anticipation) is helpful in successfully employing the block shot. With experience, some racquetball players sometimes manage to so block the ball that it is hit softly and dies near the front wall.

Kill Shots

The skilled paddleball player usually possesses a large repertoire of kill shots. With practice and concentration the beginning player can soon hit kill shots with fair success. The basic kill shot is made by playing the ball from the front court position after the ball has bounced from the floor. The player should assume a crouched position with the knees and hips flexed. Ideally, the ball should be stroked when it is no higher than the knees and preferably only six inches to a foot above the floor. Contacting the ball when it is even with, or (preferably) somewhat in front of the body, enhances the probability of making a successful kill. The point of aim on the front wall should be approximately six inches above the floor. If the player has sufficient time, he should take a backswing, forward swing, and follow-through of some length in order to

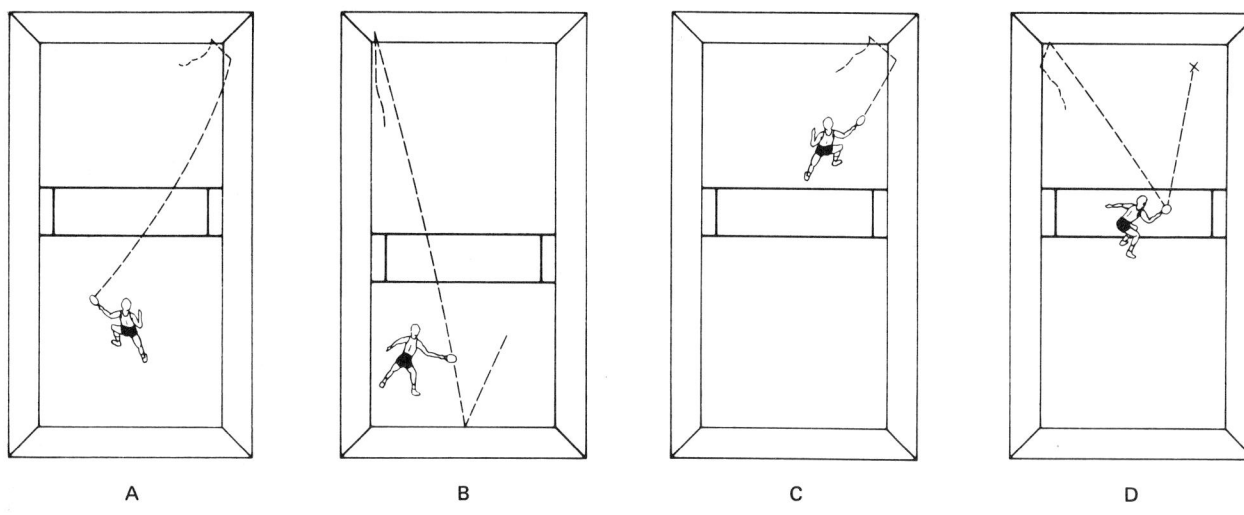

Figure 19-8. (a) Back-court kill. (b) Kill off back wall. (c) Soft kill. (d) Fly kill.

establish the correct path of the racket during the forward swing. If rushed, the player can mainly use a wrist-action stroke, but this is apt to decrease his accuracy.

Some players, when attempting to kill the ball from the front half of the court, chop or cut down slightly on the ball while keeping the racket at a neutral angle, aiming at the junction of the front wall and the floor. This chopping action of the racket causes the ball to rise enough to cause it to hit the front wall only a few inches above the floor.

Considerations When Attempting a Kill Shot. For all kill shots the player should give himself as much time as possible to get into the proper court and body positions, and he should let the ball descend to as low a point as is practical before stroking it. Rarely, if ever, should the player attempt a kill shot when the ball is shoulder height or above, and only rarely should he attempt a kill shot when the ball is as high as his waist. This is true because the higher the ball is contacted, the sharper the angle downward in order for the kill shot to hit low on the front wall. If this downward angle is in error by a few degrees, the ball will hit the floor before hitting the front wall or else it will hit high on the front wall. On the other hand, if the ball is contacted when it is low, the path of ball travel is almost parallel with the floor, and a few degrees of error will probably not result in a loss of point (or serve).

Aiming the Kill Shot. With most kill shots, the safest aiming point is to direct the ball to one of the corners. If the corner is aimed at, it does not matter too much whether the front wall or side wall is hit first or if the ball hits the corner squarely, causing it to crotch and die with very little bounce. If the side wall is contacted first, the right-handed player should usually aim to hit the right side wall. Because the natural spin imparted to the ball by the racket will cause it to hop somewhat toward the front wall, if the left side wall is hit first, the ball tends to be retarded in its forward travel to the front wall. Consequently, the ball cannot be hit very far back from the front wall if it is to travel on the fly to the front wall for a kill. If the opponent is standing to one side of the court, the kill shot is often aimed at the other corner.

In some situations it is better to avoid a corner kill and instead attempt to so kill the ball that it does not strike the side wall at all before it dies after its first bounce. This is particularly true in a singles game if the opponent is standing to one side and the ball can be killed toward the other side of the court. The player is actually attempting a combination kill shot-pass shot. In doubles play if both partners are up, then at least one of them should have a chance to make a play for the ball when a corner kill shot is attempted, unless the kill shot is exceedingly low. In this situation it is probably better to make a drive-type kill in order that only one opponent has a chance to make a play at the hard-hit ball.

Back-court Kills. As the player's ability to kill the ball improves, he may want to attempt kill shots when in the back court. However, in singles play this can be a dangerous court position from which to attempt to kill because an opponent in the front court has an easy return shot (if he can get the ball) and the player must quickly run to the front court in order to retrieve the opponent's possible return of the kill shot. Nevertheless, an occasional kill shot from the back court is usually unexpected and disconcerting, especially if a low kill with very little bounce is made. In doubles play if one partner is forward in order to protect the front court, a kill from the back court is less risky. However, returning it with a low pass shot down the side wall can result in the loss of a point or serve. Consequently, a kill from the back court is not considered a routine shot.

Racquetball and Paddleball

Back-wall Kill. A kill shot that advanced players use with marked success is to hit the kill shot as the ball rebounds off the back wall. The player quickly runs to the hitting area and faces the side wall, preferably taking a position from which a forehand shot can be executed. The player should get into hitting position ahead of time in order that he does not have to rush his shot. He waits until the ball drops to knee height or lower before stroking it. If possible, the ball is hit after it is even with, or slightly in front of him. Although considerable wrist action may be utilized to stroke the ball low to the front wall, a considerable backswing and follow-through are helpful in establishing the correct plane of motion for aiming the kill shot.

Soft Kill. The soft kill shot (in which the ball is softly hit and is lobbed to the front wall and quickly dies) can be a potent offensive shot, if practiced, because it is difficult to anticipate. To be effective the soft kill should be made when the opponent(s) is in the back court or is moving backward. The soft kill shot should usually be aimed at the corner. Some advanced players execute a soft kill shot from the overhead stroking position by cutting the ball so that it will travel forward softly and slowly, descending until it strikes quite low on the front wall. When mixed with the hard-hit drive shot, the soft kill is useful in keeping the opponent off-balance and upsetting his anticipation.

Fly Kill. The skilled racquetball player often hits (or kills) the ball before it has taken its first bounce from the floor. The fly hit often catches the opponent out of position, giving him little time to get set for his return shot. With practice a fly kill shot can be hit about as accurately as a regular kill. As for any return, the player should immediately anticipate where he is going to stroke the ball and get into that position as soon as possible. He should wait for the ball to descend, waiting until it is knee level or lower before stroking it. The fly kill can be hit with either a forehand or a backhand stroke.

Playing Position on Court

Whether playing singles, cut-throat or doubles the player(s) should always attempt to maintain or return to the basic court playing position.

Singles Play. For singles play the basic court position is located near the center of the court from each side wall and slightly toward the backhand shot side wall in order to favor slightly the forehand shot possibilities. This position is usually between the service line and the short line; a player with speed and fast reactions can play slightly forward of this position. Each time after stroking the ball the player should immediately start to return to his basic court position. He does not necessarily always need to arrive at this court position after each shot, but he should be moving toward it so that he can cover all portions of the court equally well. If he moves to this position with too much speed, the opponent may hit the ball to the spot just vacated, making it impossible for him to recover in time to return the ball.

The basic playing position is modified according to the court position occupied by the opponent. If the opponent is near one side wall then the basic court position must be moved somewhat toward the side where the opponent is located. This is true because the opponent can return a ball straight down that side wall in a minimum of time,

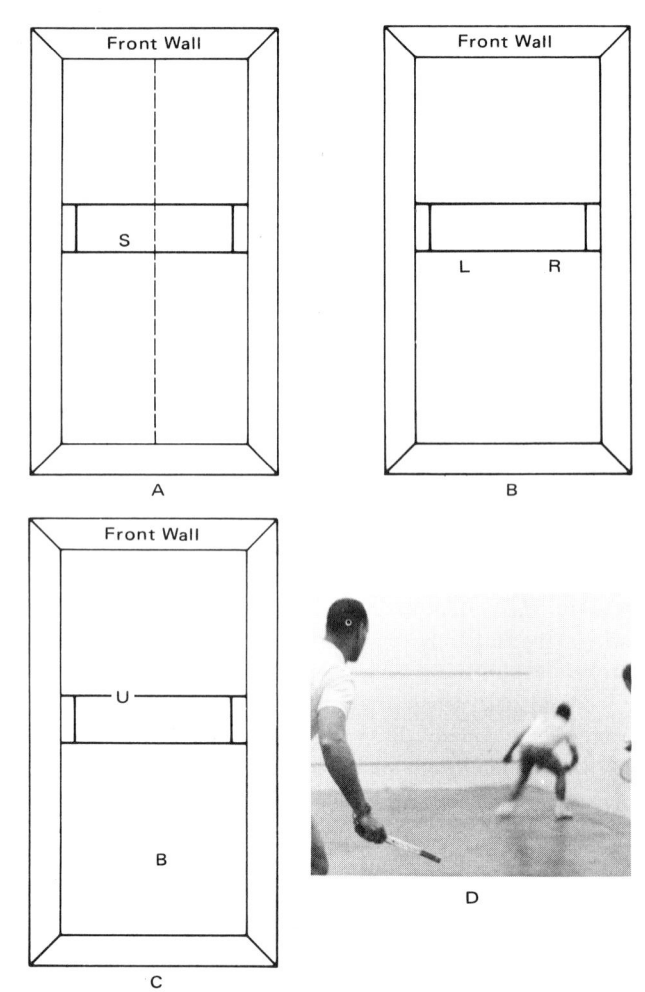

Figure 19-9. (a) Basic court position for singles play. (*Note*: A right-handed player plays somewhat toward his backhand side where his reach is restricted. Also, the player will assume a position toward whatever side of the court from which the opponent is playing the ball. Rarely should the singles player move behind the short line except to play the ball.) (b) The side-by-side doubles court playing position. (This is the usual doubles court formation during play. For two right-handed players, the left-court player will play the majority of the shots.) (c) The up-and-back method. (This formation is sometimes used if the two partners are unequal in ability. The strongest or best player usually plays up in the front court.) (d) Playing position on court.

whereas if he angles the ball toward the other side wall the player can, by either moving forward or backward, get to it while it is some distance away from the far side wall.

Doubles Play. In doubles play the usual court position is side-by-side and, if both players are right-handed, the left-court player often stands one or two steps forward of the right-court player because he has the forehand shot for all returns coming down the middle of the court. Therefore, as a rule the stronger partner plays the left side. The side-by-side system has the disadvantage that the ball can be played almost constantly to the weakest partner. A few players play in an up-and-back position, with the better player taking the front-court position. This arrangement makes a team liable to passing shots down the side wall, particularly those shots that do not travel too far to the back court. This often forces the front-court man to play almost all shots, and it is almost impossible for him to cover well-aimed shots to both side walls.

Only by playing together a considerable time can the partners learn to coordinate their efforts and instinctively know when they should let the ball go and when they should hit it. The considerable teamwork required demands that the partners talk to each other frequently during play. As soon as a player knows that he is going to take the ball he should quickly call for it by saying "Mine." If he thinks his partner should take it he quickly yells "Yours." When a player has a difficult shot, his partner should attempt to back him up or call for the ball if he has a better shot than his partner.

RACQUETBALL STRATEGY

The skillful use of strategy in paddleball play can do much to overcome playing deficiencies caused by a lack of natural speed, experience, or racquetball skills. Racquetball is a thinking man's game, and successful play demands much more than just continually returning the ball or going for a kill shot whenever possible. The application of the correct strategy in singles, cut-throat, and doubles play often determines whether a game or match is won or lost. The racquetball player should constantly review his plays after each volley, attempting to determine how he could have improved his strategy, game play, or game plan.

As in most games it is highly important to study the type of game played by the opponent in order to discover his weaknesses and strengths. Every attempt must be made to avoid playing the opponent's strong game. Instead, whenever possible, the play should be directed to his weak points. In most instances a player's backhand is weaker than his forehand; therefore, the majority of shot attempts will be made toward his backhand side.

The player should constantly analyze his game in order to discover his strengths and weaknesses. He should practice occasionally the strong points of his game in order to keep these perfected, and he should constantly practice the weak elements of his game in order to strive to eliminate them from being exploited by his opponent.

General Strategy

The basic strategy of singles play also applies to doubles play. When the opponent(s) is back, kill the ball; when the opponent(s) is up, pass him with high lobs, pass shots down the side wall, or ceiling shots in order to make him run and force him to go to the back court. In cut-throat play the server, who is playing by himself, must employ doubles strategy against the opponents; his opponents, who are playing a doubles game between them, must employ singles strategy against the lone server.

Regardless of the game being played, it is always wise to be patient in playing racquetball. This means that a kill should not be attempted on every shot but only on those shots in which the ball and the player are in the proper positions. By merely returning the ball each time, the player often can force his opponent into making numerous errors because he tries to end the game with a difficult-to-make shot that has little chance of succeeding. Instead, when out of position, or when stroking the ball without being set, the player should generally make a defensive shot that is designed to (1) move the opponent, (2) enable the player to recover to a basic court position, and (3) reduce to a minimum the possibility of committing an error. The defensive shot should be a safe one (ceiling, high lob, pass, drive, or angle) that will still hit the front wall if the ball is poorly stroked.

As a rule the ball should be hit hard only when there is a sound reason for doing so. The racquetball player who is able to play a fast game with accuracy can force the opponent to hurry and often to be in a poor playing position from which to make his return shots. However, the player must not fall into the pattern of indiscriminately hitting hard, high shots, especially those that rebound some distance off the back wall, giving the opponent plenty of time to get set for his return shot.

In playing racquetball the speed of the shot should be varied. This enables the player to avoid establishing a constant tempo for the game, and he can often confuse his opponent by not permitting him to get set for succeeding shots and causing him to make mistakes in anticipating the speed of the returns.

Because the rules do not prohibit consecutively serving to the same side of the court or to the same person, the server usually directs the serve to the weak receiver or the weak side court (backhand side). However, it is a wise idea occasionally to change the type and direction of the serve, which may disconcert the receiver and cause him difficulty in anticipating the serve placement. The objective of the serve is to force the receiver to make a weak return that the server may put away while the receiver is still out of position, or else force the receiver to make a difficult return.

Forcing the opponent to run as much as possible soon tires him (them). When fatigued, many players have a tendency to rush their shots (often hitting the ball while it is high above the floor) or not go to the proper court position; thus, their chances of making an effective return is markedly decreased.

When no better shot is apparent, an angled return, in which the ball bounces off one of the side walls and crisscrosses the court once or twice, confuses the opponent and forces him to delay in selecting the court position from which he will stroke the ball.

Singles Strategy

By using peripheral vision to watch the opponent, some idea can be gained as to where he is and perhaps in what direction he is moving just before the player strokes the ball. A highly effective shot to use occasionally is to hit where the opponent has been moving from. Driving the ball directly at the opponent when he is playing in the front court will sometimes force him to make an error or a weak return.

The player should be constantly alert to notice whether an opponent plays to one side of the court in order to offset a back hand weakness because such a court playing position opens him for a passing shot down the right-hand side (if he is right handed). A sidearm stroking action, which speeds the ball along the right-hand wall, can be highly effective in passing an opponent who has pulled to the left side of the court.

Doubles Strategy

The usual strategy in doubles play is to play to the weakest opponent as much as possible. The majority of hits should be directed at him or to the side of the court where he is playing in order that the strong partner cannot play the ball unless he gets out of position. If this happens, a winning return can often be made by hitting the ball to the area recently vacated by the strong opponent.

In doubles play, particularly, it is often wise to cut the ball off, hitting it while on the fly in order that the opponents do not have time to attain a proper court position or get set for the return shot. Attention must be given to backing up the partner in case he misses the ball and to coordinate team efforts closely so that the player in the best court position can take the shot.

COMMON ERRORS AND THEIR CORRECTIONS

One of the most fundamental errors in racquetball play is the failure to have the body in the proper position at the time the ball is stroked. When time permits, the left shoulder of a right-handed player should be pointed toward the front wall when the forehand stroke is made, and the right shoulder should be facing the front wall when the backhand stroke is made. In addition the body should be in a slightly crouched position, the legs flexed, and the weight resting primarily on the balls of the feet. As the stroke is made the body should move in the direction of the front wall. In correcting this error the player should move as quickly as possible into the proper stroking position.

A basic error that often leads to an improper stroking position is the failure to move rapidly to the correct court position. Beginning players often find themselves in a poor court position because after stroking the ball they remain standing where they are and watch the opponent play the ball. Instead of being a spectator, the racquetball player must, as soon as he strokes the ball, immediately move into the best court position in terms of the type of shot he hit, where his opponent is standing, and where the return hit is apt to be directed.

Both of the preceding two errors are frequently caused by the player's failure to anticipate where and how the opponent will play the ball. The player needs to anticipate the shot placement and watch his opponent in order to get an early start to the court area where he will probably play the next shot.

Another error frequently made by beginners is a failure to shift the racket from a forehand grip to a backhand grip or vice versa. This failure results in the racket face being slanted in the incorrect position when the backhand shot is made, thus causing the ball to be misdirected. Whether the racket is shifted or the forearm rotated, it is essential that the racket face be parallel to the front wall when the shot is made. If the nongrasping hand holds the throat of the racket, it can easily rotate the racket to the proper position whenever the need arises. The beginning player needs to concentrate on rotating the racket to the proper position for each stroke until the movement becomes automatic and no longer requires conscious thought.

A failure to hold the racket in an essentially neutral position can sometimes result in errors, especially when the player is in the front half of the court and has little time to react to the bass or move the racket into position for the stroke. For most players the neutral position is directly below the hitting shoulder and at about knee level. A slight backhand position is preferred by many because it takes less time to get the racket to a forehand stroke position than does moving from a forehand to a backhand position.

Until considerable experience is gained, many paddleball players will need to focus their attention on squeezing the racket handle as they stroke the ball. This will prevent the racket slipping in the hand.

An error frequently committed by many racquetball players, including experienced ones, is to loaf in moving to the ball, timing their arrival to the stroking location at the same time that the ball arrives there. Although this procedure works successfully most of the time, the player is in trouble whenever the ball takes an odd bounce or behaves in some fashion other than that anticipated by the player. The correction, or course, is to hustle as quickly as possible in getting to the spot where the ball is to be stroked. This permits adequate time in which to adjust to any last-second deviations in the ball's anticipated path.

Becoming impatient in trying to end the rally when the ball is in a poor position for a put-away kill shot often leads to errors and attempts at shots that have a low percentage for success. The racquetball player must discipline himself to the point where he waits until he has a high percentage shot before attempting a winning shot.

Some racquetball players often commit the common error of attempting to kill the ball when in the back court, but when the opponent(s) is in the front court position and can easily make a short return kill shot before the player can recover to a front-court position.

Some players frequently play the same type of game continuously, permitting the opponent to anticipate successfully the pattern of play or where the next shot will be hit. The type of play should be varied enough that the opponent is not too successful in anticipating playing patterns and shot placements.

In doubles play a common error is the failure of the partners to coordinate their movements and team play. The main correction for that is simply to play together against a variety of opponents to become accustomed to each other's idiosyncracies and styles of play.

SPECIFIC TRAINING METHODS

Because racquetball play demands excellent circulorespiratory endurance, quick reactions, the ability to sense and play a proper court position, anticipating the opponent's return, and the employment of winning strategy, the racquetball player can utilize several methods of training to enhance his playing ability. Regularly engaging in various types of running practice will help the racquetball player develop the stamina necessary to continue to play at top efficiency for a three-game match. Distance running is an excellent training medium. Short sprints of from fifty to one hundred yards, interspersed with short walking periods, is a type of interval training that gives excellent results. It closely simulates actual racquetball playing conditions.

Various calisthenic exercises that help improve flexibility, agility, and strength can be regularly performed in order to improve certain aspects of racquetball playing ability. Stretching exercises should be performed for a minimum of fifteen to twenty repetitions, during which the range of joint motion is gradually extended. Exercises that involve the shoulder joints, hip joints, and twisting and bending movements along the spine are especially valuable. The player can also practice agility exercises and drills in which he seeks to develop quick starting and turning movements in each direction. When practicing these movements, the player should concentrate on his footwork, insuring that he does not cross his legs in making the initial start.

The development of skillful and precisely controlled racquetball shots and strokes can be supplemented by repeating the same type of shot a number of times when the player is practicing by himself or with a partner who repeatedly hits certain shots to him. The player should devote considerable practice toward developing the proper footwork, body positions, and stroke techniques (especially for backhand shots) from all positions on the court. He should particularly strive to develop the ability to run to the back court and still get into the proper body position to execute a backhand stroke. The player should regularly practice deliberately getting to the site on the court where he intends to stroke the ball ahead of the time so that he can easily get into the proper position.

A worthwhile series of drills includes tossing or hitting the ball easily off the front wall, getting into position, and stroking the ball on its first bounce when it falls below knee level. This shot should be repeated from ten to fifty times on the forehand side and also on the backhand side. After the player has practiced this he can so hit the ball that it goes either to the backhand or forehand side and thus practice getting into the correct body position for each type of shot. The player can then practice a number of successive hits off the back wall in which he gets into correct position with his left side facing the front wall and practices hitting the ball when it is slightly in front of his body and below knee height. Again, these shots should be practiced both on the forehand side and on the backhand side and then alternately on either side. This type of practice, in which the player faces no competition or pressure, will enable him to develop rapidly the ability to wait until he is in the proper body and court position for stroking the ball. It also should enhance his ability to place the ball where he desires. When practicing such shots the player should alternate the type of returns he makes. He can attempt several passing shots in succession, then several high-lob shots, several front-wall kills, and several corner kills to either corner. This practice of a series of the same type of shot should be interspersed with regular game play, in which a variety of shots appears in no set sequence in order that this practice may be integrated into regular racquetball play.

Another helpful training method is to play a certain type of game rather than play to win the game. For example, the player can attempt only backhand kills, attempt only to pass the opponent to win, or deliberately play a close front-court position.

As the player's game improves he can impose additional handicaps on his play by playing a singles game against two opponents who play a doubles game against him. Another handicap is to spot an opponent a certain number of points in order to make the game quite close. Playing a superior opponent can be frustrating, but it forces the player to hustle to his utmost ability and to analyze in detail his own game and the strategy and skills employed by the superior player.

ADVANCED TECHNIQUES AND SKILLS OF RACQUETBALL

High Lob Shot

Although the kill shot is the most spectacular shot in racquetball, the high lob shot is extremely safe, can be hit from any court position, is frequently used to move the opponent out of position while gaining time to regain the proper court position, and can well be a winning shot if directed to die in a back corner. For these reasons the high lob shot is widely employed by advanced players and perhaps should be considered an advanced skill.

Late-ceiling Shot

A difficult shot to read and return is a high, hard-hit shot that, after rebounding from the front wall, strikes the ceiling on its backward flight. The ball then drops almost straight down toward the floor and does not rebound toward the rear of the court at the expected angle. This forces the opponent to shift his court position quickly and to hurry his stroke. This shot requires considerable practice to master, but it is often a winning one.

Crotch Serve

Some players with long practice develop the ability to so serve the ball that it lands at the junction of the side wall and the floor and crotches after striking the front wall. An expert player can do this quite frequently, and often directs the serve to the receiver's backhand side in order to further complicate his return. Even if the receiver is able to return a crotch serve, his weak return often offers a set-up that the server can put away for a point.

Crotch Kill Shot

Some players develop the knack of making a crotch kill with amazing regularity. The crotch kill is usually so aimed that the ball, after hitting the front wall, simultaneously strikes the floor and side wall only a few feet in back of the front wall. Because the ball rebounds at an unexpected angle, this shot is difficult to return; usually only a weak, uncontrolled return is possible.

Soft Kill Shot

The soft kill shot in which the ball is softly lobbed toward a front corner should not be tried too regularly, but as a change in pace it can be quite effective in throwing the opponent off-stride and upsetting his anticipation. A "cutting down" or a "coming over the ball," which places an overspin on it, can be used to propel the ball slowly to the front wall. This shot should be attempted when the opponent is in the back court.

Far-back Side-wall Kill Shot

With practice some players develop the ability to kill the ball by rebounding it off the right side wall (or left side wall) from ten or so feet in back of the front wall, thus causing it to rebound to the center or far side of the front wall. The ball strikes the front wall only a few inches above the floor and then quickly dies. This shot usually causes the opponent to move first toward the side wall off which the ball has been hit. Usually he is unable to recover in time to return the shot. This shot is also useful when playing doubles and an opponent blocks out a direct kill shot to the front wall. This kill shot seems to work best on the right wall for a right-handed player.

Squash Kill Shot

The player who hits the ball with considerable force can successfully attempt a squash kill in which an angled ball strikes the front wall near one corner about two feet above the floor. It then rebounds to a side wall and flies through the air to the next side wall. Upon striking the second side wall the ball rebounds from it at about a 90° angle and usually has little or no bounce after hitting the floor. Its unexpected angle of flight aids in making it difficult to return. If the ball strikes the floor before striking the second side wall, it has been legally played; hence, a squash kill shot is a safe low-risk shot to attempt.

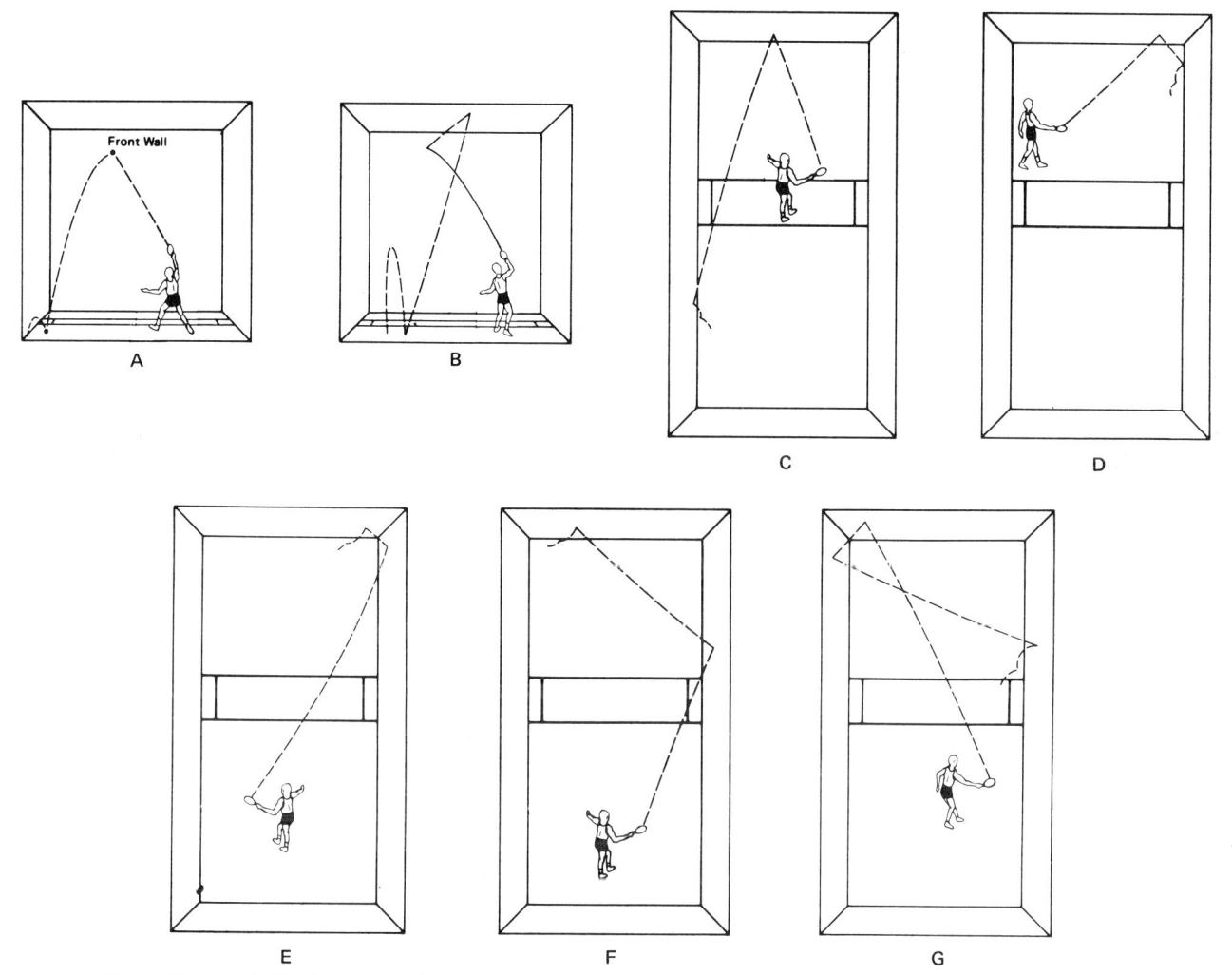

Figure 19-10. (a) High lob shot. (The high lob shot may be stroked with an underhand, sidearm or overhead stroking action; thus, it can be hit when the ball is at various heights.) (b) Late ceiling shot. (c) Crotch serve. (d) Crotch kill. (e) Soft kill. (f) Far-back side-wall kill. (g) Squash kill.

SELF-EVALUATION

The racquetball player can evaluate his progress and compare his degree of skill by a variety of methods. However, the player must remember that improvement does not occur at a steady pace; instead, it follows an erratic curve. On some days one may feel faster and more accurate and can play a better game than on other days. These individual day-to-day variations must be expected and should not cause one to become discouraged.

When practicing by himself the player can repeat a number of the same type of shots and note or keep a record of what percentage of shots he makes within an established criterion. For example, he can try twenty back-wall kill shots to the right corner and record how many of those were hit six inches or lower on the front wall, and how many hit the front wall before hitting the floor. Such charting can be particularly valuable in overcoming weaknesses in certain types of strokes or certain phases of play.

Another evaluative method is to play other players of about equal skill and keep a won-lost record. If in a class or club situation, various types of tournaments, such as single elimination, round robin, and pyramid, or ladder, can be held. These are probably the most valuable devices because regular games can be played and enjoyment derived while comparing one's progress and degree of skill to the rest of the class or group.

Racquetball and Paddleball

Glossary of Terms

Ace: A legal serve that eludes the receiver.
Backhand: Hitting the ball on the opposite side from which arm the stroke is made.
Backswing: The preliminary backward swing of the racket before taking the forward swing to hit the ball.
Block: Blocking the opponent from hitting the ball (or blocking the ball) by interjecting some part of the body between the opponent and the ball.
Crotch ball: A ball that strikes the floor and a wall simultaneously.
Dead ball: A ball no longer in play.
Doubles: A game in which a team of two players plays two other players.
Drive shot: Hitting the ball low to the front wall with considerable speed.
Error: A failure to legally return a ball during play.
Fault: An infraction of the service rules.
Follow-through: Continuing the swing of the paddle after the ball has been hit.
Foot fault: Illegal position of the server's foot (feet) during the serve.
Hinder: Unintentional interference with the opponent during play, which results in the replay of the point.
Illegal serve: A failure to serve the ball according to the serving rules.
Kill: A ball hit so low on the front wall that it is unplayable.
Let: A point that is replayed.
Lob: A high-hit ball with little force that rebounds in a high arc toward the back wall.
Pass shot: A ball hit to one side or above and out of the reach of the opponent.
Rally: The play occurring between the serve and the end of the play.
Screen: Interference with the vision of the player when he is attempting to play the ball.
Serve-out: A loss of serve in accordance with the rules.
Service box: The area in which the server's partner must remain in doubles play until the serve has passed the short line.
Service zone: The area between and including the service line and the short line.
Shadow serve: A served ball passing so close to the server's body on the rebound from the front wall that the receiver is unable to follow the flight of the ball.
Short: A serve failing to rebound past the short line. A short serve is not a legal serve.
Short line: In four-wall racquetball, a line midway between and parallel with the front and back walls; in one-wall racquetball, a line parallel to and sixteen feet from the front wall.
Side lines: The lines marking the left- and right-hand boundaries of the court in one-wall and three-wall racquetball.
Side out: Loss of service by a player in singles or both players in doubles play.
Straddle ball: A ball in play that passes between the legs of a player after it hits the front wall. A hinder is called on all straddle balls.

Selected References

BOOKS

Allsen, Philip E., and Alan Witbeck. *Racquetball/Paddleball.* Dubuque, Iowa: Wm. C. Brown, 1972.
The second book dealing exclusively with the games of racquetball and paddleball. It offers sound advice concerning the basic playing skills and the strategies involved in the game.

Kozar, Andrew J., Rodney J. Grambeau and Earl N. Riskey. *Beginning Paddleball.* Belmont, Calif.: Wadsworth, 1967.
This book, the first paddleball book to be written, covers all phases of the game of paddleball and it is well illustrated. The authors are all veteran paddleball players.

PERIODICALS

Racquetball. Published by the International Racquetball Association, 4101 Dempster St., Skokie, Ill. 60076.
Grambeau, Rodney J. *Official Paddleball Rules.* Ann Arbor, Michigan: Cushman and Maloy Printing Company, latest.

CHAPTER 20

Riflery
*Thomas W. Stoll**
St. Stephen's School

HISTORY

The specific origin of firearms is not known. The use of firearms was first recorded in 1247, but it was more than a century later when the first small arms came into use. The first firearm to be widely used was the matchlock, which appeared in around 1470. This was followed by the wheellock, which was developed in Germany in about 1510. In the mid-1600s, the flintlock rifle was developed in France; it remained an important weapon for some two hundred years.

The Kentucky rifle, a distinctly American firearm, evolved in about the middle of the eighteenth century. This rifle was a long, deeply rifled, muzzle-loaded flintlock. During the nineteenth century, percussion arms came into widespread use. The bolt-action rifle was introduced in the nineteenth century, with the first practical rifle appearing in 1867. In 1938, the United States armed services adopted the semiautomatic Garand rifle, the M1, which was named after John C. Garand, a United States inventor. At the present time, the M16 is widely used by the United States service.

DESCRIPTION OF EQUIPMENT AND ITS CARE

The equipment used in riflery consists of .22 caliber rifles, sights, slings, .22 caliber ammunition, targets, shooting coats, shooting gloves, shooting mats, ammunition blocks, kneeling pads, spotting scopes, and a scoring gauge—and, of course, a range on which the firing is done. Ranges already exist in many schools and communities. Complete plans for constructing permanent and portable ranges are available from the National Rifle Association (NRA). Only a minimum of the preceding equipment is needed for a beginner. Rifles and ammunition can usually be obtained, at a greatly reduced cost, from the Director of Civilian Marksmanship. The NRA is an excellent source for material pertaining to equipment.

The Rifle

The rifle most frequently used in riflery is the .22 caliber rimfire, with a heavier barrel than that used on most hunting rifles. A heavy barrel is advantageous as it gives increased accuracy and consistency and it improves the holding qualities of the rifle. The Model 52C and 52D Winchester and the Model 40X Remington are good examples of suitable target rifles that are reasonably priced.

The rifle consists of three major assembly groups: the action, stock, and barrel. The action, which is the heart of the rifle, is the part to which the stock and barrel are attached. It contains the functional parts that load and fire the cartridge and eject the used cartridge case. The stock is nothing more than the handle with which the rifle is held. The barrel is the metal tube through which the bullet passes when the rifle is fired. The hole through the barrel is called the bore.

Ammunition

The ammunition used in riflery should be .22 caliber long rifle, standard velocity (a muzzle velocity of 1,100 to

---

*B.S., Wisconsin State University; M.A., University of Iowa. Mr. Stoll is a former riflery instructor, at the University of Iowa and at the St. Mark's School of Dallas, Texas, and is a Certified Rifle Instructor, National Rifle Association (NRA). He is currently the riflery instructor and athletic director at St. Stephen's School, Bradenton, Fla.

1,200 feet per second). This is rimfire ammunition, in contrast to centerfire ammunition, which is used in high-powered cartridges.

Targets

For class or group use, the recommended target is one with ten bulls plus an extra sighting bull. The A-17 fifty-foot gallery rifle target, with eleven bulls, makes an excellent target.

Care of Rifles

Modern .22 rimfire ammunition utilizes what is known as noncorrosive priming compounds and lubricated bullets. Consequently, if this ammunition is used, it is necessary to clean the bore of the rifle only occasionally. The other parts of the rifle will be well preserved if a few drops of light oil are periodically applied to them. Care should be taken to not overoil the action; only a few drops should be used. The wooden parts should not be oiled. Too much oil can do as much harm as too little, because an excessive amount of oil or grease in the chamber or bore causes higher-than-ordinary pressures to be created. A clean, oily rag used to spread a light film of oil over the metal parts after each use of the rifle will prevent rust.

If the rifle is to be stored for a long time, it should first be thoroughly cleaned and then stored under a lock. The ammunition should be stored separately.

SAFETY

The death rate due to firearm accidents has decreased considerably during the last few years. This reduction is due in part at least to the success of safety education programs devised and promoted by the NRA in cooperation with state conservation departments, the National Safety Council, the Sporting Arms and Ammunition Manufacturers Institute, and the National Education Association. Safety with guns must be learned and practiced until it becomes a habit. Accidents do not just happen—they are caused by ignorance or the disregard of safe procedures. Riflery is one of the safest of modern sports; obedience to the rules of safety and range commands has enabled thousands to participate in it without any accidents. One accident on a range is too many and, therefore, should be avoided.

The following safety rules, which were formulated by the NRA, should be observed automatically whenever firearms are handled:

1. Treat every gun as if it were loaded until you have personally proven otherwise.
2. Keep the muzzle pointed in a safe direction at all times.
3. Always keep the action open.
4. Know your gun and ammunition.
5. Be sure of your backstop.
6. Be sure of your target.
7. Never mix alcohol and gunpowder.
8. Obey all firing-line commands instantly.

BASIC SHOOTING SKILLS

Breathing

The rifle moves with each breath the shooter takes; therefore, controlled breathing is necessary for accurate shooting. After the shooter's position is steady and comfortable and the sight picture is correct, the attention of the shooter should be on his breathing. In order to have an adequate reserve of air during the trigger squeeze, the shooter takes a full breath and slowly exhales half of it. He should, without effort, retain the remaining air until after the trigger squeeze is completed. If the breath is held for too long a period, the body suffers from oxygen deficiency and sends out signals to resume breathing. This will, in turn, produce slight involuntary movements that interfere with shooting accuracy. Generally speaking, eight to ten seconds is the maximum period for which the breath should be held.

Trigger Squeeze

The trigger squeeze is the most important step in producing an accurate shot; the success of the shooter

Figure 20-1. Riflery equipment.

depends on his mastering it. The correct trigger squeeze calls for a slow, steady increase of pressure on the trigger until the rifle fires. The trigger squeeze should not disturb the aim; they should be so coordinated that the rifle will be fired when a proper sight picture exists.

No part of the index or trigger finger should contact the stock. The trigger is squeezed at, or just in front of, the first joint of the index finger. The pressure must be applied directly to the rear—in line with the bore. Any pressure to either side can spoil the aim by moving the rifle to one side.

Follow-through

The purpose of the follow-through is to insure that the rifle is not moved until the bullet is well on its way. The follow-through in riflery, just as in archery, consists of continuing to hold steady during and well past the actual firing.

Rhythm

Rhythm is essential to a good shooting performance. The shooter must learn to do the same thing in the same way and at the same speed at all times. This means that a smooth, regular cadence should be developed for the firing of each shot.

USE OF THE SLING

A properly adjusted sling relieves the muscles of considerable strain and it helps to steady the rifle, thus permitting the firer to concentrate on the correct aim and a proper trigger squeeze. The sling has a nook and a clamp (or keeper) that hold it at the desired adjustment. The following steps should be followed by a right-handed person when adjusting or using the sling:

1. Place the rifle butt on the right hip and cradle the rifle with the right arm.
2. Make a loop large enough to fit the left arm.
3. Turn the sling a half turn to the left.
4. Insert the left arm in the loop and place the loop well up on the arm.
5. Slide the clamp, or keeper, against the left arm in order to hold the loop in place.
6. Place the left hand over the sling and then under the rifle.
7. The sling should be so adjusted that the rifle butt has to be forced into the right shoulder. (See Figure 20-2.)

Figure 20-2. Use of the sling.

SIGHTING AND AIMING

The modern rifles in use today have built-in accuracy. However, it remains for the shooter to aim and fire with a reasonable degree of consistency. The fundamentals of good shooting are best learned with the use of an iron sight rather than a telescopic sight.

A rifle is aimed by aligning the front sight and rear sight with the target. Regardless of the type of sight used, the principle of aligning the front sight in the center of the rear sight is the same. Many rifles are equipped with post front sights with which excellent results can be obtained. After aligning the front post in the rear sight, the target is made to appear to sit on top of the post. When using an aperture front sight, however, the target is centered in the front aperture.

An excellent exercise to determine the correctness of the sight picture is called triangulation. With the rifle set on a firm rest, a marker holds a movable target directly in front of a piece of blank paper located some distance away. As the shooter sights the rifle, he directs the marker to move the movable target until he obtains what he considers to be the correct sighting alignment. The marker removes the target after the center of the bull's eye has been marked on the blank paper; thus, it is necessary for the shooter to realign the target each time. Once the rifle is placed on whatever support is used, it should not be moved or even touched until three marks have been made. The smallness of the triangle that results when the three marks are connected indicates an understanding and application of the correct sight picture. (See Figure 20-3.)

Riflery

Figure 20-3. Triangulation.

BASIC SHOOTING POSITIONS

In order to be efficient, a shooting position must be steady and it must require a minimum of muscular effort during firing. Consequently, the use of bones rather than muscles to support the rifle is a necessity for a steady and relaxed position. The shooting position should allow the rifle to be aimed naturally and without effort at the target. The shooter should not "muscle" the rifle on the target. The butt of the rifle is always placed firmly against the shoulder before sighting and firing. The directions given in the following sections are for the right-handed shooter; the left-handed shooter must reverse them.

Prone Position

The prone position is the steadiest and the most natural shooting position to assume and hold. It is also the best position in which to learn the fundamentals of aiming, breathing, the trigger squeeze, and the follow-through.

When firing from the prone position the following points should be observed:

1. The body is positioned at an angle of between 10 and 40° with the line of aim.
2. The spine is straight and the body relaxed.
3. The ankles are relaxed; the toes point outward.
4. The weight of the upper body is supported by the triangle formed by the trunk and the upper arms.
5. The left wrist is straight and the left hand is relaxed.
6. The left elbow is positioned directly under the rifle.
7. The sling is snug on the left arm, and the left hand is against the upper sling swivel.
8. The shoulders are approximately parallel with the ground.
9. The rifle butt is placed well in on the shoulder and close to the neck.
10. The right leg is slightly flexed.
11. The right thumb is placed over the stock.
12. The trigger finger touches only the trigger.
13. The neck is relaxed and the cheek is in contact with the stock and the right thumb.
14. Elevation adjustments are made by moving the rifle butt up or down.
15. Right and left adjustments are made by shifting the body while keeping the left elbow stationary.
16. Muscular relaxation is essential! (See Figure 20-4.)

Sitting Position

The sitting position is the second-most steady of all shooting positions. When firing in this position the sling is usually shortened. The three variations of the sitting position include the (1) crossed-legs, (2) crossed-ankle, and (3) open-leg.

To shoot with accuracy and consistency from the sitting position, the shooter should heed these requirements:

1. The body is positioned at an angle to the line of aim.
2. The body leans forward until the elbows are just over the knees.
3. The left wrist is straight and the hand is relaxed.
4. The left elbow is under the rifle.
5. The sling is snug on the left arm, and the left hand is against the upper sling swivel.
6. The rifle butt is placed well in the right shoulder.
7. The right thumb is placed over the stock.
8. The trigger finger touches only the trigger.
9. The neck is relaxed and the cheek is in contact with the stock and right thumb.

Figure 20-4. Prone position.

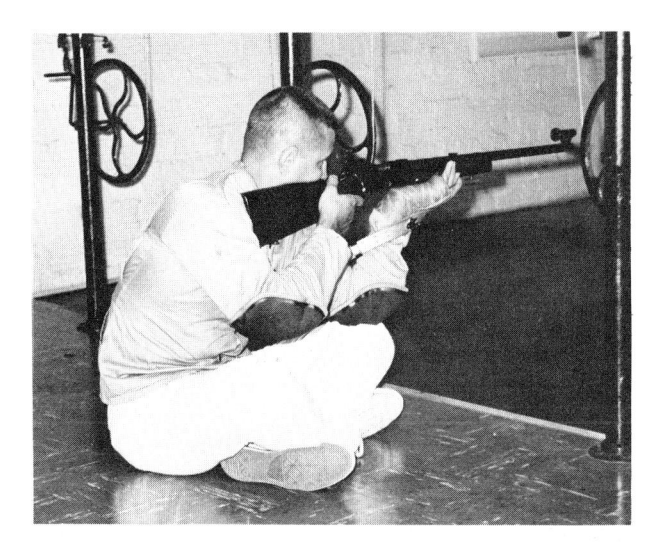

Figure 20-5. Sitting position.

Figure 20-6. Kneeling position.

10. The rifle should naturally point at the center of the target.
11. The upper body is relaxed. (See Figure 20-5.)

Kneeling Position

Recent refinements in the shooting techniques utilized while in the kneeling position have enabled shooters to shoot scores that are within 1 to 2 per cent of their prone-position scores. The same basic principles of support are used in the kneeling position as for other shooting positions.

When shooting from the kneeling position, the following points should be observed:

1. A kneeling cushion can be placed under the right ankle.
2. The right leg is at an approximately 45° angle to the line of fire.
3. The shooter sits on his right heel.
4. The left foot is parallel to the right leg.
5. The left leg is perpendicular to the floor or ground.
6. The back is kept as straight as possible.
7. About 70 per cent of the body weight is distributed to the right foot and cushion; about 25 per cent to the left foot; and about 5 per cent to the right knee.
8. The left knee supports the left arm at a spot immediately above the elbow.
9. The right shoulder and elbow are relaxed.
10. The shoulders are positioned in the same vertical plane as the hips.
11. The hands are used in the same way as when firing in the prone position. (See Figure 20-6.)

Standing Position

Because of the high center of gravity and the relatively small area of support, the standing position is the most difficult and complicated position from which to shoot. It is almost impossible to hold the rifle motionless while in this position; therefore, the shooter should concentrate on keeping the movement of the muzzle to a minimum.

When in the standing position:

1. The weight is evenly distributed on both feet.
2. The legs are straight and the knees are relaxed.
3. The hips are fairly level and positioned directly over the feet.
4. The compound back bend is used in which the back bends away from the target and to the shooter's rear.
5. The shoulders are level and relaxed.
6. The left elbow is directly below the rifle.
7. The left elbow can be placed against the body or rested on the hip.
8. The left thumb is placed on the trigger guard and the fingers are extended along the fore end of the stock.
9. The neck muscles should not be strained.
10. Both eyes must be kept open and relaxed. (See Figure 20-7.)

SCORING

The use of a scoring gauge when scoring targets greatly simplifies the task of the scorer, and its use also removes doubt on close hits. Scoring gauges are available in every

Riflery

Figure 20-7. Standing position.

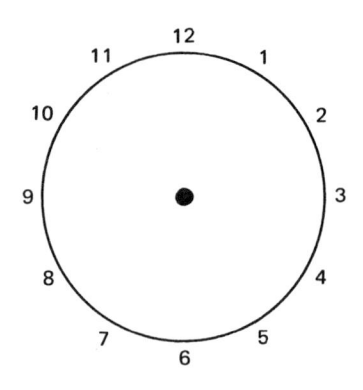

Figure 20-9. Clock system.

commonly used caliber. When the eleven-bull target is used, it is customary to score each bull separately; when this is completed, the total score is obtained. A common practice consists of placing the obtained score directly under each bull and placing the differences between that score and ten points to the right of each bull. This method of scoring is illustrated in Figure 20-8. Using this method, it is a simple task to obtain the total score for the very good as well as the very poor shooter.

To describe the location of hits on the target, the numerals on a clock dial are related to the target. The hits are located and called by using the imaginary figures on the clock face as shown in Figure 20-9.

Using this system, the hit in Figure 20-8 would be called eight ring at three o'clock.

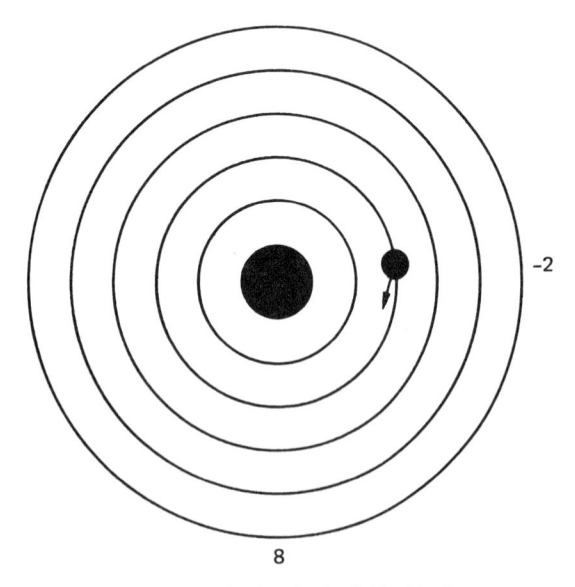

Figure 20-8. Scoring individual bulls.

For a complete list of scoring rules, a current smallbore rifle rule book, published by the NRA should be consulted. The following list includes a few of the basic rules.

1. A hot hole, the leaded edge of which comes in contact with the outside of the bulls' eye or scoring rings of a target, is given the higher value.
2. Hits outside the scoring rings are scored as misses.
3. When more than the required number of shots are fired at one bulls'-eye and a fewer number than required are fired at another bulls'-eye on the same target card—and, thus, not more than the required total number of shots are fired at the target card—the competitor will be given the actual value of his score, minus a penalty of one point for each shot fired at the wrong bulls'-eye.
4. If a competitor fires more than the required number of shots at his own target card, he will be scored on only the required number of hits of the lowest value, minus a penalty of one point for each hit in excess of the required number.
5. Penalty points should be deducted from the remaining hit or hits of the highest value. Thereafter these shall be scored as the actual value (after deduction). A 10X or a 10 so penalized becomes a 9.

COMMON ERRORS AND THEIR CAUSES

The rifles and ammunition of today are of such excellent quality that shooters should look for other causes if shooting errors occur. The utilization of targets analysis offers valuable information for this purpose. The shooter must recognize that the holes in the target indicate where the rifle was pointed when the bullet left the barrel!

The following list includes some common shooting errors and their causes:

1. Vertical errors: Indicates improper breathing or a change in eye relief from shot to shot.

310 *Individual and Team Sports*

2. Horizontal errors: Caused by canting the rifle.
3. No definite groupings: Caused by aiming on the target rather than on the front sight.
4. Six o'clock errors: Sling may be becoming loose with each shot.
5. Nine o'clock errors: Indicates too much finger on the trigger or squeezing the trigger at an angle.
6. Three to five o'clock errors: Indicates a jerked trigger or the left elbow not being under the rifle.
7. Ten to eleven o'clock errors: The shooter is not following through.

Glossary of Terms

Aperture: An opening or hole.
Bore: The hole through the barrel.
Dewar course: A course of fire consisting of twenty shots.
Entry: The act of declaring intent to shoot in a match, and the paying of the required fee to the proper official.
Eye relief: The distance between the eye and rear sight.
Fouling or waring shots: Shots fired for the purpose of cleaning the bore of cleaning solution and to "settle the barrel," preparatory to sighting and recording shots.
Framing targets: The act of placing smallbore targets on the frames and thus making them ready for firing.
Hold: A satisfactory hold consists of pointing the rifle in such a manner that its sights remain in proper alignment with the target for a sufficient length of time to permit the application of a correct technique in firing it.
Lands: The ridges of metal standing between the grooves of the bore.
Match: A complete event as indicated in the program. It may consist of one or of several stages.
Postal match: A match in which the competitors fire on their home ranges using targets that have been properly identified. The fired targets and scores are then exchanged by mail.
Rifling: Spiral grooves running the length of the bore.
Round: One complete cartridge ready for firing.
Sighting shots: The shots fired at a target provided for that purpose and used to obtain information relative to adjusting the sights.
Target butt: A general term referring to that end of the range that receives the bullets. It is the opposite of the other end of the range (referred to as the firing line) from which the bullets are sent.
Target pits: The trench in which target frames are mounted and in which the scorers work.
Target spotters: Cardboard disks, white on one side and black on the other, provided with a wooden or metal pin or hook that can be inserted into a bullet hole in the target. The target spotters can be seen easily from the firing point.
Telegraphic matches: Same as postal matches, except that the scores are exchanged by telegram.
Windage: Horizontal or side-to-side movement.
"X" ring: An inner circle placed inside the bulls'-eye of many targets. It is used to decide the scores.
Zero point: The sight adjustment that places the shots in the center of the bulls'-eye.

References

BOOKS

Handbook of Free Rifle Shooting. Washington, D. C.: Department of the Army. Current.
Individual Weapons and Marksmanship. Washington, D. C.: Headquarters, Department of the Army. Current.
Basic Rifle Marksmanship. Washington, D. C.: NRA, 1966.
National Rifle Association Illustrated Shooting Handbook. Washington, D. C.: NRA, 1966.
National Rifle Association Smallbore Rifle Rules. Washington, D. C.: NRA, 1966.
Encyclopedia Americana Small Arms. New York: Americana Corporation.
Shooter's Bible. Ed. by John Olson. South Hackensack, N. J.: Shooter's Bible, Inc., 1969.
Stephens, William L., Jr. *Rifle Marksmanship.* New York: A. S. Barnes, 1966.
Wilkinson, Frederick. *Small Arms.* New York: Hawthorn, 1966.

PERIODICALS

The American Rifleman. Washington, D. C.: NRA. Monthly.

CHAPTER 21

Rugby   *Peter R. Francis**
Iowa State University

HISTORY

The inscription on a stone at Rugby School, Warwickshire, England, reads as follows:

> This stone commemorates the exploit of William Webb Ellis who with fine disregard for the rules of football as played in his time first took the ball in his arms and ran with it, thus originating the distinctive feature of the Rugby game. A.D. 1823.

Ball games resembling football have been played in England ever since their introduction by the Romans two thousand years ago. During most of this period rules were almost nonexistent, and the games were played with such ferocity that a ban was periodically placed on such dangerous conflicts. It was in one of the select public schools during some form of soccer match that Ellis committed a breach of the rules and thus unwittingly originated the game that has since borne the name of his school. Although his action was not immediately approved, the innovation was soon made part of the football laws of the school (most public schools had their own unique rules). An exciting account of a game played under those rules appears in the classical book, *Tom Brown's Schooldays*, written in 1857. "The Schoolhouse Match" chapter describes a wild game involving more than one hundred participants.

---

*Certificate of Education, University of Leeds, England; Diploma in Physical Education, Carnegie College, England; B. Sc., University of Durham, England; and M.A., University of Iowa, Iowa City. Mr. Francis, who was a lecturer at University of London, Goldsmiths College, has been playing rugby for twenty years. In England he played for the West Hartlepool Rugby Club and Wasps, and while attending the University of Iowa in pursuit of the Ph.D. degree, he was a key player on the University of Iowa Rugby Club team. His rugby classes (and other sports classes as well) were extremely popular with the students at the University.

Variations in rugby rules persisted until 1863, when a uniform set was formulated at the University of Cambridge. Eight years later the Rugby Football Union was formed in London. This organization is still the governing body of rugby football in Britain.

The game soon spread to many countries. The first recorded game played in the United States under Rugby Union rules was between Harvard and McGill University in 1874. In 1876 Princeton, Yale, and Columbia also adopted Rugby Union rules. The game soon underwent many independent changes; the number of players on each team was reduced to eleven and the dimensions of the field were so altered that most football stadiums in the United States are now too narrow for rugby. Protective clothing, time-outs, and substitutions were permitted and many of the tactical decisions became the responsibility of nonplaying coaches. The game of American football now bears few resemblances to its forerunner, rugby football.

The game of rugby football is being played increasingly throughout the world. Over the years several traditions, which reflect the essentially amateur nature of the sport, have become associated with the game. The aim of the game must be to win, within the spirit of the laws, and at the same time to derive a great deal of enjoyment from vigorous activity. After the game, players attempt to show their appreciation for the efforts of their opponents by shaking their hands and then perhaps applauding them. The referee is thanked and it is customary to show hospitality to visiting teams. Spectators are expected to show appreciation for good play from either side, and to respect the decisions of the referee.

DESCRIPTION OF THE GAME

The object of rugby football is to touch the ball down ("score a try") beyond the opponent's goal line or, less

312 *Individual and Team Sports*

frequently, to drop kick the ball over the goal. When a try has been scored (four points), a player from the scoring side attempts to gain two extra points by kicking the ball over the crossbar of the goal from any point on a line perpendicular to the place on the goal line where the try was scored. Any of the players on either side can catch, pass laterally, kick, or run with the ball at any time. The opposing side attempts to stop the ball being touched down by tackling the opponent in possession of the ball.

Fifteen men compose a team, eight forwards and seven backs; no substitutes are permitted (even if an injury occurs). Play is continuous until a player scores, breaks one of the laws of the game, or the ball leaves the field of play.

If a serious breach of the laws has occurred the innocent team is awarded a penalty. They can take a drop kick or a place kick at the goal and, if successful, are awarded three points. For a minor breach of the laws, the game is restarted by the innocent team putting the ball into a tunnel made up by the forwards from each side, who interlock to form a *scrum*. Both sets of forwards attempt to heel the ball backward and, hence, gain possession for their side. The successful team then attempts to move the ball toward the opponent's goal line.

If the ball goes out of bounds ("into touch") the game is restarted by a "line-out." A player throws the ball between parallel lines of opposing forwards, who stand opposite a point where the ball was judged by the line umpire to have left the field of play. Once again the forwards attempt to gain possession of the ball in order that their team may ultimately advance it toward the opponent's goal line.

All players are prohibited from throwing the ball in a forward direction. It is also illegal to hold the ball after a tackle, or to tackle or block a player not in possession of the ball. Under certain conditions a player may be offside, and if this is judged to be an interference with legal play, he will be penalized.

The game is controlled by a single referee whose duties include time keeping. His decisions are absolute and irrevocable. Two touch judges assist by indicating the positions where the ball goes into touch and confirming the success or failure of kicks at goal.

UNIQUE VALUES

Although professional rugby is played in some countries, the game is essentially for amateur players. The spirit of the game is directed toward enjoyment by its participants. In addition to the strength and agility developed as a result of training for and playing rugby, the continuous nature of the game places demands on the cardiovascular endurance of the athlete. The skills of rugby are readily improved with meaningful practice, and a large number of participants continue playing at all levels of ability long after leaving college.

After retiring from active play, the former player can referee, manage, or coach a team, or he can serve on a selection committee for as long as he desires.

PURCHASE AND MAINTENANCE OF EQUIPMENT

One reason for the popularity of rugby football is the relatively inexpensive equipment it requires. The majority of players wear only a shirt, a pair of shorts and athletic supporter, stockings, and rugby shoes. The wearing of shin pads and a soft leather or cloth scrum cap (to protect the ears of the forwards in the scrum) are optional. Many experienced players also wear a headband made of adhesive tape to keep the tops of the ears safely against the sides of the head.

The most important part of the player's equipment are the rugby shoes. The careful selection of the footwear cannot be overemphasized because ill-fitting shoes can lead to great discomfort and avoidable accidents. It is difficult to justify the saving of a few dollars at the price of badly blistered feet or serious ankle injuries. New shoes should be fitted over the pair or two pairs of stockings worn during games. New shoes should not be used to play a full game until they have been broken in gradually in practice sessions. Having shoes custom made for a player offers several advantages. These cost about $30.00 in England. The European style of soccer shoe is worn by some rugby players.

No matter how much has been paid for shoes, full satisfaction will be assured only if they are correctly treated before and after use. The uppers of new shoes should be treated with a good quality hard, neutral dubbin (oil); the outside area can be polished with a black wax polish. After use, excess mud should be carefully scraped off with a blunt knife, and the remainder washed off, using a brush and a minimum of water. *Never* immerse the shoes in water, or use hot water. Allow the shoes to dry naturally, away from all artificial heat. When dry, dub (and polish) them again. Regularly check to see that the studs are firmly attached and that no dangerous nails or screws project from the soles.

Rugby stockings are traditionally knee length and require support in the form of tape or elastic below the knee. However, if the support is too tight, the circulation may be restricted, leading to discomfort during the game. Foot powders keep the feet dry and less liable to the problems of blisters and fungus infections. The shorts and athletic supporter should be strong and comfortable; if equipped with hip pockets the hands can be kept warm during periods of inactivity. Strong, well-stitched shirts are preferred because they normally last for many games of strenuous play. Any small tear should be repaired as soon as possible, because the grasp of a tackle may enlarge it beyond repair.

The rugby ball should be in good condition if it is to be handled well, kicked accurately, and not handicap the players in executing their skills. After use the ball should be cleaned with a damp cloth, deflated slightly, and left to dry naturally in a temperature of not more than 60°F. Before using the ball again, its seams should be treated with dubbin and the pressure increased to the recommended poundage.

LAWS OF RUGBY

Only selected aspects of those laws essential to a sound understanding of rugby appear in this section. The enthusiastic player should possess an up-to-date copy of the laws and study them to avoid misunderstandings and to increase his enjoyment of the game.

Law One deals with the dimensions of the field, which are depicted in Figure 21-1.

Law Four stipulates that a rugby ball must be between eleven and eleven and one-quarter inches in length; thirty to thirty-one inches in end-to-end circumference; twenty-four to twenty-five and one-half inches in width circumference; and between thirteen and one-half and fifteen ounces in weight. American footballs can be used for practice but they are unsuitable for competitive use.

Law Five describes players' clothing and specifies the dimensions of the shoe's cleats. Most American football cleats are too small in diameter for rugby play.

Law Seven lists the values of the scores of the game.

A try	4 points
A goal (a converted try)	6 points
A goal from a free kick (see Law 23) or penalty kick	3 points
A dropped goal	3 points

Law Eight states that an international match rugby game lasts for two periods of forty minutes. In most other instances the duration of play is actually fixed by the respective teams. The timing of the periods is uninterrupted, the only allowance being made for injury time. At half time the teams change ends, and the time-out interval does not exceed five minutes.

Law Nine states that the captains toss a coin for the right to kick off or the choice of ends.

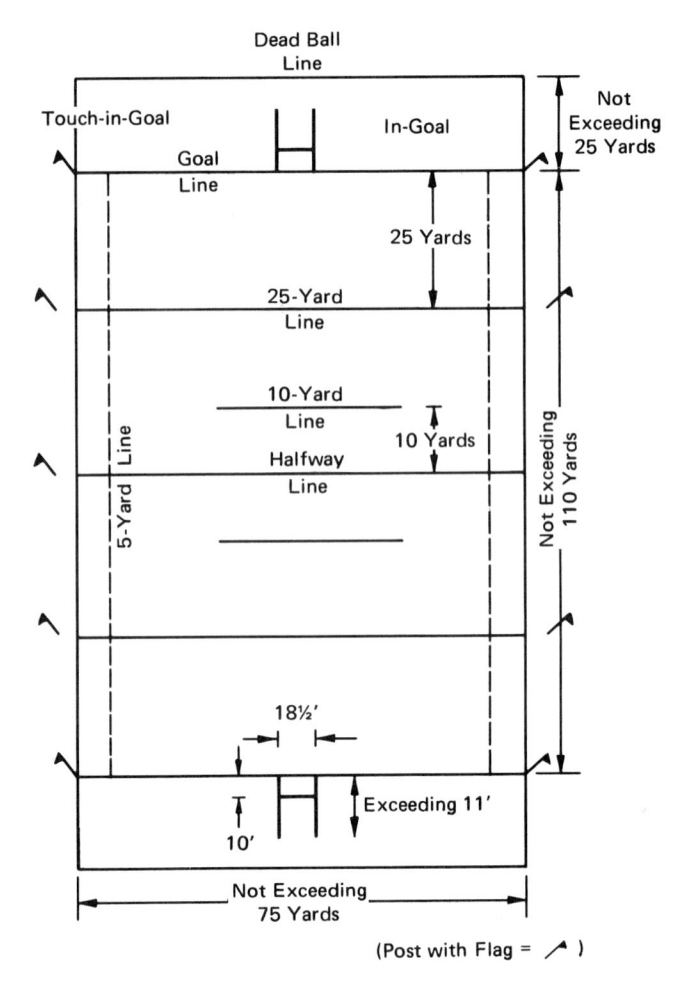

Figure 21-1. Dimensions of the rugby field.

Law Ten states that the referee is in complete control of the game and his decisions are irrevocable.

Law Eleven specifies that the two touch judges assist the referee at his discretion. They indicate, by raising a flag, the time and place at which the ball goes into touch.

Law Twelve limits the number of players to fifteen per side, and it prohibits substitution.

Law Fourteen gives the following definitions:

1. A *knock-on* occurs when the ball is propelled by the hand or arm of a player in the direction of his opponent's dead ball line. This includes a bounce from the hand or arm in a forward direction.
2. A *throw-forward* occurs when the ball in the possession of a player is thrown in the direction of his opponent's dead ball line.

If the knock-on or throw-forward is unintentional, a scrummage is formed at the place of infringement, unless

1. A fair catch has been allowed (see Law 23).
2. The opposing team gains an advantage.

3. The ball has been knocked-on by a player who is in the act of charging down an opponent's kick.
4. The ball is knocked-on by a player who is in the act of catching it directly from a kick, and it is recovered by that player before it has touched the ground or another player.
5. The knock-on is no more than a movement of the ball in the player's grasp without loss of control. (This must be an adjustment with two hands.)

Law Fifteen defines the rules governing scrummaging. Two types of scrummage are recognized at different phases of the game.

1. A *loose scrummage* is formed by one or more players from each time in physical contact and standing on their feet, closing around the ball when it is on the ground between them.
2. A *set scrummage* is formed by players from each team closing up in readiness to allow the ball to be put on the ground between them.

A set scrum must have three players in the front row—that is, in contact with the opponent's scrum. The middle player of the front row, known as the *hooker*, must hold the players on either side of him. All other players must bind (hold) with at least one arm and hand around another player of the same team. The scrum half normally puts the ball into the scrum. He must stand one yard away from the scrum, and the ball must travel straight along the middle line of the tunnel formed by the front rows. When the ball has touched the ground beyond the first *prop*, any of the front-row players can attempt to heel the ball backward, provided that they do not raise both feet from the ground, or lower or twist the body. The positions of the forwards in a set scrummage are depicted in Figure 21-2.

In all scrummages it is illegal for a player either to handle the ball or to deliberately cause the scrum to collapse. An infringement of any of the rules governing scrummaging always results in a penalty kick to the non-offending team.

Law Sixteen describes a tackle as follows: A tackle occurs when a player in possession of the ball is so held by one or more players of the opposing team that:

1. There is a moment when he cannot pass or otherwise play the ball.
2. The ball comes in contact with the ground.

When a player is tackled he must immediately release the ball and move away from it. An infringement of this law results in a penalty kick.

Figure 21-2. Position of forwards in a set scrummage (arms omitted for clarity).

Rugby

Law Eighteen is the off-side law, which is a confusing aspect of the game of rugby. A player is in an off-side position if the ball has been kicked or touched, or is being carried, by one of his own teammates *behind him*. However, the off-side player will *not* be penalized if:

1. He does not play the ball.
2. He does not interfere with an opponent.
3. He does not approach within ten yards of an opponent waiting to play the ball.

The penalty for off-side gives to the nonoffending team the choice between a penalty kick at the place of infringement, or a scrummage at the place where the ball was last played by the offending team.

If a player in an off-side position cannot avoid being touched by the ball or a ball carrier, he is "accidentally off-side" and a scrummage is formed where he was touched.

The ways in which a player can become off-side are summarized in Figures 21-3 and 21-4. The defending players are symbolized by squares; attacking players (who are attacking toward the top of the page) by circles; the player in an off-side position, a solid circle. The location of the hindmost foot of the rear player determines the "scrummage off-side line" (SOSL) for that team—that line is represented by a broken line.

1. A player is off-side if he enters any type of scrummage from his opponent's side.
2. In a loose scrummage a player who is *not* part of the scrummage must immediately move behind the ball; if he does not then join the scrummage he must not cross the scrummage off-side line.
3. A player (other than the scrum half) who is not part of a set scrummage must immediately move behind the scrummage off-side line. He must remain there until the scrummage has ceased.
4. The scrum half must not advance either foot in front of the ball while it is in the scrum.

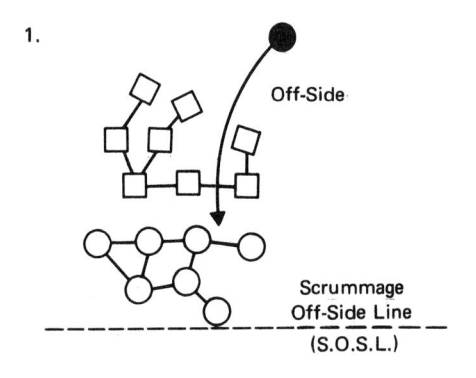

1.

Entering Scrum from Opponents' Side
Penalty Kick

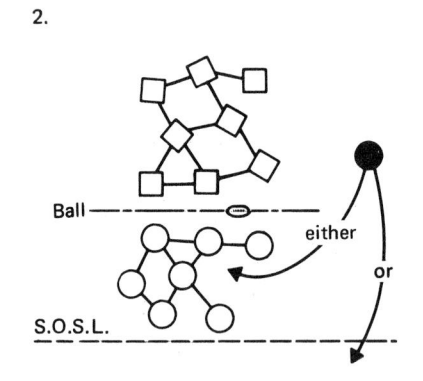

2.

Player in Off-Side Position Returning to On-Side

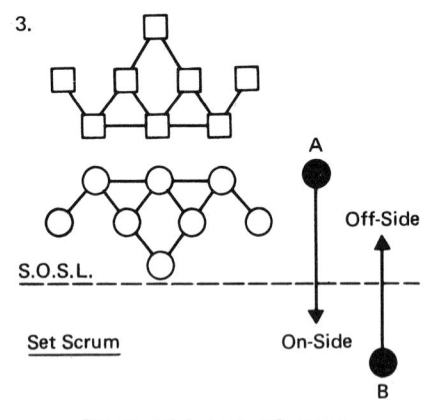

3.

Penalty Kick Against Player B
(Neither *A* nor *B* Is the Scrum Half)

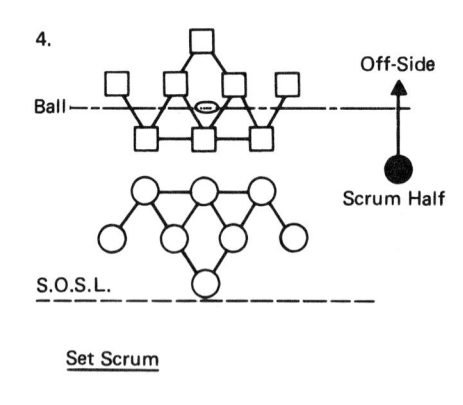

4.

Penalty Kick Against Scrum Half

Figure 21-3.

316 *Individual and Team Sports*

Players can also be off-side at a line out. An imaginary line at right angles to the touch line, through the point where the ball went into touch, is the center line of the line out.

5. The players must not cross the center line before the ball has touched a player or the ground. (See Figure 21-4.)
6. A player who is not carrying the ball must not advance in front of the ball after it has touched a player or the ground.
7. While a line out is taking place those players not participating must not be within ten yards of the center line. (Players "participating in the line out" are the parallel lines of forwards, scrum halves, and the player who is throwing the ball into the line out and his opposite number.) (See Figure 21-4.)

Law Nineteen defines on-side. A player who is off-side under Law 18 can become on-side again by the following means:

1. When one of his teammates has run in front of him carrying the ball.
2. When one of his teammates has run in front of him after having kicked the ball when behind him.
3. When he has retired (run back) behind the player of his own team who last played the ball.
4. When an opponent who has gained possession of the ball has run five yards in any direction.
5. When the ball has been kicked or passed by an opponent.
6. When an opponent has *intentionally* touched the ball but has failed to catch it.

Law Twenty states that charging and blocking an opponent who is not carrying the ball are illegal, as are foul play and misconduct. All these offenses result in a penalty kick or even a penalty try being awarded.

Law Twenty-one specifies that for a kickoff the kicker's team must all remain behind the ball until it has been kicked, and the opponents must remain behind their ten-yard line.

From a kickoff the ball must reach the ten-yard line unless first played by an opponent.

If the ball is kicked off and goes into touch without a bounce, the opposing team can accept the kick, have the ball kicked off again, or have a scrummage formed at the center.

A place kick is taken from the center of the halfway line:

1. At the beginning of the game.
2. After the half-time interval.
3. After a goal has been kicked.

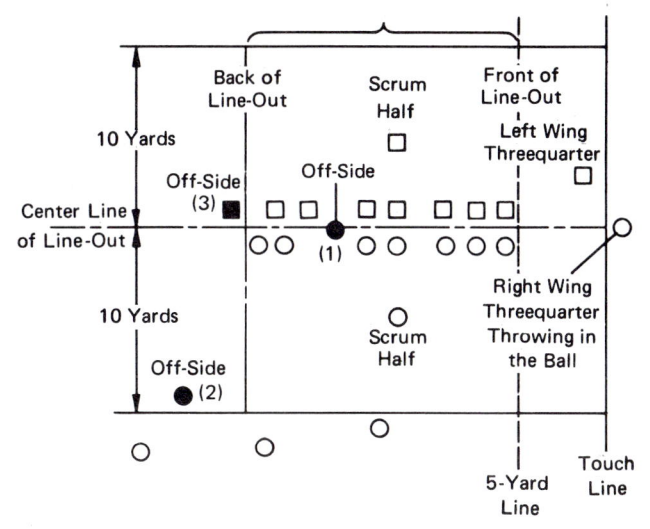

Figure 21-4. Line-out showing three possible ways of being off-side.

The game is restarted by a drop kick if the kick at goal has been unsuccessful.

Law Twenty-two defines a *drop-out* as a drop kick taken by the defending team after a touchdown (*not* a try) or after the ball has crossed the touch-in-goal, or dead-ball line. The kick is taken anywhere on or behind the twenty-five-yard line. The players on the kicker's team must remain behind the ball; the opponents must not cross the twenty-five-yard line until the kick has been taken.

Law Twenty-three states that a "free kick" is a kick allowed for a fair catch. A fair catch is obtained when a player clearly catches the ball direct from a kick, knock-on, or throw forward by one of the opposing team. At the same time the catcher must make a mark on the ground with his heel and should "Mark!"

The free kick can be a place kick, drop kick, or punt taken at, or directly behind, the mark. When the kick is taken the kicker's team must stand behind the kicker. The opponents can stand up to the line that runs through the mark and parallel to the goal lines. The kicker customarily steps back a few yards in order to kick over the heads of the forward opponents.

Law Twenty-four states that a penalty kick can be a place kick, drop kick, or punt. All players of the opposing team must retire immediately behind a line parallel to the goal lines and ten yards from the mark.

Law Twenty-five specifies that after a try has been scored, the scoring team has the right to take a place kick or drop kick at the goal. The ball can be kicked from any point on a line running parallel to the touch lines and passing through the point where the try was obtained.

All the kicking team must be behind the ball when it is kicked. The opposing team must remain behind the goal

Rugby 317

line until the kicker begins his run. If the opposing team succeeds in touching the ball before it crosses the crossbar of the goal, the kick is void.

Law Twenty-six defines certain confusing terms:

1. A try is scored by the act of an attacking player first grounding the ball in his opponent's in-goal area. (3 points are awarded.)
2. A touchdown is obtained by the act of a *defending* player first grounding the ball in his own in-goal area. (The game is restarted by a twenty-five-yard drop-out.)

Law Twenty-seven states that the ball is "in touch" when

1. It touches or crosses a touch line.
2. When a player carrying the ball touches or crosses a touch line.

The game is restarted by an opponent of the player who was last in contact with the ball. The ball must be thrown in from the spot where it went into touch. The line-out consists of at least two players from each team lining up in single parallel lines opposite this spot. The nearest player in the line-out must be beyond the five-yard line, and the line-out stretches to the farthest player of the team throwing in the ball. (See Figure 21–4.) (In most cases all eight forwards will participate in the line-out.)

Law Twenty-eight awards a penalty kick to the opposing team if a player willfully knocks or throws the ball into touch, touch-in-goal, or over his own dead-ball line.

Law Thirty specifies that if a player in possession of the ball in in-goal is so held that he cannot ground the ball, a scrummage is formed. The scrummage takes place five yards from the line opposite the place where he was held. The attacking team puts in the ball.

Law Thirty-one states that a five-yard scrum is also awarded if a defending player last contacts the ball before it is touched down by another defending player. (A dropout is awarded if an attacking player last touches the ball before it is touched down.)

SAFETY

One of the first concerns of the rugby player is that enjoyment and general welfare are not impaired by injury to either himself or his fellows. With reasonable precautions a large number of accidents can be avoided.

Shin pads and a scrum cap are permitted for additional protection and should be worn, but buckles, wrist watches, rings, and other forms of adornment are illegal. The rugby cleats must be a regulation size; the cleats used in American football may not satisfy the requirements. (See Law Five.)

A regular inspection of the field of play and its immediate surroundings is essential. Deep footprints made in wet weather are a potential hazard when the ground dries. A light roller will eradicate most irregularities, but some deep depressions may require the addition of top soil or turf. Small stones and other objects can cause unpleasant abrasions on unprotected knees; hence, constant inspections are vital.

Goal posts should be padded with mats or sponge rubber to head height. The posts bearing the flags marking significant zones of the pitch (field) should be well away from the touch line and of sufficient height to insure that a player cannot fall on top of them.

All spectators, coaches, and other nonplayers should be restricted a safe distance from the boundary lines. Whenever possible a qualified and experienced doctor or trainer should be immediately available, as should adequate first-aid equipment and means of communication with medical facilities.

FUNDAMENTAL SKILLS

The basic skills of rugby, as for most games, are best acquired when practiced for relatively short periods on many occasions. The skilled performer realizes that constant repetition of running, passing, catching, kicking, and tackling is necessary to bring his skill to the highest possible level.

Running

All running drills should be practiced while the player carries a ball so that he can learn to hold it with control and confidence under game conditions. Although natural speed is one of the greatest assets of a rugby player, acceleration and maintaining balance while running are essential for successful play. Considerable time may need to be spent in improving these aspects of running—they should of course be learned as early as possible. Advice can be sought from expert players, track coaches, and other knowledgeable persons.

Once running balance has been developed to a satisfactory level, acceleration can be improved by constant training. Improvement in performance is a long-term proposition; progressive resistance training with weights during the off-season can be beneficial.

In addition to sheer speed it is possible to evade a tackle by a body swerve, a side-step, or a change in the pace of running. Some players develop these skills without formal coaching, but practice will improve anyone's skills. Observing experts and analyzing films are helpful, but a critical analysis of running performance in practice is most valuable. Working in pairs, the player attempts to avoid being touched by a partner while sprinting across the field. Another practice drill is to run to alternate sides of posts that are spaced about fifteen feet apart. The turn method of changing direction while running (see Figure 21-5) can be continuously practiced. This type of drill enables the player to become aware that he probably has a favorite direction, either to the left or to the right, for these maneuvers. In a game a skillful opponent is quick to spot the man who can only "break" in one direction. Thus, every player should try to be equally competent in changing direction off either foot.

Running is one of the most vital skills of rugby football, and it must be practiced constantly. In addition, the game demands great stamina; thus running practice achieves two ends simultaneously; while practicing running skills, a player also develops circulorespiratory endurance.

Adequate footwear should be worn at all times. Outdoor work requires cleats suitable for the condition of the ground.

Passing and Receiving

It has been said that rugby is "a game in which we run forward and pass backward." Two-handed passing is more accurate than one-handed passing while running at speed; therefore, all members of a team must practice this skill. The passer should hold the ball vertically with the fingers opened and positioned approximately parallel to the seams. The hands are placed at the sides of and slightly behind the center of the ball. In order to throw an accurate two-hand pass, the passer must turn his head and look at the receiver. When the pass is made the chest is so turned toward the receiver that the arms are drawn away from the target. The ball is delivered by swinging it across the body and following through in the direction of the pass with the hands. Although the swing of the ball is pendulumlike, the elbows and wrists are relaxed naturally so that during the throwing delivery an accelerated extension of the arms and fingers occur. A long pass is preceded by a strong leading rotation of the upper body, which is rapidly followed by a vigorous arm swing and wrist extension. Improved balance is achieved if the pass is timed to be delivered when in the running stride the leg nearest the receiver is back.

The pass is first practiced by throwing from a standing position to a stationary partner, particular emphasis being devoted to the head position, grip on the ball, and follow-through.

When some accuracy is achieved the partners repeat the drill while walking. The speed of the partners' run is gradually increased, but a tendency to try to pass too far in the early stages must be discouraged. The pair should never be more than ten feet apart. Most players find increased success in passing to the left or to the right. The earlier that the player is aware of his weakness in passing to the opposite side, the sooner he can begin practice to remedy this deficiency.

When passing is practiced while moving, care must be taken to pass the ball in a backward direction (forward passes are illegal), at a point in front of the receiver, to allow for his forward movement. As the running speed increases, the ball must be aimed increasingly in front of the receiver. This causes him to accelerate onto the ball. In a game situation it is essential that the ball be moved toward the opponent's goal line at the fastest possible speed.

Nothing is more frustrating in the game of rugby than to see a skillful handling movement stopped by a dropped pass. The catcher must not take his eyes from the ball until it is held firmly in his grasp. Both hands are out to guide the ball, which is immediately drawn into the chest.

When passing and catching have been practiced in pairs, groups of threes can be employed. Eventually, the drill is continued using the whole three-quarter line or the entire pack of forwards.

Under game conditions insufficient time frequently exists for a pass to be made with the deliberation and form described here. The experienced player relies heavily on very fast, short passes in which most of the force is derived from the action of the wrists and fingers. Under these circumstances a catch can be rapidly followed by a pass; in such cases handling is done with the hands alone and the ball never touches the chest.

On occasions, one-handed passes *may* occur. The player who first masters the basic catching and passing skills in

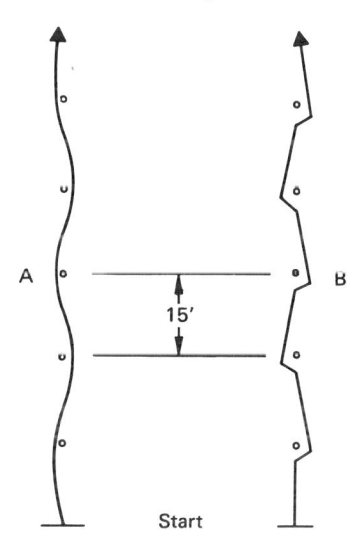

Figure 21-5. Direction of player's run: (A) bodyswerving (B) sidestepping. Series of posts 15 feet apart, using alternate sides.

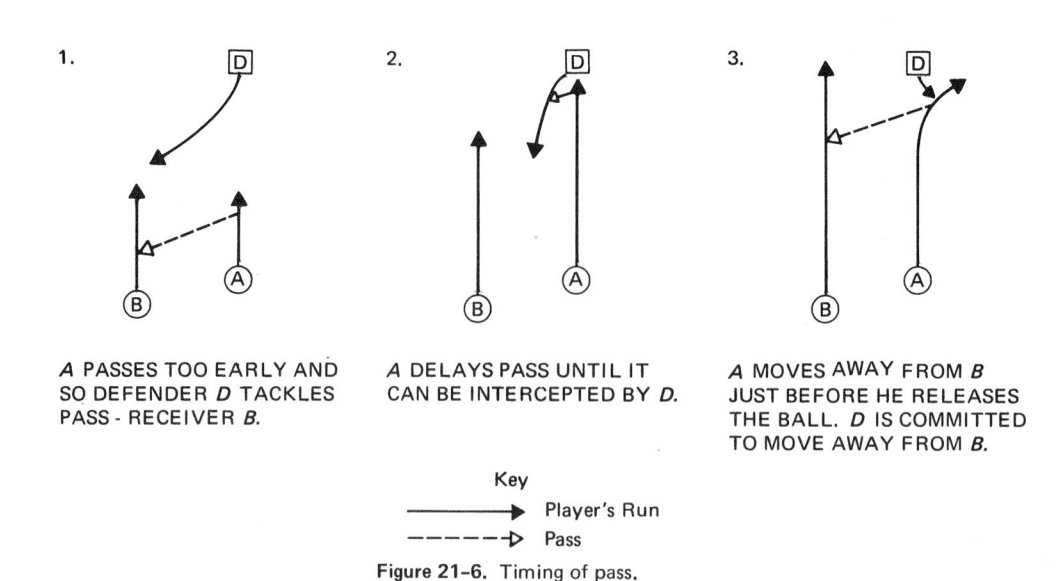

1.

A PASSES TOO EARLY AND SO DEFENDER *D* TACKLES PASS-RECEIVER *B*.

2.

A DELAYS PASS UNTIL IT CAN BE INTERCEPTED BY *D*.

3.

A MOVES AWAY FROM *B* JUST BEFORE HE RELEASES THE BALL. *D* IS COMMITTED TO MOVE AWAY FROM *B*.

Key
→ Player's Run
--▷ Pass

Figure 21-6. Timing of pass.

which a deliberate form is employed usually develops the control and confidence necessary to succeed with the difficult forms of handling the ball. However, players must not conform to a rigid style of performing the basic skills. Rugby is a game for the free and adventuresome athlete; spontaneous forms of play give the game its exciting character.

The object of the pass is to transfer the ball from the possession of one player to the hands of a teammate. If this is successfully accomplished with unfailing regularity, the player can hardly be validly criticized. But the player should remember that the man who drops a pass or throws an inaccurate pass to a teammate can be criticized if the failure results from utilizing an unorthodox technique. Whenever possible the basic techniques of catching and throwing should be practiced in the early stages by all players so that they will be confident of their abilities in these necessary skills.

The next stage in developing increased skill in the fundamentals is to practice them against opposition. The players can work in threes, in which one of the group offers passive resistance to the passing movement. The passer walks toward the defending player and, before being touched by the defender, passes to the receiver. This drill is then practiced while running. During all the practice stages of passing and catching, the passer must watch the receiver, and the receiver must watch the ball; both should be aware of the defender's position by use of their peripheral vision. The correct timing of the pass is extremely important. The three illustrations depicted in Figure 21-6 emphasize the need for great care when passing. (1) If the pass is made too early the defender will ignore the passer and take out the receiver. See Figures 21-6 (1) and 21-7. (2) If the pass is delayed too long the defender will intercept the pass or tackle the passer. See Figures 21-6 (2) and 21-8. (3) A compromise in timing the pass should be

Figure 21-7. The white player has passed too soon, hence the defender (back to camera) has already moved in to tackle the receiver.

Figure 21-8. Player in possession has held the ball too long and has been "smothered" before he can pass.

made so that the defender will be committed to take the passer, who then moves the ball to his partner before an interception is possible. (See Figure 21-6). If just before releasing the ball the passer moves away from the receiver, the defender will tend to be drawn onto the wrong foot, thus leaving him with little opportunity for catching the receiver. The passer must avoid moving toward the receiver as he passes, because this allows the defender to continue running without a drastic change of direction, enabling him to take out both players.

An efficient man-to-man defense is difficult to penetrate through the use of straight running and passing movements; a switch in the direction of the attack, however, may result in a breakdown of the defensive pattern. This directional change can be effected with the *reverse pass*. The intended receiver, who is on one side of the passer, suddenly crosses behind the ball carrier and is then given a pass in the opposite direction from the expected one. The movement should first be practiced without opposition until a degree of confidence is achieved. The following essential points should be remembered:

1. The move will only be successful if it is unexpected; therefore, the receiver must move as if he is to take a pass in the orthodox manner—the change in direction must be very fast and as late as possible.
2. The catcher must not lose sight of the ball; consequently, the passer must so handle the ball that his body never comes between it and the receiver.
3. There is a natural tendency for the receiver to run across the field when he receives the ball, but in order to advance toward the opponent's goal line he must run on an arc, as shown in Figure 21-9.

The *dummy pass* can be used to beat a defender who tends to follow the ball instead of his opposite number. As illustrated in Figure 21-10, the player must try to perform the passing action in order that

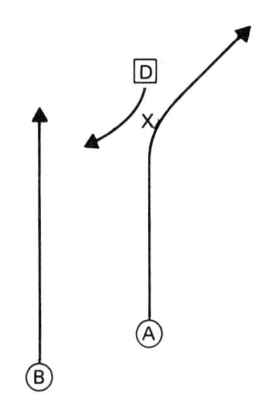

Figure 21-10. *A makes a dummy pass at point X and D follows the expected path of the ball. A then accelerates away from B and D.*

1. Movements of the body are indistinguishable from his normal passing movements, except that he keeps a firm grip on the ball.
2. He accelerates past the defender to complete the break.

The dummy and reverse passes are infrequently used methods of penetrating a defense, the element of surprise being the key to their success. Of prime importance is the fact that the passed ball can travel faster than a running man; hence, the accurate well-timed pass is the most important skill to be mastered.

Following the two-against-one passing drill, groups of five practice the dummy and reverse pass in three-against-two situations. The practice is first performed at a walking pace. It will soon become apparent that the first attacker must release the ball sooner than he did in the previous drill; otherwise, before having a chance to pass to the third attacker, the middle attacker will be smothered by his opposite number. (See Figure 21-11). If the two

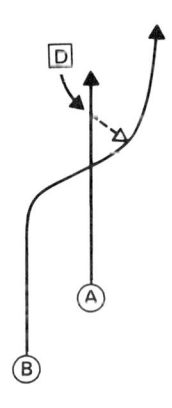

Figure 21-9. *B runs as though expecting an orthodox pass. He accelerates behind A and receives the pass while obscured from D by A.*

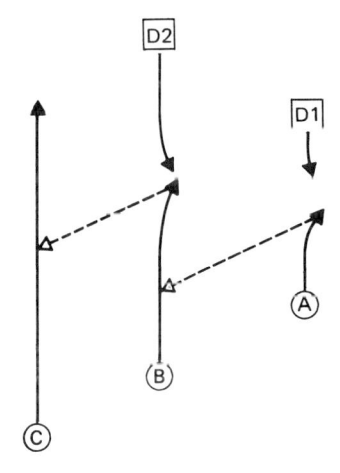

Figure 21-11. *Three-against-two drill. (A has passed the ball earlier than he would in a two-against-one drill. This gives B sufficient time to catch the ball, commit D2, and pass to C.)*

Rugby 321

lines of opposing players begin at a steep angle to each other, the outside men have a longer distance in which to plan their strategy and to catch or pass the ball. In all drills of this nature the members of the opposition are expected to enter into the spirit of the practice. They must allow the attack to succeed if it is adequately performed. They are not required to tackle, because a beginner has his mind fully occupied while learning new skills. As the attack improves, the opposition must increase their efforts to break down the attack by either touching a man in possession of the ball or else intercepting a pass.

As the skills are perfected and the teamwork improves, the numbers on each side can be increased. Eventually, all the skills learned so far can be practiced and consolidated by playing touch rugby.

Correcting Common Errors in the Basic Pass

If the passer persists in throwing inaccurate or lobbed passes, it is first essential to check to see that the hands are gripping the ball correctly, as described perviously. Next check to see that the arms are neither bent too much at the elbows, nor locked stiff. Before the ball is delivered it must be drawn away from the target and then swung across the body. The final momentum is derived from the flexion of the hand and fingers at the wrist. Just before the ball is passed, the chest is turned toward the target, but the hips and feet face forward. A very common cause of inaccurate passing is that the passer watches his opponent and not the target.

Similarly, if the receiver does not watch the ball he will frequently drop good passes. Passes can also be dropped because the receiver spreads his hands too wide apart and/or does not relax his hands and arms. To correct passing faults, the appropriate skills should be practiced unopposed until the player has confidence and has developed the correct technique for accurate passing.

A player may frequently mistime a pass, resulting either in that player being tackled before he releases the ball or the receiver being tackled by the same defender who made the passer release the ball. In both cases the player must practice the three drills outlined on page 319. When he fully appreciates the need for a compromise in the timing of his pass, it will be only a matter of sustained practice before he is ready to return from the drill to the competitive situation. Another cause of a badly timed pass may be due to the passer's difficulty in throwing the ball a considerable distance; hence, the receiver should not be too far away from the passer.

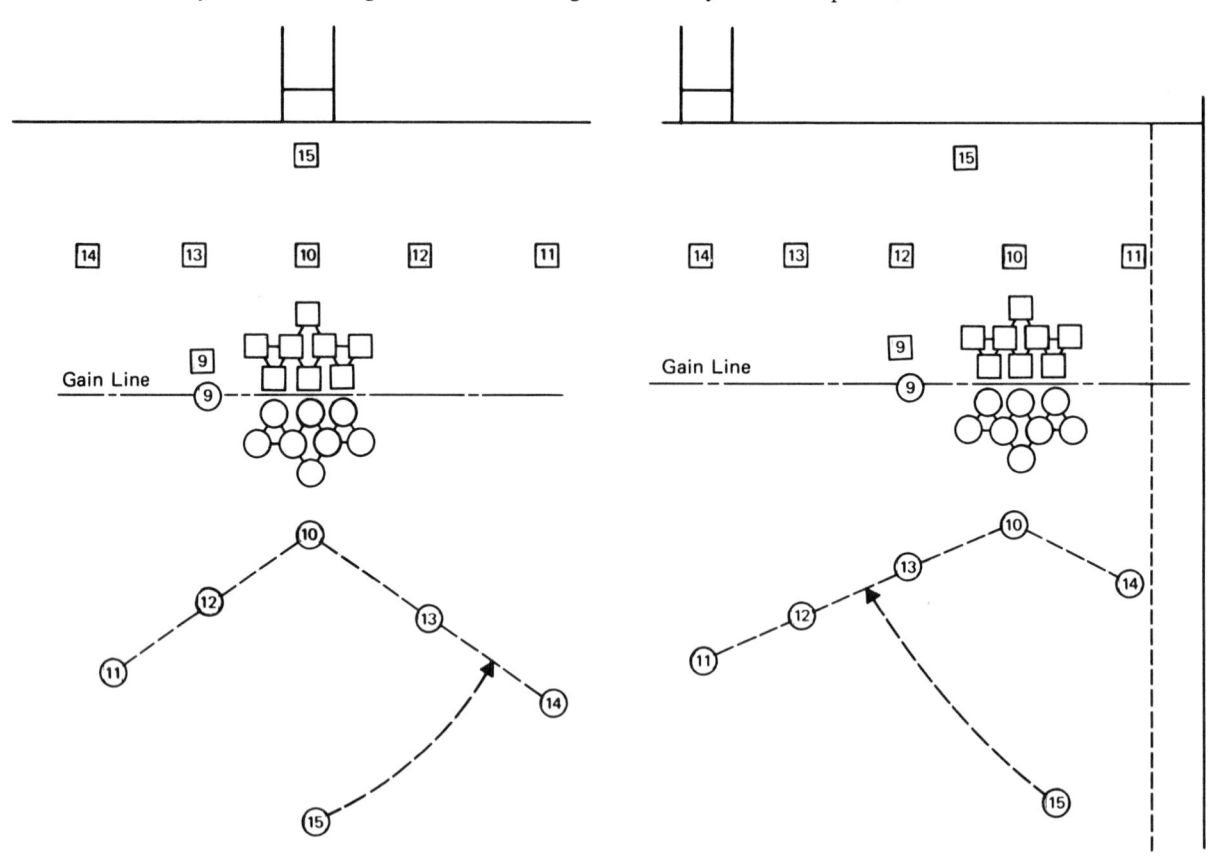

Figure 21-12. Fullback can come up into the three-quarter line to assist the attack 15.

Touch Rugby

Before playing a game, the teams practice spontaneously or at prearranged signals all running and ball-handling skills. The available space and number of players will dictate the best number per team, but about five per side seems to be practical in many cases. Goal lines are designated; these can be at each end of a gymnasium or a twenty-yard strip across a rugby pitch. Thus, by using flags to mark five separate twenty-yard strips on a pitch one hundred yards in length, up to fifty players could actively play touch rugby on a single rugby field.

The rules for touch rugby follow:

1. All passes must be lateral passes. (A player must move rapidly in order to be *behind* the ball whenever his side has possession, otherwise a pass cannot be made to him.)
2. A player must pass *immediately* if he is touched while carrying the ball. If this is not possible he must drop the ball and move back five yards toward his own goal line before he can play the ball or a man again. Play continues when the ball is dropped.
3. If the ball is either passed or accidently dropped forward, if a player holds the ball after he is touched, or if the ball goes out of the area of play, the offending team goes back five yards and the game is restarted by a free pass by the nonoffending side.
4. Points are scored by crossing the opponents' goal line. The game is restarted from the center of the pitch by a free pass by the nonscoring side. The scoring side must stand ten yards back from the center of the pitch.

Touch rugby provides skill practice and is an excellent game for any group of athletes wishing to develop circulorespiratory endurance.

Kicking and Catching the Kicked Ball

The modern trend in rugby is to restrict kicking in order to keep possession of the ball; tries can only be scored when a side is in possession of the ball. Each team, however, usually includes at least one kicking specialist who may be called on to attempt penalty kicks and conversions. In addition, when a team is defending close to its own goal line a prudent safety measure is frequently to punt the ball away from the goal line and "into touch." At the resulting line-out the defensive formation can be reorganized at a distance of increased safety from the vulnerable goal line. At any time in the game any player can score 3 points by drop kicking the ball over the goal. Tactical kicking is engaged in by specialists, but it is obvious that all players must be skilled in performing the drop kick and the punt.

Figure 21-13. Punt. (During the follow-through the weight is kept forward and the head is down.)

Punting (Figure 21-13). When practicing punting, precision should be stressed rather than brute force because accuracy is more important than great distance. The following should be remembered:

1. Watch the ball at all times; do not lift the head.
2. The ball is usually held in two hands with the long axis pointing to the chest, but some experienced kickers tilt the ball sideways in order to impart a stabilizing spin to it. The ball is dropped onto the instep of the kicking foot.
3. If the ball is raised upward to chest height before it falls to the foot, the kicker will have increased time in which to coordinate the swing of the leg and the fall of the ball.
4. The knee is extended just before the ball is contacted.
5. Keep the weight of the body over the ball.
6. Follow through with the kicking leg while keeping the head down.

Punting drills are carried out in pairs so that each player has the maximum time for practice. The pair should remain close together; only when form and accuracy have been developed is there a need to increase the kicking distance. A player who can use only one foot for kicking will be at a great disadvantage in 50 per cent of all game situations. Practice punting with alternate feet from the beginning.

Drop Kick. Many of the coaching points outlined for the punt apply to the drop kick; consequently, drop-kicking practice should be delayed until the player is reasonably competent at punting. When drop kicking, the leg swing is so delayed that impact with the ball is made an instant after the point of the ball has touched the ground. Because of its shape, a rugby ball must be dropped with great accuracy in order that it does not rebound at an angle away from the foot. The ball should be kicked as soon as possible after the rebound begins, at which time the ball has rebounded a minimum distance from the ground. In certain circumstances the game is restarted by a drop kick, and in such situations the ball should be kicked to an optimum height so that it will "float" long enough for the kicking team to reach the place where the ball will descend. The drop kick is practiced in pairs; the emphasis is on control and accuracy.

Place Kick. Although the place kick usually is performed by a specialist, the team with several expert place kickers has insurance in the event of the removal of a single specialist because of injury.

Because the use of a kicking tee is not permissible in rugby, the player must instead depend on an indention made in the turf by the heel of a shoe. To avoid spoiling the surface of the pitch, place-kick practice should be conducted away from the playing surface. For place kicks requiring height and accuracy, the ball should be placed vertically; when greater distance is necessary, the ball should be tilted toward the target. The optimum approach is found by trial and error. When place kicking remember

1. To watch the ball.
2. That the nonkicking foot should land close to the side of the ball before impact.
3. The weight of the body should remain over the ball.
4. To follow through and keep the head down.

Correcting Common Errors in Kicking. If the punt is inaccurate or frequently miskicked, the fault usually lies in poor coordination of the kicking leg with the descent of the ball. The kicker should first check to see that the ball is not being thrown into the air before the kick is initiated. The ball must be dropped with control and accuracy onto the instep. (See page 323.) A further common fault is committed when the kicker persists in lifting the head to watch the flight of the ball. He must instead keep his head down for a count of three before looking for the kicked ball. The kicker should also check to see that the kicking ankle is stretched (foot pointed away from the knee) when the foot contacts the ball, because this prevents the ball from rotating end over end in the air. Barefoot kicking with a plastic ball may remedy the fault of the kicker who does not stretch the ankle. The follow-through by the kicking leg is an important aid in achieving distance and accuracy. A kicker who finds it difficult to keep the ball low and who lacks power in the punt should make certain that he is not leaning back, thus taking his momentum away from the direction of the kick and causing the ball to be lifted. To correct this fault the kicker must keep his weight over the ball and concentrate on accuracy and form before he attempts to increase his kicking distance.

Many of the faults noticed in the drop kick can be corrected by improving punting form. Another possibility for error is not dropping the ball at the correct angle, which is on the point with the top pointing toward the kicker. To correct this fault the kicker must practice dropping the ball without actually kicking it. At first the follow-through should be short, but at all times the player must keep his head down and his weight over the ball.

The place kick is a specialized skill and the specialist is encouraged to practice frequently under the supervision of a capable coach. To save time and effort a large collection of correctly inflated balls is desirable. Beginning place kickers frequently stab at the ball; the practice of place kicking from a standing position usually improves the follow-through. The kicker tries to kick *through* the ball. The approach run varies in length for different players and must be found by trial and error. The nonkicking foot must be positioned at the side of the ball and slightly behind it or else the kicker will lose length. The foot must be held at a right angle to the kicking leg when the toe strikes the ball. If the ankle joint is loose the kicker can strengthen the muscles controlling movement of the ankle by means of selected weight-training exercises. The place kicker should also learn what is necessary to counteract the effects of wind.

Catching the Kicked Ball. Catching is practiced by the kicker's partner, who then becomes the kicker in all the drills so far presented. The following points are to be remembered when catching:

1. Because the ball usually bounces at an unpredictable angle, whenever possible it should be caught before a bounce.
2. The feet should be in a firm comfortable position immediately before the catch; during the actual catch the knees are bent to cushion the impact of the ball.
3. The arms are lifted until the hands are at least chin height, and the ball is then guided into the safety of the hands, arms, and chest. Keep the elbows close to the body.

During the initial phase of catching practice, the ball is caught after being thrown into the air. As both catching and kicking improve, the partner's kicks are caught. Later, a third player can chase the kicks so that the catcher is trying to return kicks under the pressure of opposition.

Correction of Common Errors in Catching the Ball. The catcher must watch the unpredictable bounce of a rugby ball and be convinced that he must make every effort to get underneath the ball before it bounces. The failure to do so may be due to the player's lack of speed or fitness; if so, extra running practice is essential. The failure to anticipate correctly the spot where a ball will drop can be overcome with constant practice with a partner. Many beginners fail to lift the hands to guide the ball into the arms and chest. The catcher must lift his arms prior to catching the ball thrown up by the coach or another player and, with additional practice, a ball kicked by a partner. The beginner will frequently fail to catch a high kick because of anxiety about the impact of the falling ball. Learning to bend his legs at the knees in order to help absorb the momentum of the ball will instill confidence necessary for the game situation.

Tackling

Because of a lack of protective clothing there is a reluctance to tackle with maximum efficiency during the training sessions. However, an awareness of certain safety precautions will quickly enable the player to develop the confidence and skill necessary for this vital part of the game. Tackling from the side is the least dangerous technique, and it should be learned first.

1. The impact of the tackler's shoulder on the "victim's" thigh is the most important factor in a successful tackle. The momentum for this impact is gained by diving with both feet clear of the ground.
2. Try to dive *through* the target, not at it!
3. Keep the head behind the victim's thigh in order that when he falls forward his head will be free. (See Figure 21-14.)
4. When tackling the hands should be locked to ensure that the victim cannot wriggle free of the tackle.

Figure 21-14. Tackle from the side. The shoulder is in contact with the hip; the head is kept at the rear.

The introductory drills to tackling must build confidence; therefore, tackling practice should take place on soft ground that is covered with a heavy growth of grass. Protecting the elbows and knees with clothing is helpful for the beginner. The use of either a sponge-rubber high-jump pit or a deep pile of gymnastic matting is also helpful during the initial practice stages. A suspended dummy or rolled mat can be substituted for a partner. In the later stages of practice, pairs of players should develop tackling skill at a walking pace; ultimately, tackling is practiced while both players are running. Tackling from the front and rear is largely a matter of confidence in which the most important point is to watch the target—the hips.

Correcting Common Tackling Errors. If a player frequently fails to tackle, the most obvious reason is that he is afraid of being hurt by the impact. Confidence can be developed by learning the safest tackling technique (which is described here). A failure to tackle may be the result of the tackler being caught off balance by the opponent. To correct this fault the player must learn how to take the weight of the body on the balls of the feet, how to shepherd the attacker into the best position for a tackle (frequently toward the touch line), and how to accelerate into the tackle. The tackler must watch the hips of the opponent, and not his head or hands. A tackler who takes off from two feet loses a split second. This is corrected by practicing the one-footed take-off at a tackling bag. A player may perform an apparently adequate tackle but be unable to hold the opponent. This is corrected by using the arms after the impact, in which the tackler maintains a firm grip, holding the opponent close to the chest until both are stationary on the ground. Another cause for not holding the opponent is that the tackler may be diving *at* his target and not *through* it. To correct this fault the player drives a tackling bag backward for a specified distance. The thrust of the tackle is through the shoulder and not the arms. Driving a tackling bag backward is also excellent practice for the player who insists in tackling around the upper body. A strong player can carry a lighter man a considerable distance, but the strongest runner can be stopped if his thighs are bound together by the tackler's arms.

Dribbling and Dropping on the Ball

The laws of rugby allow a player to kick the ball forward in soccer fashion. However, if this is done indiscriminately there is the danger of players from one's own team being off-side, or of the opposite team gaining possession of the ball. Under some circumstances a controlled dribbling movement by the forwards can advance the ball for many valuable yards. Therefore, dribbling, and consequently the method of stopping the dribble, are skills that must be practiced by all rugby players.

Dribbling

1. The ball must be kept close to the feet, where it can be controlled. The ball should never be more than half a yard from the dribbler.
2. The ball will roll in a straight line only if it rolls point-over-point.
3. The ability to use both feet is vital.
4. Watch the ball!

Dribbling practice is first done individually while concentrating on the preceding points. Speed is not as important as control. Later, small groups, and eventually the whole pack, work to support a dribbler; if he loses control of the ball the player nearest to it resumes the dribble. If the ball should bounce into the hands of one of the players, the drill continues with increased speed as a passing movement.

Correcting Common Dribbling Errors. Many players lose control of the ball while dribbling; often this occurs because the ball has been kicked too far in front of the dribbler. In order to control the dribble it is essential to run with the body leaning over the ball, and not run in an upright position.

Dropping on the Ball. One of the most exciting sights in the game of rugby is to see a single player courageously stopping a full pack of forwards by dropping on the ball. Because any player on a team may be required to drop on the ball when the line is under pressure, every participant must be able to do so without much danger of injury.

1. Watch the ball, not the feet of the dribbler.
2. So time the drop that the ball will have just left the dribbler's foot; he will have no control of it for a brief instant.
3. The player so falls on the ball that he rolls with his *back* to the oncoming dribbler, thus protecting himself.
4. As soon as a loose scrum begins to form around the ball, the player must crawl or roll clear in order not to interfere with the play. He keeps his head protected with his arms while rolling clear.

The player is introduced to the skill by falling onto a ball rolled by hand toward him. When he is dropping safely, he repeats the procedure with a ball dribbled by a single dribbler. As his confidence increases, he progresses to dropping on a ball that is being dribbled by the whole pack.

STRATEGY

The emphasis in modern rugby is on handling the ball whenever possible and, therefore, on retaining possession. The forwards work as a unit and not as eight individuals. Through cooperative effort the pack endeavors to gain possession from scrums and line-outs. Once possession has been gained, the ball is either advanced by a passing movement by the forwards themselves or passes quickly and cleanly to the backs.

Passing movements by the forwards must be unexpected, tight assaults that involve short, rapid passes. Because the forwards are often confronted with a man-to-man defense, it is essential that each forward combines as follows:

1. Receive the ball, *drive forward,* and commit at least one opponent to the tackle.
2. Turn into the tackle to shield the ball from the opponents.
3. Pass quickly and accurately to a moving teammate who is in a position to advance the ball farther.
4. The forward should then get onto his feet (if necessary) and move rapidly to combine again with his advancing pack.

Passing movements by the backs must be preceded by intelligent service from the forwards. If the ball is knocked back indiscriminately by the forwards, the opposing players will immediately run through from the line-out or scrum and harass the halfbacks. If a forward catches the ball cleanly in a line-out and then is immediately assisted by the other forwards of his team, the ball will be protected. Each forward must bind with members of his team to form a loose scrum. The opponents must either join the loose scrum or retire behind the back foot of the scrummage, which delays them in reaching the attacking backs when the ball is released. (See Figure 21-15.)

When the backs do receive the ball they must rapidly advance it by running and passing. If one of the backs is tackled with the ball in his possession, he must release it immediately; once more the forwards come into the game. The pack must seek *second-phase possession.* That is,

Figure 21-15. Loose scrummage. Striped forwards have bound around the man with the ball and are protecting him from the opponents. (By permission of *Northern Daily Mail*, Hartlepool, England.)

they must attempt to reach the loose ball before the opposition does. If they are sufficiently fast, they pick up the ball and continue the passing movement. If they arrive at the loose ball at the same time as the opposing forwards, they must combine to drive *over* the ball by binding and forming a loose scrummage, and then heeling the ball to the halfbacks.

When playing defense, the two objectives of a team are to halt the progress of the side having possession of the ball and then to regain possession of it. Great care must be taken that enthusiasm for harassing the opposition does not lead to infringements of the off-side law. As soon as the ball leaves a scrummage, the defending players can cross the scrummage off-side line. When the ball leaves a line-out the forwards can cross the center line of the line-out. The defending backs can also move forward from the line ten yards behind the line-out. Until the attacking team has advanced the ball to a point level with the center of a scrum or line-out (known strategically as the *gain line*), they have gained no advantage from the scrum or line-out. The defenders must make every effort to stop the ball from reaching this line, if possible, by tackling an opponent in possession. As soon as he is tackled, the defending forwards drive in to seek second-phase possession.

It is important that any back who is involved in a loose scrummage return to his position in the back formation as soon as possible. Back play is strictly man-to-man defense; if one side is able to tackle an opposing back and then move the ball to its own backs before the tackled man is on his feet, the attacking side has an extra back. Unless a forward temporarily replaces the missing back, the defending side is at a disadvantage.

Fast, open rugby is a pleasure to watch and is exciting for the players. However, there are times when the line is threatened and it may be wise to attempt to punt the ball up the field and into touch. This tactic is frequently employed behind a team's own twenty-five-yard line, and it is often successful if that team's forwards are dominating line-out play.

POSITIONAL PLAY

All rugby players need to develop the basic skills of the game. As a player improves these skills and becomes familiar with the laws of the game, he will no doubt realize that his own particular talents equip him best to play a specific team position. This is possibly a wiser approach than to choose a position and attempt to adapt to the demands of that role.

In order to assist the beginner, a list of the qualities required by each position is given. One of the attractions of

Figure 21-16. Scrum half passing the ball from a set scrum. (By permission of *Northern Daily Mail,* Hartlepool, England.)

rugby is that many variations in physique and talent are combined into a successful team.

Fullback (15). An outstanding kicker with either foot, safe hands, and a fearless tackler.

Wing Three Quarter (11 and 14). Sheer speed plus determination and agility. He normally throws the ball into the line-out; therefore, he must be able to throw an accurate torpedo pass.

Center Three Quarter (12 and 13). A powerful runner with outstanding acceleration, excellent handling, and sound defense.

Outside Half (10). A key player with the temperament and intelligence to dictate tactics. An ideal position for the captaincy. A strong runner and outstanding kicker.

Scrum Half (9). A tough gymnast with a long, fast pass, acceleration, and fearless dropping on the ball. (See Figure 21-16.)

Prop Forward (1 and 3). A tough, thick-set player with strength and stamina.

Hooker (2). A strong and agile player with fast reactions.

Flanker (6 and 7). Fast and fearless. He must have the determination and stamina to harass the backs and also the skill to continue passing moves from second-phase possession.

Lock Forward (4 and 5). Height and weight are essential. He must be able to jump and catch in the line-out and push hard in the scrum. (See Figure 21-17.)

Number 8 (8). The same qualities as desired in the flankers; extra weight can be useful.

A knowledge of the strengths and weaknesses of fellow players produces the understanding that is vital for competitive situations. The scrummage should be as comfortable and efficient as possible. Once eight players have been selected to fill the forward positions, it is essential that they practice as a unit. Figure 21-2 shows the best positions for the forwards in a set scrum. Note that the push of the flankers is so directed as to stabilize the scrummage and also to allow them to break rapidly.

Figure 21-17. Second-row forward (a lock) jumping in a line-out; the remaining forwards are preparing to assist him. (By permission of *Northern Daily Mail*, Hartlepool, England.)

The backs must also practice together and should be capable of receiving and passing the ball rapidly and accurately. In an attacking position the backs lie in a spearhead formation. The attack starts from a line-out or scrummage near a touch line. Note that the defensive team has moved up in an attempt to break up the attack before it reaches the gain line.

TRAINING FOR RUGBY

Due to the continuous nature of play in rugby football, the development of a high degree of cardio-vascular endurance should be a prime concern of all participants. It is essential that the players begin the season with the stamina necessary to endure eighty minutes of activity. Preseason training should include work to improve the speed of the players, but in addition there must be sustained training sessions in order to develop endurance. Many of the drills outlined in this chapter are ideally suited for this type of training.

Much of the team practice time must be spent on group and team skills. Each player has the responsibility of achieving an adequate level of fitness. Because fitness is specific, the obvious method of becoming fit for rugby is to play rugby. Few training sessions should be completed without a game of touch or tackle rugby. The practice of rugby skills when somewhat fatigued simulates the physical and mental stress encountered by the player when in competition.

SELF-EVALUATION

A player's relative level of over-all proficiency becomes apparent in the competitive situation. However, improvement in specific rugby skills can be evaluated by means of the following drills, which are particularly useful in the preseason training sessions.

Running

All drills are performed with a ball and in full rugby clothing.

Speed. The player should keep a record of his performances for a timed fifty-yard sprint. Consideration should be given to the condition of the ground and the direction of the wind.

Acceleration. The players are spread side-by-side across the field. They walk for about twenty-five yards and upon a whistle signal they trot for twenty-five yards, staying in line abreast. On a second whistle they accelerate and sprint an additional twenty-five yards. The drill, which continues up and down the length of the field, is a measure of endurance.

Running Agility. Posts are set out as in Figure 21-5. Motivation can be provided either by running in and out of the obstacles against a stop watch, or in relay races against other teams.

Passing and Catching

Both passing and catching are practiced and evaluated in a two-against-one situation. A player should aim for a very high percentage of successes even against an experienced defender. Passing and catching (and running speed) can be tested by pairs of players running the length of the field and continuously passing to each other.

Kicking

The kicking proficiency of each foot should be evaluated.

For Accuracy. At a convenient distance, pairs of players attempt to kick so accurately that the partner can catch the ball without moving his feet, which is awarded three points. For a catch within two strides, one point is awarded.

For Distance. Standing on opposite ten-yard lines a pair of players face each other. One player attempts to kick a ball to the other's goal line. The second player catches the ball as quickly as possible and attempts, from the point where the ball was caught, to kick to the first player's goal line. The game continues until one player has driven the other one back over his own goal line. This also tests catching skill.

Individual and Team Sports

Tackling

Working in pairs, players tackle each other from each side, front and back. Later, the ball carrier is allowed to hand-off the tackler with a straight arm and open hand.

An entire team can play a game known as British Bulldog. A limited area is designated—a gymnasium floor covered with matting, a patch of sandy beach, or a well-grassed area. One member of the team stands in the center of the area, while the other players attempt to run from one side to the other. If the original player succeeds in tackling another, *both* players stand in the center and the remaining players again attempt to cross the area. This continues until all the players except one are in middle; that player is declared the winner and the game is restarted with him in the center.

Glossary of Terms

Backs: The halfbacks, three-quarter backs, and full-back. These are the players who do not usually form into the set scrummage.

Break: To evade the player in direct opposition by speed or cunning.

Drop kick: A kick in which the ball strikes the ground at the same moment, or just an instant before, it is being propelled by the foot.

Drop-out: See Law 22.

Dropping on the ball: The act of throwing oneself onto the ball to prevent its being kicked by the opponents.

Fair-catch: See Law 23.

Free kick: See Law 23.

Gain line: The imaginary line beyond which gain in distance is made toward the goal line of the opponents. This is a line through the center of a scrum or line-out.

Into touch: Any point that is not on the field of play.

Knock-on and **throw-forward**: See Law 14.

Match: A game of rugby.

Mark: The place at which a free kick or penalty is awarded.

Pitch: The field of play.

Pack: The forwards. This term is suggestive of the cooperative foraging of the hard-working forwards.

Second-phase possession: Possession of the ball gained following the breakdown of a previous movement.

Every rugby player ought to possess a copy of the laws. Several small publications are available to supplement and clarify the laws. None of them costs more than $1 and they are excellent values for the money.

1. "Laws of the Game and Notes on the Laws."
2. "Case Laws."
3. "Rugby Football Union Handbook."
4. "History of the Laws of Rugby Football."
5. "Why the Whistle Went."

Three books deal with the practical side of the game:

6. "The Basic Skills."
7. "Training for Rugby Football."
8. "Coaching of Rugby Footballers."

These booklets are available from The Secretary, Rugby Football Union, Twickenham, England.

Selected References

A Guide for Coaches. Rugby Football Union.
   This is composed of a series of pamphlets dealing with all aspects of rugby and costs about $6.
Herbert, John. *Rugby.* London: Weidenfeld and Nicholson.
Higham, E. S. and W. J. Higham. *High Speed Rugby.* London: Heinemann, 1960.
Hudson, D. C. N. and P. S. Dyer. *Your Book of Rugger.* London: Faber.
Owen, O. L. *The History of the Rugby Football Union.* London: The Rugby Union.
Reid, J. Gavin. *Rugby.* Dubuque, Iowa: Brown.
Rugger—How to Play the Game. New York: Manhattan Rugby Football Club.
Williams, Gerwyn. *Modern Rugby.* London: Stanley Paul.
———. *Schoolboy Rugby.* London: Stanley Paul.
Williams, Leo. *Rugby: Skills, Training, and Tactics.* London: Stanley Paul.
Venables, Cedric. *Instructions to Young Rugger Players.* London: Museum Press.

A valuable periodical is the *Rugby World* which is published in England.

CHAPTER 22

Soccer

*David Bunker**
Loughborough College, England

HISTORY

The World Cup finals were played in England in 1966. Entries for the competition were received from more than sixty countries, and qualifying rounds took place in five continents to bring together the sixteen finalists. The competition was followed with keen interest all over the world—millions of people were privileged to watch the games "live" or on television while journalists' reports were quickly dispatched to other countries. Sixty-nine nations have entered the 1970 World Soccer Cup tournament, the finals of which was held in Mexico City.

Modern soccer, with all the acoutrements, is believed by many writers to date from Greek and Roman times, but it is doubtful whether any team games were played that involved kicking a ball.

The Middle Ages

The game of *footeballe* was widely played during the Middle Ages, but it was looked on as a distasteful and rowdy pastime of the masses. Local clerics and sheriffs issued proclamations forbidding the game to be played because it was extremely dangerous: whole towns became involved—kicking, hacking, running, tripping—all were allowed as one "team," containing as many as five hundred players, striving to drive their opponents and the ball beyond a predetermined limit. Fighting often occurred, windows were broken, legs also—no holds barred was the order of the day. These games were no more than violent mob battles, and yet they provided the raw material from which the modern game of soccer emerged.

The 1800s

The students of a number of public schools in England played a game in the 1800s that included ball-handling and kicking skills in which their own local rules were imposed according to the available facilities. The game filtered into the universities of Oxford and Cambridge and from there to the Clubs.

Many codes of rules existed and the concern and efforts of early authorities to establish the game led to the formation of the Football Association, in 1863. This year is one of the historic landmarks of the game, for it heralds the beginning of organized soccer. The newly formed Association had many teething troubles; after a great deal of bitter argument, handling and hacking were omitted from Association rules, with the result that a number of clubs resigned from the Association and eventually formed the Rugby Union in 1871.

The game developed rapidly in the early years of the Football Association. Large crowds attended football matches, particularly when the Football Association Knockout Cup was introduced (45,000 people watched a Cup Final in Manchester, England, in 1893). Inevitably, professionalism arrived and with it the formation of the Football League, an association of clubs that has done much to increase the social status of the professional footballer in England.

---

*DLC, Loughborough College, England; Certificate, University of Nottingham, England. Mr. Bunker was a member of the first Association Football (Soccer) team (of which he was captain) while attending Loughborough College. He also played for the English Universities' Leicestershire and Rutland County Soccer team and was later offered a contract to play with a professional soccer team in Chicago, Ill. In addition to being a highly successful soccer coach in England, his extensive knowledge of, and skills technique in, soccer caused his classes at The University of Iowa to be most popular. He is currently a lecturer in Physical Education at Loughborough College.

330 *Individual and Team Sports*

FIFA and the Olympic Games

The idea of the Federation Internationale de Football Association (FIFA) was proposed in 1902 and formalized in 1904 at a meeting of the representatives of six European countries. The game was soon well established in many European countries and emigrants introduced the game into more distant lands where it was received with immediate approval and recognition. International contests between countries were frequent events; consequently, it was decided to include soccer in the official program of events for the Olympic Games of 1908.

England won two Olympic competitions by 1920, but then withdrew from membership in the FIFA. The United States entered a team in the 1924 Olympics; Uruguay surprised many people by winning the tournament.

It soon became clear that international football could not be held within the confines of the amateur Olympic competitions. The professional game had prospered and many countries were unable to be represented by their best players. The Olympic competition continues but it is overshadowed by the World Cup, which began in Uruguay in 1932.

The World Cup

The World Cup is the shop window of soccer: the best players in the world take part, and the top coaches devise new styles of play, methods, and tactics. Competition is severe and to win brings fame to the players and prestige to a country.

The pendulum of international superiority has swung freely since the World Cup started. Uruguay enjoyed the initial period of dominance, then Italy. After World War II the competition was held in Brazil in 1950 and again Uruguay was the winner. In this tournament the United States caused a major upset by defeating England, now reinstated with FIFA. In 1954, the West German team finally overcame the great Hungarian side, while Brazil gave notice of their approaching successes in 1958 and 1962. In 1966, England, the host nation, was successful: the unknown North Koreans created a surprise by eliminating Italy and qualifying for the quarter-final stage.

Soccer is the most international of all games—at the present time people in 118 countries play the game. Its audience increases every year, and further exciting developments are taking place in the United States and Asia, where widespread efforts to launch the game are meeting success.

DESCRIPTION OF THE GAME

The game of soccer is played between two teams with a maximum of eleven players on each side. The field of play is rectangular in shape with a goal at each end. The primary aim is to score goals. The game is started by a player kicking the ball into his opponents' half of the field and into the path of one of his own players; after this the game is continuous and goes on uninterrupted until the ball goes out of play or the referee stops the game.

When the ball goes out of play (that is, over the touch line or goal line), the game is restarted as quickly as possible by a throw-in, goal kick, or corner kick, depending on the circumstances of play. Frequent interruptions to play are caused by the infringement of the laws of the game. The more serious offenses are punished by a direct free kick, and when committed inside the penalty area a penalty kick is awarded against the offending player. A minor infringement results in the award of an indirect free kick.

The two teams play in different colored shirts with numbers on the back to help spectators to identify the players. For many years a number indicated a player's function in the team: for example, number seven was always the outside right, who would be found patrolling the right touch line. In today's game, however, number seven might be an important link in midfield play or an integral part of defense.

The goalkeeper's jersey is a different color from that of the two teams. Although no other player may intentionally use the arms and hands to play the ball, the goalkeeper is allowed to handle the ball within his own penalty area and needs to be easily distinguishable from other players.

The two referees are in complete control of the game, and they are assisted by two linesmen. It is often said that a competent referee is inconspicuous in the game. An important part of his task is to ensure that the rhythm of the game is maintained, for this increases the enjoyment of both the players and the spectators.

After the game it is customary to shake hands with the opponents and for the captains to thank the referees for their services.

UNIQUE VALUES OF SOCCER

The basic rules of soccer are simple and few, and a minimum of equipment is required to play the game. A great deal of organization is required to stage a full-scale match, but spontaneous practice games, with any number of players taking part, arouse similar feelings and are equally valuable in improving individual skills and creating game situations.

Soccer is the only major game in which a concentrated coordination between the eyes and the feet is a requisite.

Soccer

Most other team games require only the basic movements of hitting, throwing, and catching and develop eye-hand coordination.

The medium of soccer presents a student with many opportunities to achieve general fitness objectives. The wide range of skills utilized in soccer play creates situations in which timing, balance, and poise are improved. More important, participation in the game helps to prepare the body to meet the needs of every day life.

DESCRIPTION OF EQUIPMENT AND ITS CARE

The equipment necessary to practice safely the fundamental skills of soccer is inexpensive and readily accessible. A ball of any kind and a vacant lot or grassy area permit the soccer enthusiast to practice and gain an appreciation of the skills involved: dribbling, kicking, passing, trapping, and heading. Many of the world's top soccer players began in a humble way: for example, in the back streets where the lamp post served as a floodlight and goal post, in a cleared patch of forest, or on a dusty and exposed airstrip. They have graduated from these environments to display their talent in front of many thousands of people in the large stadiums of the world.

The equipment required for soccer depends on the conditions encountered; for example, studded or cleated shoes are not necessary if the games are played on hard surfaces (players in some African countries play the game barefooted); the styles of the shirt worn will differ with the temperature.

The student who plays the game competitively should possess the following equipment:

A Track Suit (or Sweatsuit). An important garment for the soccer player is a track suit. It should be waterproof and windproof for use when training in cold weather. It is worn at the beginning of the practice to enhance the effect of warm-up exercises.

Shirts. Many styles of shirts are marketed. They are manufactured in a variety of fabrics and are available in different colors.

Shorts. The better-quality shorts are made of nylon/terylene, are well tailored, and allow the player to move freely.

Socks. Knee-length socks (with turn-down tops) are made of nylon and other synthetic yarns. The sock gives some protection to the shin bone.

The preceding items of equipment should all be laundered regularly.

Shin Guard. Most modern professional clubs insist that their players wear shin guards (worn inside the sock) to protect the vulnerable shin bone. The latest design is molded to the shape of the leg, is light in weight, and is made of polystyrene or a similar material.

Tie-up. Socks and shin guards are kept in position by the use of a length of bandage tied just below the knee. Care should be taken not to tie it too tightly, as this will interfere with blood circulation and cause a cramp in the calf muscle.

Soccer Shoes. Soccer or football shoes are the most important item in the soccer player's wardrobe. Two pairs of shoes, one pair with studs for playing on soft ground, the other with a molded rubber sole for hard surfaces, are desirable. Shoes with interchangeable studs can be purchased to offset the expense of buying two pairs, but the thread in the screw-in socket is liable to be damaged when the studs are changed regularly. Basketball shoes are ideal for indoor training sessions. The shoes, which may cost as much as $30, should be light, with soft, supple leather for cushioning around the ankle and below the foot. They should be thoroughly cleaned after use—all excess dirt should be removed, using a knife and then a wet cloth. After the shoes have dried naturally, a neutral dubbin (or oil) should be applied in order to maintain the suppleness of the leather. The cleats (studs) should be inspected regularly and any sharp, dangerous edges should be corrected.

LAWS OF THE GAME

Many different codes of soccer rules existed in the early 1800s. As a result of the formation of the Football Association, a set of laws was accepted nationally and, although new laws have been introduced and consequent amendments made, the laws of today are not too different from those of one hundred years ago.

There are seventeen laws of the game. Each one is presented here in simplified form in order to facilitate understanding and interpretation.

Law One deals with the dimensions of the field of play as illustrated in Figure 22-1.

Law Two states that the ball should be spherical, not more than twenty-eight inches or fewer than twenty-seven inches in circumference and weigh not more than sixteen ounces or fewer than fourteen ounces.

Law Three pertains to the number of players—the game is played by two teams of eleven players on each side. Substitutes are allowed if permission has been obtained and an agreement reached by the two teams.

Law Four on players' equipment has been alluded to previously. The usual equipment of a player consists of a shirt, shorts, socks, and shoes. A goalkeeper must wear colors that distinguish him from the other players. Special mention is made of the types of cleats (studs) that are permitted.

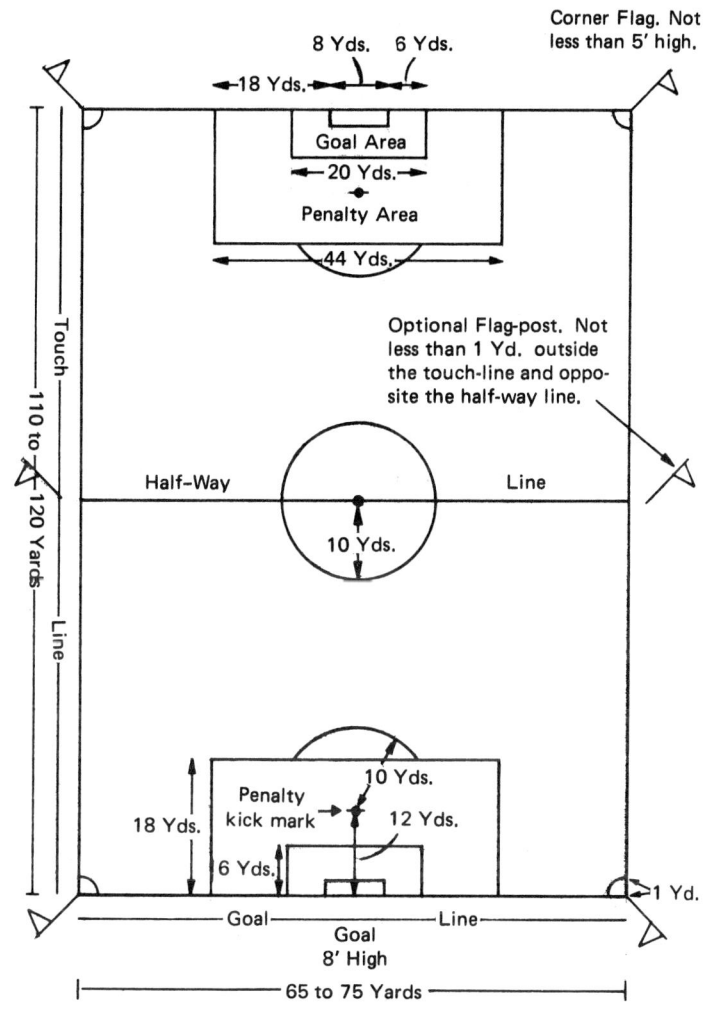

Figure 22-1. Field of play.

Law Five details the many functions of the referees in the game.

Law Six states that two linesmen are appointed to assist the referees when the ball is out of play. They help the referee to apply the offside rule and to decide which team restarts the game from a goal kick, corner kick, or throw in.

Law Seven governs the playing time. The duration of the game shall be four equal periods of twenty-two minutes, unless otherwise mutually agreed on. The half-time interval shall not exceed ten minutes except by consent of the referee. There shall be a one-minute interval between quarters and overtime periods for the purpose of changing ends.

Law Eight states that the game is started by a player taking a place kick from the center of the field of play. The ball is kicked forward and is not in play until it has rolled the distance of its own circumference. The kicker may not play the ball again on the kickoff until it has been touched or played by another player. All opposing players must be at least ten yards from the ball. The game is restarted in the same way after a goal has been scored or after the interval when the teams change ends.

Law Nine says that the ball is out of play

1. When its whole area passes over the goal line or touch line.
2. When the game has been stopped by the referee.
3. When it touches a referee.

Law Ten states that a goal is scored when the ball has passed *completely* over the goal line, between the goal posts, and under the crossbar—provided it has not been thrown, carried, or propelled by hand or arm, or carried by a player of the attacking side.

Law Eleven states that "a player is off-side if he is nearer his opponent's goal line than the ball *at the moment the ball is played* unless

1. He is in his own half of the field of play.

Soccer 333

2. There are two of his opponents nearer to their goal line than he is.
3. The ball last touched an opponent or was last played by him.
4. He receives the ball directly from a goal kick, a corner kick, a throw-in, or when it is dropped by the referee.

A player in an off-side position shall not be penalized unless, in the opinion of the referee, he is interfering with the play or with an opponent, or he is seeking to gain an advantage by being in an off-side position."

Law Twelve describes all the fouls and misconduct that can occur and for which a direct or indirect free kick may be awarded. A direct free kick is given if a player commits one of the following offenses:

1. Kicks or attempts to kick an opponent.
2. Trips an opponent; that is, throws or attempts to throw him by the use of the legs or by stopping in front of or behind him.
3. Jumps at an opponent.
4. Charges an opponent in a violent or dangerous manner.
5. Charges an opponent from behind, unless the latter is obstructing.
6. Strikes or attempts to strike an opponent.
7. Holds an opponent with his hand or any part of his arm.
8. Pushes an opponent with his hand or any part of his arm.
9. Handles the ball; that is, carries, strikes, or propels the ball with his hand or arm. (This does not apply to the goalkeeper within his penalty area.)

A penalty kick is awarded if the offense occurs within the penalty area.

Play is restarted by an indirect free kick when

1. Playing in a manner considered by the referee to be dangerous.
2. Charging fairly; that is, with the shoulder, when the ball is not within playing distance and the players are not trying to play the ball.
3. Intentionally obstructing an opponent when not playing the ball.
4. Charging the goalkeeper except when he
   a. Is holding the ball.
   b. Is obstructing an opponent.
   c. Has passed outside his goal area.
5. While playing as the goalkeeper, carrying the ball; that is, taking more than four steps while holding the ball without bouncing it on the ground.

A *caution* (the player's name is taken by the referee) is administered when a player

1. Enters the field of play to join or rejoin his team after the game has commenced, without first having received a signal from the referee.
2. Persistently infringes the laws of the game.
3. Shows by word or action dissent from any decision given by the referee.
4. Is guilty of ungentlemanly conduct.

A player is sent off the field when

1. He is guilty of violent conduct.
2. He persists in misconduct after having received a caution.

Law Thirteen explains the difference between the "direct free kick," from which a goal can be directly scored, and the "indirect free kick," when a goal cannot be scored unless the ball is played or touched by a player other than the kicker. Law thirteen itemizes the penalties for all the fouls and misconducts described in Law Twelve.

Law Fourteen states that a penalty kick is taken from any place on the penalty mark line. All players with the exception of the player taking the kick and the opposing goalkeeper must be at least ten yards from the ball and within the field of play. The opposing goalkeeper must stand on the goal line and must not move until the ball is kicked.

Law Fifteen states that when the ball goes out of play over the touch line, the game is restarted by taking a throw-in. The thrower uses two hands from over his head to propel the ball into play; at the moment of release a part of each foot must be in contact with the ground on or behind the touch-line.

Law Sixteen states that a goal kick results when the ball goes over the goal line (excluding that portion between the goal posts) and was last played or touched by a member of the attacking team. The ball is kicked beyond the penalty area from that half of the goal area nearest to where the ball went out of play.

Law Seventeen awards a corner kick to the attacking team when the ball goes over the goal line (excluding that portion between the goal posts) and was last played or touched by a member of the defending team. The kick is taken from within the quarter circle at the nearest corner flag post. A goal can be directly scored from a corner kick.

The laws of soccer can be applied to players of school age with the following modifications:

1. Size of the playing field.
2. Size and weight of the ball.

3. Dimensions of the goal.
4. Duration of play.

All students of soccer should possess a copy of the Official National Collegiate Athletic Association Soccer Guide. This booklet is inexpensive and contains much sound advice to the player.

SAFETY

The laws of the game of soccer, conceived in 1863, aim to make the game safe on the field of play. Law Four on players' equipment states that "a player shall not wear anything which is dangerous to another player" including rings, wrist watches, and medallions. Law Twelve, Fouls and Misconduct, deals specifically with the maintenance of discipline, and Law Thirteen prescribes punishments for offenders. Law Five delegates responsibility for the interpretation and enforcement of the laws to the referees appointed to officiate in each game. The referees make an inspection of the playing field to ensure that it is safe for play, and at the same time check that the goal posts are secure and that the corner flags conform to the regulation minimum height of five feet.

A qualified trainer or doctor should be in attendance or immediately available at every game.

SKILLS AND TECHNIQUES

The modern game of soccer relies on the ability of all players to attack and defend whenever necessary; therefore, it is important that all players achieve a high level of performance in the basic skills of kicking, passing, trapping, dribbling, tackling, and heading. (The position of goalkeeper appears as a separate skill later.)

Three important considerations must be included when planning a program to prepare players for competitive soccer play. The development of group and team play, and specific fitness training methods are included in later sections. In the sections that immediately follow, certain game skills are analyzed and drills are suggested that will enable the beginner to develop individual techniques on his own, with a partner, with a group of players, or under the direction of a coach—but without the distraction or interference of actual match conditions.

Kicking

A ball can be kicked in several ways: the skillful player selects a suitable kicking technique in view of the immediate game situation, but frequently adjustments are necessary in order to make a hasty clearance, to evade a tackle, or to accept an opportunity to shoot at the goal. The ball can be kicked with any surface of the foot. The instep is utilized for the low drive and the volley type of kick; the sole for pushing an awkwardly bouncing ball to a nearby teammate; and sometimes even the toe of the foot for prodding the ball past an opponent when it is nearly out of the player's reach.

A most important point to remember is that any player who can only kick the ball with one foot is kicking at 50 per cent efficiency; it is essential that the soccer player learns to kick the ball accurately with either foot.

The Low Drive (Figure 22-2). The instep is used to strike the ball firmly. At the time of impact the knee must be directly over the ball. Any tendency to project the knee too far forward will cause the instep to strike the ball into the ground, or if the knee is behind the ball the ball will be lifted into the air. The body weight must be over the ball and the nonkicking foot placed alongside it. Other points or techniques that should be observed when executing a low-drive kick are

1. Keep the eyes fixed firmly on the ball when making contact.
2. Power is obtained by a vigorous extension at the hips and the knee joint.
3. When distance is required, follow through—kick through the ball.

At first two players, standing five to ten yards apart, practice the low drive by kicking a stationary ball to each other. As progress is made the distance between the players is increased, and the stationary ball is now kicked "first-time." A third player is introduced and the ball is moved between them while the direction and distance are varied.

The Push Pass (Figure 22-3). The push with the inside of the foot is easy to perform and has proved a reliable

Figure 22-2. Low drive.   **Figure 22-3.** Push pass.

and accurate means of kicking the ball over short distances. The foot is everted—that is, turned outward—and it swings through near to the ground. A player will often tend to "measure" or "telegraph" this pass; consequently, the chances of an interception are much greater than if the *flick pass with the outside of the foot* is used. When making a flick pass the player stands to one side of the ball and is sideways to the direction of the pass. The lower leg, ankle, and foot straighten successively to produce the kicking action. The flick is most useful when evading a tackle, pushing the ball past an opponent while dribbling, or disguising the direction of a pass.

Lofted Pass

Lofted Drive. The lofted drive is a powerful kick that is intended to clear the heads of one or more opponents. The approach to the ball is made from an angle in order for an increased leg swing and, hence, increased kicking distance to be obtained. The nonkicking foot is placed to one side of and behind the ball, while the inside of the kicking instep strikes the ball below its center. The follow-through should be concentrated on when kicking long distances.

The Chip. The main object of the *chip* is to get the ball to rise steeply from the ground. The nonkicking foot is placed alongside the ball with the body weight well forward of it. The ball is struck as low as possible by stabbing the kicking toe underneath the ball. A quick extension of the kicking leg scoops the ball into the air. The follow-through is quite limited. A player can practice a chip over the head of a player and to a teammate who is twenty yards away. The distance between the players is increased in order to practice the lofted drive. These drills are first practiced when the ball is stationary, and later when it is moving.

The Volley (Figure 22-4). In the volley the ball is kicked while it is in the air, the contact being made with the instep. The position of the ball at impact helps to determine the direction and distance of the kick. A powerful leg swing is possible when the ball is near the ground. The kicking technique is similar to that of the low drive. At times a short volley kick, in which any part of the foot except the toe is used, can be utilized to pass the ball to a nearby teammate. Because the body position when executing a volley allows a full range of movement, the instep or outside of the foot is the favored kicking area of most players. On occasions the volley must be kept low; for example, when shooting at the goal. A *falling-away* technique is used, which involves moving the body sideways to allow a powerful leg movement and to enable the kicking foot to strike the ball above the midline (Figure 22-5).

The Half Volley. For a half volley the ball is kicked as it touches the ground. The trajectory of the ball will depend on the position of the body at the moment of impact. (Refer to the *low drive* and the *lofted pass*.) Beginners should begin practice of this skill by dropping the ball from the hands to volley (or half volley) to a partner. With practice, a skillful group of players can keep the ball off the ground by a succession of short volley passes.

Other ways of kicking a soccer ball are to swerve it by striking to the left or right of its vertical center line. The back-heel, scissors, and overhead kick can be employed to good effect; but the margin for error is small. Such kicks should not be overused during competition.

Passing

The two skills of kicking and passing are difficult to separate. In the previous section the various methods of kicking the ball were explained, and simple practice drills were suggested in which direction, distance, trajectory,

Figure 22-4. Volley: high ball.

Figure 22-5. Low volley.

and, above all, accuracy were considered. These points should continually be heeded when developing and practicing interpassing movements.

Ball Control or "Trapping." The most efficient way to play soccer is to keep the ball on the ground. However, it frequently goes into the air and, therefore, players must practice controlling it with different parts of the body, thus causing it to stop or drop to the feet. The following points are common to all ball-control techniques: (1) Take up a position as close as possible to the line of flight of the ball. (2) The controlling surface—that is, the instep, thigh, chest, or foot—should be relaxed and withdrawn in order to cushion the ball on impact.

The various methods of trapping with the foot follow:

1. *Sole of the foot:* The ball is wedged between the undersurface of the foot and the ground. The sole of the foot slopes upward at an approximate angle of 45°.
2. *Inside of the foot:* The "trap" is formed by the inside surface of the foot and ankle joint and the ground. The player leans in the direction in which he expects to drag the ball when it is under control.
3. *Outside of the foot:* The ball is trapped in a similar manner as when the inside of the foot is used, except that the ball is played in front of the body.

In the preceding three traps when receiving a lofted pass the foot and the ball make simultaneous contact with the ground.

Trapping drills can be practiced in groups of twos or threes with one player serving the ball—at first along the ground and later in the air. When some skill has been achieved the server, after throwing the ball, moves to tackle. The receiver traps the ball and takes evasive action.

Dribbling

The skill of dribbling takes place when a player attempts to pass one or more opponents while keeping possession of the ball. Many different plays can be used to beat the opponent by dribbling.

Change of Pace. At times a change of pace, involving quick acceleration, will be sufficient to beat an opponent. The dribbler deceives the defender by slowing down or quickly stopping and then accelerating.

Body Swerve. Few defenders will be beaten consistently by a change of pace. All forwards should practice the body swerve, which involves a slight shift in direction while running with the ball. The shift causes the opponent to be off-balance momentarily, and if the movement is performed at speed, there is little chance the tackler will have time to recover.

Feint Plays. The success of a feint depends on the player's ability to manipulate the ball and to pretend to play the ball one way and then to move it in another direction. The following practice drills are suggested:

1. Approach an opponent while controlling the ball with the inside of the foot. Take the foot over the ball in order to move it with the outside of the foot in another direction.
2. Feint as if to kick the ball, but at the last moment draw the ball back with the inside of the kicking foot.
3. Pretend to back-heel the ball, but allow it to continue moving in the same direction.

All feint plays at the ball are accompanied by a change of direction and/or sudden acceleration in order to beat an opponent.

Screening the Ball (Figure 22-6). A player screens the ball by placing his body between an opponent and the ball while keeping it within playing distance. This is a difficult skill because the eyes are turned away from the ball and toward the opponent to ascertain his movements. Screening is used at various times by all players, particularly forwards who are often outnumbered by the opposing defense but need to keep possession of the ball while waiting for support from their teammates. A recommended screening drill is one-on-one. The continuous nature of this drill makes it quite fatiguing; the ability to screen the ball will provide an opportunity for rest while keeping possession.

Player Decoy. A teammate supports the player in possession of the ball by taking a position to receive a pass. The dribbler feints to make the pass but instead decides to dribble past his opponent.

Artificial drills that are designed to improve dribbling skill are of limited value. It is necessary to engage in competitive game situations in order to gain experience and

Figure 22-6. Screening the ball.

learn the reactions of various opponents to different dribbling techniques. All dribbling skills involve running with the ball at different speeds and keeping the body over the ball while maintaining close control of it. Running and dribbling the ball are important elements in the fitness-training methods that are described in a later section.

Tackling

The ability to tackle effectively is most important when players frequently change position. A front-block tackle (Figure 22-7) is made by a defender when confronted by an opponent head-on. The inside of the foot blocks the ball. The knees are slightly flexed in order to absorb the impact and to lower the center of gravity, hence, a more effective tackling position is produced. The ball is struck near its center and possession is gained by rolling it over the opponent's foot, forcing the ball between his legs, or using a legal shoulder charge.

A most important feature of forward play is to recover quickly to tackle back to gain, or regain, possession of the ball. The nontackling foot is placed in line with the ball, the position of which enables the body to pivot and to assume the front-block tackle position and help resist the forward momentum of the player in possession of the ball.

The sliding tackle (Figure 22-8) is used in defense as a last resort to clear the ball from a dangerous position near the goal. The outside leg swings across to play the ball with the instep while the body weight is supported by the arm, thigh, and leg nearest the ball.

Skill in tackling, like dribbling, can only be acquired during scrimmage conditions when one player is as determined to evade the tackle as another is to effect it. When tackling drills are practiced, the ground should be soft to lessen the risk of possible injury. At first, all tackles should be practiced while the players are standing still; progression is made to a walking pace, running speed, and finally to a game situation, when the techniques have been properly mastered and confidence established at the preceding stage.

Tackling involves ways and means of gaining possession of the ball. The good player anticipates the direction of a pass, makes an interception, and launches a quick counter-attack to expose an opposition defense. When an interception is not possible, the player should attempt to tackle as an opponent receives the ball. At times a defender is confronted by more than one opponent; (for example, a two-in-one situation). The defender must employ delaying tactics or "jockey" in order to allow other defending players sufficient time to take up covering positions and thus minimize the danger if a tackle fails. Feinting movements to tackle can upset an opponent's control but, despite this continual battle of wits, a defender must tackle when he has retreated as far as the edge of the penalty area.

Heading

Heading, unlike kicking, is an unnatural skill. When the ball is headed incorrectly, the player can sustain an injury that causes him to lose confidence in his heading skill. The following points of technique should be remembered when heading:

1. The flat, frontal part of the forehead strikes the ball.
2. The eyes watch the ball onto the forehead.
3. The feet form a wide base to allow the trunk to move backward and then forward to generate extra power and to gain increased control of the ball.
4. The heading action starts with a vigorous extension of the leg muscles and continues with a powerful flexion of the trunk and neck muscles—that is, a jackknife movement.

Figure 22-7. Front-block tackle.    **Figure 22-8.** Sliding tackle.

Figure 22-9. Heading the ball.

338 *Individual and Team Sports*

Figure 22-10. Jumping to head the ball.

Jumping to head the ball in the air (Figure 22-10) presents other difficulties.

1. The take-off is from one foot and is similar to the take-off stride in the high jump.
2. After the take-off, the body assumes an arched position, which aids the later jackknife movement.
3. The player should so time the jump as to head the ball correctly at his maximum height. When the player wants to deflect the ball, or to head the ball in a different direction, the trunk and hips are so rotated that the ball is contacted with the forehead.

During the initial practice stages a football bladder or a rubber ball is helpful in gaining confidence in heading. Practice in pairs, one player serving the ball for a partner to head back. As the distance increases between the two players, increased attention is devoted to developing a powerful heading action. An additional player is used as a target when practicing heading in various directions. All these drills should be repeated, using a regulation soccer ball.

Goalkeeping

A goalkeeper enjoys special privileges in that he is allowed to control the ball with his hands when he is inside the penalty area, but he is subject to the same treatment as any other player once he moves outside of the penalty area. A goalkeeper must be confident, fearless, agile, and possess strong arms and hands in order to deal with shots from any angle and distance. A cardinal rule is safety first. He must keep his eyes on the ball and use two hands to catch the ball whenever possible. His body must be behind the line of the ball to stop a hard low drive, intercept an intended through pass, or move out of his goal to smother the ball at the feet of an oncoming forward.

Figure 22-11. Goalkeeping: fielding a ground shot.

At times it is difficult for the goalkeeper to catch the ball. A high centering pass dropping beneath the crossbar invites an immediate challenge from opposing forwards. In this situation the ball is palmed over the crossbar by the goalkeeper. When several players challenge for a high ball, the goalkeeper punches the ball toward the wings, using two fists if possible.

Although the goalkeeper is the last line of defense he is the first line of attack; hence, he needs to master all kicking and passing techniques. An accurate pass to an unmarked teammate can lead to a goal being scored at the other end. A quick throw of shallow trajectory, using the javelin or overarm style, is the style generally used by goalkeepers.

Most players like to practice "shots-in" at the goalkeeper: indiscriminate shooting is of limited value to him. Organized practice, however, improves a goalkeeper's

Figure 22-12. Goalkeeping: catching a high ball.

Soccer 339

Figure 22-13. Goalkeeping: The dive.

speed of reaction and gives him experience in narrowing the angle—that is, presenting the smallest possible shooting target. (See Figure 22-13.)

COMMON ERRORS AND THEIR CORRECTION

The accepted method of skill analysis—that is, the evaluation of techniques such as passing and heading—tends to divorce one skill from another. A player's ability to control the ball in the minimum of time depends on an accurate pass, which, in turn, depends on the correct application of the kicking technique.

A number of faults, common to most skills, can result in poor performance; for example:

1. The player fails to move into position to play the ball.
2. The eyes are taken off the ball at the moment of impact.
3. A momentary hesitation forces a difficult skill adjustment to be made.

Kicking and Passing

The need for accuracy in passing cannot be overemphasized. A team often loses possession of the ball by means of a misdirected pass, and a team without the ball cannot score goals. As a rule, inaccurate passing means inefficient kicking of the ball.

Quite often an intended ground pass—a low drive or a push pass—is lifted into the air. This frequently occurs because the ball has been struck below its center instead of on it, which in turn is caused by the body being positioned behind the ball (instead of beside it), causing the foot to be swinging upward at the time of impact. The low drive pass often lacks sufficient power and accuracy to reach its destination. The amount of power placed on the ball depends on the speed of the kicking foot. The ankle of the kicking foot is extended and held firm. In long, accurate passing movements, the follow-through is important because the longer the foot moves in the intended direction of the ball, the more accurate the pass tends to be.

An intended lofted pass may lack sufficient height to clear an opponent. Lifting the head tends to cause the player to straighten his body too soon; thus, the foot strikes too high on the ball. To remedy this fault the head is kept down and the eyes continue looking down after contact with the ball has been made. A lofted pass often lacks power and may be a result of positioning the non-kicking foot too far behind the ball. The development of power depends in part on the transfer of body weight from the kicking action into the follow-through. A ball kicked with too much height and insufficient distance was probably contacted too far below its mid-line.

The volley and half volley are difficult skills to master because the ball is kicked while it is in flight. A failure to judge accurately the flight path of the ball results in loss of timing and causes the player to lose control of the volley or half-volley kick. The more common faults in volleying are related to the incorrect positioning of the body. The higher the ball on impact, the more the body "leans away" to make room for the kicking foot to strike the ball at a point level with or above its midline. When a volley lacks power, the ankle should be checked so that it remains firm and extends in order to kick the ball with the instep. In the half volley a failure to keep the ball low implies that the kicker has wrongly addressed the ball. The body must be located over the ball with the head kept down and the nonkicking foot positioned close to the ball as it touches the ground.

Ball Control/Trapping

The most common failing in trapping the ball, whether on the ground or in the air, is an inability to relax and absorb the force of the ball. Unless the player cushions the ball it will bounce away out of control. When the ball is on the ground, the trapping angle between the foot and the ground may be too large or too small. There is no specific angle to trap the ball but, with practice, the player quickly develops an appreciation of the correct angle. The ability to absorb the impact is most important when controlling a ball in the air. Quite often a player anticipates a trap. Consequently, when the ball arrives the controlling surface is stationary, causing the ball to bounce out of playing distance.

Dribbling

The ability to dribble the ball past an opponent is an invaluable asset, but too often a player with great skill in

340 *Individual and Team Sports*

dribbling nullifies his own ability by trying to beat more than one opponent. The dribbler must remember to release the ball to take maximum advantage of the immediate situation.

Too many players try to beat an opponent by employing the same dribbling technique—for example, a change of pace or a feint movement to the left. A good defender will anticipate the movement and will be in position to make an effective tackle. The dribbler must practice a variety of methods that can be employed with equal effectiveness against an opponent.

A player who continually loses possession while dribbling should check to see that the ball is under close control and that the body weight is forward—this is the most difficult position for an opponent to tackle.

Tackling

Many players attempt to tackle when the ball is not within playing distance. A lunge at the ball prevents the player from transferring the body weight into the tackle and, more important, a serious injury can result from an outstretched leg taking the full force of the tackle.

A failure to win possession of the ball after a block tackle might have been caused by the tackler being too tall or too far over the ball. The player must lower his center of gravity in order to assume a sitting position behind the ball; in this way force can be applied to and through the ball.

A reluctance to tackle can mean that the player is afraid of physical contact. The player must learn the correct way to tackle and remember that there is little likelihood of injury if the tackle is made with determination.

Heading

A fear that it hurts to head a football often causes beginners to close the eyes, to hunch the shoulders (retract the muscles of the neck), and to let the ball bounce on top of the head. The use of plastic balls or soft rubber balls will help overcome any reluctance to head and will encourage the beginner to use the flat frontal part of the forehead, to keep his eyes open, and to employ his neck muscles to produce a nodding action. If the heading action lacks power, the feet may be placed too wide apart, or the powerful movement of the large muscles of the legs and trunk may be lacking.

Headed passes and attempts at goal are frequently misdirected because of a lack of timing. The players may fail to make an accurate assessment of the flight of the ball and take off too early or too late to make proper contact with it. This is a most difficult skill to perform well; it requires long hours of practice on the training ground or practice field.

Goalkeeping

A goalkeeper must be confident of his own ability. If this confidence is lost, he may be unwilling to leave his goal line. This situation requires patient understanding and careful preparation in planning a program of suitable practices. The more difficult goalkeeping skills must be introduced at the correct time, as is true of the reintroduction of the goalkeeper to match conditions.

A goalkeeper cannot afford to make a mistake, because it often results in a goal being scored. A failure to catch the ball can mean that the goalkeeper's body has not been behind the ball or that his attention has been distracted by a challenging forward. Some goalkeepers lack constructive ability—long punts down the field present the opponents with a good chance of regaining possession, whereas a short, accurate pass or throw retains possession and is important in the development of attacking movements. When a goalkeeper delays parting with the ball he gives the opposition time to recover its defensive positions.

STRATEGY IN TEAM PLAY

Attack

Soccer is a team game played by eleven individuals, and skillful play depends on the coordination of individual talent. In the early formative years the game was played with eight forwards, but gradually players have been withdrawn to concentrate on defense. A change in the off-side law, in 1925, led to the introduction of the *WM* formation. (See Figure 22-14.) In this formation the center half was committed to a defensive role as a third back with the special responsibility of guarding the opposing center forward. The *WM* became widely accepted as a team formation because of its numerical equality in attack and defense. The center half, or "stopper," created many problems for the attacking team.

The 4-2-4 system (Figure 22-15) was developed to counteract the use of two center forwards against the center half, and to prevent wingers from creating goal-scoring opportunities. A mid-field player was withdrawn to mark the other center forward and the fullbacks were employed to mark wingers tightly. The three diagrams that follow (Figures 22-16, 22-17, and 22-18) show that the trend toward defensive formations has continued with the 4-3-3, "bolt" systems, and catenaccio.

Styles of Play. A reoccurring skill pattern establishes a style of play. The *WM* is suited to the long pass, whereas more tightly grouped formations invite the short pass of from ten to twenty yards. The "push and run" requires highly mobile players to support the player with the ball; the "retreating defense" rules out the tackle in mid-field, although teams in many countries play "possession" football.

Figure 22-14. *WM* formation.

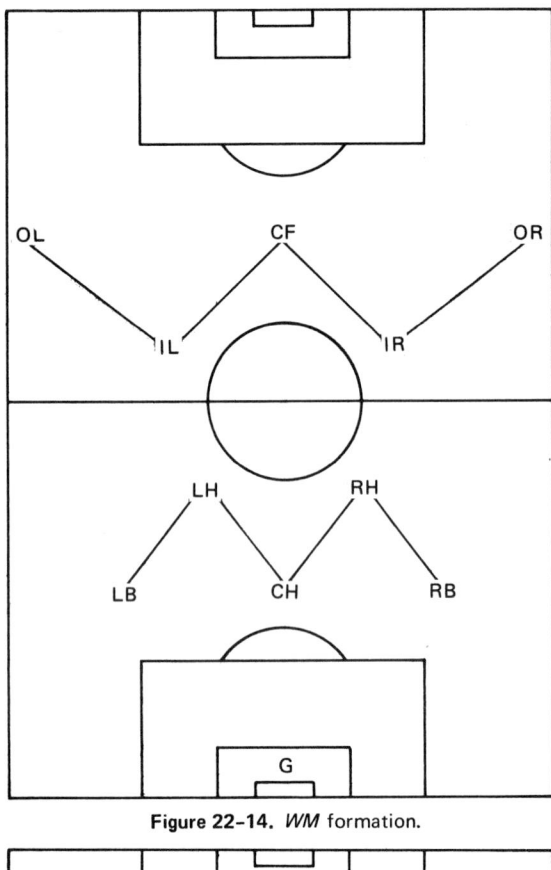

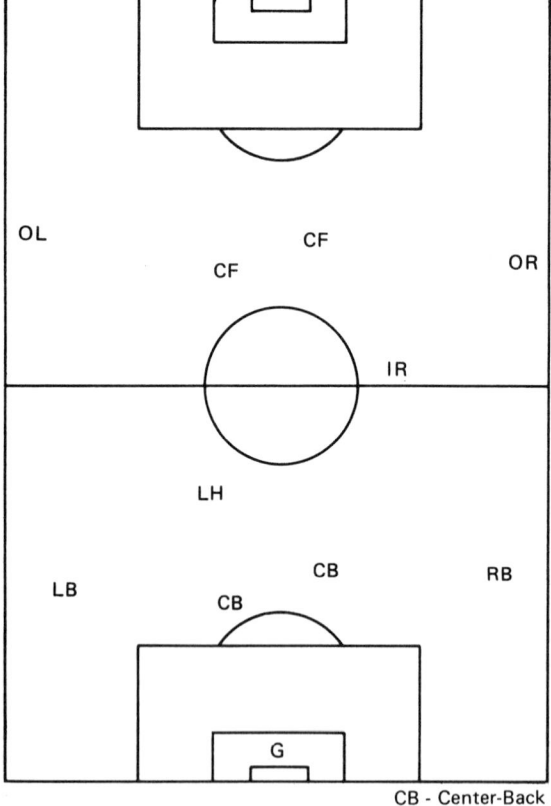

Figure 22-15. 4-2-4 formation.

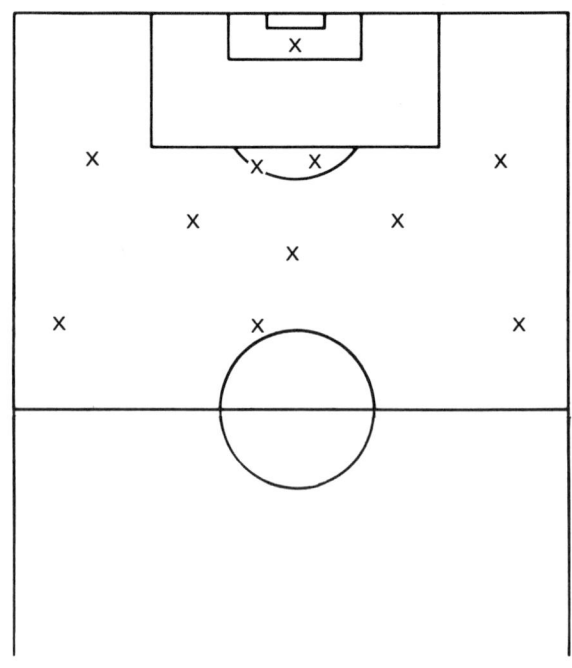

Figure 22-16. The 4-3-3 formation.

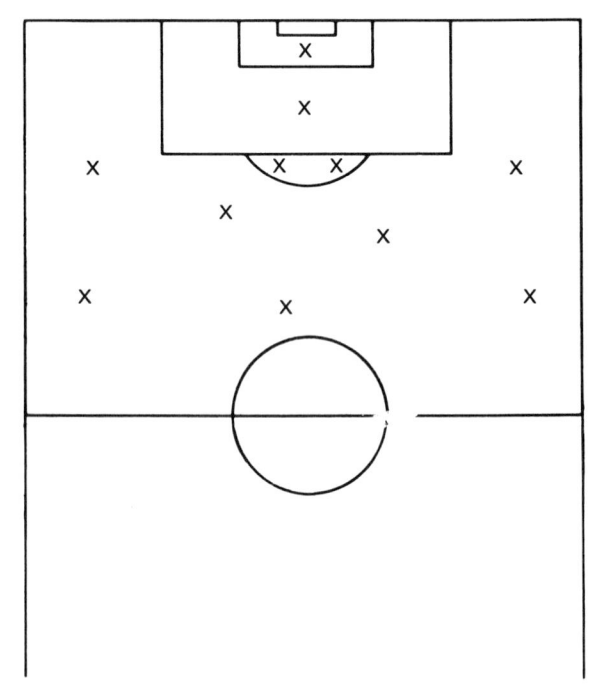

Figure 22-17. The bolt systems.

Attack. The following basic principles of attacking play are closely interrelated in the development of intelligent approaches on the goal.

1. *Mobility:* Most defenses will use a system of partial man-to-man marking—for example, the center forward marked by the center half. It is easy for a well-organized defense to contain an attack in which

342 *Individual and Team Sports*

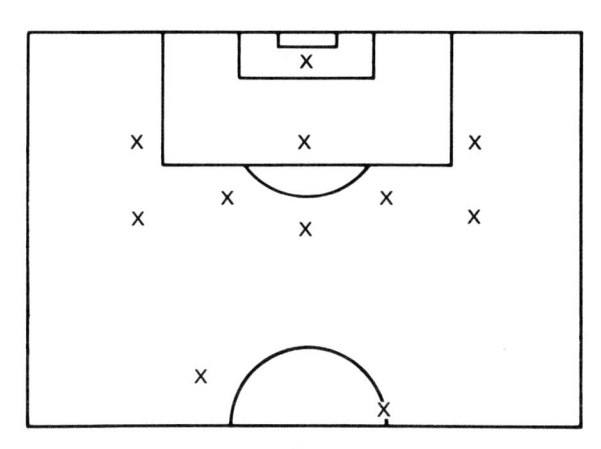

Figure 22-18. Catenaccio.

the forwards retain their position "along the touch line" or "down the middle." Attacking players create goal-scoring opportunities by movement off the ball in all directions and by rapid change and interchange of position.

2. *Space:* Highly mobile forwards will create space; so too will the dribbler who beats an opponent consistently. Movement into space will give a forward increased time to make a pass or to shoot at the goal while denying a defender the opportunity of making an interception or an effective tackle.
3. *Depth:* The effectiveness of an attack is limited when the forwards move toward the goal and develop a straight-line formation. In this situation passing alternatives are restricted to a "square ball," but when an attack moves in depth, numerous passing opportunities are created. See Figures 22-19 (*a*) and 22-19 (*b*).
4. *Width:* All attacks should develop on a wide front in order to spread the defense. The best shooting angle is directly in front of the goal (near the penalty spot), but defenses are numerically strong in the danger area. Forwards must avoid the temptation to run toward the goal, irrespective of the game situation. An intelligent run to a wing position can take a defender out of the danger area and create space for a teammate to make an accurate pass or to shoot at the goal.

Defense

All soccer teams use defensive methods involving man-to-man marking, zone defense, or a combination of both.

Man-to-man marking sets a defender to mark an attacker throughout the game. However, it is not a good idea to commit the whole defense to a marking function. When a forward beats his immediate opponent, another defender must cover and attempt to delay the forward in order to enable the beaten defender to recover and resume a new defensive position. The defense must work as a unit and not as individuals.

In *zone defense* a defender maintains his position on the field and marks any attacker who enters his zone. The system breaks down when two or three forwards confront the defender.

The great majority of teams use a *combination of the two methods* to establish a defensive pattern, using either method according to the game situation. At times a destructive defender is delegated to mark a particularly dangerous forward; that is, play man-to-man. Zone methods are utilized to maintain balance in the defense and prevent the opening up of large areas of space in which attacks can develop.

Cover in depth is greatly needed in the defense. A straight line of defenders, or a square defense, presents an attack with numerous opportunities to exploit the open spaces behind the defense. The responsibility for giving cover rests with one of the last line of defenders as illustrated in Figure 22-20.

The influence of competition and big money rewards has made teams defensive minded, but given the oppor-

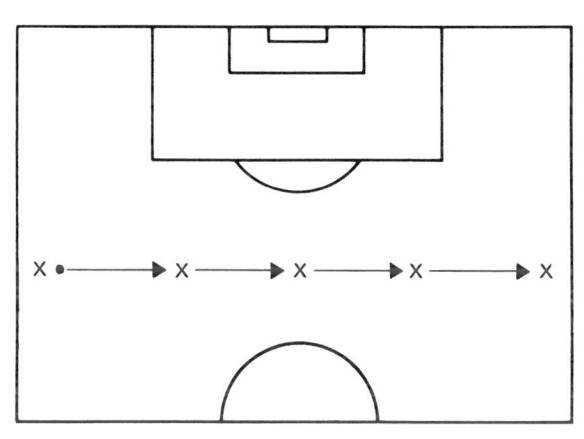

Figure 22-19(*a*). Attack: no depth.

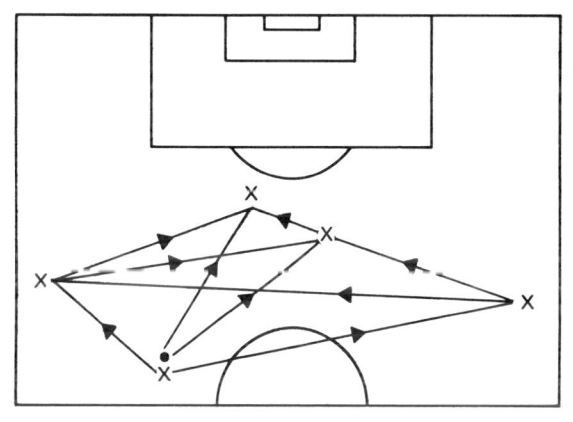

Figure 22-19(*b*). Attack in depth.

Soccer 343

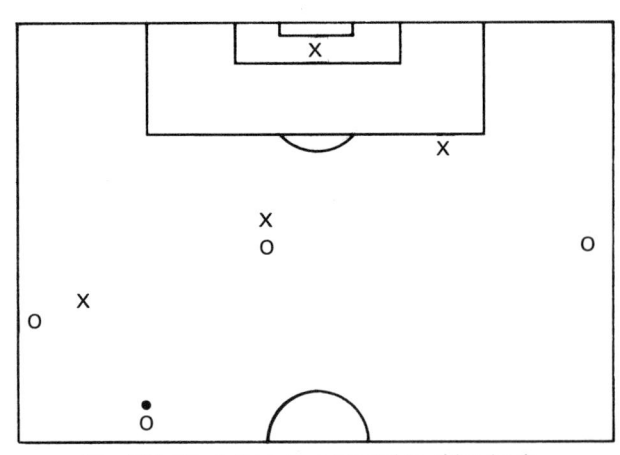

tunity, good defenders initiate attacks by long accurate passes in an attempt to catch the opposition out of position.

A few teams prevent goals from being scored (and gain possession of the ball) by trapping a forward in an off-side position. This is a completely negative tactic and is dangerous to the defending side, owing to the slight difference between an on-side and off-side position.

SPECIFIC TRAINING METHODS

The game of soccer demands a level of fitness that will enable the player to run strongly, to move quickly off the mark in any direction, to control and pass accurately, and to tackle effectively throughout the game. It is important that the training conditions simulate game conditions. All players should wear the appropriate equipment and train on a full-sized soccer field whenever possible.

Selected Running Drills

Shuttle Relay. The players alternate in pairs in running between three or four set markers with the ball under control at all times.

One-versus-one Competition. Each player plays every other player on the team. All games are played in a confined area and are of three-minutes duration with a one-minute interval between each game. The competition is won by the player who scores the most goals.

Team Game. Two teams are composed of five players, numbered 1 through 5. Player number 1 attempts to pass to number 2, number 2 to number 3, and so on until the team not in possession wins the ball. If player number 4 gains possession for the opposing team, he tries to pass to teammate number 5, and number 5 to number 1. The highest number of consecutive passes made are counted to find the winning team. The players are allowed to move freely in an area approximately half the size of a regulation soccer field.

Pressure Training

A simple pressure practice is one involving three players and two soccer balls. One player stands in the middle and receives a high ball, which he heads back to the server. The middle player then quickly turns to face the third player who serves a low ball for a return pass. This pattern is repeated. Increased pressure is brought about by increasing the speed with which the balls are served. In pressure training it should be remembered that the skill factor is less important than the intensity of work.

The *WM.* The left-back covers and provides depth in defence. The two full-backs pivot on the center half depending on the direction of attack.

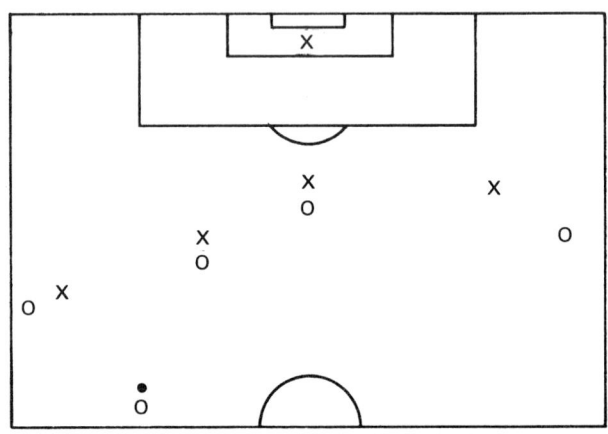

The *4-2-4 System.* One of the center-backs gives cover. Allowing the full-backs to mark the wingers tightly.

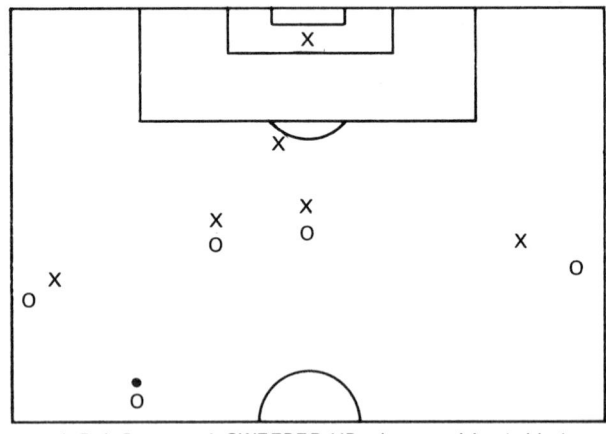

A *Bolt* System. A *SWEEPER UP* takes a position behind the line of 4 defenders to give maximum cover.

Figure 22-20. Covering in defense.

Play the Game

Other activities such as calesthenics, weight training, running, squash racquets, swimming, and basketball are valuable in adding variety to a training program but because fitness is specific, the obvious way to become fit for soccer is to play the game. A player spends approximately eighty-five minutes of each game without the ball. Consequently, in the preseason conditioning period such general training methods as cross-country running, circuit training, interval running, and weight training should be included to develop speed, strength, and cardiorespiratory endurance.

SELF-EVALUATION

The true measure of skill in soccer can be judged only when these skills are subjected to the pressure of competition, but self-evaluation drills are valuable in that objective assessments are possible and individual deficiencies are made apparent. The use of self-evaluation drills increases the meaning and applicability of individual and group practice and motivates the performer to improve his skills and techniques. A few self-evaluation drills are outlined here:

Kicking and Passing Drills

1. A penalty-kick competition is popular among players and provides an excellent opportunity for the goalkeeper to display anticipation and agility. A group of players take turns in shooting at the goal from the penalty spot, and the number of successful kicks are counted.
2. The ball is placed on the edge of the penalty area in front of the goal. An attempt is made to kick the ball into the empty goal. Competition develops as the distance is increased or the shooting angle is made increasingly difficult.
3. A wall, marked with numbers at different heights, can be utilized to evaluate accuracy in kicking and passing. The player tries to hit the numbers consecutively and, as skill improves, he kicks the ball "first time."
4. In a two-on-one situation, the number of consecutive passes is recorded before the defender wins the ball by making a tackle or an interception.

Dribbling and Ball-control Drills

1. Several players, each with a ball, move freely within a confined area keeping the ball under control and evading the other players. The difficulty of the drill is increased by increasing the number of players and decreasing the movement area.

2. Small-sided game: One-on-one. A limited area is used (twenty-five yards by fifteen yards). A player "scores a goal" by beating his opponent and kicking the ball between two poles or flags placed one yard apart.
3. Ball control. See "Heading Drills."

Tackling Drills

The ability to win the ball by tackling can be accessed in any small-sided game in which there is an equal number of players on each side. A system of man-to-man marking is used, which provides frequent opportunities for players to tackle.

Heading Drills

Apart from using predetermined targets, a game of "head tennis" enables an assessment to be made of skill in heading. The rules of the game are as follows:

1. There are five players on either side of a net, which is approximately five feet in height.
2. There are no specific "court" dimensions.
3. The ball is headed over the net.

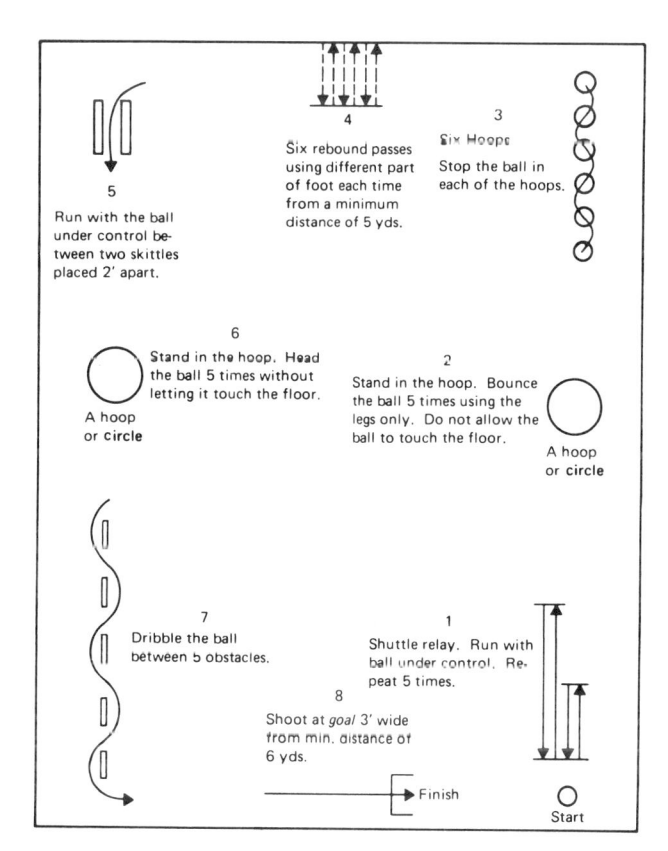

Figure 22-21. Soccer skills circuit.

4. The ball must not touch the ground more than once on either side.
5. All parts of the body (except the hands) are used to keep the ball off the ground.
6. Play starts when, by heading, the ball is served from the back of the court, over the net, and into the opponent's court.
7. Any point scoring system can be used.

It is possible to modify the rules to suit the individual players, such as raising or lowering the height of the net, for example.

A *skills circuit* is an interesting and enjoyable means of self-evaluation. A number of skills are performed in sequence (in a circuit) in the shortest time possible. (See Figure 22-21.)

Glossary of Terms

Back-heel kick: A backward kick of the ball made with the heel of the foot.
Drop ball: The referee drops the ball between a player from either side to restart the game.
First-time: In one movement the player controls the ball and also passes or shoots it.
Head-on: Face to face.
Instep: The part of the foot used for most kicking; that portion covered by the laces of the shoes.
Marking: Guarding or covering the player with the ball when he moves into your area of play.
Movement vocabulary: To develop awareness of movement possibilities in a game situation.
Pitch: The field of play.
Shuttle relay: To run to and fro between set marks.
To jockey: To determine an opponent's direction of movement.
To measure a pass: To be deliberate in judging distance.
Two-touch: The player touches the ball only twice in controlling and passing or shooting it.

Selected References

BOOKS

A "coach yourself" series of seven booklets describes the functions of each position in a team: (1) center forward, (2) goalkeeper, (3) full back, (4) wing half, (5) wing forward, (6) inside forward, and (7) center half. All the publications are obtainable from the Football Association, 16 Lancaster Gate, London, W.2., England.
Collaghan, John. *Soccer*. Pacific Palisades, Calif.: Goodyear, 1969.
Docherty, Tommy. *Better Soccer for Boys*. London: Nicholas Kaye, 1966.
Joy, Bernard. *Soccer Tactics*. London: Phoenix House, 1956.
Liss, Howard. *Soccer, International Game*. New York: Funk, 1967.
Moore, Alan C., and Melvin R. Schmid. *Soccer Anthology*. Chiefland, Fla.: Citizens Publishing Co., 1965
Nelson, Richard L. *Soccer*. Dubuque, Iowa: Brown, 1966.
Schmid, Irwin R., John L. McKeon, and Melvin R. Schmid. *Skills and Strategies of Successful Soccer*. Englewood Cliffs, N.J.: Prentice-Hall, 1968.
Wade, Allen. *The F.A. Guide to Training and Coaching*. London: Heinemann, 1967.
Winterbottom, Walter. *Modern Soccer*. London: Educational Productions, 1958.
   Soccer Coaching. London: Heinemann, 1959.
   Training for Soccer. London: Heinemann, 1960.

PERIODICALS

F.A. News. Football Association, 16 Lancaster Gate, London, England. A Football Association monthly publication.
National Collegiate Athletic Association Soccer Guide. Phoenix, Ariz.: College Athletics Publishing Service, annual $1.
World Soccer. London: Echo Publications Ltd. Sutherland House, 5-6 Argyll St., London W.1. England, monthly. Contains many interesting articles on soccer in different countries.

CHAPTER 23

Softball

*Gus Pappas**
Glendale High School

HISTORY

The game of softball as it is played today is the outgrowth of a combination of names and games. In the past it has been called mush ball, "four old cat," indoor, kittenball, diamond ball, and other names. Softball is an adaptation of baseball; consequently, the two share a common history. Baseball evolved from rounders and other early ball games, with most of the present rules of baseball having been adopted and standardized in around 1839. The exact origin of softball has not been clearly established, but it is believed to have been initiated in 1887 by George W. Hancock, a gymnasium instructor at the Chicago Farragut Boat Club.

The game of softball, first called indoor, grew slowly in popularity until the late 1920s, when it became widely played in Canada because it was played outdoors. In the United States the popularity of the game was given impetus through the sponsorship of the National Recreation Congress, which, in 1923, appointed a committee to standardize the rules and playing regulations. In 1926, Walter Hokanson of the Denver YMCA christened the game softball.

During the Depression years, softball made a significant growth in the United States; thousands of softball teams were organized through the Works Projects Administration. In 1933, a worldwide softball tournament was conducted during the Chicago World's Fair under the guidance of Leo S. Fisher and M. J. Pauley. These same men led the movement to organize the National Softball Association and Joint Rules Committee, which standardized the rules of play and supervised the sport.

The fact that softball can be capably played with enjoyment by relatively unskilled players, as compared to baseball, has added to the popularity of the game. This has been an important factor in the growth of softball, which now has more than ten million active participants. It is estimated that over 600,000 teams participate in the state and local tournaments that lead to the World's Championship Softball Tournament. The inclusion of softball into the recognized sports agenda for the Olympic Games is a future possibility.

VALUES OF SOFTBALL

The game of softball has a wide appeal because through an adjustment of the rules and the size of the balls and bats it can be so adapted that it can be safely played by both sexes and by all ages. Thus, it is popular in schools, city leagues, and industrial leagues; at family gatherings; and when camping and at other outings. Softball provides a healthful, invigorating activity in which a full range of movement through running, stretching, sliding, batting, catching, and throwing is involved. It allows for individual achievements, but requires that all players work together if the team is to be successful. Therefore, opportunities abound for developing leadership, fellowship, social adjustment, respect for authority, self-control, and other important qualities. Decisions must be made and acted on in fractions of seconds; constant mental alertness is necessary for each team member. Practicing the basic skills of softball, whether two or three players or both complete teams are participating, provides enjoyment for each person.

---

*B.A., University of Northern Iowa, Cedar Falls; M.A., University of Iowa, Iowa City. Mr. Pappas has taught physical education and coached a variety of sports during the past sixteen years. He has played semipro softball, coached varsity baseball teams at the high school level, and has taught softball classes at the University of Iowa. He is presently at Glendale H.S., in Glendale, Arizona, where he is the head baseball coach.

Softball 347

Softball is not as strenuous as basketball, soccer, or most team games, but it develops physical skills, coordination, and to some extent cardiorespiratory endurance. The fact that it is not as strenuous as other team sports may be one of the greatest values of the game for many participants who are not in good physical condition. In summary, softball, when placed in any sports program, provides a team game with more carry-over values than most team sports.

EQUIPMENT AND ITS CARE

The only equipment essential for playing softball is a bat and ball. The official softball bat, which is smaller and lighter than the baseball bat, is made of hardwood and is round in shape with the diameter at the largest point not exceeding two and one-quarter inches. Its length should not exceed thirty-four inches. The bat should have a safety grip of cork, tape, or composition material, which should not be less than ten inches long and located no more than fifteen inches from the small end of the bat.

The ball is approximately twelve inches in circumference and is made either of cork or kapok and rubber. These are wrapped with wool yarn that is covered with top-grade horsehide, cowhide, or rubber. The seams are smooth or concealed. The weight of the ball is between six and six and three-quarter ounces. In some leagues, such as a slow-pitch league, a softer ball, fourteen or sixteen inches in circumference, is used for a modified game.

The official rules require the catcher to wear a mask. It is highly recommended that this rule always be observed because of the safety afforded his face. A chest protector is also recommended for the catcher. Gloves, caps, spiked or rubber-cleated shoes, and uniforms can be worn by the players, but these are not necessary. The catcher and first baseman may use mitts; the other players can wear fielders' gloves, providing protection against injury to their hands.

The field should be a large rectangular area with one corner for a diamond or infield. The home plate should be made of rubber or another suitable material, a five-sided figure that is seventeen inches wide across the edge facing the pitcher. The pitcher's plate should be made of wood or rubber, twenty-four inches long and six inches wide. The bases, other than home plate, should be fifteen inches square and made of canvas or another suitable material.

The quality of equipment purchased should be the best that can be afforded. If possible, top-grade cowhide gloves should be purchased, and they should be oiled when put away after a season. Bats with narrow, close,

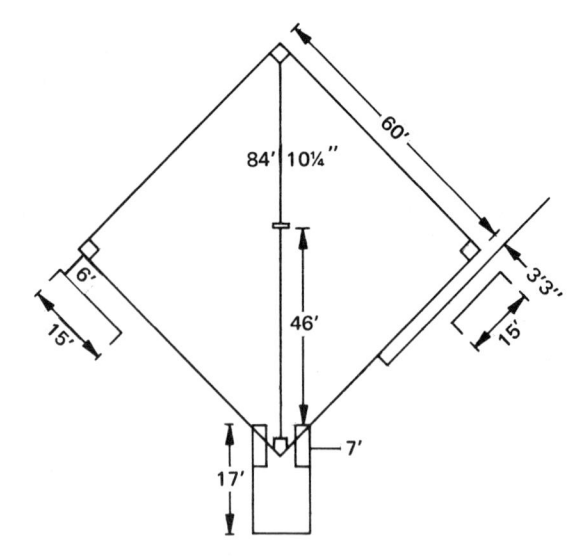

Figure 23-1. Softball diamond.

straight grains should be selected. Bats should be stored in an upright position and not be exposed to excessive moisture or dryness. A favorite bat can be protected against weathering by boning the hitting surface. Shoes made of kangaroo leather are the best, but they are expensive. Selected calfskin or cowhide shoes are economical. When wet, shoes should be allowed to dry naturally. A leather preservative helps to preserve the softness of the leather. If a uniform is purchased, a 50 per cent wool and 50 per cent cotton fabric should be selected for the most serviceable material.

BASIC RULES AND PLAYING COURTESIES

Because softball is patterned after baseball, only a minimum of difference exists between the two games and the rules governing them. Differences in playing areas, pitching techniques, and size of the ball exist between the two games:

1. The distance between bases is sixty feet for softball; ninety feet for baseball.
2. The pitching distance in softball is forty-six feet for softball and sixty feet, six inches for baseball.
3. The regulation softball is approximately twelve inches in circumference; a baseball is nine and one-quarter inches.
4. The official softball bat is shorter, smaller in circumference, and lighter than the baseball bat.
5. A regulation softball game consists of seven innings; nine constitute a baseball game.
6. In softball play the ball must be pitched underhanded, not thrown, with the wrist and follow-

through of the pitching hand passing a straight line of the body prior to the release of the ball. A pause of one second is required before the pitch is made. An illegal pitch is a *balk* and is treated as it is in baseball.
7. In softball the base runner must remain on his base until the ball is released by the pitcher; in baseball he can lead off.

During softball play sportsmanship should be displayed at all times and the following courtesies should be observed.

1. The decision of the umpires is final. If a rule violation occurs, the team manager or captain should calmly discuss the situation with the umpire.
2. The base runner should never deliberately spike a defensive player.
3. When feasible, the defensive player should inform the base runner when a possible play at the base is going to occur. This protects both the offensive and defensive player from possible injury.
4. Personal abuse toward an opponent should not be tolerated.
5. Each player should run on and off the field after a side has been retired. This moves the game along and is a courtesy to the spectators.

An up-to-date guide to softball play, which includes the current rules, appears in a yearly "Official Guide," published and distributed by the Amateur Softball Association, Skirvin Tower, Oklahoma City, Oklahoma 73102.

SAFETY

Certain safety precautions should be observed during softball play and practice sessions even though softball is not considered a hazardous sport. Injuries are always a possibility; therefore, the following precautions should be taken by all players and instructors:

1. The playing field should be kept clear of rocks, depressions, dangerous areas, and obstructions. When possible, the infield should be dampened at least twice a day.
2. Bases must be anchored to the ground.
3. Sliding techniques should be perfected, but avoid unnecessary slides.
4. The players should be acquainted with the correct procedures for calling for fly balls, covering the bases to avoid collisions with the base runner, laying down the bat after batting, and other safety precautions that are designed to avoid injury.

5. Balls that are relatively soft should be used when playing without gloves.
6. A glove should be utilized for effective catching and to lessen the possibility of hand and finger injuries.
7. Catchers should always wear a mask and chest protector when working behind the plate.
8. Bats that have a nonslip gripping handle should be used.
9. An adequate warmup is important; all players should be completely warmed up before they attempt hard throwing.
10. When players are playing catch, bunting, or hitting, they should form two lines facing each other.
11. Bats should never be scattered—a player could trip over them.

FUNDAMENTAL SKILLS AND TECHNIQUES

The basic fundamentals and techniques of softball must be practiced and learned by each participant if the game is to be played with any degree of skill. As the mechanics of softball are mastered, the enjoyment derived from participating in the game will increase the desire to strive to attain the maximum of one's efficiency in the sport.

Throwing the Ball

(The directions for performing the fundamental skills and techniques of softball are given for right-handed players.)

Throwing is one of the most important skills in softball; the ability to throw accurately is a prerequisite to successful team play. The type of throw used in softball varies with the playing situation. The outfielders and the infielders will basically use the overhand throw, but the infielders can also use the sidearm and underhand throw.

Grip on the Ball (Figure 23-2). Regardless of the type of throw employed, the grip on the ball should be the same if maximum control of the ball is to be attained. Of the many methods utilized for throwing the *tripod grip* is considered the most accurate. For this grip the thumb is placed under the ball, the index and middle fingers are spread slightly on top of the ball, and the third and fourth fingers are placed toward the side of the ball.

Overhand Throw. The overhand throw is the fastest and will go the greatest distance of all throws. The ball is raised to about ear level and carried well behind the head. This cocking position results when the forearm is held approximately at right angles to the upper arm and the elbow is raised about shoulder high. The throwing arm is

Figure 23-2. Tripod grip.

moved backward as the player transfers his weight to the rear foot. The momentum of the throw is increased by rotating the trunk clockwise until the shoulder of the non-throwing arm points toward the target. To complete the throw, as the weight is shifted to the left foot, the forearm is brought upward, forward, and downward with a full arm swing. The arm is extended and the wrist and fingers are forcefully snapped as the ball is released. To retain his balance, the player swings his rear leg forward to a position even with the forward leg and shoulder-width apart.

Sidearm Throw. For the sidearm throw the starting position is the same as in the overhand throw, but the arm is brought to the front of the body with a sideward motion rather than a forward and downward motion. The direction of the arm swing is parallel to the ground. As the ball is released and the arm is extended, the wrist is snapped, and the weight is shifted exactly as in the overhand throw.

Underhand Throw (Figure 23-3). The underhand throw is utilized by infielders when there is insufficient time to straighten up for a throw. In the underhand throw, the forearm passes through an arc below the waist as the arm goes forward in the delivery.

To be an outstanding thrower one must (1) use the same correct grip each time; (2) step properly; (3) receive the maximum whipping action from the forearm and wrist; (4) follow through and let the hip and foot come through with each throw in order not to impede the throw.

Catching and Fielding

Softball is largely a defensive game. Therefore, every participant must be a good fielder. Skill in catching and fielding takes more than natural ability—it takes constant practice of the fundamentals.

Stance of Infielder and Outfielder (Figure 23-4). The basic stance used for fielding a ball is a semicrouched position with the legs spread about shoulder width apart and bent slightly at the knee joint, and the hands hanging in front of the body. The outfielder uses the same stance, but the hands rest on the knees. As the ball is pitched, the outfielder so shifts his body weight forward that it rests on the balls of his feet. The player's eyes are focused on the ball and his body is kept low and well balanced so that he can be ready to move quickly in any direction.

If the ball is hit directly at the fielder, he should watch it closely and, if possible, move toward it and field it at the top of the bounce with the left foot placed slightly ahead of the right foot.

If the ball is hit to the left of the player, he should pivot on the left foot and cross the right foot over the left foot in order to shift into fielding position. On a ball hit to the right, the pivot is on the right foot, and the left foot is crossed over the right foot to move into position.

Fielding Mechanics. The fielder will be able to field most balls in the recommended position (in which the hands are out in front of the body and the feet are in a stride position). The goal is to keep the body low because it is easier to come up for a ball than to go down for one. Bend the legs at the knee and the hip joints, and lower the back of the glove until it is close to the ground. Keep the

Figure 23-3. Underhand throw.

Figure 23-4. Basic infielder's stance.

350 *Individual and Team Sports*

palm out and the fingers down. The ball is fielded out in front of the body with the elbow and hands away from the body. The fielder should use both hands in fielding the ball whenever possible. When the ball is fielded in front of the body, the body is used to block the ball in case the fielder misses the ball with his glove.

Throwing Mechanics. The throwing of the fielded ball is very important. The correct mechanics of throwing previously described should be utilized, as should the proper footwork involved with the throw. The fielder should be able to throw the ball hard by taking just one step. If time allows, the fielder should come to an erect position and step in the direction of the intended throw. If a hurried throw is necessary, the fielder should come to a partially erect position and throw with a sidearm motion. For a long throw, the right foot is so planted that a full push-off can be taken. This gives increased momentum to the throw.

Flyball. To catch a flyball the fielder should maneuver into position before the ball arrives. The catch should be made at head height with the thumbs together and both palms opened and directed toward the ball. The hands and wrists should be semirelaxed and should "give" with the ball as it is caught. At the time of the catch, the fielder should be in the throwing position in order to make an immediate throw to the proper base. A ball below the waist is best caught with the little fingers together, palms away from the body, and the fingers forming a cup position. The hands and wrists should give when the ball is caught in order to relieve the impact of the ball on the glove and hand.

Batting

Because the most important tool for batting is the bat, it is extremely important that the batter select the right bat. The bat should be of the proper length and weight to give the batter a feeling of control. It should be heavy enough for a good, solid swing and light enough so that it can be whipped around by the use of a strong wrist action.

In softball the pitched ball often arrives at the plate in less than a second; therefore, a keen eye and excellent timing are necessary for batting success. These attributes can be achieved only if the correct basic batting position is taken.

Plate Coverage. The most difficult concept for a hitter to understand is how far he should stand from the plate. To establish this distance he should walk up to the plate, lean over, drop the tip of the bat to the farthest corner of the plate, and straighten up to a natural hitting position.

Stance. Two words best describe the correct batting stance: be comfortable. The batter should be relaxed physically, yet remain mentally alert. The batter stands with his right (or back) foot at a 90° angle to the pitching line; his left (or front) foot is at a 45° angle to this line. This "opens" the batter's position, leaving a distance of approximately twelve inches from the inside of the front foot. An imaginary straight line drawn from the toes of both feet would extend to the pitcher. Assuming a stance in which the toes are on this line is the secret of initiating a successful stride. From this position, the batter can step toward the plate on an outside pitch and guard it completely.

Grip (Figure 23-6). To grip the bat correctly, the knuckles of both hands are aligned with the hands coming together in contact to form a flat surface. This position enables a vigorous wrist snap and follow-through to be made. Three batting grips are commonly used for softball play: the standard, the choke, and the long grip. For the standard grip the hands are together and located an inch or two above the end of the handle. This hand position on the bat is a compromise that gives maximum power and control. The choke grip, which is utilized to hit balls thrown with considerable speed, is employed by many softball players. The bat is gripped about three to four inches above the end of the handle toward the trademark.

Figure 23-5. Batting position.

Figure 23-6. Batting grip.

Softball 351

The power hitter uses the long grip by holding his hands together at the extreme end of the handle. Regardless of the grip used, the hands are kept together and the trademark is always facing up. The bat should be held rather loosely with the grip tightened just before contact is made with the ball. If the batter tenses or becomes tight, his timing and coordination will be affected; he must attempt to remain relaxed while waiting for the pitch. The bat is often held about chest high in a more vertical position than that recommended for baseball play.

Stride. The stride taken during the batting swing should be short, with the weight of the body shifting into the swing in such a way that the stride does not prevent a smooth, level swing from being made. As the bat is swung, the batter steps toward the pitcher and slightly bends his rear leg at the knee joint, while keeping his front leg firm. The stride is not the same on every pitch—the closer the pitch, the shorter the stride. Understriding rather than overstriding is recommended.

Hitting Action. Because of the speed at which the pitched ball travels in the short distance from the pitcher's mound, the three-quarter or "punch" swing is recommended, rather than the full swing. The front shoulder remains facing the pitcher until just before the swing is initiated. The hands are whipped into the swing as the arms are extended. The hips and shoulders are kept in a level position. To maintain a level swing that is parallel to the ground, the elbow of the rear arm (opposite the pitcher) should be kept close to the body.

Follow-through (Figure 23-7). A follow-through helps to insure that many, if not all, of the preceding fundamentals have been observed. The body should lean in the direction in which the ball is hit, and the end of the bat should contact the middle of the hitter's back at the completion of the swing.

Eyes. The batter must turn his head toward the pitcher and keep it motionless; his eyes must remain focused on the ball from the time that the ball is pitched until it is contacted by the bat.

Common Batting Errors. The common errors in batting are (1) crossing the hands, which results in an awkward swing, (2) placing the feet too close together or too far apart, (3) hugging both elbows to the body, (4) dropping or moving the head, (5) overcrouching at the plate, and (6) swinging at poor pitches. These errors can be corrected only if the batter is aware of them. Each batter should be observed and checked on the various points of batting, and the necessary corrections should be made.

Bunting

Bunting is an extremely important part of softball. One run wins many games, and the bunt may be the weapon to produce that run. The sacrifice bunt is utilized to advance a runner, whereas the base-hit bunt is an attempt to get a runner on first base.

Just before the pitcher releases the ball the sacrifice bunt position is assumed by shifting from the normal ready position for batting. The player turns to face the pitcher by pivoting on the balls of both feet. The rear foot can be stepped forward to square the stance, but the batter must not step on the plate or out of the batter's box. The bat is not swung, but is extended over the plate and held stationary and parallel to the ground. The batter grips the bat by keeping the left hand in its original position while the right hand is moved upward to a spot near the trademark. The fingers, which are behind the bat, loosely support the bat. The bat gives as it meets the ball in order to "cushion" the impact. To direct the bunt, the batter turns the bat at a right angle to the area in which the bunted ball is intended to travel.

When bunting for a base hit, the body movements should be the same as in batting until the pitcher releases the ball. The batter then steps slightly toward the pitch with his front foot and pushes the ball with the top hand, which controls the bat, thus directing the ball in the desired

Figure 23-7. Batting follow-through.

Figure 23-8. Sacrifice bunt position.

352 *Individual and Team Sports*

direction. This bunt is usually attempted against poor fielding pitchers or when the third baseman is playing deep. A "drag" bunt is usually attempted by a left-handed batter who allows his arms to drag behind his body, thus placing the ball toward a position between the pitcher and first baseman as the bunter takes his first steps toward first base.

Such common bunting errors as pushing the bat at the ball, using a half swing, attempting to bunt any pitch, and turning too soon (and thus giving away the intention to bunt) are all faults that can be corrected by practice. Again, observations must be made and the appropriate corrections practiced.

Base Running

Heads-up, correctly executed base running is a vital part of the offensive play in softball; it begins as soon as a batter hits the ball. After the hit, a quick start is initiated as the swing carries the batter around and away from first base. At this point, the weight is placed on the left foot for a fast start. The left foot starts the drive by pushing off, with the first step coming on the right foot. On all hits the runner must run at full speed, because an error is possible on every play. During the run to first base the runner should watch for the signals of the base coach. If the play at first base is going to be close, the runner moves along the foul line in a straight path toward the bag. He runs through the base without jumping or overstriding during the final steps. If an extra base hit is made, the runner should take a swing about twelve to fifteen feet from the bag, turning toward second base and, without breaking stride, touch the inside corner with either foot.

The base runner in softball is not permitted to "take a lead," as in baseball. Therefore, he should be prepared to advance to the next base with every pitch or play. The runner assumes a stance with the left foot against the edge of the bag, and the right leg one stride ahead with the toe pointing toward the next base. The knees are flexed and the body weight is shifted forward. The runner watches

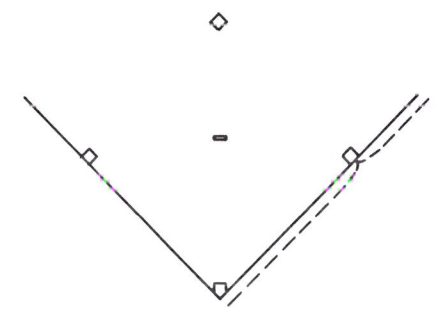

Figure 23-9. Running out a hit.

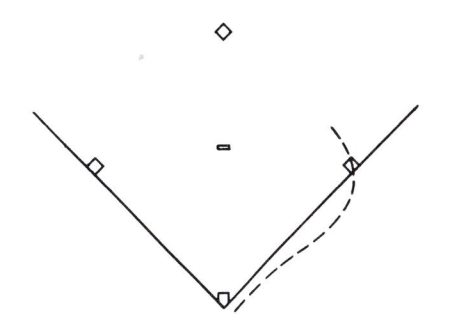

Figure 23-10. Extra base hit.

the pitcher and as the ball is released, short choppy strides are made with the arms pumping back and forth. If the steal is on, the runner drives hard toward the next base. If the runner is not attempting to steal, he must be ready to stop, pivot, and hustle quickly back to the base without being "picked off."

Sliding

The purpose of the slide is twofold: (1) to allow the runner to come into a base at full speed and (2) to avoid being tagged out by a fielder. Various slides, such as the hook, head-first, straight-in, bent-leg, and feet-first slide, are utilized in softball play. Whatever slide is used, the runner should never change his mind at the last minute— nor should he jump into a slide. A slide should be attempted only when the player's legs are properly protected.

Hook Slide (Figure 23-11). The hook slide is a feet-first slide that is most often used to evade a tag by the fielder. The runner, when sliding to the left of the bag, executes the following mechanics in the hook slide. The runner should take off on his right foot and semiextend both legs, keeping them slightly bent. Most of the landing force is absorbed by the runner's left hip, as both feet are kept several inches above the ground to avoid catching the

Figure 23-11. Hook slide.

Softball 353

heel spikes on the ground. The runner does not go into his hook-leg position immediately. The left leg is maintained in a slightly bent position throughout the slide, whereas the left foot is kept several inches above the ground. The right leg is semibent and the right foot is so pointed that the top part of the toes will contact the base. As the base is contacted by the runner's right foot, his momentum continues to carry him past the base and the slide is completed with the right foot hooked to the base. As the runner goes into the slide, the elbows are raised off the ground, the arms are bent, and the fingers are cupped. The runner's neck is stretched slightly forward so that he can watch his target (the base).

Bent-leg Slide (Figure 23-12). The bent-leg slide is a feet-first slide in which mechanics are utilized that enable the runner to slide, quickly raise his body to an erect position, and continue on to the next base if the opportunity presents itself. Because of the speed with which it can be executed, this slide is widely used because it gives the runner the opportunity to advance to another base if an error is made.

The runner takes off from either foot and lands on his right hip with his right leg bent underneath his body. During the slide the left foot is kept in the air. Throughout the slide the runner should continue to focus his vision on the bag. The moment that the bag is contacted by the runner's left foot, he pushes with his right foot and leg, thus coming to a standing position. The runner's body should be kept extended with the weight farther forward than for the hook slide.

Feet-first Slide. This is simply a straight-in slide that is used to get back to a bag quickly. The runner must make sure that the spikes are kept off the ground. The slide is on the backside, with the arms off the ground and the neck flexed to keep the head in a forward position.

Common Sliding Errors. The most common errors in sliding are jumping into a slide and hesitating before a slide. These are mental errors that can result in a possible injury unless the proper techniques are employed for the various slides.

Figure 23-12. Bent-leg slide.

PLAYING POSITIONS IN SOFTBALL

Pitcher

In no other team sport is the key to the success or failure of the team more dependent on one individual than in softball. The pitcher not only pitches, but he is a fielder as well, and he must be able to field balls that might otherwise go past him for hits. Speed is essential, not only for the pitcher who can throw a fast ball the pitching distance of forty-six feet in one-half second, but also for the "junk" pitcher who develops "stuff" on the ball that makes it do tricks. The "junker," especially, must be an exceptional fielder with good speed.

Pitching Rules. Before the windup is started, the ball must be held in both hands in front of the pitcher's body, and both feet must be on the ground in contact with the pitcher's plate. The pivot foot (the right foot for a right-handed pitcher) must remain on the ground until the ball has been released. Only one step in a forward direction toward the batter is allowed. The ball must be thrown underhanded and cannot be sidearmed. The wrist cannot be farther away from the body than the elbow.

The three distinct styles of pitching deliveries are (1) the "windmill," (2) the "slingshot," and (3) the straight underhand.

Windmill (Figure 23-13). This type of delivery, which is often used as a variety pitch, is intended to upset the batter's timing when he attempts to swing at the pitch. The windmill is started with both feet parallel on the pitching rubber. They are parallel and twelve to fourteen inches apart. The ball is held in both hands with the arms resting lightly against the hips. The delivery is started as the arm is swung forward and upward in a circular motion, and the left foot is moved to the left of the plate to maintain balance. At the highest point of the circular motion of the arm the forearm should be straight; it should be in

Figure 23-13. Windmill delivery.

that position during the backward and downward sweep of the arm. At the same time the left leg steps forward in order to maintain the body's balance. When the ball is released, the pitching arm is extended and the body weight is shifted rapidly from the right to the left leg.

Slingshot (Figure 23-14). The slingshot delivery begins from the basic starting point, from which position the ball travels back and up to the layback position. The pitching arm then whips down and forward to complete the pitching motion. The wrist is cocked at the top of the backswing, and as the arm comes down the body weight pushes forward over the left foot, with the body weight pivoting toward the plate. The important part of the delivery, along with the whipping arm action, is the snap of the wrist as the release point is reached. These actions place the pitcher's weight and power behind the pitch, which is concluded with a follow-through that enables the right foot to so swing forward that the pitcher comes to a comfortable, balanced fielding position.

Straight Underhand. To make a straight underhanded pitching delivery, the pitcher grips the ball in a tripod fashion with the tips of the middle fingers just over the seams of the ball and the thumb placed across the top seams of the ball. With his shoulders aligned with a line running between first and third base, the pitcher stands on the plate with his feet parallel to each other and slightly separated. Before starting the backswing the ball is held motionless, for one second, in both hands. The ball is first brought forward away from the body, and then the pitching arm is extended downward and backward. A counterclockwise rotation of the trunk permits a lengthened backswing. The forward arm motion is started with the trunk being rotated clockwise until the body is directly facing the batter, and the arm is swung forward in a plane parallel to the body. A forward step is taken with the left foot and the ball is released off the ends of the fingers. On the follow-through the arm is straight with no bend at the elbow joint. The right foot should then move forward until it is parallel to the left foot. This position of the feet permits the correct fielding stance to be assumed naturally. At the same time the legs should be bent slightly at the knee joint.

Regardless of the windup used, a smooth delivery and good control are necessities for pitching success. Through constant practice the ability to put the pitch where it is desired can usually be developed. Many pitchers make the error of repeatedly overpowering the batter with a fast ball, believing that this pitch alone is sufficient. This is not true and soon these pitchers find that their straight fast ball (when this is the only pitch used) is being hit regularly. Thus, a mastery of a variety of pitches is a necessity for successful pitching.

Types of Pitches. The most popular pitch is the fast ball, which requires only sheer power and control. The following pitches should be mastered in order to achieve pitching success.

Straight Pitch (Figure 23-15)

1. *Grip:* With the palm up, hold the ball in a tripod fashion with the thumb and first two fingers.
2. *Release:* Release the ball from the finger tips and thumb.

Outcurve (Figure 23-16)

1. *Grip:* Same as for the straight pitch.
2. *Release:* Supinate (turn counterclockwise) the wrist to a position in which the palm faces downward. The ball is released from between the thumb and forefinger.

Incurve (Figure 23-17)

1. *Grip:* Same as for the straight pitch.
2. *Release:* Rotate the wrist clockwise and release the ball from between the thumb and the first finger.

Drop ball (Figure 23-18)

1. *Grip:* Hold the ball, palm up, thumb to the right, with the first three fingers together and under the ball. The little finger, which is separated from the other fingers, also grips the ball.

Figure 23-14. Slingshot delivery.

Figure 23-15. Straight pitch (top) grip; (bottom) release.

Softball 355

Figure 23-16. Outcurve pitch (top) grip; (bottom) release.

Figure 23-17. Incurve pitch (top) grip; (bottom) release.

Figure 23-18. Drop-ball pitch (top) grip; (bottom) release.

2. *Release:* Release the ball in an upward motion of the hand by so flexing the wrist that the ball rolls off the first three fingers.

Rise (Figure 23-19)

1. *Grip:* The thumb points downward and all fingers are on top of the ball. The ball is gripped with the tips of the thumb and fingers.
2. *Release:* The palm is in a downward position. Bring the hand forward and keep the knuckles facing toward the batter. Snap or flex the wrist upward, almost to a right angle to the ground, while pushing the thumb against the ball in order to put a backspin on it. At the completion of the delivery the knuckles are facing upward and the fingers are pointing toward the batter.

Catcher

The mainstay of the softball team is the catcher. He keeps his teammates, particularly the pitcher, informed of the current situation and the play to be made, and he signals the type of pitch that he wants his "battery" mate to throw.

Stance. The catcher must stand within the boundaries of the catcher's box. The position taken should be one close behind the batter that will not interfere with the bat during the swing. The crouched position is taken with the legs flexed at the knee joint and the weight distributed evenly on the toes of both feet. A good target is presented to the pitcher as the catcher moves his mitt to the area where he wants to receive the pitch. As the pitched ball comes toward him, the catcher should make certain that the palm of his bare hand is facing the pitcher in order to prevent any injury to the fingers if a foul tip is hit. It is very important for the catcher to get as squarely in front of the pitch as possible. The catcher should be in readiness with his weight so controlled that he can catch practically any pitch in such a way that he can quickly get into position to make any play that may arise.

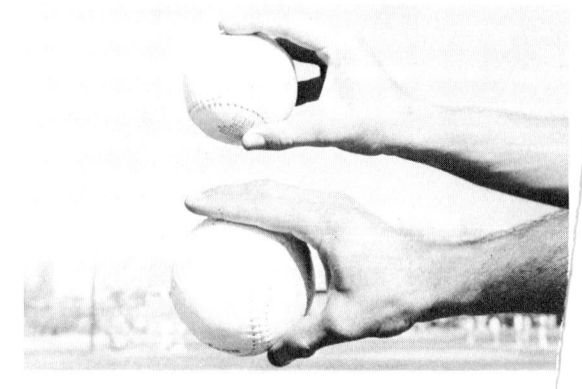

Figure 23-19. Rise-ball pitch (top) grip; (bottom) release

356   *Individual and Team Sports*

When making a throw the catcher must bring the ball up to a position behind the ear. One step is taken forward with the left foot, and the right hand is then extended forward from the ear position with the wrist snapping as the ball is released. All base throws should be directed toward the base at knee-level height.

Catching flyballs and fielding bunts must be practiced with great intent by the catcher. When catching a pop fly, the catcher should remove his mask, toss it in the opposite direction from which he is moving, and get under the ball as fast as possible. A catcher should remember that, because of the rotation of the ball, a foul fly ball will always curve toward the infield, provided there is no wind. When a ball is bunted or slowly hit in his area, the catcher should immediately start for it. If a ball is bunted to either side in the direction of the pitcher's mound, the catcher fields the ball off his right side by placing the gloved hand in front of the ball and scooping it into the glove. If the ball is rolling, he places the right foot as close to the rolling ball as possible, so that he will have plenty of room to handle it.

Bunted balls along either base line should be permitted to roll whenever the batter-runner cannot be thrown out at first base. If the ball rolls foul, it should be touched immediately before it has a chance of rolling fair.

Through signals the catcher and pitcher carry on a running conversation that determines the pattern of the game. There are many ways in which the catcher can give signals to his pitcher. They can be given with the right hand on the inside of the leg and well hidden near the crotch. The fingers, hands, and glove can all be utilized to give signals.

Infield Positions

The majority of the plays in softball are made by the infielders. Consequently, they should be exceptionally good ground-ball fielders, be able to throw fast and accurately, and be able to catch spinning pop flies. Infield play requires a two-handed catch whenever possible, the one-handed catch should be used only when a two-handed catch is impossible.

Position or Stance. The infielder should assume a ready position, which is a semicrouched stance with the legs spread about shoulder width, the legs slightly bent at the knee joint, and the hands hanging in front of the knees. During the pitch the eyes of the fielder are focused on the batter. As the ball is pitched, the weight is shifted forward to the balls of the feet. The body is kept low and on balance, and the infielder is ready to move in any direction.

First Baseman. In softball the first baseman plays much closer to home plate than in baseball because the bunt is widely used as an offensive tactic by many softball teams. The first baseman must therefore always be alert to field bunts on any pitch. His position is approximately thirty to forty feet from home plate, which he takes when there is no runner on first base. If a runner is on first base, the first baseman plays about ten to fifteen feet from first base in order that he will be able to cover the base in the event of a double play.

The first baseman should straddle the bag in order to present the best target for the infielder's throw. The proper footwork is a necessity for catching the throw. On throws to the right, the left foot is shifted to the right with the left foot in contact with the bag. The foot positions are reversed for a throw to the left.

When a bunt is made to his area the first baseman charges the bunt, stepping with the left foot first. If the play is made to second base for a possible double play, the throw is made to the inside of the diamond so that the ball is received at chest height by the shortstop. At times the third strike is dropped by the catcher and a throw to first base is necessary if it is not occupied by a runner. The target for this type of throw is in foul territory.

Second Baseman. The normal infield position for the second baseman is three or four steps to the outside of the base line between first and second base and approximately twelve to fifteen feet on the first-base side of second base. The exact spot, however, varies according to the play situation.

The second baseman must attempt to field all balls hit to the right side of the infield. When he is to cover first base, he should come to the bag from the outside of the diamond, touching the bag with his left foot in order to avoid a possible collision. On fly balls he should float back and attempt to catch unless the outfielder is in a better position than he is.

The double-play throw should be made without taking a step, directing the throw to the base at about chest height. If he is to cover for the double play, the second baseman should come to the bag with the pivot foot. If the throw is outside, the bag should be touched with the left foot, stepping back on the right foot for the throw.

The second baseman must cover first base on bunts, and in softball play he will be required to do this quite often. He also covers second base on an attempted steal whenever the batter is right handed.

Shortstop. The shortstop's normal playing position is comparable to that of the second baseman's, except that the shortstop is on the third-base side of second base. The shortstop covers second base on all bunts attempted by a left-handed batter, and when an attempt is made to steal second base. The shortstop should make an attempt to field all balls hit on the left side of second base.

Whenever possible the shortstop should field a ground ball in front of his body and throw from a set position. On a fielded ground ball with a man on second, a fake is utilized to hold the runner before throwing to first base. To receive the double-play throw, the shortstop should come in a direct line to the bag, receiving the throw and touching the bag during his pivot throw. If the throw comes outside of the bag, the base is touched with his left foot as he steps back on the right foot and throws.

Keystone Combination. The second baseman and shortstop form the keystone combination. These two work as a team and operate closely with each other at all times. When a double-play situation arises, they should both take two or three steps toward home to shorten the distance for fielding ground balls. It is their responsibility to at least put out the lead runner when attempting a double play. These two players plan how attempted steals will be covered as well as the defensive strategy for stopping a possible double steal. For example, on a double steal, the shortstop is the cutoff man with a lefthander at bat; the second baseman with a righthander at bat. The cutoff man goes to the front of second base and in about thirty feet. The other player covers the base. The second baseman decides whether to let the ball go through or to play for the runner on third base.

Third Baseman. The "hot corner" man has to field many hard-hit balls that come into his defensive area. The third baseman plays about thirty-five to forty feet from home plate and about four to five feet from the third-base foul line. The third baseman should take any ball hit to his left that he can get because his momentum will aid his throw for the put out at first base. Many times the ball is hit so hard to the third baseman that he is unable to hold it, but if he is alert he may be able to recover it and still throw the runner out.

When a possible bunt situation appears, the third baseman should charge in to receive the bunt or slow roller: he completes the play by throwing in a continuous motion. The double play is another defensive situation that the third baseman must cover. With runners on first and second the throw should be made to second base unless the ball is hit directly over the third-base bag, in which case the ball goes to the third base and then to first base. The throw to second base should arrive there at chest height. It is vital that the third baseman cover second base if both the shortstop and second baseman go for a "Texas Leaguer."

Common Errors in Playing the Infield. Infielders commonly commit the mistakes of (1) covering the base or moving with a base runner instead of fielding the batted ball, and (2) standing on the base line in a runner's path. The infielder should always go after a bad throw rather than just reach out to catch it.

Outfielders

The outfielders must be so located that they can cover their areas. The outfielder's stance is the same as that of the infielder's except that the hands are placed on the knees. The overhand throw is always used in returning the ball to the infield. When fielding ground balls the right knee is often placed on the ground in order to help block the ball and prevent it from rolling past the outfielder. When catching fly balls the glove should be positioned in front of the outfielder's face with the fingers up and the thumb hand placed next to the glove. The fielder places his left foot forward in order to make a quick return to the infield after the catch is completed. For fly balls that must be caught below belt level, the glove is positioned with the fingers pointing downward. On line drives the glove is placed in the same position as when playing catch. Each fielder should know the pitcher's capabilities and what type of balls are usually hit off the different pitches.

The outfielder should always know ahead of time where he will throw the ball on each play; thus, he will be able to field the ball and return it immediately to the infield. Each outfielder should check the direction and velocity of the wind at the start of each inning. The outfielder should play deep rather than close because it is easier and faster for him to come in than it is to go back.

Common Errors in Playing the Outfield. The outfielder should never take his position in the same spot on the outfield for each play; instead, each time he must consider the weather, batter, and possible play situations that may occur before selecting his spot. The outfielder must remember to call out fly balls, back up the infielders, and return the ball to the correct base or infielder immediately after fielding it.

DEFENSIVE SITUATIONS

The correct defensive play requires a high degree of cooperation among the defensive players in order to best combat the plays of the offensive team.

Double Play

The double play is a successful method of pulling the defense out of a tight spot because it affords an opportunity to obtain two outs instead of the usual one out per play. The double play can be started or completed by any member of the team as long as a base runner is occupying a base. The double play becomes a possibility if an outfielder, after catching a fly ball, throws the ball to a base and catches the runner before he has made his return.

The "keystone" double-play situations follow:

Feed Throw. If the baseman is only a step or two from the base when he fields the ball, he should step on the base rather than throw the ball to the pivot man. If the fielder is moving toward the base and he is fairly close to it, he should feed the ball to the baseman with an underhanded toss. If he is several feet away, the feed throw should be an overhand snap throw that is received at about chest height by the base coverer.

Pivot Footwork. There are numerous ways of making the pivot for a double play. Regardless of which pivot is used or which keystone member uses it, it is important that the pivot man come into the base at an angle at which he is squarely facing the thrower and is in line with the throw.

For the second baseman perhaps the easiest type of pivot involves the "step-and-off" methods. On the first step-and-off pivot, the second baseman steps on the base with the right foot as the ball is caught; he then steps toward first base with the left foot during the throw. This simple, effective pivot is preferred whenever the second baseman has sufficient time and the runner is not bothering him. However, because the second baseman is stepping into the path of the ball, the runner, if he is close, can slide into the second baseman's left foot. To avoid this possibility on a close play, the second step-and-off method should be utilized in which the second baseman steps on the base with the left foot and pushes off it by first stepping toward first base with the left foot. This action will bring the second baseman to a position back and away from the base line, from which position he has a clear throw to first base.

Another pivot method is the step-and-in pivot, which is executed with the second baseman stepping on the base with his right foot and then stepping to the inside of the diamond and toward first base with his left foot as he makes the throw.

The shortstop will probably use the "straddle drag" pivot because it is faster and much safer than any other method. It enables the shortstop to evade the possibility of being upended by the oncoming runner. As the shortstop catches the ball he steps over the bag with the left foot. He should then hop and drag the right foot against the corner of the base and step toward first base with the left foot as the throw is made.

Cutoffs and Relays

The purpose of the cutoff is to prevent another runner from taking an extra base when the throw is obviously too late to put out the lead runner. The cutoff man is also valuable in providing a target to which the outfielder can aim the throw. The relay man is the one who goes out to receive the outfielder's return throw after he fields a long-hit ball.

Single with a Man on First (Figures 23-20, 23-21, and 23-22). On a single to left field with no runner on first or second (or a fly ball where the throw should go to second), the shortstop covers the bag and the second baseman backs him up. The second baseman covers second base on a ball hit to right field.

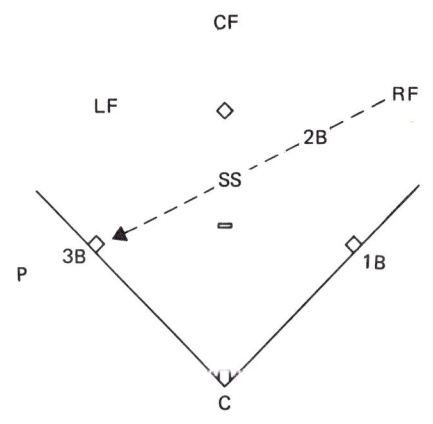

Figure 23-20. Single to right with a runner on first.

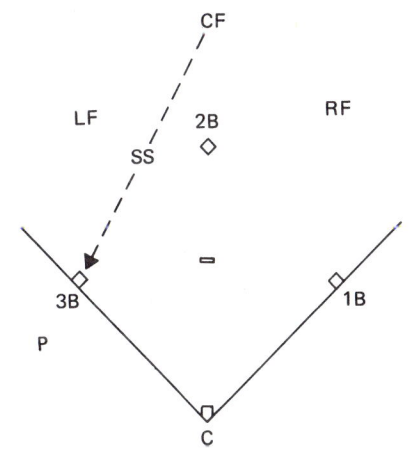

Figure 23-21. Single to center with runner on first.

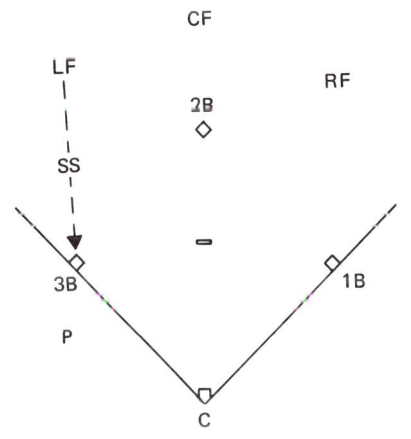

Figure 23-22. Single to left with runner on first.

Softball 359

Single with Man on Second (Figures 23-23, 23-24, and 23-25). (Throw right through the cutoff man.) The second baseman is the relay man on a long hit to right and right-center. The shortstop is the relay man on a long hit to left and center, except on a double base hit down the right field in which the first baseman should act as the relay man.

Trapping a Runner. When a runner is trapped between two bases, the infielders must cover all bases as the player with the ball moves the runner back to the base from which he started. A limited number of throws should be made, and if possible, only one throw should be employed to make the put-out.

Tagging the Runner. The methods of tagging the runner differ for each base, but for all methods the infielder will probably straddle the base and face the incoming throw. If the throw is accurate and the ball is caught, the infielder continues his motion and positions the ball in front of the bag, allowing the runner to slide into the ball.

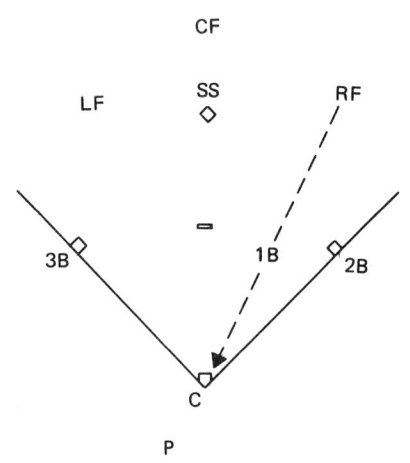

Figure 23-23. Single to right with runner on second.

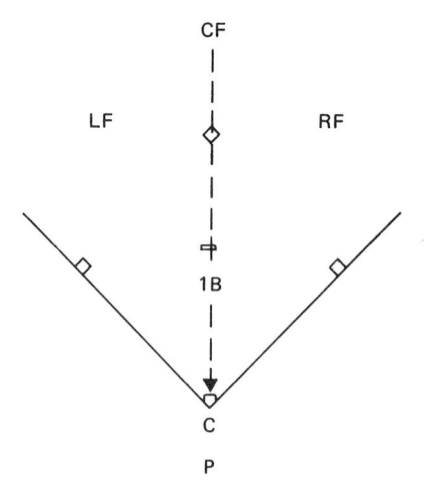

Figure 23-24. Single to center with runner on second.

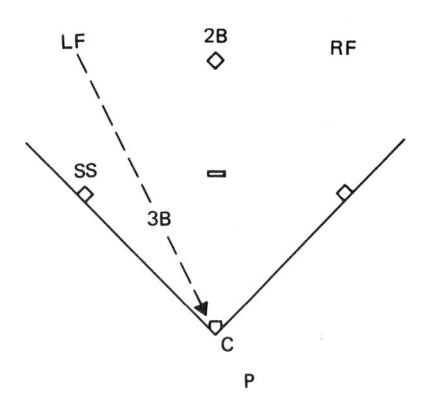

Figure 23-25. Single to left with runner on second.

If the throw is poor, the fielder should leave the base to catch the ball and then attempt to tag the runner as he passes by.

Defense Against the Bunt

In softball the bunt is a potent offensive weapon and every defensive team must be prepared to cope with the various bunt situations.

Bunt with Man on First (Figure 23-26). The first and third basemen charge the plate for the bunt. If they do not field the ball, they return to their positions. The second baseman covers first, and the shortstop covers second. The catcher is responsible for third base if the third baseman fields the ball.

Bunt with Men on First and Second (Figure 23-27). The pitcher moves to cover the third-base line, while the third baseman covers the bag. The shortstop fakes the runner back to second and covers first, while the first baseman charges the plate. If possible, the play should go to third and then to first base.

Bunt with Man on Third (Squeeze Play). The best defense against the squeeze play is an unbuntable pitch, which should be thrown in order to catch the runner trying to score. The recommended pitch in this situation is

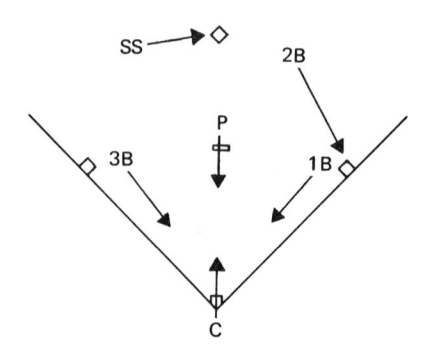

Figure 23-26. Bunt defense with runner on first.

360 *Individual and Team Sports*

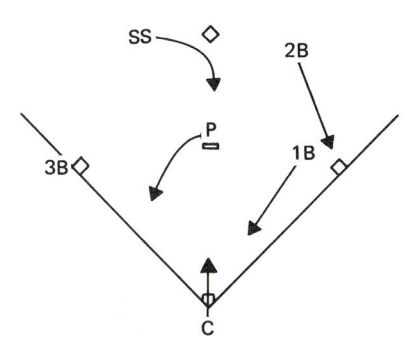

Figure 23-27. Bunt defense with runners on first and second.

one high and inside to a right-handed batter or high and outside to a left-handed batter. If a squeeze is attempted with runners on second and third, the play has to be made at first. The infielders should be alert in case the runner on second continues on to the plate.

OFFENSIVE STRATEGY

Game strategy is varied according to a given situation. What one coach regards as good strategy may be considered poor strategy by another coach. Nonetheless, basic offensive plays must be practiced and mastered. Each team should understand and be able to execute the following plays.

Sacrifice Bunt

The aim of the sacrifice bunt is to put a runner in better scoring position and to prevent the possibility of a double play. The sacrifice bunt is employed where there are no outs, when the score is close, and when first or both first and second bases are occupied. It is also used late in the game when a runner is on second base.

Squeeze Play

With less than two outs and the score tied, a squeeze play is often initiated during which the runner on third base attempts to score on the bunt. The runner starts for home as the pitch is made, and the batter bunts the ball on the ground. A double squeeze play may be attempted in which the runners on second and third base both try to score.

Hit and Run

The hit-and-run play is usually attempted by the team that leads or when the score is close with one or no outs. As the pitch is made, the runner starts for the next base and the batter attempts to punch the ball behind the runner and through the hole. This is most often attempted with a runner on first base, in which case the batter places the ball between first and second base and behind the runner.

Double Steal

On a given signal the runners on first and second base both leave with the pitch in hopes of stealing to the next bases. The batter often swings to protect the runners and to delay the catcher. A double steal may also occur when runners are on first and third base. If the catcher throws the ball through to second base in an effort to retire the runner coming from first, the runner on third then attempts to score. The runner on third must be alert for the cutoff play, which enables the defense to make a play for him at home.

Delayed Steal

This play begins after the catcher has caught the ball and has started his motion to return the ball to the pitcher. The runner breaks for the next base just as the catcher releases the ball. This is a dangerous play, but it can be successful because it requires the pitcher to catch, turn, and accurately relay the ball to the proper base in time.

Base Coaching and Signals

There are two base coaches—one at first base and the other at third base. The base coach stands in the coach's box and performs two types of duties: he is the eyes and mind of the base runner, and he relays the signals to the runner as well as to the hitter.

To perform his first duty the coach must be in a position to see for the runner while the runner is concentrating on the bases. The hitter must not watch the ball after he hits it until he is in a safe position to do so. The first-base coach will inform the hitter whether he is to make the turn at first, run it out, or slide. If a wild ball is thrown to first, the base coach is in the best position to decide if the runner should try to advance an extra base.

The third-base coach will be of greatest assistance to the runner if he informs the runner, as he nears second base, whether to advance to third or stop at second. This coach also indicates to the runner if he should make the turn at third base.

The signals used by the base coach are given either by voice or by use of the hands. Voice signals are used to direct the runners when they advance from one base to another. Hand signals are utilized to direct base runners as well as batsmen. The manager or coach can make up his own set of signals to indicate when he wants a bunt, squeeze play, steal, and so on.

Softball **361**

TRAINING METHODS

The utilization of drills during practice periods is vital for successful team play with a minimum of errors. Specific drills should be employed for infield, outfield, and individual practice. The drills selected must benefit the players; this, in turn, is dependent on their abilities and the amount of past practice. The following drill, which is illustrated in Figure 23-28, is considered to be a valuable, multiple-purpose drill, which includes offensive and defensive fundamentals that can be practiced on the playing field.

Procedure

The batting order and pitching assignments are selected in advance. The pitchers are to throw at one-half to three-fourths speed and are replaced every fifteen minutes by another pitcher who has been warming up on the sidelines.

The squad members are placed in their respective playing positions, with the first man on the batting list being the first hitter, the second man being the second hitter, and so on. The second hitter stands in the on-deck circle and swings a weighted bat while awaiting his turn. Standing behind third base in foul territory is the third hitter who bats fly balls to the outfielders who field and return them to the fourth hitter who acts as a feeder for the fungo hitter. The fifth hitter acts as a feeder for the pitcher. When the first hitter completes his batting turn, the feeder to the pitcher is replaced by the player who follows him on the batting list, and the original first hitter becomes the feeder for the fly-ball hitter. The fly-ball feeder becomes the fly-ball hitter and the fly-ball hitter then becomes the on-deck man with the on-deck man moving to the plate to hit. This procedure continues throughout the batting practice.

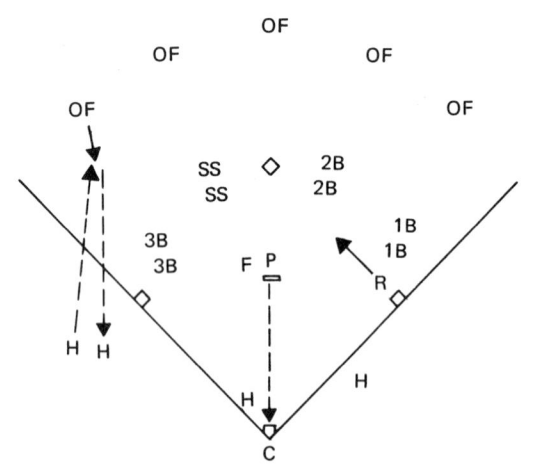

Figure 23-28. Multiple-purpose drill.

Instructions Given to Batters and Runners. The hitters are to sacrifice bunt two pitches, one down the first base line and the other down the third base line. They then have six swings, with the infielders and outfielders making plays on the ball. The seventh swing is a drag bunt, which they run out. They then remain on first base as a runner. The second batter takes his turn at bat with the runner at first base being ready to steal second base. On the first pitch the hitter attempts to protect the runner by swinging at but not making contact with the ball. As in game situations the catcher throws and the shortstop or second baseman (depending on whether it is a right- or left-handed batter) covers the second-base bag. The runner stays on second base. The next pitch is laid down for a bunt with the runner advancing to third where he remains as a runner. The hitter bunts for the second time as if the squeeze play were being attempted, and the runner on third base tries to score while the defense attempts the put-out at the plate.

The runner now takes a fielding position and the batter takes his six swings, bunting the last pitch and following the procedure of the first batter. This same procedure continues through the entire practice session, which enables the instructor or coach to see his players in action. He can then make corrections and suggestions concerning the various phases of softball that are covered in this drill.

A player must be in good physical condition in order to play his best softball. Therefore, preseason and seasonal conditioning should include running activities and training with weights. A device called the Exer-Genie is useful for increasing strength in the wrists, forearms, and shoulders and can be utilized to develop a level swing, which is so important for batting success.

Glossary of Terms

Assist: A fielding credit for a player who throws or deflects a batted or thrown ball in such a way that a put-out occurs, or would have occurred except for a subsequent error by a teammate.
Bag: A base.
Ball: A pitched ball not swung at by the batter and ruled outside of the strike zone.
Base: The four stations on a diamond that the runners on the offensive team must safely touch in succession before scoring.
Base hit: A ball hit in the fair area of the playing field that enables the hitter to reach first base safely.
Battery: The pitcher and the catcher.
Control: The ability of a pitcher to throw the ball to a desired area when pitching.

Cutoff: A throw from the outfield that is intercepted by an infielder.

Delivery: The motions made by the pitcher in pitching the ball to the batter.

Diamond: The infield; the playing field.

Double play: Two consecutive put-outs made between the time the pitcher delivers the ball to the batter and the time the ball is returned to the pitcher's rubber.

Error: A misplay or mistake by the defensive team that aids the team that is batting.

Feeder: A player or coach who stands behind the pitching area and supplies the batting-practice pitcher with baseballs. A player tossing or throwing the ball to another player.

Fungo: A ball hit to the fielder during practice. The ball is not pitched, but is thrown a short distance into the air by the batter and then hit.

Hit: A batted ball that goes fair (and no misplay is made by the defensive team) and that permits the batter to reach first base safely.

Hole: An area on the playing field that is not covered by a defensive player.

Hot corner: The third-base area.

Infield fly: With runners on first and second, or first, second, and third; with less than two outs: a fly-ball hit that can be handled by the infielders. The batter is automatically out.

Inning: The portion of the game in which both teams are each at bat for three outs.

Keystone: Shortstop and second baseman.

Mound: The pitching area.

Passed ball: A pitched ball that the catcher fails to catch or stop and that permits a base runner to advance.

Pivot man: The player who makes the force-out in a double play.

Rubber: The rubber slab on the pitcher's mound with which the pitcher's feet must be in contact when he delivers the ball.

Strike-out: Three strikes by the hitter—which puts him out.

Tag: A base runner is touched with the ball by a defensive player.

Texas Leaguer: A fly ball hit over the heads of the infielders that falls safely between the infield and outfield.

Wild pitch: A legally pitched ball delivered by the pitcher that goes so wide of the plate that the catcher cannot handle it.

Selected References

BOOKS

Allen, Ethan. *Baseball Play and Strategy.* New York: Ronald, 1959.

A complete theory of baseball techniques and presentation of fundamentals are covered. The book gives an exceptional presentation of offensive and defensive strategy.

Anderson, Clary. *Make the Team in Baseball.* New York: Grosset, 1966.

Designed for the beginning player, the fundamentals of fielding, hitting, bunting, and throwing are covered. The techniques of baseball are explained in easily understood detail.

Kneer, Marian, Dan Lupinski, and Jimmy Walsh. *Softball.* New York: Sterling, 1965.

Excellent photographs and illustrations on the fundamentals and techniques of softball are included. The chapter on pitching is excellent.

Noren, Arthur T. *Softball.* New York: A. S. Barnes, 1966.

An excellent guide for the beginning player who wants to improve his skill, this text covers each position and has a chapter dealing with rules.

Official Guide and Rule Book. Newark, N. J.: Amateur Softball Association and the International Joint Rules Committee for Softball.

This yearly publication reveals the rules, regulations, and changes for the coming softball season.

Spackman, Robert R. *Baseball.* Annapolis, Md.: U. S. Naval Institute, 1963.

The text is designed for teaching basic skills, footwork, and techniques required for playing baseball. The chapter on conditioning contains much other valuable information.

PERIODICALS

AAHPER Journal. 1201 16th Street, N. W., Washington, D. C. 20036.

Athletic Journal. Athletic Journal Publishing Company, 1719 Howard Street, Evanston, Illinois 60201.

The Coach and Athlete. 1905 Piedmont Road, N. E., Atlanta, Georgia 30300.

Scholastic Coach. Scholastic Magazine Inc., 50 W. 44th Street, New York, New York 10036.

CHAPTER 24

Speedball
*Donald D. Klotz**
The University of Iowa

HISTORY

Speedball, one of the youngest of the team games, was invented in 1920, by Elmer D. Mitchell while he was a professor of physical education at the University of Michigan, Ann Arbor, Michigan. He combined many of the best features of basketball and soccer and added the punt, drop kick, and kickoff from football. The name *speedball* was well chosen, for it accurately indicates the intensity of action characteristic of the game. Speedball received a favorable reception and quickly spread across the nation. It is now included in many physical education and intramural sports programs.

VALUES

Economy

The only essential items of equipment needed for speedball are a ball and a field on which to use it. Regulation goals can be made from inexpensive fir two-by-fours if it is deemed desirable to have them.

Skill Development

Because many of the fundamental skills of several sports are utilized in speedball, the game offers a many-sided approach to skill development for participants at all grade levels. Most of our popular American games involve the throwing, batting, catching, or kicking of a ball, which in turn aid in the development of depth perception, and hand-eye and bilateral coordination. Moreover, speedball demands that all four of these fundamental skills be used repeatedly. In addition, many of the other skills used or developed in speedball are carried over directly to other sports. For example, the overhand throw of speedball has identical elements to the tennis serve and the overhead smash of badminton, tennis, and paddleball. Similarly, the sidearm throw is closely allied to the forehand drives of the racket games. The footwork employed in speedball is similar to that used in many games and sports.

Conditioning Value

As a developer of cardiovascular endurance, speedball has few equals, because all players except the goalkeeper participate fully in playing the ball. Whether the ball is being played on the ground or in the air the players are constantly running. The challenge of competition encourages the players to exert themselves to their limit and still have fun doing it.

Adaptability

Although a definite set of rules governs the play of speedball, the players are free to adopt variations which better suit their capacities and/or the limitations of the playing area. For example, if more intense action and ball handling is desired, the number of players per team can be reduced from the regulation eleven to seven players. The size of the field can be changed to meet various situations. The scoring system can also be modified according to the degree of skill possessed by the players. Although scoring by means of a goal from kicking the ball into the end zone and a touchdown from a forward pass is suitable for elementary players, this system is too simple (and,

---

*B.S., University of Northern Iowa, Cedar Falls; M.A., Ph.D., University of Iowa, Iowa City. Dr. Klotz has taught speedball to professional classes of male physical education students at The University of Iowa for more than twenty years. In addition, he has written a multitude of sports articles for various publications.

364 *Individual and Team Sports*

hence, presents little challenge) for advanced players, who can be limited to scoring only by a place kick under the crossbar or a drop kick over the crossbar. In short, the game can be modified at will to fit the facilities and the players involved. Such modifications apparently cause none of the attraction of the game to be lost.

EQUIPMENT

Ball

It is customary to use the official soccer ball for both soccer and speedball. Rubber volleyballs can be used if no soccer balls are available.

Shoes

Only high-cut, rubber-soled shoes of the basketball type should be worn when playing speedball. The rough soles provide satisfactory traction and the uppers, if laced tightly, give strong ankle support. Because about 50 per cent of speedball is played like soccer, leather soles and opponents' shins will not be compatible.

Goal Posts

If speedball is played on a football field the posts are automatically provided. If it is played on a field without goal posts, the players can use two volleyball standards for a goal, substituting a clothesline cord for a crossbar. Even two jackets placed on the goal line six yards apart can adequately serve as goals.

Safety

A safe margin must be allowed on all sides of the playing area and on any obstructions near it, especially at the ends of the field where the momentum of a player can carry him some distance out-of-bounds. Irregularities in the surface of the field can cause sprained ankles. Because falls can be expected in the playing of the game, particularly on grassy fields that may be damp, all stones and broken glass should be removed from the field.

The rule against kicking an aerial ball is to be strictly observed. Any careless and unnecessarily hard kicking of the ball is dangerous because of possible injury to the faces of other players (some of whom may be wearing glasses). As the players tire they increasingly tend to substitute physical power for skill in playing their opponents and rough body contact may occur. If the game is not being officiated, the players must take on themselves the responsibility for good sportsmanship.

THE GAME

General Description

The game of speedball is played by two teams of eleven men each on a football field. The kickoff is made to the receiving team from the center of the field. All players of the kicking team must be behind the ball when it is kicked and they may not touch the ball until it has gone forward ten yards or has been touched by a player of the receiving team. Until the ball is kicked all players on the receiving team must be behind the ten-yard restraining line.

The ball can be advanced along the ground by kicking it, by playing it off the body, or by heading it, as in soccer play. Once the ball is kicked into the air it can be caught and then passed as in basketball. The game is divided into four twelve-minute quarters. There is a two-minute rest period between the first and second quarters; a ten-minute rest period between halves; and another two-minute rest period between the third and fourth quarters.

Scoring

Field Goal. A field goal, which counts three points for the offensive team, is scored whenever a ball crosses the goal line between the goal posts and under the crossbar because of being kicked along the ground or forced over the line by any part of the player's body.

Drop Kick. A drop kick over the crossbar from the field of play outside the penalty area scores two points.

Forward Pass. A forward pass from the field of play or penalty area to a teammate in the end zone scores one point.

End Goal. An end goal counting one point is scored by kicking the ball across the end line from the penalty area.

Penalty Kick. A penalty kick from the twelve-yard line that passes under the crossbar and over the end line scores one point.

Ground Ball

Whenever the ball strikes the ground it automatically becomes a ground ball and must be played, as in soccer, with the feet, the head, or any part of the body except the hands or arms. A bouncing ball is a ground ball.

Aerial Ball

A ground ball can be kicked in the air directly to a teammate or to the kicker himself. If it is caught on the fly it becomes an aerial ball and can be passed with the hands as in basketball. Each player is permitted one air dribble after receiving a pass. The air dribble is performed by tossing the ball into the air in any direction and is then

Speedball

caught by the same player. He can take any number of steps in running to catch the ball. After catching it he must stop within two steps. He can then pass or kick the ball to a teammate. In handling aerial balls, the two-step rule of basketball applies in moving the feet after receiving a pass, except that this rule should be liberalized if the game is being played on damp grass to prevent bad falls, which may result from the slippery footing.

The Goalkeeper

In speedball the goalkeeper has no special privileges. He must play the ball in exactly the same manner as all other players in all parts of the field.

Body Contact

When playing aerial balls the body-contact rules of basketball apply. When playing ground balls, the body-contact rules of soccer are in force. During a speedball game no tackling or blocking is permitted as is done in football.

Tie Balls

If two or more opponents grasp the ball at the same time, simultaneously touch a ball that is going out of bounds, or commit a double foul, the ball is declared a tie ball and it is tossed up between them for a jump ball, as in basketball. All other players must remain five yards away until the jump ball is tapped by one of the jumpers. A touchdown cannot be scored from a jump ball that is tapped directly to a teammate located in the end zone.

Out-of-bounds

If a player causes a ball to pass out-of-bounds over one of the sidelines, any opponent can put the ball back in play using any type of pass that he wishes. A ball that passes out of bounds over an end line can be either kicked or passed into play by an opponent.

Penalty Kick

A penalty kick is a free kick taken from within the penalty area (from the twelve-yard line). Only the kicker and the goalkeeper are involved; all other players must remain outside the penalty area.

Officials

The game of speedball is officiated by one referee and two linesmen. The referee has the final authority in decisions concerning the conduct of the game.

Violations of the Rules

The following actions constitute a violation of the rules and call for a penalty to be assessed:

1. Traveling with the ball.
2. Intentional touching of a ground ball with the hands or arms.
3. Double air dribble.
4. Kicking or kneeing a fly ball before catching it (with the exception noted under aerial ball).
5. Causing a ball to go out-of-bounds.
6. Interfering with a kickoff or jump ball.
7. Interfering with a penalty kick.
8. Illegal interference with a player when he is putting the ball in play from out-of-bounds.

Penalties for Violations

1. If the violation is committed outside the end zone, the ball goes to the opponents out-of-bounds.
2. If the violation is committed within the penalty area (end zone) one penalty kick is given with the ball in play if the kick does not directly result in a score.

Technical Fouls

1. Illegal substitutions.
2. Unsportsmanlike conduct.
3. Unnecessary delay of the game.
4. Taking more than three time-outs.
5. Having more than eleven players on the field of play when time is in.

Penalties for Technical Fouls

1. One penalty kick is awarded the opposing team if the technical foul is committed outside the penalty area. If the kick is missed the ball is dead and immediately goes to opponents out-of-bounds.
2. If the technical foul is committed inside the penalty area, one penalty kick is awarded, with a follow-up if the kick is missed.

Personal Fouls

1. Pushing, holding, kicking, tripping, charging, or blocking.
2. Unnecessary roughness.

Penalties for Personal Fouls

1. If the personal foul is committed by the defending team in its own penalty area, the opponents are awarded two penalty kicks with a follow-up permitted after the second kick if it is missed.

2. If the personal foul is committed by a team in the field of play, one penalty kick is awarded. The ball is dead if the kick is missed and the ball is awarded to the opponents out-of-bounds.

FUNDAMENTAL SKILLS AND TECHNIQUES

Dribble and Pass

The dribble with the feet is the basic technique utilized for moving a ground ball. Practice of this dribble should begin with short passes in which the ball is chiefly contacted with the inside of either foot. The outside of the foot or the heel can be used occasionally. Two players can develop footwork skills by kicking the ball back and forth to each other, gently at first and from a distance of no more than ten feet. Each player traps the ball with the sole of his foot, then gently passes it back to his teammate. As the skill of each improves they move an increased distance from each other, kicking the ball with increased force. An alternate method is for the player to check the ball with the inside of the foot and then pass it back to his teammate. The next step in improving ball-handling skills is for two players to trot slowly down the field in a parallel formation, perhaps fifteen feet apart, dribbling the ball for two or three steps, and then passing it.

A more advanced drill involves two offensive players attempting to pass and drive past one defensive opponent as they run down the field. With additional practice three offensive men practice against two defensive players, who attempt to intercept the passes and dribbles.

Trapping the Ball

The speedball player should early learn to trap the ball with either his feet, shins, thighs, or any other part of his body as determined by the height of the bounce as he contacts the ball. When trapping the ball at any height he must quickly learn to so give with the ball as it strikes his body that it will fall dead at his feet. Initial skill in trapping the ball is probably best learned by the beginner by trapping a tossed ball that is thrown from close range and that bounces at various heights. The height, speed, and angle of the tossed ball are increased as rapidly as the player's improvement in skill will allow.

Heading

A high-bouncing ball is occasionally handled best by heading it, as in soccer. The player who is learning to head the ball should initially practice with a ball tossed to him from a distance of perhaps ten feet in which the ball travels above head height in a gentle arc. The neck should be kept in line with the spine, and the eyes should be focused on the ball until the ball is struck by the head at about the hairline. The ball is given a firm nudge as it strikes the head of the player who then directs the ball back to the tosser. This heading drill should be practiced until the beginner acquires confidence in his ability to control the direction of the headed ball.

Passing and Related Skills

In speedball the player can use effectively all the basketball passes once the ball is kicked into his hands and thus becomes an aerial ball. A few beginners, because of a lack of previous instruction and practice, may have to learn the correct mechanics of throwing properly. For example, when throwing with the right hand, step with the left foot in the direction of the throw; when throwing with the left hand, step with the right foot.

Punting

The football punt is an effective method of quickly moving the ball a considerable distance down the field. When performing the football punt the player should hold the ball well out in front of the body with both hands and drop it directly over the kicking foot. For a right-footed kicker, one step is taken with the left foot before the kick is made, and the ball is kicked with the top of the instep of the kicking foot.

Drop Kicking

The drop kick is an effective method of scoring and should be practiced intensively. To execute a drop kick the player holds the ball with both hands well out in front of the body and slightly below the waist. Flexing his body forward, he steps once with the left foot and then kicks the ball with the right foot, striking the ball with the instep just after it rebounds off the ground. The initial drop-kicking practice should begin at a close range to the goal posts.

Kick-up

Because aerial balls, which can be passed with the hands, are easier to control than kicked balls, it is desirable to convert ground balls to aerial balls at the earliest possible moment. This is often done by means of a kick-up. A player can kick the ball up to himself or to a teammate. A rolling or bouncing ball can be lifted into the hands by simply putting a foot under the ball as it approaches, and as it rolls or rebounds on top of the foot the ball is gently kicked into the player's hands. A stationary ball can be

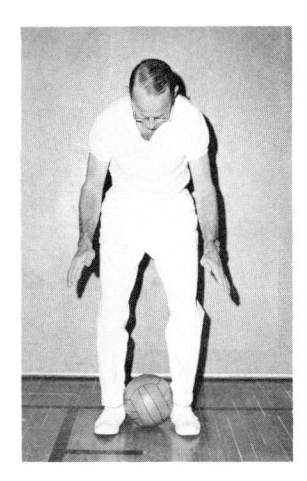

Figure 24-1(a). Two-foot kick-up of stationary ball.

Figure 24-1(b). Two-foot kick-up of stationary ball.

Figure 24-2(a). One-foot kick-up of stationary ball.

Figure 24-2(b). One-foot kick-up of stationary ball.

kicked or lifted to a teammate by carefully placing the upper surface of the toes under the ball and giving it a forward and upward lift. It can also be given a sharp kick in which the ball is struck with the kicking toe at a point just above ground level.

A player can make a simple kick-up to himself by placing his feet on either side of the middle of the ball, pressing inward with his ankles, flexing his knees, and then jumping straight upward with both legs, lifting the ball as he jumps. This is depicted in Figures 24-1 (a) and 24-1 (b).

Another type of kick-up can be made by the player to himself if he places the toes of one foot behind and under the ball and bends forward until his hands are about one foot above the ground, with his palms facing the ball. A gentle kick, chiefly made by flexing the ankle, delivers the ball directly into the player's hands as illustrated in Figures 24-2 (a) and 24-2 (b).

The roll pick-up is effective but somewhat difficult to learn. A stationary ground ball is located about two feet in front of the pickup foot, which is then placed on top of the ball and drawn quickly backward and down, coming to rest on the ground just behind the rolling ball. If the foot is kept flat on the ground for just an instant the backspin of the ball will cause it to roll up on the player's toes, at which time it can be tossed up to the hands by a quick flip of the foot. The roll pick-up is illustrated in Figures 24-3 (a) and 24-3 (b).

TEAMWORK

Defense

Because of the large area to be covered in speedball play a man-to-man defense is the most effective type. The defensive man who assumes the guarding stance of basketball generally plays between his opponent and the goal.

Figure 24-3(a). One-foot roll and kick-up of stationary ball.

Figure 24-3(b). One-foot roll and kick-up of stationary ball.

An efficient defense demands excellent physical condition because an opponent cannot be covered if a player cannot keep up with him. The players can switch defensive assignments, as is done in man-to-man defense in basketball, if the opposing players are crisscrossing in their offensive plays and a man is blocked off from the opponent he is guarding. The defensive patterns illustrated in the chapter on soccer are applicable to speedball.

Offense

A basic principle for the offensive team is to keep spread out. An inexperienced player tends to follow the ball rather than to play in his own position or his own area of the playing field. This type of play results in a disorganized mob instead of a cohesive team. The kickoff generally should be deep, with the defensive front line driving down the field fast in order to intercept the ball as soon as possible. The backs should follow closely behind the front

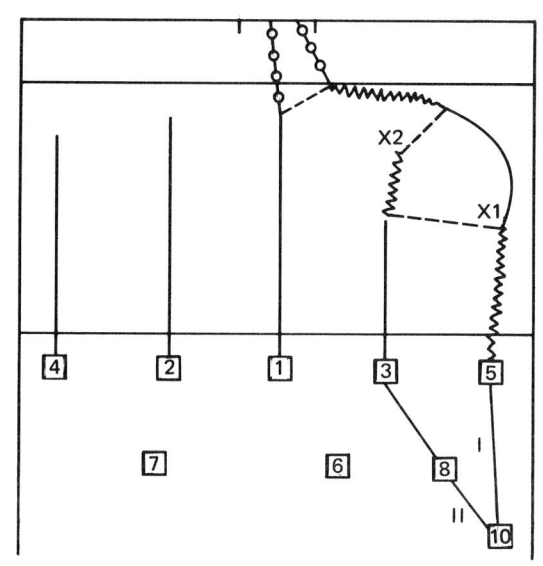

Plays After Interception—Option I: *10* intercepts and passes to *5* who dribbles down field until blocked by X1. *5* passes to *3* who dribbles until stopped by X2, then passes back to *5* who dribbles into the end zone and either kicks for goal or passes to *1* for goal kick.

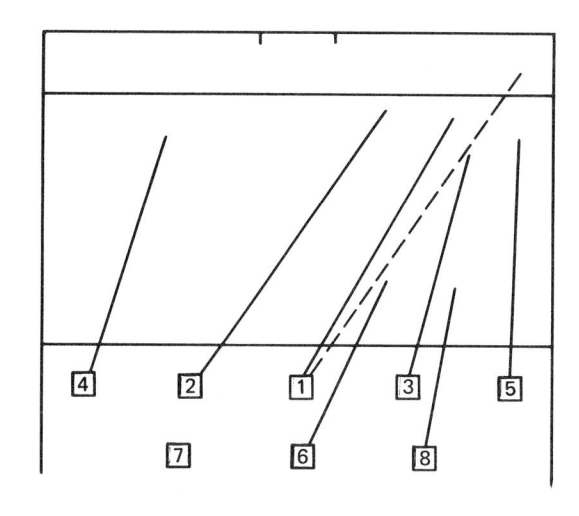

Kick-off Play: *1* kicks off to the corner. *1, 2, 3,* and *5* converge on the opponents to try to intercept deep in opponents' end of field. *4* stays wide for quick break toward goal to score. *6* follows to be in good position for drop kick.

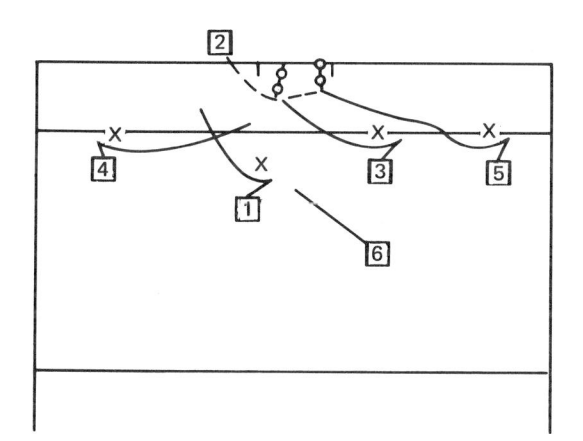

Out-of-Bounds at End: *1, 3, 4,* and *5* fake as indicated to shake guards. *1* and *4* cross-cross. *2* may kick to *3* for goal kick or pass to *5*. *4* or *1* may elude guards to take pass. Pass may go to *6* for drop kick.

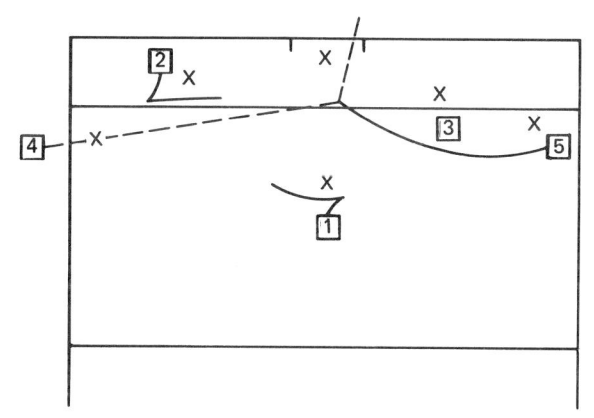

Out-of-bounds, Offensive End: *4* takes ball out. *2* and *1* fake and hold position. *3* serves as screen for *5* who cuts fast to near goal to head pass from *4* into goal for score.

Figure 24-4. Various offensive plays.

line for support and to serve as ball feeders to the forwards and ends, once the ball is intercepted. The backs will have numerous opportunities for making forward passes to the forwards and for attempting drop kicks.

Whenever the ball is intercepted it should be passed immediately to a forward or to an end who will advance it down the field. If the offensive players remain approximately in their own positions, their teammates will know where to look for them and the offense will have a better chance at functioning smoothly. Various offensive plays can be developed as the players become familiar with the game and with one another. The general offensive patterns illustrated in the chapter on soccer are of value in speedball offensive play.

Selected References

Mitchell, E. D. *Sports for Recreation.* New York: A. S. Barnes, 1952.

Shaw, John H., et al. *Selected Team Sports for Men.* Philadelphia: Saunders, 1952.

Speedball

CHAPTER 25

Swimming
Robert H. Allen*
The University of Iowa

HISTORY

The skill of propelling oneself through the water, either at the surface or underneath it, is at least as old as written history. Reference is made in the Bible to Egyptians bathing in the Nile River. Carvings recovered from the ruins of Pompeii depict swimmers using a stroke similar to the side stroke.

European swimming associations were formed in around 1860 to promote interest in swimming through swimming exhibitions. The first game of water football was played in London in 1874. The game, as it developed, and as additional rules were established, became known as water polo, now a popular event in the Olympic Games.

The first modern Olympic Games held in Athens, Greece, in 1896, included swimming. Alfred Hajos of Hungary won the 100-meter free-style event in one minute, twenty-two and two-tenths seconds. Americans became interested in swimming as a sport in about 1900. Charles Daniels was the first American to win an Olympic swimming championship by winning the 220-yard and the 440-yard events in 1904. During the same games E. G. Sheldon of the United States won the diving event in the Olympic Games. Commodore Wilbert Longfellow, a pioneer in water safety in the United States, started the Life Saving Service of the American Red Cross in 1914.

---

*B.S. and M.A., University of Iowa, Iowa City. Mr. Allen, an All-American in swimming and honorable mention in football while in college, has been coaching swimming for thirty years, the last fifteen as the varsity swimming coach at The University of Iowa. He is a past president of the College Swimming Coach's Association and for sixteen years has served as a member of the executive committee of the Swimming Clinic that this Association holds each year in Fort Lauderdale, Florida. The students in his classes consider him to be a master teacher of swimming. His devotion to this sport is in part evidenced by the fact that he is a co-editor of the book, Swimming and Diving, C. V. Mosby, St. Louis, which is in its sixth edition.

After World War I, public beaches and pools were built throughout the country. Swimming facilities were erected in the colleges and high schools and swimming was added to the physical education curriculum. After World War II, swimming continued to gain in popularity both as a recreational activity and as a competitive sport. This was accompanied by a large increase in swimming pool construction; motel operators built swimming pools as a service to their guests; and having one's own pool in the back yard became a prestige symbol. During the past few years the increased amount of leisure time available to Americans has resulted in the increased use of natural water facilities. Boating, fishing, water skiing, sailing, and scuba and skin diving have increased in popularity. But in order to participate safely in the many recreational aspects of water activity available today, it is extremely important to know how to swim—and in order for this participation to be of maximum enjoyment, one must be past the beginning swimming level.

VALUES DERIVED FROM SWIMMING

Participation in swimming is not limited by sex, age, or level of skill; it can be enjoyed by the whole family. Perhaps the greatest value derived from the ability to swim well is the knowledge that one can participate in a vast number of aquatic activities with confidence and safety. Swimming makes a large contribution to the physical fitness of the participant, for the activity is such that most of the muscles of the body are brought into play. Moreover, there is very little chance of injury such as is incurred in contact sports. To many handicapped people swimming has proven to be a highly stimulating therapeutic exercise. Competitive swimmers that follow a well-planned conditioning program enjoy the esthetic value of a symmetrical, well-muscled body.

WATER SAFETY RULES

1. Everyone should be able to swim with sufficient skill and endurance to survive in deep water should an unforeseen emergency occur.
2. For maximum security swim in a supervised swimming area in which a lifeguard is on duty.
3. Never swim alone, regardless of swimming ability.
4. Lake swimmers may find themselves in an area filled with weeds. If momentarily ensnarled by weeds *do not panic* and do not use rapid movements, which tend to cause the weeds to wrap more tightly around the struggling swimmer. Instead, relax, go into a float position, and slowly remove the weeds from the legs and arms.
5. Avoid swimming during electrical storms.
6. Avoid swimming in areas that are known to have undertows (a current that flows beneath the surface away from the shore). If caught in an undertow do not panic; do swim the breast stroke in the direction of the flow and diagonally toward the surface.
7. A strong flexion or extension movement may result in a muscular cramp. The most common cramp in swimming occurs in the calf of the leg and in the foot. If a cramp occurs, do not panic. Instead, take a breath and assume a ball-type float position. If the cramp is in the calf, reach down with the hands and pull the foot and toes up toward the knee—keep the foot in this upward position while using the arms to get to the shore or side of the pool.
8. Understand the safety rules before engaging in such aquatic sports as skin diving, scuba diving, water skiing, sailing, canoeing, and boating.
9. Avoid swimming in close proximity to the area where diving boards are located.
10. When diving be familiar with the depth of the water and the possibility of any foreign objects beneath the water surface. The arms and hands should be extended to protect the head in all head-first dives.
11. Nonswimmers should not depend on inflated objects to support them in deep water.
12. Everyone should be familiar with safe and simple methods of assisting another swimmer in distress. The extending of a pole, plank, branch, or similar device, or the throwing of a ring buoy, rope, or floating object involves the rescuer in no personal danger.

WATER ORIENTATION

The nonswimmer entering the water for the first time will experience several new sensations. However, by knowing what to expect prior to entering the water, he can be better prepared to cope with the situation and thus the new sensations will tend to be less frightening. The rapid loss of body heat when in the water may momentarily chill the bather. He will soon learn that if he moves about in the water he will relax and feel more comfortable than if he stands still. When standing chest deep in the water, he may experience difficulty in maintaining his balance. This is a result of an apparent loss of most of his body weight because of the buoyancy of the water lifting his body toward the surface; however, by slowly bouncing up and down and then turning in circles the beginning swimmer learns to control his balance in a matter of minutes. The first time the body is completely submerged, water will enter the outer ears; this may add to the sensation of a loss of balance.

The first attempt to open the eyes while underwater may prove unsuccessful. Reflex action will normally cause the eyes to remain shut during the first or second trial. Nevertheless, it is very unusual for a person not to be able to learn this new skill after three or four attempts. Care should be taken not to rub the eyes after submersion; instead, a slight pressure to the closed eyes with the finger tips, followed by a blinking of the eyes several times, will eliminate any irritation caused by the water. When the beginning swimmer has learned to control his movements and balance and has learned to recover to a standing position, underwater activity will become a pleasant experience and his swimming progress will be rapid.

BASIC WATER SKILLS

The following set of water skills is presented in a logical, progressive series. Practicing them should enable the beginner to relax in the water, to gain confidence in his mastery of the water, and to learn the basic fundamentals of swimming.

Balance Control

Learning to control the balance of the body while in the water is accomplished by bouncing up and down in a circular direction in waist-deep water. This is done with the assistance of a partner, and then alone.

Breath Control

Completely submerge and hold the breath for ten seconds. Repeat this several times with the partner giving support, and then alone.

Swimming 371

Rhythmic Breathing

Inhale through the mouth, lower the face beneath the water surface, and exhale through the mouth. Repeat, but exhale through the nose. Repeat several times, continuously exhaling in the most natural way.

Opening Eyes Underwater

Submerge with the eyes shut, open the eyes slowly, and attempt to identify objects underwater. If reflex action causes the eyes to shut, stay submerged and try again.

Regaining a Standing Position from a Prone Float

From a prone float position (stomach-down position) with the head in the water and the arms extended forward beyond the head, flex the knees and draw them toward the chest. Press downward with both arms, keeping the elbows straight; elevate the head and continue to press it backward as the knees are extended and the feet are planted on the bottom of the pool. The first few attempts should be made with the support of a partner holding the extended hands.

Spread Reach Float

Stand with the feet spread wide. Take a deep breath and bend forward slowly, sliding the hands down to the ankles from a position above the knees. As the hands reach the ankles the feet will lift from the pool bottom. To recover, slide the hands upward toward the knees, lift the back and head, and plant the feet on the pool bottom.

Ball Float

Take a deep breath and lower the head and upper body beneath the water surface. Bring the knees to the chest and wrap the arms around the lower legs—the body will tilt forward while in a tucked position. Recover by releasing the legs and then elevating the back and head and pressing the hands down and back, finally planting the feet on the pool bottom.

Ball Float and Extension

From a ball-float position extend the arms forward and the legs backward in order to assume a prone-float position. Hold the extended position momentarily, then return to the ball float. Recover as before and stand up.

Body Spin

Assume the ball-float position. Release the right arm from holding the legs. Bend the right elbow and reach back in a clockwise movement as far as the right arm will go. Straighten the elbow and pull in a counterclockwise movement to the original position. This action should result in a clockwise spin of the body. Repeat the skill using the left arm to spin in a clockwise direction. Then perform the skill, using both arms and attempting to spin the body in a half spin to the rear.

Prone Float and Glide

Standing in waist-deep water, bend the knees slightly, lowering the head into the water with the arms extended in front as far as possible. Forcefully extend the knees and push the body forward so that it is parallel to the surface of the water. Repeat several times, attempting to glide an increased distance with each trial.

Prone Glide with Leg Kick

Do a prone float and glide and immediately add an alternating up-and-down movement of the legs. The kick is initiated in the hip joint, with only a slight bend of the knee. The toes and feet press downward away from the knee.

Windmill Crawl Drill

As soon as a prone float with a leg kick is started, an alternating straight-arm action is added. The arms resemble two opposite blades of a windmill. The elbow remains straight as one arm presses slowly downward and backward. The hand is lifted high as it comes out of the water and the arm is straight—it is not bent at the elbow joint. Stop when air is needed and regain a standing position.

Regaining a Standing Position from a Back-floating Position

From a back-floating position with the arms extended sideward beyond the head and with the palms facing downward, press the chin downward toward the chest. This action should cause the hips to drop. Compliment this action with a downward pressure on the hips and a rounding of the back. Draw the heels down toward the buttocks and the knees toward the chest. Press the arms downward and then upward in a circular movement. Then place the feet on the bottom of the pool and stand up. A partner should assist during the first few attempts in learning this skill.

Back Float

In waist-deep water bend the knees until the head is at surface level. Lay the back of the head beneath the water surface until the ears are submerged. Extend the arms slowly overhead keeping them underwater. Arch the back and push the feet slowly from the bottom until the body is in a back-floating position. If the legs have a tendency to drop, allow the knees to bend, keeping the thighs up toward the surface of the water. Press the air downward from the chest cavity into the abdomen. Keep the pelvis tilted upward.

Sculling

From a back-float position with the arms positioned at the sides of the body and the palms facing the pool bottom, elevate the little finger side of each hand 40°. Press the arms and hands downward and away from the body until they reach a point approximately fifteen inches away from the hip. Reverse the position of the palms in order that the thumb side of the palm is elevated 40° from the horizontal plane and press the hands downward and toward the body returning to the starting position. The complete cycle of action results in a continuous force being applied downward, which will help to support the upward position of the hips when in the back float.

Back-float Sculling with Leg Kick

From a back-float position, with the ears beneath the water surface and the eyes directed upward, scull with the arms and add an up-and-down alternating kick. Initiate the kick in the hip joint and keep the toes and feet pressed away from the knee. Attempt to kick the water out of the pool on the upbeat, keep the knees beneath the surface at all times, inhale through the mouth, and exhale through the nose.

ELEMENTARY BACKSTROKE

When skill in floating on the back and the ability to regain the feet from a back-float position have been developed, the beginner is ready to learn the elementary backstroke. The balanced, simple timing action of the arms and legs, plus the head position with the face above the water surface make this stroke relatively easy to learn.

Inverted Breast-stroke Kick

Three variations of the inverted breast-stroke kick can be used for the elementary backstroke. One student will find a certain method to be more natural and easier for him to execute than any other, whereas his classmate may prefer a different kicking method.

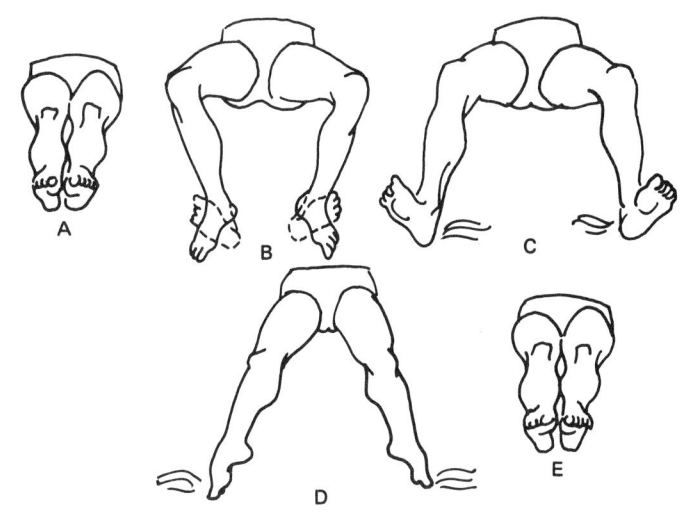

Figure 25-1. Inverted breast stroke wedge, orthodox or frog kick. (a) Glide position. (b) Knees bend laterally. The feet are elevated toward the knees, following the knee bend. (c) Pressure is to the soles of the feet as they press outward in a circular, clockwise manner. (d) The legs are powerfully adducted. (e) Glide position.

Wedge Kick

Recovery. From a back-floating position with the legs extended and joined, the legs are flexed and so drawn sideward that the right knee is facing the right side of the pool and the left knee is facing the left side of the pool. During the flexing of the legs (knees) and outward rotation of the thighs, the lower portion of the legs is relaxed as the feet spread to a distance of approximately twelve inches.

Propulsion. At this point the feet are flexed or elevated toward the knees, followed by an outward circular motion of the lower legs and feet. When the feet reach a position well outside of the knees, the circular action of the feet continues, but the force is now exerted inward. Pressure is felt on the feet as the adductor muscles of the thighs squeeze the legs together to the starting position.

Whip Kick

Recovery. From a back-floating position with the legs extended and joined, the heels are pressed downward toward the bottom of the pool until the lower portion of the legs is at an angle of 90° to the thighs. The feet are turned outward, attempting to have the toes of the right foot facing the right side of the pool and the toes of the left foot facing the left side of the pool. The ankle is so flexed that the sole of the foot is parallel to the bottom of the pool.

Propulsion. The feet describe an outward circular motion as they move outside of the knees and are whipped back to the starting position.

Modified Whip Kick

The kick is identical to the whip kick, except that the knees are permitted to spread to a greater degree during the recovery of the legs.

Swimming 373

A   B   C   D   E

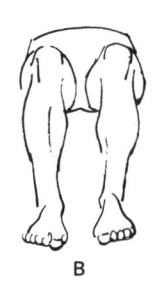

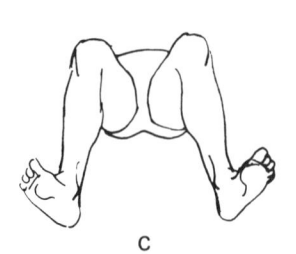

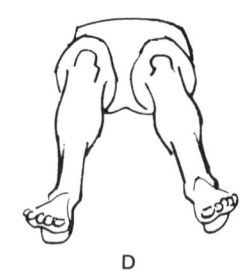

Figure 25-2. Inverted breast stroke whip kick. (a) The glide position. (b) The heels and lower legs are depressed to a point perpendicular to the water surface. (c) The feet have been abducted and are moving outward in a circular manner well outside of the knee position. (d) The feet and legs are adducted forcefully. (e) The glide position.

Arm Action

Recovery. The starting position is a back-float position with the arms resting at the sides of the body. The elbows flex and are drawn sideward to a point just beyond shoulder level. During this action the arms slide outward and are so rotated that the palms are extended. The arms are then so rotated that the little finger faces the pool bottom.

Propulsion. The elbows remain extended and pressure is felt on the palms as the arms squeeze back and toward the body.

Timing

The timing of the elementary backstroke is simple because the arms and legs work in unison. When the knees bend in the recovery of the legs, the elbows bend in the recovery of the arms. As the feet move to a position outside of the knees, the hands move to a point just beyond the shoulders. The propulsive effort is applied by the arms at the same time that it is applied by the legs.

Body Position and Glide

The efficiency of the stroke is dependent on the distance traveled during the glide. Immediately following the propulsive thrust of the arms and legs the body is stretched with the shoulders pressed backward and downward. The head is held in line with the spine, with the ears beneath the water surface and the eyes looking toward the ceiling. The hips are pressed upward. The legs are together with the feet extended in a streamlined position. The arms are extended and pressed to the sides of the body.

Breathing

While swimming, the elementary backstroke breathing is relatively simple because the nose and mouth are above the surface of the water at all times. It is recommended that once during each stroke cycle air be inhaled through the mouth and exhaled through the nose. The inhalation should take place just prior to the recovery of the arms and legs.

Helpful Suggestions

1. Recover the arms and legs slowly—a fast recovery will tend to drop the hip and cause water to be washed over the face.
2. Do not bend the elbow or wrist during the arm pull.
3. Keep the pelvic girdle tilted upward during the glide.
4. Do not hold the breath for several strokes; instead, breathe regularly.
5. Keep the knees and hands beneath the water at all times.

SIDE STROKE

The side stroke was a racing speed stroke in the early days of competitive swimming. In the evolution of speed swimming it was succeeded by the overarm side stroke, the trudgen stroke, the trudgen crawl, and finally the modern crawl stroke. The side stroke is a restful stroke and is popular for recreational distance swimming. It is the basis for the cross-chest carry in life saving. The side-stroke

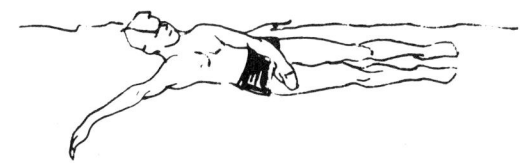

(1) The starting and glide position.

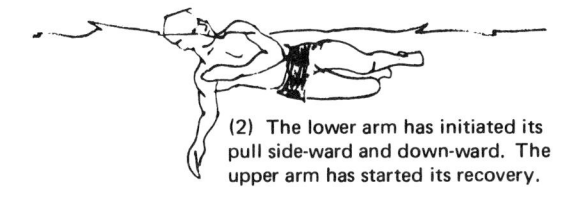

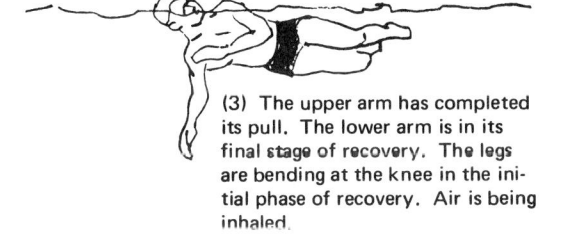

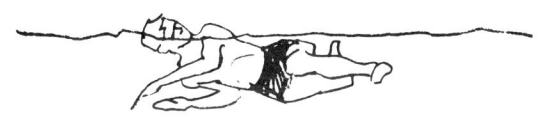

(2) The lower arm has initiated its pull side-ward and down-ward. The upper arm has started its recovery.

(3) The upper arm has completed its pull. The lower arm is in its final stage of recovery. The legs are bending at the knee in the initial phase of recovery. Air is being inhaled.

(4) The lower arm has completed its pull and is in position to be extended forward. The upper arm is positioned for the start of its propulsive phase. The legs are in the final state of their spread.

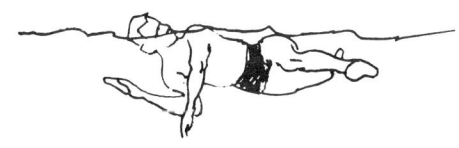

(5) The lower arm is being extended. The upper arm is pulling to the rear as the legs start the powerful squeezing action.

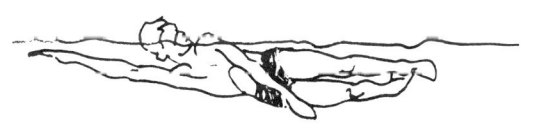

(6) The final stage of the leg kick and upper arm pull.

Figure 25-3. Side Stroke.

kick can be used in treading water as well as for performing several other aquatic skills. During the early learning stages it is beneficial to learn the side-stroke technique on both sides of the body.

Scissors Kick

The side-stroke kick is called the scissors kick because it resembles the action of the blades of a scissors. The starting position is one in which the swimmer is on his side with the legs extended, one directly above the other. The initial movement is to draw the heels backward toward the buttocks as the knees flex and move forward. From an imaginary line drawn down the center length of the body, the top leg continues to move forward until the thigh is at a right angle to the trunk. The lower thigh reaches backward, attempting to reach a position equidistant from the center line. At this stage the top leg from the knee on down continues to move forward, and the foot is fully flexed until it reaches a point just prior to a full extension of the knee. The lower leg from the knee on down continues to move backward and to be equidistant with the foot stretching in an extended position.

Propulsion. As the legs reach a position just prior to a full extension of the knees, the propulsive force of the kick is initiated. After the feet execute a final reaching movement, the extended feet change direction and are forcefully squeezed together.

Arm Action

In the starting position the body is on its side. The lower arm is stretched forward in line with the body, and the palm is facing downward just beneath the surface of the water. The lower arm presses slowly downward until it is perpendicular to the shoulder. The lower arm is recovered by flexing the elbow and drawing the hand upward to a position directly under the head. With the palm down the fingers are then directed forward, and the lower arm is stretched forward to its starting position.

In the starting position the upper arm is straight and is held close to the body with the palm pressed against the front of the top thigh. The elbow flexes as the hand is recovered under the water close to the chest to a point in front of the eyes. During the propulsion phase of the upper-arm action, the palm is forcefully pressed downward and backward toward the feet, coming to rest in the starting position. The elbow extends early in the pull. The pull is parallel to the front of the body.

Timing

The legs and upper arm move coincidentally with each other and in opposition to the underarm. The stroke is initiated with the pull of the lower arm and the simultaneous recovery of the legs and upper arm. Then, as the underarm extends toward the glide position, the legs and upper arm propel the body forward. Each stroke is followed by a glide. As the swimmer becomes skilled in the

Swimming 375

side stroke, the timing described here is changed. The legs and upper arm delay their action until the lower arm reaches a point in its pull where it is perpendicular to the shoulder.

The Glide. The propulsive power of the strong scissors kick combined with the pull and push action of the upper arm moves the body through the water with considerable speed. The streamlined position of the body, with the lower arm extended and the upper arm held in front of the top thigh, is held until the forward movement of the body has almost stopped.

Breathing

Air should be exchanged during each stroke cycle. This is done by inhaling during the downward press of the lower arm and exhaling toward the end of the glide. The head position, with the face always above the water, simplifies the breathing techniques used in the side stroke.

Helpful Suggestions

1. Do not allow the knee of the lower leg to drop during the recovery of the legs. Do keep the legs in a plane parallel to the surface throughout the kicking action.
2. Do not kick the feet outward in the recovery. Do think of the kick as a bend, reach, and forceful squeeze action.
3. Do not pull the top arm shallow and away from the body, because this action tends to roll the body away from the desired side position.
4. Do not pull the lower arm beyond a point perpendicular to the shoulder. An overpull may result in a bobbing up-and-down movement of the body, which hinders forward progress.
5. The lower arm should be considered as a stabilizer rather than a prime mover. The top arm is the power arm and as such contributes more forward motion to the body than does the lower arm.

BACK-CRAWL STROKE

The back crawl is one of the competitive swimming strokes listed on the Olympic Games program. Records for the back-crawl event date back to 1910. Adolph Kiefer, of Chicago, won the national backstroke championship nine times, and at one time held every listed world's record for the event.

Leg Kick

Because of its similarity to the front-crawl kick, the leg action of the back-crawl stroke is often referred to as the inverted crawl kick or the inverted flutter kick. The body is on its back in an extended position with the hips up. The leg movement is initiated in the hip joint and consists of an alternating up-and-down action. The six-beat kick is most widely used—three beats of the legs to each arm stroke or six beats for each complete arm cycle. The feet are extended and the toes are pointed downward away from the knee throughout the kicking cycle. As the leg starts its downward movement the knee is extended and pressure should be felt on the sole of the foot. The knee flexes as the lower leg continues downward. Immediately before the point where the foot reaches its deepest position in the water, the thigh (upper leg) initiates the upward movement followed by the upward whip of the lower leg. The action is similar to the action involved in cracking a whip. The knees and feet remain below the surface at all times. However (when executed properly) the strong upbeat will tend to throw water above the surface, giving the illusion that the foot emerges above the surface of the water.

Arm Stroke

The arm stroke utilized in the back-crawl stroke can be described as an alternating arm stroke in which the emphasis is placed on an opposition rhythm. The arms can be compared with the top and bottom blades of a windmill. As they rotate, one blade is always in an opposite position to the other. The application of this principle to the arms results in a propulsive force being applied by one arm or the other at any given time. When one arm is pulling, the other arm is recovering.

The arm is recovered by lifting the shoulder, while keeping the entire arm extended, the wrist relaxed, and the palm facing downward. The arm swings upward and slightly away from the body and continues to the point of entry approximately six inches outside of the shoulder line and above it. The arm does not pause prior to the entry but goes directly into the water.

Straight-arm Pull. The straight-arm pull is recommended when learning the backstroke. As the hand enters the water it presses downward to a depth of four to six inches below the surface. The palm faces toward the feet as the arm pulls from the shoulder, similar to an oar of a racing scull. When the hand reaches a point directly opposite the shoulder, a very slight bend in the elbow occurs during the transition from the pull to the push phase of the arm stroke. The palm rotates to a downward position during the final pushing thrust of the arm action.

376 *Individual and Team Sports*

Bent-arm Pull (Figure 25-4). The bent-arm (elbow) pull action is favored by most competitive swimmers. Bending the elbow shortens the lever arm, thus requiring less force to move the arm and permitting a faster turnover of the arms. The initial entry is the same as for the straight-arm pull. However, just after the start of the pull, the elbow is bent or flexed sharply and dropped to a point perpendicular to the body. The degree of bend varies with the individual swimmer. The bending of the arm at the elbow joint permits a whipping action of the forearm and hand. The stroking action is similar to the action involved in throwing a baseball down toward the feet.

Timing

Attempting to time the position of the feet with the position of the arms tends to add to the confusion in learning the back-crawl stroke. The important factor is to maintain a balance between the action of the arms and the legs. Many students have had success by counting 1-2-3 during one arm's propulsive action and 4-5-6 during the other. Each count is synchronized with a beat of the leg kick, thus resulting in a six-beat kick for a complete arm cycle.

Body Position

During the back-crawl stroke the body is extended on its back. The head is in line with the spine, with the ears beneath the water surface. The body is stretched from head to toes, which presses the hips upward. The rotation of the body along its longitudinal axis compliments the high recovery of the shoulders and arms. However, a lateral (side-to-side) swaying of the hips, which is normally caused by overreaching with the arms, should be avoided.

Breathing

Because the face is above the water, breathing while swimming the backstroke is not difficult. However, to avoid building up an oxygen debt, the backstroker should strive to inhale and exhale during each stroke cycle. Many teachers of swimming advocate inhaling through the mouth and exhaling through the nose, contending that should a wave pass over the swimmer's face any potential discomfort would be eliminated. Other swimming teachers teach mouth breathing only because of the possibility that exhalation through the nose could be a contributing factor in sinus infections.

(1) The right arm is entering the water as the left arm starts its recovery. The lifting action is initiated in the shoulder.

(2) The shoulders roll to accomodate the arm recovery. The right arm has initiated its pull.

(3) The right arm has completed its pull and is starting its push action. The left arm shows the high vertical recovery.

(4) The left arm is entering the water, palm downward. The right shoulder has lifted for the recovery.

(5) The left arm is completing the pull phase as the right arm rotates for the entry.

(6) The left arm is pushing. The right arm is beginning its downward drive in the entry.

Figure 25-4. Backstroke.

Helpful Suggestions

1. When swimming the backstroke avoid assuming a sitting position in the water. Keep the back of the head and ears under the water and the hips up.
2. Do not allow the elbow to bend during the arm recovery. This action often results in pushing the upper part of the arm through the water (and thus creating added resistance), rather than lifting it above the water surface.
3. Initiate the arm recovery in the shoulder, not the hand. A quick lifting of the hand will tend to throw water into the face. Do not recover the arm across the center of the body for the same reason.
4. The pull is shallow and the fingers should face the side of the pool, not the bottom. Avoid a deep pull. Use the arms to move the body backward, not to lift it.
5. Remember that the whole leg, including the thigh, is involved in the kick, not just the lower leg from the knee down. Keep the knees under the water at all times.

BREAST STROKE

The breast stroke was the first stroke to be used in competitive swimming and is still being used at all competitive levels. It is a basic stroke in survival swimming, and it is used in life saving. Women and older swimmers enjoy swimming the breast stroke because it is relaxing when executed properly; the head can be maintained above the water surface constantly if desired.

Leg Kick

The three methods of kicking the legs when swimming the breast stroke are the wedge kick, the whip kick, and the modified whip kick. These were described in their inverted form earlier in the chapter in the section concerning the elementary backstroke. See page 373.

Arm Stroke

The swimmer starts from a prone-float position with his arms extended forward and near each other. The palms are facing downward and are so rotated inward that the thumbs are facing downward. The initial movement of the arms is laterally downward and backward to a position just in front of the shoulders and underneath them. The hands are then brought together under the chest and extended forward to the glide position.

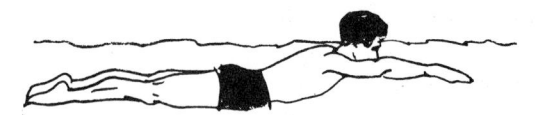

(1) The starting glide position.

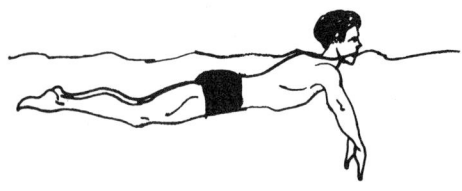

(2) The arms have completed the pull. Air is being inhaled.

(3) The arms and legs have started the recovery action.

(4) The arms are positioned for their forward thrust.

(5) The feet are turned outward initiating the powerful kick action. Arms are reaching the final stage of recovery.

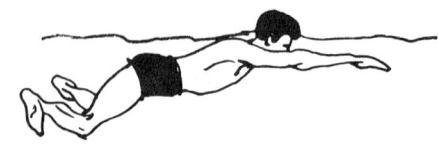

(6) The legs are half way through the propulsive phase.

Figure 25-5. Breast stroke.

Timing

From the starting glide position, execute the arm pull while the legs remain extended and streamlined. When the elbows bend at the start of the arm recovery, bend the knees and recover the legs. As the legs drive together in their propulsive phase, simultaneously extend the arms forward to the starting position.

378 *Individual and Team Sports*

Body Position and Glide

When swimming a long distance, or for relaxed recreational swimming, a long glide is recommended. In a breast-stroke race, the glide is almost eliminated, as the competitor strives to maintain a constant velocity rather than a stop-and-go type of stroke. The ideal body position is one in which the body is as close to being parallel to the water surface as possible. The hips are held high, but not to the extent that the heels break the water surface during their recovery.

Breathing

In learning the breast stroke it is well to inhale through the mouth during the propulsive phase of the arm action. The head is elevated and the chin moved forward at the very start of the arm pull. The head is lowered as the arms extend in their recovery. Buoyant swimmers can exhale through the mouth following inhalation. Nonbuoyant swimmers are advised to hold their breath during the glide and exhale quickly and forcefully immediately before the arm pull begins. One breath is taken with each stroke cycle; however, in a race one breath can be taken on each stroke, every second stroke, or every third stroke, depending on the distance of the race.

Helpful Suggestions

1. Do not pull the arms beyond (below) the shoulders. The recovery from an overpull causes the body to sink, resulting in another long overpull in order to regain the surface.
2. Attempt to lift only the head to inhale rather than elevate the whole body above the surface.
3. During the glide press the forward part of the body forward and downward in order to help elevate the hips.
4. Do not pull with the arms as soon as they are fully extended. If necessary, hold the hands together to insure a coast or glide.
5. Care should be taken to avoid dropping one knee during the kick recovery. Dropping the knee results in a scissor kick, which is illegal in the breast-stroke event.

FRONT-CRAWL STROKE

The front-crawl stroke is the fastest swimming stroke yet devised; it is often called the freestyle stroke in competitive swimming. There are variations of the crawl stroke such as the Japanese crawl, the Australian crawl, the American crawl, and the drag-kick crawl. Basically they all employ the alternating out-of-the-water recovery of the arms. Variations occur in the number of kicks per arm cycle, the recovery of the arms, and the technique of the arm action.

Leg Kick

A two-beat, four-beat, six-beat, or eight-beat kick can be used in swimming the crawl stroke. However, the six-beat kick—one complete arm cycle to six kicks of the legs—is by far the most widely used. In learning the correct kicking action, the first attempts should be made with the legs (knees) straight and the toes and feet extended—pointed away from the knees—and with the legs moving up and down from the hips. To fully utilize the potential of the leg kick, the knees must bend in order to achieve a whip-like action of the feet. The knee bend occurs toward the end of the upstroke of the leg, during which the foot and lower leg continue their movement upward as the knee drops and the upper part of the leg (thigh) initiates the downward drive. The lower leg and foot belatedly follow the upper leg downward, resulting in the whipping action. Similarly, the upper part of the leg will start its upward move before the foot has reached its lowest point. The vertical spread between the feet at their widest point is from eighteen to twenty-six inches.

Arm Stroke

The alternating arm action involves the recovery of one arm above the surface of the water while the other arm first pulls and then pushes beneath the water surface. The hand enters the water directly in line with its shoulder. The elbow is slightly bent in order to allow the hand to precede the elbow in entering the water. Once the hand is in the water, the arm is completely straightened while the hand, with the palm facing downward, presses forward and downward. The arm then pulls downward and backward to a point below the chin where the pulling action ends and the pushing action begins. Prior to the transition from the pull to the push, the arm bends at the elbow, giving the arm the appearance of a boomerang as it continues to push backward toward the feet.

Recovery. At the end of the push the elbow bends as it is lifted high out of the water. The forearm is relaxed as it pivots about the elbow in an outward circular movement to the entry into the water.

Body Position

During the learning process the freestyle swimmer has the tendency to press downward on his arms and hands in

(1) The right hand is about to enter the water short of a full arm extension. The elbow is high and the palm is facing downward.

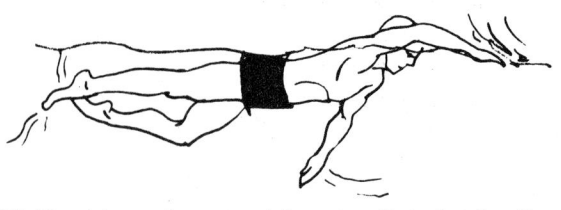

(2) The right arm has entered the water. Note that the elbow is higher than the wrist, and the wrist is higher than the finger tips.

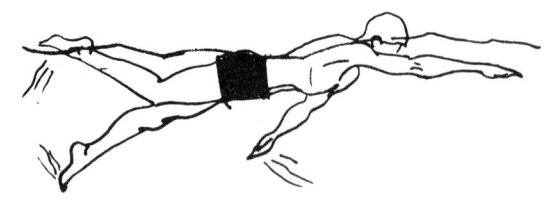

(3) The right arm is executing the *support* which assists in maintaining proper body position.

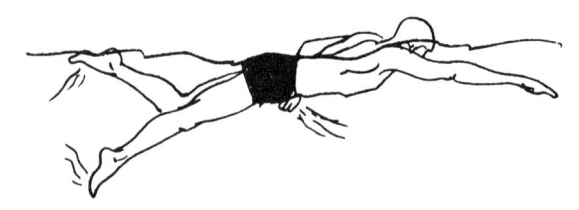

(4) The right hand has started the *catch*, the beginning of the pull.

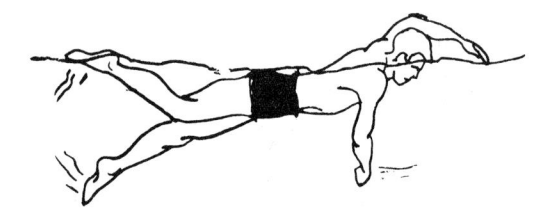

(5) The right arm has completed the pull and is starting the pushing action. The elbow is bent with the forearm almost parallel to the water surface.

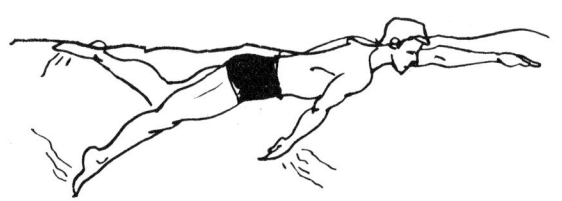

(6) The right arm and hand are pushing backward and outward.

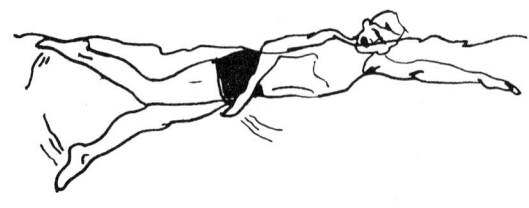

(7) Breath is taken during the release of the right arm.

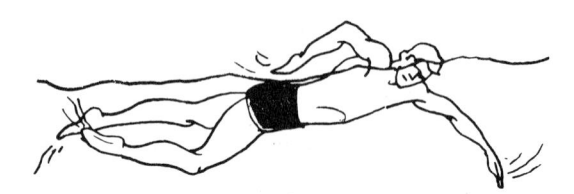

(8) The right arm is initiating the recovery action. The lower arm will swing forward and outward in a circular movement.

Figure 25-6. Crawl stroke.

order to lift the upper part of his body and head. This results in a lowering of the hips and legs, which causes increased water resistance, requires an excessive effort, and produces little forward motion. If the swimmer can think of himself as swimming downhill—that is, pressing forward and downward from his waist upward while lifting his hips and legs upward so that his buttocks break the water surface—his body will be in its most streamlined position. He can then use his arms to pull and push himself forward, and at the same time the problem of breathing properly will be reduced.

Breathing

When swimming the crawl stroke the face is in the water except when the head is turned to the left (or right) to inhale air. The head is positioned in the water with the chin comfortably extended forward from the chest. The eyes are beneath the water surface and are looking forward, not downward. Just as the hand of the breathing arm enters the water—the arm opposite to the direction in which the head is turned is called the breathing arm—the head turns away from the breathing arm. As the head turns sideward the chin should maintain its position below the forehead;

the chin should not be elevated; it remains lower than the forehead. Air is quickly taken in through the mouth, and the head returns to its forward position as the arm opposite the breathing arm recovers. Just after inhalation, exhale through the mouth so that air is exchanged during each arm-stroke cycle. During the learning process many swimmers tend to overinhale and then fail to exhale soon enough, creating breathing problems. The daily practice of breathing exercises while bobbing should help the student to overcome this difficulty.

Helpful Suggestions

1. Before attempting to breathe properly, learn the correct body position for the front-crawl stroke while using only the arms and legs.
2. Use the whole leg in kicking; do not kick only from the knee on down.
3. Make certain that the hand enters the water before the elbow. Keep the elbow high during the arm recovery.
4. Allow the water to support the body and use the arms to propel the body forward, not to elevate the head and shoulders.
5. Relax and attempt to achieve a slow rhythm. Do not overkick.

THE DOLPHIN BUTTERFLY STROKE

The dolphin butterfly stroke was created in 1935 at the University of Iowa by Coach David A. Armbruster, who was assisted by one of his swimmers, Jack Sieg. The stroke is the newest competitive swimming stroke, and it is second in speed to the front-crawl stroke. It utilizes a simultaneous out-of-water recovery of the arms, which is combined with a fishtail kick.

Leg Kick

The dolphin fishtail kick is the fastest leg kick in swimming in terms of propelling the swimmer through the water. The action is identical to that described for one leg of the crawl-stroke kick (page 379), except that the legs move up and down as a unit—rather than alternate in opposition to each other.

Arm Stroke

The arms start the stroke from the point of entry, in which the hands enter the water in front of and slightly outside the shoulders. The hands briefly press outward and downward and then inward and downward, which is followed by a strong backward push. The pattern that the hands follow is similar to the shape of an old-fashioned keyhole ( ). At the end of the underwater propulsive phase, the completely extended arms are lifted from the water and are thrown forward, traveling parallel to the water surface. During the recovery the thumbs lead the hands and arms to the point of entry.

Timing

The legs kick down as the arms enter the water. During the pull of the arms the legs whip up. The powerful push of the arm is accompanied by a strong downkick of the legs. As the arms recover above the water surface the legs complete the second upbeat, resulting in two upbeats and downbeats of the legs to each arm cycle.

Body Position

When learning the dolphin butterfly stroke the wiggle should be mastered before attempting the whole stroke. The wiggle is an exaggerated, undulating kicking movement that is initiated in the shoulder girdle. As the swimmer becomes skilled in the wiggle, the movement of the arms is added to the stroke, and the movement of the shoulders is minimized while emphasis is placed on the action of the legs. The ideal body position is one that is as parallel to the water surface as possible, while permitting the arms and legs to work with maximum efficiency.

Breathing

Air is inhaled through the mouth during the end of the push action of the arms. The exhalation will normally start with the beginning of the arm pull.

Helpful Suggestions

1. The most common error in technique in swimming the dolphin butterfly stroke is to use the arms to lift the body up for air early in the arm pull. Instead, the arm should move the body forward, and the intake of air should be delayed until the end of the propulsive action of the arms.
2. Avoid kicking the legs down and pausing; instead, kick down and then immediately up in order to achieve a whip action of the legs and feet.
3. During the entry the elbows should not be allowed to drop and thus enter the water before the hands.
4. The hands should push until the arms are completely extended to the rear. A common error is to recover the arms too soon.
5. As the arms enter the water the hips should press upward toward the water surface.

Swimming

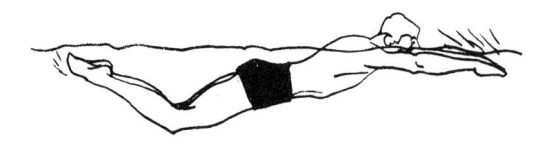

(1) The arms have entered the water and the legs are about to kick down.

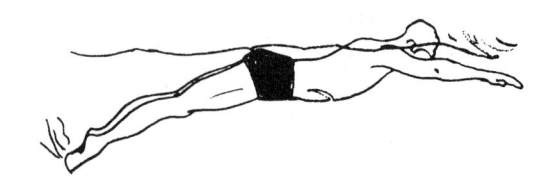

(2) The arms are in the support phase; the legs have completed the down beat.

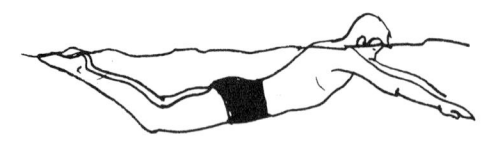

(3) The arms are pulling outward and downward. The legs are finishing the up beat.

(4) The hands are pressing downward and inward in preparation for the powerful push action.

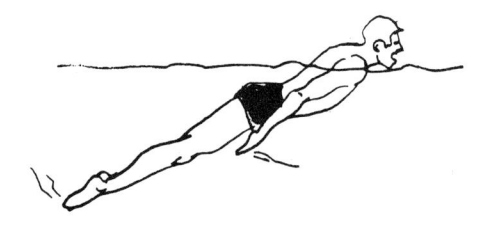

(5) The completion of the arm push and leg down kick. Air is inhaled at this point.

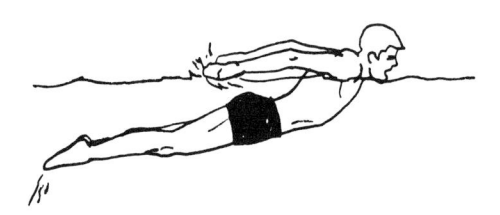

(6) The recovery of the arms.

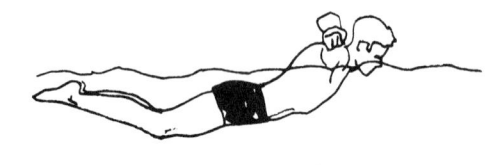

(7) The recovery of the arms.

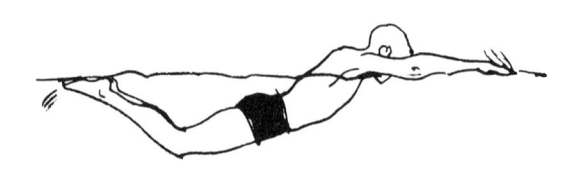

(8) The recovery of the arms.

Figure 25-7. Dolphin butterfly stroke.

References

American National Red Cross. *Swimming and Water Safety*. Washington, D. C., 1968.
Armbruster, David A., Robert H. Allen, and Hobert S. Billingsley. *Swimming and Diving*. St. Louis, Mo.: Mosby, 1973.
Barr, A. R., B. F. Grady, and John (Bud) Higgins. *Swimming and Diving*. Annapolis, Md.: U. S. Naval Institute, 1950.
Gabrielsen, Alexander M., Betty Spears, and B. S. Gabrielsen. *Aquatics Handbook*. Englewood Cliffs, N. J.: Prentice-Hall.
Kiputh, Robert J., and Harry M. Burke. *Basic Swimming*. New Haven, Conn.: Yale.
Mann, Matthew, and Charles C. Fries. *Swimming Fundamentals*. Englewood Cliffs, N. J.: Prentice-Hall, 1949.
Smith, Ann Avery. *Skillful Swimming*. Ann Arbor, Mich.: J. W. Edwards, 1954.
Torney, John A. *Swimming*. New York: McGraw-Hill, 1950.

CHAPTER 26

Table tennis
*Jay McGrew**
Luther College

HISTORY

The origin of table tennis is obscure, although it is believed to have originated in the early 1880s as a miniature version of tennis, in England. Hollow, banjolike rackets, rectangular millboard rackets, and rubber and cork balls were used during the first few years of the game.

In 1890, an Englishman, James Gibb, first introduced the lively celluloid ball, permitting increased control of it by the player, and from 1899 to 1904, table tennis enjoyed a wave of popularity in the English-speaking nations. The simplicity of the game, which was limited by inferior equipment and a lack of standardized rules, soon caused its popularity to wane. In 1902, E. C. Goode, of London, introduced the rubber-faced racket, permitting an increased variety of strokes and spins to be placed on the ball.

The International Table Tennis Federation was formed in Berlin, in 1926, at which time it sponsored the first world tournament in London and adopted uniform rules and standardized implements of play. This organization created widespread interest in table tennis. Interest in table tennis in the United States increased rapidly again in the mid-1920s. The American Ping Pong Association was formed in 1930 under the encouragement of the Parker Brothers of Salem, Massachusetts, who had earlier patented the name *ping pong* and were the only manufacturers of official ping pong equipment in America. Other manufacturers, who called their products table tennis equipment, sponsored the formation of the United States Table Tennis Association, which was the name adopted in 1934 when the two associations merged.

GENERAL DESCRIPTION OF THE GAME

Two (singles) or four (doubles) players can play table tennis. The player who initiates the play is called the server and the player who receives the serve is called the receiver or striker-out. To begin play, the server so strikes the ball with his racket that it lands first on his side of the net. The receiver, in turn, strikes the ball with his racket after the ball has bounced once on his side of the table. The two players endeavor to keep the ball in play until one or the other fails to make a valid return (a ball that crosses over the net and lands on the opponent's side). A point is scored by the opponent when a player fails to make a legal (good) return (or service).

DESCRIPTION OF EQUIPMENT AND ITS CARE

Table

The standard table tennis table is nine feet long and five feet wide, with the playing surface located thirty inches from the floor. A white line one-eighth to one-fourth of an inch runs lengthwise down the center of the playing surface and divides the table into two halves. This line is used officially only in doubles play, but it is helpful in locating the neutral playing position in singles play.

---

*B.A., University of Northern Iowa, Cedar Falls; M.A., University of Iowa, Iowa City. Jay McGrew has long excelled as a table tennis player and instructor. Among his titles are those of State of Iowa and University of Iowa Singles and Doubles Champion and Winner of the Des Moines, Iowa, Open Table Tennis Tournament; the Quad Cities Open; and the Peoria, Illinois, Open. His classes in table tennis at Central High School, Davenport, Iowa, at the University of Iowa, and Luther College, Decorah, Iowa, have always been popular and several of his students have entered table tennis tournament play because of his encouragement and coaching. Mr. McGrew is presently the faculty advisor to the table tennis club at Luther College.

Table Tennis

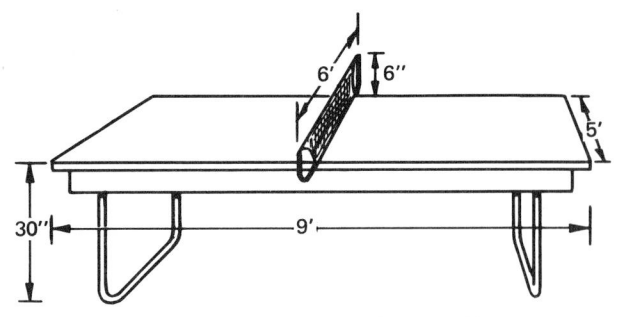

Figure 26-1. Dimensions of tennis table.

Extreme care should be taken to avoid striking the table with the racket, because the resulting holes and dents on the playing surface will cause the table tennis ball to bounce in an unpredictable direction.

Ball

Table tennis balls approved by the United States Table Tennis Association or the International Table Tennis Federation are of superior quality. Extreme care should be taken to check that the ball is round. A test of roundness is to spin the ball on a flat surface; if the ball wobbles the slightest bit, it should be discarded. The ball should weigh between thirty-seven and forty-one grains, and it should be between four and one-half and four and three-fourths inches in circumference.

Net and Posts

The total length of the net is six feet, which consists of five feet for table width and a six-inch extension on each side of the table. The posts are six and three-quarter inches high; the net is suspended by a cord that is connected to the posts exactly six inches above the table top.

Racket

An official racket can be of any size, shape, or weight, but it can be covered only by two different materials: (1) ordinary pimpled rubber with the pimples turned outward or (2) a layer of cellular (sponge) rubber surface turned either inward or outward. A sponge racket with the pimpled rubber turned inward is called an inverted sponge and is generally the racket most used by experienced players. The beginning student, however, is advised to purchase a racket of ordinary pimpled rubber, because this type of racket facilitates increased control of the ball on all strokes. The sponge racket is quite lively, causing the ball to react to it with increased speed and spin. This may seem to be an advantage, but the beginning player is often not able to control the ball under such fast conditions. After the player has attained a fair degree of proficiency, he can then profitably experiment with the sponge racket.

Care of the Racket. The playing surface of the racket should be covered when not in use. A racket cover can be purchased; often one is given free with the purchase of a new racket. The playing surface should not be rubbed against a surface that might cause part of the rubber to be torn off, because the condition of the surface affects the flight of the ball. Players who use an inverted sponge racket commonly wipe the surface with a wet towel in order to get the best hold on the ball during the stroke, thus producing the most effective spins possible.

Attire

The wearing of proper clothing can aid the player in playing his best game. Tennis shoes are an absolute necessity; tightly fitting sweat socks should be worn to help prevent blisters, which sometimes result because of the numerous quick stops and starts required in table tennis play. The other clothing should be sufficiently loose that complete freedom of movement is permitted for all shots. In tournament play the players are often required to wear a black or dark-colored shirt in order to help the opponent follow the ball.

BASIC RULES

Singles

Scoring. On each valid serve a point is awarded the player who made the last legal return of the ball. The server serves until 5 points have been scored between the two players. After 5 points the receiver of the serve (striker-out) becomes the server and the server the striker-out, and so on after each 5 points. If the score becomes 20-all, the serve alternates after each point until the game ends. A game is won by the player who first wins 21 points. If the score is 20-all, the winner is the player who first scores two points more than his opponent.

Serving (Figure 26-2). The service must be delivered by the server, who releases the ball without imparting any spin

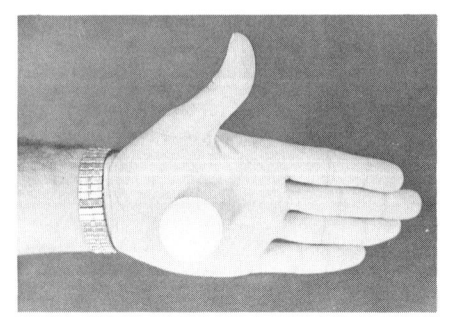

Figure 26-2. Service hand.

384 *Individual and Team Sports*

to it. The server must then so stroke the ball that it first touches the server's court and then, passing directly over the net, touches the striker-out's court. On the service any form of spin imparted to the ball by any agency but the racket is prohibited. The service must be made with the serving hand open and flat, fingers straight and together, and the thumb free. The ball must be *thrown up* by the serving hand before it can be struck. A recent rule change now allows the server to serve the ball outside an imaginary continuation of the side lines of the table, but at the instant that the ball is struck, the serving hand and the racket must be behind the end line of the server's court.

Ball in Play. After a successful serve, the ball must be so struck by one player and then by his opponent that it passes directly over or around the net. The ball must land on the table before it can be struck, and it must be so hit that it next touches the opponent's side of the table.

Doubles

Serving. The service in doubles must be made from the right-hand court of the server to the right-hand court of the striker-out (receiver). The first five services can be delivered by either partner of the pair who has the serve and they can be received by either partner of the opposing pair. The second set of five services is delivered by the striker-out of the first five services and received by the partner of the server of the first five services. The original server's partner delivers the third set of five services, which are received by the partner of the original striker-out. For the fourth set of five services the partners of the server and the striker-out for the second set are in action. The fifth set of five services is delivered as the first five services. The order of service is that after a player serves his five services, he should change places with his partner. However, his opponents remain in the same position with the receiver of the last set of serves becoming the new server. If the score becomes 20-all, the sequence of serving and striking-out is uninterrupted, but each player serves only one service in turn.

Ball in Play. The only difference between doubles and singles play is that in doubles the partners must alternate in hitting the ball.

ETIQUETTE

The following rules of etiquette are generally followed among table tennis players.

1. Before serving, make certain that the opponent is ready to receive.
2. Do not try to upset your opponent by the use of unsportsmanlike conduct.
3. If a player commits an infraction of the rules of which his opponent is unaware, the player should call the infraction at once.
4. If an opponent's stroke is interfered with by a spectator, a player, or a ball from another table, play the point over.
5. Wait until the players on any adjoining tables have completed a point before retrieving a stray ball.
6. Refrain from any abusive language or other unsportsmanlike conduct.
7. If a point is won by a lucky shot, be generous enough to indicate regret with an appropriate remark such as, "Sorry."
8. Do not attempt to distract the opponent's attention in any way.
9. Do not make excuses for defeats.
10. When a spectator at a table tennis match, refrain from making loud noises or moving about during actual play.

FUNDAMENTAL SKILLS AND TECHNIQUES

The instructions given in this chapter for performing the skills and techniques of table tennis are for a right-handed player.

Grip

The western grip has several variations but the basic grip is easy to learn. With his nonplaying hand, the player should hold the racket by its blade and then grasp the handle with his playing hand as if shaking hands with it. In this position the blade rests between the index finger and the thumb of the playing hand. The remaining fingers curl around the handle, securing it in the palm of the hand. The racket now forms an extension of the arm and hand. A firm grip should be taken on the racket; however, the player should avoid gripping it too tightly. If the racket is held firmly, the impact of a hard shot will register through the fingers and will permit control of, and

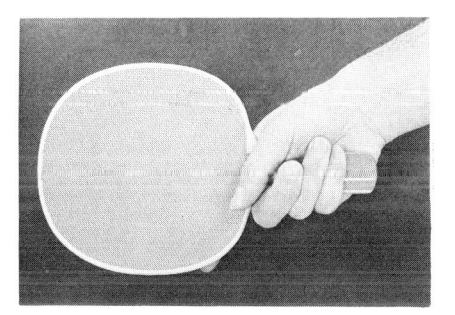

Figure 26-3. Forehand grip.

Table Tennis 385

Figure 26-4. Backhand grip.

Figure 26-6. Forehand position.

precision in, the return. A grip that is too tight, however, hampers the shot perception and touch. The pen-holder grip, which is popular with certain groups of table tennis players, is not recommended for the beginner.

Body Position

One of the most neglected aspects of table tennis, yet probably one of the most important, is that of proper body position. The three positions basically employed in table tennis play are the (1) neutral, (2) forehand, and (3) backhand positions.

Neutral Position (Figure 26-5). To assume the neutral position the player should directly face the table with his legs slightly flexed, his feet spread about eighteen inches apart, and his body in a crouched position. The weight should rest on the balls of the feet. When the ball is in play, the neutral position directly behind the center of the table should be assumed after each return, regardless of the distance that the player retreats behind the table. The player should always start from the neutral position, move into the correct position for a particular shot, and then immediately return to the neutral position. Because the opponent may drive any shot to the left or right side of the table, the player must assume a position that enables him to reach to either side with equal ease.

Forehand Position (Figure 26-6). The forehand position is used when hitting shots from the right of forehand side of the table. To assume this position, the player should move his right foot backward and so turn on his left foot that his body is at about a 45° angle with the table and his left side is facing the table.

Backhand Position (Figure 26-7). The backhand position, which is used to hit shots on the backhand (or left) side of the table is the reverse of the forehand position. Shots directly in front of or to the left of the player should be hit with the backhand side of the racket. The player should assume either a forehand or a backhand position when hitting shots that are to his right or left because the weight should always shift from the back to the front foot (toward the direction of the shot).

Footwork. The correct footwork should be used when moving from shot to shot. When shifting from the neutral position to the forehand or backhand position, the player can either drop one foot back and turn on the heel of his front foot or he can step forward with one foot and turn on the ball of his rear foot. The important point to remember is that the player must not cross his legs while changing position as this causes him to be off-balance and thus increases the difficulty of executing the strokes correctly.

Putting Spin on Ball

The spinning of the ball plays an important role in table tennis play. Every ball hit or received has some spin imparted to it, and this rotary action prevents the ball from rebounding normally and following an arc of normal trajectory. The strokes of table tennis and the spin imparted to the ball are inseparably related. The

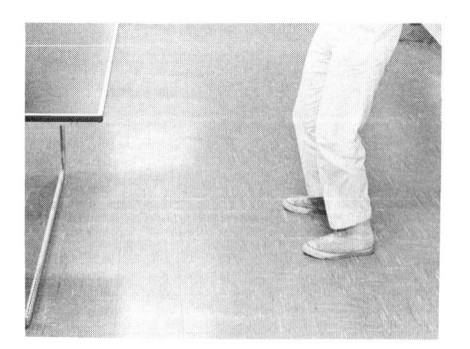

Figure 26-5. Neutral position.

Figure 26-7. Backhand position.

386 *Individual and Team Sports*

three basic kinds of spin are (1) backspin, (2) topspin, and (3) sidespin.

Backspin. When backspin is applied, the ball revolves in a counterclockwise direction as it moves forward. This can be illustrated by placing the ball on the table and pressing down on it behind its top. The ball will spring forward a short distance and then roll backward because of its backspin. When backspin is applied during a stroke, the ball will float through the air with a comparatively straight, flat trajectory, or if hit with sufficient force the ball will rise during its flight. As the ball hits the table top, its forward motion is impeded and it will bounce higher than, but not as far as, it would were it not spinning. A ball with backspin, when struck by a racket, will dive downward toward the hitter's side of the table or into the net if the backspin is not taken into account. The stroke used to impart backspin is the chop stroke, which is discussed later.

Topspin. When topspin is applied, the ball rotates clockwise as it moves forward. This causes the ball to descend or dive sharply onto the opponent's side of the table, and as the ball hits the table it scoots or "takes off." When a ball with topspin is struck with the racket, it will fly into the air and over the net in a high arc unless the topspin is taken into account. The stroke used to impart topspin is the drive, which is discussed later.

Sidespin. When sidespin is applied to the ball, it will rotate from side to side. The direction of rotation depends on whether the ball was stroked from right to left or left to right. A sidespin shot hitting the table will hop either to the right or to the left, depending on the direction in which the ball rotates.

Returning Backspin and Topspin Shots. In order to return backspin and topspin shots successfully the player must know which of the spins the opponent is imparting to the ball. With experience and by watching closely the player will be able to determine which stroke his opponent is using. If the opponent starts his racket high and brings it down and under the ball, he is placing backspin on the ball. If he starts his racket low, comes up and forward with it, and his racket finishes in an overhead position, he is putting topspin on the ball. If the opponent applies backspin, the player should tilt the blade of his racket back and push the ball forward and upward. If the opponent applies topspin, the player should tilt the top of his racket down and not follow through.

Returning Sidespin Shots. Sidespin is mainly imparted to the ball during the serve. In returning such a serve, the beginning player should use only the block or push shot. If the player is receiving the serve, he should tilt his racket and follow through in the direction to the side opposite to the path of the server's stroke. For example, if the server strokes from his left to his right, the player should then aim to the server's left because the path of the server's stroke was to the right. This rule can be applied in returning any ball that has sidespin placed on it. During play the beginner should not attempt to place sidespin on the ball because it is difficult to control the ball and correctly apply sidespin to it. The deliberate placing of sidespin on the ball should be delayed until the player becomes advanced in his skills. An understanding of how to return a ball that has sidespin on it will, however, enhance his ability to cope successfully with such shots.

Serving

In modern table tennis, so many restrictions have been placed on the service that for the advanced player little, if any, advantage accrues from serving rather than receiving the serve. Consequently, the serve should be primarily regarded as a means of safely putting the ball into play, although for nonadvanced players, having the serve is often a distinct advantage.

The five fundamental serves are the (1) forehand chop, (2) backhand chop, (3) forehand topspin, (4) backhand topspin, and (5) sidespin. Except for the sidespin serve, these serves are executed with actions similar to those used in stroking ordinary drives and chops; that is, by bringing the racket either over or under the ball as it is stroked forward.

Forehand and Backhand Topspin Serves. Topspin serves must be kept low in order that the striker-out cannot "kill" them on his return. The racket blade should be kept almost parallel to the table top, and the stroking motion should be in a forward and upward direction. A downward stroking action results in a serve with a high bounce, thus enabling the opponent to make a return kill. On the serve the ball should first hit an area near the server's end of the table, thus lessening the possibility that the ball will go into the net or long. For the forehand topspin serve the player should assume the forehand position and hold his racket with the blade tilted forward and in a position a little below and behind the ball. The ball is then thrown up and, with a sweeping upward motion, the racket should brush behind and above the ball. The ball should be hit when it is approximately waist high. The backhand topspin serve is made with the same motion as is the forehand topspin serve.

Forehand Chop Serve. The forehand chop serve is started from the forehand position. The racket is shoulder high, with the top of the blade directed back at about a 45° angle. The ball should be tossed vertically in the air to about shoulder height. The racket should then be brought forward and downward so that the blade is drawn across and a little below the center of the back of the ball.

This is done when the ball is slightly above table level. The wrist should be relaxed and the racket should pass well underneath the ball in order to give it the necessary backspin.

Backhand Chop Serve. The backhand chop serve is executed in approximately the same way as the forehand chop serve except that the player assumes the backhand position and the racket is started from a position in front of the shoulder of the nonstroking arm. The swing is made across the body and the follow-through is made by extending the forearm at the elbow joint.

Sidespin Serves. A sidespin serve can be made from either a forehand or a backhand position. The racket blade is angled slightly forward and the side stroking action starts sideward toward the center of the body with only a slight forward motion of the racket.

THE STROKES

Defensive Strokes

Defensive strokes are used to keep the ball in play until the opponent makes an error or executes a weak return. The beginner should learn defensive play first, because with a sound defense he can force the opponent to be the aggressor, in which type of play there are additional chances for errors to be made. The three defensive strokes are (1) the block or half-volley stroke, (2) forehand chop stroke, and (3) backhand chop stroke.

Block Stroke (Figure 26-8 and 26-9). The block is the basic defensive stroke; it has many uses and should be learned and perfected as soon as possible. The beginner can use it as a means of becoming acquainted with the game by developing proper timing and the ability to keep his eyes focused on the ball. It is an excellent way of learning how to neutralize spin on the ball, and it helps the beginner to develop accuracy and the "feel" of making a good return. It is particularly useful in maintaining consistency and ball control, which are among the most important aspects of skilled table tennis play.

The block is made by intercepting the ball just after it starts its upward bounce from the table top. The racket is not brought forward to strike the ball because the rebound from a hard drive has sufficient force to carry the blocked ball back across the net. The backhand side of the racket is usually used in executing the block stroke; however, a few champion players also use a forehand block. For the backhand block the right foot is slightly ahead of the left, with the weight equally distributed on both feet. The stroking arm should be bent at the elbow and the wrist should remain firm throughout the blocking action. The player should stand close to the table, holding the blade of the racket parallel with the end line. Because most block shots are made in front of the body, body position is less important for this stroke than for the other strokes.

The block shot can be effectively used to return topspin drives. The top of the blade should be tilted forward for such returns; the racket should be retracted by motion at the elbow and shoulder joints just before it contacts the ball. It is beneficial to grip the racket loosely when returning an extremely hard drive.

Advanced Defensive Strokes. The more advanced defensive strokes are the forehand and backhand chop strokes. When the player plays an opponent who consistently hits the ball hard, the defensive man's reactions are usually not fast enough to move the racket into the correct position for block returns of a series of drives. Instead, when returning hard-hit drives, the ball must sometimes be returned from a considerable distance (ten to twenty-five feet) behind the table. This increased distance gives the player increased time in which to get into the proper defensive position; it also enables him to hit the ball after its speed has diminished. By using a chop stroke, the player can (1) largely counteract the topspin placed on the ball with the drive stroke and (2) put backspin on his return shot, thus creating increased difficulty for his opponent in returning the ball.

Forehand Chop Stroke (Figure 26-10). The forehand chop is executed from a forehand position. The arm should be bent slightly at the elbow, the wrist kept straight, the legs bent, and the weight resting primarily on the right foot. The stroke is started with the racket blade tilted back at about a 45° angle. The forehand chop stroke is made with a forward and downward chopping action that begins at about shoulder height and ends at about knee height. The blade of the racket should be drawn across the ball so that the ball is stroked from below and behind its center. As contact with the ball is made the weight is shifted from the right to the left foot

Figure 26-8. Backhand block.   **Figure 26-9.** Forehand block.

Figure 26-10. Forehand chop.

Figure 26-11. Backhand chop.

and the weight is accompanied by an increase in the flexing of the legs and trunk. The follow-through should be toward the net and in the direction that the player wants the ball to go. The ball should be hit after it has passed the top of its bounce, which is the point at which the speed of the ball has perceptively diminished.

Backhand Chop Stroke (Figure 26-11). Standing in the backhand position, the stroke is started with the racket in front of the left shoulder; the wrist is straight and the arm flexed. The path of the racket is forward and downward; the blade of the racket is at a 45° angle to the table top. The face of the racket should be drawn across the ball, striking it below and behind its center. The arm should stay flexed and close to the body until the follow-through, when the arm is completely straightened and forms a continuous straight line with the blade of the racket, all pointing toward the opponent. The racket should continue on forward while underneath the ball; this follow-through differs from the follow-through action of the forehand chop stroke. The weight transfer, however, is the same as for the forehand chop stroke.

Offensive Strokes

The three offensive or attacking strokes are the (1) push shot, (2) forehand drive, and (3) backhand drive.

Push Shot (Figure 26-12). The push shot is the most elementary offensive stroke. It is executed in the same manner as the block shot except that when the ball is hit a slight push and follow-through action are applied to the ball by the action of the stroking arm. As with all offensive strokes the player should definitely wait for the ball to bounce to its highest point from the table before stroking it. The pushing action, which comes from extending the forearm until the arm is straight, must be applied because the ball has little momentum from the opponent's return. The forearm should swing freely forward with the elbow acting as a hinge joint. The stroking action should be smooth, not jerky. A jerky stroke is frequently caused by overanxiousness, which may result in poor timing.

The beginner should use the push shot to return the backspin shots of his opponent. For such returns the top of the blade should be tilted back and the stroking action

Table Tennis 389

Figure 26-12. Push shot.

directed forward and upward. The stroke should be somewhat more forceful than when returning a ball with little spin on it. The upward stroke gives a lift to the ball, which is necessary to counteract the effect of the backspin on it.

Drive Shot. The drive shot has a twofold purpose: (1) to cause the opponent to err by forcing him to make his return shot with a minimum of time or (2) to give the attacking player a setup, which can be killed, thus earning a point by direct placement.

Forehand Drive Stroke (Figure 26-13). Because extensive use of the body is made in the forehand drive it is a more powerful stroke and is used more than the backhand drive. In executing the forehand drive a forehand position is taken and the body is slightly crouched, bringing the eyes closer to the level of the ball. The stroking arm is bent slightly at the elbow; the racket is fairly close to the body at about waist height. The wrist should be firm and fairly straight, and the blade of the racket should be an extension of the wrist. The degree of racket tilt is dependent on how much backspin the opponent imparts to the ball. As the opponent's shot comes across the net, the weight is shifted to the right foot and the racket is brought back. This is followed by a forward and upward swing of the racket with the follow-through finishing in a position above the forehead. The wrist should not be bent or turned but should remain fairly firm throughout the stroke. The arc of the swing forms somewhat of a flattened half circle, starting about waist high and ending near and above the forehead. At the point of contact the weight shifts from the right to the left foot, giving added power to the shot. The ball should be hit at the highest point of its bounce with the racket rubbing over the back and partly over the top of the ball, imparting maximum topspin to it. The arm remains semiflexed—the arm is never straight when the ball is hit.

Figure 26-13. Forehand drive.

390 *Individual and Team Sports*

Figure 26-14. Backhand drive.

Backhand Drive Stroke (Figure 26-14). The ball is contacted in front of, or slightly to the left of, the body when executing the backhand drive. The proper body position depends on where the ball is contacted. The wrist should be fairly firm but not rigid, and the elbow should be bent. The stroke should be started from a waist-high position with the forearm positioned across the body in a line parallel with the waist. The weight is on the left foot and the stroke starts with a slight backward motion as the opponent's shot comes over the net. The stroking action then swings forward and upward, with the weight shifting to the right foot. At the peak of the bounce, the racket is drawn across the back and slightly over the top of the ball. The follow-through is upward with the racket finishing in a position above the head. The wrist should be turned over at the height of the follow-through, an action that helps impart topspin to the ball.

COMMON ERRORS AND THEIR CORRECTIONS

Block Shot

The most common error in executing the block shot is tilting the top of the blade back. The block shot is used almost exclusively against drive shots (which impart considerable topspin on the ball); consequently, the racket blade must be perpendicular with the table top or even tilted forward, depending on the speed of the drive and the amount of topspin on the ball. Another error in executing the block shot is holding the racket blade too high off the table top. The racket blade must be held close to the table top in order to intercept the ball the instant after its bounce.

Forehand Chop

Several common errors are frequently committed when first attempting the forehand chop stroke. The most common error is hitting across the ball rather than following through toward the net. Returns that are too high indicate that the player is scooping under the ball. The stroke should travel forward and downward, rather than straight forward on a path parallel to the table top. The beginner invariably attempts to get too much of a chopping action at first. Consistency and ball control are much more important than a heavy chop.

Backhand Chop

The main fault in executing the backhand chop is hitting the ball while it is too far in front of the body, causing a jerky, punching type of stroke rather than a smooth stroke. The stroke must be made across the body because it is taken on the left side. If the ball is coming toward the player's midsection, he should, by the use of proper footwork, move quickly to his right.

Push Shot

The most common error in executing the push shot is stroking across the ball, which makes ball control difficult because of the resulting curve produced by the side spin on the ball. The stroke should be made with a straight, forward action that is smoothly performed.

Forehand Drive

Four common errors in the forehand drive shot follow:

1. Swinging the racket too straight forward and not sufficiently upward. (The upward swing should be exaggerated; the swing starts in a forward direction

Table Tennis

but when the ball is contacted, the swing shifts sharply upward.)
2. Rotating the forearm over in order to impart topspin. (Topspin should instead be imparted by the upward motion of the racket.)
3. Prematurely shifting the body weight forward, throwing the player off-balance.
4. Trying to hit the ball too hard before learning the correct mechanics of the swing. (The player should work for consistency, not speed.)

Backhand Drive

Two common errors in the backhand drive are (1) hitting the ball while keeping the wrist straight. (The wrist should be turned over at the top of the stroke, which places topspin on the ball and allows a harder shot.) (2) Turning the wrist over prematurely. (The wrist should be rotated as the stroke is completed, not when it is beginning.)

DRILLS FOR ELEMENTARY TABLE TENNIS SKILLS

The following drills can be used to practice the elementary skills of table tennis. The drills are divided into groups in which the partners can each practice a different skill.

Drills for Developing Push Shots and Chop Shots

1. Standing behind his right-hand court, player A practices forehand chop to the middle of the far side. Player B returns with push shots.
2. Standing behind his left-hand court, player A practices backhand chops to the middle of player B's side, who returns with push shots.
3. Alternating backhand and forehand chops, player A practices chop shots to any portion of the far side of the table. Player B returns with push shots.

Drills for Developing Drives and Blocks

1. Player A practices forehand drives and player B returns with block shots. Player A stands behind his right-hand court and directs all drives to the middle of player B's side of the table.
2. Player A, standing behind his left-hand court, practices backhand drives to the middle of the far side of the table, and player B returns with block shots.
3. By alternating backhand and forehand drives, player A practices drive shots to anywhere on the far side of the table, and player B returns with block shots.

ADVANCED STROKES AND RELATED SKILLS

Drives Against Hard Chops

When a hard chop is used to return the ball, it has a tendency to dive down immediately after it contacts the opponent's racket. In order to lift a hard-chopped ball over the net, the opponent must emphasize the upward motion of his swing, and the racket blade should be perpendicular with the table top rather than tilted forward. Less wrist action is used in the backhand drive than usual because the hand is normally turned over at the top of the swing to help impart topspin.

Ball control is the key to playing against hard chops. The low, heavily chopped ball should not be killed, because it will generally go into the net. The player should patiently return each ball as low as is safe and wait before attempting a kill shot until he has forced his opponent into making a higher return.

Backhand Flick

The backhand flick is a variation of the backhand drive. It is the only shot in table tennis that necessitates the use of considerable wrist action. The backhand flick is used to return balls that have landed so close to the net that there is insufficient time to employ the full motion needed for a drive or chop. Its chief attributes are the quickness with which it is executed and the element of surprise that it offers. In reality the backhand flick is a half-volley shot played as a topspin drive; the ball is not hit at the top of its bounce but as it begins its rise.

The body position from which the backhand flick is executed is the same as that used for the backhand drive, and the entire stroke is made with the forearm and wrist moving very rapidly. As the ball begins its upward bounce, by turning the hand over it is hit with the backhand side of the racket. On the follow-through the palm of the hand is facing upward. The stroke is quickly executed and the swing is short.

Chiseling

Many players needlessly lose points because they do not know how to employ a chop shot to return a chop. This stroke, which is commonly called a chisel stroke, not only serves to keep the opponent off-balance but is invaluable in returning short, low shots that cannot be driven back.

Individual and Team Sports

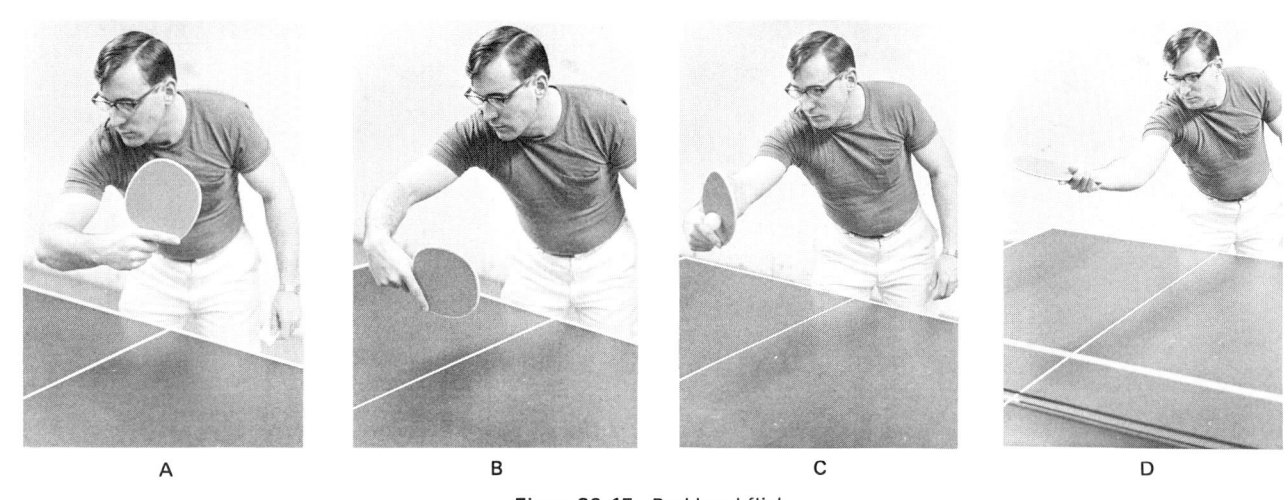

Figure 26-15. Backhand flick.

It is usually impractical to use a push or block shot to return a chop shot because the angle of the racket must continually be changed, which often results in a "sitter" (setup) for the opponent.

The chisel stroke is the same as the regular forehand and backhand chops except that there is no downward motion. The blade of the racket should go completely under the ball so that the stroking action is parallel with the table top. Sometimes it is necessary to stroke up slightly if the opponent has chopped the ball particularly well.

Counterhitting

Counterhitting is returning a topspin drive with a topspin drive. Counterhitting can be successfully employed against a hard, steady driver who has too much speed and accuracy for a player's defense, or against a player who has a particularly poor defense. The element of surprise in the counterdrive may enable a player to gain a point outright, as this sometimes catches an opponent off-balance.

The forehand or backhand can be used for counterhitting. The player should make certain that he is in the correct position and that he does not attempt the shot while off-balance. The normal drive stroke should be used, except that the movement of the stroke and follow-through should be in an almost horizontal direction instead of upward—the ball does not have to be lifted. The blade of the racket should be angled forward and the ball is stroked as it rises from the bounce—the sooner-than-usual timing adds to the element of surprise.

Figure 26-16. Backhand chisel.

Table Tennis 393

A   B   C

Figure 26-17. Chop smash.

Chop Smash

A chop smash is used against a high, short return that contains little backspin. It is usually executed from the forehand side from either a forehand or a neutral position. The ball is hit as it reaches its highest point. The regular forehand chop stroke is used except that the direction of the stroking action is almost all downward—very little of it is forward. The swing originates from the elbow; the wrist action does not come into play until the stroke is nearly completed. Because the backspin applied by the chopping action will cause the ball to soar while in flight the ball should be so hit that it lands fairly short in the opponent's court. The chop smash is a valuable stroke in one's repertoire. The opponent expects a hard smash, but instead the ball approaches him at a slower-than-usual speed, which often catches him off-balance because of the soaring of the ball.

Drop Shot

A drop shot is a short return with a small bounce, which is placed only a few inches on the other side of the net. It is mainly used by the attacker after he has hit a number of hard drives and has the defender far behind the end of the table. The defender expects another drive but instead the attacker barely taps the ball over the net.

The drop shot serves to keep the defender off-balance. An awareness of the attacker's potential drop shot may cause the defender to play too close to the table, giving the attacker a definite advantage. If the defender can get to and return the drop shot, he will many times be off-balance and give the attacker a setup or an opportunity to drive the ball past the defender before he regains his balance. A hard drive coupled with a delicate drop shot is a tremendous offensive combination because the defender must play sufficiently behind the table to return the drives

A   B   C   D

Figure 26-18. Loop.

394   *Individual and Team Sports*

but still be sufficiently close to catch the drop shots in time.

The drop shot is most effective against low, short returns that contain backspin. Because the drop shot may be taken on either the forehand or backhand side, the body position varies. The drop shot is started with the same motion as that used for the normal topspin drive, but instead of hitting the ball the player slides the racket under the ball as soon as possible after it bounces. The blade of the racket should be tilted back and the ball should be slightly scooped. The grip should be relaxed so that the ball will just barely fall over the net. Because the motion of the stroke is suddenly stopped, no follow-through occurs—the player lets the ball hit the racket rather than hitting the ball with the racket.

The Loop

The loop, a relatively new stroke in table tennis, is probably the most difficult stroke to perfect. Because of the extraordinary topspin that is placed on the ball, the loop can be performed effectively only with an inverted sponge racket. A well-executed loop shot is difficult to return and if successfully returned the returned ball usually travels back in a high arc and can be killed easily. Like the drop shot, the loop is used primarily against low, heavily chopped balls; however, the chopped balls returned by the looper land near the end of the table rather than near the net.

The loop is performed on the forehand side of the racket and is very similar to the forehand drive stroke; however, the feet are at a 90° rather than a 45° angle with the table and the player is facing in a direction parallel with the endline of the table. The racket is held about waist high, and as the ball approaches the looper's side of the table he should bring the racket down to knee level with the legs flexing at the knee. The stroke starts with the extended stroking arm bringing the blade of the racket straight upward. When the ball is contacted at about waist height, the arm flexes at the elbow. The follow-through should continue above and to the right of the head. In the loop shot the racket blade is positioned at a 90° angle to the table top (rather than tilted forward as in the forehand drive) and the racket has no forward travel. Contact should be made at the back of the ball so that the ball is barely brushed in the upward sweep of the stroke.

COMMON ERRORS IN ADVANCED STROKES

Drives Against Hard Chops

The most common mistake in driving heavily chopped balls is not getting enough lift in the stroke, that is, not emphasizing the upward part of the stroke. In order to counteract the backspin of the chop the racket must be brought up more vigorously and sooner than against a ball without backspin. A second error in driving hard chops is trying to hit the ball too hard. The low, heavily chopped ball should not be killed because it will usually go into the net. When playing a hard chop the player should patiently return each ball and keep his returns low, waiting until he has forced his opponent into making a high return before attempting a kill shot.

Backhand Flick

Not turning the hand completely over at the time of contact or turning it over after the contact is a common error in the backhand flick. This prevents the ball from dropping, causing it to go off the end of the table. Turning the wrist over before the ball is contacted is an error that causes the ball to go into the net.

Chiseling

A common fault made in counterhitting is stroking in an upward direction instead of a horizontal one. A second common mistake is waiting until the ball has risen to the top of its bounce rather than hitting the ball as it rises from the bounce.

Chop Smash

The chop smash is used against a high, short return. It should not be attempted against balls that land near the end of the table.

Drop Shot

The most common fault in executing the drop shot is the player's "telegraphing" of his intentions. Because surprise is one of the main values of the shot, the player should attempt to mask the shot by waiting until the last instant before attempting it.

Loop

The difficulty of the loop stroke causes many errors to be made by the players who attempt it. These mistakes include

1. Stroking forward, rather than straight up (any forward motion will cause the ball to go long).
2. Tilting the top of the racket blade forward (the blade must remain at a 90° angle throughout the stroke).

3. Contacting the topside of the ball (it must be contacted at its backside in order to obtain maximum topspin).
4. Incorrect body position (the feet should be parallel with the end line).

DRILLS FOR ADVANCED TABLE TENNIS SKILLS

The following drills can be used to practice the various skills and techniques of advanced table tennis. Innumerable variations of these drills can be used profitably.

Drills for Developing Consistency and Ball Control

1. Standing behind his right-hand court, player A practices forehand drives to the right-hand court of player B, who returns with forehand chops.
2. Standing behind his left-hand court, player A practices forehand drives to the left-hand court of player B, who returns with backhand chops.
3. From the left-court position player A practices backhand drives to the left-hand court of player B, who returns with backhand chops.
4. Player A practices backhand drives to the right-hand court of player B, who returns with forehand chops.

Drills for Developing Skill in Mixing Shots

5. Using forehand drives, player A plays his first return to player B's right-hand corner, his second to the left-hand corner, and then to either corner. Player B should attempt to return his shots to player A's forehand side.
6. Repeat drill 5 with player A using his backhand drive and player B returning his shots to the backhand side of player A.
7. Repeat drill 5 except that player A employs both forehand and backhand drives.
8. Player A mixes his forehand and backhand drives with forehand and backhand chops.

Drill for Developing the Backhand Flick

9. Repeat drill 3. Player A returns the appropriate shots with backhand flicks.

Drills for Developing Skill in Chiseling

10. Both players return each other's shots with the forehand chop, and they attempt to place each shot on the opponent's forehand side.
11. Both players return each other's shots with the backhand chop, placing each shot on their opponent's backhand side.

Drill for Counterhitting

12. Repeat drill 1, except that player B occasionally returns a forehand drive with a forehand drive.

Drill for Developing the Chop Smash

13. Player B returns the serve with a high arching shot that lands short on player A's side. Player A responds with the chop smash, using a straight-armed underhand stroke similar to the motion involved in tossing a ball with underhanded motion.

Drill for Developing the Drop Shot

14. Repeat drills 1 and 2 with player A using drop shots.

Drill for Developing the Loop

15. Repeat drill 1. Player A loops the appropriate shot.

PLAYING STRATEGY

The introduction of sponge rackets into table tennis has created a change in tactics. Sponge, especially inverted sponge, makes it possible to produce an increased variety of spins and chopping action. The most significant factor, however, is that inverted sponge has brought about a much faster game and the loop shot, both of which make it extremely advantageous to take the offense. There are now few defensive artists among the top players. The game has changed from a battle of offensive drives against defensive chops to a battle of offensive power with the player having the harder and more consistent drives usually being the winner. Many average tournament players, however, still play a defensive chopping game along with an offensive driving game when the opportunity arises.

Singles

The strategy employed by a singles player should depend mainly on his style of play and that of his opponent. If the player excels at the forehand drive, he will naturally use it at every opportunity, and if his opponent has a specific weakness he will try to direct his shots at that weakness. A good player should have a complete mastery of the different skills and techniques of table tennis play and he should be consistent. A player can indirectly gain points by forcing his opponent into an error and directly gain points by placing a shot out of his opponent's reach. Keeping the ball on the table by skillful ball control is preferable to hitting a beautiful drive that often misses.

Doubles

Doubles play in table tennis is unique in that the partners must alternate shots. Otherwise, the strong player could play all the returns because he could easily cover the entire table. The table tennis player should choose a complimentary partner who basically plays the same type of game. If an offensive player teams with a defensive player, the rhythm of their game will be broken because neither player can play his own type of game. The partners should also have similar temperaments.

A common mistake made by doubles partners is not getting out of their partner's way after playing a shot. The player should not wait to see where the ball that he has stroked is returned, but should step briskly to the side or rear or continue running past his court area after he has returned the ball. The doubles partner should not return to the position from which he started his stroke because this will obscure his partner's view of the ball.

A singles player often relies heavily on his defense to win a match; however, in doubles the team that has the better offense usually has the advantage. The team controlling the drives has few problems in getting out of each other's way—this, however, is a frequent problem for the defensive team, because they do not know where the ball will go until the last instant. The doubles team may gain the offensive by counterdriving, which allows the defender little time to get into position for the return. The counterdrive should be directed at the opponent who last hit the ball because that opponent's partner must now also gain that position. The offense can be gained by driving the service. This is not difficult because the striker-out knows the serve must be made to his right-hand court. The server, in order to avoid this, should keep his serves short and low. Gaining the offense in doubles is a definite advantage if not forced. The player should not smash blindly but should work up his drives and wait for the setup.

Glossary of Terms

Angle shot: A return so angled that it normally bounces from the table top to one side rather than to the end of the table.
Attacking stroke: An aggressive or offensive stroke; usually the drive, smash, or surprise drop shot.
Backhand: A stroke executed with the back of the hand facing the net; the position to the left side of the right-handed player.
Backswing: The preliminary backward movement of the racket to a position from which it is brought forward to stroke the ball.
Bat: The racket.
Blade: The face of the racket or the striking surface.
Block shot: A shot made by placing the racket on or near the table top and returning the ball with a half volley.
Chop: A return made with a forward and downward motion similar to that used in chopping with an axe.
Defensive stroke: The opposite of an attacking stroke, usually a chop or block shot.
Drop shot: A short shot played close to the net.
English: Spin applied to the ball with the racket.
Flick: An attacking backhand shot made primarily with wrist action, usually played against short returns.
Follow-through: That part of the stroke that follows the striking of the ball by the racket.
Foot position: The position of the feet while executing a shot.
Forehand: A stroke made with the palm of the stroking hand facing toward the net.
Half volley: A return played by stroking the ball at the instant that it bounces off the table top.
Let: An obstruction of the ball in some way specified in the rules—a served ball, otherwise good, that touches the net, or a ball that a player is, by accident, prevented from serving or returning.
Net: A fabric six inches high used as a barrier to divide the tennis table into two equal sections; also, a return that goes into the net.
Overspin: The clockwise motion of the ball.
Penholder grip: A method of gripping the racket similar to that used in holding a writing pen.
Ping pong: Another name for table tennis; a name registered by Parker Brothers of Salem, Massachusetts.
Rally: A series of strokes exchanged between players before the point is won.
Rest: A series of repeated or uninterrupted returns.
Setup: A return in such a position that it is easy to score a point.
Sidespin: The rotary motion of the ball from one side to the other.
Sitter: A setup; an easy return.
Slice: An undercut stroke similar to a chop.
Smash: A drive hit as flat as possible for the purpose of scoring a point; an attacking shot.

Spin: A revolving or whirling motion of the ball.
Squaring off: Turning the body squarely into position to hit the ball.
Tennis grip: A method of gripping the racket similar to that used in gripping a tennis racket.
Topspin: Same as overspin.
Underspin: Same as backspin.
Wristed shot: A backhand shot made with considerable wrist action.

Selected References

BOOKS

Carrington, Jack. *Modern Table Tennis.* New York: A. S. Barnes, 1963.

Cartland, Douglas. *Table Tennis Illustrated.* New York: A. S. Barnes, 1953.

Leach, Johnny. *Table Tennis Complete.* New York: A. S. Barnes, 1960.

Miles, Richard. *The Game of Table Tennis.* Philadelphia: Lippincott, 1967.

Rowe, Diana. *Rowe Table Tennis.* London: Stanley Paul, 1965.

Stanley, K. *Table Tennis: New Approach.* London: Nicholas Kaye, 1959.

Varner, Margaret, and J. Rufford Harrison. *Table Tennis.* Dubuque, Iowa: Brown, 1967.

Venner, Harry. *Instructions in Table Tennis.* London: London Museum, 1960.

PERIODICALS

Table Tennis Topics. Newark, Del.: United States Table Tennis Association.

CHAPTER 27

Tennis
*Dave Snyder**
University of Texas

HISTORY

The history of tennis in its early form can be traced back to the pre-Christian era in Greece when players used bare hands to bat a ball against a wall. During the Middle Ages players in England added gloves to their equipment and finally a racket in order to gain an increased reach. The French played a game in A.D. 1300 called Jeu de Paume, which was similar to modern tennis. The name *tennis* was probably derived from a French command, "Tenez," which literally means, "Take it! Play."

Mary Ewing Outerbridge is credited with bringing lawn tennis to the United States. Miss Outerbridge was introduced to the game in 1874 while vacationing in Bermuda. She returned to the United States with the necessary equipment and set up a court on the grounds of the Staten Island Cricket and Baseball Club.

In 1881, differences in the playing rules, ball specifications, net-height regulations, and other matters relating to tennis were settled at a convention in New York. An outgrowth of this convention was the formation of the United States Lawn Tennis Association (USLTA), which presently governs amateur tennis competition. Coinciding with the 1881 convention, the first National Lawn Tennis Championship was held at the Casino in Newport, Rhode Island. The National Championships were moved to the West Side Tennis Club in Forest Hills, Long Island, New York, in 1915, but the Casino continues to host a large grass court championship annually, and it is the site of the Tennis Hall of Fame Museum.

Sixteen different sectional associations in the continental United States combine to make up the USLTA. Each section holds its own championship tourney and ranks players on the basis of their results. In addition to the sectional championships, various open tournaments offer a tennis enthusiast the opportunity to compete against others in his age division.

In 1900, Dwight Davis donated a cup, which bears his name, to be awarded to the winner of an international match between the United States and England. The competition now includes many other nations; thus, the Davis Cup is a symbol of world supremacy in men's tennis. Davis Cup competition is a truly international event in which more than fifty different countries participate yearly. The Australians, under their famous coach Harry Hopman, and the Americans have dominated the Cup competition in the sixties and early seventies, but Italian, Brazilian, Rumanian, and Mexican teams have lately made strong bids to capture the coveted title.

In addition to the Davis Cup competition, many important amateur tournaments are staged internationally. Undoubtedly the most famous international amateur tournament is the All-England Championship in Wimbledon, England; this tourney and the French, Italian, and American Championships comprise the four most important tourneys. Only Don Budge of the United States and Rod Laver of Australia have managed a Grand Slam in tennis by winning all four of these men's singles titles in a single year.

---

*B.S., University of Texas, Austin; M.Ed., University of Arizona, Tucson; Ph.D., The Ohio State University, Columbus. Dave Snyder held national men's tennis rankings in both singles and doubles when active as a participant. He coached at the University of Arizona for twelve years where his teams were in the top ten nationally eight times. Currently, he is tennis coach at the University of Texas. Snyder coached the United States Junior Davis Cup Team in 1962. Twice he has served as chairman of the NCAA Tennis Committee. In 1969, he coached the United States Tennis Team in the World University Games in Turin, Italy. He has been ranked as the number two college tennis coach in the United States.

TENNIS—THE GAME

There are two slightly different games of tennis: singles and doubles. The singles game is a contest between two players on opposite sides of the net on a court 78 feet long and 27 feet wide. (See Figure 27-1.) To begin a point the server stands behind the base line and tosses the ball up, striking it with his racket so that it travels diagonally into his opponent's service court. The receiver attempts to return the ball after the first bounce, and the rally continues back and forth across the net until one person fails to return the ball or to keep the ball within the court boundaries. The server begins serving from the right-hand side of the court but alternates thereafter from side to side until the game is over, at which time he becomes the receiver. After the receiver plays the ball on the first bounce, either player can hit the ball on the fly (a volley) or on the first bounce. The points total up to games, games to sets, and sets to a match.

The doubles game is played by four people, two on each side of the net. Either partner can legally hit the ball during play. In doubles the serve rotates among the members of the teams with each player having a turn every fourth game within a set. Although the doubles court is 4½ feet wider on each side than the singles court, the rules for both are basically the same.

UNIQUE VALUES OF TENNIS

Tennis is a recreational sport that can be played as late in life as one's physical condition allows (King Gustavus of Sweden played until he was in his eighties). The playing of tennis aids in maintaining physical fitness—a vigorous workout requires as little as an hour. A person's size need not prevent his excelling in the game, as attested by the success of two outstanding professionals—"Pancho" Gonzales (6 feet, 4 inches) and Kenny Rosewall (5 feet, six inches). A single opponent or a foursome for doubles is easily acquired; the intensity of the action can vary from a "hit and giggle" social affair to an international Davis Cup match played before twenty thousand spectators. Only the abilities and desires of the participants need dictate the caliber of competition.

Tennis provides an excellent opportunity to meet others in a social or competitive situation. Mixed doubles is always a popular activity for couples who have a common interest in sports. Tennis demands the utmost in sportsmanship, as each player is on his honor to decide whether his opponent's shots land in- or out-of-bounds. The unwritten rule is that on a close call the opponent should receive the benefit of the doubt.

In the past local racket and country clubs were the hubs of tennis activity. Now tennis is no longer considered a rich man's sport, and many of the current champions are the products of park and school instructional programs.

EQUIPMENT

The use of the proper equipment helps assure the prospective tennis player of the opportunity to perform at his best and to make rapid improvement. The basic items of tennis equipment include a well-strung racket, fresh tennis balls, and proper attire.

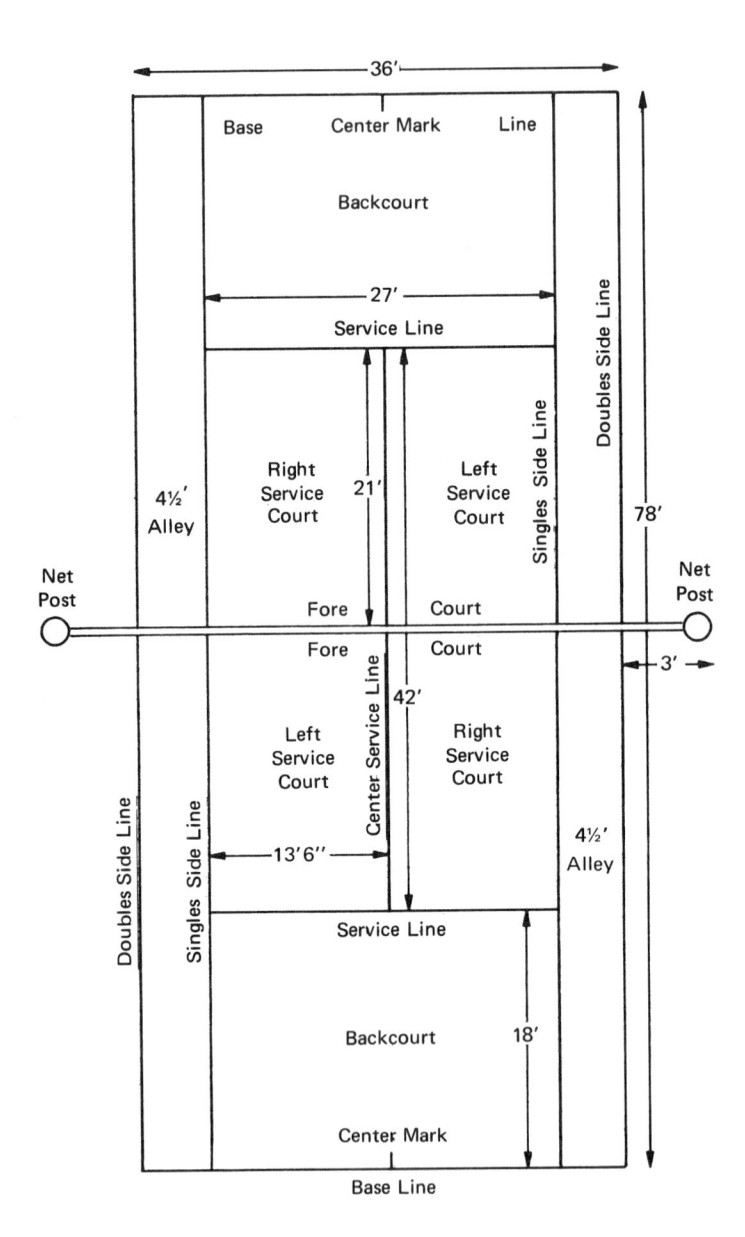

Figure 27-1. Diagram of court.

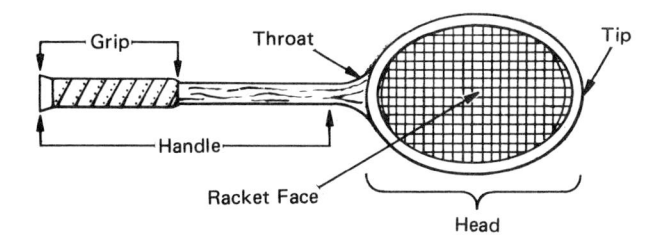

Figure 27-2. Diagram of racket.

Racket

The important parts of a racket are labeled in Figure 27-2. A person's strength and hand size should determine the size and weight of the racket used. The strong individual usually uses a racket of increased weight. A grip of the correct size is one in which the tip of the thumb overlaps the middle finger by a joint's measurement when the racket is gripped. The chart below will assist the reader in selecting a racket of the appropriate size.

Boys and most men	Medium weight (12 1/4–13 3/4 oz.; 4 5/8–4 3/4 in. grip size)
Exceptionally strong men	Heavy weight (14–15 oz.)

A good rule of thumb is to swing several rackets and buy the one that feels best and is evenly balanced. The beginner should probably choose a racket that has nylon strings because nylon is less expensive than gut and is not affected by moisture.

Ball

Tennis balls are made by cementing together two wool-covered, molded rubber cups. The USLTA has weight and bounce specifications that a manufacturer must meet before he can advertise his ball as "USLTA approved." A player should buy an unopened, airtight can of tennis balls to assure himself of fresh balls that will bounce well. Balls not meeting the USLTA standards are referred to as "seconds" and can be bought at a lower price.

Racket Covers and Presses

In those regions of the country where the climate is relatively humid, racket covers and presses are standard tennis equipment. The waterproof cover serves to protect the strings and racket head from moisture; the wooden press, screwed evenly and tightly, prevents the wooden racket from warping. The press and cover can be removed safely before taking the racket to the tennis courts.

Attire

The traditional color of clothing for tennis players is white. Men ordinarily wear a short-sleeved knit shirt and shorts. The shoes are rubber-soled, flat low cuts; the white socks are usually wool or some other highly absorbent material.

Care of Equipment

Observing the following suggestions will help to insure that one's equipment will last a maximum time while retaining its quality.

1. Keep the racket protected by a waterproof cover.
2. Keep the racket in a press between matches in a humid climate. Tighten all screws evenly.
3. Avoid scraping the racket against the court surface whenever possible. A thin strip of tape applied across the top of the racket head will protect it.
4. Do not hit rocks or other sharp objects with the racket strings.
5. Do not open a can of tennis balls until they are to be used. A pronounced hiss of escaping air should be heard when the can is opened. If the hiss does not occur, return the can and balls to the dealer for a free replacement.

RULES OF LAWN TENNIS[1]

Dimensions and Equipment

The dimensions of the singles and doubles tennis court are illustrated in Figure 27-1. The net is three feet high in the center of the court and three feet, six inches at each net post.

Server and Receiver

The opposing players stand on opposite sides of the net; the person putting the ball into play is the server, the other the receiver. The choice of sides and the right to be server or receiver in the first game shall be decided by a spin of the racket or the toss of a coin. The player winning the toss can choose between the two options or require his opponent to choose.

Delivery of Service

The server must make his delivery from behind the base line. He has two service attempts to put the ball into play.

[1] For the latest official rules, consult the "Rules of Lawn Tennis," by the USLTA, 51 East 42nd Street, New York, New York 10017.

Tennis

To make the serve, the ball is tossed in the air and struck with the racket before it hits the ground. Throughout the delivery of the service the server cannot change his position by walking or running, nor can either foot touch the base line or the court inside the base line before his racket contacts the ball. (Such a violation is termed a *foot fault.*)

Faults. The serve is a fault if the server:

1. Commits a foot fault.
2. Misses the ball while attempting to strike it.
3. Does not hit the ball into the proper service court.
4. Hits his doubles partner with the ball.

Lets. (1) A let is a legally served ball that touches the net and then falls into the proper service court. (2) A let is called when play is interrupted because of some interference. The rule demands that when a let occurs on the service, only that one serve can be repeated; however, if it is an interruption in playing a point, the entire point is replayed (two serves allowed).

Loss of Point

A player loses a point if

1. He touches or strikes the ball in play with his racket more than once.
2. He volleys the ball before it passes the net.
3. The ball in play touches him or anything he wears or carries, except his racket while in his hand or hands.
4. He throws his racket at the ball and touches it.
5. He fails to hit the ball before it has bounced twice consecutively on the ground.

Good Returns

It is a good return if

1. The ball lands on the proper boundary line.
2. The ball rebounds off the net and into the proper court.
3. A player contacts the ball on his side of the net but his racket follows through over the net (without touching the net).

When Players Change Sides

Players are required to change sides at the end of the first, third, and each subsequent alternate game of each set.

Order of Service in Doubles

The team that is to serve in the first game of each set decides which partner will serve; the opposing pair similarly decides for the second game. The partner of the player who served in the first game serves in the third; the partner of the player who served in the second game serves in the fourth, and so on in the same order in all subsequent games of a set.

Order of Receiving in Doubles

The order of receiving serves remains the same once a team begins receiving. The pair receiving decides which partner will receive the first serve; that partner continues to receive from that side (forehand or backhand) for the remainder of the set. The receiving or serving order can be changed at the end of a set.

Scoring

Points are designated 15, 30, 40, and game. The score of 40-40 is called deuce, and play continues until one player wins two consecutive points beyond deuce. Scoring after deuce is reached proceeds: advantage server or advantage receiver, depending on which player wins the point. It then returns to deuce, unless the player with the advantage wins the following point and, thus, the game.

The first person to win six games and to be two games ahead of his opponent wins the set. In the event that the player who first wins six games is not two games ahead of his opponent, play continues until one person attains a two-game lead and thus wins the set. Thus, a set score could be 6-0, 6-1–up to 6-4. A five-out-of-nine-point tie-breaker is normally played at 6-6.

In most tournaments the player who wins two out of three sets wins the match, but in Eastern-circuit tournaments or national championships, the semifinal and final victors are usually decided by a three-out-of-five set match.

Tennis Courtesies

1. Cross behind a court only between points.
2. Begin a point with at least two balls in your hand or possession.
3. Wait until the opponent is ready before serving.
4. If a ball lands in the proper court, say nothing; if the ball is out, call "Out."
5. Do not talk while play is in progress.
6. Recognize a good shot by your opponent.
7. Do not return or retrieve first serves that are faults.
8. When a foreign ball enters your court during play, ask to play the point over.
9. Encourage your doubles partner.
10. When others are waiting, do not monopolize the courts. If playing singles, limit play to a set or play doubles with those waiting.

402 Individual and Team Sports

11. Offer to assist and practice with players of less-developed skill.
12. At the conclusion of a match, shake hands with your opponent and thank him for the match.
13. Tennis spectators should applaud good play (never errors) after a point is completed.

FUNDAMENTAL SKILLS AND TECHNIQUES

The first few attempts at trying to stroke a tennis ball over the net may be somewhat frustrating because it is not as easy to do as it looks to be. However, with some practice of the correct stroking techniques, a player will usually find himself hitting the ball over the net with increased regularity.

Ground Strokes

Ordinarily, the student will learn to hit the ground strokes first—the forehand and backhand strokes. For a right-hander the forehand is the shot that is hit on the right side of the body and the backhand is the shot hit on the left side of the body. Because the instruction presented throughout this chapter assumes that the hitter is a right-hander, a left-handed player should remember to reverse the directions. A ground stroke involves hitting a ball after it bounces, usually, but not necessarily, from a position near the base line; the ball should be at about waist height when it is stroked. The ball is usually hit upward with the racket in order to enable it to clear the net and then drop into the court boundaries on the other side of the net.

Racket Grip (Figure 27-3). Learning the proper grip is essential to hitting the forehand well. The three types of forehand grip are the eastern, the western, and the continental. The *eastern forehand grip* is the most popular grip and is the one used by most champion tennis players. It is often described as the "shake-hands grip" because the hand on the handle is in a position that resembles a handshake. The V between the thumb and first finger is on the top level of the racket, the thumb wraps around the handle and touches the middle finger, and the index finger is extended, forming a "trigger finger" slightly up the handle. The entire hand is ordinarily positioned at the bottom of the leather handle, although a beginner may choke up on the handle somewhat while learning the stroke.

Once a student learns the proper grip he can begin to concentrate on the swing, which can be divided into three phases:

1. The backswing.
2. Contact with the ball.
3. The follow-through.

Forehand Swing (Figures 27-4, 27-5, and 27-6). The backswing is begun soon after the player determines to which side of his body the ball is coming. The racket is

Figure 27-4. Forehand backswing.

Figure 27-5. Contact with ball.

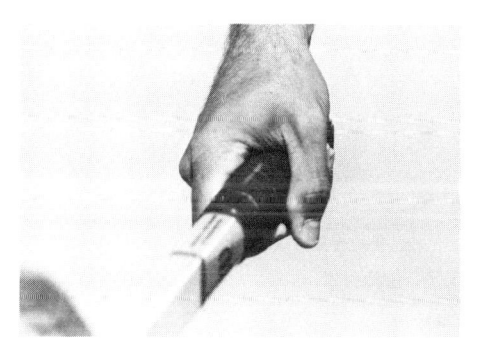

Figure 27-3. Proper grip for forehand.

Figure 27-6. Follow-through.

Tennis 403

taken back to a point behind the body and slightly above waist height. At the end of the backswing, the racket often describes a slight hairpin turn in order to bring it down and under the ball. On the forward swing the racket comes up and forward, contacting the back of the ball thus causing it to rebound forward, up, and over the net. When hitting the ball the arm is completely extended to its full length, but the elbow joint is not locked; the wrist is firm as the ball is met. The follow-through of the racket continues in an upward direction sending the ball in the desired forward and upward direction. As the shot is completed the racket should be at about shoulder height and pointing across the net at about the spot where the shot will land.

Footwork. Proper footwork is the final important segment of the forehand stroke to be mastered. This involves getting to the ball at the correct instant while positioning one's body sideways to the net. The correct body position when hitting the ball is sideways, much like a baseball batter's position when in the batter's box. To get into position for a forehand shot, the right-handed player first pivots on the right foot, then steps forward with the left foot as illustrated in Figure 27-7. The racket goes back as the left foot goes forward and the swing completes the action. A common drill for beginning tennis classes is to practice these movements at the instructor's command (that is, pivot, step, swing). Soon, these phases of the forehand stroke become automatic and the proper reactions are intuitive.

Backhand Stroke. The progression for the backhand is basically the same as for the forehand except that the grip is different and the right-hander pivots on the left foot and steps forward to the right foot. For the backhand grip, as illustrated in Figure 27-8, the hand is turned a quarter of a turn counterclockwise and the knuckle of the index

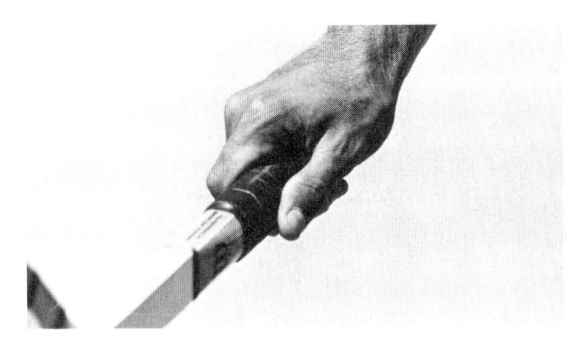

Figure 27-8. Proper grip for backhand.

finger is on top of the handle. This change in hand position is important because it allows the wrist to be behind the racket, thus allowing increased power to be put into the stroke. The thumb acts as a brace if it is positioned diagonally behind the grip. The following actions are important components to remember when learning the backhand stroke:

Grip. The racket is rotated a quarter turn, counterclockwise from the eastern forehand grip.

Swing

Backswing (Figure 27-9). The racket is taken back behind the body at about waist height (help take the racket back with the left hand to get the shoulders turned properly). Hairpin turn the racket at the end of the backswing.

Forward Swing. Pull the racket around to meet the ball when it is slightly in front of the body.

Ball Contact (Figure 27-10). Contact with the ball is made at about waist height, even with (or slightly ahead of) the front foot.

Follow-through (Figure 27-11). The backhand swing finishes with the racket at about shoulder height, pointing across the net.

Footwork. Pivot on the left foot, and with the right foot, step forward in the direction that the ball is to be hit, as illustrated in Figure 27-12.

Positioning for Balls to One Side (Figure 27-13). The next skill that the beginner should learn is to align himself

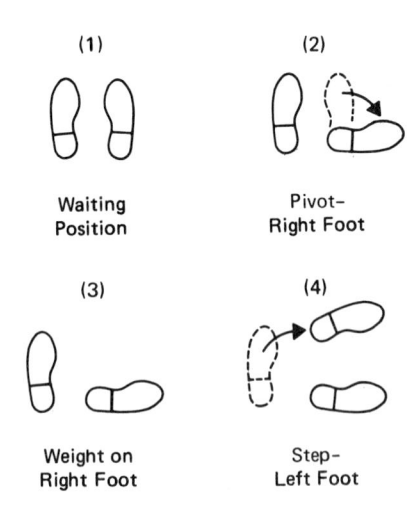

(1) Waiting Position
(2) Pivot- Right Foot
(3) Weight on Right Foot
(4) Step- Left Foot

Figure 27-7. Proper forehand footwork.

Figure 27-9. Backhand backswing.

404 *Individual and Team Sports*

Figure 27-10. Backhand contact.

Figure 27-11. Backhand follow-through.

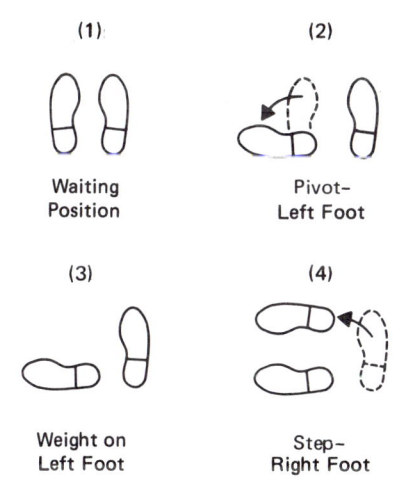

(1) Waiting Position
(2) Pivot–Left Foot
(3) Weight on Left Foot
(4) Step–Right Foot

Figure 27-12. Proper backhand footwork.

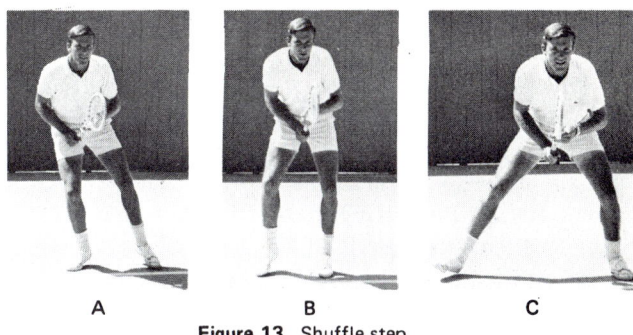

Figure 13. Shuffle step.

properly to stroke a ball that is bouncing to one side or the other. When the ball is just a few feet away, the hitter should make a shuffle or skip step in a sideward direction. This action is similar to the moves made by a defensive basketball player, who is careful not to cross his legs. If the ball cannot be reached with the shuffle step, the player should pivot and break into a run directly toward the ball. This maneuver is so judged and timed that the back foot is an arm's length to one side of the ball. The player steps toward the net with the front foot as the stroking arm begins its forward motion.

Importance of Ground Strokes. The importance of ground strokes cannot be overemphasized because they, along with the serve and volley, constitute the major shots in tennis. In playing a match, many points are a series of ground strokes made from the base line—if the player cannot hit the forehands and backhands consistently and accurately, his chance of winning is diminished considerably. As a player improves, he will hope to do more than just keep the ball in play and will begin hitting the ball away from the opponent, forcing him into an error or making an occasional placement of the ball that the opponent cannot reach in time. A ground stroke that clears the net by about four feet will usually land near the opponent's base line and keep him in a defensive position.

Ground-stroke Drills

The following ground-stroke drills are helpful in practicing both forehand and backhand strokes.

Drop-and-hit Drill. With the left hand, drop a ball and hit it toward a fence, backboard, or across the net.

1. *Beginners:* Line up sideways before the drop and hit drill.
2. *More advanced:* Face the net and add a pivot and step to the hitting action.
3. *Self-testing:* Aim for a target on a fence, wall, or area across the net.

Three- (or four-) man Drop-and-hit Drill

Beginners.

1. The hitter stands sideways at the base line with the racket back, ready to swing.
2. The tosser stands to the side of the hitter and so drops a ball that it bounces up for the hitter to strike.
2. The retriever(s) recovers the balls struck over the net and rolls them back under the net to the tosser. (The net can be held up by S hooks.) After several strokes by the hitter the positions are rotated.

Tennis 405

More Advanced. The hitter faces the net and adds a pivot and step before making the ground stroke.

Still More Advanced. The tosser throws a ball underhand to the waiting hitter. At first the tosser will stand only ten to fifteen feet in front of and slightly to the side of the hitter, but gradually he can move farther away as the hitter increases in proficiency. A ball-tossing machine can feed the hitter if such a machine is available.

Most Advanced. The tosser throws the ball to alternate sides, making the hitter move laterally before stroking.

Self-testing. The hitter will try to get a certain percentage of his shots to clear the net and land in the court, aiming for the back-court area across the net.

Rally. Two players pair up across the net from each other and try to keep hitting the ball over the net.

More Advanced. Allow the ball to take just one bounce and try to keep the ball within the court boundaries.

Service

The service is used to put the ball in play. The overhead arm action resembles that of a pitcher's throw. The three types of serves are the *slice* (used most often), the *American twist,* and the *flat* or *cannonball serve.* Two different motions involved in serving are the tossing or placing of the ball in the air with the left hand and the overarm hitting action with the right hand. These two aspects of the serve must be closely coordinated.

The server lines up behind the base line and slightly to the side of the center hash mark. A right-handed server positions his left foot forward at a 45° angle, with his right foot twelve to fourteen inches behind his left foot, as comfortable. The tennis ball is gripped with the fingertips of his left hand. He tosses the ball up in the air—the height of the toss will depend on his height and reach. The ball should go straight up, slightly in front of the body and left shoulder. The student should practice moving his left hand in a straight upward direction, so releasing the ball that it continues upward when the arm is fully extended.

Half-swing Serve (Figure 27-14). The beginner normally uses a forehand grip when serving, and, will probably experience increased success at first if he serves with the half swing. This action is started with the serving arm bent at the elbow joint and the racket laid back in a cocked position. The racket swings upward to strike the ball at the top of the reach. On the sliced serve the racket should come up and over the upper right side of the ball, causing it to spin forward.

Full-service Swing (Figures 27-15, 27-16, 27-17, 27-18, and 27-19). Once the beginner has mastered the half-swing serve, he should progress to the complete service swing. Using a pendulum motion, the server brings the racket close to the right side of the body; the palm is down until the end of the backswing, at which time the wrist is turned and the racket is rotated to the cocked or "back-scratching" position used in the half swing. The racket then is swung up and forward and meets the ball at the top of the server's reach. After contacting the ball the racket is brought down, finishing on the left side of the left foot. The right leg may swing around and into the court with the serve as the server puts his full body weight into the shot. Timing and rhythm are important in serving; the hitter should attempt to keep the racket moving and thus avoid a break or hitch in the serving action.

Figure 27-14. Serve—half-swing.

Figure 27-15. Service backswing.

Figure 27-16. Service toss.

Figure 27-17. Service cocked position.

Figure 27-18. Service contact with ball.

Figure 27-19. Service follow-through.

Advanced players often rotate their serving grip counterclockwise (from the forehand toward the backhand), keeping the thumb wrapped around the racket. This grip enables increased power to be obtained from the resultant increased range of wrist action.

Service Drills

1. The beginner begins practicing his half-swing by hitting toward a fence or backboard located twenty to thirty feet away from him.

2. An advanced drill is to stand at the base line and serve to the service court across the net, using first the half-swing serve with the forehand grip. In the next stage a full-swing serve with the grip positioned halfway between a forehand and backhand grip is used.

Self-testing. Attempt to place a high percentage of serves into the proper court. A class contest can be held in which the number of serves landing in the proper service court are counted.

A challenge for advanced players is to serve at targets such as towels or tennis cans that are strategically placed in the corners of the service court.

The Volley

The volley shot is from the net position as a rule. Because the volleyer intercepts the ball in flight before it bounces, there is insufficient time for a long backswing; therefore, the volleyer merely "punches" the ball, employing very little backswing or follow-through. The better volleyer slices the high volley—from a position above the ball the racket is brought forward and down through the ball, giving it a slight undercut or backspin.

Grip. Two popular theories exist concerning what constitutes the proper volley grip. (1) The player should change grips at the net, using the same grips (forehand and backhand) as for the groundstrokes. (2) The Australian tennis stars have had marked success, however, with an in-between grip that resembles the continental forehand; consequently, they do not have to switch grips in the fast exchanges at the net.

Stance. The stance at the net should be low with the feet spread wide apart, knees bent, and the body weight forward on the balls of the feet. The racket is held at the throat with the left hand to assure a fast racket motion to the side and improved shoulder position. In this position the player can see the ball well, is best prepared to handle difficult low volleys, and is in the best position mechanically to push off quickly when lateral movement is required. The volleyer's distance from the net is typically six to eight feet. This varies, however, according to the type of shot the opposing groundstroker is hitting, the lobbing ability of his opponent, and the ability of the volleyer to pivot and run back for lobs.

Footwork (Figure 27-20). The footwork for the volleyer is ordinarily the same as that used for ground strokes. In hitting a forehand volley a right-hander pivots on the ball of the right foot, steps forward to the left foot, and then punches the ball with a forward and downward action. The racket goes to the side of the ball as the forward step is made. The action resembles a first baseman's reach for

Tennis 407

Figure 27-20. Forehand volley.

the baseball. As the ball is about to be hit, the volleyer should squeeze the racket tightly, causing the wrist to be firm during the contact. The wrist can break as the ball leaves the strings, however. The racket travels forward only about fourteen to eighteen inches to enable the volleyer to quickly ready himself for continuing action.

Backhand Volley (Figure 27-21). The backhand volley is executed in a similar manner as the forehand volley except that the player contacts the ball on his left side. The footwork for a backhand volley is a pivot with the left foot and a step forward with the right foot as the ball is punched. Here again, from a position above the ball the racket is brought down into the ball in a slicing action.

High and Low Volleys. On shoulder-high volleys the net is cleared with increased ease; hence, once a player gains confidence at the net these higher volleys are turned into kill shots. The low volley is one of the most difficult shots in tennis. The ground stroker usually tries to force it on his volleying opponent. The best advice to follow in hitting a low volley is to bend the knees and so get the racket underneath the ball that it can be hit upward. This low volley cannot be hit forcefully; instead, it should be aimed at the opponent's weakest ground stroke or away from him so that he has to run to retrieve it. Hopefully, the next ball passing over the net will not be as difficult to handle and the volleyer can play a more aggressive shot.

Figure 27-21. Backhand volley.

Anticipation. The ability to anticipate successfully is a knack mastered by the great volleyers in the game. Here, the champion studies his opponent's ground strokes (forehand down the line, forehand cross-court, backhand down the line, and backhand cross-court) and his ability to use each one in different situations. He also studies his opponent's footwork and hitting mannerisms and learns to anticipate where the opponent will hit the potential passing shot before that opponent actually hits the ground stroke. This anticipation allows a player to get a quick start and thus reach more balls than usual.

Volley Drills

Two-man Volley Drill. Probably the simplest volley drill is for a tosser with several balls to make underhand throws to a volleyer across the net. The toss need only be fifteen or twenty feet away. To make it easier, the volleyer can turn sideways to begin with and practice all forehands or all backhands. Later, the volleyer can add a pivot and step as a slow-floating ball comes toward him. The tossers and hitters take turns retrieving balls and throwing to each other.

One Up and One Back. This drill involves one player at the base line ground stroking a ball to his partner just across the net. The ground stroker should feed his partner slow, high shots so that he can gain confidence in his volley. Turns are taken at the net position. Eventually a rally of several shots can be kept going.

Both at the Net. In this drill two advanced volleyers are both stationed at the net (about thirty feet apart). They try to keep the ball rebounding from racket to racket without its touching the court or landing in the net. Because it is difficult to include the proper footwork in this drill, it is suggested that a player be proficient at volleying before attempting it. It is a challenging drill and one that Davis Cuppers use to improve their reactions.

Pepper Drill. This drill resembles the familiar baseball drill. One center man volleys to two or more opposing volleyers. When he makes an error the center volleyer is replaced by the player volleying to him.

The Overhead

The overhead is a vital shot in the game of tennis. It is the answer to the opponent's arching lob when a player is at the net position. The overhead, or smash as it is often called, resembles the serve except that the player must play the ball wherever it happens to be coming down within the court; therefore, the ability to get into the correct position is of great importance.

Proper footwork will enable the player to move to the ball quickly and to arrive in a good ready position. From

Individual and Team Sports

Figure 27-22. Overhead backswing.

Figure 27-23. Overhead follow-through.

the proper net stance facing the net, the player first pivots on the left foot and then steps back with the right foot. He next runs backward, watching the ball over the left shoulder. The run should be in line with the ball and if possible the smasher should get back before the ball arrives, plant his right foot, and step forward toward the net with his left foot while hitting the ball.

Because the overhead will be hit above the head, the contact procedure should resemble that of the serve. Several differences exist, however. A forehand grip is recommended on the overhead because less side spin is needed because of the extended court area that is available as a target. A half swing is easier to coordinate than the full swing and is therefore recommended. While waiting with the racket in the back-scratching, half swing position, point at the ball with the left hand. Meet the ball in front of the body with the stroking arm extended. The body weight should be transferred from the back foot to the front foot as the ball is met. If the smashing form is correct, the hitter is balanced and can quickly run back to his original net position.

At times the lob is a high one that is coming straight down. When this is the case the recommended procedure is to let the ball first bounce and then smash it as it comes down the second time.

The Lob

The lob is a strategy shot employed against the net player. The offensive lob is an arching shot that is intended to barely clear the opponent's outstretched racket as he attempts to run back for his smash. The defensive lob is hit much higher than the offensive lob in order to allow the lobber time to run back into a good court position and hopefully be able to return the oncoming smash. The ideal lob is one hit with top spin; thus, if allowed to bounce it will continue toward the back fence, making it difficult to retrieve. The lob is executed very similarly to the ground stroke, except that the racket must be dropped even farther below the ball on the backswing so that the ball can be hit upward. The more effectively the lobber can disguise his intention by not revealing with his racket movement whether a lob or a drive is forthcoming, the more effective his shots will be.

Drill. A beginner should have the ball tossed to him from the opposite service line. He takes a position just inside the base line and, emphasizing the position of his body under the ball, racket back and ready for the hit, he strokes the ball upward. The height and distance of the lob are increased as the player's skill improves. A simple and effective drill for both lob and overhead shots is for two players to take turns hitting lobs and overheads to each other.

Half Volley

The half volley is not hit in the air as its name indicates but rather is a pick-up shot that is hit just after the ball bounces. It is usually hit from around the service line area as a player approaches the net. The half volley is a difficult shot to execute and should be avoided if possible. The necessity to use it often indicates slowness or laziness on the part of the half volleyer who is caught out of position, although it may be just a case of having to handle an exceptionally fine, low, accurate return from an opponent. The half volley is usually hit with a shortened backswing and follow through; the racket face is tilted slightly forward, and the ball is contacted very soon after it strikes the ground. The player should bend the knees and stay low until after the shot is made. The ball is hit rather softly with the angle of the racket face controlling the trajectory of the ball. The ball should be lifted over the net by means of an upward movement of the racket. Generally, the player will merely try to return the ball as deep as possible.

A player with exceptional ability will, in hitting a half volley, roll the racket over the top portion of the ball. The knees should be bent, legs spread, and the body weight moving forward as the player contacts the ball on the rise. Because the timing and the motion of rolling the wrist over the ball are difficult, the shot is ordinarily played deep to the center or to a corner of the court. The half volley is not intended to be hit for a winner.

Drill. One common drill for practicing the half volley is for two players to stand on or around the service line on each side of the net and take turns hitting half volleys to each other in continuous action if possible. The same practice can be gained by one player hitting low drives from the base line to his half-volleying partner who is positioned back from the net around the service line where half volleys are most often hit.

SAFETY

Safety is not a major concern in tennis as it is in many sports; however, several safety factors should be considered when playing tennis.

The proper preparation for any serious match involves warming up or stretching the muscles. An experienced player will usually do several stretching exercises before taking the court. The rally previous to any match will exercise the muscles involved in the playing of the game and thus serve as a formal warm-up. The serve and overhead stroke involve the same arm and shoulder muscles that a baseball pitcher so carefully warms up. Most tennis players consciously hit several of these shots at less than full speed when beginning their practice serves before a match.

The playing court and surrounding area in which a player may be running should be free of obstructions. Loose sand on a hard court or wet lines on clay courts can cause falls that could injure the knees and ankles. Articles of clothing or racket covers and presses should be left near a net post or against a backstop. In a doubles match inexperienced partners sometimes collide. An understanding of who is to hit shots coming down the middle, calling for lobs when in doubt, and much practice together should eliminate this danger.

COMMON ERRORS AND THEIR CORRECTIONS

Ground-stroking Errors

Improper Foot Position. Improper foot position causes the body to be off-balance when hitting a ground stroke. Two common footwork errors are a failure to pivot sideways (allowing the toes of both feet to point toward the net) and overstepping with the left foot.

Correction. So align the feet that a line drawn from the right toe to the left toe will form a straight line toward

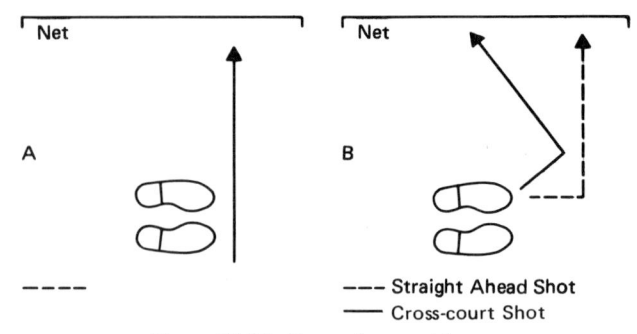

Figure 27-24. Proper foot positions.

the net. (See Figure 27-24A.) To hit the ball cross-court (to the left), meet the ball ahead of the body and the angle of the racket will direct the ball cross-court. A straight or down-the-line shot is not contacted early, but when the ball is about even with the front foot, as illustrated in Figure 27-24B.

Failure to Place the Body Weight into the Ground Stroke. A great deal of power can be gained by getting the body, especially the shoulder and hips, into the ground stroke.

Correction. Go to the ball quickly and get set to hit it. Take the racket back with the left hand—this tends to turn the shoulders into a position from which they are ready to turn with the racket during the forward swing. The weight moves from the back foot to the front foot as the ball is hit. During practice, holding the follow-through allows a player to check his body position.

Hitting the Ball into the Net. If the net is a basket that collects more shots than it should, some adjustment must be made.

Correction. A lower backswing and a higher follow-through on top-spin ground strokes will usually cure this fault. Even the national champions intend to clear the net by two or four feet on most ground strokes. Hitting the ball at the top of its bounce allows the net to be cleared with increased ease and permits the ball to be hit down with increased force. Conversely, if too great a percentage of shots are traveling long (out of the court), the swing should be leveled out and a lower follow-through made. Concentration on keeping the front knee bent can also help correct this fault.

Missing Low Shots. A ball that is contacted close to the ground is a very difficult shot for anyone to hit effectively. However, if a low shot seems to be a player's nemesis, several hints may solve the problem.

Correction. Concentrate on the low ball and watch it even closer than usual. The knees and waist have to be bent in order for a sidearm tennis stroke to be executed. If no bending occurs, an underhand, golflike shot results. Make certain that the front leg is so bent at the knee that on the follow-through the racket does not come up too high and cause the ball to carry long. A player must realize that a low ball cannot ordinarily be hit hard and still remain in the playing court.

Being Out of Position for the Next Ground Stroke. Perhaps the opponent is hitting an exceptional number of placements, but if a player will concentrate on being in the correct court position each time, he should not see nearly so many balls whiz past him before he can swing.

Correction. Upon finishing a shot, immediately move back toward the center of the court. A player's position should bisect the possible angle of his opponent's return.

Failing to Hit the Ball in the Center of the Racket. This frustrating experience is a universal one among tennis players. The feel of some solid hits in the center of the racket will again restore interest in the game.

Correction. Watch the ball. Concentrate the full attention on it. If the opponent is at the net watch the ball even more closely. The previous advice of getting prepared early for the shot applies, but even the old pros have to keep reminding themselves to concentrate and WATCH THE BALL.

Inability to Control Shots on a Windy Day. Playing in the wind is not much fun for anyone. Remember, the opponent is not going to enjoy the wind either unless he is given good reason to relish it.

Correction. First of all, hit the ball harder when hitting into the wind. An experienced player will hit more slice shots if these are in his repertoire because the sliced ball glides longer and supplies added depth that is often needed. Often a player will have increased success if he lobs against the wind. A drop shot is also very effective against the wind. Hitting the ball with the wind can be an advantage if the wind is allowed for and the ball is not hit too hard.

Service Errors

Serving into the Net or Beyond the Service Line. When a series of serves miss the service court and are consistently either long or short, the left hand may be laying the ball up either too far in front of or behind the body.

Correction. If the serves are all hitting the net, try tossing the ball up more directly above the body than in front of it. If the serves are landing beyond the service court, toss the ball in front of the body and hit down on top of the ball.

Inability to Hit a Powerful Serve. A serve does not have to be hard to be successful, but the better players do win many points by hitting a fast-moving serve. A beginner has to start with medium-speed serves initially. However, later, when the service cannot be hit as hard as desired, it is time to study the service motion for possible improvements.

Correction. Try to attain a rhythm in which the speed of the racket continues to increase until the point of contact. The elbow should be sharply bent on the backswing and then, keeping the elbow high, throw the racket at the ball. Attempt to hit the ball at or near the height of the reach.

Looking into the Sun on a Serve. This is a common occurrence in midday matches.

Correction. Try adjusting the stance slightly to the right or left. Experiment until a position is found in which the ball is not tossed directly toward the sun.

Volley Errors

Low Volleys Netted or Hit Too Long. The low volley is the most difficult one for most participants to hit.

Correction. Once a player accepts the fact that he is limited in the speed in which he can hit a low volley and still keep it in court, his next major task is to bend the knees and get the racket down under the ball so that it can be chipped up. A low waiting position at the net prepares a volleyer for a low return by an opponent.

Faulty Footwork at the Net. Two common footwork faults in hitting volleys are not stepping into the ball or stepping back before stepping into the ball.

Correction. If possible, a right-hander steps toward the net with the left foot on the forehand shot and with the right foot on the backhand shot. There is no need or time to step back—merely step forward at the net. If the ball is wide to the side, take a crossover step. If the ball comes so fast that no step can be made, at least try to turn the shoulders previous to blocking the ball, while tightly holding the racket.

What if the ball is hit directly at a player? He should use the backhand volley. The racket can be drawn across the front of the body much more naturally with the backhand than with the forehand, where the arm comes into the body. Even though the first few experiences of seeing a ball heading straight for the midsection are a bit frightening, satisfaction from the eye-hand coordination and the backhand can be achieved and the sense of self-preservation will be there.

STRATEGY

Singles Strategy

Being a sound tennis strategist implies that one has the ability to recognize what tactics will win, together with the courage to follow this correct course of action. The server generally has to decide whether to go to the net and hopefully win with his volleys and overheads or to remain in the backcourt and rely on his ground strokes.

Tennis 411

In the decision to rush the net several important questions must be pondered by the player:

1. Are the volleys and overheads reliable?
2. Will the serve and/or approach shots pave the way for arrival at the net in a good volleying position?
3. What are the passing and lobbing capabilities of the opponent? Can he hit both the forehand and backhand effectively to either side of the court? If not, how can this be capitalized on?
4. Does the court favor the net rusher? A slow court (clay or rough cement) allows the passer to get to high-bouncing balls and hit down, forcing difficult volleys. A fast court (cement, wood) yields more low, sliding bounces that put the base liner at a disadvantage when the player is entrenched at the net.
5. Is sufficient speed possessed to get to the net and take the proper net position?

In deciding to remain on the base line a player must answer these questions:

1. Can the ball be kept in play without too many errors?
2. How do the ground strokes of the two players compare?
3. Can a fair share of points be won through lobbing and passing shots if the opponent comes to the net?
4. Does the court favor the ground stroker? Here again, a court that produces high bounces that slow the speed of the ball usually favors base-line huggers.
5. Will the player's physical condition permit him to excel on the base line? Increased stamina and conditioning are required to play primarily a ground-stroking game, especially if the players are well matched and the opponent stays back and forces long rallies.

An unwritten rule in tennis is to change a losing game and never change a winning game. If the pattern of play is definite and obvious, consider these possibilities. If one is losing by remaining at the base line and relying on ground strokes, the two options are (1) to go to the net and attempt to begin winning with volleys and overheads and (2) to hit more short balls or drop shots that just clear the net, forcing the opponent to come to the net and volley.

If rushing the net is a losing tactic, consider (1) staying back on the base line and attempting to defeat the opponent by trading ground strokes with him or (2) staying on the base line and drawing the opponent to the net in the hope of winning by passing and lobbing.

The decisions are not usually so obvious as the preceding paragraph would indicate, because veteran players can be expected to mix their tactics. With an all-court game a player can change his strategy at will—a strong reason why a beginner should learn and practice all the various tennis shots.

Specific Situations: Singles

In a beginning tennis class the most consistent winner is the person who can keep returning the ball over the net without committing numerous errors. In advanced play and competition for boys and men the ability to hit the various shots without numerous errors remains very important, but these players must add net play and fast drives and serves to their repertoire. Utilizing these advanced tactics of power tennis, the stars make more placements and draw errors from the opposition when they get their favorite shots.

Specific situations occur in a match that call for a particular strategy.

Serving

1. Hit a large percentage of the first serves in the court if possible, even if it means hitting the ball with less speed. The best servers hit around 70 per cent of their first serves in the proper service court.
2. Serve mainly to an opponent's backhand, although he should be "kept honest" by an occasional forehand serve. A serve at the opponent's body is also effective at times.
3. A beginner should not attempt to run to the net as soon as he serves. A player of moderate experience will occasionally run to the net after serving. A very experienced player may do so quite often if the courts are to his liking.
4. The first serve is usually hit with increased speed and, thus, is likely to elicit a weak return from the opponent, which offers the opportunity to make a "put-away shot," especially if the server has run to the net.
5. A server should consider the success an opponent has in returning the various serves (different speeds, spins, directions) hit to him. He should recognize which serves have the best chance of drawing errors and winning points.

Going to the Net

1. A relative beginner will ordinarily remain at the base line after serving. He should run to the net only after his opponent hits an exceptionally short and easy-to-hit shot that can be hit from well inside the base line. If he has learned to volley and has some confidence in these shots, the beginner may decide to charge the net whenever he believes he has a good chance of winning the point.

2. To follow a serve to the net effectively, hit the ball with some spin (rather than flat) in order to have time to take the four or five steps necessary to be in a good volleying position inside the service court. A server can advance toward the net behind a flat serve if he expects an unusually soft, easy-to-put-away return.
3. The approach shot should ordinarily be hit to drive the opponent deep behind his base line.
4. When running to the forecourt, a net rusher should go to the side of the court to which the ball has been hit.
5. A ground stroker making an approach shot from one side of the court has the choice of a straight-ahead, down-the-line shot or an angled cross-court shot. In making this decision he should—all things being equal—hit the ball down the line because it will mean fewer steps for him in gaining his proper net position. (See Figure 27-25.)
6. As illustrated in Figure 27-25, the volleyer positions himself at the net on a line that bisects the possible angles of returns that an opponent may execute. Remember that a cross-court passing shot will have to clear the net several feet inside the sideline if it is going to land in bounds—not all shots that clear the net must be reached.
7. In deciding whether to go to the net, try to make an approach shot with the most effective ground stroke, attempting to hit it to the opponent's weakest ground stroke or to a spot where he will have to run a considerable distance to reach the ball. For a beginner this often means hitting a forehand to an opponent's backhand.
8. In hitting the approach shot, do not expect or attempt to hit an outright winner. The same may be true for the first volley that follows a rather long run to the net. A smart player knows when he has a good chance to put the ball away or to draw errors. He tries to keep his own errors to a minimum.
9. An effective net rusher is usually fast and gets as close to the net as he can without leaving himself wide open for the lob. From a position close to the net he can hit down on an increased percentage of his volleys.

Rallying from the Back Court

1. When both players are exchanging ground strokes from the back court there are three good reasons for hitting the ball cross-court rather than straight down the line. First, the inbounds distance diagonally is longer; therefore, the ball can be hit longer and harder and still land within the boundaries. Secondly, the net is six inches lower in height at the center; thus, the clearance height is lower for the angling cross-court. Thirdly, the ball continues to angle after it bounces, which draws the opponent farther to one side of the court. This results in his being out of position for receiving the next return. (See Figure 27-26.)
2. Because the ball has so far to travel on a ground stroke, a formidable opponent can usually retrieve all but the most exceptional of them. Sound percentage tennis requires that the ground stroker not risk errors trying to make placements when both opponents are back, but rather that he use the ground stroker to draw errors or to move the opponent out of position in order to approach the net with a good chance of winning the point from there.
3. Because the better players are often jockeying for position from the back court with hopes of rushing to the net, there is a definite advantage in driving the ball deep into the opponent's court—if he attempts to approach the net, his run will be a long one.

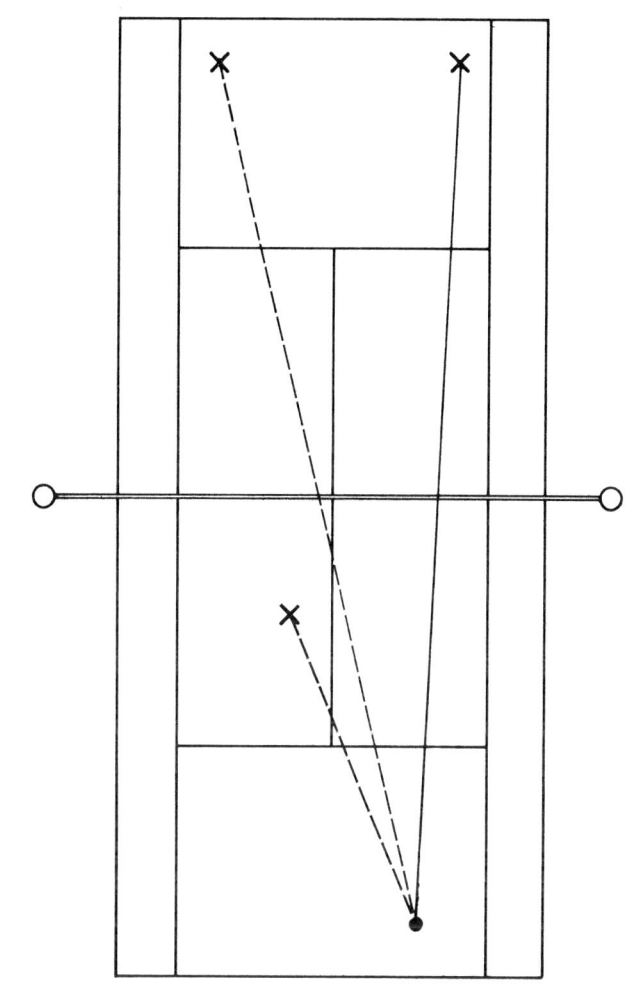

Figure 27-25. Net approach alternatives.

Tennis 413

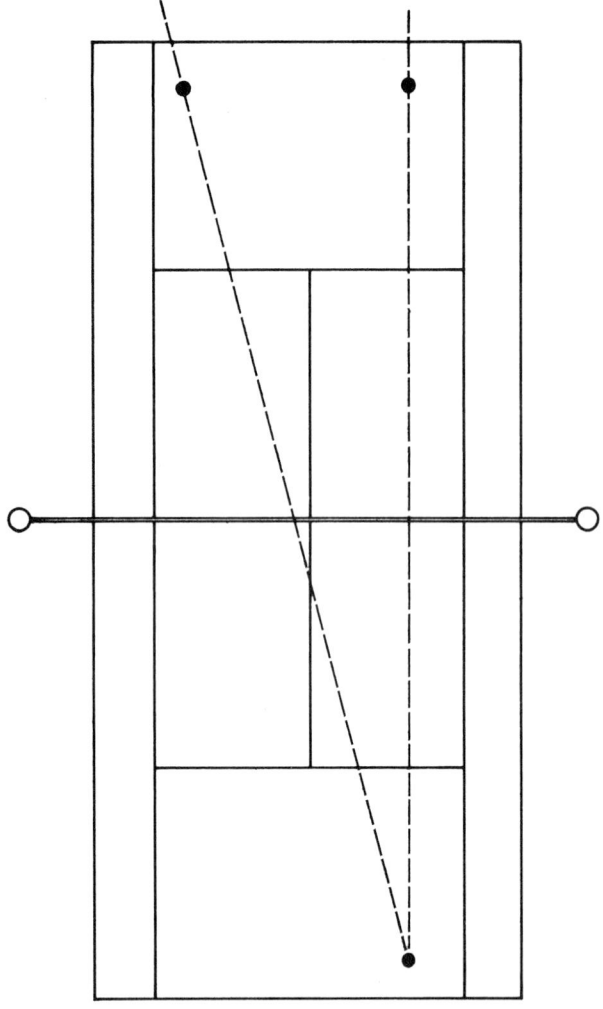

Figure 27-26. Cross-court return advantages.

4. When out of position a player needs increased time to return to the center position just in back of the base line. If the opponent is remaining in the back court an arching cross-court shot is the proper strategy.
5. When an exceptional ground stroke is made or the ball is placed to an opponent's inferior ground stroke, move toward the net a step or two in anticipation of a weak return that can be capitalized on.
6. If a short, weak return is coming, move well into the court to hit down on the ball and to play it aggressively. An approach shot or possible placement should be forthcoming. A ground stroker must be ready to move up and back as well as from side to side in positioning himself to stroke the ball.
7. If an opponent covers up for a weak ground stroke (for example, a backhand) by running around it, then it may be necessary to hit purposely to his strong side in order to pull him off to one side and open up the court for a return play to his weakness.

8. An opponent may hit one shot (for example, a forehand) very hard, but he may be erratic and miss the court quite often with this stroke. A smart player will mentally note the direction and consistency of his opponent's strokes and play his weaknesses accordingly.

Opposing a Net Man

1. If the ball is played from deep in the court, do not expect to pass the opponent outright. Instead, lob or attempt to drive the ball low, so that the opponent has to volley upward.
2. Most passing shots are made from inside the base line. The ground stroker should attempt to run in and hit down on balls landing in midcourt.
3. Attempt to make the volleyer "hit up." Low drives draw errors and put pressure on a net man.
4. The advantages of the cross-court passing shot are that it clears the low part of the net and tends to make the opponent volley toward the passer. The cross-court passing shot should be aimed at the outside corner of the service court, as illustrated in Figure 27-27.
5. The down-the-line passing shot has a shorter distance to travel before passing a net man and is often used when a fast-moving shot cannot be reached by the volleyer. This passing shot can be effective when hit deep in the court as well as when hit into the service court.
6. Lobs are quite effective when the opponent is getting too close to the net. They should be used frequently.
7. Mixing the direction of the passing shots and lobs and paying particular attention to watching the ball rather than the opponent are vital to countering the volleyer successfully.

Returning the Serve

1. Attempt to keep the service return in play. If many returns are missed, the server has no chance to make errors.
2. Attempt to hit downward on high-bouncing serves. An expert player may even hit the ball as it rises.
3. If the opponent does not come to the net after serving, keep the ball in play by returning his serve deep down the middle or to his backhand. Once in a ground-stroke rally, the advantage of the serve is gone and the returnee has an equal opportunity to win the point.
4. If an unusual number of returns are being missed, slightly vary the receiving position up or back. Concentrate on watching the ball, beginning with the time the server contacts it with his racket.

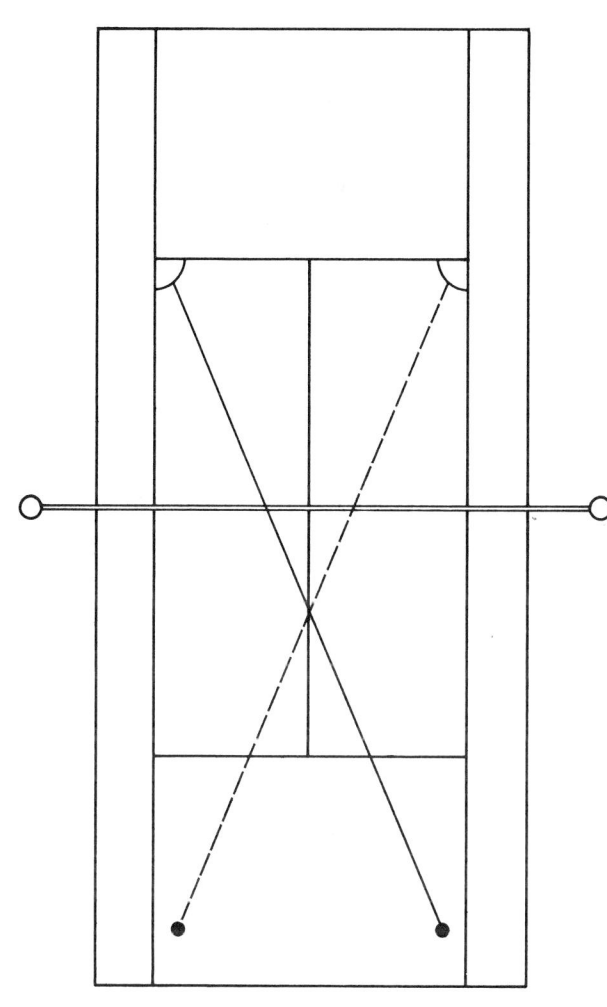

Figure 27-27. Cross-court passing shot.

Doubles Strategy

Because of the enjoyable teamwork involved in doubles play, many tennis enthusiasts prefer doubles to singles. With four players the strategy increases in complexity and thus generates increased interest.

Doubles Service Advice

1. Get the first serve in a majority of the time.
2. Serve to the receiver's backhand most of the time.
3. A doubles team holding the net position has an advantage; consequently, the server will hit a three-quarter speed serve and join his partner at the net. (See Figure 27-28.)
4. The server should get inside the service court from which he will hit the first volley. Unless it is an easy put-away, he should aim the first volley deep down the middle of the opponent's court. (See Figure 27-29.)
5. Once a team is stationed at the net, any high volley should be hit decisively for a winner or to draw an error. This involves angling the volleys cross-court, between opponents, or past the net man. A knowledge of which of the opponents' ground strokes are most subject to error is valuable in order to hit to that weakness.

Receiving Team Tactics

1. Doubles strategy for beginners usually involves the returning side remaining at the base line and hitting low returns or lobs at the opponents, who are at the net.

Figure 27-28. Server joining his doubles partner at net.

Tennis 415

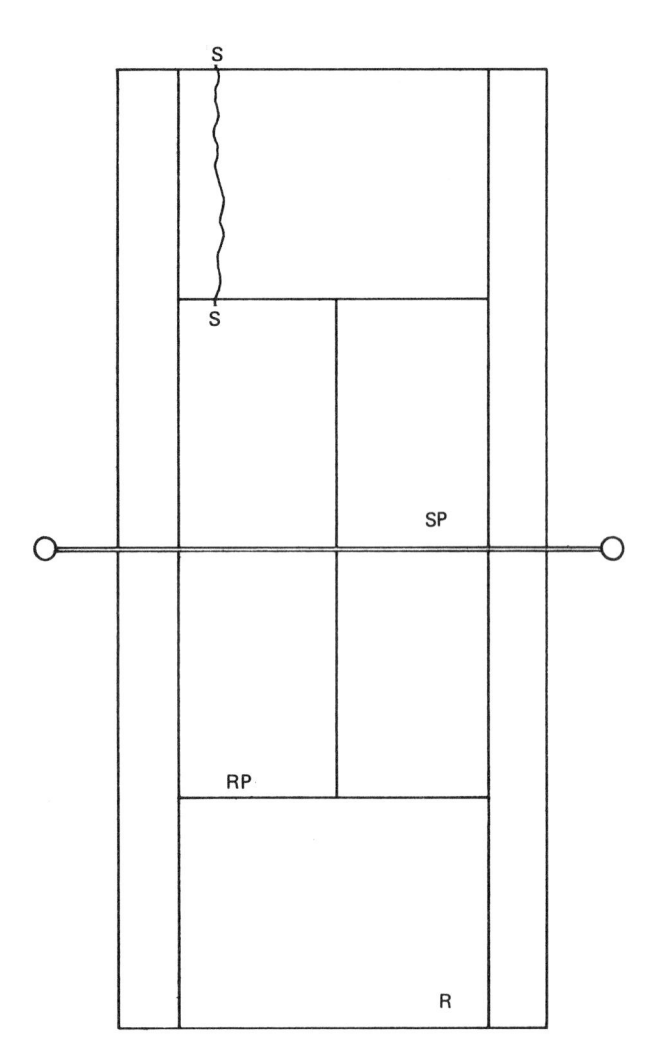

S - Server
R - Receiver
SP - Server's Partner
RP - Receiver's Partner

Figure 27-29. Service strategy diagram.

2. The low drives and lobs should be played at the opponents' weaknesses. If they give up their net positions the receivers should attempt to take over the forecourt position by driving the ball deep and approaching the net while side by side.

Other Doubles Advice

1. When a ball comes down the middle the player with a forehand usually hits it, assuming that right-handed players have paired up.
2. Help cover part of the partner's area if he is drawn out of court while making a return. (See Figure 27-30.)
3. Doubles partners ordinarily play side-by-side except for the service line-up. A continuous one-up-one-back position leaves a wide, vulnerable area down the middle.
4. If a player retrieves a lob that is over his partner's head and is out of reach for him, the partner in turn should cross over and take the other side of the court.

ADVANCED TECHNIQUES OF PARTICIPATION

Singles Techniques

Most advanced male tennis players employ the serve-and-rush-the-net strategy; this strategy is dependent on the server's having a superior serve and volley to gain the advantage for him. The server knows where his service is aimed and what type spin it has on it. An experienced net rusher will win many more games when serving than he will lose. The deciding factor in winning is which player can consistently win his own serve and put together several effective service returns and passing shots in order to break the serve of the opponent. A singles player ideally attempts to hit his strongest shots to the opponent's weakest shots.

DRILLS TO IMPROVE NET-RUSHING TECHNIQUES

Two Against One

The *overload principle* can be incorporated when two players oppose one. The two can either be volleyers while the backcourt man attempts difficult passing shots, or two players in the backcourt can attempt to pass the net man who has two men firing at him.

Aussie Put-away-volley Drill[2]

A drill utilized by the Australian Davis Cup Squad to sharpen their game is to have the net man cover one side of the court and attempt to make winning "put-away volleys" against his opponent, who is covering one-half of the court across the net. Lobs as well as passing shots are used against the net man. If both players struggle to retrieve every ball this drill has great conditioning value. Twenty-five to thirty tennis balls are recommended for use in this drill. The players rotate between the volley and back-court position and to the sides of the court for which they will be aiming.

[2] Roy Emerson, "A Method of Conditioning," *World Tennis*, Vol. 14, No. 7 (Dec., 1966), pp. 60-61.

Figure 27-30. Helping with court coverage when partner is drawn wide.

Coach's Feeding Drill

Using a box of balls a coach or other player can "feed" a player a series of volleys and overheads as fast as he can make his shots. The volleyer should be attentive to using good form. The volleyer should alternate forehand, backhand ground strokes, forehand, backhand volleys, and lobs.

DOUBLES TECHNIQUES

Advanced doubles teams in tennis concentrate their efforts on getting to the net.

Advice for the Server

In championship doubles the server, immediately after serving, almost invariably joins his partner, who is positioned at the net. The first serve should go into the service court a great majority of the time. Once a successful serve is made the server should

1. Run fast and get inside the service court if possible before preparing to make a first volley.
2. Ordinarily hit the first volley back across the net and down the middle of the opponent's court.
3. Volley low returns back to the opponent farthest away from the net. If all four opponents are at the net, hit the low ball softly or at an angle, causing it, after clearing the net, to drop at the opponent's feet. If the opposition in turn hits a high ball, then a put-away shot should be forthcoming.
4. Any high return that is close to the net should be hit hard with the intent of making a placement or forcing an error.

Advice for the Receiver

In championship doubles play, the receiver's partner stands inside the service court on his side while the receiver attempts a low cross-court return of the serve, which is directed at the oncoming server. Upon returning the serve, he dashes to the net. Good doubles teams vary the speed and angle of their returns plus confusing the opposition with lobs in their attempt to break the serve.

Other Doubles Advice

1. The partners usually decide which side each will play according to their ability to return serves from a particular side. They often prefer their weakest ground stroke to be in the middle of the court where their partner can help take some of the shots. The partner with the best overhead should play on the left side of the court because this person (right-handed) is in the best position to hit lobs down the middle of the court.
2. The person with the forehand shot usually hits the ball down the middle—unless one partner is definitely closer to the net, in which case he usually hits the volley.
3. Experienced doubles teams try to help each other by shouting "Out" if an opponent's ball is going out of court, and "Mine" if they believe they are in the best position to hit a lob down the middle. They help each other in court coverage if one is pulled wide to a side or a lob gets over their partner's head before he can hit it.

Tennis 417

DRILLS TO IMPROVE DOUBLES TECHNIQUES

Serve, Return, First-volley Drill

Simulating a doubles situation with a server and returner, the server serves and runs for the net. The returner angles a cross-court shot as both converge from opposite sides of the net. The server can volley from close range at the net while two new players come in to repeat the action.

Two, Three, or Four Volleying at the Net

In this drill either two, three, or four practice volleys from inside the service court.

Converging Drill

Both players stand at the base line, one hits the ball straight up the middle of the court and both immediately converge at the net. This drill emphasizes (1) moving toward the net as the ball leaves the racket and (2) keeping the ball so low to the opponent that he will have to volley upward.

TRAINING METHODS

Beginners usually train in organized group drills aimed at giving progression to the learning experience. The student, by choking up on the racket or hitting with a shorty racket, can at first progress with increased speed. Swinging, footwork, and hitting drills help the student simplify the rather difficult task of hitting the ball over the net.

The serious player will attempt to improve his various strokes through drills, rallies, and practice sets. The drills presented earlier are excellent for this purpose. When rallying, the participants try to keep the ball in play without the pressure of trying to win. It is important, however, to hustle, to watch, and to hit the ball as in a match situation when rallying.

Practice sets simulate somewhat the match situation except that the concentration should be focused on hitting the shots properly—winning is not the objective. In practice sets one can purposely expose some of his weaknesses in order to get increased practice in hitting the shots found to be most difficult.

Physical conditioning is an important aspect of the preparation for playing serious tennis. The exercises listed subsequently are often used by better players to prepare for strenuous matches.

Sit-ups.
Kangaroo jumps (jump high, tucking knees to try to touch chin).
Squeezing a rubber ball.
Rope skipping.
Tattoo running (run in place as fast as possible in ten-second bursts; rest ten seconds; repeat).
Swing a racket with a press on it.
Volley a ball against a backboard (try it with a racket cover on the racket head).
Side skipping (back and forth on signal).
Sprints and long-distance running.

SELF-EVALUATION

The primary objectives in playing tennis are enjoyment, exercise, and the challenge of competing against others. During the initial learning stages, especially, it is encouraging to measure one's progress and, if possible, diagnose the shots that need additional practice. Several individual tests can aid in this diagnosis:

1. Bounce the ball on the floor, using the forehand grip—try for fifty or one hundred consecutive bounces.
2. Bounce the ball in the air with the racket—try for fifty or one hundred bounces without the ball touching the ground.
3. Dribble the ball (basketball style) twenty yards and back.
4. Bounce and hit the ball from the base line to the back-court area across the net. Try forehand and backhand shots—ten out of twenty is a reasonable goal for beginners.
5. Serve into the right and left service court. Fifty per cent success with good form is a good score for beginners. Advanced players hit for targets (towels or tennis cans placed in the service court corner).
6. Rally ground strokes in an attempt to see how many consecutive shots can be hit after the first bounce into the opponent's court. This is a challenging contest for a tennis student with several weeks of practice. Advanced players can hit ground strokes and volleys at targets placed on the court.

Glossary of Terms

Ace: A good service that is not touched by the receiver.
Advantage: The point after deuce. "Advantage in" refers to the server winning the point; "advantage out" refers to the receiver winning the point.
Alley: Strip of court lying between the singles side line and the side line on a doubles court.

Approach shot: A shot made just previous to running to the net.
Back court: Area of the court between the base line and the service line.
Backhand: Stroke used to hit balls on the left side of a right-handed player (right side of a left-handed player).
Base-line game: A strategy in which a player remains near his own base line and attempts to win by hitting ground strokes; in contrast to the net game.
Center strap: Two-inch-wide strip of canvas that holds the net down at the center.
Chop: Shot in which the racket is swung down sharply under the ball, giving it backspin.
Cross-court: Phrase indicating a ball hit diagonally from one corner across the net to the opposite corner.
Deuce: Even game score when each side has three or more points.
Double fault: Loss of a point by the server for failing to hit either of his two consecutive service attempts into the proper service court.
Drive: A shot from the back court hit with a full swing.
Drop shot: A safely-hit shot having backspin that barely clears the net and does not bounce very high.
Error: A point lost due to a mistake on the part of the hitter.
Fault: Failure to serve the ball into the proper court.
Flat: A shot or serve hit with little or no spin.
Foot fault: A service violation, usually consisting of stepping on the line while serving.
Forcing shot: A deep, hard shot intended to maneuver the opponent out of position.
Forecourt: Area of the court between the service line and the net.
Forehand: Stroke used to hit balls on the right side of a right-handed player (left side of a left-handed player).
Game: Unit of a set completed by winning four points, or by winning two consecutive points after deuce.
Ground stroke: Stroke made by hitting the ball after it bounces.
Half volley: A stroke used to hit the ball immediately after it hits the ground.
Kill: A hard-hit, well-placed shot that the opponent cannot return.
Let: A point that is to be replayed because of some type of interference or a serve that strikes the top of the net and drops into the proper service court.
Lob: A high arching shot that is intended to land near the opponent's base line.
Love: Term used to mean zero score.
Match: A contest usually consisting of two out of three sets.
Match point: Point that, if won by the player ahead, allows him to win the match.
Mixed doubles: Competition in which a boy and girl play as partners on a side.
Net game: A strategy in which a player attempts to win by reaching the forecourt in order to utilize his volleys and overheads.

Net man: Player in doubles who positions himself near the net.
Overhead smash: The overhead stroke resembling the serve that is used to counter the lob.
Passing shot: A shot hit to the side of an opponent at the net.
Placement: An accurately hit shot that the opponent cannot reach.
Rally: A term used to describe play from the serve to the conclusion of the point. Also used to describe a series of ground strokes hit in practicing.
Return: A ball hit back to the opponent; can be used specifically to refer to the return of service.
Service: Putting the ball into play.
Service break: When the server fails to win the game he is serving.
Set: Unit of a match completed by winning six games, or by gaining a two-game lead after each side has won five games.
Set point: The point that, if won by the player ahead, wins the set.
Singles: Competition with one person on each side of the net.
Slice: Stroke in which the ball is hit with backspin; when applied to a serve, the ball is hit with sidespin.
Tape: The strip of canvas that covers the cable at the top of the net.
Tie-Breaker: A sudden-death procedure of ending the set by playing five out of nine points when the game score reaches 6-6.
Topspin: A forward spin given a ball by hitting up behind it.
USLTA: United States Lawn Tennis Association.
Volley: A ball hit in the air before it bounces.

Selected References

BOOKS

Budge, J. Donald. *Budge on Tennis.* Englewood Cliffs, N.J.: Prentice-Hall, 1949.
   A book written by a former men's champion covering various instructional points. Some excellent pictures showing Don Budge's winning strokes are included.
Editors of *Sports Illustrated. Sports Illustrated Book of Tennis.* Philadelphia: Lippincott, 1961.
   A collection of several instructional articles written and published in *Sports Illustrated* magazine.
Everett, Peter, and Virginia Dumas. *Beginning Tennis.* Belmont, Calif.: Wadsworth, 1968.
   One of the Wadsworth Activity Series books covering the fundamentals of tennis. Includes skill tests and written exams.
Harmon, Bob, and Keith Monroe. *Use Your Head in Tennis.* New York: Crowell, 1950.
   A book specializing in practical and common-sense advice to tennis players, regardless of their sex, ability, or age.

How to Play Tennis the Professional Way. Ed. by Alan Trengrove. New York: Simon & Schuster, 1964.

Several current playing professionals give inside tips. The contributors include Ken Rosewall, Pancho Gonzales, Lew Hoad, Rod Laver, Tony Trabert, and Pancho Segura.

Murphy, William, and Chet Murphy. *Tennis Handbook.* New York: Ronald, 1962.

A series of 59 different articles by experts on the various facets of the game organized into a helpful book. Many of the great players up to the 1960s have contributed to this book.

Talbert, William, and Bruce Old. *The Game of Singles in Tennis.* Philadelphia: Lippincott, 1962.

A thorough study of "percentage tennis" strategy by a former Davis Cup captain. Most meaningful for the more advanced players.

Talbert, William, and Bruce Old. *The Game of Doubles in Tennis.* New York: Holt, 1956.

Former Davis Cup captain Billy Talbert co-authors a book describing doubles strategies used by the champions. Many diagrams and play situations are included.

United States Lawn Tennis Association. *USLTA Official Yearbook.* 51 East 42nd Street, New York, New York 10017.

This yearbook gives the current sectional and national rankings. Many tennis records, Davis Cup scores, plus the USLTA rules are included.

PERIODICALS

Tennis, U.S.A. P. O. Box 2248, South Hackensack, N.J. 07606.

A periodical sent to USLTA members informing them of recent tournament results, sectional news, and coming events. (Published by USLTA.)

World Tennis Magazine. 8100 Westglen, Houston, Texas 77042.

A monthly magazine with helpful articles on playing tennis, on various national tournaments, and on results of recent tournaments.

CHAPTER 28

Track and field

Gordon Coker*
Northwestern State University

Bill Kozar†
Texas Technological University

HISTORY

Unlike most sports, the origin of track (and field) arose from man's natural competitive urges; running races is as old as man himself.

Various track and field events formed an integral part of the ancient Olympic and other Pan-Hellenic Games, which were held regularly in ancient Greece for approximately 1,200 years. The forerunner of modern track, which for many years was termed *athletics,* was born in England and quickly spread to Europe and America. Informal running led to group running; impromptu races led to planned games; and local games led to national and then international games, such as the Scotland Highland Games, Caledonia Society Festivals, and First Olympian Games. In England, *pedestrianism,* or professional racing, dates back to the early years of the eighteenth century. It involves running or walking over any distance from fifty yards to the distance from New York to San Francisco. Pedestrianism was especially popular from the 1840s through the 1880s, but died with the development of bicycle racing and the development of amateur track and field meets.

The first intercollegiate track and field meet in America was held in 1874 and involved athletes from Harvard, Yale, Princeton, and Columbia.

DESCRIPTION

Track is an ancient sport in which primitive big-muscle activities such as running, jumping, and throwing are involved. Track and field provide the individual athlete many opportunities to use his special abilities and talents. In some events speed is the primary factor; in others, circulorespiratory endurance; and in some field events power is foremost. Coordination, timing, and a competitive attitude are important in all track and field events. Performance in this sport is measured and judged chiefly by means of a stop watch or tape measure; thus, the track and field performer competes individually against his own best performance as much as against other competitors. Success or failure depends on the competitor himself more than on the performance of teammates.

SPRINTS

The sprints include all races in which the contestant runs at or near full speed over the entire distance. Included are the 100-, 220-, and 440-yard dash. The 40-, 50-, 60-, 70-, and 80-yard dashes are run in indoor competition.

---

*B.S. and M.S. from the University of Tennessee, Knoxville; Ph.D., The University of Iowa; has taught track and field classes at Atlantic Christian College, The University of Iowa and Northwestern State University. He was head track and cross-country coach at Karns High School, Knoxville, Tennessee, and Atlantic Christian College, North Carolina, for eleven years. He competed in several sports while in high school and college. He is presently chairman of the division of undergraduate physical education at Northwestern State University.

†B.S. and M.S., Western Illinois University Macomb; Ph.D., The University of Iowa, Iowa City; was a cross-country and track competitor of national renown while competing in Canada, California, and for Western Illinois University. He was coached for one year by Mihaly Igloi, the great Hungarian coach. He was the National Association of Intercollegiate Athletics (NAIA) mile champion in 1961, and ran the mile in 4:07.1 in 1962 at the National AAU Championship meet. He has taught track and field classes at The University of Iowa; served as track coach at Sargent Park Junior High School in Winnipeg, Manitoba, Canada; and was assistant track and cross-country coach at Western Illinois University. He is presently the director of the motor learning laboratory at Texas Tech University.

The Start

A quick, effective start is extremely important in a short race. The three types of starts are the bunch, medium, and elongated.

Bunch. The bunch start position is one in which the toe of the back foot is placed in line with the heel of the front foot while in a standing position. Experimental evidence indicates that this type of foot spacing, which is the narrowest generally employed, permits the runner to get out of the blocks fastest.

Medium. In the medium start the knee of the back leg is, while in a kneeling position, placed opposite the front of the arch of the front foot.

Elongated. While kneeling, the elongated start results in the knee of the back leg being placed opposite the heel of the front foot. This starting position generally results in the longest foot spread assumed by sprinters. The experimental evidence available to date indicates that this starting position results in the slowest start of the three types of starts.

Spacing of Feet. The height of the runner is the determining factor in the positioning of the feet from the starting line. In the following table appears the approximate distance the feet should be from the starting line when in the different types of starts.

Start	Front Foot, inches	Back Foot, inches
Bunch	18–20	28–30
Medium	14–16	33–35
Elongated	12–14	40–42

Position of Hands and Arms. When assuming the starting position the hands are so positioned that considerable body weight rests on the thumbs and (1) the second joint of the fingers or (2) the knuckles of the hands. The hands should be as close to the starting line as possible, with the fingers and thumb forming an arch parallel to the starting line. The comfort of the sprinter should be the main consideration in determining the position of the hands and fingers. The arms should come straight down from the shoulders and the elbows should not be locked.

Starting

The starting commands for sprinters are "Starters ready" (interval of five seconds), "Get on your marks" (interval of ten to twelve seconds), "Set" (interval of not less than two seconds), and then the gun shot or the command "Go" is given. The sprinter should breathe normally until the command "Set" is given, at which time the breath is held until the starting signal sounds. After the command "Set," the contestant has four points of contact with the ground—both hands and both feet.

Upon hearing the pistol report or voiced "Go," the contestant, who has been concentrating on the starting signal, drives both legs vigorously against the starting blocks and swings the arms energetically in order to maintain balance. If holes in the track are used instead of starting blocks, it is important that they be dug deeply enough to provide a solid back surface. The size of the foot will determine the depth of the hole.

Run

The length of the first step is usually between eighteen and twenty-eight inches in front of the starting line. The succeeding steps gradually increase in length, and the forward body angle increases from the horizontal as the first four or five steps are taken. When the athlete is sprinting at full speed, his trunk is inclined forward at about 25° from the vertical. Breathing throughout the sprint is done through both the nose and the mouth. On each running step the knees are brought rather high in front, the head and eyes are directed straight forward, and contact with the ground is made with a pawing-back motion of the foot. The foot contacts the ground directly under or only slightly behind the center of body weight. Power is developed through the leg and the hip thrust and is exerted against the ground. During the entire sprint the runner should continually strive to relax to achieve his top running speed. A proper type of arm action that aids in maintaining good balance and relaxation generally is more important than forceful and exaggerated arm action. The head should at all times remain in line with the body because this aids in lessening any tension in the upper body. The sprinter should run on the balls of the feet, never with a heel-toe rock-up.

400-Yard Dash

The 440-yard dash, one of the most grueling races in track, was at one time considered to be a middle-distance run. However, improvements in running ability and training technique have caused it to be classified as a sprint; great emphasis is placed on speed, endurance, and pace in this event. Consequently, the starting technique and running form remain the same as in shorter races. The start is from a staggered position, and the entire race is usually run in lanes. Running in a lane permits the runner to plan a *unit-type* race in which both halves of the race are run in the same time. This helps ensure that the correct pace and timing will be used, making it possible to run the same type of race in any lane.

When running the curve, an important phase of this event, the quarter-miler must lean into the turn and run relaxed. This requires considerable practice and timing. The last 110 yards of the race are usually the slowest because the runner's muscles begin to tighten; hence, he must especially concentrate on relaxing during this final phase of the race.

The beginners should first run the 440-yard distance at a slow pace to learn the distance involved and how much effort is needed to perform well.

THE 880-YARD RUN

Speed, endurance, and strength are the physical components that a runner must possess in order to perform well in the 880-yard run. The runner must learn the length of stride, knowledge of pace, start and finish, and check the marker at which the break for the pole is made if he is to be consistently successful in this race.

A successful 880-yard runner must plan his own race and run his own pace. During practice he should time himself at several points during the 880-yard run. This will help to prepare him mentally for the race, as well as give him confidence in what he is capable of doing during all phases of the race.

The standing start is best for the half-miler. One foot (whichever is more comfortable) is placed close to the starting line while the opposite foot is back. If the left foot is forward, then the right arm is back and in a flexed position for running. The runner must run with a smooth, long stride, avoiding a short, jerky stride, which will tighten his muscles and make it impossible to finish the race with a fast sprint.

The 880-yard run is usually started from a staggered position from which the contestants break for the pole (inside lane) after the first turn. The observance of the following *DO'S* and *DON'TS* should enable the half-miler to continue to improve.

1. Know the track and check the marker at which the break for the pole (inside lane) can first be made.
2. Do not pass on the curve; instead, it is best to pass at the beginning of a straightaway.
3. If leading the race and the opponent attempts to pass on the curve, increase his speed, forcing the opponent to run wide or lag behind. This maneuver also gives the lead runner a psychological advantage over the opponent.
4. Avoid getting boxed. When running behind someone, the left shoulder is in line with the middle of the back of the runner in front.
5. At all times stay within eight to ten yards of the leader.

MILE RUN

Distance running has progressed greatly within the last few years. Breaking the four-minute mile in 1954 was one of the most exciting happenings in track. Since then the times for all distance races have continued to improve. The mile run is often called the glamour event of a track meet. Speed, strength, strategy, endurance, and a positive mental attitude are all prerequisites for success. Most good milers spend considerable time running with a stop watch in order to learn to pace themselves evenly throughout the race. Other milers depend on their speed and endurance, running against the opponent rather than the watch.

The mile runner should start from a standing position in which the foot is placed close to the starting line while the other foot is back. Which foot is in front is a matter of individual preference. If the left foot is forward, the right arm is back in a flexed position. Regardless of the starting method or racing strategy employed, the miler must run relaxed and easy and without any unnecessary strain. The jaw must be loose and the fingers relaxed. He can run with his hands open or closed, but they should not be tight or tense.

When passing an opponent, it is best to ease by him instead of turning on a sudden burst of speed (unless it is near the end of the race). Putting on a burst of speed will at any time cause a change in the stride and increased use of much-needed energy. When being passed, a good runner should hold his own pace and not be concerned about the pace of his opponent. Many times a runner tightens or tenses when being passed. Instead it is important that he stay relaxed and run easily.

Tactics can play a very important role in distance running. As in the 880, the runner must plan his own race. If he has a good kick he should try to slow the pace and finish with a sprint. If the runner has no kick at the finish, he must set a fast, steady pace that can be held the entire distance.

In a track meet a common practice among teams having more than one entry is to run a *decoy* to set a fast pace. This tactic is not effective against an experienced runner. *Boxing* is another tactic that a team with two or more runners can employ. To prevent being boxed, when running behind someone, the left shoulder should be in line with the middle of the back of the runner in front.

RELAY RACING

One of the most exciting events in track and field is relay racing, which involves both competitive running and baton exchanging. The first three members of each team must, after having run their specified distance, pass the baton to their teammates within a designated twenty-two yard zone or be disqualified. In theory the members of a sprint relay team should run in the following order:

1. The fastest starter runs first.
2. The fastest runner runs second.
3. The second fastest runner runs last.

Traditionally, the fastest sprinter runs the anchor leg, but the placement of the team members can vary according to the competition available.

Methods of Baton Exchange

Although a number of methods of passing (exchanging) the baton have been developed, only two commonly used ones are described. The experience of the team and the distance of the relay mainly determine the type of baton exchange to be made. Regardless of the method of exchange used, the pass must be well timed and executed smoothly while running at a steady speed. Both athletes should be running at approximately the same speed when the exchange is made to eliminate the possibility of the passer coming abreast of, or going by, the receiver.

Blind Pass. The blind pass is the best exchange for the sprint relays (440 and 880 yards) because it can be executed at maximum speed. The receiver does not look at the baton when the exchange is made, which enables him to run in a sprint position during the transfer. The success of this exchange depends on the accurate location of the check mark, the location of which must be measured from the back line of the exchange zone. Experimentation and practice are the best ways to find the correct placement for this check mark. For beginners, Figure 28-1 depicts the locations of the check marks for the 440-yard and the 880-yard relays.

The extended-arm method of the blind exchange is best suited for sprint relays. This method permits a safety zone to be maintained between the two athletes at the time and point of exchange.

Right-to-right-hand Exchange. During the last few years many teams have used the right-to-right-hand exchange with great success. The theory is that because most athletes are right handed this exchange enables them to have improved control and timing at the exchange. Additionally, because the athlete does not have to change the baton from one hand to the other, this practically eliminates the chances of dropping the baton and also permits the runner to maintain continuous and smooth arm action.

The fundamentals of the right-to-right-hand exchange follow:

1. With the left foot back and facing the curb of the track, the receiving athlete stands inside the back line of the eleven-yard buffer zone.
2. When the teammate's foot strikes the check mark, the receiver starts sprinting at maximum speed. A verbal signal ("Go," "Hut," or "Ho") is also given by the incoming runner, which tells the receiver that the incoming runner can catch him at maximum speed. Practice is the only way to perfect this timing.
3. In the exchange zone there will be a spot at which the receiver extends his right arm backward. The outstretched hand is just above the waist, the palm is up, and the thumb is to the side and out of the way.
4. The incoming runner runs to the outside of his lane, which positions his left foot close to and behind the right foot of the receiver. The baton is placed into the receiver's right hand with a downswing of the passer's right arm. This action should be smooth with the receiver never slowing down or risking being run past. Many practice exchanges are the only way to perfect this skill.

Alternate-hand Exchange. The alternate-hand exchange used by several world-record-setting teams is recommended by some authorities because of the following advantages:

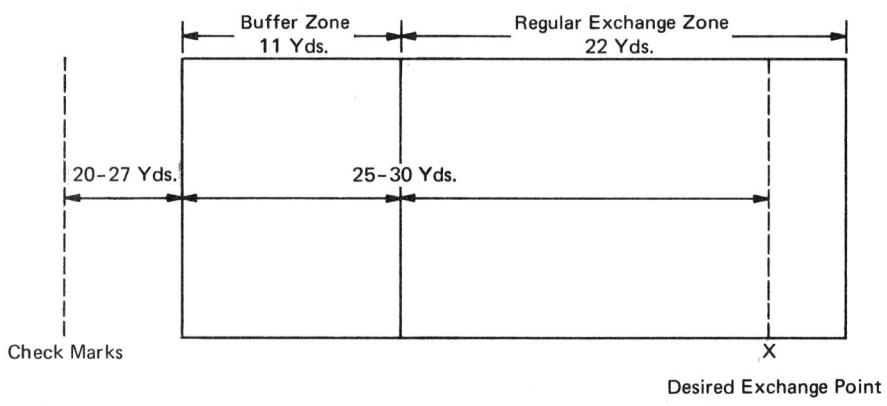

Figure 28-1. Check marks for 440- and 880-yard relays.

424 *Individual and Team Sports*

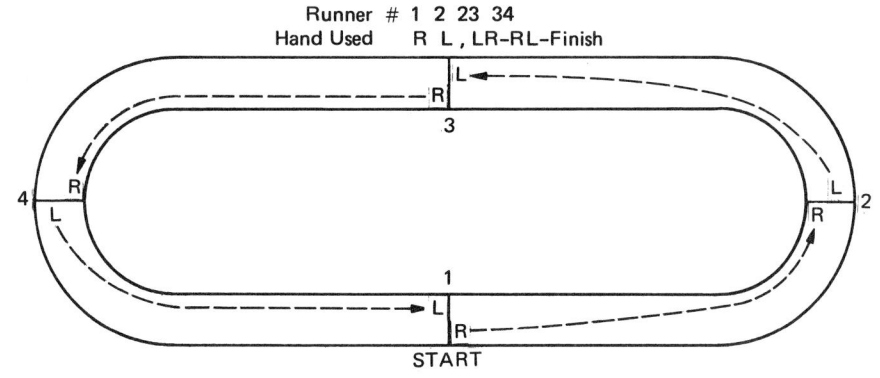

Figure 28-2. Alternate-hand exchange.

1. The baton is never changed from one hand to another.
2. The baton is never exchanged across the body.
3. The outside lane position is taken advantage of for the second and the fourth runners; there is less curve to run.

The exchange proceeds as diagramed in Figure 28-2.

Visual Exchange. The visual exchange is best suited for the one-mile, two-mile, distance-medley, and four-mile relay. The receiver is at the back line of the exchange zone, facing the curb. His left foot should be back so that he will be in position to watch his incoming teammate.

The receiver will start running when his teammate hits the check mark. The success of the exchange is the responsibility of the receiver, whose speed will be determined by the strength of his teammate's finish. When he starts his run the receiver can look forward until he has run about eleven yards. However, it is preferable for him to look at his teammate from the time he starts his run until he receives the baton. Because the receiver is anxious to get a good start, the visual method gives him an opportunity to force his teammate to run and, at the same time, not run off and leave him.

As the receiver watches his teammate approach him, he extends the left hand back with the palm down, as shown in Figure 28-3. His teammate carries the baton in his right

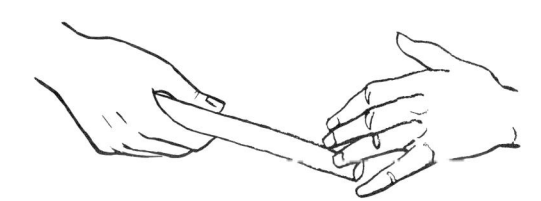

Figure 28-3. Handing off the baton.

hand and, with an upward motion, places it into the receiver's open palm. The transfer should be made at the midpoint of the exchange zone as depicted in Figure 28-4. The receiver will change the baton from the left to the right hand after he runs several steps.

HURDLES

The start for the hurdles event is the same as for any sprint race.

Low Hurdles

The 180-yard hurdles event has eight hurdles, thirty inches high, spaced twenty yards apart. It is a sprint race in which the hurdles are crossed with a high-striding action, rather than a gliding action. Form in clearing the low hurdles is important but is of less value than in crossing the high hurdles.

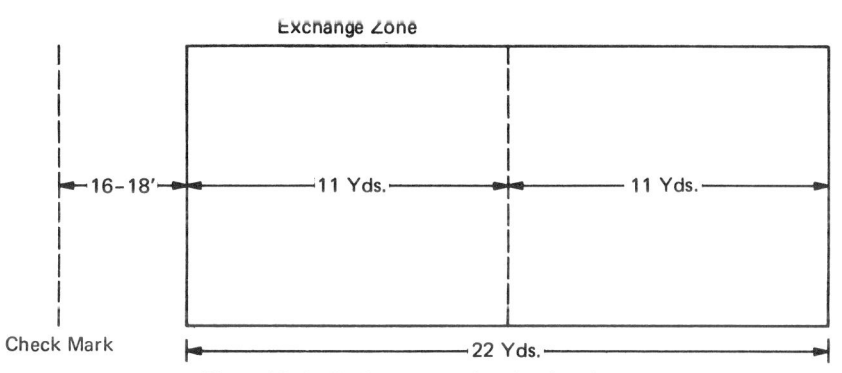

Figure 28-4. Exchange zone for visual exchange.

Track and Field

Figure 28-5. Form in crossing a low hurdle.

Strides

A set, preplanned number of strides should be taken between hurdles in order to run the event in the shortest time possible. Because the first few strides from the starting line are relatively short, more strides are needed to reach the first hurdle than the succeeding hurdles. If the left foot is the take-off foot, ten strides are required for most runners to clear the first hurdle. If more are needed, the runner can assume a starting position with the left foot in the rear position and use eleven strides to get to the first hurdle.

Seven strides are the most effective number to use between hurdles, assuming that the runner takes off on the same foot to clear each hurdle. If he cannot reach the hurdle in seven strides, an even number of strides (eight in most cases) can be used and the take-off foot can be alternated (left foot for the first hurdle, right foot for the second hurdle). Two reasons mitigate against the eight-stride plan, however. Many hurdlers tend to favor one foot and find it difficult to learn to alternate the take-off foot. In addition, most runners discover that through practice the length of the stride can be increased sufficiently to use the seven-stride plan effectively. This allows them to cover the same distance in one less stride—requiring less time than when the eight-stride plan is followed. The important point in determining the stride plan to follow from the start to the finish is that the hurdler must decide the combination cadence that works best for him and permits him to run the hurdles in a fast time.

Clearing the Hurdle

The twenty yards to the first hurdle gives the runner sufficient distance to gain the momentum needed to cross the hurdle rapidly. Little time is required to prepare for the take-off over the low hurdle; thus, a high striding action is taken with less concern given to staying low over the crossbar as it is cleared.

For the average low hurdler the take-off foot is "planted" seven feet, nine inches from the first hurdle and about eight feet for the others. During this instant the trunk leans forward slightly in order to maintain momentum and balance. When the lead foot is within fifteen inches of the hurdle, a cut-down action is quickly initiated to prevent floating across the hurdle and in order to resume a running position as quickly as possible.

As the trailing leg leaves the ground, the knee is raised and flexed so that the medial (inside) sides of the foot, ankle, and thigh are almost horizontal as they cross the hurdle.

The angle of the trunk throughout the clearance of the hurdle is less pronounced than in the high hurdles. However, if the runner tends to float or drift across the hurdle, he needs to increase his forward lean only enough to correct the error—an exaggerated lean results in a waste of energy and time.

The position of the arms is less significant in the low hurdles clearance than in the high hurdles. The runner needs only to maintain the arms in a good running position, spreading them slightly for balance. However, he must thrust forward the arm opposite the lead leg in order to continue the quick action of that leg.

After clearing the hurdle, the lead foot touches the ground as quickly as possible. The average distance from the hurdle that the lead foot touches the ground is four feet, three inches for the first hurdle and four feet for other hurdles. One reason for this quick action is to get into sprinting position immediately, thus making for an improved time. In addition, this quick action enhances improved striding; hence, the take-off for the next hurdle occurs at a point that permits the preparatory stride to be full, rather than choppy.

By the time the runner reaches the last hurdle, he is tired and may anticipate the finish, causing a tendency to hit the hurdle. To prevent this he should deliberately attempt to clear the hurdle a little higher than he believes is necessary. Better yet, he should refrain from anticipating the finish. The burst to the finish line is the same as for any sprint race.

High Hurdles

The high hurdles event is 120 yards in length; it contains hurdles spaced ten yards apart, and the first and last hurdles are fifteen yards from the starting and finish lines. In general, because the high hurdle is higher than the low hurdle (forty-two inches for collegiate and thirty-nine inches for high school), the form in clearing the high hurdles is more important than that for the low hurdles. Consequently, increased time is required to clear the high hurdle. Most runners should take off about seven feet, three inches from the first hurdle and cut the lead leg down about five feet beyond it. On succeeding hurdles, the take-off is about five inches longer, and the cut-down is about five inches shorter than for the first hurdle. Most high hurdlers take eight strides to the first hurdle and three strides between hurdles. If this combination proves ineffective, adjustments are made in the same manner as for the low hurdles.

On the take-off the lead leg is vigorously straightened and is in line with the shoulder to achieve an effective push from the ground. As this move is made, both arms are quickly swung forward. The arm opposite the lead leg is parallel and close to it; the other arm is flexed and swung backward slightly. The body leans forward substantially in order to maintain momentum and to keep the center of gravity low, which prevents floating.

When the lead leg is approximately a foot from the hurdle, a vigorous cut-down action is begun. To wait longer results in floating and the cut-down is farther from the hurdle, both of which adversely affect the take-off point for the next hurdle. During the cut-down action, the foot extends and reaches for the ground in order to effect a pawing action on contact. As the lead leg is lowered, the knee of the trail leg is flexed and quickly raised while the toes of the foot point toward the knee. The trailing leg and foot are in a horizontal position when clearing the hurdle. They then move as quickly as possible into running position.

Training for the Hurdles

The following pointers should be observed when training for hurdle racing.

1. Several flexibility exercises should be done daily and with progression: Toe touches, trunk twisting, bicycling, stationary hurdling, and toe touching with the take-off leg bent and the knee resting on the crossbar of the hurdle.
2. Train often with sprinters.
3. The runner should first practice with one hurdle. When he feels confident, a second one can be added, then a third one. The form and technique can be learned readily using only a few hurdles; therefore, practicing using all the hurdles of the race is fatiguing.
4. Check the footprints for the take-off and cut-down to determine if the toes are pointed ahead and are in line with the stride footprints. If out of line, the arm movement can be exaggerated during the hurdle clearance.
5. When clearing the high hurdles, the hand opposite the lead leg reaches as if it were untying a shoelace or scratching the sole of the lead foot.

DISCUS THROW

Handhold

The grasp is made with the palm down. The discus is held with the end (or first) joints of the fingers of the throwing hand hooked over the edge of the metal rim of the discus. The little finger and the ring finger are spread somewhat. The little finger and the thumb are utilized chiefly to provide lateral support. The thumb lies flat on the face of the discus and should be fairly close to the index finger. The hand should be so cupped that only the part of the fingers curled over the rim of the discus actually touch the discus, which should rest on the wrist and the thumb.

The best method of grasping the discus depends on the size of the hand. In Figure 28-6(a) finger positions for a discus thrower with a large hand are depicted, and in Figure 28-6(b) the finger position for a person with a small hand is shown. Discus throwers who have large hands will grasp slightly behind the center of weight of the discus and those with small hands will have the palm over the center of the discus.

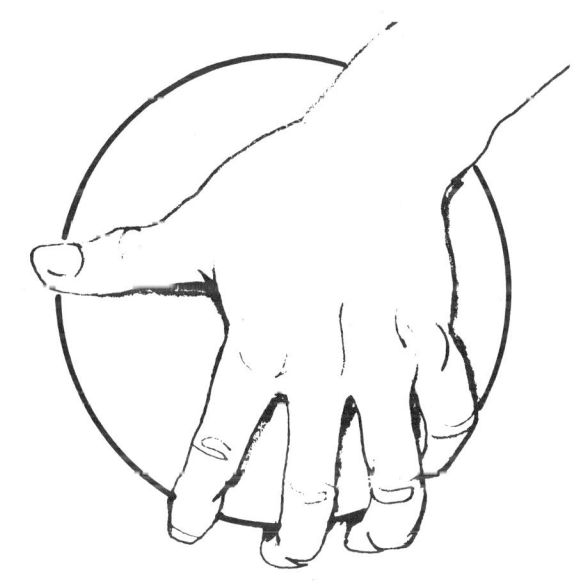

Figure 28-6(a). Finger positions on discus for large hands.

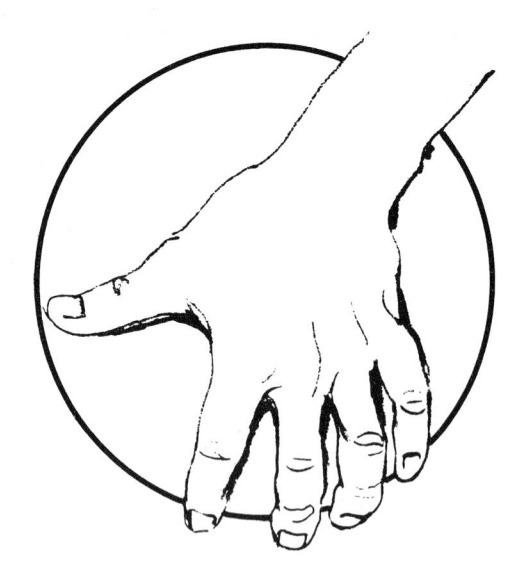

Figure 28-6(b). Finger position on discus for small hand.

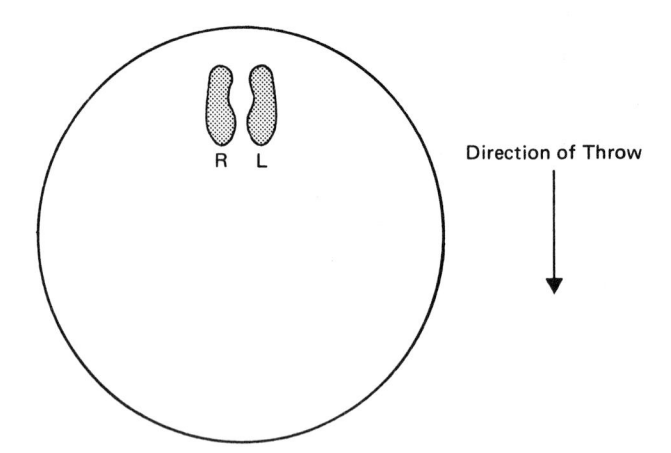

Figure 28-7(a). Delivery from stationary position.

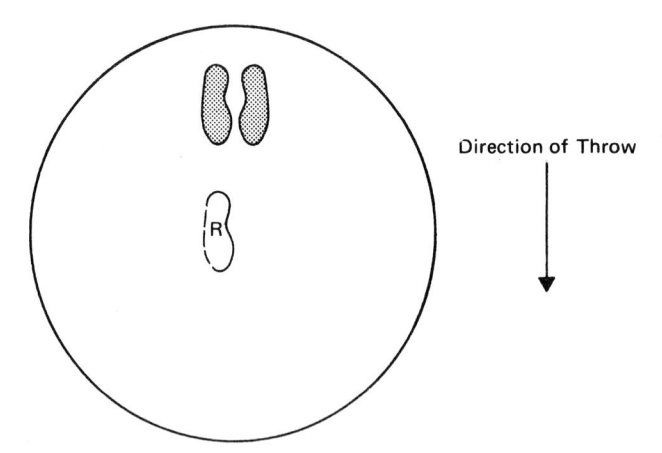

Figure 28-7(b). Step-and-throw delivery.

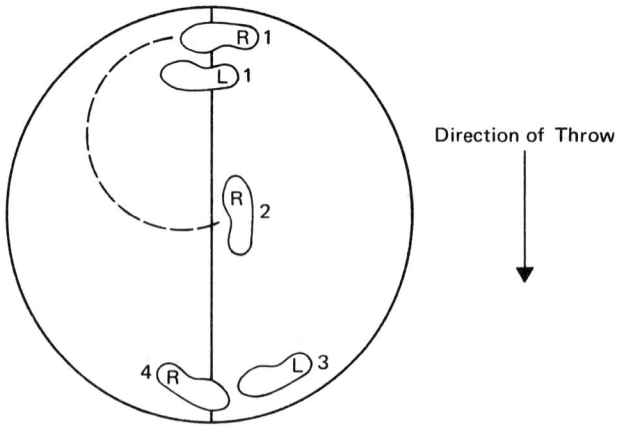

Figure 28-7(c). One and one-half turn delivery.

Delivery

The delivery is made off the index finger with a forward and upward swing of the arm. The impetus from the index finger will cause the discus to rotate clockwise for the right-handed thrower. If the discus has a tendency to "pancake" (travel through the air broadside), the thumb should be positioned closer to the index finger.

Proper Form

After learning the handhold one must then learn to sail the discus correctly. This requires considerable practice and should first be done from a stationary position and without any turn of the body as illustrated in Figure 28-7(a). The next transition is to the step-and-throw delivery, which is diagramed in Figure 28-7(b). The starting position in this delivery is more erect, with the feet pointed in the direction of the throw. Two or three preliminary swings are taken to insure the proper rhythm and balance. When the discus comes to the end of the backswing, the performer steps approximately fifteen inches forward with his right foot and assumes the delivery position. When this position has been attained the delivery is then completed as from the stationary throwing position.

One and One-half Turn

After the step-and-throw technique has been mastered, the turning technique should be integrated with the throw. See Figure 28-7(c). The one and one-half turn is probably the best turning technique with which to begin. The

428 *Individual and Team Sports*

technique for taking the one and one-half turn involves the following:

1. A line is drawn through the center of the discus circle that runs in the direction of the intended throw.
2. With the left side facing the throwing direction the thrower assumes a position at the rear of the circle. The stance is balanced and relaxed.
3. The ball of the right foot and the heel of the left foot are placed on the center line of the circle. The feet are shoulder width apart and the hips and knees are slightly bent.
4. Several preliminary swings are made with the discus, with the swinging action started by shifting the weight from one foot to the other.
5. When the discus reaches the end of the backswing, the left foot turns in the direction of the throw. As the body begins pivoting to the left, the weight is transferred to the left foot by driving off the right foot, which should remain in contact with the ground as long as possible. As the knee of the right leg swings around it should remain close to the left leg. The throwing arm, fully extended, stays behind the right shoulder and hip, keeping the discus "on the drag" (to the rear as much as possible) throughout the turning action.
6. The weight of the body is transferred to the right foot as it lands just beyond the center of the circle, and the final half turn is started. At this instant the right toes point somewhat toward the rear of the circle. The second part of the turn is executed like the first part, with the left knee close to the right leg and leading the body as it rotates. The throwing arm stays behind the hip and the shoulder.
7. As the left foot comes around to complete the second turn, the thrower quickly assumes the delivery stance. If the pivot over the right foot has been properly balanced no direct effort is needed to place the left foot. Instead, it is, without conscious direction, in correct alignment just inside the front of the circle and about twelve inches to the left of the center line. At this point delivery is executed as described for the stationary throw.

SHOTPUT

Two requisites for the aspiring shotputter are a knowledge of the rules, which will help him understand the correct position of the shot and the feet throughout the entire shotputting sequence, and having a safe, accident-free place in which to practice. Flipping the shot from one hand to the other will give the beginner the feel of the shot and aid him in obtaining a correct holding position.

The shot is held high on the fingers and does not touch the palm of the hand. The fingers are spread with the thumb to the front to help hold the shot in a high position. The shot is held under the jaw and against the side of the neck. The elbow of the putting arm should be pointed outward and downward, and the elbow of the nonputting arm should be pointed outward in a relaxed position at shoulder height.

Stationary Put

The beginner should first practice shotputting by making a large number of stationary puts.

1. The stance is at a right angle to the direction of the throw, and the performer is in a crouch position that is natural and balanced.
2. During the initial phases of the delivery the right elbow remains behind the right foot and the trunk remains erect.
3. The shot is put forward and upward. Both feet remain on the ground when the delivery is executed, and no conscious thought is given to the reverse.
4. In order to obtain the best leverage and most explosiveness, the performer, from the start, stays behind and under the shot.

Step and Put

1. The athlete, facing in the direction of the put, assumes an erect, balanced, and relaxed stance at the rear of the circle.
2. The right-handed shotputter points his left arm, which is flexed at the elbow outward. The left arm is at shoulder height and relaxed.
3. The athlete next takes a step forward, placing the heel of his right foot at the center of the circle and pointing his toes to the front of the circle. As this step is being made, the athlete lowers his body into the delivery position.
4. His left foot is then placed at the front of the circle and close to the center of the toe board.
5. The putting stance is completed at this instant, and the athlete makes the delivery as part of a continuous step-and-put action.

Advanced Technique

When the athlete has partially mastered the step-and-put technique he should proceed to practice the most advanced

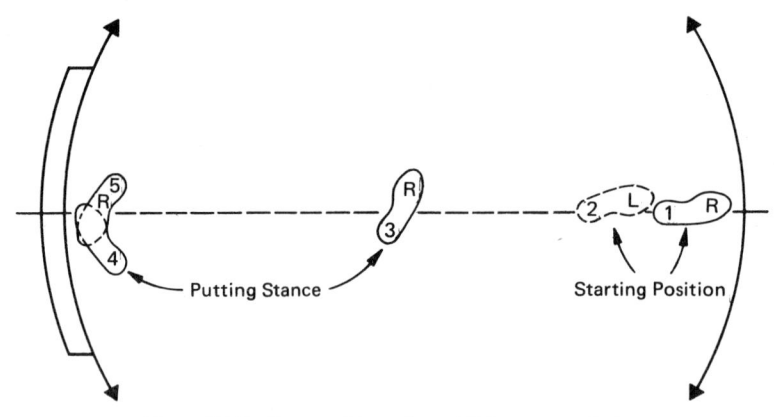

Figure 28–8. Feet position when shifting across circle.

shotputting technique, which is described subsequently. (See Figure 28–8.)

Initial Stance. The athlete should be in an erect stance that is close to and facing the rear of the circle. The right foot is pointed away from the toe board. The weight is over the right leg; for balance the toes of the left foot barely touch the ground.

The Shift Across the Circle. To begin the shift across to the putting action, the athlete should flex the right leg and lower the chest until it touches his knees. With the left foot raised, the left leg is thrust strongly toward midcircle. Simultaneously, the right leg is straightened, powerfully driving the putter across the circle. This movement, which involves power and a kick, produces a low, fast glide across the circle. The right foot trails behind the body during the glide and it lands near the center of the circle, pointing at a 35 to 45° angle to the rear. At this point the putter is in approximately the same position as that in which he started, and with his weight over the right foot. When the right foot lands at the midcenter of the circle, the left foot is thrust (jammed) down sideways against the board with the toes at the center of the board. As the body begins to rise, because of the extension of the right leg and back, the athlete rotates his hips and shoulders to the left. From the right leg the weight is shifted to and over the partially flexed left leg. The complete shift across the circle is done in a continuously rapid movement.

Putting Action. When the weight is over the left leg, the shot is thrust up and out at a 45° angle. At this point the right arm should be fully extended, with the shoulder, elbow, and hand forming a straight line. The follow-through forces a reversal of the feet position, which is necessary to maintain balance at the conclusion of the shotput. The reverse is made by quickly shifting the right foot to the toe board and swinging the left leg backward.

HIGH JUMP

The lift off from the ground and the efficient clearance of the crossbar are the two basic considerations in high jumping. In the roll forms of jumping the inside foot (the foot nearer the bar) is the take off foot, and the outside foot makes the kick. Most authorities believe that for most high jumpers, the *roll form* is the best style to utilize in clearing the crossbar. The *western* and *straddle* are the two basic forms of the roll.

Approach

The high jumper starts his approach about thirty to forty feet from the crossbar, approaching it at a 45° angle, which brings him close to the bar and places him in good position for the take-off. In the approach a relaxed, bouncy stride is used with a gradual decrease of speed until the last three steps, after which an increase of speed and lengthening of stride occurs in order to provide a sufficient upward thrust for the kicking leg. During the last three strides, the legs are bent at the knees in order to lower the body into a crouched position for the upward spring. Simultaneously, with the final stride, the jumper leans backward away from the bar in order to get additional upward drive from the next-to-last step as well as from the take-off.

Take-off

The better jumpers take off twenty-three to twenty-five inches from the bar. The point of take-off varies from jumper to jumper because of the speed of approach, the length of the legs, and the direction of the approach run. In addition, the take-off point is adjusted as the jumping height increases during competition. When taking off, the jumper first hits the ground with the back of his heel and then rocks up on his toes as he leaves the point of take-off.

Kick and Lift

The jumper's take-off leg represents the hour hand of the clock; his lead leg, the minute hand. In developing the proper kicking action, the jumper should kick in a six o'clock direction, which provides sufficient momentum to carry the jumper directly upward. A kick in the 6:15 direction causes the jumper to ride along the bar. After approaching the bar and planting the take-off foot, he drives his lead leg straight upward past the 6:15 position and toward the six o'clock direction before the toes of his take-off foot leave the ground.

Rolling Action

As the jumper leaves the ground, he should thrust his left arm forward while keeping his right arm passive. This prevents him from jumping into the bar. A strong kick with the right leg and a strong lead with the left arm should enable the rolling action to come easily for the jumper. At the highest point of the jump, the jumper's trunk and lead leg are immediately above and parallel to the bar. At this instant the jumper is rolling, causing his right arm and leg to lead his fall into the pit. This rolling action keeps his trail leg from hitting or knocking off the bar.

Differences in Roll Forms

The approach, the gather, the take-off, and the kick are the same in both the western and the straddle rolls. The difference between the two styles occurs when the jumper is above the crossbar. In the western roll the jumper pulls his trail leg (take-off leg) under him, clearing the bar while on his right take-off leg side.

LONG JUMP

The successful long jumper must develop the following qualities: (1) speed for the take-off, which gives momentum for the jump; (2) good height in order to stay in the air and travel as far as possible before landing; and (3) legs fully extended during the ascent in order to get as much distance as possible from the jump.

Practice for the Beginner

The beginning long jumper should practice with an easy, relaxed run-through that is started about eight strides away from the pit. The jumper should make several run-throughs, striving to develop easy, smooth strides and without taking any jumps. After the run-through becomes consistent, the jumper, with the aid of another person, should locate a spot within jumping distance from the pit where the take-off foot consistently hits. This spot is marked as the take-off point.

The jumper proceeds to practice the "pop-up" (a short jump stressing height rather than distance) from the previously marked take off point. Beginning eight strides from the take-off point, the jumper takes his run and, without using the take-off board, pops-up into the pit. After several run-throughs and pop-ups have been practiced, the jumper measures for distance from his take-off point.

Run

The length of the run for the long jump varies from 100 to 150 feet. During the run the jumper should be relaxed and should take smooth, even strides.

To determine the length of run, the jumper should first stand about twelve feet behind (on the pit side) the take-off board at the edge of the pit. He should next jog forward, hitting the board with his take-off foot and sprinting full stride up the runway. When he attains his top speed, a teammate or coach marks where his take-off foot lands. Starting from this mark the direction of the sprint is then reversed in order to recheck the steps and to determine if the take-off foot hits the take-off board exactly right.

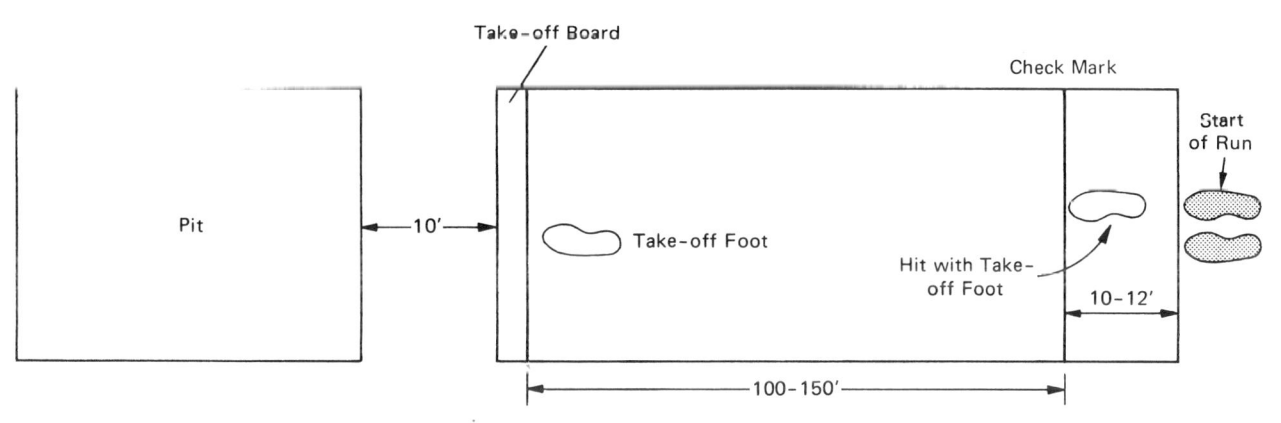

Figure 28-9. Check marks for long jump.

Track and Field

Take-off

At the time of the take-off, the take-off foot should be directly under the jumper's body and pointed straight ahead; emphasis is placed on achieving height. The take-off leg is flexed slightly at the knee on the last step in order to give the jumper an opportunity to develop a powerful push-off as the leg is straightened. As the lift starts, the take-off leg is vigorously straightened while the knee of the free leg is thrust upward to help obtain increased height.

Flight

During the flight the jumper should avoid dropping his feet too early; this action would decrease his jumping distance. Keeping the feet high enables the jumper to travel an increased distance, especially when combined with one of the two types of action used while the jumper is in the air.

Tuck Technique

The tuck action consists of pulling the knees up toward the chest and then straightening the legs. At the same time the arms are swung forward to help lift the body and to keep it balanced.

Hitch-kick Technique

In the hitch-kick technique, the jumper takes off from the left foot while moving his right leg forward. With the arms remaining in a high position during the entire flight, the jumper next reverses the position of his legs, moving the right leg backward and the left leg forward. Keeping the left leg forward, the jumper brings the right leg forward to a position alongside the left leg. Both legs are extended forward for the landing.

TRIPLE JUMP

In order to achieve success the triple jumper must possess or develop the characteristics of a long jumper: strong and resilient muscles and speed, agility, and spring. In addition, the triple jumper should have a thorough knowledge of the emphasis that must be placed on each phase of the event, be well trained in the mechanics of the triple jump, and strive for complete coordination and unity throughout his performance.

Early Practice

The triple-jump event places tremendous strain on the muscles and tendons of the knee and leg that are used in jumping and hopping. Therefore, a considerable portion of the early season training must be devoted to strengthening and developing their strength, power, and resiliency. Specific formal exercises that are useful include:

1. Long jumping, taking off from the weak leg.
2. Hopping in series, working toward the ability to hop several 50-yard series.
3. Running in a series of high bounding steps.
4. Practicing with a short hop, a long step, and a high long jump, increasing the length of the hop as strength and power are gained.

Run

The run is almost identical to that used for the long jump. The check marks are moved back farther from the take-off board because the hop-and-step part of the event are done on the runway in front of the jumping pit.

Take-off

The importance of a relaxed, well-balanced take-off for running at full momentum cannot be overemphasized. As in the take-off for the long jump, the body weight must be shifted over the take-off foot—if proper balance is not achieved on the hop, the later phases of the event will suffer. As a general principle, the take-off for the hop should be made from the same leg as is used in the long jump. Thus, if the take-off for the hop is from the left foot, the take-off for the step is also from the left foot, followed by the jump, which is taken from the right foot. If the right leg is stronger, the take-off hop should be from the right foot.

Flight in the Hop

The aim during the hop is to move, hence the body is not kept as erect as in the long jump. If the take-off is made from the left foot, then the right leg is driven forward and up at take-off and brought down and back as the left leg is carried forward with a high knee lift. The hands and arms are used naturally to maintain proper balance.

Step

The step is begun by bringing the free right leg forward with the knee high. This position is held until just before landing when the right foot is placed down for the landing.

Jump

The jump is the same as that used in the long jump, which was described earlier in this chapter. Whatever momentum the performer has must be put to good use by obtaining as much height and distance as possible in this final phase of the event.

Distance Ratio of the Hop, Step, and Jump

Most beginners make the mistake of starting with a very long hop, which causes them to take a very short step and a medium jump. Whenever one part of the event is overemphasized the other two parts suffer; therefore, the jumper must properly proportion his efforts to obtain the best distance possible from all three phases combined. Although there is no one best ratio for the three parts of the triple jump, the evidence from research has shown that some ratios are better than others. In the following table, adapted from Eng Yoon Tan, various distances for the 10:8:9 ratio system are listed; the table is used by a number of top-flight triple jumpers. This ratio is provided as a guide only. As the jumper practices and accumulates experience he must find the ratio that is best for him in the triple-jump event.

10:8:9 Ratio for the Triple Jump*

Distance, feet	Hop	Step	Jump
34	12'6-1/2"	10' 1-1/2"	11'4"
36	13'3-1/2"	10' 8-1/2"	12'0"
38	14' 1/2"	11' 3-1/2"	12'8"
40	14'9-1/2"	11'10-1/2"	13'4"
42	15'6-1/2"	12' 5-1/2"	14'0"
44	16'3-1/2"	13' 1/2"	14'8"
46	17' 1/2"	13' 7-1/2"	15'4"
48	17'9-1/2"	14' 2-1/2"	16'0"
50	18'6-1/2"	14' 9-1/2"	16'8"
52	19'3-1/2"	15' 4-1/2"	17'4"
54	20' 1/2"	15'11-1/2"	18'0"
56	21'9-1/2"	16' 6-1/2"	18'8"

*Eng Yoon Tan, "Research into the Hop Step and Jump," presented as thesis at the Loughborough Training School, England, and published in *Clinic Notes*, National Collegiate Track Coaches Association, 1959, pp. 16-41.

POLE VAULT

History

Pole vaulting was utilized for centuries to clear obstacles too great to cross by means of the running broad jump. The concept of pole vaulting for distance prevailed both during early times and when the pole vault first became a competitive event. By 1877, when the pole vault was added to the American track and field program, height had replaced distance as the primary goal. An Englishman soon afterward ended the American domination of this event by a method in which he literally climbed the pole hand over hand until the pole reached a vertical position. In 1890, the American rules were changed to prohibit climbing the pole; later, this rule was adopted for the Olympic Games.

Evolving from poles of virgin wood that were sharpened on the lower end, the first competitive poles of ash, hickory, or spruce were equipped with an iron tip or tripod. These were succeeded by the bamboo pole with an iron tip and later a plug shaped like a mushroom. Steel poles were an even later development, until, more recently, extremely flexible fiberglass poles have enabled increased heights to be vaulted. By 1900, a hole was being dug in which to plant the pole; a wooden trough was in use in 1924; and since World War II the metal trough has become popular.

In the 1950s, the introduction of the fiberglass pole, which somewhat catapults the vaulter, practically revolutionized the pole vault. As a result, the sixteen-foot height was quickly achieved, and today vaulters are attempting to break the nineteen-foot barrier—a far cry from the record of nine feet, seven inches set in 1877.

Qualities Needed

In order to vault well the performer should be well coordinated and should possess or develop good speed, endurance, leg power, arm and shoulder strength, and space orientation. Considerable practice and intense concentration can enable many performers to become reasonably good pole vaulters with a command of the proper techniques.

Handhold

The placement of the handhold on the pole depends on the vaulter, the height of the crossbar, and the distance of the spread of the hands on the pole. The vaulter who is tall, speedy, and strong can assume a higher grasp on the pole than one who is shorter and not as well developed. With the crossbar at a low height the beginner can grasp the pole with the right hand at a height greater than the crossbar; at middle heights (ten or eleven feet) the grasp on the pole may be at the same height as the crossbar; at great heights the grasp will be lower than the height of the crossbar. However, the grasp is not changed each time that the crossbar is raised; instead, the changes are made from low, to medium, to high elevations.

Arm Position

The right arm is almost fully extended as the reverse grasp is made. The left hand, with the palm down, is

Track and Field 433

Figure 28-10. Arm and hand positions on pole.

placed on the pole in line with the left shoulder, the forearm forming approximately a right angle to the upper arm.

Carry of the Pole

The position of the hands varies according to the type of carry preferred. The low, middle, and high carries refer to the relationship of the pole to the ground. In all these carries the pole is in line with the approach direction. In the low carry, the pole is held at approximately a 25° angle; in the high carry, the pole is held at about a 45° angle. In the cross-body carry, the pole is held crossways to the trunk of the performer and is approximately parallel with the ground. Experimentation and practice are the basis for selecting the type of carry one uses. In general, when the types of carries are compared, fewer errors occur in the pole plant in the low carry, greater speed is attained during the approach in the middle carry, better pole balance is gained in the high carry, and more speed is gained in the initial part of the approach in the cross-body carry.

Approach

Because the purpose of the approach is to gain optimum momentum for the vault, the performer must experiment in order to determine which stride plan is best for him. Most approaches utilize sixteen (the most popular) or eighteen strides to cover a distance of 100 to 125 feet. The goal is to attain near-maximum speed in the least number of strides while carrying the pole.

Like any jumping event that is preceded by a run, the approach in the pole vault begins at a speed requiring approximately one half of maximum effort and increases to nearly maximum effort. Because the body must be under full control for the vault, the performer should not reach full speed during the approach.

The pole plant is made when the vaulter is nine or ten feet from the trough. At this point he lowers the pole and slides it down the middle of the trough. This is done with the arms bent in order to absorb the shock when the end of the pole strikes the back of the trough.

The vaulter must coordinate the hand shift and the foot stamp with the pole thrust. He must also slightly shorten the last two or three strides in order to prepare for the spring.

Take-off and Swing

As the pole slides into the trough, the left hand slides near or next to the right hand. This left-hand shift enables both arms to hold the weight of the body and it also permits a smooth swing-up, an effective pull-up, and a high push-up. As the hand shift is made, the hands are moved above the head, and the arms are held at right angles at the elbows in order to absorb the impact of the pole stopping at the trough.

Simultaneously with the above actions the foot stamp is made by forcefully hitting the ground flat footed with the left foot while the left leg is slightly bent at the knee. The body weight is then quickly transferred to the left toes in order to effect a rock-up. A maximum spring from the left leg must be obtained for an effective swing-up to be made. The foot stamp and the swing-up are continuous actions or else some momentum will be lost. As the rock-up is executed with the left foot, the knee of the right leg is raised, which is immediately followed by raising the left leg (which is swung close to the right leg and on the right side of the pole). Both legs, which are close to the pole, are then extended briefly. The knees are then raised when the hips are even with the pole.

Pull-up and Turn

The pull-up, which is vigorously made in order to raise the body, and during which the body remains close to the pole, begins when the hips are at least level with the shoulders. By this time the pole is approaching a vertical line. During the initial part of the pull-up both legs are bent, then the right leg is extended for the swing. Near the completion of the pull-up, the extended right leg is swung sufficiently high so that the right foot is above the crossbar. This swing initiates a counterclockwise body turn—a half turn toward the pole. At the peak of the upward swing of the right leg, the left leg is thrust vigorously upward and parallel to the right leg.

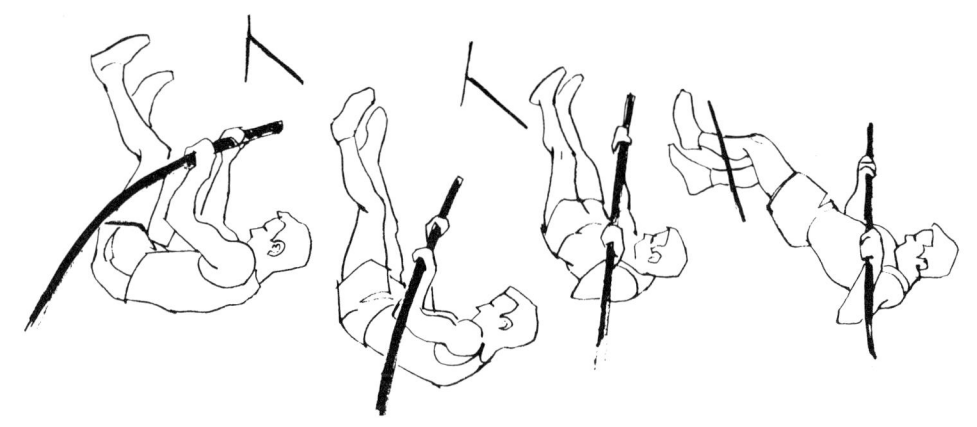

Figure 28-11. Pull-up and beginning of turn.

Push-up

The last phase before clearing the crossbar is the push-up, which is initiated at the end of the pull-up when the pole is in a vertical position. For this the arms are extended vigorously, raising the body high enough to move over the crossbar. The legs are apart only enough to maintain balance.

As the body moves over the crossbar, the legs and hips continue to elevate as high as possible. A moderate pike position is then taken in which the trunk is bent at the hips, and the feet are lowered to the level of the hands. The vaulter's body is then facing the bar.

Pole Release

The pole can be released either by both hands simultaneously or by the left hand first and then the right hand. The latter method has the advantage of permitting the left arm, which is the lower arm, to be moved out of the way early to avoid hitting the crossbar while the right hand continues to apply force on the pole. Either method is effective and both enable the vaulter to push the pole away from the crossbar.

Landing

Even though extremely soft canvas bags or portable foam rubber pits are available on which to land, the descent and landing are still important elements of the pole vault. After the crossbar is cleared, the vaulter relaxes and initiates the equivalent of a back drop to a trampoline bed. During the descent the trunk is gradually flexed, and the body rotation is such that by the time the descent is completed, the landing is made on the back. The vaulter remains in a controlled state of relaxation until any bouncing motion ceases. If sawdust or similar material is used in the landing pit, the vaulter must descend feet first and, upon landing, flex the legs in order to absorb the landing impact.

Training Suggestions

1. Perform gymnastic activities to develop strength, power, and endurance. Push-ups from a handstand in a corner are particularly beneficial.
2. Follow the training schedule for sprinters in order to develop speed for the approach.

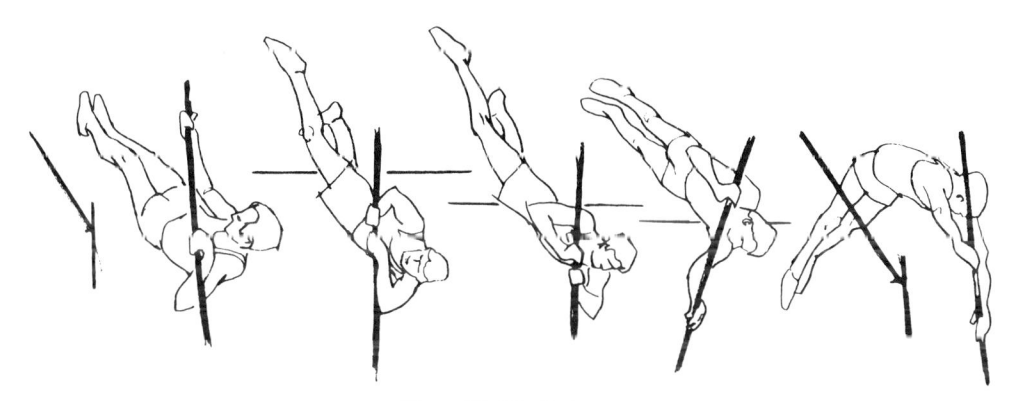

Figure 28-12. Push-up.

Track and Field

3. Repeatedly practice pull-ups on a fixed vertical pole and practice rope climbing.
4. Place the crossbar about three feet higher than the regular height and practice by kicking off the crossbar during the vault.

Selected References

Cretzmeyer, Francis X., Louis E. Alley, and Charles M. Tipton. *Bresnahan and Tuttle's Track and Field Athletics*. St. Louis, Mo.: Mosby, 1974.

A classic in track and field, which dates back to 1937, this book has long been popular in many foreign countries. In addition to discussing techniques and listing various track standards and records, the latest research findings and facts concerning the physiology of training are included. A chapter is devoted to each of the major events in track and field. 317 pp.

Doherty, J. Kenneth. *Modern Track and Field*. Englewood Cliffs, N.J.: Prentice-Hall, 1963.

This well accepted book on track and field events and techniques is written by a long-time, highly successful coach of the sport. In it are covered the hows, whats, and whys; up-to-date training methods; and many sequence drawings of champion performers. 557 pp.

CHAPTER 29

Trampolining
*Donald R. Casady**
The University of Iowa

HISTORY

The forerunner of the modern trampoline appears to have been the safety net employed by most circus trapeze flyers. Almost two hundred years ago a Frenchman named du Trampolin discovered that he could do many entertaining stunts on the safety net itself; consequently, he abandoned flying on the trapeze and developed a rebounding act on the safety net. Other performers followed his example and this device was used to generate considerable height and perform many of the stunts still done on the trampoline today. The size of the net area was gradually reduced, and in the twentieth century the practice of suspending a small net by springs was evolved by circus and vaudeville performers. Perhaps the most famous performer of this era was the late Joe E. Brown, who perfected a triple back somersault on such a hand-made trampoline and later enjoyed fame as a comedian in Hollywood movies.

Trampolines were first manufactured for commercial sale by two former University of Iowa gymnasts, Larry Griswold and George Nissen, who toured the country giving trampoline acts and selling trampolines between performances. The United States Navy Flight Program, in which the trampoline was extensively used to accustom potential Naval aviators to unusual body positions, did much to popularize the trampoline. Soon after World War II ended, trampolining was accepted as a collegiate gymnastics event; it soon became an event in the NCAA and AAU national championships and in high school gymnastics meets.

In the late 1950s and early 1960s trampoline centers were widespread throughout the United States. Because of poor supervision and lack of instruction, these centers acquired the reputation of being dangerous and the centers became commercially unfeasible.

At the present time competition on the trampoline is held in many high schools and at the national and international level, but it is not one of the events in college gymnastics.

BRIEF DESCRIPTION OF TRAMPOLINING

The novice trampolinist, after taking several preliminary bounces, generally performs a single skill, or only a few consecutive skills, before stopping. In trampoline competition a single routine is done in which the performer is permitted ten contacts with the trampoline bed after performing his first stunt. The routine is concluded with the tenth bounce. Ordinarily, the trampolinist performs a stunt before each landing, with one or two landings on his back or stomach.

POTENTIAL VALUES OF TRAMPOLINING

Bouncing on the trampoline, whether a single stunt is performed or a series of trampolining skills is performed, is a unique experience that is virtually unduplicated in any other type of activity. Because of the kinetic energy present in the springs or shock cords surrounding the trampoline bed, the performer does not have to exert much effort when bouncing in order to generate considerable

---

*While a member of The University of Iowa gymnastics team, this writer first competed on the trampoline. While varsity gymnastics coach at Georgia Military Academy, Atlanta, and later as freshman gymnastics coach at The University of Iowa, Casady helped coach several prominent trampolinists. While diving coach at The University of Iowa, he often utilized the trampoline to help train the members of the diving squad. In addition, he has taught many trampolining classes to college students and has co-authored a book on gymnastics.

height. This yields an extremely exhilarating sensation if fear is not an inhibiting factor.

Because of the small effort required and because retaining proper balance on the trampoline can usually be quickly mastered, an infinite variety of skills or series of stunts can be performed on the trampoline with only a reasonable amount of practice and instruction. This creates a feeling of achievement. Moreover, the trampolining student is constantly challenged to master skills, perform combinations of stunts, or combine them into a routine of his own devising, which affords opportunities to express ingenuity and creativity.

One research study indicated that a definite increase in ankle flexibility resulted from the regular practice of trampolining. Bouncing regularly on the trampoline commonly aids in developing most of the muscles of the legs, particularly the calves and thighs. The sense of balance is increased and the ability to think quickly and make decisions rapidly can be enhanced, as can cardiorespiratory and general endurance.

TRAMPOLINE EQUIPMENT AND ITS CARE

Trampolines are equipped with crash pads on top of all four sides, which cushion the impact force if the trampolinist lands on the trampoline frame. These should always be in place before a trampoline is used. Almost all modern-day trampolines can be folded for storage. Folding a trampoline when it is not in use relieves the pressure on the trampoline bed and on its springs or shock cords. A trampoline should be unfolded slowly and carefully in order not to drop it and sprain the frame. The leg supports should be securely fastened in place before the trampoline is used.

Beginning trampolinists, especially, should wear pants of sufficient length to protect the knees and shirt sleeves to protect the elbows and prevent skin abrasions during landings. The trampolinist should not use a trampoline when barefooted, but should wear socks (which can slip on the bed) or, preferably, gymnastics slippers with rubber soles.

Several different kinds of safety devices are available to help safeguard the beginning trampolinist when attempting new skills. The overhead safety belt, for which the trampolinist wears a safety belt around his waist and from which a rope is attached on either side that passes through ceiling pulleys and down to a spotter, is probably the most universally used spotting device. Hand safety belts are also available for use by spotters who are standing on the frame of the trampoline.

Trampolines come in a variety of sizes. The most common bed sizes are six feet wide by twelve feet long or seven feet wide by fourteen feet long. The bed is usually made of webbed nylon strips that are one inch in width and interwoven. Because shock cord deteriorates with age and in the sun, most trampolines are equipped with springs, which are quite durable.

PRELIMINARY SKILLS

Getting on and off the trampoline safely is the first step in acquiring trampolining skill. The trampolinist should get onto the trampoline by rolling sideways over the springs and onto the bed. He can also grasp a spring with each hand, place one knee on a crash pad, rock up on the frame, place the other foot on the bed, and walk to the center of the bed. To dismount from the trampoline the trampolinist faces away from the trampoline and sits on the edge of the bed with both legs dangling. He then pushes with both hands and jumps to his feet. Another method of dismounting is to lie face down on the frame pads and slide the feet down while swinging the head toward the center of the trampoline. The trampolinist should avoid the temptation to jump off the trampoline while still bouncing.

Bouncing Correctly on the Trampoline

In order to maintain his balance at all times and to be the best prepared to perform a skill on the trampoline, the beginning student should first learn the correct method of bouncing on the trampoline. Several different actions are involved; the beginner will probably need to first concentrate on one and then another, gradually coordinating and integrating all of them until they require no conscious thought.

Bouncing Skills. Beginning with his first efforts the trampolining student should attempt to land near the center of the trampoline bed after each bounce, keeping traveling from side to side or end to end at a minimum. During each bounce the head should be erect and in line with the rest of the body. While bouncing, the eyes should be either focused on one end of the trampoline or at an eye-level spot on the wall. As the upward bounce begins the arms should swing forward and then upward to about shoulder height or somewhat higher. The arms pause at this height while being brought sideward. As the descent begins the arms are swung downward and in line about even with the sides of the body. As the landing is made the downward swing of the arms is continued in order to help push down on the trampoline bed. Using knee and ankle action to push down on the bed, the performer, when the bed pushes back, extends his legs and feet, pushing off the balls of the feet. The arm action of the trampolinist is a clockwise action of the right arm and a counterclockwise action of the left arm in a movement resembling the letter *D*.

Check Bounce. Simultaneously with learning to bounce correctly on the trampoline, the beginning trampolinist must learn how to check (kill or stop entirely) his bounce. This safety skill can prevent an accident if the performer is off-balance and must kill his bounce to avoid being thrown by the rebounding bed. The principle followed in checking a bounce is that the body's center of gravity must be going downward while the trampoline bed is coming upward. Thus, the two actions nullify each other. This nullifying action is performed by bending the legs quickly at the knees and flexing the hips while keeping the head up. The skill of killing the bounce completely should be so overlearned that it is automatically applied any time an off-balance landing is made.

Spotters

If the beginner progresses at his own rate, attempts new stunts and series only after he can visualize them in his mind, and is confident that he can perform them, spotters around the sides of the trampoline would still occasionally be needed to help prevent a possible accident. As a rule the minimum number of spotters should be four—one at each side and one at each end of the trampoline. If the performer is using a safety belt, only an operator of the safety belt is needed.

Spotters (normally other members of the trampoline class or another trampolinist) have the chief duty of insuring that the trampolinist does not come off the trampoline. Therefore, whenever the trampolinist appears to be rebounding off the bed or landing on the springs or frame, the spotter must make every effort to push the trampolinist back upon the bed before he lands. If this is impossible, the spotter should protect the trampolinist's upper body (especially the head) by grasping his shoulders or upper arms or catching him. The spotter must be constantly alert even though his services are rarely needed. If his help is needed he must not close his eyes or shy away.

Use of the Overhead Safety Belt

The trampolinist must be familiar with how to use the overhead safety belt. The belt should be fitted tightly around the waist to prevent chafing the skin. The ropes to the belt should be of equal length from their pulley, and the pulleys should be in line with the center of the trampoline so that the belt will pull the trampolinist there when lift is applied. The trampolinist should ignore the belt when bouncing; he should never grasp the ropes coming from the belt.

The spotter manipulating the overhead safety belt ropes must keep the slack out of the ropes without providing lift to the trampolinist. This enables the spotter to quickly stop the trampolinist at whatever height danger is perceived. A loose spotting rope delays the spotting action and causes the trampolinist to be jerked about considerably. Most trampolining students can learn to be competent spotters with an overhead safety belt if they conscientiously practice this skill. They should first practice spotting a performer who is merely bouncing up and down, stopping him at selected times or when called out by the trampolinist.

PRINCIPLES OF TRAMPOLINING

The trampolining student should keep several principles in mind whenever he is performing on the trampoline. A complete mental picture of what is planned before attempting a skill or series of skills is a necessity. If performing a routine the trampolinist should be able to go completely through it in his mind before performing it on the trampoline. This may necessitate breaking the routine into parts and practicing each part separately, concentrating on mastering the difficult parts before performing the complete series.

Whenever the trampolinist is not confident that he can safely complete a dangerous stunt, he should use a safety belt until the stunt has been mastered. The beginner should not over-rely on the belt, but it should be used to avoid unnecessary risks. If the trampolinist is unsure about completing part of a series of skills, that phase can be practiced in a safety belt until the necessary skill and confidence are acquired.

When performing on the trampoline the eyes should be open. Because it is impossible to see and consciously note everything passing before the eyes, the performer must be quite selective in what he attempts to focus his vision on. For example, when doing a backward somersault the room appears to turn over or make a full revolution—a disconcerting sight. Instead of receiving such a confusing impression the trampolinist keeps his eyes open but ignores most of what he sees and looks only for the trampoline bed to appear. In a double back somersault, the trampolinist should only note the bed appearing once and then a second time just before landing. Skill in selectively focusing the vision and excluding part of what is seen usually develops rapidly if practiced.

Through practice the trampolinist develops skill and a sense of timing to know about how long it takes to complete a particular stunt and on what targets he should focus his eyes. Although an experienced trampolinist could probably perform many skills with his eyes closed, relying on an acute sense of timing and skill, the beginner

Trampolining 439

should always look for his spotting target in order to adjust his timing if needed. The ability to "see" only certain objects when performing is particularly important whenever a poor take-off or *throw* is made and the regular timing may not be correct. At all times the trampolinist should attempt to work from a fair amount of height in order to have sufficient time to complete each trick and to be able to drop from a height with control and with adequate time to adjust his landing. From the very beginning, the student should strive to maintain a constant height of bounce after each landing. He will have to exert some effort each time because the rebound of the trampoline bed is insufficient by itself.

On the other hand the trampolining student should avoid the tendency to try to obtain maximum height on each bounce. Making a maximum effort often causes him to be off-balance, making it doubly difficult to perform with safety on the trampoline. Instead, the trampolinist should bounce with at least fair height and "coast" somewhat on the last bounce preceding the performance of a skill or routine.

Once a trampolinist starts to perform a skill, he should always complete it; he should not change his mind after the take-off and quit. This will leave him blind and not knowing where the trampoline bed is located. Should a bad take-off or an inadequate beginning be made, the performer should "ride through" the stunt. If a tucking action is involved, he should quickly go into a tight tuck. Once a stunt has been started the beginner will find it almost impossible to stop, open up, and locate his position in time to make a controlled landing. When practicing routines, the beginning trampolinist must not hesitate to stop the routine without completing it if he feels off-balance and thus cannot fully control his amount of lean or angle of take-off. The routine should be stopped before the take-off for the next skill is made.

RATIONALE FOR PRESENTATION OF TRAMPOLINING

Skills and Routines

The trampolining skills and routines presented in this section are placed in an approximate ascending order of difficulty. However, different individuals will find that they are able to master some types of skills and sequences more easily than others. For this reason the trampolining student should not necessarily attempt to learn the skills in the order they are presented.

A question that the trampolining student should answer is, "What is my purpose in using the trampoline?" Does he plan to do sequences of skills in a routine or does he only want to perform individual skills, as is done in springboard diving? The skills in this chapter are presented mainly in the form of a short routine; a new skill is included in each sequence. Because both gymnastics and trampolining competition involve routines only, most students will probably want to learn sequences of trampolining skills. Because the sequence of skills is presented in an order that affords maximum safety and permits an orderly progression in which the learned skills serve as stepping stones to acquiring new skills, the beginner may want to learn the skills in the order in which they are presented. However, the sequences of skills in this chapter serve as examples of what the trampolinist might do; he should profit from creating routines of his own devising. Moreover, the competitive trampolining approach followed in this chapter facilitates learning control and form while learning trampolining skills.

In each routine the instruction given is primarily for the new skill and not for the complete routine. The most commonly used names are given in describing each trampolining skill comprising a routine. When more than one name commonly exists for the same skill, the second name is listed in parenthesis.

ELEMENTARY TRAMPOLINING SKILLS

(1) Three Feet Bounces, Three Tuck Bounces, Check Bounce (Breakfall)

The performer does three regular bounces on the trampoline, attempting to swing his arms forward and upward as he bounces upward and then swings his arms sideward and downward as he descends to the bed. He then does three tuck bounces in which he keeps his upper body in an erect position and brings his knees to his chest, grasping his forearms around his knees at the top of each of the tuck bounces. Upon landing after the third tuck bounce he immediately does a check bounce by bending his legs and hips—thus nullifying the rebound of the trampoline bed. The bounces should be done without traveling, with each landing being located on the center of the trampoline bed where the vertical and horizontal lines intersect.

(2) Three One-half Pirouettes, Check Bounce (Breakfall)

After doing a few feet bounces the performer, as soon as he takes off, does a one-half twist, initiating the action by first turning his head to face the opposite end of the trampoline and then bringing both hands to the shoulder toward which the face was turned. Upon landing, another one-half pirouette is made and then a third one before the bounce is killed.

(3) Three Knee Drops, Three Seat Drops, Kill Bounce (Breakfall)

When doing knee drops the performer keeps his entire body straight except for flexing his lower legs behind him. When landing his feet are pointed but his weight is mainly supported by the knees, not the top of the insteps. The performer should keep his head in line with his body but can look down at the trampoline bed when landing in the knee-drop position. He should not lean forward or backward but should keep his body weight positioned directly over his knees.

When performing seat drops the performer must, as he starts upward from the trampoline bed, swing his extended legs forward while slightly piking at the hips. He should land in a straight-body sitting position with the legs extended and the arms at the sides where the hands contact the trampoline bed beside his hips. The fingers should *face forward* in the same direction that he is facing in order that the elbow joint is not locked against the body. As the performer rebounds upward from the seat drop, he leans forward with his upper body and head, pushes vigorously off the trampoline bed with his hands, and tucks his legs, coming to a standing or feet-bounce position.

In performing this sequence of skills, the performer alternates knee or seat drops with coming to his feet; thus, after each knee (or seat) drop he does a feet bounce.

(4) Knee Drop, Hand-and-knee Drop, Front Drop, Hand-and-knee Drop, Knee Drop, Check Bounce

Immediately after doing the knee drop, and as soon as he leaves the trampoline bed, the performer slowly bends forward with his upper body until, as he is coming down, his trunk is parallel with the trampoline bed. His knees should be positioned directly below his hips and his hands directly below his shoulders. Keeping his head somewhat forward, the performer lands simultaneously on his hands, knees, and insteps. The hand-and-knee drop should be practiced until several can be done in succession.

After doing a hand-and-knee drop with his body parallel with the bed, the performer, as he rebounds from the bed, extends his legs behind him and brings his hands to a position near each shoulder, extending his elbows sideward. Keeping his head forward and his chin up, the performer lands flat on the trampoline bed. When doing the front drop the performer should not travel forward or backward on the bed. The skill of proceeding from a hand-and-knee drop to a front drop should be practiced several times. (See Figure 29-1.)

The performer then does a front drop, and as he rebounds from the bed, he goes to a hand-and-knee drop and then to a knee drop. The entire routine is then practiced.

(5) Three Alternate Front Drops

To do a front drop from a feet bounce, the performer starts to rebound upward and slowly flexes his upper body forward at the waist while keeping his legs and feet vertical and directly underneath his hips. By the time he has achieved the peak of his height his upper body is flexed forward at almost a 90° angle and is almost parallel to the trampoline bed. As he descends the performer rather slowly extends his legs behind him. When he lands on the bed his body is in a horizontal position and is parallel to the trampoline bed. The performer should land with his hands positioned near his shoulder in somewhat of a push-up position and with his head arched back so that he is looking forward. Some trampolinists prefer to land with their lower legs flexed at the knees. The performer should aim to land with his hips on the bed where his feet were on the last bounce. This eliminates any tendency to travel and prevents the possibility of abrading the skin from sliding on the bed.

After landing, the performer pushes vigorously with his hands as if he were doing a fast push-up and, as he comes off the trampoline bed, he tucks his legs under him. This should cause his body to rotate a one-fourth somersault backward, from which position he extends his legs and comes to an erect position, ready to do a feet bounce.

The last step is front drops in swing time, building up to doing three successive front drops with a feet bounce between each.

(6) Three Alternate Back Drops

Before attempting this sequence the performer must first master a back drop, landing with the legs flexed. The initial step is to stand in a semicrouched position on the trampoline with the chin on the chest, and the hands on the thighs. From this position the performer falls off-balance backward and at the same time kicks one leg upward as high as possible while bending the other leg to

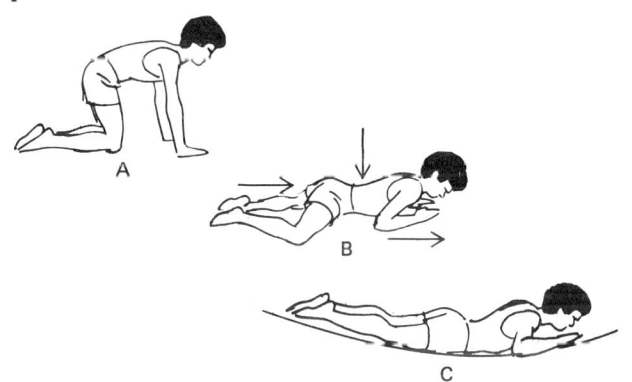

Figure 29-1. Hand-and-knee drop to front drop.

Trampolining 441

almost a 90° angle. This action should cause him to land flat on his back with his head flexed forward. When this action is performed correctly, the kicking leg is aimed almost directly straight upward toward the ceiling.

When this type of elementary back drop can be done several times without error, the next step is to perform a back drop from a very low feet bounce. For this, as the upward bounce begins, both legs are raised upward rather slowly and with the legs bent at the knees. The landing should be squarely on the back with the thighs pointed almost directly toward the ceiling and the lower legs almost parallel with the trampoline bed. The arms are also pointing somewhat toward the ceiling.

From this elementary back drop, the performer proceeds to a regular back drop in which he increases the height of his bounce and lands flat on his back with his legs flexed. As he starts to rebound off the bed, he flexes his head forward and kicks vigorously forward toward the end of the bed. This causes a forward somersault action from which the performer tucks his legs underneath him and comes to a standing position.

(7) Back Drop, Feet Bounce, Knee Drop, Seat Drop, Front Drop, Feet Bounce, Breakfall

The performer should have mastered all the skills comprising this routine. He now combines them without any intervening feet bounces. He may want first to attempt doing only two and then three of the skills in sequence before putting the entire routine together, working toward performing it without a break.

(8) Seat Drop, Knee Drop, Front Drop, Check Bounce

This sequence involves moving from a front drop to a back drop—one half of a back somersault—and may require some practice. After landing in the front drop, the performer pushes vigorously with his hands, forcefully thrusts his head backward, and quickly sweeps his knees through to a tuck position. He holds this position until he is almost parallel with the trampoline bed where he opens up to a regular back-drop position with his legs partially flexed.

(9) Back Drop, Feet Bounce, Knee Drop, Seat Drop, Half Twist, Seat Drop, Feet Bounce, Check Bounce

The new skill is called swivel hips, which is a seat drop, half twist, seat drop. When performing the swivel hips the legs should pass directly under the hips when the half twist is done. After landing in the seat-drop position the

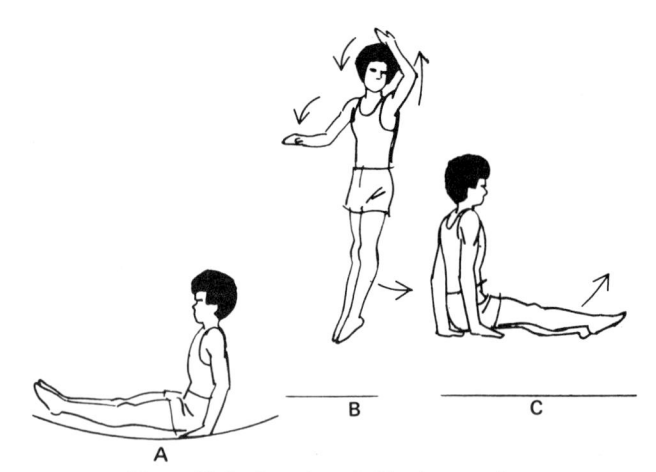

Figure 29-2. Seat drop, half twist, seat drop.

performer pushes upward vigorously with his hands and leans forward slightly with his upper body. As quickly as possible he vigorously swings his legs to the rear; as they pass underneath his hips he vigorously swings his arms upward, overhead, and behind. At the same time he twists with his head and body, completing a half twist while his body is in an erect position. He then comes to a seat-drop landing. The performer should not try to move his legs directly sideward in a circular motion when doing a swivel hips because this is a difficult and limiting technique. (See Figure 29-2.)

(10) Swivel Hips, Hand-and-knee Drop, Front Drop, One-half Turntable, Front Drop, Check Bounce

The one-half turntable is executed from a front drop in which, as the body rises off the trampoline bed, no pushing action is made with the hands in order to eliminate any somersaulting motion. Instead, by not pushing and by piking his body slightly as he rises from the bed, the performer will be able to return to a front-drop position by unpiking as he comes down. When this has been mastered, a sideward revolution of the body is made by pushing sideward with both hands and pulling in the opposite direction with the head as the rebound begins. The performer then quickly tucks, holding the tuck until his body has revolved 180°. He then extends his body and comes down to a front drop, landing with his hand facing the opposite end of the trampoline. (See Figure 29-3.)

(11) Full Pirouette, Seat Drop, Front Drop, One-half Turntable, Check Bounce

A full pirouette entails doing a complete 360° revolution of the body while keeping the feet directly under the body and maintaining an erect position. The performer

Figure 29-3. Half turntable.

initiates the twisting action by raising his arms forward and upward in the usual fashion. Just as he leaves the bed he vigorously brings both arms toward one shoulder, and at the same time he vigorously twists his head sideward toward the same shoulder. During the time that the twisting action is taking place the legs must be together and extended and the body must be completely straight. The performer should look for the same end of the trampoline or the same wall he was facing before initiating the pirouetting action.

(12) Feet Bounce, One-half Twist to Back Drop, One-half Twist to Front Drop, Hand-and-knee Bounce, Feet Bounce, Check Bounce

The two new skills introduced in this sequence are highly similar movements. The performer takes off as if to do a front drop but keeps his body extended throughout the skill. As he nears the top of the bounce, the performer looks away from the trampoline bed and toward the ceiling with a twisting action of the head. At the same time he brings both hands close to the shoulder toward which his head is facing, pulling hard with the elbow facing behind him. This causes a slow twisting movement. When he has rotated 180° he extends his arms sideward and drops to a flat back-drop landing, contacting the trampoline bed with the back of his head, shoulders, hips, calves, and ankles simultaneously. Without any somersaulting action, his body should rebound in an extended position from which he again lands flat on the trampoline bed.

When this skill has been mastered, as he rebounds from the trampoline bed, the performer brings both hands to one shoulder, pulls back with one elbow, and at the same time turns his head toward the same shoulder. Thus, his body is rotated a one-half twist until he is facing the trampoline bed. He drops to a front drop.

(13) Back Drop, Forward to Front Drop, Backward to Back Drop, Kill Bounce

Two types of somersaulting action—forward and backward—are introduced in this sequence. For the first part the performer should do a high back drop in which most of his weight is on his upper back and his legs are flexed. As he begins to rebound from the trampoline he thrusts his legs forward toward the far end of the trampoline and then tucks his body while flexing his head forward. He holds this tucked position until he revolves 180° and then extends and lands in a front-drop position. He then pushes vigorously with his hands, thrusts his head backward, and quickly thrusts his knees toward his chest, holding this tuck position until he is in position for a back-drop landing.

(14) Knee Drop, Roundoff, Knee Drop, Feet Bounce, Seat Drop, Front Drop, Back Drop, Check Bounce

From the knee-drop landing, the performer, who has his hands raised overhead, vigorously whips his arms forward and downward onto the trampoline bed directly in front of him. He places one hand close to his body and the other one in line with and about two feet in front of it. As his knees, hips, and body rebound upward, the performer comes to a handstand position, from which he pivots a one-half turn and pikes his body downward, coming to a knee drop. First learning a roundoff on the tumbling mat will facilitate learning this skill. (See Figure 29-4.)

(15) Knee Drop, Front Over to Seat Drop, Feet Bounce, Swivel Hips, Check Bounce

The front over described here is actually a low, three-quarter forward somersault. This action is simple and safe

Trampolining 443

Figure 29-4. Roundoff—knees to knees.

Figure 29-5. Front over to seat drop.

(16) Seat Drop, Full Twist, Seat Drop, Front Drop, Half Turntable, Front Drop, Check Bounce

The full-twisting seat drop is performed with the body completely extended. As the trampolinist starts to rebound, he vigorously lifts his hips and completely extends his body, coming to a position in which his head is somewhat higher than his hips. As soon as complete body extension is attained, the performer brings his hands to one shoulder and simultaneously turns his head sharply toward that shoulder. He holds this twisting position until he has rotated a full 360° turn. He then pikes and comes down to a seat-drop landing while looking toward the end of the trampoline. (See Figure 29-6.)

(17) Back Drop, One-half Turn Forward with One-half Twist, Back Drop, One-quarter Turn Forward with One-half Twist to Feet-Landing Position

The first part of this sequence is known as the cradle. The performer executes this skill as if he were going to turn forward to a front drop from a back-drop landing. When more than halfway through the one-half forward turn, and as he is falling toward a front-drop landing, he quickly does a one-half twist and lands in a back drop

and is usually quickly learned by most beginners. From a front-drop landing in which the arms are overhead and are semiextended, the performer, keeping his body straight, leans forward slightly as he starts to take off from the bed. He then swings his arms forward and downward, simultaneously bringing his head and his hands to his knees. He somersaults forward until his head is clear of the trampoline bed. Keeping his eyes open, he then goes from a tuck to a pike position. The bed of the trampoline should be seen before the seat-drop landing occurs. (See Figure 29-5.)

Figure 29-6. Seat drop, full twist, seat drop.

444   *Individual and Team Sports*

with his legs flexed. Repeating this action, the performer does a one-half twist just before landing on his feet.

(18) Consecutive Full Turntables

From a front-drop landing the performer vigorously flexes his head to one side, pushes with one arm, and pulls with the other one. Tucking as tightly as possible and holding it for a full 360°, the performer continues to attempt to pull with his head. He then extends for the landing and immediately attempts a second turntable—and, if possible, a third one. Some trampolinists grasp the edge of the trampoline bed with the hand with which they are going to pull in an attempt to obtain increased leverage in performing the turntable action. Considerable practice is sometimes necessary for success, but if only a three-quarter turntable is done, the performer should land safely on the middle of the trampoline bed, especially if he flexes his lower legs and keeps his head up.

(19) Consecutive Full-twisting Back Drops

The performer does a back-drop landing with his body completely extended. As he begins to rebound he twists as for a full pirouette while keeping his body as straight as possible. As soon as he again sees the ceiling, he brings his arms to either side and lands in a straight-body back drop.

(20) Consecutive Full-twisting Front Drops

The performer repeats the same action as is done for the full-twisting back drops, being careful that as he leaves the trampoline bed he performs only a twisting action and does nothing to initiate any forward or backward somersaulting. The performer looks to the side until he again sees the trampoline bed, at which time he extends his arms sideward and comes down to a front-drop landing.

(21) Front Drop to Front Cody, Back Drop, Seat Drop, Check Bounce

The front cody to a back drop involves a front somersaulting action. Although it is not difficult to perform, it

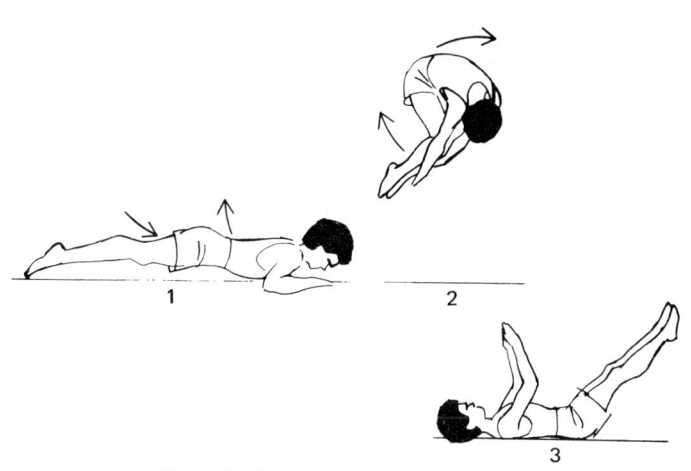

Figure 29-7. One-half front cody.

causes an eerie feeling the first few times it is attempted simply because the performer somersaults so slowly. As soon as he starts to leave the bed, after landing in a front drop, he thrusts his hips as high as possible and simultaneously pulls his arms, chest, and head back under his hips. Piking his hips forward, he comes to a back-drop landing. When beginning, the performer can look down and see the bed and, if short, can place his hands down on the bed, coming to a momentary tucked handstand and then doing a forward roll. During his take-off the performer must be especially careful not to push down at all with his hands or do anything to initiate a back somersaulting action. (See Figure 29-7.)

(22) Back Drop, Back Pullover to Feet, Knee Drop, Swivel Hips, Check Bounce

To perform a back pullover the performer, from a low bounce, drops into a high back-drop position in which most of his weight is resting on his upper shoulders. His legs are flexed and before he rebounds from the trampoline bed he very vigorously thrusts them directly overhead and toward the end of the trampoline in which his head is pointing. This action should cause a back somersaulting action sufficient to bring him to his feet.

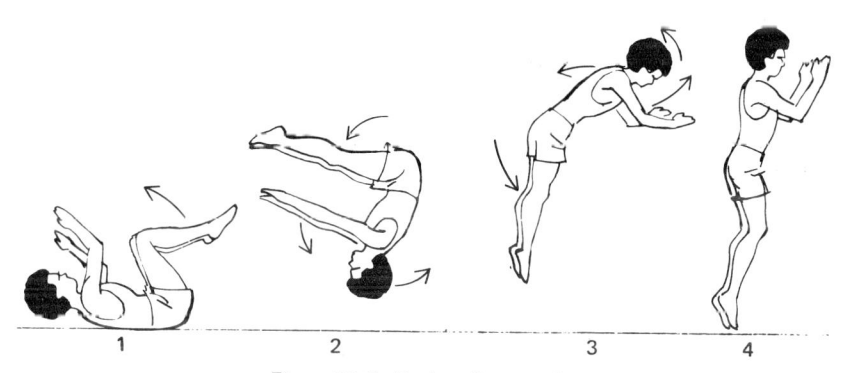

Figure 29-8. Back pullover to feet.

Trampolining 445

As a safety measure, he should position his thumbs alongside the top of his head in order to help support his weight with his arms in case his head does not completely clear the trampoline bed. The movement performed here is highly similar to that done in a backward extension roll on the tumbling mat, which should have been mastered previously. The more vigorously the legs are thrust backward and the tighter the tuck is taken immediately after the leg-thrusting action, the more quickly will the performer rotate in the back somersaulting action.

A variation of this skill can be performed by landing somewhat off-balance in a tucked, sitting position on the bed. The action of the trampoline bed rebounding upward causes the tucked performer to do a partial back somersault. This technique is easier to do but does not aid the performer in learning a true back somersaulting action. (See Figure 29-8.)

(23) Back Drop, Forward Somersault to Back Drop, One-quarter Turn Forward with Half Twist to Feet, Full Pirouette, Check Bounce

The full forward somersault is safely introduced by performing it from a high back-drop landing in which the legs are flexed. As the rebound begins the legs are thrust forward, the head and arms are brought toward the knees, and the body is tucked tightly. Keeping the eyes open to determine when he has revolved past the bed, the trampolinist opens into a back-drop landing.

(24) Back Pullover to Back Drop, One-half Turn Forward to Front Drop, Full Turntable, Check Bounce

The full backward somersault is initiated from a back-drop landing in the same manner as for a back pullover. The backward extension of the legs is more vigorous and the tight body tuck is held longer. Once the performer somersaults past his feet, he opens to a back-drop landing with his legs flexed.

(25) Cradle with One-half Twist, One-half Turn Backward to Back Drop, Back Pullover to Feet

The twisting movements in this routine are the same type utilized in all forward somersaults with twists. The performer lands in a high back-drop position and initiates a forward somersaulting action. He revolves forward until upright and from where he can see the bed. He then initiates a twisting movement while his body is completely extended. Instead of doing a half twist, he holds his twisting position and continues turning his head and pulling with his arms until he can again see the trampoline bed. At this time he opens for a front drop. The performer must wait until his body is almost vertical; his body must be extended, and he must continue his twisting action until he can see the trampoline bed. The performer should never rush into the twisting movement but should always first initiate somersaulting movement. (See Figure 29-9.)

ADVANCED TRAMPOLINING STUNTS AND SEQUENCES

The dividing point between advanced and elementary trampolining skills and routines is arbitrary. The emphasis has been on performing sequences of trampolining skills, thus enabling the beginning trampolinist to acquire a feel for performing a routine. In the advanced section the emphasis is placed on performing single stunts; however, the trampolinist should, as soon as he masters a single stunt, attempt to work it into a routine. As a general rule, once a new stunt is mastered, it should usually go near the beginning or end of a routine.

(26) Three-quarter Forward Somersault from Feet

This skill is almost identical to the three-quarter forward somersault from a knee drop, except that it is initiated from a regular bounce and it is usually done with increased

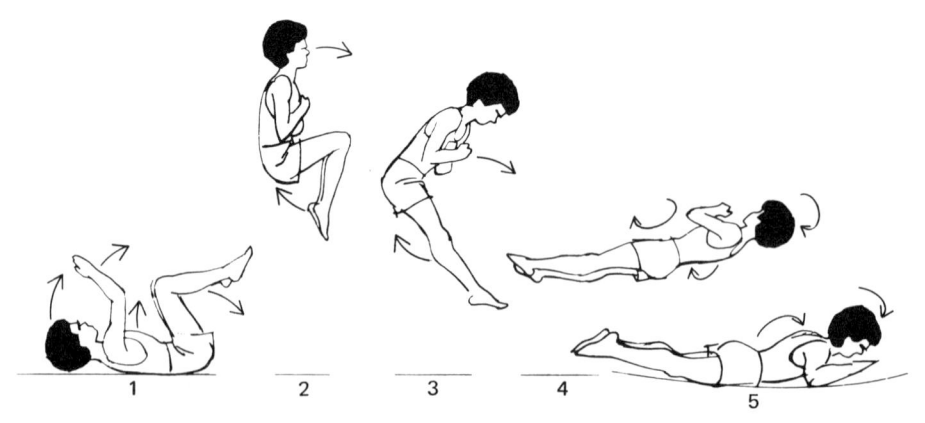

Figure 29-9. Cradle with one-half twist.

height. The performer should have his arms raised and flexed so that his hands are positioned above his ears. As he starts upward from the bed he throws his hands and arms forward and downward, and at the same time flexes his upper body and head downward. His hips should feel that they are being lifted straight upward. Not too much somersaulting action is required for the performer to revolve three quarters of a turn forward and land in a seat-drop position. The trampolinist looks for the tramploline bed and then immediately pikes to slow the somersaulting action.

(27) Forward Somersault from a Knee Drop

From a knee-drop landing the performer, with his arms flexed and overhead, initiates a forward somersaulting action as he takes off. Excess forward lean, which causes forward travel, should be avoided during the take-off. He should have a fair amount of height when going to the knee drop, and he should throw the somersaulting action vigorously, holding the tuck for an increased period of time. The performer should keep his chin on his chest and look down in order to see the bed as soon as it appears in his line of sight. Upon seeing the bed he thrusts his feet directly underneath himself. In case of an off-balance landing, a check bounce should be done immediately.

(28) Forward Somersault to Feet

The forward somersaulting action for this skill is initiated from a regular bounce, which gives the performer additional height, allowing this skill to be easily completed. (See Figure 29-10.)

(29) Crash Dive

The crash dive is commonly employed to initiate trampolining stunts—such as a cannon ball—that are done from the high back-drop position. The crash dive should be a simple skill to learn for the trampolinist who has mastered the forward somersault. However, because any landing that involves an upside-down position is potentially dangerous, the trampolinist must be quite sure of what he should do before attempting the crash dive. A slow forward somersaulting action is initiated in which the hips quickly go overhead. Watching the trampoline bed at all times, the performer then extends his body until coming downward. Although he is some distance above the trampoline bed he ducks his head and lands on his shoulders and upper back. With practice the trampolinist will be able to do a crash dive in which he comes down while almost upside down and does not duck his head until he is fairly close to the bed.

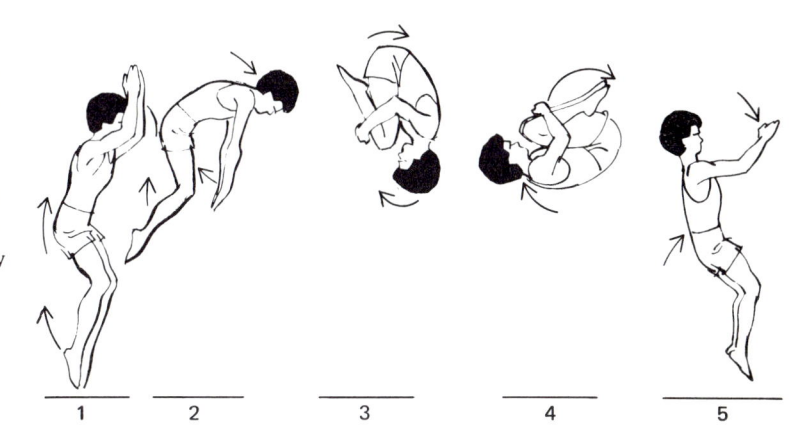

Figure 29-10. Front somersault.

(30) Backward Somersault from Feet

The performer by this time should have experienced the sensation of doing a complete back somersault from a back drop to a back drop. Therefore, the transition from feet to feet should be relatively simple. Because of a natural fear of falling backward—an element involved in this skill—it is recommended that the beginner wear a safety belt until he feels it is no longer needed. A hand spot for the next few attempts is also recommended.

Because the performer can see his landing site soon after the take-off, the backward somersault is an easier skill to perform and control than is the forward somersault. During the take-off, the performer should look straight ahead in order to retain his sense of balance and body position and not lean backward and off-balance.

The backward somersaulting action is initiated on the take-off by vigorously lifting the arms forward and upward until they are almost overhead. At the same time the performer vigorously lifts his tucked legs upward, attempting to bring his knees completely overhead to his waiting hands. The performer then tucks by grasping his knees and extends his head backward, looking for the trampoline bed. He holds his tuck position until he can extend his legs directly under his body and come to a controlled landing while maintaining his balance. During the first few landings, a check bounce should automatically be done. (See Figure 29-11.)

(31) Backward Somersault, Forward Somersault

Once the performer has mastered the forward and backward somersaults, he can combine them in a short routine.

Trampolining 447

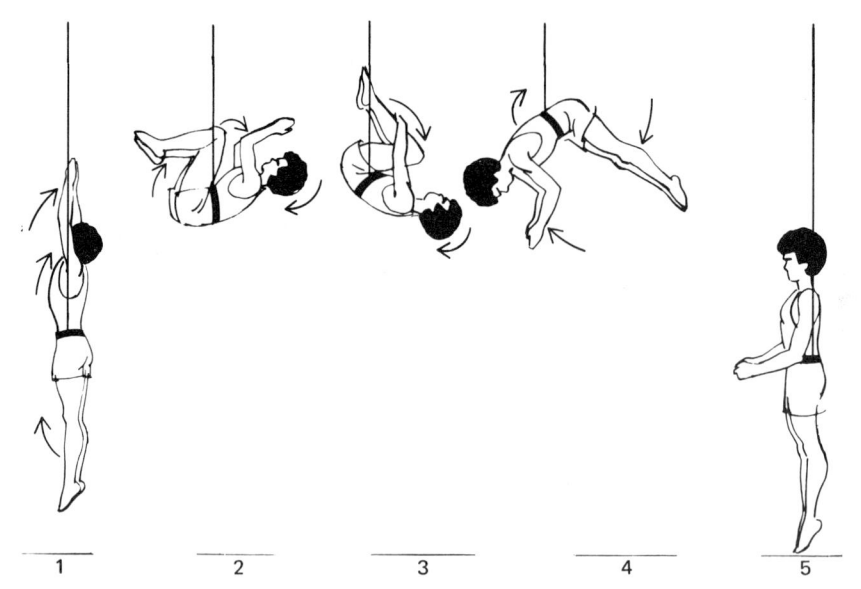

Figure 29-11. Back somersault.

(32) Three-quarter Backward Somersault

Once the backward somersault has been mastered, proficiency in performing a three-quarter backward somersault can be soon acquired. The first step is to learn to do a backward somersault while in an approximate layout position; that is, with the body extended. During the take-off, the arms are vigorously lifted forward, upward, and backward; the hips are forcefully thrust forward and upward; the body is arched; and the head is extended backward as far as possible. Because the body is extended, about twice as much effort is required to do the backward somersault in a layout position. The performer may need to pike his legs underneath his body during the first few attempts in order to complete the somersaulting action. Once this is mastered, the three-quarter back somersault is initiated in the same manner, but with somewhat less force. No leg pike occurs, but instead the trampolinist quickly looks for the bed while keeping his body extended; he then "floats" down to a front-drop landing. It is recommended that the performer be spotted closely during his first few attempts. (See Figure 29-12.)

(33) Three-quarter Backward Somersault with One-half Twist

A regular three-quarter backward somersault (layout position) is thrown, and as the performer sees the bed and is coming down to a front-drop landing, he does a quick one-half twist while his body is extended. To do the one-half twist he should look for the ceiling and pull both arms toward the side to which he is looking. He lands with his body extended and with his chin on his chest.

(34) Knee Drop, Forward Somersault to Feet, Front Drop, Half Turntable, One-half Turn Backward to Back Drop, Cradle, Feet, One-half Twist to Front Drop, Feet, Back Somersault

This routine is typical of a full-length routine that a trampolinist might perform, utilizing the skills previously described in this chapter.

(35) Baroni (Barani)

The Baroni is a forward somersault with an early one-half twist, and is almost the only twisting somersault per-

Figure 29-12. Three-quarter backward somersault.

448 *Individual and Team Sports*

Figure 29-13. Baroni.

formed with an early instead of a late twist. The early twisting action enables the trampolinist to see the trampoline bed throughout the complete stunt; thus it can be performed with safety and a controlled landing. The performer should think in terms of starting a vigorous layout front somersault and then, when upside down, doing a one-half twist while watching the middle of the bed. To initiate the Baroni the performer, with his flexed arms in an overhead position, throws his arms, head, and chest forward and downward so that they point toward the spot on the bed where his feet were. At the same time he lifts his hips and his legs upward as vigorously as possible. When the trampolinist is upside down he performs a one-half twist by continuing to look at the center of the trampoline bed and by rotating his hips a half turn while keeping his arms pointing down toward the center of the trampoline bed. The half twist is almost an automatic movement, as is landing on the feet. The important factors to remember are (1) to throw a complete forward somersaulting action so that the body can make a full 360° somersaulting turn with the body in a partial layout position and (2) to have the legs and hips pass directly above the body instead of to one side of it. (See Figure 29-13.)

(36) Backward Somersault with One-half Twist

The backward somersault with a half twist is probably easier to learn than is the Baroni, but it is more difficult to land in good balance and with full control. A regular layout back somersault is first thrown and held until the trampoline bed can be seen. At this point a one-half twist is done by rotating both arms and the head to one side, pulling with them, and looking for the opposite end of the trampoline. Because the trampolinist is upside down, or nearly so when the one-half twist occurs, he may be disoriented the first few times concerning which end of the trampoline is which. With practice, however, he will gain the ability to determine which end of the trampoline he should look toward. Having someone at the correct end of the trampoline bed yell "Here" as the trampolinist completes one half of the backward somersault usually aids in helping him learn which end of the trampoline bed to turn toward. When the backward somersault with the delayed half twist has been mastered the performer should practice doing the twist earlier, attempting to do it when exactly upside down. For a one-half twist, one end of the trampoline bed will seem to revolve a 180° turn.

(37) Baroni, Backward Somersault One-half Twist

The performer should do the Baroni with some height and in good balance.

(38) Backward One and One-quarter Somersault

This routine can be done to either a seat-drop or a backdrop landing, but the first few times it should be taken to a seat drop. The performer throws a regular backward somersault and tucks tightly. When he sees the trampoline bed, instead of extending his feet directly under him, he remains in a tucked position until his hips are directly under his chest, at which time he goes to a piked position and lands in a seat drop. When this has been mastered the performer can initiate the backward somersault with

Trampolining 449

additional force or height and, keeping his eyes open, can watch the trampoline bed in order to come to a back-drop landing.

(39) Forward One and One-quarter Somersault

The trampolinist should learn to do a forward somersault to his feet, extending out of the tuck while some distance above the bed. Then, throwing a regular forward somersault with slightly more force, or from slightly more height than usual, the tuck position is held a bit longer while watching very closely for the trampoline bed. Once the bed is seen the tuck is held until about a one-eighth revolution past a feet-landing position. At this instant the legs are extended to the rear and the performer drops down to a front-drop landing.

(40) Forward One and One-quarter Somersault with One-half Twist

When the performer has almost completed a high forward one and one-quarter somersault and his body is almost extended, he quickly cat twists by rotating both arms and his head toward one shoulder and looking for the ceiling. He should land in a regular back-drop position with his legs semiflexed. (See Figure 29-14.)

Other Skills

Many other advanced trampolining skills can be performed if the student has progressed to this stage. Competent coaching and spotting while learning advanced skills and routines are highly desirable.

Figure 29-14. Forward one and one-quarter somersault with one-half twist.

SELF-EVALUATION

Trampolining Skills Test Score Sheet

Name_____ Semester_____ Year_____

	Skill	0	1	2	3
1.	Three Feet Bounces, Three Tuck Bounces, Check Bounce (Breakfall)				
2.	Three One-half Pirouettes, Check Bounce (Breakfall)				
3.	Three Knee Drops, Three Seat Drops, Kill Bounce (Breakfall)				
4.	Knee Drop, Hand-and-knee Drop, Front Drop, Hand-and-knee Drop, Knee Drop, Check Bounce				
5.	Three Alternate Front Drops				
6.	Three Alternate Back Drops				
7.	Back Drop, Feet Bounce, Knee Drop, Seat Drop, Front Drop, Feet Bounce, Breakfall				
8.	Seat Drop, Knee Drop, Front Drop, Back Drop, Check Bounce				
9.	Back Drop, Feet Bounce, Knee Drop, Seat Drop, Half Twist, Seat Drop, Feet Bounce, Check Bounce				
10.	Swivel Hips, Hand-and-knee Drop, Front Drop, One-half Turntable, Front Drop, Check Bounce				
11.	Full Pirouette, Seat Drop, Front Drop, One-half Turntable, Check Bounce				
12.	Feet Bounce, One-half Twist to Back Drop, One-half Twist to Front Drop, Hand-and-knee Bounce, Feet Bounce, Check Bounce				
13.	Back Drop, Forward to Front Drop, Backward to Back Drop, Kill Bounce				
14.	Knee Drop, Roundoff, Knee Drop, Feet Bounce, Seat Drop, Front Drop, Back Drop, Check Bounce				
15.	Knee Drop, Front-over to Seat Drop, Feet Bounce, Swivel Hips, Check Bounce				
16.	Seat Drop, Full Twist, Seat Drop, Front Drop, Half Turntable, Front Drop, Check Bounce				
17.	Back Drop, One-half Turn Forward with One-half Twist, Back Drop, One-quarter Turn Forward with One-half Twist to Feet-Landing Position				
18.	Consecutive Full Turntables				
19.	Consecutive Full-twisting Back Drops				
20.	Consecutive Full-twisting Front Drops				
21.	Front Drop to Front Cody, Back Drop, Seat Drop, Check Bounce				
22.	Back Drop, Back Pullover to Feet, Knee Drop, Swivel Hips, Check Bounce				
23.	Back Drop, Forward Somersault to Back Drop, One-quarter Turn Forward with Half Twist to Feet, Full Pirouette, Check Bounce				
24.	Back Pullover to Back Drop, One-half Turn Forward to Front Drop, Full Turntable, Check Bounce				

450 *Individual and Team Sports*

Skill	0	1	2	3
25. Cradle with One-half Twist, One-half Turn Backward to Back Drop, Back Pullover to Feet				
26. Three-quarter Forward Somersault from Feet				
27. Forward Somersault from a Knee Drop				
28. Forward Somersault to Feet				
29. Crash Dive				
30. Backward Somersault from Feet				
31. Backward Somersault, Forward Somersault				
32. Three-quarter Backward Somersault				
33. Three-quarter Backward Somersault with One-half Twist				
34. Knee Drop, Forward Somersault to Feet, Front Drop, Half-turntable, One-half Turn Backward to Back Drop, Cradle, Feet, One-half Twist to Front Drop, Feet, Back Somersault				
35. Baroni (Barani)				
36. Backward Somersault with One-half Twist				
37. Baroni, Backward Somersault One-half Twist				
38. Backward One and One-quarter Somersault				
39. Forward One and One-quarter Somersault				
40. Forward One and One-quarter Somersault with One-half Twist				

Total Points _____

0 = failed
1 = completed with poor form and at least one break.
2 = completed with fair form and no breaks.
3 = completed with good form and no breaks.

A = 70 points and above
B = 55–69 points
C = 35–54 points
D = 15–34 points
F = 0–14 points

Selected References

Griswold, Larry, and Glenn Wilson. *Trampoline Tumbling Today.* New York: A. S. Barnes, 1970.

This book first appeared in 1948. Larry Griswold is a world-famous trampolinist who has for many years presented an immensely popular trampolining act in Europe and in the United States and on TV. The basic skills of trampolining are described in detail and are profusely illustrated. The co-author, Glenn Wilson, is a former national champion and is now a college gymnastics coach.

La Due, Frank, and Jim Norman. *This Is Trampolining.* Cedar Rapids, Iowa: Nissen Trampoline Co., 1960.

Written by two former University of Iowa National Trampoline Champions, this book includes advanced trampolining stunts. Sections on the mechanics of trampolining and mechanical analysis of several stunts, and fundamentals are included. The book is unique in that 15 stunts are shown by multiple-flip pictures in which action is depicted by flipping the pages rapidly. 167 pp.

Musker, Frank F., Donald R. Casady, and Leslie W. Irwin. *A Guide to Gymnastics.* New York: Macmillan, Inc., 1968.

All aspects of gymnastics preparation, training, and skill learning are covered in this book, in which chapter 6 is devoted to trampolining. Each of the skills, which proceed through an elementary level, is illustrated. 256 pp.

Szypula, George. *Beginning Trampolining.* Belmont, Calif.: Wadsworth, 1968.

In this booklet a variety of elementary and intermediate trampolining skills are explained and illustrated. Rules for safety and training are also presented by the author, who has been the gymnastics coach at Michigan State University for several years. 57 pp.

CHAPTER 30

Tumbling and balancing
*D. R. Casady**
The University of Iowa

HISTORY

Man has apparently engaged in tumbling and balancing activities for countless generations. A number of written works mention that the ancient Greeks and Romans engaged in these activities. The jesters of the Middle Ages frequently utilized tumbling and balancing as a form of entertainment in the courts of kings and lords, as did traveling troupes who journeyed from town to town. Tumbling and balancing activities still possess a high degree of entertainment value as evidenced by the popularity of one-, two- and three-man balancing and tumbling acts on television and in night clubs and other show places.

For many years tumbling was a competitive event in the United States at both the high school and college level. However, several years ago it was eliminated as a college competitive event so that the gymnastics rules followed in the United States would agree with those of the Federated International Gymnastics Association, which includes floor exercise as a competitive event. Floor exercise is mainly comprised of tumbling, balancing, and strength and flexibility skills that are combined into a graceful sequence of rhythmic movements. For this reason neither tumbling nor balancing activities alone has ever been a competitive event in the modern Olympic Games.

Tumbling and balancing activities often are included as two components in gymnastics classes. For convenience, tumbling and balancing activities have been placed in a separate chapter in this publication because they frequently are taught in a class separate from gymnastics apparatus activities.

Because tumbling and balancing require little or no special equipment or areas in which to perform them, and because they can be engaged in safely by quite young participants, these activities are considered by many to be a foundation from which skills are developed for regular participation in gymnastics apparatus events.

DESCRIPTION OF TUMBLING AND BALANCING ACTIVITIES

The urge to hold balanced positions of various kinds and to do leaping, somersaulting, and twisting movements seems to be inherent in man, who eons ago must have discovered the inherent appeal of these activities. Most tumbling movements involve performing precise and sometimes rather complex movements, usually immediately after leaping off the floor and in a short space of time. Balancing skills combine varying degrees of balancing ability with at least a fair amount of strength and skill. A particular balancing feat is normally held for at least a few seconds in order to demonstrate control and mastery. A large variety of balancing and tumbling skills can be performed in a team effort by more than one participant.

UNIQUE VALUES OF TUMBLING AND BALANCING

Regular participation in tumbling and balancing activities brings to the performer a sense of accomplishment, a sense of enjoyment and fun, and a sense of having special control over one's body. New tumbling or balancing skills and new combinations or sequences of these activities can

---

*Dr. Casady has been long intrigued with tumbling and balancing activities. He first engaged seriously in these activities while in the Armed Services and later was a member of The University of Iowa gymnastics team. During the past several years he has taught tumbling and balancing activities to a large number of high school and college students. He is also the co-author of the book, *A Guide to Gymnastics,* which was published by Macmillan, Inc., in 1968.

452 *Individual and Team Sports*

usually be practiced, which further challenge the participant.

Tumbling activities involve the ability to do precise movements in an extremely short amount of time; they develop the ability to generate an explosive force or power; and they can help to develop strength, flexibility, and agility. Regular participation in balancing activities can develop a high amount of strength, a well-developed sense of balance, and additional flexibility. Skill in tumbling and balancing may enable one to avoid a serious injury in case an accident occurs.

EQUIPMENT

No special equipment is needed to engage in tumbling or balancing activities. Insulite or other types of mats are helpful in cushioning the landing shock and are especially valuable when tumbling stunts are being learned. Special extra-thick mats have recently been developed to aid in absorbing much of the landing force when learning new tumbling stunts. The safety belt (either the overhead or the hand-held type) is frequently utilized when advanced tumbling skills are practiced.

Balancing activities can be performed on a variety of gymnastics apparatus and once mastered many can be done on a bare floor. Those described in this chapter require no special equipment, but again mats provide an extra safety factor and should be used during all stages of learning.

TECHNIQUES OF PARTICIPATION

Safety

During the learning stages, in addition to having mats under the performer, at least one spotter, who has been trained in correct spotting procedures, should be present when tumbling or balancing skills are being learned. If the performer falls or loses control, his upper body, especially his head, should be protected by the spotter from landing on the mat or floor. This is usually accomplished by grasping solidly with both hands the neck, shoulder, or upper arm of the performer and lifting. During the performance of a moving or revolving tumbling skill, the spotter should step very close and place his hands on the upper back or chest of the performer, ready to give assistance and lift as needed. In case a stunt is overthrown, or if the performer loses his balance after landing, the spotter may need to give physical assistance to help the performer regain his balance. All members of a tumbling and balancing class should closely observe the spotting procedures used by their instructor and should work under his tutelage in acquiring skill in spotting other students.

Because tumbling and balancing activities can be quite strenuous and may strain the muscles, the performer should thoroughly warm up and stretch before performing difficult skills. Reviewing mentally the tumbling or balancing skill or sequence of skills that is to be performed is another recommended safety measure. In addition, the performer should anticipate what saving techniques (saves) he can use should he lose his balance, get lost, or otherwise encounter difficulty in completing the planned skill or sequence of skills.

Specific Training Methods for Acquiring Skill in Tumbling and Balancing

The tumbling and balancing student should practice one skill only so long as he can give his full attention and effort to it. As soon as his attention or concentration lags, he should start to review or practice other skills. In many cases lead-up skills can be mastered in order to aid in learning a difficult or complicated skill.

The performer is urged to concentrate his efforts during his early learning stages to doing sequences of skills or a short routine. Thus, although individual skills are mainly presented in this chapter, suggestions will occasionally be given on combining them into short routines.

The tumbling and balancing skills contained in this chapter should be practiced repeatedly until the performer can do them with good form. When performing balancing activities the performer should be aware of his body position: the toes and feet are pointed away from the legs; the legs are together and straight; and the legs hold correct form throughout the entire performance of the skill or sequence. While learning a new skill, the performer must be conscious of his form and try to maintain correct body form at all times. When sitting, or in other positions, practice in pointing the feet and toes and keeping the legs squeezed together and straight will help this to become a habit that requires little conscious effort or thought when performing.

For the doubles balancing and tumbling activities, it is helpful to first practice a stunt with a partner who is sufficiently strong and skillful to give active help. Once the skill is mastered, the performer may want to practice it with a variety of partners.

Regularly engaging in flexibility exercises is also a helpful training device for success in tumbling and balancing. The successful performance of tumbling activities requires an above-average amount of explosive power; in some instances balancing activities require an above-average degree of strength. The novice can enhance his acquisition of tumbling and balancing skills by engaging in weight-training activities, which are described in Chapter 32 of this book.

TUMBLING AND BALANCING SKILLS

Introduction

For the sake of convenience and for ease of understanding the activities in this chapter are divided into four parts: (1) one-man (single) tumbling activities, (2) two-man (doubles) tumbling activities, (3) one-man (single) balancing activities, and (4) two-man (doubles) balancing activities. To increase variety, to avoid boredom, and to exercise all parts of the body, it is suggested that all these activities be engaged in during each class period or exercise session.

Even though the skills and sequences contained in this chapter are representative and somewhat typical of what might be included at an elementary- or an advanced-level class they are by no means inclusive. Instead they are only representative—many variations of these skills exist, as do many other skills that are not mentioned.

When a single skill is presented and described, two or three skills of approximately equal difficulty are presented in one grouping. This is done in order to accommodate individual aptitudes and interests. This arrangement permits the student to at least learn, after a reasonable amount of practice, one of the skills included in the group. The ambitious student will probably attempt to master all the skills in each group. In general, the skills are listed in order of difficulty.

The nomenclature and terms employed to describe various tumbling and balancing skills are not standardized throughout the United States. The commonly used names for such skills are therefore employed in this chapter.

SINGLES TUMBLING SKILLS

Forward Roll
Backward Roll

Forward Roll. The performer squats and places his hands in front of his feet about shoulder width apart. Tucking his chin on his chest, he lifts his hips forward, and pushes forward while tucking his body. His arms support his weight until the back of his head and upper back contact the mat. He continues rolling forward while tucked until he can come to his feet in a squat position.

Backward Roll. From a squatting position the performer thrusts his body backward while keeping his body tucked. He rolls to his hips, back, and then supports his weight with his arms (hands under the shoulders) while upside down. He remains tucked, pushes with his hands, and comes to his feet in a low squat position.

Shoulder Roll (Football Roll)
Side Roll
Straddle Roll-Up

Shoulder Roll (Figure 30-1). The performer bends over and places his left (right) forearm on the mat. He pushes forward and tucks his body while his weight is successively supported by his left shoulder, upper back, right hip, right knee, and feet. With practice the shoulder roll can be done quickly from a run.

Side Roll. This can be attempted first from a stationary hand-and-knee position on the mat. The performer rolls directly to one side and his weight transfers to that shoulder and hip, to his back, to the other shoulder and hip, and then to his original position. When done from a run, the performer jumps to a sideward position and starts the roll with his weight supported by one hand and foot.

Straddle Roll-up (Figure 30-2). A vigorous forward roll is initiated and, as the last half begins, the legs are extended and spread wide. While the weight is on the hips and the body is piked, the hands are placed on the mat near the crotch and they push forcefully while the performer leans forward and comes to a straddle stand.

Five-foot Dive and Roll (2 points maximum)
Eight-foot Dive and Roll (3 points maximum)

The forward roll and the dive and roll should first be practiced from a standing position. Once a performer masters a simple forward roll he next leans and reaches his hands forward some distance in front of his feet. As his

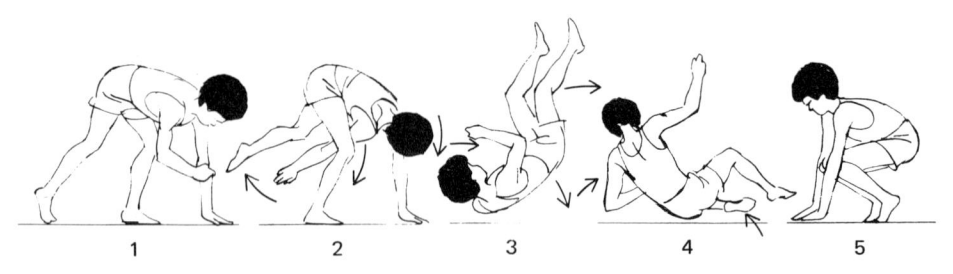

Figure 30-1. Shoulder roll.

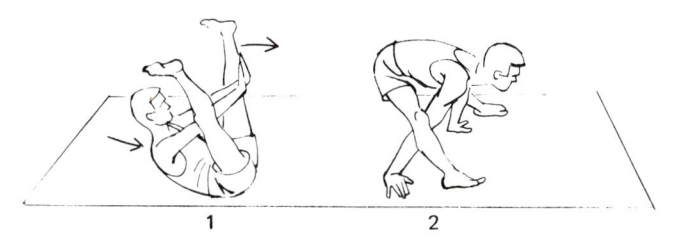

Figure 30-2. Straddle roll-up.

hands begin to contact the floor he pushes vigorously with his feet, thrusting his hips to a position above or past his hands. He then ducks his head, tucks his body, and holding the tuck rolls forward, coming to his feet. This phase can be practiced profitably by diving over a rolled-up mat or other soft small object. Proceeding from a standing dive and roll, the next step is a slow short run and jump to a two-footed landing and then a somewhat high dive and roll. During the initial learning stages of the dive and roll, the performer should be closely spotted by a spotter who grasps the performer's shoulder and upper arm and insures that the performer goes past a piked handstand position and into a tucked position with the head ducked. The performer should closely watch the mat during the dive until after his hands actually make contact with the mat and he flexes his arm and starts to tuck his head and body. To increase the distance of the dive and roll an increase is made in the speed of the run and the force of the leap.

Cartwheel
Roundoff

Cartwheel (Figure 30-3). In a cartwheel the action is similar to that of a wheel turning. The performer travels directly sideward while keeping his arms and legs spread wide apart and extended; his body is slightly arched; his head is flexed backward; and he is looking toward his hands as they contact the mat. From a sideward stand on the mat, the performer vigorously bends downward and sideward and places one hand on the mat close to his near foot. He then pushes vigorously off the mat with both feet as he brings the other hand down to the mat in a line directly sideward to the position of the first hand. This places him in an upside-down position, similar to a spread-arm handstand. The performer then whips one leg sideward and down to the mat and in line with the line formed by his two hands. He pushes off the mat with the near hand and then the far hand, bringing the other foot to the mat. With practice, cartwheels can be initiated from a short run and a hop or skipping step.

Roundoff (Figure 30-4). The roundoff is usually started from a run and is used to convert forward running speed to backward momentum. It begins somewhat like a cartwheel but requires an additional one-quarter twist while upside down. Practicing first from a stand, the performer, facing the length of the mat, raises one knee fairly high. With his hands directly overhead and extended, the performer snaps his raised leg down to the mat; at the same time he flexes sharply forward at the waist and brings his extended arms forward and downward so that they contact the mat in front of his forward leg. The hands are about shoulder width apart and form a straight line with the forward foot. The legs are thrust upward, at which time the position is similar to the cartwheel except that the legs are together. At this instant the performer pikes his leg and quickly snaps them toward the mat to a position past his hands. At the same time the performer pushes vigorously with his shoulders and arms and thrusts his upper body upward while his legs are piking down toward the mat. The performer comes to a stand facing the opposite end of the mat from which he initiated the roundoff. Practicing the snap-down movement from a semihandstand position is especially helpful in mastering the roundoff.

When done from a short run, skip on one foot (the skip or hop step is often done with the left foot) while raising the other leg until the knee is as high as the hip.

Figure 30-3. Cartwheel.

Tumbling and Balancing

Figure 30-4. Roundoff.

As the skip is completed, the raised leg is forcefully stomped down on the mat and the performer quickly snaps his upper body to the mat by flexing at the waist and swinging his extended arms forward and downward to the mat and doing a fast roundoff. A quick second jump and twist can then be done upon landing in order to control the fast backward movement.

Backward Extension Roll
Back Roll to Chest Roll

Backward Extension Roll. In the initial learning stages, the performer squats and allows his body to fall backward, pushing backward vigorously with his legs while keeping his body tucked. His hands are so positioned that his thumbs are alongside the sides of his head. As the performer comes to an almost upside-down position, he supports his weight primarily with his arms while keeping his head flexed. At this stage he thrusts his legs upward and slightly backward while extending his arms, thus coming to a momentary handstand position. He shortly thereafter snaps down as in the roundoff, coming to a standing position if possible. The more vigorously the initial backward movement is taken, the less effort will be needed to complete the backward extension roll.

Back Roll to Chest Roll (Figure 30-5). Once the backward extension roll is learned, the chest roll is executed after coming to a momentary but slightly overbalanced handstand with the head flexed back. Watching the mat, the performer arches his body and lowers it as it slowly falls toward his stomach. His chest contacts the mat and, keeping his body arched as much as possible, he rolls from his chest to his stomach, hips, thighs, and knees.

Sequence: Forward Roll, Dive and Roll, One-half Pirouette, Backward Roll, Backward Extension Roll to Stand

The performer should have mastered all the preceding skills and should practice combining them in this routine or other combinations. The rolls should be done with good form and adequate speed to proceed without a break to the next skill.

Three Cartwheels, Roundoff, Backward Extension Roll

To do a series of cartwheels well, the performer must whip vigorously into each cartwheel movement and continue the cartwheeling by pushing with his arms and legs.

Figure 30-5. Back roll to chest roll.

456   *Individual and Team Sports*

Forward Neckspring from Rolled-up or Stacked Mat
Forward Headspring from Rolled-up or Stacked Mat
Forward Handspring from Rolled-up or Stacked Mat

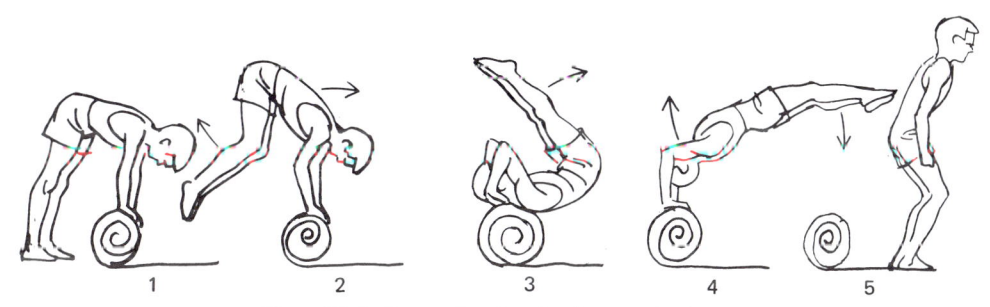

Forward Neckspring from a Raised Mat (Figure 30-6). The tumbler does a kipping movement from an elevated body position, which raises his center of gravity and thus eases the task of getting his feet under him. The raised mat should be securely held by another performer or spotter. The tumbler stands in front of the rolled-up or stacked mat, bends over, and places his hands and the back of his head and upper shoulders on top of it. Keeping his body tucked, the tumbler starts to roll forward and, as his hips pass over his shoulders and he starts to fall forward, he rapidly thrusts his legs forward and forcefully arches his body while pushing vigorously with his arms. The kipping and pushing action should rotate his body while raising his hips, bringing his feet underneath him to where at least a squat landing can be made. Once a standing neckspring has been learned, the tumbler can walk or slowly run to the mat and quickly perform the kipping action after he passes an upside-down position. The spotter grasps the performer's upper arm and can assist him by pushing on his back.

Forward Headspring from a Raised Mat. The forward neckspring is a natural lead-up to the forward headspring, which is about as easy to learn. The performer starts from a stand, walk, or slow run, taking a skipping or hopping step immediately before reaching the raised mat. First, the flexed, raised leg vigorously stomps down just behind the mat, while the other leg whips behind and overhead. At the same time he flexes sharply and forcefully at the waist, bringing his hands and head down to the top of the raised mat. He quickly comes to somewhat of a headstand position with his hands alongside his head and with his body piked. As he falls forward off-balance, he whips both legs forward and downward, coming from the piked body position to an arched body position or to a squat position. At the same time the performer pushes vigorously with his hands and attempts to come to a squat or arched position on his feet.

A Forward Handspring from a Raised Mat. For this skill the arms remain straight but the action otherwise is almost identical to that for a headspring. Starting from a run and skip, the handspring is done with increased speed, in which the performer attempts to come to a standing position.

Forward Headspring
Forward Handspring

The actions for the forward headspring and handspring are identical to those used with a raised mat, except that the movements must be done with increased speed and force.

Kip (Snap-up), Forward Roll, Forward Headspring

The kip, or snap-up, is quite similar to a forward neckspring. The tumbler may go into the snap-up position by performing a partial backward roll, rolling backward until his body weight is on his shoulders. He is in a tight tuck and his hands are resting on the mat alongside his head. The tumbler then vigorously thrusts his feet upward and forward at about a 45° angle and at the same time pushes vigorously with his arms. As his body rotates he flexes his knees, placing his feet underneath his hips and landing in a squat position. Once this has been mastered, the performer can do a forward roll, doing a snap-up during its latter stages.

Forward Roll, Cartwheel, Roundoff, Backward Roll to Momentary Headstand, Forward Roll, Dive and Roll, Headspring

By this time all the stunts contained in this sequence of skills should have been mastered; the performer has the task of combining them into this or a similar routine.

Figure 30-6. Forward neckspring from a raised mat.

Tumbling and Balancing

Forward Somersault

(See Figure 29-10.) The front somersault progression can be learned with almost complete safety, and the height of the somersault can be gradually increased until a feet landing is attained. When learning the front somersault, the landing surface should be quite soft. An eight-inch soft-landing mat, several mats piled on top of one another, or an all-cotton mattress can be used. Standing just off or on one end of the mat the performer places his hands above his head with his hands slightly above his ears. Leaning slightly forward off-balance, he jumps vigorously upward and simultaneously whips his hands and arms forward and downward, while flexing sharply forward at the waist, tucking his body downward. While performing these actions he should attempt to jump his hips upward and then bring his heels to them. He should land on his back or seat with his head tucked forward in order to see the landing surface. The performer must tuck his arms, head, and upper body with considerable speed and force.

Once this phase is mastered and the movements are well coordinated, the tumbler performs the front somersault from a run, hop, and throw from a two-footed take-off. He takes off with his hands above his head and his body straight. He should land in at least a sitting position and hopefully in a squatting position. With some practice he should proceed to a semisquat landing. He then practices a forward somersault on a level mat.

During all the learning phases, the performer can easily be spotted by a spotter who places a hand on the back of the performer's neck or upper back and insures that he somersaults well past his head.

Back Handspring

Several lead-up skills for learning the action of a back handspring (back flipflop) appear in the doubles tumbling section. Practicing these skills should enable the tumbler to learn a back handspring rapidly and safely. The performer should have trained for some time in achieving maximum shoulder (arm overhead) and upper-back flexibility to the rear. Back bends and similar stretching movements are helpful. The back flipflop should be first attempted on a soft mat with one or two spotters present.

Initiating a sitting-down action, the tumbler swings his extended arms behind him a short distance. As he falls backward off-balance, he forcefully swings his outstretched arms forward, upward, and above and behind his head. At the same time he jumps upward and backward thrusting his hips upward while arching his body and extending his head backward. Pulling his hands (which are about shoulder width apart and facing in the direction his feet were pointing) forcefully underneath his head while looking at the mat, the tumbler lands in a fast-moving handstand from which he does a vigorous snap-down. The spotter should lift the performer's hips up and back during the first few tries. (See Figure 30-7.)

Because the back handspring and the back somersault involve different types of body action, one of them should be learned before the other is attempted so that negative transfer, which inhibits learning, does not occur.

Back Somersault

(See Figure 29-11.) The standing performer swings his outstretched arms (extended forward to the front) down and back and simultaneously dips his body, primarily by flexing his legs at the knees. His arms are quickly swung forward, upward, and overhead while he leaps as high as possible, thrusting his hips up and bringing his knees (legs tucked) to his hands. He tucks tightly while extending his head back, looking for the landing spot on the mat, to which he guides his feet. He lands in a semicrouched position. During the first attempts the spotter should lift, help rotate, and guide the tumbler.

Figure 30-7. Back handspring.

Figure 30-8. Two-man rolls.

DOUBLES TUMBLING SKILLS

Many of the doubles tumbling skills presented in this section are variations of some of the singles tumbling skills presented in the last section. Otherwise, they are lead-up skills for learning handspringing and somersaulting movements.

Two-man Rolls—Two Forward and Two Backward
Triple Rolls (Monkey Rolls)

Two-man Rolls (Figure 30-8). When performing two-man forward rolls each performer should have the feeling of doing a short dive and roll. One partner lies on his back with his hands near his shoulders. The other partner, facing the same direction, stands close to the shoulders of the supine man, who pikes his legs and grasps each ankle of the standing man. Grasping the supine man's ankles firmly, the standing man does a short dive, placing the feet of the bottom man shoulder width apart and as near his own hips as possible. As the feet of the bottom man contact the mat, the standing man ducks his head as he flexes his arms and contacts the mat with his upper back. He then rolls forward as vigorously as possible in order to pull his partner to a standing position. The man who is now standing up then repeats this action. The supine man should relax his legs and let the top man control them.

Two-man backward rolls are similar to a backward roll and a backward extension roll. Starting as for the two-man forward roll, the standing man does as compact a backward roll as is possible for him. At the same time he pulls very vigorously on the legs of the man lying down in order to pull him to his feet. The man lying down simultaneously performs the action of the backward extension roll. With some practice two-man rolls can be done quite rapidly.

Triple Rolls (Figure 30-9). The three performers either do all side rolls or a combination of forward rolls and dive and rolls (all described earlier). When learning the sequence of movements, side rolls should first be done.

The performers line up on the mat in a hand-and-knee position, all facing the same direction toward one side of the mat. One outside man does a side roll to his hands and knees, coming to the middle position. At the same time the center man leaps over him and to the outside by quickly extending his legs and thrusting with his arms. The man who performed the side roll to the middle then leaps over the other outside man who is doing a side roll into the center position. This action is continued with the outside man doing a side roll into the middle and the center man always leaping above the incoming man and going to the outside.

The sequence of action for forward rolls and dives and rolls is the same except that the outside man always does a tight forward roll to the middle while the center man simultaneously is doing a dive and roll over the incoming forward-rolling outside man. As soon as the outside man has done a forward roll to the center he comes to his feet

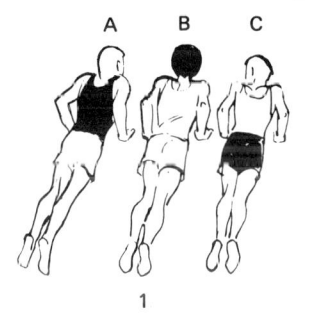

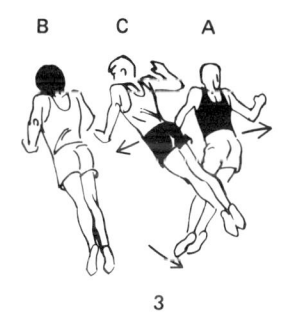

Figure 30-9. Triple roll.

Tumbling and Balancing 459

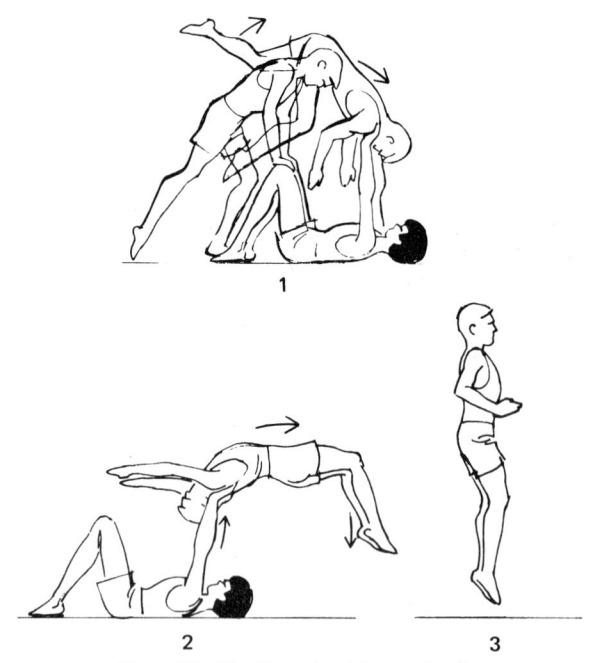

Figure 30-10. Knee-shoulder handspring.

Knee-shoulder Handspring (Figure 30-10). The bottom man supplies considerable lift and somersaulting action to the top man to aid him in landing on his feet. The top man should keep his head and shoulders forward so that they are directly above the head and shoulders of the bottom man. Starting from a standing position, the top man places a hand on either knee of the bottom man, bends forward, and quickly whips one leg and then the other leg upward and forward. At the same time the bottom man, who is lying on his back with his knees flexed, reaches upward and grasps and supports the shoulders or upper portion of the back of the top man. As the top man passes a handstand position and starts to come to his feet with his body arched, the bottom man pushes upward and backward on the top man's shoulders. When performing this skill the top man should avoid the tendency to do it as for a forward roll; instead, he should keep his body arched and his head flexed back as long as possible. As his legs whip toward the mat, he flexes his head forward, and looks down his chest at his landing site. An experienced bottom man can be immensely helpful in facilitating the learning of a shoulder-knee handspring.

and immediately does a dive and roll over the other outside man, who is doing a tight forward roll into the middle. The performers should signal when they want to quit performing the three-man rolls and all should stop at the same time.

Front Headspring over Partner
Knee-shoulder Handspring

Front Headspring over Partner's Back. The partner assumes a hands-and-knees position crossways on the mat. The tumbler does an overbalanced headstand against one side of the partner, rolling over onto his back to a squat position in a forward-roll-type action. Later, the tumbler can do a slow run and skip, placing the back of his neck against the partner's side and doing a bent-arm handspring to his feet.

Straddle-lift Front Somersault
Wheelbarrow Pitch Front Somersault
Ankle-lift Front Somersault

Straddle-lift Front Somersault (Figure 30-11). The standing performer spreads his legs, bends forward, and positions his forearms between his legs. His partner stands behind him and grasps his wrists. At the count of three (dipping with each count), the performer jumps up and rotates forward while keeping his legs spread and staying in a semitucked position. The bottom man forcefully lifts on the performer's wrist until after he lands in a semi-squat position.

Wheelbarrow Pitch Front Somersault (Figure 30-12). With the top man in a push-up position with his legs

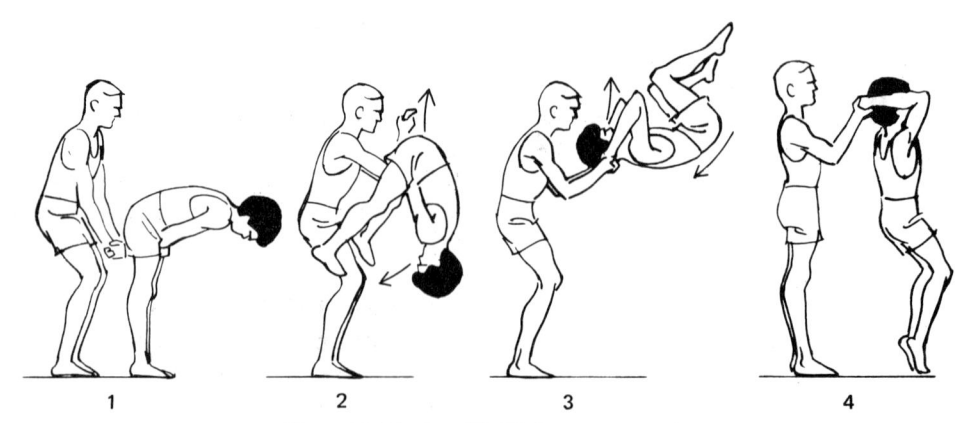

Figure 30-11. Straddle-lift front somersault.

460   *Individual and Team Sports*

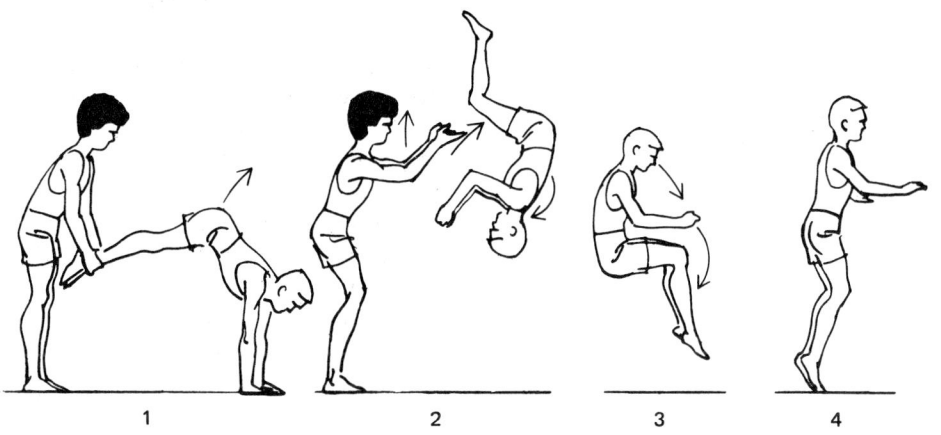

Figure 30-12. Wheelbarrow pitch front somersault.

spread, his ankles are grasped by the bottom man. On the count of three, the bottom man lifts vigorously as the top man, keeping his arms straight, pikes his hips upward and forward while resisting the lifting action on his legs. He then tucks his heels to his buttocks, flexes his head forward, tucks, and opens to a bent-leg landing when he sees the mat.

Ankle-lift Front Somersault (Figure 30-13). With the instep of his flexed leg grasped by the bottom man, who is immediately behind him, the top man keeps his flexed knee as far forward as possible, dips, leaps upward, tucks, and does a front somersault (described in the previous section). The bottom man lifts as high as possible when the top man takes off. The lift and timing for this skill can be practiced by the top man jumping as high as possible but not somersaulting.

Back-to-back Pullover
Foot-push Back Handspring

Back-to-back Pullover (Figure 30-14). Standing back to back the partners interlock elbows. The bottom man posi-

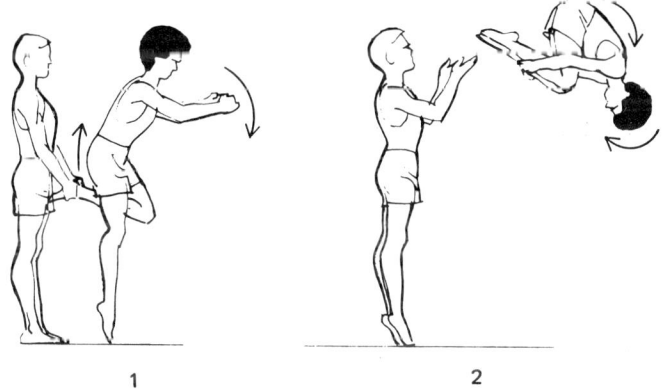

Figure 30-13. Ankle-lift front somersault.

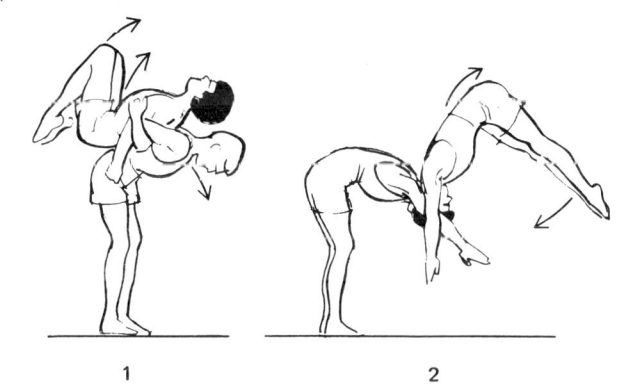

Figure 30-14. Back-to-back pullover.

tions his hips under those of the top man, and on the count of three he pulls hard with his arms while flexing forward quickly until his back is parallel to the mat. As the pull begins the top man flexes his legs overhead and rides on his partner's back until he can pike to the mat. With practice and sufficient snap, the partners can release their arms well before the landing.

Foot-push Back Handspring (Figure 30-15). Lying on his back, the bottom man places his feet against his partner's buttocks. The top man drops back into an arch, pulling back and down with his arms and head until he can place his hands on the mat beyond his partner's head. With his feet the bottom man supports the top man's weight until his hands almost touch the mat. At this time the top man's weight is overbalanced and the bottom man pushes upward and backward with his feet after first catching the top man's shoulders. The top man then pikes down to a feet landing.

Side-pitch Back Somersault
Sitting-pitch Back Somersault
Toe-pitch Back Somersault

Side-pitch Back Somersault. Assuming the position depicted in Figure 30-16, the top man dips and jumps

Tumbling and Balancing

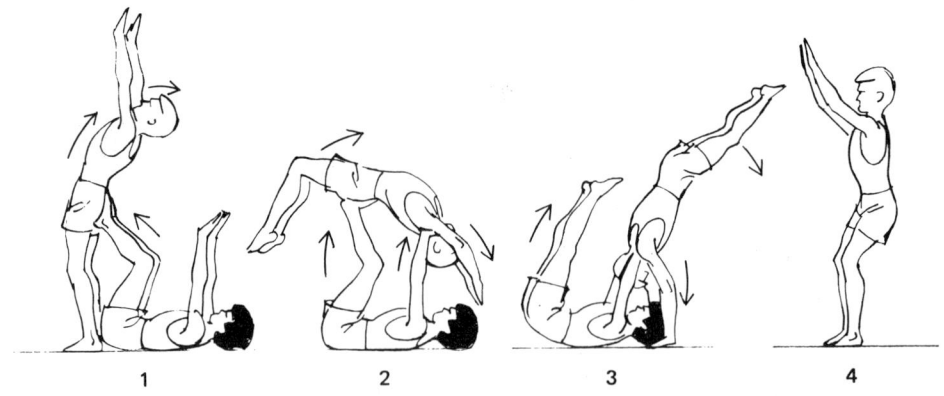

Figure 30-15. Foot-push back handspring.

Figure 30-16. Side-pitch back somersault.

upward. He first pushes down with his raised leg and then tucks, completing a back somersault action as described in the singles tumbling section. The bottom man lifts straight up with his legs and both arms.

Sitting-pitch Back Somersault (Figure 30-17). Facing the seated bottom man who has his legs spread, the top man steps on his hands. On the signal he jumps up and performs a back somersault while the bottom man lifts vigorously.

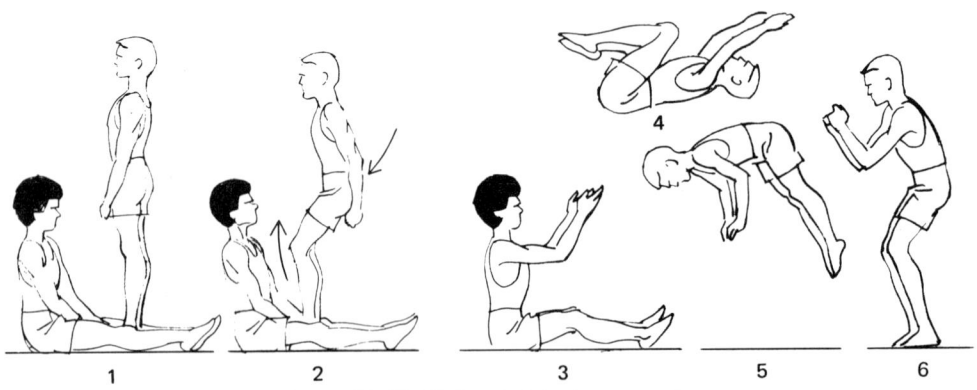

Figure 30-17. Sitting-pitch back somersault.

462 *Individual and Team Sports*

Figure 30-18. Toe-pitch back somersault.

Toe-pitch Back Somersault (Figure 30-18). The top man walks to the bottom man, flexes a leg (the right one, if right handed), and steps into the bottom man's interlocked hands. They dip together and the top man jumps up, pushing his foot hard against the bottom man's hands before tucking sufficiently to complete a back somersault. Again, the bottom man lifts vigorously.

SINGLES BALANCING SKILLS

Squat Handstand

The squat handstand, crab stand, or tip-up balance is a basic balance in which the performer supports his entire body weight on his hands. The performer squats, places the palms of his hands flat on the mat, and rests his knees on his arms just above his elbows. Keeping his head tilted back and looking forward, the performer supports his weight on his hands and knees and gradually tips forward until his toes leave the mat. By experimenting, the performer will learn to control his balance through his hands or by moving his head up or down, moving it up (or pushing with his finger tips) when he begins to overbalance and moving it downward (or placing his weight to the heels of the hands) when he underbalances.

Head-and-hand Stand

The head-and-hand stand, commonly called the headstand, is a basic three-point balance in which the two hands and the forehead form an equilateral triangle. By keeping his center of gravity within this triangle, the performer should be able to maintain a headstand for several seconds. The performer places his hands on the mat about shoulder width apart and then places his forehead, at about the hairline, an equal distance ahead of his hands. From this squatting position he slowly raises both legs upward, keeping them tucked until his hips are directly over his shoulders. He then extends his legs, holding them straight, squeezing them together, and pointing his feet and toes.

Head-in-hand Stand (10 seconds)
Forearm Stand (10 seconds)

Head-in-hand Stand (Figure 30-19). This is identical with the headstand except that the performer's forehead is placed in his cupped hands, which are placed one above the other. The resulting equilateral triangle has a small base, requiring the balance to be carefully controlled.

Figure 30-19. Head-in-hand stand.

Tumbling and Balancing

Forearm Stand. The forearms (including elbows and palms) are placed on the mat about shoulder width apart and parallel. Keeping his head forward, the performer extends one leg behind and overhead as high as possible. He then slowly kicks the other alongside it, and moves slowly into the forearm stand. If he begins to overbalance, he presses forcefully with his finger tips; if he begins to underbalance, he increases the arch of his body, flexes his upper arms, and moves his shoulders and upper body forward from his elbows.

V Balance
Straddle Stance

V Balance Holding Feet (Balance Seat) (Figure 30-20). Sitting tucked on the floor, the performer raises and extends his legs while holding his ankles, coming to a balanced V position. If he has sufficient strength, flexibility, and balance, he can release his ankles and extend his arms directly sideward.

Straddle Stance (Figure 30-21). The performer straddles as wide as possible, leans forward until his body is parallel to the floor, and extends his arms sideward, holding this position several seconds.

Double-arm Planche
Half Lever on Floor

Double-arm Planche. From a kneeling position the performer places his elbows, which are several inches apart, firmly against his sides. Leaning forward he places his hands, fingers out, under his hips and tips forward until balanced on his hands with his body extended and slightly arched.

Half Lever on Floor (L Position). Sitting with his hands flat on the floor, the performer pushes with his arm and shoulder muscles, contracts his abdominal and hip flexor muscles and lifts clear of the floor, keeping his legs extended and his feet pointed.

Front Scale
Side Scale

Front or Swan Scale (Figure 30-22). The performer pikes forward at the hips until his slightly arched body is

Figure 30-20. V balance holding feet.

Figure 30-21. Straddle stance.

parallel to the floor and he is looking directly in front of him. At the same time he raises one extended leg behind him until the heel is at least as high as his head; he then extends his arms sideward. He holds this position several seconds without moving his supporting foot.

Side Scale. Assuming a front scale position the trunk and head are turned 90° to face to one side, the bottom arm points directly forward away from the raised leg, and the top arm is placed alongside the upper side and hip of the body.

Squat Handstand, Knee-elbow Headstand, Headstand, Forward Roll, Straddle Stance, Front Scale, Half Lever

Each balanced position should be held a sufficient length of time (at least five seconds) to demonstrate full control before proceeding to the next balanced position.

Back Bend
Straddle Sit

Back Bend. Lying on his back the performer places his feet next to his hips, and, fingers pointing toward his feet, places his hand immediately above his shoulders. He then does a high bridge, arching his body and looking down at his hands. The next step is to stand with the feet wide apart, the head back, and the arms overhead and back. Keeping his balance the performer arches back into a back

Figure 30-22. Front or swan scale.

464 *Individual and Team Sports*

bend while being spotted. The flexibility needed to do a back bend usually requires considerable practice.

Straddle Sit. The performer sits on the floor or mat, spreading his extended legs as far to the side as possible. An advanced version of this is to do a complete straddle in which the legs form a nearly straight line. The arms are extended sideward and the performer flexes forward until his chin touches the floor.

Handstand
Handwalk
Press-up to Handstand

Handstand. The handstand has a small base of support; success requires a delicate sense of balance and early, accurate, corrective actions. The handstand position is often started by bending forward at the waist, placing both hands on the mat about shoulder width apart, and pointing straight ahead. One leg is then kicked backward and then upward vigorously; the other one is then positioned alongside it. Much practice is generally necessary before the performer has a sensitive enough feel of his balance that a steady, stationary handstand is held.

If the performer begins to overbalance he should press vigorously with his fingers and thrust his head forward. If these measures do not succeed, one or two handwalking steps can be taken. If he begins to underbalance, the performer can attempt to straighten and stretch his body upward as much as possible and quickly transfer his weight to the heels of his hands. A more successful correction is often to lower the body by flexing the arms at the shoulders and elbows. When coming out of a handstand position the performer should keep one leg above his hips while he flexes the other leg down behind him, reversing this procedure for getting up into the handstand. If he overbalances, he can place his weight on one hand, pivot 180°, and then flex one or both legs downward to the mat.

Being held in a handstand position by a spotter helps to attain a feeling for the correct position. This skill can first be practiced in a corner or against a wall.

Handwalk. When handwalking, the performer deliberately overbalances; he lifts one hand and places it forward, thus momentarily regaining the balance before again moving into an overbalanced position.

Press to Handstand. The ability to press to a handstand requires more-than-average strength and balance. The performer can start from a squat handstand or from a headstand.

From the headstand position, the performer brings his hands somewhat forward so that they are in a line not too far behind his forehead on the mat. The performer overbalances slightly and, just before losing his balance, begins a pressing movement with his hands, which he continues until his arms are straight and he is in a handstand.

Regardless of his starting position the performer should as soon as possible flex his head back and look down and slightly ahead of his hands. At first he may need to kip his legs upward to aid his pressing effort. The performer can attempt a handstand press while his feet are held overhead. This skill can also be practiced in a corner or against the wall.

Press to Handstand, Chest Roll to Handstand, Forward Roll, Backward Extension Roll to Handstand

This sequence combines the tumbling skills and balancing skills described previously. On the forward chest roll, the performer rocks forward moving to his thighs, hips, waist, and chest. As soon as possible the performer places his hands alongside his hips and presses vigorously with his hands as he is rocking forward on his chest. He then tucks his chin and rocks up to a headstand.

On the back extension roll the performer should thrust his legs almost directly upward in a vigorous movement. He presses forcefully with his arms while positioning his head between them and looking at his hands.

DOUBLES BALANCING SKILLS

For most doubles balancing skills a special grip is employed in which each performer grasps the other's hand with the index and middle finger on either side of the wrist just beyond the heel of the hand. In all two-man balancing stunts the top man must allow the bottom man to hold the balance. The top man should remain quite steady throughout the balance and not attempt to secure the balance for himself; this will counteract the efforts of and confuse the bottom man.

Swan Balance
Chest Balance
Sitting Balance

Swan Balance on Partner's Feet (Flying Angel) (Figure 30-23). The top man stands near the hips of the bottom man, facing him. The bottom man carefully places his feet diagonally across the pelvic girdle of the top man, keeping his heels fairly close together. Grasping the top man's hands, the bottom man slowly supports the weight of the top man and brings him forward until the legs of the bottom man are perpendicular. The top man should maintain an arched position with his feet together, toes pointed and head extended upward. When balanced, the partners release hands, and the top man extends his arms sideways.

Tumbling and Balancing

Figure 30-23. Flying Angel.

Figure 30-25. Sitting balance on partner's feet.

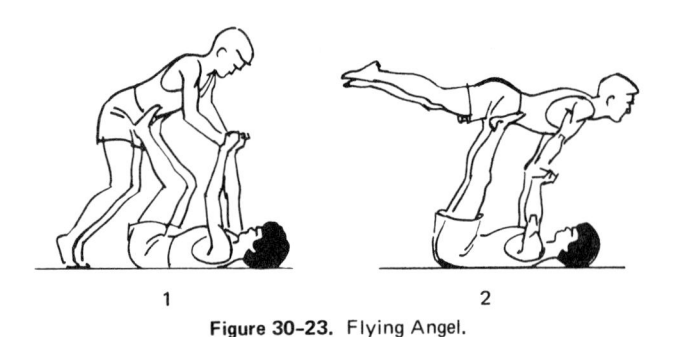

Chest Balance on Partner's Back (Figure 30-24). The top man stands facing the bottom man who is in a knee-hand position. The top man places both hands underneath the chest and stomach and his upper arms and shoulders on the back of the bottom man. With his chin extended past the side of the bottom man, the top man tucks his legs and slowly pushes them upward into a shoulder-stand position. He reverses the procedures to come to his feet.

Sitting Balance on Partner's Feet (Figure 30-25). The bottom man lies on his back, flexes his legs, and places his feet against the buttocks of the top man, who is standing with his back to the bottom man. Grasping hands, the top man sits back until he is balanced on the feet of the bottom man, who then straightens his legs. When his balance is sufficiently controlled, the top man releases his grasp and holds his arms sideward. For the dismount the mounting actions are reversed.

Thigh Stand
Foot-to-hand Stand

Thigh Stand (Figure 30-26). The top man stands with his legs spread fairly wide apart. Standing directly behind him, the bottom man squats and places his head between the legs of the top man and slowly comes erect while holding the legs of the top man. With the top man sitting on his shoulders, the bottom man flexes his body until he is in a semisitting position. The top man places his feet on the thighs of the bottom man who holds the thighs of the top man, just above the knee caps, while the top man straightens his legs. The bottom man ducks his head and leans back and the top man leans forward slightly while keeping his body arched until a balanced position is achieved. To come down from the thigh stand, the top man straightens his legs and pushes slightly forward against the bottom man and jumps forward a short distance.

Foot-to-hand Stand. The bottom man lies on his back, positioning the back of his hands on the man next to his shoulders and raises his legs upright. The top man steps onto the hands of the bottom man and grasps his feet. On the count of three, the top man jumps directly upward and the bottom man presses vigorously and completely extends his arms while balancing the top man. Once the top man has attained his balance he releases one and then the other foot of the bottom man and stands erect. The bottom man maintains the balance of the top man at all times. If the bottom man has at least fair strength this skill can be mastered quickly. When ready to descend, the

Figure 30-24. Chest balance on partner's back.

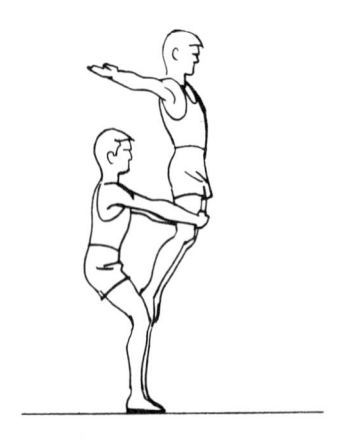

Figure 30-26. Thigh stand.

466   *Individual and Team Sports*

bottom man raises his legs. The top man grasps them, leans forward slightly, and jumps forward, landing in a straddle over the bottom man's legs. An advanced method of going into a foot-to-hand stand is for the top man to jump upward while the bottom man, who presses vigorously with his arms, keeps his legs on the mat. A spotter on either side of the top man should be present during the first few attempts.

Shoulder Mount

The shoulder mount can be done with a minimum of strength if the partners work closely together, coordinate their movements, and the top man stays close to the center axis of the bottom man. The right-handed partners each place the back of the right hand against their forehead. They shake hands with their left hands and move their right hands forward until they can grasp each other's hands. The top man places the sole of his left foot (toes pointed inward) as high as possible on the top of the bottom man's left thigh. On the count of three, lifting upward slightly with the right hand on each count, the bottom man lifts very vigorously upward and overhead with the right hand while pulling steadily with the left hand. At the same time the top man steps quickly upward with the left leg, swings his right leg close around the back of the bottom man's back, and places his right foot on the right shoulder of the top man. The top man quickly swings his left foot onto the left shoulder of the bottom man, straightens his body, and looks forward. The bottom man first moves one hand to the back of the top man's calf (just below the back of the knee) and pulls downward vigorously. He then transfers the other hand to the other calf. The bottom man keeps his neck stiff and his head erect; the top man stands erect, looks forward, and keeps his knees close together and presses his shins against the back of the bottom man's head. To descend from the shoulder stand, the partners grasp hands, one at a time. The bottom man keeps his arms extended in a pressing type of movement while the top man, who also presses with his arms, jumps forward slightly and comes to the floor in front of the bottom man. (See Figure 30-27).

In the *hand-to-hand shoulder mount,* the action is similar to a walk-up except that the bottom man grasps the top man's left foot in his left hand. With practice some partners may be able to do a *jump-up shoulder mount.* Assuming the starting position used for the walk-on mount, on the count of three the top man jumps upward as high as possible and presses vigorously with his arms. At the same time the bottom man lifts and presses forcefully with his arms, attempting to straighten them overhead. He simultaneously does a quarter turn to his right while turning his partner a quarter turn. The top man lands in a squat position and then comes erect.

Knee-and-shoulder Stand
Low Shoulder-to-shoulder Stand

Knee-and-shoulder Stand (Figure 30-28). The bottom man lies on his back and positions his feet underneath his knees, keeping his feet and knees about shoulder width apart; he extends his arms directly upward. Facing the bottom man, the top man places his feet between those of the bottom man and then places his hands on the bottom man's knees. He leans forward until the bottom man can grasp his shoulders. With both partners keeping their

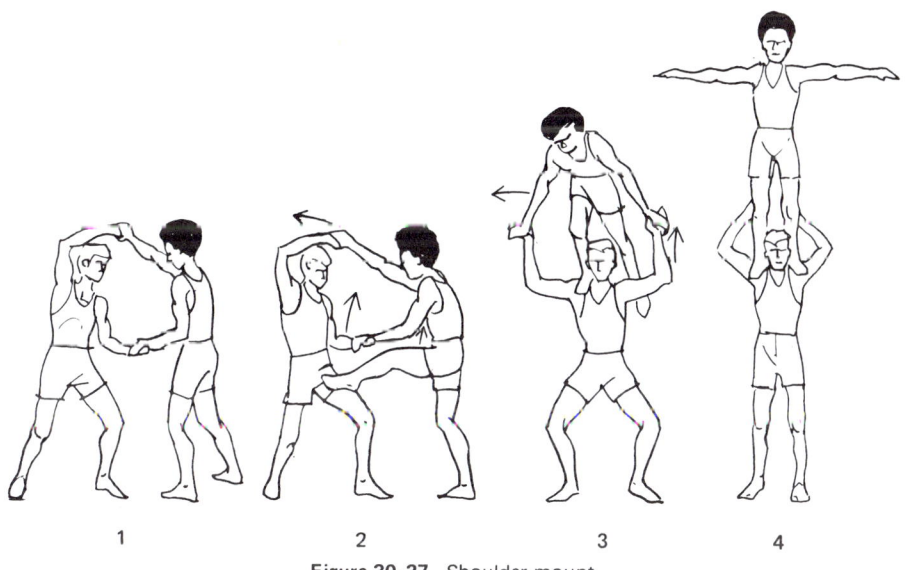

Figure 30-27. Shoulder mount.

Tumbling and Balancing

Figure 30-28. Knee-and-shoulder stand.

arms extended, and with the top man keeping his head upward so that he can look at the bottom man's face, the top man then kicks one leg upward and then the other, coming to a low knee-shoulder stand. The top man can also tuck his legs and press up to a knee-shoulder stand position. Again, the top man should keep his body extended and permit the bottom man to shift him about in order to obtain and maintain a balanced position. To come down, the top man flexes one leg downward while keeping the other leg above his hips. He must be careful that he comes down to one side of the bottom man's legs or else places one foot between the bottom man's feet.

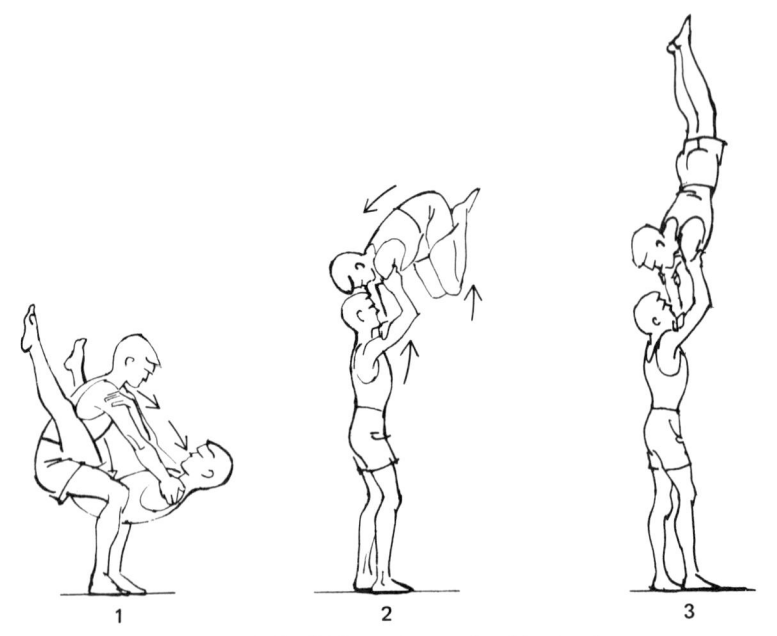

Low Shoulder-to-shoulder Stand. The top man usually kicks one leg alongside the other raised leg or else slowly tucks his legs and presses into position. The top man shifts his weight forward until hardly any weight is supported with his hands on the knees of the bottom man. When he feels that he is in balance and directly over the shoulders of the bottom man, the top man moves one hand to a position around the bottom man's upper arm. When his balance is regained, the top man then moves his other hand to the bottom man's upper arm.

Low Shoulder-to-shoulder Stand, Forward Roll High Shoulder-to-shoulder Stand
Low Wrist-to-wrist Stand

High Shoulder-to-shoulder Stand (Figure 30-29). This requires no more balancing skill for either partner than does the low shoulder-to-shoulder stand. However, getting into a high shoulder-to-shoulder stand position requires a strong bottom man. The usual method of getting into a high shoulder-to-shoulder stand is for the two partners to stand facing each other and grasping each other's upper arms. On the count of three, the top man jumps and encircles the waist of the bottom man with his thighs. The bottom man bends forward at the waist, flexes his legs slightly, and then straightens vigorously, lifting and pressing upward on the upper arms of the top man. As the bottom man starts his upward and backward motion, the top man tucks his knees tightly to his chest and swings up to a tuck position above the bottom man, who is arched back slightly and looking upward. The top man then extends his legs overhead, coming to a high shoulder-stand position directly above the bottom man. If the top man loses his balance, the bottom man retains his grasp and

Figure 30-29. High shoulder-to-shoulder stand.

Individual and Team Sports

Figure 30-30. Low wrist-to-wrist stand.

guides him to his feet. If the top man overbalances, the bottom man quickly pivots 180° so that the top man falls toward his stomach and can pike his legs under him.

Low Wrist-to-wrist Stand (Figure 30-30). The bottom man lies on the mat. Standing near his shoulders, the top man faces the bottom man's feet. They grasp each other's wrists with the thumb and fingers on opposite sides. Keeping his head forward, the top man can kick one leg up and then the other one, coming to a low wrist-to-wrist stand. Another method of getting into the stand is for the top man to tuck and then press up to a stand.

Routine: Shoulder Mount, Half Lever, Lower Top Man to Stand, Low Shoulder-to-shoulder Stand, Low Wrist-to-wrist Stand

SELF-EVALUATION

Tumbling and Balancing Skills Test Score Sheet

Skill	0	1	2	3
Singles Tumbling Skills				
1. Forward Roll, Backward Roll				
2. Shoulder Roll, Side Roll, Straddle Roll-up				
3. Five-foot Dive and Roll, Eight-foot Dive and Roll				
4. Cartwheel, Roundoff				
5. Backward Extension Roll, Back Roll to Chest Roll				
6. Forward Neckspring from Rolled-up or Stacked Mat, Forward Headspring from Rolled-up or Stacked Mat, Forward Handspring from Rolled-up or Stacked Mat				

Skill	0	1	2	3
7. Forward Headspring, Forward Handspring				
8. Forward Somersault				
9. Back Handspring				
10. Back Somersault				
Doubles Tumbling Skills				
11. Two-man Forward Rolls, Two-man Backward Rolls, Triple Rolls				
12. Front Headspring over Partner, Knee-shoulder Handspring				
13. Straddle-lift Front Somersault, Wheelbarrow Pitch Front Somersault, Ankle-lift Somersault				
14. Back-to-back Pullover, Foot-push Back Handspring				
15. Side-pitch Back Somersault, Sitting-pitch Back Somersault, Toe-pitch Back Somersault				
Singles Balancing Skills				
16. Squat Handstand				
17. Head-and-hand Stand				
18. Head-in-hand Stand, Forearm Stand				
19. V Balance, Straddle Stance				
20. Double-arm Planche, Half Lever on Floor				
21. Front Scale, Side Scale				
22. Back Bend, Straddle Sit				
23. Handstand, Handwalk, Press to Handstand				
Doubles Balancing Skills				
24. Chest Balance, Swan Balance, Sitting Balance				
25. Thigh Stand, Foot-to-hand Stand				
26. Walk-up Shoulder Mount, Hand-to-hand Shoulder Mount, Jump-up Shoulder Mount				
27. Knee-and-shoulder Stand, Low Shoulder-to-shoulder Stand				
28. High Shoulder-to-shoulder Stand, Low Wrist-to-wrist Stand				

Total Points _____

0 = failed
1 = completed with poor form or did not hold more than 4 seconds.
2 = completed with fair form or did not hold more than 8 seconds.
3 = completed with good form and held 12 seconds or more.
A = 66 points and above
B = 50–65 points
C = 29–49 points
D = 15–28 points
F = 0–14 points

Selected References

Bailey, James A. *An Illustrated Guide to Tumbling.* Boston: Allyn, 1968.
This book, which is written primarily for the novice, contains a large variety of tumbling and floor-exercise skills. A large number of sequential photographs depict faithfully the several actions involved in various tumbling stunts. Several films and magazine articles on tumbling as well as suppliers of equipment are listed. 170 pp.

Kenney, Charles J. *Fundamental Tumbling Skills Illustrated* (with Floor Exercises). New York: Ronald, 1966.
Written for the beginning tumbler by a long-renowned college gymnastics coach, this volume thoroughly covers the common skills of tumbling and floor exercise. Corrections for common errors are also given. 97 pp.

Musker, Frank F., Donald R. Casady, and Leslie W. Irwin. *A Guide to Gymnastics.* New York: Macmillan, Inc., 1968.
All aspects of gymnastics preparation, training, and skill learning are covered in this book, in which Chapter 5 is devoted to "Single and Dual Tumbling Stunts" and Chapter 7 to "Balancing and Flexibility Stunts." Each of the skills, which proceed through to an intermediate level, is illustrated. 256 pp.

Szypula, George. *Tumbling and Balancing for All.* Dubuque, Iowa: Brown, 1957.
Both balancing and tumbling activities are covered in this book, which is written by a long-time college gymnastic coach.

CHAPTER 31

Volleyball

*James White**
University of California, San Diego

Donald R. Casady[†]
The University of Iowa

HISTORY

The sport of volleyball was invented in 1895 by William J. Morgan of the Holyoke, Massachusetts, YMCA. He wanted to devise a game that would provide an opportunity for large numbers of businessmen to enjoy interesting exercise and have some recreation and relaxation. A tennis net was raised to the height of six feet, over which a basketball bladder was batted. This ball proved to be too light and, consequently, a special ball was designed by A. G. Spaulding and Brothers, which proved satisfactory. The ball used today conforms to those original specifications.

In July 1896, the first article on this new game appeared in the publication, *Physical Education*. It described how the game was played and listed ten specific rules to guide anyone interested in playing the new sport. In 1922, at the Central YMCA in Brooklyn, New York, the first National Volleyball Championship was held, and in 1928 the United States Volleyball Association was formed.

Volleyball was played in the 1955 Pan-American Games, which were held in Mexico City. The 1956 World Volleyball Championships in Paris drew teams from twenty-seven countries and filled the Palais des Sportes on several occasions with crowds of more than twenty-five thousand people. It continues to have a strong spectator attraction.

The importance of volleyball as a team sport is evident in its being approved as an event in the 1964 Olympic Games; more than thirty teams competed in the sport.

In the United States volleyball is increasingly being played as a club or interscholastic and intercollegiate sport, with many women's teams being fielded. Volleyball is a growing sport in secondary schools, colleges, recreation centers and playgrounds, public and private clubs, camps, and beaches. It is played in more than sixty countries by more than fifty million people each year and is so popular that it is ranked third in the world

Figure 31-1. A volleyball team in action. (Note the spiker's cocked arm and the three-man block being formed.) Acknowledgment is gratefully extended to Dr. Leonard B. Stallcup, official photographer of the U.S. Volleyball Association, for the use of this photograph.)

---

*Dr. White is presently an associate supervisor at the University of California at San Diego and has been active in organizing, teaching, and playing volleyball in the Midwest and in California. He was assistant director of the 1970 and 1973 National Volleyball Championships held in San Diego. Dr. White received his B.A. from Graceland College, Lamoni, Iowa, his M.A. from The University of Iowa, Iowa City, and his Ph.D. from the University of Southern California, Los Angeles.

[†]Dr. Casady has been teaching and playing volleyball since he was an undergraduate in college, at which time he played on two all-university championship volleyball teams. Since that time he has been a member of several different championship teams and has encouraged a large number of students to participate in this sport.

in popularity as a recreational team game. The exposure of millions of TV viewers to the superb volleyball play of both men and women at the 1972 Olympic Games added immeasurably to the popularity of this sport.

BRIEF DESCRIPTION OF VOLLEYBALL PLAY

Volleyball is similar to tennis (or badminton) in that a ball is played back and forth over a net, the top of which is eight feet above the floor. A volleyball team is composed of six players, who use their hands and arms as striking implements, and they must hit the ball before it touches the floor. One team serves the ball over the net to commence play. Thereafter, the teams try to make the ball touch the opponent's court, generally using the legal maximum of three hits before volleying the ball back over the net or entering the opponent's court. The serving team scores a point (the receiving team wins the serve) when the other team fails to return the ball legally according to the rules. The winning team is the one first scoring 15 points (with a 2-point advantage) or the one that has the most points after eight minutes of play.

VALUES OF VOLLEYBALL

The sport of volleyball is excellent for developing quick movement, rapid adaptation to the opponent's style of play, and reliance on skillful team performance and coordinated effort rather than impulsive individual reactions to the game situation. All these traits require the discipline and training of the muscles and body so that nearly instantaneous correct responses are made to game situations.

Volleyball play emphasizes planned strategy, correct application of defensive and offensive maneuvers under varying conditions, and an accurate execution of the varied movements required in the game. To defend successfully against the opponent's attack demands heightened powers of observation and skill. The ball may be hit so hard on a spike that it approaches the defensive man at speeds of nearly one hundred miles per hour. At such times the defensive man must quickly position himself to block or receive and subsequently pass the ball to the appropriate teammate.

Volleyball, properly played, is sufficiently vigorous to develop organic power; it calls for the development of a high degree of neuromuscular coordination. As a leisure-time activity it can be ranked near the top in any list of games or sports because it can be played during a long period of one's life.

VOLLEYBALL EQUIPMENT

Court

The outside dimensions of the volleyball court are sixty by thirty feet and the ceiling height should be at least twenty-six feet. This area is divided by a net that is three feet wide, the top of which is eight feet from the floor. A center line under the net (four inches wide) divides the court into two playing areas each thirty by thirty feet. Ten feet on each side of the center line is the spiking line for the back-court players. The outer boundary lines and spiking lines are marked by two-inch wide lines of color in contrast to the color of the floor. The markings of a volleyball court are depicted in Figure 31-2.

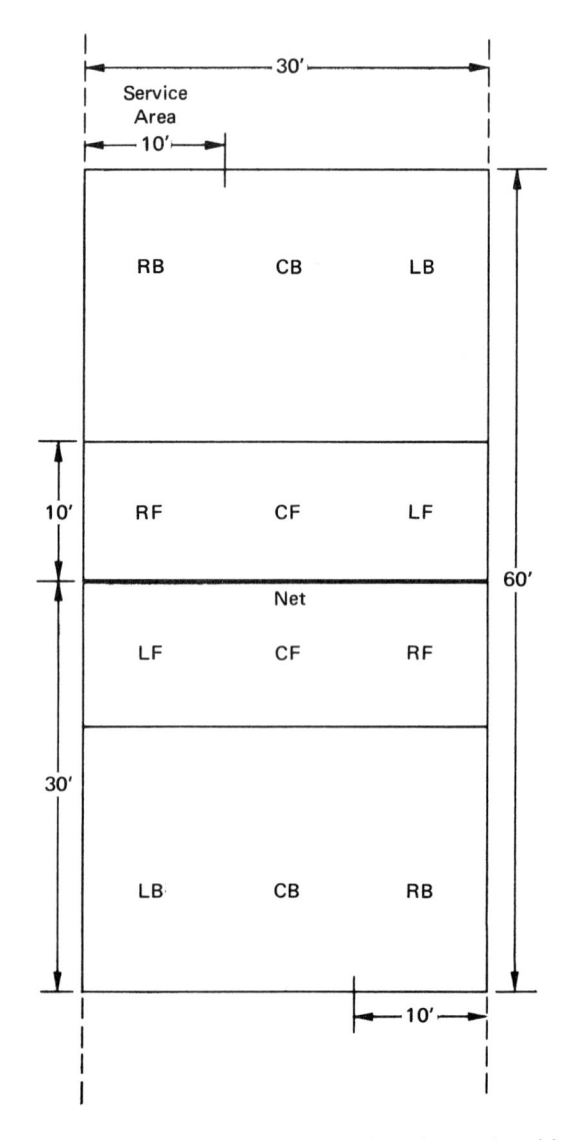

Figure 31-2. Volleyball court showing dimensions and positions of the players. (All lines are two inches wide except the center line which is four inches wide.)

472 *Individual and Team Sports*

Net

The net is thirty-two feet in length when stretched and is made of four-inch square mesh of black or dark brown, which is topped with a double white tape, two inches wide. A steel cable or rope is run through the top and bottom of the net to secure it to the uprights, which should be at least three feet outside the court. The bottom of the net should be drawn taut by special ropes located at each end.

Ball

The spherical ball should have a laceless cover made of twelve or more pieces of leather. Practice games can be played with a rubber covered ball. The ball should not be fewer than twenty-five inches nor more than twenty-seven inches in circumference and should weigh not less than nine ounces (250 grams) or more than ten ounces (280 grams). The pressure in a leather ball should be between seven and eight pounds; in a rubber ball, five to seven pounds. When dropped from a height of one hundred inches onto a concrete floor, the ball should rebound vertically sixty to sixty-five inches.

SELECTED RULES GOVERNING VOLLEYBALL PLAY

The official rules governing volleyball play in the United States are formulated and published each year by the United States Volleyball Association (P.O. Box 109, Berne, Indiana 46711). In this section a brief synopsis of the important rules is included that the volleyball player needs to know.

Players

An official volleyball team consists of six players, each of whom is responsible for covering the playing floor in his area of the court. Three players cover the front half of the court and the other three cover the back area. The six positions are designated left forward, center forward, right forward, right back, center back, and left back. For elementary volleyball teams, with elementary playing skill, the players are often divided into pairs; each pair performs specific duties when playing in the front line. One of the players is known as the *set man* and the other is known as the *spiker*. The set man is responsible for the proper placement of the ball above and near the net so that the spiker can hit it over the net and into the opponents' court with sufficient speed and placement to make it difficult to return.

Playing Position on Court

Prior to the serve each player must be in his relative court position. After the ball is served the players can switch to any position on their side of the court. The only restriction after a switch is that a back lineman cannot spike the ball inside the line ten feet behind the center line. A player can leave the playing area to retrieve a ball provided he does not step over the center line or an extension of the center line when he plays the ball. Players can change positions before beginning a game but not during the game. Substitutions can be made at any time that the ball is dead. During the third game of a match, the teams automatically change playing areas either (1) after one team has scored 8 points, or (2) as soon after four minutes of ball-in-play time has elapsed and the ball becomes dead.

Rotating Court Positions

After each side out, the team awarded the serve rotates one player position in a clockwise direction.

Scoring Points

Only the serving team can score points. A point is scored by the serving team if the receiving team commits a foul or fails to return the ball legally to the serving team's playing area. The team scoring 15 points with a 2-point advantage wins the game. If the game is played under a time-limit rule, the team that has scored the most points the first time the ball becomes dead after *eight* minutes of play is the winner. The team first winning two games out of three wins the match.

Serving Rules

The server must serve from within the serving area (illustrated in Figure 31-1) and must not touch the lines bounding this area or the floor outside this area at the instant the ball is contacted when hit for the serve. (However, part of the server's body can be in the air over or beyond these lines.) An out-of-turn service, if verified while that player is still serving, causes the points made on this service to be canceled and a side-out declared. The players of the team in error must regain their proper court positions before play is resumed. The losing team has the privilege of serving first for the next game.

All players, other than the server, must be within their playing area and in serving order, with each of the forward line players in front of his respective back-line player, at the instant the ball is contacted for a serve. When determining the serving order and the front and rear lines, no part of a player's body touching the floor

Volleyball **473**

may overlap any part of another player's body that touches the floor. After the ball is contacted, when hit for the serve, the players can move from their respective positions.

Playing the Ball

The ball can be hit by any part of the player's body that is above, and also including, the waist. When a ball only partially crosses the net and is then contacted by an opponent, it is considered to have crossed the net. Backline players may not attempt to block the ball at the net.

A player may not make successive contacts with the ball except that, when playing a hard-driven spiked ball not already touched by a teammate, a player can make successive contacts if they constitute one attempt to play the ball. A player may not play the ball twice in succession. The following three plays are exempt from this rule:

1. Simultaneous contacts by teammates.
2. Successive contacts by blockers (multiple block).
3. Simultaneous contacts by opponents.

In any such plays any participating player can also participate in the next play.

Players may not engage in unsportsmanlike conduct, such as stamping their feet or shouting at an opponent who is about to play or is in the act of playing.

Legal Plays

1. A ball can be played off the net except on the service or after three hits.
2. If a ball (other than on the serve) hits the net and goes over the net, the ball is in play.
3. The ball must pass over the net within the side boundaries.

Fouls and Penalties

If a foul is committed by the serving team they lose the serve; if a foul is committed by the receiving team, the serving team scores a point. In determining fouls, a play is not considered completed until each player participating in the play has regained equilibrium and full physical control. (A teammate may help a player regain his equilibrium.)

A *foul* is committed when any of the following occurs:

1. The server steps on or over the back line while serving.
2. A player steps over the center line that is located under the net. (A player can step on the center line without penalty, however.)
3. A player touches the net or supporting uprights with any part of his body while the ball is in play (unless the force of the ball drives the net against a player).
4. A player reaches over the net, except after spiking or when blocking a spiked ball. On a block, the spiker must spike the ball before a blocker can contact the ball on the spiker's side of the net.
5. A player scoops, lifts, shoves, throws, or follows the ball, or allows it to come to rest momentarily in his hands. The ball must be clearly batted.
6. A player plays the ball twice in succession. (The present rule, however, permits a defensive player to have multiple contacts with a hard-driven spiked ball.)
7. The ball is hit four or more times. (The ball must be returned over the net in a maximum of three plays.) However, if two opposing players simultaneously contact a ball above the net, this contact does not constitute a hit for the side on whose court the ball falls.
8. A player serves out of turn. Points scored while the incorrect server is serving do not count.
9. A player reaches under the net and interferes with the ball while his opponents are playing it.
10. A player playing a back position spikes a ball and alights in front of the ten-foot line. (However, a back-court player can spike the ball in front of the ten-foot line if the ball is below net level.)

Derogatory remarks about or to the officials or opponents can result in the referee penalizing the offending team.

THE SKILLS OF VOLLEYBALL

The Serve

Rules of Serving. The serve is the act of putting the ball in play by the right-back player. The server must serve from within the serving area (illustrated in Figure 31-2) and must not touch the lines bounding this area or the floor inside this area at the instant he contacts the ball on the serve. The server puts the ball in play by hitting it with his hand, fist, or arm. The ball must be hit over the net and into the opponents' playing area; it must not touch the net. Prior to a serve, the receiving team is allowed a reasonable amount of time in which to return to their playing positions.

A served ball is dead, a side-out is called on the serving team, and the serve is awarded the receiving team if the serve:

1. Touches the floor of the serving team's court, a teammate of the server, or the net.

2. Passes under the net or crosses the net entirely outside the markers on the sides of the net.
3. Touches the ceiling or any obstructions or objects before contacting an opponent or the floor of the opponents' playing area.
4. Lands out-of-bounds without touching or being touched by a receiving team player.

Importance of the Serve. Effective serves are very important in volleyball. A team with effective servers has an advantage in retaining the serve and thus keeping its offensive, or point-making, system in play. An effective server can often force the opponents to play the ball the way he wishes. His serves can be played to the weaker receivers, who may miss the ball entirely, commit errors or fouls in playing the ball, or make poor or misdirected passes.

Overhand Serve. The overhand serve can be very effective because of its speed and accuracy. Returning the overhand serve is considerably more difficult than returning the underhand serve; however, either serve can be learned in about the same period of time.

The techniques for executing the overhand serve for a right-handed player are as follows:

1. The body should be so positioned that it squarely faces the net; the feet are in a stride stance, with the front of the left foot two inches behind the rear line and the heel of the left foot ten to twelve inches in front of the toe of the right foot. However, some players prefer a square stance (feet parallel) for serving.
2. The ball is held in the upraised palm of the left hand. With the left upper arm touching the body, the left hand is held a few inches in front of the right shoulder. The right hand rests lightly on top of the ball, in order to help stabilize and balance it.
3. With both hands, the ball is so thrown vertically upward that it rises one to three feet above the head and directly in front of the right shoulder. In this action the left hand supplies most of the lifting force, and the right hand quickly leaves the ball and is brought behind the right ear and close to the head. The right elbow is so bent that the right upper arm is parallel to the floor and the right hand is cupped.
4. The weight of the body is shifted forward just before the ball is contacted. The right wrist is snapped forward and the cupped hand (the fingers, lateral edge side of the thumb, and heel of the palm, but not the palm itself) strikes the ball, contacting it when it is in front of the right shoulder and just above the head. This action results in a no-spin served ball, commonly called a floater.

Figure 31-3. Overhand Serve. (Acknowledgment is gratefully extended to Dr. Leonard B. Stallcup, official photographer of the U.S. Volleyball Association, for the use of this photograph.)

5. After completing the serve, the player should square his body with the net and quickly advance to his playing area.
6. Another serving method is to toss the ball directly over the right shoulder with the right fingers, and hit it toward its top. This imparts a forward spin to the ball, causing it to dive downward after it crosses the net. This serve is quite similar to the action used in spiking the ball, which will be discussed later.

Points to Remember When Serving

1. The advantages of scoring are with the serving team. All servers should be certain that the serves are within the opponents' playing area, are deep, and are to the far corners of the playing area.
2. The ball should be served to the opponents' weakest back lineman.
3. Fast and slow balls can be served interchangeably in order to attempt to confuse the opponent.

Selected Serving Drills

Elevating Drill. In this drill the individual practices correctly tossing the ball to the desired position preparatory to serving the ball.

Wall-serving Drill. Standing ten to twenty feet away from a wall, the player practices serving the ball against the wall as depicted here. (A curved line indicates a served ball; *X* indicates the player.)

Class-serving Drill. The servers on one side of the net serve to the players on the opposite side. The first few serves can be practiced from behind the line located ten

Volleyball 475

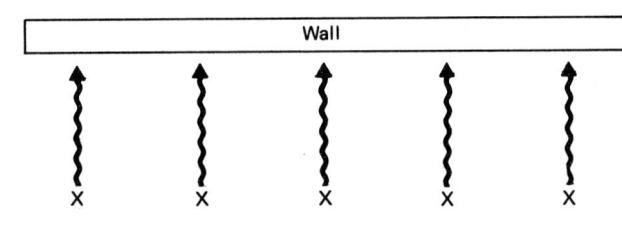

Figure 31-4.

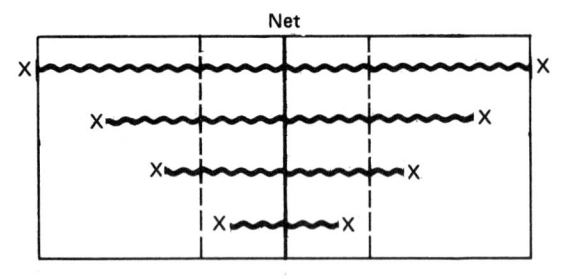

Figure 31-5.

feet behind the center line. As depicted here, as the servers gain proficiency, they gradually can move toward the end line until all serves are made from the regular serving position.

Chest Pass

Any member of the receiving team may have to receive the ball coming from the opponents' court, and there is no way to avoid this responsibility. This means that every member of the receiving team must be able to pass the ball accurately and correctly. The skill of passing is very important, as it initiates the attack; if it is done poorly it reduces the effectiveness of the offensive play. The main objective when receiving the ball is to reduce the speed of the ball, remove any spin, and then pass the ball high and accurately to the setup man. The chest pass (so-named because the ball is contacted somewhat above chest height), is the usual method of passing to a teammate. However, if receiving a chest pass, or if playing a spike or a ball low to the floor, other types of passes must be employed. These are discussed in a later section in this chapter.

Chest-pass Techniques. The skillful passer learns to maneuver his body quickly into the correct passing position. His legs are spread wide for support, they are slightly flexed at the knees and hips, and one foot is forward. The passer does not hesitate to squat down or even drop to one or both knees in order to get into the correct position for passing a low ball. As the ball approaches the passer, he extends his arms toward the ball, raising his elbows sideways to a point below the line of the shoulders, extending his wrists in line with the forearms, and rotating his arms, wrists, and hands inward and positioning them at shoulder height. The thumbs are pointing downward and the fingers are spread and extended in an upward direction toward the fingers of the opposite hand. The thumb and index finger approach the thumb and index finger of the opposite hand and may contact them. The fingers and thumb form an irregular circle, which can be used by the passer to sight through at the ball, thus accurately positioning the thumbs and fingers in order to help insure a well-hit pass. The ball is contacted predominently with the distal (far) tip of the thumb and the tips of the index and middle fingers of each hand. To emphasize the three-finger pass, the ring and little finger can be flexed tightly so that they will never contact the ball. Whenever the ball is contacted with the heel or palm of the hand or the proximal joints of the fingers, the resulting pass is illegal and is referred to as a carry.

As the ball is received, most of the speed at impact is absorbed by allowing the hands and fingers to give toward the body, and in one continuous movement the ball is clearly batted with the fleshy distal tip of the fingers and thumbs. The ball is released with a finger snap, which initiates a full-arm extension and a coordinated follow-through of the body.

Points to Remember

1. The passer must move quickly to the position where the ball will drop and be contacted by him.
2. An attempt should be made to play any ball while it is above the shoulders, even if this makes it necessary for the player to kneel, squat, or even sit on the floor.

Figure 31-6. Regular chest pass. (Acknowledgment is gratefully extended to Dr. Leonard B. Stallcup, official photographer of the U.S. Volleyball Association, for the use of this photograph.)

3. The passer should contact the ball with his finger tips above his shoulders and in front of his face.
4. The passer should face the player to whom the resultant pass is being directed.
5. An attempt should be made to pass the ball to a height of approximately fifteen feet and in such an arc that it will drop down toward the head of the intended receiver.

Inverted Bump Pass. When receiving a serve or spike that is chest to head height, a special type of bump pass is used in order to avoid carrying the ball. The inverted bump pass permits the defensive player to avoid the dangerous (because it may be called illegal) chest pass in passing to the setup player. Starting with the arms in position for a regular bump pass (this is described in the next section), the elbows are flexed completely, bringing the hands (palms facing each other and the fingers flexed and resting on each other) in front of the face. The ball is then bumped upward and forward with the outside edges of the wrists or forearms (or even the hands). The forearm action is coordinated closely with an extension of the legs and body. The inverted bump pass, which is depicted below, requires considerable practice before consistency and accuracy can be obtained.

Chest-passing Drills

Bounce-and-pass Drill. Each player throws the ball ten to fifteen feet into the air, and as it bounces from the floor he positions himself under the ball and passes it straight up, letting it bounce again and continuing to pass after each bounce. In a group situation this drill can be performed by passing to a teammate.

Wall-pass Drill. Each player practices ten repetitions of passing the ball against a spot located fifteen feet high on a wall.

Wall-tap Drill. Each player practices passing the ball against the wall for one minute. The first few passes may go fifteen feet high, but as the player gains confidence, the passing height is reduced in order that repeated passes can be rapidly made with the goal of developing speed and coordination.

Individual Pass Through a Basketball Hoop. Each player attempts to pass the ball through the basketball hoop. If the ball fails to pass through the hoop, the player continues to pass the rebound, before it touches the floor, until the basket is made. The player, after completing the basket, tosses the ball up for the next player, who then attempts to basket his pass as soon as possible.

The Below-chest Recovery Pass (Bump, Bounce, or Dig Pass)

A well-played ball is often driven with some speed to a position below or to either side of the chest, thus making it impossible to use the chest pass for passing the ball. When this happens the receiver must use a recovery pass in his attempt to regain control of the ball. The recovery pass can be played with one or both hands and is referred to as the below-chest recovery pass or *bounce pass*. Its most common names are the *bump pass* if two arms are used, or the *dig pass* if only one is used. In games that are called by a referee, the serve must ordinarily be handled by means of a bump or dig pass. Consequently, many volleyball players form the habit of automatically playing all serves, spikes, and low balls with a recovery pass.

Two-arm Bump or Bounce Pass. When a ball is driven directly toward the receiver and at such an angle or height that it is impossible to lower the body and use the chest pass, the two-arm bump or bounce pass should be used. The hands are quickly clasped or placed next to each other so that the thumbs, wrists, forearms, and upper arms are parallel. The wrists and hands are often rotated down toward the floor to help prevent the arms from bending at the elbows. The elbows are so supinated (turned inward) and elevated that the flat broad portion of the forearm contacts the ball. The forearms, which are in line with the upper arms, are placed near the floor in a position to receive the ball, and both arms are held at an angle that will cause the ball to rebound vertically (or nearly so) from the forearms.

The clasped hands should not be used to strike the ball, because they are narrower than the forearms and present many irregular areas because of the thumbs and knuckles. For the most effective bounce pass, the ball is contacted dead center at a spot on the forearms near the elbow.

An effective two-arm bounce pass often can be played as easily by the setup man or by the spike man as a setup pass. Considerable practice is needed to develop the skill to move into the correct court position and to make a bump pass with accuracy.

Figure 31-7.

Volleyball

Figure 31-8. Two-hand bump pass with the forearms. (Acknowledgment is gratefully extended to Dr. Leonard B. Stallcup, official photographer of the U.S. Volleyball Association, for the use of this photograph.)

One-arm Bounce Pass. The one-arm bounce pass, usually referred to as a dig pass, involves the same principles as the two-arm bounce pass. The solid surface of either hand, preferably the heel, wrist, or forearm, is placed in the path of the ball. The ball must be watched closely so that it can be struck squarely in its center. The fingers of the striking hand are slightly closed, like those of a relaxed hand, with the thumb so flexed that the ball cannot contact the palm of the hand. The body should be in a ready, crouched position, with the weight resting on the balls of the feet and with the knees slightly flexed in order to allow the body to be extended simultaneously with the contact of the ball.

The one-arm bounce pass can be executed with a closed fist, in which case the ball is hit on the combined surface of the heel of the hand and the clenched fingers. Although the closed fist pass is less accurate than the relaxed hand pass, it allows the ball to be contacted with increased force.

Figure 31-9. A one-hand "dig" pass. (Going into the roll after recovering the ball.) (Acknowledgment is gratefully extended to Dr. Leonard B. Stallcup, official photographer of the U.S. Volleyball Association, for the use of this photograph.)

Japanese Roll (Save). At times, especially in retrieving hard spikes, the defensive player is unable to position himself in line with the ball. In order to make a successful save of the ball (using a two-arm dig or, more often, a one-arm dig) the player must leave his feet and dive to the ball. After he hits the ball he is faced with the urgent problem of avoiding any possible injuries by either *absorbing* the force of his dive to the floor by doing a quick push-up in reverse or else distributing this force by doing a quick roll. Because an equally important goal is to get back into playing position as quickly as possible, a rolling action is preferred in order to come back quickly to the feet.

If the dive is directly forward (and especially if the player is close to the floor), his only choice is often to attempt to do a push-up in reverse with his arms while arching his back, keeping his head up, and sliding on the floor on his chest, belly, and thighs. As soon as possible, he rolls sideways, tucks his legs in, pushes with his arms, and comes to a stand. If the dive is forward and to one side, the player can do a quick shoulder roll similar to that done by football players. If the dive is to the side, a side roll should be performed. Such rolls are sometimes termed *Japanese rolls.* Their purpose is to round the body in the direction of the roll and to prevent any portion of the body from hitting the floor squarely. Instructions for performing these rolls are presented in Chapter 30. These rolls and saves should be practiced many times on mats before attempting them on the hard floor.

Points to Remember

1. All serves and balls directed below the chest, or to either side of or deep behind the receiver, should be played with below-chest recovery passes.
2. The hands must be clenched in such a manner that the palm of the hand does not contact the ball.
3. The forearms must be held at an angle that will cause the ball to rebound in a nearly vertical direction.
4. The heel of the hand should be placed directly behind the center of the ball, and the ball should be punched with an easy wrist action in order to send it high in an arc toward the intended receiver.

Net Recovery Pass

It is possible, most of the time, to recover and play balls hit into the net (other than on the third hit). The one- or two-arm bounce pass is generally the most effective pass for this play. To effectively recover balls rebounding from the net, a fundamental knowledge of the action of the rebounding ball is necessary. A ball striking the cable at the top of the net will usually drop straight down; a ball striking midway in the net will be pushed out by the recoiling net and will drop a foot or two away from the net; a ball striking near the rope through the bottom of the net will be held by the net and will rebound well away from the net before dropping. Players should test the net before each game, because the rebound pattern varies with the tension of the connecting cables. If the net recovery is only the second contact, the ball should be bounced back away from the net and high. This will guard against the common fault of hitting the ball back into the net and will place the ball high for a teammate to spike or make a deliberate placement. By being alert and watching where the ball strikes the net, an effective recovery position can be taken to one side of the ball and close to the floor. A recovery that is made near the floor is generally more effective than one in which the ball is recovered directly out of the net. A ball hit into the net at a high speed will rebound farther out of the net than a slowly hit ball.

Recovery Drills

Wall-volley Bounce-pass Drill. Standing five feet from the wall, the player practices the one- and two-arm bounce pass, volleying the ball as many times in succession as possible.

Net Recovery Bounce-pass Drill. The instructor tosses the volleyball into the net at different heights and at different speeds. The player attempts a one- or two-arm net recovery bump pass as the ball rebounds from the net.

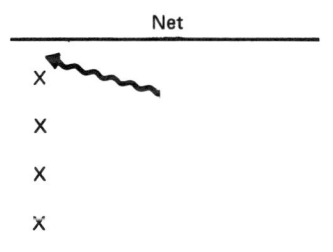

Figure 31-10.

The Setup

The purpose of the setup is to place the ball in a position above and slightly behind the net from which it can most effectively be spiked. Volleyball authorities do not agree on what constitutes the best height, the best direction, the best distance from the net, the best arc of fall, and the best floor target toward which the setter should direct the pass because each individual spiker has his own preference for the particular setup that best meets his requirements. Therefore, the best setup ball is the one that satisfies the needs of the spiker receiving the setup pass.

The setup man must be alert and agile and must move quickly to different areas in the court. Serves of great speed are often received by the setup man's teammate, who consequently may make a poorly controlled pass to the setup man. Regardless of the poor passes that may be directed toward him, an effective setup man is able to consistently set the ball up in a position that meets the needs of the spiker.

The setup man executes the setup pass in the same manner as the *chest pass* except that he must

1. Move quickly to the ball, keeping his back arched and his hands at or above head level.
2. Aim the ball upward at an increased vertical angle because the spiker will be positioned closer to him and thus he does not travel many feet in distance.
3. Accurately place the ball in a specific area because most spikers are unsuccessful if they are required to make unnecessary movements or have to move to an unexpected spot before or during their spiking action.
4. Pass the ball to a height of twelve to twenty feet (the actual height of the setup depends on the experience, ability, and wishes of the particular spiker).
5. Set the ball in front of the spiker and in a position that is above and approximately two or three feet behind the net.
6. Get out of the spiker's path after setting the ball up for him and be in a position to recover the ball in case the spiked ball is blocked by the opponents.

Behind-the-head Setup (Back Set). When the setup player is located in the front-center playing area, he can use the behind-the-head setup to set up to the spiker behind him. He should position himself when receiving a pass so that the ball is dropping directly toward his face (or chest). In order to direct the ball upward and behind him, he uses significantly less arm, wrist, and finger extension than in the chest pass. Thus, as the ball leaves his fingers, his arms are still bent and his wrists and fingers

Figure 31-11. The setup.

Volleyball

Figure 31-12. Behind-the-head setup. (Acknowledgment is gratefully extended to Dr. Leonard B. Stallcup, official photographer of the U.S. Volleyball Association, for the use of this photograph.)

remain flexed, but considerable body thrust is used. The arms move upward and backward, instead of upward and forward. The setup should travel directly upward and to his rear; hence, his back should be squarely toward the spot to which the ball is aimed. To avoid "tipping" the direction of the setup in advance, the setter's initial body position and actions should be identical for either the forward or backward setup.

Low, Quick Setups. For advanced play, a low setup that travels only one or two feet above the height or level at which it is spiked is sometimes utilized. This permits a quick spike to be made before the defensive team players can position themselves properly. The low setup is made in the same manner as a regular setup, except that less force is employed. In order to be most effective, it should, until the ball is hit, look exactly like a regular setup.

Setup Drills

Toss and Setup Drills. Standing near the net, the instructor (or another player) tosses the ball to the setup man who attempts a high vertical setup pass back to the instructor. After setting up the ball for the instructor, each player returns to the rear of the line and repeats the setup, in turn, several times.

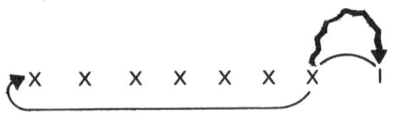

Figure 31-13.

Single-file Setup Drill. Player A sets up the ball high over his head; then player B positions himself under the ball and sets it up again, high overhead, for player C.

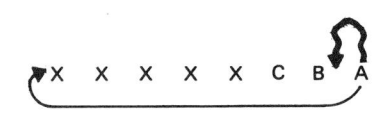

Figure 31-14.

After setting up the ball, each player returns to the rear of the line and repeats the setup, in turn, several times.

Accuracy-scoring Setup Drill. Each player, after receiving a pass from the instructor, sets up five separately passed balls to the target area in front of him. He is awarded points according to the placement of the ball in the target area, which is marked as follows: the center circle has a one-foot diameter and each of the surrounding circles has a radius of an additional foot.

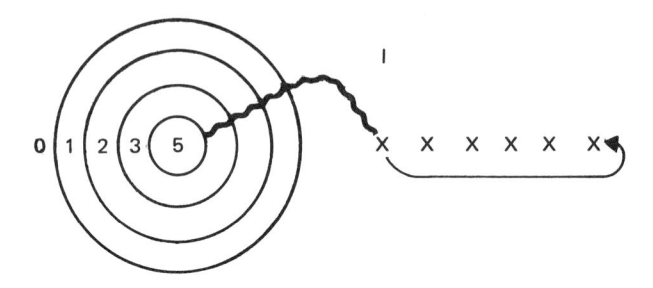

Figure 31-15.

The Spike

The third and final play of the traditional offensive attack in volleyball is known as the spike, and it is the most spectacular and colorful part of the game. The spiker jumps high into the air and coordinates his movements in order to hit a moving ball over the eight-foot-high net with such force and direction that it will evade the opposition. The skill of spiking requires strength, jumping power, agility, timing, coordination, perception, balance, and concentration.

An important factor in executing the spike is a knowledge of how to hit the ball correctly. To develop the greatest arm power for striking the ball requires that the spiking arm be initially in a flexed position. As in serving, the right hand is cocked behind the right ear, close to the head. The elbow is so bent that the right forearm is parallel to the floor, and the right upper arm is in a vertical position. The hyperextended wrist is rapidly flexed forward just before the open hand contacts the ball at a position in front of the right shoulder and above the head. The wrist must be relaxed just before contacting the ball. As the ball is contacted, the hand becomes rigid and the fingers are slightly flexed in order to form a cupped hand position. The ball should be driven downward into the opponent's court. Snapping the hand by means of relaxed wrist action adds velocity and an increased downward angle to the flight of the ball.

The spot on the ball that is hit by the hand and the angle from which the ball is hit will determine the direction of the spiked ball. The line of motion of the spiking force must be applied from an angle above the back dead center of the ball and in the desired direction. In order to get his hand above the ball, the spiker should make a vertical jump that enables him to reach with his hand to the top portion of the ball. The direction in which the spiked ball travels is determined by the position of the hand at the instant of impact. If the hand is in the normal flexed striking position the ball will rebound from it in a line nearly perpendicular to the forearm. However, if the wrist is either inwardly or outwardly rotated, the ball will rebound from the hand in a line to the right or to the left of the forearm.

At the time that the ball is spiked, it should be twelve to eighteen inches in front of the spiking shoulder and about two feet behind the net. The optimum distance of the ball from the net during the spike is a matter of individual preference; spikers who learn to spike at various distances from the net have an advantage over those who cannot spike well except at a set distance from the net.

Most spikers start their movement toward the net from a position eight to twelve feet behind the net. The approach is made squarely toward the net and, as the double-legged take-off is executed, the opponents' court should be scanned to note the position of the defensive players. As the legs are extended, both arms are vigorously extended upward to assist in the lift from the floor. Both arms are moved overhead and in a semistriking position, so that either hand can be used for the spike. The non-spiking arm is then brought downward and to the side and the spiking shoulder is rotated toward the net. While in the air the body is erect and does not travel toward the net. The ball must be contacted approximately one to two feet in front of the body (depending on the amount of wrist action and the distance from the net), and the spiking arm should be approximately 20 to 45° forward from the vertical when the ball is contacted.

The beginning spiker should practice the spike while remaining in a standing position. This is done by holding the ball in the opposite hand, striking it, and observing its path when struck from different angles. The unskilled spiker should regularly use the wall-spiking drill that will be described later to improve his spiking skill and the force of his hit.

After the beginning spiker has acquired the ability to hit the ball downward with force, he moves to the net; the toss-and-spike drill should be used with the top of the net lowered to a height of six and one-half feet. As the spiker gains confidence and proficiency in spiking, the net should gradually be raised. As the net is raised, the vertical jump should be introduced. The three-step approach, and finally the controlled run, should supply the speed required to generate the force needed for the high vertical jump and spike.

Points to Remember

1. Using an open hand is more effective than using the closed fist for the spike.
2. The approach for the spike should ordinarily be made squarely toward the net, and the double-legged take-off should be executed with sufficient control and vertical lift to keep the spiker from jumping into the net, stepping over the center line, passing any part of his body over the net, or touching the net with his hand.
3. The ball must be contacted from an overhead position and in front of the right shoulder in order to place the proper downward angle on it. If the ball is contacted when it is directly above the body the

Figure 31-16. Spike.

Figure 31-17. Spike and follow-through. (Note the two-man block.) (Holtzman of UCLA is spiking; Tom Madison and Kirk Kilgour are setting up the block.) (Acknowledgment is gratefully extended to Dr. Leonard B. Stallcup, official photographer of the U.S. Volleyball Association, for the use of this photograph.)

Volleyball 481

ball cannot be hit at a downward angle with any force, considerable wrist action is required, and to attempt to do so may result in an illegal spike called a carry.

4. A ball that is hit with *great* speed and at an angle that is sufficiently downward so that it hits in the front half of the opponent's court is referred to as a spike. A ball that is hit with *sufficient* speed but at such an angle that it hits in the back half of the opponents' court is referred to as either a volley or a spike.

5. After spiking the ball, the spiker should land on both feet, facing the net squarely and in a crouched position, with his elbows close to his body and his hands in position to recover the ball with a bounce pass if the spike is blocked.

6. Although tall players have an advantage in spiking, regardless of a player's height, if he is able to jump high enough to extend his wrist and hand above the net, he can learn to spike the ball effectively.

Dink Shot (Soft Spikes). If the spiker always plays a regular or hard spike, this simplifies the task of the blockers and defensive players in anticipating his spike and in recovering it. One method used to deceive the defensive players is for the spiker, as he is spiking the ball, to flex his hand to the right or to the left, instead of only downward. This wrist action will deflect the ball to one side of its apparent path.

Another deceptive action on the spike is to execute a dink shot (soft spike) instead of the usual hard spike. The dink shot is a softly played lob shot or drive that quickly falls to the floor. It is usually directed (1) over the blockers' hands and immediately behind them, (2) in front of the other front-line players, or (3) to one of the rear corners.

Preparation for the dink should look exactly as if a spike is going to be attempted. At the last second, however, the spiker stiffens his wrist and extends his fingers, striking the ball with the finger tips only or with a semifist. The striking action resembles a soft, semipushing motion that is derived from a straightening of the forearm at the elbow. Care must be taken not to carry the ball when making a dink shot.

Multiple Spiking Attack (Quick Spike). Individual and (especially) multiple-player defensive skills and strategy have been sufficiently advanced by the better players so that advanced offensive strategy has had to improve correspondingly. Much of this improvement has been created by adding the element of deception and increased speed to the attack. Occasionally, a team will spike the ball on their second hit. Some back-line players have developed the ability to spike effectively from behind the ten-foot line. Both of these modes of attack attempt to surprise the defensive players.

Much more frequently used, however, is the multiple spiking attack, in which a back-line player moves to a center front position and sets up the ball for one of the three front-line spikers. This permits the spiking attack to come from any spot behind the thirty-foot net. In order to add deception by hiding the point of the attack until the last second, the setter often makes a low, quick setup. At the same time, all spikers run forward and jump, expecting the setup. This type of attack, when well executed, makes it extremely difficult for the defensive team to establish a two- or three-man block in time.

Another type of setup that is successfully utilized by some teams is to station the setter at one of the front corners. He sets up the ball low (one to two feet above the net), parallel with it and about two feet behind it, causing it to travel to the other corner. One or more spikers can run to the ball and spike it from a variety of locations. Again, this is difficult to defend against, but the running spiker must have great coordination and timing. This is usually gained through practice.

Spiking Drills

Wall-spiking Drill. Standing ten feet away from the wall, each player so spikes the ball that it strikes the floor three to five feet in front of the wall and rebounds ten to fifteen feet upward. As the ball bounces off the floor the player again spikes the ball in a similar fashion.

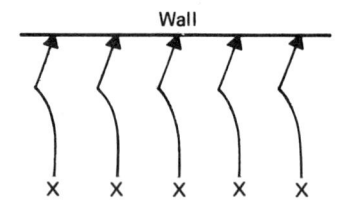

Figure 31-18.

Vertical Jump Drill. The player practices imaginary spiking, starting his approach ten feet behind the net, executing the two-legged take-off, and spiking an imaginary ball when he has attained his maximum height.

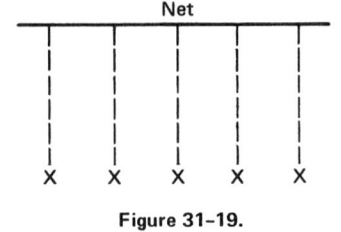

Figure 31-19.

Toss-and-spike Drill. The instructor (or another player) tosses the ball two feet above a six-foot high net. The player takes one or two steps, jumps, and spikes the ball.

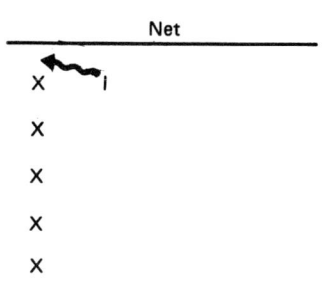

Figure 31-20.

As the player gains confidence and ability in spiking the net is elevated a few inches at a time.

Dual Spiking Drill. Player A passes to player B; player B sets up the ball for player A, who approaches the net, jumps, and spikes the ball.

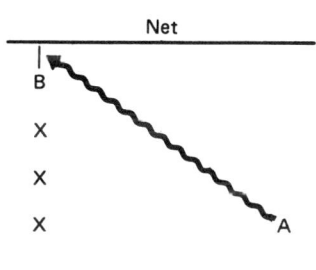

Figure 31-21.

OFFENSIVE TEAM STRATEGY

A well-planned offense cannot be effective unless the team is superior in ball handling. The members of a team must perfect the ever-important first pass (recovery or bump pass) and setup and must spend a majority of this practice time in drilling on these skills.

A successful team offense depends on teamwork and cooperation. Many of the plays in volleyball begin from different points, with the offensive players in different relative positions and facing a different defensive pattern by the opposing team. Because of these factors, and because, as the play develops, there are so many other rapid changes in the situation, no specific offensive pattern can be prescribed. In attempting to develop the best style of play for a particular team, the abilities and weaknesses of the team members themselves must be analyzed. Experience, height, speed, and ball-handling ability must be considered.

Generally speaking, the offensive play is effective only as long as the setup man is able to set up the ball well. The value of a top-flight setter cannot be overemphasized.

One of the most important ingredients of a team's offense is their reception of the serve and the subsequent first pass of the ball. All players should be alert and ready to receive different types of serves (which may curve, drop, or float) and serves of varying speeds and heights above the net. In receiving a serve a player is occasionally drawn out of position. In such instances, he should return to his normal playing position as quickly as possible.

Team Offensive Formations

When a team is composed of an equal number of setters and spikers an offensive formation termed the 3-3 is used. This formation alternates a setup man between each pair of spikers (and vice versa). The following diagrams depict the 3-3 formation: (X = spiker and O = setup man.)

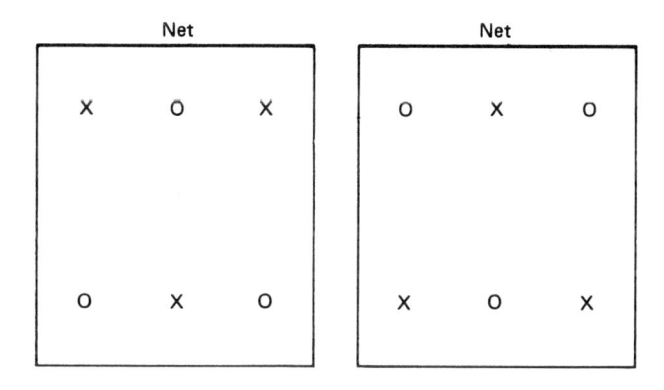

Figure 31-22.

When using the 3-3 formation, alternate rotations cause the spiker to rotate into the center-forward position. Here he is flanked by setup men, which provides two distinct offensive possibilities. First, with no switch, the spiker always has the same setup man setting up to him; thus, they get used to each other's playing traits. Because the center spiking position is also advantageous for angling the spiked ball to all areas of the opponents' court, it is also considered a strong position from which to spike. Secondly, the setup man will always be in the front-center position so that he can always go out after the ball that has been passed forward by the first player. If the setup man is in the center-forward position as a result of the normal rotation there is no problem. However, if, due to the rotation, he is in either forward corner, a switch—which is made as soon as the ball is served—is necessary to get him back into the center-forward position. The advantage of always having the setup man in the front-center position is the fact that, regardless of who receives the ball from the opponent, the receiver knows that the ball will always be passed to the center-forward position. Another advantage is that the distance the ball must travel is generally reduced when the setup man is in the

Volleyball 483

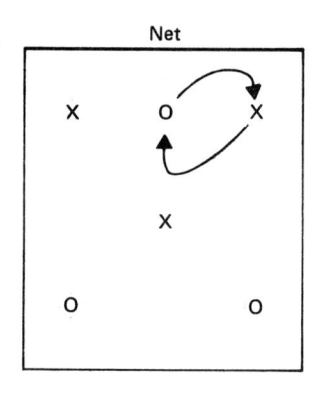

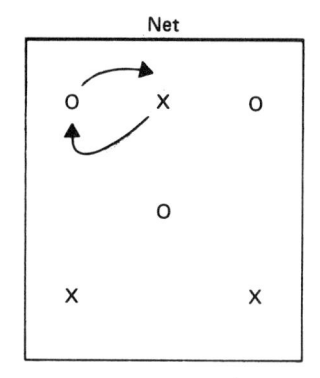

Figure 31-23.

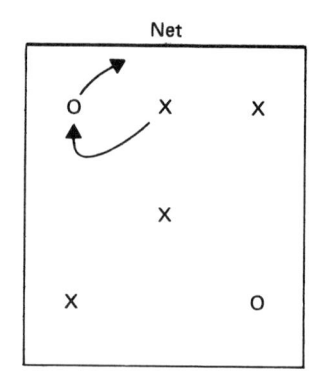

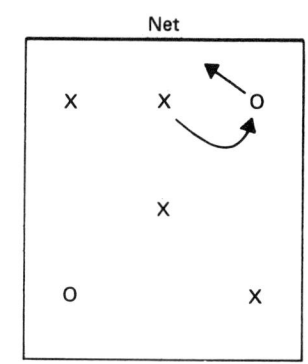

Figure 31-25.

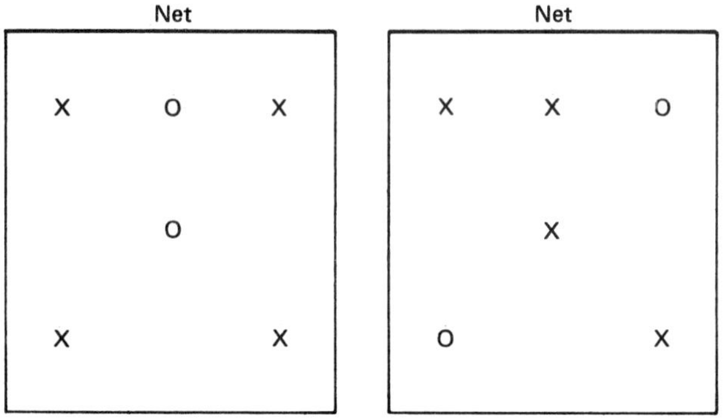

Figure 31-24.

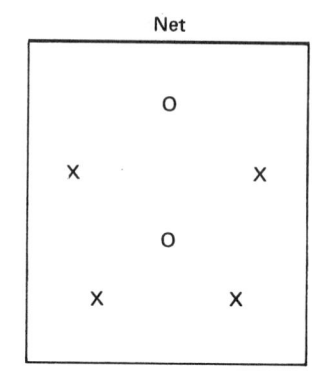

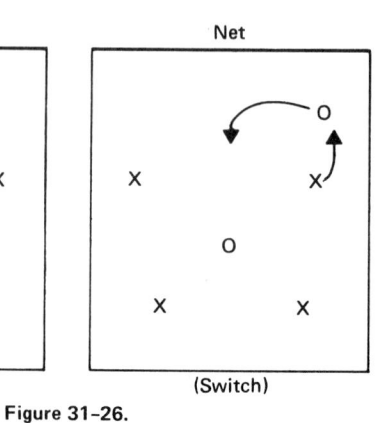

Figure 31-26.

front-center position, rather than in the right-forward position. Figure 31-23 demonstrates the 3-3 switch.

A team composed of more spikers than setters would probably use an offensive formation called the 4-2, which is considered a strong offensive team formation. This formation alternates a setup man between pairs of spikers. Figure 31-24 depicts the 4-2 formations.

When using the 4-2 formation, two of the three rotations cause the setup man to be rotated out of the center-forward position. To get the setup man back into the center position it is necessary to switch the setup man and the appropriate spiker. Here again, the same two distinct offensive possibilities appear as in the 3-3 formation. Is it better to have the spiker always receive from the same setup man, or is it better to always locate the setup man in the center-forward position? These questions are best answered after assessing the abilities of the players. Figure 31-25 demonstrates the 4-2 switch.

Receiving the Serve

As a result of the effectiveness of the overhand serve, certain receiving patterns have been devised to help the receiving team. Front-line players, excluding the setup man, step back and toward each side line. Back linemen, excluding the center back, step back to a position approximately seven or eight feet in front of the back line. The setup man stands near the net and faces his teammates. He may follow the direction of the ball by watching the eyes and hands of his teammates. The center back stands twelve to fifteen feet from the back line and generally tries to receive the majority of serves. Figure 31-26 demonstrates the 3-3 receiving formation and the switch that may take place if it is advantageous to place the setup man in the center-front position.

Figure 31-27 demonstrates the 4-2 receiving formation and the switch.

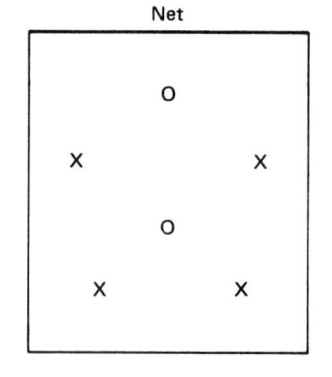

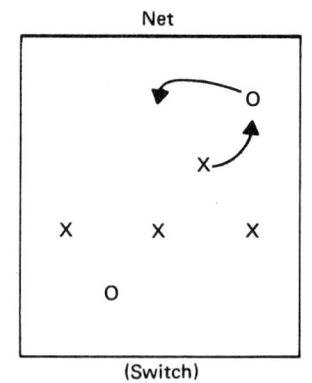

Figure 31-27.

484 *Individual and Team Sports*

Points to Remember

1. The majority of practice time should be spent in ball handling.
2. The best style of play depends on the team's experience, height, speed, and ball handling.
3. When a player is drawn out of position, he should return to his normal court position as quickly as possible.
4. The setup man should be switched into the center position if he will then be in a position to set the ball up to the best spiker.

6-2 Formation

Advanced volleyball players frequently use what is known as the 6-2 offensive formation. This is also called a 6-0 formation. The 6 refers to the fact that all six players on the team can spike effectively. The 2 indicates that the team has two skilled setters. Thus, all three front-line players are spikers, which increases the variety of the offensive attacks. The setup player in the back line, as soon as the serve is made, moves to the front-center position, in order to set up to any of the three spikers. In order to deceive the defensive team so they will not form a multiple block, a low, quick setup is made to any of the three spikers. As the setup is being initiated, all three spikers move straight forward and jump, with the setup going to any of them. Although this requires a high degree of timing and practice to execute well, it is most difficult to defend against.

The 0 in the 6-0 designation indicates that all six of the players can act as the setter. Thus, any player (usually a back-line player, however) can switch to the front-line position and set the ball up for the spike.

Offensive Drills

The 3-3, the 4-2, and the 6-0 formations can be formed and appropriate switches can be made with a verbal command, "Switch." After the switch has been learned, actual practice in receiving the serve in conjunction with the switch should be practiced. During this time the players must remember to be in their normal rotating positions prior to the serve.

DEFENSIVE TEAM TECHNIQUES

Two fundamental principles of defensive volleyball play are always to face squarely toward the attack (the point from which the ball is hit over the net) and to keep the eyes and concentration focused on the ball at all times. In preparing to receive an oncoming ball when no block is planned, each player should have a firm, wide stance that will enable him to move in any direction. To achieve this stance, the legs are flexed at the knees, the body is tilted forward at the hips, and the hands are placed in front of the body with the forearms parallel with the floor (in readiness to make the one- or two-arm dig pass). If the oncoming ball is above the shoulders, then the chest pass can be used. However, in championship play the dig pass is habitually used to recover all spikes. It is more effective to keep the hands low and then bring them up for the chest pass then it is to keep them high and be forced to lower them for the dig.

Blocking the Ball

A more effective way to meet a spiking attack than the dig is the use of the two- or three-man block. The block is a defensive play close to the net. It involves a coordinated, simultaneous jump by all the blocking players in which they jump just after the spiker leaves the floor. The blockers attempt to be in a position approximately eighteen inches behind the net, from which they can form a solid screen of hands above and slightly behind the top of the net. The shoulders of the blockers should contact one another, the fingers should be spread with the thumbs touching each other, and the heels of the hands should be pressed forward, with the hands and fingers flexed backward. All blockers should make their first moves to get close to the net and then shift along the net in order to meet the oncoming ball. If the blockers lunge forward from a distance, their hands tend to go into or over the net. Players who do lunge also run the risk of touching the net or crossing over the center line. Again, it should be emphasized that the blockers can reach over the net for the block, providing that they do not touch the net or contact the ball until after it is spiked. In fact, some blockers attempt to simulate catching the ball just as it is spiked in order to block it most effectively.

All arm motion should be executed in front of the body because not much elbowroom exists when the blockers are in their correct positions. The hands should be two to four inches from the net. If the hands are more than four inches away from the net the spike can be driven down between the net and the hands. Tilting the hands back prevents injury to the fingers, lessens the danger of the finger tips going over the net, and allows the blocked ball to come back high on the blocking team's side of the net.

During the setup, the blockers should not watch the ball but, instead, should watch the angle in which the opposing spiker is facing the the angle of the spiker's arm. This will assist the blockers in detecting the direction of the spiked ball. After the direction is observed the blockers should focus their attention on the ball. At the moment the ball is spiked, the blockers should stiffen their arms to offset the shock of the drive, but it is necessary

Volleyball

Figure 31-28. One-man block (side view).

Figure 31-30. Multiple block. (Note that the spiker has jumped higher and sooner than the three blockers, who have jumped simultaneously.) (Acknowledgment is gratefully extended to Dr. Leonard B. Stallcup, official photographer of the U.S. Volleyball Association, for the use of this photograph.)

to tilt the hands back and thus gain better control of the spiked ball. After the spiked ball has been blocked, the hands and arms should be brought down to the normal position and each player should be properly situated and in readiness for the next play.

In essence, effective team blocking consists of the individual players moving as a team to the correct positions. The blocking team must shift positions quickly and in unison in order to be at the net at the desired moment to meet the spiked ball. Proper timing is essential, and adequate practice time must be scheduled in order to master blocking skills.

There are two types of blocks: (1) the hard block, in which the hands and fingers are kept rigid in an attempt to force the ball back into the spiker's court and, (2) the soft block, in which the fingers and hands are tilted backward and are relaxed in an effort to so block the ball that its rebound is played on the blocker's side of the court. The soft block is ordinarily the preferred block.

Points to Remember. Good blocking techniques include

1. The ability of the blockers to move as a unit to all points along the net in time to obtain proper position.
2. The ability to study a spiker and the setup and anticipate whether the spiker will cut, hit straightaway, or hit down the line.
3. The ability to recover court position and play all balls that fall off the block.
4. Teamwork on the part of the nonblockers in covering the court. This gives the blockers confidence and enables them to concentrate on blocking the ball.

Two-man Block. When two players are blocking, they position themselves on either side of the spiker in order to cover a maximum area. Both blockers jump at the same time, just after the spiker leaves the floor. The blockers should be in a position approximately eighteen inches behind the net with their fingers spread in order to meet the oncoming spike. Generally, the center-front-court player and the front-side-court player nearest the spiker join to form the blocking team. The other players, who are not involved in the block, drop into a position forming a near semicircle around the blockers from which they can retrieve the ball after it rebounds from the blockers or else retrieve a spike that angles around or over the blockers. Figure 31-31 demonstrates the two-man blocking formation.

Figure 31-29. Spike and one-man block. (Acknowledgment is gratefully extended to Dr. Leonard B. Stallcup, official photographer of the U.S. Volleyball Association, for the use of this photograph.)

Individual and Team Sports

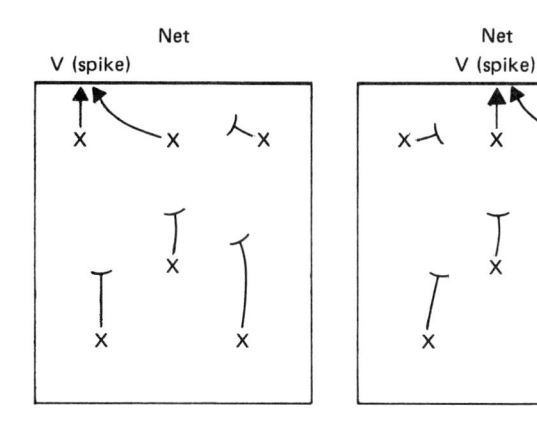

Figure 31-31.

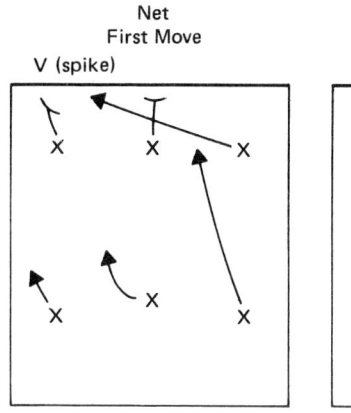

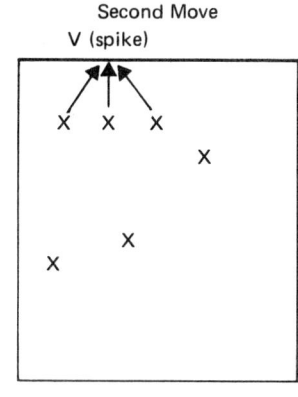

Figure 31-33.

Two-man Blocking Drill. The players stand in their normal court positions until the spiker's location is designated by the instructor. The blockers approach the designated point of attack and form a two-man block, using the center-front-court player and the front-side-court player nearest the spiker. The instructor can designate any location along the net, and the proper players move to the location to meet the spiked ball. The players not involved move to form a semicircle around and behind the block. (See Figure 31-32.)

Three-man Block. When three players are blocking, the center player blocks directly in front of the spiker. The center man is trying to position his hands parallel to the net, in line with the probable direction of the spike. The players on either side angle in to keep the ball from deflecting off their hands and out-of-bounds. The end result is a slightly concave barrier of six hands, located about two to four inches from the net, that attempts to intercept the spiked ball and, at the same time, keep it from skewing off to one side. The blockers' hands must be close together to prevent the ball from passing through.

To achieve the three-man block requires that the three front-line players move in to the appropriate court positions, because back-line players may not block at the net.

The timing of the block is accomplished after the three front-line players move into position. Figure 31-33 illustrates the three-man blocking formation.

Three-man Blocking Drill. The players stand in their normal court positions until the spiker's location is designated by the instructor. The blockers (the three front-line players) approach the designated point of attack and form a three-man block. The instructor can designate any location along the net and the proper players move to the location to meet the spiked ball.

The two-man and three-man blocking drills can be used against an actual spiker after the players have gained confidence and skill in forming the blocking formation. (See Figure 31-34.)

SELF-EVALUATION

The various drills presented in this chapter are excellent devices for assessing how well one is mastering the skills that comprise volleyball. The results can be analyzed in order to discover weaknesses to which additional practice and coaching can be directed.

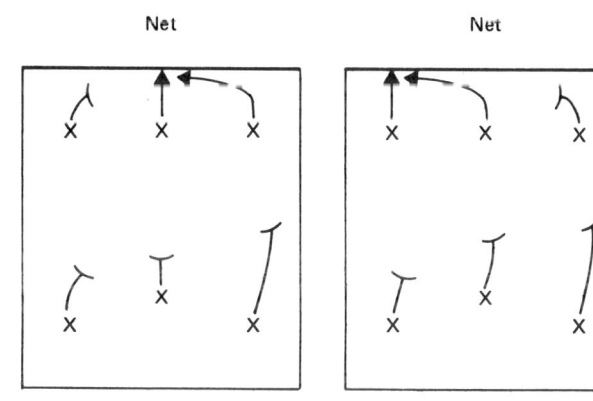

Figure 31-32.

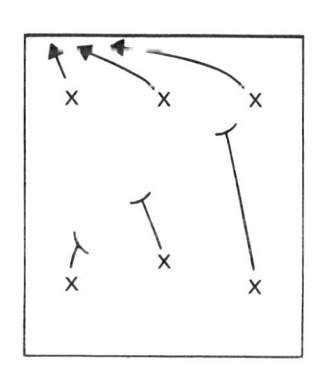

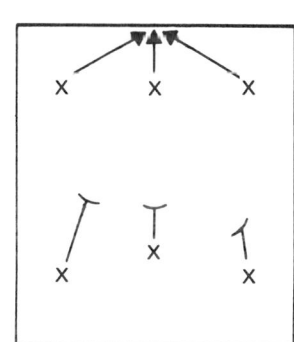

Figure 31-34.

Volleyball 487

Selected Definitions of Playing Terms

Ball in play: The ball is in play from the first contact for the serve until an error or foul has been committed or play is suspended for any other reason (dead ball).

Blocking: A defensive play close to the net in which the defensive players attempt to intercept the ball after it crosses the net or to prevent it from doing so. Reaching over the net is permitted when blocking.

Contacted ball: A ball that touches or is touched by any part of a player's body (or his clothing). This constitutes a hit. However, a multiple contact by one player or more (if together) on the block of a hard-driven spike is considered to be only one hit.

Court: The playing area marked off on either side of the net.

Error: A failure to play the ball properly as permitted under the rules. An error normally results in a foul.

Foul: A breaking of the rules or a failure to play the ball legally. It results in a side-out, if committed by the serving team, and a point, if committed by the receiving team.

Hit ball: The ball must be clearly hit. If the proper official believes the ball visibly comes to rest at contact, a foul is called.

Officials: The officials in an official match are the referee, umpire, timekeeper, and either two or four linesmen.

Out-of-bounds: The ball is out-of-bounds when it touches any object or surface outside the court or touches the net outside the court side line. If any part of the ball touches a boundary line or net side marker, or if it is contacted by a player before landing out-of-bounds, it is not out-of-bounds.

Playover: The act of putting the ball in play again, by the last server, without awarding point or side-out. A playover occurs whenever a double foul is called or when the referee stops the play.

Screening: Screening occurs if a player conceals the start of a teammate's serve by obstructing in any way an opponent's line of sight. Screening is illegal if it masks the server's action and results in a foul being called.

Simultaneous contacts: Contacts made at the same instant.

Spiked ball: A ball forcefully hit (other than on the serve) from a height not less than that of the top of the net.

Selected References

BOOKS

Egstrom, Glen H. *Volleyball.* (physical Education Activities Series). Dubuque, Iowa: Brown, 1966.

Keller, Val. *Point, Games, Match!* Hollywood, Calif.: Creative Sports, 1968.

Laveaga, Robert E. *Volleyball.* New York: Ronald, 1960.

Odeneal, William T., Harry E. Wilson, and Mary Frances Kellam. *Beginning Volleyball.* Belmont, Calif.: Wadsworth, 1969.

Sandefur, Randy. *Volleyball.* Pacific Palisades, Calif.: Goodyear, 1970.

Slaymaker, Thomas, and Virginia H. Brown. *Power Volleyball.* Philadelphia: Saunders, 1970.

Welch, J. Edmund. *How to Play and Teach Volleyball.* New York: Association Press, 1963.

PERIODICALS

International Volleyball Review, published by Harry E. Wilson, P.O. Box 554, Encino, Calif., 91316.

The Annual Official Volleyball Rules and Reference Guide of the United States Volleyball Association. (Robert Reid, editor). P.O. Box 169, Berne, Indiana, 46711 (published annually).

CHAPTER 32

Weight training and Weight lifting[1]

Donald R. Casady[*]
The University of Iowa

Edward F. Chui[†]
University of Hawaii

HISTORY

Man has engaged in the lifting of weights for sport or exercise for at least as long as he has kept a written history. This type of weight lifting has varied from the exercising with *halteres* (dumbbell-like objects) performed by the ancient Greeks to improve their strength, athletic prowess, and military proficiency to contests of lifting boulders by the Irish. The late nineteenth century might be termed the *era of the strong man*, both in Europe and the United States. At that time professional strong men gave demonstrations and waged contests in a wide variety of odd lifts in which each person specialized in a few favorite lifts in which he excelled. For example, George Hackenschmidt of Germany at that time was considered by many to be one of the strongest men in the world; one of his favorite feats of strength was to bend coins with his fingers. Eugene Sandow of England developed a well-proportioned muscular physique and traveled throughout Europe and the United States staging shows and exhibitions of strength. He was more renowned for his build than for his strength, however. Because many of these old-time strong men were gluttons and hence quite fat, they presented a poor body image to the public; consequently, weight training and weight lifting never became popular with the masses during this era.

The inclusion of weight lifting, in 1896, at the first Olympic Games, and in each succeeding Olympics, was probably a prime factor in the current popularity of weight lifting and weight training. In 1928, the present three lifts (the two-handed press, snatch, clean and jerk) were, for the first time, the only lifts included in Olympic competition.

In the United States, the use of such weight training equipment as barbells and dumbbells to develop strength and the size of the muscles has increased greatly during the last two decades. There are two factors that were responsible for this increase: progressive resistance exercises (dumbbells, barbells, or pulley weights) were used successfully in rehabilitation centers during and after World War II; and reports from research studies, many of which were completed in the 1950s, indicated that weight training is an efficient method of training athletes and others for improved physical performance. During the last ten years many famous athletes have regularly engaged in weight-training exercises in order to enhance their athletic performance. Perry O'Brien, the shotputting champion, and Bob Richards, the pole vaulting champion, are two forerunners in adopting this form of special training supplement.

---

[1] Part of the material for this chapter has been adapted from *Handbook of Physical Fitness Activities*, by D. Casady, P. Mapes, and L. Alley, chap. 8, pp. 51–66. Acknowledgment is gratefully given to Macmillan, Inc., for permission to use this material.

[*] Professor Casady first engaged in weight training while serving as a physical training instructor in the Army Air Force. He continued this training while a basketball and gymnastics team member in college and afterward, winning two all-university weight lifting championships while at The University of Iowa. He has taught many weight training classes and has coached several weight training teams. One of his team members won the 123 pound Southeastern AAU weight lifting championship and another later won the "Mr. Florida" physique contest.

[†] Professor Chui first engaged in weight training during his high school days in the early 1940s. His interest and participation continued throughout his college years to the extent that his M.A. thesis and his Ph.D. dissertation involved studies, in part, dealing with weight training technology. He has taught many weight training classes and has employed weight training in his athletics coaching.

DESCRIPTION OF WEIGHT TRAINING AND WEIGHT LIFTING

Exercises that primarily involve the lifting of weight are usually performed for one or all of the following three purposes.

Weight Training

Weight training is concerned with the development of increased physical capacity; that is, increased muscular strength, power, and often speed of movement. Weight training involves the systematic exercising of the various muscle groups by repeatedly subjecting them to progressively increased exercise loads in order to enhance their development. Weight training is frequently one of the exercise mediums employed in physical rehabilitation programs.

Weight Lifting

Weight lifting is concerned with how much weight the performer is able to lift. Competition is held for several different body-weight divisions and the winner in each division is determined by the total poundage lifted in each lift or the combined poundage lifted in different types of lifts. For many years, weight lifting—that is, the three Olympic lifts (which consist of the two-hands press, snatch, and clean and jerk)—has been a competitive athletic event at state, national, and international levels, including the Olympic Games. In addition, odd-lift contests, in which competition is held in such lifts as the bench press or the dead lift, are frequently held.

Body Building

Body building is concerned with increasing the size of the muscles and developing a well-proportioned body. Contests for body builders are held regularly to determine the person with the best physique, the best build, and the most muscularly developed body. Titles such as Mr. California, Mr. America, and Mr. Universe are awarded to the winners of such contests.

UNIQUE VALUES OF WEIGHT TRAINING

Many research studies have been conducted since World War II in which the effects of regularly engaging in weight training were investigated. These effects have often been compared with the gains resulting from engaging in other types of physical activity for a similar period of time—usually six weeks to a semester. For almost all studies a greater gain in over-all strength and in the strength of selected muscle groups occurred in the weight training groups than in the control groups (nonweight training groups). In addition, the weight training groups often were found to have made a larger gain in speed of movement and in power than did the control groups (when these factors were investigated). Other benefits that have been found to accrue from engaging in a weight training program are (1) an increase in local muscular endurance (which is usually a concomitant of increased muscular strength) and (2) an increase in the flexibility of certain joints (when weight training exercises involve a complete range of motion). Increasing evidence is being accumulated that weight training is a valuable means for improving performance in almost all sports, and numerous examples can be found of athletes who have testified that their participation in weight training aided their performance in such sports as football, basketball, swimming, track and field, baseball, gymnastics, golf, tennis, and diving.

Some of the reasons why weight training appeals to many young males follow:

1. Weight training exercises involve essentially simple skills and, hence, are easy to learn.
2. Only a minimum of basic weight training equipment is needed; and this equipment is ordinarily available at any college, YMCA, or similar organization. If purchased, equipment is rather inexpensive, but it is quite durable.
3. Weight training exercises can be selected to develop specific muscles or areas of the body.
4. A large variety of weight training exercises can be included in a program, thus permitting the weight trainer to change his program of exercises as often as he desires in order to avoid monotony and boredom.
5. Engaging in a weight training program can be very satisfying because the weight trainer can easily observe the gains made in strength and muscular development. By keeping a record of the amount of weight lifted for each exercise, the weight trainer has a built-in motivator because he knows exactly how much progress he is making.

No evidence has been produced to support the concept that participating in weight training causes muscle boundness (lack of flexibility and loss of coordination and timing).

For most people weight training is a supplement to participation in other sports and is not an end in itself. Participation in weight training does little, if anything, to develop increased coordination, timing, or motor skills; nor does it often bring much immediate satisfaction or fun. Consequently, most people will want to combine other activities such as running, swimming, games, and sports with their weight training program.

WEIGHT TRAINING EQUIPMENT AND ITS CARE

Weight training equipment ranges from inexpensive, homemade barbells, made by inserting the ends of iron pipes into cement-filled cans or buckets, to special precision-machined, chrome-plated equipment of various kinds placed in carpeted, air-conditioned, commercial gymnasiums or studios. The following weight training equipment is frequently encountered.

Bar

The bar is steel and ranges from one to one and one-eighth inches in diameter and from one to seven feet in length (five and six feet are the most common lengths). With collars attached, the five foot bar weighs approximately twenty-five pounds and the six-foot bar weighs approximately thirty pounds. The middle section of the surface of the bar is usually knurled to provide increased friction for the one-hand and two-hand grip.

Plates

The plates are metal discs (plastic plates are increasing in popularity) with a center hole of sufficient diameter to accommodate the insertion of the bar. The weight of the plate is generally imprinted on each of its sides. Plates are usually available in poundages ranging from one and one-quarter, to two and one-half, to five, ten, and up to seventy-five pounds.

Collars

Four metal collars (two inside and two outside) usually encircle each bar and are used to hold the plates in place on the bar.

Barbell

The bar with collars and plates attached makes up the barbell, which is the only essential piece of weight training equipment. The poundage on most barbells can be adjusted by changing the plates.

Dumbbell

The dumbbell can best be described as a short barbell, eight to twenty inches in length. Most dumbbells are cast in one piece and have round- or hexagonal-shaped ends; the poundage of this type of dumbbell is fixed.

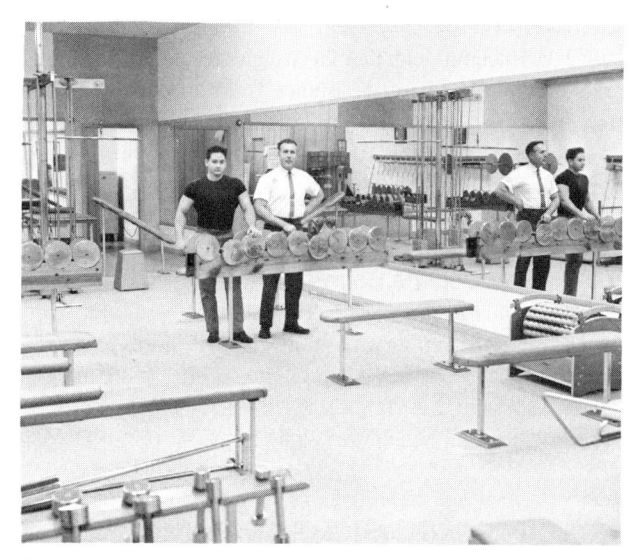

Figure 32-1. Colonial Health Studios, Chattanooga, Tennessee. (Acknowledgment is gratefully extended to *Strength and Health Magazine,* York, Pennsylvania, for permission to reproduce this photograph.)

Iron Boots

Iron boots are attached to the feet with straps in order to perform exercises designed to strengthen the muscles controlling leg movements at the knee or hip joints. Each boot contains a center hole through which a short metal bar is inserted and to which plates are attached in order to increase the weight of the boot to the desired poundage.

Head Strap

The head strap is a device made of canvas webbing; it is worn like a cap around the top of the head. Plates are attached to a chain that is fastened to the head strap. The head strap is primarily used to develop the muscles of the neck.

Benches

Padded metal or wooden benches are commonly twelve to sixteen inches in height, ten to sixteen inches in width, and four to six feet in length. The weight trainer lies on the bench when performing certain exercises.

Standards

For convenience in performing certain exercises, metal standards are used to support the barbell at a desired height from the floor.

Leg-press Machine

The leg-press machine is chiefly used for developing the extensor (thigh) muscles of the legs.

Lat Machine

The lat machine enables the weight trainer to bring his arms downward against resistance from an overhead position in order to exercise the latisimus dorsi muscles, the development of which creates the appearance of a broad upper back.

Incline and Decline Boards

Incline and decline boards are padded boards that support the weight trainer's body at an angle sloping upward or downward from a horizontal position. Their use enables the weight trainer to exercise various muscle groups at a variety of angles and body positions.

PRINCIPLES OF WEIGHT TRAINING AND WEIGHT LIFTING

Preliminary Conditioning

The beginning weight trainer should use a lighter-than-normal exercise load during the first five-or-so weight training workouts in order to permit his muscles and body to adjust to unaccustomed movements and to avoid in large part the muscular soreness and stiffness that might otherwise result. This preliminary conditioning period will also permit him to learn the correct form for performing the weight training exercises before he begins to perform them with a near-maximum load.

Warm-up

Before lifting heavy poundages the weight trainer should warm up by using a light weight to exercise most of the major muscle groups of his body (if he has not already warmed up as a result of participating in other vigorous physical activity). The warm-up exercise (described later in this chapter) is excellent for this purpose.

Safety

The beginning weight trainer should not exercise with or lift heavy weights without first practicing for several periods the exercises or lifts with a light load he can easily control. When in doubt as to his ability to handle a weight safely, the weight trainer should ask one or two spotters to assist him. Before performing an exercise with a barbell the weight trainer should first check to see that the outside collars on the barbell are securely fastened—a loose collar will permit the plates to slide off the end of the bar if it is tilted. Although the weight trainer, if he retains his grasp on the bar, is in no danger of the plates dropping on his feet, the plates could drop on someone nearby and also cause the weight trainer to lose control of the barbell. When straining for several seconds to lift a maximum load, it is essential that the weight trainer not hold his breath; in rare instances, this action can result in loss of consciousness.

Basic Body Position When Exercising

When lifting a heavy weight the weight trainer should (1) keep his back as straight as possible, or even slightly arched, to allow the stronger muscles of the legs to do the work, thus avoiding straining the weaker muscles of the back; (2) keep the bar close to his body when lifting the barbell to his chest; (3) keep his feet flat on the floor for improved balance and to spread the load over a wide area of support; and (4) keep his feet spread approximately shoulder width in order to maintain a comfortable stance and proper balance while performing an exercise.

Correct Form

For maximum gains, and to avoid the possibility of injury, the beginning weight trainer should strive to use correct form throughout the performance of each weight training exercise.

Control All Exercise Movements

During all phases of a weight training exercise, whether working against or with gravity, the weight trainer should forcefully control his exercise movements.

Order of Exercises

The beginning weight trainer should perform his weight training workout in a sequence that will cause one area of the body to be exercised for the first exercise, another area of the body for the second exercise, and so on. The advanced weight trainer, however, may want to perform a series of exercises in which the muscles of only one area of the body are heavily exercised, before performing a series involving another area.

Number of Repetitions

The amount of weight used for a weight training exercise will depend on the performer's strength and the number of repetitions that he wants to perform. To effectively develop both strength and local muscular endurance, it is recommended that for most exercises the beginning weight trainer employ a load with which he can perform from seven to eleven repetitions. During his first few workouts, by trial and error, the beginner can establish this training load for each exercise.

Strength Development. Six executions-maximum have been found superior to two or ten executions-maximum for the development of strength. To develop strength rapidly, the beginner should perform three sets of each exercise, six repetitions of each set.

Local Muscular Endurance. A minimum of fifteen executions-maximum seems to be required for the effective development of local muscular endurance, and as many as thirty executions-maximum is sometimes used. The usual range of repetitions is from fifteen to twenty-five for each exercise.

Number of Sets

During the first few workouts the beginning weight trainer should do only one set of each exercise. In the following workouts he should attempt to do a minimum of two sets. If time permits, three sets of each exercise are preferable; this produces greater gains in strength than does performing only one set or even two sets.

Frequency of Workout

For beginners, performing weight training exercises three times a week or every other day produces more effective results than working out every day or only once or twice a week. Beginning weight trainers will probably profit most if they have approximately forty-eight hours of rest between weight training workouts.

Duration of Workout

Depending on the amount of rest taken between exercise bouts, the number of exercises and sets included in each workout and the number of persons with which the equipment is shared, the beginning weight trainer can usually complete his workout in from thirty to fifty minutes. As his strength, the exercise load, and the length of rest period increase, the weight trainer may require as long as two hours to complete a full workout.

Overloading

When the desired number of repetitions of an exercise can be performed during the first set, the poundage used for that exercise should be increased by approximately 2 or 3 per cent (five pounds is the most common increase in poundage) for the next workout.

FUNDAMENTAL TECHNIQUES OF WEIGHT TRAINING

The most important basic techniques of weight training and weight lifting follow.

Basic Stance

The basic stance for performing weight training exercises from the standing position is one in which the head is held erect, the back is straight, the feet are spread about hip width and aligned with each other, and the feet are flat on the floor.

Grips

When grasping the barbell, the hands should be placed approximately shoulder width apart on the bar; they should be spaced equidistant from the inside collars.

Regular or Pronated Grip. The regular grip is used when performing most barbell exercises. The palms of the hands face down and back when grasping a bar resting on the floor. At all times the thumbs are adjacent to each other and encircle the bar in a direction opposite to that in which the fingers are pointing.

Reverse or Supinated Grip. The reverse grip is used for only a few barbell exercises and is the opposite of the regular grip. The fifth or little fingers are adjacent to each other.

Combination or Alternate Grip. For the combination grip, which enables the lifter to retain his grasp when lifting heavy weights, the regular grip is taken with one hand and the reverse grip is taken with the other.

Body Positions

Crouch or Dead-lift Position. The crouch position is used when lifting a heavy barbell from the floor. In this position the bar, the hips, and the feet are in line with the weight trainer's shoulders. The body is crouched, the knees and hips are flexed, the back is straight, the neck and head are extended slightly backward, and the eyes are focused straight ahead.

Front-hang or Front-thigh-rest Position. In the front-hang position, the body and arms are straight, and the barbell is held in front of, and resting against, the thighs.

Supine Position. The weight trainer lies on his back in a horizontal position when in the supine position.

Chest-rest Position. In the chest-rest position, the bar is in contact with the chest, the arms are flexed, and the arms are under the bar.

Shoulder-rest Position. In the shoulder-rest position, the barbell is behind the weight trainer's neck and is resting on his shoulders and upper back. He grasps the bar with his hands located several inches on either side of his shoulders.

Movements

The two primary movements used in weight training exercises are *flexion* and *extension*.

Weight Training and Weight Lifting

Flexion. Flexion is movement in which two parts of the body connected at a joint are brought closer together, as exemplified by a curling movement.

Extension. Extension is the straightening or unfolding of two parts of the body, as exemplified by a pressing movement.

Use of Barbells and Dumbbells. For most exercises a barbell or a pair of dumbbells can be utilized to perform the exercise movements. When dumbbells are utilized, they can be moved together, in opposition, or alternately.

Identification of Exercised Muscles

For the specific weight training exercises described in this chapter, only the primary muscles and the muscle groups that strongly function when a movement is performed are identified. Two methods by which the weight trainer can identify the muscle groups involved in an exercise follow:

1. The muscles that cause movement to occur at a joint are usually located immediately above the joint (toward the center part of the body). For example, when the forearm is flexed or extended at the elbow joint, the muscles responsible for these movements are located between the elbow joint and the shoulder joint.
2. By having someone resist his movement in a certain direction, the weight trainer can feel or manipulate his surface muscles near the joint where movement occurs. The hard muscles are the contracted, working muscles and the soft and yielding muscles are the relaxed, nonworking muscles.

As a further aid in muscle identification, the weight training exercises in this chapter are arranged according to the muscle groups that are primarily exercised. The major surface muscles primarily developed by specific weight training exercises are depicted in Figure 32-2.

COMMON WEIGHT TRAINING TERMS

The terms identified in this section are frequently used in weight training; hence, an understanding of them will enable the reader to understand better the **instructions** concerning the principles, techniques, and rules of weight training.

1. Load: The actual poundage lifted during each movement of a weight training exercise.
2. Repetitions: One repetition of a weight training exercise is executed each time the complete movement cycle is performed. When engaging in a weight training workout, the poundage and the number of repetitions are generally indicated for each exercise.
3. Ten executions-maximum: This term refers to the maximum number of repetitions of an exercise that

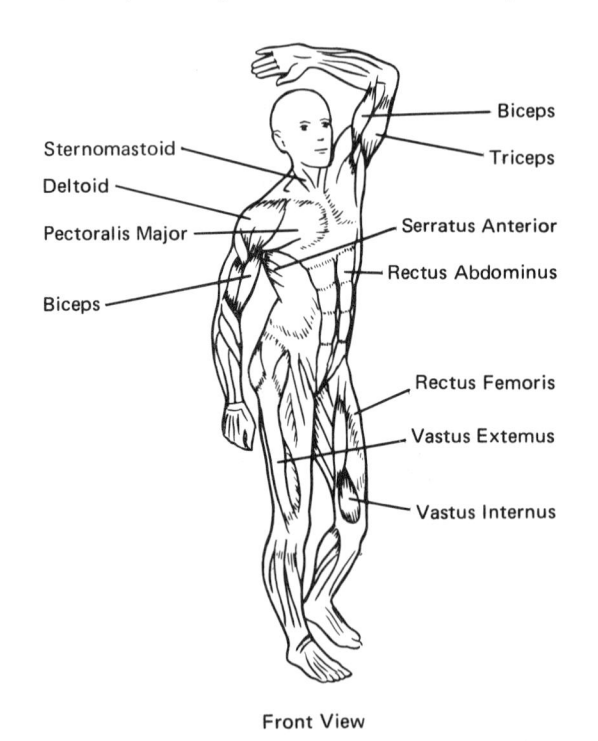

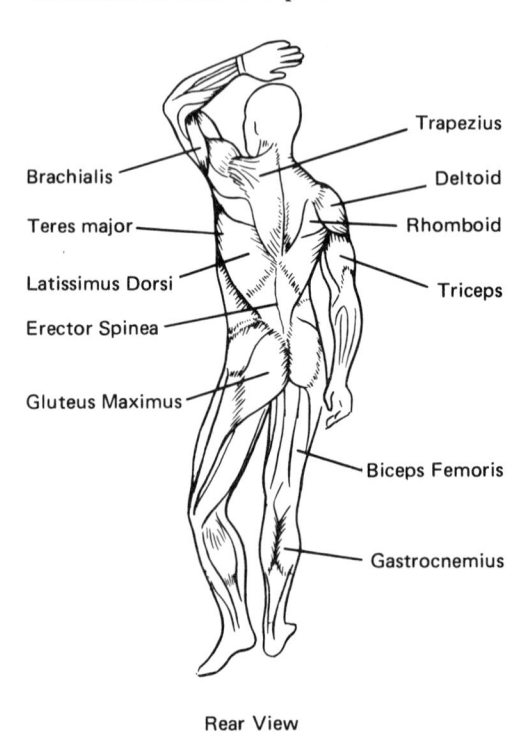

Figure 32-2. Major surface muscles. (Reproduced from *Handbook of Physical Fitness Activities,* Courtesy of Macmillan, Inc.)

494 *Individual and Team Sports*

the weight trainer can perform with a specified poundage. Ten executions-maximum means that the weight trainer cannot perform more than ten repetitions using a given poundage. A corollary of this term is *six repetitions-minimum,* which indicates that the poundage for an exercise should be such that the weight trainer can do at least six repetitions.

BASIC WEIGHT TRAINING EXERCISES

When all the variations of the same type of exercise are included with all the various types of exercises possible, there are literally hundreds of weight training exercises that can be performed. However, the number of *basic* weight training exercises is considerably less. Only those weight training exercises that are commonly used and whose values have been demonstrated by long usage are included in this chapter. The selection includes exercises that can be utilized to develop all the major muscle groups of the body. For most exercises the most descriptive or more common name is listed; but for a few exercises, more than one name is listed. The type of grip to be used for an exercise is specified only when the regular grip should not be used.

Warm-up Exercise with Barbell

From a crouch position the weight trainer in one slow, continuous motion first straightens his body and legs; with his arms he then raises the barbell completely overhead to an extended-arm position. He then slowly lowers the barbell to the starting position. (See Figure 32-3.)

Figure 32-3. Warm-up exercise with barbell.

Figure 32-4. Wrist curl.

Forearm Muscles that Flex Wrist and Fingers

Wrist Curl (Figure 32-4). The performer sits on a bench and, with his wrists extended beyond his knees, rests his forearms on his thighs. He holds a dumbbell (barbell) in each hand in a reverse grip (the regular grip can also be used). Without moving his forearm, he curls or flexes his hands upward as high as possible. He then lowers the dumbbells to the starting position.

Upper Arm Muscles that Flex Forearm (Biceps, Brachii, Brachialis, Brachioradialis, and Pronator Teres)

Regular Curl with Barbell (Figure 32-5). From a front-hang position with a reverse grip, the weight trainer, keep-

Figure 32-5. Regular curl with barbell. (Courtesy of *Strength and Health Magazine,* York, Pennsylvania.)

Weight Training and Weight Lifting 495

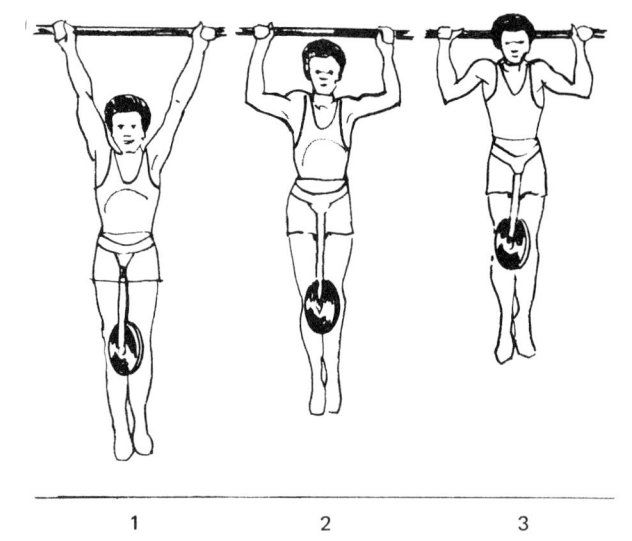

Figure 32-6. Pull-up with weight.

ing his elbows at his sides and flexing his forearms, raises the barbell (dumbbells) through an arc until the bar touches his chest. He then lowers the barbell to the starting position. The reverse curl is performed when the regular grip is used.

Pull-up with Weight (Figure 32-6). Pull-ups (chins) are performed in the usual manner, except that overloading is obtained by resting a barbell behind the knees while the legs remain flexed, or else plates can be chained to a belt fastened around the waist. A variation of this exercise is to thrust the head forward and touch the back of the neck to the bar as the pull-up is being completed.

Muscles of the Upper Arm that Extend the Forearms (Triceps)

Military Press (Figure 32-7). From a chest-rest position, the weight trainer, looking straight ahead throughout the exercise and being careful not to bend his back or legs, presses the barbell to an overhead position in which his arms are completely extended. The starting position can be the shoulder-rest position, in which case the exercise is then called the press-behind-the-neck.

Supine Press on Bench (Figure 32-8). From a supine position with the barbell held at arm's length above the chest, the weight trainer lowers the barbell to his chest and then pushes (presses) it back to the starting position.

Figure 32-7. Press from behind neck. (Reproduced by courtesy of *Strength and Health Magazine,* York, Pennsylvania.)

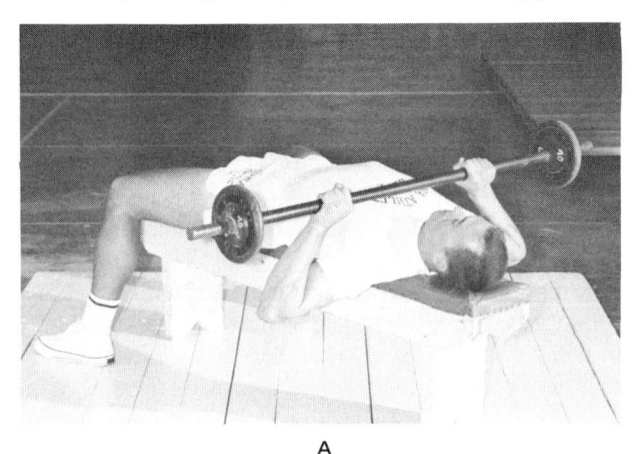

Figure 32-8. Supine press on bench.

496 *Individual and Team Sports*

Figure 32-9. Triceps press.

The hands are usually spaced considerably more than shoulder width apart. Similar exercises can be performed on inclined or declined boards or with dumbbells.

Forearm Extension from Behind Neck (Triceps Press or French Curl) (Figure 32-9). Using a reverse grip, the weight trainer assumes the basic stance and then supports the barbell in a position behind his neck. His elbows point directly upward. Without moving his upper arms, he extends or raises his forearms overhead. He then reverses the movement of the barbell and lowers it to the starting position. This exercise can be performed alternately with a dumbbell in each hand or it can be performed from a sitting position or a supine position on a bench.

Dip with Weight (Figure 32-10). Stationary dips are performed on the parallel bars in the usual manner except that an overload is attained by (1) placing a barbell behind the knees and flexing the legs; (2) placing a barbell across the top of the feet and flexing the feet upward; or (3) placing a chain through plates and fastening the chain to a belt worn around the waist.

Muscles Surrounding the Shoulders that Move the Upper Arms (Deltoids, Pectoralis Major, Latissimus Dorsi, and Teres Major)

Exercises that develop the muscles of the shoulders also develop to some degree the muscles of the back, chest, and upper arm. Persons with an unstable shoulder joint should be cautious in performing the exercises described in this section. Such persons, including those who are subject to chronic shoulder dislocations, should not do exercises involving the shoulder joint until the approval of a physician or an orthopedist has been obtained.

Upright Rowing with Barbell (Figure 32-11). From a front-hang position with both hands placed near the middle of the bar and within a few inches of each other and keeping his elbows higher than the bar throughout the exercise, the weight trainer raises the barbell (dumbbells) until it is in line with or touches his chin. He then lowers the barbell to the starting position.

Forward Raise with Barbell (Figure 32-12). From a front-hang position and keeping his arms straight, the weight trainer raises the barbell forward and upward through an arc until the weight is overhead (or else to shoulder height). He then slowly lowers the barbell to the starting position.

Lateral Raise with Dumbbells (Figure 32-13). Standing in the basic stance, the weight trainer holds a dumbbell to the side of each thigh. Keeping his arms straight, he raises his arms sideward (laterally) and upward until the dumbbells are overhead (or to shoulder height). He then lowers

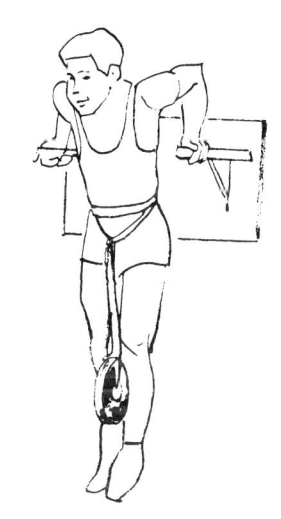

Figure 32-10. Dip with weight.

Figure 32-11. Upright rowing with barbell. (Courtesy of *Strength and Health Magazine*, York, Pennsylvania.)

Figure 32-12. Forward raise with barbell. (Courtesy of *Strength and Health Magazine*, York, Pennsylvania.)

Figure 32-14. Lateral raise with dumbbells with trunk flexed.

the dumbbells through the same arc to the starting position.

Lateral Raise with Dumbbells with Trunk Flexed (Figure 32-14). The trunk is flexed forward until it is approximately parallel with the floor. A dumbbell is held in each hand, and the extended arms are hanging directly below the shoulders. The weight trainer raises the dumbbell sideward and outward to at least shoulder height. The dumbbells are then slowly lowered to the starting position.

Other Shoulder Exercises. The military press, supine press on bench, and dips on the parallel bars are also useful for developing the shoulder muscles.

Muscles of the Upper Back that Move the Shoulders and Upper Arms (Trapesius, Latissimus Dorsi, Rhomboids, and Teres Major)

Bent-over Rowing (Figure 32-15). The weight trainer assumes a basic stance, flexes his trunk forward until it is parallel with the floor, and grasps a barbell, which is resting on the floor underneath his shoulders. Remaining in the bent-over position, the weight trainer raises the bar-

Figure 32-13. Lateral raise with dumbbells.

Figure 32-15. Bent-over rowing.

498   *Individual and Team Sports*

bell to his chest and then lowers it to the starting position. He attempts to keep his head and upper trunk stationary during the entire exercise movement. The barbell can be moved in a straight up-and-down or in a circular motion. This exercise can be performed with a dumbbell held in one hand while the other hand rests on a bench.

Shoulder Shrug (Figure 32-16). Keeping his arms straight, the weight trainer, who has the barbell in a front-hand position, lifts the barbell (dumbbells) by raising his shoulders, shrugging them as high as possible, while attempting to touch his shoulder tips to his ears. He then lowers his shoulders (and barbell) to the starting position. Up-and-down or circular movements—either clockwise or counterclockwise—can be performed while doing this exercise.

Bent-arm Pull-over (Figure 32-17). The weight trainer takes a supine position on a bench with the back of his head resting on the edge of the bench, below which a barbell is placed on the floor. With his arms flexed at about a 90° angle, the weight trainer reaches overhead and grasps the barbell with his hands spaced only a few inches apart. He then raises the bar overhead in an arc, maintaining his arms in a flexed position throughout the movement. After the bar passes over his face and touches his chest, the weight trainer reverses the movement, returning the barbell through the original arc to the floor. The pull-over exercise can also be performed with the arms completely extended throughout the exercise.

Other Upper-back Exercises. Pull-ups, upright rowing, and the forward raise with dumbbells or barbell are somewhat beneficial in developing the muscles of the upper back.

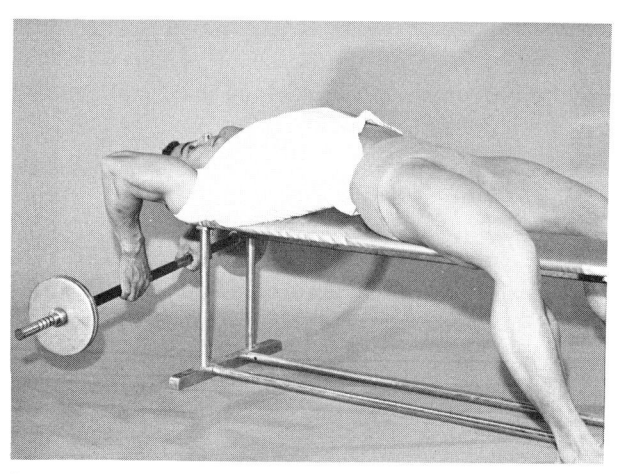

Figure 32-17. Bent-arm pull-over. (Courtesy of *Strength and Health Magazine,* York, Pennsylvania.)

Muscles of the Chest that Move the Upper Arms (Pectoralis Major)—Serratus Anterior, Indirectly

Supine Lateral Raise with Dumbbells (Figure 32-18). The weight trainer assumes a supine position on a bench with his arms straight and extended sideward in line with his shoulders. Starting with the dumbbells resting on the floor, and keeping his arms straight, he raises the dumbbells upward and over his chest until they touch. He then lowers them to the starting position. After the dumbbells are raised over the chest, a variation is to continue the original arm movements until the arms are crossed and the dumbbells touch the opposite sides of the chest. This exercise can also be performed with the arms bent at an angle of about 120°.

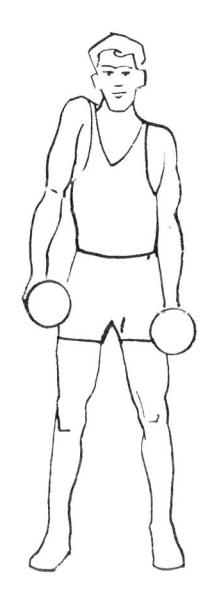

Figure 32-16. Shoulder shrug.

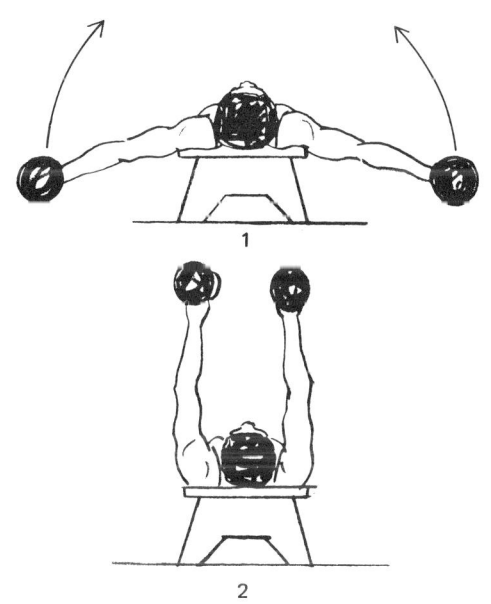

Figure 32-18. Supine lateral raise with dumbbells.

Weight Training and Weight Lifting 499

Other Chest Exercises. The bent- and straight-arm pullover, supine press on bench, dip on parallel bars, and pull-up can effectively contribute to the development of the muscles of the chest.

Muscles of the Neck

Exercises for the specific purpose of developing the muscles of the neck are infrequently included in a weight training program. Extension, flexion, and circular movements of the head when plates are fastened to a chain attached to the front or back of a head strap placed on the head are effective exercises for developing the muscles of the neck. Pull-overs or supine presses from the wrestler's bridge position are sometimes used for this purpose.

Muscles of the Lower Back and Hips that Extend the Trunk or Thighs (Extensors of the Trunk and Thighs: Erector Spinea and Gluteus Maximus)

Anyone with a history of low-back pain or difficulty with a knee joint should not do the exercises in this section without prior approval from an orthopedist or a physician.

Regular Dead Lift (Figure 32-19). Using a regular or a combination grip, starting from a crouch position and keeping his arms and back straight throughout the exercise, the weight trainer raises to an erect standing position. He then returns to the starting position. The barbell can be straddled during the dead lift, in which event the lift is called the straddle or Jefferson lift. If a light poundage is lifted, the legs can be kept straight throughout the exercise; the movement of the trunk is created by extension and flexion of the lower back. This exercise, called the stiff-leg dead lift, is an excellent developer of the muscles of the lower back and hips. The regular dead lift is considered by many to be one of the best single weight training exercises because it develops many muscle groups, including those of the legs, back, shoulder, forearms, and hands.

Flat-footed Squat with Barbell (Figure 32-20). With the barbell in a shoulder-rest position, the weight trainer rests his heels on a one- or two-inch high board for increased support. Keeping his back straight and head erect, the weight trainer squats by flexing his legs and lowering his hips until his thighs are parallel with the floor. He then returns to the starting position. Deep squats, in which the buttocks are lowered until they touch the heels, can be performed, but some authorities believe that this movement may have a detrimental effect on the knee joint, as may the walking squat. However, squatting movements in which the body is lowered to a sitting position on a bench place less strain on the knee joints and, hence, are highly recommended. Squat jumps, in which a dumbbell is held in each hand and a jump is performed after each squatting movement, can also be performed. Because heavy poundages are often used for squatting exercises, the weight trainer may want to place padding on the back of his neck and shoulders before resting the barbell on that area. Squatting movements require considerable energy and, for this reason, should probably be scheduled among the first few exercises in the weight training program.

Abdominal and Other Muscles of the Lower Trunk that Flex the Trunk or Thighs (Flexors and Rotators of the Trunk: Ilio-psoas, Rectus Abdominus, Internal and External Obliques)

Sit-up on Inclined Board (Figure 32-21). The weight trainer assumes a supine position on an inclined board with his feet held in place by straps and a dumbbell or

Figure 32-19. Regular dead lift. (Courtesy of *Strength and Health Magazine,* York, Pennsylvania.)

Figure 32-20. Flat-footed squat with barbell.

500   *Individual and Team Sports*

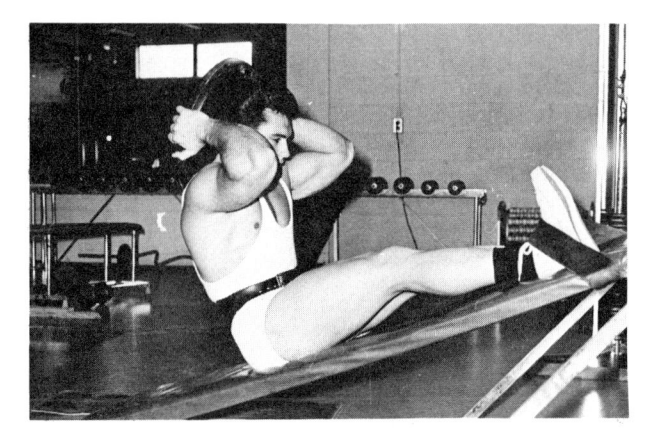

Figure 32-21. Sit-up on inclined board. (Courtesy of *Strength and Health Magazine,* York, Pennsylvania.)

plate held behind the head with both hands. He curls to a sitting position by flexing his trunk, touches an elbow to the opposite knee, and returns to the starting position. Each knee should be alternately touched. Sit-ups can be performed on a level surface, or with the hips resting crossways on a bench. They also can be performed without holding a weight behind the head. Many weight training instructors recommend that a minimum of twenty executions of the sit-up movement be performed in order to develop adequately the endurance and definition of the abdominal muscles.

If sit-ups are performed with the legs straight, the hip flexors often do more work than the abdominal muscles. For this reason, sit-ups with the legs held in a bent or partially flexed position are recommended, particularly for those whose lower backs curve considerably when they do a sit-up with their legs straight.

Side Bend (Figure 32-22). The weight trainer grips the barbell with a wide grasp and rests it on his shoulders, taking a wider-than-usual stance. He then bends the trunk directly to one side as far as possible and then returns to the starting position from where he repeats the movement to the opposite side. These movements can be performed while holding a dumbbell in one hand and performing several repetitions. A minimum of twenty repetitions of this exercise is recommended if the weight trainer wishes to slim his waistline.

Muscles of the Hips and Thighs that Flex the Thigh (Ilio-psoas and Rectus Femoris) and Extend the Lower Leg (Quadriceps—Vastus Internus, Vastus Intermedius, Vastus Externus, and Rectus Femoris)

Forward Leg Raise with Iron Boot (Figure 32-23). From a supine position on an inclined board or a hanging

Figure 32-22. Side bend.

Figure 32-23. Forward leg raise with iron boots.

position from a horizontal bar, the weight trainer, keeping the legs straight, raises them until they are at right angles to his trunk. He then slowly lowers them to the starting position. One leg at a time can be raised and lowered in alternate order or the legs can be flexed at the knees throughout the exercise movement.

Lower Leg Extension with Iron Boot (Figure 32-24). From a sitting position with the exercised lower leg hanging down just past the edge of the padded table, the weight trainer extends or raises his lower leg until it is in line with the thigh and the entire leg is straight. He then slowly lowers it.

Weight Training and Weight Lifting **501**

Figure 32-24. Lower leg extension with iron boot.

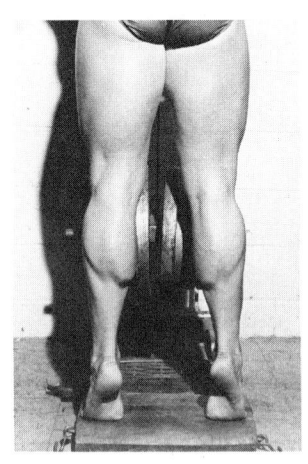

Figure 32-25. Rise on toes. (Photograph by courtesy of *Strength and Health Magazine,* York, Pennsylvania.)

Other Exercises. All variations of the squat and the regular dead lift are particularly useful exercises for developing the quadriceps muscles.

Muscles of the Hips and Thighs that Extend the Thigh (Gluteus Maximus and Hamstrings) and Flex the Leg (Hamstring Muscles— Biceps Femoris)

Leg Curl with Iron Boot. Standing on the foot on which the iron boot is not secured and grasping a support for improved balance, the weight trainer raises the booted foot backward and upward until his heel touches or almost touches his buttock. The leg is then lowered to the starting position. The exercise is then repeated with the other leg. Both feet can be exercised simultaneously if leg curls are performed from a prone position on a bench or inclinded board.

Other Exercises for Developing the Thigh Extensors. Squat exercises aid the development of the extensor muscles of the thigh.

Muscles of the Leg that Extend the Foot (Calf Muscle—Gastrocnemius and Soleus)

Rise on Toes (Heel Raise) (Figure 32-25). With the barbell in a shoulder-rest position and with the balls of the feet positioned on a board two inches in height, the weight trainer raises his heels off the floor as high as possible and holds that position momentarily. He then lowers his heels to the floor. Because heavy poundages are often used for this exercise, the weight trainer can, for increased comfort, place padding between the bar and his upper back and shoulders.

Other Exercises for the Lower Leg. Squat jumping with dumbbells, or straddle hops performed with a barbell in the shoulder-rest position, help in developing the muscles of the lower leg.

WEIGHT TRAINING PROGRAMS FOR BEGINNERS

Reproduced here is a weight training exercise chart developed at the University of Iowa for use by students who are beginning a weight training program. It serves merely as an example of some of the exercises that might be included in a program designed to improve the general, over-all muscular development of an inexperienced weight trainer.

ADVANCED TECHNIQUES OF PARTICIPATION

Strength Exercises

The exercises described in the previous section are performed primarily to increase rapidly the strength of selected or specific muscle groups or for over-all strength gains. Normally, the weight trainer does not engage in any strength exercises until after he has completed a basic course in weight training, which is generally two to three months in duration.

502 *Individual and Team Sports*

Weight Training Exercise Chart for Beginners

Name _____ Section Number _____ Station Number _____

1. As a rule, the range of repetitions (*reps.*) for most weight training exercises is minimum, 7 times; maximum, 11 times. However, for increased endurance, do 15 to 20 repetitions (*reps.*).
2. Do 30 repetitions for heel raises (10 with toes pointed inward, 10 with toes pointed outward, and 10 with toes pointed straight ahead).
3. The fraction listed for each exercise is the percentage of your body weight that, in pounds, should be the weight of the barbell used for that exercise during your first workout.
4. When the maximum number of repetitions is achieved, encircle the poundage used in that exercise and increase the barbell weight by 5 pounds for that exercise in the next training period.
5. The first exercise (warm-up exercise) should be omitted from your workout if you have just performed calisthenics or are thoroughly warmed up.

	Exercise		Wt.	Reps.	Wt.	Reps.	Wt.	Reps.	Wt.	Reps.	Wt.	Reps.	Wt.	Reps.	Wt.	Reps.
1.	Warm-up exercises	1/4														
2.	Regular two-arm curl	1/3														
3.	Military press	1/3														
4.	Flat-footed squats	1/3														
5.	Pull-over on bench	1/10														
6.	Bent-over rowing	1/2														
7.	Heel raising (30 reps.)	1/2														
8.	Regular dead lift	1/2														
9.	Supine press on bench	1/2														
10.	Inclined sit-ups (20 reps)															

Remember: *Regular Workouts Are the Key to Success*

Weight Training and Weight Lifting 503

The basic principle followed when performing strength exercises is to do a minimum of three sets to as many as five sets of an exercise, performing only a few repetitions per set. The range of repetitions generally varies from three to as many as six. In some cases weight trainers perform specific strength exercises with a starting poundage of 80 to 85 per cent of their maximum, doing as many repetitions as possible, with 90 per cent of their maximum poundage. This is repeated with 95 per cent of their maximum one-repetition poundage, and then with a 100 per cent load, which usually consists of one repetition. A final attempt to perform the exercise is then made with from 102 to 105 per cent of the heaviest weight with which the exercise has previously successfully been lifted.

In some instances the weight trainer, instead of working up, may work down in the poundage lifted. This means that after a thorough warm-up, he attempts to do at least one repetition with a weight that is 100 to 105 per cent of his maximum. He works down in the poundage lifted until the weight is 80 to 85 per cent of the one-repetition maximum, but with each poundage he does as many repetitions as possible. Many weight trainers, however, prefer to begin with a poundage that is 80 to 90 per cent of their one-repetition maximum, performing as many repetitions as possible with this starting load. Quite often, a maximum-poundage lift is only attempted once a week, or even less often.

When performing strength exercises only, the weight trainer commonly finds that he must concentrate his efforts and possess considerable determination in order to muster sufficient will power to exert a maximum effort each time that he performs a set of repetitions of a specific exercise. As a rule the weight trainer will want to concentrate his strength exercises on those muscle groups (1) that are underdeveloped in strength compared with his over-all strength, (2) in which he purposely wants to develop additional strength, such as in the muscles that extend the forearms, (3) that are directly involved in the three Olympic lifts, or (4) that involve some of the odd lifts.

Endurance Exercises

As for weight training exercises primarily directed toward developing increased strength, the basic techniques of weight training can be utilized for enhancing endurance, particularly local muscular endurance. The weight trainer should, however, be cautioned that endurance exercises performed with weights do not enhance to any extent his over-all circulorespiratory endurance—which requires that the pulse rate be almost doubled, usually by engaging in some type of running activity.

In performing endurance exercises through the medium of weight training, the guiding principle is to do a considerable number of repetitions of each exercise. This means a minimum of fifteen repetitions—twenty is a number commonly performed, but sometimes as many as twenty-five or thirty repetitions of an exercise are performed. This of course means that the weight trainer must use a light poundage if he is to perform correctly a large number of repetitions. When performing endurance exercises the weight trainer may want to confine his efforts to only one set of repetitions per exercise—he should do only two sets at the most. The weight trainer should be judicious in selecting the exercises he will perform to enhance his endurance, and he should have sound reasons for developing the endurance of any muscle groups.

Flexibility Exercises

The use of dumbbells and barbells is ideal for increasing the range of movement at various joints because of the added pull of gravity that aids in overcoming the natural resistance of the body parts. Selected weight training exercises can be performed to enhance the flexibility at most of the joints of the body. For example, to increase the forward flexibility of the trunk and spine, stiff-legged dead lifts are performed while standing on a bench. The barbell can be lowered below the level of the surface on which the feet are resting. Springboard divers often perform this exercise and frequently develop the ability to lower the barbell approximately one foot below the level of the feet. In the same way, the range of motion at the shoulder joint can be increased by slowly lowering the dumbbells sideward with extended arms until they are below the surface of the bench on which the weight trainer is in a supine position. If the bench is a rather high one—twenty to twenty-four inches in height—the weight trainer will find that his shoulder and chest muscles are stretched and the range of motion of the shoulder joint is soon increased in this plane of movement.

Figure 32-26. Developing forward flexibility by performing stiff-legged dead lifts on bench. (Photograph by courtesy of *Strength and Health Magazine,* York, Pennsylvania.)

By giving some thought to the type of exercises that will be useful for his purposes, the ingenious weight trainer will discover a variety of flexibility exercises that will enable him to increase his range of motion and, hence, his flexibility at many of his joints. When performing flexibility exercises the weight trainer should take care that (1) he uses only slow movement, (2) that the weight used is not too heavy, and (3) that when the maximum range of motion has been reached, this position is held approximately five seconds before moving from it.

Super Sets

Some advanced weight trainers and body builders perform what is sometimes termed *super sets* of weight training exercises. When doing super sets they perform two to four different exercises that involve only the muscles of one area of the body—perhaps only one major muscle or a set of antagonistic muscles, such as the biceps and triceps of the arm.

Although the performance of super sets is quite exhausting, the exercised muscles are so strenuously exercised as to be almost completely fatigued, thus enhancing a rapid development of the muscular bulk and strength of the muscle groups involved. The principle of super sets can be utilized by doing all upper-body exercises every other day and doing only leg exercises on the alternate days. The theory is that the exercised muscles will receive approximately forty-eight hours of rest between exercise sessions; yet, the advanced weight trainer or body builder can do a strenuous workout each day.

Isometric Exercises

Isometric exercises, which involve flexing the muscles against an immovable object, and which are described and illustrated in the companion to this book,[2] are sometimes used to supplement weight training exercises. The values of isometric exercises are that they do not require a great expenditure of energy; they require only a short period of recuperation; they require little special equipment and can be done anywhere at any time; and a full workout can be completed in a short time. In addition, isometric exercises can involve an exertion of the muscles at different angles than is possible in weight training or body building. Although the use of isometric exercises can be a valuable supplement for the beginning weight trainer or body builder, they appear to be of less value to the advanced weight trainer or body builder. However, when weights are not available while on vacation or when traveling, for example, an isometric exercise program can be substituted for the regular weight training program.

Specific Weight Training Exercises for Athletes in Various Sports[3]

A practice that is becoming more and more common is for athletes from a large variety of sports to utilize weight training to enhance their performance in their particular sport. Swimmers, track and field athletes, basketball players, football players, gymnasts, tennis players, golfers, and other athletes frequently engage in selected weight training exercises. The use of weight training exercises seems to be particularly valuable as a preseason or a postseason training method.

Regardless of the sport, the principle underlying the selection of the weight training exercises to be performed is that the athlete should perform those exercises that duplicate the plane-of-motion movements frequently utilized in performing the sport. Thus, the muscles that are to be strengthened are exercised in the same range or plane of movement that is used in performing the skills comprising the sport. A baseball pitcher who wants to increase the muscular development, strength, and speed of the throwing arm, for example, would use a range of movements that simulates the three-quarter overarm throw. Dumbbells and barbells are frequently used to do movements of this kind; pulley or cable weights and isometric exercises in which, at various points along the throwing motion, the throwing arm exerts force against an immovable handle attached to a stationary cable are especially valuable for this purpose. The pulling motion used in the swimming stroke; the shoulder and arm muscles used in pressing to a handstand by the gymnast; the leg and trunk muscles used by the football lineman in his charge or blocking action; the leg muscles used in jumping and rebounding by the basketball players; the leg, trunk, shoulder, arm, and wrist muscles used in the golf swing; and other such movements are duplicated against a heavy or immovable resistance so that the athlete can enhance his performance in his sport.

As long as regular workouts and practice of the sport are performed concurrently with the weight training or other type of resistance exercises, no appreciable drop-off of skill, precision, or over-all athletic performance should result. Most athletes seem to prefer to perform weight training exercises after the regular workout has been completed so that the factor of fatigue does not adversely affect their practice. Also, most athletes prefer not to do any weight training exercises within the last two to four days before competition takes place.

---

[2] D. Casady, D. Mapes, and L. Alley, *Handbook for Physical Fitness* (New York: Macmillan, Inc., 1965).

[3] An excellent reference in this area is *Weight Training in Sports and Physical Education* (Washington, D.C.: American Association for Health, Physical Education and Recreation, 1962).

OLYMPIC LIFTS

The three Olympic lifts—those used in the modern Olympic Games and in other weight lifting competitions—are a very popular means of testing one's strength, timing, coordination, skill, speed of movement, and ability to exert power in an explosive manner. The weight lifter, of course, practices quite conscientiously many variations of these three lifts, as well as other exercises designed to improve his performance in these lifts. Many body builders and weight trainers also enjoy practicing the Olympic lifts and attempting to better their previous records.

In the Olympic lifts the contestant is permitted three different attempts for each type of lift, and he is credited with the heaviest poundage successfully lifted in each of them. For each lift the contestant must between the first and second attempt increase his poundage by ten pounds and he must between the second and third attempt increase it by at least five pounds. For this reason many lifters commonly attempt their first lift with a poundage they know they are capable of lifting so that they do not lose one of the three lifts because of three unsuccessful attempts.

Figure 32-27. Two-hands clean and press.

Table 32-1
Recent World Records in the Olympic Lifts

Bodyweight Class (lbs.)	Press (lbs.)	Snatch (lbs.)	Clean & Jerk (lbs.)	Total (lbs.)
123-1/2	259	239	307-1/2	787-3/4
132-1/4	282	271	336	876
148-3/4	315	298	370-1/4	953-1/4
165-1/4	326	309-1/2	391-1/4	986-1/4
181-3/4	352-1/2	325	412-1/4	1,052-1/2
198-1/4	370-1/4	328-1/4	418-3/4	1,074-1/2
Heavyweight	436-3/4	380-1/4	479-1/2	1,278-1/4

Two-hands Clean and Press

The two-hands clean and press is a lift that primarily requires strength and the ability to press a weight overhead from the chest-rest position. To perform the two-hands press, the weight lifter quickly, and with as little extraneous effort as possible, lifts (cleans) the barbell to a chest-rest position. In this position the barbell is touching the chest, and the weight lifter should stand with his head looking straight ahead and have his feet spread about shoulder width apart. In actual competition the lifter holds this position until the referee signals him to start his pressing movement. At this time, upon his own volition, and without hunching his body or legs, the lifter presses the weight to a straight-arm position overhead. During the pressing movement the lifter cannot seesaw the weight upward with one arm and then the other, nor can he sway his body or arch backward during the actual press. He is, however, permitted to have a body arch before starting his pressing movement; most good lifters employ this technique. During the pressing movement the lifter must stand flat footed; he cannot move his feet or raise up on his toes; nor can he move his hand position on the bar. After his arms are completely extended, the lifter must hold his position (for two seconds) until given the signal to lower the weight. This lift, as well as the other lifts, is usually judged by three referees. The chief referee makes known the referee's decision or else signal lights are flashed simultaneously.

Weight lifters commonly train for the two-hands press by jerking (jumping) overhead a weight that is too heavy for them to press; they then lower it as slowly as possible to the chest-rest position. Another training technique for the press is to practice starting a heavy weight upward, pressing it as high as possible even though the lifter is not capable of pressing it completely overhead.

Two-hands Snatch

The two-hands snatch requires more speed, timing, balance, and coordination than any of the other Olympic lifts. To perform the two-hands snatch the lifter must in one continuous motion lift the barbell from a resting position on the platform to an overhead position in which the arms are completely extended. The most efficient snatching technique involves starting the snatching movement with a jumping motion and raising the barbell as high as possible while keeping the wrists above the bar.

Figure 32-28. Two-hands snatch.

Without pausing, the lifter then quickly squats under the weight and completely extends his arms while thrusting his head forward so that the bar is even with or slightly behind the back of the neck and the shoulders. For all snatching movements the arms are spaced as widely apart as possible. The squatting technique of snatching is considered to be most efficient if the lifter has a good sense of balance and timing. He can place his body lower with the squatting movement than he can with the other technique, which involves a splitting movement of his legs.

In the split type of snatch the lifter lifts the barbell as high as possible; as it is still moving upward, he splits under it by moving one leg forward as far as possible while bending the knee and extending the other nearly extended leg as far to the rear as possible. When the lifter has perfected his splitting technique the knee of the rear leg is only two or three inches above the surface of the platform. While the splitting technique of snatching does not require an extraordinary sense of balance, considerable speed as well as power is needed if heavy poundages are to be successfully snatched.

The rules governing the two-hands snatch insist that no part of the snatcher's body, except his feet, can touch the platform during the snatch and that the lifter's arm must be completely extended when he completes the snatching movement; he is not permitted to finish by pressing the barbell overhead. The lifter must then come to an erect position in which his legs are straight and fairly close together. Although the lifter can move about the platform in gaining control of the weight after completing the snatching movement, he cannot step off the platform and he must come to a stationary position and hold it for at least two seconds.

Any exercises that increase the strength of the legs, back, or the arms in performing an upward motion are beneficial in improving a person's ability to snatch. Several specific exercises are practiced to enhance the ability to lift heavy weights by means of the snatch technique. One of these is to start with a heavy weight in the chest-rest position and to leap upward with it while quickly moving to a split or squat position, repeating this movement a number of times. A very helpful exercise is to practice lifting a resting barbell upward as high as possible, but without performing a splitting or squatting movement. Another one is to practice repetition snatches, beginning the snatching movement as soon as the last lift is lowered sufficiently so that the plates of the barbell just touch the lifting platform.

In all splitting movements the weight trainer is quite close to the barbell, which is resting directly underneath his shoulders and very close to his legs. The snatcher must avoid a tendency to stand back from the barbell or to attempt to lift it with a forward direction in a needless effort to avoid hitting his legs. While grazing the shins with the barbell appears to be a danger, this is not the case. When lifting the barbell upward the snatcher must lift it as high as he possibly can. While it is still moving upward because of inertia, he quickly moves his body under it in either a splitting or squatting movement. When the snatch is properly performed the lifter should get the feeling of very fast speed instead of a vast exertion of strength.

Two-hands Clean and Jerk

The two-hands clean and jerk is the lift in which almost all lifters lift the heaviest weight overhead. For this reason it involves a considerable expenditure of energy. The clean and jerk is performed in two distinct phases. The lifter first lifts the barbell, which is resting on the platform, to a chest-rest position. After gaining control of the barbell the lifter at his own volition jumps the weight upward, straightens his arms, and comes to an erect position in which the weight is held overhead with the arms completely extended.

For the clean and jerk the lifter starts with his hands spread fairly wide apart, although not quite so wide as for the two-hands snatch. The lifter stands quite close to the barbell in a semisquat position with his back straight, his head erect, and looking forward in order to maintain his balance. On the first lifting movement, the lifter attempts to lift the weight just as high as possible, preferably almost to chest height. As he is still lifting the weight upward the lifter must quickly get his forearms, hands, and chest under the weight, bringing it to a chest-rest position. A squatting or a splitting movement is employed to "get under" the barbell—both movements are highly similar to the movements used on completing the two-hands snatch. From the chest-rest position, the lifter then jumps the weight upward and again gets under the weight with a

Weight Training and Weight Lifting 507

Figure 32-29. (A) Two-hands clean (squat style); (B) two-hands jerk (squat style).

semisquat or a semisplit movement. Most lifters, especially those who have strong legs, are capable of jerking any weight overhead that they can clean to their chest.

The rules for the two-hands clean and jerk are similar to those for the snatch. The lifter must not violently touch any part of the barbell to his thighs during the jerk. He must get the weight completely overhead during the jerking movement, he must not use any apparent effort from the shoulders, and he must remain on the platform. He must hold the weight overhead for two seconds or until the chief referee gives him permission to lower the weight.

Repetition cleans and repetition jerks in which the barbell is immediately lifted as soon as it attains the resting position are valuable exercises for increasing the poundage lifted in the clean and jerk. Regular dead lifts and one-half squats in which the lifter squats only halfway down are other beneficial exercises.

Odd Lifts

Odd lift and power lift contests are frequently held at weight lifting meets and/or at physique contests. The two-hands bench press (supine press), the squat, and sometimes the two-hands curl and the two-hands clean-and-press-behind-the-neck or the two-hands dead lift (lifts that are not part of the three Olympic lifts) are included in an odd lift contest.

SELF-EVALUATION

Several methods can be used by the weight trainer, weight lifter, or body builder in evaluating his progress or standing in his specialty. The power index (Table 32-2) can be computed periodically to determine what progress is being achieved.

Table 32-2
Power Index

Name _____

	Poundage	No. of Executions	Total (No. of Exec. x lb.)
1. Regular curl	(e.g., 60 lbs)	(e.g., 15)	(900)
2. One-half squat			
3. Jerk			
4. Sit-ups	(e.g., 10 lbs)	(e.g., 35)	(350)
5. Dead lift			

Body Weight _____   Total =

5 times body weight = _____ Power Index =
(Divide total by 5 times body weight.)

Because the power index will vary according to the poundage used in each of the exercises, it is important that the lifter use the same poundage each time he computes his index. In this way multiplying the poundage lifted by the number of repetitions is not subject to the variation introduced by varying the poundage for each exercise on different occasions. For a beginning weight training student a power index of 3.00 is good. While periodically maintaining his weight training chart, the weight trainer can easily compute the poundage increase and percentage of increase for the various weight training exercises in which the same number of repetitions of the exercises are performed. The beginner commonly finds that he will make rapid improvement for a few weeks but that this gradually tapers off until he reaches a plateau and may not progress in the poundage lifted for at least two or three weeks. In these cases it is often helpful to change to other kinds of weight training exercises in order to introduce variety and to avoid monotony in an effort to overcome the slump.

Another common method of evaluating one's progress in weight lifting is to keep a record of the highest poundage lifted in each of the three Olympic lifts and of the highest total poundage lifted in all three Olympic lifts. The same record can be maintained for the various odd lifts, such as the individual and total poundage lifted in the bench press, the dead lift, and upright rowing motion.

Body builders frequently keep a chart of the various measurements of different areas of the body. The areas commonly measured are the circumferences of the biceps, calves, thighs, hips, waist, and chest. As a result of regular training most body builders noticeably increase the size of these muscles; however, because of a loss of adipose tissue in the area of the waist and hips, some loss of circumference may occur in these locations.

Selected References

BOOKS

Leighton, Jack R. *Progressive Weight Training.* New York: Ronald, 1961.
This book is written for both men and women and presents sections concerning weight training equipment and facilities, exercise programs and their conduct and evaluation, special exercises, and weight lifting. 143 pp.

Massey, Benjamin H., et al. *The Kinesiology of Weight Lifting.* Dubuque, Iowa: Brown, 1959.
Information concerning the following topics is presented in this book: a discussion of several aspects of weight lifting (weight training) and the human machine; the background and the physiological basis of the sport; lifting and training techniques; exercises; competitive lifting; weight lifting in athletics; organizing weight lifting groups; and measurement. 175 pp.

O'Shea, John P. *Scientific Principles and Methods of Strength Fitness.* Corvallis, Ore.: Oregon State University Book Stores, 1966.
This manual presents important physiological principles, methods and techniques of strength development, and weight training. Also included are circuit training, isometric exercise training, and competitive Olympic lifting as well as how to train for the "quick" lifts. Included with the manual are some excellent drawings, photographs, and charts. 135 pp.

Rasch, Philip J. *Weight Training.* Dubuque, Iowa: Brown, 1966.
This booklet differentiates between various types of weight training, presents the physiologic principles of weight training, and discusses selected health factors. Other chapters deal with a basic weight training program, advanced training methods, dumbbell usages, taking measurements, and weight training for athletes. 77 pp.

Ruff, Wesley K. *Physical Conditioning Through Weight Training.* Palo Alto, Calif.: National Press Publications, 1966.
This booklet contains material concerning the following topics: resistance, isometric and eccentric exercises, starting a program, safety, diet, training for sports, tips for athletes, developmental exercises, specialized training, exercises for prominent muscle groups, the Olympic lifts, and evaluative procedures. 57 pp.

Weight Training in Sports and Physical Education. Washington, D.C.: The American Association for Health, Physical Education, and Recreation, 1962.
More than twenty contributors wrote portions of this book. Among the areas covered are the history of weight training in the United States, the principles and scientific basis of weight training, the role of weight training in athletics, representative programs of weight training, weight training programs for selected sports, safety factors, rehabilitation and prevention of athletic injuries, measurement and evaluations, and weight training exercises and equipment. 173 pp.

PERIODICALS

Weight Lifting (AAU Official Rules). The Amateur Athletic Union of the United States. 231 West 58th Street, New York, New York 10019, annual.
In addition to the AAU rules of weight lifting, this publication contains information about scoring and organizing weight lifting meets, championship meet results, weight lifting records, and the rules for odd lifts and power lifts.

CHAPTER 33

Wrestling
David McCuskey*
The University of Iowa

HISTORY

Amateur wrestling as it is practiced today is a mixture of wrestling styles that has evolved since prehistoric times. Many rules and techniques have been handed down from the ancient Assyrians, Egyptians, Greeks, Chinese, and Japanese, as well as from the early Europeans and Americans.

The men of the Stone Age had to develop physical skills and strength to protect themselves against other men in warfare and against the wild beasts with which they came into conflict and that they hunted. Friends and families would grapple with one another to learn those skills that would be most effective, and crude wrestling contests were held. At the dawn of civilization wrestling was highly developed. Scenes depicting wrestlers were sculptured on the walls of Egyptian tombs. These scenes date back more than 5,000 years and show many of the wrestling holds that are in use today.

---

*B.S., University of Northern Iowa, Cedar Falls; M.A., Columbia University, New York City. Mr. McCuskey is an associate professor and head wrestling coach at The University of Iowa where he has coached since 1952. His records achieved in the sport of wrestling include the coaching of the United States Olympic Freestyle Wrestling Team in 1956; former chairman of the United States Olympic Wrestling Committee; former president of the American Wrestling Coaches and Officials Association; and former editor of the American Wrestling Coaches and Officials News Letter. Prior to coming to The University of Iowa he coached wrestling at Northern Iowa University from 1930 to 1952, during which time he coached one NCAA Championship team, three NAAU Championship teams, seventeen individual national champions, five Olympic team members, and one Olympic champion. While head wrestling coach at The University of Iowa he coached eight individual national champions, two Olympic team members, one Olympic champion, and two Big-Ten Championship teams.

The Chinese are believed to have been the first in Asia to participate in wrestling; the sport later became popular in Japan, where wrestling tournaments were held as early as 25 B.C. The first recorded history of wrestling in Japan refers to Sumo wrestling as a method of combat. The object was to kill the opponent or cause him to surrender unconditionally. This was done by kicking, trampling, or otherwise using the powerful legs of the Sumo wrestler. As the Japanese people became more enlightened they gradually began to regard these vicious practices as cruel and savage. The first rules in wrestling came as an Imperial Order in the eighth century. They prohibited any wrestling that resulted in the death of an opponent and listed kicking and striking with the hand or fist as fouls. This marked the beginning of a great advance in the art of wrestling. Many of the lifts and trips used in Judo, Jujitsu, and Sumo, as practiced by the Japanese, are now used by amateur wrestlers all over the world.

The early Greeks stressed athletic competition not only to train soldiers to be physically fit but to develop strong, robust, and symmetrical bodies, which have never since been excelled in beauty. The wrestler was one of their most admired athletes, surpassed only by the discus thrower. Wrestling was rated by the Greeks with running and jumping as a natural form of athletics. They considered it an excellent method of building muscles and improving health.

After the Roman conquest of Greece, the Roman style of wrestling was blended with the Grecian style. This was the origin of the Greco-Roman style of wrestling, which is still used in many European countries and which is included in the American Wrestling Tournaments of the Amateur Athletic Union, in the World Wrestling Championships, and in the Olympic Games. The Greco-Roman style permits arm holds above the waist only; and the legs cannot be used in any way to trip the opponent or to block or counter an attempted hold or movement.

The American Indians were holding wrestling matches long before the first settlers arrived. Later, wrestling matches were popular entertainment at the social gatherings of the early settlers.

Wrestling in high schools in the United States enjoyed a tremendous surge in popularity in the early 1900s, and it has continued to grow. Wrestling is now being included in many of the junior high and grade school programs on both an intramural and interscholastic basis. In recent years, the increase in the number of high schools and colleges participating in wrestling has been phenomenal. Much of the growth of interscholastic and intercollegiate wrestling is the result of the recognition by athletic directors and other school officials of its many values and worthwhile benefits to the participants.

VALUES OF WRESTLING

Wrestling, an individual combative activity, develops self-confidence, self-reliance, sportsmanship, and respect for others. Because all the muscles of the body are involved, it is one of the best sports for achieving all-around physical fitness. It develops strength, endurance, agility, alertness, and quickness of response time. Wrestling is mentally stimulating because there are many different moves, maneuvers, holds, combinations of holds, blocks, and countermoves to learn, and new ones are continually being conceived. With every change of position a new situation arises that must be met with a countermove. This maintains a constant challenge to the mind in order to achieve a winning strategy.

Wrestlers of any height, weight, or build can participate in wrestling with enjoyment, thus making it an invaluable sport in any athletic program. It is also a sport in which the blind and other physically handicapped youths can competitively participate with enjoyment.

EQUIPMENT AND UNIFORMS

The regulation size for a square wrestling mat is twenty-four feet by twenty-four feet; for a circular mat, a diameter of twenty-eight feet. All mats should have a supplemental mat five feet in width located around its perimeter for the protection of the wrestlers. Even a mat twelve feet by twelve feet can be used for wrestling if proper safety precautions are taken. If a regulation-sized wrestling mat is unavailable, smaller mats can be fastened together. A plastic-covered mat that can be washed and disinfected daily is recommended. The mat should be made of a soft, resilient material.

Regulation gym clothing can be worn for wrestling, except that buckles on shorts or protruding metals of any kind must be eliminated. When wrestling on soft mats with vinyl plastic covers very few skin abrasions or bruises occur; therefore, wearing knee pads, tights, sweat pants, or long-sleeved sweat shirts is optional.

RULES

Amateur wrestling rules are subject to change each year by rules committees; therefore, no attempt is made to list any here. It is recommended that reference be made to the *NCAA Intercollegiate and Interscholastic Guide* and the *AAU Official Wrestling Guide*—these inexpensive rule books are published yearly. Information for procuring these books can be obtained by writing to the National Collegiate Athletic Association Bureau, Box 757, Grand Central Station, New York, New York 10017, or by contacting the Amateur Athletic Union of the United States, 251 West 58th Street, New York, New York 10019.

The NCAA rules govern what is known as free-style or catch-as-catch-can wrestling. The AAU rules govern the international styles of wrestling, which include free-style as well as the Greco-Roman style. The NCAA and AAU free-style wrestling rules differ in some respects; however, there is a trend toward standardizing these rules. Each country has its own style of wrestling, and their rules may differ from those of other countries or the international rules. However, any country that participates in the world championships or the Olympic Games must do so under the international rules.

Many changes have been made in amateur wrestling rules over the years. The rules committees have made every attempt to attain the following:

1. To prevent injuries.
2. To make the sport enjoyable for the participants.
3. To increase spectator interest.

By making dangerous holds illegal, the contestant can safely perform with increased speed and skill. The more action that there is in a wrestling match, the more enjoyable it is for both the participant and the spectators.

SAFETY DEVICES

All possible precautions should be exerted to insure that no hazards exist in the wrestling area. Heating devices, pipes, and projections into this area should be padded. Supplemental mats should extend five feet on each side of the main mat. Whenever the mat area extends near a wall, wall mats five feet in height should be hung to the floor. If the wrestling mat is made up of smaller ones, it is important that they be held close together with no cracks in between.

WARM-UP PROCEDURES

Because wrestling is a strenuous activity that requires the use of all the muscles, a complete warm-up before competing is a necessity. This applies whether the competition is during a physical education class, a team practice, or a varsity bout. Body bending and twisting and bending the legs and arms utilized as warm-up exercises are useful for any sport. The wrestler also needs to stretch and to strengthen his back and neck by doing bridging exercises. Tumbling exercises such as forward rolls, backward rolls, and headstands are excellent because they develop agility, which is an essential trait for a wrestler to possess. Lifting exercises in which a partner is lifted off the mat with body holds and crotch holds develops strength; they should be practiced at the end of the warm-up period.

BASIC WRESTLING FUNDAMENTALS AND MANEUVERS

These are the four basic wrestling maneuvers:

1. Take-downs.
2. Escapes and reversals.
3. Breakdowns.
4. Pinning combinations.

For every maneuver listed in each of the four classifications, there are several countermoves or blocks that can be used to avoid or escape the maneuver. These counters and blocks should be learned as soon as some proficiency has been acquired in the specific offensive maneuver.

In order for the beginning wrestler to participate quickly in matches, he should first learn one take-down, one escape, a breakdown, and a pinning combination. This will enable him to grasp the over-all aspects of wrestling from the start of his instruction.

After the wrestling student has learned an offensive maneuver, he should learn the countermove or the correct defense. He should progress as rapidly as possible in learning the maneuvers, making certain he wrestles often enough so that he knows that the fundamentals he has learned will work in a wrestling match.

When the fundamentals and maneuvers presented in this section are learned to the point of being used without having to think through the actions involved, the wrestling student will have advanced beyond the level of the beginner.

Figure 33-1. Square stance.

WRESTLING FROM A STANDING POSITION

Open Stance (Neutral Position—No Contact)

Square Stance (Figure 33-1). The feet are in line, far enough apart for a solid base, and flat on the mat with the weight centered on the balls of the feet. The knees are slightly bent. The trunk is bent slightly forward at the waist, the back is straight, and the head is up.

Lead-foot Stance (Figure 33-2). The position for the lead-foot stance is the same as for an open stance, except that one foot is forward; this puts the wrestler in a position to drive forward off his back foot without having to shift his feet first in order to get a power leg to the rear.

Setup for Take-downs from an Open Stance. In setting up an opponent for a take-down, the wrestler attempts to get him to so react to certain movements that he is vulnerable to an attack. From an open stance the following methods can be used to attempt to set up an opponent:

1. Feint with the hands, body, head, eyes, or feet, or any combination of these, in order to make the opponent believe that one form of attack is planned. This will cause him to leave himself open for a different attack. He may react to a feint to the head and expose his legs, or in countering a feint to the

Figure 33-2. Lead-foot stance.

legs he may become exposed to an arm drag or some other maneuver.

2. Retreat so that the opponent will follow—then attack him as he is moving forward.
3. Watch the opponent's mannerisms. He may have a tendency to relax, straighten up to take a deep breath, or otherwise leave himself open for attack. This may happen after he has been on the offensive and has concluded that no offensive attack is planned against him. Be ready to attack at the proper psychological time.
4. Circle the opponent or move laterally. When he shifts position in order to face any possible attack, time your attack for that instant when all his weight is on one foot.
5. An attempted take-down should be made from a distance no farther than an arm's length. In order to become a skilled take-down artist, a wrestler must practice attacking from this close a distance. He must make certain that he can also protect himself from this close position.

Closed Stance

The closed-stance position (Figure 33-3) is the same as described for the open stance, except that the wrestler makes contact with his hands or arms on the arms, hands, or neck of the opponent. To set up a take-down, push or pull the opponent, causing him to resist the force exerted against him. Apply the pressure so that resistance is met in a forward, backward, or lateral direction. When the resistance occurs, release quickly and allow the opponent to move in the direction toward which he is forcing. The opponent is off-balance and vulnerable to attack whenever he resists. As a general rule a wrestler should try to keep a position in which his arms are inside the opponent's arms so that a closed position can be taken safely in preparation for an attack.

Figure 33-4. Neck and elbow.

Hook-up Positions from a Closed Stance

Neck and Elbow (Figure 33-4).

1. The palm of the hand is on top of the opponent's neck, the wrist is close in, and the elbow is positioned toward the center of the chest.
2. Keeping his thumb on the outside, the wrestler grasps the opponent's elbow with his opposite hand.

Neck and Inside Arm (Figure 33-5).

1. The hand is on the neck of the opponent as shown in Figure 33-4.
2. With his opposite hand, the wrestler grasps, just above the elbow with his thumb down, from the inside of the arm of the opponent. The opponent's arm is so controlled that his hand is removed from and held away from the wrestler's neck.

Double Inside-arm Position (Figure 33-6).

1. With both hands inside of the opponent's arms, the wrestler, with his thumbs down, grasps the opponent's arms just above the elbow.
2. He forces the opponent's arms in and down.
3. The wrestler should keep his head in the center of the opponent's chest so that he can attack either

Figure 33-3. Closed stance.

Figure 33-5. Neck and inside arm.

Wrestling 513

Figure 33-6. Double inside-arm position.

Figure 33-7. Hand or wrist control.

right or left. The opponent's reaction to the force applied will determine the course and direction of the action to be taken.

Hand or Wrist Control (Figure 33-7).

1. One hand grasps each wrist or hand of the opponent.
2. Attack the opponent after quickly jerking on one or both of his hands or whenever he attempts to pull or twist his hands free. Other hook-up positions that are not illustrated follow:

Double Underarm Hook. Both arms are under the opponent's arms in this position and force is exerted, thus causing him to straighten up to an erect position.

Double Wrist Hold. Both hands grasp one of the opponent's wrists in this position and he is forced off-balance by jerking his wrist down and forward. If the opponent resists by pulling away, or if he is forced to step forward, he is then vulnerable for a leg tackle.

Single Underarm Hook. One arm is placed under the opponent's arm in this position, and the opponent's opposite arm is controlled by grasping his wrist with the free hand. Force is then exerted with the underarm hook to straighten the opponent and pull him forward, thus forcing him open for a leg attack.

Any one of the many hook-up positions may be taken when setting up the opponent for a take-down. The actual take-down used will depend upon the reaction of the opponent to the hook-up.

TAKE-DOWNS

Double-leg Drop

1. The wrestler first gets the opponent moving toward him and then, with his back straight and head up, drops on both knees close to the opponent.
2. He keeps his head outside of the opponent's leg.
3. He wraps his arms around both the opponent's legs, pulling them together as he lifts him off the mat.
4. He lifts the opponent's legs, pulls them across his chest, and forces against the opponent with his head, taking him to the mat. (See Figure 33-8).

If there is difficulty in lifting the opponent because he is standing in an erect position, the wrestler should step outside and in back of the opponent's heel, tripping him directly backward to the mat.

If the opponent moves his legs back and puts so much weight forward that he cannot be lifted, the wrestler should hold on to the leg nearest his head and release the other leg. He then lifts his head, sits through halfway, and comes back to his knees as he pivots behind the opponent.

A B C D

Figure 33-8. Double-leg drop.

514 *Individual and Team Sports*

Figure 33-9. Sprawl and front double bar.

Counters for the Double-leg Drop

Sprawl and Front Double Bar (Figure 33-9). As the opponent drops and reaches for the legs, the wrestler jumps backward with his feet far apart and places both arms underneath and in front of the opponent's shoulders, forcing the opponent away as he moves his legs backward to free them from the opponent's grasp.

Sprawl, Overarm Bar, and Cross Face (Figure 33-10). The wrestler moves his legs back and apart, overhooks the opponent's arm with one arm, and places the other arm across the opponent's face, forcing him backward as he moves his own legs back to free them from the opponent's grasp.

Figure 33-10. Sprawl, overarm bar, and cross face.

Single-leg Drop

1. When attacking the opponent's right leg, the wrestler, keeping his right hand and left foot on the mat, drops close to the opponent's right knee. With his left arm the wrestler traps the opponent's right leg, driving his head inside of the opponent's leg.
2. He spins behind the opponent and stands up while lifting the leg of the opponent off the mat.
3. Lifting the opponent's leg high in front of his body, the wrestler steps his left leg in front of the opponent's left leg and trips him to the mat.

Counter for the Single-leg Drop

Sprawl and Overarm Bar (Figure 33-11). As the opponent drops for the wrestler's leg, the wrestler jumps backward with his feet wide apart and applies pressure with the overarm bar. Keeping his body in front of the opponent, the wrestler, forcing the opponent's head down, extends his leg backward and frees it from the opponent's grasp.

Duck Under

The duck under take-down works especially well if the opponent is rapidly moving his legs backward and is sprawling in order to counter leg drops (Figure 33-12).

1. The wrestler pushes forward from a closed-stance position until the opponent resists the pressure by forcing toward him. When this occurs, the wrestler pulls forward on the opponent's neck and arm, releases the opponent's arm, steps forward with his outside foot, and drops to his inside knee as he ducks his head under the opponent's arm.

Figure 33-11. Sprawl and overarm bar.

Wrestling 515

Figure 33-12. Duck under

2. The wrestler forces his head against the opponent's upper arm and continues to pull the opponent's head forward toward the mat.
3. The wrestler pivots on his inside knee and goes behind the opponent, bringing him to the mat.

Counters for the Duck Under

Double Underarm Bar. To prevent the opponent from ducking under his arm the wrestler places both arms under and in front of the opponent's arms and lifts.

Open Stance (Figure 33-13). The wrestler tries to avoid hooking up close with the opponent. If the wrestler is successful in thus preventing the opponent from controlling his neck and upper arm it will be difficult to set up the duck under.

Sprawl with Elbows In (Figure 33-14). When he is in a closed-stance position, the wrestler keeps his elbows close

Figure 33-13. Open stance.

Figure 33-14. Sprawl with elbows in.

to his body and his hands inside the opponent's arms. If the opponent starts to duck under, the wrestler jumps back, sprawls, and pulls the opponent's head down to the mat.

Fireman's Carry

To employ the fireman's carry (Figure 33-15) the opponent must again be "set up" by getting him to force forward—at that instant:

1. The wrestler reaches over the top of the opponent's forearm and grasps his elbow or biceps muscle. The wrestler drops in close on his knees as he ducks his head under the opponent's arm that is being controlled.

Figure 33-15. Fireman's carry.

516 *Individual and Team Sports*

2. The wrestler reaches his free arm inside the opponent's crotch. As the wrestler straightens his back he lifts the opponent off the mat.
3. As he takes him over his shoulder to the mat the wrestler pivots toward the opponent's head and finishes the take-down by placing the opponent on his back. The offensive wrestler is in a top position with an arm lock and an inside crotch hold. From this position he can quickly move into a pinning combination before the opponent can get off his back.

Counters for the Fireman's Carry

Double Underarm Bar. To prevent the opponent from using the fireman's carry the wrestler places both arms under and in front of the opponent's arms. Unless he can control the opposite arm the wrestler *never* places only one arm under the opponent's arm, as this gives the opponent an excellent setup for the fireman's carry.

Sprawl and Block Opponent's Free Arm (Figure 33-16). When the opponent controls the arm and drops under for the fireman's carry, the wrestler sprawls by jumping backward with his feet wide apart, forcing the opponent's head to the mat. The wrestler then places his free hand in front of the opponent's opposite arm, keeping the opponent's head on the mat until the opponent's grip on his upper arm can be freed.

Arm Drag

The arm drag (Figure 33-17) is used to set up single- and double-leg drops. It can also be combined with a forward trip or a back heel trip and, hence, can be utilized as a complete take-down.

1. With his left hand the wrestler grasps the opponent's right wrist and simultaneously reaches across, grasping high on the opponent's right upper arm.
2. The wrestler jerks hard with his right arm, pulling the opponent forward and forcing his right arm across to the right side of the wrestler's body, thus making the opponent expose his legs to an attack.
3. Releasing the opponent's wrist as his arm is pulled across, the wrestler executes a single- or a double-leg drop as previously described.
4. To execute the arm-drag trip variation, the wrestler goes to a sitting position to his left and with his right lower leg trips the opponent's left leg. At the same time he grasps the opponent's right leg from the rear with his left hand and pulls him forward and down to the mat. The wrestler must make certain that his right hand is under the opponent's armpit and around his arm. He should move forward as the drag is started in order to get close to the opponent. He should get a top position on the opponent's shoulder, thus leaving him less chance to step across and counter.

Figure 33-16. Sprawl and block opponent's free arm.

Figure 33-17. Arm drag.

Wrestling 517

Counters for the Arm Drag

Elbows Close, Hands in Motion. When in an open stance the wrestler keeps his elbows close to his body. He does not reach out to contact the opponent but waits for the opponent to reach out and make contact with him. The wrestler tries to prevent the opponent from grasping his wrists or arms by keeping them in motion.

Redrag (Figure 33-18). When the opponent is successful in starting the arm drag, the wrestler places the hand of the arm being controlled or dragged on the upper arm of the opponent and drags the opponent's shoulder past his own, getting a top position on the opponent's shoulder. He then spins behind him, using the arm-drag motion in bringing him to the mat.

The Crossover (Figure 33-19). If the opponent is attempting an arm-drag trip, the wrestler throws his body across the opponent's body, drops to his knees, and controls one of the opponent's legs with his free hand.

WRESTLING FROM THE KNEES

Wrestlers who are poor in defending against the take-downs when standing on their feet should instead drop to their knees and attempt take-downs from a kneeling position. Whenever a wrestler drops to his knees, the opponent should also go to his knees and remain in a kneeling position until contact is made. When some measure of control is gained after hooking up, the wrestler who comes to a stand on his feet has an advantage because he has a wider base than the wrestler who stays on his knees. In addition, he has increased mobility and can exert increased force. However, the man who remains on his knees can probably better defend himself from this position than he could were he on his feet; therefore, he has nothing to lose by staying down on his knees.

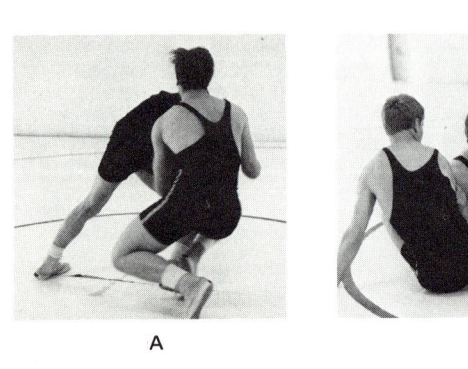

An opportunity to wrestle an opponent who is on his knees also occurs whenever he has attempted a take-down such as a single- or a double-leg drop. After the attempted take-down is blocked, and while the opponent is still on his knees, it is possible to hook up and keep the opponent off-balance until the wrestler can successfully utilize one of the take-downs from the knees.

Figure 33-18. Redrag.

Figure 33-19. The crossover.

TAKE-DOWNS FROM THE KNEES

Snap-down

1. The wrestler places his right hand on top of the opponent's neck, his left hand on top of the opponent's upper arm, and then quickly comes to a standing position.
2. The wrestler pushes his opponent straight to his rear or to either side. When the wrestler feels resistance to this pressure, he immediately snaps the opponent's head forward and down to the mat.

A   B   C   D

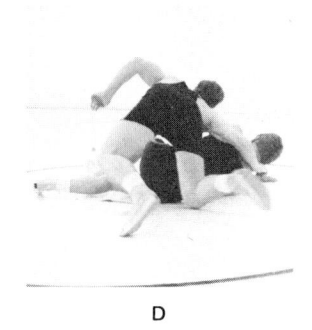

Figure 33-20. Snap-down.

3. As the opponent's head is snapped downward, the wrestler puts his weight down on the opponent's shoulders, spinning behind him to either the right or left, depending on the direction that his head was snapped. (See Figure 33-20.)

Counters for the Snap-down from the Knees

Inside Top-position Hook-up. The wrestler hooks up with his hands inside and in a top position on his opponent's neck or arms. He should not let his opponent get the inside top position. If the wrestler does not get the hook-up he wants he ducks out and clears all contact with his opponent.

Hook-up and Stand-up. If the wrestler drops to his knees to get contact with his opponent, the wrestler hooks up and quickly gets to his feet in order to have a solid base and increased mobility.

Pancake

The pancake (Figure 33-21) is an efficient maneuver with which to get a take-down and near-fall points quickly, because the opponent is taken directly to his back.

1. When the opponent attempts a take-down by dropping for the legs, the wrestler quickly moves his feet back to counter and catches under the opponent's right arm with his left arm. The wrestler's left hand should be on the opponent's upper back in order to bar his arm upward. With his right hand the wrestler simultaneously grasps the opponent's left upper arm.

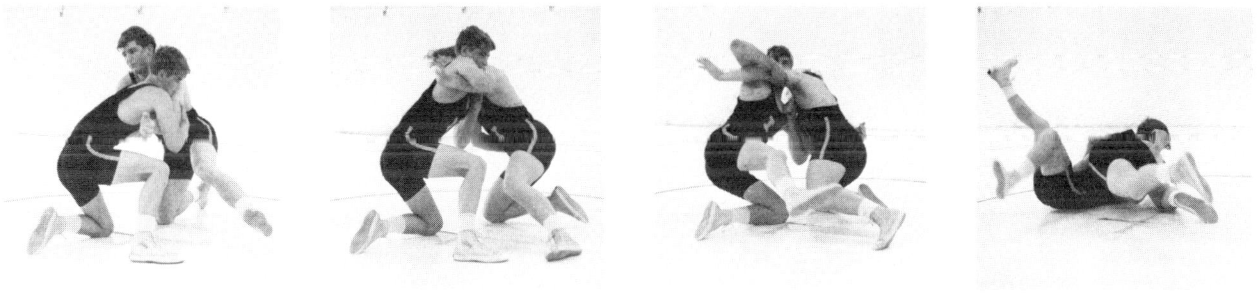

2. The wrestler forces the opponent's body to an erect position by driving forward. The wrestler then steps up and drives off his left foot, lifting the opponent's right arm with his left arm and pulling in toward his chest.

3. The wrestler turns the opponent to his right and onto his back, locking the opponent's arms tightly. He then sits through by driving his left leg under his right leg in order to prevent the opponent from bridging and turning off his back.

Counters for the Pancake

Arm Bar and Stand-up. If the wrestler allows his opponent to get an arm under one of his arms (single underarm bar), the wrestler locks over the arm, steps up first with his foot opposite the bar and gets to both feet as quickly as possible.

Recovery from Missed Leg Drops. To prevent his opponent from using the pancake after a missed leg drop, the wrestler gets his head up quickly and with his hands controls the opponent's arms while coming to a standing position. The wrestler never remains on his knees with his head down after an unsuccessful attempt to take the opponent down.

Referee's Position on the Mat

When a wrestler gains control he is said to be in the position of advantage or in the top position. The wrestler who is underneath is the down or bottom man. The wrestlers are started from the referee's position, in which

A   B   C   D

Figure 33-21. Pancake.

Wrestling 519

Figure 33-22. Referee's position on the mat.

they are on their hands and knees; (1) at the beginning of the second and third periods or, (2) if one of them has control at the time when the clock is stopped. (See Figure 33-22.)

ESCAPES AND REVERSALS

Stand-up

The stand-up (Figure 33-23) is a safe method of escaping from the bottom position because the shoulders are never exposed to the mat. A wrestler who can escape and who is better at take-downs than his opponent has an advantage because a take-down scores 2 points and an escape scores only 1 point. Consequently, some wrestlers concentrate on the take-down, let-up style to accrue points over their opponent. The following maneuvers are for a stand-up:

1. The bottom man pushes off the mat with both hands and simultaneously brings his elbows backward, close to his ribs. He raises his head and trunk, steps out forward with either foot, and protects his rear legs and foot—which are still on the mat—by sitting on them. The action of covering the foot prevents the top man from grasping the bottom man's ankle or stepping over his near leg.

2. The bottom man grasps the opponent's hands and spreads them apart while continually driving back into him. The top man has to drive forward and thus force the bottom man to a standing position or else be pushed over backward.

3. When the top man forces against the bottom man and both men have come to a standing position, the bottom man continues to spread his opponent's hands apart and turns to face him.

Counters for the Stand-up

Far-ankle Pick-up (Figure 33-24). Starting from the referee's position on the mat, the top man releases the body hold and grasps the far ankle of the bottom man.

Near-ankle Pick-up (Figure 33-25). Starting from the referee's position, the top man releases the near arm, moves backward, and grasps the near ankle of the bottom man.

Forward Jam (Figure 33-26). The top man keeps the body and near-arm hold and jams the bottom man forward to prevent him from standing up.

Body Lock and Forward Trip (Figure 33-27). If the bottom man gets to his feet, the top man, using the wrestler's grip, clasps his hands around the bottom man's body, steps outside and in front of the bottom man's near leg, and trips him forward.

Pick-up. If the bottom man stands up, the top man takes a body hold, picks the bottom man off the mat, and twists the bottom man's body so that he may be brought safely down to the mat on his side.

Sit-out and Turn-in

The sit-out is an escape that is executed by the following actions:

1. The top man is on the left side and has his right arm around the waist of the bottom man.
2. The bottom man steps forward with his right foot and shifts his weight to his right foot and left hand.

A   B   C   D

Figure 33-23. Stand-up.

Figure 33-24. Far-ankle pick-up.

Figure 33-26. Forward jam.

Figure 33-25. Near-ankle pick-up.

Figure 33-27. Body lock and forward trip.

3. He then shoots his left leg forward as far as possible and drops to his left elbow.
4. He completes the escape by pivoting on his left knee and elbow, turning onto his knees, and facing the top man.
5. After escaping, the bottom man brings his arms out in front of him, ready to stop any countermove by the top man. (See Figure 33-28.)

Sit-out and Turn-out

The top man has his right arm around the opponent's waist.

1. The bottom man steps out with his right foot and shoots his left foot forward.
2. He turns to his right and lands on his hip, bringing his right elbow down forcefully to free himself from the opponent's arm that is around his waist.
3. The bottom man completes the escape by pivoting on his right knee, completing his turn to the right.
4. He finishes on his knees, facing his opponent with his hands out in front and ready for action. (See Figure 33-29.)

Counters for Sit-outs

Far-ankle Pick-up. From the referee's position, starting on the left side of the bottom man, the top man quickly

A   B   C   D

Figure 33-28. Sit-out and turn-in.

Wrestling 521

A   B   C   D

Figure 33-29. Sit-out and turn-out.

releases the body hold and with his right hand grasps the far ankle of the bottom man.

Near-ankle Pick-up. The top man quickly releases the bottom man's near arm, moves back, and grasps his near ankle.

Body Hold and Near Arm (Figure 33-30). If the top man moves more quickly than the bottom man when the starting signal is given, the top man can use the waist hold and near-arm breakdown.

The Drop (Figure 33-31). If the bottom man sits out, the top man slides his hands from the rear up under and to the bottom man's armpits and jerks the shoulders of the bottom man to the mat. The top wrestler can then change to a pinning hold or move around behind the bottom man in order to maintain the top position.

Arm Hook and Spin (Figure 33-32). If, when working on the left side of the bottom man, he sits out and turns in, the top man slides his right hand under the right armpit of the bottom man. He then jerks the right arm of the bottom man back and the top man moves to his own left to spin behind the bottom man and retain control.

Figure 33-30. Body hold and near arm.

Figure 33-31. The drop.

Switch

The switch (Figure 33-33) is used to reverse the opponent; that is, to go from the bottom to the top position and to gain control.

1. The top man is on the left side with his right arm around the bottom man's waist and his left hand holding the bottom man's left arm.
2. The bottom man releases the top man's hold on his left arm by twisting his elbow to the inside and back, moves his left hand across to the right, and places his left hand on the mat in front of his right hand where it is out of reach of the top man.
3. The bottom man places all his weight on his left hand and right foot and raises his right knee.
4. The bottom man pivots and brings his left leg through to the right. At the same time he throws his right arm over the top man's right arm and grasps inside the top man's right thigh.

Figure 33-32. Arm hook and spin.

522   *Individual and Team Sports*

A B C D

Figure 33-33. Switch.

5. The bottom man shifts his hips away and puts pressure backward and downward on the shoulder of the top man until he frees himself from the waist hold. The bottom man then places his left arm around the top man's left leg from the rear and pivots to his knees, completing the reversal.

Counters for the Switch

Far-ankle Pick-up. The top man, working on the left side in a referee's position, releases the body hold and grasps the bottom man's far ankle with his right hand.

Limp Arm (Figure 33-34). The top man, by rotating his hand backward and letting the arm go limp, slips his arm out of the bottom man's grasp before he can put pressure on it. The top man then pulls his arm out and reaches back to grasp one of the opponent's legs.

Legs Away and Behind (Figure 33-35). The top man moves his legs away and behind the bottom man as the switch is started. As the top man moves behind he slides both of his hands under the bottom man's armpits from behind and attempts to jerk the bottom man's shoulders back toward the mat.

Step-over (Figure 33-36). After the switch is started, the top man forces his arm deep around the bottom man's waist, pulls the hips of the bottom man toward him, and steps across the bottom man's legs. With his free arm the top man controls one of the bottom man's legs and takes his other arm out of the switch.

Reswitch (Figure 33-37). The reswitch is used by the top man when the bottom man has almost completed his switch but is not yet free of the body hold. As the bottom man raises his shoulders to complete the reversal, the top man sits under, using the same switch motion that was used by the bottom man.

A B

C

Figure 33-34. Limp arm.

Figure 33-35. Legs away and behind.

Figure 33-36. Step-over.

Wrestling 523

A   B

C

Figure 33-37. Reswitch.

Side Roll

The side roll (Figure 33-38) is a reversal. The top man is on the left side with his right arm around the bottom man's waist. With his right hand, the bottom man grasps the top man's right wrist, holding it around his body.

1. The bottom man turns his upper body to the left, driving his right knee to the left until it is under the top man.
2. The bottom man continues to turn and drops his right elbow to the mat, at which time he lifts with his left leg, which is positioned in the top man's crotch. The bottom man turns the top man onto his back.
3. The bottom man moves his body to a position perpendicular to the top man, puts his weight on his right foot, shoots his left leg back under his right leg, and turns onto his stomach, thus securing the position of advantage in which he is chest to chest with the top man, who is lying on his back.

Counters for the Side Roll

Far-ankle Grasp. In order to use a side roll the bottom man must lock the top man's arm around his waist. The top man removes his arm from the bottom man's waist and quickly grasps the far ankle.

Step-across (Figure 33-39). As the bottom man locks the wrist of the top man and starts to roll, the top man moves his legs and body across the bottom man's body, and then with his free hand the top man controls one of the legs of the bottom man.

Roll-through. If the top man is caught in a roll he grapevines the bottom man's leg, reaches around the body with his free hand, and grasps the far wrist of the bottom man. He continues to roll the bottom man on through.

MAINTAINING CONTROL

In order to maintain control of the bottom man, the top man must maintain his balance. Speed and fast reaction time are important factors in maintaining balance. Many believe that some wrestlers have natural balance. The wrestler who appears to have natural balance, however, is one who responds quickly and gets into a position in which he is in balance. The move that enables him to maintain his balance and control may be for only one or two inches. The move may be a change of position that, because of suppleness or the ability to relax or turn and twist, may shift his weight and thus prevent him from being thrown over. The surest way to maintain control of an opponent is by means of holds on his body, legs, or arms—or a combination of two of these—that break him down from a position on his hands and knees. Breaking the opponent down to his stomach, side, or back not only makes it easier to control him but permits pinning holds to be applied with increased safety.

A   B   C   D

Figure 33-38. Side roll.

A   B

C

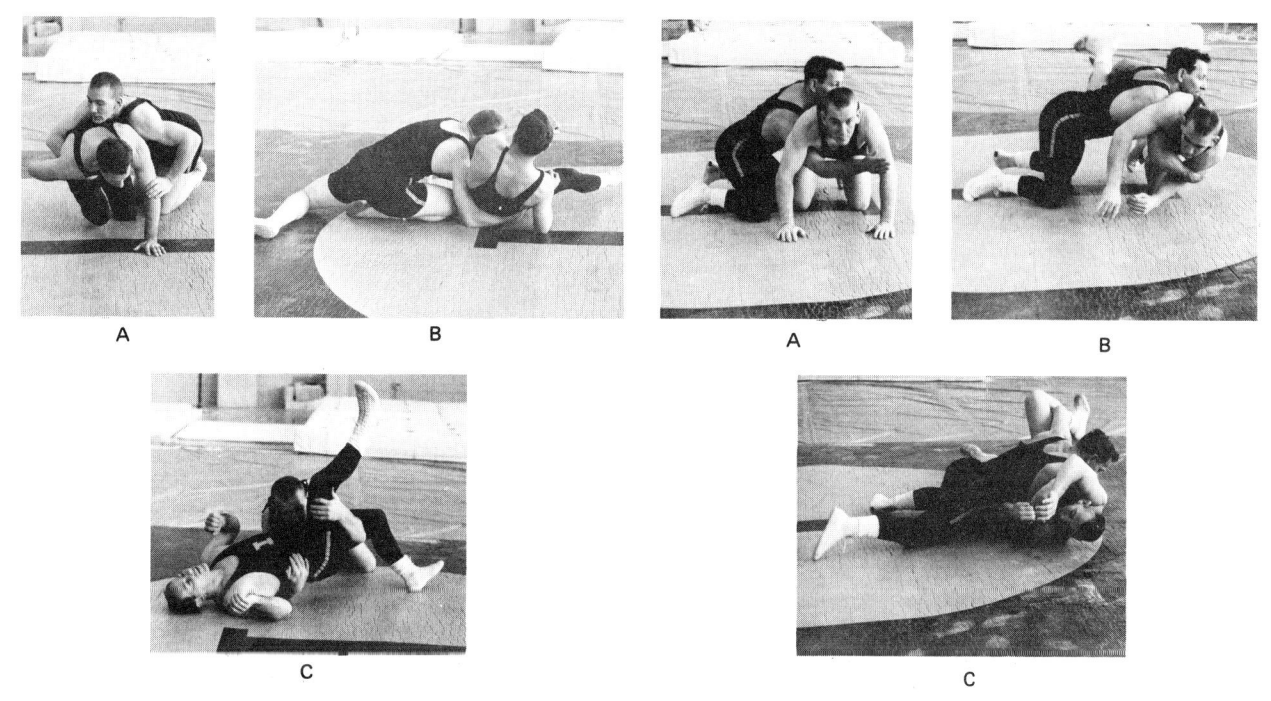

Figure 33-39. Step-across.

A   B

C

Figure 33-40. Far arm and near leg.

BREAKDOWNS

In all the illustrations of breakdowns, the top man is on the left side and his right arm is around the bottom man's waist.

Far Arm and Near Leg

1. With his left hand the top man reaches behind the left arm and under the body of the bottom man and grasps his right arm just above the elbow.
2. The right hand of the top man drops from the position around the waist to the opponent's left leg and lifts it up.
3. The top man pulls the right arm of the bottom man across the bottom man's chest; he continues to lift the left leg of the bottom man and drives him to the right and onto his back (See Figure 33-40.)

Counter for Far-arm, Near-leg Breakdown (Figure 33-41). As the top man, working from the left side, reaches for the right arm of the bottom man, the bottom man lowers his left shoulder and moves his right arm away. The bottom man can then use his left arm to lock the left arm of the top man and roll him to the left.

Head Lever

1. While driving his head in behind the armpit of the bottom man's left arm, the top man moves his left hand downward and grasps the bottom man's left wrist.
2. Pulling the bottom man's wrist outward, the top man drives his right hand back into an inside crotch pry and lifts the right leg of the bottom man.
3. The top man continues to drive with the lever and crotch pry as he flattens the bottom man to his stomach. (See Figure 33-42.)

Figure 33-41. Counter for far-arm, near-leg breakdown.

Wrestling 525

Figure 33-42. Head lever.

Figure 33-43. Far ankle and near arm to chicken wing.

Counter for the Head-lever Breakdown. As the top man attempts to grasp the wrist of the bottom man and to lower his head behind the bottom man's near shoulder, he lowers that shoulder and pushes his arm out to the front to prevent the top man from pulling the arm back.

Far Ankle and Near Arm to Chicken Wing

1. With his right hand the top man grasps the bottom man's right instep and then places his left hand on the bottom man's left arm at the elbow.
2. The top man then lifts the bottom man's right leg and pulls his left arm back, driving forward and to the left.
3. The top man betters his position by driving his right hand through and onto the bottom man's upper left arm. This type of arm bar is known as the chicken wing. (See Figure 33-43.)

Counter for Far Ankle and Near Arm to Chicken Wing.
Ankle Release. As the top man reaches for the bottom man's far ankle, the bottom man either sits back on that ankle or straightens his far leg to keep the ankle free of the top man's grasp.
Arm Release. To prevent the top man from getting the chicken wing, the bottom man straightens his arm and moves it forward.
Near Side Roll and Step-over. If the chicken wing is applied from the left side, the bottom man rolls to his left, puts pressure on the top man's left arm, rolls the top man, and steps across his body.

Far Ankle to Inside Crotch Hold

The hold is very effective for maintaining control of the bottom man; it is sometimes used as a stalling hold because it is difficult to break. (See Figure 33-44.)

1. With his right arm the top man picks up the bottom man's right instep, pulls it up, and allows the right leg of the bottom man to straighten.
2. The top man steps up onto his right foot and pulls the bottom man's right leg across his own right thigh.
3. With his upper right arm holding the bottom man's right upper leg across his own right thigh, the top man reaches through with his right hand and from the outside grasps the bottom man's left leg.
4. The top man drives forward and to the left, moves his right arm inside the crotch of the bottom man and tips him over onto his back.

There are other methods of getting into this hold: for example, when the bottom man is moving to escape, the top man has many chances to drive an arm into his crotch and stop his movement.

Counter for Far Ankle to Inside Crotch. If the top man grasps the bottom man's far ankle, the bottom man extends his right leg and sits back on his own foot. He then grasps

526   *Individual and Team Sports*

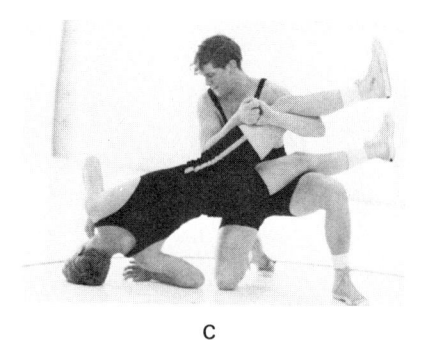

A   B   C   D

Figure 33-44. Far ankle to inside crotch hold.

the top man's hand, forcing the top man to release the ankle hold. If the bottom man attempts to straighten his leg in order to release his ankle, the inside crotch (over and under) is set up for the top man.

PINNING HOLDS

The objective of an offensive wrestler should be to secure a fall. He has prepared himself to do this by first learning to take his opponent to the mat, to break him down, and to counter his attempted escapes. Too many wrestlers prefer to win by edging the opponent on points instead of working for a fall. This tends to make a match dull and uninteresting, especially if the wrestlers are not skilled.

The leverages used to pin are not learned quickly; therefore, if a wrestler is going to learn to pin, he must regularly practice pinning holds. He should try for a fall every time that he wrestles a match, during practice as well as during competition.

Half-nelson and Crotch Hold

1. The top man flattens the bottom man to the mat, using one of the breakdowns described earlier. He places his left hand under the bottom man's left arm and onto the back of his neck (this is a half nelson).

2. With his right hand the top man grasps the bottom man's left leg. The top man then drives forward to the right with his left arm and with his right hand lifts the bottom man's left leg.

3. Continuing to turn the bottom man onto his back, the top man encircles his left arm as far around the bottom man's neck as possible. The top man takes an inside crotch hold with his right hand. (See Figure 33-45.)

Counters for the Half-nelson Crotch Hold

Near Wing-lock and Step-over. When the top man applies the half nelson from the left side while the bottom man is still on his knees, the bottom man locks the top man's left arm above the elbow, rolls to the left, and steps across the top man's body.

Elbow to Body, Turning Head Away. If the bottom man is flat on his stomach when the top man applies the half nelson from the left side, the bottom man forces his left elbow to his left side, turns his body toward the top man, turns his face to the right, and lifts his head.

Bridge and Turn-in. If the bottom man is turned onto his back with the half-nelson crotch hold from the left side, he bridges high and turns away from the top man. He then places his right hand between his body and that of the top man, drops down from the bridge, drives his right arm between their two bodies, and turns to his stomach.

A   B   C   D

Figure 33-45. Half-nelson and crotch hold.

Wrestling 527

A B C D

Figure 33-46. Near cradle.

Near Cradle

The cradle hold (Figure 33-46) is one of the most effective methods of pinning the shoulders of the opponent to the mat. It can be applied from many different positions, and if properly executed there is little chance of losing the position of advantage.

1. The top man is on the left side. As the bottom man starts to stand up by raising his left knee off the mat, with his right arm the top man grasps the bottom man's left knee from behind and encircles the bottom man's head with his left arm, locking his hands together.
2. The top man now has his arms wrapped around the bottom man's head and left knee and has forced them tightly together. He then drives the bottom man to the right and forward, exposing the bottom man's shoulders to the mat.
3. The bottom man's left arm and shoulder may be in an "up" or raised position under the top man's chest. To get the bottom man's left shoulder exposed to the mat, the top man loosens his hold with his hands and drops his left shoulder back and down, getting it in front of the bottom man's left shoulder. The top man then turns the bottom man onto his back for the fall.

Counters for the Near Cradle

Extend Body and Leg. If the top man attempts the near cradle from the left side, the bottom man flattens out, turns to his left side, extends his left leg, and raises his head.

Sit-through. When the top man has applied the near cradle from the left side, the bottom man sits under and to the left side of the top man; the bottom man raises his head and straightens his leg to break the cradle hold.

Far Cradle

The far cradle hold (Figure 33-47) is sometimes called the cross-face cradle. As with the near cradle, this hold can be applied from several different positions. For example, when the bottom man sits out, the top man can employ it as a countermove. He may wait until the bottom man steps with his right or outside foot before attempting a far cradle, or he may force the bottom man into an exposed position by first breaking him down onto his stomach, as described subsequently.

1. The top man is on the left side of the bottom man. After breaking the bottom man down until he is flat on his stomach on the mat, the top man reaches his left hand in front of the bottom man's right arm

A B C D

Figure 33-47. Far cradle.

528 *Individual and Team Sports*

just above the elbow. The top man immediately places his right hand on the mat directly behind the bottom man's right knee in order to prevent him from moving it back.

2. The top man then shifts his body to the left and forces the bottom man to double up by driving his head down to his knees. The top man then locks his hands together.
3. The top man drops to his left side and pulls the bottom man's shoulders back to the mat. If any difficulty occurs in forcing the bottom man's right shoulder to the mat, the top man should drive his left knee into the bottom man's ribs, forcing the bottom man's body away and thus causing his shoulders to be exposed to the mat.

Counters for the Far Cradle

Extend Body and Leg. When the top man attempts to apply the far cradle from the left side, the bottom man extends or straightens his body and right leg and lifts his head.

Overhook Foot and Kick Free. When the top man has locked the right leg and head of the bottom man in a far cradle, the bottom man hooks his left leg over his own right foot, kicks hard, and straightens his body in order to break the hold.

Guillotine

There are many types of pinning holds that require the use of the legs for their successful execution. The guillotine (Figure 33-48), which is described here, is effectively used by wrestlers who make maximum use of their legs when pinning their opponents.

1. The top man, working from the left side of the bottom man, steps behind him, putting his weight on the bottom man's hips by leaning against them with his stomach. The top man quickly steps forward with his left leg, drives his left foot inside of the bottom man's left leg, and grapevines (entwines or wraps around) it with his left leg.

2. The top man reaches across the bottom man's back with his left arm and places it around the bottom man's right arm from behind, hooking his right elbow. With his right hand the top man next grasps the bottom man's right wrist.
3. The top man pulls the bottom man's right arm upward and over his head. The top man immediately drops to his left side, pulling the bottom man's right shoulder toward the mat.
4. The top man quickly places his left hand under and around the bottom man's neck, releases his right wrist, and locks both hands around the bottom man's head. The top man then applies pressure with his legs, drives his hip against the bottom man's back, and pulls on the bottom man's head, forcing his shoulders to the mat.

Counters for the Guillotine. It is difficult to escape from this pinning hold once the top man has completely secured it. Rather than concentrate on methods of breaking the hold after it has been obtained, it is more important to strive to avoid it.

The wrestler needs to counter the hold by stages; for example: if the top man is not able to grapevine the leg, the guillotine cannot be applied. The bottom man moves his knees forward or his elbows back in order to block out the legs of the top man and prevent the grapevine.

If the top man does secure the grapevine on the left leg of the bottom man, the bottom man sits out, scoots his hips forward, straightens his leg to break the grapevine, grasps the top man's left leg in both arms, and pulls it overhead to escape.

If the top man has secured the leg grapevine on the bottom man's left leg and reaches across the body and behind the bottom man's right arm, the bottom man extends his right arm, grasps the top man's wrist with his left hand, and puts pressure back on the top man's arm until the top man flattens out on his stomach. The bottom man then releases the wrist and spins to the top position for a reversal.

A   B   C   D

Figure 33-48. Guillotine.

Selected References

BOOKS

Clayton, Thomas. *A Handbook of Wrestling Terms and Holds.* South Brunswick, N.Y.: A.S. Barnes, 1968.

Dratz, John P., Manly Johnson, and Terry McCann. *Winning Wrestling.* Englewood Cliffs, N.J.: Prentice-Hall, 1966.

Kenney, Harold E., and Newt Law. *Wrestling.* New York: McGraw-Hill, 1952.

Leeman, Gerald, and T. Ralph Williams. *Learn Wrestling: A Functional Wrestling Notebook.* Bethlehem, Pa.: 1966.
    Available through Gerald Leeman, wrestling coach, Lehigh University, Bethlehem, Pennsylvania.

Macias, Rummy. *Learning How to Wrestle.* Mankato, Minn.: Creative Education Press, 1965.

Unback, Arnold W., and Warren R. Johnson. *Successful Wrestling.* St. Louis, Mo.: Mosby, 1953.

PERIODICALS

Amateur Wrestling News. P.O. Box 1936, Oklahoma City, Oklahoma 73101.

Scholastic Wrestling News. 1904 Grace, Worland, Wyoming 82401.

FILMS

Championship Wrestling on Film—Basic Holds and Techniques. Cliff Keen Wrestling Products, 2895 Overridge Drive, Ann Arbor, Michigan.